WEST HAM UNITED
THE COMPLETE RECORD

I dedicate this book to my special daughter Louise who has always shown
a keen interest and given me her support and encouragement.

John Northcutt

To my 5-month-old grandson Jasper Mills.
Football will play a big part in your life as you grow older, whether its supporting Crystal Palace like
your dad or following West Ham United like your grandad. May you Hammer the Eagles as time goes by.

Steve Marsh

WEST HAM UNITED
THE COMPLETE RECORD

by JOHN NORTHCUTT and STEVE MARSH

First published as a hardback by deCoubertin Books Ltd in 2015.

deCoubertin Books, Basecamp, Studio N, Baltic Creative Campus, Liverpool, L1 OAH

www.decoubertin.co.uk
First Hardback Edition.

ISBN: 978-1-909245-27-3
Special Edition ISBN: 978-1-909245-31-0

A CIP catalogue record for this book is available from the British Library.
Cover design by Thomas Regan at Milkyone Creative.
Special Edition Design by Leslie Priestley.
Typeset design by Leslie Priestley.
Layout by Thomas Regan at Milkyone Creative.

Printed and bound by Standart.

Every effort has been made to contact copyright holders for photographs used in this book. If we have overlooked you in any way, please get in touch so that we can rectify this in future editions.

CONTENTS

Introduction

Back in 1895 the workers at the ship building firm Thames Ironworks formed a football team. They played at the Hermit Road ground in Canning Town with the ground being surrounded by a moat and with canvas sheeting used for the fencing.

Looking back to their humble beginnings we wonder what the players and supporters would think of today's all-seater stadiums, sponsorship deals and live televised games. As the club look to move into the magnificent Olympic Stadium in 2016 the Ironworks players would have been proud of the progress that the club has made.

It will be a sad day when West Ham play their final game at the Boleyn Ground as it holds so many memories for our supporters. Such fine players have graced the Upton Park turf, the famous 1966 World Cup trio Bobby Moore, Geoff Hurst and Martin Peters, the elegant Trevor Brooking, the exciting skills of Paolo Di Canio and the leadership of Billy Bonds who played 386 games on home soil more than any other player. West Ham United is more than a football club – it is a way of life.

This book aims to become the definitive reference book on the club. Every competitive game has been included, and every effort has been made to ensure that the facts in this book are correct. Various discrepancies from earlier publications have been identified and corrected. Due to enemy action during the Second World War many of the club records were destroyed and we are pleased to be able to resurrect our proud history.

Finally, we hope that this book evokes memories for all those Hammers supporters who have stood on the terraces or sat in the stand urging on their heroes.

John Northcutt and Steve Marsh
London
July 2015

PART ONE

SEASON BY SEASON RECORDS

THE EARLY YEARS
1895-1896 TO 1899-1900

The foundation of West Ham United FC

can be traced back to the shipbuilding firm, the **Thames Ironworks & Shipbuilding Company**. The works were situated at the mouth of the River Lea in East London. In 1860 they built **HMS Warrior** which, at the time, was **the largest warship in the world**. The works were successful and by the time of their closure in 1912 **they had built around 1,000 vessels**.

The company's owner **Arnold Hills** was keen to look after the welfare of his workers and suggested to his foreman Dave Taylor that he should organise a works football team. Hills had previously been a top-class footballer himself, having represented England against Scotland in 1879 while playing for Old Harrovians FC.

In the local area there had been other club sides such as Old Castle Swifts, St Luke's, Upton Park and South West Ham. Some of their players were employed at the Ironworks and it was those players who became the nucleus of the first Thames Ironworks team. A ground was found at Hermit Road, Canning Town. It was surrounded by a moat, with canvas sheeting used for fencing.

In that first season of 1895/96 they did not enter a league but played friendly fixtures instead. They did, however, enter the West Ham Charity Cup and the FA Cup. The first friendly was a home game against Royal Ordnance on 7 September 1895. The game ended at 1–1 with the distinction of scoring the first ever goal for the club going to Arthur Darby. Three successive victories followed, before the team travelled to Kent to play Chatham in the FA Cup. There was an attendance of 3,000 to see the more experienced Kent side proceed to the next round by beating the Ironworks 5–0.

A unique experiment took place in December as Thames decided to play a game under electric light. The lights were provided by dynamo machines, which were powered by batteries, and the game was played on 16 December against

Season **1895-96**
Match Details

	Date		Competition	Venue	Opponents		Results		Attendance	Scorers
1	Oct 12	Sat	FAC Q1	A*	Chatham		L	0-5	3,000	

* Thames Ironworks were first out of the hat, but waived the right to stage the game at their Hermit Road ground

Old St Stephen's, who were beaten 3–1. Ten lights were suspended on poles around the pitch and at various times play had to be halted as the generator failed. Undeterred, the club tried again in January when Barking Woodville were the visitors. This time there were no generator breakdowns and the experiment was voted a success. The Ironworks were easy 6–2 winners, with Charlie Dove scoring a hat-trick. Two more games were played under lights and the attendances of up to 3,000 suggested the experiment was a success.

The success of the matches under lights prompted Thames to play two further games in this way and an excited crowd came along to see Football League sides Woolwich Arsenal and West Bromwich Albion. Although both games were lost, the club had benefitted from extra revenue and the players had gained valuable experience.

In the West Ham Charity Cup, Park Grove were beaten in the semi-final and, following two drawn games, Barking were defeated 1–0 in the final. It had been a successful first season with them winning the majority of their friendly fixtures and being rewarded with some silverware as well.

Arnold Hills

Appearances & Goals 1895-96

	FA Cup	
	Starts	Goals
DARBY Arthur	1	0
FREEMAN Thomas	1	0
FRENCH Barnabas	1	0
LINDSAY Jamie	1	0
PARKS Walter	1	0
SAGE George	1	0
STEWART Johnny	1	0
TULL Henry	1	0
WATSON John	1	0
WILLIAMS A.	1	0
WOODS John	1	0
TOTALS	**11**	**0**

Team Line-Ups

DARBY Arthur	FREEMAN Thomas	FRENCH Barnabas	LINDSAY Jamie	PARKS Walter	SAGE George	STEWART Johnny	TULL Henry	WATSON John	WILLIAMS A.	WOODS John
11	10	5	9	6	8	4	2	1	3	7

1896-97

Story of the season

For the 1896-97 season the club entered the London League and new players arrived in the form of **Edward Hatton, Johnny Morrison, Fred Chalkley** and **Frank Dandridge.**

The campaign started well as Vampires were beaten 3–0 at home in the opening game. Another home win followed when the 1st Scots Guards were beaten 2–0. This was the last match played at Hermit Road; the club had found a new ground at Browning Road, East Ham.

Appearances & Goals 1896-97

Player	London League Starts	London League Goals	FA Cup Starts	FA Cup Goals	London Senior Cup Starts	London Senior Cup Goals	Essex Senior Cup Starts	Essex Senior Cup Goals	Total Starts	Total Goals
BARNES T.	1	0	0	0	0	0	1	0	2	0
BIRD Richard	9	0	1	0	6	1	0	0	16	1
BUTTERWORTH H.	6	4	0	0	0	0	0	0	6	4
CHALKLEY Frederick	7	0	0	0	5	0	1	0	13	0
CHAPMAN William	1	0	0	0	0	0	0	0	1	0
CHARSLEY A.J.	2	0	0	0	1	0	0	0	3	0
COOPER T.	2	2	0	0	0	0	0	0	2	2
COWIE Andrew	2	1	0	0	0	0	0	0	2	1
DANDRIDGE Frank	10	0	1	0	4	1	0	0	15	1
DARBY Arthur	0	0	0	0	2	0	0	0	2	0
DAVIE Peter	4	0	1	0	4	0	0	0	9	0
DOVE Charles	10	1	0	0	7	2	1	0	18	3
DUFF Alex	4	0	0	0	5	0	0	0	9	0
FURNELL David	1	0	0	0	0	0	0	0	1	0
GRAHAM Hugh	3	0	0	0	1	0	0	0	4	0
GRESHAM George	10	2	1	0	6	4	0	0	17	6
HATTON Edward	4	3	1	0	0	0	0	0	5	3
HICKMAN William	1	0	0	0	2	0	1	0	4	0
HOLSTOCK Albert	2	0	1	0	0	0	0	0	3	0
HURST Joseph	1	0	0	0	0	0	0	0	1	0
JONES	1	0	0	0	0	0	0	0	1	0
MORRISON John	9	1	1	0	7	2	0	0	17	3
MORTON William	6	0	0	0	3	0	1	0	10	0
NEIL George	1	0	0	0	0	0	0	0	1	0
NICHOLS Albert	1	0	1	0	0	0	0	0	2	0
OLIVANT A.	3	0	0	0	0	0	0	0	3	0
READ Charles	3	0	0	0	1	0	0	0	4	0
RIDGES Victor	0	0	0	0	1	0	0	0	1	0
ROSSITER H.	4	1	1	0	6	1	0	0	11	2
SAGE George	1	1	0	0	1	0	1	0	3	1
SOUTHWOOD	0	0	1	0	0	0	0	0	1	0
STARES Colin	0	0	0	0	5	1	1	0	6	1
STEVENSON Robert	4	0	1	0	4	3	1	1	10	4
STEWART Johnny	0	0	0	0	0	0	1	0	1	0
TAYLOR William	1	0	0	0	1	0	1	0	3	0
TRANTER Walter	6	0	0	0	4	0	0	0	10	0
WILLIAMS A.	1	0	0	0	0	0	0	0	1	0
WOODS W.	0	0	0	0	1	0	1	0	2	0
own goal		1				1		1		3
TOTALS	121	17	11	0	77	16	11	2	220	35

Thames Ironworks holders of the West Ham Charity Shield 1896
Back row: Arnold Hills (Chairman Thames Iron Works), Barnabas French, Hugh Graham, Francis Payne (Secretary), John Woods, William Hickman and Tom Robinson (Trainer).
Middle row: Frederick Chamberlain, George Sage, Robert Stevenson, William Chapman, William Barnes.
Front row: Johnny Stewart and Thomas Freeman.

The FA Cup brought a trip to Kent where the Ironworks were overwhelmed, losing 8–0 to Sheppey United, although an injury to Hatton caused them to play with ten men for most of the game.

In the West Ham Charity Cup first Claremont Athletic were beaten 2–0, followed by another 2–0 victory over Manor Park in the semi-final. Thames were then paired with West Ham Garfield in the final. As current holders, Thames were

the favourites, but they relinquished their hold on the trophy after losing 1–0. A further competition entered was the London Senior Cup, where they scored victories over West Norwood, Marcians, Wandsworth and Barking Woodville. Up next were Bromley and after two draws the Kent club came through, winning 2–0 on their ground.

In the league, Thames were doing well after wins against Vampires and Ilford but this all changed on 1 April following a 5–0 defeat against 3rd Grenadier Guards. The Guards eventually won the league while Thames finished as runners-up. It was announced by owner Arnold Hills that he would help fund the building of a new ground, which would also be used for athletics and cycling. The work was soon completed and in June 1897 the company held a gala day for the opening. There were 8,000 present to see the enclosure, which was named the Memorial Grounds.

For the opening game at the new ground, Thames had arranged a friendly with Northfleet. The attendance was disappointing, with just over 200 present to witness the 1–1 draw. However, a week later there was an improved attendance of 1,000 for the visit of Brentford in the London

London League Final Table 1896-1897

	P	W	D	L	F	A	Pts
3rd Grenadier Guards	12	9	1	2	32	13	19
Thames Ironworks	**12**	**7**	**2**	**3**	**17**	**17**	**16**
Barking Woodville	12	6	3	3	20	11	15
Ilford	12	7	1	4	26	14	15
Crouch End	12	4	2	6	14	19	10
Vampires	12	3	1	8	10	28	7
London Welsh	12	0	2	10	9	26	2

London Welsh were suspended and as a result Thames Ironworks were awarded two wins.
The 1st Scots Guards withdrew and their record was deleted.

Season **1896-97** London League
Match Details

Manager **Committee responsible for team selection**   Final League Position **2nd**

	Date		Competition	Venue	Opponents	Results		Attendance	Scorers
1	Sep 19	Sat	Lond	H	Vampires	W	3-0		Hatton 2, Gresham
2	Oct 8	Sat	Lond	H	1st Scots Guards	W	2-0		Gresham, Rossiter
3	Oct 10	Thu	FAC 1Q	A	Sheppey United	L	0-8		
4	Oct 17	Sat	LSC	A	West Norwood	W	2-1		Rossiter, Stevenson [pen]
5	Oct 22	Thu	Lond	A	3rd Grenadier Guards	L	1-4		Sage
6	Oct 24	Sat	Lond	A	Crouch End	W	1-0		Hatton
7	Nov 11	Wed	LSC	A	Marcians	W	4-0		Gresham 2, Bird, 1 untraced
8	Nov 28	Sat	Lond	A	Ilford	D	2-2		Dove, (og)
9	Dec 5	Sat	ESC	H	Leyton	L	2-3		Stevenson, 1 untraced
10	Jan 9	Sat	LSC	H	Wandsworth	W	3-1		Stevenson 2, Gresham
11	Jan 16	Sat	LSC	H	Barking Woodville	W	2-0		Dove, Morrison
12	Jan 30	Sat	LSC	H	Bromley*	D	3-3		Dandridge, Dove, Stares
13	Feb 6	Sat	LSC	A	Bromley	D	2-2		Gresham, Morrison
14	Feb 13	Sat	LSC Replay	A	Bromley	L	0-2		
15	Feb 27	Sat	Lond	A	Vampires	W	2-1		Butterworth, Morrison
16	Mar 6	Sat	Lond	H	Ilford	W	3-2	1,500	Read 2, Butterworth
17	Mar 13	Sat	Lond	A	Barking Woodville	L	0-1		
18	Apr 1	Thu	Lond	H	3rd Grenadier Guards	L	0-5		
19	Apr 3	Sat	Lond	H	Crouch End	W	4-1		Butterworth 2, Cooper 2
20	Apr 8	Thu	Lond	H	Barking Woodville	D	1-1		Cowie

* Stopped in extra time due to bad light

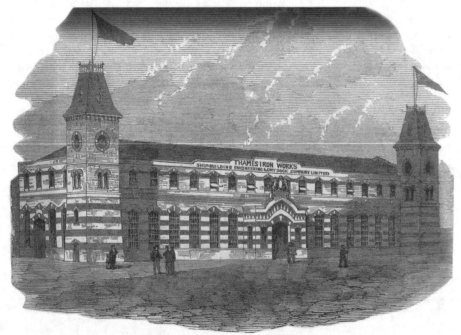

Thames Iron Works and Ship Building
Company, Orchard Yard, Blackwall

Team Line-Ups

BARNES T.	BIRD Richard	BUTTERWORTH H.	CHALKLEY Frederick	CHAPMAN William	CHARSLEY A.J.	COOPER T.	COWIE Andrew	DANDRIDGE Frank	DARBY Arthur	DAVIE Peter	DOVE Charles	DUFF Alex	FURNELL David	GRAHAM Hugh	GRESHAM George	HATTON Edward	HICKMAN William	HOLSTOCK Albert	HURST Joseph	JONES	MORRISON John	MORTON William	NEIL George	NICHOLS Albert	OLIVANT A.	READ Charles	RIDGES Victor	ROSSITER H.	SAGE George	SOUTHWOOD	STARES Colin	STEVENSON Robert	STEWART Johnny	TAYLOR William	TRANTER Walter	WILLIAMS A.	WOODS W.	#
1						5					6	7			11	9		3			10	4					8				2							1
	4		1			5					6				10	9		3			11		7				8				2							2
	4					5					6				10	9		3			11		7				8		1		2							3
			1								9	3			11		5				10	4					7	8	6		2							4
	6					5						7	1		10	9		3			11	4					8				2							5
	4					5					10	6		1		9					11				3		7				2					8		6
	4										10	5		1	8						11						9	7	6		2	3						7
	6		2			5					10	9		1	8						11	4					7								3			8
1		2										7							6		4						8					11	9	10	3		5	9
	6		2								9			1	8		5				10						7				4	11			3			10
	4		2							5	8	9		1							10						7				6	11			3			11
	4		2								11	9		1	8						10						7								3	6		12
	6		2							5	11	9		1	8						10	4					7								3			13
	6		2							5	11	9		1	8						10	4			3		7											14
	4	9	2							5	11	1			10						8	6					7								3			15
	4	9	2							5	11	1			10						8	6					7								3			16
		9	2							5	11	1			10					4	8	6					7								3			17
	6	11	2	8	1										4	9	5				10						7								3			18
	6	9	2	10	7	5						4	1		8						11														3			19
	6	9	2	10	7	5						4	1		8						11														3			20

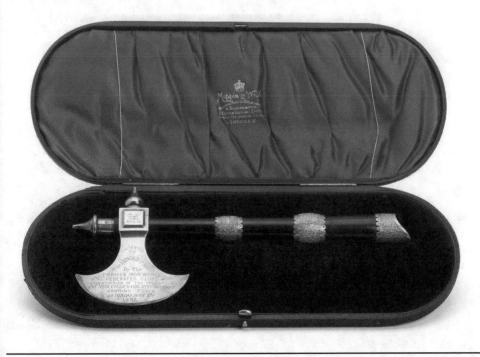

Presented to Mrs Arnold F. Hills by the Thames Iron Works Federated Clubs on the occasion of the opening of The new Cycle & Athletic Grounds Canning Town Saturday June 19th 1897

League. New signing Jimmy Reid scored the Thames goal in a 1–0 victory.

The FA Cup began and Redhill were beaten 3–0 at home, with Chisholm scoring twice. Next up in the Cup was another home tie with Royal Engineers, who were beaten 2–1. Unfortunately further progress in the FA Cup was

1897-98
Story of the season

The start of the 1897-98 season saw several new signings – **Simon Chisholm**, a half-back, and two forwards, **James Reid** and **Percy Mills**.

Appearances & Goals 1897-98

	London League		FA Cup		London Senior Cup		Total	
	Starts	Goals	Starts	Goals	Starts	Goals	Starts	Goals
BIRD Richard	1	0	0	0	1	0	2	0
BONE J.	1	1	0	0	0	0	1	1
CHALKLEY Frederick	2	0	3	0	0	0	5	0
CHISHOLM Simon	15	0	2	2	2	0	19	2
COOPER T.	0	0	0	0	1	1	1	1
COX Francis	1	0	0	0	0	0	1	0
DANDRIDGE Frank	2	0	3	0	2	0	7	0
DENHAM	1	0	0	0	0	0	1	0
DOVE Charles	10	0	3	0	1	0	14	0
EDWARDS A.	12	6	3	0	2	0	17	6
FITZJOHN J.	1	0	0	0	0	0	1	0
FOSS L.	2	0	0	0	0	0	2	0
FURNELL David	10	0	3	0	2	0	15	0
GILLIES	11	1	1	0	0	0	12	1
GRESHAM George	16	12	3	0	2	1	21	13
HATTON Edward	2	1	3	1	0	0	5	2
HEATH Robert	6	0	0	0	0	0	6	0
HICKMAN William	1	0	0	0	0	0	1	0
HIRD Henry	12	5	1	0	0	0	13	5
HOUNSELL Robert	10	8	0	0	1	1	11	9
MILLS Percy	1	0	0	0	1	0	2	0
MORRISON John	0	0	0	0	2	0	2	0
NEIL George	14	1	0	0	2	0	16	1
NICHOLS Albert	1	0	0	0	0	0	1	0
OLDER	0	0	2	0	0	0	2	0
OXSPRING Arthur	3	0	0	0	0	0	3	0
REID Jimmy	16	10	3	1	1	0	20	11
ROOFF J.	2	0	0	0	0	0	2	0
TAYLOR William	10	0	1	0	0	0	11	0
TRANTER Walter	12	0	2	0	2	0	16	0
WOODCOCK A.	1	0	0	0	0	0	1	0
own goal		2		1		1		4
	176	47	33	5	22	4	231	56

Thames Ironworks 1897-98
Back: George Neil, David Furnell, Walter Tranter,
Centre: Gillies, William Taylor, Simon Chisholm,
Front: Henry Hird, Jimmy Reid, Robert Hounsell, George Gresham, A. Edwards

halted when Thames lost 2–0 to St Albans.

In the league in October, the 3rd Grenadier Guards were beaten 1–0 and local rivals Leyton were thrashed 4–0. During November and December the team remained

London League Final Table 1897-1898

	P	W	D	L	F	A	Pts
Thames Ironworks	16	12	3	1	47	15	27
Brentford	16	12	2	2	43	17	26
Leyton	16	8	4	4	41	33	20
3rd Grenadier Guards	16	7	3	6	34	33	17
Ilford	16	5	7	4	33	25	17
Stanley	16	5	4	7	22	22	14
Barking Woodville	16	2	6	8	16	37	10
Bromley	16	4	2	10	20	49	10
2nd Grenadier Guards	16	0	3	13	17	42	3

unbeaten, with a 3–0 victory against Barking Woodville and the 2nd Grenadier Guards being beaten 5–1, following a hat-trick from Edwards. In the New Year the impressive league form continued with hat-tricks for Gresham against Stanley, who were beaten 3–0, and a further hat-trick for Edwards in the 7–3 victory over Bromley. By April there were only two clubs in contention to win the league, with Thames having just one more point than Brentford. The two teams met at Brentford before a crowd of 3,000, boosted by a party of 200 from Thames who had arrived by boat. It was a fast and furious encounter which saw Brentford triumph by 1–0. The final day of the season arrived with Thames at home to the 2nd Grenadier Guards. Despite an injury to Dove and having to play with ten men, Thames won 3–1. There were joyous scenes as the news came through that Brentford had been beaten, which meant that Thames were London League champions.

Season **1897-98** London League
Match Details

Manager **Committee responsible for team selection**   Final League Position **1st**

	Date		Competition	Venue	Opponents	Results		Attendance	Scorers
1	Sep 11	Sat	Lond	H	Brentford	W	1-0	1,000	Reid
2	Sep 18	Sat	FAC Q1	H	Redhill	W	3-0	1,000	Chisholm 2, (og)
3	Sep 25	Sat	FAC Q2	H	Royal Engineers Training Battalion	W	2-1	1,200	Hatton, Reid
4	Oct 2	Sat	Lond	H	Leyton	W	4-0	2,500	Reid 2, Gresham, Hatton
5	Oct 16	Sat	FAC Q3	A	St. Albans	L	0-2	1,000	
6	Oct 23	Sat	Lond	A	3rd Grenadier Guards	W	1-0		Reid
7	Oct 30	Sat	Lond	A	Leyton	W	3-1	3,000	Gresham, Hird, Hounsell
8	Nov 13	Sat	Lond	H	Barking Woodville	W	3-0		Gresham 2, Reid
9	Nov 27	Sat	LSC	A	Novocastrians	W	3-1		Cooper, Hounsell, (og)
10	Dec 2	Thu	Lond	H	2nd Genadier Guards	W	5-1		Edwards 3, Gresham, Hird
11	Dec 11	Sat	Lond	A	Ilford	D	3-3		Hird 2, Reid
12	Jan 1	Sat	Lond	H	Ilford	W	4-0		Bone, Gresham, Reid, (og)
13	Jan 8	Sat	Lond	H	Stanley	W	4-2	600	Gresham 3, (og)
14	Jan 15	Sat	Lond	H	Bromley	W	7-3		Edwards 3, Hounsell 2, Gillies, Gresham
15	Jan 22	Sat	LSC	H	Ilford	L	1-3		Gresham
16	Feb 26	Sat	Lond	A	Stanley	D	1-1	3,000	Gresham
17	Mar 12	Sat	Lond	A	Barking Woodville	D	0-0	1,500	
18	Mar 19	Sat	Lond	A	Bromley	W	5-1		Reid 3, Hird, Hounsell
19	Apr 2	Sat	Lond	H	3rd Grenadier Guards	W	3-1		Hounsell 2, Neil
20	Apr 23	Sat	Lond	A	Brentford	L	0-1	3,000	
21	Apr 30	Sat	Lond	A*	2nd Genadier Guards	W	3-1		Hounsell 2, Gresham

LSC = London Senior Cup* Played at Memorial Grounds

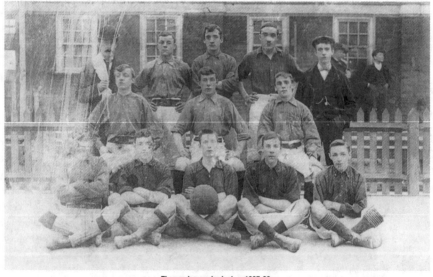

Thames Ironworks Juniors 1897-98
Back: F. Barr, D. Trollope, T. Barr, G. Pearson, R.J. Gardner
Centre: J. Conjuite, C. Willacy, W. Bentley Front: J. Ballantyne, D. Ballantyne, H. Ruffell, W. Loman (Capt), D. Southgate

Team Line-Ups

BIRD Richard	BONE J.	CHALKLEY Frederick	CHISHOLM Simon	COOPER T.	COX Francis	DANDRIDGE Frank	DENHAM	DOVE Charles	EDWARDS A.	FITZJOHN J.	FOSS L.	FURNELL David	GILLIES	GRESHAM George	HATTON Edward	HEATH Robert	HICKMAN William	HIRD Henry	HOUNSELL Robert	MILLS Percy	MORRISON John	NEIL George	NICHOLS Albert	OLDER	OXSPRING Arthur	REID Jimmy	ROOFF J.	TAYLOR William	TRANTER Walter	WOODCOCK A.	
6		2	4			5		3	10			1		8	9					7						11					1
		2	6			5			4	11		1		10	8									7		9		5	3		2
		2	6			5			4	11		1		10	8									7		9		5	3		3
		2	6			5	7		4	11		1		8	9								3			10					4
		2				5			4	11		1	6	8	9			7								10			3		5
			6						4	7		1	11	9				8					2			10		5	3		6
			6						4			1	7	10			11	9					2			8		5	3		7
			6						4			1	11	8				9					2	7		10		5	3		8
			6	8		5			4	7		1		10						9	11	2							3		9
			6						2	11		1	4	10				7	9				2			8		5	3		10
			6						4	11		1	10	8				7					2			9		5	3		11
	9								7		11	1	4	10			6						2			8		5	3		12
			6							11		1	4	8				7	9				2			10		5	3		13
			5	4					8			1	6	11				7	9				2			10			3		14
4			6	5					11			1		8				9			7		2			10			3		15
			6						11	9				5	10		1	7					2			8		4	3		16
			4						11				6	8			1	7	9				2			10	3	5			17
			6						11				4				1	7	9				2			8	3	5			18
			6						4	11				10			1	7	9				2		5	8			3		19
			6						4					10			1	7	9				2		5	8			3	11	20
			6						4		11			10			1	7	9				2		5	8			3		21

Thames Ironworks 1898-99 versus Royal Engineers Training Battalion 1st October 1898
Back: George Neil, David Lloyd, Thomas Moore, Walter Tranter
Centre: Henry Hird, Sam Hay, F. Adams, Roderick McEachrane, R. Cobb Front: Simon Chisholm, George Gresham

1898-99

Story of the season

For this season the football committee persuaded the owner Arnold Hills that the club should **consider their players to be professionals** and pay them accordingly. They then entered two leagues - the Southern League Division Two and the Thames and Medway Combination.

Kicking off the season in the Southern League, Thames won 3–0 at Shepherds Bush with new goalkeeper Tommy Moore in fine form. Sadly this success did not extend to the Thames and Medway Combination, as the first five games ended in defeat.

During October the FA Cup began with the Royal Engineers

Appearances & Goals 1898-99

	League		Test		FA Cup		Total	
	Starts	Goals	Starts	Goals	Starts	Goals	Starts	Goals
ADAMS F.	2	1	0	0	3	0	5	1
ATKINSON W.	2	2	0	0	0	0	2	2
BIRD Richard	1	0	0	0	0	0	1	0
BRETT Frank	1	0	0	0	0	0	1	0
BULLER	1	0	0	0	0	0	1	0
CHISHOLM Simon	16	1	1	0	3	0	20	1
COBB R.	2	0	0	0	3	0	5	0
DOVE Charles	15	3	0	0	2	0	17	3
DUNN Thomas	12	0	1	0	0	0	13	0
FOSS L.	1	0	0	0	0	0	1	0
GILMORE Henry	1	1	0	0	0	0	1	1
GRESHAM George	14	4	1	0	3	1	18	5
HAY Sam	6	2	0	0	1	0	7	2
HENDERSON R.	9	7	1	0	0	0	10	7
HIRD Henry	19	3	0	0	3	1	22	4
HITCH Alf	3	0	0	0	2	0	5	0
HOUNSELL Robert	2	1	0	0	0	0	2	1
LEONARD Patrick	11	7	1	0	0	0	12	7
LLOYD David	12	12	1	1	3	0	16	13
MARJERAM Arthur	8	0	0	0	0	0	8	0
McEACHRANE Roderick	23	1	1	0	3	1	27	2
McEWAN L.	8	2	0	0	0	0	8	2
McMANUS Peter	5	0	1	0	0	0	6	0
MOORE Thomas	22	0	1	0	3	0	26	0
NEILL George	2	0	0	0	1	0	3	0
REID George	6	1	0	0	0	0	6	1
REID Jimmy	14	9	0	0	0	0	14	9
REYNOLDS J.	13	5	1	0	0	0	14	5
TRANTER Walter	21	0	1	0	3	0	25	0
WENHAM	1	1	0	0	0	0	1	1
own goal		1						1
TOTALS	**253**	**63**	**11**	**1**	**33**	**3**	**297**	**68**

being beaten 2–0 at home. The next round saw Thames travelling to Brighton United where they drew 0–0. In the replay at the Memorial Grounds it was Brighton who came out on top, winning 4–1.

In November there was a fine 4–1 victory at St Albans with centre-forward David Lloyd scoring a hat-trick. Lloyd followed it up with two more as Watford were beaten 2–1 at home. A 3–0 victory at Chesham on Christmas Eve was followed by a game at Maidenhead on New Year's Eve. Goalkeeper Tommy Moore missed the train and Charlie Dove showed his versatility by taking his place and not conceding a goal in the 4–0 win. Lloyd was on target again with two goals as Wycombe were beaten 4–1; Thames were now unbeaten in eight league games. The game at Wolverton in January was played in a hurricane and with the wind in their favour the home team took a three-goal lead. In the second half, however, it was Thames who had the benefit of the conditions, which enabled them to fight back with three goals to draw 3–3. A week later the luckless Chesham were beaten 8–1 in an excellent performance before 2,000 at the Memorial Grounds. In February new boy Henderson scored all four goals in the 4–0 win against Uxbridge and continued with both goals at Southall in a 2–0 victory. A 1–0 win at Fulham in April saw Thames go into the final match of the season on an undefeated run of 17 games. Maidenhead were the visitors and were crushed 10–0, with Leonard scoring four and Lloyd getting a hat-trick.

Southern League Division Two Final Table 1898-99

	P	W	D	L	F	A	Pts
Thames Ironworks	22	19	1	2	64	16	39
Wolverton	22	13	4	5	88	43	30
Watford	22	14	2	6	62	35	30
Brentford	22	11	3	8	59	39	25
Wycombe Wanderers	22	10	2	10	55	57	22
Southall	22	11	0	11	44	55	22
Chesham	22	9	2	11	45	62	20
St. Albans	22	8	19	11	45	59	19
Shepherds Bush	22	7	3	12	37	53	17
Fulham	22	6	4	12	36	44	16
Uxbridge	22	7	2	13	29	48	16
Maidenhead	22	3	2	17	33	86	8

Thames were worthy winners of the league by a margin of nine points. However to determine who were to win the overall title, there needed to be a playoff with Cowes, who were the winners of the South West Section of Division Two. The game was played at East Ferry Road, the home of Millwall, where Thames beat the Isle of Wight club 3–1. To win promotion, however, Thames had to play a Test Match against Sheppey United from the First Division. The match played at Chatham ended 1–1 and before a replay could take place the Southern League committee decided to expand the First Division and accepted both clubs

THOMAS DUNN

Tommy came down from Scotland to sign for Wolverhampton Wanderers in 1891. He was a strong full-back and soon established himself in the First Division side.

In 1896 he was in the Wolves side that was beaten by Sheffield Wednesday in the FA Cup Final. After six seasons at Molineux where he played in 102 games Tommy left to sign for Burnley in 1897. He only made seven appearances for the Lancashire club before coming south to join Chatham in 1898 to play in the Southern League. It was only a short spell with the Kent side as he was transferred to Thames Ironworks in 1899, where he was in the team that won the Southern League Division Two. He played in 13 games that season and was never on the losing side. The following season he was a regular in the side, playing in 21 league games and 7 FA Cup ties.

After returning to Scotland in 1899 he took up an undertakers business and died in June 1938.

Season **1898-99** Southern League Division Two
Match Details

Manager **Committee responsible for team selection**   Final League Position **1st**

	Date		Competition	Venue	Opponents	Results		Attendance	Scorers
1	Sep 10	Sat	SL Div 2	A	Shepherd's Bush	W	3-0	1,500	Atkinson 2, Adams
2	Sept 24	Sat	SL Div 2	H	Brentford	W	3-1	1,200	Hay 2, Dove
3	Oct 1	Sat	FAC Q1	H	Royal Engineers Training Battalion	W	2-0	1,000	Gresham, McEachrane
4	Oct 8	Sat	SL Div 2	A	Uxbridge	L	1-2	2,000	Gresham
5	Oct 15	Sat	FAC Q2	A	Brighton United	D	0-0	2,000	
6	Oct 19	Wed	FAC Q2 Rep	H	Brighton United	L	1-4	2,000	Hird
7	Oct 29	Sat	SL Div 2	A	Wycombe Wanderers	L	1-4	1,000	Reid J.
8	Nov 5	Sat	SL Div 2	H	Shepherd's Bush	W	1-0	1,000	Wenham
9	Nov 12	Sat	SL Div 2	A	St. Albans	W	4-1	800	Lloyd 3, Reid J.
10	Nov 26	Sat	SL Div 2	A	Watford	D	0-0	1,000	
11	Dec 3	Sat	SL Div 2	H	Fulham	W	2-1	2,000	Gresham, Reynolds
12	Dec 17	Sat	SL Div 2	H	Watford	W	2-1	1,500	Lloyd 2
13	Dec 24	Sat	SL Div 2	A	Chesham	W	3-0	1,000	Hird 2, Hounsell
14	Dec 31	Sat	SL Div 2	A	Maidenhead	W	4-0	2,000	Hird, McEwan, Reid J., Reynolds
15	Jan 14	Sat	SL Div 2	H	Wycombe Wanderers	W	4-1	1,000	Lloyd 2, McEwan, Keen (og)
16	Jan 21	Sat	SL Div 2	A	Wolverton	W	4-3	200	Leonard 2, Chisholm, Dove
17	Jan 28	Sat	SL Div 2	H	Chesham	W	8-1	2,000	Gresham 2, Reynolds 2, Dove, Lloyd, McEachrane, Reid J.
18	Feb 11	Sat	SL Div 2	A	Brentford	W	2-0	2,000	Leonard, Reynolds
19	Feb 18	Sat	SL Div 2	H	Uxbridge	W	4-0	1,500	Henderson 4
20	Mar 4	Sat	SL Div 2	A	Southall	W	2-0	4,000	Henderson 2
21	Mar 11	Sat	SL Div 2	H	St. Albans	W	1-0	2,000	Reid J.
22	Mar 18	Sat	SL Div 2	H	Wolverton	W	2-1	1,000	Reid J. 2
23	Mar 25	Sat	SL Div 2	H	Southall	W	2-0	3,000	Gilmore, Reid G.
24	Apr 8	Sat	SL Div 2	A	Fulham	W	1-0	3,000	Lloyd
25	Apr 15	Sat	SL Div 2	H	Maidenhead	W	10-0	3,000	Leonard 4, Lloyd 3, Reid J. 2, Henderson
26	Apr 22	Sat	SL CD	N	Cowes*	W	3-1	1,000	Henderson, Leonard, Lloyd
27	Apr 29	Sat	Test Match	A	Sheppey United**	D	1-1	2,000	Lloyd

* Championship Decider (against champions of Second Division South West Section - played at Millwall)
** No replay: Thames Ironworks promoted and Sheppey United retained their place

Team Line-Ups

ADAMS F.	ATKINSON W	BIRD Richard	BRETT Frank	BULLER	CHISHOLM Simon	COBB R.	DOVE Charles	DUNN Thomas	FOSS L.	GILMORE Henry	GRESHAM George	HAY Sam	HENDERSON R	HIRD Henry	HITCH Alf	HOUNSELL Robert	LEONARD Patrick	LLOYD David	MARJERAM Arthur	McEACHRANE Roderick	McEWAN L.	McMANUS Peter	MOORE Thomas	NEILL George	REID George	REID Jimmy	REYNOLDS J	TRANTER Walter	WENHAM	
10	9		8		4		5		11					7					3	6			1					2		1
	9				4		11				10	8		7	5			3		6			1					2		2
10					4	11					9	8		7				3		6			1	5				2		3
9					4	11	3				10	8		7	5			2		6			1							4
9					4	11	2				10			8	5		7			6			1					3		5
9					4	11	2				10			8	5		7			6			1					3		6
			11		4		3				10	9		7	5					6			1			8		2		7
			11		4						10							3		6	5		1			8	7	2	9	8
					6						10			7			9		3	11	5		1	4		8		2		9
					4						10	9		7				3		6	5		1			8	11	2		10
					6		4				10	9		7				3		11	5		1			8		2		11
					4						10	6		8			9	3		11	5		1			7		2		12
							4				11			7		10	9	3		6	5		1			8		2		13
							1				11			5	8			9	2	6	4			3	10	7				14
								3			10			4		11	9			6	5		1			8	7	2		15
				5			4	3			10			8		11	9			6			1			7		2		16
							4	2			8			6			7	9		5			1			10	11	3		17
				5			4	3					9				11			6			1		10	8	7	2		18
							5	3					10	4			11			6			1		9	8	7	2		19
							4	5	3					9			11			6			1		10	8	7	2		20
							4	3						9	7		11			6		5	1		10	8		2		21
							4	3						9	7		11			6		5	1		10	8		2		22
		8					4	3	11					9	7					6		5	1		10			2		23
							4	3			10			9	7		11	8		6		5	1					2		24
							4	3						9	7		11	8		6		5	1		10			2		25
							4	5	3					9			11	8		6			1		10	7		2		26
							4	3			10			9			11	8		6		5	1			7		2		27

1899-1900
Story of the season

As the season started, club secretary Francis Payne retired and George Neil took over. There were **four new signings** with forward Albert Carnelly arriving from Bristol City and three experienced players from Tottenham, Harry Bradshaw, Bill Joyce and Kenny McKay. There was a 1–0 defeat at Reading on the opening day but a week later **Chatham were beaten 4-0** with two goals each from new boys Carnelly and McKay. The FA Cup began with a preliminary-round tie with the Royal Engineers. The army side were defeated by 6–0 with **Bill Joyce claiming a hat trick**.

A trip to Grays in the next round saw Thames progress, winning 4–0 despite McManus missing a penalty. Following a narrow 1–0 league victory against Bedminster, two more FA Cup ties were played. First came a home game against Sheppey United, who were beaten 4–2 with Carnelly and Joyce grabbing two goals each. Then came a visit to Dartford where the Kent side were overwhelmed in a 7–0 victory where again Carnelly scored twice. In the league Thames travelled to Tottenham and it was a disaster as they lost 7–0. They did have to play with ten men, however, as Dunn went off injured and Joyce and McManus were left limping due to knee injuries. Back to the FA Cup, and after a goalless draw at Dartford Thames won the replay 2–0 with Tommy Moore saving a penalty. In the next round

Appearances & Goals 1899-1900

	League		Test		FA Cup		Total	
	Starts	Goals	Starts	Goals	Starts	Goals	Starts	Goals
ADAMS F.	6	1	0	0	2	0	8	1
ALLAN Robert	21	1	1	0	0	0	22	1
BIGDEN James	11	0	0	0	2	0	13	0
BRADSHAW Thomas	5	0	0	0	7	2	12	2
CARNELLY Albert	27	8	1	0	6	6	34	14
CORBETT Fred	3	0	0	0	0	0	3	0
CRAIG Charles	17	0	1	0	4	0	22	0
DOVE Charles	15	0	1	0	5	0	21	0
DUNN Thomas	21	0	1	0	7	0	29	0
GENTLE	1	0	0	0	1	0	2	0
GILMORE Henry	4	0	0	0	0	0	4	0
HIRD Henry	1	0	0	0	3	0	4	0
JANES W.	2	0	0	0	0	0	2	0
JOYCE William	27	8	1	3	7	7	35	18
KING Syd	16	0	0	0	7	0	23	0
McEACHRANE Roderick	28	0	1	0	7	2	36	2
McKAY Kenny	28	8	1	0	7	5	36	13
McMANUS Peter	5	0	0	0	4	1	9	1
MOORE Thomas	27	0	1	0	7	0	35	0
REID Jimmy	1	0	0	0	1	1	2	1
STEWART William	16	0	1	1	0	0	17	1
SUNDERLAND H.	1	0	0	0	0	0	1	0
TAYLOR Frank	14	1	1	0	0	0	15	1
TURNER	4	0	0	0	0	0	4	0
WALKER Len	7	0	0	0	0	0	7	0
OWN GOALS		3		1				4
TOTALS	**308**	**30**	**11**	**5**	**77**	**24**	**396**	**59**

there was a clash with local rivals Millwall, which drew a crowd of 13,000 to the Memorial Grounds. It was a tight affair but the Lions came out on top, winning 2–1.

December proved to be a poor month with five league defeats as Millwall triumphed again, winning 2–0, and Queens Park Rangers beat Thames home and away over the Christmas period. There was sad news when it was announced that team captain Harry Bradshaw had died on Christmas Day from the result of a rupture of a blood vessel. Further defeats followed in January against Chatham, Reading and Gravesend, but Thames did manage to beat Sheppey United 3–0. During February and March there was only one victory, when Carnelly scored twice in a 2–1 win against Gravesend in March. There was further joy on Easter Monday when Bill Joyce scored a hat-trick in the 4–1 defeat of Southampton and a week later Sheppey United were beaten 4–2.

To avoid a relegation playoff Thames had to win their final game of the season and also hope that Chatham would lose their last game. The final game was at Millwall and hundreds of Thames supporters made the trip. They came away happy after Kenny McKay scored the only goal of the game. However, Chatham also won their game so this meant Thames had to take part in a playoff Test Match against Fulham, who had finished as runners-up in Division Two. The game was played at neutral White Hart Lane before an attendance of 600. Thames were in control throughout and won 5–1 with Bill Joyce scoring a hat-trick.

As the season ended it was announced that a new limited company would be formed and shares issued to employees of the ship-building company and to members of the public. Thames Ironworks FC was wound up in June 1900 and on 5 July West Ham United Football Club was registered as a company.

WILLIAM JOYCE

Bill began his career at Greenock Morton in 1893 playing as a centre forward.

He then joined Bolton Wanderers in 1894 where he spent three seasons, playing in 30 league games and scoring 16 goals. That total would have been more had he not had the misfortune in 1896 to suffer a broken leg. He joined Tottenham in 1897 where he had an amazing goalscoring record, netting 63 goals in 83 league appearances. This included four goals against both Southampton and Wolverton. Bill joined Thames Ironworks in season 1899–1900, missing only one game in that campaign. He was joint top scorer in the league with eight goals and scored hat-tricks in the FA Cup against Royal Engineers and in the Test Match with Fulham. After one season with Thames he left to join Portsmouth for one season, scoring 16 goals in his 21 matches. Bill was then transferred to Second Division side Burton United, where in two seasons he played in 52 league games, scoring 16 goals.

Southern League - Division One Final Table 1899-1900

	P	HOME					AWAY					Pts
		W	D	L	F	A	W	D	L	F	A	
Tottenham Hotspur	28	13	1	0	42	8	7	3	4	25	18	44
Portsmouth	28	14	0	0	39	5	6	1	7	20	24	41
Southampton	28	11	0	3	52	14	6	1	7	18	19	35
Reading	28	10	2	2	25	6	5	0	9	16	22	32
Swindon Town	28	12	1	1	30	11	3	1	10	20	31	32
Bedminster	28	9	1	4	27	18	4	1	9	17	27	28
Millwall Athletic	28	9	0	5	25	17	3	3	8	11	20	27
Queens Park Rangers	28	8	2	4	29	20	4	0	10	21	38	26
Bristol City	28	9	0	5	33	23	0	7	7	11	24	25
Bristol Rovers	28	9	2	3	31	16	2	1	11	15	39	25
New Brompton	28	7	3	4	26	17	2	3	9	13	32	24
Gravesend United	28	7	4	3	28	25	3	0	11	10	33	24
Chatham	28	9	1	4	26	16	1	2	11	12	42	23
Thames Ironworks	**28**	**6**	**4**	**4**	**19**	**13**	**2**	**1**	**11**	**11**	**32**	**21**
Sheppey United*	28	1	5	8	10	25	2	2	10	14	41	13
Brighton United**	22	0	0	0	0	0	0	0	0	0	0	0
Cowes**	13	0	0	0	0	0	0	0	0	0	0	0

* Relegated ** Resigned

Season **1899-1900** Southern League Division One

Match Details

Manager **Committee responsible for team selection**   Final League Position **14th**

	Date		Competition	Venue	Opponents	Results		Attendance	Scorers
1	Sep 16	Sat	SL Div 1	A	Reading	L	0-1	3,000	
2	Sep 18	Mon	SL Div 1	H	Chatham	W	4-0	1,000	Carnelly 2, McKay 2
3	Sep 23	Mon	FAC Pre	H	Royal Engineers	W	6-0	1,000	Joyce 3, McEachrane, McKay, Reid
4	Sep 30	Sat	FAC Q1	A	Grays United	W	4-0	750	Carnelly, Joyce, McKay, McManus
5	Oct 7	Sat	SL Div 1	H	Bedminster	W	1-0	3,000	Joyce
6	Oct 14	Sat	FAC Q2	H	Sheppey United	W	4-2	2,000	Carnelly 2, Joyce 2
7	Oct 28	Sat	FAC Q3	A	Dartford	W	7-0	1,200	Carnelly 2, McKay 2, Bradshaw, Joyce, McEachrane
8	Nov 4	Sat	SL Div 1	A	Tottenham Hotspur	L	0-7	7,000	
9	Nov 11	Sat	SL Div 1	H	New Brompton	D	0-0	2,000	
10	Nov 18	Sat	FAC Q4	A	New Brompton	D	0-0	3,000	
11	Nov 23	Thur	FAC Q4 Rep	H	New Brompton	W	2-0	3,000	Carnelly, McKay
12	Nov 25	Sat	SL Div 1	H	Swindon Town	W	1-0	2,000	Adams
13	Dec 2	Sat	SL Div 1	A	Bristol City	L	0-2	3,000	
14	Dec 9	Sat	FAC Q5	H	Millwall Athletic	L	1-2	13,000	Bradshaw
15	Dec 16	Sat	SL Div 1	A	Southampton	L	1-3	4,000	McKay
16	Dec 23	Sat	SL Div 1	H	Millwall Athletic	L	0-2	12,000	
17	Dec 25	Mon	SL Div 1	A	Queens Park Rangers	L	0-2	4,000	
18	Dec 30	Sat	SL Div 1	H	Queens Park Rangers	L	1-2	4,000	McKay
19	Jan 6	Sat	SL Div 1	A	Chatham	L	1-3	5,000	Carnelly
20	Jan 13	Sat	SL Div 1	H	Reading	L	0-1	4,000	
21	Jan 15	Mon	SL Div 1	A	Bristol Rovers	D	1-1	6,000	McKay
22	Jan 20	Sat	SL Div 1	A	Sheppey United	W	3-0	4,000	Carnelly, Joyce, McKay
23	Jan 24	Wed	SL Div 1	A	Gravesend United	L	1-2	1,200	Carnelly
24	Feb 10	Sat	SL Div 1	A	Bedminster	L	1-3	2,000	Carnelly
25	Feb 17	Sat	SL Div 1	H	Bristol Rovers	D	0-0	4,000	
26	Feb 24	Sat	SL Div 1	A	Portsmouth	L	0-2	2,000	
27	Mar 10	Sat	SL Div 1	H	Tottenham Hotspur	D	0-0	9,000	
28	Mar 17	Sat	SL Div 1	A	New Brompton	L	1-3	2,000	Atherton (og)
29	Mar 24	Sat	SL Div 1	H	Gravesend United	W	2-1	3,500	Carnelly 2
30	Mar 31	Sat	SL Div 1	A	Swindon Town	L	1-3	3,000	Menham (og)
31	Apr 5	Thur	SL Div 1	H	Portsmouth	L	2-4	5,000	Joyce 2
32	Apr 7	Sat	SL Div 1	H	Bristol City	D	0-0	5,000	
33	Apr 9	Mon	SL Div 1	H	Southampton	W	4-1	4,000	Joyce 3, Allan
34	Apr 17	Tue	SL Div 1	H	Sheppey United	W	4-2	3,000	Joyce, McKay, Taylor, Hulford (og)
35	Apr 28	Sat	SL Div 1	A	Millwall Athletic	W	1-0	8,000	McKay
36	Apr 30	Mon	Test Match	N	Fulham*	W	5-1	600	Joyce 3, Stewart, Howland (og)

* Played at Tottenham Hotspur

Team Line-Ups

ADAMS F.	ALLAN Robert	BIGDEN James	BRADSHAW Thomas	CARNELLY Albert	CORBETT Fred	CRAIG Charles	DOVE Charles	DUNN Thomas	GENTLE	GILMORE Henry	HIRD Henry	JANES W.	JOYCE William	KING Syd	McEACHRANE Roderick	McKAY Kenny	McMANUS Peter	MOORE Thomas	REID Jimmy	STEWART William	SUNDERLAND H.	TAYLOR Frank	TURNER	WALKER Len	No.
			11	10	7		4	2					9	3	6	8	5	1							1
			11	10	7		4	2					9	3	6	8	5	1							2
			11				4	2			7		9	3	6	8	5	1	10						3
			11	10			4	2			7		9	3	6	8	5	1							4
			11	10			4	2			7		9	3	6	8	5	1							5
			11	10			4	2			7		9	3	6	8	5	1							6
			11	10		7	4	2					9	3	6	8	5	1							7
			11	10		7	4	2					9	3	6	8	5	1							8
			11	9		2	5		4			7		3	6	8		1	10						9
		5	11	10			4	2			7		9	3	6	8		1							10
7		5	11	10			4	2					9	3	6	8		1							11
7		5		10			4	2					9	3	6	8		1						11	12
		4	9		7	2							10	3	6	8	5				1			11	13
7			11	10			4	5	2				9	3	6	8		1							14
3	7	5	9				2		4				10		6	8		1						11	15
3	7	5	9				2		4				10		6	8		1						11	16
3	7	5	9				2			4			10		6	8		1						11	17
3	7		9				2			4			10		6	8		1				5		11	18
3	7		10							4			9	2	6	8		1				5		11	19
	7	4		10				2					9	3	6	8		1		5		11			20
	7	4						2					9	3	6	8		1		5		11	10		21
	10	4	7			6		2					8	3	11	9		1		5					22
	7	4		10		6		2					9	3	11	8		1		5					23
	7			10			4	2					9	3	6	8		1		5		11			24
	7			10			4	2					9	3	6	8		1		5		11			25
	7	4		10				2					9	3	6	8		1		5		11			26
	7			10			4	2					9	3	6	8		1		5		11			27
	7	4		10				2	3				9		6	8		1		5		11			28
		4		10				2				7	9		6	8		1		5		11	3		29
	7			10		3	4	2					9		6	8		1		5		11			30
	7			10		3	4	2					9		6	8		1		5		11			31
	7			10		3	4	2					9		6	8		1		5		11			32
	7			10		3	4	2					9		6	8		1		5		11			33
	7			10		3	4	2					9		6	8		1		5		11			34
	7			10		3	4	2					9		6	8		1		5		11			35
	7			10		2	4	3					9		6	8		1		5		11			36

THE MODERN ERA
1900-1901 TO 2014-2015

1900-01
Story of the season

It was goodbye to the Ironworks as the Hammers began the season under their **new name of West Ham United**. Most of the former Ironworks players were retained but there were also seven new signings. Among those, were two Scots - goalkeeper **Hugh Monteith** and inside forward **Billy Grassam**.

The opening game of the season saw Gravesend United beaten 7–0 at home with Grassam scoring four goals. The 2,000 attendance was a disappointment as many more were expected to see the club's new beginning. However, there was a marked improvement through the turnstiles for the next home game with Southampton. A crowd of 7,500 went home happy as the Hammers won 2–0 with goals from Reid and Grassam. In October the team met local rivals Tottenham Hotspur at White Hart Lane and thanks to Monteith in goal they came away with a creditable goalless draw. The qualifying rounds of the FA Cup were played in November and after amateur side Olympic were beaten 1–0 at home, a clash with New Brompton saw West Ham win 4–1 in a replay following a 1–1 draw in Kent.

Appearances & Goals 1900-01

	League		FA Cup		Total	
	Starts	Goals	Starts	Goals	Starts	Goals
ALLAN Robert	24	0	3	0	27	0
CORBETT Fred	21	7	2	2	23	9
CRAIG Charles	25	0	6	0	31	0
DOVE Charles	13	0	3	0	16	0
FENTON Frederick	14	2	5	1	19	3
GRASSAM William	20	12	3	3	23	15
HUNT Fergus	27	3	6	1	33	4
KAYE Albert	14	2	6	3	20	5
KELLY William	19	0	3	0	22	0
KING Syd	22	0	6	0	28	0
McEACHRANE Roderick	28	1	6	0	34	1
MONTEITH Hughie	24	0	6	0	30	0
MOORE Thomas	4	0	0	0	4	0
NEILL George	1	0	0	0	1	0
PINDER A.	1	0	0	0	1	0
PUDAN Richard	2	0	0	0	2	0
RAISBECK Luke	2	0	2	0	4	0
RATCLIFFE Geroge	17	4	1	0	18	4
REID James	13	5	6	0	19	5
TAYLOR Frank	12	4	0	0	12	4
TRANTER Walter	4	0	2	0	6	0
WALKER Len	1	0	0	0	1	0
Totals	**308**	**40**	**66**	**10**	**374**	**50**

George Ratcliffe was signed from Grimsby Town and scored on his debut against Reading. The 1–0 win lifted the side to fifth in the table. Next up was the FA Cup tie with local side Clapton. The game attracted a season's-best attendance of 10,000 to the Memorial Grounds. In a hard-fought contest the teams drew 1–1.In the replay it was another close game but a hat-trick from Billy Grassam gave the Hammers a 3–2 victory. In the next round, West Ham were drawn at home to Liverpool, who would finish Football League champions that season. The Hammers played with pride and passion but the Merseysiders came out on top, winning 1–0. Back to the league and there were three successive wins in the New Year against Swindon, Watford and Luton. The eagerly awaited clash with Tottenham proved to be a disaster as the North London side ran out 4–1 winners following a poor show from goalkeeper Tommy Moore.

There was an unbeaten run of eight games, which included a 1–0 win against bitter rivals Millwall. The final game of the season was a 2–0 home win against New Brompton, which saw the Hammers finish in a creditable sixth position in the Southern League.

WILLIAM GRASSAM

Billy started his career in junior soccer in Glasgow with Redcliffe Thistle and Glasgow Maryhill in 1897.

He came south in 1899 to play for Burslem Port Vale where, playing at inside right, he scored 5 goals in his 31 appearances for the club. Billy joined West Ham in 1900 and became a firm favourite with the fans after scoring four goals against Gravesend on his debut. He became the first Hammer to score a hat-trick in the FA Cup, a feat he achieved against Clapton in December 1900. Billy spent three seasons at the Memorial Grounds where he was top goalscorer in each campaign.

In 1904 he signed for Manchester United and in his initial season in Division Two he became joint top goalscorer with 11 goals. In his two seasons with the Lancashire club he scored 14 goals in 37 appearances. Following short spells at Celtic and Leyton, Billy returned to West Ham in 1905, where he spent a further four seasons. He retired in 1909 after scoring 68 goals during his 179 appearances for West Ham.

Southern League - Division One Final Table 1900-01

	P	HOME					AWAY					Pts
	P	W	D	L	F	A	W	D	L	F	A	Pts
Southampton	28	13	1	0	44	12	5	4	5	14	14	41
Bristol City	28	12	2	0	40	6	5	3	6	14	21	39
Portsmouth	28	12	2	0	33	6	5	2	7	23	26	38
Millwall Athletic	28	11	1	2	36	10	6	1	7	19	22	36
Tottenham Hotspur	28	12	1	1	35	8	4	3	7	20	25	36
West Ham United	**28**	**10**	**2**	**2**	**28**	**10**	**4**	**3**	**7**	**12**	**18**	**33**
Bristol Rovers	28	10	3	1	29	8	4	1	9	17	27	32
Queens Park Rangers	28	9	1	4	18	17	2	3	9	15	31	26
Reading	28	7	2	5	16	10	1	6	7	8	15	24
Luton Town	28	9	1	4	32	20	2	1	11	11	29	24
Kettering Town	28	7	4	3	21	12	0	5	9	12	34	23
New Brompton	28	5	4	5	20	19	2	1	11	14	32	19
Gravesend United*	28	5	5	4	23	27	1	2	11	9	58	19
Watford	28	6	3	5	17	16	0	1	13	7	36	16
Swindon Town	28	3	6	5	15	18	0	2	12	4	29	14
Chatham*	10	0	0	0	0	0	0	0	0	0	0	0

*Resigned

Season **1900-01** Southern League - Division One
Match Details

Manager **Committee Responsible For Team Selection**   Final League Position **6/16**

	Date		Competition	Venue	Opponents	Results		Attendance	Scorers
1	Sep 1	Sat	SL Div 1	H	Gravesend United	W	7-0	2,000	Grassam 4, Reid 2, Hunt
2	Sep 8	Sat	SL Div 1	A	Millwall Athletic	L	1-3	10,000	Reid
3	Sep 15	Sat	SL Div 1	H	Southampton	W	2-0	7,500	Reid, Grassam
4	Sep 29	Sat	SL Div 1	H	Bristol City	L	1-2	5,000	Kaye
5	Oct 6	Sat	SL Div 1	A	Swindon Town	W	1-0	2,000	Corbett
6	Oct 13	Sat	SL Div 1	H	Watford	W	2-0	4,000	Corbett, Fenton
7	Oct 20	Sat	SL Div 1	A	Luton Town	L	0-2	4,000	
8	Oct 27	Sat	SL Div 1	A	Tottenham Hotspur	D	0-0	6,000	
9	Nov 3	Sat	FAC 3Q	H	Olympic	W	1-0	3,000	Fenton
10	Nov 10	Sat	SL Div 1	A	Portsmouth	L	2-3	5,000	Reid, Kaye
11	Nov 17	Sat	FAC 4Q	A	New Brompton	D	1-1	1,200	Corbett
12	Nov 21	Wed	FAC 4Q Rep	H	New Brompton	W	4-1	4,000	Kaye 2, Corbett, Hunt
13	Nov 24	Sat	SL Div 1	A	Bristol Rovers	L	0-2	3,000	
14	Dec 1	Sat	SL Div 1	H	Reading	W	1-0	4,000	Ratcliffe
15	Dec 8	Sat	FAC 5Q	H	Clapton	D	1-1	10,000	Kaye
16	Dec 12	Wed	FAC 5Q Rep	A	Clapton	W	3-2	5,000	Grassam 3
17	Dec 15	Sat	SL Div 1	A	Gravesend United	D	0-0	1,000	
18	Dec 29	Sat	SL Div 1	A	Southampton	L	2-3	4,000	Hunt, Fenton
19	Jan 5	Sat	FAC Sup	H	Liverpool	L	0-1	6,000	
20	Jan 12	Sat	SL Div 1	A	Bristol City	L	0-1	2,500	
21	Jan 19	Sat	SL Div 1	H	Swindon Town	W	3-1	4,000	Corbett 2, Grassam
22	Jan 26	Fri	SL Div 1	A	Watford	W	1-0	2,000	Grassam
23	Feb 9	Sat	SL Div 1	H	Luton Town	W	2-0	1,000	Corbett, Taylor
24	Feb 16	Sat	SL Div 1	H	Tottenham Hotspur	L	1-4	5,500	Grassam
25	Feb 23	Sat	SL Div 1	A	Queens Park Rangers	W	2-0	6,000	Grassam, Taylor
26	Mar 2	Sat	SL Div 1	H	Portsmouth	D	1-1	3,000	McEachrane
27	Mar 9	Sat	SL Div 1	A	New Brompton	D	1-1	2,000	Hunt
28	Mar 16	Sat	SL Div 1	H	Bristol Rovers	W	2-0	4,000	Grassam, Corbett
29	Mar 21	Wed	SL Div 1	H	Millwall Athletic	W	1-0	2,500	Corbett
30	Mar 23	Sat	SL Div 1	A	Kettering Town	W	1-0	1,000	Grassam
31	Mar 30	Sat	SL Div 1	H	Kettering Town	D	1-1	1,000	Taylor
32	Apr 5	Thur	SL Div 1	H	Queens Park Rangers	W	2-1	4,000	Ratcliffe 2
33	Apr 10	Wed	SL Div 1	A	Reading	L	1-3	1,000	Grassam
34	Apr 20	Sat	SL Div 1	H	New Brompton	W	2-0	2,000	Ratcliffe, Taylor

Team Line-Ups

ALLAN Robert	CORBETT Fred	CRAIG Charles	DOVE Charles	FENTON Frederick	GRASSAM William	HUNT Fergus	KAYE Albert	KELLY William	KING Syd	McEACHRANE Roderick	MONTEITH Hughie	MOORE Thomas	NEILL George	PINDER A.	PUDAN Richard	RAISBECK Luke	RATCLIFFE George	REID James	TAYLOR Frank	TRANTER Walter	WALKER Len	
		3	4	11	8	7	10			6	1					5		9		2		1
7		3	4	11	8		10			6		1				5		9		2		2
4		3	5	11	8	7	10			6		1						9		2		3
4	8	3	5	11		7	10			6	1							9		2		4
4	8	3	5	11		7	10		2	6	1							9				5
	8	3	5	11		7	10		2	6		1	4					9				6
4	8	2	5	11		7	10		2	6	1							9				7
4	8	3	5	11		7	10		2	6	1							9				8
7		3	5	11		9	10		2	6	1						4	8				9
4	8	3	5	11		7	10		2	6	1							9				10
4	9	5		11		7	10		3	6	1							8		2		11
	9	5		11		7	10		3	6	1						4	8		2		12
4	8	3		11		7	9	5	2	6	1										10	13
4		3		11	8	7		5	2	6	1						10	9				14
4		3		11	8	7	10	5	2	6	1							9				15
		3	5	11	8	7	10	4	2	6	1							9				16
		3	4	11	8	7	10	5	2	6	1							9				17
		3	4	11		7	10	5	2	6	1						9	8				18
		3	5		8	7	11	4	2	6	1							10	9			19
4					8	7	11	5	2	6	1				3			10	9			20
4	9				8	7		5	2	6	1				3			10		11		21
4	9	3			8	7		5	2	6	1							10		11		22
4	9	3			8	7		5	2	6	1							10		11		23
4	9	3			8	7		5	2	6		1						10		11		24
4	9				8	7		5	2	6	1		3					10		11		25
4	9	3			8	7		5	2	6	1							10		11		26
4	9	3			8	7		5	2	6	1							10		11		27
4	9	3			8	7		5	2	6	1							10		11		28
4	9	3		11	8	7		5	2	6	1							10				29
4	9	3			8	7	11	5	2	6	1							10				30
4	9	3			8	7		5	2	6	1							10		11		31
4	9	3			8	7		5	2	6	1							10		11		32
4	9	2	3		8	7		5		6	1							10		11		33
4	9	2	3		8	7		5		6	1							10		11		34

1901-02
Story of the season

There were new additions to the squad as the second season got underway. **Jimmy Bigden**, a half back, came from Gravesend together with **Bill Linward**, a winger from Doncaster Rovers.

For this campaign the club decided that, in addition to their Southern League fixtures, they would also enter the Western League and London League. The team made a positive start and by the end of September they were leading the Southern League courtesy of four wins and a draw. Included in those games was a victory against Brentford, who were beaten 2–0 with Billy Grassam scoring both goals. Also among the goals was Freddie Corbett with a hat-trick against Wellingborough in a 4–2 win. There were four goals scored against both Northampton and Luton but what followed next was a disappointing run of six defeats with only one goal scored. Due to an administrative error,

Appearances & Goals 1901-02

	League		FA Cup		Total	
	Starts	Goals	Starts	Goals	Starts	Goals
ALLAN Robert	18	1	1	0	19	1
AMBLER Charlie	1	0	1	0	2	0
BIGDEN James	28	0	0	0	28	0
CORBETT Fred	12	6	0	0	12	6
CRAIG Charles	28	0	1	0	29	0
FAIR Aubrey	0	0	1	0	1	0
GRASSAM William	29	10	1	0	30	10
HITCHENS J.	1	0	1	0	2	0
HUNT Fergus	15	6	0	0	15	6
JENKINSON William	19	2	0	0	19	2
JONES William	15	0	0	0	15	0
KELLY William	12	0	0	0	12	0
KING Syd	28	0	1	0	29	0
KYLE Peter	1	0	2	0	3	0
LINWARD William	30	3	1	1	31	4
McDONALD Alex	4	2	0	0	4	2
McEACHRANE Roderick	25	4	1	0	26	4
McGEORGE Robert	0	0	2	0	2	0
MONTEITH Hughie	29	0	1	0	30	0
PINDER A.	0	0	1	0	1	0
PUDAN Richard	5	0	2	0	7	0
RATCLIFFE Geroge	24	10	1	0	25	10
TAYLOR Frank	0	0	1	1	1	1
WALLACE James	1	0	1	0	2	0
WARD Tommy	0	0	1	0	1	0
YENSON William	5	0	1	0	6	0
own goal		1				1
Totals	**330**	**45**	**22**	**2**	**352**	**47**

the team had to fulfil an FA Cup tie against Leyton on the same day as they were due to play Tottenham in a league match. To resolve this, the reserve team were sent to Leyton, where they won 1–0, and the first team entertained Tottenham. Before a crowd of 17,000 the Hammers lost 1–0 to their London rivals.

A home tie in the FA Cup followed against local side Grays United, ending in a giant-killing as the village team won 2–1. The side was inconsistent – during December and January there was a run of three games without a win followed by three straight victories. However, this all changed as the team remained unbeaten during the last two months of the campaign. Fergus Hunt scored twice against Luton and got two more in the 4–0 defeat of Queens Park Rangers. Fellow striker George Ratcliffe also hit form as he scored nine goals in the last ten games including two against both Watford and Queens Park Rangers. There was an excellent 2–1 victory at Tottenham, where goalkeeper Hugh Monteith was the star performer. The backbone of the side had been four Scots: forward Billy Grassam, half-back Rod McEachrane, full-back Charlie Craig and goalkeeper Hugh Monteith. It had been a good campaign with the team finishing in fourth position in the Southern League but off the field the club struggled with their finances.

Southern League - Division One Final Table 1901-02

		HOME					AWAY					
	P	W	D	L	F	A	W	D	L	F	A	Pts
Portsmouth	30	11	4	0	35	5	9	3	3	32	19	47
Tottenham Hotspur	30	11	2	2	42	11	7	4	4	19	11	42
Southampton	30	12	2	1	54	10	6	4	5	17	18	42
West Ham United	30	10	2	3	27	13	7	4	4	18	15	40
Reading	30	10	4	1	38	9	6	3	6	19	15	39
Millwall Athletic	30	9	3	3	33	13	4	3	8	13	18	32
Luton Town	30	8	5	2	16	10	3	5	7	15	26	32
Kettering Town	30	9	4	2	31	12	3	1	11	13	27	29
Bristol Rovers	30	11	1	3	37	10	1	4	10	6	29	29
New Brompton	30	10	2	3	27	8	0	5	10	12	30	27
Northampton Town	30	7	4	4	40	28	4	1	10	13	37	27
Queens Park Rangers	30	7	4	4	22	16	2	2	11	12	39	24
Watford	30	7	2	6	21	19	2	2	11	15	39	22
Wellingborough Town	30	8	2	5	23	18	1	1	13	11	54	21
Brentford	30	7	2	6	23	21	0	4	11	11	40	20
Swindon Town	30	2	3	10	13	27	0	0	15	4	65	7

WILLIAM JONES

A capable defender who was born in the small Rhondda mining village of Penrhiwceiber, Jones started his football career with Aberdare Athletic in 1898 playing in the Welsh League.

In 1901 he was selected for Wales and played in internationals against Scotland and England. That same year, he was transferred to Kettering in the Southern League. Bill never settled at Kettering and after nine appearances he joined West Ham in 1901; he made his debut in December in a 2–1 home win against Swindon Town. He became a regular in the side and his good form saw him gain further international caps in March 1902 when again he played against England and Scotland. Bill therefore had the honour of being the first West Ham player to be capped by his country. After 15 games for the Hammers he returned to Wales to play for Aberamen, who he helped reach the final of the Welsh Cup. In 1904 he left to join Rogerstone in the South Wales League where he played for two seasons before retiring. During World War One, Bill was a member of the Royal Welsh Fusiliers. In May 1918 he was killed in action in Macedonia and was buried in the Doiran military cemetery in the north of Greece.

Season **1901-02** Southern League - Division One
Match Details

Manager **Committee Responsible For Team Selection**   Final League Position **4/16**

	Date		Competition	Venue	Opponents	Results		Attendance	Scorers
1	Sep 7	Sat	SL Div 1	A	Bristol Rovers	W	2-0	5,000	Corbett, Grassam
2	Sep 14	Sat	SL Div 1	H	Brentford	W	2-0	4,500	Grassam 2
3	Sep 21	Sat	SL Div 1	A	New Brompton	D	0-0	4,000	
4	Sep 28	Sat	SL Div 1	H	Kettering Town	W	1-0	6,000	Grassam
5	Sep 30	Mon	SL Div 1	H	Wellingborough Town	W	4-2	2,000	Corbett 3, Grassam
6	Oct 5	Sat	SL Div 1	A	Northampton Town	W	4-3	2,000	Grassam 2, McEachrane, Bennett (og)
7	Oct 12	Sat	SL Div 1	H	Luton Town	W	4-1	6,000	Corbett 2, Linward, Ratcliffe
8	Oct 19	Sat	SL Div 1	A	Watford	D	0-0	4,000	
9	Oct 26	Sat	SL Div 1	H	Millwall Athletic	L	0-2	9,000	
10	Nov 2	Sat	SL Div 1	H	Tottenham Hotspur	L	0-1	17,000	
11	Nov 2	Sat	FAC 3Q	A	Leyton	W	1-0	2,000	Taylor
12	Nov 9	Sat	SL Div 1	A	Queens Park Rangers	L	1-2	4,000	Linward
13	Nov 16	Sat	FAC 4Q	H	Grays United	L	1-2	2,000	Linward
14	Nov 23	Sat	SL Div 1	A	Reading	L	0-3	5,000	
15	Dec 7	Sat	SL Div 1	A	Southampton	L	0-4	4,000	
16	Dec 14	Sat	SL Div 1	H	Swindon Town	W	2-1	2,000	Linward, McEachrane
17	Dec 21	Sat	SL Div 1	H	Bristol Rovers	W	2-0	2,000	McDonald 2
18	Dec 27	Fri	SL Div 1	A	Wellingborough Town	W	2-0	2,500	Allan, McEachrane
19	Jan 4	Sat	SL Div 1	H	New Brompton	D	0-0	2,000	
20	Jan 11	Sat	SL Div 1	A	Kettering Town	L	0-1	2,000	
21	Jan 18	Sat	SL Div 1	H	Northampton Town	L	0-1	5,000	
22	Jan 25	Sat	SL Div 1	A	Luton Town	W	3-0	5,000	Hunt 2, Grassam
23	Feb 1	Sat	SL Div 1	H	Watford	W	3-2	2,000	Ratcliffe 2, Grassam
24	Feb 8	Sat	SL Div 1	A	Millwall Athletic	D	1-1	3,000	Ratcliffe
25	Feb 15	Sat	SL Div 1	A	Tottenham Hotspur	W	2-1	8,000	Jenkinson, McEachrane
26	Feb 22	Sat	SL Div 1	H	Queens Park Rangers	W	4-0	4,000	Hunt 2 Ratcliffe 2
27	Mar 3	Mon	SL Div 1	A	Brentford	W	2-0	500	Hunt, Jenkinson
28	Mar 8	Sat	SL Div 1	H	Reading	W	2-1	6,000	Hunt, Ratcliffe
29	Mar 15	Sat	SL Div 1	A	Portsmouth	D	0-0	6,000	
30	Mar 22	Sat	SL Div 1	H	Southampton	W	2-1	7,000	Grassam, Ratcliffe
31	Mar 29	Sat	SL Div 1	A	Swindon Town	W	1-0	1,000	Ratcliffe
32	Apr 12	Sat	SL Div 1	H	Portsmouth	D	1-1	6,000	Ratcliffe

Team Line-Ups

ALLAN Robert	AMBLER Charlie	BIGDEN James	CORBETT Fred	CRAIG Charles	FAIR Aubrey	GRASSAM William	HITCHENS J.	HUNT Fergus	JENKINSON William	JONES William	KELLY William	KING Syd	KYLE Peter	LINWARD William	McDONALD Alex	McEACHRANE Roderick	McGEORGE Robert	MONTEITH Hughie	PINDER A.	PUDAN Richard	RATCLIFFE Geroge	TAYLOR Frank	WALLACE James	WARD Tommy	YENSON William	
7		4	9	3		8					5	2		11	6			1			10					1
7		4	9	3		8					5	2		11	6			1			10					2
7		4	9	3		8					5	2		11	6			1			10					3
7		4	9	3		8					5	2		11	6			1			10					4
7		4	9	3		8					5	2		11	6			1			10					5
7		4	9	3		8					5	2		11	6			1			10					6
7		4	9	3		8					5	2		11	6			1			10					7
7		5	9	3		8	10					2		11	6			1						4		8
7		4	9	3		8			10		5	2		11	6			1								9
		4	9	3		8		7			5	2		11	6			1			10					10
7	1				2	10							9				4		6	3	11	8		5		11
4	1		7	3		8					5	2	9	11	6						10					12
			5			8						2	9	11	6		4	1		3	10			7		13
				3		7			9		5	2		11	6			1			10		8	4		14
7		4	9	3		8			6		5			11				1		2	10					15
7		4				8			9	5	2			11	6			1		3	10					16
7		4		3		8			10	5		2		11	9	6		1								17
7		4		3		8		9	10	5		2		11		6		1								18
7		4		3		8		9	6	5		2		11	10			1								19
4	6			3		8		7	10	5		2		11	9			1								20
7		4		3		8				5				11	9	6		1		2	10					21
		4		3		7		9	10	5		2		11				1		6	8					22
		4		3		7		9	10	5		2		11				1		6	8					23
		4		3		7		9	10	5		2		11	6			1			8					24
		4		3		7		9	10	5		2		11	6			1			8					25
		4		3		7		9	10	5		2		11	6			1			8					26
		4		3		7		9	10			2		11	6			1			8				5	27
		4		3		7		9	10	5		2		11	6			1			8					28
7		4		3				9	10			2		11	6			1			8				5	29
		4		3		7		9	10	5		2		11	6			1			8					30
		4				7		9	10	5		2		11	6			1			8			3		31
		4		3		7		9	10	5		2		11	6			1			8					32

1902-03
Story of the season

There was an exodus of senior players as the season began, which upset the fans. Key players such as Charlie Craig, Bill Jones, Roddy McEachrane and Fergus Hunt left for pastures new. Among the **new recruits** were wing-half Joe Blythe, centre-half Tommy McAteer, full-back George Eccles and winger Billy Barnes.

The opening game of the season saw West Ham draw 1–1 with Reading at home and this was followed up with a 0–0 draw at Queens Park Rangers. A visit to Wellingborough finished with the Hammers being beaten 5–1. With no victories on the board there were complaints that the new players were not as good as those who had left.

The team responded and wins followed over Watford (3–1) and Brentford (3–0) with Billy Grassam scoring twice in both games. However, the good form did not last; visitors Millwall won 3–0 and a week later the Hammers were knocked out of the FA Cup with Lincoln City winning 2–0 at Sincil Bank. Worse was to follow with a crushing 6–0 defeat at Reading in early December. The Christmas fixtures

Appearances & Goals 1902-03

	League		FA Cup		Total	
	Starts	Goals	Starts	Goals	Starts	Goals
ALLAN Robert	10	1	1	0	11	0
BARNES William	27	4	1	0	28	4
BIGDEN James	30	2	1	0	31	2
BIGGAR William	8	0	0	0	8	0
BLYTHE Joe	29	0	1	0	30	0
BUSH Robert	2	1	0	0	2	1
CAMPBELL John	18	1	0	0	18	1
DAVIDSON Alexander	9	2	0	0	9	2
DOW James	13	0	1	0	14	0
ECCLES George	25	0	1	0	26	0
EVANS Roger	1	0	0	0	1	0
FAIR Aubrey	12	0	0	0	12	0
FARRELL John	20	3	1	0	21	3
GRASSAM William	29	19	1	0	30	19
GRIFFITHS Frederick	22	0	1	0	23	0
KELLY William	2	0	1	0	3	0
KING Syd	9	0	0	0	9	0
LINWARD William	10	0	1	0	11	0
McATEER Tommy	13	0	0	0	13	0
MIECZNIKOWSKI W	3	0	0	0	3	0
PARKINSON Harry	2	0	0	0	2	0
SUGDEN Sydney	1	0	0	0	1	0
WALLACE James	16	3	0	0	16	3
YENSON William	19	0	0	0	19	0
Totals	**330**	**36**	**11**	**0**	**341**	**35**

did not bring any cheer with a 2–1 home defeat to Southampton on Christmas Day and a 2–0 loss at Portsmouth on Boxing Day. However, the supporters morale soon changed as the team went on to record five successive home wins, with Billy Grassam scoring five times. At home West Ham remained unbeaten for the rest of the season, which gave an upsurge in the attendances resulting in a crowd of 10,000 for the final home game against Portsmouth. The remaining three games of the season were all away, which resulted in a 6–0 defeat at Reading, a 4–0 defeat at Luton and a final game 2–1 loss at rivals Millwall. It meant a final placing of 10th but the 49 goals conceded was one of the worst in the league.

GEORGE ECCLES

George was a sturdy and reliable full-back who served all his clubs with distinction.

He began his career in local football before joining Burslem Port Vale in 1893, where he made 50 league appearances in the Second Division. After breaking a collarbone in February 1896, he later joined Wolverhampton Wanderers and in two seasons played in 36 First Division league games. A move to Everton followed, which saw George play in a further 56 league games for the Lancashire side. He came south in 1902 to play for West Ham, making his debut in September 1902 in the home game with Reading. He played at the Memorial Grounds for two seasons, only missed five league games and was everpresent in season 1903/04. After playing in 59 league games and 5 FA Cup ties George joined Bolton Wanderers in 1904 where he played in six league games before retiring as a player and being appointed as Bolton trainer. He served them for many years and was granted a benefit match in 1921 when Bolton played an International XI. George died in December 1945.

Southern League - Division One Final Table 1902-03

		HOME					AWAY					
	P	W	D	L	F	A	W	D	L	F	A	Pts
Southampton	30	12	2	1	53	7	8	6	1	30	13	48
Reading	30	12	2	1	47	14	7	5	3	25	16	45
Portsmouth	30	11	2	2	36	13	6	5	4	33	19	41
Tottenham Hotspur	30	10	5	0	34	9	4	2	9	13	3	22
Bristol Rovers	30	9	5	1	33	12	4	3	8	13	22	34
New Brompton	30	9	4	2	24	9	2	7	6	13	26	33
Millwall Athletic	30	9	2	4	33	16	5	1	9	19	21	31
Northampton Town	30	7	3	5	23	19	5	3	7	16	29	30
Queens Park Rangers	30	8	3	4	25	16	3	3	9	9	26	28
West Ham United	**30**	**8**	**5**	**2**	**25**	**14**	**1**	**5**	**9**	**10**	**35**	**28**
Luton Town	30	8	3	4	28	14	2	4	9	15	30	27
Swindon Town	30	8	5	2	24	13	2	2	11	14	33	27
Kettering Town	30	5	8	2	19	12	3	3	9	14	28	27
Wellingborough Town	30	9	2	4	27	15	2	1	12	9	41	25
Watford	30	5	1	9	22	33	1	3	11	13	54	16
Brentford	30	2	1	12	10	36	0	0	15	6	48	5

Season **1902-03** Southern League - Division One
Match Details

Manager **Syd King**   Final League Position **10/16**

	Date		Competition	Venue	Opponents	Results		Attendance	Scorers
1	Sep 6	Sat	SL Div 1	H	Reading	D	1-1	7,000	Barnes
2	Sep 13	Sat	SL Div 1	A	Queens Park Rangers	D	0-0	7,000	
3	Sep 27	Sat	SL Div 1	A	Wellingborough Town	L	1-5	4,000	Grassam
4	Oct 4	Sat	SL Div 1	H	Bristol Rovers	W	1-0	6,500	Grassam
5	Oct 11	Sat	SL Div 1	A	Northampton Town	L	0-2	3,000	
6	Oct 18	Sat	SL Div 1	H	Watford	W	3-1	4,000	Grassam 2, Barnes
7	Oct 25	Sat	SL Div 1	A	Brentford	W	3-0	3,000	Grassam 2, Bigden
8	Nov 1	Sat	SL Div 1	A	Tottenham Hotspur	D	1-1	7,000	Grassam
9	Nov 8	Sat	SL Div 1	H	Millwall	L	0-3	10,000	
10	Dec 6	Sat	SL Div 1	H	Kettering Town	D	1-1	2,500	Grassam
11	Dec 13	Sat	FAC IR	A	Lincoln City	L	0-2	3,000	
12	Dec 20	Sat	SL Div 1	A	Reading	L	0-6	4,000	
13	Dec 25	Thur	SL Div 1	H	Southampton	L	1-2	6,000	Grassam
14	Dec 26	Fri	SL Div 1	A	Portsmouth	L	0-2	18,000	
15	Dec 27	Sat	SL Div 1	H	Queens Park Rangers	W	2-0	2,500	Barnes, Grassam
16	Jan 10	Sat	SL Div 1	H	Wellingborough Town	W	3-0	4,000	Barnes, Davidson, Grassam
17	Jan 17	Sat	SL Div 1	A	Bristol Rovers	D	1-1	4,000	Wallace
18	Jan 24	Sat	SL Div 1	H	Northampton Town	W	3-2	4,000	Davidson, Grassam, Wallace
19	Jan 31	Sat	SL Div 1	A	Watford	L	1-2	5,000	Campbell
20	Feb 7	Sat	SL Div 1	H	Brentford	W	2-0	3,000	Grassam 2
21	Feb 14	Sat	SL Div 1	H	Tottenham Hotspur	W	1-0	8,000	Wallace
22	Mar 7	Sat	SL Div 1	A	New Brompton	L	0-2	7,000	
23	Mar 14	Sat	SL Div 1	H	Swindon Town	D	1-1	4,000	Farrell
24	Mar 23	Mon	SL Div 1	H	New Brompton	D	1-1	1,000	Farrell
25	Mar 28	Sat	SL Div 1	H	Luton Town	W	4-1	800	Grassam 2, Bigden, Farrell
26	Apr 4	Sat	SL Div 1	A	Swindon Town	D	1-1	2,500	Grassam
27	Apr 10	Fri	SL Div 1	H	Portsmouth	D	1-1	10,000	Grassam
28	Apr 13	Mon	SL Div 1	A	Southampton	L	0-6	6,000	
29	Apr 15	Wed	SL Div 1	A	Kettering Town	D	1-1	2,000	Bush
30	Apr 18	Sat	SL Div 1	A	Luton Town	L	0-4	2,000	
31	Apr 25	Sat	SL Div 1	A	Millwall	L	1-2	3,000	Grassam

Team Line-Ups

ALLAN Robert	BARNES William	BIGDEN James	BIGGAR William	BLYTHE Joe	BUSH Robert	CAMPBELL John	DAVIDSON Alexander	DOW James	ECCLES George	EVANS Roger	FAIR Aubrey	FARRELL John	GRASSAM William	GRIFFITHS Frederick	KELLY William	KING Syd	LINWARD William	McATEER Tommy	MIECZNIKOWSKI W	PARKINSON Harry	SUGDEN Sydney	WALLACE James	YENSON William	
	10	4	1	6		7		3	2			9	8				11	5						1
	10	4	1	6		7		3	2			9	8				11	5						2
7	10	4	1	6				3	2			9	8				11	5						3
7	10	4		6					3			9	8	1		2	11	5						4
7	10	4		6					3			9	8	1		2	11	5						5
	10	4		6		7		2	3				8	1			11	5			9			6
	10			6		7		2	3			9	8	1	4		11	5						7
	10	4		6		7		2	3			9	8	1			11	5						8
	10	4		6		7		2	3			9	8	1			11	5						9
7	10	4		6	8					3			9	1		2	11	5						10
7	10	4		6				2	3			9	8	1	5		11							11
	11	8	1	6		10			3			9	7			2	5						4	12
	11	4		6		7	9		3			10	8	1		2							5	13
	11	4		6		7	9		3			10	8	1		2							5	14
	11	4		6		7	10		3			9	8	1									5	15
	11	4		6		7	9		3		2		8	1								10	5	16
	11	4		6		7	9		3				8	1		2						10	5	17
	11	4		6		7	9		3		2		8	1								10	5	18
	11	4		6		7	9		3		2		8	1								10	5	19
	11	4		6		7	9	3			2		8	1								10	5	20
	11	4		6		7	9	3			2		8	1								10	5	21
	11	4		6					3		2	9	8	1						7		10	5	22
7	11	4		6					3		2	9	8	1								10	5	23
7	11	4		6				2	3			8	9	1								10	5	24
7	11	4		6					3		2	8	9									10	5	25
7	11	4	1	6					2			9	8						3			10	5	26
7	11	4		6					3		2	8	9	1								10	5	27
		4	1	6		11		3	2			8	9								7	10	5	28
		4	1		7							8	9		5	3			11	6		10	2	29
	11	4		6	8				2	9	3			1				5	7			10		30
7	11	8	1	6				3	2				9							4		10	5	31

1903-04
Story of the season

During the close season there had been many changes to the playing staff as **eight players** had left. As replacements, **the club signed** goalkeeper Charlie Cotton, inside-forward Herbert Lyon, wing-half Tommy Allison, centre-half Ernie Watts, outside-right Bill Kirby and centre-forward Charlie Satterthwaite.

The opening game at Millwall saw the Hammers beaten 4–2. This was followed by two home victories against Kettering (4–1) and Queens Park Rangers (1–0). There were no wins in the next eight league games but in between those there had been victories in the FA Cup. In the third qualifying round Brighton were beaten 4–0 with two goals from Herbert Lyon. The same player scored another brace in the next round with a 3–0 victory against Clapton. Chatham were the opponents in the fifth qualifying round, where Charlie Satterthwaite scored a hat-trick in a 5–0 win. The FA Cup run came to an end before an attendance of 12,000 against Fulham. It was a poor performance as the visitors won 1–0.

The Christmas period brought two welcome home league wins. League leaders Southampton were beaten 2–1 and revenge for the Cup defeat was sweet as the Hammers beat

Appearances & Goals 1903-04

	League		FA Cup		Total	
	Starts	Goals	Starts	Goals	Starts	Goals
ALLISON Tommy	28	2	4	0	32	2
BARNES William	22	1	4	0	26	1
BIGDEN James	33	1	4	0	37	1
BIRNIE Alexander	1	0	1	0	2	0
BLYTHE Joe	23	0	4	0	27	0
BRIDGEMAN William	19	4	0	0	19	4
BUTCHART James	3	0	0	0	3	0
CHURCH William	2	0	0	0	2	0
COTTON Charles	8	0	1	0	9	0
EARL Arthur	1	0	0	0	1	0
ECCLES George	34	0	4	0	38	0
FAIR Aubrey	7	1	0	0	7	1
GRIFFITHS Frederick	26	0	3	0	29	0
HILSDON Jack	1	0	0	0	1	0
INGHAM William	2	0	0	0	2	0
JARVIS Len	2	0	0	0	2	0
KIRBY William	33	10	3	1	36	11
LYON Herbert	29	4	4	5	33	9
MAPLEY Percy	13	0	4	0	17	0
MERCER Frederick	7	1	0	0	7	1
OAKES William	14	0	0	0	14	0
SATTERWAITE Charles	32	13	4	5	36	18
THOMPSON Alec	9	1	0	0	9	1
WATTS Ernest	25	1	4	1	29	2
Totals	**374**	**39**	**44**	**12**	**418**	**51**

Fulham 2–0. The next victory, though, didn't come until the end of January when visitors Wellingborough lost 4–1. The gate was only 250 and was to be the club's lowest ever Southern League attendance. The team were again inconsistent – a 0–4 reverse at Bristol Rovers was followed by a 5–0 win against Brighton, where Satterthwaite scored four. In March there was a poor run of five consecutive league defeats without scoring. It was the away form that was letting the Hammers down with one draw and eleven defeats.

The West Ham directors were at this time looking to relocate the club to a new ground. They met with officials of the Boleyn Castle FC and it was decided that the two clubs would merge and West Ham would move to the Boleyn Ground at Upton Park, commencing the following season. On Good Friday there was a 3–0 home triumph over Portsmouth but this was followed by five consecutive away fixtures. Facing relegation, the team rallied and fought out two wins and two draws with only one defeat. The final home game – and the last at the Memorial Grounds – was a disappointment. Swindon Town were the visitors and won with a solitary goal, which left West Ham finishing in 12th position in the league.

Southern League - Division One
Final Table 1903-04

	P	W	D	L	F	A	W	D	L	F	A	Pts
			HOME						AWAY			
Southampton	34	12	3	2	43	15	10	3	4	32	15	50
Tottenham Hotspur	34	10	5	2	34	19	6	6	5	20	18	43
Bristol Rovers	34	11	4	2	38	12	6	4	7	26	30	42
Portsmouth	34	11	4	2	24	11	6	4	7	17	27	42
Queens Park Rangers	34	13	3	1	34	12	2	8	7	19	25	41
Reading	34	8	6	3	27	15	6	7	4	21	20	41
Millwall	34	10	2	5	41	20	6	6	5	23	22	40
Luton Town	34	12	4	1	23	9	2	8	7	15	24	40
Plymouth Argyle	34	8	5	4	27	16	5	5	7	17	18	36
Swindon Town	34	7	7	3	18	14	3	4	10	12	28	31
Fulham	34	7	6	4	23	15	2	6	9	11	21	30
West Ham United	34	8	4	5	26	14	2	3	12	13	30	27
Brentford	34	8	4	5	25	18	1	5	11	9	30	27
Wellingborough Town	34	7	4	6	34	25	4	1	12	10	38	27
Northampton Town	34	8	4	5	22	20	2	3	12	14	40	27
New Brompton	34	4	10	3	18	15	2	3	12	8	28	25
Brighton & Hove Albion	34	5	6	6	27	29	1	6	10	19	40	24
Kettering Town*	34	6	4	7	23	23	0	3	14	16	53	19

* Resigned

CHARLES SATTERTHWAITE

The inside-forward began his career at Bury in 1895, playing in four league games before joining Burton Swifts in 1897.

He played eight games in two seasons at Burton before transferring to Liverpool in 1899. With the Merseysiders he played for three campaigns, scoring 12 goals in his 46 appearances. Coming south in 1902 he enjoyed a short spell at New Brompton before joining West Ham in 1903. He was an immediate success, scoring on his debut against Millwall and finishing the season as the Hammers' top scorer with 18 goals. His best achievements were his four goals against Brighton in the league and a hat-trick against Chatham in the FA Cup. In 1904 the lure of First Division football with newly promoted Woolwich Arsenal prompted Charlie to leave West Ham. With the Gunners he scored their first goal in the First Division and was leading scorer in two of his first three seasons. He scored 48 goals in his 141 total appearances before retiring in 1910. He later became a publican in Workington and died in May 1948 aged 70.

Season **1903-04** Southern League - Division One
Match Details

Manager **Syd King**   Final League Position **12/18**

	Date		Competition	Venue	Opponents	Results		Attendance	Scorers
1	Sep 5	Sat	SL Div 1	A	Millwall	L	2-4	10,000	Kirby, Satterthwaite
2	Sep 7	Mon	SL Div 1	H	Kettering Town	W	4-1	1,000	Lyon 2, Allison, Bigden
3	Sep 12	Sat	SL Div 1	H	Queens Park Rangers	W	1-0	6,000	Satterthwaite
4	Sep 19	Sat	SL Div 1	A	Plymouth Argyle	L	0-2	5,000	
5	Sep 24	Thur	SL Div 1	H	Luton Town	D	0-0	3,000	
6	Sep 26	Sat	SL Div 1	H	Reading	D	1-1	10,000	Satterthwaite
7	Oct 10	Sat	SL Div 1	H	Bristol Rovers	L	1-4	5,000	Watts
8	Oct 17	Sat	SL Div 1	A	Brighton & Hove Albion	L	2-3	4,000	Fair, Satterthwaite
9	Oct 31	Sat	FAC Q3	H	Brighton & Hove Albion	W	4-0	5,000	Lyon 2, Satterthwaite, Watts
10	Nov 7	Sat	SL Div 1	H	Brentford	L	0-1	2,000	
11	Nov 14	Sat	FAC Q4	A	Clapton	W	3-0	4500	Lyon 2, Satterthwaite
12	Nov 21	Sat	SL Div 1	A	Tottenham Hotspur	L	1-2	8,000	Kirby
13	Nov 28	Sat	FAC Q5	A	Chatham	W	5-0	5,000	Satterthwaite 3, Kirby, Lyon
14	Dec 5	Sat	SL Div 1	A	New Brompton	D	0-0	4,000	
15	Dec 12	Sat	FAC IR	H	Fulham	L	0-1	12,000	
16	Dec 25	Fri	SL Div 1	H	Southampton	W	2-1	10,000	Kirby, Satterthwaite
17	Dec 26	Sat	SL Div 1	A	Portsmouth	L	1-2	14,000	Barnes
18	Dec 28	Mon	SL Div 1	H	Fulham	W	2-0	2,000	Kirby, Satterthwaite
19	Jan 2	Sat	SL Div 1	H	Millwall	L	0-1	10,000	
20	Jan 9	Sat	SL Div 1	A	Queens Park Rangers	L	1-2	7,000	Kirby
21	Jan 16	Sat	SL Div 1	H	Plymouth Argyle	D	1-1	8,000	Kirby
22	Jan 30	Sat	SL Div 1	H	Wellingborough Town	W	4-1	250	Kirby 2, Thompson, Satterthwaite
23	Feb 6	Sat	SL Div 1	A	Bristol Rovers	L	0-4	2,000	
24	Feb 13	Sat	SL Div 1	H	Brighton & Hove Albion	W	5-0	3,000	Satterthwaite 4, Lyon
25	Feb 27	Sat	SL Div 1	H	Northampton Town	W	2-0	4,000	Kirby, Lyon
26	Mar 2	Wed	SL Div 1	A	Reading	L	0-1	1,000	
27	Mar 5	Sat	SL Div 1	A	Brentford	L	0-2	4,000	
28	Mar 12	Sat	SL Div 1	A	Swindon Town	L	0-1	3,000	
29	Mar 19	Sat	SL Div 1	H	Tottenham Hotspur	L	0-2	9,500	
30	Mar 26	Sat	SL Div 1	A	Luton Town	L	0-1	5,000	
31	Apr 1	Fri	SL Div 1	H	Portsmouth	W	3-0	8,000	Satterthwaite 2, Bridgeman
32	Apr 2	Sat	SL Div 1	H	New Brompton	D	0-0	5,000	
33	Apr 4	Mon	SL Div 1	A	Southampton	D	1-1	10,000	Bridgeman
34	Apr 7	Thur	SL Div 1	A	Northampton Town	W	3-1	1,000	Allison, Kirby, Mercer
35	Apr 9	Sat	SL Div 1	A	Kettering Town	W	1-0	1,000	Bridgeman
36	Apr 20	Wed	SL Div 1	A	Wellingborough Town	L	0-3	3,000	
37	Apr 23	Sat	SL Div 1	A	Fulham	D	1-1	4,000	Bridgeman
38	Apr 30	Sat	SL Div 1	H	Swindon Town	L	0-1	4,000	

Team Line-Ups

ALLISON Tommy	BARNES William	BIGDEN James	BIRNIE Alexander	BLYTHE Joe	BRIDGEMAN William	BUTCHART James	CHURCH William	COTTON Charles	EARL Arthur	ECCLES George	FAIR Aubrey	GRIFFITHS Frederick	HILSDON Jack	INGHAM William	JARVIS Len	KIRBY William	LYON Herbert	MAPLEY Percy	MERCER Frederick	OAKES William	SATTERWAITE Charles	THOMPSON Alec	WATTS Ernest	
	11	4		6				1		3	2		9			7	8				10		5	1
6	11	4					8	1		3	2					7	9				10		5	2
6	11	4					8	1		3	2					7	9				10		5	3
6	11	4					8	1		3	2					7	9				10		5	4
6	11	4						1		2			8			7	9	3			10		5	5
6	11	4						1		2	3		9			7	8				10		5	6
6	10	4			8			1	11	2						7	9	3					5	7
4	11	8		6				1		2			9			7		3			10		5	8
4	11	8		6				1		2						7	9	3			10		5	9
4	11	5	8	6						2	1					7	9	3			10			10
4	11	8		6						2	1					7	9	3			10		5	11
4	11	8		6						2	1					7	9	3			10		5	12
4	11	8		6						2	1					7	9	3			10		5	13
4	11	8		6						2	1					7	9	3			10		5	14
4	11	8	7	6						2	1						9	3			10		5	15
4	11	8		6	9					2	1					7		3			10		5	16
4	11	8		6	7					2	1					9		3			10		5	17
4	11	8		6	7					2	1					9		3			10		5	18
4		8		6	7					2	1					9		3	11		10		5	19
	11	4		6						2	1					7	8	3			10	9	5	20
	11	4		6						2	1					7	8	3			10	9	5	21
5	11	4		6						2	1					7	8	3			10	9		22
5	11	4		6						2	1					7	8				10	9	3	23
5	11	4		6						2	3	1				7	8				10	9		24
5		4		6	11					2	1					7	8			3	10	9		25
5		4		6	11					2	1					7	8			3	10	9		26
5		4		6	11					2	1					7	8			3	10	9		27
5		4		6	9		11			2	1					7	8			3	10			28
5		4		6	9		11			2	1					7	8			3	10			29
5		4		6	9					2	1					7	8		11	3	10			30
6		4			9					2	1					7	8		11	3	10		5	31
		4			9					2	1				6	7	8		11	3	10		5	32
		4			9					2	1				6	7	8		11	3	10		5	33
6		4			9					2	1					7	8		11	3	10		5	34
6		4			9					2	1					7	8		11	3	10		5	35
4	11			6	9					2	1					7	8			3	10		5	36
	11	4		6	9					2	1					7	8			3	10		5	37
4	11	7		6	9					2	1						8			3		10	5	38

1904-05
Story of the season

All the supporters were looking forward to attending a match at the **new ground**. There was a **covered grandstand** holding 2,000 people on one side of the ground and opposite was a **covered terrace** which could hold 3,000.

After a poor showing the previous season only five players were retained. Among the new recruits were goalkeeper Matt Kingsley, full-backs Tommy Bamlett and Dave Gardner, half-back Frank Piercy and forwards Chris Carrick and Charlie Simmons.

The opening league game was at home to rivals Millwall. The Hammers put on a good performance by winning 3–0 with two goals from Billy Bridgeman and another from Jack Flynn. The improved form continued with only one defeat in the first seven games. Both Luton and Swindon had been beaten 2–0, with Jack Fletcher scoring in both games. Fletcher was the man in form and so it proved when he grabbed a hat-trick in the 4–0 home victory with Wellingborough. After beating Plymouth 2–1 in November the team were in fourth place in the table and looking for a successful campaign. What followed was a disastrous run

Appearances & Goals 1904-05

	League		FA Cup		Total	
	Starts	Goals	Starts	Goals	Starts	Goals
ALLISON Tommy	30	2	1	0	31	2
BAMLETT Herbert	18	0	1	0	19	0
BLACKWOOD John	4	1	0	0	4	1
BRIDGEMAN William	27	11	1	0	28	11
BRUNTON Fred	1	0	0	0	1	0
CARRICK Christopher	18	6	0	0	18	6
COTTON Charles	5	0	0	0	5	0
FAIR Aubrey	9	0	1	0	10	0
FLETCHER Jack	25	7	1	0	26	7
FLYNN Jack	20	3	1	1	21	4
GARDNER David	29	0	0	0	29	0
HAMILTON John	5	0	0	0	5	0
HAMMOND Sidney	10	0	0	0	10	0
HILSDON George	7	4	0	0	7	4
JARVIS Len	22	0	0	0	22	0
KINGSLEY Matthew	29	0	1	0	30	0
McCARTNEY William	28	3	1	0	29	3
MILNES Frederick	2	0	0	0	2	0
PIERCY Frank	33	2	1	0	34	2
RUSSELL John	16	0	1	0	17	0
SIMMONS Charles	34	8	1	0	35	8
SMITH Sidney	2	1	0	0	2	1
Totals	**374**	**48**	**11**	**1**	**385**	**49**

of eight consecutive defeats with only one goal scored. Six of those defeats were by 1–0, which indicated that it was the forwards who were to blame. During that period the Hammers were also knocked out of the FA Cup after a 2–1 defeat to Brighton.

In late January things turned for the better when visitors Luton Town were thrashed 6–2, with Chris Carrick scoring a hat-trick. An improved run gave only one defeat in six games (albeit the defeat was by 3–0 away to bottom of the league Wellingborough). Following a 2–0 home defeat to Reading in early April the team were third from bottom. However, in the remaining five games there were three wins and two draws, resulting in an improved final position of 11th. Off the field there had been success, as the move to the Boleyn Ground had attracted bigger crowds and increased revenue.

Southern League - Division One Final Table 1904-05

		HOME					AWAY					
	P	W	D	L	F	A	W	D	L	F	A	Pts
Bristol Rovers	34	13	4	0	51	11	7	4	6	23	25	48
Reading	34	13	3	1	36	12	5	4	8	21	26	43
Southampton	34	9	4	4	29	21	9	3	5	25	19	43
Plymouth Argyle	34	14	3	0	38	11	4	2	11	19	28	41
Tottenham	34	10	3	4	34	15	5	5	7	19	19	38
Fulham	34	10	5	2	32	9	4	5	8	14	25	38
Queens Park Rangers	34	10	2	5	36	19	4	6	7	15	27	36
Portsmouth	34	12	1	4	39	19	4	3	10	22	37	36
New Brompton	34	8	7	2	25	13	3	4	10	15	27	33
Watford	34	12	0	5	30	19	3	3	11	14	26	33
West Ham United	**34**	**9**	**3**	**5**	**30**	**15**	**3**	**5**	**9**	**18**	**27**	**32**
Brighton & Hove Albion	34	9	2	6	25	15	4	4	9	19	30	32
Northampton Town	34	8	4	5	26	17	4	4	9	17	37	32
Brentford	34	5	7	5	17	14	5	2	10	16	24	29
Millwall	34	7	6	4	26	17	4	1	12	12	30	29
Swindon Town	34	11	2	4	30	17	1	3	13	11	42	29
Luton Town	34	11	1	5	35	18	1	2	14	10	36	27
Wellingborough Town*	34	4	3	10	16	37	1	0	16	9	70	13

* Resigned

MATTHEW KINGSLEY

Goalkeeper Kingsley began his career in 1895 with the Second Division side, Darwen where he made 70 appearances.

He joined Newcastle United in 1898 and established himself as one of the top goalkeepers in the country. He was selected three times for the Football League and gained one England cap against Wales in 1901. Kingsley spent six seasons with the Tyneside club, playing in a total of 189 games.

Matt joined West Ham in 1904 and made his debut in the first ever match at the Boleyn Ground against Millwall. At Brighton in March, there was an incident which resulted in him being sent off – after serving his suspension he never played for the club again.

After 30 games for West Ham he left to play for Queens Park Rangers, where he played 20 games in season 1905–06. He later had spells with Rochdale and Barrow.

Season **1904-05** Southern League - Division One
Match Details

Manager **Syd King**   Final League Position **11/18**

	Date		Competition	Venue	Opponents	Results		Attendance	Scorers
1	Sep 1	Thur	SL Div 1	H	Millwall	W	3-0	10,000	Bridgeman 2, Flynn
2	Sep 3	Sat	SL Div 1	A	Brentford	D	0-0	7,000	
3	Sep 10	Sat	SL Div 1	H	Queens Park Rangers	L	1-3	14,000	Allison [pen]
4	Sep 17	Sat	SL Div 1	A	Millwall	D	1-1	10,000	Fletcher
5	Sep 24	Sat	SL Div 1	H	Tottenham Hotspur	D	0-0	16,000	
6	Oct 1	Sat	SL Div 1	A	Luton Town	W	2-0	4,000	Bridgeman, Fletcher
7	Oct 8	Sat	SL Div 1	H	Swindon Town	W	2-0	6,000	Fletcher, Flynn
8	Oct 15	Sat	SL Div 1	A	New Brompton	L	0-3	7,000	
9	Oct 22	Sat	SL Div 1	H	Wellingborough Town	W	4-0	5,000	Fletcher 3, Flynn
10	Oct 29	Sat	SL Div 1	A	Southampton	D	2-2	4,000	Bridgeman, McCartney
11	Nov 5	Sat	SL Div 1	H	Fulham	D	0-0	8,000	
12	Nov 19	Sat	SL Div 1	H	Plymouth Argyle	W	2-1	10,000	Simmons 2
13	Nov 26	Sat	SL Div 1	H	Bristol Rovers	L	0-2	7,000	
14	Dec 3	Sat	SL Div 1	A	Reading	L	0-1	5,000	
15	Dec 10	Sat	FAC Q6	H	Brighton & Hove Albion	L	1-2	6,000	Flynn
16	Dec 17	Sat	SL Div 1	A	Northampton Town	L	0-1	4,000	
17	Dec 26	Mon	SL Div 1	A	Portsmouth	L	1-4	16,000	Blackwood
18	Dec 27	Tue	SL Div 1	H	Brighton & Hove Albion	L	0-1	12,000	
19	Dec 31	Sat	SL Div 1	H	Brentford	L	0-1	8,000	
20	Jan 7	Sat	SL Div 1	A	Queens Park Rangers	L	0-1	8,000	
21	Jan 21	Sat	SL Div 1	A	Tottenham Hotspur	L	0-1	12,000	
22	Jan 28	Sat	SL Div 1	H	Luton Town	W	6-2	5,000	Carrick 3, Bridgeman 2, Simmons
23	Feb 4	Sat	SL Div 1	A	Swindon Town	D	3-3	3,000	Bridgeman, Fletcher, Piercy
24	Feb 11	Sat	SL Div 1	H	New Brompton	W	2-0	6,000	Hilsdon, Simmons
25	Feb 18	Sat	SL Div 1	A	Wellingborough Town	L	0-3	1,500	
26	Feb 25	Sat	SL Div 1	H	Southampton	W	2-1	1,500	Hilsdon, McCartney
27	Mar 11	Sat	SL Div 1	H	Watford	W	2-0	3,000	Bridgeman, Carrick
28	Mar 18	Sat	SL Div 1	A	Plymouth Argyle	L	0-2	7,000	
29	Mar 25	Sat	SL Div 1	A	Brighton & Hove Albion	L	1-3	5,000	Bridgeman
30	Apr 1	Sat	SL Div 1	H	Reading	L	0-2	5,000	
31	Apr 8	Sat	SL Div 1	A	Bristol Rovers	D	2-2	5,000	Hilsdon, McCartney [pen]
32	Apr 15	Sat	SL Div 1	H	Northampton Town	W	5-1	7,000	Carrick 2, Simmons 2, Bridgeman
33	Apr 17	Mon	SL Div 1	A	Fulham	W	3-0	1,000	Allison, Hilsdon, Simmons
34	Apr 21	Fri	SL Div 1	H	Portsmouth	D	1-1	6,000	Bridgeman
35	Apr 25	Tue	SL Div 1	A	Watford	W	3-0	1,000	Piercy, Simmons, Smith

Team Line-Ups

ALLISON Tommy	BAMLETT Herbert	BLACKWOOD John	BRIDGEMAN William	BRUNTON Fred	CARRICK Christopher	COTTON Charles	FAIR Aubrey	FLETCHER Jack	FLYNN Jack	GARDNER David	HAMILTON John	HAMMOND Sidney	HILSDON George	JARVIS Len	KINGSLEY Matthew	McCARTNEY William	MILNES Frederick	PIERCY Frank	RUSSELL John	SIMMONS Charles	SMITH Sidney	
4	2		9					8	11	3					1	7		5	6	10		1
4	2		9					8	11	3					1	7		5	6	10		2
4	2		9					8	11	3					1	7		5	6	10		3
4	2		9					8	11	3					1	7		5	6	10		4
4	2		9					8	11	3					1	7		5	6	10		5
4	2		9					8	11	3					1	7		5	6	10		6
4	2		9		7			8	11	3				5	1				6	10		7
4			9		7		2	8	11	3					1			5	6	10		8
4			9					8	11	3					1	7	2	5	6	10		9
4			9					8	11	3					1	7	2	5	6	10		10
	2		9					8	11	3				4	1	7		5	6	10		11
	2		9		10		3		11					4	1	7		5	6	8		12
4	2		9		10		3		11						1	7		5	6	8		13
4	2		9				3	10	11						1	7		5	6	8		14
4	2		9				3	8	11						1	7		5	6	10		15
4	2		9				3	10	11						1	7		5	6	8		16
4	2	9					3	8	11		7			6	1			5		10		17
		9		4			2	8	11	3	7			6	1			5		10		18
4	2	9				1			11	3	8			6		7		5		10		19
4	2	9						8	11	3	7			6	1			5		10		20
4			9	11				8		3		2		6	1	7		5		10		21
4			9	11				8		3		2		6	1	7		5		10		22
4	2		9					8	11	3				6	1	7		5		10		23
4	2			11				8		3			9	6	1	7		5		10		24
4	2			11				8		3			9		1	7		5		10		25
4				11				8		3		2	9	6	1	7		5		10		26
4			9	11				8		3		2		6	1	7		5		10		27
4			9	11				8		3		2		6	1	7		5		10		28
4			9	11			2			3			8	6	1	7		5		10		29
4			9	11				8		3		2		6	1	7		5		10		30
4			9	11						3		2	8	6	1	7		5		10		31
4			9	11	1					3		2	8	6		7		5		10		32
4			9	11	1		2			3			8	6		7		5		10		33
4			9	11	1					3		2		6		7		5		10	8	34
			9	11	1					3	7	2		4				5	6	10	8	35

1905-06
Story of the season

Once again there was an **exodus of players** and in their place arrived full-back Alex McCartney, goalkeeper George Kitchen and forwards Lionel Watson and Fred Blackburn.

The opening game at the Boleyn was against Swindon Town and in a close contest the Hammers won 1–0, the goal being a penalty scored by goalkeeper Kitchen.

Both Brentford and league leaders Plymouth were beaten at home but these were the only victories in the next nine games. By early December the team were third from bottom in the league, but there was an improvement after the purchase of two new forwards. Former player Billy Grassam returned, together with the promising amateur Harry Stapley. They rejuvenated the team, and there were 1–0 home wins against New Brompton, Portsmouth and Millwall. In the first round of the FA Cup West Ham travelled to First Division side Woolwich Arsenal.

Appearances & Goals 1905-06

	League		FA Cup		Total	
	Starts	Goals	Starts	Goals	Starts	Goals
ALLISON Tommy	28	1	2	0	30	1
BLACKBURN Fred	31	5	2	0	33	5
BRIDGEMAN William	26	4	2	1	28	5
BUSH Robert	18	0	1	0	19	0
COTTON Charles	5	0	0	0	5	0
FEATHERSTONE Arthur	17	0	0	0	17	0
FORD William	7	1	0	0	7	1
GARDNER David	34	0	2	0	36	0
GRASSAM William	14	3	0	0	14	3
HAMMOND Sidney	4	0	0	0	4	0
HILSDON George	9	3	2	0	11	3
HINDLE Harry	3	0	0	0	3	0
JACKSON James	24	0	0	0	24	0
JARVIS Len	27	2	2	0	29	2
KITCHEN George	29	3	2	1	31	4
MACKIE Charles	10	3	0	0	10	3
McCARTNEY Alex	6	0	0	0	6	0
MILNES Frederick	0	0	2	0	2	0
PIERCY Frank	24	0	2	0	26	0
STAPLEY Harry	13	9	0	0	13	9
WATSON Lionel	22	6	2	1	24	7
WILKINSON Henry	13	2	1	0	14	2
WINTERHALDER Arthur	6	0	0	0	6	0
WINTERHALDER Herbert	4	0	0	0	4	0
Totals	**374**	**42**	**22**	**3**	**396**	**45**

Goalkeeper George Kitchen again scored from the penalty spot and the game ended 1–1. In the replay there were 12,000 present to see the Hammers put up a gallant fight but eventually lose 3–2. The side were playing well at home, with victories over Norwich (6–1) and Southampton (3–0), but as usual it was the away form that was causing concern. Four goals were conceded at Plymouth and in early March there was a 6–1 defeat at Reading.

Aside from beating Northampton 4–1, the remaining games of the season – with four goalless draws – were drab affairs. The mid-table finishing position of 11th was the same as the previous season, with the goalscoring being the problem.

GEORGE KITCHEN

He was considered to be one of the finest uncapped goalkeepers in the country.

Starting out at Stockport County in 1897, he played in eight league games before joining Everton in 1898. By 1903 he was the first-choice keeper and went on to play in 90 games for the Goodison club. George signed for West Ham in 1905 and on his debut scored a penalty against Swindon Town in a 1–0 victory. During his time at Upton Park he went on to score five more goals from penalties, which earned him fame around the country. He served the Hammers well, playing in a total of 205 games in six seasons before being transferred to Southampton in 1912. His stay with Saints lasted two seasons, where he played in 37 games. He must have enjoyed the south coast as on retiring he became a golf professional in Bournemouth.

Southern League - Division One Final Table 1905-06

	P	HOME W	D	L	F	A	AWAY W	D	L	F	A	Pts
Fulham	34	10	7	0	22	6	9	5	3	22	9	50
Southampton	34	13	2	2	32	11	6	5	6	26	28	45
Portsmouth	34	13	3	1	39	11	4	6	7	22	24	43
Luton Town	34	13	2	2	45	13	4	5	8	19	27	41
Tottenham Hotspur	34	13	2	2	36	11	3	5	9	10	18	39
Plymouth Argyle	34	11	3	3	32	13	5	4	8	19	20	39
Norwich City	34	8	8	1	30	12	5	2	10	16	26	36
Bristol Rovers	34	11	1	5	37	23	4	4	9	19	33	35
Brentford	34	11	3	3	28	19	3	4	10	15	33	35
Reading	34	9	7	1	34	15	3	2	12	19	31	33
West Ham United	**34**	**12**	**2**	**3**	**30**	**9**	**2**	**3**	**12**	**12**	**30**	**33**
Millwall	34	9	4	4	26	16	2	7	8	12	25	33
Queens Park Rangers	34	9	3	5	39	14	3	4	10	19	30	31
Watford	34	7	6	4	28	20	1	4	12	10	37	26
Swindon Town	34	6	4	7	21	23	2	5	10	10	29	25
Brighton & Hove Albion	34	8	5	4	24	24	1	2	14	6	31	25
New Brompton	34	5	5	7	10	20	2	3	12	10	42	22
Northampton Town	34	5	4	8	17	22	3	1	13	15	57	21

Season **1905-06** Southern League - Division One
Match Details

Manager **Syd King**   Final League Position **11/18**

	Date		Competition	Venue	Opponents	Results		Attendance	Scorers
1	Sep 2	Sat	SL Div 1	H	Swindon Town	W	1-0	10,000	Kitchen [pen]
2	Sep 9	Sat	SL Div 1	A	Millwall	L	0-1	6,500	
3	Sep 16	Sat	SL Div 1	H	Luton Town	L	1-2	10,000	Blackburn
4	Sep 23	Sat	SL Div 1	A	Tottenham Hotspur	L	0-2	12,000	
5	Sep 30	Sat	SL Div 1	H	Brentford	W	2-0	8,000	Blackburn, Wilkinson
6	Oct 7	Sat	SL Div 1	A	Norwich City	L	0-1	6,000	
7	Oct 14	Sat	SL Div 1	H	Plymouth Argyle	W	2-1	5,000	Blackburn, Mackie
8	Oct 21	Sat	SL Div 1	A	Southampton	L	0-1	6,000	
9	Oct 28	Sat	SL Div 1	H	Reading	L	2-3	7,000	Allison, Ford
10	Nov 4	Sat	SL Div 1	A	Watford	L	1-3	4,000	Bridgeman
11	Nov 11	Sat	SL Div 1	H	Brighton & Hove Albion	W	2-0	8,000	Mackie, Wilkinson
12	Nov 18	Sat	SL Div 1	A	Northampton Town	L	1-2	5,000	Mackie
13	Nov 25	Sat	SL Div 1	A	Fulham	L	0-1	12,000	
14	Dec 2	Sat	SL Div 1	H	Queens Park Rangers	W	2-0	7,500	Hilsdon, Watson
15	Dec 9	Sat	SL Div 1	A	Bristol Rovers	L	1-2	5,000	Hilsdon
16	Dec 16	Sat	SL Div 1	H	New Brompton	W	1-0	6,000	Jarvis
17	Dec 23	Sat	SL Div 1	H	Portsmouth	W	1-0	8,000	Stapley
18	Dec 30	Sat	SL Div 1	A	Swindon Town	W	3-2	4,000	Blackburn, Jarvis, Watson
19	Jan 6	Sat	SL Div 1	H	Millwall	W	1-0	15,000	Watson
20	Jan 13	Sat	FAC 1	A	Woolwich Arsenal	D	1-1	18,000	Kitchen [pen]
21	Jan 18	Thur	FAC 1 Rep	H	Woolwich Arsenal	L	2-3	12,000	Bridgeman, Watson
22	Jan 20	Sat	SL Div 1	A	Luton Town	D	1-1	5,000	Stapley
23	Jan 27	Sat	SL Div 1	H	Tottenham Hotspur	L	0-1	16,500	
24	Feb 10	Sat	SL Div 1	H	Norwich City	W	6-1	6,000	Stapley 2, Watson 2, Grassam, Kitchen [pen]
25	Feb 17	Sat	SL Div 1	A	Plymouth Argyle	L	2-4	3,000	Grassam, Kitchen [pen]
26	Feb 26	Mon	SL Div 1	H	Southampton	W	3-0	5,000	Stapley 2, Bridgeman
27	Mar 3	Sat	SL Div 1	A	Reading	L	1-6	5,000	Watson
28	Mar 10	Sat	SL Div 1	H	Watford	D	0-0	7,000	
29	Mar 17	Sat	SL Div 1	A	Brighton & Hove Albion	D	0-0	5,000	
30	Mar 24	Sat	SL Div 1	H	Northampton Town	W	4-1	4,000	Bridgeman 2, Stapley 2
31	Mar 31	Sat	SL Div 1	H	Fulham	D	0-0	12,000	
32	Apr 7	Sat	SL Div 1	A	Queens Park Rangers	W	1-0	10,000	Stapley
33	Apr 14	Sat	SL Div 1	H	Bristol Rovers	W	2-0	9,000	Blackburn, Hilsdon
34	Apr 21	Sat	SL Div 1	A	New Brompton	D	0-0	3,000	
35	Apr 23	Mon	SL Div 1	A	Brentford	L	1-3	2,000	Grassam
36	Apr 28	Sat	SL Div 1	A	Portsmouth	L	0-1	5,000	

Team Line-Ups

ALLISON Tommy	BLACKBURN Fred	BRIDGEMAN William	BUSH Robert	COTTON Charles	FEATHERSTONE Arthur	FORD William	GARDNER David	GRASSAM William	HAMMOND Sidney	HILSDON George	HINDLE Harry	JACKSON James	JARVIS Len	KITCHEN George	MACKIE Charles	McCARTNEY Alex	MILNES Frederick	PIERCY Frank	STAPLEY Harry	WATSON Lionel	WILKINSON Henry	WINTERHALDER Arthur	WINTERHALDER Herbert	
	11	7				8	3				4		6	1	9	2		5		10				1
	11	9				7	3				4		6	1	8	2		5		10				2
	11	9	4				3	2					6	1	8			5			10	7		3
4	11	9					3	2					6	1	8			5			10	7		4
4	10	8	6				3	2	9					1				5			11	7		5
4	10	8	6				3	2	9					1				5			11	7		6
4	10	8	6			7	3							1	9	2		5			11			7
4	10	8	6			7	3							1	9	2		5			11			8
4	10	8	6			7	3			5				1	9	2					11			9
4	10	8		7			3						6	1	9	2		5			11			10
4	10	8	6	7			3					2	5	1	9						11			11
4	10	8	6	7			3					2	5	1	9						11			12
4	11	8	6	7			3			9		2	5	1						10				13
4		8	6	7			3			9		2	5	1						10	11			14
4		8	6	7			3			9		2	5	1						10	11			15
4	11		6	7			3			9		2	5	1						10	8			16
4	11		6	7			3	8				2	5	1					9	10				17
4	11			7			3	8				2	5	1				6	9	10				18
4	11			7			3	8				2	5	1				6	9	10				19
4	11	7	8				3			9			5	1			2	6		10				20
4	11	8					3			9			5	1			2	6		10	7			21
			4	7			3	8				2	5	1				6	9	10		11		22
	11		4	7			3	8				2	5	1				6	9	10				23
4	11	7					3	8				2	5	1				6	9	10				24
4	11	8		7			3	9				2	5	1				6		10				25
4	11	8	6	7			3					2	5	1					9	10				26
4	11	8	6	7			3					2	5	1					9	10				27
4	10			7			3			5		2		1				6	9	8		11		28
	11		6	7			3	8	4			2		1				5	9	10				29
4	11	7					3	8				2	6	1				5	9	10				30
4	11	7			1		3	8				2	6					5	9	10				31
4	11	7					3	8				2	6	1				5	9	10				32
4	10	8			1	7	3			9		2	6					5				11		33
4	11	7			1		3	8				2	6					5		10		9		34
4	10	9			1	7	3	8				2	6					5				11		35
4	11	7			1		3	8				2	6					5		10		9		36

1906-07
Story of the season

For once, **there were no huge changes** to the playing staff for the new campaign. **Four players left** and in their place came forwards David Lindsay and Fred Kemp.

There were also two new full-backs in Bill Wildman and Bill Taylor. It was a good start to the season as the Hammers came away from Tottenham after a 2–1 triumph. At home the Hammers were again in command, beating Swindon 2–0 and Luton Town 5–1 with Lionel Watson claiming a hat-trick. In September there were two goals from Billy Grassam in a 3–0 home win over Leyton. A week later he scored a hat-trick at Portsmouth – but unfortunately the home side scored four. The away form improved, with creditable draws at Plymouth, Reading and Gillingham. During November there was an excellent 4–1 victory at Fulham in which Lionel Watson grabbed a hat-trick to inflict Fulham's first home defeat of the season. The Christmas period brought two further wins at home; Southampton were beaten 1–0, followed by a satisfying 4–2 triumph against London rivals Tottenham. Young Arthur

Appearances & Goals 1906-07

	League		FA Cup		Total	
	Starts	Goals	Starts	Goals	Starts	Goals
ALLISON Tommy	36	2	2	0	38	2
BLACKBURN Fred	29	4	0	0	29	4
BLYTH James	3	0	0	0	3	0
BOURNE Stanley	1	0	0	0	1	0
CLARKE David	1	0	0	0	1	0
FAIR Aubrey	3	0	0	0	3	0
FEATHERSTONE Arthur	2	0	0	0	2	0
GARDNER David	14	0	1	0	15	0
GRASSAM William	37	10	2	0	39	10
HAMMOND Sidney	16	0	1	0	17	0
HORN George	4	0	0	0	4	0
JARVIS Len	30	1	2	0	32	1
KEMP Fred	8	0	0	0	8	0
KITCHEN George	37	0	2	0	39	0
LINDSAY David	37	4	2	0	39	4
PIERCY Frank	37	0	2	0	39	0
RANDALL Tommy	1	1	0	0	1	1
STAPLEY Harry	35	20	2	2	37	22
TAYLOR William	4	0	0	0	4	0
WATSON Lionel	32	12	2	0	34	12
WILDMAN William	37	0	2	0	39	0
WINTERHALDER Arthur	12	6	2	1	14	7
WOODARDS Dan	2	0	0	0	2	0
Totals	**418**	**60**	**22**	**3**	**440**	**63**

Winterhalder scored a hat-trick, with Harry Stapley adding the other goal.

In the FA Cup, First Division side Blackpool were the visitors and went away beaten 2–1. In the next round Everton, another First Division side, proved too strong for the Hammers as they won 2–1 at the Boleyn Ground. There was a big crowd of 16,000 for the visit of Millwall. It was a disappointing day as the visitors won 1–0, which left the Hammers in sixth place in the table. After this there was a five-match unbeaten run including home victories over Queens Park Rangers (2–1), and Portsmouth (3–0). Now up to third in the league, the Easter period brought further wins against Reading at home (2–0), and a 3–2 win at Southampton. The final home game of the season was against Fulham, who had already been crowned champions. The home faithful ended the season on a high as the Hammers won 4–1 to finish fifth in the table.

Southern League - Division One Final Table 1906-07

	P	HOME					AWAY					Pts
		W	D	L	F	A	W	D	L	F	A	
Fulham	38	13	5	1	34	12	7	8	4	24	20	53
Portsmouth	38	15	3	1	45	11	7	4	8	19	25	51
Brighton & Hove Albion	38	12	4	3	33	16	6	5	8	20	27	45
Luton Town	38	12	4	3	37	22	6	5	8	15	30	45
West Ham United	38	12	5	2	39	12	3	9	7	21	29	44
Tottenham Hotspur	38	13	4	2	46	12	4	5	10	17	33	43
Millwall	38	14	3	2	53	12	4	3	12	18	38	42
Norwich City	38	9	6	4	34	21	6	6	7	23	27	42
Watford	38	9	7	3	31	18	4	9	6	15	25	42
Brentford	38	14	3	2	39	16	3	5	11	18	40	42
Southampton	38	9	6	4	31	18	4	3	12	18	38	35
Reading	38	12	3	4	42	11	2	3	14	15	36	34
Leyton	38	9	6	4	26	23	2	6	11	12	37	34
Bristol Rovers	38	10	4	5	41	21	2	5	12	14	33	33
Plymouth Argyle	38	7	9	3	26	14	3	4	12	17	36	33
New Brompton	38	9	4	6	30	21	3	5	11	17	38	33
Swindon Town	38	11	7	1	28	8	0	4	15	15	46	33
Queens Park Rangers	38	9	5	5	32	16	2	5	12	15	39	32
Crystal Palace	38	7	4	8	29	28	1	5	13	17	38	25
Nothampton Town	38	5	8	6	22	25	0	1	18	7	63	19

FRED BLACKBURN

Fred was not only born in Blackburn but he started his career as a player with Blackburn.

He was a creative ball-playing winger and first appeared for the Lancashire club in 1897. He then went on to make a total of 240 appearances, scoring 30 goals. While with Rovers he was capped three times for England, against Scotland twice and Ireland. He came south in May 1905 to join West Ham. A switch to wing-half saw Fred play in a total of 237 games and score 28 goals. In 1911 he gained a well-deserved benefit match against Coventry City, where the proceeds of the league game were shared jointly with goalkeeper George Kitchen.

He retired from playing in 1913 and joined the Merchant Navy. Fred later returned to the game as a coach at Barking and died at Ilford in March 1951 aged 72.

Season **1906-07** Southern League - Division One
Match Details

Manager **Syd King** Final League Position **5/20**

	Date		Competition	Venue	Opponents	Results		Attendance	Scorers
1	Sep 1	Sat	SL Div 1	A	Tottenham Hotspur	W	2-1	17,000	Stapley, Watson
2	Sep 8	Sat	SL Div 1	H	Swindon Town	W	2-0	10,000	Stapley, Watson
3	Sep 15	Sat	SL Div 1	A	Norwich City	L	2-3	10,000	Blackburn, Stapley
4	Sep 22	Sat	SL Div 1	H	Luton Town	W	5-1	13,000	Watson 3, Lindsay, Stapley
5	Sep 24	Mon	SL Div 1	A	Bristol Rovers	L	0-3	3,000	
6	Sep 29	Sat	SL Div 1	A	Crystal Palace	D	1-1	10,000	Winterhalder A.
7	Oct 6	Sat	SL Div 1	H	Brentford	W	3-1	12,000	Allison, Grassam, Stapley
8	Oct 13	Sat	SL Div 1	A	Millwall	D	1-1	15,000	Stapley
9	Oct 15	Mon	SL Div 1	H	Bristol Rovers	L	0-1	4,000	
10	Oct 20	Sat	SL Div 1	H	Leyton	W	3-0	12,000	Grassam 2, Stapley
11	Oct 27	Sat	SL Div 1	A	Portsmouth	L	3-4	12,000	Grassam 3
12	Nov 3	Sat	SL Div 1	H	New Brompton	D	1-1	7,000	Stapley
13	Nov 10	Sat	SL Div 1	A	Plymouth Argyle	D	0-0	10,000	
14	Nov 17	Sat	SL Div 1	H	Brighton & Hove Albion	D	0-0	5,000	
15	Nov 27	Tue	SL Div 1	A	Reading	D	2-2	4,000	Grassam, Lindsay
16	Dec 1	Sat	SL Div 1	H	Watford	D	1-1	7,000	Stapley
17	Dec 8	Sat	SL Div 1	A	New Brompton	D	2-2	5,000	Stapley, Watson
18	Dec 22	Sat	SL Div 1	A	Fulham	W	4-1	10,000	Watson 3, Blackburn
19	Dec 25	Tue	SL Div 1	H	Southampton	W	1-0	20,000	Stapley
20	Dec 29	Sat	SL Div 1	H	Tottenham Hotspur	W	4-2	14,000	Winterhalder A. 3, Stapley
21	Jan 5	Sat	SL Div 1	A	Swindon Town	L	0-2	5,000	
22	Jan 12	Sat	FAC 1	H	Blackpool	W	2-1	13,000	Stapley, Winterhalder A.
23	Jan 19	Sat	SL Div 1	H	Norwich City	W	3-1	7,000	Stapley 2, Lindsay
24	Jan 26	Sat	SL Div 1	A	Luton Town	D	1-1	4,000	Stapley
25	Feb 2	Sat	FAC 2	H	Everton	L	1-2	14,000	Stapley
26	Feb 9	Sat	SL Div 1	A	Brentford	D	0-0	6,000	
27	Feb 16	Sat	SL Div 1	H	Millwall	L	0-1	16,000	
28	Feb 23	Sat	SL Div 1	A	Leyton	D	0-0	10,000	
29	Feb 25	Mon	SL Div 1	H	Queens Park Rangers	W	2-1	4,000	Grassam, Watson
30	Mar 2	Sat	SL Div 1	H	Portsmouth	W	3-0	11,000	Stapley 2, Lindsay
31	Mar 7	Thur	SL Div 1	A	Northampton Town	D	0-0	2,000	
32	Mar 16	Sat	SL Div 1	H	Plymouth Argyle	D	0-0	6,000	
33	Mar 23	Sat	SL Div 1	A	Brighton & Hove Albion	L	0-2	6,000	
34	Mar 25	Mon	SL Div 1	H	Crystal Palace	D	1-1	3,000	Winterhalder A.
35	Mar 30	Sat	SL Div 1	H	Reading	W	2-0	6,000	Allison, Blackburn
36	Apr 1	Mon	SL Div 1	A	Southampton	W	3-2	8,000	Jarvis, Stapley, Watson
37	Apr 6	Sat	SL Div 1	A	Watford	L	0-2	4,000	
38	Apr 13	Sat	SL Div 1	H	Northampton Town	W	4-0	2,500	Grassam 2, Stapley 2
39	Apr 20	Sat	SL Div 1	A	Queens Park Rangers	L	0-2	5,000	
40	Apr 27	Sat	SL Div 1	H	Fulham	W	4-1	10,000	Blackburn, Randall, Watson, Winterhalder A.

Team Line-Ups

ALLISON Tommy	BLACKBURN Fred	BLYTH James	BOURNE Stanley	CLARKE David	FAIR Aubrey	FEATHERSTONE Arthur	GARDNER David	GRASSAM William	HAMMOND Sidney	HORN George	JARVIS Len	KEMP Fred	KITCHEN George	LINDSAY David	PIERCY Frank	RANDALL Tommy	STAPLEY Harry	TAYLOR William	WATSON Lionel	WILDMAN William	WINTERHALDER Arthur	WOODARDS Dan	
4	11						3	8			6		1	7	5		9		10	2			1
4	11						3	8			6		1	7	5		9		10	2			2
4	11	2					3	8			6		1	7	5		9		10				3
4	11						3	8			6		1	7	5		9		10	2			4
4	11						3	8			6		1	7	5				10	2	9		5
6		4					3	8					1	7	5		9		10	2	11		6
4							3	8			6	11	1	7	5		9		10	2			7
4								8	3		6	11	1	7	5		9		10	2			8
4								8			6	11	1	7	5		9	3	10	2			9
4	11							8	3		6		1	7	5		9		10	2			10
4	11						3	8			6		1	7	5		9		10	2			11
4	11	6					3	8				10	1	7	5		9			2			12
4	11						3	8		6			1	7	5		9		10	2			13
4	11						3	8			6		1	7	5		9		10	2			14
4								8	3	6		10	1	7	5		9			2			15
4	11		6					8	3			10	1	7	5		9			2			16
4	11						3	8		6			1	7	5		9		10	2			17
4	11							8	3		6		1	7	5		9		10	2			18
4	11							8	3		6		1	7	5		9		10	2			19
4					1			8	3		6			7	5		9		10	2	11		20
4						7	9		3		6		1	8	5				10	2	11		21
4								8	3		6		1	7	5		9		10	2	11		22
4							3	8			6		1	7	5		9		10	2	11		23
4							3	8			6		1	7	5		9		10	2	11		24
4							3	8			6		1	7	5		9		10	2	11		25
4	6							8					1	7	5		9	3	10	2	11		26
4				3				8			6		1	7	5		9		10	2	11		27
4	11			3		7		8			6		1		5		9		10	2			28
4	11			3				8			6		1	7	5		9		10	2			29
4	10							8	3		6		1	7			9		5	2	11		30
4	10							8			6		1	7	3		9		5	2	11		31
4	11							8	3		6	10	1	7	5		9			2			32
	11							8	3		6	10	1	7	5		9			2		4	33
	10							8	3		6		1	7	5		9			2	11	4	34
4	11							8	3		6		1	7	5		9		10				35
4	11							8			6		1	7	5		9	3	10	2			36
4	11							8			6		1	7	5		9	3	10	2			37
4	11							8	3		6		1	7	5		9		10	2			38
4	11							8	3		6		1	7	5		9		10	2			39
4	10								3	6			1	7	5	8			9	2	11		40

1907-08
Story of the season

After finishing 5th in the previous campaign **there was optimism** that this would be a good season. The usual player movement during the summer saw five players leave.
New recruits were full backs Archie Taylor and James Gault, together with forwards William Brown, Alf Harwood and Tommy Lee.

The opening home game was disappointing as the visitor Swindon Town won 2–1, with the Hammers' Frank Piercy being sent off.

What followed was a run of seven undefeated games, which included five clean sheets. This consistency didn't last as during November, there was a fine 4–1 win at home to Brentford but the next home game brought a poor 2–0 defeat to lowly Leyton. This trend continued as on Christmas Day New Brompton, who finished bottom that season, won 2–1 at the Boleyn Ground. On Boxing Day Queens Park Rangers who won the league that campaign, were beaten 3–0.

Appearances & Goals 1907-08

	League		FA Cup		Total	
	Starts	Goals	Starts	Goals	Starts	Goals
ALLISON Tommy	29	0	0	0	29	0
BLACKBURN Fred	36	4	2	1	38	5
BOURNE Stanley	3	0	0	0	3	0
BROWN William	18	4	0	0	18	4
CLARKE David	15	0	0	0	15	0
FEATHERSTONE Arthur	5	1	1	0	6	1
FROST James	13	3	1	0	14	3
GAULT James	34	0	2	0	36	0
GRASSAM William	32	9	2	0	34	9
HAMMOND Sidney	2	0	1	0	3	0
HARWOOD Alf	3	0	0	0	3	0
HORN George	4	0	1	0	5	0
JARVIS Len	29	2	1	0	30	2
KEMP Fred	2	0	0	0	2	0
KITCHEN George	23	0	2	0	25	0
LEE Thomas	6	0	0	0	6	0
LINDSAY David	14	0	0	0	14	0
PIERCY Frank	23	0	2	0	25	0
RANDALL Tommy	7	1	0	0	7	1
ROBERTSON	1	0	0	0	1	0
SHEA Danny	13	3	2	0	15	3
STAPLEY Harry	23	10	2	0	25	10
TAYLOR Archie	25	0	1	0	26	0
WATSON Lionel	22	8	0	0	22	8
WILDMAN William	2	0	0	0	2	0
WOODARDS Dan	1	0	0	0	1	0
YOUNG Robert	33	1	2	0	35	1
own goal		1				1
Totals	**418**	**47**	**22**	**1**	**440**	**48**

The FA Cup began with a visit from Rotherham Town. The Midland League side played well but a goal from Fred Blackburn took West Ham through to the next round. The second-round match saw the Hammers travel to Newcastle United, where a crowd of 47,000 were in attendance. West Ham gave a spirited display, with goalkeeper George Kitchen in fine form until he suffered a foot injury. Playing with ten men, the Hammers could not hold out and lost 2–0.

After beating Portsmouth and Bradford it was disappointing to lose 2–0 at home to Millwall and 4–0 at Brentford. The supporters were frustrated as the team continued to win two then lose two. There were five games remaining, with four of these being away from home. In the game at the Boleyn with Southampton, Billy Brown scored twice in a 4–2 victory. However, the away games were a disaster, with defeats in all four games without scoring. Among those was a poor 3–0 defeat at bottom club New Brompton. The campaign ended with a mid-table position of tenth being five places lower than the previous season.

Southern League - Division One
Final Table 1907-08

	P	W	D	L	F	A	W	D	L	F	A	Pts
			HOME						AWAY			
Queens Park Rangers	38	12	4	3	46	26	9	5	5	36	31	51
Plymouth Argyle	38	13	5	1	33	13	6	6	7	17	18	49
Millwall	38	11	5	3	25	9	8	3	8	24	23	46
Crystal Palace	38	10	4	5	35	28	7	6	6	19	23	44
Swindon Town	38	12	6	1	41	12	4	4	11	14	28	42
Bristol Rovers	38	11	5	3	36	19	5	5	9	23	37	42
Tottenham Hotspur	38	11	2	6	33	18	6	5	8	26	30	41
Northampton Town	38	9	5	5	30	17	6	6	7	20	24	41
Portsmouth	38	14	1	4	43	19	3	5	11	21	33	40
West Ham United	**38**	**9**	**6**	**4**	**27**	**16**	**6**	**4**	**9**	**20**	**32**	**40**
Southampton	38	11	5	3	32	21	5	1	13	19	39	38
Reading	38	12	1	6	38	18	3	5	11	17	32	36
Bradford Park Avenue	38	6	7	6	30	27	6	5	8	23	27	36
Watford	38	9	4	6	31	22	3	6	10	16	37	34
Norwich City	38	10	4	5	31	16	2	5	12	15	33	33
Brentford	38	13	3	3	38	15	1	2	16	11	38	33
Brighton & Hove Albion	38	9	6	4	29	19	3	2	14	17	40	32
Luton Town	38	9	4	6	21	17	3	2	14	12	39	30
Leyton	38	6	6	7	30	31	2	5	12	22	43	27
New Brompton	38	7	3	9	24	29	2	4	13	20	46	25

ROBERT YOUNG

Robert joined West Ham in 1907 after starting has career in Scotland with St Mirren.

Playing as a centre-half, he made his debut against Tottenham in a 1–1 draw in September 1907. He soon established himself in the side and as a utility man he played in most of the defensive positions. He made a total of 33 league appearances that season, his one goal coming in the 3–0 victory over Norwich City. The following campaign found his appearances scarcer and after a 6–3 defeat at Norwich he was transferred to Middlesbrough. He stayed on Teeside for two seasons, where he became the club's penalty-taker, scoring four times from the spot in 1910. He played in 37 games before joining Everton in 1910 for a fee of £1,200. Again he took the penalties and scored four in season 1910–11. With the Blues he completed 41 games before leaving in 1911 to join Wolverhampton Wanderers for a fee of £200. He played in 33 games for Wolves, scoring 7 goals, up to 1914 when injury and ill health ended his career.

Season **1907-08** Southern League - Division One
Match Details
Manager **Syd King**   Final League Position **10/20**

	Date		Competition	Venue	Opponents	Results		Attendance	Scorers
1	Sep 2	Mon	SL Div 1	H	Swindon Town	L	1-2	8,000	Grassam [pen]
2	Sep 7	Sat	SL Div 1	H	Tottenham Hotspur	D	1-1	13,000	Blackburn
3	Sep 14	Sat	SL Div 1	A	Swindon Town	D	1-1	5,000	Grassam [pen]
4	Sep 21	Sat	SL Div 1	H	Crystal Palace	W	1-0	8,000	Grassam
5	Sep 28	Sat	SL Div 1	A	Luton Town	W	3-0	7,000	Stapley 2, Grassam
6	Oct 5	Sat	SL Div 1	H	Brighton & Hove Albion	D	0-0	7,000	
7	Oct 12	Sat	SL Div 1	A	Portsmouth	W	2-0	12,000	Blackburn, Watson
8	Oct 19	Sat	SL Div 1	H	Bradford Park Avenue	D	0-0	12,000	
9	Oct 26	Sat	SL Div 1	A	Millwall	L	0-1	13,000	
10	Nov 2	Sat	SL Div 1	H	Brentford	W	4-1	6,000	Stapley 2, Grassam, Randall
11	Nov 9	Sat	SL Div 1	A	Bristol Rovers	L	0-1	10,000	
12	Nov 16	Sat	SL Div 1	H	Leyton	L	0-2	8,000	
13	Nov 23	Sat	SL Div 1	A	Reading	W	1-0	6,000	Watson
14	Nov 30	Sat	SL Div 1	H	Watford	W	2-0	6,000	Stapley, Watson
15	Dec 7	Sat	SL Div 1	A	Norwich City	D	1-1	4,500	Grassam
16	Dec 14	Sat	SL Div 1	H	Northampton Town	D	1-1	4,000	Stapley
17	Dec 21	Sat	SL Div 1	A	Southampton	D	0-0	6,000	
18	Dec 25	Wed	SL Div 1	H	New Brompton	L	1-2	10,000	Floyd (og)
19	Dec 26	Thur	SL Div 1	H	Queens Park Rangers	W	3-0	17,000	Grassam 2, Featherstone
20	Dec 28	Sat	SL Div 1	H	Plymouth Argyle	D	1-1	10,000	Shea
21	Jan 4	Sat	SL Div 1	A	Tottenham Hotspur	L	2-3	12,000	Stapley 2
22	Jan 11	Sat	FAC 1	H	Rotherham Town	W	1-0	9,500	Blackburn
23	Jan 18	Sat	SL Div 1	A	Crystal Palace	W	3-1	8,000	Shea, Stapley, Watson
24	Jan 25	Sat	SL Div 1	H	Luton Town	W	1-0	8,000	Watson
25	Feb 1	Sat	FAC 2	A	Newcastle United	L	0-2	47,000	
26	Feb 8	Sat	SL Div 1	H	Portsmouth	W	2-1	10,000	Frost, Watson
27	Feb 15	Sat	SL Div 1	A	Bradford Park Avenue	W	1-0	9,000	Watson
28	Feb 22	Sat	SL Div 1	H	Millwall	L	0-2	12,000	
29	Feb 29	Sat	SL Div 1	A	Brentford	L	0-4	4,000	
30	Mar 7	Sat	SL Div 1	H	Bristol Rovers	D	0-0	6,000	
31	Mar 14	Sat	SL Div 1	A	Leyton	D	2-2	11,000	Brown 2
32	Mar 21	Sat	SL Div 1	H	Reading	W	2-1	6,000	Grassam, Watson
33	Mar 25	Wed	SL Div 1	A	Brighton & Hove Albion	L	1-3	1,500	Jarvis
34	Mar 28	Sat	SL Div 1	A	Watford	W	3-2	3,000	Frost, Jarvis, Stapley
35	Apr 4	Sat	SL Div 1	H	Norwich City	W	3-0	6,000	Blackburn, Frost, Young
36	Apr 11	Sat	SL Div 1	A	Northampton Town	L	0-4	6,000	
37	Apr 17	Fri	SL Div 1	A	New Brompton	L	0-3	6,000	
38	Apr 18	Sat	SL Div 1	H	Southampton	W	4-2	8,000	Brown 2, Blackburn, Shea
39	Apr 20	Mon	SL Div 1	A	Queens Park Rangers	L	0-4	11,000	
40	Apr 25	Sat	SL Div 1	A	Plymouth Argyle	L	0-2	4,000	

Team Line-Ups

ALLISON Tommy	BLACKBURN Fred	BOURNE Stanley	BROWN William	CLARKE David	FEATHERSTONE Arthur	FROST James	GAULT James	GRASSAM William	HAMMOND Sidney	HARWOOD Alf	HORN George	JARVIS Len	KEMP Fred	KITCHEN George	LEE Thomas	LINDSAY David	PIERCY Frank	RANDALL Tommy	ROBERTSON	SHEA Danny	STAPLEY Harry	TAYLOR Archie	WATSON Lionel	WILDMAN William	WOODARDS Dan	YOUNG Robert	
4	11							8				6		1		7	5				9	3	10	2			1
4	11							8						1		7	5				9	3	10	2	6		2
	11	9					2	8				6		1		7	5					3	10		4		3
4	11						2	8				6		1	7						9	3	10		5		4
4	6		7					8						1	10	8					5	3	11		2		5
4	10						2	8						1	11	7					9	3	5		6		6
4	11						2	8				6		1		7					9	3	10		5		7
4	11						2	8				6		1		7	5				9	3	10		6		8
4	11						2							1		7	5	8			9	3	10		6		9
4	11						2	8				6	10	1			5	7			9	3					10
4	11						2	8				6	10	1			3	7			9				5		11
4	11		10				2	8				6		1			3	7			9				5		12
4	11						2	8		3				1		7	5				9		10		6		13
4	11						2	8				6		1		7	5				9		10		3		14
4	10						2	8				6		1		7	5	11		9					3		15
4	11						2	7				6		1			5	10		8	9				3		16
	10						2	8				6		1	11	7	5		9		3				4		17
4	11						2	8		3		6		1		7					9		10		5		18
	11	3			7		2	10			4	6		1						8	9				5		19
	11	3			7		2	10			4			1						8	9			6	5		20
	11	3			7		2	10			4	6		1						8	9				5		21
	11				7		2	10	3		4			1			5			8	9				6		22
4	11						2							1		7	5			8	9	3	10		6		23
4	11					7			2					1			5			8	9	3	10		6		24
	11					7	2	10				6		1			5			8	9				4		25
	11		8	1		7	2	9				6					5					3	10		4		26
4	11		8	1		7	2	9				6					5					3	10				27
	11		10	1		7	2					6					5			8		3	9		4		28
	11		10	1		7	2				4	6					5			8	9	3					29
	11		10	1		7	2					6					5			8	9	3			4		30
4	11		10	1		7	2	8				6					5					3				9	31
4			10	1		7	2	8				6			11		5					3	9				32
4	11		10	1		7	2	8				6										3	9		5		33
4	11		10	1		7	2	8				6									9	3			5		34
4	11		10	1		7	2	8				6										3	9		5		35
4	11		10	1		7	2	8				6					3						9		5		36
4	11		10	1		7	2	8	3			6											9		5		37
4	11		9	1	7		2	10				6								8		3			5		38
4	11		9	1	7		2	8				6									10	3			5		39
4			9	1			2	10		3		6				7		11		8					5		40

1908-09
Story of the season

In need of new players, the club signed three forwards, David Waggott, Walter Miller and right winger Herbert Ashton. Also to **bolster the defence** they bought full back Fred Shreeve and half back Bill Yenson. **The Hammers made an excellent start** after beating current champions Queens Park Rangers 2-0 at the Boleyn. Jack Foster scored one of the goals and he scored again at Brighton in a 3-2 defeat.

Luton Town were beaten 4-0 at home, with another two goals from Foster. He was certainly the man in form as Portsmouth came to the Boleyn and were defeated 3-1 with Foster claiming a hat-trick. It was the same old story again as the Hammers were winning their home games but losing away. They were leading 3-1 at half-time at Norwich but finished up losing 6-3. By Christmas the away record was one draw and nine defeats, so it was crucial to keep winning at home. On Christmas Day a goal from Fred

Appearances & Goals 1908-09

	League		FA Cup		Total	
	Starts	Goals	Starts	Goals	Starts	Goals
ALLISON Tommy	5	0	0	0	5	0
ASHTON Herbert	27	1	2	0	29	1
ATKINS C.	2	1	0	0	2	1
BLACKBURN Fred	40	6	6	0	46	6
BOURNE Stanley	3	0	2	0	5	0
BROWN William	2	0	0	0	2	0
BURTON John	15	3	4	0	19	3
CHALKLEY George	7	0	4	0	11	0
CLARKE David	1	0	0	0	1	0
COSTELLO Frank	12	3	0	0	12	3
DAWSON C.	4	0	0	0	4	0
DYER James	3	0	0	0	3	0
EASTWOOD Henry	6	0	0	0	6	0
FOSTER Jack	15	9	0	0	15	9
FROST James	7	1	4	0	11	1
GAULT James	13	0	0	0	13	0
GRASSAM William	8	2	1	0	9	2
HARWOOD Alf	9	0	0	0	9	0
JARVIS Len	23	0	2	0	25	0
KITCHEN George	35	0	6	0	41	0
MILLER Walter	11	5	6	1	17	6
PIERCY Frank	26	2	0	0	26	2
RANDALL Tommy	17	1	0	0	17	1
SHEA Danny	35	16	6	4	41	20
SHREEVE Frederick	19	1	6	0	25	1
TAYLOR Archie	35	0	6	0	41	0
TIRRELL Patrick	13	1	3	0	17	1
WAGGOTT David	8	2	1	0	9	2
WEBB George	4	2	0	0	4	2
YENSON William	26	0	6	0	32	0
YOUNG Robert	9	0	0	0	9	0
Totals	**440**	**56**	**65**	**5**	**506**	**61**

Blackburn ensured a 1–0 home win over Southampton, but on Boxing Day, before a crowd of 20,000 at Leyton, the team slumped again and lost 1–0. It was back to the Boleyn for the visit of Plymouth Argyle, which saw Danny Shea score all four goals in the 4–0 victory.

The FA Cup began with a trip to Queens Park Rangers where the teams drew 0–0, with the Hammers winning the replay 1–0 courtesy of a goal from Danny Shea. The next round brought another away tie at Leeds City. This was drawn 1–1 and in the replay it was Danny Shea again who scored twice in a 2–1 win. In the third round it was First Division Newcastle United who travelled to London. It was a hard-fought game that ended goalless, with the replay being played before an attendance of 36,500. Despite another goal from Shea, West Ham were beaten 2–1.

In between the cup games there had been four away defeats, with the Hammers losing 4–1 at Portsmouth and suffering a 6–0 defeat at Northampton. Luckily the home form

continued, with Shea scoring a hat-trick against Swindon in a 4–2 win. This was followed up with two more home wins against Southend (4–0) and Exeter City (4–1). The season ended with two more away defeats at Reading and Exeter, which gave a final placing of seventeenth. The difference between the home and away results was remarkable. In away games there were 3 draws and 17 defeats from the 20 games played, while at home there had been 16 victories with only 3 lost.

HERBERT ASHTON

A diminutive outside-right, he began his career at Preston North End, playing in four league games in 1905.

He then joined Accrington and helped them win the Lancashire Combination in 1906. He moved to West Ham in 1908 and quickly became a favourite with the fans with some sparkling performances. He was not a prolific scorer but set up many goals for his partner Danny Shea. Their best season together was in 1910–11 when they scored 31 goals between them. In his seven seasons at Upton Park he played in 224 Southern League games, more than any other West Ham player. In October 1914 he represented the Southern League against the Irish League and a month later he played his last Southern League game for the club at Watford. Herbert became ill and did not play another match that season. As the Great War continued, in 1915 Herbert joined the Royal Flying Corps as a mechanic. He did however manage to play in 87 wartime games, playing in the London Combination.

Southern League - Division One Final Table 1908-09

	P	HOME					AWAY					Pts
		W	D	L	F	A	W	D	L	F	A	
Northampton Town	40	15	3	2	55	14	10	2	8	35	31	55
Swindon Town	40	18	0	2	68	15	4	5	11	28	40	49
Southampton	40	13	4	3	44	26	6	6	8	23	32	48
Portsmouth	40	13	5	2	42	17	5	5	10	26	43	46
Bristol Rovers	40	13	5	2	39	20	4	4	12	21	43	43
Exeter City	40	13	2	5	37	28	5	4	11	19	37	42
New Brompton	40	12	2	6	30	22	5	5	10	18	37	41
Reading	40	7	9	4	33	19	4	9	7	27	38	40
Luton Town	40	16	1	3	45	15	1	5	14	14	45	40
Plymouth Argyle	40	9	6	5	28	16	6	4	10	18	31	40
Millwall	40	14	3	3	38	17	2	3	15	21	44	38
Southend United	40	12	6	2	33	14	2	4	14	19	40	38
Leyton	40	13	3	4	35	12	2	5	13	17	43	38
Watford	40	12	7	1	37	16	2	2	16	14	48	37
Queens Park Rangers	40	10	6	4	41	24	2	6	12	11	26	36
Crystal Palace	40	10	4	6	42	23	2	8	10	20	39	36
West Ham United	**40**	**16**	**1**	**3**	**43**	**13**	**0**	**3**	**17**	**13**	**47**	**36**
Brighton & Hove Albion	40	11	4	5	46	20	3	3	14	14	41	35
Norwich City	40	11	8	1	44	18	1	3	16	15	57	35
Coventry City	40	10	4	6	44	37	5	0	15	20	54	34
Brentford	40	10	5	5	40	26	3	2	15	19	48	33

Season **1908-09** Southern League - Division One
Match Details

Manager **Syd King**   Final League Position **17/21**

	Date		Competition	Venue	Opponents	Results		Attendance	Scorers
1	Sep 1	Tue	SL Div 1	H	Queens Park Rangers	W	2-0	7,000	Blackburn, Foster
2	Sep 5	Sat	SL Div 1	A	Brighton & Hove Albion	L	2-3	6,000	Burton, Foster
3	Sep 12	Sat	SL Div 1	H	Crystal Palace	L	0-1	10,000	
4	Sep 19	Sat	SL Div 1	A	Brentford	L	0-1	6,000	
5	Sep 26	Sat	SL Div 1	H	Luton Town	W	4-0	3,000	Foster 2, Ashton, Piercy
6	Sep 30	Wed	SL Div 1	A	Watford	L	1-2	3,000	Shea
7	Oct 3	Sat	SL Div 1	A	Swindon Town	L	0-3	6,000	
8	Oct 10	Sat	SL Div 1	H	Portsmouth	W	3-1	8,000	Foster 3
9	Oct 17	Sat	SL Div 1	A	Queens Park Rangers	L	0-3	6,000	
10	Oct 24	Sat	SL Div 1	H	Northampton Town	W	2-1	9,000	Shreeve [pen], Tirrell
11	Oct 31	Sat	SL Div 1	A	New Brompton	L	1-2	6,000	Miller
12	Nov 7	Sat	SL Div 1	H	Millwall	W	1-0	14,000	Foster
13	Nov 14	Sat	SL Div 1	A	Southend United	D	0-0	6,000	
14	Nov 21	Sat	SL Div 1	H	Coventry City	W	2-0	6,000	Foster, Randall
15	Nov 28	Sat	SL Div 1	A	Bristol Rovers	L	0-1	8,000	
16	Dec 5	Sat	SL Div 1	A	Plymouth Argyle	L	0-2	7,000	
17	Dec 12	Sat	SL Div 1	A	Norwich City	L	3-6	4,500	Burton 2, Grassam
18	Dec 19	Sat	SL Div 1	H	Reading	W	2-1	5,000	Blackburn, Grassam
19	Dec 25	Fri	SL Div 1	H	Southampton	W	1-0	15,000	Blackburn
20	Dec 26	Sat	SL Div 1	A	Leyton	L	0-1	20,000	
21	Dec 28	Mon	SL Div 1	H	Plymouth Argyle	W	4-0	10,000	Shea 4
22	Jan 2	Sat	SL Div 1	H	Brighton & Hove Albion	D	1-1	5,000	Waggott
23	Jan 9	Sat	SL Div 1	A	Crystal Palace	D	2-2	5,000	Shea 2
24	Jan 16	Sat	FAC 1	A	Queens Park Rangers	D	0-0	17,000	
25	Jan 20	Wed	FAC 1 Rep	H	Queens Park Rangers	W	1-0	11,400	Shea
26	Jan 23	Sat	SL Div 1	H	Brentford	W	3-0	7,000	Frost, Miller, Waggott
27	Jan 30	Sat	SL Div 1	A	Luton Town	L	0-1	3,000	
28	Feb 6	Sat	FAC 2	A	Leeds City	D	1-1	31,500	Miller
29	Feb 11	Thur	FAC R2 Rep	H	Leeds City	W	2-1	13,000	Shea 2
30	Feb 13	Sat	SL Div 1	A	Portsmouth	L	1-4	5,000	Miller
31	Feb 20	Sat	FAC 3	H	Newcastle United	D	0-0	17,00	
32	Feb 24	Wed	FAC 3 Rep	A	Newcastle United	L	1-2	36,500	Shea
33	Feb 27	Sat	SL Div 1	A	Northampton Town	L	0-6	5,000	
34	Mar 6	Sat	SL Div 1	H	New Brompton	L	0-1	3,000	
35	Mar 8	Mon	SL Div 1	H	Swindon Town	W	4-2	4,000	Shea 3 [2 pens], Costello
36	Mar 13	Sat	SL Div 1	A	Millwall	L	0-3	9,000	
37	Mar 20	Sat	SL Div 1	H	Southend United	W	4-0	9,000	Atkins, Costello, Piercy, Shea
38	Mar 27	Sat	SL Div 1	A	Coventry City	L	1-3	7,000	Shea
39	Apr 1	Thur	SL Div 1	H	Exeter City	W	4-1	4,000	Blackburn 2, Miller 2
40	Apr 3	Sat	SL Div 1	H	Bristol Rovers	L	0-2	7,000	
41	Apr 9	Fri	SL Div 1	H	Leyton	W	1-0	13,000	Webb
42	Apr 10	Sat	SL Div 1	H	Watford	W	3-1	7,000	Shea 2, Costello
43	Apr 12	Mon	SL Div 1	A	Southampton	D	2-2	7,500	Shea, Webb
44	Apr 17	Sat	SL Div 1	H	Norwich City	W	2-1	5,000	Blackburn, Shea
45	Apr 21	Wed	SL Div 1	A	Exeter City	L	0-1	7,000	
46	Apr 24	Sat	SL Div 1	A	Reading	L	0-1	2,500	

Team Line-Ups

ALLISON Tommy	ASHTON Herbert	ATKINS C.	BLACKBURN Fred	BOURNE Stanley	BROWN William	BURTON John	CHALKLEY George	CLARKE David	COSTELLO Frank	DAWSON C.	DYER James	EASTWOOD Henry	FOSTER Jack	FROST James	GAULT James	GRASSAM William	HARWOOD Alf	JARVIS Len	KITCHEN George	MILLER Walter	PIERCY Frank	RANDALL Tommy	SHEA Danny	SHREEVE Frederick	TAYLOR Archie	TIRRELL Patrick	WAGGOTT David	WEBB George	YENSON William	YOUNG Robert	
	7		11			10					8		9		2			6	1		5				3				4		1
	7		11			10					8		9		2			6	1		5				3				4		2
			11										9	7	2			6	1		5		8		3		10		4		3
			11								10			7	2				1		5		8		3	4		9	6		4
	7		11			10							9				3		1		5		8		2	6			4		5
	7		11			10							9				3	6	1		5		8						4		6
	7		11			10							9				3	6	1		5		8		2				4		7
			11		10							7	9				3	6	1		5		8		2	4					8
			11		10							7					3	6	1	9	5		8		2	4				5	9
			11									7	9			8		6	1		5		10	2	3	4			4		10
			11									7							1	9	5	8	10	2	3	4				6	11
			11									7	9		2	10		6	1		5	8			3				4		12
	7		11										9		2			6	1		5	10	8		3				4		13
	7		11										9		2			6	1		5	10	8		3				4		14
	7		11										9		2	10		6	1		5		8		3				4		15
	7		11		10											8		6	1	9	5			2	3				4		16
	7		11		10								9		2	8		6	1		5				3				4		17
4	7		11		10											8	3	6	1		5		9		2						18
			11	5	10							7				8	3	6	1				9		2				4		19
	7		11	5	10											8	3	6	1				9		2				4		20
			11	5									9	7	2				1				8		3	6	10		4		21
			11	5									9	7	2				1				8		3	6	10		4		22
			11	5										7		2			1	9			8		3	6	10		4		23
			11	5	10									7						9			8	2	3	6			4		24
			11	5										7						9			8	2	3	6	10		4		25
			11	5										7						9			8	2	3	6	10		4		26
			11	5										7						9			8	2	3	6	10		4		27
			11	5	10									7						9			8	2	3	6			4		28
			11	5	10									7						9			8	2	3	6			4		29
	7		11															5	1	9			8	2	3	6	10		4		30
	7	6	11														10	4	1	9			8	2	3				5		31
	7	6	11			10												4	1	9			8	2	3				5		32
	7		11			10				1					2		3	4		9		6	8						5		33
	7		11	2					10	1								4		9		6	8		3				5		34
	7		11		9				10	1								4			2	6	8		3				5		35
	7		11			10			9	1								4				6	8	2	3				5		36
	7	9	11						10										1		5	6	8	2	3				4		37
	7	9	11						10										1		5	6	8	2	3				4		38
4	7		11						10										1	9	5	6	8	2	3						39
4	7		11						10										1	9	5	6	8	2	3						40
4	7		11						10										1		5	6	8	2	3		9				41
4	7		11						10													6	8	2	3		9		5		42
	7		11						10												5	6	8	2	3		9		4		43
	7	3	11						10												5	6	8	2			9		4		44
	7		11		8				10	1											5	6	9	2	3				4		45
	7	3	11		10													5	1				8	2		6		9	4		46

1909-10
Story of the season

After a poor season in 1908 fresh players were needed. In came **winger Tommy Caldwell**, centre-forward Vincent Haynes, full-back Robert Fairman **and three players from Norwich**, Robert Whiteman, George Wagstaffe and William Silor.

It proved to be a good start as Exeter City were beaten 2–1 on the opening day followed by a 3–1 win at Norwich City. The team were overjoyed to win an away game at last and the fine form continued when Danny Shea scored a hat-trick in the 3–2 home victory over Brentford. Shea scored two more in the 3–0 away win at Reading and Tommy Caldwell grabbed a hat-trick as Bristol Rovers were beaten 5–0 at the Boleyn Ground.

The team were benefitting from having a settled side and the goals continued to flow. At home Plymouth Argyle were beaten 4–1 and Croydon Common suffered a 5–1 defeat. The man in form was Danny Shea, who scored twice in

Appearances & Goals 1909-10

	League		FA Cup		Total	
	Starts	Goals	Starts	Goals	Starts	Goals
ASHTON Herbert	42	4	5	0	47	4
BLACKBURN Fred	42	3	5	3	47	6
BOURNE Stanley	4	0	1	0	5	0
BUTCHER George	3	1	0	0	3	1
CALDWELL Thomas	35	8	5	0	40	8
CANNON Frank	3	1	1	0	4	1
CURTIS Frank	3	2	0	0	3	2
DAWSON C	2	0	0	0	2	0
FAIRMAN Robert	37	0	3	0	40	0
GEGGUS John	4	0	0	0	4	0
HAYNES Vincent	15	5	0	0	15	5*
KITCHEN George	36	0	5	0	41	0
LAVERY William	2	0	2	0	4	0
MASSEY Frederick	20	0	3	0	23	0
PIERCY Frank	29	0	5	0	34	0
RANDALL Tommy	39	1	5	1	44	2
SCANES Albert	3	3	0	0	3	3
SHEA Danny	38	28	5	3	43	31
SHREEVE Frederick	41	3	4	0	45	3
SILOR William	6	0	0	0	6	0
WAGGOTT David	2	1	0	0	2	1
WAGSTAFF Edward	3	0	0	0	3	0
WEBB George	18	7	4	5	22	12
WHITEMAN Robert	33	1	2	0	35	1
WOODARDS Dan	2	0	0	0	2	0
Own goal		1				1
Totals	**462**	**69**	**55**	**12**	**517**	**81**

both games. December proved to be a poor month, with three defeats and two draws, but there was relief in January when Norwich City were thrashed 5–0 at home.

The FA Cup brought a home tie with Lancashire Combination side Carlisle United. The Hammers underestimated their opponents and the tie ended at 1–1. Carlisle, mindful of the extra revenue, requested that the replay be played at Upton Park. This time, West Ham played better, winning 5–0 with Fred Blackburn scoring twice. In the next round, away to Football League side Wolverhampton Wanderers, the Hammers were sensational, winning 5–1. George Webb scored a hat-trick and Shea claimed the other two. The cup draw then brought a trip across London to play Queens Park Rangers, where the Hammers forced a 1–1 draw. It was a disappointing replay, with the visitors winning 1–0 after extra time.

After this, the team's league form suffered, with only one win coming in the next eight games. There was better fortune at Easter as Crystal Palace were beaten both home and away. April only brought one victory, though, and the season ended with a poor 5–0 defeat at Swindon Town. After being second in the table in November it was a disappointing finish that saw the team end up in ninth place.

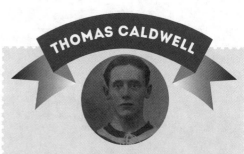

THOMAS CALDWELL

A Londoner by birth, Tommy played seven games for Clapton Orient in 1907.

A speedy outside-left, he signed for West Ham in 1909 and made his debut at the Boleyn Ground against Exeter City. He proceeded to make 32 consecutive appearances before he was injured. Included in that run was a 5–0 victory at home to Bristol Rovers, where he scored a hat-trick. The following season he was ever-present and became a hero when scoring the winning goal which knocked Manchester United out of the FA Cup. He was with the club for three seasons, making 96 appearances in the claret and blue. Joining Gillingham in 1912, he was with the Kent side for three campaigns, playing in 56 games.

Southern League - Division One Final Table 1909-10

	P	HOME					AWAY					Pts
		W	D	L	F	A	W	D	L	F	A	
Brighton & Hove Albion	42	18	2	1	50	11	5	11	5	19	17	59
Swindon Town	42	15	3	3	63	20	7	7	7	29	26	54
Queens Park Rangers	42	12	5	4	41	28	7	8	6	15	19	51
Northampton Town	42	16	3	2	66	11	6	1	14	24	33	48
Southampton	42	11	7	3	39	25	5	9	7	25	30	48
Portsmouth	42	13	5	3	43	17	7	2	12	27	46	47
Crystal Palace	42	13	3	5	48	20	7	3	11	21	30	46
Coventry City	42	11	6	4	50	24	8	2	11	21	36	46
West Ham United	**42**	**10**	**7**	**4**	**43**	**23**	**5**	**8**	**8**	**26**	**33**	**45**
Leyton	42	11	4	6	45	22	5	7	9	15	24	43
Plymouth Argyle	42	14	5	2	40	8	2	6	13	21	46	43
New Brompton	42	16	2	3	52	21	3	3	15	24	53	43
Bristol Rovers	42	13	5	3	25	8	3	5	13	12	40	42
Brentford	42	13	5	3	33	13	3	4	14	17	45	41
Luton Town	42	10	7	4	45	34	5	4	12	27	58	41
Millwall	42	9	6	6	24	17	6	1	14	21	42	37
Norwich City	42	11	5	5	42	26	2	4	15	17	52	35
Exeter City	42	12	4	5	45	22	2	2	17	15	47	34
Watford	42	8	8	5	32	24	2	5	14	19	52	33
Southend United	42	10	4	7	26	17	2	5	14	25	73	33
Croydon Common	42	8	2	11	29	38	5	3	13	23	58	31
Reading	42	7	6	8	27	25	0	4	17	11	48	24

Season 1909-10 Southern League - Division One
Match Details

Manager **Syd King**   Final League Position **9/22**

	Date		Competition	Venue	Opponents	Results		Attendance	Scorers
1	Sep 2	Thur	SL Div 1	H	Exeter City	W	2-1	5,000	Shea 2 [1 pen]
2	Sep 4	Sat	SL Div 1	A	Norwich City	W	3-1	7,000	Blackburn, Haynes, Shea
3	Sep 11	Sat	SL Div 1	H	Brentford	W	3-2	10,000	Shea 3
4	Sep 13	Mon	SL Div 1	H	Portsmouth	L	0-2	6,000	
5	Sep 18	Sat	SL Div 1	A	Coventry City	D	2-2	8,000	Haynes, Shea
6	Sep 25	Sat	SL Div 1	H	Watford	W	2-0	10,000	Randall, Shea
7	Sep 29	Wed	SL Div 1	A	Portsmouth	D	1-1	2,000	Haynes
8	Oct 2	Sat	SL Div 1	A	Reading	W	3-0	3,000	Shea 2, Webb
9	Oct 4	Mon	SL Div 1	H	Bristol Rovers	W	5-0	4,000	Caldwell 3, Shea, Webb
10	Oct 9	Sat	SL Div 1	H	Southend United	D	0-0	10,000	
11	Oct 16	Sat	SL Div 1	A	Leyton	W	2-1	13,000	Caldwell, Webb
12	Oct 23	Sat	SL Div 1	H	Plymouth Argyle	W	4-1	10,000	Shea 2, Webb 2
13	Oct 25	Mon	SL Div 1	A	Bristol Rovers	L	0-1	2,000	
14	Oct 30	Sat	SL Div 1	A	Southampton	D	2-2	7,000	Haynes, Shea
15	Nov 6	Sat	SL Div 1	H	Croydon Common	W	5-1	10,000	Shea 2 [2 pens], Ashton, Caldwell, Whiteman
16	Nov 13	Sat	SL Div 1	A	Millwall	D	0-0	10,000	
17	Nov 20	Sat	SL Div 1	A	Plymouth Argyle	D	0-0	8,000	
18	Nov 27	Sat	SL Div 1	A	Northampton Town	L	1-3	7,000	Webb
19	Dec 4	Sat	SL Div 1	H	Queens Park Rangers	L	1-2	12,000	Shreeve [pen]
20	Dec 11	Sat	SL Div 1	A	Luton Town	L	2-4	3,000	Ashton, Shea
21	Dec 18	Sat	SL Div 1	H	Swindon Town	D	2-2	10,000	Blackburn, Shreeve [pen]
22	Dec 25	Sat	SL Div 1	H	Brighton & Hove Albion	D	1-1	15,000	Shea
23	Dec 27	Mon	SL Div 1	A	Brighton & Hove Albion	L	0-3	10,000	
24	Jan 1	Sat	SL Div 1	H	New Brompton	D	2-2	7,000	Caldwell, Shea
25	Jan 8	Sat	SL Div 1	H	Norwich City	W	5-0	6,000	Cadwell 2, Shea 2, Cannon
26	Jan 15	Sat	FAC 1	H	Carlisle United	D	1-1	11,000	Blackburn
27	Jan 20	Thur	FAC 1 Rep*	H	Carlisle United	W	5-0	7,000	Blackburn 2, Randall, Shea, Webb
28	Jan 22	Sat	SL Div 1	A	Brentford	D	0-0	4,000	
29	Jan 29	Sat	SL Div 1	H	Coventry City	W	3-2	6,000	Ashton, Haynes, Shea
30	Feb 5	Sat	FAC 2	A	Wolverhampton Wanderers	W	5-1	17,000	Webb 3, Shea 2
31	Feb 12	Sat	SL Div 1	H	Reading	D	1-1	8,000	Shreeve [pen]
32	Feb 19	Sat	FAC 3	A	Queens Park Rangers	D	1-1	31,000	Webb
33	Feb 24	Thur	FAC 3 Rep	H	Queens Park Rangers	L	0-1	18,000	
34	Feb 26	Sat	SL Div 1	H	Leyton	D	0-0	10,000	
35	Mar 2	Wed	SL Div 1	A	Watford	L	1-2	1,000	Butcher
36	Mar 5	Sat	SL Div 1	A	Exeter City	L	0-1	6,500	
37	Mar 12	Sat	SL Div 1	H	Southampton	D	1-1	4,000	Blackburn
38	Mar 19	Sat	SL Div 1	A	Croydon Common	D	1-1	6,000	Webb
39	Mar 25	Fri	SL Div 1	H	Crystal Palace	W	3-1	15,000	Shea 2, Bulcock (og)
40	Mar 26	Sat	SL Div 1	H	Millwall	L	1-2	12,000	Shea
41	Mar 28	Mon	SL Div 1	A	Crystal Palace	W	4-2	20,000	Scanes 2, Ashton, Shea
42	Mar 29	Tue	SL Div 1	A	Southend United	W	1-0	1,200	Shea
43	Apr 2	Sat	SL Div 1	A	New Brompton	L	0-1	5,000	
44	Apr 9	Sat	SL Div 1	H	Northampton Town	W	1-0	10,000	Scanes
45	Apr 16	Sat	SL Div 1	A	Queens Park Rangers	D	3-3	7,000	Curtis, Shea, Waggott
46	Apr 23	Sat	SL Div 1	H	Luton Town	L	1-2	4,000	Curtis
47	Apr 30	Sat	SL Div 1	A	Swindon Town	L	0-5	4,000	

*West Ham United and Carlisle United agree to stage the replay at the Boleyn Ground

Team Line-Ups

ASHTON Herbert	BLACKBURN Fred	BOURNE Stanley	BUTCHER George	CALDWELL Thomas	CANNON Frank	CURTIS Frank	DAWSON C	FAIRMAN Robert	GEGGUS John	HAYNES Vincent	KITCHEN George	LAVERY William	MASSEY Frederick	PIERCY Frank	RANDALL Tommy	SCANES Albert	SHEA Danny	SHREEVE Frederick	SILOR William	WAGGOTT David	WAGSTAFF Edward	WEBB George	WHITEMAN Robert	WOODARDS Dan	
7	10			11				3		9	1			5	6		8	2					4		1
7	10			11				3		9	1			5	6		8	2					4		2
7	10			11				3		9	1			5	6		8	2					4		3
7	10			11				3		9	1			5	6		8	2					4		4
7	10			11				3		9	1			5	6		8	2					4		5
7	10			11				3			1			5	6		8	2				9	4		6
7	10			11				3		9	1			5	6		8	2					4		7
7	10			11				3			1			5	6		8	2				9	4		8
7	10			11				3			1			5	6		8	2				9	4		9
7	10			11				3			1			5	6		8	2				9	4		10
7	10			11				3			1			5	6		8	2				9	4		11
7	10			11				3			1			5	6		8	2				9	4		12
7	10			11				3		9	1			5	6			2				8	4		13
7	10			11				3		9	1			5	6		8	2					4		14
7	10			11				3		9	1			5	6		8	2					4		15
7	10			11			1	3						5	6		8	2				9	4		16
7	10			11				3		9	1			5	6		8	2					4		17
7	10			11				3			1			5	6		8	2				9	4		18
7	10			11				3			1			5	6		8	2				9	4		19
7	10			11				3			1	2			6		8				5	9	4		20
7	10	3		11							1		6	5			8	2				9	4		21
7	10	3		11							1		6	5			8	2				9	4		22
7	10			11				3		9	1			5	6		8	2					4		23
7	10			11	9			3			1		4	5	6		8	2							24
7	10	2		11	9						1		4	5	6		8	2							25
7	10	3		11	9						1	2		5	6		8						4		26
7	10			11							1	3	4	5	6		8	2				9			27
7	10			11	9						1	3	4	5	6		8	2							28
7	10	3		11						9	1		4	5	6		8	2							29
7	10			11				3			1		4	5	6		8	2				9			30
7	10			11				3			1			5	6		8	2				9	4		31
7	10			11				3			1		4	5	6		8	2				9			32
7	10			11				3			1			5	6		8	2				9	4		33
7	10			11				3		9	1		4	5	6		8	2							34
7	10		8	11				3		9	1		4	5	6			2							35
7	10			11			1	3						5	6		8	2	9				4		36
7	10			11				3				1	4		6		8	2		5		9			37
7	10		8					3	1				4					2		5	11	9			38
7	10							3				1		5	6		8	2			11	9	4		39
7	10							3				1		5	6		8	2			11	9	4		40
7	10			11				3				1		5	6	9	8	2					4		41
7	10							3				1		5	6		8	2			11		4		42
7	10					9		3				1		5	6		8	2			11		4		43
7	10			11				3				1		5	6	9	8	2					4		44
7	10					9		3				1		5	6		8	2			11		4		45
7	10			11		9		3	1					5	6		8	2					4		46
7	10		8					3	1	9			4				2			11		6	5	47

1910-11
Story of the season

After **finishing ninth** in the **previous campaign** there were only a couple of **new signings**. Centre-forward Bill Kennedy was purchased together with full-back Jim Rothwell.

On the opening day at the Boleyn against Southend United, West Ham raced into a three-goal lead after 12 minutes and a big win looked likely, but the team became too casual and the game ended as a 3–3 draw. Following 2–0 wins over Queens Park Rangers and Gillingham there was a trip to old rivals Millwall. This resulted in another 2–0 victory and it was the first time that West Ham had won at Millwall in the Southern League. As in previous seasons the trend of winning at home then losing away continued, but in December there was an improvement. Two goals from Herbert Ashton came in a 3–0 home win over Leyton and this was followed by a 4–0 victory at the Boleyn against Plymouth Argyle. Danny Shea hit form by scoring twice at Watford in a 3–1 triumph and followed this up by scoring four at Southend as the Hammers romped to a 6–0 victory. The FA Cup began with a home tie against First Division

Appearances & Goals 1910-11

	League		FA Cup		Total	
	Starts	Goals	Starts	Goals	Starts	Goals
ASHTON Herbert	37	6	4	0	41	6
BLACKBURN Fred	16	2	0	0	16	2
BOURNE Stanley	1	0	0	0	1	0
BUTCHER George	26	2	4	2	30	4
CALDWELL Thomas	38	3	4	1	42	4
CURTIS Frank	3	2	0	0	3	2
FAIRMAN Robert	33	0	4	0	37	0
FROST Alf	2	0	0	0	2	0
GEGGUS John	14	0	0	0	14	0
HARRISON Fred	5	2	0	0	5	2
KENNEDY William	10	4	0	0	10	4
KITCHEN George	24	2	4	0	28	2
LAVERY William	15	0	0	0	15	0
MASSEY Frederick	13	0	0	0	13	0
MEILLEAR Joe	1	0	0	0	1	0
PIERCY Frank	32	2	4	0	36	2
RANDALL Tommy	34	1	4	0	38	1
REDWARD Frank	1	0	0	0	1	0
ROTHWELL James	22	2	4	0	26	2
SHEA Danny	35	25	4	3	39	28
SHREEVE Frederick	5	0	0	0	5	0
WEBB George	19	10	4	3	23	13
WHITEMAN Robert	27	0	4	0	31	0
WOODARDS Dan	5	0	0	0	5	0
Totals	**418**	**63**	**44**	**9**	**462**	**72**

Nottingham Forest. Despite playing in the fog the Hammers won 2–1, with both goals from Shea. The next round brought another home tie with Preston North End, another top-flight side. The Hammers turned in an excellent performance in winning 3–0. Star of the show was centre-forward George Webb, who scored a hat-trick. Now in fine form, there were home wins over Norwich City and Luton Town. There was huge excitement as the draw for the third round of the FA Cup saw West Ham paired with Manchester United at home. The game attracted a record crowd of 27,000 and turned out to be a classic. The Hammers took the lead though Shea but United equalised soon after. Just three minutes from the end Tommy Caldwell was on hand to score the winning goal. The Hammers were through to the quarter-finals.

Good fortune played a part as West Ham were again drawn at home in the FA Cup, this time to Preston North End. Despite a gallant fight and two goals from George Butcher, the Hammers were beaten 3–2. The FA Cup run against four First Division opponents had brought acclaim and admiration from the footballing public. There were honours for three players as George Webb was chosen to represent England against Wales and Scotland, and Danny Shea and George Kitchen played for the Southern League side.

The Easter period saw West Ham beating Southampton both home and away but true to form this was followed by 3–0 defeats at Leyton and Brighton. It had been a good campaign as the team finished fifth in the league and reached the last eight of the FA Cup.

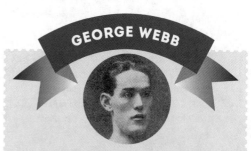

GEORGE WEBB

A strong centre-forward, he kept his amateur status throughout his career.

He made his debut for the Hammers in April 1909 and scored the winning goal against Leyton. George saved his best displays for the FA Cup when scoring hat-tricks against Wolverhampton Wanderers in 1910 and Preston North End in 1911.

International honours came his way in 1911 when he was capped five times by England at amateur level. That year he also became the first West Ham player to win a full international cap for England when selected to play against Scotland and Wales. As an amateur he had busy outside interests: he was a freemason and a toy manufacturer. He made 62 appearances, scoring 32 goals before joining Manchester City in July 1912. After playing in two league games for City he discovered that they had paid a fee for his transfer; this went against his amateur beliefs and he left the club. It was a great shock to his former colleagues in March 1915 to learn that he had died aged 28 of consumption.

Southern League - Division One
Final Table 1910-11

	P	HOME					AWAY					Pts
	P	W	D	L	F	A	W	D	L	F	A	Pts
Swindon Town	38	16	2	1	54	9	8	3	8	26	22	53
Northampton Town	38	14	3	2	39	7	4	9	6	15	20	48
Brighton & Hove Albion	38	15	2	2	41	12	5	6	8	17	24	48
Crystal Palace	38	11	5	3	35	23	6	8	5	20	25	47
West Ham United	**38**	**12**	**6**	**1**	**44**	**17**	**5**	**5**	**9**	**19**	**29**	**45**
Queens Park Rangers	38	11	6	2	37	16	2	8	9	15	25	40
Leyton	38	13	3	3	37	15	3	5	11	20	37	40
Plymouth Argyle	38	10	6	3	37	14	5	3	11	17	41	39
Luton Town	38	13	4	2	42	18	2	4	13	25	45	38
Norwich City	38	12	5	2	31	13	3	3	13	15	35	38
Coventry City	38	12	4	3	47	21	4	2	13	18	47	38
Brentford	38	12	5	2	32	13	2	4	13	9	29	37
Exeter City	38	8	5	6	31	28	6	4	9	20	25	37
Watford	38	10	5	4	32	23	3	4	12	17	42	35
Millwall	38	8	3	8	21	20	3	6	10	21	34	31
Bristol Rovers	38	6	6	7	24	23	4	4	11	18	32	30
Southampton	38	8	3	8	25	28	3	5	11	17	39	30
New Brompton	38	10	5	4	19	15	1	3	15	15	50	30
Southend United	38	7	4	8	28	26	3	5	11	19	38	29
Portsmouth	38	6	10	3	21	15	2	1	16	13	38	27

Season **1910-11** Southern League - Division One
Match Details
Manager **Syd King**   Final League Position **5/20**

	Date		Competition	Venue	Opponents	Results		Attendance	Scorers
1	Sep 3	Sat	SL Div 1	H	Southend United	D	3-3	15,000	Ashton, Blackburn, Webb
2	Sep 10	Sat	SL Div 1	A	Coventry City	L	0-3	6,000	
3	Sep 12	Mon	SL Div 1	A	Queens Park Rangers	W	2-0	7,000	Shea 2
4	Sep 17	Sat	SL Div 1	H	New Brompton	W	2-0	12,000	Shea, Webb
5	Sep 24	Sat	SL Div 1	A	Millwall	W	2-0	10,000	Blackburn, Shea
6	Oct 1	Sat	SL Div 1	H	Queens Park Rangers	W	3-0	20,000	Curtis 2, Shea
7	Oct 8	Sat	SL Div 1	A	Norwich City	L	0-2	8,000	
8	Oct 15	Sat	SL Div 1	A	Luton Town	D	1-1	8,000	Shea
9	Oct 22	Sat	SL Div 1	H	Portsmouth	W	3-1	10,000	Ashton, Kitchen, Shea
10	Oct 29	Sat	SL Div 1	A	Northampton Town	L	0-2	6,000	
11	Nov 5	Sat	SL Div 1	H	Brighton & Hove Albion	W	3-1	14,000	Kennedy, Kitchen [pen], Shea
12	Nov 12	Sat	SL Div 1	A	Exeter City	D	0-0	6,000	
13	Nov 19	Sat	SL Div 1	H	Swindon Town	W	1-0	12,000	Shea
14	Nov 26	Sat	SL Div 1	A	Bristol Rovers	D	1-1	6,000	Shea
15	Dec 3	Sat	SL Div 1	H	Crystal Palace	D	1-1	10,000	Shea
16	Dec 10	Sat	SL Div 1	A	Brentford	L	0-3	5,000	
17	Dec 17	Sat	SL Div 1	H	Leyton	W	3-0	7,000	Ashton 2, Shea
18	Dec 24	Sat	SL Div 1	A	Watford	W	3-1	2,000	Shea 2, Piercy
19	Dec 26	Mon	SL Div 1	H	Plymouth Argyle	W	4-0	14,000	Webb 2, Rothwell [pen], Shea
20	Dec 27	Tue	SL Div 1	A	Plymouth Argyle	L	0-1	8,000	
21	Dec 31	Sat	SL Div 1	A	Southend United	W	6-0	3,000	Shea 4, Caldwell, Kennedy
22	Jan 7	Sat	SL Div 1	H	Coventry City	D	1-1	11,000	Webb
23	Jan 14	Sat	FAC 1	H	Nottingham Forest	W	2-1	12,000	Shea 2
24	Jan 21	Sat	SL Div 1	A	New Brompton	D	1-1	5,000	Ashton
25	Jan 28	Sat	SL Div 1	H	Millwall	D	2-2	8,000	Randall, Webb
26	Feb 4	Sat	FAC 2	H	Preston North End	W	3-0	12,000	Webb 3
27	Feb 11	Sat	SL Div 1	H	Norwich City	W	2-1	12,000	Rothwell, Webb
28	Feb 18	Sat	SL Div 1	H	Luton Town	W	2-0	8,000	Kennedy, Piercy
29	Feb 25	Sat	FAC 3	H	Manchester United	W	2-1	27,000	Caldwell, Shea
30	Mar 4	Sat	SL Div 1	H	Northampton Town	L	1-2	10,000	Butcher
31	Mar 11	Sat	FAC 4	H	Blackburn Rovers	L	2-3	20,000	Butcher 2
32	Mar 18	Sat	SL Div 1	H	Exeter City	W	4-1	8,000	Webb 3, Shea
33	Mar 25	Sat	SL Div 1	A	Swindon Town	L	1-4	6,000	Kennedy
34	Mar 29	Wed	SL Div 1	A	Portsmouth	D	0-0	2,000	
35	Apr 1	Sat	SL Div 1	H	Bristol Rovers	D	2-2	5,000	Caldwell, Shea
36	Apr 8	Sat	SL Div 1	A	Crystal Palace	L	1-4	10,000	Shea
37	Apr 14	Fri	SL Div 1	H	Southampton	W	4-1	12,000	Ashton, Caldwell, Harrison, Shea
38	Apr 15	Sat	SL Div 1	H	Brentford	W	2-0	8,000	Butcher, Shea
39	Apr 17	Mon	SL Div 1	A	Southampton	W	1-0	8,000	Harrison
40	Apr 22	Sat	SL Div 1	A	Leyton	L	0-3	10,000	
41	Apr 26	Wed	SL Div 1	A	Brighton & Hove Albion	L	0-3	4,000	
42	Apr 29	Sat	SL Div 1	H	Watford	D	1-1	5,000	Shea

Team Line-Ups

Ashton Herbert	Blackburn Fred	Bourne Stanley	Butcher George	Caldwell Thomas	Curtis Frank	Fairman Robert	Frost Alf	Geggus John	Harrison Fred	Kennedy William	Kitchen George	Lavery William	Massey Frederick	Meillear Joe	Piercy Frank	Randall Tommy	Redward Frank	Rothwell James	Shea Danny	Shreeve Frederick	Webb George	Whiteman Robert	Woodards Dan	#
7	10			11		3					1		4	5	6				8	2	9			1
7	10			11		3					1	2	4	5	6				8		9			2
7	10			11	9	3					1	2	4	5	6				8					3
7	10			11		3					1	2	4	5	6				8		9			4
7	10	3		11							1	2	4	5	6				8		9			5
7	10			11	9	3					1	2	4	5	6				8					6
7	10			11	9	3					1	2	4	5	6				8					7
7	10			11		3					1	2			6				8		9	4	5	8
7	10			11		3					1	2			6				8		9	4	5	9
7			10	11		3					1	2			6				8		9	4	5	10
7	10			11		3				9	1	2		5	6				8			4		11
7	10			11		3				9	1	2		5	6				8			4		12
7	10			11		3		1		9		2		5	6				8			4		13
7			10	11		3		1		9		2		5	6				8			4		14
7			10	11		3					1	2		5	6				8		9	4		15
7			10	11		3		1						5	6			2	8		9	4		16
7			10	11		3		1					4	5	6			2	8		9			17
7			10	11		3		1					4	5	6			2	8		9			18
7			10	11		3		1					4	5	6			2	8		9			19
7			10	11		3		1					4		6			2	8		9		5	20
7			10	11						9	1	2			6				8	3		4	5	21
7			10	11		3		1						5	6			2	8		9	4		22
7			10	11		3		1						5	6			2	8		9	4		23
7			10	11		3		1						5	6			2	8		9	4		24
7			10	11		3		1						5	6			2	8		9	4		25
7			10	11		3		1						5	6			2	8		9	4		26
7			10	11		3		1					6	5				2	8		9	4		27
7			10	11		3	8			9	1			5	6			2				4		28
7			10	11		3		1						5	6			2	8		9	4		29
			10	11		3	8			9	1				6	7		2				4	5	30
7			10	11		3		1						5	6			2	8		9	4		31
7			10	11		3		1						5	6			2	8		9	4		32
7			10	11				1	9					5	6		4	2	8	3		4		33
7			10	11				1	9					5	6			2	8	3		4		34
7	6		10	11				1	9					5				2	8	3		4		35
7			10	11		3		1						5	6			2	8		9	4		36
7	6		10	11		3		1	9					5				2	8			4		37
7			10	11		3		1	9					5	6			2	8			4		38
7			10	11		3		1	9					5	6			2	8			4		39
7			10	11		3		1	9					5	6			2	8			4		40
7	8		10	11		3		1	9					5	6			2				4		41
7	8		10	11		3		1						5	6			2			9	4		42

1911-12
Story of the season

After **finishing fifth in the previous campaign** the team looked to make a significant **challenge for the title**. With a good set of players the only signing was that of full-back Vic Glover.

It was a poor start with only one victory in the first seven games, this being a 5–0 home win against Reading. At Exeter in October Danny Shea scored twice in a 3–3 draw and followed this up a week later with a hat-trick against Brentford. There were plenty of goals in the Brentford match as Bill Kennedy also scored a hat-trick in the 7–4 victory. November saw two home wins, the first being against Millwall. The attendance for this match was 23,000

Appearances & Goals 1911-12

	League		FA Cup		Total	
	Starts	Goals	Starts	Goals	Starts	Goals
ASHTON Herbert	33	3	5	1	38	4
BELL George	2	0	0	0	2	0
BLACKBURN Fred	22	0	5	0	27	0
BOURNE Stanley	1	0	0	0	1	0
BRADFORD T.	1	0	0	0	1	0
BURRILL Frank	7	0	0	0	7	0
BUTCHER George	16	2	3	1	19	3
CALDWELL Thomas	11	1	3	0	14	1
DAWSON Harold	10	1	0	0	10	1
FAIRMAN Robert	21	0	5	0	26	0
FROST Alf	2	0	0	0	2	0
GEGGUS John	13	0	0	0	13	0
GLOVER Victor	29	0	5	0	34	0
HARRISON Fred	30	13	4	3	34	16
HUGHES Joseph	25	0	5	0	30	0
KENNEDY William	11	6	2	0	13	6
MACKESY Jack	1	1	0	0	1	1
MASSEY Frederick	5	0	0	0	5	0
MEILLEAR Joe	2	0	1	0	3	0
MORRISON Jack	15	1	0	0	15	1
PIERCY Frank	10	1	1	0	11	1
RANDALL Tommy	23	1	0	0	23	1
REDWARD Frank	6	0	3	0	9	0
REDWOOD George	3	0	0	0	3	0
ROTHWELL James	23	2	0	0	23	2
SHEA Danny	36	24	5	0	41	24
WALDEN George	2	0	0	0	2	0
WEBB George	11	4	2	1	13	5
WHITEMAN Robert	27	1	2	0	29	1
WOODARDS Dan	20	2	4	0	24	2
own goal		1				1
Totals	**418**	**64**	**55**	**6**	**473**	**70**

and the majority went home happy after seeing the Hammers win 2–1. The away form was causing concern, at Stoke West Ham raced into a two-goal lead. Unfortunately an injury to Randall saw the Hammers go down to ten men and they finally lost 4–3. After beating Leyton 2–0 at home on Christmas Day there was a shock a few days later when visitors Crystal Palace won 6–1.

The FA Cup brought the usual excitement and West Ham started well by beating Gainsborough Trinity 2–1 at home. It was a tougher contest in the next round as the Hammers travelled to First Division side Middlesbrough. It was a hard-fought match but West Ham drew 1–1 and won the replay 2–1 with ten men after an injury to Bill Kennedy. The FA Cup run had lifted spirits and there were league wins over New Brompton and Exeter City. Danny Shea was in fine form and scored twice in both games. Swindon Town, the current Southern League champions, were the next opponents in the FA Cup. At the Boleyn Ground the Hammers took the lead but Swindon equalised to force a

replay, and it was a disaster at the County Ground as the home side ran out 4–0 winners.

Days later the league leaders Queens Park Rangers came across London and were hit by three goals in 12 minutes, with the Hammers going on to win 3–0. The local derby at Millwall attracted a crowd of 28,500 but the Hammers slumped to a 5–1 defeat. Danny Shea came to the rescue, scoring twice in a 6–2 victory over Bristol Rovers and grabbing a hat-trick in the 4–0 home win against Norwich City. It was a poor ending to the season with not a single win in the remaining seven games, which gave a final placing of 13th.

JOSEPH HUGHES

The young goalkeeper signed for West Ham in 1911 and was given a baptism of fire.

He was chosen to play in the fierce London derby with Millwall and acquitted himself well in the 2–1 victory. He kept his place in the side and over the next four seasons he gave the club excellent service, playing in 105 games. In 1916 he signed for Chelsea and played for them during World War One, appearing in 89 matches. He was always sure of a good reception when Chelsea played at the Boleyn Ground. After the war ended Joe went north to Bolton Wanderers where he played in 41 games for the First Division side.

He returned to London in 1921 to play for Charlton in the Third Division. This was Charlton's first season as a league club and he played in their opening game against Exeter City. That was to be his only season with Charlton, where he played in 19 league games. He later joined Clapton Orient but did not make a first-team appearance.

Southern League - Division One Final Table 1911-12

		HOME					AWAY					
	P	W	D	L	F	A	W	D	L	F	A	Pts
Queens Park Rangers	38	12	5	2	36	14	9	6	4	23	21	53
Plymouth Argyle	38	16	2	1	42	7	7	4	8	21	24	52
Northampton Town	38	16	2	1	57	15	6	5	8	25	26	51
Swindon Town	38	14	3	2	52	19	7	3	9	30	31	48
Brighton & Hove Albion	38	15	2	2	54	12	4	7	8	19	23	47
Coventry City	38	14	3	2	46	15	3	5	11	20	39	42
Crystal Palace	38	11	5	3	43	14	4	5	10	27	32	40
Millwall	38	11	6	2	43	19	4	4	11	17	38	40
Watford	38	10	5	4	35	20	3	5	11	21	48	36
Stoke City	38	11	4	4	35	25	2	6	11	16	38	36
Reading	38	10	7	2	35	14	1	7	11	8	45	36
Millwall	38	8	10	1	27	17	2	4	13	13	43	34
West Ham United	**38**	**10**	**3**	**6**	**40**	**27**	**3**	**4**	**12**	**24**	**42**	**33**
Brentford	38	10	5	4	43	18	2	4	13	17	47	33
Exeter City	38	8	6	5	30	22	3	5	11	18	40	33
Southampton	38	9	3	7	29	27	1	8	10	17	36	31
Bristol Rovers	38	7	8	4	24	18	2	5	12	17	44	31
New Brompton	38	7	6	6	23	23	4	3	12	12	49	31
Luton Town	38	7	5	7	33	28	2	5	12	16	33	28
Leyton	38	6	8	5	15	19	1	3	15	12	43	25

Season **1911-12** Southern League - Division One
Match Details

Manager **Syd King**   Final League Position **13/20**

	Date		Competition	Venue	Opponents	Results		Attendance	Scorers
1	Sep 2	Sat	SL Div 1	A	Crystal Palace	L	0-1	14,000	
2	Sep 9	Sat	SL Div 1	H	Southampton	D	2-2	8,000	Harrison, Kennedy
3	Sep 16	Sat	SL Div 1	A	Plymouth Argyle	D	0-0	9,000	
4	Sep 23	Sat	SL Div 1	H	Reading	W	5-0	10,000	Piercy, Rothwell [pen], Shea, Webb, Whiteman
5	Sep 30	Sat	SL Div 1	A	Watford	L	0-2	6,000	
6	Oct 7	Sat	SL Div 1	H	New Brompton	D	0-0	5,000	
7	Oct 14	Sat	SL Div 1	A	Exeter City	D	3-3	8,000	Shea 2, Webb
8	Oct 21	Sat	SL Div 1	H	Brentford	W	7-4	10,000	Kennedy 3, Shea 3, Harrison
9	Oct 28	Sat	SL Div 1	A	Queens Park Rangers	L	1-4	16,000	Webb
10	Nov 4	Sat	SL Div 1	H	Millwall	W	2-1	23,000	Harrison 2
11	Nov 11	Sat	SL Div 1	H	Luton Town	W	3-0	9,000	Harrison, Shea, Webb
12	Nov 18	Sat	SL Div 1	A	Bristol Rovers	D	1-1	7,000	Shea
13	Nov 25	Sat	SL Div 1	H	Swindon Town	L	0-2	11,000	
14	Dec 2	Sat	SL Div 1	A	Northampton Town	L	2-3	6,000	Harrison, Morrison
15	Dec 9	Sat	SL Div 1	H	Brighton & Hove Albion	W	1-0	7,000	Shea
16	Dec 16	Sat	SL Div 1	A	Stoke City	L	3-4	8,000	Kennedy 2, Randall
17	Dec 23	Sat	SL Div 1	H	Coventry City	L	0-1	7,000	
18	Dec 25	Mon	SL Div 1	H	Leyton	W	2-0	17,000	Ashton, Butcher
19	Dec 30	Sat	SL Div 1	H	Crystal Palace	L	1-6	8,000	Shea
20	Jan 6	Sat	SL Div 1	A	Southampton	W	2-1	3,000	Shea 2
21	Jan 13	Sat	FAC 1	H	Gainsborough Trinity	W	2-1	14,400	Harrison, Webb
22	Jan 20	Sat	SL Div 1	H	Plymouth Argyle	L	0-2	10,000	
23	Jan 27	Sat	SL Div 1	A	Reading	L	1-3	4,000	Ashton
24	Feb 3	Sat	FAC 2	A	Middlesbrough	D	1-1	12,327	Harrison
25	Feb 8	Thu	FAC 2 Rep	H	Middlesbrough	W	2-1	10,000	Ashton, Harrison
26	Feb 10	Sat	SL Div 1	A	New Brompton	W	3-0	5,000	Shea 2, Butcher
27	Feb 17	Sat	SL Div 1	H	Exeter City	W	3-2	10,000	Shea 2, Harrison
28	Feb 24	Sat	FAC 3	H	Swindon Town	D	1-1	20,000	Butcher
29	Feb 28	Wed	FAC 3 Rep	A	Swindon Town	L	0-4	13,328	
30	Mar 2	Sat	SL Div 1	H	Queens Park Rangers	W	3-0	10,000	Ashton, Caldwell, Shea
31	Mar 9	Sat	SL Div 1	A	Millwall	L	1-5	28,400	Harrison
32	Mar 11	Mon	SL Div 1	H	Watford	L	1-3	4,000	Rothwell [pen]
33	Mar 16	Sat	SL Div 1	A	Luton Town	L	1-2	6,000	Harrison
34	Mar 23	Sat	SL Div 1	H	Bristol Rovers	W	6-2	4,000	Harrison 2, Shea 2, Dawson, Woodards
35	Mar 27	Wed	SL Div 1	A	Brentford	W	2-1	4,000	Harrison, Spratt (og)
36	Apr 5	Fri	SL Div 1	H	Norwich City	W	4-0	10,000	Shea 3, Harrison
37	Apr 6	Sat	SL Div 1	H	Northampton Town	L	0-2	10,000	
38	Apr 8	Mon	SL Div 1	A	Norwich City	D	2-2	12,000	Shea, Woodards
39	Apr 9	Tue	SL Div 1	A	Leyton	L	1-3	3,000	Shea
40	Apr 13	Sat	SL Div 1	A	Brighton & Hove Albion	L	0-2	5,000	
41	Apr 20	Sat	SL Div 1	H	Stoke City	D	0-0	8,000	
42	Apr 22	Mon	SL Div 1	A	Swindon Town	L	1-3	2,000	Mackesy
43	Apr 27	Sat	SL Div 1	A	Coventry City	L	0-2	5,000	

Team Line-Ups

ASHTON Herbert	BELL George	BLACKBURN Fred	BOURNE Stanley	BRADFORD T.	BURRILL Frank	BUTCHER George	CALDWELL Thomas	DAWSON Harold	FAIRMAN Robert	FROST Alf	GEGGUS John	GLOVER Victor	HARRISON Fred	HUGHES Joseph	KENNEDY William	MACKESY Jack	MASSEY Frederick	MEILLEAR Joe	MORRISON Jack	PIERCY Frank	RANDALL Tommy	REDWARD Frank	REDWOOD George	ROTHWELL James	SHEA Danny	WALDEN George	WEBB George	WHITEMAN Robert	WOODARDS Dan	
7							11		3		1		10							5	6			2	8		9	4		1
7							11		3		1		10		9					5	6			2	8			4		2
7									3		1		10		9				11	5	6			2	8			4		3
7						10					1	3							11	5	6			2	8		9	4		4
7	6					10	11				1									3				2	8		9	4	5	5
7						10	11				1	3								5	6	2			8		9	4		6
7									2		1	3	10			5			11		6				8		9	4		7
7									2		1	3	10		9	5			11		6				8			4		8
7									3		1		10			5			11		6			2	8		9	4		9
7												3	10	1					11		6			2	8		9	4	5	10
7												3	10	1					11		6			2	8		9	4	5	11
7												3	10	1	9				11	5	6			2	8			4		12
7												3	10	1					11	5	6			2	8		9	4		13
7						10						3	8	1	9				11	5	6			2				4		14
7	5											3	10	1	9				11		6			2	8			4		15
7	5											3	10	1	9				11		6			2	8			4		16
7	6											3	10	1					11					2	8		9	4	5	17
7	6					10	11					3		1										2	8		9	4	5	18
7	6						11					3	10	1	9								5	2	8			4		19
7	6					10			2			3	11	1	9	5									8			4		20
7	6					10			2			3	11	1						5					8		9	4		21
7	6					10			2			3	11	1	9		4			5	6				8					22
7	6						11		2			3	9	1	10										8			4	5	23
7	6								2			3	11	1	10										8		9	4	5	24
7	6						11		2			3	9	1	10								4		8				5	25
	6					10	11		2	9	1	3						7					4		8				5	26
	6					10	11		2	1	3	9						7					4		8				5	27
	6					10	11		2		3	9	1										4		8				5	28
7	6					10	11		2		3		1						9				4		8				5	29
7	6		9			10	11		2		3		1										4		8				5	30
7	6					10	11				3	9	1										4	2	8				5	31
	6					10					3	9	1						11					2	8	7		4	5	32
7	6					10		11	2		3	9	1										4		8				5	33
7	6			8				11	2		3	9	1												10			4	5	34
	4			8				11	2		3	9	1										6		10	7			5	35
7	6			8				11	2		3	9	1												10			4	5	36
7	9	6		8				11	2		3		1												10			4	5	37
7		3		8				11					9	1									6	2	10			4	5	38
7				8						1	3		9						11				6	2	10			4	5	39
7	4			8				11			3		9	1									6	2	10				5	40
	4		7	8				11			3		9	1									6	5	2		10			41
7	9	4		8				11			3			1					10				6	5	2					42
7	4							11	2	8	1	3	9										6		10				5	43

1912-13
Story of the season

The directors decided to retire trainer Tommy Robinson, who had been at the club since the Thames Ironworks days. In his place came reserve trainer **Charlie Paynter**.

Danny Shea began the season well, scoring twice against Exeter City in the opening 4–0 victory. He continued his success by getting two more in a 3–1 win at Southampton. By mid-October there had only been one defeat in the seven games played. Gillingham came to the Boleyn and left beaten 4–0 and a week later the Hammers scored three at Northampton – but unfortunately the home side scored four. In December there were four successive wins, including home victories against Swindon Town by 4–1 and a 5–0 win over Stoke City on Christmas Day. The return game with Stoke on Boxing Day was won 1–0 but days later came a 4–1 defeat at Coventry City. The New Year kicked off with a 2–0 home win over Watford, after which came startling news that upset the supporters. It was announced that leading scorer Danny Shea was being sold to Blackburn

Appearances & Goals 1912-13

	League		FA Cup		Total	
	Starts	Goals	Starts	Goals	Starts	Goals
ASHTON Herbert	36	5	4	0	40	5
ASKEW Leslie	30	2	2	0	32	2
BAILEY Daniel	10	2	0	0	10	0
BLACKBURN Fred	2	0	0	0	2	0
BURRILL Frank	2	1	0	0	2	1
BURTON Frank	5	0	0	0	5	0
BUTCHER George	4	3	2	0	6	3
CARTER Henry	9	0	0	0	9	0
CASEY Jack	24	3	4	0	28	3
CATON Harry	3	0	0	0	3	0
DAWSON Harold	12	2	0	0	12	2
DENYER Albert	29	11	4	1	33	12
FORSTER Harry	25	0	4	0	29	0
HARRISON Fred	19	4	4	1	23	5
HILSDON George	32	13	4	4	36	17
HUGHES Joseph	29	0	4	0	33	0
IRVINE George	16	0	0	0	16	0
MACKESY Jack	1	0	0	0	1	0
PUDDEFOOT Syd	4	1	0	0	4	1
RANDALL Tommy	35	2	4	0	39	2
ROTHWELL James	32	0	4	0	36	0
SHEA Danny	22	15	0	0	22	15
WHITEMAN Robert	8	0	0	0	8	0
WOODARDS Dan	29	1	4	0	33	1
Totals	**418**	**66**	**44**	**6**	**462**	**69**

Rovers. He had scored 111 goals in his 179 appearances and would be greatly missed. While he was with the Lancashire club he won a First Division championship medal and gained two England caps.

The FA Cup saw the Hammers travel to the Midlands to face First Division side West Bromwich Albion. Fred Harrison scored for West Ham in the 1–1 draw. In the replay the Albion raced into a two-goal lead but George Hilsdon then scored twice to force another replay. Before this took place the Hammers had to play away to Merthyr Town, and to avoid fatigue seven changes were made to the side; at one stage in the game West Ham were leading 2–1 but finally lost 6–2. The cup replay at West Bromwich proved to be a shock for the Midland side as the Hammers won 3–0, to face a return trip to Birmingham for an away tie with Aston Villa. The Hammers were well beaten by 5–0 on the day and the Villa went on to win the FA Cup that year.

Southern League - Division One
Final Table 1912-13

		HOME					AWAY					
	P	W	D	L	F	A	W	D	L	F	A	Pts
Plymouth Argyle	38	15	2	2	47	9	7	4	8	30	27	50
Swindon Town	38	13	5	1	44	16	7	3	9	22	25	48
West Ham United	38	11	6	2	39	15	7	6	6	27	31	48
Queens Park Rangers	38	14	4	1	33	10	4	6	9	13	26	46
Crystal Palace	38	13	3	3	38	13	4	8	7	17	23	45
Millwall	38	14	0	5	36	17	5	7	7	26	26	45
Exeter City	38	13	3	3	29	16	5	5	9	19	28	44
Reading	38	12	3	4	34	20	5	5	9	25	35	42
Brighton & Hove Albion	38	12	5	2	39	19	1	7	11	9	28	38
Northampton Town	38	11	4	4	42	17	1	8	10	19	31	36
Portsmouth	38	11	5	3	28	15	3	3	13	13	34	36
Merthyr Town	38	9	8	2	27	17	3	4	12	16	43	36
Coventry City	38	9	4	6	42	27	4	4	11	11	32	34
Watford	38	8	5	6	28	24	4	5	10	15	26	34
Gillingham	38	7	7	5	19	21	5	3	11	17	32	34
Bristol Rovers	38	9	6	4	37	23	3	3	13	18	41	33
Southampton	38	7	7	5	28	25	3	4	12	12	47	31
Norwich City	38	8	7	4	26	17	2	2	15	13	33	29
Brentford	38	10	3	6	27	17	1	2	16	15	38	27
Stoke City	38	8	3	8	21	17	2	1	16	18	58	24

After being knocked out of the FA Cup the league became a priority and the team then went on an amazing run of 14 undefeated games. They finished third in the league, just two points behind champions Plymouth Argyle. For the supporters it had been an excellent campaign but many thought that by keeping Shea they would have won the title.

GEORGE HILSDON

George played as an amateur with Clapton Orient and Luton Town before coming to West Ham in 1904.

In two seasons he scored 7 goals in 16 Southern League appearances and was not able to command a regular place in the side. In 1906 he was allowed to leave on a free transfer to Chelsea, a decision the club would later regret. He made a sensational start, scoring five goals as Chelsea beat Glossop 9–2, and finished as top scorer that season with 27 goals, which helped Chelsea win promotion to the First Division. He was also the top goalscorer the following season, when he scored four goals against Bristol City in the league and six goals against Worksop Town in the FA Cup as Chelsea won 9–1. It was this form that led him to win eight international caps for England. In six seasons he scored 107 goals in 164 league and cup appearances. George returned to Upton Park in 1912, where he spent three seasons before World War One broke out. He did better on his return, scoring 28 goals in his 74 games. When the war ended he had spells with Gillingham and Chatham. He died in Leicester in 1941 aged 56.

Season **1912-13** Southern League - Division One
Match Details

Manager **Syd King**   Final League Position **3/20**

	Date		Competition	Venue	Opponents	Results		Attendance	Scorers
1	Sep 2	Mon	SL Div 1	H	Exeter City	W	4-0	9,000	Shea 2, Dawson, Harrison
2	Sep 7	Sat	SL Div 1	H	Coventry City	L	1-2	12,000	Ashton
3	Sep 14	Sat	SL Div 1	A	Watford	W	2-0	5,000	Harrison, Shea
4	Sep 21	Sat	SL Div 1	H	Merthyr Town	D	1-1	7,000	Shea
5	Sep 28	Sat	SL Div 1	A	Crystal Palace	D	1-1	15,000	Hilsdon [pen]
6	Oct 5	Sat	SL Div 1	H	Plymouth Argyle	W	3-1	8,000	Dawson, Hilsdon, Shea
7	Oct 12	Sat	SL Div 1	A	Southampton	W	3-1	9,000	Shea 2, Hilsdon [pen]
8	Oct 19	Sat	SL Div 1	H	Reading	L	1-2	15,000	Hilsdon [pen]
9	Oct 26	Sat	SL Div 1	A	Norwich City	L	0-2	7,000	
10	Oct 30	Wed	SL Div 1	A	Exeter City	D	0-0	2,000	
11	Nov 2	Sat	SL Div 1	H	Gillingham	W	4-0	10,000	Denyer 2, Hilsdon 2 [1 pen]
12	Nov 9	Sat	SL Div 1	A	Northampton Town	L	3-4	6,000	Burrill, Casey, Shea
13	Nov 16	Sat	SL Div 1	H	Queens Park Rangers	W	1-0	14,000	Denyer
14	Nov 23	Sat	SL Div 1	A	Brentford	L	1-5	7,000	Shea
15	Nov 30	Sat	SL Div 1	H	Millwall	D	1-1	16,000	Hilsdon
16	Dec 7	Sat	SL Div 1	A	Bristol Rovers	L	1-2	8,000	Denyer
17	Dec 14	Sat	SL Div 1	H	Swindon Town	W	4-1	14,000	Denyer 2, Hilsdon 2
18	Dec 21	Sat	SL Div 1	A	Portsmouth	W	2-1	10,000	Ashton, Shea
19	Dec 25	Wed	SL Div 1	H	Stoke City	W	5-0	8,000	Shea 2, Ashton, Askew, Denyer
20	Dec 26	Thu	SL Div 1	A	Stoke City	W	1-0	5,000	Shea
21	Dec 28	Sat	SL Div 1	A	Coventry City	L	1-4	7,000	Shea
22	Jan 4	Sat	SL Div 1	H	Watford	W	2-0	10,000	Harrison, Shea [pen]
23	Jan 13	Mon	FAC 1	A	West Bromwich Albion	D	1-1	20,000	Harrison
24	Jan 16	Thu	FAC 1 Rep	H	West Bromwich Albion	D	2-2	15,000	Hilsdon 2 [1 pen]
25	Jan 18	Sat	SL Div 1	A	Merthyr Town	L	2-6	4,000	Butcher 2
26	Jan 22	Wed	FAC 1 : 2 Rep	N*	West Bromwich Albion	W	3-0	27,075	Hilsdon 2, Denyer
27	Jan 25	Sat	SL Div 1	H	Crystal Palace	D	1-1	14,000	Butcher
28	Feb 1	Sat	FAC 2	A	Aston Villa	L	0-5	50,000	
29	Feb 8	Sat	SL Div 1	A	Plymouth Argyle	W	2-0	8,000	Denyer, Woodards
30	Feb 15	Sat	SL Div 1	H	Southampton	D	1-1	5,000	Harrison
31	Mar 1	Sat	SL Div 1	H	Norwich City	W	2-1	8,000	Hilsdon 2 [1 pen]
32	Mar 8	Sat	SL Div 1	A	Gillingham	D	2-2	5,000	Casey 2
33	Mar 15	Sat	SL Div 1	H	Northampton Town	D	0-0	9,000	
34	Mar 21	Fri	SL Div 1	H	Brighton & Hove Albion	D	1-1	15,000	Puddefoot
35	Mar 22	Sat	SL Div 1	A	Queens Park Rangers	W	1-0	10,000	Denyer
36	Mar 24	Mon	SL Div 1	A	Brighton & Hove Albion	D	0-0	11,000	
37	Mar 29	Sat	SL Div 1	H	Brentford	W	2-1	7,000	Denyer, Hilsdon
38	Apr 5	Sat	SL Div 1	A	Millwall	W	3-1	24,000	Ashton, Bailey, Randall
39	Apr 12	Sat	SL Div 1	H	Bristol Rovers	W	3-1	8,000	Askew, Hilsdon, Randall
40	Apr 19	Sat	SL Div 1	A	Swindon Town	D	1-1	9,000	Denyer
41	Apr 23	Wed	SL Div 1	A	Reading	D	1-1	2,000	Denyer
42	Apr 26	Sat	SL Div 1	H	Portsmouth	W	2-1	8,000	Ashton, Bailey

* 2nd Replay at Stamford Bridge

Team Line-Ups

ASHTON Herbert	ASKEW Leslie	BAILEY Daniel	BLACKBURN Fred	BURRILL Frank	BURTON Frank	BUTCHER George	CARTER Henry	CASEY Jack	CATON Harry	DAWSON Harold	DENYER Albert	FORSTER Harry	HARRISON Fred	HILSDON George	HUGHES Joseph	IRVINE George	MACKESY Jack	PUDDEFOOT Syd	RANDALL Tommy	ROTHWELL James	SHEA Danny	WHITEMAN Robert	WOODARDS Dan	No.
7	5									11	9	3	10		1	2			6		8	4		1
7	5									11	9	3	10		1	2			6		8	4		2
7	5									11		3	10	9	1	2			6		8	4		3
7	5									11		3	10	9	1	2			6		8	4		4
7	5									11		3	9	10	1				6	2	8	4		5
7	5				3					11			9	10	1				6	2	8	4		6
7	5				3					11			9	10	1				6	2	8	4		7
7	5									11		3	9	10	1	2			6		8	4		8
7	5									11	4		9	10	1	3			6	2	8			9
7	5		10								9		11		1	3			6	2	8	4		10
7	5								11		9		10		1	3			6	2	8	4		11
7	5		10						11		9				1	3			6	2	8	4		12
7	5									11	9		10		1	3			6	2	8	4		13
7	5									11	9		10		1	3			6	2	8	4		14
7	5								11		9		10		1	3			6	2	8	4		15
7				5					11		10			9	1	3			6	2	8	4		16
7	5								11		9		10		1	3			6	2	8	4		17
7	5								11		9	3	10		1				6	2	8	4		18
7	5								11		9	3	10		1				6	2	8	4		19
7	5								11		9	3	10		1				6	2	8	4		20
7	5				6				11		9	3	10		1					2	8	4		21
7	5								11		10			9	1	3			6	2	8	4		22
7	5								11		8	3	9	10	1				6	2		4		23
7	5								11		8	3	9	10	1				6	2		4		24
			6			8			7	11	9		5			1	3	10		2		4		25
7						8			11		9	3	5	10	1				6	2		4		26
7						8			11		9	3	5	10	1				6	2		4		27
7						8			11		9	3	5	10	1				6	2		4		28
						8	1		11	7	9	3	5	10					6	2		4		29
7					2	8	1		11		9	3	5	10					6			4		30
7									11		8	3	5	10	1			9	6	2		4		31
7									11		8	3	5	10	1			9	6	2		4		32
7		8							11			3	5	10	1			9		2		6	4	33
7	5	8							11			3		10	1			9	6	2			4	34
7	5	8							11		9	3		10	1				6	2			4	35
7	5	8						1	11		9	3		10					6	2		4		36
11	5	8			3		1		7		9		4	10					6	2				37
7	5	8						1	11		9	3		10					6	2		4		38
7	5	8						1	11		9	3		10					6	2		4		39
7	5	8						1	11		9	3		10					6	2		4		40
7	5	8						1	11		9	3		10					6	2		4		41
7	5	8						1	11		9	3		10					6	2		4		42

1913-14
Story of the season

The club was now **in a better financial position** and during the close season **a new grandstand was built** to replace the one erected in 1904. There were two new recruits, full-back Tommy Brandon and forward Alf Leafe.

There was a creditable 1–1 draw at Millwall on the opening day followed by a 3–2 home defeat to Swindon Town. New boy Alf Leafe scored twice against Swindon and scored again in the next three games. In between defeats at Plymouth and Reading was a fine 5–1 home win against Southampton. A trip to Coventry City in November produced a 4–2 victory, with Leafe claiming a hat-trick. The centre-forward was on top of his form and scored in each of the victories against Gillingham, Brighton and

Appearances & Goals 1913-14

	League		FA Cup		Total	
	Starts	Goals	Starts	Goals	Starts	Goals
ASHTON Herbert	35	3	4	1	39	4
ASKEW Leslie	38	0	4	0	42	0
BAILEY Daniel	19	6	4	3	23	9
BEALE Robert	1	0	0	0	1	0
BOURNE William	1	0	0	0	1	0
BRANDON Thomas	31	0	3	0	34	0
BURRILL Frank	8	1	0	0	8	1
BURTON Frank	19	2	4	0	23	2
BUTCHER George	4	0	0	0	4	0
CARTER Henry	1	0	0	0	1	0
CASEY Jack	31	7	3	0	34	7
CATON Harry	3	0	0	0	3	0
DENYER Albert	17	5	0	0	17	5
DENYER Frank	2	0	0	0	2	0
FORSTER Harry	15	0	0	0	15	0
GODDARD James	1	0	0	0	1	0
HILSDON George	17	6	0	0	17	6
HUGHES Joseph	15	0	4	0	19	0
IRVINE George	5	0	0	0	5	0
LEAFE Alfred	33	20	4	1	37	21
LONSDALE Thomas	21	0	0	0	21	0
MACKESY Jack	3	0	0	0	3	0
PUDDEFOOT Syd	16	9	4	7	20	16
RANDALL Tommy	28	1	3	0	31	1
ROTHWELL James	10	0	3	0	13	0
STALLARD Arthur	2	1	0	0	2	1
TIRRELL Alfred	1	0	0	0	1	0
TRESADERN Jack	4	0	0	0	4	0
WHITEMAN Robert	7	0	0	0	7	0
WOODARDS Dan	30	0	4	0	34	0
Totals	**418**	**61**	**44**	**12**	**462**	**73**

Portsmouth. There was a poor 4–1 defeat at Swindon that saw Tom Brandon sent off.

In early January the Hammers fans were in for a treat as 14 goals were scored in successive home games. First up were Bristol Rovers who were beaten 6–1, with Syd Puddefoot scoring a hat-trick. Next was an FA Cup tie with Chesterfield of the Midland League. Fresh from his earlier hat-trick, centre-forward Puddefoot went better by scoring five in the 8–1 demolition. The second round of the FA Cup saw Crystal Palace beaten 2–0, with both goals being scored by Dan Bailey. The next round brought Liverpool to Upton Park, where the teams fought out a 1–1 draw. The Merseysiders were too strong in the replay, winning 5–1 before an attendance of 45,000.

In the league there were seven successive wins, pushing the side up to third in the table. There was a shock in April when the Hammers played at Watford. The home side,

languishing near the bottom of the league, won 6–0. This was a setback and only one win was recorded in the remaining games of the season. It was a good win, however, beating old rivals Millwall 3–2 at home. The campaign ended with a 5–1 defeat at Portsmouth, which saw the side finish in sixth position.

JACK TRESADERN

Jack started out at Barking before joining West Ham in 1913. He didn't enjoy the best of debuts as the Hammers were beaten 6–0 at Watford in the Southern League.

He was only able to make a few more appearances in the side before World War One broke out in 1914. During the war he managed to play in 20 games for West Ham in the wartime competitions. Playing at half-back he made up for his lack of height with his pace and terrier-like tackling.

After the war the Hammers were now in the Football League and he had an excellent season in 1922/23 as the Hammers were promoted to the First Division. In that campaign he also played in the first Wembley Cup Final when West Ham lost 2–0 to Bolton Wanderers. His fine form attracted the attention of the England selectors and he was capped against Scotland and Sweden.

In October 1924, after 166 games in the claret and blue, he joined Burnley. He was only with the Lancashire club for one season, playing in 23 matches, before he became player-manager at Northampton Town. He was later the manager at Crystal Palace, Tottenham, Plymouth Argyle, Chelmsford City ,Hastings and finally Tonbridge

Southern League - Division One Final Table 1913-14

	P	W	D	L	F	A	W	D	L	F	A	Pts
			HOME						**AWAY**			
Swindon Town	38	14	3	2	57	11	7	5	7	24	30	50
Crystal Palace	38	12	5	2	41	13	5	11	3	19	19	50
Northampton Town	38	11	8	0	31	11	3	11	5	19	26	47
Reading	38	14	4	1	32	12	3	6	10	11	24	44
Plymouth Argyle	38	11	6	2	25	12	4	7	8	21	30	43
West Ham United	**38**	**9**	**7**	**3**	**39**	**22**	**6**	**5**	**8**	**22**	**38**	**42**
Brighton & Hove Albion	38	12	5	2	30	16	3	7	9	13	29	42
Queens Park Rangers	38	10	6	3	28	14	6	3	10	17	29	41
Portsmouth	38	10	7	2	31	13	4	5	10	26	35	40
Cardiff City	38	10	6	3	27	11	3	6	10	19	31	38
Southampton	38	11	2	6	36	23	4	5	10	19	31	37
Exeter City	38	7	8	4	21	11	3	8	8	18	27	36
Gillingham	38	10	6	3	35	15	3	3	13	13	34	35
Norwich City	38	7	10	2	34	19	2	7	10	15	32	35
Millwall	38	10	6	3	34	20	1	6	12	17	36	34
Southend United	38	7	7	5	29	28	3	5	11	12	38	32
Bristol Rovers	38	10	5	4	32	25	0	6	13	14	42	31
Watford	38	9	4	6	37	20	1	5	13	13	36	29
Merthyr Town	38	7	7	5	23	18	2	3	14	15	43	28
Coventry City	38	4	8	7	28	28	2	6	11	15	40	26

Season **1913-14** Southern League - Division One
Match Details

Manager **Syd King**   Final League Position **6/20**

	Date		Competition	Venue	Opponents	Results		Attendance	Scorers
1	Sep 1	Mon	SL Div 1	A	Millwall	D	1-1	12,000	Hilsdon
2	Sep 6	Sat	SL Div 1	H	Swindon Town	L	2-3	25,000	Leafe 2
3	Sep 13	Sat	SL Div 1	A	Bristol Rovers	W	2-1	10,000	Denyer, Leafe
4	Sep 20	Sat	SL Div 1	H	Merthyr Town	W	3-1	15,000	Ashton, Casey, Leafe
5	Sep 27	Sat	SL Div 1	A	Queens Park Rangers	D	2-2	12,000	Denyer, Leafe
6	Oct 4	Sat	SL Div 1	A	Plymouth Argyle	L	0-3	10,000	
7	Oct 11	Sat	SL Div 1	H	Southampton	W	5-1	6,000	Hilsdon 2, Ashton, Burton, Casey
8	Oct 18	Sat	SL Div 1	A	Reading	L	0-2	8,000	
9	Oct 25	Sat	SL Div 1	H	Crystal Palace	L	1-2	13,000	Casey
10	Nov 1	Sat	SL Div 1	A	Coventry City	W	4-2	7,000	Leafe 3, Denyer
11	Nov 8	Sat	SL Div 1	H	Watford	D	1-1	10,000	Denyer
12	Nov 15	Sat	SL Div 1	A	Norwich City	L	0-1	7,000	
13	Nov 22	Sat	SL Div 1	H	Gillingham	W	3-1	10,000	Burrill, Leafe, Puddefoot
14	Nov 29	Sat	SL Div 1	A	Northampton Town	D	0-0	5,000	
15	Dec 6	Sat	SL Div 1	H	Southend United	L	0-1	10,000	
16	Dec 13	Sat	SL Div 1	A	Brighton & Hove Albion	W	1-0	6,000	Leafe
17	Dec 20	Sat	SL Div 1	H	Portsmouth	W	3-2	9,000	Denyer, Leafe [pen], Puddefoot
18	Dec 25	Thu	SL Div 1	H	Exeter City	D	1-1	18,000	Puddefoot
19	Dec 26	Fri	SL Div 1	A	Exeter City	D	1-1	7,000	Leafe
20	Dec 27	Sat	SL Div 1	A	Swindon Town	L	1-4	8,000	Puddefoot
21	Jan 3	Sat	SL Div 1	H	Bristol Rovers	W	6-1	14,000	Puddefoot 3, Bailey, Casey, Leafe
22	Jan 10	Sat	FAC 1	H	Chesterfield	W	8-1	16,000	Puddefoot 5, Ashton, Bailey, Leafe
23	Jan 17	Sat	SL Div 1	A	Merthyr Town	W	2-1	6,000	Casey, Puddefoot
24	Jan 24	Sat	SL Div 1	H	Queens Park Rangers	W	4-1	11,000	Casey 2, Bailey, Leafe
25	Jan 31	Sat	FAC 2	H	Crystal Palace	W	2-0	18,000	Bailey 2
26	Feb 7	Sat	SL Div 1	H	Plymouth Argyle	W	2-1	8,000	Leafe, Puddefoot
27	Feb 14	Sat	SL Div 1	A	Southampton	W	3-2	7,000	Bailey, Burton [pen], Leafe
28	Feb 21	Sat	FAC 3	H	Liverpool	D	1-1	16,000	Puddefoot
29	Feb 25	Wed	FAC 3 Rep	A	Liverpool	L	1-5	45,000	Puddefoot
30	Feb 28	Sat	SL Div 1	A	Crystal Palace	W	2-1	12,000	Ashton, Bailey
31	Mar 7	Sat	SL Div 1	H	Coventry City	W	1-0	14,000	Leafe
32	Mar 21	Sat	SL Div 1	H	Norwich City	D	1-1	6,000	Leafe
33	Mar 23	Mon	SL Div 1	H	Reading	D	0-0	5,000	
34	Mar 28	Sat	SL Div 1	A	Gillingham	L	1-3	7,000	Randall
35	Apr 1	Wed	SL Div 1	A	Watford	L	0-6	4,000	
36	Apr 4	Sat	SL Div 1	H	Northampton Town	D	1-1	10,000	Leafe
37	Apr 10	Fri	SL Div 1	A	Cardiff City	L	0-2	12,000	
38	Apr 11	Sat	SL Div 1	A	Southend United	D	1-1	7,000	Bailey
39	Apr 13	Mon	SL Div 1	H	Cardiff City	D	1-1	15,000	Leafe
40	Apr 14	Tue	SL Div 1	H	Millwall	W	3-2	15,000	Hilsdon 2, Stallard
41	Apr 18	Sat	SL Div 1	H	Brighton & Hove Albion	D	1-1	10,000	Hilsdon
42	Apr 25	Sat	SL Div 1	A	Portsmouth	L	1-5	8,000	Bailey

Team Line-Ups

ASHTON Herbert	ASKEW Leslie	BAILEY Daniel	BEALE Robert	BOURNE William	BRANDON Thomas	BURRILL Frank	BURTON Frank	BUTCHER George	CARTER Henry	CASEY Jack	CATON Harry	DENYER Albert	DENYER Frank	FORSTER Harry	GODDARD James	HILSDON George	HUGHES Joseph	IRVINE George	LEAFE Alfred	LONSDALE Thomas	MACKESY Jack	PUDDEFOOT Syd	RANDALL Tommy	ROTHWELL James	STALLARD Arthur	TIRRELL Alfred	TRESADERN Jack	WHITEMAN Robert	WOODARDS Dan	#
7	5	8								11		9		3		10	1					6	2						4	1
7	5	8								11				3		10	1	9				6	2						4	2
7	5				2					11		8		3		10	1	9				6							4	3
7	5				2					11		8		3		10	1	9				6							4	4
7	5				2					11		8		3		10	1	9				6							4	5
7	5				2					11		8		3		10	1	9				6							4	6
7	5						6			11		10		3		8	1	9							2			4		7
7	5									11		10		3		8	1	9				6	2					4		8
7	5									11		10		3		8		9	1			6	2						4	9
	5				2	8				11	7	9		3					10	1		6							4	10
	5				2	8				11	7	9		3	1				10			6							4	11
7	5				2	8				11				3		9	1		10			6							4	12
7	5				2	8			1	11				3					10			9	6						4	13
7	5				2	8				11				3					10	1		9	6						4	14
7	5				2	8				11				3					10	1		9	6						4	15
11	5				2					7						8		3	10	1		9	6						4	16
11	5				2					7						8		3	10	1		9	6						4	17
7	5	8			2				10	11								3		1		9	6						4	18
7	5				2					11						10		3	8	1		9	6						4	19
7	5	8			2		6			11					3				10	1		9							4	20
7	5	8			2		6			11									10	1		9			3				4	21
7	5	8					3			11							1		10			9	6		2				4	22
7	5	8			2		6			11							1		10			9			3				4	23
	5	8			2		6			11	7						1		10			9			3				4	24
7	5	8			2	6				11							1		10			9			3				4	25
7	5	8			2		6			11							1		10			9			3				4	26
7	5	8			2		6			11		9					1		10						3				4	27
7	5	8			2		3			11							1		10			9	6						4	28
7	5	8			2		6										1		10			9	11	3					4	29
7	5	8			2														10	1	11	9	6				3		4	30
7	5				2		3									8			10	1	11	9	6						4	31
7	5	8			2		3					9							10	1	11		6						4	32
7	5	10	11		2		3	8				9									1		6						4	33
7	5	9			2		3	8		11									10		1		6						4	34
7	5					9	3	8							2				10	1	11				6				4	35
7	5	8			2		3			11						9	1		10			6							4	36
7	5	8								11		9	2						10	1		6						4		37
7	5	8			2		3			11		9	4						10	1		6								38
7	5	8			2		3			11									10	1		9	6						4	39
7	5	8			2		3			11									10	1					9			6	4	40
7	5	8			2		3			11									10	1					9			6	4	41
7	5	8	1		2		3			11									10			9						6	4	42

1914-15
Story of the season

Before the season kicked off in September **World War One had already broken out**, but the Southern League, along with the Football League, **decided to continue with their fixtures**.

New players were goalkeeper Joe Webster, full-backs Bill Cope and George Speak, and Alf Fenwick, a forward. In the first two home games Syd Puddefoot scored twice in victories against Gillingham and Luton Town but away from home it was the same story with three successive defeats. There were home draws against Swindon and Queens Park Rangers and the away form improved with victories at Southend, Croydon Common and Watford. Inside-forward Alf Leafe scored in five successive games to bring his total to seven. Due to the war there were many restrictions, and attendances were poor. On Boxing Day Brighton were beaten 2–1 at home, with Puddefoot scoring twice. He went one better a few days later when scoring a hat-trick against Exeter City in a 4–1 victory at the Boleyn.

Appearances & Goals 1914-15

	League		FA Cup		Total	
	Starts	Goals	Starts	Goals	Starts	Goals
ASHTON Herbert	14	0	1	0	15	0
ASKEW Leslie	36	0	2	0	38	0
BAILEY Daniel	20	5	0	0	20	5
BRANDON Thomas	2	0	0	0	2	0
BURTON Frank	26	2	2	0	28	2
BUTCHER George	9	1	0	0	9	1
CARR James	9	1	0	0	9	1
CASEY Jack	19	2	2	1	21	3
CATON Harry	4	0	0	0	4	0
COPE William	31	0	2	0	33	0
FENWICK Alfred	19	1	2	0	21	1
HILSDON George	20	5	1	0	21	5
HUGHES Joseph	21	0	2	0	23	0
LEAFE Alfred	30	13	2	3	32	16
MACKESY Jack	5	1	0	0	5	1
PUDDEFOOT Syd	35	18	2	0	37	18
RANDALL Tommy	5	0	0	0	5	0
SPEAK George	13	0	0	0	13	0
STALLARD Arthur	11	7	0	0	11	7
TIRRELL Alfred	6	0	0	0	6	0
TRESADERN Jack	2	0	0	0	2	0
WEBSTER Joseph	17	0	0	0	17	0
WHITEMAN Robert	34	1	2	0	36	1
WOODARDS Dan	20	0	2	0	22	0
WRIGHT Percy	10	1	0	0	10	1
Totals	**418**	**58**	**22**	**4**	**440**	**62**

The FA Cup brought an exciting clash with Newcastle United which saw Alf Leafe score twice in a 2–2 home draw. Alf scored again in the replay but the Geordies progressed by winning 3–2 before 28,130 fans. Portsmouth and Southend were beaten at home and following the 1–1 draw with Millwall the team were undefeated in nine games and up to second in the league. However, despite home wins against Cardiff City and Watford, there were three away defeats which left the team in fourth place as the season ended.

The next four seasons saw the club compete in wartime competitions as hostilities continued. There were many West Ham players who fought for their country and Arthur Stallard paid the ultimate price. The following former West Ham players were also killed in action: Frank Cannon, Frank Costello, Fred Griffiths, Sydney Hammond, William Jones, William Kennedy and William Kirby.

WILLIAM COPE

Bill Cope was a full-back whose football career spanned 19 years. He joined Second Division Burslem Port Vale in 1904 and in three seasons he made 80 appearances, scoring one goal.

After the club resigned from the league in 1907 he was transferred to Stoke City where he played in 31 games in season 1907–08. Stoke also resigned from the league and he then moved on to Second Division Oldham Athletic, appearing in the side that won promotion to the First Division in 1910. He spent six years at Boundary Park, playing in 65 matches, before coming south to join West Ham in 1914.

Playing in the Southern League, he made 33 appearances in that campaign played during the first year of World War One. In five seasons playing in wartime football he played in 111 games and was in the side that won the London Combination in 1917. After the war West Ham had been elected to the Football League and Bill was able to play in a further 77 matches in the Second Division. For season 1922–23 he was at Wrexham, where he finished his footballing career, playing in 13 games. He died in Stoke in February 1937 aged 52.

Southern League - Division One Final Table 1914-15

	P	HOME					AWAY					Pts
		W	D	L	F	A	W	D	L	F	A	
Watford	38	12	4	3	37	15	10	4	5	31	31	52
Reading	38	12	4	3	37	16	9	3	7	37	27	49
Cardiff City	38	16	1	2	51	12	6	3	10	21	26	48
West Ham United	38	14	4	1	42	18	4	5	10	16	29	45
Northampton Town	38	11	5	3	37	22	5	6	8	19	29	43
Southampton	38	14	3	2	56	28	5	2	12	22	46	43
Portsmouth	38	10	5	4	26	14	6	5	8	28	28	42
Millwall	38	9	4	6	28	23	7	6	6	22	28	42
Swindon Town	38	11	5	3	55	21	4	6	9	22	38	41
Brighton & Hove Albion	38	11	5	3	29	16	5	2	12	17	31	39
Exeter City	38	10	3	6	32	16	5	5	9	18	25	38
Queens Park Rangers	38	8	4	7	30	28	5	8	6	25	28	38
Norwich City	38	10	6	3	33	16	1	8	10	20	40	36
Luton Town	38	6	3	10	27	34	7	5	7	34	39	34
Crystal Palace	38	8	4	7	24	25	5	4	10	23	36	34
Bristol Rovers	38	12	2	5	42	28	2	1	16	11	47	31
Plymouth Argyle	38	8	7	4	34	25	0	7	12	17	36	30
Southend United	38	8	5	6	27	20	2	3	14	17	44	28
Croydon Common	38	7	6	6	28	18	2	3	14	19	45	27
Gillingham	38	6	7	6	32	29	0	1	18	11	54	20

West Ham United were elected into the Football League Division 2 after the Second World War

Season **1914-15** Southern League - Division One
Match Details
Manager **Syd King**   Final League Position **4/20**

	Date		Competition	Venue	Opponents	Results		Attendance	Scorers
1	Sep 1	Tue	SL Div 1	H	Gillingham	W	2-1	5,000	Puddefoot 2
2	Sep 5	Sat	SL Div 1	A	Exeter City	L	1-3	4,000	Puddefoot
3	Sep 9	Wed	SL Div 1	A	Gillingham	L	0-4	2,000	
4	Sep 12	Sat	SL Div 1	H	Luton Town	W	3-0	5,000	Puddefoot 2, Hilsdon
5	Sep 19	Sat	SL Div 1	A	Portsmouth	L	1-3	7,000	Hilsdon
6	Sep 26	Sat	SL Div 1	H	Swindon Town	D	1-1	11,000	Puddefoot
7	Oct 3	Sat	SL Div 1	A	Southend United	W	1-0	5,000	Leafe
8	Oct 10	Sat	SL Div 1	H	Queens Park Rangers	D	2-2	12,000	Leafe, Puddefoot
9	Oct 17	Sat	SL Div 1	A	Millwall	L	1-2	15,000	Puddefoot
10	Oct 24	Sat	SL Div 1	H	Bristol Rovers	W	4-1	10,000	Bailey, Burton [pen], Leafe, Wright
11	Oct 31	Sat	SL Div 1	A	Croydon Common	W	2-1	5,000	Bailey, Leafe
12	Nov 7	Sat	SL Div 1	H	Reading	W	3-2	10,000	Bailey, Leafe, Puddefoot
13	Nov 14	Sat	SL Div 1	A	Southampton	L	1-3	5,000	Leafe
14	Nov 21	Sat	SL Div 1	H	Northampton Town	W	1-0	8,000	Leafe
15	Nov 28	Sat	SL Div 1	A	Watford	W	1-0	2,000	Bailey
16	Dec 5	Sat	SL Div 1	H	Plymouth Argyle	W	2-0	6,000	Butcher, Carr
17	Dec 12	Sat	SL Div 1	H	Crystal Palace	L	1-2	5,000	Mackesy
18	Dec 19	Sat	SL Div 1	A	Norwich City	D	0-0	4,000	
19	Dec 25	Fri	SL Div 1	A	Brighton & Hove Albion	D	0-0	1,000	
20	Dec 26	Sat	SL Div 1	H	Brighton & Hove Albion	W	2-1	9,600	Puddefoot 2
21	Jan 2	Sat	SL Div 1	H	Exeter City	W	4-1	7,000	Puddefoot 3, Fenwick
22	Jan 9	Sat	FAC 1	H	Newcastle United	D	2-2	15,000	Leafe 2
23	Jan 16	Sat	FAC 1 Rep	A	Newcastle United	L	2-3	28,130	Casey, Leafe
24	Jan 23	Sat	SL Div 1	H	Portsmouth	W	4-3	3,000	Leafe 2, Burton [pen], Casey
25	Jan 30	Sat	SL Div 1	A	Swindon Town	D	1-1	3,000	Casey
26	Feb 6	Sat	SL Div 1	H	Southend United	W	3-1	5,000	Puddefoot 2, Leafe
27	Feb 13	Sat	SL Div 1	A	Queens Park Rangers	D	1-1	5,000	Whiteman
28	Feb 20	Sat	SL Div 1	H	Millwall	D	1-1	17,000	Puddefoot
29	Feb 27	Sat	SL Div 1	A	Bristol Rovers	L	0-1	3,000	
30	Mar 6	Sat	SL Div 1	H	Croydon Common	W	1-0	5,000	Hilsdon
31	Mar 10	Wed	SL Div 1	A	Luton Town	W	2-1	7,000	Bailey, Leafe
32	Mar 13	Sat	SL Div 1	A	Reading	L	1-3	7,000	Leafe
33	Mar 20	Sat	SL Div 1	H	Southampton	W	3-0	8,000	Hilsdon [pen], Leafe, Stallard
34	Mar 27	Sat	SL Div 1	A	Northampton Town	D	1-1	1,500	Stallard
35	Apr 2	Fri	SL Div 1	H	Cardiff City	W	2-1	13,000	Stallard 2
36	Apr 3	Sat	SL Div 1	H	Watford	W	2-0	10,000	Hilsdon [pen], Puddefoot
37	Apr 5	Mon	SL Div 1	A	Cardiff City	L	1-2	10,000	Stallard
38	Apr 10	Sat	SL Div 1	A	Plymouth Argyle	L	0-1	5,000	
39	Apr 17	Sat	SL Div 1	A	Crystal Palace	L	1-2	4,000	Stallard
40	Apr 24	Sat	SL Div 1	H	Norwich City	D	1-1	3,000	Stallard

Team Line-Ups

ASHTON Herbert	ASKEW Leslie	BAILEY Daniel	BRANDON Thomas	BURTON Frank	BUTCHER George	CARR James	CASEY Jack	CATON Harry	COPE William	FENWICK Alfred	HILSDON George	HUGHES Joseph	LEAFE Alfred	MACKESY Jack	PUDDEFOOT Syd	RANDALL Tommy	SPEAK George	STALLARD Arthur	TIRRELL Alfred	TRESADERN Jack	WEBSTER Joseph	WHITEMAN Robert	WOODARDS Dan	WRIGHT Percy	
7	5	8							2	4			10		9	6	3		1					11	1
7	5	8							2	4			10		9	6	3		1					11	2
7	5	8	6						2				10		9		3		1				4	11	3
7	5	8							2	6	10				9		3		1			4		11	4
7	5	8	2						3	6	10				9				1			4		11	5
7	5	8	3			11			2	6	10				9				1			4			6
7	5	8	3			11			2	6			10		9				1			4			7
7	5	8	3			11			2	6			10		9				1			4			8
7	5		3			11			2		8		10		9					6	1	4			9
7	5	8	3						2	6			10		9				1					11	10
	5	8	2			11		7		6			10		9			3	1			4			11
7	5	8	2			11				6			10		9			3	1			4			12
7	5	8	2			11				6			10		9			3	1						13
7	5		2	8		11							10		9	6		3	1			4			14
7	5	9	2	8		11								10		6		3	1			4			15
	5	7	2	8		11								10	9	6		3	1			4			16
	5	7	2	8		11								10	9			3		6	1	4			17
	5	9	2	8			11		3	10		1	7									4	6		18
	5	9	2	8			11		3	10		1	7									4	6		19
	5		2	8			11		3	10		1	7		9							4	6		20
	5		2				11		3	10	8	1	7		9							4	6		21
	5		2				11		3	10	8	1	7		9							4	6		22
7	5		2				11		3	10		1	8		9							4	6		23
	5		2				11		3	8	10	1	7		9							4	6		24
			2	8		7	11		3	5	10	1			9							4	6		25
			2	8			11		3	5	10	1	7		9							4	6		26
	5		2				11	7	3		10	1	8		9							4	6		27
	5		2				11	7	3		10	1	8		9							4	6		28
	5		2				11	7	3		10	1	8		9							4	6		29
	5		2				11		3		10	1	7		8			9				4	6		30
	5	10	2				11		3			1	7		8			9				4	6		31
	5	10	2				11		3	6		1	7		8			9				4			32
	5						11		2		10	1	7		8		3	9				4	6		33
	5						11		2		10	1	7		8		3	9				4	6		34
	5								2		10	1	7		8		3	9				4	6	11	35
	5				4				2		10	1	7		8		3	9					6	11	36
	5								2		10	1	7		8		3	9				4	6	11	37
	5						11		2			1	7		8		3	9				4	6	10	38
	5								2		10	1	7	11	8		3	9				4	6		39
	5	7							2		10	1		11	8		3	9				4	6		40

1915-16
Hammers in Wartime

West Ham United **played a commendable part** in providing the public with some diversion during **two world wars**.

Appearances & Goals 1915-16

	Total	
	Starts	Goals
APPLEBY [Guest]	2	0
ASHTON Herbert	16	1
ASKEW William	28	0
BAILEY Daniel	4	1
BOURNE [Guest]	6	0
BURGE W. [Guest]	1	1
BURRILL Frank	2	0
BURTON Frank	22	0
BURTON John	4	2
BUTCHER George	1	0
CAMERON [Guest]	2	0
CASEY Jack	20	4
CATON Harold	18	1
COPE William	29	0
CROSS [Guest]	1	0
CUNNINGHAM Andrew [Guest]	5	2
FENWICK Alfred	19	3
GIBBS [Guest]	1	0
HARROLD James [Guest]	1	0
HIGGS William [Guest]	3	0
HUFTON Edward	19	0
HUGHES Joseph	4	0
LEAHY Edward [Guest]	13	0
MACKESY Jack	20	6
MASTERMAN Wallace [Guest]	6	4
McGINN Alex [Guest]	2	0
PARKER H. [Guest]	1	0
PIGGOTT [Guest]	28	1
PUDDEFOOT Syd	31	25
SHEA Danny	27	17
SPEAK George	3	0
STALLARD Arthur	17	11
TIRRELL Alfred	1	0
TOUGH H. [Guest]	1	0
TRESADERN Jack	1	0
WHITEMAN Robert	3	0
WOODARDS Dan	32	0
Totals	**394**	**79**

During World War One, the Hammers not only achieved a great deal in taking people's minds, momentarily at least, off the conflict, they also earned themselves sufficient status to win a place in the Football League once the fighting was over.

In 1915, Syd King was in his 16th year with the club and he was to skilfully guide Hammers through the testing times ahead. In the summer of that year it was decided that all League and Cup football should be suspended in favour of local, regionalised tournaments for which there would be no prizes and no professionalism.

The suspension of players' contracts for the duration meant that individuals were given virtual freedom to play where they liked and West Ham, in particular, benefitted from the arrangement. A host of famous names soon began to appear in Hammers' colours.

From the start of the wartime programme, in September 1915, Syd King took full advantage of this and players from provincial clubs, who found themselves stationed nearby, were drafted into the Hammers' teams. The garrisons at Woolwich and Colchester were particularly happy hunting grounds.

The first season, Hammers enjoyed the skills of Ted Hufton, Danny Shea (then still a Blackburn player), Bill Masterman (like Hufton from Sheffield United) and Andy Cunningham, the Glasgow Rangers player destined to win a number of caps after the war.

Yet it was a local boy, Syd Puddefoot, who did most to lift Hammers to fourth place in the London Combination Championship. His 25 goals put him amongst the country's leading marksmen.

The new league comprised five Football League clubs and seven from the Southern League and although the players were unpaid, pride was still at stake and Hammers had their share of offenders as vigour sometimes overstepped the mark. Between November 1915 and September 1916 four West Ham players were sent off.

Bill Askew, Danny Shea (along with Clapton Orient's Hinds), and Alf Fenwick all fell foul of referees. Perhaps the most unlikely wrongdoer was Herbert Ashton, who was dismissed in the home game against Watford. Before he reached the dressing-room the visitors goalkeeper, Williams intervened and won Ashton a reprieve.

On a happier note, Puddefoot scored five in the 8-2 thrashing of Arsenal on Boxing Day and also recorded two hat-tricks that season; also among the goals was Danny Shea who finished with 17 goals.

London Combination Principal Tournament Final Table 1915-16

	P	W	D	L	F	A	Pts
Chelsea	22	17	3	2	71	18	37
Millwall	22	12	6	4	46	24	30
Arsenal	22	10	5	7	43	46	25
West Ham United	**22**	**10**	**4**	**8**	**47**	**35**	**24**
Fulham	22	10	4	8	45	37	24
Tottenham Hotspur	22	8	8	6	38	35	24
Brentford	22	6	8	8	36	40	20
Queens Park Rangers	22	8	3	11	27	41	19
Crystal Palace	22	8	3	11	35	55	19
Watford	22	8	1	13	37	46	17
Clapton Orient	22	4	6	12	22	44	14
Croydon Common	22	3	5	14	24	50	11

London Combination Supplementary Tournament Final Table 1915-16

	P	W	D	L	F	A	Pts
Chelsea	14	10	1	3	50	15	21
West Ham United	**14**	**9**	**2**	**3**	**32**	**16**	**20**
Tottenham Hotspur	14	8	3	3	32	22	19
Fulham	14	9	0	5	38	19	18
Millwall	14	8	2	4	30	22	18
Crystal Palace	14	8	2	4	41	29	18
Watford	14	5	3	6	22	20	13
Brentford	14	5	2	7	29	33	12
Croydon Common	14	4	3	7	28	27	11
Clapton Orient	14	3	4	7	17	27	10
Arsenal	14	3	4	7	19	31	10
Luton Town	14	4	1	9	31	44	9
Queens Park Rangers	14	2	5	7	14	37	9
Portsmouth	14	2	2	8	23	64	8

Season **1915-16** London Combination Principal Tournament
Match Details

Manager **Syd King**   Final League Position **4/12**

	Date		Venue	Opponents	Results		Attendance	Scorers
1	Sep 4	Sat	A	Brentford	L	1-2	2,000	Shea
2	Sep 11	Sat	H	Chelsea	D	0-0	12,000	
3	Sep 18	Sat	H	Tottenham Hotspur	D	1-1	8,000	Stallard
4	Sep 25	Sat	A	Crystal Palace	L	0-2	2,500	
5	Oct 2	Sat	H	Queens Park Rangers	W	2-1	4,000	Burton J., Puddefoot
6	Oct 9	Sat	A	Fulham	L	0-1	7,000	
7	Oct 16	Sat	H	Clapton Orient	W	5-2	6,500	Shea 2, Ashton, Burton J., Casey
8	Oct 23	Sat	A	Watford	W	3-2	3,000	Bailey, Mackesy, Puddefoot
9	Oct 30	Sat	H	Millwall	W	2-1	12,000	Shea, Stallard
10	Nov 6	Sat	A	Croydon Common	D	1-1	2,000	Puddefoot
11	Nov 13	Sat	H	Brentford	W	4-1	3,000	Puddefoot 2, Mackesy, Shea
12	Nov 20	Sat	A	Chelsea	L	2-5	12,000	Burge, Puddefoot
13	Nov 27	Sat	A	Tottenham Hotspur	L	0-3	5,000	
14	Dec 4	Sat	H	Crystal Palace	W	3-1	3,000	Puddefoot 3
15	Dec 11	Sat	A	Queens Park Rangers	D	1-1	2,000	Casey
16	Dec 18	Sat	H	Fulham	L	2-3	4,000	Masterman, Puddefoot
17	Dec 25	Sat	H	Arsenal	W	8-2	5,500	Puddefoot 5, Masterman 2, Shea
18	Dec 27	Mon	A	Arsenal	L	2-3	8,869	Fenwick, Stallard
19	Jan 1	Sat	A	Clapton Orient	W	2-1	2,000	Fenwick, Stallard
20	Jan 8	Sat	H	Watford	W	5-1	5,000	Shea 3, Masterman, Mackesy
21	Jan 15	Sat	A	Millwall	L	0-1	8,000	
22	Jan 22	Sat	H	Croydon Common	W	3-0	5,000	Caton, Fenwick, Stallard

London Combination Supplementary Tournament
Match Details

Manager **Syd King**   Final League Position **2/14**

	Date		Venue	Opponents	Results		Attendance	Scorers
1	Feb 5	Sat	H	Tottenham Hotspur	W	2-0	7,000	Stallard 2
2	Feb 12	Sat	A	Millwall	L	0-1	6,000	
3	Feb 19	Sat	H	Chelsea	W	2-0	9,000	Mackesy, Puddefoot
4	Mar 4	Sat	H	Brentford	W	4-2	2,000	Stallard 3, Shea
5	Mar 11	Sat	A	Reading	W	4-0	4,000	Puddefoot 3, Shea
6	Mar 18	Sat	H	Millwall	W	2-1	12,000	Puddefoot 2
7	Mar 25	Sat	A	Chelsea	L	0-4	8,000	
8	Apr 1	Sat	H	Watford	D	2-2	8,000	Shea 2
9	Apr 8	Sat	A	Brentford	W	3-1	3,000	Mackesy 2, Puddefoot
10	Apr 15	Sat	H	Reading	W	7-0	5,500	Cunningham 2, Puddefoot 2, Shea 2, Casey
11	Apr 21	Fri	A	Clapton Orient	L	1-3	6,000	Casey
12	Apr 22	Sat	H	Clapton Orient	W	2-1	10,000	Piggott, Puddefoot
13	Apr 29	Sat	A	Tottenham Hotspur	D	1-1	7,000	Stallard
14	May 6	Sat	A	Watford	W	2-0	3,500	Shea 2

Team Line-Ups

1	2	3	4	5	6	7	8	9	10	11	
Leahy	Cope	Burton F.	Fenwick	Askew	Woodards	Caton	Shea	Puddefoot	Butcher	Casey	1
Leahy	Cope	Burton F.	Fenwick	Askew	Woodards	Ashton	Shea	Stallard	Puddefoot	Mackesy	2
Leahy	Cope	Burton F.	Piggott	Askew	Harold	Ashton	Shea	Stallard	Puddefoot	Casey	3
Leahy	Cope	Speak	Whiteman	Askew	Burton F.	Caton	Shea	Stallard	Puddefoot	Ashton	4
Leahy	Cope	Speak	Whiteman	Askew	Woodards	Ashton	Shea	Puddefoot	Burton J.	Casey	5
Leahy	Cope	Burton F.	Fenwick	Askew	Woodards	Ashton	Shea	Puddefoot	Burton J.	Casey	6
Leahy	Cope	Burton F.	Piggott	Askew	Woodards	Ashton	Shea	Puddefoot	Burton J.	Casey	7
Leahy	Cope	Fenwick	Piggott	Askew	Woodards	Ashton	Shea	Bailey	Puddefoot	Mackesy	8
Leahy	Cope	Fenwick	Piggott	Askew	Woodards	Ashton	Shea	Stallard	Puddefoot	Mackesy	9
Hughes	Cope	Bourne	Piggott	Fenwick	Woodards	Ashton	Shea	Bailey	Puddefoot	Mackesy	10
Hughes	Cope	Bourne	Piggott	Fenwick	Woodards	Ashton	Shea	Bailey	Puddefoot	Mackesy	11
Hughes	Cope	Burton F.	Piggott	Fenwick	Woodards	Caton	Appleby	Burge	Puddefoot	Casey	12
Leahy	Tirrell	Fenwick	Burton J.	Askew	Woodards	Caton	Bailey	Bourne	Puddefoot	Mackesy	13
Leahy	Burton F.	Bourne	Piggott	Askew	Woodards	Caton	Hilsdon	Puddefoot	Mackesy	Casey	14
Hughes	Burton F.	Bourne	Piggott	Fenwick	Woodards	Caton	Hilsdon	Puddefoot	Gibbs	Casey	15
Hufton	Burton F.	Bourne	Piggott	Woodards	Tresadern	Stallard	Appleby	Puddefoot	Masterman	Cross	16
Hufton	Burton F.	Cope	Piggott	Fenwick	Woodards	Stallard	Shea	Puddefoot	Masterman	Mackesy	17
Hufton	Burton F.	Cope	Piggott	Fenwick	Woodards	Stallard	Shea	Puddefoot	Masterman	Casey	18
Hufton	Burton F.	Fenwick	Piggott	Askew	Whiteman	Stallard	Shea	Puddefoot	Masterman	Mackesy	19
Hufton	Burton F.	Fenwick	Piggott	Askew	Woodards	Caton	Shea	Stallard	Masterman	Mackesy	20
Hufton	Burton F.	Fenwick	Piggott	Askew	Woodards	Caton	Shea	Stallard	Masterman	Casey	21
Leahy	Burton F.	Cope	Piggott	Askew	Woodards	Caton	Mackesy	Stallard	Fenwick	Casey	22

Team Line-Ups

1	2	3	4	5	6	7	8	9	10	11	
Hufton	Burton F.	Cope	Piggott	Askew	Woodards	Caton	Fenwick	Stallard	Burill	Casey	1
Hufton	Burton F.	Cope	Piggott	Askew	Fenwick	Caton	Burill	Stallard	Macesy	Casey	2
Hufton	Burton F.	Cope	Piggott	Askew	Woodards	Caton	Shea	Puddefoot	Macesy	Casey	3
Hufton	Higgs	Cope	Piggott	Askew	Woodards	Caton	Shea	Stallard	Puddefoot	Casey	4
Hufton	Burton F.	Cope	Piggott	Askew	Woodards	Caton	Shea	Puddefoot	McGinn	Cameron	5
Hufton	Burton F.	Cope	Piggott	Parker	Woodards	Caton	Shea	Puddefoot	Macesy	Casey	6
Hufton	Burton F.	Cope	Piggott	Askew	Woodards	Caton	Shea	Puddefoot	Cunningham	Casey	7
Hufton	Woodards	Cope	Piggott	Askew	Ashton	Caton	Shea	Puddefoot	McGinn	Cameron	8
Leahy	Caton	Cope	Piggott	Askew	Woodards	Ashton	Shea	Puddefoot	Macesy	Casey	9
Hufton	Higgs	Cope	Woodards	Askew	Mackesy	Ashton	Shea	Puddefoot	Cunningham	Casey	10
Hufton	Cope	Speak	Piggott	Askew	Woodards	Ashton	Puddefoot	Stallard	Mackesy	Casey	11
Hufton	Fenwick	Cope	Piggott	Askew	Woodards	Ashton	Shea	Puddefoot	Cunningham	Casey	12
Hufton	Tough	Cope	Piggott	Askew	Woodards	Stallard	Shea	Puddefoot	Cunningham	Mackesy	13
Hufton	Higgs	Cope	Ashton	Askew	Woodards	Stallard	Shea	Puddefoot	Cunningham	Mackesy	14

1916-17

Appearances & Goals 1916-17

	Total	
	Starts	Goals
ASHTON Herbert	27	3
BAILEY Daniel	1	0
BAVERSTOCK H. [Guest]	1	0
BOLTON [Guest]	1	0
BROWN W. [Guest]	2	0
BURTON Frank	14	0
CARLESS J. [Guest]	2	0
CASEY Jack	8	1
CHEDGZOY Sam [Guest]	22	10
COOK H. [Guest]	1	1
COPE William	31	0
CRABTREE J. [Guest]	2	0
CURRY J. [Guest]	1	0
DAVIES S. [Guest]	10	0
DAY J. [Guest]	3	0
DIVERS John [Guest]	2	0
FEEBURY J. [Guest]	7	0
FENWICK Alfred	2	0
HARRISON George [Guest]	16	3
HEMSHALL Horace [Guest]	2	0
HODSON James [Guest]	16	0
HUFTON Edward	4	0
KAY George	18	5
KEARNS J. [Guest]	3	0
KINNAIRD [Guest]	1	0
KIRSOPP William [Guest]	9	0
KNIGHT J. [Guest]	3	0
LEAHY Edward [Guest]	34	0
MACKESY Jack	11	4
MacLACHLAN Albert [Guest]	20	0
MACONNACHIE Jock [Guest]	6	0
MANNING J. [Guest]	4	0
McBEAN Robert [Guest]	3	0
McDOUGALL Robert [Guest]	23	16
MOORE [Guest]	1	0
MORTON J. [Guest]	2	0
PIGGOTT [Guest]	12	0
PUDDEFOOT Syd	34	24
ROSS W. [Guest]	1	0
ROTHWELL James	2	0
SHEA Danny	32	32
SMITH Percy [Guest]	3	0
STALLARD Arthur	7	6
STEEL [Guest]	1	0
TAYLOR W. [Guest]	3	0
WALTERS Joe [Guest]	3	1
WATSON [Guest]	2	1
WOODARDS Dan	25	0
WRIGHT Percy	2	2
own goal		1
Totals	**440**	**110**

Amidst all this, of course, the fighting in France and Belgium continued and Hammers fans were given a sharp reminder when the Athletic News reported the death of Bill Kennedy who lost his life serving with the London Scottish Regiment. He had spent two years at Upton Park between 1910 and 1912, mainly as understudy to George Webb. The London Combination had been split for this campaign into two tournaments, the Principal Tournament which ran from September to January and the Supplementary Tournament which ran from February until May.

In 1916/17, West Ham won the London Combination title with seven points to spare. They used 49 players in the season, 30 of whom were 'guests'. One 'well-known' (yet still unknown) full-back requested anonymity and appeared under the name, J.Day'.

Hammers began the season in blistering style, going nine games before their first defeat, and another 18 before their second. In only three games did they fail to score.

Regular players included four of Everton's 1914-15 Football League Championship winning team — Harrison, Chedgzoy, Macconachie and Kirsopp. Walters and Hodson, members of the Oldham Athletic team that finished

London Combination
Final Table 1916-17

	P	W	D	L	F	A	Pts
West Ham United	40	30	5	5	110	45	65
Millwall	40	26	6	8	85	48	58
Chelsea	40	24	5	11	93	48	53
Tottenham Hotspur	40	24	5	11	112	64	53
Arsenal	40	19	10	11	62	47	48
Fulham	40	21	3	16	102	63	45
Luton Town	40	20	3	16	101	82	43
Crystal Palace	40	14	7	17	68	72	35
Southampton	40	13	8	18	57	80	34
Queens Park Rangers	40	10	9	20	48	86	29
Watford	40	8	9	22	69	115	25
Brentford	40	9	7	24	56	99	25
Portsmouth	40	9	4	27	58	117	22
Clapton Orient	40	6	7	27	49	104	19

runners-up to Everton, also played for Hammers, and Blackburn Rovers, who finished third, provided Danny Shea and Percy Smith.

For the first time West Ham exceeded 100 goals in a season and Puddefoot and Shea between them contributed 56 of the 110 goals West Ham scored in 40 matches. The best win of the season was the 4-1 victory at runners up Millwall

Soon after the outbreak of war, letters had appeared in newspapers accusing the football authorities of almost treasonable behaviour in allowing the game to continue whilst thousands more, less talented, young men were suffering the horrors of trench warfare. The Athletic News responded with regular mentions of sportsmen who had volunteered for military service, and in December 1914, the so-called Footballers' Battalion had been formed as part of the Middlesex Regiment.

Yet not all footballers were fit for the army. Bill Masterman, who had played for Sheffield United in the 1915 FA Cup Final and who turned out for Hammers the following season, was rejected for military service because he was deaf.

Others, including Puddefoot, worked long, exhausting and often dangerous shifts in munitions factories. In November 1915, for instance, a Bromley amateur called Burge made an eventful appearance for West Ham at Stamford Bridge. He scored once, missed two other chances at crucial times, and West Ham went down 5-2. Later it was revealed that he had completed a night shift at the Woolwich Arsenal only hours before the game and, at its conclusion, hurried off to begin another.

The course of the war meant that troops were continually on the move and King's task in raising a team became more difficult. In March 1917, scratching around for a side to play an important match against Spurs, he heard that MacLachlan (Aberdeen) and McDougal (Liverpool) would be returning from Ireland to their units in Wiltshire.

King wired the men's officer requesting their services, and MacLachlan and McDougal arrived just in time to help West Ham end Spurs' unbeaten run of 20 games.

Season **1916-17** London Combination
Match Details
Manager **Syd King**   Final League Position **1/14**

	Date		Venue	Opponents	Results		Attendance	Scorers
1	Sep 2	Sat	H	Arsenal	W	2-1	3,000	Chedgzoy, McDougall
2	Sep 9	Sat	A	Luton Town	W	4-3	3,000	Chedgzoy, McDougall, Puddefoot, Shea
3	Sep 16	Sat	H	Reading	W	5-1	5,000	Shea 4, Chedgzoy
4	Sep 23	Thu	A	Millwall	W	4-2	7,000	Ashton, Chedgzoy, McDougall, Wright
5	Sep 28	Sat	A	Tottenham Hotspur	W	2-1	3,000	Kay, Puddefoot
6	Sep 30	Mon	H	Watford	D	2-2	8,000	McDougall, Wright
7	Oct 7	Sat	A	Clapton Orient	W	4-0	4,500	Puddefoot 3, Shea
8	Oct 14	Sat	H	Fulham	W	2-0	10,000	McDougall. Shea
9	Oct 21	Sat	A	Queens Park Rangers	W	4-0	3,000	McDougall 2, Shea 2
10	Oct 28	Sat	A	Southampton	L	0-3	5,000	
11	Nov 4	Sat	H	Tottenham Hotspur	W	5-1	8,000	Kay 3, Shea 2
12	Nov 11	Sat	A	Crystal Palace	W	8-1	2,000	Shea 3, Chedgzoy 2, McDougall 2, Cook
13	Nov 18	Sat	H	Brentford	W	4-0	1,800	Shea 2, Ashton, Walters
14	Nov 25	Sat	A	Arsenal	W	2-0	7,000	McDougall, Shea
15	Dec 2	Sat	H	Luton Town	W	2-0	7,000	Kay, McDougall
16	Dec 9	Sat	A	Portsmouth	W	2-1	5,000	Shea, Stallard
17	Dec 23	Sat	A	Watford	W	3-1	500	McDougall 2, Puddefoot
18	Dec 25	Mon	A	Chelsea	D	1-1	20,000	McDougall
19	Dec 26	Tue	H	Chelsea	W	2-0	8,000	Puddefoot 2
20	Dec 30	Sat	H	Clapton Orient	W	6-1	6,000	Shea 3, Puddefoot 2, Mackesy
21	Jan 6	Sat	A	Fulham	W	2-0	8,000	Puddefoot, Shea
22	Jan 13	Sat	H	Queens Park Rangers	W	5-3	4,000	Shea 3, Puddefoot 2
23	Jan 20	Sat	H	Southampton	D	1-1	3,000	Shea
24	Jan 27	Sat	A	Tottenham Hotspur	D	0-0	7,000	
25	Feb 3	Sat	H	Crystal Palace	W	1-0	3,000	Puddefoot
26	Feb 10	Sat	A	Brentford	D	1-1	1,500	Harrison
27	Feb 17	Sat	H	Southampton	W	5-2	6,000	Stallard 2, Ashton, Chedgzoy, Mackesy
28	Feb 24	Sat	A	Clapton Orient	W	4-3	5,000	Chedgzoy 2, Puddefoot, Watson
29	Mar 3	Sat	A	Crystal Palace	L	1-3	5,000	Shea
30	Mar 10	Sat	H	Arsenal	L	2-3	6,000	Shea, Stallard
31	Mar 17	Sat	A	Portsmouth	W	5-2	5,000	Harrison 2, Stallard 2, Mackesy
32	Mar 24	Sat	H	Tottenham Hotspur	W	3-0	12,000	Chedgzoy, Puddefoot, Shea
33	Mar 31	Sat	A	Southampton	W	2-1	8,000	Puddefoot, Shea
34	Apr 6	Fri	H	Brentford	W	2-0	7,000	Puddefoot, Amos (og)
35	Apr 7	Sat	H	Clapton Orient	W	2-0	8,000	McDougall, Shea
36	Apr 9	Mon	A	Brentford	W	2-1	4,000	Mackesy, Puddefoot
37	Apr 10	Tue	H	Millwall	L	0-2	6,000	
38	Apr 14	Sat	H	Crystal Palace	W	2-1	7,000	Puddefoot 2
39	Apr 21	Sat	A	Arsenal	L	1-2	4,000	Puddefoot
40	Apr 28	Sat	H	Portsmouth	W	5-2	5,000	Puddefoot 2, Casey, McDougall, Shea

Team Line-Ups

1	2	3	4	5	6	7	8	9	10	11	
Hufton	Baverstock	Cope	Piggott	Kay	Maclachlan	Chedgzoy	Shea	Puddefoot	McDougall	Knight	1
Hufton	Cope	Hodson	Maclachlan	Kay	Woodards	Casey	Puddefoot	Chedgzoy	McDougall	Shea	2
Hufton	Maconnachie	Crabtree	Kay	Woodards	Chedgzoy	Shea	Puddefoot	Ashton	Casey	Hodson	3
Hufton	Hodson	Cope	Piggott	Kay	Maclachlan	Ashton	Chedgzoy	Puddefoot	McDougall	Wright	4
Leahy	Cope	Divers	Piggott	Kay	Woodards	Ashton	Shea	Puddefoot	Mackesy	Chedgzoy	5
Leahy	Hodson	Cope	Maclachlan	Maconnachie	Woodards	Ashton	Shea	Puddefoot	McDougall	Wright	6
Leahy	Hodson	Cope	Woodards	Kay	Maclachlan	Chedgzoy	Shea	Puddefoot	McDougall	Ashton	7
Leahy	Hodson	Burton	Woodards	Kay	Maclachlan	Chedgzoy	Shea	Puddefoot	McDougall	Ashton	8
Leahy	Hodson	Cope	Piggott	Woodards	Ashton	Chedgzoy	Shea	McDougall	Brown	Walters	9
Leahy	Hodson	Steel	Piggott	Kay	Woodards	Ashton	Smith	Puddefoot	Shea	Casey	10
Leahy	Hodson	Cope	Woodards	Kay	Maclachlan	Chedgzoy	Shea	Puddefoot	Mackesy	Hemshall	11
Leahy	Hodson	Maconnachie	Woodards	Kay	Maclachlan	Chedgzoy	Shea	Cook	McDougall	Hemshall	12
Leahy	Hodson	Burton	Woodards	Kay	Maclachlan	Chedgzoy	Shea	Puddefoot	Walters	Ashton	13
Leahy	Hodson	Cope	Morton	Kay	Maclachlan	Brown	Shea	Puddefoot	McDougall	McBean	14
Leahy	Hodson	Cope	Smith	Kay	Maclachlan	Chedgzoy	Shea	Puddefoot	McDougall	McBean	15
Ross	Hodson	Cope	Morton	Crabtree	Maclachlan	McBean	Shea	Stallard	McDougall	Casey	16
Leahy	Hodson	Cope	Woodards	Burton	Mackesy	Ashton	Shea	Puddefoot	McDougall	Casey	17
Leahy	Hodson	Cope	Woodards	Kay	Maclachlan	Chedgzoy	Shea	Puddefoot	McDougall	Ashton	18
Leahy	Rothwell	Cope	Woodards	Kay	Burton	Chedgzoy	Shea	Puddefoot	McDougall	Ashton	19
Leahy	Rothwell	Cope	Woodards	Kay	Maclachlan	Ashton	Shea	Smith	Puddefoot	Mackesy	20
Leahy	Burton	Cope	Woodards	Kay	Piggott	Chedgzoy	Shea	Puddefoot	McDougall	Ashton	21
Leahy	Divers	Cope	Ashton	Woodards	Piggott	Chedgzoy	Shea	Puddefoot	McDougall	Harrison	22
Leahy	Kearns	Cope	Woodards	Kay	Piggott	Ashton	Shea	Puddefoot	Kirsopp	Harrison	23
Leahy	Kearns	Cope	Piggott	Burton	Mackesy	Chedgzoy	Kirsopp	Stallard	Puddefoot	Harrison	24
Leahy	Kearns	Burton	Woodards	Davies	Piggott	Ashton	Chedgzoy	Puddefoot	Kirsopp	Harrison	25
Leahy	Knight	Burton	Davies	Manning	Curry	Ashton	Mackesy	Puddefoot	Kirsopp	Harrison	26
Leahy	Feebury	Cope	Davies	Manning	Woodards	Ashton	Chedgzoy	Stallard	Mackesy	Harrison	27
Leahy	Knight	Cope	Davies	Manning	Woodards	Ashton	Chedgzoy	Puddefoot	Watson	Harrison	28
Leahy	Feebury	Cope	Moore	Burton	Woodards	Ashton	Shea	Watson	Mackesy	Casey	29
Leahy	Feebury	Cope	Davies	Woodards	Ashton	Chedgzoy	Shea	Stallard	Puddefoot	Harrison	30
Leahy	Feebury	Cope	Bolton	Taylor	Carless	Kirsopp	Shea	Stallard	Mackesy	Harrison	31
Leahy	Day	Cope	Davies	Burton	Maclachlan	Chedgzoy	Shea	Puddefoot	McDougall	Harrison	32
Bailey	Feebury	Cope	Davies	Burton	Maclachlan	Kirsopp	Shea	Puddefoot	McDougall	Harrison	33
Leahy	Maconnachie	Cope	Piggott	Burton	Maclachlan	Kirsopp	Shea	Puddefoot	McDougall	Harrison	34
Leahy	Day	Cope	Davies	Fenwick	Maclachlan	Ashton	Shea	Puddefoot	McDougall	Harrison	35
Leahy	Day	Feebury	Piggott	Taylor	Davies	Casey	Mackesy	Stallard	Puddefoot	Kirsopp	36
Leahy	Burton	Cope	Davies	Taylor	Fenwick	Ashton	Puddefoot	Stallard	Mackesy	Harrison	37
Leahy	Maconnachie	Cope	Ashton	Burton	Woodards	Walters	Shea	Puddefoot	McDougall	Harrison	38
Leahy	Feebury	Maclachlan	Ashton	Manning	Carless	Kirsopp	Shea	Puddefoot	McDougall	Harrison	39
Leahy	Maconnachie	Cope	Woodards	Kinnaird	Maclachlan	Ashton	Shea	Puddefoot	McDougall	Casey	40

1917-18

Appearances & Goals 1917-18

	Total	
	Starts	Goals
ALLEN Percy	1	0
ASHTON Herbert	30	6
BELL [Guest]	3	0
BLYTHE [Guest]	1	0
BRENNAN J. [Guest]	3	0
BRIDGEMAN Willian [Guest]	2	0
BROWN W. [Guest]	2	0
BROWNLIE James [Guest]	1	0
BURKE [Guest]	7	6
BURTON Frank	4	0
BUTCHER George	1	0
CAMPBELL Alec [Guest]	5	0
CASEY Jack	2	1
COPE William	25	0
COWLESS [Guest]	1	1
CUNNINGHAM Andrew [Guest]	7	6
DODDS G. [Guest]	1	0
FERRIS [Guest]	2	0
GODDARD J. [Guest]	2	1
HAMILTON [Guest]	23	1
HEBDEN George [Guest]	2	0
HILSDON George	1	0
HODSON James [Guest]	28	0
HUFTON Edward	10	0
ISLIP Ernie [Guest]	4	0
JOHNSTONE [Guest]	28	2
KENLAN [Guest]	1	0
KIRBY [Guest]	1	0
KIRSOPP William [Guest]	11	6
LANGFORD [Guest]	1	0
LARCOMBE [Guest]	2	1
LAWTON [Guest]	1	0
LEAHY Edward [Guest]	15	0
LEE, [Guest]	4	0
MACKESY Jack	24	1
MACONNACHIE Jock [Guest]	9	0
MANNING J. [Guest]	16	0
MASSEY [Guest]	2	0
McDOUGALL Robert [Guest]	1	0
PIGGOTT [Guest]	1	0
PUDDEFOOT Syd	35	35
ROBERTS Frank [Guest]	13	14
SHEA Danny	14	15
STEVENSON [Guest]	14	0
TANNER [Guest]	1	0
TEMPEST [Guest]	2	0
TIRRELL Alfred	9	0
TRESADERN Jack	6	1
TUFNELL Harry [Guest]	6	3
TURLEY [Guest]	1	0
WILLIAMS [Guest]	3	0
WILLIAMS B. [Guest]	3	0
WOODARDS Dan	1	0
WRAY J. [Guest]	1	0
WRIGHT Percy	2	2
own goal		1
Totals	**396**	**103**

One criticism of West Ham was that they had won the title with 'northern imports', but the Athletic News congratulated them for taking the Championship despite having to make so many team changes.

In the third wartime season, West Ham scored at an even greater rate. Although the 103 goals were fewer than the previous season, they came from a reduced fixture list caused by travelling problems. Southampton, Luton, Portsmouth and Watford were forced out and Hammers longest journey was now to Brentford. The clubs played each other four times each, giving a 36-match league programme.

West Ham had nothing to show for topping the 100-goal mark again. They used 56 different players and for the third time in four seasons Puddefoot was top scorer, with 35 goals. Shea (15) and Manchester City's Frank Roberts (15 in only 14 appearances) trailed him.

Shea, who ended his association with West Ham after the December fixture with Brentford, scored four in the opening game, against Fulham. Puddefoot netted a hat-trick in the next game, at QPR, and by mid-November, Hammers had scored 36 goals in 11 games. Puddefoot claimed 14 of them and by the season's end he could boast a ten-match scoring sequence, ending with seven against Crystal Palace to equal a Combination record.

In that match, Hammers' outside-left, Jack Mackesy, was sent-off by referee Albert Neale. Some years later Mr Neale was to collapse and die whilst refereeing a Combination match between Charlton and West Ham at The Valley.

In 1917/18, matches between West Ham and Brentford gave special value for money. One-quarter of Hammers' goals that season were scored against the Bees who themselves contributed 11. The four games between the clubs produced 35 goals.

West Ham used six goalkeepers that season, the best-known being Third Lanark's Scottish international, James Brownlie. The youngest was 16-year-old England Schoolboy international, George Hebden. After the war he spent many years with Leicester City and, later, Gillingham.

The saddest event of 1917/18 was the death of Arthur Stallard, who was killed in action in France during the last week in November, seven months after his final game in Hammers' colours.

West Ham called upon 62 players in 1918/19, a club record. Two goalkeepers turned up for one game, against Arsenal in November, but the problem was solved when Hufton, the regular 'keeper, agreed to play at right-back.

The reason for the high number of players was a happy one — nine weeks after the start of the new season, the war came to an end. Servicemen were not released immediately, but travel became easier and many more professional players became available.

George Kay, absent from the whole of the previous season recovering from shell-shock, reappeared briefly; and another returnee was Ted Hufton, who had found himself in the front line as the war drew to its close. Of the newcomers, the most important was wing-half James McCrae from Scottish League club, Clyde.

It was McCrae who was the innocent victim of a stone-thrower during a Combination game at Stamford Bridge. McCrae apprehended the person and then had to receive police protection from the hostile home supporters.

London Combination Final Table 1917-18

	P	W	D	L	F	A	Pts
Chelsea	36	21	8	7	82	39	50
West Ham United	36	20	3	7	103	51	49
Fulham	36	20	7	9	75	60	47
Tottenham Hotspur	36	22	2	12	86	56	46
Arsenal	36	16	5	15	76	57	37
Brentford	36	16	3	17	81	94	35
Crystal Palace	36	13	4	19	54	83	30
Queens Park Rangers	36	14	2	20	43	73	30
Millwall	36	12	4	20	52	74	28
Clapton Orient	36	2	4	30	34	104	8

Season **1917-18** London Combination
Match Details
Manager **Syd King**   Final League Position **2/10**

	Date		Venue	Opponents		Results	Attendance	Scorers
1	Sep 1	Sat	H	Fulham	W	6-1	5,000	Shea 4, Roberts 2
2	Sep 8	Sat	A	Queens Park Rangers	W	3-0	5,000	Puddefoot 3
3	Sep 15	Sat	H	Clapton Orient	L	1-2	6,000	Goddard
4	Sep 22	Sat	A	Millwall	W	3-2	10,000	Kirsopp 2, Ashton
5	Sep 29	Sat	H	Tottenham Hotspur	W	1-0	6,000	Roberts
6	Oct 6	Sat	A	Chelsea	L	3-4	12,000	Casey, Hamilton, Puddefoot
7	Oct 13	Sat	H	Brentford	W	8-3	5,000	Shea 4, Roberts 3, Puddefoot
8	Oct 20	Sat	A	Arsenal	D	2-2	6,000	Puddefoot, Shea
9	Oct 27	Sat	A	Fulham	D	1-1	10,000	Puddefoot
10	Nov 3	Sat	H	Queens Park Rangers	W	4-0	4,500	Puddefoot 2, Shea 2
11	Nov 10	Sat	A	Clapton Orient	W	4-1	5,000	Roberts 2, Shea 2
12	Nov 17	Sat	H	Millwall	D	0-0	7,000	
13	Nov 24	Sat	A	Tottenham Hotspur	L	0-2	9,000	
14	Dec 1	Sat	H	Chelsea	D	1-1	8,000	Shea
15	Dec 8	Sat	A	Brentford	L	2-3	2,000	Puddefoot, Shea
16	Dec 15	Sat	H	Arsenal	W	3-2	5,000	Roberts 2, Puddefoot
17	Dec 22	Sat	H	Fulham	L	0-3	6,000	
18	Dec 25	Tue	H	Crystal Palace	W	2-1	7,000	Kirsopp, Puddefoot
19	Dec 26	Wed	A	Crystal Palace	L	0-4	5,000	
20	Dec 29	Sat	A	Queens Park Rangers	D	1-1	3,000	Cowless
21	Jan 5	Sat	H	Clapton Orient	W	3-0	8,000	Roberts 2, Puddefoot
22	Jan 12	Sat	A	Millwall	W	1-0	5,000	Puddefoot
23	Jan 19	Sat	H	Tottenham Hotspur	D	2-2	8,000	Johnstone, Wright
24	Jan 26	Sat	A	Chelsea	D	2-2	8,000	Kirsopp, Puddefoot
25	Feb 2	Sat	H	Brentford	W	7-2	5,000	Kirsopp 2, Ashton, Mackesy, Puddefoot, Roberts, Yenson (og)
26	Feb 9	Sat	A	Crystal Palace	D	1-1	4,000	Larcombe
27	Feb 16	Sat	A	Fulham	L	1-3	5,000	Puddefoot
28	Feb 23	Sat	H	Queens Park Rangers	W	4-0	5,000	Ashton, Cunningham, Puddefoot, Tresadern
29	Mar 2	Sat	A	Clapton Orient	W	3-1	4,000	Burke, Puddefoot, Tufnell
30	Mar 9	Sat	H	Millwall	W	2-0	6,000	Cunningham, Puddefoot
31	Mar 16	Sat	A	Tottenham Hotspur	W	5-0	10,000	Cunningham 2, Ashton, Puddefoot, Roberts
32	Mar 23	Sat	H	Chelsea	D	2-2	14,000	Cunningham, Puddefoot
33	Mar 29	Fri	H	Arsenal	W	4-1	10,000	Tufnell 2, Burke, Puddefoot
34	Mar 30	Sat	A	Brentford	W	7-3	4,000	Puddefoot 3, Ashton, Burke, Johnstone, Wright
35	Apr 1	Mon	A	Arsenal	W	3-1	6,000	Puddefoot 2, Burke
36	Apr 6	Sat	H	Crystal Palace	W	11-0	4,000	Puddefoot 7, Burke 2, Ashton, Cunningham

Team Line-Ups

1	2	3	4	5	6	7	8	9	10	11	
Leahy	Hodson	Cope	Manning	Campbell	Maconnachie	Ashton	Shea	Roberts	Puddefoot	McDougall	1
Leahy	Hodson	Maconnachie	Manning	Hamilton	Ferris	Ashton	Shea	Puddefoot	Mackesy	Casey	2
Leahy	Hodson	Maconnachie	Manning	Hamilton	Woodards	Ashton	Shea	Puddefoot	Goddard	Burton	3
Leahy	Hodson	Cope	Manning	Goddard	Maconnachie	Ashton	Kirsopp	Roberts	Puddefoot	Mackesy	4
Leahy	Hodson	Cope	Manning	Johnstone	Maconnachie	Ashton	Shea	Roberts	Puddefoot	Mackesy	5
Leahy	Hodson	Ferris	Johnstone	Manning	Hamilton	Ashton	Shea	Puddefoot	Mackesy	Casey	6
Lawton	Hodson	Tanner	Johnstone	Manning	Hamilton	Kirsopp	Shea	Roberts	Puddefoot	Ashton	7
Williams	Hodson	Cope	Johnstone	Manning	Hamilton	Ashton	Shea	Puddefoot	Kirsopp	Mackesy	8
Leahy	Maconnachie	Hodson	Johnstone	Manning	Hamilton	Kirsopp	Shea	Puddefoot	Butcher	Ashton	9
Leahy	Hodson	Cope	Johnstone	Manning	Hamilton	Kirby	Shea	Puddefoot	Hilsdon	Mackesy	10
Leahy	Hodson	Cope	Johnstone	Manning	Hamilton	Ashton	Shea	Roberts	Puddefoot	Mackesy	11
Leahy	Hodson	Cope	Johnstone	Manning	Hamilton	Ashton	Shea	Dodds	Puddefoot	Mackesy	12
Leahy	Hodson	Maconnachie	Johnstone	Manning	Hamilton	Ashton	Shea	Roberts	Puddefoot	Williams B.	13
Williams	Maconnachie	Cope	Johnstone	Brennan	Hamilton	Ashton	Shea	Puddefoot	Islip	Tempest	14
Leahy	Hodson	Maconnachie	Brennan	Manning	Mackesy	Ashton	Shea	Roberts	Puddefoot	Williams B.	15
Leahy	Hodson	Cope	Johnstone	Hamilton	Mackesy	Ashton	Kirsopp	Roberts	Wray	Puddefoot	16
Leahy	Hamilton	Cope	Johnstone	Manning	Brennan	Ashton	Kirsopp	Puddefoot	Mackesy	Williams B.	17
Leahy	Hodson	Cope	Johnstone	Hamilton	Tresadern	Ashton	Kirsopp	Puddefoot	Mackesy	Bridgeman	18
Hebden	Cope	Hodson	Tresadern	Hamilton	Johnstone	Bridgeman	Stevenson	Kenlan	Blythe	Allen	19
Hebden	Hodson	Cope	Hamilton	Stevenson	Tresadern	Ashton	Kirsopp	Puddefoot	Cowless	Mackesy	20
Hufton	Tirrell	Cope	Johnstone	Stevenson	Tresadern	Turley	Hamilton	Roberts	Puddefoot	Mackesy	21
Williams	Tirrell	Hodson	Hamilton	Stevenson	Johnstone	Burke	Langford	Puddefoot	Tufnell	Mackesy	22
Lee	Tirrell	Cope	Johnstone	Stevenson	Hamilton	Burke	Kirsopp	Puddefoot	Brown	Wright	23
Lee	Cope	Hodson	Hamilton	Stevenson	Johnstone	Mackesy	Puddefoot	Brown	Kirsopp	Ashton	24
Lee	Cope	Tirrell	Manning	Stevenson	Hamilton	Ashton	Kirsopp	Roberts	Puddefoot	Mackesy	25
Hufton	Tirrell	Cope	Campbell	Stevenson	Johnstone	Islip	Puddefoot	Larcombe	Tufnell	Ashton	26
Brownlie	Hodson	Cope	Johnstone	Stevenson	Campbell	Ashton	Cunningham	Roberts	Puddefoot	Islip	27
Hufton	Hodson	Cope	Hamilton	Stevenson	Tresadern	Ashton	Cunningham	Puddefoot	Tufnell	Islip	28
Hufton	Cope	Tirrell	Johnstone	Stevenson	Hamilton	Burke	Cunningham	Puddefoot	Tufnell	Mackesy	29
Hufton	Hodson	Cope	Johnstone	Stevenson	Campbell	Ashton	Cunningham	Larcombe	Puddefoot	Tempest	30
Hufton	Hodson	Cope	Johnstone	Stevenson	Campbell	Ashton	Cunningham	Puddefoot	Roberts	Mackesy	31
Hufton	Hodson	Cope	Johnstone	Bell	Tresadern	Ashton	Cunningham	Puddefoot	Roberts	Mackesy	32
Hufton	Hodson	Burton	Johnstone	Stevenson	Massey	Ashton	Burke	Puddefoot	Tufnell	Mackesy	33
Hufton	Hodson	Tirrell	Johnstone	Bell	Burton	Ashton	Burke	Puddefoot	Mackesy	Wright	34
Lee	Cope	Tirrell	Johnstone	Burton	Massey	Ashton	Burke	Puddefoot	Tufnell	Mackesy	35
Hufton	Hodson	Tirrell	Johnstone	Bell	Piggott	Ashton	Burke	Puddefoot	Cunningham	Mackesy	36

1918-19
Story of the season

Appearances & Goals 1918-19

	Total	
	Starts	Goals
ADAMS [Guest]	1	0
ALLEN Percy	2	0
ASHMORE [Guest]	2	0
ASHTON Herbert	14	1
BAKER [Guest]	2	0
BELL [Guest]	4	1
BEST E. [Guest]	25	5
BRANDON Thomas	2	0
BRITTON [Guest]	1	1
BURKE [Guest]	10	1
BURKINSHAW J. [Guest]	1	0
BUTCHER George	3	2
CAMPBELL Alec [Guest]	14	1
CHEDGZOY Sam [Guest]	6	4
COPE William	26	0
COWNLEY F. [Guest]	7	0
CUNNINGHAM Andrew [Guest]	5	1
DILLEY Ernie [Guest]	4	1
DODD [Guest]	11	7
FENWICK Alfred	1	0
FISHER [Guest]	1	0
GREEN Tommy	1	0
HAMILTON [Guest]	6	0
HARRISON George [Guest]	2	0
HILSDON George	1	0
HODSON James [Guest]	5	0
HOLMES [Guest]	3	3
HUFTON Edward	21	0
HUGHES Joseph	4	0
JOHNSTONE [Guest]	10	0
KAY George	5	0
KIRSOPP William [Guest]	19	6
LANE Harry	20	0
LEAFE Richard	5	0
LEWIS T. [Guest]	1	1
LOWE [Guest]	1	0
MASSEY [Guest]	1	0
McCRAE James	22	3
McCULLOCH [Guest]	2	0
McDOUGALL Robert [Guest]	1	0
MOORE [Guest]	9	0
MOYES James	6	4
NEWTON [Guest]	1	0
PEARCY [Guest]	2	0
PIGGOTT [Guest]	1	0
PROCTOR [Guest]	1	0
PUDDEFOOT Syd	14	16
ROBERTS Frank [Guest]	6	4
SMITH Percy [Guest]	1	0
STEELE [Guest]	2	0
STEVENSON [Guest]	17	1
TATE [Guest]	2	0
TIRRELL Alfred	30	0
TRESADERN Jack	13	0
TURLEY [Guest]	1	0
TYLER [Guest]	1	0
WALDEN George	2	0
WEBSTER [Guest]	2	0
WEIR [Guest]	2	1
WILLIAMS [Guest]	5	0
WOODS [Guest]	4	0
YELLOP Jimmy [Guest]	2	0
own goal		1
Totals	**396**	**65**

The fact that West Ham's 1918-19 season was not nearly as impressive as previous campaigns mattered little as the country celebrated the restoration of peace. Only 65 goals were scored and Puddefoot alone reached double figures.

After the Armistice in November 1918, attendances at football matches increased dramatically and by the end of the season almost a quarter of a million people had passed through the Upton Park turnstiles. In January 1919, Hammers beat Clapton Orient 7-0 at home to record their 13th win in 16 wartime matches with the Homerton men.
In the spring of 1919, West Ham applied for the Football League and, with the backing of a significant number of established League clubs, they won their place, finishing second behind Coventry City in the poll. Coventry, incidentally, had finished fifth in the Southern League Second Division in 1914/15.

The Southern League clubs and officials were not impressed at Hammers' move and only Swindon Town sent a congratulatory telegram, Syd King, meanwhile, considered West Ham's elevation as the most important and satisfying achievement of his long career.

London Combination
Final Table 1918-19

	P	W	D	L	F	A	Pts
Brentford	36	20	9	7	94	46	49
Arsenal	35	20	5	11	85	54	45
West Ham United	**36**	**17**	**7**	**12**	**65**	**51**	**41**
Fulham	36	17	6	13	70	55	40
Queens Park Rangers	36	16	7	13	69	60	39
Chelsea	36	13	11	12	70	53	37
Crystal Palace	36	14	6	16	66	73	34
Tottenham Hotspur	36	13	8	15	52	72	34
Millwall	36	10	9	17	50	67	29
Clapton Orient	36	3	6	27	35	123	12

Season **1918-19** London Combination
Match Details

Manager **Syd King**   Final League Position **3/10**

	Date		Venue	Opponents	Results		Attendance	Scorers
1	Sep 7	Sat	A	Brentford	L	0-2	4,000	
2	Sep 14	Sat	H	Clapton Orient	W	3-1	5,000	Ashton, Best, Weir
3	Sep 21	Sat	H	Tottenham Hotspur	L	0-1	8,000	
4	Sep 28	Sat	A	Chelsea	L	1-3	12,000	Puddefoot
5	Oct 5	Sat	H	Arsenal	L	1-4	6,500	Moyes
6	Oct 12	Sat	A	Crystal Palace	D	0-0	4,000	
7	Oct 19	Sat	H	Queens Park Rangers	W	4-1	7,000	Best, Kirsopp, Moyes, Puddefoot
8	Oct 26	Sat	A	Fulham	D	2-2	5,000	Kirsopp, Roberts
9	Nov 2	Sat	H	Brentford	L	1-3	6,000	Roberts
10	Nov 9	Sat	A	Clapton Orient	W	5-1	5,000	Puddefoot 2, Roberts 2, McCrae
11	Nov 16	Sat	A	Tottenham Hotspur	W	4-1	6,000	Best 2, Kirsopp, McCrae
12	Nov 23	Sat	H	Chelsea	W	3-1	12,000	Moyes 2, Cunningham
13	Nov 30	Sat	A	Arsenal	W	2-0	7,000	Best, Kirsopp
14	Dec 7	Sat	H	Crystal Palace	W	2-0	10,000	Kirsopp, Stevenson
15	Dec 14	Sat	A	Queens Park Rangers	L	0-1	8,000	
16	Dec 21	Sat	H	Fulham	W	2-1	10,000	Puddefoot 2
17	Dec 25	Wed	A	Millwall	W	2-0	12,000	Dodd, Puddefoot
18	Dec 26	Thu	H	Millwall	W	2-0	16,000	Dodd, Puddefoot
19	Dec 28	Sat	A	Brentford	L	1-3	10,000	Puddefoot
20	Jan 4	Sat	H	Clapton Orient	W	7-0	8,000	Dodd 3, Holmes 2, Burke, Campbell
21	Jan 11	Sat	H	Tottenham Hotspur	W	2-0	13,000	Dodd, Puddefoot
22	Jan 18	Sat	A	Chelsea	D	0-0	25,000	
23	Jan 25	Sat	H	Arsenal	L	1-2	18,000	Kirsopp
24	Feb 1	Sat	A	Crystal Palace	L	0-3	4,000	
25	Feb 8	Sat	H	Queens Park Rangers	L	0-4	12,000	
26	Feb 15	Sat	A	Millwall	D	2-2	25,000	Holmes, McCrae
27	Feb 22	Sat	H	Brentford	W	2-1	16,000	Dodd, Bullock (og)
28	Mar 1	Sat	A	Clapton Orient	D	0-0	15,000	
29	Mar 8	Sat	A	Tottenham Hotspur	W	1-0	17,000	Puddefoot
30	Mar 15	Sat	H	Chelsea	D	3-3	26,000	Chedgzoy 2, Puddefoot
31	Mar 22	Sat	A	Arsenal	L	2-3	20,000	Bell, Chedgzoy
32	Mar 29	Sat	H	Crystal Palace	L	1-3	15,500	Dilley
33	Apr 5	Sat	A	Queens Park Rangers	W	3-1	7,000	Chedgzoy, Lewis, Puddefoot
34	Apr 12	Sat	H	Millwall	W	3-2	25,000	Butcher 2, Britton
35	Apr 18	Fri	A	Fulham	D	1-1	15,000	Puddefoot
36	Apr 21	Mon	H	Fulham	W	2-1	16,000	Puddefoot 2

Team Line-Ups

1	2	3	4	5	6	7	8	9	10	11	
Williams	Cope	Tirrell	Turley	Johnstone	Moore	Burke	Kirsopp	Roberrts	Hamilton	Best	1
Fisher	Cownley	Tirrell	Johnstone	Burkinshaw	Moore	Ashton	Burke	McCulloch	Weir	Best	2
Williams	Hodson	Tirrell	Hamilton	Stevenson	Moore	Ashton	Kirsopp	Proctor	Weir	Best	3
Williams	Cownley	Tirrell	Johnstone	Stevenson	Massey	Ashton	Burke	Puddefoot	Best	Kirsopp	4
Williams	Hodson	Tirrell	Johnstone	Stevenson	Hamilton	Ashton	Moyes	McCulloch	Yellop	Best	5
Williams	Cownley	Tirrell	Johnstone	Stevenson	Moore	McCrae	Moyes	Burke	Kirsop	Best	6
Woods	Cownley	Tirrell	Johnstone	Stevenson	Moore	Allen	Moyes	Puddefoot	Kirsop	Best	7
Woods	Cownley	Tirrell	Piggott	Hamilton	Moore	Allen	Burke	Roberrts	Kirsop	Best	8
Woods	Hodson	Cope	Johnstone	Campbell	Moore	Burke	Hamilton	Roberrts	Kirsop	Best	9
Hufton	Lowe	Cope	Johnstone	Stevenson	Campbell	Kirsopp	Roberts	Puddefoot	Best	McCrae	10
Hufton	Cope	Tirrell	Lane	Stevenson	McCrae	Kirsopp	Moyes	Baker	Cunningham	Best	11
Hufton	Cope	Tirrell	Johnstone	Stevenson	McCrae	Kirsopp	Moyes	Baker	Cunningham	Best	12
Woods	Hufton	Hodson	Moore	Hamilton	McCrae	Kirsopp	Moyes	Leafe	Cunningham	Best	13
Hufton	Cope	Tirrell	Lane	Stevenson	McCrae	Burke	Leafe	Kirsopp	Cunningham	Best	14
Hufton	Cope	Tirrell	Lane	Stevenson	McCrae	Burke	Kirsopp	Leafe	Cunningham	Best	15
Hufton	Cope	Tirrell	Johnstone	Stevenson	Lane	Ashton	Kirsopp	Puddefoot	McCrae	Best	16
Hufton	Cope	Tirrell	Campbell	Stevenson	McCrae	Ashton	Kirsopp	Puddefoot	Dodd	Best	17
Hufton	Cope	Tirrell	Campbell	Stevenson	McCrae	Ashton	Kirsopp	Puddefoot	Dodd	Best	18
Hufton	Hodson	Cope	Campbell	Stevenson	McCrae	Yellop	Lane	Puddefoot	Dodd	Best	19
Hufton	Cownley	Tirrell	Campbell	Stevenson	Tresadern	Ashton	Dodd	Burke	Holmes	Best	20
Webster	Cope	Tirrell	Lane	Campbell	McCrae	Kirsopp	Dodd	Puddefoot	Holmes	Ashton	21
Hufton	Cope	Tirrell	Lane	Campbell	McCrae	Kirsopp	Dodd	Puddefoot	Roberts	Best	22
Hufton	Cope	Tirrell	Lane	Stevenson	Campbell	Kirsopp	Dodd	Roberrts	McCrae	Best	23
Hufton	Cope	Tirrell	Lane	Campbell	Stevenson	Ashton	Dodd	Smith	Tresadern	Best	24
Hufton	Cope	Tirrell	Lane	Fenwick	Moore	Best	Hilsdon	Burke	Tresadern	Steele	25
Hufton	Cope	Tirrell	Lane	Campbell	Tresadern	Walden	Dodd	Dilley	Holmes	McCrae	26
Hufton	Cope	Tirrell	Lane	McCrae	Tresadern	Ashton	Dodd	Dilley	Leafe	Steele	27
Hufton	Cope	Tirrell	Lane	Campbell	Tresadern	Ashton	Dodd	Dilley	McCrae	Pearcy	28
Hufton	Cope	Tirrell	Lane	Campbell	Tresadern	Ashmore	Newton	Puddefoot	McCrae	Best	29
Hufton	Cope	Tirrell	Lane	Kay	Tresadern	Ashmore	Chedgzoy	Puddefoot	Adams	Pearcy	30
Webster	Cope	Tirrell	Lane	Campbell	Tresadern	Leafe	Chedgzoy	McDougall	Bell	McCrae	31
Hufton	Cownley	Tirrell	Lane	McCrae	Tresadern	Ashton	Chedgzoy	Dilley	Butcher	Harrison	32
Hughes	Cope	Tirrell	Lane	Kay	McCrae	Chedgzoy	Lewis	Puddefoot	Bell	Harrison	33
Hughes	Cope	Tirrell	Ashton	Kay	Tresadern	Walden	Butcher	Britton	Bell	Tyler	34
Hughes	Cope	Brandon	Tresadern	Kay	Lane	Tate	Bell	Puddefoot	Butcher	Chedgzoy	35
Hughes	Brandon	Cope	Tresadern	Kay	Lane	Chedgzoy	Green	Puddefoot	McCrae	Tate	36

There were **20,000 inside the ground** to see Jimm[y] Moyes score West Ham's first ever league goal in the 1–[1] draw. Making his debut was goalkeeper Ted Hufton, wh[o] went on to play 402 games for the club. There was a shoc[k] in the next fixture at Barnsley as the Hammers were beaten[?]

1919-20
Story of the season

The club's **application to join the Football League was successful** and the Hammers started the season in Division Two, where **they played host to Lincoln City.**

Appearances & Goals 1919-20

	League		FA Cup		Total	
	Starts	Goals	Starts	Goals	Starts	Goals
ALLEN Percy	4	0	1	0	5	0
ALLEN Robert	1	1	0	0	1	1
BAILEY Daniel	27	9	3	1	30	10
BIGGIN Horace	2	0	0	0	2	0
BIRCHENOUGH Frank	1	0	0	0	1	0
BRADSHAW Harry	13	0	1	0	14	0
BURTON Frank	34	2	4	0	38	2
BUTCHER George	33	8	4	2	37	10
CARTER George	13	0	3	0	16	0
COPE William	29	0	4	0	33	0
CUMMING James	10	0	0	0	10	0
FENWICK Alfred	2	0	0	0	2	0
GREEN Tommy	3	0	0	0	3	0
HUFTON Edward	38	0	4	0	42	0
JOHNSON William	2	0	0	0	2	0
KAY George	27	3	4	0	31	3
LANE Harry	9	0	0	0	9	0
LEAFE Alfred	15	0	0	0	15	0
LEE Alf	17	0	0	0	17	0
MACKESY Jack	5	0	0	0	5	0
McCRAE James	35	0	4	0	39	0
MORRIS Robert	3	0	0	0	3	0
MOYES James	2	1	0	0	2	1
MURRAY Frank	2	0	0	0	2	0
PALMER James	12	1	0	0	12	1
PHIPPS Cecil	1	0	0	0	1	0
PUDDEFOOT Syd	39	21	4	5	43	26
ROBERTS Vivian	1	0	0	0	1	0
SMITH David	1	0	0	0	1	0
SMITH Stephen	23	0	4	1	27	1
SMITHURST Edgar	2	0	0	0	2	0
STANLEY Thomas	1	0	0	0	1	0
TIRRELL Alf	1	0	0	0	1	0
TRESADERN Jack	35	0	4	0	39	0
TURNER Cyril	3	1	0	0	3	1
WEBSTER Joe	2	0	0	0	2	0
WOODARDS Dan	9	0	0	0	9	0
WOODBURN John	4	0	0	0	4	0
YOUNG John	1	0	0	0	1	0
Totals	**462**	**47**	**44**	**9**	**506**	**56**

7–0. Centre-forward Syd Puddefoot was the man in form as he scored twice in the 4–1 victory in the return game with Lincoln City. He then scored a goal in four successive matches. One feature of this season was that in the majority of cases clubs played each other at home and away on successive Saturdays. After the debacle at Barnsley the defence improved and there were many low-scoring games. At home Grimsby and Leicester were beaten 1–0, followed by 2–0 victories against Coventry and Bristol City.

In the FA Cup, after a 0–0 draw at Southampton the Saints were beaten 3–1 in the replay. The next round brought Bury to the Boleyn and with Syd Puddefoot scoring a hat-trick the Lancashire club were beaten 6–0. Puddefoot followed this up a week later with another hat-trick in the 3–1 home win over Port Vale. The goals then dried up as none were scored in the next four league games leading up to the FA Cup tie at Tottenham. Spurs were unbeaten at home and the Hammers unsurprisingly bowed out of the cup, losing

3–0 before a crowd of 47,646. There was some revenge a week later in the league game at the Boleyn. This occasion saw West Ham beat Tottenham 2–1, with Puddefoot scoring both goals. Dan Bailey contributed to the goal tally as he scored in six out of the next seven games, and leading scorer Puddefoot grabbed four more in the 5–1 win against Wolverhampton Wanderers. Being the club's first season in the league, it was an excellent effort to finish seventh.

EDWARD HUFTON

Possibly West Ham's greatest goalkeeper, he began his career at Sheffield United in 1912, playing in 12 matches before war broke out.

Ted joined the Coldstream Guards and was wounded in action in France. After recovering he played in 54 wartime games for West Ham as a guest. After hostilities ceased, in 1919 he joined West Ham on a permanent basis for a fee of £350. He was in the Hammers side that lost 2–0 to Bolton Wanderers in the first FA Cup final at Wembley in 1923.

His fine form saw him gain international honours and he went on to play six times for England, with his debut coming against Belgium in 1923. For 13 seasons Ted was West Ham's first-choice keeper, making a total of 402 appearances. In 1932 he joined Watford for a short spell but only played twice in their colours before retiring as a player. After World War Two he returned to Upton Park and worked as a steward in the press room. Ted later moved to Swansea, where he died in February 1967.

Football League - Division Two Final Table 1919-20

	P	HOME					AWAY					Pts
		W	D	L	F	A	W	D	L	F	A	
Tottenham Hotspur	42	19	2	0	60	11	13	4	4	42	21	70
Huddersfield Town	42	16	4	1	58	13	12	4	5	39	25	64
Birmingham	42	14	3	4	54	16	10	5	6	31	18	56
Blackpool	42	13	4	4	40	18	8	6	7	25	29	52
Bury	42	14	4	3	35	15	6	4	11	25	29	48
Fulham	42	11	6	4	36	18	8	3	10	25	32	47
West Ham United	**42**	**14**	**3**	**4**	**34**	**14**	**5**	**6**	**10**	**13**	**26**	**47**
Bristol City	42	9	9	3	30	18	4	8	9	16	25	43
Stoke City	42	13	3	5	37	15	5	3	13	23	39	42
Hull City	42	13	4	4	53	23	5	2	14	25	49	42
Barnsley	42	9	5	7	41	28	6	5	10	20	27	40
Port Vale	42	11	3	7	35	27	5	5	11	24	35	40
Leicester City	42	8	6	7	26	29	7	4	10	15	32	40
Clapton Orient	42	14	3	4	34	17	2	3	16	17	42	38
Stockport County	42	11	4	6	34	24	3	5	13	18	37	37
Rotherham County	42	10	4	7	32	27	3	4	14	19	56	34
Nottingham Forest	42	9	4	8	23	22	2	5	14	20	51	31
Wolverhampton Wanderers	42	8	4	9	41	32	2	6	13	14	48	30
Coventry City	42	7	7	7	20	26	2	4	15	15	47	29
Lincoln City	42	8	6	7	27	30	1	3	17	17	71	27
Grimsby Town	42	8	4	9	23	24	2	1	18	11	51	25

Season **1919-20** Football League - Division Two
Match Details

Manager **Syd King**   Final League Position **7/22**

	Date		Competition	Venue	Opponents	Results		Attendance	Position	Scorers
1	Aug 30	Sat	Div 2	H	Lincoln City	D	1-1	20,000	12	Moyes
2	Sep 1	Mon	Div 2	A	Barnsley	L	0-7	6,000	16	
3	Sep 6	Sat	Div 2	A	Lincoln City	W	4-1	6,000	13	Puddefoot 2, Burton [pen], Butcher
4	Sep 8	Mon	Div 2	H	Barnsley	L	0-2	14,000	16	
5	Sep 13	Sat	Div 2	A	Rotherham County	W	1-0	6,000	12	Puddefoot
6	Sep 20	Sat	Div 2	H	Rotherham County	W	2-1	20,000	12	Butcher, Puddefoot
7	Sep 27	Sat	Div 2	A	Stoke City	L	1-2	12,000	12	Puddefoot
8	Oct 4	Sat	Div 2	H	Stoke City	D	1-1	23,000	14	Puddefoot
9	Oct 11	Sat	Div 2	A	Grimsby Town	W	1-0	6,000	11	Turner
10	Oct 18	Sat	Div 2	H	Grimsby Town	W	1-0	20,000	10	Palmer
11	Oct 25	Sat	Div 2	A	Birmingham	W	1-0	25,000	9	Kay
12	Nov 1	Sat	Div 2	H	Birmingham	L	1-2	20,000	11	Allen R.
13	Nov 8	Sat	Div 2	A	Leicester City	D	0-0	14,000	9	
14	Nov 15	Sat	Div 2	H	Leicester City	W	1-0	23,000	9	Burton [pen]
15	Nov 22	Sat	Div 2	A	Fulham	W	2-1	20,000	7	Puddefoot 2
16	Nov 29	Sat	Div 2	H	Fulham	L	0-1	20,000	9	
17	Dec 6	Sat	Div 2	A	Coventry City	D	0-0	15,000	9	
18	Dec 13	Sat	Div 2	H	Coventry City	W	2-0	15,000	8	Bailey, Butcher
19	Dec 20	Sat	Div 2	A	Huddersfield Town	L	0-2	6,000	9	
20	Dec 25	Thu	Div 2	H	Bristol City	W	2-0	20,000	6	Bailey, Butcher
21	Dec 26	Fri	Div 2	A	Bristol City	D	0-0	12,000	8	
22	Dec 27	Sat	Div 2	H	Huddersfield Town	D	1-1	25,000	7	Butcher
23	Jan 3	Sat	Div 2	A	Blackpool	D	0-0	7,000	7	
24	Jan 10	Sat	FAC 1	A	Southampton	D	0-0	12,000		
25	Jan 15	Thu	FAC 1 Rep	H	Southampton	W	3-1	25,000		Puddefoot 2, Butcher
26	Jan 17	Sat	Div 2	H	Blackpool	W	1-0	26,000	6	Bailey
27	Jan 24	Sat	Div 2	H	Bury	W	1-0	20,000	5	Kay
28	Jan 31	Sat	FAC 2	H	Bury	W	6-0	27,000		Puddefoot 3, Bailey, Butcher, Smith S.
29	Feb 7	Sat	Div 2	H	Port Vale	W	3-1	23,000	5	Puddefoot 3
30	Feb 11	Wed	Div 2	A	Bury	L	0-1	5,000	5	
31	Feb 14	Sat	Div 2	A	Port Vale	L	0-1	15,000	5	
32	Feb 21	Sat	FAC 3	A	Tottenham Hotspur	L	0-3	47,646		
33	Feb 28	Sat	Div 2	A	Clapton Orient	L	0-1	25,000	8	
34	Mar 4	Sat	Div 2	H	Clapton Orient	L	0-1	15,000	8	
35	Mar 13	Sat	Div 2	H	Tottenham Hotspur	W	2-1	30,000	7	Puddefoot 2
36	Mar 20	Sat	Div 2	A	South Shields	L	0-3	18,000	8	
37	Mar 22	Mon	Div 2	A	Tottenham Hotspur	L	0-2	25,000	8	
38	Mar 27	Sat	Div 2	H	South Shields	W	1-0	18,000	7	Bailey
39	Apr 2	Fri	Div 2	H	Nottingham Forest	W	5-1	20,000	6	Puddefoot 4, Bailey
40	Apr 3	Sat	Div 2	A	Wolverhampton Wanderers	D	1-1	15,000	7	Bailey
41	Apr 5	Mon	Div 2	A	Nottingham Forest	L	1-2	10,000	7	Bailey
42	Apr 10	Sat	Div 2	H	Wolverhampton Wanderers	W	4-0	16,000	7	Butcher 2, Puddefoot 2
43	Apr 17	Sat	Div 2	A	Hull City	D	1-1	8,000	7	Bailey
44	Apr 24	Sat	Div 2	H	Hull City	W	2-1	18,000	7	Bailey, Puddefoot [pen]
45	Apr 26	Mon	Div 2	A	Stockport County	L	0-1	5,000	7	
46	May 1	Sat	Div 2	H	Stockport County	W	3-0	15,000	7	Butcher, Kay, Puddefoot

Team Line-Ups

ALLEN Percy	ALLEN Robert	BAILEY Daniel	BIGGIN Horace	BIRCHENOUGH Frank	BRADSHAW Harry	BURTON Frank	BUTCHER George	CARTER George	COPE William	CUMMING James	FENWICK Alfred	GREEN Tommy	HUFTON Edward	JOHNSON William	KAY George	LANE Harry	LEAFE Alfred	LEE Alf	MACKESY Jack	McCRAE James	MORRIS Robert	MOYES James	MURRAY Frank	PALMER James	PHIPPS Cecil	PUDDEFOOT Syd	ROBERTS Vivian	SMITH David	SMITH Stephen	SMITHURST Edgar	STANLEY Thomas	TIRRELL Alf	TRESADERN Jack	TURNER Cyril	WEBSTER Joe	WOODARDS Dan	WOODBURN John	YOUNG John	#
					11				2	5			1		4			3	6	10		8				9		7											1
	8								2	5	11		1			4	7		6	10						9					3								2
						5	8		2				1	4			7				3		10	11		9						6							3
							8		2				1	4	5		7				3		10	11		9						6							4
						4	8		2			10	1		5		7	3	11							9						6							5
					11	4		10	2				1		5		7				3	8				9						6							6
					11			10	3				1		5	4	7					8				9									6	2			7
	7				11	4			3			10	1		5				6							9										2			8
					11	3	8		2				1		5	4	10							7											6	9			9
	7					3	8		2				1		5	4	10				6			11		9													10
	7					3	8		2				1		5		10				6			11		9												4	11
7	8				11	3			2				1		5	4	10				6					9													12
	7				11	3	8		2				1		5	4	10				6					9													13
7									3	8		2	1			5	10				6								11				4						14
	8								3	10	7	2	1			5					6			11		9							4						15
	8								3	10	7	2	1			5					6			11		9							4						16
	8									10	7	2	1			5		3			6					9			11				4						17
	8									10	7	2	1			5		3			6					9			11				4						18
	8								11	2	10	7	1			5		3			6					9							4						19
	8				11				3	10	7	2	1			5					6					9							4						20
	8								3	10	7	2	1			5					6					9			11				4						21
	8								3	10	7	2	1			5					6					9			11				4			1			22
8									11	3	7	2	1			5					6							10					4						23
	8								3	10	7	2	1			5					6					9			11				4						24
	8								3	10	7	2	1			5					6					9			11				4						25
	8								3	10	7	2	1			5					6					9			11				4						26
	8								3	10	7	2	1			5					6					9			11				4						27
	8								3	10	7	2	1			5					6					9			11				4						28
	8								3	10	7	2				5					6					9			11				4	1					29
7	8								3				1			5		2			6	10				9			11				4						30
	9				11				3	8	7	2	1			5					6							10					4						31
	7				11				3	8		2	1			5					6					9		10					4						32
	8								3	10		2	1			5	9	7			6											11	4						33
									3	8	2	7	1								6			10		9			11				4				5		34
	8								3				1					2			6			10		9			11	7			4				5		35
	8								3				1					2			6			10		9			11	7			4				5		36
	8								2			7	1					3			6			10		9			11				4				5		37
	8								3	10		7	1					2			6					9			11				4				5		38
	8								3	10		7	1					2			6					9			11				4				5		39
	8								3	10		7	1					2			6					9			11				4				5		40
	8		1						3			7					10	2			6					9			11				4				5		41
	8								3	10		7	1					2			6					9			11				4				5		42
	8								3	10			1			7		2			6					9			11				4				5		43
	8								3	10		7	1					2			6					9			11				4				5		44
	8									10		7	1					2			6					9	1		11		3		4				5		45
	8								3	10		7	1			5		2			6					9							4					11	46

1920-21
Story of the season

The Hammers would once again **rely on Syd Puddefoot to score the goals and he was on target in the opening game** with Hull City and then **scored three goals** in home and away victories over Wolverhampton Wanderers.

October was a poor month, with only one win in six matches, this being a 1–0 success at Coventry City. The goals flowed in November, however, with nine goals netted in two home games. Sheffield Wednesday were beaten 4–0, with Puddefoot scoring all four goals and netting two more in the 5–0 defeat of Stockport County. In this game Alf Leafe was also on target with a hat-trick. The team seemed

Appearances & Goals 1920-21

	League		FA Cup		Total	
	Starts	Goals	Starts	Goals	Starts	Goals
ALLEN Percy	28	0	1	0	29	0
BAILEY Daniel	8	0	0	0	8	0
BISHOP Syd	21	3	1	0	22	3
BRADSHAW Harry	1	0	0	0	1	0
BROWN William	1	0	0	0	1	0
BURTON Frank	30	0	1	0	31	0
BUTCHER George	1	0	0	0	1	0
CALLADINE John	1	0	0	0	1	0
CARTER George	20	1	1	0	21	1
COPE William	36	0	1	0	37	0
COWELL Herbert	1	0	0	0	1	0
CROWTHER George	3	0	0	0	3	0
CUMMING James	5	0	0	0	5	0
GATLAND Bill	1	0	0	0	1	0
HAMPSON Tommy	4	0	0	0	4	0
HART Joseph	1	0	0	0	1	0
HEBDEN Jack	1	0	0	0	1	0
HUFTON Edward	38	0	1	0	39	0
JAMES William	18	3	0	0	18	3
KAY George	36	1	1	0	37	1
LANE Harry	10	0	0	0	10	0
LEAFE Alfred	13	7	1	0	14	7
LEE Alf	9	0	0	0	9	0
McCRAE James	15	0	0	0	15	0
PALMER James	1	0	0	0	1	0
PUDDEFOOT Syd	38	29	1	0	39	29
ROBINSON Leslie	5	1	0	0	5	1
SHEA Danny	16	1	0	0	16	1
SIMMONS Jim	18	1	0	0	18	1
SMITH Stephen	1	0	0	0	1	0
SMITHURST Edgar	1	0	0	0	1	0
TRESADERN Jack	30	0	1	0	31	0
WATSON Victor	9	2	0	0	9	2
WOODARDS Dan	7	0	0	0	7	0
YOUNG John	34	0	1	0	35	0
own goal		2				2
Totals	462	51	11	0	473	51

to play well in alternate months, as there were no wins in December but on New Year's Day Coventry City were thrashed 7–0 at the Boleyn, with Puddefoot claiming four goals.

A week later the Hammers were knocked out of the FA Cup after losing 1–0 at Sheffield Wednesday. In the league the side were still inconsistent; four wins, which included a Puddefoot hat-trick against Leeds, were followed by three defeats with no goals being scored. The season continued in a similar vein with the side relying too much on Puddefoot scoring.

The campaign ended with a respectable fifth-place finish, some ten points behind champions Birmingham City.

JACK YOUNG

Jack came to West Ham in 1920 from Southend United and made his debut in the home game with Hull City in August that year.

He played as an outside-left for two seasons before being converted to a left-back with some success. In 1923 he was in the side that was promoted to the First Division and he also played against Bolton Wanderers in the first Wembley FA Cup final. Jack's daughter donated his Cup Final shirt to the club in 1993. In February 1924 West Ham lost 3–2 at home to champions elect Huddersfield Town, with Jack scoring his first two goals for the club. After 138 appearances he left to join Queens Park Rangers in 1926, where he became the club captain. In three seasons at Loftus Road he played in 91 games, scoring 12 goals before leaving to join Accrington Stanley, where he played four games in 1929. On retiring he ran a farm in the northeast, and died in 1952 aged 57.

Football League - Division Two
Final Table 1920-21

	P	HOME					AWAY					Pts
		W	D	L	F	A	W	D	L	F	A	
Birmingham City	42	16	4	1	55	13	8	6	7	24	25	58
Cardiff City	42	13	5	3	27	9	11	5	5	32	23	58
Bristol City	42	14	3	4	35	12	5	10	6	14	17	51
Blackpool	42	12	3	6	32	19	8	7	6	22	23	50
West Ham United	42	13	5	3	38	11	6	5	10	13	19	48
Notts County	42	12	5	4	36	17	6	6	9	19	23	47
Clapton Orient	42	13	6	2	31	9	3	7	11	12	33	45
South Shields	42	13	4	4	41	16	4	6	11	20	30	44
Fulham	42	14	4	3	33	12	2	6	13	10	35	42
Sheffield Wednesday	42	9	7	5	31	14	6	4	11	17	34	41
Bury	42	10	8	3	29	13	5	2	14	16	36	40
Leicester City	42	10	8	3	26	11	2	8	11	13	35	40
Hull City	42	7	10	4	24	18	3	10	8	19	35	40
Leeds United	42	11	5	5	30	14	3	5	13	10	31	38
Wolverhampton Wanderers	42	11	4	6	34	24	5	2	14	15	42	38
Barnsley	42	9	10	2	31	17	1	6	14	17	33	36
Port Vale	42	7	6	8	28	19	4	8	9	15	30	36
Nottingham Forest	42	9	6	6	37	26	3	6	12	11	29	36
Rotherham County	42	8	9	4	23	21	4	3	14	14	32	36
Stoke City	42	9	5	7	26	16	3	6	12	20	40	35
Coventry City	42	8	6	7	24	25	4	5	12	15	45	35
Stockport County	42	8	6	7	30	24	1	6	14	12	51	30

Season **1920-21** Football League - Division Two
Match Details

Manager **Syd King**   Final League Position **5/22**

	Date		Competition	Venue	Opponents	Results		Attendance	Position	Scorers
1	Aug 28	Sat	Div 2	H	Hull City	D	1-1	26,000	13	Puddefoot
2	Aug 30	Mon	Div 2	A	Wolverhampton Wanderers	W	2-1	20,000	6	Puddefoot 2
3	Sep 4	Sat	Div 2	A	Hull City	L	1-2	12,000	12	Simmons
4	Sep 6	Mon	Div 2	H	Wolverhampton Wanderers	W	1-0	15,000	6	Puddefoot
5	Sep 11	Sat	Div 2	A	Fulham	D	0-0	30,000	5	
6	Sep 18	Sat	Div 2	H	Fulham	W	2-0	20,000	4	Kay, Puddefoot
7	Sep 25	Sat	Div 2	A	Cardiff City	D	0-0	30,000	3	
8	Oct 2	Sat	Div 2	H	Cardiff City	D	1-1	26,000	4	Shea
9	Oct 4	Mon	Div 2	A	Coventry City	W	1-0	8,000	2	Watson
10	Oct 9	Sat	Div 2	A	Leicester City	L	0-1	17,000	5	
11	Oct 16	Sat	Div 2	H	Leicester City	L	0-1	25,000	7	
12	Oct 23	Sat	Div 2	A	Blackpool	L	0-1	10,000	8	
13	Oct 30	Sat	Div 2	H	Blackpool	D	1-1	20,000	7	Puddefoot
14	Nov 6	Sat	Div 2	A	Sheffield Wednesday	W	1-0	30,000	7	Puddefoot
15	Nov 13	Sat	Div 2	H	Sheffield Wednesday	W	4-0	20,000	6	Puddefoot 4 [1 pen]
16	Nov 20	Sat	Div 2	A	Stockport County	L	0-2	9,000	8	
17	Nov 27	Sat	Div 2	H	Stockport County	W	5-0	20,000	6	Leafe 3, Puddefoot 2
18	Dec 4	Sat	Div 2	A	Stoke City	L	0-1	10,000	7	
19	Dec 11	Sat	Div 2	H	Stoke City	W	1-0	18,000	7	Puddefoot
20	Dec 25	Sat	Div 2	H	Birmingham	D	1-1	23,000	7	Bishop
21	Dec 27	Mon	Div 2	A	Birmingham	L	1-2	65,000	8	Puddefoot
22	Jan 1	Sat	Div 2	H	Coventry City	W	7-0	8,000	6	Puddefoot 4, Leafe 2, Bishop
23	Jan 8	Sat	FAC 3	A	Sheffield Wednesday	L	0-1	49,125		
24	Jan 15	Sat	Div 2	A	Clapton Orient	W	1-0	20,000	6	Bishop
25	Jan 22	Sat	Div 2	H	Clapton Orient	W	1-0	27,000	6	James
26	Jan 29	Sat	Div 2	A	Leeds United	W	2-1	15,000	5	Carter, Puddefoot
27	Feb 5	Sat	Div 2	H	Leeds United	W	3-0	23,000	4	Puddefoot 3 [1 pen]
28	Feb 12	Sat	Div 2	A	Bury	L	0-1	10,000	5	
29	Feb 19	Sat	Div 2	H	Bury	L	0-1	20,000	6	
30	Feb 26	Sat	Div 2	A	Bristol City	L	0-1	20,000	6	
31	Mar 5	Sat	Div 2	H	Bristol City	W	1-0	20,000	6	Puddefoot
32	Mar 12	Sat	Div 2	A	Barnsley	D	1-1	13,000	6	Puddefoot
33	Mar 19	Sat	Div 2	H	Barnsley	W	2-1	18,000	5	James, Gittins (og)
34	Mar 25	Fri	Div 2	H	Notts County	L	0-2	25,000	6	
35	Mar 26	Sat	Div 2	H	Nottingham Forest	W	3-0	20,000	5	Puddefoot 2, Leafe
36	Mar 28	Mon	Div 2	A	Notts County	D	1-1	22,000	5	Puddefoot
37	Apr 2	Mon	Div 2	A	Nottingham Forest	L	0-1	22,000	5	
38	Apr 9	Mon	Div 2	H	Rotherham County	W	1-0	20,000	5	Leafe
39	Apr 16	Mon	Div 2	A	Rotherham County	L	0-2	10,000	5	
40	Apr 23	Mon	Div 2	H	Port Vale	D	1-1	15,000	5	Robinson
41	Apr 30	Mon	Div 2	A	Port Vale	W	2-1	12,000	5	James, Watson
42	May 2	Wed	Div 2	H	South Shields	W	2-1	15,000	5	Puddefoot, Walker (og)
43	May 7	Mon	Div 2	A	South Shields	D	0-0	15,000	5	

Team Line-Ups

ALLEN Percy	BAILEY Daniel	BISHOP Syd	BRADSHAW Harry	BROWN William	BURTON Frank	BUTCHER George	CALLADINE John	CARTER George	COPE William	COWELL Herbert	CROWTHER George	CUMMING James	GATLAND Bill	HAMPSON Tommy	HART Joseph	HEBDEN Jack	HUFTON Edward	JAMES William	KAY George	LANE Harry	LEAFE Alfred	LEE Alf	McCRAE James	PALMER James	PUDDEFOOT Syd	ROBINSON Leslie	SHEA Danny	SIMMONS Jim	SMITH Stephen	SMITHURST Edgar	TRESADERN Jack	WATSON Victor	WOODARDS Dan	YOUNG John	
					3				2		7						1		5				6		9		8	10			4			11	1
					3				2		7						1		5				6		9		8	10			4			11	2
					3				2		7						1		5				6		9		8	10			4			11	3
					3				2		10						1		5				6		9		8	7			4			11	4
			11		3				2		10						1		5				6		9		8	7			4				5
					3				2		10						1		5				6		9		8	7			4			11	6
					3				2								1		5				6		9		8	7			4	10		11	7
					3				2								1		5				6		9		8	7			4	10		11	8
					3				2								1		5				6		9		8	7			4	10		11	9
					3				2								1		5				6		9		8	7			4	10		11	10
					3		10		2								1		5				6		9		8			7	4			11	11
	8								2		7						1		5			3	6		9		10				4			11	12
	10							3			7						1		5	2			6		9		8				4			11	13
	10			5				7	3								1		2				6		9		8				4			11	14
4	10			5				7	3								1		2				6		9		8							11	15
4	10			5				7	3								1		2						9		8				6			11	16
4								7	3								1		5	2	10				9			8			6			11	17
4								7	3								1		5	2	10				9			8			6			11	18
4	8							7	2								1		5	3	10				9						6			11	19
4			10					7	3								1		5	2					9			8			6			11	20
4	8						2		3								1		5	10					9				7		6			11	21
4	8						2	7	3								1		5	10					9						6			11	22
4	8						2	7	3								1		5	10					9						6			11	23
4	8						2	7	3				1						5	10					9						6			11	24
4	8						2	7	3								1	10	5						9						6			11	25
4	8	3						7	2								1	10	5						9						6			11	26
4	8	3						7	2								1	10	5						9						6			11	27
4	8	3						7	2								1	10	5						9						6			11	28
4	8	3						7	2								1	10	5						9						6			11	29
4	8	6					3	7	2								1	10	5						9									11	30
4	8	6					3		2								1	10	5						9				7					11	31
4	8						3		2								1	10	5						9				7			6		11	32
4	8						3		2								1	10	5										7		6	9		11	33
7	4						2										1	10	5			3						8			6	9		11	34
4	8						2		7								1	11	5	10		3			9							6			35
4	8						2		7					1				11	5	10		3			9							6			36
4	8								7									11	5	2	10	3										9	6		37
4	6								7	8							1	11	5	2	10	3			9										38
4	6						2		7								1	11	5	10		3			9	8									39
4											3	2					1	11		7					9	8		10			6		5		40
4	5								2								1	10			7	3				8					6	9		11	41
4	5								2				7				1	11				3			9	8					6	10			42
4						10		7	3						1	2			5					6	9	8								11	43

1921-22
Story of the season

Since joining the Football League **the team had shown a steady improvement** and promotion to the First Division was the aim.

They now had an experienced defence and it was hoped that young Vic Watson would be able to contribute with the goalscoring to ease the burden on Puddefoot. Once again it was the usual pattern of losing away and winning at home. There were five successive away defeats, while at home Stoke, Port Vale and Bristol City were all beaten with a 3–0 scoreline. The first away win came in October at Bristol City, where Syd Bishop scored in a 1–0 victory, and he repeated the feat in November at Wolverhampton, scoring the only goal of the game. At home the Hammers were particularly strong and Puddefoot scored a brace in each of

Appearances & Goals 1921-22

	League		FA Cup		Total	
	Starts	Goals	Starts	Goals	Starts	Goals
ALLEN Percy	42	5	3	0	45	5
BISHOP Syd	36	4	3	0	39	4
BROWN William	7	0	0	0	7	0
CARTER George	3	0	0	0	3	0
COPE William	41	0	3	0	44	0
GURKIN John	1	0	0	0	1	0
HAMPSON Tommy	9	0	0	0	9	0
HEBDEN Jack	19	0	0	0	19	0
HENDERSON William	12	0	0	0	12	0
HODGSON Tommy	1	0	0	0	1	0
HUFTON Edward	33	0	3	0	36	0
JACKSON Thomas	3	1	0	0	3	1
JAMES William	36	4	3	0	39	4
KAY George	39	5	3	0	42	5
LEAFE Alfred	3	0	0	0	3	0
LEE Alf	0	0	2	0	2	0
MACKESY Jack	1	0	0	0	1	0
PUDDEFOOT Syd	26	14	3	0	29	14
ROBINSON Leslie	10	0	0	0	10	0
RUFFELL James	14	0	1	0	15	0
SIMMONS Jim	9	0	0	0	9	0
SMITH Stephen	3	0	0	0	3	0
THIRLAWAY William	33	2	3	0	36	2
TRESADERN Jack	28	3	2	0	30	3
TURNER Cyril	4	0	0	0	4	0
WATSON Victor	37	12	3	1	40	13
WAUGH William	6	0	1	0	7	0
WILLIAMS William	1	1	0	0	1	1
YOUNG John	5	0	0	0	5	0
own goal		1				1
Totals	**462**	**52**	**33**	**1**	**495**	**53**

he successive home victories against Barnsley, Coventry City and Derby County. January proved to be a poor month, with no wins in the league and a FA Cup defeat at Swansea Town.

t was a huge shock in February when leading scorer Puddefoot was sold to Falkirk for £5,000. It was a large fee at the time and the club said that they had a ready replacement in Vic Watson. There were three successive wins in March and after beating Sheffield Wednesday 2–0 in April the team lay third in the table. Unfortunately, not a single win came in the remaining seven games, leaving the side to finish fourth in the league. In the final game of the season at Blackpool, Billy Williams scored on his debut.

Football League - Division Two
Final Table 1921-22

	P	HOME					AWAY					Pts
		W	D	L	F	A	W	D	L	F	A	
Nottingham Forest	42	13	7	1	29	9	9	5	7	22	21	56
Stoke City	42	9	11	1	31	11	9	5	7	29	33	52
Barnsley	42	14	5	2	43	18	8	3	10	24	34	52
West Ham United	42	15	3	3	39	13	5	5	11	13	26	48
Hull City	42	13	5	3	36	13	6	5	10	15	28	48
South Shields	42	14	5	2	41	8	4	4	13	16	30	45
Fulham	42	14	5	2	41	8	4	4	13	16	30	45
Leeds United	42	10	8	3	31	12	6	5	10	17	26	45
Leicester City	42	11	6	4	30	16	3	11	7	9	18	45
Sheffield Wednesday	42	12	4	5	31	24	3	10	8	16	26	44
Bury	42	11	3	7	35	19	4	7	10	19	36	40
Derby County	42	11	3	7	34	22	4	6	11	26	42	39
Notts County	42	10	7	4	34	18	2	8	11	13	33	39
Crystal Palace	42	9	6	6	28	20	4	7	10	17	31	39
Clapton Orient	42	12	4	5	33	18	3	5	13	10	32	39
Rotherham County	42	8	9	4	17	7	6	2	13	15	36	39
Wolverhampton Wanderers	42	8	7	6	28	19	5	4	12	16	30	37
Port Vale	42	10	5	6	28	19	4	3	14	15	38	36
Blackpool	42	11	1	9	33	27	4	4	13	11	30	35
Coventry City	42	8	5	8	31	21	4	5	12	20	39	34
Bradford Park Avenue	42	10	5	6	32	22	2	4	15	14	40	33
Bristol City	42	10	3	8	25	18	2	6	13	12	40	33

WILLIAM HENDERSON

Billy was from County Durham but started his career with Aberdare, who were then in the Second Division.

Playing as a full-back, he appeared in 19 games for the Welsh club in 1921/22. He then came to London to sign for West Ham, making his debut in March 1922 in the 2–0 home win against Crystal Palace. The following season he was in the side that won promotion to the First Division and he also played in every game as the Hammers reached the FA Cup final, where they lost 2–0 to Bolton Wanderers.

He was selected for the FA against the Army and for the Professionals versus the Amateurs in 1923. Billy was at Upton Park for seven seasons, playing in 183 matches and scoring one goal. It was an amazing coincidence that his only goal was scored against his former club Aberdare. After retiring in 1928 he was affected by poor health and died of tuberculosis in 1934.

Season **1921-22** Football League - Division Two
Match Details

Manager **Syd King**   Final League Position **4/22**

	Date		Competition	Venue	Opponents	Results		Attendance	Position	Scorers
1	Aug 27	Sat	Div 2	A	Stoke City	L	0-2	20,000	21	
2	Aug 29	Mon	Div 2	H	Bradford Park Avenue	W	1-0	20,000	16	Dickinson (og)
3	Sep 3	Sat	Div 2	H	Stoke City	W	3-0	20,000	5	Allen, Jackson, Puddefoot [pen]
4	Sep 5	Mon	Div 2	A	Bradford Park Avenue	L	0-2	7,000	11	
5	Sep 10	Sat	Div 2	H	Port Vale	W	3-0	15,000	6	Puddefoot 2, Watson
6	Sep 17	Sat	Div 2	A	Port Vale	L	1-2	10,000	10	Watson
7	Sep 24	Sat	Div 2	H	South Shields	D	1-1	18,000	8	Puddefoot
8	Oct 1	Sat	Div 2	A	South Shields	L	0-1	14,000	10	
9	Oct 3	Mon	Div 2	A	Coventry City	L	0-2	12,000	12	
10	Oct 8	Sat	Div 2	H	Bristol City	W	3-0	18,000	10	Puddefoot 2, Watson
11	Oct 15	Sat	Div 2	A	Bristol City	W	1-0	10,000	6	Bishop
12	Oct 22	Sat	Div 2	H	Nottingham Forest	W	1-0	20,000	5	Watson
13	Oct 29	Sat	Div 2	A	Nottingham Forest	L	0-2	15,000	8	
14	Nov 5	Sat	Div 2	H	Wolverhampton Wanderers	W	2-0	16,000	8	Kay, Tresadern
15	Nov 12	Sat	Div 2	A	Wolverhampton Wanderers	W	1-0	11,000	4	Bishop
16	Nov 19	Sat	Div 2	H	Barnsley	W	4-0	18,000	3	Puddefoot 2, Bishop, Watson
17	Nov 26	Sat	Div 2	A	Barnsley	D	1-1	9,000	4	Thirlaway
18	Dec 10	Sat	Div 2	H	Coventry City	W	3-0	18,000	5	Puddefoot 2 [1 pen], Watson
19	Dec 17	Sat	Div 2	H	Derby County	W	3-1	20,000	5	Puddefoot 2 [1 pen], James
20	Dec 24	Sat	Div 2	A	Derby County	L	1-3	10,000	5	Kay
21	Dec 26	Mon	Div 2	A	Bury	W	1-0	20,000	4	Allen
22	Dec 27	Tue	Div 2	H	Bury	W	3-2	20,000	3	Puddefoot 2, Bishop
23	Dec 31	Sat	Div 2	H	Leicester City	W	1-0	20,000	2	Tresadern
24	Jan 7	Sat	FAC 1	A	Swansea Town	D	0-0	26,000		
25	Jan 11	Wed	FAC 1 Rep	H	Swansea Town	D	1-1	20,000		Watson
26	Jan 14	Sat	Div 2	A	Leicester City	L	1-2	17,000	3	Watson
27	Jan 16	Mon	FAC 1 2nd Rep	A	Swansea Town	L	0-1	8,976		
28	Jan 21	Sat	Div 2	A	Leeds United	D	0-0	7,000	3	
29	Jan 28	Sat	Div 2	H	Leeds United	D	1-1	20,000	2	James
30	Feb 4	Sat	Div 2	A	Hull City	D	0-0	8,000	3	
31	Feb 11	Sat	Div 2	H	Hull City	D	1-1	20,000	4	Kay
32	Feb 25	Sat	Div 2	H	Notts County	W	2-1	20,000	3	Watson 2
33	Mar 4	Sat	Div 2	A	Crystal Palace	W	2-1	10,000	4	Allen, Watson
34	Mar 11	Sat	Div 2	A	Crystal Palace	W	2-0	23,000	3	Tresadern, Watson
35	Mar 18	Sat	Div 2	H	Rotherham County	L	1-2	20,000	3	Kay
36	Mar 25	Sat	Div 2	A	Rotherham County	W	1-0	10,000	3	James
37	Mar 29	Wed	Div 2	A	Notts County	D	1-1	7,000	3	Watson
38	Apr 1	Sat	Div 2	H	Sheffield Wednesday	W	2-0	20,000	3	Allen, Kay
39	Apr 8	Sat	Div 2	A	Sheffield Wednesday	L	1-2	7,000	3	Tresadern
40	Apr 14	Fri	Div 2	H	Clapton Orient	L	1-2	30,000	3	James
41	Apr 15	Sat	Div 2	H	Fulham	W	1-0	25,000	3	Allen
42	Apr 17	Mon	Div 2	A	Clapton Orient	D	0-0	27,000	3	
43	Apr 22	Sat	Div 2	A	Fulham	L	0-2	10,000	4	
44	Apr 29	Sat	Div 2	H	Blackpool	L	0-2	18,000	4	
45	May 6	Sat	Div 2	A	Blackpool	L	1-3	12,000	4	Williams

Team Line-Ups

ALLEN Percy	BISHOP Syd	BROWN William	CARTER George	COPE William	GURKIN John	HAMPSON Tommy	HEBDEN Jack	HENDERSON William	HODGSON Tommy	HUFTON Edward	JACKSON Thomas	JAMES William	KAY George	LEAFE Alfred	LEE Alf	MACKESY Jack	PUDDEFOOT Syd	ROBINSON Leslie	RUFFELL James	SIMMONS Jim	SMITH Stephen	THIRLAWAY William	TRESADERN Jack	TURNER Cyril	WATSON Victor	WAUGH William	WILLIAMS William	YOUNG John	
4	6	7		3	5		2			1		10					9	8										11	1
4	8			3			2			1		6	5				9	10				11	7						2
4	6			3			2			1	8	11	5				9					10	7						3
4	8			3			2			1	10	6	5				9					11	7						4
4	6			3		1	2					11	5				9	8					7		10				5
4	6			3		1	2					11	5				9	8					7		10				6
4	6	8		3			2			1		11	5				9						7		10				7
4	6	8		3			2			1		11	5				9						7		10				8
4	6	8		3			2			1		11	5				9						7		10				9
4	8			3			2			1		6	5				9						7		10		11		10
4	8			3		1	2					6	5				9						7		10		11		11
4	6			3		1	2					10	5				8						7		9		11		12
4	8			3		1	2					6	5				9						7		10		11		13
4	8			3		1	2					11	5				9						7	6	10				14
4	8			3		1	2					11	5				9						7	6	10				15
4	8			3			2			1		11	5				9						7	6	10				16
4	8			3			2			1		11	5				9						7	6	10				17
4	8			3			2			1		11	5				9						7	6	10				18
4	8			3			2			1		11	5				9						7	6	10				19
4	8			3						1		11	5				9						7	6	10	2			20
4	8			3						1		11	5				9						7	6	10	2			21
4	8	5		3						1							9		11				7	6	10	2			22
4	5			3						1		8					9		11				7	6	10	2			23
4	8			2						1		6	5	3			9		11				7		10				24
4	8			2						1		11	5	3			9						7	6	10				25
4				3						1		8	5		7	10			11					6	9	2			26
4	8			2						1		11	5				9						7	6	10	3			27
4				3						1			5		7	10			11	8				6	9	2			28
2	4			3						1	10	11	5				9			8			7	6					29
4	8			3						1		11	5				9						7	6	10	2			30
4	10			3						1		11	5							8			7	6	9	2			31
4	8			3						1		10	5						11				7	6	9	2			32
4	8			3						1		10	5						11				7	6	9	2			33
4	8			3					2	1		10	5						11				7	6	9				34
4	8			3					2	1		10	5						11				7	6	9				35
4	10			3					2	1		11	5								8		7	6	9				36
4	10			3					2	1		11	5		6						8		7		9				37
4	10			3					2	1		11	5								8		7	6	9				38
4	10			3					2	1		11	5								8		7	6	9				39
4	8			3					2	1		10	5						11				7	6	9				40
4	10			3					2	1			5					8	11				7	6	9				41
4	10			3					2	1			5					8	11				7	6	9				42
4	8			3					2	1		10	5						11				7	6	9				43
4	8	10		3					2	1			5						11				7	6	9				44
4			8			1		3	2				5						11				7	6	9			10	45

1922-23
Story of the season

The Hammers began the season with high hopes of achieving **promotion to the First Division.** With this in mind **there were new signings made.** Inside-forward **Billy Moore** came from Sunderland in addition to wingers **Dick Richards** and **Billy Charlton.**

It was a disastrous start, with West Ham winning ju three of their opening 14 matches with Billy Moore scorir twice against Rotherham in a 4–0 victory and Vic Watsc doing the same in a 2–0 win against Blackpool. After losin 3–1 at Leeds on 4 November the Hammers went on a amazing run where they only lost one game in 36 league an cup matches. Unlike previous seasons, the team wer winning away games. Watson scored a hat-trick at Coventr in a 3–1 victory, Billy Moore scored three at Leicester in remarkable 6–0 win, then in successive away matches Vi Watson scored six goals in total as Crystal Palace wer beaten 5–1 followed by a 5–2 win against Bury.

On the final day of the season West Ham were top of th league on goal difference from Leicester City and Nott County. The Hammers were at home to Notts Count

Appearances & Goals 1922-23

	League		FA Cup		Total	
	Starts	Goals	Starts	Goals	Starts	Goals
ALLEN Percy	6	0	1	0	7	0
BISHOP Syd	34	2	8	0	42	2
BROWN William	26	9	8	3	34	12
BURGESS Daniel	2	0	0	0	2	0
CARTER George	10	0	4	0	14	0
CHARLTON William	8	0	0	0	8	0
CROSSLEY Charlie	15	1	1	0	16	1
EDWARDS William	1	0	0	0	1	0
FLETCHER Albert	1	0	0	0	1	0
HAMPSON Tommy	3	0	0	0	3	0
HEBDEN Jack	9	0	0	0	9	0
HENDERSON William	34	0	9	0	43	0
HODGSON Tommy	11	0	0	0	11	0
HORLER George	5	0	2	0	7	0
HUFTON Edward	39	0	9	0	48	0
KAY George	36	0	5	0	41	0
MACKESY Jack	4	0	0	0	4	0
MOORE William	42	15	9	5	51	20
RICHARDS Dick	34	5	9	1	43	6
ROBINSON Leslie	3	1	0	0	3	1
RUFFELL James	33	6	9	1	42	7
THIRLAWAY William	2	0	0	0	2	0
TRESADERN Jack	37	2	9	0	46	2
WATSON Victor	41	22	9	5	50	27
WILLIAMS William	1	0	0	0	1	0
YOUNG John	25	0	7	0	32	0
Totals	**462**	**63**	**99**	**15**	**561**	**78**

while Leicester played Bury. At the Boleyn Ground it was a tense affair as County scored after seven minutes and held on to win 1–0. There was dejection at Upton Park until the news came through that Leicester had also lost 1–0. Then there were joyous scenes as the supporters celebrated promotion to the First Division.

The FA Cup also brought fame as the Hammers reached the final, which was the first to be played at the new Wembley Stadium. In earlier rounds Hull City, Brighton, Plymouth and Southampton were beaten to set up a semi-final against Derby County at Stamford Bridge. Before a crowd of 50,795, Derby were overwhelmed as the Hammers won 5–2 with two goals each from Billy Moore and Billy Brown, and one from Jimmy Ruffell. The FA Cup final with Bolton Wanderers was to become famous for events off the pitch rather than the game itself. Thousands of fans climbed the gates to get in and descended on the pitch. There were chaotic scenes as police and officials tried to control the crowds and clear the area, with the now-legendary 'white horse' prominent in the proceedings. The match itself was ruined as a spectacle as on occasions the crowd around the touchline spilled on to the pitch. The Bolton team handled the conditions better, scored after two minutes and eventually won 2–0. In any event it had been an excellent campaign in winning promotion and taking part in the first ever Wembley Cup Final.

Football League - Division Two Final Table 1922-23

	P	HOME					AWAY					Pts
		W	D	L	F	A	W	D	L	F	A	
Notts County	42	16	1	4	29	15	7	6	8	17	19	53
West Ham United	**42**	**9**	**8**	**4**	**21**	**11**	**11**	**3**	**7**	**42**	**27**	**51**
Leicester City	42	14	2	5	42	19	7	7	7	23	25	51
Manchester United	42	10	6	5	25	17	7	8	6	26	19	48
Blackpool	42	12	4	5	37	14	6	7	8	23	29	47
Bury	42	14	5	2	41	16	4	6	11	14	30	47
Leeds United	42	11	8	2	26	10	7	3	11	17	26	47
Sheffield Wednesday	42	14	3	4	36	16	3	9	9	18	31	46
Barnsley	42	12	4	5	42	21	5	7	9	20	30	45
Fulham	42	10	7	4	29	12	6	5	10	14	20	44
Southampton	42	10	5	6	28	21	4	9	8	12	19	42
Hull City	42	9	8	4	29	22	5	6	10	14	23	42
South Shields	42	11	7	3	26	12	4	3	14	9	32	40
Derby County	42	9	5	7	25	16	5	6	10	21	34	39
Bradford City	42	8	7	6	27	18	4	6	11	14	27	37
Crystal Palace	42	10	7	4	33	16	3	4	14	21	46	37
Port Vale	42	8	6	7	23	18	6	3	12	16	33	37
Coventry City	42	12	2	7	35	21	3	5	13	11	42	37
Clapton Orient	42	9	6	6	26	17	3	6	12	14	33	36
Stockport County	42	10	6	5	32	24	4	2	15	11	34	36
Rotherham County	42	10	7	4	30	19	3	2	16	14	44	35
Wolverhampton Wanderers	42	9	4	8	32	26	0	5	16	10	51	27

WILLIAM MOORE

He was born in Newcastle in 1894 but began his career with their northeast rivals Sunderland in 1913.

He spent seven seasons with the Roker Park club, scoring 11 goals in 47 appearances. The inside-forward joined West Ham in 1922 and was ever-present that season as the Hammers won promotion to the First Division and were runners-up to Bolton Wanderers in the first Wembley FA Cup final. His left-wing partnership with Jimmy Ruffell saw them contribute 21 league goals between them that season. Billy's fine form saw him capped for England against Sweden in 1923 and he scored two goals in England's 4–2 victory. He remained at Upton Park until 1929, playing in 202 games and scoring 48 goals. After retiring as a player he became the club's trainer and remained in that capacity until his retirement in 1960. Living in the area, he was a frequent visitor to the ground on match days until 1968, when he sadly died aged 73.

Season **1922-23** Football League - Division Two
Match Details
Manager **Syd King**   Final League Position **2/22 Promoted to Division 1**

	Date		Competition	Venue	Opponents	Results		Attendance	Position	Scorers
1	Aug 26	Sat	Div 2	H	Bradford City	L	1-2	27,000	18	Watson
2	Aug 28	Mon	Div 2	H	Derby County	D	0-0	16,000	13	
3	Sep 2	Sat	Div 2	A	Bradford City	W	1-0	20,000	14	Ruffell
4	Sep 4	Mon	Div 2	A	Derby County	L	1-2	9,000	14	Moore
5	Sep 9	Sat	Div 2	H	Rotherham County	W	4-0	14,000	11	Moore 2, Ruffell, Watson
6	Sep 16	Sat	Div 2	A	Rotherham County	D	2-2	9,000	11	Robinson, Watson
7	Sep 23	Sat	Div 2	H	Stockport County	L	0-1	15,000	14	
8	Sep 30	Sat	Div 2	A	Stockport County	L	1-2	16,000	16	Moore
9	Oct 7	Sat	Div 2	H	Southampton	D	1-1	20,000	16	Crossley
10	Oct 14	Sat	Div 2	A	Southampton	L	0-2	17,000	17	
11	Oct 21	Sat	Div 2	H	Blackpool	W	2-0	18,000	16	Watson 2
12	Oct 28	Sat	Div 2	A	Blackpool	L	1-4	14,000	17	Moore
13	Nov 4	Sat	Div 2	A	Leeds United	L	1-3	12,000	18	Moore
14	Nov 11	Sat	Div 2	H	Leeds United	D	0-0	15,000	18	
15	Nov 18	Sat	Div 2	H	Clapton Orient	W	1-0	20,000	18	Watson
16	Nov 25	Sat	Div 2	A	Clapton Orient	W	2-0	20,000	18	Watson 2
17	Dec 2	Sat	Div 2	H	South Shields	W	1-0	15,000	11	Moore
18	Dec 9	Sat	Div 2	A	South Shields	D	0-0	7,000	11	
19	Dec 16	Sat	Div 2	A	Wolverhampton Wanderers	W	4-1	10,000	11	Brown 2, Moore, Watson
20	Dec 23	Sat	Div 2	H	Wolverhampton Wanderers	W	1-0	15,000	9	Watson
21	Dec 25	Mon	Div 2	A	Manchester United	W	2-1	17,500	7	Brown, Moore
22	Dec 26	Tue	Div 2	H	Manchester United	L	0-2	20,000	10	
23	Dec 30	Sat	Div 2	A	Coventry City	W	3-1	14,000	7	Watson 3
24	Jan 6	Sat	Div 2	H	Coventry City	W	1-0	16,000	8	Tresadern
25	Jan 13	Sat	FAC 1	A	Hull City	W	3-2	14,000		Watson 2, Moore
26	Jan 20	Sat	Div 2	A	Port Vale	W	3-1	17,000	7	Bishop, Richards, Ruffell
27	Jan 27	Sat	Div 2	H	Port Vale	D	0-0	17,000	7	
28	Feb 3	Sat	FAC 2	A	Brighton & Hove Albion	D	1-1	19,531		Watson
29	Feb 7	Wed	FAC 2 Rep	H	Brighton & Hove Albion	W	1-0	20,000		Moore
30	Feb 10	Sat	Div 2	H	Leicester City	D	2-2	16,000	7	Brown, Richards
31	Feb 15	Thu	Div 2	A	Leicester City	W	6-0	12,000	5	Moore 3, Richards, Ruffell, Tresadern
32	Feb 17	Sat	Div 2	H	Barnsley	D	0-0	20,000	4	
33	Feb 24	Sat	FAC 3	H	Plymouth Argyle	W	2-0	30,525		Richards, Moore
34	Mar 3	Sat	Div 2	H	Sheffield Wednesday	W	2-1	16,000	4	Brown, Moore
35	Mar 10	Sat	FAC 4	A	Southampton	D	1-1	21,960		Watson
36	Mar 14	Wed	FAC 4 Rep	H	Southampton	D	1-1	28,000		Watson
37	Mar 17	Sat	Div 2	A	Hull City	D	1-1	14,000	5	Ruffell
38	Mar 19	Mon	FAC 4 2nd Rep	N*	Southampton	W	1-0	22,184		Brown
39	Mar 24	Sat	FAC SF	N**	Derby County	W	5-2	50,795		Brown 2, Moore 2, Ruffell
40	Mar 30	Fri	Div 2	H	Bury	D	0-0	31,000	8	
41	Mar 31	Sat	Div 2	A	Crystal Palace	W	5-1	16,000	6	Watson 4, Brown
42	Apr 2	Mon	Div 2	A	Bury	W	5-2	25,000	5	Watson 2, Moore, Richards, Ruffell
43	Apr 7	Sat	Div 2	H	Crystal Palace	D	1-1	25,000	5	Watson
44	Apr 9	Mon	Div 2	H	Hull City	W	3-0	18,000	3	Brown 2, Richards
45	Apr 14	Sat	Div 2	A	Fulham	W	2-0	30,000	2	Bishop, Moore
46	Apr 16	Mon	Div 2	A	Barnsley	L	0-2	10,000	2	
47	Apr 18	Wed	Div 2	A	Notts County	L	0-2	15,000	2	
48	Apr 21	Sat	Div 2	H	Fulham	W	1-0	20,000	2	Watson
49	Apr 28	Sat	FAC Final	N***	Bolton Wanderers	L	0-2	126,047		
50	Apr 30	Mon	Div 2	A	Sheffield Wednesday	W	2-0	10,000	1	Brown, Watson
51	May 5	Sat	Div 2	H	Notts County	L	0-1	26,000	2	

* Villa Park   ** Stamford Bridge   *** Wembley Stadium

Team Line-Ups

ALLEN Percy	BISHOP Syd	BROWN William	BURGESS Daniel	CARTER George	CHARLTON William	CROSSLEY Charlie	EDWARDS William	FLETCHER Albert	HAMPSON Tommy	HEBDEN Jack	HENDERSON William	HODGSON Tommy	HORLER George	HUFTON Edward	KAY George	MACKESY Jack	MOORE William	RICHARDS Dick	ROBINSON Leslie	RUFFELL James	THIRLAWAY William	TRESADERN Jack	WATSON Victor	WILLIAMS William	YOUNG John	
4	6				7	8						2	3	1	5		10	11					9			1
4					7	8				3		2		1	5		10	11				6	9			2
	4		8	7						3		2		1	5		10			11		6	9			3
	4		8	7						3		2		1	5		10			11		6	9			4
4	5			7						3		2		1			10		8	11		6	9			5
	4			7						3		2		1	5		10		8	11		6	9			6
	4			7								2		1	5		10		8	11		6	9	3		7
	4	8		7								2		1	5		10			11		6	9	3		8
8	7		4		10				2	3				1	5		11					6	9			9
		4	5		10				2	3				1			11	7				6	8	9		10
			4		10					3		2		1	5		8	7		11		6	9			11
			4		10					3		2		1	5		8	7		11		6	9			12
			4		10					3		2		1	5		8	7		11		6	9			13
	4				10				2	3				1	5		8	7		11		6	9			14
	4	9				8			2	3				1	5		10			11	7	6	8			15
	4	8										2		1	5		10	7		11		6	9		3	16
	4	8										2		1	5		10	7		11		6	9		3	17
	4	8										2		1	5		10	7		11		6	9		3	18
	4	8										2		1	5		10	7		11		6	9		3	19
	4	8										2		1	5		10	7		11		6	9		3	20
	4	8										2		1	5		10	7		11		6	9		3	21
	4	8										2		1	5		10	7		11		6	9		3	22
	4					8						2		1	5		10	7		11		6	9		3	23
	4					8						2		1	5		10	7		11		6	9		3	24
	4					8						2		1	5		10	7		11		6	9		3	25
	4					8						2		1	5		10	7		11		6	9		3	26
	4					8						2	3	1	5		10	7		11		6	9			27
	4	8										2	3	1	5		10	7		11		6	9			28
4		8	5									2	3	1			10	7		11		6	9			29
4		8	5		11							2	3	1			10	7				6	9			30
		4	5		8							2	3	1			10	7		11		6	9			31
4		8	5									2	3	1			10	7		11		6	9			32
	4	8	5									2		1			10	7		11		6	9		3	33
	4	8	5									2		1			10	7		11		6	9		3	34
	4	8	5									2		1			10	7		11		6	9		3	35
	4	8	5									2		1			10	7		11		6	9		3	36
	4	8	6									2		1	5		10	7		11		6	9		3	37
	4	8										2		1	5		10	7		11		6	9		3	38
	4	8										2		1	5		10	7		11		6	9		3	39
	4	8										2		1	5		10	7		11		6	9		3	40
	4	8					7					2		1	5	6	10	11					9		3	41
	4	8										2		1	5		10	7		11		6	9		3	42
	4	8										2		1	5		10	7		11		6	9		3	43
	4	8										2		1	5	6	10	7		11			9		3	44
	4	8						9				2		1	5	6	10	7		11					3	45
	4	8				10						2		1	5		11	7				6	9		3	46
	4	8										2		1	5	11	10	7				6	9		3	47
	4	8							1			2			5		10	7			11	6	9		3	48
	4	8										2		1	5		10	7		11		6	9		3	49
	4	8							1			2			5		10	7		11		6	9		3	50
	4	8							1			2			5		10	7		11		6	9		3	51

1923-24
Story of the season

The **opening game in the First Division** saw the Hammers gain a creditable 0–0 draw at Sunderland. Two days later there were **25,000 inside the Boleyn Ground to see Arsenal beaten 1–0** with a goal from Albert Fletcher.

Goals were hard to come by, with only five being scored in the first eleven games. In November Birmingham City were beaten 4–1 at home but this was followed up with a 5–1 defeat at Burnley. The Christmas and New Year period brought three home wins against Nottingham Forest, Aston Villa and Liverpool.

In the FA Cup Third Division side Aberdare Athletic were the visitors and, with Billy Brown scoring twice, the Welsh side were beaten 5–0. Cup hopes were ended in the next round with a 1–0 replay defeat at Leeds United, which followed a 1–1 draw at home.

Appearances & Goals 1923-24

	League		FA Cup		Total	
	Starts	Goals	Starts	Goals	Starts	Goals
BISHOP Syd	31	0	0	0	31	0
BROWN William	26	6	3	2	29	8
CADWELL Albert	29	0	3	0	32	0
CAMPBELL John	11	4	0	0	11	4
CARTER George	16	0	3	0	19	0
COLLINS Jimmy	5	1	0	0	5	1
EDWARDS William	25	3	2	0	27	0
FLETCHER Albert	7	1	0	0	7	1
GIBBINS Vivian	3	1	0	0	3	1
HAMPSON Tommy	27	0	3	0	30	0
HEBDEN Jack	2	0	0	0	2	0
HENDERSON William	42	0	3	1	45	1
HODGES Harry	2	1	0	0	2	1
HODGSON Tommy	5	0	0	0	5	0
HUFTON Edward	15	0	0	0	15	0
KAY George	40	3	3	1	43	4
MOORE William	36	9	3	1	39	10
PROCTOR Norman	7	1	0	0	7	1
RICHARDS Dick	9	0	1	0	10	0
RICHARDSON Frank	10	2	1	0	11	2
ROBINSON Leslie	1	0	0	0	1	0
RUFFELL James	39	2	3	0	42	2
THIRLAWAY William	1	0	0	0	1	0
TRESADERN Jack	10	0	0	0	10	0
WATSON Victor	11	3	0	0	11	3
WILLIAMS William	5	0	2	1	7	1
YEWS Tommy	12	1	0	0	12	1
YOUNG John	35	2	3	0	38	2
Totals	**462**	**40**	**33**	**6**	**495**	**43**

The defence were playing well, with full-backs Henderson and Young behind half-backs Bishop, Kay and Cadwell. It was the forwards who were struggling, hence the five draws in the next six games. The season ended with home and away defeats to Manchester City, which resulted in a mid-table position of 13th.

Football League - Division One
Final Table 1923-24

		HOME				AWAY					
	P	W	D	L	F	A	W	D	L	F	A	Pts
Huddersfield Town	42	15	5	1	35	9	8	6	7	25	24	57
Cardiff City	42	14	5	2	35	13	8	8	5	26	21	57
Sunderland	42	12	7	2	38	20	10	2	9	33	34	53
Bolton Wanderers	42	13	6	2	45	13	5	8	8	23	21	50
Sheffield United	42	12	5	4	39	16	7	7	7	30	33	50
Aston Villa	42	10	10	1	33	11	8	3	10	19	26	49
Everton	42	13	7	1	43	18	5	6	10	19	35	49
Blackburn Rovers	42	14	5	2	40	13	3	6	12	14	37	45
Newcastle United	42	13	5	3	40	21	4	5	12	20	33	44
Notts County	42	9	7	5	21	15	5	7	9	23	34	42
Manchester City	42	11	7	3	34	24	4	5	12	20	47	42
Liverpool	42	11	5	5	35	20	4	6	11	14	28	41
West Ham United	**42**	**10**	**6**	**5**	**26**	**17**	**3**	**9**	**9**	**14**	**26**	**41**
Birmingham	42	10	4	7	25	19	3	9	9	16	30	39
Tottenham Hotspur	42	9	6	6	30	22	3	8	10	20	34	38
West Bromwich Albion	42	10	6	5	43	30	2	8	11	8	32	38
Burnley	42	10	5	6	39	27	2	7	12	16	33	36
Preston North End	42	8	4	9	34	27	4	6	11	18	40	34
Arsenal	42	8	5	8	25	24	4	4	13	15	39	33
Nottingham Forest	42	7	9	5	19	15	3	3	15	23	49	32
Chelsea	42	7	9	5	23	21	2	5	14	8	32	32
Middlesbrough	42	6	4	11	23	23	1	4	16	14	37	22

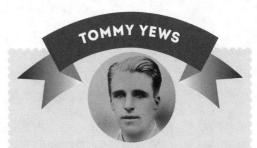

TOMMY YEWS

After some sparkling displays in 39 games for Hartlepool in the Third Division, a fee of £150 brought Tommy to Upton Park.

He made his debut at Cardiff in September 1923 and soon established himself in the side, playing at outside-right. With Jimmy Ruffell on the opposite wing they provided many goals for centre-forward Vic Watson.

Tommy was a provider rather than a goalscoring winger but his scoring record improved as he developed and he netted 11 goals in 1927/28 and 13 the following season. He spent ten seasons with West Ham, scoring 51 goals in his 361 appearances, before joining Clapton Orient in 1933. With the Orient he only played three league games before retiring as a player. He later worked as a charge hand at the Ford Motor Company and died in August 1966.

Season **1923-24** Football League - Division One
Match Details
Manager **Syd King**   Final League Position **13/22**

	Date		Competition	Venue	Opponents	Results		Attendance	Position	Scorers
1	Aug 25	Sat	Div 1	A	Sunderland	D	0-0	32,000	12	
2	Aug 27	Mon	Div 1	H	Arsenal	D	1-0	25,000	6	Fletcher
3	Sep 1	Sat	Div 1	H	Sunderland	L	0-1	25,000	12	
4	Sep 8	Sat	Div 1	H	Cardiff City	D	0-0	30,000	16	
5	Sep 10	Mon	Div 1	A	Arsenal	L	1-4	40,000	16	Hodges
6	Sep 15	Sat	Div 1	A	Cardiff City	L	0-1	37,000	20	
7	Sep 22	Sat	Div 1	H	Middlesbrough	D	1-1	20,000	20	Brown
8	Sep 29	Sat	Div 1	A	Middlesbrough	W	1-0	20,000	17	Yews
9	Oct 6	Sat	Div 1	H	Newcastle United	W	1-0	30,000	14	Brown
10	Oct 13	Sat	Div 1	A	Newcastle United	D	0-0	30,000	14	
11	Oct 20	Sat	Div 1	A	Chelsea	D	0-0	45,000	15	
12	Oct 27	Sat	Div 1	H	Chelsea	W	2-0	25,000	13	Brown, Kay
13	Nov 3	Sat	Div 1	H	Birmingham	W	4-1	20,000	9	Brown, Kay, Moore, Richardson
14	Nov 10	Sat	Div 1	A	Birmingham	L	0-2	30,000	12	
15	Nov 17	Sat	Div 1	A	Burnley	L	1-5	9,000	14	Moore
16	Nov 24	Sat	Div 1	H	Burnley	D	0-0	20,000	13	
17	Dec 1	Sat	Div 1	A	Bolton Wanderers	D	1-1	22,592	13	Brown
18	Dec 8	Sat	Div 1	H	Bolton Wanderers	L	0-1	30,000	14	
19	Dec 15	Sat	Div 1	A	Nottingham Forest	L	1-2	10,000	15	Edwards
20	Dec 22	Sat	Div 1	H	Nottingham Forest	W	3-2	15,000	14	Moore 2, Kay
21	Dec 25	Tue	Div 1	A	Aston Villa	D	1-1	40,000	13	Richardson
22	Dec 26	Wed	Div 1	H	Aston Villa	W	1-0	30,000	11	Moore
23	Dec 29	Sat	Div 1	A	Liverpool	L	0-2	20,000	12	
24	Jan 1	Tue	Div 1	A	Sheffield United	W	2-0	30,000	11	Brown, Gibbins
25	Jan 5	Sat	Div 1	H	Liverpool	W	1-0	25,000	11	Moore
26	Jan 12	Sat	FAC 1	H	Aberdare Athletic	W	5-0	23,000		Brown 2, Henderson, Moore, Williams
27	Jan 19	Sat	Div 1	A	Blackburn Rovers	D	0-0	5,000	11	
28	Jan 26	Sat	Div 1	H	Blackburn Rovers	L	0-1	20,000	11	
29	Feb 2	Sat	FAC 2	H	Leeds United	D	1-1	30,123		Kay
30	Feb 6	Wed	FAC 2 Rep	A	Leeds United	L	0-1	31,071		
31	Feb 9	Sat	Div 1	H	Tottenham Hotspur	D	0-0	20,000	11	
32	Feb 16	Sat	Div 1	A	Huddersfield Town	D	1-1	10,000	12	Ruffell
33	Mar 1	Sat	Div 1	A	Notts County	D	1-1	10,000	13	Collins
34	Mar 8	Sat	Div 1	H	Notts County	D	1-1	20,000	12	Proctor
35	Mar 15	Sat	Div 1	H	Everton	W	2-1	22,000	11	Campbell, Edwards
36	Mar 22	Sat	Div 1	A	Everton	L	1-2	28,000	12	Moore
37	Mar 27	Thu	Div 1	H	Huddersfield Town	L	2-3	15,000	12	Young 2
38	Mar 29	Sat	Div 1	H	West Bromwich Albion	W	1-0	18,000	11	Ruffell
39	Apr 5	Sat	Div 1	A	West Bromwich Albion	D	0-0	12,000	11	
40	Apr 12	Sat	Div 1	H	Preston North End	W	3-1	18,000	10	Edwards, Moore, Watson
41	Apr 19	Sat	Div 1	A	Preston North End	L	1-2	15,000	11	Watson
42	Apr 21	Mon	Div 1	H	Sheffield United	D	2-2	18,000	11	Campbell 2
43	Apr 22	Tue	Div 1	A	Tottenham Hotspur	W	1-0	25,000	11	Campbell
44	Apr 26	Sat	Div 1	H	Manchester City	L	1-2	18,000	11	Moore
45	May 3	Sat	Div 1	A	Manchester City	L	1-2	12,000	13	Watson

Team Line-Ups

BISHOP Syd	BROWN William	CADWELL Albert	CAMPBELL John	CARTER George	COLLINS Jimmy	EDWARDS William	FLETCHER Albert	GIBBINS Vivian	HAMPSON Tommy	HEBDEN Jack	HENDERSON William	HODGES Harry	HODGSON Tommy	HUFTON Edward	KAY George	MOORE William	PROCTOR Norman	RICHARDS Dick	RICHARDSON Frank	ROBINSON Leslie	RUFFELL James	THIRLAWAY William	TRESADERN Jack	WATSON Victor	WILLIAMS William	YEWS Tommy	YOUNG John	
4	8										2		3	1	5	10		7			11		6	9				1
4	8						9		1		2		3		5	10		7			11		6					2
4	8						9		1		2		3		5	10		7			11		6					3
4	8						9				2		3	1	5	10		7			11		6					4
4							8		1		2	9	3		5	10		7			11		6					5
4	8						9	3			2			1	5	10					11		6			7		6
4	10						9	3						1	5		8				11		6			7	2	7
4	8										2			1	5		10				11		6	9		7	3	8
4	8										2			1	5	10					11		6	9		7	3	9
6	8		4								2			1	5		10				11			9		7	3	10
	8	6	4								2			1	5	10					11			9		7	3	11
6	8		4								2			1	5	10			9		11					7	3	12
4	8		6								2			1	5	10			9			11				7	3	13
6	8		4								2			1	5	10			9		11					7	3	14
4	8	6				7					2			1	5	10			9		11						3	15
4	8	6				7			1		2				5	10			9		11						3	16
4	8	6				7					2			1	5	10			9		11						3	17
4	8	6				7					2			1	5	10			9		11						3	18
	8	6				7		9			2			1	5	10					11		4				3	19
	8	6	4			7			1		2				5	10			9		11						3	20
	8	6	4			7			1	3	2				5	10		11	9									21
	8	6	4			7		9	1		2				5	10					11						3	22
	8	6	4			7			1		2				5	10			9		11						3	23
	8	6	4			7		9	1		2				5	10					11						3	24
	8	6	4			7			1		2				5	10					11				9		3	25
	8	6	4			7			1		2				5	10					11				9		3	26
	8	6	4			7			1		2				5	10					11				9		3	27
		6	4			7			1		2				5	10				8	11				9		3	28
	8	6	4			7			1		2				5	10					11				9		3	29
	8	6	4			7			1		2				5	10		7	9		11						3	30
		6	4	8	7				1		2	9			5						11			10			3	31
4	9	6		8	7				1		2				5						11			10			3	32
4		6		9	7	8			1		2				5	10					11						3	33
4		6		9	7				1		2				5	10	8				11						3	34
4		6		9	8	7			1		2				5	10					11						3	35
4		6		9	7				1		2				5	10	8				11						3	36
4		6		9	7				1		2				5	10	8				11						3	37
4		6		9	7				1		2				5	10	8				11						3	38
4		6		9	7				1		2				5	10				8	11						3	39
4		6		9	7				1		2				5	10					11			8			3	40
4		6	5	9	7				1		2					10					11			8			3	41
4		6	5	9	7				1		2					10					11			8			3	42
4		6		9					1		2				5	10					11			8		7	3	43
4		6		9					1		2				5	10					11			8		7	3	44
4		6		9					1		2				5	10					11			8		7	3	45

1924-25
Story of the season

To add some firepower to the Hammers attack inside-forward Stan Earle was bought from Arsenal. **There was only one defeat in the first eight games** and Earle scored the goals in 1–0 victories against Blackburn and Arsenal.

However, only one win followed in a further nine games culminating in a 5–0 defeat at Bolton Wanderers. In December Sunderland were beaten 4–1 at home, with Bill Moore scoring twice against his old club. Vic Watson also scored two goals in that game, which started him on an amazing run where he scored in ten successive league games, a club record that still stands.

London rivals Arsenal were the visitors at home in the FA Cup, and after a goalless first game the teams also drew 2– in the replay. The second replay took place at Stamford Bridge and a single goal from George Kay put the Hammers

Appearances & Goals 1924-25

	League		FA Cup		Total	
	Starts	Goals	Starts	Goals	Starts	Goals
BARRETT Jim	5	0	0	0	5	0
BISHOP Syd	14	0	0	0	14	0
CADWELL Albert	40	0	6	0	46	0
CAMPBELL John	10	3	0	0	10	3
CARTER George	19	0	5	0	24	0
COLLINS Jimmy	2	0	1	0	3	0
COWPER Peter	2	0	0	0	2	0
EARLE Stanley	18	6	0	0	18	6
EASTMAN George	1	0	0	0	1	0
EDWARDS William	7	0	0	0	7	0
GIBBINS Vivian	1	0	0	0	1	0
HAMPSON Tommy	27	0	6	0	33	0
HEBDEN Jack	4	0	3	0	7	0
HENDERSON William	41	0	6	0	47	0
HODGSON Tommy	1	0	0	0	1	0
HORLER George	15	0	0	0	15	0
HUFTON Edward	8	0	0	0	8	0
JENNINGS Samuel	9	3	0	0	9	3
KAINE Bill	7	0	0	0	7	0
KAY George	41	2	6	1	47	3
MOORE William	32	10	6	0	38	10
RUFFELL James	42	9	6	3	48	12
TRESADERN Jack	4	0	0	0	4	0
WATSON Victor	41	22	6	1	47	23
WILLIAMS William	15	4	6	0	21	4
YEWS Tommy	33	1	6	1	39	2
YOUNG John	23	1	3	0	26	1
own goal		1				1
Totals	**462**	**62**	**66**	**6**	**528**	**68**

hrough. Round two saw West Ham win 2–0 away to Nottingham Forest to set up a home tie with Second Division Blackpool, but after a 1–1 draw at the Boleyn the Hammers crashed 3–0 in the replay.

A few days later West Ham found themselves losing 5–1 at half-time at Burnley. In a remarkable comeback, goals from Jennings, Moore and Watson gave the Hammers hope, but Burnley held out to win 5–4. In March London neighbours Arsenal were beaten 2–1 away followed by a 1–1 draw at Tottenham. There was a good ending to the season as in successive home games Sheffield United were beaten 6–2 followed by a 4–1 win against Everton. Only two games were lost at home but with only three away wins the team finished in 13th place, the same as the previous campaign.

Football League - Division One Final Table 1924-25

		HOME					AWAY					
	P	W	D	L	F	A	W	D	L	F	A	Pts
Huddersfield Town	42	10	8	3	31	10	11	8	2	38	18	58
West Bromwich Albion	42	13	6	2	40	17	10	4	7	18	17	56
Bolton Wanderers	42	18	2	1	61	13	4	9	8	15	21	55
Liverpool	42	13	5	3	43	20	7	5	9	20	35	50
Bury	42	13	4	4	35	20	4	11	6	19	31	49
Newcastle United	42	11	6	4	43	18	5	10	6	18	24	48
Sunderland	42	13	6	2	39	14	6	4	11	25	37	48
Birmingham	42	10	8	3	27	17	7	4	10	22	36	46
Notts County	42	11	6	4	29	12	5	7	9	13	19	45
Manchester City	42	11	7	3	44	29	6	2	13	32	39	43
Cardiff City	42	11	5	5	35	19	5	6	10	21	32	43
Tottenham Hotspur	42	9	8	4	32	16	6	4	11	20	27	42
West Ham United	42	12	7	2	37	12	3	5	13	25	48	42
Sheffield United	42	10	5	6	34	25	3	8	10	21	38	39
Aston Villa	42	10	7	4	34	25	3	6	12	24	46	39
Blackburn Rovers	42	7	6	8	31	26	4	7	10	22	40	35
Everton	42	11	4	6	25	20	1	7	13	15	40	35
Leeds United	42	9	8	4	29	17	2	4	15	17	42	34
Burnley	42	7	8	6	28	31	4	4	13	18	44	34
Arsenal	42	12	3	6	33	17	2	2	17	13	41	33
Preston North End	42	8	2	11	29	35	2	4	15	8	39	26
Nottingham Forest	42	5	6	10	17	23	1	6	14	12	42	24

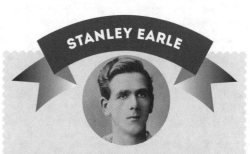

STANLEY EARLE

Inside-forward Earle was playing as an amateur for Clapton when he also played four games for Arsenal, scoring on his debut against Preston in 1923 and twice in his second game against West Ham.

With Clapton he gained two England Amateur caps and was in the Clapton team that won the FA Amateur Cup in 1924. Stan joined West Ham in 1924 and after making his debut (again against Preston North End) he later turned professional. Stan set up an excellent partnership with Vic Watson and had the ability both to score goals and to set up chances. His fine form in 1927 led to him being selected for England against Northern Ireland. He spent eight seasons with the Hammers, scoring 58 goals in his 273 appearances. He later spent season 1932–33 playing 16 games for Clapton Orient in the Third Division. After retiring as a player he became the coach at Walthamstow and later managed Leyton. He passed away at Brightlingsea in September 1971.

Season **1924-25** Football League - Division One
Match Details

Manager **Syd King**   Final League Position **13/22**

	Date		Competition	Venue	Opponents	Results		Attendance	Position	Scorers
1	Aug 30	Sat	Div 1	H	Preston North End	W	1-0	25,000	8	Jennings
2	Sep 6	Sat	Div 1	A	Blackburn Rovers	W	1-0	25,000	9	Earle
3	Sep 8	Mon	Div 1	H	Newcastle United	D	0-0	20,000	6	
4	Sep 13	Sat	Div 1	H	Huddersfield Town	D	0-0	30,000	6	
5	Sep 17	Wed	Div 1	A	Newcastle United	L	1-4	25,000	11	Watson
6	Sep 20	Sat	Div 1	A	Aston Villa	D	1-1	30,000	10	Watson
7	Sep 22	Mon	Div 1	A	Sheffield United	D	1-1	10,000	7	Watson
8	Sep 27	Sat	Div 1	H	Arsenal	W	1-0	35,000	4	Earle
9	Oct 4	Sat	Div 1	A	Manchester City	L	1-3	45,000	10	Cookson (og)
10	Oct 11	Sat	Div 1	H	Bury	D	1-1	15,000	10	Young
11	Oct 18	Sat	Div 1	A	Nottingham Forest	L	1-2	18,000	13	Jennings
12	Oct 25	Sat	Div 1	H	Burnley	W	2-0	18,000	12	Moore, Ruffell
13	Nov 1	Sat	Div 1	A	Leeds United	L	1-2	14,000	15	Watson
14	Nov 8	Sat	Div 1	H	Birmingham	L	0-1	30,000	15	
15	Nov 15	Sat	Div 1	A	West Bromwich Albion	L	1-4	16,000	17	Watson
16	Nov 22	Sat	Div 1	H	Tottenham Hotspur	D	1-1	28,000	17	Watson
17	Nov 29	Sat	Div 1	A	Bolton Wanderers	L	0-5	25,977	17	
18	Dec 6	Sat	Div 1	H	Notts County	W	3-0	18,000	17	Williams 2, Watson
19	Dec 13	Sat	Div 1	A	Everton	L	0-1	15,000	18	
20	Dec 20	Sat	Div 1	H	Sunderland	W	4-1	20,000	16	Moore 2, Watson 2
21	Dec 25	Thu	Div 1	H	Cardiff City	W	3-2	27,000	15	Kay, Moore, Watson
22	Dec 26	Fri	Div 1	A	Cardiff City	L	1-2	30,000	16	Watson
23	Dec 27	Sat	Div 1	A	Preston North End	L	2-3	15,000	16	Watson, Williams
24	Jan 3	Sat	Div 1	H	Blackburn Rovers	W	2-0	16,000	14	Moore, Watson
25	Jan 14	Wed	FAC 1	H	Arsenal	D	0-0	26,000		
26	Jan 17	Sat	Div 1	A	Huddersfield Town	W	2-1	14,000	13	Ruffell, Watson
27	Jan 21	Wed	FAC 1 Rep	A	Arsenal	D	2-2	34,160		Ruffell 2
28	Jan 24	Sat	Div 1	H	Aston Villa	W	2-0	20,000	11	Watson, Williams
29	Jan 26	Mon	FAC 2nd Rep	N*	Arsenal	W	1-0	36,955		Kay
30	Jan 31	Sat	FAC 2	A	Nottingham Forest	W	2-0	10,590		Ruffell, Yews
31	Feb 7	Sat	Div 1	H	Manchester City	W	4-0	25,000	11	Moore 2, Ruffell, Watson
32	Feb 14	Sat	Div 1	A	Bury	L	2-4	20,000	12	Watson, Yews
33	Feb 21	Sat	FAC 3	H	Blackpool	D	1-1	30,000		Watson
34	Feb 25	Wed	FAC 3 Rep	A	Blackpool	L	0-3	15,190		
35	Feb 28	Sat	Div 1	A	Burnley	L	4-5	10,000	14	Jennings, Moore, Ruffell, Watson
36	Mar 7	Sat	Div 1	H	Leeds United	D	0-0	15,000	13	
37	Mar 14	Sat	Div 1	A	Birmingham	D	1-1	20,000	13	Campbell
38	Mar 21	Sat	Div 1	H	West Bromwich Albion	W	2-1	25,000	13	Kay, Ruffell
39	Mar 23	Mon	Div 1	A	Arsenal	W	2-1	10,000	10	Campbell, Ruffell
40	Mar 28	Sat	Div 1	A	Tottenham Hotspur	D	1-1	35,000	10	Watson
41	Apr 2	Thu	Div 1	H	Nottingham Forest	D	0-0	5,000	9	
42	Apr 4	Sat	Div 1	H	Bolton Wanderers	D	1-1	20,000	11	Campbell
43	Apr 10	Fri	Div 1	A	Liverpool	L	0-2	30,000	12	
44	Apr 11	Sat	Div 1	A	Notts County	L	1-4	10,000	12	Ruffell
45	Apr 13	Mon	Div 1	H	Liverpool	L	0-1	15,000	13	
46	Apr 14	Tue	Div 1	H	Sheffield United	W	6-2	12,000	12	Ruffell 2, Watson 2, Earle, Moore
47	Apr 18	Sat	Div 1	H	Everton	W	4-1	15,000	11	Earle 2, Moore, Watson
48	Apr 25	Sat	Div 1	A	Sunderland	D	1-1	10,000	11	Earle

* Stamford Bridge

Team Line-Ups

BARRETT Jim	BISHOP Syd	CADWELL Albert	CAMPBELL John	CARTER George	COLLINS Jimmy	COWPER Peter	EARLE Stanley	EASTMAN George	EDWARDS William	GIBBINS Vivian	HAMPSON Tommy	HEBDEN Jack	HENDERSON William	HODGSON Tommy	HORLER George	HUFTON Edward	JENNINGS Samuel	KAINE Bill	KAY George	MOORE William	RUFFELL James	TRESADERN Jack	WATSON Victor	WILLIAMS William	YEWS Tommy	YOUNG John	
4	6						8		7		1		2				10		5		11		9		3		1
	6						8		7		1		2				10		5		11	4	9		3		2
	6						8		7	9	1		2						5		11	4	10		3		3
	6						8		7		1		2				10		5		11	4	9		3		4
	6						8		7		1		2				10		5		11	4	9		3		5
	6		4				8				1		2						5	10	11		9		3		6
	6		4				8				1		2		3				5	10	11		9			7	7
	6		4				8				1		2		3				5	10	11		9			7	8
	6		4				8		7		1		2						5	10	11		9		3		9
	6		4			7	8				1		2						5	10	11		9		3		10
6			4			7							2				8	1	5	10	11		9		3		11
	6	9	4										2					1	5	10	11		8		7	3	12
	6	9	4								1		2						5	10	11		8		7	3	13
4	6	9											2						5	10	11		8		7	3	14
	6		4				8				1		2						5	10	11		9		7		15
	6		4				8				1	3	2						5	10	11		9		7		16
4	6						8				1		2				10		5		11		9		7	3	17
4	6										1		2				8		5		11		9	10	7	3	18
4	6										1		2				8		5		11		9	10	7	3	19
4	6										1		2						5	8	11		9	10	7	3	20
4	6										1		2						5	8	11		9	10	7	3	21
4	6										1		2						5	8	11		9	10	7	3	22
	6		4				8				1		2						5		11		9	10	7	3	23
	6		4								1		2						5	8	11		9	10	7	3	24
	6		4								1		2						5	8	11		9	10	7	3	25
	6		4								1		2						5	8	11		9	10	7	3	26
	6		4								1		2						5	8	11		9	10	7	3	27
6			4								1	3	2						5	8	11		9	10	7		28
	6		4								1	3	2						5	8	11		9	10	7		29
	6		4								1	3	2						5	8	11		9	10	7		30
	6		4								1	3	2						5	8	11		9	10	7		31
	6		4								1	3	2						5	8	11		9	10	7		32
	6			4							1		2						5	8	11		9	10	7	3	33
	6		4								1	3	2						5	8	11		9	10	7		34
	6			4							1		2				10		5	8	11		9		7	3	35
	6		4										2		3	1			5	8	11		9	10	7		36
	6	9	4										2		3	1			5	8	11			10	7		37
	6	9	4										2		3		1		5	8	11			10	7		38
	6	9		4										2	3	1			5	8	11			10	7		39
4	6	9											2		3	1			5		11		8	10	7		40
4	6												2		3	1			5	8	11		9	10	7		41
4	6	9											2		3	1			5	8	11			10	7		42
4	6	9											2		3	1			5	8	11			10	7		43
4	6	9											2		3	1			5	8	11			10	7		44
4	6						8						2		3	1			5	10	11		9		7		45
4	6						8						2		3	1			5	10	11		9		7		46
4	6						8	5					2		3	1				10	11		9		7		47
4	6						8						2		3	1			5	10	11		9		7		48

1925-26
Story of the season

The season started well and after five games including three home wins **West Ham were undefeated** until a trip to Leeds saw them beaten 5–2.

In October worse was to follow as Arsenal won 4–0 at the Boleyn Ground followed by a 7–1 defeat away to West Bromwich Albion. There were home wins over Manchester City and Blackburn with Moore, Earle and Watson scoring but it was the defence that was letting them down, especially away from home. On their travels four goals were conceded at Tottenham, Sunderland and Bury. There was some cheer on Christmas Day as Stan Earle scored a hat-trick against Aston Villa in a 5–2 home win.

The FA Cup was a disaster as West Ham were knocked out of the competition following a 5–0 defeat at Tottenham Hotspur. For the visit of Leeds United, centre-half Jim Barrett was played at centre-forward and the experiment

Appearances & Goals 1925-26

	League		FA Cup		Total	
	Starts	Goals	Starts	Goals	Starts	Goals
BAILLIE David	3	0	0	0	3	0
BARRETT Jim	42	6	1	0	43	6
BISHOP Syd	14	1	1	0	15	1
CADWELL Albert	18	0	0	0	18	0
CAMPBELL John	6	4	0	0	6	4
CARTER George	29	0	0	0	29	0
COLLINS Jimmy	24	0	1	0	25	0
EARL Alfred	8	0	1	0	9	0
EARLE Stanley	37	9	1	0	38	9
EASTMAN George	1	0	0	0	1	0
EDWARDS William	4	0	0	0	4	0
GIBBINS Vivian	1	2	0	0	1	2
HEBDEN Jack	24	0	0	0	24	0
HENDERSON William	17	0	1	0	18	0
HODGSON Tommy	16	0	0	0	16	0
HORLER George	5	0	0	0	5	0
HUFTON Edward	38	0	1	0	39	0
KANE Alex	1	0	0	0	1	0
KAY George	18	1	0	0	18	1
MOORE William	30	4	0	0	30	4
RUFFELL James	40	12	1	0	41	12
WATSON Victor	38	20	1	0	39	20
WEALE Robert	3	0	0	0	3	0
WILLIAMS William	12	3	1	0	13	3
YEWS Tommy	32	1	1	0	33	1
YOUNG John	1	0	0	0	1	0
Totals	**462**	**63**	**11**	**0**	**473**	**63**

proved a success as he scored a hat-trick in a 4–2 win. At home the goals began to flow as Bolton Wanderers were thrashed 6–0 and West Bromwich Albion were beaten 3–0. The away form was poor with only one win all season, a dismal record that still stands today. There was an eighteenth place finish and only by winning 14 home games were the club saved from relegation to the Second Division.

JIM BARRETT

As a youngster he played as a forward and gained two Schoolboy caps playing for England.

He joined West Ham in 1923 and made his debut in April 1925 in the 1–1 draw at Tottenham. The following two seasons he was ever-present, showing his versatility by playing in many positions. While switching to the centre-forward position in January 1926 he scored a hat-trick against Leeds United. Jim provided the backbone of the Hammers defence over the next 15 seasons. A great character, he filled every defensive position in his time with the club. In October 1928 he was selected to play for England against Northern Ireland at Goodison Park, but unfortunately an injury forced him to retire from the game after only four minutes. His next appearance at Goodison was a happier one as in April 1929 the Hammers won 4–0 there – still their biggest victory on Merseyside.

Up until 1939 when World War Two broke out he played in a total of 467 games, scoring 53 goals. During the war he played in a further 86 games and on one occasion in November 1941 he played in goal against Crystal Palace. His last game for the club was a remarkable home game with Brighton in January 1944. The Hammers were losing 4–1 with 30 minutes remaining when they scored four goals to win 5–4. He later coached the juniors at Upton Park and was able to see his son Jimmy graduate to the first team. He died following a long illness in November 1970.

Football League - Division One Final Table 1925-26

	P	W	D	L	F	A	W	D	L	F	A	Pts
		HOME					**AWAY**					
Huddersfield Town	42	14	6	1	50	17	9	5	7	42	43	57
Arsenal	42	16	2	3	57	19	6	6	9	30	44	52
Sunderland	42	17	2	2	67	30	4	4	13	29	50	48
Bury	42	12	4	5	55	34	8	3	10	30	43	47
Sheffield United	42	15	3	3	72	29	4	5	12	30	53	46
Aston Villa	42	12	7	2	56	25	4	5	12	30	51	44
Liverpool	42	9	8	4	43	27	5	8	8	27	36	44
Bolton Wanderers	42	11	6	4	46	31	6	4	11	29	45	44
Manchester United	42	12	4	5	40	26	7	2	12	26	47	44
Newcastle United	42	13	3	5	59	33	3	7	11	25	42	42
Everton	42	9	9	3	42	26	3	9	9	30	44	42
Blackburn Rovers	42	11	6	4	59	33	4	5	12	32	47	41
West Bromwich Albion	42	13	5	3	59	29	3	3	15	20	49	40
Birmingham	42	14	2	5	35	25	2	6	13	31	56	40
Tottenham Hotspur	42	11	4	6	45	36	4	5	12	21	43	39
Cardiff City	42	8	5	8	30	25	8	2	11	31	51	39
Leicester City	42	11	3	7	42	32	3	7	11	28	48	38
West Ham United	42	14	2	5	45	27	1	5	15	18	49	37
Leeds United	42	11	5	5	38	28	3	3	15	26	48	36
Burnley	42	7	7	7	43	35	6	3	12	42	73	36
Manchester City	42	8	7	6	48	42	4	4	13	41	58	35
Notts County	42	11	4	6	37	26	2	3	16	17	48	33

Season **1925-26** Football League - Division One
Match Details

Manager **Syd King**   Final League Position **18/22**

	Date		Competition	Venue	Opponents	Results		Attendance	Position	Scorers
1	Aug 29	Sat	Div 1	H	Manchester United	W	1-0	25,630	8	Earle
2	Aug 31	Mon	Div 1	H	Cardiff City	W	3-1	16,129	1	Watson 2, Earle
3	Sep 5	Sat	Div 1	A	Liverpool	D	0-0	28,267	3	
4	Sep 7	Mon	Div 1	A	Cardiff City	W	1-0	19,462	2	Watson
5	Sep 12	Sat	Div 1	H	Burnley	W	2-0	24,188	1	Ruffell 2
6	Sep 19	Sat	Div 1	A	Leeds United	L	2-5	16,433	3	Watson 2
7	Sep 21	Mon	Div 1	A	Arsenal	L	2-3	24,800	5	Ruffell, Watson
8	Sep 26	Sat	Div 1	H	Newcastle United	W	1-0	24,722	4	Watson
9	Oct 3	Sat	Div 1	A	Bolton Wanderers	L	0-1	20,923	5	
10	Oct 5	Mon	Div 1	H	Arsenal	L	0-4	18,769	7	
11	Oct 10	Sat	Div 1	H	Notts County	W	1-0	21,401	6	Williams
12	Oct 17	Sat	Div 1	H	Sheffield United	L	1-3	19,940	8	Earle
13	Oct 24	Sat	Div 1	A	West Bromwich Albion	L	1-7	18,014	11	Ruffell
14	Oct 31	Sat	Div 1	H	Manchester City	W	3-1	16,172	7	Bishop, Earle, Ruffell
15	Nov 7	Sat	Div 1	A	Tottenham Hotspur	L	2-4	35,259	9	Barrett, Yews
16	Nov 14	Sat	Div 1	H	Blackburn Rovers	W	2-1	21,029	8	Moore, Watson
17	Nov 21	Sat	Div 1	A	Sunderland	L	1-4	17,667	12	Watson
18	Nov 28	Sat	Div 1	H	Huddersfield Town	L	2-3	13,914	13	Ruffell, Watson
19	Dec 5	Sat	Div 1	A	Everton	L	0-2	17,337	14	
20	Dec 12	Sat	Div 1	H	Birmingham	D	2-2	12,766	16	Ruffell, Watson
21	Dec 19	Sat	Div 1	A	Bury	L	1-4	12,564	18	Watson
22	Dec 25	Fri	Div 1	H	Aston Villa	W	5-2	22,218	16	Earle 3, Watson, Williams
23	Dec 26	Sat	Div 1	A	Aston Villa	L	0-2	45,538	17	
24	Jan 2	Sat	Div 1	A	Manchester United	L	1-2	29,612	19	Ruffell
25	Jan 9	Sat	FAC 3	A	Tottenham Hotspur	L	0-5	49,800		
26	Jan 16	Sat	Div 1	H	Liverpool	L	1-2	13,009	21	Watson
27	Jan 23	Sat	Div 1	A	Burnley	D	2-2	10,304	20	Barrett, Williams
28	Jan 30	Sat	Div 1	H	Leeds United	W	4-2	17,246	15	Barrett 3, Moore
29	Feb 6	Sat	Div 1	A	Newcastle United	L	1-4	27,034	18	Barrett
30	Feb 13	Sat	Div 1	H	Bolton Wanderers	W	6-0	24,062	17	Gibbins 2, Ruffell 2, Watson 2
31	Feb 27	Sat	Div 1	A	Sheffield United	D	1-1	19,800	18	Moore
32	Mar 6	Sat	Div 1	H	West Bromwich Albion	W	3-0	23,030	17	Watson 2, Moore
33	Mar 13	Sat	Div 1	A	Manchester City	L	0-2	36,400	19	
34	Mar 20	Sat	Div 1	H	Tottenham Hotspur	W	3-1	29,423	19	Kay, Ruffell, Watson
35	Mar 22	Mon	Div 1	A	Notts County	D	1-1	4,278	17	Ruffell
36	Mar 27	Sat	Div 1	A	Blackburn Rovers	L	0-1	16,152	19	
37	Apr 2	Fri	Div 1	H	Leicester City	D	1-1	24,028	18	Watson
38	Apr 3	Sat	Div 1	H	Sunderland	W	3-2	21,942	18	Campbell 2, Earle
39	Apr 5	Mon	Div 1	A	Leicester City	D	1-1	19,269	18	Campbell
40	Apr 10	Sat	Div 1	A	Huddersfield Town	L	1-2	21,116	17	Earle
41	Apr 17	Sat	Div 1	H	Everton	W	1-0	15,866	17	Campbell
42	Apr 24	Sat	Div 1	A	Birmingham	L	0-1	12,571	18	
43	May 1	Sat	Div 1	H	Bury	L	0-2	15,347	18	

Team Line-Ups

BAILLIE David	BARRETT Jim	BISHOP Syd	CADWELL Albert	CAMPBELL John	CARTER George	COLLINS Jimmy	EARL Alfred	EARLE Stanley	EASTMAN George	EDWARDS William	GIBBINS Vivian	HEBDEN Jack	HENDERSON William	HODGSON Tommy	HORLER George	HUFTON Edward	KANE Alex	KAY George	MOORE William	RUFFELL James	WATSON Victor	WEALE Robert	WILLIAMS William	YEWS Tommy	YOUNG John	#
	5	6			4			8					3	2		1			10	11	9			7		1
	5	6			4			8					3	2		1			10	11	9			7		2
	5	6			4			8		7			3	2		1			10	11	9					3
	5	6			4			8					3	2		1			10	11	9			7		4
	5	6			4			8					3	2		1			10	11	9			7		5
	5	6			4			8						2		1			10	11	9			7	3	6
	5	6			4			8						2	3	1			10	11	9			7		7
	5	6			4			8					3	2		1			10	11	9			7		8
	5	6			4			8					3	2		1				11	9		10	7		9
	5	6	9		4			8		7			3	2		1				11	10					10
	5	6			4			8				2	3			1				11	9	7	10			11
	5	6			4			8				2		3		1			10	11	9	7				12
	4	8	6									2		3		1		5	10	11	9			7		13
	5	8	6					9					3	2		1			10	11				7		14
	5	8	6		4								3	2		1			10	11	9			7		15
	5	4	6					8					3	2		1			10	11	9			7		16
	5	4	6					8					3	2		1			10	11	9			7		17
1	5	4	6					8					3	2					7	11	9		10			18
1	5				4	6		8				2		3					7	11	9		10			19
	5				4	6		7				2		3		1			8	11	9		10			20
	5	6			4			8				2		3		1				11	9	7	10			21
	5	6			4	3		8				2				1				11	9		10	7		22
	5	6			4	3		8				2				1				11	9		10	7		23
	5	6			4	3		8				2				1				11	9		10	7		24
	5	6			4	3		8				2				1				11	9		10	7		25
	6				4	3		8				2				1		5		11	9		10	7		26
	9	6			4	3						2				1		5		11	8		10	7		27
	9	6			4	3						2				1		5	10	11	8			7		28
	9	6			4	3						2				1		5	10	11	8			7		29
	4					6	3	8			9	2				1		5		11			10	7		30
1	3		9		4	6		8				2						5	10	11				7		31
	3				4	6		8				2				1		5	10	11	9			7		32
	3	10			4	6		8				2				1		5			9		11	7		33
	3				4	6		8				2				1		5	10	11	9			7		34
	3				4	6		8				2				1		5	10	11	9			7		35
	3				4	6		8				2				1		5	10	11	9			7		36
	3				4	6		8				2				1		5	10	11	9			7		37
	3		9		4	6		8				2				1		5	10	11				7		38
	3		9		4	6		8				2				1		5	10	11				7		39
	3				4	6		8				2				1		5	10	11	9			7		40
	3		9		4	6		8	5			2				1				11			10	7		41
	3		9		4	6		8		7		2				1		5		11			10			42
	3				4	6		8		7		2				1		5	10	11	9					43

1926-27
Story of the season

In a reversal of previous seasons, **a good 3–0 win at Everton** was followed by a 5–1 home defeat to Blackburn Rovers. In fact **the team did not win a home game** until 30 October, when **Manchester United were beaten 4–0.**

Vic Watson was in good form, having scored nine goals in the first twelve games. There was a 5–1 home win against Aston Villa which brought a hat-trick from Watson, and the home form continued with wins over Burnley, Leeds and Birmingham City.

The FA Cup saw the Hammers once again drawn against Tottenham, but this time West Ham triumphed, winning 3–1 with another Watson hat-trick. The cup run did not last long, however, as Brentford knocked West Ham out in the next round in a replay. In February two of the top teams, Huddersfield and Sunderland, were both beaten 3–2, but this was followed up with a 4–1 defeat at Blackburn and a 2–1 home defeat to bottom club West Bromwich Albion.

There were only 11,764 spectators in the ground for the visit of London rivals Arsenal, but they were all in for a

Appearances & Goals 1926-27

	League		FA Cup		Total	
	Starts	Goals	Starts	Goals	Starts	Goals
BAILLIE David	1	0	0	0	1	0
BARRETT Jim	42	1	3	0	45	1
BISHOP Syd	9	0	0	0	9	0
CADWELL Albert	13	0	0	0	13	0
CAMPBELL John	0	0	1	0	1	0
CARTER George	26	0	3	0	29	0
COLLINS Jimmy	42	1	3	0	45	1
DOWSEY John	1	0	0	0	1	0
EARL Alfred	1	0	0	0	1	0
EARLE Stanley	42	13	3	0	45	13
GIBBINS Vivian	22	4	1	0	23	4
HEBDEN Jack	39	0	3	0	42	0
HODGSON Tommy	16	0	0	0	16	0
HORLER George	20	0	3	0	23	0
HUFTON Edward	40	0	3	0	43	0
HULL Archie	1	0	0	0	1	0
JOHNSON Joseph	14	7	0	0	14	7
KANE Alex	1	0	0	0	1	0
MOORE William	12	2	1	0	13	2
PAYNE John	1	0	0	0	1	0
RUFFELL James	37	13	3	1	40	14
WATSON Victor	42	34	3	3	45	37
WILLIAMS William	1	0	0	0	1	0
YEWS Tommy	39	8	3	0	42	8
own goal		3				3
Totals	**462**	**86**	**33**	**4**	**495**	**90**

reat as the Hammers romped to a 7–0 victory. Vic Watson was again on target, grabbing another hat-trick, and the Arsenal defenders helped out with two own goals. The goals were flowing now with 15 being scored in the next four games. Both Sheffield United and Manchester United were beaten 3–0 and there was an exciting 4–4 home draw with Bolton Wanderers. Aston Villa were beaten 5–1 at Villa Park with a further two goals from Watson. Flying winger Jimmy Ruffell had been contributing to the goals and he scored his twelfth of the season in a fine 3–1 victory at Tottenham. Finishing the season in sixth place was an excellent achievement and was due to a settled side and the goalscoring of Vic Watson. Ever-present in the league **were** im Barrett, Stan Earle, Jimmy Collins and Vic Watson.

Football League - Division One
Final Table 1926-27

		HOME				AWAY					
	P	W	D	L	F	A	W	D	L	F	A	Pts
Newcastle United	42	19	1	1	64	20	6	5	10	32	38	56
Huddersfield Town	42	13	6	2	41	19	4	11	6	35	41	51
Sunderland	42	15	3	3	70	28	6	4	11	28	42	49
Bolton Wanderers	42	15	5	1	54	19	4	5	12	30	43	48
Burnley	42	15	4	2	55	30	4	5	12	36	50	47
West Ham United	**42**	**9**	**6**	**6**	**50**	**36**	**10**	**2**	**9**	**36**	**34**	**46**
Leicester City	42	13	4	4	58	33	4	8	9	27	37	46
Sheffield United	42	12	6	3	46	33	5	4	12	28	53	44
Liverpool	42	13	4	4	47	27	5	3	13	22	34	43
Aston Villa	42	11	4	6	51	34	7	3	11	30	49	43
Arsenal	42	12	5	4	47	30	5	4	12	30	56	43
Derby County	42	14	4	3	60	28	3	3	15	26	45	41
Tottenham Hotspur	42	11	4	6	48	33	5	5	11	28	45	41
Cardiff City	42	12	3	6	31	17	4	6	11	24	48	41
Manchester United	42	9	8	4	29	19	4	6	11	23	45	40
The Wednesday	42	15	3	3	49	29	0	6	15	26	63	39
Birmingham	42	13	3	5	36	17	4	1	16	28	56	38
Blackburn Rovers	42	9	5	7	40	40	6	3	12	37	56	38
Bury	42	8	5	8	43	38	4	7	10	25	39	36
Everton	42	10	6	5	35	30	2	4	15	29	60	34
Leeds United	42	9	7	5	43	31	2	1	18	26	57	30
West Bromwich Albion	42	10	4	7	47	33	1	4	16	18	53	30

VIVIAN GIBBINS

Playing as an amateur with Clapton, this inside-forward enjoyed a successful time.

He signed for West Ham in 1923 but kept his amateur status, thus allowing him to play for both West Ham and Clapton. He made his debut for the Hammers at Nottingham Forest in December 1923. He was one of the last amateurs to gain full England recognition when he was capped against France in 1924 and 1925, scoring three times in the two matches. In those same two years he won FA Amateur Cup winners medals with Clapton. Between 1925 and 1932 he also won eight England international amateur caps. Viv spent nine seasons with West Ham, scoring 63 goals in his 130 appearances before joining Brentford in February 1932. He left at the end of that season after playing in only eight games and then spent a successful season at Bristol Rovers where he was their top scorer with 15 goals, including hat-tricks against Brighton and Clapton Orient. He later played a couple of games for Southampton before ending his career in non-league football at Leyton and Catford Wanderers.

After retiring as a player he became a headmaster at a school in West Ham. Viv died in November 1979 at Herne Bay, Kent.

Season **1926-27** Football League - Division One
Match Details
Manager **Syd King**   Final League Position **6/22**

	Date		Competition	Venue	Opponents	Results		Attendance	Position	Scorers
1	Aug 28	Sat	Div 1	H	Leicester City	D	3-3	20,615	13	Earle, Ruffell, Watson
2	Sep 4	Sat	Div 1	A	Everton	W	3-0	26,957	8	Watson 2, Moore
3	Sep 6	Mon	Div 1	A	The Wednesday	L	0-1	18,602	10	
4	Sep 11	Sat	Div 1	H	Blackburn Rovers	L	1-5	20,680	18	Watson
5	Sep 18	Sat	Div 1	A	Huddersfield Town	L	1-2	16,809	20	Watson
6	Sep 25	Sat	Div 1	H	Sunderland	L	1-2	20,778	20	Yews
7	Oct 2	Sat	Div 1	A	West Bromwich Albion	W	3-1	18,256	19	Earle, Ruffell, Watson
8	Oct 4	Mon	Div 1	H	The Wednesday	D	1-1	9,770	18	Earle
9	Oct 9	Sat	Div 1	H	Bury	L	1-2	18,541	19	Watson
10	Oct 16	Sat	Div 1	A	Arsenal	D	2-2	35,534	19	Gibbins, Watson
11	Oct 23	Sat	Div 1	A	Sheffield United	W	2-0	20,373	18	Ruffell 2
12	Oct 30	Sat	Div 1	H	Manchester United	W	4-0	19,733	14	Gibbins, Watson, Yews, Mann (og)
13	Nov 6	Sat	Div 1	A	Bolton Wanderers	L	0-2	13,934	18	
14	Nov 13	Sat	Div 1	H	Aston Villa	W	5-1	7,647	16	Watson 3, Earle, Yews
15	Nov 20	Sat	Div 1	A	Cardiff City	W	2-1	10,736	13	Watson, Yews
16	Nov 27	Sat	Div 1	H	Burnley	W	2-1	19,634	10	Gibbins, Watson
17	Dec 4	Sat	Div 1	A	Newcastle United	L	0-2	35,079	12	
18	Dec 11	Sat	Div 1	H	Leeds United	W	3-2	20,924	11	Gibbins, Ruffell, Watson
19	Dec 18	Sat	Div 1	A	Liverpool	D	0-0	24,563	10	
20	Dec 25	Sat	Div 1	H	Birmingham	W	1-0	27,984	8	Earle
21	Dec 27	Mon	Div 1	A	Birmingham	W	2-0	39,204	7	Ruffell, Watson
22	Dec 28	Tue	Div 1	A	Derby County	L	0-3	21,888	7	
23	Jan 1	Sat	Div 1	H	Derby County	L	1-2	20,882	7	Watson
24	Jan 8	Sat	FAC 3	H	Tottenham Hotspur	W	3-2	44,417		Watson 3
25	Jan 15	Sat	Div 1	A	Leicester City	L	0-3	21,861	9	
26	Jan 22	Sat	Div 1	H	Everton	W	2-1	11,235	9	Moore, Watson
27	Jan 29	Sat	FAC 4	H	Brentford	D	1-1	40,000		Ruffell
28	Feb 2	Wed	FAC 4 Rep	A	Brentford	L	0-2	25,000		
29	Feb 5	Sat	Div 1	H	Huddersfield Town	W	3-2	19,087	7	Johnson, Watson, Yews
30	Feb 12	Sat	Div 1	A	Sunderland	W	3-2	17,088	7	Earle, Watson, Yews
31	Feb 14	Mon	Div 1	A	Blackburn Rovers	L	1-4	10,443	8	Yews
32	Feb 19	Sat	Div 1	H	West Bromwich Albion	L	1-2	18,231	9	Watson
33	Feb 26	Sat	Div 1	A	Bury	W	2-1	13,509	9	Johnson, Yews
34	Mar 7	Mon	Div 1	H	Arsenal	W	7-0	11,764	8	Watson 3, Johnson, Ruffell, Parker (og), John (og)
35	Mar 12	Sat	Div 1	H	Sheffield United	W	3-0	19,520	5	Earle 2, Watson
36	Mar 19	Sat	Div 1	A	Manchester United	W	3-0	18,347	4	Watson 2, Johnson
37	Mar 26	Sat	Div 1	H	Bolton Wanderers	D	4-4	17,752	5	Ruffell 2, Earle, Watson
38	Apr 2	Sat	Div 1	A	Aston Villa	W	5-1	22,413	4	Watson 2, Earle, Johnson, Ruffell
39	Apr 9	Sat	Div 1	H	Cardiff City	D	2-2	14,777	4	Earle, Watson
40	Apr 15	Fri	Div 1	A	Tottenham Hotspur	W	3-1	42,010	4	Ruffell 2, Earle
41	Apr 16	Sat	Div 1	A	Burnley	L	1-2	20,333	4	Watson
42	Apr 18	Mon	Div 1	H	Tottenham Hotspur	L	1-2	21,354	5	Earle
43	Apr 23	Sat	Div 1	H	Newcastle United	D	1-1	29,722	6	Ruffell
44	Apr 30	Sat	Div 1	A	Leeds United	L	3-6	10,997	6	Watson 2, Johnson
45	May 7	Sat	Div 1	H	Liverpool	D	3-3	10,225	6	Barrett, Collins, Johnson

Team Line-Ups

BAILLIE David	BARRETT Jim	BISHOP Syd	CADWELL Albert	CAMPBELL John	CARTER George	COLLINS Jimmy	DOWSEY John	EARL Alfred	EARLE Stanley	GIBBINS Vivian	HEBDEN Jack	HODGSON Tommy	HORLER George	HUFTON Edward	HULL Archie	JOHNSON Joseph	KANE Alex	MOORE William	PAYNE John	RUFFELL James	WATSON Victor	WILLIAMS William	YEWS Tommy	
	5	4				6		3	8		2			1				10		11	9		7	1
	3	4			5	6			8		2			1				10		11	9		7	2
	3	4			5	6	7		8		2			1				10			9	11		3
	3	4			5	6			8	9	2			1				11	7		10			4
	3	4			5	6			8	10	2			1						11	9		7	5
	3	4			5	6			8	10	2			1						11	9		7	6
	3	4			5	6			8	9	2			1				7		11	10			7
	3	4			5	6			8	9	2			1				10		11			7	8
	3	4			5	6			8		2			1				10		11	9		7	9
	5				4	6			8	10	2		3	1						11	9		7	10
	5				4	6			8	10	2		3	1						11	9		7	11
	5				4	6			8	10	2		3	1						11	9		7	12
	5				4	6			8		2		3	1				10		11	9		7	13
	5				4	6			8	10	2		3	1						11	9		7	14
	5				4	6			8	10	2		3	1						11	9		7	15
	5				4	6			8	10	2		3	1						11	9		7	16
	5				4	6			8	10	2		3	1						11	9		7	17
	5				4	6			8	10	2		3	1						11	9		7	18
	5				4	6			8		2		3	1				10		11	9		7	19
	5				4	6			8	10	2		3	1						11	9		7	20
	5				4	6			8	10	2		3	1						11	9		7	21
	5				4	6			8	10	2		3	1						11	9		7	22
	5				4	6			8	10	2		3	1			1			11	9		7	23
	5				4	6			8	10	2		3	1						11	9		7	24
	5				4	6			8	10	2		3	1						11	9		7	25
	5				4	6			8		2		3	1					10	11	9		7	26
	5			9	4	6			8		2		3	1					10	11	9		7	27
	5				4	6			8		2		3	1						11	10		7	28
	5				4	6			8		2		3	1		10				11	9		7	29
	5				4	6			8		2		3	1		11			10		9		7	30
	5				4	6			8		2		3	1		10				11	9		7	31
	5					6			8	10	2		3	1			4			11	9		7	32
	5	6			4				8		2		3	1		11			10		9		7	33
1	5	6			4				8		2		3			10				11	9		7	34
	5	6			4				8		2		3	1		10				11	9		7	35
	5	6			4				8	10	2		3	1						11	9		7	36
	5	6			4				8		2		3	1		10				11	9		7	37
	5	6			4				8		2		3	1		10				11	9		7	38
	5	6			4				8		2		3	1		10				11	9		7	39
	5	6			4				8	10	2		3	1						11	9		7	40
	5	6			4				8		2		3	1		10				11	9		7	41
	5	6			4				8	10	2		3	1						11	9		7	42
	5	6			4				8		2		3	1		10				11	9		7	43
	5	6			4				8		2		3	1		10				11	9		7	44
	5	6			4				8		2		3	1		10				11	9		7	45

1927-28
Story of the season

The goals were flowing as the season started with **21 goals in the first seven games**, inside-forward **Stan Earle scoring six times.**

By mid-October there had only been two defeats as the team travelled to play Everton. It was a shock as the Hammers were crushed 7–0, and they let in a further five in the next away game at Tottenham. Four goals were scored at home against Middlesbrough – but five were conceded.

In this period regular goalkeeper Ted Hufton had been injured, which left reserve keepers Baillie and Tate to endure a torrid time. On Christmas Eve Newcastle were beaten 5–2 at home, with Viv Gibbins claiming a hat-trick, but two days later there came a 6–2 defeat at Sheffield United.

Appearances & Goals 1927-28

	League		FA Cup		Total	
	Starts	Goals	Starts	Goals	Starts	Goals
BAILLIE David	10	0	0	0	10	0
BARRETT Jim	34	5	0	0	34	5
CADWELL Albert	27	0	2	0	29	0
CAMPBELL John	1	0	0	0	1	0
COLLINS Jimmy	42	0	2	0	44	0
COX William	26	0	2	0	28	0
EARL Alfred	33	0	2	0	35	0
EARLE Stanley	31	11	1	0	32	11
GIBBINS Vivian	25	14	2	2	27	16
HEBDEN Jack	12	0	0	0	12	0
HENDERSON William	16	0	2	0	18	0
HODGSON Tommy	5	0	0	0	5	0
HORLER George	2	0	0	0	2	0
HUFTON Edward	25	0	2	0	27	0
JACKSON William	2	0	0	0	2	0
JOHNSON Joseph	1	0	0	0	1	0
LOUGHLIN James	10	4	0	0	10	4
MOORE William	23	2	1	0	24	2
NORRINGTON Cyril	13	0	0	0	13	0
ROBSON George	1	0	0	0	1	0
RUFFELL James	39	18	2	1	41	19
SMITH Harold	1	0	0	0	1	0
SMITH William	1	0	0	0	1	0
TATE Isaac	7	0	0	0	7	0
WATSON Victor	33	16	2	0	35	16
YEWS Tommy	42	11	2	0	44	11
Totals	**462**	**81**	**22**	**3**	**484**	**84**

The FA Cup brought a 2–0 victory at Portsmouth but in the next round there was a 2–1 defeat at Huddersfield. The team were struggling in mid-table but results improved in March. Vic Watson scored a hat-trick in the 4–0 home win against Leicester City and followed this up with two more goals in a fine 5–1 victory at Cardiff City. The month ended with Jimmy Ruffell scoring twice in the 4–3 defeat of Blackburn Rovers, but there were no further wins in the remaining seven games of the campaign. It had been a disappointing season which ended with a seventeenth place finish.

Football League - Division One Final Table 1927-28

| | P | HOME | | | | | AWAY | | | | | Pts |
		W	D	L	F	A	W	D	L	F	A	
Everton	42	11	8	2	60	28	9	5	7	42	38	53
Huddersfield Town	42	15	1	5	57	31	7	6	8	34	37	51
Leicester City	42	14	5	2	66	25	4	7	10	30	47	48
Derby County	42	12	4	5	59	30	5	6	10	37	53	44
Bury	42	13	1	7	53	35	7	3	11	27	45	44
Cardiff City	42	12	7	2	44	27	5	3	13	26	53	44
Bolton Wanderers	42	12	5	4	47	26	4	6	11	34	40	43
Aston Villa	42	13	3	5	52	30	4	6	11	26	43	43
Newcastle United	42	9	7	5	49	41	6	6	9	30	40	43
Arsenal	42	10	6	5	49	33	3	9	9	33	53	41
Birmingham	42	10	7	4	36	25	3	8	10	34	50	41
Blackburn Rovers	42	13	5	3	41	22	3	4	14	25	56	41
Sheffield United	42	12	4	5	56	42	3	6	12	23	44	40
The Wednesday	42	9	6	6	45	29	4	7	10	36	49	39
Sunderland	42	9	5	7	37	29	6	4	11	37	47	39
Liverpool	42	10	6	5	54	36	3	7	11	30	51	39
West Ham United	**42**	**9**	**7**	**5**	**48**	**34**	**5**	**4**	**12**	**33**	**54**	**39**
Manchester United	42	12	6	3	51	27	4	1	16	21	53	39
Burnley	42	12	5	4	55	31	4	2	15	27	67	39
Portsmouth	42	13	4	4	40	23	3	3	15	26	67	39
Tottenham Hotspur	42	12	3	6	47	34	3	5	13	27	52	38
Middlesbrough	42	7	9	5	46	35	4	6	11	35	53	37

JIMMY COLLINS

He began his career at non-league level, having spells at Clapton, Chelmsford and Leyton before joining West Ham in 1921.

He made his debut as an inside-forward against Tottenham in February 1924 and later changed to playing at wing-half.

Collins was a model of consistency as from December 1925 until April 1929 he played in a total of 158 consecutive league and cup matches. A valuable member of the team, he played for 13 seasons, scoring three goals in his 336 appearances. After retiring as a player in 1936 he went into the horticultural trade and he also owned greyhounds.

Jimmy and his wife were season ticket holders at Upton Park until his death in May 1977 at the age of 74.

Season **1927-28** Football League - Division One
Match Details

Manager **Syd King**   Final League Position **17/22**

	Date		Competition	Venue	Opponents	Results		Attendance	Position	Scorers
1	Aug 27	Sat	Div 1	A	Derby County	W	3-2	18,538	5	Barrett, Gibbins, Watson
2	Sep 1	Thu	Div 1	H	Sunderland	L	2-4	19,037	12	Ruffell 2
3	Sep 3	Sat	Div 1	H	Huddersfield Town	W	4-2	23,925	10	Earle 2, Loughlin, Yews
4	Sep 10	Sat	Div 1	H	Portsmouth	W	4-2	24,729	5	Loughlin 2, Earle, Ruffell
5	Sep 17	Sat	Div 1	A	Leicester City	W	3-2	25,482	5	Earle, Ruffell, Yews
6	Sep 24	Sat	Div 1	H	Liverpool	W	3-1	26,876	3	Earle. Gibbins, Ruffell
7	Oct 1	Sat	Div 1	A	Arsenal	D	2-2	34,931	2	Earle, Gibbins
8	Oct 8	Sat	Div 1	H	Burnley	W	2-0	27,467	1	Gibbins 2
9	Oct 15	Sat	Div 1	A	Bury	L	1-3	20,110	4	Ruffell
10	Oct 22	Sat	Div 1	A	Everton	L	0-7	20,151	8	
11	Oct 29	Sat	Div 1	H	Manchester United	L	1-2	21,972	10	Watson
12	Nov 5	Sat	Div 1	A	Tottenham Hotspur	L	3-5	35,099	12	Barrett, Earle, Ruffell
13	Nov 12	Sat	Div 1	H	Cardiff City	W	2-0	18,189	9	Watson, Yews
14	Nov 19	Sat	Div 1	A	Blackburn Rovers	L	0-1	14,040	12	
15	Nov 26	Sat	Div 1	H	Middlesbrough	L	4-5	14,666	16	Yews 2, Gibbins, Watson
16	Dec 3	Sat	Div 1	A	The Wednesday	L	0-2	22,796	17	
17	Dec 10	Sat	Div 1	H	Bolton Wanderers	W	2-0	18,926	12	Watson 2
18	Dec 17	Sat	Div 1	A	Birmingham	W	2-1	18,206	12	Ruffell, Yews
19	Dec 24	Sat	Div 1	H	Newcastle United	W	5-2	19,296	10	Gibbins 3, Ruffell 2
20	Dec 26	Mon	Div 1	A	Sheffield United	L	2-6	23,591	11	Gibbins, Yews
21	Dec 27	Tue	Div 1	H	Sheffield United	D	1-1	20,434	9	Yews
22	Dec 31	Sat	Div 1	H	Derby County	D	2-2	17,702	9	Ruffell, Watson
23	Jan 2	Mon	Div 1	A	Sunderland	L	2-3	27,542	11	Gibbins 2
24	Jan 7	Sat	Div 1	A	Huddersfield Town	L	2-5	10,972	18	Watson, Yews
25	Jan 14	Sat	FAC 3	A	Portsmouth	W	2-0	27,692		Gibbins, Ruffell
26	Jan 21	Sat	Div 1	A	Portsmouth	L	1-2	17,656	18	Gibbins
27	Jan 28	Sat	FAC 4	A	Huddersfield Town	L	1-2	27,000		Gibbins
28	Feb 4	Sat	Div 1	A	Liverpool	W	3-1	23,897	15	Ruffell 2, Watson
29	Feb 11	Sat	Div 1	H	Arsenal	D	2-2	28,086	16	Watson 2
30	Feb 18	Sat	Div 1	A	Burnley	D	0-0	14,663	15	
31	Feb 25	Sat	Div 1	H	Bury	L	1-2	19,903	17	Ruffell
32	Mar 3	Sat	Div 1	H	Everton	D	0-0	31,997	15	
33	Mar 10	Sat	Div 1	A	Manchester United	D	1-1	21,577	18	Earle
34	Mar 12	Mon	Div 1	H	Leicester City	W	4-0	6,211	11	Watson 3, Yews
35	Mar 17	Sat	Div 1	H	Tottenham Hotspur	D	1-1	33,908	12	Ruffell
36	Mar 24	Sat	Div 1	A	Cardiff City	W	5-1	14,529	8	Earle 2, Watson 2, Yews
37	Mar 31	Sat	Div 1	H	Blackburn Rovers	W	4-3	12,504	6	Ruffell 2, Earle, Moore
38	Apr 6	Fri	Div 1	H	Aston Villa	D	0-0	31,469	7	
39	Apr 7	Sat	Div 1	A	Middlesbrough	D	2-2	21,860	7	Moore, Ruffell
40	Apr 9	Mon	Div 1	A	Aston Villa	L	0-1	31,059	8	
41	Apr 14	Sat	Div 1	H	The Wednesday	L	1-2	14,580	9	Barrett
42	Apr 21	Sat	Div 1	A	Bolton Wanderers	L	0-4	8,520	12	
43	Apr 28	Sat	Div 1	H	Birmingham	D	3-3	17,917	13	Barrett 2, Loughlin
44	May 5	Sat	Div 1	A	Newcastle United	L	1-3	17,909	17	Gibbins

Team Line-Ups

BAILLIE David	BARRETT Jim	CADWELL Albert	CAMPBELL John	COLLINS Jimmy	COX William	EARL Alfred	EARLE Stanley	GIBBINS Vivian	HEBDEN Jack	HENDERSON William	HODGSON Tommy	HORLER George	HUFTON Edward	JACKSON William	JOHNSON Joseph	LOUGHLIN James	MOORE William	NORRINGTON Cyril	ROBSON George	RUFFELL James	SMITH Harold	SMITH William	TATE Isaac	WATSON Victor	YEWS Tommy	
	5	6	4		3		8	10	2				1							11				9	7	1
	5	6	4		3		8		2				1				10			11				9	7	2
1	5	6	4		3		8		2						10	9				11					7	3
	5	6	4		3		8	10	2				1			9				11					7	4
	5	6	4		3		8		2				1				10			11				9	7	5
	5	6	4		3		8	9	2				1				10			11					7	6
	5	6	4		3		8	9	2				1				10			11					7	7
	5	6	4		3		8	9	2				1				10			11					7	8
	5	6	4		3		10		2				1				8			11				9	7	9
1	5	6	4		3		10		2								8			11				9	7	10
1	5		4	6			8		2	3							10			11				9	7	11
1	5		4	6			8	9	2	3							10			11					7	12
1	5		4	6	2		8	10										3		11				9	7	13
1	5		4	6	2		8	10										3		11				9	7	14
1	5		4	6	2		8	10										3		11				9	7	15
1	5		4	6	2		8	10										3		11				9	7	16
	5		4	6	2		8										10	3		11			1	9	7	17
	5		4	6	2			9									10	3		11			1	8	7	18
	5		4	6	2			9									10	3		11			1	8	7	19
	5		4	6	2			9						11			10	3					1	8	7	20
	5		4	6	2		8	9						11				3					1	10	7	21
	5	9	4	6	2												10	3		11			1	8	7	22
	5		4	6	2			9									10	3		11			1	8	7	23
	5		4	6	2			9					1				10			11	3			8	7	24
		6	4	5	3			9	2				1				10			11				8	7	25
		6	4	5	3			9	2				1				10			11				8	7	26
		6	4	5	3		8	9	2				1							11				10	7	27
		6	4	5	3		8		2				1				10			11				9	7	28
		6	4	5	3		8		2				1				10			11				9	7	29
		6	4	5	3		8		2				1				10			11				9	7	30
		6	4	5	3		8		2				1				10			11				9	7	31
	5		4	6	3			9	2				1				10			11				8	7	32
		6	4	5	3		8	9	2				1				10			11					7	33
1		6	4	5	3		8		2								10			11				9	7	34
	3	6	4	5			8		2				1				10			11				9	7	35
	5	6	4		3		8		2				1				10			11				9	7	36
1	5	6	4		3		8				2						10			11				9	7	37
	5	6	4		3		8				2		1				10			11				9	7	38
	5	6	4		3		8				2		1				10			11				9	7	39
	5	6	4		3		8	10			2		1							11				9	7	40
	5	6	4		3		8	10			2		1				11							9	7	41
	3	6	4	5	2		8						1				10			11				9	7	42
	10	6	4	5	2		8						1			9			3	11					7	43
		6	4	5	2		10						1			9			3	11		8			7	44

1928-29
Story of the season

As in the previous season **the team started well** with a **4–0 home victory** against Sheffield United and a **4–1 home win** over Aston Villa.

Vic Watson was in good form, scoring seven goals in the first five games. Again the good start came to an end, a 5–0 defeat at Leicester City being followed by a 4–1 reverse at Leeds United.

The team were so inconsistent: champions elect Sheffield Wednesday were beaten 3–2 at home, followed a week later by a 6–0 defeat at Derby County. In December winger Jimmy Ruffell scored twice in the 3–3 home draw with Sunderland, the third time that he had scored two in a match that season.

The FA Cup began with a narrow 1–0 home win against Sunderland, and this was followed by a 3–0 home victory

Appearances & Goals 1928-29

	League		FA Cup		Total	
	Starts	Goals	Starts	Goals	Starts	Goals
BAILLIE David	2	0	1	0	3	0
BARRETT Jim	22	1	2	3	24	4
CADWELL Albert	40	0	5	0	45	0
COLLINS Jimmy	39	1	5	0	44	1
COSHALL John	2	0	0	0	2	0
COX William	20	0	2	0	22	0
DIXON Robert	2	0	0	0	2	0
EARL Alfred	32	0	5	0	37	0
EARLE Stanley	41	6	5	2	46	8
GIBBINS Vivian	29	11	2	0	31	11
HODGSON Tommy	28	0	5	0	33	0
HUFTON Edward	31	0	4	0	35	0
HULL Archie	1	0	0	0	1	0
MOORE William	6	0	1	0	7	0
NORRINGTON Cyril	14	0	0	0	14	0
NORRIS Fred	6	0	0	0	6	0
PAYNE John	3	1	0	0	3	1
ROBSON George	5	1	0	0	5	1
RUFFELL James	37	20	5	0	42	20
SHONE Danny	12	5	0	0	12	5
SMAILES Matthew	7	0	3	0	10	0
SMITH William	1	0	0	0	1	0
TATE Isaac	7	0	0	0	7	0
WATSON Victor	34	29	5	1	39	30
YEWS Tommy	41	10	5	3	46	13
own goal		1		1		2
Totals	**462**	**86**	**55**	**10**	**517**	**96**

against the amateur team Corinthians. Round five saw a trip to Bournemouth and a 1–1 draw. The replay was won 3–1 but the cup run was ended after a 3–2 quarter-final defeat at Portsmouth.

Following a good 3–2 win at Manchester United there was an amazing home game with Leeds United. After an hour the score was 2–2, and then the goal glut began as the Hammers won 8–2 with Vic Watson scoring six. The good home form continued throughout March with victories over Leicester, Birmingham and Burnley, and there was an excellent 4–0 win at Everton where Viv Gibbins claimed a hat-trick. In April there was a trip to league leaders Sheffield Wednesday that ended in a 6–0 defeat; a final-day placing of seventeenth was achieved to equal the previous campaign.

Football League - Division One
Final Table 1928-29

	P	HOME					AWAY					Pts
		W	D	L	F	A	W	D	L	F	A	
The Wednesday	42	18	3	0	55	16	3	7	11	31	46	52
Leicester City	42	16	5	0	67	22	5	4	12	29	45	51
Aston Villa	42	16	2	3	62	30	7	2	12	36	51	50
Sunderland	42	16	2	3	67	30	4	5	12	26	45	47
Liverpool	42	11	4	6	53	28	6	8	7	37	36	46
Derby County	42	12	5	4	56	24	6	5	10	30	47	46
Blackburn Rovers	42	11	6	4	42	26	6	5	10	30	37	45
Manchester City	42	12	3	6	63	40	6	6	9	32	46	45
Arsenal	42	11	6	4	43	25	5	7	9	34	47	45
Newcastle United	42	15	2	4	48	29	4	4	13	22	43	44
Sheffield United	42	12	5	4	57	30	3	6	12	29	55	41
Manchester United	42	8	8	5	32	23	6	5	10	34	53	41
Leeds United	42	11	5	5	42	28	5	4	12	29	56	41
Bolton Wanderers	42	10	6	5	44	25	4	6	11	29	55	40
Birmingham	42	8	7	6	37	32	7	3	11	31	45	40
Huddersfield Town	42	9	6	6	45	23	5	5	11	25	38	39
West Ham United	**42**	**11**	**6**	**4**	**55**	**31**	**4**	**3**	**14**	**31**	**65**	**39**
Everton	42	11	2	8	38	31	6	2	13	25	44	38
Burnley	42	12	5	4	55	32	3	3	15	26	71	38
Portsmouth	42	13	2	6	43	26	2	4	15	13	54	36
Bury	42	9	5	7	38	35	3	2	16	24	64	31
Cardiff City	42	7	7	7	34	26	1	6	14	9	33	29

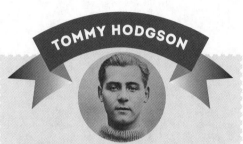

TOMMY HODGSON

Full-back Hodgson was working as a miner when West Ham signed him in 1921.

He made his debut in May 1922 on the final day of the season at Blackpool and played for the Hammers for the next seven years, making 92 appearances, a figure that would have been far more had he not suffered numerous injuries. Tommy's final game for the club was in December 1929 against Blackburn Rovers at Upton Park.

He then joined Luton Town in 1930, where he would be connected with the club for more than 50 years. First as a player, where he was the captain and made 67 appearances before injuries ended his career. Then in a remarkable achievement he became director, manager, chairman and president of the club until 1984 when he moved to the south coast. He had the honour of leading the team out at Wembley in the 1959 FA Cup final against Nottingham Forest. Tommy passed away in 1989.

Season **1928-29** Football League - Division One
Match Details

Manager **Syd King**   Final League Position **17/22**

	Date		Competition	Venue	Opponents	Results		Attendance	Position	Scorers
1	Aug 25	Sat	Div 1	H	Sheffield United	W	4-0	23,683	9	Ruffell 2, Barrett, Shone
2	Sep 1	Sat	Div 1	A	Bury	W	3-0	15,709	7	Watson 2, Ruffell
3	Sep 3	Mon	Div 1	A	Burnley	D	3-3	17719	1	Watson 2, Yews
4	Sep 8	Sat	Div 1	H	Aston Villa	W	4-1	26,110	1	Watson 2, Collins, Ruffell
5	Sep 10	Mon	Div 1	A	Cardiff City	L	2-3	17,189	3	Ruffell, Watson
6	Sep 15	Sat	Div 1	A	Leicester City	L	0-5	24,652	4	
7	Sep 17	Mon	Div 1	H	Cardiff City	D	1-1	13,750	4	Watson
8	Sep 22	Sat	Div 1	H	Manchester United	W	3-1	20,788	2	Shone 2, Payne
9	Sep 29	Sat	Div 1	A	Leeds United	L	1-4	29,423	6	Watson
10	Oct 6	Sat	Div 1	H	Liverpool	D	1-1	25,583	6	Earle
11	Oct 13	Sat	Div 1	A	Arsenal	W	3-2	43,327	4	Earle, Ruffell, Shone
12	Oct 20	Sat	Div 1	H	Everton	L	2-4	33,221	8	Gibbins, Shone
13	Oct 27	Sat	Div 1	A	Blackburn Rovers	L	0-2	18,496	9	
14	Nov 3	Sat	Div 1	H	Manchester City	W	3-0	22,572	6	Ruffell 2, Yews
15	Nov 10	Sat	Div 1	A	Birmingham	D	2-2	17,323	6	Earle, Gibbins
16	Nov 17	Sat	Div 1	H	Portsmouth	L	0-1	18,520	8	
17	Nov 24	Sat	Div 1	A	Bolton Wanderers	L	1-4	12,371	12	Gibbins
18	Dec 1	Sat	Div 1	H	The Wednesday	W	3-2	18,536	11	Yews 2, Watson
19	Dec 8	Sat	Div 1	A	Derby County	L	0-6	15,284	12	
20	Dec 15	Sat	Div 1	H	Sunderland	D	3-3	16,206	12	Ruffell 2, Robson
21	Dec 22	Sat	Div 1	A	Huddersfield Town	L	0-4	11,509	13	
22	Dec 25	Tue	Div 1	H	Newcastle United	W	1-0	23,794	11	Gibbins
23	Dec 26	Wed	Div 1	A	Newcastle United	L	0-1	43,237	11	
24	Dec 29	Sat	Div 1	A	Sheffield United	D	3-3	21,547	13	Ruffell, Watson, Yews
25	Jan 5	Sat	Div 1	H	Bury	L	2-3	11,801	15	Watson, Yews
26	Jan 12	Sat	FAC 3	H	Sunderland	W	1-0	35,000		Earle
27	Jan 19	Sat	Div 1	A	Aston Villa	L	2-5	28,838	18	Ruffell, Watson
28	Jan 26	Sat	FAC 4	H	Corinthian	W	3-0	42,000		Earle, Watson, Yews
29	Feb 2	Sat	Div 1	A	Manchester United	W	3-2	12,020	17	Gibbins, Ruffell, Watson
30	Feb 9	Sat	Div 1	H	Leeds United	W	8-2	18,055	16	Watson 6, Gibbins, Yews
31	Feb 16	Sat	FAC 5	A	Bournemouth	D	1-1	11,346		Yews
32	Feb 20	Wed	FAC 5 Rep	H	Bournemouth	W	3-1	30,217		Barrett, Yews, Isherwood (og)
33	Feb 23	Sat	Div 1	H	Arsenal	L	3-4	28,931	18	Ruffell 2, Watson
34	Mar 2	Sat	FAC QF	A	Portsmouth	L	2-3	39,088		Barrett 2
35	Mar 4	Mon	Div 1	H	Leicester City	W	2-1	8,603	16	Wearle, Ruffell
36	Mar 9	Sat	Div 1	H	Blackburn Rovers	D	3-3	24,379	15	Yews 2, Watson
37	Mar 12	Tue	Div 1	A	Liverpool	L	1-2	11,387	16	Watson
38	Mar 16	Sat	Div 1	A	Manchester City	L	2-4	32,157	17	Ruffell, Watson
39	Mar 23	Sat	Div 1	H	Birmingham	W	2-1	15,257	16	Earle, Watson, Yews
40	Mar 29	Fri	Div 1	H	Burnley	W	4-0	20,926	13	Ruffell 2, Gibbins, Yews
41	Mar 30	Sat	Div 1	A	Portsmouth	L	0-3	21,450	15	
42	Apr 6	Sat	Div 1	H	Bolton Wanderers	W	3-0	20,973	15	Earle, Gibbins, Watson
43	Apr 10	Wed	Div 1	A	Everton	W	4-0	7,996	13	Gibbins 3, Kelly (og)
44	Apr 13	Sat	Div 1	A	The Wednesday	L	0-6	22,596	13	
45	Apr 20	Sat	Div 1	H	Derby County	D	2-2	15,068	12	Watson 2
46	Apr 27	Sat	Div 1	A	Sunderland	L	1-4	9,469	13	Watson
47	May 4	Sat	Div 1	H	Huddersfield Town	D	1-1	13,005	17	Ruffell

Team Line-Ups

BAILLIE David	BARRETT Jim	CADWELL Albert	COLLINS Jimmy	COSHALL John	COX William	DIXON Robert	EARL Alfred	EARLE Stanley	GIBBINS Vivian	HODGSON Tommy	HUFTON Edward	HULL Archie	MOORE William	NORRINGTON Cyril	NORRIS Fred	PAYNE John	ROBSON George	RUFFELL James	SHONE Danny	SMAILES Matthew	SMITH William	TATE Isaac	WATSON Victor	YEWS Tommy	#
	5	6	4					8		2	1			3				11	10				9	7	1
	5	6	4					8		2	1			3				11	10				9	7	2
	5	6	4					8		2	1			3				11	10				9	7	3
	5	6	4					8		2	1			3				11	10				9	7	4
	5	6	4							2	1			3	8			11	10				9	7	5
	5	6	4					8		2				3				11	10			1	9	7	6
	5	6	4	3				8	10	2								11				1	9	7	7
		6	4	5				8		2				3				11	10			1	9	7	8
		6	4	5				8		2				3				11	10			1	9	7	9
1	5	6	4	3				8		2								11	10				9	7	10
	5	6	4	3		2		8	9		1							11	10					7	11
	5	6	4	3		2		8	9		1							11	10					7	12
		6	4	5		3		8	9	2	1							11	10					7	13
		6	4	5		3		8	9	2	1		10					11						7	14
		6	4	5		3		8	9	2	1		10					11						7	15
		6	4	5		3		8	9	2	1		10			11		11						7	16
		6	4	3		5	2	8	10		1							11					9	7	17
		6	4	5		3		8	10		1							11					9	7	18
		6	4	2		5	3	8	10		1					7		11					9		19
		6	4	3		5			10	2	1						8	11					9	7	20
			4	2	3	5			10		1	6					8	11					9	7	21
		6	4	5		3		8		2	1							11					9	7	22
		6	4	5		3		8	10	2								11					9	7	23
		6	4	5		3		8	10	2			2					11					9	7	24
		6	4	5		3		8	10				2					11					9	7	25
		6	4	5		3		8		2	1		10					11					9	7	26
		6	4	5		3		8			1		10					11			2		9	7	27
		6	4	5		3		8		2	1							11					9	7	28
		6	4	5		3		8		2	1							11					9	7	29
		6	4			3		8		2	1							11	5				9	7	30
		6	4			3		8	10	2	1							11	5				9	7	31
1	10	6	4			3		8		2								11	5				9	7	32
1	10	6	4			3		8		2								11	5				9	7	33
	10	6	4			3		8		2	1							11	5				9	7	34
	9	6	4			3		8	10	2								11	5			1		7	35
		6	4			3		8	10	2								11	5			1	9	7	36
		6	4			3		8	10	2			11						5			1	9	7	37
	10	6	4			1	3	8		2								11	5				9	7	38
	5	6	4			1	2	8					10	3				11					9	7	39
	5	6	4				2	8	10		1			3				11					9	7	40
	5	6	4				2	8	10		1			3				11					9	7	41
	2	6	4				3	8	10		1							11	5				9	7	42
	2	6	4				3	8	9		1				5		10						11	7	43
	2	6	4				3	8	9		1				5		10						11	7	44
	5	6					3	8	10	2	1				4			11					9	7	45
	5	6					3	8	10	2	1				4			11					9	7	46
	5	6						8	9	2	1			3	4		10	11						7	47

1929-30
Story of the season

Ten goals were scored in the first two home games as both Middlesbrough and Newcastle United conceded five. New signing inside-left **John Ball** came from Bury and **scored twice in both matches**.

He was on form and went on to score eight goals in h[...] first ten games. Centre-forward Vic Watson was also prolif[...] as he scored twice in the 3–1 victory at Leeds United an[...] grabbed a hat-trick in a 5–2 home win against Aston Villa i[...] early December. Huddersfield Town won both games ov[...] the Christmas period and these came in a run of fi[...] successive defeats.

There was a comfortable 4–0 home win against Not[...] County in the FA Cup, and the next round saw another wi[...] 4–1 against Leeds United, Vic Watson scoring all four goal[...] Round five brought another home tie, with local riva[...] Millwall the visitors. The in-form Watson scored twice in [...] 4–1 victory. Sadly the cup run ended in the quarter-fina[...] again as Arsenal won 3–0 at the Boleyn Ground. A wee[...] later at the same venue Arsenal were beaten 3–2, with th[...]

Appearances & Goals 1929-30

	League		FA Cup		Total	
	Starts	Goals	Starts	Goals	Starts	Goals
BALL John	15	9	0	0	15	9
BARRETT Jim	40	7	4	1	44	8
CADWELL Albert	38	0	4	0	42	0
COLLINS Jimmy	21	0	4	0	25	0
COX William	32	0	4	0	36	0
DIXON Robert	12	0	0	0	12	0
EARL Alfred	38	0	4	0	42	0
EARLE Stanley	36	3	4	0	40	3
GIBBINS Vivian	18	3	3	2	21	5
HODGSON Tommy	4	0	0	0	4	0
HUFTON Edward	30	0	4	0	34	0
NORRIS Fred	19	0	0	0	19	0
POLLARD Walter	7	0	0	0	7	0
ROBSON George	10	1	1	0	11	1
RUFFELL James	40	13	4	0	44	13
St PIER Wally	4	0	0	0	4	0
WADE Reg	2	0	0	0	2	0
WADE William	11	0	0	0	11	0
WATSON Victor	40	42	4	8	44	50
WOOD Jimmy	4	1	0	0	4	1
YEWS Tommy	41	3	4	1	45	4
own goal		4				4
Totals	**462**	**86**	**44**	**12**	**506**	**98**

...an Watson again scoring twice. To add to his goal tally he scored another hat-trick in the 3–0 home win against Leeds. Now the Leeds defenders must have feared Vic Watson. Last season he scored seven league goals against them and this season he netted five league goals and four in the FA Cup.

The campaign ended with three home victories and a good 6–2 win at Aston Villa, where Watson yet again claimed a hat-trick. A position of seventh in the table was a vast improvement and was due to the amazing scoring of Vic Watson, who scored 42 league goals and eight in the FA Cup.

JOHN BALL

Playing at inside-left, Ball was a prolific scorer at Bury. In five seasons at Gigg Lane between 1923 and 1928 he scored 99 goals in his 217 appearances.

In 1927 he was chosen to play for England against Ireland in Belfast, and in goal for England was Ted Hufton, the West Ham keeper. Hufton was injured in the first half and Ball took over in goal for the remainder of the game, which England lost 2–0. He left Bury in 1929 to sign for West Ham, where he scored on his debut at Blackburn Rovers in a 3–3 draw. He made an early impression at Upton Park, scoring five goals in his first four games. The early promise did not continue, though, as he only played in 15 games that season and was subsequently sold to Coventry City. He played one season at Highfield Road, scoring four goals in 29 appearances, before going into non-league football at Stourbridge. John died in Birmingham in May 1989 aged 89.

Football League - Division One Final Table 1929-30

	P	HOME					AWAY					Pts
		W	D	L	F	A	W	D	L	F	A	
Sheffield Wednesday	42	15	4	2	56	20	11	4	6	49	37	60
Derby County	42	16	4	1	61	32	5	4	12	29	50	50
Manchester City	42	12	5	4	51	33	7	4	10	40	48	47
Aston Villa	42	13	1	7	54	33	8	4	9	38	50	47
Leeds United	42	15	2	4	52	22	5	4	12	27	41	46
Blackburn Rovers	42	15	2	4	65	36	4	5	12	34	57	45
West Ham United	42	14	2	5	51	26	5	3	13	35	53	43
Leicester City	42	12	5	4	57	42	5	4	12	29	48	43
Sunderland	42	13	3	5	50	35	5	4	12	26	45	43
Huddersfield Town	42	9	7	5	32	21	8	2	11	31	48	43
Birmingham	42	13	3	5	40	21	3	6	12	27	41	41
Liverpool	42	11	5	5	33	29	5	4	12	30	50	41
Portsmouth	42	10	6	5	43	25	5	4	12	23	37	40
Arsenal	42	10	2	9	49	26	4	9	8	29	40	39
Bolton Wanderers	42	11	5	5	46	24	4	4	13	28	50	39
Middlesbrough	42	11	3	7	48	31	5	3	13	34	53	38
Manchester United	42	11	4	6	39	34	4	4	13	28	54	38
Grimsby Town	42	8	6	7	39	39	7	1	13	34	50	37
Newcastle United	42	13	4	4	52	32	2	3	16	19	60	37
Sheffield United	42	12	2	7	59	39	3	4	14	32	57	36
Burnley	42	11	5	5	53	34	3	3	15	26	63	36
Everton	42	6	7	8	48	46	6	4	11	32	46	35

Season **1929-30** Football League - Division One
Match Details

Manager **Syd King**   Final League Position **7/22**

	Date		Competition	Venue	Opponents	Results		Attendance	Position	Scorers
1	Aug 31	Sat	Div 1	A	Blackburn Rovers	D	3-3	21,817	14	Ball, Watson, Jones (og)
2	Sep 4	Wed	Div 1	A	Birmingham	L	2-4	13,301	16	Watson 2
3	Sep 7	Sat	Div 1	H	Middlesbrough	W	5-3	22,760	11	Ball 2, Ruffell 2 [1 pen], Watson
4	Sep 9	Mon	Div 1	H	Newcastle United	W	5-1	15,536	4	Ball 2, Yews 2, Watson
5	Sep 14	Sat	Div 1	A	Liverpool	L	1-3	29,087	10	Watson
6	Sep 16	Mon	Div 1	H	Birmingham	L	0-1	13,265	12	
7	Sep 21	Sat	Div 1	H	Derby County	W	2-0	26,601	5	Barrett, Ruffell
8	Sep 28	Sat	Div 1	H	Manchester United	W	2-1	20,695	6	Ball, Watson
9	Oct 5	Sat	Div 1	A	Grimsby Town	D	2-2	15,542	7	Ball, Watson
10	Oct 12	Sat	Div 1	H	Leicester City	L	1-2	23,525	12	Watson
11	Oct 19	Sat	Div 1	A	Manchester City	L	3-4	34,568	14	Ball, Ruffell, Yews
12	Oct 26	Sat	Div 1	H	Portsmouth	L	0-1	20,493	17	
13	Nov 2	Sat	Div 1	A	Arsenal	W	1-0	44,828	13	Watson
14	Nov 9	Sat	Div 1	H	Everton	W	3-1	24,801	10	Ruffell 2, Watson
15	Nov 16	Sat	Div 1	A	Leeds United	W	3-1	18,582	7	Watson 2, Milburn (og)
16	Nov 23	Sat	Div 1	H	Sheffield Wednesday	D	1-1	18,753	8	Watson
17	Nov 30	Sat	Div 1	A	Burnley	D	1-1	6,640	7	Barrett
18	Dec 7	Sat	Div 1	H	Sunderland	D	1-1	16,456	7	Watson
19	Dec 14	Sat	Div 1	A	Bolton Wanderers	L	1-4	11,421	9	Watson
20	Dec 21	Sat	Div 1	H	Aston Villa	W	5-2	14,624	8	Watson 3, Gibbins, Ruffell
21	Dec 25	Wed	Div 1	H	Huddersfield Town	L	2-3	28,390	10	Gibbins, Watson
22	Dec 26	Thu	Div 1	A	Huddersfield Town	L	0-3	21,657	12	
23	Dec 28	Sat	Div 1	H	Blackburn Rovers	L	2-3	23,901	14	Ruffell, Watson
24	Jan 1	Wed	Div 1	A	Sheffield United	L	2-4	16,361	16	Ball, Ruffell
25	Jan 4	Sat	Div 1	A	Middlesbrough	L	0-2	17,767	18	
26	Jan 11	Sat	FAC 3	H	Notts County	W	4-0	28,384		Watson 2, Barrett, Gibbins
27	Jan 18	Sat	Div 1	H	Liverpool	W	4-1	21,788	16	Barrett, Robson, Watson, Davidson (og)
28	Jan 25	Sat	FAC 4	H	Leeds United	W	4-1	34,000		Watson 4
29	Feb 1	Sat	Div 1	A	Manchester United	L	2-4	15,424	18	Earle, Watson
30	Feb 5	Wed	Div 1	A	Derby County	L	3-4	10,723	18	Watson 2, Barker (og)
31	Feb 8	Sat	Div 1	H	Grimsby Town	W	2-0	15,034	17	Ruffell, Watson
32	Feb 15	Sat	FAC 5	H	Millwall	W	4-1	24,000		Watson 2, Yews, Gibbins
33	Feb 20	Thu	Div 1	A	Leicester City	W	2-1	13,156	16	Watson, Wood
34	Feb 22	Sat	Div 1	H	Manchester City	W	3-0	21,860	14	Barrett, Gibbins, Watson
35	Mar 1	Sat	FAC QF	H	Arsenal	L	0-3	40,492		
36	Mar 8	Sat	Div 1	H	Arsenal	W	3-2	31,268	11	Watson 2, Earle
37	Mar 12	Wed	Div 1	A	Portsmouth	L	1-3	11,245	11	Ruffell
38	Mar 15	Sat	Div 1	A	Everton	W	2-1	27,953	10	Watson 2
39	Mar 22	Sat	Div 1	H	Leeds United	W	3-0	18,351	9	Watson 3
40	Mar 29	Sat	Div 1	A	Sheffield Wednesday	L	1-2	25,092	11	Watson
41	Apr 5	Sat	Div 1	H	Burnley	W	1-0	12,092	10	Barrett
42	Apr 12	Sat	Div 1	A	Sunderland	L	2-4	20,459	11	Barrett, Ruffell
43	Apr 18	Fri	Div 1	H	Sheffield United	W	1-0	19,633	11	Watson
44	Apr 19	Sat	Div 1	H	Bolton Wanderers	W	5-3	12,837	8	Watson 2, Barrett, Earle, Ruffell
45	Apr 26	Sat	Div 1	A	Aston Villa	W	3-2	18,047	6	Watson 3
46	May 3	Sat	Div 1	A	Newcastle United	L	0-1	39,389	7	

Team Line-Ups

BALL John	BARRETT Jim	CADWELL Albert	COLLINS Jimmy	COX William	DIXON Robert	EARL Alfred	EARLE Stanley	GIBBINS Vivian	HODGSON Tommy	HUFTON Edward	NORRIS Fred	POLLARD Walter	ROBSON George	RUFFELL James	St PIER Wally	WADE Reg	WADE William	WATSON Victor	WOOD Jimmy	YEWS Tommy	
10	5	6	4			3	8			1				11			2	9		7	1
10	5		4	6		3	8			1				11			2	9		7	2
10	5	6	4			3	8			1				11			2	9		7	3
10	5	6	4			3	8			1				11			2	9		7	4
	5	6	4			3	8			1		10		11			2	9		7	5
10	5	6	4			3	8			1				11			2	9		7	6
10	5	6	4			3	8		2	1				11				9	7		7
10	5	6				3	8		2	1	4			11				9		7	8
10	5	6				3	8		2	1	4							9		7	9
10	5			6		3	8			1				11	4		2	9		7	10
10	5	6	3			2	8			1				11	4			9		7	11
10	5	6	3			2	8			1	4			11				9		7	12
	5	6	3			2	8	10		1	4			11				9		7	13
	5	6	3			2	8	10		1	4			11				9		7	14
	5	6	3			2	8	10		1	4			11				9		7	15
	5	6	3			2	8	10		1	4			11				9		7	16
	5	6	3			2	8	10		1	4							9	11	7	17
	5	6	3			2	8	10		1	4			11				9		7	18
		6	3			2	8	10		1	4			11	5			9		7	19
	5	6	3			2		10		1	4		8	11				9		7	20
	5	6	3					10		1	4		8	11			2	9		7	21
	5	6	3					10		1	4		8	11			2	9		7	22
10	5	6	3						2	1	4		8	11				9		7	23
10	5	6	3					9		1	4		8	11			2			7	24
	5	6	3			2		10		1	4		8					9		7	25
	5	6	4	3		2	8	10		1								9		7	26
	5	6	4			2	8			1			10			3		9		7	27
	5	6	4	3		2	8			1			10					9		7	28
	5	6	4	3	1	2	8						10					9		7	29
	5	6	3			2	8			1	4		10					9		7	30
	5	6	3			2	8			1			10					9		7	31
	5	6	4	3		2	8	10		1				11				9		7	32
10		6	3		1	2	8		5		4							9	11	7	33
	5	6	4	3	1	2	8	10						11				9		7	34
	5	6	4	3		2	8	10		1				11				9		7	35
	5	6	4	3		2	8	10		1				11				9		7	36
10	5	6	4	3		2	8			1				11				9		7	37
	5	6	4	3	1	2	8				10			11				9		7	38
	5	6	4	3	1	2	8	10						11				9		7	39
	5	6	3		1	2	8	10						11				9	7	4	40
	5	6	4	3	1	2	8	9				10		11						7	41
	5	6	4	3	1	2	8					10		11				9		7	42
	5	6	4	3	1	2	8					10		11				9		7	43
	5	6	3		1	2	8					10		11				9		7	44
	5	6	4		1	2	8					10		11		3		9		7	45
			4	6	1	2	8					10		11	5		3	9		7	46

1930-31
Story of the season

The Hammers **got off to a blistering start as nine goals were scored** in home wins against Huddersfield Town and Liverpool. **The Merseysiders crashed 7–0 to a rampant West Ham** led by Vic Watson in sparkling form.

The Merseysiders crashed 7–0 to a rampant West Ham led by Vic Watson in sparkling form. After two goals against Huddersfield he scored four against Liverpool. The early promise was soon shattered as five days later the Hammers crashed 6–1 at Aston Villa and two days after that were beaten 3–0 at home by Middlesbrough. With Watson scoring in the next three games it was a huge blow when he got injured at Newcastle and missed the next four months of the season. In his absence Viv Gibbins did well and in October he was on hand to hit a hat-trick against Manchester United in a 5–1 home victory. Following that game there

Appearances & Goals 1930-31

	League		FA Cup		Total	
	Starts	Goals	Starts	Goals	Starts	Goals
BARRETT Jim	40	4	1	0	41	4
CADWELL Albert	31	0	1	0	32	0
COLLINS Jimmy	38	0	1	0	39	0
COX William	2	0	0	0	2	0
DIXON Robert	28	0	1	0	29	0
EARL Alfred	38	0	1	0	39	0
EARLE Stanley	36	8	1	0	37	8
ENGLAND Ernest	5	0	0	0	5	0
EVANS Arthur	1	0	0	0	1	0
FRYATT William	1	0	0	0	1	0
GAMBLE Frederick	2	2	0	0	2	2
GIBBINS Vivian	21	18	1	1	22	19
GOODACRE Reg	6	0	0	0	6	0
HARRIS Jimmy	5	1	0	0	5	1
HUFTON Edward	14	0	0	0	14	0
JAMES Wilf	36	7	1	0	37	7
MUSGRAVE Joe	7	1	0	0	7	1
NORRIS Fred	16	2	0	0	16	2
POLLARD Walter	5	1	0	0	5	1
ROBSON George	1	0	0	0	1	0
RUFFELL James	37	13	1	0	38	13
St PIER Wally	6	0	0	0	6	0
WADE Reg	28	0	1	0	29	0
WATSON Victor	18	14	0	0	18	14
WOOD Jimmy	3	1	0	0	3	1
YEWS Tommy	37	7	1	0	38	7
Totals	**462**	**79**	**11**	**1**	**473**	**80**

as a run of nine games unbeaten, ended by a 6–1 defeat at
underland. In early January Boleyn Ground customers
ere treated to ten goals as the Hammers and Aston Villa
rew 5–5.

week later the FA Cup hopes faded as Chelsea won 3–1
n a third-round tie at Upton Park. Flying winger Jimmy
uffell scored a hat-trick against Grimsby Town but
rimsby went away with the points after winning 4–3.This
as the start of a very poor run as the Hammers won only
ne game in the next ten fixtures; a disappointing final
acing of eighteenth was achieved.

Football League - Division One Final Table 1930-31

	P	HOME					AWAY					Pts
		W	D	L	F	A	W	D	L	F	A	
Arsenal	42	14	5	2	67	27	14	5	2	60	32	66
Aston Villa	42	17	3	1	86	34	8	6	7	42	44	59
Sheffield Wednesday	42	14	3	4	65	32	8	5	8	37	43	52
Portsmouth	42	11	7	3	46	26	7	6	8	38	41	49
Huddersfield Town	42	10	8	3	45	27	8	4	9	36	38	48
Derby County	42	12	6	3	56	31	6	4	11	38	48	46
Middlesbrough	42	13	5	3	57	28	6	3	12	41	62	46
Manchester City	42	13	2	6	41	29	5	8	8	34	41	46
Liverpool	42	11	6	4	48	28	4	6	11	38	57	42
Blackburn Rovers	42	14	3	4	54	28	3	5	13	29	56	42
Sunderland	42	12	4	5	61	38	4	5	12	28	47	41
Chelsea	42	13	4	4	42	19	2	6	13	22	48	40
Grimasby Town	42	13	2	6	55	31	4	3	14	27	56	39
Bolton Wanderers	42	12	6	3	45	26	3	3	15	23	55	39
Sheffield United	42	10	7	4	49	31	4	3	14	29	53	38
Leicester City	42	12	4	5	50	38	4	2	15	30	57	38
Newcastle United	42	9	2	10	41	45	6	4	11	37	42	36
West Ham United	**42**	**11**	**3**	**7**	**56**	**44**	**3**	**5**	**13**	**23**	**50**	**36**
Birmingham	42	11	3	7	37	28	2	7	12	18	42	36
Blackpool	42	8	7	6	41	44	3	3	15	30	81	32
Leeds United	42	10	3	8	49	31	2	4	15	19	50	31
Manchester United	42	6	6	9	30	37	1	2	18	23	78	22

FRED NORRIS

Born in Birmingham in 1903, he joined his local club Aston Villa in 1925, scoring twice in nine league games for the Midlands side over three seasons.

He joined West Ham in 1928 and made his debut in a 3–2 defeat at Cardiff in September. A versatile player, he alternated between a wing-half and a forward with some success. While playing in the forward line he scored a hat-trick against Oldham Athletic at the Boleyn Ground in October 1932.

After five seasons at Upton Park, playing in 65 games, he was transferred to Third Division side Crystal Palace in 1933. He scored on his debut against Southend United and played in 11 games that season before retiring.

Season **1930-31** Football League - Division One
Match Details

Manager **Syd King**   Final League Position **18/22**

	Date		Competition	Venue	Opponents	Results		Attendance	Position	Scorers
1	Aug 30	Sat	Div 1	H	Huddersfield Town	W	2-1	18,023	5	Watson 2
2	Sep 1	Mon	Div 1	H	Liverpool	W	7-0	11,682	1	Watson 4, Earle 2, James
3	Sep 6	Sat	Div 1	A	Aston Villa	L	1-6	35,897	6	Watson
4	Sep 8	Mon	Div 1	H	Middlesbrough	L	0-3	13,597	8	
5	Sep 13	Sat	Div 1	H	Chelsea	W	4-1	31,334	7	Watson 2, Earle, James
6	Sep 17	Wed	Div 1	A	Middlesbrough	D	2-2	14,778	7	James, Watson
7	Sep 20	Sat	Div 1	A	Newcastle United	L	2-4	18,971	12	Earle, Watson
8	Sep 27	Sat	Div 1	H	Sheffield Wednesday	D	3-3	26,487	10	Gibbins, Ruffell, James
9	Oct 4	Sat	Div 1	A	Grimsby Town	L	0-4	14,423	15	
10	Oct 11	Sat	Div 1	H	Manchester United	W	5-1	20,003	11	Gibbins 3, Barrett, Ruffell
11	Oct 18	Sat	Div 1	H	Blackburn Rovers	W	4-3	22,114	9	Yews 2, Gibbins, Ruffell
12	Oct 25	Sat	Div 1	A	Arsenal	D	1-1	51,918	9	Pollard
13	Nov 1	Sat	Div 1	H	Sheffield United	W	4-1	19,740	8	Gibbins 2, Barrett, Earle
14	Nov 8	Sat	Div 1	A	Birmingham	W	2-0	20,171	8	Yews 2
15	Nov 15	Sat	Div 1	H	Leeds United	D	1-1	16,612	7	Norris
16	Nov 22	Sat	Div 1	A	Derby County	D	1-1	12,092	6	Gibbins
17	Nov 29	Sat	Div 1	H	Leicester City	W	2-0	17,670	5	Ruffell 2
18	Dec 6	Sat	Div 1	A	Blackpool	W	3-1	12,115	5	Earle, Gibbins, Ruffell
19	Dec 13	Sat	Div 1	H	Manchester City	W	2-0	19,875	3	Ruffell 2
20	Dec 20	Sat	Div 1	A	Sunderland	L	1-6	20,846	6	Gibbins
21	Dec 25	Thu	Div 1	H	Portsmouth	W	4-3	27,718	4	Gibbins 2, James, Norris
22	Dec 26	Fri	Div 1	A	Portsmouth	L	0-2	25,442	6	
23	Dec 27	Sat	Div 1	A	Huddersfield Town	L	0-2	13,830	6	
24	Jan 3	Sat	Div 1	H	Aston Villa	D	5-5	18,810	6	Gibbins 2, Barrett, Harris, Yews
25	Jan 10	Sat	FAC 3	H	Chelsea	L	1-3	21,000		Gibbins
26	Jan 17	Sat	Div 1	A	Chelsea	L	1-2	40,011	7	Gibbins
27	Jan 26	Mon	Div 1	H	Newcastle United	W	3-2	9,090	6	Earle, Gibbins, James
28	Jan 31	Sat	Div 1	A	Sheffield Wednesday	L	3-5	16,796	6	James, Watson, Yews
29	Feb 7	Sat	Div 1	H	Grimsby Town	L	3-4	15,559	7	Ruffell 3
30	Feb 14	Sat	Div 1	A	Manchester United	L	0-1	9,745	9	
31	Feb 21	Sat	Div 1	A	Blackburn Rovers	L	0-1	9,680	11	
32	Feb 28	Sat	Div 1	H	Arsenal	L	2-4	30,361	13	Earle, Watson
33	Mar 7	Sat	Div 1	A	Sheffield United	W	2-1	13,315	11	Ruffell, Yews
34	Mar 16	Mon	Div 1	H	Birmingham	L	1-2	8,521	11	Watson
35	Mar 21	Sat	Div 1	A	Leeds United	L	0-3	11,611	12	
36	Mar 28	Sat	Div 1	H	Derby County	L	0-1	16,658	14	
37	Apr 3	Fri	Div 1	H	Bolton Wanderers	L	1-4	19,116	16	Wood
38	Apr 4	Sat	Div 1	A	Leicester City	D	1-1	13,808	16	Gamble
39	Apr 6	Mon	Div 1	A	Bolton Wanderers	L	2-4	20,229	17	Barrett, Gamble
40	Apr 11	Sat	Div 1	H	Blackpool	W	3-2	15,514	18	Gibbins, Musgrave, Ruffell
41	Apr 18	Sat	Div 1	A	Manchester City	D	1-1	13,737	16	Gibbins
42	Apr 25	Sat	Div 1	H	Sunderland	L	0-3	10,118	17	
43	May 2	Sat	Div 1	A	Liverpool	L	0-2	14,523	18	

Team Line-Ups

BARRETT Jim	CADWELL Albert	COLLINS Jimmy	COX William	DIXON Robert	EARL Alfred	EARLE Stanley	ENGLAND Ernest	EVANS Arthur	FRYATT William	GAMBLE Frederick	GIBBINS Vivian	GOODACRE Reg	HARRIS Jimmy	HUFTON Edward	JAMES Wilf	MUSGRAVE Joe	NORRIS Fred	POLLARD Walter	ROBSON George	RUFFELL James	St PIER Wally	WADE Reg	WATSON Victor	WOOD Jimmy	YEWS Tommy	No.
5	6	4	3	1	2	8									10					11			9		7	1
5	6	4		1	2	8									10					11		3	9		7	2
5	6	4		1	2	8									10					11		3	9		7	3
5	6	4		1	2	8									10					11		3	9		7	4
3	6	4			2	8								1	10					11	5		9		7	5
3	6	4			2	8								1	10					11	5		9		7	6
	6	4	3		2	8								1	10					11	5		9		7	7
3	6	4			2	8					9			1	10					11	5				7	8
3	6	4			2	8	7				9			1	10					11	5					9
5	6	4		1	2	8					9				10					11		3			7	10
5	6	4		1	2	8					9				10					11		3			7	11
5	6			1	2	8					9						4	10		11		3			7	12
5	6			1	2	8					9				10		4			11		3			7	13
5	6			1	2	8					9				10		4			11		3			7	14
5	6	4		1	2	8									10	9				11		3			7	15
5	6	4		1	2	8					9				10	7				11		3			7	16
5		4		1	2	8					9				10	6				11		3			7	17
5	6	4		1	2	8					9				10					11		3			7	18
9	6	4		1	2	8									10	5				11		3			7	19
5	6	4		1	2	8					9				10					11		3			7	20
5	6	4		1	2							8	10		9					11		3			7	21
5	6	4		1	2						9		11		10				8			3			7	22
5	6	4		1	2	8					9		11		10							3			7	23
5	6	4		1	2	8	3				9		11		10										7	24
5	6	4		1	2	8					9				10					11		3			7	25
5		4		1	2	8					9				10	6				11		3			7	26
5		4			2	8	3				9			1	10	6				11					7	27
5	6	4		1	2	8									10					11		3	9		7	28
5	6			1	2		3				8				10		4						9		7	29
5		4				8						2		1	10	6				11		3	9		7	30
	6	4													10					11	5	3	9		7	31
5	6	4		1	2	8									10					11		3	9		7	32
5		4		1	2	8									10	6				11		3	9		7	33
5		4		1		8	3								10	6				11		2	9		7	34
5		4		1		8	3					2			10	6							9		7	35
5	6	4				8		3			9	2		1						11			10		7	36
5	6	4			3	8						2		1	10					11			9		7	37
5	6	4			3	8					9	2		1				10		11					7	38
5	6	4			3						9	2	11	1				8							7	39
5		4			2	8					9			1	10	6				11		3			7	40
5		4			2						9			1	10	6		8		11		3			7	41
5		4		1	2						9				10	6		8		11					7	42
5		4			2	8								1	10	6				11		3	9		7	43

1931-32
Story of the season

Two wins against Bolton and Chelsea and a goal in each game from Vic Watson gave **the Hammers' faithful hope for the season.** The bubble burst in September with a 6–0 defeat at Sheffield United followed by a 5–2 reverse at Aston Villa.

To relieve the gloom there were narrow wins ov Manchester City and Portsmouth but the defensive worr soon returned as both Derby County and West Bromwi Albion gained 5–1 victories. There was a mini-revival December with a fine 4–2 win at Blackburn Rovers and week later Jimmy Ruffell scored a hat-trick in a 4–2 hor win over eventual champions Everton.

The FA Cup began with a 2–1 win at Charlton but ended the next round as for the second year running the Hamme were knocked out by Chelsea, who won 3–1 at Stamfo

Appearances & Goals 1931-32

	League		FA Cup		Total	
	Starts	Goals	Starts	Goals	Starts	Goa
BARRETT Jim	38	3	2	0	40	3
CADWELL Albert	26	1	2	0	28	1
CHALKLEY Alfred	29	1	2	0	31	1
COLLINS Jimmy	35	0	2	0	37	0
COX William	9	0	0	0	9	0
DIXON Robert	20	0	2	0	22	0
EARL Alfred	30	0	2	0	32	0
EARLE Stanley	17	0	0	0	17	0
GIBBINS Vivian	9	5	0	0	9	5
GOODACRE Reg	10	0	0	0	10	0
HARRIS Jimmy	2	0	0	0	2	0
HUFTON Edward	22	0	0	0	22	0
JAMES Wilf	4	0	0	0	4	0
MORTON John	5	1	0	0	5	1
MUSGRAVE Joe	3	0	0	0	3	0
NORRIS Fred	17	1	0	0	17	1
PHILLIPS Wilf	21	3	2	0	23	3
POLLARD Walter	7	0	0	0	7	0
PUDDEFOOT Syd	7	0	0	0	7	0
RUFFELL James	39	15	2	0	41	15
St PIER Wally	7	0	0	0	7	0
WADE Reg	2	0	0	0	2	0
WADE William	5	0	0	0	5	0
WATSON Victor	38	23	2	2	40	25
WELDON Anthony	20	3	2	1	22	4
WOOD Jimmy	17	2	0	0	17	2
YEWS Tommy	23	2	2	0	25	2
own goal		2				2
Totals	**462**	**62**	**22**	**3**	**484**	**65**

...ridge. Inside-forward Viv Gibbins left to join Brentford ...d was later replaced after a ten-year absence by former ...vourite Syd Puddefoot. Despite a string of poor ...erformances, by mid-March the team stood fifteenth in ...e table. Then came trouble as defeats at Sheffield ...ednesday (6–1), bottom of the table Blackpool (7–2) and ...verton (6–1) sent West Ham plummeting down the league. ...ne final game of the season saw the Hammers travel to ...helsea, where they played badly and lost 3–2. They ...nished bottom of the league, having conceded 107 goals, ...d were relegated to the Second Division.

JOHN MORTON

Right-winger Morton signed for West Ham in 1932 after the club bought him for £600 from Gainsborough Trinity.

John could play on either wing and became a regular in the side for eight seasons, which was only halted by the outbreak of war. After making his debut against Arsenal in March 1932 he went on to play in a total of 275 games, scoring 57 goals. In 1935 he played in two unofficial England games held in respect of the King George V Jubilee Trust Fund. He played against the Anglo-Scots at Highbury and against Scotland at Hampden Park. A full England cap came his way in 1937 when he was selected to play against Czechoslovakia at White Hart Lane. John scored one of the goals in England's 5–4 victory. During World War Two Morton served in the Royal Air Force and afterwards became a bookmaker. He died in March 1986 at the age of 72.

Football League - Division One Final Table 1931-32

	P	HOME					AWAY					Pts
		W	D	L	F	A	W	D	L	F	A	
...verton	42	18	0	3	84	30	8	4	9	32	34	56
...rsenal	42	14	5	2	52	16	8	5	8	38	32	54
...heffield Wednesday	42	14	4	3	60	28	8	2	11	36	54	50
...uddersfield Town	42	11	8	2	47	21	8	2	11	33	42	48
...ston Villa	42	15	1	5	64	28	4	7	10	40	44	46
...est Bromwich Albion	42	12	4	5	46	21	8	2	11	31	34	46
...heffield United	42	13	3	5	47	32	7	3	11	33	43	46
...rtsmouth	42	14	2	5	37	21	5	5	11	25	41	45
...rmingham	42	13	5	3	48	22	5	3	13	30	45	44
...verpool	42	13	4	4	56	38	6	2	13	25	55	44
...ewcastle United	42	13	5	3	52	31	5	1	15	28	56	42
...helsea	42	12	4	5	43	27	4	4	13	26	46	40
...underland	42	11	4	6	42	29	4	6	11	25	44	40
...anchester City	42	10	5	6	49	30	3	7	11	34	43	38
...erby County	42	13	5	3	51	25	1	5	15	20	50	38
...ackburn Rovers	42	12	3	6	57	41	4	3	14	32	54	38
...olton Wanderers	42	15	1	5	51	25	2	3	16	21	55	38
...iddlesbrough	42	12	3	6	41	29	3	5	13	23	60	38
...icester City	42	11	3	7	46	39	4	4	13	28	55	37
...ackpool	42	9	4	8	42	40	3	5	13	23	62	33
...rimsby Town	42	11	4	6	39	28	2	2	17	28	70	32
West Ham United	42	9	5	7	35	37	3	2	16	27	70	31

Season **1931-32** Football League - Division One
Match Details

Manager **Syd King**   Final League Position **22/22 Relegated to Division 2**

	Date		Competition	Venue	Opponents	Results		Attendance	Position	Scorers
1	Aug 29	Sat	Div 1	A	Bolton Wanderers	W	1-0	15,740	9	Watson
2	Aug 31	Mon	Div 1	H	Chelsea	W	3-1	28,338	3	Norris, Watson, Weldon
3	Sep 5	Sat	Div 1	H	Middlesbrough	L	0-2	23,129	6	
4	Sep 7	Mon	Div 1	A	Sheffield United	L	0-6	11,055	9	
5	Sep 12	Sat	Div 1	A	Huddersfield Town	L	1-3	11,986	17	Watson
6	Sep 19	Sat	Div 1	H	Newcastle United	W	2-1	21,558	15	Ruffell, Watson
7	Sep 21	Mon	Div 1	H	Sheffield United	L	1-2	12,075	15	Ruffell
8	Sep 26	Sat	Div 1	A	Aston Villa	L	2-5	39,619	18	Wood, Tate (og)
9	Oct 3	Sat	Div 1	H	Leicester City	L	1-4	20,196	20	Gibbins
10	Oct 10	Sat	Div 1	A	Liverpool	D	2-2	23,819	21	Gibbins, Weldon
11	Oct 17	Sat	Div 1	A	Manchester City	W	1-0	18,310	17	Ruffell
12	Oct 24	Sat	Div 1	H	Portsmouth	W	2-1	18,092	15	Gibbins 2
13	Oct 31	Sat	Div 1	A	Derby County	L	1-5	10,424	18	Watson
14	Nov 7	Sat	Div 1	H	West Bromwich Albion	L	1-5	20,685	18	Ruffell
15	Nov 14	Sat	Div 1	A	Arsenal	L	1-4	41,028	18	Watson
16	Nov 21	Sat	Div 1	H	Blackpool	D	1-1	14,800	19	Ruffell
17	Nov 28	Sat	Div 1	A	Blackburn Rovers	W	4-2	8,426	17	Barrett, Gibbins, Phillips, Watson
18	Dec 5	Sat	Div 1	H	Everton	W	4-2	34,109	14	Ruffell 3, Wood
19	Dec 12	Sat	Div 1	A	Birmingham	L	1-4	19,725	18	Watson
20	Dec 19	Sat	Div 1	H	Sunderland	D	2-2	6,505	18	Barrett [pen], Watson
21	Dec 25	Fri	Div 1	A	Grimsby Town	L	1-2	15,132	19	Watson
22	Dec 26	Sat	Div 1	H	Grimsby Town	W	3-1	23,859	16	Ruffell 2, Watson
23	Jan 2	Sat	Div 1	H	Bolton Wanderers	W	3-1	15,997	17	Watson 2, Ruffell
24	Jan 9	Sat	FAC 3	A	Charlton Athletic	W	2-1	26,500		Watson 2
25	Jan 16	Sat	Div 1	A	Middlesbrough	L	2-3	8,287	18	Watson 2
26	Jan 23	Sat	FAC 4	A	Chelsea	L	1-3	36,657		Weldon
27	Jan 30	Sat	Div 1	A	Newcastle United	D	2-2	31,942	18	Cadwell, Watson
28	Feb 1	Mon	Div 1	H	Huddersfield Town	D	1-1	8,631	17	Watson
29	Feb 6	Sat	Div 1	H	Aston Villa	W	2-1	25,438	16	Phillips, Yews
30	Feb 18	Thu	Div 1	A	Leicester City	L	1-2	9,983	18	Ruffell
31	Feb 20	Sat	Div 1	H	Liverpool	W	1-0	15,721	17	Ruffell
32	Mar 2	Wed	Div 1	H	Manchester City	D	1-1	13,524	17	Chalkley
33	Mar 5	Sat	Div 1	A	Portsmouth	L	0-3	14,031	18	
34	Mar 12	Sat	Div 1	H	Derby County	W	2-1	19,635	14	Watson 2, Ruffell
35	Mar 19	Sat	Div 1	A	West Bromwich Albion	L	1-3	19,002	17	Phillips
36	Mar 25	Fri	Div 1	H	Sheffield Wednesday	L	1-2	25,759	17	Ruffell
37	Mar 26	Sat	Div 1	H	Arsenal	D	1-1	34,852	17	Watson
38	Mar 28	Mon	Div 1	A	Sheffield Wednesday	L	1-6	14,848	17	Watson
39	Apr 2	Sat	Div 1	A	Blackpool	L	2-7	13,092	19	Morton, Watson
40	Apr 9	Sat	Div 1	H	Blackburn Rovers	L	1-3	10,136	19	Watson
41	Apr 16	Sat	Div 1	A	Everton	L	1-6	26,997	20	Cresswell (og)
42	Apr 23	Sat	Div 1	H	Birmingham	L	2-4	10,983	20	Watson, Weldon
43	Apr 30	Sat	Div 1	A	Sunderland	L	0-2	13,528	21	
44	May 7	Sat	Div 1	A	Chelsea	L	2-3	24,386	22	Barrett, Yews

Team Line-Ups

BARRETT Jim	CADWELL Albert	CHALKLEY Alfred	COLLINS Jimmy	COX William	DIXON Robert	EARL Alfred	EARLE Stanley	GIBBINS Vivian	GOODACRE Reg	HARRIS Jimmy	HUFTON Edward	JAMES Wilf	MORTON John	MUSGRAVE Joe	NORRIS Fred	PHILLIPS Wilf	POLLARD Walter	PUDDEFOOT Syd	RUFFELL James	St PIER Wally	WADE Reg	WADE William	WATSON Victor	WELDON Anthony	WOOD Jimmy	YEWS Tommy	#
5	6	3				2	8				1				4				11				9	10		7	1
5	6	3				2					1				4		8		11				9	10		7	2
5	6	3				2					1				4		8		11				9	10		7	3
5	6	3				2	8				1				4				11				9	10		7	4
5			6	3		2					1				4		8		11				9	10		7	5
5			6	3		2	8				1				4				11				9	10		7	6
5			6	3		2	8				1				4				11				9	10	7		7
5			6	3	1	2	8								4				11				9	10	7		8
5			6	3		2	7	9			1				4				11				8	10			9
			6			2		9			1	8			4				11	5		3		10		7	10
			4				8	9	2		1				6				11	5		3		10		7	11
			4					9	2		1				6		8		11	5		3		10		7	12
			4				8		2		1				6				11	5		3	9	10		7	13
6			4	3			8		2		1								11	5			9	10		7	14
6			4		3				2		1	10							11	5			9	8		7	15
5			4	6	1	2	8	9											11			3		10		7	16
5	6	3	4		1	2		9								8			11				10			7	17
5	6	3	4		1	2		10								8			11				9			7	18
5	6	3	4		1	2		10								8			11				9			7	19
5	6	3	4		1	2		10								8			11				9			7	20
5	6	3	4		1	2						10				8			11				9			7	21
5	6	3	4		1	2						10				8			11				9			7	22
5	6	3	4		1	2										8			11				9	10		7	23
5	6	3	4		1	2										8			11				9	10		7	24
5	6	3	4		1	2										8			11				9	10		7	25
5	6	3	4		1	2										8			11				9	10		7	26
5	6	3	4		1	2	8			11					10								9			7	27
5	6	3	4		1	2	8			11					10								9			7	28
5	6	3	4		1	2	8								10				11				9			7	29
5	6	3	4		1	2	8								10				11				9			7	30
5	6	3	4		1		8								10				11		2		9			7	31
5	6	3	4		1	2									10		8		11				9			7	32
5	6		4	3	1	2									10		8		11				9			7	33
5	6	3	4		1	2									10		8		11				9			7	34
5	6	3	4		1				2						10		8		11				9			7	35
5	6	3	4								1				10		8		11		2		9			7	36
5		3	4								1		7	6			8	10	11		2		9				37
5		2	4	3							1		7	6	10		8		11				9				38
5	6	3	4			2	8				1		7		10				11				9				39
5	6	3	4			2					1		7					10	11				9		8		40
5	6	3						2			1		11		4	10							9		8	7	41
5		3	6			2	8				1				4				11				9	10		7	42
5	6	3			1	2									4		8		11				9	10		7	43
10		3				2								6	4				11	5			9		8	7	44

1932-33
Story of the season

Starting life in the Second Division, **the Hammers struggled** as Bradford City won 4–2 at the Boleyn Ground, and in the return a week later the Yorkshire side won 5–1. **A good 3–0 victory at home against old rivals Millwall was welcome,** but this was soon followed by a 6–0 defeat at Lincoln City.

The home faithful were then treated to five successi home wins where the team scored 24 goals. There were ha tricks for Fred Norris against Oldham and for Vic Watso against Burnley. After Grimsby Town were beaten 5– there was an excellent 7–3 home win over neighbou Charlton Athletic.

The long-serving manager, Syd King, had been warn several times over his drink-related conduct and followi an emergency board meeting in November 1932 he w suspended for three months. In January 1933 he w informed that his contract had been terminated. Days lat he drank a cocktail of alcohol and disinfectant, and h passed away on 12 January in St Mary's hospital, Plaisto He had been at the club since the Thames Ironworks da

Appearances & Goals 1932-33

	League		FA Cup		Total	
	Starts	Goals	Starts	Goals	Starts	Goal
BARRETT Jim	40	8	6	0	46	8
CADWELL Albert	10	0	2	0	12	0
CHALKLEY Alfred	34	0	6	0	40	0
COCKROFT Joe	6	0	0	0	6	0
COLLINS Jimmy	33	0	6	0	39	0
DEACON Dickie	3	0	0	0	3	0
DIXON Robert	3	0	0	0	3	0
EARL Alfred	11	0	0	0	11	0
FENTON Edward	6	0	0	0	6	0
FRYATT William	2	0	0	0	2	0
GOODACRE Reg	4	0	0	0	4	0
GOULDEN Len	7	1	0	0	7	1
JOHNSON William	5	0	0	0	5	0
McMAHON Pat	13	0	1	0	14	0
MILLS Hugh	7	3	0	0	7	3
MORTON John	36	11	6	2	42	13
MUSGRAVE Joe	23	0	4	1	27	1
NORRIS Fred	7	3	0	0	7	3
POLLARD Walter	18	2	6	2	24	4
PUDDEFOOT Syd	15	3	0	0	15	3
RUFFELL James	8	0	0	0	8	0
St PIER Wally	7	0	0	0	7	0
WALKER Albert	33	0	6	0	39	0
WATSON George	26	0	5	0	31	0
WATSON Victor	35	24	6	4	41	28
WILSON Arthur	27	13	6	2	33	15
WOOD Jimmy	11	2	1	0	12	2
YEWS Tommy	32	2	5	0	37	2
own goal		3		1		4
Totals	**462**	**75**	**66**	**12**	**528**	**87**

playing as full-back until April 1903. He was replaced by club trainer Charlie Paynter.

Throughout December there was only one defeat in seven games and it was hoped that this fine form would continue into the New Year. Non-league Corinthians were beaten 2–0 in the FA Cup and this brought a home tie against West Bromwich Albion. West Brom lay seventh in the First Division but the Hammers beat them 2–0. A fifth-round tie with Brighton was the reward, but a week before that West Ham were beaten 6–1 at Bury. The Brighton tie attracted a record crowd of 32,310 to the Goldstone Ground. In an exciting tie the teams drew 2–2 and the Hammers won the resultant replay by 1–0. Forgetting about their lowly league position they brushed aside Birmingham City in the quarter-final as they won 4–0 at the Boleyn Ground. The semi-final was against Everton at Wolverhampton's Molineux ground. The teams were drawing 1–1 with seven minutes remaining when Everton grabbed the winner.

League form was still poor and by Good Friday, after a 1–0 defeat at Chesterfield, the team were bottom of the league. After that, though, four successive games were won and relegation was narrowly avoided. They had enjoyed an exciting FA Cup journey but by finishing in 20th place the team had almost been relegated to the Third Division.

JOE COCKROFT

Cockcroft was a wing-halfback who joined West Ham in 1932 from non-league side Gainsborough Trinity.

After making his debut at Chesterfield in April 1933 he played in 208 consecutive league games up to March 1938, an amazing achievement which endeared him to the fans. Up to the outbreak of war in 1939 Joe played in a total of 263 games for the club, missing only seven league games in that period. During the war he played in 29 regional games and was in the team that won the Football League War Cup when beating Blackburn Rovers 1–0 at Wembley in 1940.

Later during the war his London home was blitzed and he came to live in Yorkshire and joined Sheffield Wednesday. League soccer resumed when the war ended and he was a consistent performer, playing in 97 games up until 1949 when he was transferred to Sheffield United. His spell with the Blades was brief and after playing 12 games for them he became player-manager for Wisbech Town.

He later became a publican and also worked as a printer. He died in King's Lynn aged 82 in February 1994.

Football League - Division Two Final Table 1932-33

		HOME					AWAY					
	P	W	D	L	F	A	W	D	L	F	A	Pts
Stoke City	42	13	3	5	40	15	12	3	6	38	24	56
Tottenham Hotspur	42	14	7	0	58	19	6	8	7	38	32	55
Fulham	42	12	5	4	46	31	8	5	8	32	34	50
Bury	42	13	7	1	55	23	7	2	12	29	36	49
Nottingham Forest	42	9	8	4	37	28	8	7	6	30	31	49
Manchester United	42	11	5	5	40	24	4	8	9	31	44	43
Millwall	42	11	7	3	40	20	5	4	12	19	37	43
Bradford Park Avenue	42	13	4	4	51	27	4	4	13	26	44	42
Preston North End	42	12	2	7	53	36	4	8	9	21	34	42
Swansea Town	42	17	0	4	36	12	2	4	15	14	42	42
Bradford City	42	10	6	5	43	24	4	7	10	22	37	41
Southampton	42	15	3	3	48	22	3	2	16	18	44	41
Grimsby Town	42	8	10	3	49	34	6	3	12	30	50	41
Plymouth Argyle	42	13	4	4	45	22	3	5	13	18	45	41
Notts County	42	10	4	7	41	31	5	6	10	26	47	40
Oldham Athletic	42	10	4	7	38	31	5	4	12	29	49	38
Port Vale	42	12	3	6	49	27	2	7	12	17	52	38
Lincoln City	42	11	6	4	46	28	1	7	13	26	59	37
Burnley	42	8	9	4	35	20	3	5	13	32	59	36
West Ham United	42	12	6	3	56	31	1	3	17	19	62	35
Chesterfield	42	10	5	6	36	25	2	5	14	25	59	34
Charlton Athletic	42	9	3	9	35	35	3	4	14	25	56	31

Season **1932-33** Football League - Division Two
Match Details

Manager **Syd King** (to October) **Charlie Paynter** (from November 1)   Final League Position **20/22**

	Date		Competition	Venue	Opponents		Results	Attendance	Position	Scorers
1	Aug 27	Sat	Div 2	A	Swansea Town	L	0-1	15,247	22	
2	Aug 29	Mon	Div 2	H	Bradford City	L	2-4	10,964	19	Mills, Pollard
3	Sep 3	Sat	Div 2	H	Notts County	D	1-1	10,656	21	Puddefoot
4	Sep 7	Wed	Div 2	A	Bradford City	L	1-5	17,137	22	Watson
5	Sep 10	Sat	Div 2	A	Port Vale	L	0-4	9,582	22	
6	Sep 17	Sat	Div 2	H	Millwall	W	3-0	25,496	21	Watson 2, Morton
7	Sep 24	Sat	Div 2	A	Southampton	L	3-4	11,636	21	Morton 2, Watson
8	Oct 1	Sat	Div 2	H	Bury	L	0-1	12,848	22	
9	Oct 8	Sat	Div 2	A	Lincoln City	L	0-6	9,887	22	
10	Oct 15	Sat	Div 2	H	Oldham Athletic	W	5-2	13,161	21	Norris 3, Morton, Watson
11	Oct 22	Sat	Div 2	A	Preston North End	L	1-4	8,525	21	Mills
12	Oct 29	Sat	Div 2	H	Burnley	D	4-4	12,009	21	Watson 3, Morton
13	Nov 5	Sat	Div 2	A	Bradford Park Avenue	L	0-3	14,861	22	
14	Nov 12	Sat	Div 2	H	Grimsby Town	W	5-2	11,481	21	Wilson 2, Watson, Yews, Jacobson (og)
15	Nov 19	Sat	Div 2	A	Stoke City	D	0-0	11,225	22	
16	Nov 26	Sat	Div 2	H	Charlton Athletic	W	7-3	18,347	20	Watson 2, Wilson, 2, Barrett, Morton, Yews
17	Dec 3	Sat	Div 2	A	Nottingham Forest	D	2-2	7,399	20	Watson, Wilson
18	Dec 10	Sat	Div 2	H	Manchester United	W	3-1	13,435	19	Watson 2, Wilson
19	Dec 17	Sat	Div 2	A	Tottenham Hotspur	D	2-2	45,129	18	Morton, Whatley (og)
20	Dec 24	Sat	Div 2	H	Plymouth Argyle	D	2-2	21,312	18	Barrett, Morton
21	Dec 26	Mon	Div 2	A	Fulham	L	2-4	26,932	18	Puddefoot, Watson
22	Dec 27	Tue	Div 2	H	Fulham	D	1-1	32,237	19	Watson
23	Dec 31	Sat	Div 2	H	Swansea Town	W	3-1	16,876	17	Watson 2, Barrett
24	Jan 7	Sat	Div 2	A	Notts County	L	0-2	11,437	18	
25	Jan 14	Sat	FAC 3	A	Corinthian	W	2-0	16,421		Pollard, Watson
26	Jan 21	Sat	Div 2	H	Port Vale	W	5-0	13,908	16	Watson 2, Wilson 2, Barrett
27	Jan 28	Sat	FAC 4	H	West Bromwich Albion	W	2-0	37,222		Watson, Wilson
28	Jan 30	Mon	Div 2	A	Millwall	L	0-1	4,063	16	
29	Feb 4	Sat	Div 2	H	Southampton	W	3-1	16,521	16	Wilson 2, Watson
30	Feb 11	Sat	Div 2	A	Bury	L	1-6	7,516	17	Barrett
31	Feb 18	Sat	FAC 5	A	Brighton & Hove Albion	D	2-2	32,310		Musgrave, Watson
32	Feb 22	Wed	FAC 5 Rep	H	Brighton & Hove Albion	W	1-0	36,742		Morton
33	Mar 4	Sat	FAC QF	H	Birmingham	W	4-0	44,232**		Morton, Pollard, Wilson, Barkas (og)
34	Mar 6	Mon	Div 2	H	Preston North End	D	1-1	8,648	18	Puddefoot
35	Mar 11	Sat	Div 2	A	Burnley	L	0-4	10,771	18	
36	Mar 13	Mon	Div 2	A	Oldham Athletic	L	2-3	7,159	19	Mills, Wood
37	Mar 18	Sat	FAC SF	N*	Everton	L	1-2	37,936		Watson
38	Mar 20	Mon	Div 2	H	Bradford Park Avenue	W	2-1	7,258	18	Wilson 2
39	Mar 25	Sat	Div 2	A	Grimsby Town	L	1-2	8,546	20	Wilson
40	Mar 27	Mon	Div 2	H	Lincoln City	D	0-0	9,836	19	
41	Apr 1	Sat	Div 2	H	Stoke City	L	1-2	19,104	20	Barrett
42	Apr 8	Sat	Div 2	A	Charlton Athletic	L	1-3	21,487	20	Barrett
43	Apr 14	Fri	Div 2	A	Chesterfield	L	0-1	11,974	22	
44	Apr 15	Sat	Div 2	H	Nottingham Forest	W	4-3	16,925	20	Barrett, Goulden, Morton, Wood
45	Apr 17	Mon	Div 2	H	Chesterfield	W	3-1	18,394	20	Pollard, Watson, Wilson
46	Apr 22	Sat	Div 2	A	Manchester United	W	2-1	14,958	20	Morton, Wilson
47	Apr 29	Sat	Div 2	H	Tottenham Hotspur	W	1-0	31,706	19	Wilson
48	May 6	Sat	Div 2	A	Plymouth Argyle	L	1-4	10,444	20	Hardie (og)

* Played at Molineux ** West Ham United have often repudiated this attendance figure, as the occupants of the "Chicken Run" that day were counted twice in the final reckoning. The club had a "transfer ticket" system in operation at that time; the total was therefore nearly 4,000 less.

Team Line-Ups

BARRETT Jim	CADWELL Albert	CHALKLEY Alfred	COCKROFT Joe	COLLINS Jimmy	DEACON Dickie	DIXON Robert	EARL Alfred	FENTON Edward	FRYATT William	GOODACRE Reg	GOULDEN Len	JOHNSON William	McMAHON Pat	MILLS Hugh	MORTON John	MUSGRAVE Joe	NORRIS Fred	POLLARD Walter	PUDDEFOOT Syd	RUFFELL James	St PIER Wally	WALKER Albert	WATSON George	WATSON Victor	WILSON Arthur	WOOD Jimmy	YEWS Tommy	
5		3		4		1	2							9		6			10	11					8		7	1
5		3		4	10		2							9		6		8		11			1				7	2
5		3		4		1	2							9		6		8	10	11							7	3
5		3		4			2	8								6			10	11				9			7	4
5		3		4			2	8								6			10	11			1	9			7	5
6		3					2	8			11						4		10		5		1	9			7	6
6		3					2	8			11						4		10		5		1	9			7	7
6	2			4				8	3		11								10		5		1	9			7	8
5	6	2		4					3					7					10	11			1	9		8		9
							2					5		9	11	6	8				4	3	1		10		7	10
							2					5		9	11	6	8				4	3	1		10		7	11
5	6	2	4											9	11			8				3	1		10		7	12
5		2	4					8						9	11	6			10			3	1				7	13
5	2		4												11	6		8				3	1	9	10		7	14
5	2		4												11	6		8				3	1	9	10		7	15
5	2		4												11	6		8				3	1	9	10		7	16
5	2														11	6	4	8				3	1	9	10		7	17
5	2		4												11	6		8				3	1	9	10		7	18
5	2		4												11	6		8	9			3	1		10		7	19
5	2		4												11	6		8				3	1	9	10		7	20
5			4							2					11	6		8	10			3	1	9			7	21
5			4							2					11	6		8				3	1	9	10		7	22
5			4							2					11	6		8				3	1	9	10	7		23
5			4							2					11	6		8				3	1	9	10	7		24
5	2		4												11	6		8				3	1	9	10		7	25
5	2		4													6		8		11		3	1	9	10		7	26
5	6	2	4												11			8				3	1		10		7	27
5	6	2	4												11			8	9			3	1		10		7	28
5	6	2	4												11			8				3	1	9	10		7	29
5	6	2	4												11			8				3	1	9	10		7	30
5	2		4												11	6		8				3	1	9	10		7	31
5	2		4												11	6		8				3	1	9	10		7	32
5	2		4										1		11	6		8				3		9	10		7	33
5	2		4										1		11	6		8				3		9	1		7	34
5	2		4										1		11	6		8				3		9	10		7	35
5	2		8										1	9	11	6					4	3			10		7	36
5	6	2	4												11			8				3	1	9	10		7	37
5	6	2	4												11							3	1	9	10	8	7	38
5	6	2	4										1		11							3		9	10	8		39
5	6	2	4										1		11			8				3		9	10			40
5	6	2	4										1		11			8				3		9	10		7	41
8	6	2	4								10		1		7					11	5	3		9				42
5	2	6	4								10		1		11							3		9		8	7	43
5	2	6	4								10		1		11							3		9		8	7	44
5	2	6	4								10		1		11			8				3		9			7	45
5	2	6	4								10		1		11							3		9		8	7	46
5	2	6	4								10		1		11							3		9		8	7	47
5	2	6	4		9						10		1		11							3				8	7	48

1933-34
Story of the season

After two disastrous campaigns **the Hammers were looking to improve** and they began the season well. **Bolton Wanderers were beaten at home 4–2 on the opening day** and then came an exciting 4–4 draw at Plymouth Argyle.

Away from home there were two 4–1 reverses at Brentford and Oldham Athletic, but at home the goals flowed. Vic Watson was back on form, scoring two in the 5–1 victory over Plymouth and a hat-trick as Preston North End were crushed 6–0 at the Boleyn Ground. Following a creditable 2–2 draw with Millwall at the Den, Vic Watson did it again with another hat-trick in the 4–1 defeat of Lincoln City. The Christmas period brought two 1–1 draws with Swansea Town and the Hammers ended the year losing 5–1 at Bolton Wanderers.

A home tie in the FA Cup brought a 3–2 win against Bradford City but in the next round at Tottenham the

Appearances & Goals 1933-34

	League		FA Cup		Total	
	Starts	Goals	Starts	Goals	Starts	Goals
ANDERSON Edward	24	0	2	0	26	0
BARRETT Jim	38	5	2	0	40	5
CHALKLEY Alfred	37	0	2	0	39	0
COCKROFT Joe	42	0	2	0	44	0
COLLINS Jimmy	17	0	0	0	17	0
ETTE Cliff	1	1	0	0	1	1
FENTON Edward	12	5	0	0	12	5
GOULDEN Len	40	5	2	1	42	6
INNS Tommy	4	0	0	0	4	0
LANDELLS Jack	21	4	1	0	22	4
McMAHON Pat	3	0	0	0	3	0
MILLS Hugh	4	2	0	0	4	2
MORTON John	42	6	2	0	44	6
MUSGRAVE Joe	1	0	0	0	1	0
ROBSON William	3	0	0	0	3	0
RUFFELL James	22	8	2	0	24	8
RUTHERFORD Jack	33	0	2	0	35	0
THORPE Percy	3	0	0	0	3	0
TIPPETT Thomas	21	8	1	0	22	8
WALKER Albert	37	0	2	0	39	0
WATSON George	6	0	0	0	6	0
WATSON Victor	30	26	2	3	32	29
WILSON Arthur	2	1	0	0	2	1
WOOD Jimmy	16	4	0	0	16	4
YOUNG Len	3	0	0	0	3	0
own goal		3				3
Totals	**462**	**78**	**22**	**4**	**484**	**82**

Hammers crashed out 4–1. There were four successive defeats before the biggest crowd of the season, 24,335, turned up at the Boleyn to see local rivals Millwall gain a point in the 1–1 draw. Twenty-year-old Ted Fenton had been drafted into the side at centre-forward and he responded with a hat-trick in the 3–1 home win over Bury. Two weeks later at Easter he was scoring the winner at Old Trafford as the Hammers triumphed 1–0, and the following day the London derby with Fulham was won 5–1, with Watson scoring three. The season ended with narrow wins against Port Vale and Nott County, which resulted in a final placing of seventh in the table.

Football League - Division Two Final Table 1933-34

	P	HOME					AWAY					Pts
		W	D	L	F	A	W	D	L	F	A	
Grimsby Town	42	15	3	3	62	28	12	2	7	41	31	59
Preston North End	42	15	3	3	47	20	8	3	10	24	32	52
Bolton Wanderers	42	14	2	5	45	22	7	7	7	34	33	51
Brentford	42	15	2	4	52	24	7	5	9	33	36	51
Bradford Park Avenue	42	16	2	3	63	27	7	1	13	23	40	49
Bradford City	42	14	4	3	46	25	6	2	13	27	42	46
West Ham United	42	13	3	5	51	28	4	8	9	27	42	45
Port Vale	42	14	4	3	39	14	5	3	13	21	41	45
Oldham Athletic	42	12	5	4	48	28	5	5	11	24	32	44
Plymouth Argyle	42	12	7	2	43	20	3	6	12	26	50	43
Blackpool	42	10	8	3	39	27	5	5	11	23	37	43
Bury	42	12	4	5	43	31	5	5	11	27	42	43
Burnley	42	14	2	5	40	29	4	4	13	20	43	42
Southampton	42	15	2	4	40	21	0	6	15	14	37	38
Hull City	42	11	4	6	33	20	2	8	11	19	48	38
Fulham	42	13	3	5	29	17	2	4	15	19	50	37
Nottingham Forest	42	11	4	6	50	27	2	5	14	23	47	35
Notts County	42	9	7	5	32	22	3	4	14	21	40	35
Swansea Town	42	10	9	2	36	19	0	6	15	15	41	35
Manchester United	42	9	3	9	29	33	5	3	13	30	52	34
Millwall	42	8	8	5	21	17	3	3	15	18	51	33
Lincoln City	42	7	7	7	31	23	2	1	18	13	52	26

LEN GOULDEN

Goulden was known as the prince of inside-forwards, with a magical left foot. He began his career as an amateur for West Ham in 1931 and was loaned out to both Chelmsford City and Leyton.

He made his debut against Charlton Athletic at the Valley in April 1933. Len became a fixture in the side, making 253 appearances and scoring 55 goals in seven seasons before war came in 1939. His fine form saw him make his international debut for England and scoring in the 6–0 victory against Norway in 1937. Len was capped 14 times by England and he partnered club colleague John Morton in England's 5–4 victory against Czechoslovakia in 1937 at White Hart Lane.

During the war he played in regional football for the Hammers, appearing in a further 194 games and scoring 76 goals. He was in the West Ham team in 1940 that won the War Cup. There were more England appearances as he played in six unofficial wartime internationals.

In 1945 a fee of £5,000 was agreed and he joined First Division Chelsea, where he spent five seasons and played in a total of 111 games, scoring 19 goals. After retiring as a player he managed Watford from 1952 until 1956 and later had coaching jobs at Banbury Town and Oxford United. He died in London in February 1995.

Season **1933-34** Football League - Division Two
Match Details

Manager **Charlie Paynter**   Final League Position **7/22**

	Date		Competition	Venue	Opponents	Results		Attendance	Position	Scorers
1	Aug 26	Sat	Div 2	H	Bolton Wanderers	W	4-2	24,825	5	Watson V. 2, Morton, Griffiths (og)
2	Aug 30	Wed	Div 2	A	Plymouth Argyle	D	4-4	24,312	7	Barrett [pen], Goulden, Landells, Mills
3	Sep 2	Sat	Div 2	A	Brentford	L	1-4	19,918	14	Wilson
4	Sep 4	Mon	Div 2	H	Plymouth Argyle	W	5-1	16,004	6	Tippett 2, Watson 2, Landells
5	Sep 9	Sat	Div 2	H	Burnley	L	1-2	22,087	10	Tippett
6	Sep 16	Sat	Div 2	A	Oldham Athletic	L	1-4	8,439	11	Tippett
7	Sep 23	Sat	Div 2	H	Preston North End	W	6-0	15,738	9	Watson 3, Goulden, Morton, Tippett
8	Sep 30	Sat	Div 2	A	Bradford Park Avenue	D	0-0	11,865	9	
9	Oct 7	Sat	Div 2	H	Grimsby Town	W	3-1	23,481	7	Morton, Watson, Jacobson (og)
10	Oct 14	Sat	Div 2	A	Nottingham Forest	W	1-0	9,450	5	Wood
11	Oct 21	Sat	Div 2	A	Millwall	D	2-2	28,080	6	Barrett, Watson
12	Oct 28	Sat	Div 2	H	Lincoln City	W	4-1	19,380	4	Watson 3, Reddish (og)
13	Nov 4	Sat	Div 2	A	Bury	L	1-2	9,408	5	Watson
14	Nov 11	Sat	Div 2	H	Hull City	W	2-1	19,309	3	Watson, Landells
15	Nov 18	Sat	Div 2	A	Fulham	L	1-3	18,175	4	Landells
16	Nov 25	Sat	Div 2	H	Southampton	D	0-0	18,724	6	
17	Dec 2	Sat	Div 2	A	Blackpool	D	1-1	13,882	5	Ruffell
18	Dec 9	Sat	Div 2	H	Bradford City	L	1-2	15,321	8	Barrett
19	Dec 16	Sat	Div 2	A	Port Vale	D	0-0	6,610	7	
20	Dec 23	Sat	Div 2	H	Notts County	W	5-3	16,370	7	Ruffell 2, Goulden, Morton, Watson
21	Dec 25	Mon	Div 2	H	Swansea Town	D	1-1	25,791	5	Watson
22	Dec 26	Tue	Div 2	A	Swansea Town	D	1-1	16,493	7	Goulden
23	Dec 30	Sat	Div 2	A	Bolton Wanderers	L	1-5	9,551	8	Mills
24	Jan 6	Sat	Div 2	H	Brentford	W	3-2	24,108	8	Watson 2, Tippett
25	Jan 13	Sat	FAC 3	H	Bradford City	W	3-2	28,426		Watson 2, Goulden
26	Jan 20	Sat	Div 2	A	Burnley	L	2-4	9,655	9	Barrett, Watson
27	Jan 27	Sat	FAC 4	A	Tottenham Hotspur	L	1-4	51,747		Watson
28	Feb 3	Sat	Div 2	A	Preston North End	L	1-4	14,419	11	Ette
29	Feb 7	Wed	Div 2	H	Oldham Athletic	L	1-4	8,832	12	Watson
30	Feb 10	Sat	Div 2	H	Bradford Park Avenue	L	0-1	16,630	14	
31	Feb 17	Sat	Div 2	A	Grimsby Town	D	1-1	10,627	14	Morton
32	Feb 24	Sat	Div 2	H	Nottingham Forest	W	2-1	14,594	12	Ruffell 2
33	Mar 3	Sat	Div 2	H	Millwall	D	1-1	24,335	13	Watson
34	Mar 10	Sat	Div 2	A	Lincoln City	W	2-0	5,213	12	Ruffell, Wood
35	Mar 17	Sat	Div 2	H	Bury	W	3-1	15,559	9	Fenton 3
36	Mar 24	Sat	Div 2	A	Hull City	L	0-2	7,811	11	
37	Mar 30	Fri	Div 2	A	Manchester United	W	1-0	29,114	10	Fenton
38	Mar 31	Sat	Div 2	H	Fulham	W	5-1	22,518	8	Watson 3, Goulden, Morton
39	Apr 2	Mon	Div 2	H	Manchester United	W	2-1	20,085	6	Wood 2
40	Apr 7	Sat	Div 2	A	Southampton	L	2-3	6,917	8	Barrett, Watson
41	Apr 14	Sat	Div 2	H	Blackpool	L	1-2	14,170	10	Watson
42	Apr 21	Sat	Div 2	A	Bradford City	D	2-2	6,396	9	Fenton, Ruffell
43	Apr 28	Sat	Div 2	H	Port Vale	W	1-0	9,893	7	Ruffell
44	May 5	Sat	Div 2	A	Notts County	W	2-1	4,436	7	Tippett 2

Team Line-Ups

ANDERSON Edward	BARRETT Jim	CHALKLEY Alfred	COCKROFT Joe	COLLINS Jimmy	ETTE Cliff	FENTON Edward	GOULDEN Len	INNS Tommy	LANDELLS Jack	McMAHON Pat	MILLS Hugh	MORTON John	MUSGRAVE Joe	ROBSON William	RUFFELL James	RUTHERFORD Jack	THORPE Percy	TIPPETT Thomas	WALKER Albert	WATSON George	WATSON Victor	WILSON Arthur	WOOD Jimmy	YOUNG Len	#
4	5		6				10		8	1		11		3			2	7			9				1
4	5		6				10		8	1	9	11		3			2	7							2
	5		6	4			10					11		3			2	7	1		9	8			3
	5	2	6	4			10		8			11						7	3	1	9				4
	5	2	6	4					8			11						7	3	1	9				5
4	5	2	6				10		8	1		11						7	3		9				6
4	5	2	6				10		8			11				1		7	3		9				7
4	5	2	6				10		8			11				1		7	3		9				8
4	5	2	6				10		8			11				1		7	3		9				9
4	5	2	6						8			11				1		10	3		9		7		10
4	5	2	6				10		8			11				1		7	3		9				11
4	5	2	6				10		8			11				1		7	3		9				12
4	5	2	6				10		8			11				1		7	3		9				13
4	5	2	6				10		8			11				1		7	3		9				14
4	5	2	6				10		8			11				1		7	3		9				15
4	5	2	6				10		8			7			11	1			3		9				16
4	5	2	6				10		8			7			11	1			3		9				17
4	5	2	6				10		8			7			11	1			3		9				18
4	5	2	6				10		8		9	7			11	1			3						19
4	5	2	6				10					7			11	1		8	3		9				20
4	5	2	6				10					8			11	1		7	3		9				21
	5	2	6				10	3			9	7	4		11	1		8							22
4	5	2	6					3	10		9	8			11			7		1					23
4	5	2	6				10					8			11	1		7	3		9				24
4	5	2	6				10					8			11	1		7	3		9				25
4	5	2	6				10		8			7			11	1			3		9				26
4	5	2	6				10		8			7			11	1			3		9				27
4	5	2	6		8		10					7			11	1			3		9				28
	5	2	6	4			10					7			11	1			3		9	8			29
4			6			5	10	2	8			11				1			3		9		7		30
	5		6	4		9	8	2				10			11	1			3				7		31
	5	2	6	4			8					10			11	1			3		9		7		32
	5	2	6	4			8					10			11	1			3		9		7		33
	5	2	6	4		9	8					10			11				3				7		34
	5	2	6	4		9	8					10			11	1			3				7		35
	5	2	6	4		9	8					10			11	1			3				7		36
	5	2	6	4		9	8					10			11	1			3				7		37
	5	2	6	4		8	10					11				1			3		9		7		38
	5	2	6	4		8	10					11				1			3		9		7		39
	5	2	6	4		8	10					11				1			3		9		7		40
4	5	2	6			8	10					11				1			3		9		7		41
		2	6	4		9	10					8			11				3	1			7	5	42
		2	6	4		9	10					8			11				3	1			7	5	43
		2	6	4			10					8			11	1	9		3				7	5	44

1934-35
Story of the season

The **opening four games** saw one 3–1 home victory against Nottingham Forest and three defeats. **It was a poor start,** with defeats at Burnley by 5–2 and a 4–1 loss at Brentford.

After another poor showing at Hull City where the home side won 4–0, Hugh Mills was drafted into the side at centre-forward with dramatic effect.

He scored eleven goals in the following nine games with the Hammers winning seven of them. In the tenth game he did not score and never played for West Ham in the league again. In his place came Vic Watson, who also went on a goal spree with a hat-trick in the 4–0 home win over Notts County and another two in the 4–1 home victory against Bolton Wanderers. The Christmas period saw a double over Bury and hoisted West Ham to second place in the table.

The FA Cup brought a home tie against Third Division Stockport County. Winning 1–0 with three minutes left, it was a shock when Jim Barrett scored an own-goal equaliser. In the replay the Hammers conceded after just three minutes and finally lost the tie 1–0. During February there

Appearances & Goals 1934-35

	League		FA Cup		Total	
	Starts	Goals	Starts	Goals	Starts	Goals
ANDERSON Edward	2	0	0	0	2	0
BARRETT Jim	41	5	2	0	43	5
CHALKLEY Alfred	42	0	2	0	44	0
COCKROFT Joe	42	0	2	0	44	0
COLLINS Jimmy	12	0	0	0	12	0
CONWAY Herman	41	0	2	0	43	0
FENTON Edward	32	6	1	0	33	6
FOREMAN John	21	3	2	0	23	3
FOXALL Joseph	4	2	0	0	4	2
GALL Herbert	1	0	0	0	1	0
GOULDEN Len	40	3	2	0	42	3
MANGNALL David	10	6	0	0	10	6
MARSHALL James	10	2	0	0	10	2
MILLS Hugh	10	11	2	1	12	12
MORTON John	40	7	2	0	42	7
RUFFELL James	36	20	2	0	38	20
TIPPETT Thomas	4	2	0	0	4	2
WALKER Albert	42	0	2	0	44	0
WALKER Richard	3	0	0	0	3	0
WALLBANKS Fred	0	0	1	0	1	0
WATSON George	1	0	0	0	1	0
WATSON Victor	15	9	0	0	15	9
WOOD Jimmy	12	4	0	0	12	4
YOUNG Len	1	0	0	0	1	0
Totals	**462**	**80**	**22**	**1**	**484**	**81**

were home wins over Bradford Park Avenue and Norwich City but these were followed by a 3–0 defeat at Newcastle United. In a dramatic match at Swansea Town the Hammers scored four times but Swansea scored five. Two new forwards were purchased: James Marshall from Arsenal and Dave Mangnall from Birmingham City. The new boys were soon on target as they both scored on their debuts in the 2–2 draw at Port Vale. Six wins in the next seven games saw West Ham on course for promotion, being third in the table, a point behind Bolton Wanderers. On the final day of the season Oldham Athletic were beaten 2–0 at the Boleyn Ground and Bolton drew at Blackpool. Both teams finished on 56 points but Bolton were promoted by virtue of a much better goal difference. A settled side was the main reason for success: defenders Chalkley, Cockroft and Walker were ever-present while goalkeeper Conway and centre-half Barrett only missed one game.

Football League - Division Two Final Table 1934-35

		HOME					AWAY					
	P	W	D	L	F	A	W	D	L	F	A	Pts
Brentford	42	19	2	0	59	14	7	7	7	34	34	61
Bolton Wanderers	42	17	1	3	63	15	9	3	9	33	33	56
West Ham United	42	18	1	2	46	17	8	3	10	34	46	56
Blackpool	42	16	4	1	46	18	5	7	9	33	39	53
Manchester United	42	16	2	3	50	21	7	2	12	26	34	50
Newcastle United	42	14	2	5	55	25	8	2	11	34	43	48
Fulham	42	15	3	3	62	26	2	9	10	14	30	46
Plymouth	42	13	3	5	48	26	6	5	10	27	38	46
Nottingham Forest	42	12	5	4	46	23	5	3	13	30	47	42
Bury	42	14	1	6	38	26	5	3	13	24	47	42
Sheffield United	42	11	4	6	51	30	5	5	11	28	40	41
Burnley	42	11	2	8	43	32	5	7	9	20	41	41
Hull City	42	9	6	6	32	22	7	2	12	31	52	40
Norwich City	42	11	6	4	51	23	3	5	13	20	38	39
Bradford Park Avenue	42	7	8	6	32	28	4	8	9	23	35	38
Barnsley	42	8	10	3	32	22	5	2	14	28	61	38
Swansea Town	42	13	5	3	41	22	1	3	17	15	45	36
Port Vale	42	10	7	4	42	28	1	5	15	13	46	34
Southampton	42	9	8	4	28	19	2	4	15	18	56	34
Bradford City	42	10	7	4	34	20	2	1	18	16	48	32
Oldham Athletic	42	10	3	8	44	40	0	3	18	12	55	26
Notts County	42	8	3	10	29	33	1	4	16	17	64	25

JAMES MARSHALL

The Scottish international inside-forward began his career at Glasgow Rangers in 1925 and went on to gain six Scottish Championship medals and three Scottish Cup winners medals.

While at Rangers he represented Scotland on three occasions, all against England. Marshall was a qualified doctor, having gained his medical degree in October 1933. A medical appointment in London caused him to leave Rangers and sign for Arsenal. He only played in four league games for them before joining West Ham in 1935. He made his debut at Port Vale in March that year and in three seasons at Upton Park he scored 14 goals in 59 appearances. Jimmy retired from playing at the age of 29 and then worked for Bermondsey borough council. He passed away in December 1977.

Season **1934-35** Football League - Division Two
Match Details

Manager **Charlie Paynter**   Final League Position **3/22**

	Date		Competition	Venue	Opponents	Results		Attendance	Position	Scorers
1	Aug 27	Mon	Div 2	H	Burnley	L	1-2	18,070	16	Watson V.
2	Sep 1	Sat	Div 2	H	Nottingham Forest	W	3-1	18,549	16	Wood 2, Morton
3	Sep 3	Mon	Div 2	A	Burnley	L	2-5	13,562	16	Fenton 2
4	Sep 8	Sat	Div 2	A	Brentford	L	1-4	20,818	17	Fenton
5	Sep 15	Sat	Div 2	H	Fulham	W	2-1	17,956	16	Morton, Ruffell
6	Sep 17	Sat	Div 2	A	Hull City	L	0-4	5,338	17	
7	Sep 22	Sat	Div 2	A	Bradford Park Avenue	W	3-1	7,089	14	Mills 2, Fenton
8	Sep 29	Sat	Div 2	H	Plymouth Argyle	W	2-1	20,484	11	Barrett, Mills
9	Oct 6	Sat	Div 2	A	Norwich City	W	2-1	16,316	10	Foreman, Mills
10	Oct 13	Sat	Div 2	H	Newcastle United	W	3-2	26,799	5	Barrett, Mills, Ruffell
11	Oct 20	Sat	Div 2	H	Swansea Town	W	2-0	21,227	5	Mills, Morton
12	Oct 27	Sat	Div 2	A	Manchester United	L	1-3	31,950	7	Mills
13	Nov 3	Sat	Div 2	H	Port Vale	W	3-1	19,391	6	Mills 2, Ruffell
14	Nov 10	Sat	Div 2	A	Barnsley	D	1-1	7,878	6	Mills
15	Nov 17	Sat	Div 2	H	Sheffield United	W	2-0	20,178	6	Goulden, Mills
16	Nov 24	Sat	Div 2	A	Bradford City	W	2-0	8,150	4	Foreman, Morton
17	Dec 1	Sat	Div 2	H	Notts County	W	4-0	18,390	3	Watson V. 3, Ruffell
18	Dec 8	Sat	Div 2	A	Southampton	D	2-2	8,752	4	Ruffell, Watson V.
19	Dec 15	Sat	Div 2	H	Bolton Wanderers	W	4-1	27,489	4	Ruffell 2, Watson V. 2
20	Dec 22	Sat	Div 2	A	Oldham Athletic	W	2-1	7,290	4	Ruffell, Watson V.
21	Dec 25	Tue	Div 2	A	Bury	W	4-2	15,155	4	Ruffell 2, Wood 2
22	Dec 26	Wed	Div 2	H	Bury	W	3-0	34,496	2	Ruffell 2, Watson V.
23	Dec 29	Sat	Div 2	H	Hull City	L	1-2	25,344	3	Ruffell
24	Jan 5	Sat	Div 2	A	Nottingham Forest	L	0-2	16,506	4	
25	Jan 12	Sat	FAC 3	H	Stockport County	D	1-1	26,400		Mills
26	Jan 16	Wed	FAC 3 Rep	A	Stockport County	L	0-1	17,911		
27	Jan 19	Sat	Div 2	H	Brentford	W	2-0	33,788	4	Ruffell, Tippett
28	Jan 26	Sat	Div 2	A	Fulham	L	0-3	22,582	4	
29	Feb 2	Sat	Div 2	H	Bradford Park Avenue	W	2-1	20,593	3	Morton, Ruffell
30	Feb 9	Sat	Div 2	A	Plymouth Argyle	W	1-0	10,841	3	Foreman
31	Feb 18	Mon	Div 2	H	Norwich City	W	1-0	13,296	2	Ruffell
32	Feb 23	Sat	Div 2	A	Newcastle United	L	0-3	27,439	3	
33	Mar 2	Sat	Div 2	A	Swansea Town	L	4-5	8,380	4	Foxall 2, Morton, Tippett
34	Mar 9	Sat	Div 2	H	Manchester United	D	0-0	19,718	4	
35	Mar 16	Sat	Div 2	A	Port Vale	D	2-2	12,853	3	Mangnall, Marshall
36	Mar 23	Sat	Div 2	H	Barnsley	W	4-3	27,338	3	Barrett, Goulden, Marshall, Ruffell
37	Mar 30	Sat	Div 2	A	Sheffield United	W	2-1	15,101	2	Mangnall 2
38	Apr 6	Sat	Div 2	H	Bradford City	W	1-0	28,019	2	Mangnall
39	Apr 13	Sat	Div 2	A	Notts County	W	2-0	9,721	2	Morton, Ruffell
40	Apr 19	Fri	Div 2	A	Blackpool	L	2-3	29,626	3	Barrett, Fenton
41	Apr 20	Sat	Div 2	H	Southampton	W	2-1	28,862	3	Fenton, Ruffell
42	Apr 22	Mon	Div 2	H	Blackpool	W	2-1	35,161	2	Mangnall, Ruffell
43	Apr 27	Sat	Div 2	A	Bolton Wanderers	L	1-3	34,909	2	Goulden
44	May 4	Sat	Div 2	H	Oldham Athletic	W	2-0	23,275	3	Barrett, Mangnall

Team Line-Ups

ANDERSON Edward	BARRETT Jim	CHALKLEY Alfred	COCKROFT Joe	COLLINS Jimmy	CONWAY Herman	FENTON Edward	FOREMAN John	FOXALL Joseph	GALL Herbert	GOULDEN Len	MANGNALL David	MARSHALL James	MILLS Hugh	MORTON John	RUFFELL James	TIPPETT Thomas	WALKER Albert	WALKER Richard	WALLBANKS Fred	WATSON George	WATSON Victor	WOOD Jimmy	YOUNG Len	
	5	2	6		1					10				8	11		3	4			9	7		1
	5	2	6	4	1					10				8	11		3				9	7		2
	5	2	6	8	1	9				10				11			3	4				7		3
	5	2	6	4	1	9				10				8	11		3					7		4
	5	2	6	4	1	9				10				8	11		3					7		5
	5	2	6	4	1	8				10					11		3				9	7		6
	5	2	6		1	8		11		10			9				3					7	4	7
	5	2	6	4	1		7			10			9	8	11		3							8
		2	6	4	1		7			10			9	8	11		3	5						9
	5	2	6	4	1		7			10			9	8	11		3							10
	5	2	6	4	1		7						9	8	11		3				10			11
	5	2	6	4	1		7			10			9	8	11		3							12
	5	2	6	4	1		7			10			9	8	11		3							13
	5	2	6	4	1	8	7						9	10	11		3							14
	5	2	6		1	4	7			10			9	8	11		3							15
	5	2	6		1	4	7			10			9	8	11		3							16
	5	2	6		1	4	7			10				8	11		3				9			17
	5	2	6		1	4	7			10				8	11		3				9			18
	5	2	6		1	4				10				8	11		3				9	7		19
	5	2	6		1	4				10				8	11		3				9	7		20
	5	2	6		1	4				10				8	11		3				9	7		21
	5	2	6		1	4				10				8	11		3				9	7		22
	5	2	6		1	4				10				8	11		3				9	7		23
	5	2	6		1	4	7			10				8	11		3				9			24
	5	2	6		1	4	7			10			9	8	11		3							25
	5	2	6		1		7			10			9	8	11		3		4					26
4	5	2	6		1		7			10				8	11	9	3							27
4	5	2	6		1		7			10				8	11		3							28
	5	2	6		1	4	7			10				8	11	9	3							29
	5	2	6		1	4	7			10				8	11		3				9			30
	5	2	6		1	4	7			10				8	11		3				9			31
	5	2	6		1	4	7	9	11	10				8			3							32
	5	2	6		1	4	7	9		10				8		11	3							33
	5	2	6		1	4	7	8		10				11			3				9			34
	5	2	6		1	4				10	9	8		7	11		3							35
	5	2	6		1	4				10	9	8		7	11		3							36
	5	2	6		1	4				10	9	8		7	11		3							37
	5	6	6		1	4	7			10	9	8		11			3							38
	5	2	6		1	4				10	9	8		7	11		3							39
	5	2	6		1	4				10	9	8		7	11		3							40
	5	2	6			4				10	9	8		7	11		3			1				41
	5	2	6		1	4				10	9	8		7	11		3							42
	5	2	6		1	4				10	9	8		7	11		3							43
	5	2	6		1	4				10	9	8		7	11		3							44

1935-36
Story of the season

There were two new faces in the Hammers side as they kicked off the season away to Norwich City. Inside-forward **Peter Simpson** had arrived from Crystal Palace and goalkeeper **Vince Blore** came from Derby County.

The Hammers scored three times at Norwich bu conceded four, with Blore having a nightmare debut. Dav Mangnall was brought in for the visit of Nottingham Fores and obliged with a hat-trick in a 5–2 victory. By the end of September there had been five defeats in eight games and both new boys lost their place in the side. Mangnall then went on a scoring spree, scoring nine goals in nine games a the Hammers climbed the table. At home both Swanses Town and Port Vale were beaten 4–0 while Hull City suffered a 4–1 defeat. On Boxing Day there was a good 4–2 win at Southampton, with Mangnall scoring twice, and two days later he scored another hat-trick in a 3–2 home win against Norwich City.

There was a shock in the FA Cup as Third Division Luto Town knocked the Hammers out, winning 4–0 in a replay a

Appearances & Goals 1935-36

	League		FA Cup		Total	
	Starts	Goals	Starts	Goals	Starts	Goals
BARRETT Jim	40	2	2	0	42	2
BICKNELL Charlie	7	0	0	0	7	0
BLORE Vincent	9	0	0	0	9	0
CHALKLEY Alfred	32	0	2	0	34	0
COCKROFT Joe	42	1	2	0	44	1
COLLINS Jimmy	1	0	0	0	1	0
CONWAY Herman	33	0	2	0	35	0
CONWELL Lawrence	6	1	0	0	6	1
DOWEN John	1	0	0	0	1	0
FENTON Edward	41	3	2	0	43	3
FOREMAN John	20	4	0	0	20	4
FOXALL Joseph	1	1	0	0	1	1
GOULDEN Len	38	15	2	0	40	15
LEWIS Harry	4	4	0	0	4	4
MANGNALL David	25	23	2	1	27	24
MARSHALL James	36	9	2	0	38	9
MORTON John	26	5	0	0	26	5
MUSGRAVE Joe	2	0	0	0	2	0
PARKER Reginald	2	0	0	0	2	0
RUFFELL James	30	10	2	1	32	11
SIMPSON Peter	20	9	2	0	22	9
TIPPETT Thomas	2	0	0	0	2	0
TONNER Arthur	1	0	0	0	1	0
WALKER Albert	41	0	2	0	43	0
WALKER Richard	2	0	0	0	2	0
own goal		3				3
Totals	**462**	**90**	**22**	**2**	**484**	**92**

Kenilworth Road. The league results were good, however, with six successive wins after Boxing Day including a 6–0 home win over Bury, where Harry Lewis claimed a hat-trick. In March there was a narrow 2–1 defeat to champions elect Manchester United, but this was followed up by two excellent victories. Before a crowd of 57,417 Spurs were beaten 3–1 at White Hart Lane and a week later Newcastle United were thrashed 4–1 at the Boleyn Ground. The final home game of the season against Charlton Athletic saw both teams with 50 points, with Charlton in second place and the Hammers just below in third. This crucial clash attracted an attendance of 41,254 to the ground. On the day Charlton proved to be the better team, winning 3–1 and going on to gain promotion. For West Ham, finishing fourth had been a good achievement and the 39 goals scored away from home could not be bettered by any other team in the Football League.

Football League - Division Two Final Table 1935-36

	P	HOME					AWAY					Pts
		W	D	L	F	A	W	D	L	F	A	
Manchester United	42	16	3	2	55	16	6	9	6	30	27	56
Charlton Athletic	42	15	6	0	53	17	7	5	9	32	41	55
Sheffield United	42	15	4	2	51	15	5	8	8	28	35	52
West Ham United	**42**	**13**	**5**	**3**	**51**	**23**	**9**	**3**	**9**	**39**	**45**	**52**
Tottenham Hotspur	42	12	6	3	60	25	6	7	8	31	30	49
Leicester City	42	14	5	2	53	19	5	5	11	26	38	48
Plymouth Argyle	42	15	2	4	50	20	5	6	10	21	37	48
Newcastle United	42	13	5	3	56	27	7	1	13	32	52	46
Fulham	42	11	6	4	58	24	4	8	9	18	28	44
Blackpool	42	14	3	4	64	34	4	4	13	29	38	43
Norwich City	42	14	2	5	47	24	3	7	11	25	41	43
Bradford City	42	12	7	2	32	18	3	6	12	23	47	43
Swansea Town	42	11	3	7	42	26	4	6	11	25	50	39
Bury	42	10	6	5	41	27	3	6	12	25	57	38
Burnley	42	9	8	4	35	21	3	5	13	15	38	37
Bradford Park Avenue	42	13	6	2	43	26	1	3	17	19	58	37
Southampton	42	11	3	7	32	24	3	6	12	15	41	37
Doncaster Rovers	42	10	7	4	28	17	4	2	15	23	54	37
Nottingham Forest	42	8	8	5	43	22	4	3	14	26	54	35
Barnsley	42	9	4	8	40	32	3	5	13	14	48	33
Port Vale	42	10	5	6	34	30	2	3	16	22	76	32
Hull City	42	4	7	10	33	45	1	3	17	14	66	20

CHARLIE BICKNELL

Full-back Charlie Bicknell was one of the most consistent players in the Football League.

While at Bradford City he made 224 consecutive league appearances and on joining West Ham he played in a total of 208 matches without a break. Charlie began his career with Third Division Chesterfield in 1927 where he played in 85 league and cup matches up until his £600 transfer to Bradford City in March 1930. He played for the Yorkshire club for six seasons; for four of these he was ever-present. After 254 appearances he joined West Ham in 1936, was made captain and went on that remarkable run of consecutive appearances until the outbreak of war in 1939. During the conflict he served as a Police Special but still found time to represent West Ham in regional football on 229 occasions. He skippered the side in 1940 when the Hammers won the War Cup by beating Blackburn Rovers 1–0 at Wembley.

After the war he played in a further 19 games in season 1946–47 before joining Bedford Town as their manager. He died in Cambridgeshire in September 1994 aged 88.

Season **1935-36** Football League - Division Two
Match Details

Manager **Charlie Paynter**   Final League Position **4/22**

	Date		Competition	Venue	Opponents	Results		Attendance	Position	Scorers
1	Aug 31	Sat	Div 2	A	Norwich City	L	3-4	29,779	16	Marshall, Morton, Ruffell
2	Sep 2	Mon	Div 2	A	Bradford Park Avenue	L	0-2	16,224	20	
3	Sep 7	Sat	Div 2	H	Nottingham Forest	W	5-2	27,566	14	Mangnall 3, Ruffell 2
4	Sep 9	Mon	Div 2	H	Bradford Park Avenue	W	1-0	17,709	11	Goulden
5	Sep 14	Sat	Div 2	A	Blackpool	L	1-4	22,082	14	Marshall
6	Sep 16	Mon	Div 2	H	Sheffield United	W	3-2	14,049	9	Goulden, Mangnall, Marshall
7	Sep 21	Sat	Div 2	H	Doncaster Rovers	L	1-2	26,431	17	Mangnall
8	Sep 28	Sat	Div 2	A	Bury	L	0-3	9,059	19	
9	Oct 5	Sat	Div 2	H	Barnsley	W	2-0	21,584	16	Mangnall 2
10	Oct 12	Sat	Div 2	H	Swansea Town	W	4-0	23,551	11	Goulden 2, Marshall, Lawarence (og)
11	Oct 19	Sat	Div 2	A	Plymouth Argyle	L	1-4	19,140	12	Mangnall
12	Oct 26	Sat	Div 2	H	Bradford City	D	1-1	20,703	14	Mangnall
13	Nov 2	Sat	Div 2	A	Newcastle United	D	3-3	22,873	13	Mangnall 2, Ruffell
14	Nov 9	Sat	Div 2	H	Tottenham Hotspur	D	2-2	40,245	15	Mangnall, Ruffell
15	Nov 16	Sat	Div 2	A	Manchester United	W	3-2	24,440	13	Fenton, Foreman, Simpson
16	Nov 23	Sat	Div 2	H	Hull City	W	4-0	21,114	11	Ruffell 2, Conway, Mangnall
17	Nov 30	Sat	Div 2	A	Fulham	L	2-4	23,444	11	Mangnall, Hindson (og)
18	Dec 14	Sat	Div 2	A	Charlton Athletic	D	2-2	32,170	13	Barrett, Goulden
19	Dec 21	Sat	Div 2	H	Port Vale	W	4-0	13,905	11	Goulden 2, Foreman, Mangnall
20	Dec 25	Wed	Div 2	H	Southampton	D	0-0	27,609	11	
21	Dec 26	Thu	Div 2	A	Southampton	W	4-2	19,347	10	Mangnall 2, Goulden, Sillett (og)
22	Dec 28	Sat	Div 2	H	Norwich City	W	3-2	24,438	8	Mangnall 3
23	Jan 4	Sat	Div 2	A	Nottingham Forest	W	2-0	14,035	7	Goulden, Ruffell
24	Jan 11	Sat	FAC 3	H	Luton Town	D	2-2	42,000		Mangnall, Ruffell
25	Jan 15	Wed	FAC 3 Rep	A	Luton Town	L	0-4	17,527		
26	Jan 18	Sat	Div 2	H	Blackpool	W	2-1	19,362	5	Foreman, Ruffell
27	Jan 25	Sat	Div 2	A	Doncaster Rovers	W	2-0	10,551	3	Lewis, Simpson
28	Feb 1	Sat	Div 2	H	Bury	W	6-0	26,204	4	Lewis 3, Cockroft, Morton, Simpson
29	Feb 3	Mon	Div 2	H	Burnley	D	0-0	12,212	3	
30	Feb 8	Sat	Div 2	A	Barnsley	W	2-1	13,458	3	Goulden, Morton
31	Feb 15	Sat	Div 2	A	Swansea Town	W	1-0	10,378	1	Mangnall
32	Feb 22	Sat	Div 2	H	Plymouth Argyle	W	4-2	19,518	2	Barrett, Fenton, Goulden, Morton
33	Feb 29	Sat	Div 2	A	Burnley	L	0-1	7,614	2	
34	Mar 7	Sat	Div 2	H	Manchester United	L	1-2	29,684	3	Goulden
35	Mar 14	Sat	Div 2	A	Tottenham Hotspur	W	3-1	57,417	3	Goulden, Marshall, Simpson
36	Mar 21	Sat	Div 2	H	Newcastle United	W	4-1	37,298	1	Marshall 2, Ruffell, Simpson
37	Mar 28	Sat	Div 2	A	Hull City	W	3-2	5,038	1	Goulden, Ruffell, Simpson
38	Apr 4	Sat	Div 2	H	Fulham	D	0-0	32,062	1	
39	Apr 10	Fri	Div 2	H	Leicester City	W	3-2	38,332	1	Fenton, Goulden, Simpson
40	Apr 11	Sat	Div 2	A	Bradford City	L	1-3	12,867	1	Morton
41	Apr 13	Mon	Div 2	A	Leicester City	D	1-1	24,892	3	Simpson
42	Apr 18	Sat	Div 2	H	Charlton Athletic	L	1-3	41,254	3	Simpson
43	Apr 25	Sat	Div 2	A	Port Vale	W	3-2	8,066	3	Mangnall 2, Foxall
44	May 2	Sat	Div 2	A	Sheffield United	L	2-4	16,461	4	Foreman, Marshall

Team Line-Ups

BARRETT Jim	BICKNELL Charlie	BLORE Vincent	CHALKLEY Alfred	COCKROFT Joe	COLLINS Jimmy	CONWAY Herman	CONWELL Lawrence	DOWEN John	FENTON Edward	FOREMAN John	FOXALL Joseph	GOULDEN Len	LEWIS Harry	MANGNALL David	MARSHALL James	MORTON John	MUSGRAVE Joe	PARKER Reginald	RUFFELL James	SIMPSON Peter	TIPPETT Thomas	TONNER Arthur	WALKER Albert	WALKER Richard	
5			2	6					4			10			8		7		11	9			3		1
5			2	6					4			10			8		7		11	9			3		2
5		1		6					4			10		9	8		7		11		2		3		3
5		1		6					4			10		9	8		7	3	11				2		4
5		1		6					4	7		10		9	8	11		3					2		5
5		1	2	6					4	7		10		9	8	11							3		6
		1	2	6	4							10		9	8		7		11				3	5	7
		1	2	6					4			10	8	9			7		11				3	5	8
5			2	6		1			4			10		9	8		7		11				3		9
5			2	6		1			4			10		9	8				11		7		3		10
5		1	2	6					4			10		9	8				11		7		3		11
5			2	6		1	7		4			10		9	8				11				3		12
5			2	6		1		8	4	7		10		9					11				3		13
5			2	6		1		8	4	7		10		9					11				3		14
5			2	6		1		8	4	7		10							11	9			3		15
5			2	6		1		8	4	7		10		9					11				3		16
5			2	6		1		8	4	7		10		9					11				3		17
5			2	6		1			4	7		10		9	8				11				3		18
5			2	6		1			4	7		10		9	8				11				3		19
5			2	6		1			4	7		10		9	8				11				3		20
5			2	6		1			4			10		9	8				11	7			3		21
5			2	6		1			4			10		9	8				11	7			3		22
5			2	6		1			4			10		9	8				11	7			3		23
5			2	6		1			4			10		9	8				11	7			3		24
5			2	6		1			4			10		9	8				11	7			3		25
5			2	6		1			4	7		10			8			11		9			3		26
5			2	6		1			4	7			10		8			11		9			3		27
5			2	6		1			4				10		8		7		11	9			3		28
5			2	6		1			4				10		8		7		11	9			3		29
5			2	6		1			4	7		10		9	8	11							3		30
5			2	6		1			4	7		10		9	8	11							3		31
5			2	6		1			4			10		9	8		7		11				3		32
5			2	6		1			4	7		10		9	8	11							3		33
5			2	6		1			4			10			8		7		11	9			3		34
5			2	6		1			4			10			8		7		11	9			3		35
5	2			6		1			4			10			8		7		11	9			3		36
5	2			6		1			4			10			8		7		11	9			3		37
5	2			6		1			4			10			8		7		11	9			3		38
5	2			6		1			4	7		10			8	11				9			3		39
5	2			6		1			4	7		10			8	11				9			3		40
5	2			6		1			4	7		10			8	11				9			3		41
5		2		6		1			4			10			8		7		11	9			3		42
5	2			6		1			4	7	9		10		8	11							3		43
5	2			6		1	3		4	7			10		8	11				9					44

1936-37
Story of the season

Beginning their **pursuit of promotion** the Hammers **beat Tottenham 2–1** at home on the opening day, but promptly lost the next three games.

One of these was a remarkable game at Newcastle where Hammers debutant Tudor Martin scored a hat-trick in a 5–3 defeat. Martin scored seven goals in eleven games and was then sold to Southend. The away form was causing concern; a 4–0 defeat at Coventry City was followed by a 5–0 thrashing at Fulham. The first away win came in November with a 2–0 victory at Southampton but more satisfying was the 3–2 victory at Tottenham in December. This preceded an unbeaten run of seven league games without defeat, which included a 5–1 home win over Bury.

Appearances & Goals 1936-37

	League		FA Cup		Total	
	Starts	Goals	Starts	Goals	Starts	Goals
ADAMS William	3	1	0	0	3	1
BARRETT Jim	11	1	0	0	11	1
BICKNELL Charlie	28	0	2	0	30	0
BLACK Robert	1	0	0	0	1	0
CHALKLEY Alfred	14	0	0	0	14	0
COCKROFT Joe	42	1	2	0	44	1
CONWAY Herman	7	0	0	0	7	0
CONWELL Lawrence	2	0	0	0	2	0
CORBETT David	4	0	0	0	4	0
CORBETT Norman	1	0	0	0	1	0
DELL Fred	2	0	0	0	2	0
FENTON Edward	28	1	2	0	30	1
FOREMAN John	8	0	0	0	8	0
FOXALL Joseph	25	10	2	0	27	10
GOULDEN Len	42	15	2	0	44	15
GREEN Tommy	22	3	2	0	24	3
GUEST William	3	1	0	0	3	1
HOLMES Jim	2	0	0	0	2	0
KIRKALDIE Jack	3	1	0	0	3	1
MARSHALL James	11	2	0	0	11	2
MARTIN Tudor	11	7	0	0	11	7
MORTON John	39	14	2	0	41	14
RUFFELL James	12	0	0	0	12	0
SIMPSON Peter	12	3	2	0	14	3
SMALL Sam	18	12	0	0	18	12
WALKER Albert	8	0	0	0	8	0
WALKER Charlie	34	0	2	0	36	0
WALKER Richard	27	0	2	0	29	0
WEARE Arthur	35	0	2	0	37	0
YOUNG Len	7	0	0	0	7	0
own goal		1				1
Totals	**462**	**73**	**22**	**0**	**484**	**73**

First Division Bolton Wanderers were the visitors in the FA Cup and after a goalless draw the Lancashire team won the replay 1–0. West Ham were now in fourth spot in the table and looking to overtake Leicester and Blackpool. Right-winger John Morton was in sparkling form and scored in each of the four-goal victories against Coventry, Doncaster and Southampton. In the remaining nine games the Hammers were unbeaten, but this gallant effort went unrewarded as they finished in sixth position, some seven points behind champions Leicester City.

Football League - Division Two
Final Table 1936-37

	P	HOME					AWAY					Pts
	P	W	D	L	F	A	W	D	L	F	A	Pts
Leicester City	42	14	4	3	56	26	10	4	7	33	31	56
Blackpool	42	13	4	4	49	19	11	3	7	39	34	55
Bury	42	13	4	4	46	26	9	4	8	28	29	52
Newcastle United	42	11	3	7	45	23	11	2	8	35	33	49
Plymouth Argyle	42	11	6	4	42	22	7	7	7	29	31	49
West Ham United	**42**	**14**	**5**	**2**	**47**	**18**	**5**	**6**	**10**	**26**	**37**	**49**
Sheffield United	42	16	4	1	48	14	2	6	13	18	40	46
Coventry City	42	11	5	5	35	19	6	6	9	31	35	45
Aston Villa	42	10	6	5	47	30	6	6	9	35	40	44
Tottenham Hotspur	42	13	3	5	57	26	4	6	11	31	40	43
Fulham	42	11	5	5	43	24	4	8	9	28	37	43
Blackburn Rovers	42	11	3	7	49	32	5	7	9	21	30	42
Burnley	42	11	5	5	37	20	5	5	11	20	41	42
Barnsley	42	11	6	4	30	23	5	3	13	20	41	41
Chesterfield	42	12	3	6	54	34	4	5	12	30	55	40
Swansea Town	42	14	2	5	40	16	1	5	15	10	49	37
Norwich City	42	8	6	7	38	29	6	2	13	25	42	36
Nottingham Forest	42	10	6	5	42	30	2	4	15	26	60	34
Southampton	42	10	8	3	38	25	1	4	16	15	52	34
Bradford Park Avenue	42	10	4	7	33	33	2	5	14	19	55	33
Bradford City	42	8	8	5	36	31	1	4	16	18	63	30
Doncaster Rovers	42	6	6	9	18	29	1	4	16	12	55	24

SAM SMALL

Small was a hard-working centre-forward who began his career in non-league football with Bromsgrove Rovers before joining Birmingham City in 1934.

In two seasons with the Midlands side he played in six league games before being transferred to West Ham in 1937. Making his debut against Bury in January 1937, he scored twice in the 5–1 home win. Sam became a regular in the side and by the time war brought a halt to league football in 1939 he had scored 30 goals in his 59 appearances. During the war years, playing in regional football, he managed 80 goals in 201 games. His most famous contribution to the Hammers history was scoring the goal that beat Blackburn Rovers 1–0 in the 1940 War Cup Final. Sam played for two seasons after the war ended before joining Brighton in March 1948, where he played in 38 games without scoring. He died in Birmingham in December 1993 aged 81.

Season **1936-37** Football League - Division Two
Match Details

Manager **Charlie Paynter**   Final League Position **6/22**

	Date		Competition	Venue	Opponents	Results		Attendance	Position	Scorers
1	Aug 29	Sat	Div 2	H	Tottenham Hotspur	W	2-1	31,906	4	Goulden 2
2	Aug 31	Mon	Div 2	H	Newcastle United	L	0-2	21,854	13	
3	Sep 5	Sat	Div 2	A	Blackpool	L	0-1	20,671	17	
4	Sep 9	Wed	Div 2	A	Newcastle United	L	3-5	23,560	19	Martin 3
5	Sep 12	Sat	Div 2	H	Blackburn Rovers	W	3-1	22,520	16	Goulden, Martin, Morton
6	Sep 14	Mon	Div 2	A	Sheffield United	L	0-2	14,676	20	
7	Sep 19	Sat	Div 2	A	Bury	D	1-1	17,700	19	Martin
8	Sep 26	Sat	Div 2	H	Leicester City	W	4-1	24,286	15	Marshall 2, Goulden, Martin
9	Oct 3	Sat	Div 2	A	Nottingham Forest	L	0-1	20,326	16	
10	Oct 10	Sat	Div 2	A	Norwich City	D	3-3	16,350	16	Barrett, Cockroft, Martin
11	Oct 17	Sat	Div 2	H	Plymouth Argyle	D	1-1	24,306	17	Morton
12	Oct 24	Sat	Div 2	A	Coventry City	L	0-4	28,154	20	
13	Oct 31	Sat	Div 2	H	Doncaster Rovers	W	1-0	12,814	17	Guest
14	Nov 7	Sat	Div 2	A	Fulham	L	0-5	22,281	19	
15	Nov 14	Sat	Div 2	H	Burnley	L	0-2	19,464	19	
16	Nov 21	Sat	Div 2	A	Southampton	W	2-0	17,587	19	Adams, Foxall
17	Nov 28	Sat	Div 2	H	Swansea Town	W	2-0	16,615	16	Foxall, Goulden
18	Dec 5	Sat	Div 2	A	Bradford City	L	1-2	5,821	17	Goulden
19	Dec 19	Sat	Div 2	A	Chesterfield	D	1-1	9,918	17	Morton
20	Dec 25	Fri	Div 2	A	Bradford Park Avenue	L	1-2	17,203	19	Green
21	Dec 26	Sat	Div 2	A	Tottenham Hotspur	W	3-2	34,196	17	Simpson 2, Foxall
22	Dec 28	Mon	Div 2	H	Bradford Park Avenue	W	1-0	12,901	13	Morton
23	Jan 2	Sat	Div 2	H	Blackpool	W	3-0	26,229	12	Foxall, Simpson, Blair (og)
24	Jan 9	Sat	Div 2	A	Blackburn Rovers	W	2-1	9,240	12	Goulden, Morton
25	Jan 16	Sat	FAC 3	H	Bolton Wanderers	D	0-0	42,300		
26	Jan 20	Wed	FAC 3 Rep	A	Bolton Wanderers	L	0-1	21,539		
27	Jan 23	Sat	Div 2	H	Bury	W	5-1	18,770	11	Small 2, Fenton, Foxall, Goulden
28	Feb 4	Thu	Div 2	A	Leicester City	D	2-2	12,541	11	Goulden, Small
29	Feb 6	Sat	Div 2	H	Nottingham Forest	D	2-2	26,068	11	Morton 2
30	Feb 13	Sat	Div 2	H	Norwich City	W	4-1	23,976	10	Foxall 2, Morton 2
31	Feb 20	Sat	Div 2	A	Plymouth Argyle	L	0-2	19,230	11	
32	Feb 27	Sat	Div 2	H	Coventry City	W	4-0	20,644	10	Foxall, Green, Morton, Small
33	Mar 6	Sat	Div 2	A	Doncaster Rovers	W	4-1	8,079	9	Foxall, Goulden, Morton, Small
34	Mar 13	Sat	Div 2	H	Fulham	D	3-3	29,405	9	Goulden, Morton, Small
35	Mar 20	Sat	Div 2	A	Burnley	L	1-2	8,455	10	Small
36	Mar 26	Fri	Div 2	H	Barnsley	D	0-0	28,967	10	
37	Mar 27	Sat	Div 2	H	Southampton	W	4-0	20,277	9	Goulden 2, Morton, Small
38	Mar 29	Mon	Div 2	A	Barnsley	D	0-0	21,718	8	
39	Apr 3	Sat	Div 2	A	Swansea Town	D	0-0	10,077	9	
40	Apr 10	Sat	Div 2	H	Bradford City	W	4-1	15,802	8	Small 2, Foxall, Goulden
41	Apr 17	Sat	Div 2	A	Aston Villa	W	2-0	19,908	7	Kirkcaldie, Small
42	Apr 24	Sat	Div 2	H	Chesterfield	D	1-1	16,353	7	Small
43	Apr 26	Mon	Div 2	H	Aston Villa	W	2-1	11,558	6	Goulden, Green
44	May 1	Sat	Div 2	H	Sheffield United	W	1-0	10,068	6	Morton

Team Line-Ups

ADAMS William	BARRETT Jim	BICKNELL Charlie	BLACK Robert	CHALKLEY Alfred	COCKROFT Joe	CONWAY Herman	CONWELL Lawrence	CORBETT David	CORBETT Norman	DELL Fred	FENTON Edward	FOREMAN John	FOXALL Joseph	GOULDEN Len	GREEN Tommy	GUEST William	HOLMES Jim	KIRKALDIE Jack	MARSHALL James	MARTIN Tudor	MORTON John	RUFFELL James	SIMPSON Peter	SMALL Sam	WALKER Albert	WALKER Charlie	WALKER Richard	WEARE Arthur	YOUNG Len	
5				2	6	1					4			10					8		7	11	9		3					1
5				2	6	1					4		9	10					8		7	11			3					2
				2	6	1					4			10		5			8		7	11	9		3					3
				2	6	1					4			10		5			8	9	7	11			3					4
5				2	6	1					4			10					8	9	7	11			3					5
5				2	6	1		8			4			10						9	7	11			3					6
5				2	6	1	8					7		10						9		11			3				4	7
5				2	6							7		10					8	9		11			3		1		4	8
5				2	6							7		10					8	9		11			3		1		4	9
5				2	6				4			7		10					8	9		11			3		1			10
5				2	6				4			7		10					8	9		11			3		1			11
5				2	6			8						10		11				9	7				3		1		4	12
	2				6					4		7	9	10		11			8						3		1		5	13
	2				6					4		7		10		11			8	9					3		1		5	14
5	2				6		8							10						9		11			3		1		4	15
4	2				6							7		10					8			11		9	3	5	1			16
4	2				6							7	11	10					8					9	3	5	1			17
4	2				6							7		10			8					11		9	3	5	1			18
	2				6						4	7		10			8					11		9	3	5	1			19
	2				6						4	7		10			8					11		9	3	5	1			20
	2				6						4	7		10			8					11		9	3	5	1			21
	2				6						4	7		10			8					11		9	3	5	1			22
	2				6						4	7		10			8					11		9	3	5	1			23
	2				6						4	7		10					8			11		9	3	5	1			24
	2				6						4	7		10			8					11		9	3	5	1			25
	2				6						4	7		10			8					11		9	3	5	1			26
	2				6						4	7		10			8						11	9	3	5	1			27
	2				6						4	7		10							8	11		9	3	5	1			28
	2	4			6									10							8	11		9	3	5	1			29
	2				6						4	7		10			8					11		9	3	5	1			30
	2				6						4	7		10			8					11	3	9		5	1			31
	2				6						4	7		10			8					11		9	3	5	1			32
	2				6						4	7		10			8					11		9	3	5	1			33
	2				6						4	7		10			8					11		9	3	5	1			34
	2				6						4			10			8				7	11		9	3	5	1			35
	2				6						4			10			8					11	7	9	3	5	1			36
	2				6						4			10			8	7				11		9	3	5	1			37
	2				6						4			10			8	7				11		9	3	5	1			38
	2				6						4	7		10			8					11		9	3	5	1			39
	2				6						4			10			8					11		9	3	5	1			40
	2				6						4			10			8	7				11		9	3	5	1			41
	2				6						4	7		10			8					11		9	3	5	1			42
	2				6						4	7		10			8					11		9	3	5	1			43
	2				6					4		7		10			8					11		9	3	5	1			44

1937-38
Story of the season

The big talking point as the season began was the signing of Scottish forward **Archie Macaulay** from Glasgow Rangers.

He was soon on the score sheet in the 3–1 home win against Bradford Park Avenue. More effort was shown on opponents' grounds as there were favourable draws at Swansea, Stockport and Southampton. At home the goals flowed, with Chesterfield beaten 5–0 and Barnsley 4–1. This fine home form drew an attendance of 40,547 for the visit of Coventry City in November but the teams played out a 0–0 stalemate. In contrast, a thriller at Bury in December saw the Hammers lose 4–3 before a sparse attendance of 4,724.

Appearances & Goals 1937-38

	League		FA Cup		Total	
	Starts	Goals	Starts	Goals	Starts	Goals
ATTWELL Reg	1	0	0	0	1	0
BARRETT Jim	8	1	0	0	8	1
BICKNELL Charlie	42	0	1	0	43	0
BLACK Robert	1	0	0	0	1	0
COCKROFT Joe	38	0	1	0	39	0
CONWAY Herman	20	0	1	0	21	0
CORBETT Norman	6	0	0	0	6	0
DELL Fred	2	0	0	0	2	0
FENTON Benny	3	0	0	0	3	0
FENTON Edward	32	3	1	0	33	3
FORDE Steve	6	0	0	0	6	0
FOXALL Joseph	36	10	0	0	36	10
GOULDEN Len	35	9	1	0	36	9
GREEN Tommy	15	2	1	0	16	2
KIRKALDIE Jack	6	0	1	0	7	0
MACAULAY Archibald	39	10	0	0	39	10
MORTON John	39	3	1	0	40	3
ROBERTS Bill	1	0	0	0	1	0
SMALL Sam	18	7	0	0	18	7
TURNER Charlie	6	0	0	0	6	0
WALKER Albert	1	0	0	0	1	0
WALKER Charlie	35	0	1	0	36	0
WALKER Richard	32	0	1	0	33	0
WEARE Arthur	22	0	0	0	22	0
WILLIAMS Rod	9	5	1	0	10	5
WOOD John	8	0	0	0	8	0
YOUNG Len	1	0	0	0	1	0
own goal		3				3
Totals	**462**	**53**	**11**	**0**	**473**	**53**

or the fourth successive season West Ham were beaten at
ne first attempt in the FA Cup. On this occasion it was
irst Division side Preston North End who won 3–0 at
'eepdale. The team were hovering in mid-table, winning at
ome but without an away win. Finishing the season on a
igh note, the Boleyn men had a good 1–0 victory over
Manchester United, the league leaders. Then on the final
ay the Hammers at last recorded their first away win of the
eason by beating Chesterfield 1–0 at Saltergate. A final
lace of ninth was achieved, but only registering one away
in was a huge cause for concern.

ARCHIE MACAULAY

**After service with Glasgow Rangers, where
he won a League Championship medal in
1935, Archie joined West Ham in 1937.**

The inside-forward made his debut in the 2–0
defeat at Aston Villa in August, and over the
next two seasons until the outbreak of war he
played in 75 league games, scoring 26 goals.
He was a key figure in the West Ham team
that won the Football League War Cup in
1940. After hostilities had ceased he spent a
couple of seasons with the Hammers before
being transferred to Brentford, where he
played 26 games in the First Division. He then
moved on to Arsenal, winning a League
Championship medal in his first season, and
played for Great Britain against the Rest of
the World in 1947. After making 103
appearances for the Gunners he finished his
playing career with Fulham, playing in 49
games. Archie then went into management
and guided Third Division Norwich City to the
FA Cup semi-final in 1959. He later had spells
as manager at West Bromwich Albion and
Brighton & Hove Albion. Archie died in June
1993 aged 77.

Football League - Division Two Final Table 1937-38

	P	HOME					AWAY					Pts
		W	D	L	F	A	W	D	L	F	A	
ston Villa	42	17	2	2	50	12	8	5	8	23	23	57
Manchester United	42	15	3	3	50	18	7	6	8	32	32	53
heffield United	42	15	4	2	46	19	7	5	9	27	37	53
oventry City	42	12	5	4	31	15	8	7	6	35	30	52
ottenham Hotspur	42	14	3	4	46	16	5	3	13	30	38	44
urnley	42	15	4	2	35	11	2	6	13	19	43	44
radford Park Avenue	42	13	4	4	51	22	4	5	12	18	34	43
ulham	42	10	7	4	44	23	6	4	11	17	34	43
Vest Ham United	42	13	5	3	34	16	1	9	11	19	36	42
ury	42	12	3	6	43	26	6	2	13	20	34	41
hesterfield	42	12	2	7	39	24	4	7	10	24	39	41
uton Town	42	10	6	5	53	36	5	4	12	36	50	40
lymouth Argyle	42	10	7	4	40	30	4	5	12	17	35	40
orwich City	42	11	5	5	35	28	3	6	12	21	47	39
outhampton	42	12	6	3	42	26	3	3	15	13	51	39
lackburn Rovers	42	13	6	2	51	30	1	4	16	20	50	38
heffield Wednesday	42	10	5	6	27	21	4	5	12	22	35	38
wansea Town	42	12	6	3	31	21	1	6	14	14	52	38
ewcastle United	42	12	4	5	38	18	2	4	15	13	40	36
ottingham Forest	42	12	3	6	29	21	2	5	14	18	39	36
arnsley	42	7	11	3	30	20	4	3	14	20	44	36
tockport County	42	8	6	7	24	24	3	3	15	19	46	31

Season **1937-38** Football League - Division Two
Match Details
Manager **Charlie Paynter**   Final League Position **9/22**

	Date		Competition	Venue	Opponents	Results		Attendance	Position	Scorers
1	Aug 28	Sat	Div 2	A	Aston Villa	L	0-2	50,539	22	
2	Aug 30	Mon	Div 2	H	Swansea Town	W	2-1	15,473	11	Fenton E., Foxall
3	Sep 4	Sat	Div 2	H	Bradford Park Avenue	W	3-1	22,467	7	Goulden 2, Macaulay
4	Sep 6	Mon	Div 2	A	Swansea Town	D	0-0	12,718	6	
5	Sep 11	Sat	Div 2	A	Stockport County	D	0-0	17,781	8	
6	Sep 13	Mon	Div 2	H	Chesterfield	W	5-0	15,010	4	Goulden 2, Small 2, Morton
7	Sep 18	Sat	Div 2	A	Southampton	D	3-3	19,478	4	Small 2, Foxall
8	Sep 25	Sat	Div 2	H	Blackburn Rovers	W	2-0	27,699	2	Foxall, Goulden
9	Oct 2	Sat	Div 2	A	Sheffield Wednesday	L	0-1	20,173	6	
10	Oct 9	Sat	Div 2	H	Fulham	D	0-0	33,294	6	
11	Oct 16	Sat	Div 2	H	Barnsley	W	4-1	27,291	5	Goulden 2, Foxall, Macaulay
12	Oct 23	Sat	Div 2	A	Luton Town	D	2-2	17,757	5	Small, King (og)
13	Oct 30	Sat	Div 2	H	Newcastle United	W	1-0	29,915	4	Morton
14	Nov 6	Sat	Div 2	A	Nottingham Forest	D	0-0	14,801	4	
15	Nov 13	Sat	Div 2	H	Coventry City	D	0-0	40,547	4	
16	Nov 20	Sat	Div 2	A	Tottenham Hotspur	L	0-2	47,000	5	
17	Nov 27	Sat	Div 2	H	Burnley	W	1-0	21,607	4	Williams
18	Dec 4	Sat	Div 2	A	Bury	L	3-4	4,724	6	Foxall 2, Williams
19	Dec 11	Sat	Div 2	H	Sheffield United	L	0-2	21,431	7	
20	Dec 27	Mon	Div 2	A	Norwich City	D	2-2	27,475	9	Williams 2
21	Dec 28	Tue	Div 2	H	Norwich City	D	3-3	17,087	8	Barrett, Green, Williams,
22	Jan 1	Sat	Div 2	H	Aston Villa	D	1-1	30,408	7	Cummings (og)
23	Jan 8	Sat	FAC 3	A	Preston North End	L	0-3	30,198		
24	Jan 15	Sat	Div 2	A	Bradford Park Avenue	L	1-2	8,611	9	Macaulay
25	Jan 22	Sat	Div 2	H	Stockport County	W	1-0	19,143	6	Macaulay
26	Jan 29	Sat	Div 2	H	Southampton	W	3-1	18,489	7	Foxall, Macaulay, Small
27	Feb 5	Sat	Div 2	A	Blackburn Rovers	L	1-2	13,082	9	Small
28	Feb 12	Sat	Div 2	H	Sheffield Wednesday	W	1-0	17,538	8	Macaulay
29	Feb 19	Sat	Div 2	A	Fulham	D	1-1	22,891	6	Goulden
30	Feb 23	Wed	Div 2	A	Manchester United	L	0-4	14,572	7	
31	Feb 26	Sat	Div 2	A	Barnsley	L	0-1	10,613	8	
32	Mar 5	Sat	Div 2	H	Luton Town	D	0-0	22,955	8	
33	Mar 12	Sat	Div 2	A	Newcastle United	D	2-2	22,361	9	Foxall 2
34	Mar 19	Sat	Div 2	H	Nottingham Forest	W	2-1	22,426	6	Macaulay 2
35	Mar 26	Sat	Div 2	A	Coventry City	D	1-1	22,154	6	Mason (og)
36	Apr 2	Sat	Div 2	H	Tottenham Hotspur	L	1-3	30,031	6	Morton
37	Apr 9	Sat	Div 2	A	Burnley	L	0-2	11,173	8	
38	Apr 15	Fri	Div 2	H	Plymouth Argyle	L	0-1	21,947	9	
39	Apr 16	Sat	Div 2	H	Bury	W	3-1	13,514	8	Fenton E., Green, Macaulay
40	Apr 18	Mon	Div 2	A	Plymouth Argyle	L	1-2	21,805	9	Foxall
41	Apr 23	Sat	Div 2	A	Sheffield United	L	1-3	20681	11	Fenton E.
42	Apr 30	Sat	Div 2	H	Manchester United	W	1-0	14,816	11	Goulden
43	May 7	Sat	Div 2	A	Chesterfield	W	1-0	7,202	9	Macaulay

Team Line-Ups

ATTWELL Reg	BARRETT Jim	BICKNELL Charlie	BLACK Robert	COCKROFT Joe	CONWAY Herman	CORBETT Norman	DELL Fred	FENTON Benny	FENTON Edward	FORDE Steve	FOXALL Joseph	GOULDEN Len	GREEN Tommy	KIRKALDIE Jack	MACAULAY Archibald	MORTON John	ROBERTS Bill	SMALL Sam	TURNER Charlie	WALKER Albert	WALKER Charlie	WALKER Richard	WEARE Arthur	WILLIAMS Rod	WOOD John	YOUNG Len	#
		2		6					4		7	10			8	11		9			3	5	1				1
		2		6					4		7		10		8	11		9			3	5	1				2
	5	2		6					4		7	10			8	11		9			3		1				3
	5	2		6					4		7	10			8	11		9			3		1				4
	5	2		6					4		7	10			8	11		9			3		1				5
	5	2		6					4		7	10			8	11		9			3		1				6
	5	2		6					4		7	10			8	11		9			3		1				7
		2		6					4		7	10			8	11		9			3	5	1				8
		2		6					4		7	10			8	11		9			3	5	1				9
		2		6				9	4		7	10			8	11					3	5	1				10
		2		6					4		7	10			8	11		9			3	5	1				11
		2		6					4		7		10		8	11		9			3	5	1				12
		2		6					4		7	10			8	11		9			3		1			5	13
		2		6					4		7	10			8	11		9			3	5	1				14
		2		6					4		7	10			8	11					3	5	1	9			15
		2		6					4		7	10			8	11					3	5	1	9			16
		2		6							7	10			8	11	4				3	5	1	9			17
4		2		6							7	10			8	11					3	5	1	9			18
		2		6					4		11	10		7	8						3	5	1	9			19
		2		6					4				10	7	8	11					3	5	1	9			20
4		2		6									10	7	8	11			3			5	1	9			21
4		2		6							7	10	8			11					3	5	1	9			22
		2		6	1				4			10	8	7		11					3	5		9			23
		2		6	1		9		4		7	10				11					3	5					24
		2		6	1		9		4		7		10			11					3	5					25
		2		6	1				4		7	10				11		9			3	5					26
		2		6	1				4		7	10				11		9			3	5					27
		2		6	1				4		7	10				11		9	5		3						28
		2		6	1						7	10				11		9	4		3	5					29
		2		6	1						8	10				7		9	5		3	4			11		30
		2		6	1				4				10		8	7					3	5		9	11		31
		2		6	1				4			9	10	7	8						3	5			11		32
		2		6	1	4						9	10	8	7						3	5			11		33
		2		6	1	4							10	8	9	7					3	5			11		34
		2		6	1	4	8					7	10		9	11				5	3						35
		2		1	6				4	3	7	10	8		9	11				5							36
	2		4	1	6		8			3			10		9	7				5					11		37
		2		6	1				4	3		10	8	7	9	11						5					38
		2		6	1				4	3	7	10	8		9	11						5					39
		2		6	1				4	3	7	10	8		9	11						5					40
4		2			1				6	3	7	10	8		9	11						5					41
		2		6	1				4		7	10			9	8					3	5			11		42
		2			1	6			4		7	9			8	10					3	5			11		43

1938-39
Story of the season

After **losing the first two home games** to Blackburn Rovers and Sheffield Wednesday it was **a welcome relief** to travel away to Manchester City and win 4–2.

A rare away win was just the tonic needed as the Hammers scored 15 goals in the next three home games. Coventry City were beaten 4–1 and a hat-trick from Archie Macaulay came in the 6–1 thrashing of Tranmere Rovers. Swansea Town were next to face the onslaught and with Small and Morton getting two goals each the Welsh team were beaten 5–2. Away form had improved this campaign and following a draw at Nottingham Forest and a 2–1 win at Luton there was a splendid 4–1 victory at Sheffield Wednesday.

The FA Cup brought a 2–1 victory at Queens Park Rangers after which a home tie with Tottenham followed. There were thrills and spills at the Boleyn Ground as Spurs took a 3–1 lead with 30 minutes remaining. But in that final period

Appearances & Goals 1938-39

	League		FA Cup		Total	
	Starts	Goals	Starts	Goals	Starts	Goals
BANNER Arthur	1	0	0	0	1	0
BARRETT Jim	1	0	0	0	1	0
BELL Richard	1	1	0	0	1	1
BICKNELL Charlie	41	0	5	0	46	0
BURTON Stan	1	0	0	0	1	0
COCKROFT Joe	39	1	3	0	42	1
CONWAY Herman	21	0	0	0	21	0
CORBETT Norman	31	1	4	0	35	1
FENTON Benny	18	9	1	0	19	9
FENTON Edward	12	0	3	0	15	0
FORDE Steve	1	0	0	0	1	0
FOREMAN George	6	1	0	0	6	1
FOXALL Joseph	40	14	5	5	45	19
GORE Reg	5	1	0	0	5	1
GOULDEN Len	37	4	5	0	42	4
GREEN Tommy	3	1	1	0	4	1
HUBBARD Cliff	1	1	0	0	1	1
KIRKALDIE Jack	2	0	0	0	2	0
MACAULAY Archibald	36	16	5	2	41	18
MEDHURST Harry	21	0	5	0	26	0
MORTON John	31	7	4	1	35	8
PROUDLOCK George	4	1	0	0	4	1
SMALL Sam	19	11	4	0	23	11
TURNER Charlie	5	0	0	0	5	0
WALKER Charlie	41	0	5	0	46	0
WALKER Richard	38	0	5	0	43	0
WOOD John	2	0	0	0	2	0
WOODGATE Terry	4	0	0	0	4	0
own goal		1				1
Totals	**462**	**70**	**55**	**8**	**517**	**78**

an Foxall scored twice for the Hammers to take the tie to
replay. There were 50,798 inside White Hart Lane for the
play, which in a hard-fought tussle ended 1–1. The second
play took place at Highbury and goals from Foxall and
acaulay gave West Ham a 2–1 win. The fifth round saw
e Hammers travel to First Division Portsmouth, where
o second-half goals gave the home side a 2–0 victory.

the next ten league games the Hammers failed to score
seven occasions, but Nottingham Forest were beaten
0 and Norwich City were crushed 6–2 at Carrow Road.
here were four further wins before the season ended with
est Ham in a mid-table place of eleventh. The positives
d been a decent cup run and the seven games won on
pponents' grounds.

ootball League - Division Two
inal Table 1938-39

	P	HOME					AWAY					Pts
		W	D	L	F	A	W	D	L	F	A	
ackburn Rovers	42	17	1	3	59	23	8	4	9	35	37	55
heffield United	42	9	9	3	35	15	11	5	5	34	26	54
heffield Wednesday	42	14	4	3	47	18	7	7	7	41	41	53
oventry City	42	13	4	4	35	13	8	4	9	27	32	50
anchester City	42	13	3	5	56	35	8	4	9	40	37	49
hesterfield	42	16	1	4	54	20	4	8	9	15	32	49
ton Town	42	13	4	4	47	27	9	1	11	35	39	49
ottenham Hotspur	42	13	6	2	48	27	6	3	12	19	35	47
ewcastle United	42	13	3	5	44	21	5	7	9	17	27	46
est Bromwich Albion	42	15	3	3	54	22	3	6	12	35	50	45
est Ham United	**42**	**10**	**5**	**6**	**36**	**21**	**7**	**5**	**9**	**34**	**31**	**44**
ulham	42	12	5	4	35	20	5	5	11	26	35	44
illwall	42	12	6	3	44	18	2	8	11	20	35	42
urnley	42	13	3	5	32	20	2	6	13	18	36	39
ymouth Argyle	42	9	7	5	24	13	6	1	14	25	42	38
ury	42	9	5	7	48	36	3	8	10	17	38	37
radford Park Avenue	42	8	6	7	33	35	4	5	12	28	47	35
outhampton	42	9	6	6	35	34	4	3	14	21	48	35
wansea Town	42	8	6	7	33	30	3	6	12	17	53	34
ottingham Forest	42	8	6	7	33	29	2	5	14	16	53	31
orwich City	42	10	5	6	39	29	3	0	18	11	62	31
anmere Rovers	42	6	4	11	26	38	0	1	20	13	61	17

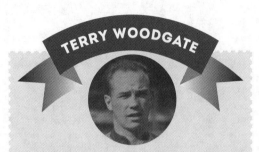

TERRY WOODGATE

Flying right-winger Woodgate came to West
Ham in 1939 and made his debut against
Bradford Park Avenue in April of that year.

He played in three league games that season
before the war interrupted his career. During
the conflict he served with the Essex Regiment
but still found time to turn out for the
Hammers on 77 occasions. Against Plymouth
Argyle in February 1946 he scored a hat-trick
within seven minutes in the 7–0 victory.

When league football resumed after the war
he became a regular in the side and played
for a further seven seasons. After playing in a
total of 275 league and cup games, scoring 52
goals, he was transferred to Peterborough in
March 1954. After retiring as a player he
became a publican in Cambridgeshire. Terry
passed away in April 1985 aged 65.

Season **1938-39** Football League - Division Two
Match Details

Manager **Charlie Paynter**   Final League Position **11/22**

	Date		Competition	Venue	Opponents	Results		Attendance	Position	Scorers
1	Aug 27	Sat	Div 2	A	Fulham	L	2-3	24,561	14	Macaulay 2
2	Aug 29	Mon	Div 2	H	Blackburn Rovers	L	1-2	15,222	15	Macaulay
3	Sep 3	Sat	Div 2	H	Sheffield Wednesday	L	2-3	21,586	18	Fenton B., Morton
4	Sep 7	Wed	Div 2	A	Manchester City	W	4-2	20,351	18	Foxall 2, Fenton B., Morton
5	Sep 10	Sat	Div 2	A	Bury	D	1-1	12,090	17	Small
6	Sep 17	Sat	Div 2	H	Coventry City	W	4-1	23,411	13	Fenton B. 2, Macaulay 2
7	Sep 19	Mon	Div 2	A	Blackburn Rovers	L	1-3	18,008	14	Fenton B.
8	Sep 24	Sat	Div 2	H	Tranmere Rovers	W	6-1	20,549	11	Macaulay 3, Cockroft, Corbett, Foxall
9	Oct 1	Sat	Div 2	A	Chesterfield	L	0-1	11,503	15	
10	Oct 8	Sat	Div 2	H	Swansea Town	W	5-2	20,992	12	Morton 2, Small 2, Foxall
11	Oct 15	Sat	Div 2	A	Nottingham Forest	D	0-0	17,449	12	
12	Oct 22	Sat	Div 2	H	Newcastle United	D	1-1	26,721	13	Ancell (og)
13	Oct 29	Sat	Div 2	A	Tottenham Hotspur	L	1-2	51,170	15	Foxall
14	Nov 5	Sat	Div 2	H	Norwich City	W	2-0	22,038	13	Fenton B., Macaulay
15	Nov 12	Sat	Div 2	A	Luton Town	W	2-1	18,331	9	Macaulay, Small
16	Nov 19	Sat	Div 2	H	Plymouth Argyle	W	2-1	22,946	7	Macaulay, Goulden
17	Nov 26	Sat	Div 2	A	Sheffield United	L	1-3	19,603	10	Foxall
18	Dec 3	Sat	Div 2	H	Burnley	W	1-0	18,759	8	Morton
19	Dec 10	Sat	Div 2	A	West Bromwich Albion	L	2-3	23,902	9	Macaulay, Small
20	Dec 17	Sat	Div 2	H	Southampton	L	1-2	14,476	11	Small
21	Dec 24	Sat	Div 2	H	Fulham	W	1-0	10,399	9	Macaulay
22	Dec 27	Tue	Div 2	H	Millwall	D	0-0	34,350	12	
23	Dec 31	Sat	Div 2	A	Sheffield Wednesday	W	4-1	29,081	11	Foxall 2, Morton, Small
24	Jan 7	Sat	FAC 3	A	Queens Park Rangers	W	2-1	22,408		Foxall, Morton
25	Jan 14	Sat	Div 2	H	Bury	D	0-0	18,165	12	
26	Jan 21	Sat	FAC 4	H	Tottenham Hotspur	D	3-3	42,716		Foxall 2, Macaulay [pen]
27	Jan 28	Sat	Div 2	A	Tranmere Rovers	D	2-2	8,456	13	Fenton B., Foxall
28	Jan 30	Mon	FAC 4 Rep	A	Tottenham Hotspur	D	1-1	50,798		Foxall
29	Feb 2	Thu	FAC 4 2nd Rep	N*	Tottenham Hotspur	W	2-1	50,468		Foxall, Macaulay
30	Feb 4	Sat	Div 2	H	Chesterfield	D	1-1	20,108	13	Macaulay
31	Feb 11	Sat	FAC 5	A	Portsmouth	L	0-2	47,614		
32	Feb 16	Thu	Div 2	A	Swansea Town	L	2-3	8,711	13	Green, Macaulay
33	Feb 18	Sat	Div 2	H	Nottingham Forest	W	5-0	15,472	12	Fenton B. 2, Foxall, Goulden, Macaulay
34	Feb 25	Sat	Div 2	A	Newcastle United	L	0-2	29,587	12	
35	Mar 4	Sat	Div 2	H	Tottenham Hotspur	L	0-2	20,832	15	
36	Mar 11	Sat	Div 2	A	Norwich City	W	6-2	15,027	13	Small 3, Foxall 2, Morton
37	Mar 18	Sat	Div 2	H	Luton Town	L	0-1	18,628	14	
38	Mar 25	Sat	Div 2	A	Plymouth Argyle	D	0-0	14,307	14	
39	Mar 27	Mon	Div 2	A	Millwall	W	2-0	9,955	13	Foreman, Proudlock
40	Apr 1	Sat	Div 2	H	Sheffield United	D	0-0	19,683	13	
41	Apr 7	Fri	Div 2	H	Bradford Park Avenue	L	0-2	23,336	14	
42	Apr 8	Sat	Div 2	A	Burnley	L	0-1	10,420	14	
43	Apr 11	Tue	Div 2	A	Bradford Park Avenue	W	2-1	9,177	13	Gore, Small
44	Apr 15	Sat	Div 2	H	West Bromwich Albion	W	2-1	13,624	12	Bell, Foxall
45	Apr 22	Sat	Div 2	A	Southampton	W	2-0	9,931	12	Foxall, Goulden
46	Apr 24	Mon	Div 2	A	Coventry City	D	0-0	12,127	12	
47	May 6	Sat	Div 2	H	Manchester City	W	2-1	21,547	11	Goulden, Hubbard

* Played at Highbury Stadium

Team Line-Ups

BARKER Albert	BARRETT Jim	BELL Richard	BICKNELL Charlie	BURTON Stan	COCKROFT Joe	CONWAY Herman	CORBETT Norman	FENTON Benny	FENTON Edward	FORDE Steve	FOREMAN George	FOXALL Joseph	GORE Reg	GOULDEN Len	GREEN Tommy	HUBBARD Cliff	KIRKALDIE Jack	MACAULAY Archibald	MEDHURST Harry	MORTON John	PROUDLOCK George	SMALL Sam	TURNER Charlie	WALKER Charlie	WALKER Richard	WOOD John	WOODGATE Terry	
	2		6		1		4					7		10				9		11			5	3		8		1
	2		6		1		4							10			7	9		11			5	3		8		2
	2		6		1		4	8				7		10				9		11			5	3				3
5	2		6		1		4	8				7		10				9		11				3				4
	2		6		1		4					7		10				8		11	9			3	5			5
	2		6		1		4	8				7		10				9		11				3	5			6
	2		6		1		4	8				7		10				9		11				3	5			7
	2		6		1		4	8				7		10				9		11				3	5			8
	2		6		1		4	8				7		10				9		11				3	5			9
	2		6		1		4					7		10				9		11	8			3	5			10
	2		6		1		4					7		10				9			8			3	5			11
	2		6		1		4	10				7						9		11				3	5			12
	2		6		1		4	8				7		10				9		11				3	5			13
	2		6		1		4	10				7						8		11				3	5			14
	2		6		1		4	10				7						8						3	5			15
	2		6		1		4	8				7		10				9		11				3	5			16
	2		6		1		4	8				7		10						11				3	5			17
	2		6		1		4					7		10				8		11				3	5			18
	2		6		1		4					7		10				8		11				3	5			19
	2		6		1		4					7		10				8		11				3	5			20
	2		6				4					7		10				8	1	11				3	5			21
	2		6				4					7		10	9			8	1	11				3	5			22
	2		6				4					7		10				8	1	11				3	5			23
	2		6				4					7		10				8	1	11				3	5			24
	2		6				4					7		10				8	1	11				3	5			25
	2		6				4					7		10				8	1	11				3	5			26
					1	6	10	4	2			9			8		7			11				3	5			27
	2		6				4					7		10				8	1	11	9			3	5			28
	2		6				4					7		10				8	1	11	9			3	5			29
	2		6				4	8				7		10				9		11				3	5			30
	2		6				4		11			7		10	9			8	1					3	5			31
	2		6						11			7		10	8			9	1				4	3	5			32
	2		6					8				7		10	9				1	11			4	3	5			33
	2		6				4	8				7		10	9				1	11				3	5			34
	2		6				4	8				7		10	9				1	11				3	5			35
	2		6				4					7		10				8	1	11	9			3	5			36
	2		6				4					7		10				8	1	11	9			3	5			37
	2		6						4		9	11		10				8	1			7		3	5			38
	2		6						4		9	11		8					1		10	7		3	5			39
	2		6						4		9	11		8					1		10	7		3	5			40
	2		6						4		9	11		8					1		10			3	5		7	41
	2		6						4		9	11		10				8	1					3	5		7	42
	2		6						4			8	11	10					1			9		3	5		7	43
10	2		6						4			7	11	8					1			9		3	5			44
3	2		6						4		9	7	11	10				8	1						5			45
	2		6						4			7	11	10					1			9		3	5		8	46
	2	7	6						4				11	10		9		8	1					3	5			47

1939-40
Hammers in Wartime

Preparations for the 1939/40 football season began in an **unreal atmosphere** as **war loomed once more.**

Appearances & Goals 1939-40

	League 'A' & 'C'		FL War Cup		Total	
	Starts	Goals	Starts	Goals	Starts	Goa
ATTWELL Reg	1	0	0	0	1	0
BARRETT Jim	31	7	2	0	33	7
BICKNELL Charlie	34	1	7	0	41	1
BROWN A.R. [Guest]	1	0	0	0	1	0
BROWN W [Guest]	1	0	0	0	1	0
BURKE [Guest]	1	0	0	0	1	0
CANN Bert [Guest]	4	0	0	0	4	0
CATER Ron	1	0	0	0	1	0
CHALKLEY Alfred	7	0	0	0	7	0
CHAPMAN Eddie [Guest]	2	0	1	0	3	0
COCKROFT Joe	17	0	9	0	26	0
CONWAY Herman	16	0	8	0	24	0
CORBETT Norman	6	0	2	0	8	0
CURTIS [Guest]	16	2	0	0	16	2
DRAKE Ted [Guest]	2	0	0	0	2	0
DUNN Richard	2	2	0	0	2	2
FENTON Edward	29	16	7	1	36	17
FLACK Doug [Guest]	2	0	0	0	2	0
FORDE Steve	2	0	2	0	4	0
FOREMAN George	34	36	9	6	43	42
FOXALL Joseph	34	15	9	4	43	19
GORE Reg	2	0	0	0	2	0
GOULDEN Len	23	5	6	2	29	7
GREEN Tommy	2	0	0	0	2	0
GREGORY Ernie	4	0	0	0	4	0
GRIFFITHS R. [Guest]	1	0	0	0	1	0
HAPGOOD Eddie [Guest]	2	0	0	0	2	0
HARRIS [Guest]	1	0	0	0	1	0
HOBBIS Syd [Guest]	2	0	0	0	2	0
HOWE [Guest]	1	0	0	0	1	0
JINKS Jimmy [Guest]	1	0	0	0	1	0
JONES [Guest]	1	0	0	0	1	0
JOY Bernard [Guest]	1	0	0	0	1	0
MACAULAY Archibald	6	3	7	5	13	8
MASSON [Guest]	4	0	1	0	5	0
McLEOD Jim [Guest]	1	0	0	0	1	0
MEDHURST Harry	7	0	1	0	8	0
PEARSON Harold [Guest]	1	0	0	0	1	0
RICHARDSON S. [Guest]	1	0	0	0	1	0
ROBINSON [Guest]	1	0	0	0	1	0
ROLES Albert [Guest]	1	0	0	0	1	0
SCOTT Laurie [Guest]	0	0	1	0	1	0
SIDEY Bill [Guest]	1	0	0	0	1	0
SMALL Sam	22	16	9	4	31	20
SMITH E.J. [Guest]	1	0	0	0	1	0
SMITH J. [Guest]	1	0	0	0	1	0
TAYLOR George	1	0	0	0	1	0
WALKER Charlie	27	0	8	0	35	0
WALKER Richard	27	2	9	0	36	2
WILKINS Ernie [Guest]	2	1	0	0	2	1
WOOD John	8	3	1	0	9	3
own goal		1		2		3
Totals	**396**	**110**	**99**	**24**	**495**	**134**

he Football League season was only three matches old when everyone's worst fears were realised and this time — like 1914 — the League programme was immediately abandoned. There was, of course, a different set of circumstances prevailing in 1939 and, fearing immediate mass air-raids, the Government introduced measures to restrict large gatherings at cinemas, race-tracks and football grounds.

Eventually, the restrictions were relaxed and, after a short period of friendly matches, the League began again in a regionalised format. And, as in World War One, West Ham enjoyed considerable success. In June 1940, they beat Blackburn Rovers 1-0 at Wembley to win the League War

Football League South 'A' Final Table 1939-40

	P	W	D	L	F	A	Pts
Arsenal	18	13	4	1	62	22	30
West Ham United	18	12	1	5	57	33	25
Millwall	18	8	5	5	46	38	21
Watford	18	9	3	6	44	38	21
Norwich City	18	7	6	5	41	36	20
Charlton Athletic	18	8	1	9	61	58	17
Crystal Palace	18	5	3	10	39	56	31
Clapton Orient	18	5	3	10	28	60	13
Tottenham Hotspur	18	5	2	11	37	43	12
Southend United	18	4	0	14	30	61	8

Football League South 'C' Final Table 1939-40

	P	W	D	L	F	A	Pts
Tottenham Hotspur	18	11	4	3	43	30	26
West Ham United	18	10	4	4	53	28	24
Arsenal	18	9	5	4	41	26	23
Brentford	18	8	4	6	42	34	20
Millwall	18	7	5	6	36	30	19
Charlton Athletic	18	7	4	7	39	56	18
Fulham	17	8	1	9	38	42	17
Southampton	17	5	3	10	28	55	13
Chelsea	18	4	3	11	33	53	11
Portsmouth	18	3	3	12	26	45	9

Cup — the semi-final against Fulham had kicked off at 6.40pm on a Saturday evening to accommodate war-workers — and although they never again tasted wartime Cup triumphs, Hammers were always well placed in the League. In seven competitions between 1939/40 and 1944/5, West Ham finished runners-up on five occasions, even though the format of the competitions was often changed. The nearest they came to further Cup glory was in 1945 when, having won their group from Queen's Park Rangers, Spurs and Aldershot, they found Chelsea too good for them in a White Hart Lane semi-final.

Although able to call on guests — and there were some very impressive ones, too, in the Arsenal trio of Drake, Hapgood and Joy, and Hearts' Tommy Walker — West Ham relied largely on their own players. Some 85 per cent of all wartime appearances were made by men who were already on Hammers' books, or who would be by 1945/46. One of the few guests was Manchester City's Northern Ireland international inside-forward Peter Doherty.

At first, Charlie Paynter had little difficulty in fielding a strong side. Several players, including Charlie Bicknell, were in the Special Constabulary, and a further group was serving in an Army unit based in East Anglia. Later, it got more difficult to field a regular side, but other clubs suffered far more than Hammers. In January 1941, Millwall's 50-year-old trainer, Bill Voisey, had to turn out against West Ham.

In the late summer of 1944, a VI flying bomb landed on the pitch at Upton Park, destroying a large part of the South Bank terracing and that end of the Main Stand. Forced to play away from home, Hammers strung together nine consecutive wins — and on their return to Upton Park in December, they lost 1-0 to Spurs. For 1945/46, Hammers found themselves in a more familiar 22-club Football League South, comprising pre-war First and Second Division clubs. Their longest journeys were to Plymouth, Nottingham and Derby and they gained 27 of their 51 points away from home in finishing a respectable seventh.

Nine pre-war players were in the side for the opening game, against Birmingham, and there was a special welcome for Charlie Walker, back home after a long spell in the Far East with the RAF. Joe Cockroft, though, would not return; he decided to remain with Sheffield Wednesday, for whom he had guested during the war. Before the season started, Len Goulden was transferred to Chelsea; and in March, George

Season **1939-40** Football League - Division Two
Match Details
Manager **Charlie Paynter**   Final League Position **Season abandoned – records expunged**

	Date		Competition	Venue	Opponents		Results	Attendance	Scorers
1	Aug 26	Sat	Div 2	A	Plymouth Argyle	W	3-1	18,000	Hubbard 2, Wood
2	Aug 28	Mon	Div 2	H	Fulham	W	2-1	15,000	Fenton, Wood
3	Sep 2	Sat	Div 2	H	Leicester City	L	0-2	13,400	Goulden, Hubbard

Season abandoned on outbreak of WWII : records expunged.

Football League War Cup

	Round	Date		Venue	Opponents		Results	Attendance	Scorers
1	R1:1	Apr 20	Sat	H	Chelsea	W	3-2	15,200	Fenton, Macaulay, O'Hare (og)
2	R1:2	Apr 27	Sat	A	Chelsea	W	2-0	14,897	Foreman, Small
3	R2:1	May 4	Sat	A	Leicester City	D	1-1	6,320	Macaulay
4	R2:2	May 11	Sat	H	Leicester City	W	3-0	15,500	Foreman 2, Foxall
5	R3	May 18	Sat	A	Huddersfield Town	D	3-3	7,550	Foreman, Foxall, Macaulay
6	R3 Rep	May 22	Wed	H	Huddersfield Town	W	3-1	20,000	Foreman, Foxall, Macaulay
7	R 4	May 25	Sat	H	Birmingham	W	4-2	18,500	Foreman, Goulden, Macaulay, Small
8	SF	Jun 1	Sat	N*	Fulham	W	4-3	32,799	Foxall, Goulden, Small, Brown (og)
9	F	Jun 8	Sat	N**	Blackburn Rovers	W	1-0	42,399	Small

* Played at Stamford Bridge   ** Played at Wembley Stadium

Football League War Cup trophy

Football League War Cup medal

eam Line-Ups

1	2	3	4	5	6	7	8	9	10	11	
Medhurst	Bicknell	Walker C.	Fenton	Walker R.	Cockroft	Burton	Macaulay	Hubbard	Goulden	Wood	1
Medhurst	Bicknell	Walker C.	Fenton	Walker R.	Cockroft	Burton	Macaulay	Hubbard	Goulden	Wood	2
Medhurst	Bicknell	Walker C.	Fenton	Walker R.	Cockroft	Burton	Macaulay	Hubbard	Goulden	Wood	3

1	2	3	4	5	6	7	8	9	10	11	
Conway	Bicknell	Walker C.	Cockroft	Walker R.	Masson	Small	Fenton	Foreman	Macaulay	Foxall	1
Medhurst	Bicknell	Walker C.	Corbett N.	Walker R.	Cockroft	Small	Fenton	Foreman	Goulden	Foxall	2
Conway	Bicknell	Walker C.	Corbett N.	Walker R.	Cockroft	Small	Macaulay	Foreman	Wood	Foxall	3
Conway	Bicknell	Walker C.	Barrett	Walker R.	Cockroft	Small	Fenton	Foreman	Wood	Chapman	4
Conway	Bicknell	Walker C.	Barrett	Walker R.	Cockroft	Small	Macaulay	Foreman	Goulden	Foxall	5
Conway	Bicknell	Scott	Fenton	Walker R.	Cockroft	Small	Macaulay	Foreman	Goulden	Foxall	6
Conway	Forde	Walker C.	Fenton	Walker R.	Cockroft	Small	Macaulay	Foreman	Goulden	Foxall	7
Conway	Forde	Walker C.	Fenton	Walker R.	Cockroft	Small	Macaulay	Foreman	Goulden	Foxall	8
Conway	Bicknell	Walker C.	Fenton	Walker R.	Cockroft	Small	Macaulay	Foreman	Goulden	Foxall	9

EMPIRE STADIUM

WEMBLEY

THE FOOTBALL LEAGUE

WAR

CUP FINAL

BLACKBURN ROVERS
V
WEST HAM UNITED

SATURDAY, JUNE 8TH, 1940

OFFICIAL PROGRAMME • SIXPENCE

otball League War Cup Final programme

Season **1939-40** Football League South 'A' Division
Match Details

Manager **Charlie Paynter**   Final League Position **2/10**

	Date		Venue	Opponents	Results		Attendance	Scorers
1	Oct 21	Sat	H	Crystal Palace	L	2-6	6,700	Foxall 2
2	Oct 28	Sat	A	Norwich City	L	3-5	2,000	Foreman 2, Foxall
3	Nov 4	Sat	H	Tottenham Hotspur	W	2-1	7,800	Goulden, Macaulay
4	Nov 11	Sat	A	Millwall	D	2-2	8,000	Dunn, Macaulay
5	Nov 18	Sat	A	Southend United	L	2-3	3,000	Dunn, Wood
6	Nov 25	Sat	H	Watford	W	5-0	5,400	Walker R. 2, Foxall, Goulden, Lewis (og)
7	Dec 2	Sat	A	Arsenal	L	0-3	10,000	
8	Dec 9	Sat	H	Charlton Athletic	W	4-3	6,850	Small 2, Barrett, Foreman
9	Dec 16	Sat	A	Clapton Orient	W	6-1	8,000	Foreman 2, Curtis, Fenton, Foxall, Small
10	Dec 25	Mon	H	Norwich City	W	4-1	6,800	Wood 2, Barrett, Foreman
11	Dec 26	Tue	A	Tottenham Hotspur	W	1-0	4,276	Foreman
12	Dec 30	Sat	H	Millwall	W	6-2	7,200	Foreman 3, Small 2, Foxall
13	Jan 6	Sat	H	Southend United	W	4-0	5,200	Foreman 2, Small 2
14	Jan 13	Sat	A	Watford	L	1-3	4,000	Foreman
15	Jan 17	Wed	A	Crystal Palace	W	3-0	896	Foxall 2, Curtis
16	Jan 20	Sat	H	Arsenal	W	3-0	8,000	Barrett, Fenton, Foreman
17	Feb 8	Thu	A	Charlton Athletic	W	5-2	1,200	Fenton 3, Foreman, Foxall
18	Feb 22	Thu	H	Clapton Orient	W	4-1	2,300	Foreman 2, Fenton, Foxall

Season **1939-40** Football League South 'C' Division
Match Details

Manager **Charlie Paynter**   Final League Position **2/10**

	Date		Venue	Opponents	Results		Attendance	Scorers
1	Feb 10	Sat	H	Tottenham Hotspur	W	2-0	7,500	Barrett, Foxall
2	Feb 17	Sat	A	Brentford	L	3-4	1,885	Barrett, Small 2
3	Feb 24	Sat	H	Portsmouth	W	4-1	1,800	Foreman 3, Small
4	Mar 2	Sat	A	Millwall	L	0-4	10,857	
5	Mar 9	Sat	H	Fulham	W	5-0	8,000	Fenton, Foreman 2, Foxall 2
6	Mar 16	Sat	A	Arsenal	W	3-2	10,731	Fenton 2, Foreman
7	Mar 22	Fri	A	Southampton	W	6-1	8,000	Foreman 2, Small 2, Fenton, Goulden
8	Mar 23	Sat	H	Charlton Athletic	W	2-0	8,000	Fenton, Foxall
9	Mar 25	Mon	H	Southampton	D	2-2	8,000	Fenton 2
10	Mar 30	Sat	A	Chelsea	W	10-3	10,000	Fenton 3, Foreman 2, Foxall, Small 4
11	Apr 6	Sat	A	Tottenham Hotspur	W	6-2	15,000	Bicknell, Foreman 4, Goulden
12	Apr 8	Mon	H	Arsenal	W	2-1	8,000	Foreman, Macaulay
13	Apr 13	Sat	H	Brentford	D	1-1	8,000	Foreman
14	Apr 29	Mon	H	Chelsea	W	4-2	5,500	Foreman 2, Goulden, Wilkins
15	May 13	Mon	A	Portsmouth	D	1-1	3,000	Barrett
16	May 27	Mon	A	Fulham	L	1-2	5,000	Barrett
17	Jun 3	Mon	H	Millwall	L	1-2	5,000	Foreman
18	Jun 5	Wed	A	Charlton Athletic	D	0-0	4,000	

eam Line-Ups

1	2	3	4	5	6	7	8	9	10	11	
Medhurst	Bicknell	Forde	Fenton	Walker R.	Cockroft	Small	Macaulay	Foreman	Goulden	Foxall	1
Medhurst	Bicknell	Walker C.	Fenton	Barrett	Corbett N.	Foxall	Macaulay	Foreman	Goulden	Wood	2
Gregory	Bicknell	Chalkley	Fenton	Barrett	Cockroft	Small	Macaulay	Foreman	Goulden	Foxall	3
Gregory	Bicknell	Chalkley	Harris	Barrett	Corbett N.	Small	Macaulay	Foreman	Dunn	Wood	4
Taylor	Bicknell	Walker C.	Fenton	Walker R.	Attwell	Foxall	Dunn	Foreman	Goulden	Wood	5
Pearson	Bicknell	Walker C.	Fenton	Sidey	Barrett	Small	Foreman	Walker R.	Goulden	Foxall	6
Cann	Bicknell	Walker C.	Brown W.	Barrett	Fenton	Small	Foreman	Walker R.	Goulden	Foxall	7
Cann	Bicknell	Walker C.	Fenton	Griffiths	Barrett	Small	Foreman	Walker R.	Goulden	Foxall	8
Cann	Bicknell	Walker C.	Fenton	Barrett	Corbett N.	Small	Curtis	Foreman	Goulden	Foxall	9
Cann	Bicknell	Chalkley	Fenton	Barrett	Cater	Foxall	Curtis	Foreman	Goulden	Wood	10
Flack	Bicknell	Chalkley	Fenton	Barrett	Walker C.	Small	Curtis	Foreman	Goulden	Foxall	11
Flack	Bicknell	Walker C.	Fenton	Walker R.	Barrett	Small	Curtis	Foreman	Goulden	Foxall	12
Medhurst	Bicknell	Walker C.	Fenton	Barrett	Cockroft	Small	Curtis	Foreman	Goulden	Foxall	13
Conway	Bicknell	Walker C.	Fenton	Barrett	Cockroft	Small	Curtis	Foreman	Goulden	Foxall	14
Conway	Bicknell	Chalkley	Fenton	Walker R.	Barrett	McLeod	Curtis	Foreman	Goulden	Foxall	15
Conway	Bicknell	Walker C.	Barrett	Walker R.	Cockroft	Foxall	Fenton	Foreman	Curtis	Wood	16
Conway	Bicknell	Walker C.	Barrett	Walker R.	Cockroft	Foxall	Curtis	Foreman	Fenton	Wood	17
Gregory	Bicknell	Chalkley	Barrett	Walker R.	Cockroft	Chapman	Fenton	Foreman	Curtis	Foxall	18

eam Line-Ups

1	2	3	4	5	6	7	8	9	10	11	
Conway	Bicknell	Walker C.	Barrett	Walker R.	Cockroft	Small	Fenton	Foreman	Wood	Foxall	1
Conway	Bicknell	Chalkley	Barrett	Walker R.	Walker C.	Small	Fenton	Foreman	Curtis	Foxall	2
Conway	Bicknell	Walker C.	Fenton	Walker R.	Corbett N.	Small	Curtis	Foreman	Goulden	Foxall	3
Conway	Bicknell	Walker C.	Barrett	Walker R.	Cockroft	Foxall	Small	Foreman	Fenton	Wood	4
Conway	Bicknell	Walker C.	Barrett	Walker R.	Cockroft	Small	Fenton	Foreman	Curtis	Foxall	5
Conway	Bicknell	Walker C.	Barrett	Walker R.	Cockroft	Small	Fenton	Foreman	Goulden	Foxall	6
Medhurst	Bicknell	Walker C.	Barrett	Walker R.	Cockroft	Small	Fenton	Foreman	Goulden	Foxall	7
Conway	Bicknell	Walker C.	Barrett	Walker R.	Cockroft	Small	Fenton	Foreman	Goulden	Foxall	8
Medhurst	Bicknell	Walker C.	Barrett	Walker R.	Cockroft	Small	Fenton	Foreman	Goulden	Foxall	9
Gregory	Bicknell	Walker C.	Barrett	Walker R.	Masson	Small	Fenton	Foreman	Curtis	Foxall	10
Medhurst	Bicknell	Walker C.	Corbett N.	Walker R.	Masson	Small	Fenton	Foreman	Goulden	Foxall	11
Medhurst	Bicknell	Walker C.	Barrett	Walker R.	Corbett N.	Foxall	Macaulay	Foreman	Curtis	Gore	12
Conway	Bicknell	Walker C.	Masson	Walker R.	Cockroft	Foxall	Fenton	Foreman	Macaulay	Gore	13
Conway	Bicknell	Walker C.	Barrett	Walker R.	Cockroft	Foxall	Wilkins	Foreman	Goulden	Hobbis	14
Conway	Bicknell	Walker C.	Barrett	Walker R.	Cockroft	Foxall	Wilkins	Foreman	Goulden	Hobbis	15
Conway	Bicknell	Roles	Barrett	Walker R.	Masson	Robinson	Chapman	Brown A.	Green	Foxall	16
Conway	Forde	Hapgood	Barrett	Walker R.	Green	Drake	Curtis	Foreman	Goulden	Foxall	17
Burke	Barrett	Smith E.	Hapgood	Joy	Howe	Drake	Richardson	Jinks	Jones	Smith J.	18

1940-41

Appearances & Goals 1940-41

	League		Football League War Cup		London War Cup		Total	
	Starts	Goals	Starts	Goals	Starts	Goals	Starts	Goal
BANNER Arthur	0	0	0	0	1	0	1	0
BARRETT Jim	21	5	5	2	6	0	32	7
BICKNELL Charlie	13	0	6	0	10	1	29	1
CHALKLEY Alfred	20	0	5	0	7	1	32	1
CHAPMAN [Guest]	10	1	0	0	1	0	11	1
COCKROFT Joe	3	0	0	0	0	0	3	0
COLLIER [Guest]	0	0	0	0	1	0	1	0
CONWAY Herman	13	0	0	0	0	0	13	0
CORBETT Norman	6	1	6	0	4	1	16	2
FENTON Edward	17	7	0	0	5	1	22	8
FERRIS A. [Guest]	1	0	0	0	0	0	1	0
FOREMAN George	23	24	6	3	10	7	39	34
FOXALL Joseph	25	14	6	1	10	2	41	17
GOULDEN Len	23	8	4	0	8	2	35	10
GREEN Tommy	0	0	1	0	3	0	4	0
GREGORY Ernie	6	0	4	0	5	0	15	0
HOBBINS Harold [Guest]	5	0	0	0	0	0	5	0
HOBBIS Syd [Guest]	6	1	6	0	9	2	21	3
JOY Bernard [Guest]	1	0	0	0	0	0	1	0
LEWIS [Guest]	13	1	0	0	3	0	16	1
MACAULAY Archibald	8	2	2	0	4	0	14	2
MEDHURST Harry	1	0	2	0	5	0	8	0
NIEUWENHUYS Berry [Guest]	6	2	1	0	1	0	8	2
OSBORNE J. [Guest]	1	1	0	0	0	0	1	1
PENNY R. [Guest]	1	0	0	0	0	0	1	0
PHYPERS Ernest [Guest]	1	0	0	0	0	0	1	0
SAVAGE R. [Guest]	6	0	1	0	2	0	9	0
SMALL Sam	22	3	6	4	10	5	38	12
WALKER Charlie	9	0	0	0	0	0	9	0
WALKER Richard	5	0	4	0	2	0	11	0
WALLER H. [Guest]	4	0	0	0	2	0	6	0
WHITTAKER Bill [Guest]	1	0	0	0	0	0	1	0
WOOD John	0	0	1	0	1	1	2	1
WOODGATE Terry	1	0	0	0	0	0	1	0
YORSTON Benny [Guest]	2	0	0	0	0	0	2	0
	274	70	66	10	110	23	450	103

oreman joined Tottenham. Before the end of the season, harlie Walker left to manage Margate, and at the final histle, Ted Fenton took up a similar post at Colchester nited, then in the Southern League.

here were compensations: Derek Parker, Ken Bainbridge, ric Parsons, Ken Wright and Eddie Chapman had all rogressed to the point where they would soon be allenging for a first-team place. Foreman's departure let in 1-year-old Mancunian, Don Travis, who scored four goals a match against Plymouth; and in the same game, Terry Voodgate emulated Syd Puddefoot's feat in World War ne football — a seven-minute hat-trick.

he FA Cup was re-started on a home and away basis up to nd including the quarter-finals and Hammers received a lum draw against Arsenal. Some 35,000, the largest Upton ark crowd since January 1939, saw the first-leg when the unners were shattered by four goals in the first 30 minutes. lammers' eventual 6-0 lead gave Arsenal an impossible isk in the second leg. In the fourth round, a 65,000 crowd Stamford Bridge saw Chelsea win 2-0., The return at pton Park began in a hailstorm and the gates closed on a 1,000 crowd. After only eight minutes they saw former lammers favourite, Len Goulden, break his collar-bone, ut Chelsea held on and Almeric Hall's goal was not enough save West Ham. The final match of the season was gainst Arsenal at White Hart Lane on 4 May 1946. After even years of war time football, everyone connected with e game could now look forward to a return to normality.

Wartime programme 1940-41 Arsenal v. West Ham United

Wartime programme 1940-41 West Ham United v. Tottenham Hotspur

ootball League South
inal Table 1940-41

	P	W	D	L	F	A	Pts
rystal Palace							26
/est Ham United	25	14	6	5	70	39	24

ere were 34 clubs in 'South' Division, with positions decided on goal average.

st Ham finished in second (behind Crystal Palave) with a goal average of 1.794

Season **1940-41** Football League South
Match Details

League competition was split into two regional leagues, one North and one South.
Many fixtures were unfulfilled and winners were decided on goal average rather than points.

	Date		Venue	Opponents	Results		Attendance	Scorers
1	Jul 31	Wed	A	Tottenham Hotspur	W	3-2	5,000	Fenton 2, Barrett
2	Sep 7	Sat	H	Tottenham Hotspur	L	1-4	3,000	Goulden
3	Sep 14	Sat	A*	Luton Town				
4	Sep 21	Sat	H	Luton Town	W	3-0	500	Barrett, Fenton, Small
5	Sep 28	Sat	A**	Clapton Orient	D	3-3	500	Foxall 2, Goulden
6	Oct 5	Sat	A	Chelsea	D	1-1	2,000	Goulden
7	Oct 12	Sat	H	Millwall	W	3-2	1,000	Fenton, Foreman, Foxall
8	Oct 19	Sat	A	Millwall	D	2-2	600	Foreman, Lewis
9	Oct 26	Sat	H	Southend United	W	11-0	5,000	Foreman 4, Foxall 3, Barrett, Fenton, Goulden, Macaulay
10	Nov 2	Sat	A	Southend United	L	1-3	1,000	Foxall
11	Nov 16	Sat	A	Brentford	W	2-0	400	Corbett, Goulden
12	Nov 23	Sat	H	Charlton Athletic	W	4-0	500	Foreman 2, Fenton, Foxall
13	Nov 30	Sat	A	Charlton Athletic	W	2-1	300	Foreman, Foxall
14	Dec 7	Sat	H	Chelsea	W	6-2	1,000	Foreman 2, Barrett, Foxall, Goulden, Macaulay
15	Dec 14	Sat	H	Clapton Orient	W	5-1	1,200	Foreman 3, Fenton, Goulden
16	Dec 21	Sat	A	Fulham	W	2-1	1,000	Foreman, Osborne
17	Dec 25	Wed	H	Arsenal	W	4-2	9,000	Foreman 2, Chapman, Foxall
18	Dec 28	Sat	H	Fulham	D	1-1	2,500	Foreman
19	Apr 14	Mon	H	Watford	W	2-0	2,000	Foreman, Foxall
20	Apr 26	Sat	H	Fulham	L	0-1	3,000	
21	May 3	Sat	H	Brentford	W	3-2	3,000	Foreman, Hobbis, Small
22	May 10	Sat	A	Reading	D	1-1	6,000	Barrett
23	May 24	Sat	H	Chelsea	D	3-3	2,500	Nieuwenhuys 2, Foxall
24	May 31	Sat	A	Queens Park Rangers	W	5-1	2,000	Foreman 3, Foxall, Goulden
25	Jun 2	Mon	H	Millwall	L	0-3	3,500	
26	Jun 7	Sat	H	Queens Park Rangers	L	2-3	2,100	Foreman, Small

* Fixture not played ** West Ham only fielded ten players

Football League War Cup

	Round	Date		Venue	Opponents	Results		Attendance	Scorers
1	R1:1	Feb 15	Sat	A	Norwich City	L	1-2	4,555	Barrett
2	R1:2	Feb 22	Sat	H	Norwich City	W	4-1	5,500	Foreman 2, Barrett, Small
3	R2:1	Mar 1	Sat	A	Southend United	L	1-2	3,500	Foxall
4	R2:2	Mar 8	Sat	H	Southend United	W	3-1	6,000	Small 3
5	R3:1	Mar 15	Sat	H	Arsenal	L	0-1	14,000	
6	R3:2	Mar 29	Sat	A	Arsenal	L	1-2	12,500	Foreman

London War Cup 'B' Division

	Date		Venue	Opponents	Results		Attendance	Scorers
1	Jan 4	Sat	A	Millwall	W	2-1	2,500	Foreman, Goulden
2	Jan 11	Sat	H	Millwall	W	2-1	3,500	Foreman, Hobbis
3	Jan 25	Sat	H	Arsenal	L	1-3	5,000	Bicknell
4	Feb 1	Sat	A	Tottenham Hotspur	W	2-1	4,690	Fenton, Small
5	Feb 8	Sat	H	Tottenham Hotspur	W	3-2	5,200	Foreman, Foxall, Small
6	Mar 22	Sat	H	Reading	D	1-1	4,000	Hobbis
7	Apr 5	Sat	A	Reading	L	1-4	5,069	Wood
8	Apr 12	Sat	H	Clapton Orient	W	8-1	3,000	Foreman 2, Small 2, Chalkley, Corbett N., Foxall, Goulden
9	Apr 19	Sat	A	Clapton Orient	W	3-2	1,000	Foreman 2, Small
10	May 17	Sat	A	Arsenal	L	0-3	7,365	

Team Line-Ups

1	2	3	4	5	6	7	8	9	10	11	
Conway	Chalkley	Walker C.	Barrett	Walker R.	Cockroft	Small	Fenton	Foreman	Goulden	Foxall	1
Medhurst	Corbett N.	Walker C.	Fenton	Barrett	Cockroft	Woodgate	Macauley	Small	Goulden	Foxall	2
											3
Conway	Chalkley	Walker C.	Fenton	Barrett	Cockroft	Chapman	Small	Foreman	Goulden	Foxall	4
Conway	Chalkley	Walker C.	Small	Fenton	Phypers	Foxall	Foreman	Goulden	Chapman		5
Conway	Chalkley	Walker C.	Fenton	Barrett	Lewis	Small	Macaulay	Chapman	Goulden	Foxall	6
Conway	Chalkley	Walker C.	Lewis	Walker R.	Barrett	Small	Fenton	Foreman	Goulden	Foxall	7
Conway	Chalkley	Walker C.	Fenton	Barrett	Lewis	Small	Chapman	Foreman	Goulden	Foxall	8
Conway	Savage	Walker C.	Fenton	Walker R.	Barrett	Small	Macaulay	Foreman	Goulden	Foxall	9
Conway	Chalkley	Savage	Fenton	Barrett	Lewis	Chapman	Macaulay	Foreman	Goulden	Foxall	10
Conway	Chalkley	Lewis	Ferris	Barrett	Corbett N.	Small	Fenton	Foreman	Goulden	Foxall	11
Conway	Bicknell	Chalkley	Savage	Barrett	Lewis	Chapman	Fenton	Foreman	Goulden	Foxall	12
Conway	Bicknell	Savage	Fenton	Barrett	Lewis	Chapman	Small	Foreman	Goulden	Foxall	13
Conway	Bicknell	Savage	Fenton	Barrett	Corbett N.	Small	Macaulay	Foreman	Goulden	Foxall	14
Conway	Bicknell	Chalkley	Savage	Barrett	Corbett N.	Small	Fenton	Foreman	Goulden	Foxall	15
Gregory	Bicknell	Chalkley	Small	Barrett	Fenton	Chapman	Osborne	Foreman	Goulden	Foxall	16
Gregory	Bicknell	Chalkley	Fenton	Barrett	Corbett N.	Chapman	Yorston	Foreman	Goulden	Foxall	17
Gregory	Bicknell	Chalkley	Small	Barrett	Fenton	Macaulay	Yorston	Foreman	Goulden	Foxall	18
Gregory	Bicknell	Chalkley	Waller	Barrett	Small	Foxall	Nieuwenhuys	Foreman	Goulden	Hobbis	19
Hobbins	Corbett N.	Chalkley	Waller	Barrett	Small	Foxall	Nieuwenhuys	Foreman	Goulden	Hobbis	20
Gregory	Bicknell	Chalkley	Waller	Walker R.	Lewis	Foxall	Small	Foreman	Macaulay	Hobbis	21
Hobbins	Bicknell	Chalkley	Barrett	Walker R.	Lewis	Foxall	Small	Foreman	Goulden	Penny	22
Hobbins	Lewis	Chalkley	Macaulay	Whittaker	Small	Foxall	Nieuwenhuys	Foreman	Goulden	Hobbis	23
Hobbins	Bicknell	Walker C.	Small	Barrett	Lewis	Foxall	Nieuwenhuys	Foreman	Goulden	Hobbis	24
Gregory	Bicknell	Walker C.	Small	Waller	Lewis	Foxall	Nieuwenhuys	Foreman	Goulden	Hobbis	25
Hobbins	Bicknell	Chalkley	Barrett	Joy	Lewis	Chapman	Nieuwenhuys	Foreman	Small	Foxall	26

1	2	3	4	5	6	7	8	9	10	11	
Medhurst	Bicknell	Savage	Small	Barrett	Corbett N.	Foxall	Macaulay	Foreman	Goulden	Hobbis	1
Gregory	Bicknell	Chalkley	Barrett	Walker R.	Corbett N.	Foxall	Small	Foreman	Goulden	Hobbis	2
Medhurst	Bicknell	Chalkley	Green	Barrett	Corbett N.	Foxall	Small	Foreman	Macaulay	Hobbis	3
Gregory	Bicknell	Chalkley	Barrett	Walker R.	Corbett N.	Foxall	Small	Foreman	Wood	Hobbis	4
Gregory	Bicknell	Chalkley	Barrett	Walker R.	Corbett N.	Foxall	Small	Foreman	Goulden	Hobbis	5
Gregory	Bicknell	Chalkley	Small	Walker R.	Corbett N.	Foxall	Nieuwenhuys	Foreman	Goulden	Hobbis	6

1	2	3	4	5	6	7	8	9	10	11	
Medhurst	Bicknell	Chalkley	Small	Barrett	Fenton	Foxall	Macaulay	Foreman	Goulden	Hobbis	1
Gregory	Bicknell	Chalkley	Small	Barrett	Fenton	Foxall	Macaulay	Foreman	Goulden	Hobbis	2
Gregory	Bicknell	Chalkley	Small	Fenton	Green	Foxall	Macaulay	Foreman	Goulden	Hobbis	3
Medhurst	Bicknell	Savage	Small	Barrett	Green	Foxall	Fenton	Foreman	Goulden	Hobbis	4
Gregory	Bicknell	Savage	Barrett	Walker R.	Green	Foxall	Small	Foreman	Fenton	Hobbis	5
Medhurst	Bicknell	Banner	Small	Corbett N.	Lewis	Foxall	Macaulay	Foreman	Goulden	Hobbis	6
Medhurst	Bicknell	Chalkley	Small	Walker R.	Corbett N.	Foxall	Wood	Foreman	Goulden	Hobbis	7
Gregory	Bicknell	Chalkley	Waller	Barrett	Corbett N.	Nieuwenhuys	Small	Foreman	Goulden	Foxall	8
Medhurst	Bicknell	Chalkley	Collier	Waller	Lewis	Foxall	Small	Foreman	Goulden	Hobbis	9
Gregory	Bicknell	Chalkley	Corbett N.	Barrett	Lewis	Foxall	Chapman	Foreman	Small	Hobbis	10

1941-42

Appearances & Goals 1941-42

	League		London War Cup		Total	
	Starts	Goals	Starts	Goals	Starts	Goals
ATTWELL Reg	9	0	2	0	11	0
BANNER Arthur	7	0	0	0	7	0
BARRETT Jim	10	1	1	0	11	1
BICKNELL Charlie	24	3	6	0	30	3
CHALKLEY Alfred	18	0	4	0	22	0
CHAPMAN [Guest]	7	6	0	0	7	6
CORBETT Norman	16	0	4	1	20	1
DUNN Richard	3	0	0	0	3	0
FENTON Edward	29	3	5	2	34	5
FORDE Steve	1	0	0	0	1	0
FOREMAN George	30	21	6	7	36	28
FOXALL Joseph	29	13	3	1	32	14
GORE Reg	0	0	2	0	2	0
GOULDEN Len	29	11	6	2	35	13
GREGORY Ernie	13	0	3	0	16	0
JOBLING Joe [Guest]	1	0	0	0	1	0
JONES [Guest]	1	0	0	0	1	0
LEWIS [Guest]	12	0	3	0	15	0
MACAULAY Archibald	15	4	0	0	15	4
MAHON J. [Guest]	1	1	3	2	4	3
MEDHURST Harry	13	0	1	0	14	0
NIEUWENHUYS Berry [Guest]	8	3	2	0	10	3
PRYDE Bob [Guest]	1	0	0	0	1	0
QUICKENDEN [Guest]	1	1	0	0	1	1
RICKETTS Horace [Guest]	1	0	1	0	2	0
SLIMAN A. [Guest]	1	0	0	0	1	0
SMALL Sam	26	11	5	1	31	12
TANN Bert [Guest]	1	0	0	0	1	0
WALKER Charlie	2	0	2	0	4	0
WALKER Richard	14	0	2	0	16	0
WALLER H [Guest]	1	0	1	0	2	0
WHATLEY William [Guest]	1	0	0	0	1	0
WOOD John	3	3	3	2	6	5
Totals	**328**	**81**	**65**	**18**	**393**	**99**

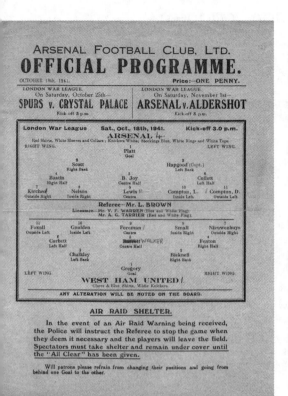

Wartime programme 1941-42 Arsenal v. West Ham United

Wartime programme 1941-42 West Ham United v. Aldershot

London League
Final Table 1941-42

	P	W	D	L	F	A	Pts
Arsenal	30	23	2	5	108	43	48
Portsmouth	30	20	2	8	105	59	42
West Ham United	**30**	**17**	**5**	**8**	**81**	**44**	**39**
Aldershot	30	17	5	8	85	56	39
Tottenham Hotspur	30	15	8	7	61	41	38
Crystal Palace	30	14	6	10	70	53	34
Reading	30	13	8	9	76	58	34
Charlton Athletic	30	14	5	11	72	64	33
Brentford	30	14	2	14	80	76	30
Queens Park Rangers	30	11	3	16	52	59	25
Fulham	30	10	4	16	79	99	24
Brighton & Hove Albion	30	9	4	17	71	108	22
Chelsea	30	8	4	18	56	88	20
Millwall	30	7	5	18	53	82	19
Clapton Orient	30	5	7	18	42	94	17
Watford	30	6	4	20	47	114	16

Season **1941-42** London League
Match Details

Manager **Charlie Paynter**   Final League Position **3/16**

	Date		Venue	Opponents	Results		Attendance	Scorers
1	Aug 30	Sat	H	Portsmouth	L	1-3	6,300	Foxall
2	Sep 6	Sat	A	Chelsea	W	8-4	6,427	Foreman 3, Foxall 2, Fenton E., Goulden, Small
3	Sep 13	Sat	A	Charlton Athletic	D	1-1	7,633	Foreman
4	Sep 20	Sat	H	Clapton Orient	W	3-1	4,500	Foreman, Foxall, Macaulay
5	Sep 27	Sat	A	Watford	W	8-0	4,000	Foreman 3, Foxall 2, Nieuwenhuys 2, Small
6	Oct 4	Sat	H	Aldershot	W	3-0	5,500	Foreman 2, Barrett
7	Oct 11	Sat	H	Millwall	W	4-2	7,500	Foreman 2, Bicknell, Nieuwenhuys
8	Oct 18	Sat	A	Arsenal	L	1-4	13,419	Foreman
9	Oct 25	Sat	H	Queens Park Rangers	W	2-0	5,300	Foreman, Macaulay
10	Nov 1	Sat	A	Reading	L	2-3	6,000	Bicknell, Macaulay
11	Nov 8	Sat	H	Brighton & Hove Albion	W	4-0	5,600	Foreman 2, Goulden 2
12	Nov 15	Sat	A	Brentford	W	5-0	5,000	Foxall 2, Small 2, Goulden
13	Nov 22	Sat	H	Crystal Palace	L	0-5	7,000	
14	Nov 29	Sat	A	Fulham	W	3-1	4,468	Small 2, Goulden
15	Dec 6	Sat	A	Tottenham Hotspur	D	1-1	8,493	Foxall
16	Dec 13	Sat	A	Portsmouth	L	0-1	6,000	
17	Dec 20	Sat	H	Chelsea	W	5-0	3,800	Fenton E., Foreman, Foxall, Goulden, Macaulay
18	Dec 25	Thu	H	Charlton Athletic	D	2-2	4,000	Bicknell, Foxall
19	Dec 27	Sat	A	Clapton Orient	L	1-3	3,000	Chapman
20	Jan 3	Sat	H	Watford	W	4-1	4,000	Wood 3, Foxall
21	Jan 10	Sat	A	Aldershot	W	5-1	3,500	Chapman 3, Forman, Quickenden
22	Jan 17	Sat	A	Millwall	W	3-1	4,000	Chapman, Foxall, Small
23	Jan 24	Sat	H	Arsenal	W	3-0	20,000	Forman 2, Goulden
24	Jan 31	Sat	A	Queens Park Rangers	L	1-2	5,000	Small
25	Feb 14	Sat	A	Brighton & Hove Albion	W	3-1	3,000	Foreman, Goulden, Small
26	Feb 21	Sat	H	Brentford	W	2-1	4,000	Goulden, Small
27	Feb 28	Sat	A	Crystal Palace	D	1-1	7,790	Small
28	Mar 7	Sat	H	Fulham	D	1-1	2,500	Goulden
29	Mar 14	Sat	H	Tottenham Hotspur	L	2-3	8,000	Fenton E., Goulden
30	Apr 25	Sat	H	Reading	W	2-1	4,500	Chapman, Mahon

London War Cup Group One

	Date		Venue	Opponents	Results		Attendance	Scorers
1	Mar 21	Sat	A	Brighton & Hove Albion	W	2-1	4,000	Foreman, Foxall
2	Mar 28	Sat	H	Arsenal	L	0-4	19,000	
3	Apr 4	Sat	H	Brighton & Hove Albion	W	6-2	4,000	Foreman 3, Mahon 2, Fenton
4	Apr 6	Mon	A	Arsenal	W	4-1	22,000	Goulden 2, Fenton E., Small
5	Apr 11	Sat	H	Clapton Orient	W	5-3	7,000	Foreman 2, Wood 2, Corbett N.
6	Apr 18	Sat	A	Clapton Orient	W	1-0	8,000	Foreman

Team Line-Ups

1	2	3	4	5	6	7	8	9	10	11	
Medhurst	Bicknell	Chalkley	Fenton E.	Walker R.	Corbett N.	Small	Macaulay	Foreman	Goulden	Foxall	1
Gregory	Bicknell	Chalkley	Fenton E.	Barrett	Lewis	Nieuwenhuys	Small	Foreman	Goulden	Foxall	2
Medhurst	Bicknell	Chalkley	Corbett N.	Walker R.	Fenton E.	Nieuwenhuys	Small	Foreman	Goulden	Foxall	3
Gregory	Bicknell	Chalkley	Small	Barrett	Fenton E.	Nieuwenhuys	Macaulay	Foreman	Goulden	Foxall	4
Medhurst	Bicknell	Chalkley	Corbett N.	Walker R.	Fenton E.	Nieuwenhuys	Small	Foreman	Goulden	Foxall	5
Gregory	Bicknell	Chalkley	Fenton E.	Barrett	Attwell	Small	Macaulay	Foreman	Goulden	Foxall	6
Medhurst	Bicknell	Chalkley	Fenton E.	Walker R.	Attwell	Nieuwenhuys	Small	Foreman	Goulden	Foxall	7
Gregory	Bicknell	Chalkley	Fenton E.	Walker R.	Corbett N.	Nieuwenhuys	Small	Foreman	Goulden	Foxall	8
Medhurst	Bicknell	Chalkley	Fenton E.	Barrett	Corbett N.	Small	Macaulay	Foreman	Goulden	Foxall	9
Gregory	Bicknell	Chalkley	Fenton E.	Walker R.	Attwell	Small	Macaulay	Foreman	Goulden	Foxall	10
Taylor	Corbett N.	Banner	Fenton E.	Barrett	Small	Nieuwenhuys	Macaulay	Foreman	Goulden	Foxall	11
Gregory	Bicknell	Chalkley	Fenton E.	Walker R.	Attwell	Small	Macaulay	Foreman	Goulden	Foxall	12
Barrett	Bicknell	Chalkley	Lewis	Fenton E.	Attwell	Nieuwenhuys	Small	Foreman	Goulden	Foxall	13
Medhurst	Bicknell	Chalkley	Fenton E.	Barrett	Corbett N.	Small	Wood	Foreman	Goulden	Foxall	14
Gregory	Walker C.	Whatley	Fenton E.	Walker R.	Corbett N.	Small	Macaulay	Foreman	Goulden	Foxall	15
Gregory	Bicknell	Jobling	Waller	Barrett	Lewis	Chapman	Fenton E.	Foreman	Goulden	Foxall	16
Medhurst	Bicknell	Banner	Fenton E.	Walker R.	Corbett N.	Small	Macaulay	Foreman	Goulden	Foxall	17
Gregory	Bicknell	Chalkley	Fenton E.	Corbett N.	Attwell	Wood	Macaulay	Foreman	Goulden	Foxall	18
Ricketts	Bicknell	Banner	Chalkley	Barrett	Corbett N.	Chapman	Small	Foreman	Fenton E.	Foxall	19
Medhurst	Corbett N.	Lewis	Fenton E.	Sliman	Attwell	Small	Wood	Foreman	Goulden	Foxall	20
Gregory	Bicknell	Lewis	Tann	Fenton E.	Macaulay	Quickenden	Chapman	Foreman	Goulden	Foxall	21
Medhurst	Bicknell	Lewis	Fenton E.	Walker R.	Macaulay	Small	Chapman	Foreman	Goulden	Foxall	22
Gregory	Bicknell	Walker C.	Fenton E.	Barrett	Macaulay	Small	Chapman	Foreman	Goulden	Foxall	23
Medhurst	Bicknell	Banner	Corbett N.	Fenton E.	Lewis	Small	Chapman	Foreman	Goulden	Foxall	24
Medhurst	Bicknell	Chalkley	Corbett N.	Fenton E.	Lewis	Small	Dunn	Foreman	Goulden	Foxall	25
Gregory	Bicknell	Forde	Pryde	Fenton E.	Lewis	Small	Dunn	Foreman	Goulden	Foxall	26
Medhurst	Chalkley	Banner	Bicknell	Walker R.	Corbett N.	Small	Fenton E.	Foreman	Goulden	Foxall	27
Medhurst	Bicknell	Lewis	Walker R.	Fenton E.	Attwell	Small	Jones	Foreman	Goulden	Foxall	28
Gregory	Corbett N.	Lewis	Attwell	Walker R.	Macaulay	Small	Fenton E.	Foreman	Goulden	Foxall	29
Taylor	Chalkley	Banner	Walker R.	Macaulay	Lewis	Chapman	Dunn	Foreman	Goulden	Mahon	30

1	2	3	4	5	6	7	8	9	10	11	
Taylor	Bicknell	Chalkley	Lewis	Fenton E.	Attwell	Small	Wood	Foreman	Goulden	Foxall	1
Gregory	Bicknell	Chalkley	Fenton E.	Walker R.	Corbett N.	Nieuwenhuys	Small	Foreman	Goulden	Foxall	2
Ricketts	Bicknell	Lewis	Waller	Barrett	Fenton E.	Mahon	Small	Foreman	Goulden	Gore	3
Gregory	Bicknell	Chalkley	Fenton E.	Walker R.	Corbett N.	Nieuwenhuys	Small	Foreman	Goulden	Foxall	4
Gregory	Bicknell	Walker C.	Corbett N.	Fenton E.	Attwell	Small	Wood	Foreman	Goulden	Mahon	5
Medhurst	Chalkley	Lewis	Bicknell	Corbett N.	Walker C.	Mahon	Wood	Foreman	Goulden	Gore	6

1942-43

Appearances & Goals 1942-43

	League		FL Cup		Total	
	Starts	Goals	Starts	Goals	Starts	Goals
AICKEN [Guest]	1	0	0	0	1	0
ATTWELL Reg	17	0	2	0	19	0
BANNER Arthur	4	0	0	0	4	0
BARRETT Jim	5	1	1	0	6	1
BARTRAM Sam [Guest]	1	0	0	0	1	0
BICKNELL Charlie	18	0	4	0	22	0
BROWN [Guest]	0	0	1	0	1	0
CHALKLEY Alfred	4	0	2	0	6	0
CHAPMAN [Guest]	2	0	0	0	2	0
CORBETT Norman	16	0	0	0	16	0
CORBETT Willie [Guest]	8	0	1	0	9	0
DAVIS C [Guest]	1	0	0	0	1	0
DUNKLEY Maurice [Guest]	1	0	0	0	1	0
DUNN Richard	11	12	3	2	14	14
FENTON Edward	21	3	0	0	21	3
FOREMAN George	28	23	6	7	34	30
FOXALL Joseph	16	8	2	0	18	8
GLADWIN G. [Guest]	1	0	6	0	7	0
GOULDEN Len	24	12	6	5	30	17
GREGORY Ernie	11	0	2	0	13	0
JONES [Guest]	1	0	0	0	1	0
KIPPAX F [Guest]	7	2	2	0	9	2
LEWIS [Guest]	25	0	6	0	31	0
MACAULAY Archibald	5	1	4	0	9	1
MAHON J. [Guest]	12	3	0	0	12	3
MEDHURST Harry	11	0	4	0	15	0
MUTTITT Ernie [Guest]	1	0	0	0	1	0
PAGE Albert [Guest]	2	0	1	0	3	0
RIORDAN J. [Guest]	1	0	0	0	1	0
SMALL Sam	25	8	4	1	29	9
TAYLOR George	4	0	0	0	4	0
TRIGG Cyril [Guest]	1	2	0	0	1	2
WALKER Richard	2	0	0	0	2	0
WALKER Tommy [Guest]	5	0	4	1	9	1
WALLER H. [Guest]	0	0	1	0	1	0
WATSON-SMITH [Guest]	1	0	0	0	1	0
WOOD John	13	3	3	1	16	4
WOODGATE Terry	1	0	1	1	2	1
WRIGHT Ken	1	0	0	0	1	0
own goal		2		1		3
Totals	**308**	**80**	**66**	**19**	**374**	**99**

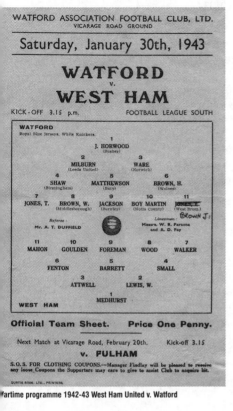

Wartime programme 1942-43 West Ham United v. Watford

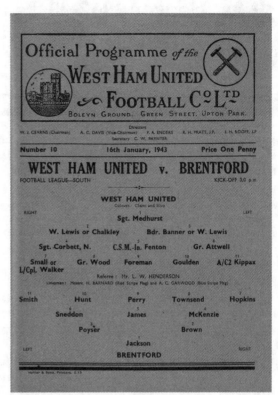

Wartime programme 1942-43 West Ham United v. Brentford

League South
Final Table 1942-43

	P	W	D	L	F	A	Pts
Arsenal	28	21	1	6	102	40	43
Tottenham Hotspur	28	16	6	6	68	28	38
Queens Park Rangers	28	18	2	8	64	49	38
Portsmouth	28	16	3	9	66	52	35
Southampton	28	14	5	9	86	58	33
West Ham United	**28**	**14**	**5**	**9**	**80**	**66**	**33**
Chelsea	28	14	4	10	52	45	32
Aldershot	28	14	2	12	87	77	30
Brentford	28	12	5	11	64	63	29
Charlton Athletic	28	13	3	12	68	75	29
Clapton Orient	28	11	5	12	54	72	27
Brighton and Hove Albion	28	10	5	13	65	73	25
Reading	28	9	6	13	67	74	24
Fulham	28	10	2	16	69	78	22
Crystal Palace	28	7	5	16	49	75	19
Millwall	28	6	5	17	66	88	17
Watford	28	7	2	19	51	88	16
Luton Town	28	4	6	18	43	100	14

Season **1942-43** League South
Match Details

Manager **Charlie Paynter**   Final League Position **6/18**

	Date		Venue	Opponents	Results		Attendance	Scorers
1	Aug 29	Sat	A	Portsmouth	W	5-4	8,000	Small 2, Foreman, Foxall, Goulden
2	Sep 5	Sat	H	Luton Town	W	3-1	6,370	Foreman 2, Barrett
3	Sep 12	Sat	H	Crystal Palace	D	2-2	7,000	Dunn, Goulden
4	Sep 19	Sat	H	Tottenham Hotspur	W	3-1	10,160	Foreman 2, Fenton E.
5	Sep 26	Sat	A	Clapton Orient	W	5-0	4,000	Dunn 2, Mahon 2, Foxall
6	Oct 3	Sat	H	Chelsea	L	0-1	10,200	
7	Oct 10	Sat	A	Brentford	L	2-6	7,000	Foreman, Foxall
8	Oct 17	Sat	A	Aldershot	L	1-5	7,500	Small
9	Oct 24	Sat	H	Watford	W	3-0	5,000	Foreman, Small, Wood
10	Oct 31	Sat	A	Fulham	W	3-2	5,500	Foreman 2, Bacuzzi (og)
11	Nov 7	Sat	A	Queens Park Rangers	L	2-5	6,852	Foreman, Foxall
12	Nov 14	Sat	H	Millwall	W	7-5	5,000	Goulden 3, Dunn 2, Foreman, Foxall
13	Nov 21	Sat	A	Brighton & Hove Albion	L	2-2	3,000	Foreman, Foxall
14	Nov 28	Sat	H	Portsmouth	W	2-1	7,000	Foxall, Wood
15	Dec 5	Sat	A	Luton Town	L	2-3	3,000	Foreman, Foxall
16	Dec 12	Sat	A	Crystal Palace	D	0-0	5,127	
17	Dec 19	Sat	A	Tottenham Hotspur	L	0-2	9,741	
18	Dec 25	Fri	H	Charlton Athletic	L	1-3	10,000	Goulden
19	Dec 26	Sat	A	Charlton Athletic	D	4-4	7,379	Goulden 3, Foreman
20	Jan 2	Sat	H	Clapton Orient	W	10-3	6,000	Dunn 3, Foreman 3, Trigg 2, Macaulay, Brooks (og)
21	Jan 9	Sat	A	Chelsea	W	3-1	8,585	Fenton, Foreman, Goulden
22	Jan 16	Sat	H	Brentford	W	4-1	7,500	Foreman 2, Kippax, Wood
23	Jan 23	Sat	H	Aldershot	W	6-3	8,000	Dunn 3, Small 2, Goulden
24	Jan 30	Sat	A	Watford	L	2-3	2,274	Goulden, Mahon
25	Feb 6	Sat	H	Fulham	W	2-1	5,200	Kippax, Small
26	Feb 13	Sat	H	Queens Park Rangers	L	1-3	6,000	Foreman
27	Feb 20	Sat	A	Millwall	D	3-3	2,000	Dunn, Fenton, Foreman
28	Feb 27	Sat	H	Brighton & Hove Albion	W	2-1	3,000	Foreman, Small

Football League (South) Cup Group One

	Date		Venue	Opponents	Results		Attendance	Scorers
1	Mar 6	Sat	H	Watford	W	6-1	2,000	Dunn 2, Foreman 2, Goulden 2
2	Mar 13	Sat	A	Brighton & Hove Albion	W	4-1	7,521	Foreman 3, Wood
3	Mar 20	Sat	H	Arsenal	L	1-3	22,000	Foreman
4	Mar 27	Sat	A	Watford	D	0-0	3,246	
5	Apr 3	Sat	H	Brighton & Hove Albion	W	7-1	5,500	Goulden 3, Foreman, Walker, Woodgate, Ball (og)
6	Apr 10	Sat	A	Arsenal	L	1-3	31,066	Small

Team Line-Ups

1	2	3	4	5	6	7	8	9	10	11	
Medhurst	Lewis	Banner	Corbett N.	Corbett W.	Attwell	Small	Dunn	Foreman	Goulden	Foxall	1
Gregory	Chalkley	Lewis	Corbett N.	Barrett	Macaulay	Mahon	Small	Foreman	Goulden	Foxall	2
Taylor	Bicknell	Lewis	Walker R.	Corbett W.	Attwell	Small	Dunn	Foreman	Goulden	Foxall	3
Gregory	Bicknell	Lewis	Corbett W.	Walker R.	Macaulay	Small	Fenton E.	Foreman	Goulden	Foxall	4
Medhurst	Bicknell	Lewis	Small	Fenton E.	Attwell	Mahon	Dunn	Foreman	Goulden	Foxall	5
Gregory	Bicknell	Lewis	Small	Barrett	Fenton E.	Mahon	Chapman	Foreman	Goulden	Foxall	6
Medhurst	Bicknell	Lewis	Small	Fenton E.	Corbett N.	Mahon	Dunn	Foreman	Goulden	Foxall	7
Gregory	Small	Lewis	Fenton E.	Corbett W.	Attwell	Mahon	Macaulay	Foreman	Goulden	Foxall	8
Medhurst	Bicknell	Attwell	Fenton E.	Corbett W.	Corbett N.	Small	Wood	Foreman	Goulden	Foxall	9
Medhurst	Bicknell	Banner	Small	Fenton E.	Corbett N.	Mahon	Dunn	Foreman	Goulden	Foxall	10
Gregory	Bicknell	Lewis	Fenton E.	Barrett	Aicken	Mahon	Small	Foreman	Wood	Foxall	11
Taylor	Attwell	Lewis	Fenton E.	Corbett W.	Corbett N.	Small	Dunn	Foreman	Goulden	Foxall	12
Medhurst	Bicknell	Banner	Small	Fenton E.	Lewis	Mahon	Chapman	Foreman	Wood	Foxall	13
Gregory	Bicknell	Lewis	Corbett N.	Corbett W.	Attwell	Small	Wood	Foreman	Goulden	Foxall	14
Gregory	Bicknell	Lewis	Corbett N.	Fenton E.	Attwell	Mahon	Wood	Foreman	Goulden	Foxall	15
Gregory	Bicknell	Macaulay	Corbett N.	Fenton E.	Attwell	Small	Wood	Foreman	Goulden	Mahon	16
Gregory	Small	Lewis	Fenton E.	Corbett N.	Attwell	Mahon	Dunn	Foreman	Goulden	Wood	17
Medhurst	Bicknell	Lewis	Corbett N.	Page	Barrett	Attwell	Wood	Foreman	Goulden	Kippax	18
Medhurst	Bicknell	Lewis	Corbett N.	Page	Barrett	Attwell	Wood	Foreman	Goulden	Kippax	19
Watson-Smith	Small	Lewis	Davis	Fenton E.	Macaulay	Walker T.	Dunn	Foreman	Goulden	Trigg	20
Bartram	Bicknell	Lewis	Fenton E.	Corbett W.	Mutitt	Small	Walker T.	Foreman	Goulden	Dunkley	21
Medhurst	Chalkley	Lewis	Corbett N.	Fenton E.	Attwell	Small	Wood	Foreman	Goulden	Kippax	22
Gregory	Bicknell	Lewis	Small	Fenton E.	Corbett N.	Walker T.	Dunn	Foreman	Goulden	Kippax	23
Medhurst	Lewis	Banner	Small	Fenton E.	Attwell	Walker T.	Wood	Foreman	Goulden	Mahon	24
Gregory	Chalkley	Lewis	Corbett N.	Fenton E.	Attwell	Small	Dunn	Foreman	Goulden	Kippax	25
Medhurst	Chalkley	Lewis	Corbett N.	Fenton E.	Attwell	Walker T.	Small	Foreman	Wood	Kippax	26
Taylor	Bicknell	Lewis	Small	Fenton E.	Riordan	Woodgate	Dunn	Foreman	Wright	Kippax	27
Taylor	Bicknell	Lewis	Gladwin	Jones	Attwell	Small	Wood	Foreman	Goulden	Foxall	28

1	2	3	4	5	6	7	8	9	10	11	
Medhurst	Chalkley	Lewis	Gladwin	Attwell	Macaulay	Small	Dunn	Foreman	Goulden	Foxall	1
Gregory	Chalkley	Lewis	Gladwin	Small	Attwell	Foxall	Walker T.	Foreman	Goulden	Wood	2
Medhurst	Bicknell	Lewis	Gladwin	Brown	Macaulay	Small	Dunn	Foreman	Goulden	Kippax	3
Gregory	Bicknell	Lewis	Waller	Page	Gladwin	Walker T.	Wood	Foreman	Goulden	Kippax	4
Medhurst	Bicknell	Lewis	Gladwin	Corbett W.	Macaulay	Woodgate	Dunn	Foreman	Goulden	Wood	5
Medhurst	Bicknell	Lewis	Gladwin	Barrett	Small	Walker T.	Macaulay	Foreman	Goulden	Wood	6

1943-44

Appearances & Goals 1943-44

	League		FL Cup		Total	
	Starts	Goals	Starts	Goals	Starts	Goals
ALDRIDGE [Guest]	1	0	0	0	1	0
ARMESON L. [Guest]	4	0	0	0	4	0
ATTWELL Reg	6	0	1	0	7	0
BICKNELL Charlie	26	0	5	1	31	1
CARDWELL Louis [Guest]	1	0	0	0	1	0
CHALKLEY Alfred	3	0	0	0	3	0
CHAPMAN [Guest]	1	0	1	0	2	0
CORBETT Norman	13	0	3	0	16	0
CORBETT Willie [Guest]	16	0	6	0	22	0
DEANS Tommy [Guest]	4	1	0	0	4	1
DUNKLEY Maurice [Guest]	10	1	0	0	10	1
DUNN Richard	9	6	2	1	11	7
FENTON Edward	18	3	5	2	23	5
FOREMAN George	30	22	5	2	35	24
FOXALL Joseph	12	4	1	0	13	4
GIBBS [Guest]	1	0	0	0	1	0
GILLESPIE Ian [Guest]	1	0	0	0	1	0
GIRLING Howard [Guest]	1	0	0	0	1	0
GOULDEN Len	28	11	6	2	34	13
GREGORY Ernie	13	0	1	0	14	0
HOBBIS Syd [Guest]	6	1	4	0	10	1
HUGHES William [Guest]	1	0	0	0	1	0
JONES [Guest]	20	0	5	0	25	0
LEWIS [Guest]	27	0	5	0	32	0
LOWES Arnold [Guest]	1	1	0	0	1	1
MACAULAY Archibald	4	2	1	0	5	2
MAHON J [Guest]	2	1	0	0	2	1
MEDHURST Harry	14	0	4	0	18	0
MUTTITT Ernie [Guest]	1	0	0	0	1	0
PARSONS [Guest]	1	1	1	0	2	1
SANDERS J. [Guest]	0	0	1	0	1	0
SMALL Sam	28	7	6	4	34	11
SMITH C [Guest]	0	0	1	1	1	1
TAYLOR George	1	0	0	0	1	0
WALKER Tommy [Guest]	6	0	0	0	6	0
WEAVER Sam [Guest]	0	0	1	1	1	1
WILSON Ron	1	0	0	0	1	0
WOOD John	16	11	1	1	17	12
WOODGATE Terry	1	0	0	0	1	0
WRIGHT Ken	1	0	0	0	1	0
own goal		2		1		3
Totals	**329**	**74**	**66**	**15**	**395**	**89**

Wartime programme 1943-44 Queens Park Rangers v. West Ham United

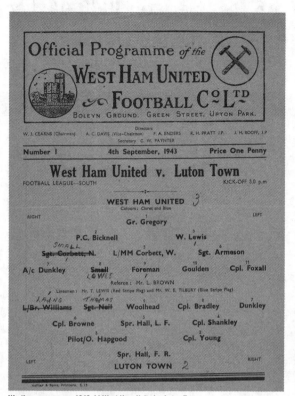

Wartime programme 1943-44 West Ham United v. Luton Town

League South
Final Table 1943-44

	P	W	D	L	F	A	Pts
Tottenham Hotspur	30	19	8	3	71	36	46
West Ham United	**30**	**17**	**7**	**6**	**74**	**39**	**41**
Queens Park Rangers	30	14	12	4	69	54	40
Arsenal	30	14	10	6	72	42	38
Crystal Palace	30	16	5	9	75	53	37
Portsmouth	30	16	5	9	68	59	37
Brentford	30	14	7	9	71	51	35
Chelsea	30	16	2	12	79	55	34
Fulham	30	11	9	10	80	73	31
Millwall	30	13	4	13	70	66	30
Aldershot	30	12	6	12	64	73	30
Reading	30	12	3	15	73	62	27
Southampton	30	10	7	13	67	88	27
Charlton Athletic	30	9	7	14	57	73	25
Watford	30	6	8	16	58	80	20
Brighton and Hove Albion	30	9	2	19	55	82	20
Luton Town	30	3	5	22	42	104	11
Clapton Orient	30	4	3	23	32	87	11

Season **1943-44** League South
Match Details
Manager **Charlie Paynter**   Final League Position **2/18**

	Date		Venue	Opponents	Results		Attendance	Scorers
1	Aug 28	Sat	A	Portsmouth	L	0-2	6,000	
2	Sep 4	Sat	H	Luton Town	W	3-2	6,000	Foreman, Lowes, Small
3	Sep 11	Sat	H	Arsenal	D	2-2	15,000	Macaulay 2
4	Sep 18	Sat	H	Tottenham Hotspur	D	3-3	20,000	Dunn, Foreman, Hobbis
5	Sep 25	Sat	A	Clapton Orient	W	4-0	6,000	Foreman 2, Foxall, Goulden
6	Oct 2	Sat	A	Crystal Palace	W	6-1	7,040	Foreman 2, Foxall 2, Goulden, Wood
7	Oct 9	Sat	H	Brentford	D	0-0	12,000	
8	Oct 16	Sat	A	Southampton	W	4-2	9,000	Dunn 2, Fenton, Foreman
9	Oct 23	Sat	H	Reading	W	1-0	10,000	Wood
10	Oct 30	Sat	A	Fulham	W	6-2	10,000	Goulden 2, Small 2, Fenton, Foreman
11	Nov 6	Sat	H	Queens Park Rangers	D	1-1	16,100	Wood
12	Nov 13	Sat	H	Millwall	W	3-0	12,000	Foreman, Goulden, Wood
13	Nov 20	Sat	A	Brighton & Hove Albion	W	2-1	5,000	Foreman, Goulden
14	Nov 27	Sat	H	Portsmouth	W	5-1	8,000	Foreman, Mahon, Small, Wood, Morgan (og)
15	Dec 4	Sat	A	Luton Town	W	1-0	4,000	Dunn
16	Dec 11	Sat	A	Arsenal	D	1-1	22,497	Foreman
17	Dec 18	Sat	H	Charlton Athletic	L	0-1	7,000	
18	Dec 25	Sat	A	Chelsea	D	3-3	16,000	Dunn, Fenton, Wood
19	Dec 27	Mon	H	Chelsea	W	3-0	12,000	Wood 2, Foreman
20	Jan 1	Sat	A	Tottenham Hotspur	L	0-1	40,067	
21	Jan 8	Sat	A	Queens Park Rangers	L	0-3	11,944	
22	Jan 22	Sat	H	Crystal Palace	W	3-0	9,500	Foreman 2, Goulden
23	Jan 29	Sat	A	Brentford	L	1-2	11,220	Foreman
24	Feb 5	Sat	H	Southampton	W	4-1	7,500	Foreman 2, Dunkley, Goulden
25	Feb 12	Sat	A	Reading	L	2-3	5,574	Foxall, Small
26	Apr 1	Sat	H	Fulham	W	3-2	5,000	Wood 2, Parsons
27	Apr 10	Mon	H	Clapton Orient	W	3-1	9,000	Foreman, Goulden, Small
28	Apr 22	Sat	A	Charlton Athletic	D	1-1	8,500	Oakes (og)
29	Apr 29	Sat	A	Millwall	W	3-1	6,000	Foreman 2, Dunn
30	May 6	Sat	H	Brighton & Hove Albion	W	6-2	4,000	Goulden 2, Deans, Foreman, Small, Wood

Football League (South) Cup Group B

	Date		Venue	Opponents	Results		Attendance	Scorers
1	Feb 19	Sat	H	Watford	L	1-2	4,500	Weaver
2	Feb 26	Sat	A	Southampton	W	2-1	14,00	Dunn, Goulden
3	Mar 4	Sat	A	Chelsea	L	0-4	15,520	
4	Mar 11	Sat	A	Watford	L	1-2	4,257	Wood
5	Mar 18	Sat	H	Southampton	W	5-1	6,500	Foreman 2, Small 2, Smith
6	Mar 25	Sat	H	Chelsea	W	6-1	11,500	Fenton 2, Small 2, Bicknell, Goulden

Team Line-Ups

1	2	3	4	5	6	7	8	9	10	11	
Medhurst	Bicknell	Lewis	Corbett W.	Morris	Armeson	Small	Wood	Foreman	Goulden	Foxall	1
Gregory	Bicknell	Lewis	Corbett N.	Corbett W.	Armeson	Dunkley	Lowes	Foreman	Goulden	Small	2
Medhurst	Bicknell	Lewis	Corbett N.	Corbett W.	Attwell	Small	Macaulay	Foreman	Wood	Foxall	3
Gregory	Bicknell	Chalkley	Lewis	Small	Armeson	Walker T.	Dunn	Foreman	Goulden	Hobbis	4
Medhurst	Jones	Chalkley	Lewis	Cardwell	Armeson	Foxall	Wood	Foreman	Goulden	Hobbis	5
Gregory	Bicknell	Jones	Small	Wright	Lewis	Walker T.	Wood	Foreman	Goulden	Foxall	6
Medhurst	Bicknell	Jones	Corbett N.	Corbett W.	Lewis	Foxall	Small	Foreman	Goulden	Hobbis	7
Gregory	Bicknell	Jones	Corbett N.	Corbett W.	Lewis	Small	Dunn	Foreman	Fenton E.	Walker T.	8
Medhurst	Bicknell	Jones	Corbett N.	Fenton E.	Small	Dunkley	Wood	Foreman	Goulden	Foxall	9
Gregory	Bicknell	Jones	Corbett N.	Corbett W.	Lewis	Small	Fenton E.	Foreman	Goulden	Dunkley	10
Medhurst	Bicknell	Lewis	Corbett N.	Fenton E.	Attwell	Small	Wood	Foreman	Goulden	Foxall	11
Gregory	Jones	Lewis	Fenton E.	Corbett W.	Corbett N.	Small	Dunn	Foreman	Goulden	Wood	12
Medhurst	Bicknell	Jones	Corbett N.	Corbett W.	Lewis	Small	Fenton E.	Foreman	Goulden	Foxall	13
Gregory	Jones	Lewis	Small	Corbett W.	Fenton E.	Walker T.	Wood	Foreman	Goulden	Mahon	14
Medhurst	Bicknell	Jones	Fenton E.	Corbett W.	Lewis	Small	Dunn	Foreman	Goulden	Foxall	15
Medhurst	Bicknell	Jones	Lewis	Corbett W.	Attwell	Dunkley	Small	Foreman	Goulden	Mahon	16
Gregory	Bicknell	Jones	Fenton E.	Small	Lewis	Dunkley	Dunn	Foreman	Goulden	Foxall	17
Gregory	Bicknell	Jones	Lewis	Corbett W.	Fenton E.	Dunkley	Dunn	Foreman	Goulden	Wood	18
Gregory	Bicknell	Jones	Fenton E.	Corbett W.	Lewis	Dunkley	Wood	Foreman	Goulden	Small	19
Medhurst	Jones	Lewis	Small	Fenton E.	Attwell	Walker T.	Wood	Foreman	Goulden	Foxall	20
Gregory	Bicknell	Chalkley	Jones	Fenton E.	Lewis	Dunkley	Dunn	Foreman	Goulden	Small	21
Medhurst	Bicknell	Jones	Macaulay	Corbett W.	Lewis	Small	Fenton E.	Foreman	Goulden	Hobbis	22
Gregory	Bicknell	Jones	Small	Corbett W.	Macaulay	Dunkley	Wood	Foreman	Goulden	Walker T.	23
Hughes	Bicknell	Jones	Small	Fenton E.	Muttitt	Dunkley	Wood	Foreman	Goulden	Hobbis	24
Medhurst	Bicknell	Jones	Corbett N.	Fenton E.	Lewis	Foxall	Small	Foreman	Goulden	Hobbis	25
Gregory	Bicknell	Lewis	Fenton E.	Corbett W.	Small	Parsons	Wood	Foreman	Goulden	Girling	26
Gibbs	Bicknell	Aldridge	Deans	Corbett N.	Wilson	Small	Gillespie	Foreman	Goulden	Lewis	27
Medhurst	Bicknell	Lewis	Deans	Attwell	Small	Chapman	Wood	Foreman	Goulden	Dunn	28
Medhurst	Bicknell	Lewis	Deans	Corbett N.	Attwell	Small	Dunn	Foreman	Goulden	Woodgate	29
Taylor	Bicknell	Lewis	Macaulay	Corbett N.	Deans	Small	Fenton E.	Foreman	Goulden	Wood	30

1	2	3	4	5	6	7	8	9	10	11	
Sanders	Jones	Lewis	Corbett N.	Corbett W.	Weaver	Small	Fenton E.	Foreman	Goulden	Hobbis	1
Medhurst	Bicknell	Jones	Small	Corbett W.	Fenton E.	Parsons	Dunn	Foreman	Goulden	Hobbis	2
Medhurst	Bicknell	Jones	Attwell	Corbett W.	Lewis	Small	Fenton E.	Foreman	Goulden	Hobbis	3
Gregory	Bicknell	Jones	Corbett N.	Corbett W.	Lewis	Small	Wood	Dunn	Goulden	Hobbis	4
Medhurst	Bicknell	Jones	Fenton E.	Corbett W.	Lewis	Small	Smith	Foreman	Goulden	Foxall	5
Medhurst	Bicknell	Corbett N.	Small	Corbett W.	Fenton	Chapman	Macaulay	Foreman	Goulden	Lewis	6

1944-45

Appearances & Goals 1944-45

	League		FL Cup		Total	
	Starts	Goals	Starts	Goals	Starts	Goal
ATTWELL Reg	4	0	0	0	4	0
BAINBRIDGE Ken	3	2	0	0	3	2
BANNER Arthur	0	0	2	0	2	0
BARRETT Jim	4	1	0	0	4	1
BELL [Guest]	1	0	0	0	1	0
BICKNELL Charlie	25	0	6	0	31	0
BRIDON [Guest]	1	0	0	0	1	0
BUCHANAN Peter [Guest]	0	0	1	0	1	0
BURKE [Guest]	1	0	0	0	1	0
BURNETT [Guest]	1	0	0	0	1	0
CHAPMAN [Guest]	1	1	0	0	1	1
CHEETHAM Tom [Guest]	1	2	0	0	1	2
CORBETT Norman	23	2	7	0	30	2
CORBETT Willie [Guest]	2	0	0	0	2	0
DEANS Tommy [Guest]	2	0	0	0	2	0
DODDS Jack [Guest]	10	11	0	0	10	11
DUNN Richard	12	3	2	0	14	3
FENTON Benny	1	1	0	0	1	1
FENTON Edward	24	3	7	0	31	3
FERRIER Bob [Guest]	1	0	0	0	1	0
FOREMAN George	11	15	4	0	15	15
FOXALL Joseph	2	1	0	0	2	1
GOULDEN Len	25	10	6	7	31	17
GREGORY Ernie	3	0	1	0	4	0
HALL Almeric	7	6	0	0	7	6
HENLEY Les [Guest]	0	0	1	0	1	0
HOPKINS Idris [Guest]	1	0	0	0	1	0
HUBBARD Cliff	1	0	0	0	1	0
HUNT Doug [Guest]	1	0	0	0	1	0
JONES [Guest]	17	0	0	0	17	0
LEWIS [Guest]	28	2	7	0	35	2
LUDFORD George [Guest]	3	3	0	0	3	3
MACAULAY Archibald	8	1	4	1	12	2
MALLETT Joe [Guest]	1	1	0	0	1	1
MEDHURST Harry	23	0	6	0	29	0
MEDLEY Leslie [Guest]	1	1	0	0	1	1
PARKER [Guest]	1	0	0	0	1	0
PRITCHARD H [Guest]	1	0	0	0	1	0
RIDYARD Alf [Guest]	1	0	0	0	1	0
ROBINSON [Guest]	1	0	0	0	1	0
SMALL Sam	7	5	2	1	9	6
SMITH C [Guest]	1	0	0	0	1	0
TAYLOR George	4	0	0	0	4	0
THOMAS DWJ [Guest]	1	1	0	0	1	1
THOMAS Robert [Guest]	1	0	0	0	1	0
TOWNSEND Laurie [Guest]	0	0	1	1	1	1
WHITCHURCH Charlie [Guest]	9	7	6	2	15	9
WILSON Ron	18	2	6	0	24	2
WOOD John	13	7	1	1	14	8
WOODGATE Terry	23	7	7	2	30	9
own goal		2		1		3
Totals	**330**	**97**	**77**	**15**	**407**	**112**

Wartime programme 1944-45 Arsenal v. West Ham United

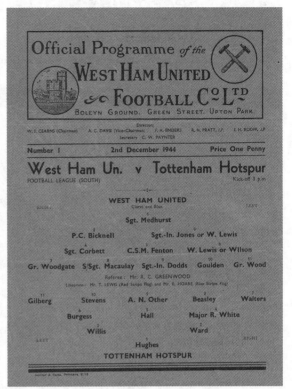

Wartime programme 1944-45 West Ham United v. Tottenham Hotspur

League South
Final Table 1944-45

	P	W	D	L	F	A	Pts
Tottenham Hotspur	30	23	6	1	81	30	52
West Ham United	30	22	3	5	96	47	47
Brentford	30	17	4	9	87	57	38
Chelsea	30	16	5	9	100	55	37
Southampton	30	17	3	50	96	69	37
Crystal Palace	30	15	5	10	74	70	35
Reading	30	12	6	10	78	68	34
Arsenal	30	12	3	13	77	67	31
Queens Park Rangers	30	10	10	10	70	61	30
Watford	30	11	6	13	66	84	28
Fulham	30	11	4	15	79	83	26
Portsmouth	30	11	4	15	56	61	26
Charlton Athletic	30	12	2	16	72	81	26
Brighton and Hove Albion	30	10	2	18	66	95	22
Luton Town	30	6	7	17	56	104	19
Aldershot	30	7	4	19	44	85	18
Millwall	30	5	7	18	50	84	17
Clapton Orient	30	5	7	18	39	86	17

Season **1944-45** League South
Match Details

Manager **Charlie Paynter**   Final League Position **2/18**

	Date		Venue	Opponents	Results		Attendance	Scorers
1	Aug 26	Sat	A	Tottenham Hotspur	D	2-2	14,000	Foreman, Wood
2	Sep 2	Sat	A	Charlton Athletic	L	2-3	4,000	Corbett, Fenton
3	Sep 9	Sat	A	Watford	D	3-3	3,842	Fenton, Foxall, Brown (og)
4	Sep 16	Sat	A	Queens Park Rangers	W	1-0	8,000	Goulden
5	Sep 23	Sat	A	Portsmouth	W	3-1	16,000	Dodds, Dunn, Macaulay
6	Sep 30	Sat	A	Brighton & Hove Albion	W	1-0	6,000	Dodds
7	Oct 7	Sat	A	Aldershot	W	3-2	4,500	Dodds, Foreman, Wood
8	Oct 14	Sat	A	Luton Town	W	4-3	5,000	Wood 2, Dodds, Dunn
9	Oct 21	Sat	A	Arsenal	W	3-0	27,800	Dodds, Goulden, Scott (og)
10	Oct 28	Sat	A	Millwall	W	3-0	5,000	Foreman 2, Woodgate
11	Nov 4	Sat	A	Clapton Orient	W	3-0	10,000	Dodds 2, Ludford
12	Nov 11	Sat	A	Fulham	W	7-4	10,359	Dodds 3, Ludfird 2, Fenton B., Goulden
13	Nov 18	Sat	A	Southampton	L	1-2	14,000	Dodds
14	Nov 25	Sat	A	Crystal Palace	L	0-3	11,600	
15	Dec 2	Sat	H	Tottenham Hotspur	L	0-1	25,000	
16	Dec 9	Sat	H	Charlton Athletic	W	2-0	9,500	Foreman, Woodgate
17	Dec 16	Sat	H	Watford	W	6-2	7,000	Goulden 2, Wood 2, Barrett, Foreman
18	Dec 30	Sat	H	Queens Park Rangers	W	4-2	9,000	Foreman 3, Woodgate
19	Jan 6	Sat	H	Portsmouth	W	4-0	9,000	Woodgate 2, Goulden, Wood
20	Jan 13	Sat	H	Brighton & Hove Albion	W	5-4	5,000	Bainbridge 2, Foreman 2, Medley
21	Jan 20	Sat	H	Aldershot	W	8-1	4,000	Foreman 4, Goulden 3, Dunn
22	Mar 24	Sat	H	Millwall	W	3-1	8,000	Wilson 2, Woodgate
23	Mar 31	Sat	H	Clapton Orient	W	1-0	8,000	Thomas
24	Apr 2	Mon	A	Chelsea	W	4-3	23,827	Whitchurch 2, Goulden, Mallett
25	Apr 14	Sat	H	Fulham	W	3-2	8,000	Chapman, Fenton, Whitchurch
26	Apr 21	Sat	H	Southampton	L	3-5	12,000	Hall, Lewis, Small
27	Apr 28	Sat	H	Crystal Palace	W	5-0	6,257	Small 3, Hall, Woodgate
28	May 5	Sat	H	Arsenal	D	1-1	9,000	Small
29	May 12	Sat	H	Luton Town	W	9-1	5,000	Hall 3, Whitchurch 3, Cheetham 2, Corbett N.
30	May 19	Sat	H	Chelsea	W	2-1	10,000	Hall, Whitchurch

Football League (South) Cup Group C

	Date		Venue	Opponents	Results		Attendance	Scorers
1	Feb 3	Sat	A	Aldershot	W	3-1	5,000	Goulden, Wood, Woodgate
2	Feb 10	Sat	H	Tottenham Hotspur	W	1-0	21,000	Goulden
3	Feb 17	Sat	A	Queens Park Rangers	D	1-1	17,000	Macaulay
4	Feb 24	Sat	H	Aldershot	W	4-0	10,000	Goulden 3, Woodgate
5	Mar 3	Sat	A	Tottenham Hotspur	L	0-4	29,838	
6	Mar 10	Sat	H	Queens Park Rangers	W	5-0	20,000	Goulden 2, Whitchurch 2, Small
SF	Mar 17	Sat	N*	Chelsea	L	1-2	35,000	Townsend

* Played at White Hart Lane

eam Line-Ups

1	2	3	4	5	6	7	8	9	10	11	
Gregory	Bicknell	Jones	Deans	Bridon	Lewis	Tgomas R.	Fenton E.	Foreman	Goulden	Wood	1
Gregory	Deans	Jones	Burke	Barrett	Corbett N.	Burnett	Macaulay	Foreman	Fenton E.	Lewis	2
Medhurst	Lewis	Bicknell	Corbett N.	Barrett	Attwell	Woodgate	Fenton E.	Hubbard	Foreman	Foxall	3
Gregory	Lewis	Bicknell	Corbett N.	Jones	Fenton E.	Foxall	Robinson	Dodds	Goulden	Wood	4
Medhurst	Bicknell	Jones	Corbett N.	Corbett W.	Lewis	Woodgate	Macaulay	Dodds	Goulden	Dunn	5
Medhurst	Bicknell	Lewis	Attwell	Fenton E.	Corbett N.	Woodgate	Macaulay	Dodds	Goulden	Dunn	6
Medhurst	Bicknell	Jones	Wilson	Attwell	Lewis	Hall	Wood	Dodds	Goulden	Foreman	7
Medhurst	Bicknell	Jones	Corbett N.	Fenton E.	Lewis	Woodgate	Dunn	Dodds	Wood	Bell	8
Medhurst	Jones	Lewis	Macaulay	Fenton E.	Corbett N.	Woodgate	Dunn	Dodds	Goulden	Wood	9
Medhurst	Bicknell	Jones	Corbett N.	Fenton E.	Lewis	Woodgate	Dunn	Foreman	Goulden	Wood	10
Medhurst	Bicknell	Jones	Wilson	Fenton E.	Lewis	Woodgate	Dunn	Dodds	Goulden	Ludford	11
Medhurst	Bicknell	Lewis	Wilson	Fenton E.	Corbett N.	Small	Fenton B.	Dodds	Goulden	Ludford	12
Medhurst	Bicknell	Lewis	Macaulay	Fenton E.	Corbett N.	Woodgate	Dunn	Dodds	Goulden	Ludford	13
Medhurst	Bicknell	Lewis	Wilson	Small	Attwell	Woodgate	Bainbridge	Dunn	Goulden	Wood	14
Medhurst	Bicknell	Jones	Corbett N.	Fenton E.	Lewis	Woodgate	Macaulay	Dodds	Goulden	Wood	15
Medhurst	Jones	Lewis	Corbett N.	Corbett W.	Wilson	Woodgate	Fenton E.	Foreman	Goulden	Wood	16
Medhurst	Jones	Lewis	Macaulay	Barrett	Wilson	Woodgate	Dunn	Foreman	Goulden	Wood	17
Medhurst	Bicknell	Jones	Corbett N.	Fenton E.	Wilson	Woodgate	Dunn	Foreman	Wood	Lewis	18
Medhurst	Bicknell	Lewis	Corbett N.	Fenton E.	Wilson	Woodgate	Dunn	Foreman	Goulden	Wood	19
Medhurst	Bicknell	Ferrier	Corbett N.	Barrett	Wilson	Whitchurch	Bainbridge	Foreman	Goulden	Medley	20
Medhurst	Bicknell	Lewis	Macaulay	Fenton E.	Corbett N.	Woodgate	Dunn	Foreman	Goulden	Wood	21
Medhurst	Bicknell	Jones	Corbett N.	Fenton E.	Lewis	Woodgate	Bainbridge	Small	Wilson	Whitchurch	22
Medhurst	Bicknell	Jones	Wilson	Fenton E.	Lewis	Woodgate	Parker	Thomas D.	Goulden	Whitchurch	23
Medhurst	Bicknell	Jones	Wilson	Ridyard	Lewis	Woodgate	Mallett	Whitchurch	Goulden	Pritchard	24
Medhurst	Bicknell	Lewis	Corbett N.	Fenton E.	Wilson	Woodgate	Hall	Chapman	Goulden	Whitchurch	25
Medhurst	Bicknell	Jones	Corbett N.	Fenton E.	Lewis	Small	Hall	Wilson	Goulden	Whitchurch	26
Taylor	Bicknell	Lewis	Corbett N.	Fenton E.	Wilson	Woodgate	Hall	Small	Goulden	Whitchurch	27
Taylor	Corbett N.	Lewis	Hunt	Fenton E.	Wilson	Hopkins	Hall	Small	Goulden	Woodgate	28
Taylor	Bicknell	Lewis	Corbett N.	Fenton E.	Wilson	Woodgate	Hall	Cheetham	Goulden	Whitchurch	29
Taylor	Bicknell	Smith	Corbett N.	Fenton E.	Wilson	Woodgate	Hall	Small	Goulden	Whitchurch	30

1	2	3	4	5	6	7	8	9	10	11	
Medhurst	Banner	Lewis	Corbett N.	Fenton E.	Wilson	Woodgate	Wood	Foreman	Goulden	Whitchurch	1
Medhurst	Bicknell	Lewis	Corbett N.	Fenton E.	Wilson	Woodgate	Henley	Foreman	Goulden	Buchanan	2
Gregory	Bicknell	Lewis	Corbett N.	Fenton E.	Wilson	Woodgate	Macaulay	Foreman	Goulden	Whitchurch	3
Medhurst	Bicknell	Lewis	Corbett N.	Fenton E.	Banner	Woodgate	Macaulay	Foreman	Goulden	Whitchurch	4
Medhurst	Bicknell	Lewis	Corbett N.	Fenton E.	Wilson	Woodgate	Macaulay	Small	Goulden	Whitchurch	5
Medhurst	Bicknell	Lewis	Corbett N.	Fenton E.	Wilson	Woodgate	Dunn	Small	Goulden	Whitchurch	6
Medhurst	Bicknell	Lewis	Corbett N.	Fenton E.	Wilson	Woodgate	Dunn	Townsend	Macaulay	Whitchurch	SF

1945-46

Appearances & Goals 1945-46

	League		FA Cup		Total	
	Starts	Goals	Starts	Goals	Starts	Goal
ATTWELL Reg	7	0	0	0	7	0
BAINBRIDGE Ken	9	3	3	1	12	4
BICKNELL Charlie	41	4	4	0	45	4
CATER Ron	21	0	4	0	25	0
CORBETT Norman	26	0	0	0	26	0
DUNN Richard	1	0	0	0	1	0
FENTON Edward	37	3	4	0	41	3
FORDE Steve	1	0	0	0	1	0
FOREMAN George	23	13	3	1	26	14
GRAY George [Guest]	1	1	0	0	1	1
HALL Almeric	34	16	4	3	38	19
HARRIS [Guest]	1	0	0	0	1	0
HOPKINS Idris [Guest]	1	0	0	0	1	0
MACAULAY Archibald	23	9	2	0	25	9
MEDHURST Harry	42	0	4	0	46	0
POWELL-BESENS Paul [Guest]	1	0	0	0	1	0
SMALL Sam	25	10	4	0	29	10
TRAVIS Don	6	7	0	0	6	7
WALKER Charlie	19	0	0	0	19	0
WALKER Richard	40	0	4	0	44	0
WHITCHURCH Charlie [Guest]	19	3	0	0	19	3
WILSON Ron	11	0	0	0	11	0
WOOD John	29	7	4	2	33	9
WOODGATE Terry	39	12	4	0	43	12
WRIGHT Ken	5	5	0	0	5	5
own goal		1				1
Totals	**462**	**94**	**44**	**7**	**506**	**101**

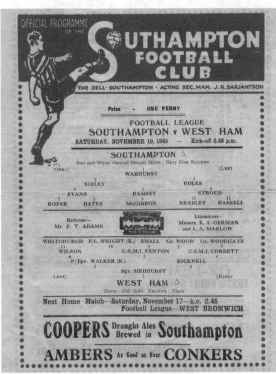

Wartime programme 1945-46 Southampton v. West Ham United

eague South
inal Table 1945-46

	P	W	D	L	F	A	Pts
rmingham City	42	28	5	9	96	45	61
ston Villa	42	25	11	6	106	58	61
harlton Athletic	42	25	10	7	92	45	60
erby County	42	24	7	11	101	62	55
est Bromwich Albion	42	22	8	12	104	69	52
olverhampton Wanderers	42	20	11	11	75	48	51
West Ham United	42	20	11	11	94	76	51
ulham	42	20	10	12	93	73	50
ottenham Hotspur	42	22	3	17	78	81	47
nelsea	42	19	6	17	92	80	44
rsenal	42	16	11	15	76	73	43
illwall	42	17	8	17	79	105	42
oventry City	42	15	10	17	70	69	40
entford	42	14	10	18	82	72	38
ottingham Forest	42	12	13	17	72	73	37
outhampton	42	14	9	19	97	105	37
wansea City	42	15	7	20	90	112	37
ston Town	42	13	7	22	60	92	33
ortsmouth	42	11	6	25	66	87	28
eicester City	42	8	7	27	57	101	23
ewport County	42	9	2	31	52	125	20
lymouth Argyle	42	3	8	31	39	120	14

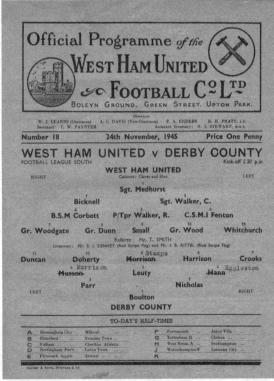

Wartime programme 1945-46 West Ham United v. Derby County

Season **1945-46** League South
Match Details

Manager **Charlie Paynter**   Final League Position **7/22**

	Date		Venue	Opponents	Results		Attendance	Scorers
1	Aug 25	Sat	A	Birmingham City	W	1-0	30,000	Bicknell
2	Aug 27	Mon	H	Arsenal	D	1-1	25,000	Whitchurch
3	Sep 1	Sat	H	Birmingham City	W	3-2	20,000	Foreman 2, Whitchurch
4	Sep 8	Sat	H	Tottenham Hotspur	D	1-1	26,000	Foreman
5	Sep 10	Mon	H	Aston Villa	L	1-2	20,000	Foreman
6	Sep 15	Sat	A	Tottenham Hotspur	W	3-2	34,778	Macaulay 2, Hall
7	Sep 22	Sat	A	Brentford	D	1-1	19,000	Hall
8	Sep 29	Sat	H	Brentford	L	0-2	23,000	
9	Oct 6	Sat	H	Chelsea	L	2-4	25,000	Foreman, Whitchurch
10	Oct 13	Sat	A	Chelsea	W	2-1	45,000	Bicknell [pen], Hall
11	Oct 20	Sat	A	Millwall	D	0-0	32,000	
12	Oct 27	Sat	H	Millwall	W	3-1	25,000	Foreman, Hall, Wood
13	Nov 3	Sat	H	Southampton	W	3-1	20,000	Small 3
14	Nov 10	Sat	A	Southampton	D	3-3	17,000	Foreman, Woodgate, Wright
15	Nov 17	Sat	A	Derby County	L	1-5	20,000	Hall
16	Nov 24	Sat	H	Derby County	L	2-3	28,000	Small 2
17	Dec 1	Sat	H	Leicester City	D	2-2	20,000	Macaulay, Small
18	Dec 8	Sat	A	Leicester City	L	1-4	12,345	Woodgate
19	Dec 15	Sat	A	Coventry City	W	5-2	11,719	Hall 2, Wright 2, Woodgate
20	Dec 22	Sat	H	Coventry City	W	6-3	14,000	Foreman 2, Wright 2, Wood, Woodgate
21	Dec 25	Tue	H	Luton Town	L	3-4	10,000	Fenton E., Foreman, Woodgate
22	Dec 26	Wed	A	Luton Town	W	4-1	14,000	Bicknell, Foreman, Small, Woodgate
23	Dec 29	Sat	A	Aston Villa	D	2-2	30,000	Bainbridge, Cummings (og)
24	Jan 12	Sat	A	Charlton Athletic	L	0-3	45,000	
25	Jan 19	Sat	H	Charlton Athletic	W	2-0	25,000	Fenton E., Foreman
26	Feb 2	Sat	A	Fulham	W	1-0	30,000	Hall
27	Feb 9	Sat	A	Plymouth Argyle	W	2-1	20,000	Foreman, Wood
28	Feb 16	Sat	H	Plymouth Argyle	W	7-0	15,000	Travis 4, Woodgate 3
29	Feb 23	Sat	H	Portsmouth	W	3-1	15,000	Bainbridge, Travis, Woodgate
30	Mar 2	Sat	A	Portsmouth	W	3-2	12,000	Bainbridge, Bicknell, Woodgate
31	Mar 9	Sat	A	Nottingham Forest	D	1-1	22,000	Bicknell [pen]
32	Mar 16	Sat	H	Nottingham Forest	L	1-3	18,000	Small
33	Mar 23	Sat	H	Newport County	W	4-1	12,000	Macaulay 2, Gray, Hall
34	Mar 30	Sat	A	Newport County	D	2-2	16,000	Hall, Macaulay
35	Apr 6	Sat	A	Wolverhampton Wanderers	D	3-3	25,000	Wood 2, Macaulay
36	Apr 13	Sat	H	Wolverhampton Wanderers	W	2-1	25,000	Travis 2
37	Apr 19	Fri	A	Swansea Town	W	3-2	25,000	Hall 2, Small
38	Apr 20	Sat	H	West Bromwich Albion	D	1-1	24,600	Macaulay
39	Apr 22	Mon	H	Swansea Town	W	3-0	14,959	Hall 2, Woodgate
40	Apr 27	Sat	A	West Bromwich Albion	W	2-1	10,000	Macaulay, Small
41	Apr 29	Mon	H	Fulham	L	3-5	28,000	Hall 2, Wood
42	May 4	Sat	A	Arsenal	L	1-2	30,000	Wood

FA Cup

	Round	Date		Venue	Opponents	Results		Attendance	Scorers
1	R3:1	Jan 5	Sat	H	Arsenal	W	6-0	35,000	Hall 2, Wood 2, Bainbridge, Foreman
2	R3:2	Jan 9	Wed	A	Arsenal	L	0-1	22,000	
3	R4:1	Jan 26	Sat	A	Chelsea	L	0-2	65,000	
4	R4:2	Jan 30	Wed	H	Chelsea	W	1-0	31,000	Hall

Team Line-Ups

1	2	3	4	5	6	7	8	9	10	11	
Medhurst	Bicknell	Walker C.	Corbett N.	Walker R.	Wilson	Woodgate	Fenton E.	Foreman	Small	Whitchurch	1
Medhurst	Bicknell	Walker C.	Corbett N.	Walker R.	Wilson	Woodgate	Hall	Foreman	Small	Whitchurch	2
Medhurst	Bicknell	Walker C.	Fenton E.	Walker R.	Wilson	Woodgate	Macaulay	Foreman	Wood	Whitchurch	3
Medhurst	Bicknell	Walker C.	Corbett N.	Walker R.	Fenton E.	Woodgate	Macaulay	Foreman	Wood	Whitchurch	4
Medhurst	Bicknell	Walker C.	Corbett N.	Walker R.	Fenton E.	Woodgate	Hall	Foreman	Wood	Whitchurch	5
Medhurst	Bicknell	Walker R.	Corbett N.	Fenton E.	Wilson	Hall	Macaulay	Foreman	Wood	Whitchurch	6
Medhurst	Bicknell	Walker R.	Attwell	Fenton E.	Wilson	Hall	Macaulay	Foreman	Wood	Whitchurch	7
Medhurst	Bicknell	Walker R.	Corbett N.	Fenton E.	Attwell	Woodgate	Hall	Foreman	Wood	Whitchurch	8
Medhurst	Bicknell	Walker C.	Corbett N.	Walker R.	Attwell	Woodgate	Hall	Foreman	Wood	Whitchurch	9
Medhurst	Bicknell	Walker C.	Corbett N.	Walker R.	Wilson	Hopkins	Hall	Foreman	Wood	Whitchurch	10
Medhurst	Bicknell	Walker C.	Corbett N.	Walker R.	Wilson	Woodgate	Hall	Foreman	Wood	Whitchurch	11
Medhurst	Bicknell	Walker R.	Corbett N.	Fenton E.	Wilson	Woodgate	Hall	Foreman	Wood	Whitchurch	12
Medhurst	Bicknell	Forde	Corbett N.	Walker R.	Wilson	Woodgate	Fenton E.	Small	Wood	Whitchurch	13
Medhurst	Walker R.	Walker C.	Corbett N.	Fenton E.	Wilson	Woodgate	Wood	Foreman	Wright	Whitchurch	14
Medhurst	Bicknell	Walker C.	Corbett N.	Walker R.	Wilson	Woodgate	Hall	Small	Foreman	Whitchurch	15
Medhurst	Bicknell	Walker C.	Corbett N.	Walker R.	Fenton E.	Woodgate	Dunn	Small	Wood	Whitchurch	16
Medhurst	Bicknell	Walker C.	Corbett N.	Walker R.	Fenton E.	Woodgate	Macaulay	Small	Wood	Wright	17
Medhurst	Bicknell	Walker C.	Harris	Fenton E.	Walker R.	Woodgate	Hall	Small	Wright	Whitchurch	18
Medhurst	Bicknell	Cater	Small	Fenton E.	Walker R.	Woodgate	Hall	Foreman	Wright	Wood	19
Medhurst	Bicknell	Cater	Small	Fenton E.	Walker R.	Woodgate	Hall	Foreman	Wright	Wood	20
Medhurst	Bicknell	Cater	Powell-Besens	Fenton E.	Walker R.	Woodgate	Hall	Foreman	Bainbridge	Whitchurch	21
Medhurst	Bicknell	Walker C.	Cater	Fenton E.	Walker R.	Woodgate	Hall	Foreman	Small	Bainbridge	22
Medhurst	Bicknell	Walker C.	Small	Fenton E.	Walker R.	Woodgate	Hall	Foreman	Bainbridge	Whitchurch	23
Medhurst	Bicknell	Cater	Small	Walker R.	Fenton E.	Woodgate	Hall	Foreman	Macaulay	Wood	24
Medhurst	Bicknell	Cater	Macaulay	Walker R.	Fenton E.	Woodgate	Hall	Foreman	Small	Wood	25
Medhurst	Bicknell	Cater	Small	Walker R.	Fenton E.	Woodgate	Hall	Foreman	Macaulay	Bainbridge	26
Medhurst	Bicknell	Walker C.	Cater	Walker R.	Fenton E.	Woodgate	Small	Foreman	Macaulay	Wood	27
Medhurst	Bicknell	Walker C.	Cater	Walker R.	Fenton E.	Woodgate	Hall	Travis	Macaulay	Bainbridge	28
Medhurst	Bicknell	Cater	Corbett N.	Walker R.	Fenton E.	Woodgate	Hall	Travis	Macaulay	Bainbridge	29
Medhurst	Bicknell	Cater	Corbett N.	Walker R.	Fenton E.	Woodgate	Hall	Small	Macaulay	Bainbridge	30
Medhurst	Bicknell	Walker C.	Corbett N.	Walker R.	Cater	Woodgate	Hall	Small	Fenton E.	Wood	31
Medhurst	Bicknell	Cater	Corbett N.	Walker R.	Fenton E.	Woodgate	Hall	Small	Macaulay	Bainbridge	32
Medhurst	Bicknell	Cater	Small	Fenton E.	Attwell	Woodgate	Hall	Gray	Macaulay	Bainbridge	33
Medhurst	Bicknell	Walker R.	Corbett N.	Fenton E.	Attwell	Woodgate	Hall	Small	Macaulay	Wood	34
Medhurst	Bicknell	Walker C.	Corbett N.	Fenton E.	Attwell	Woodgate	Hall	Travis	Macaulay	Wood	35
Medhurst	Bicknell	Cater	Fenton E.	Walker R.	Attwell	Woodgate	Hall	Travis	Macaulay	Wood	36
Medhurst	Bicknell	Cater	Fenton E.	Walker R.	Corbett N.	Woodgate	Hall	Small	Macaulay	Wood	37
Medhurst	Bicknell	Cater	Fenton E.	Walker R.	Corbett N.	Woodgate	Hall	Travis	Macaulay	Wood	38
Medhurst	Bicknell	Cater	Fenton E.	Walker R.	Small	Woodgate	Hall	Travis	Macaulay	Wood	39
Medhurst	Bicknell	Cater	Fenton E.	Walker R.	Corbett N.	Woodgate	Hall	Small	Macaulay	Wood	40
Medhurst	Bicknell	Cater	Fenton E.	Walker R.	Corbett N.	Woodgate	Hall	Small	Macaulay	Wood	41
Medhurst	Bicknell	Cater	Fenton E.	Walker R.	Corbett N.	Woodgate	Hall	Small	Macaulay	Wood	42

1	2	3	4	5	6	7	8	9	10	11	
Medhurst	Bicknell	Cater	Small	Walker R.	Fenton E.	Woodgate	Hall	Foreman	Wood	Bainbridge	1
Medhurst	Bicknell	Cater	Small	Walker R.	Fenton E.	Woodgate	Hall	Foreman	Wood	Bainbridge	2
Medhurst	Bicknell	Cater	Macaulay	Walker R.	Fenton E.	Woodgate	Hall	Foreman	Small	Wood	3
Medhurst	Bicknell	Cater	Small	Walker R.	Fenton E.	Woodgate	Hall	Macaulay	Wood	Bainbridge	4

1946-47
Story of the season

League football was resumed after the war when the fans were still able to see the **damage caused by a German V1 flying bomb** which had landed on the pitch in August 1944, **destroying a large part of the South Bank terracing** and that end of the main stand.

The Hammers celebrated the return of the Football League with a 3–2 win against Fulham in their first home game. Only four players – Bicknell, Medhurst, Walker and Macaulay – had played in the last peacetime game back in 1939. Following the Fulham victory there were three defeats but all was well when local rivals Millwall were beaten 3–1 at the Boleyn before an attendance of 30,571. The team were inconsistent: a good 3–2 win at West Bromwich Albion was followed by a 4–0 home defeat to Birmingham City. Centre forward Joe Payne was signed from Chelsea and did well scoring in five successive games, including a goal in the 4–? defeat of Plymouth Argyle. That game marked the debut

Appearances & Goals 1946-47

	League		FA Cup		Total	
	Starts	Goals	Starts	Goals	Starts	Goals
ATTWELL Reg	4	0	0	0	4	0
BAINBRIDGE Ken	35	9	1	0	36	9
BANNER Arthur	21	0	0	0	21	0
BICKNELL Charlie	19	1	0	0	19	1
CATER Ron	34	0	1	0	35	0
CORBETT Norman	35	0	1	0	36	0
DEVLIN Ernie	2	0	0	0	2	0
DUNN Richard	7	1	0	0	7	1
FORDE Steve	24	0	1	0	25	0
GREGORY Ernie	9	0	0	0	9	0
HALL Almeric	24	5	1	0	25	5
MACAULAY Archibald	8	3	0	0	8	3
MEDHURST Harry	3	0	0	0	3	0
NEARY Frank	14	15	0	0	14	15
PARKER Derek	10	1	0	0	10	1
PARSONS Eric	12	4	1	0	13	4
PAYNE Joe	10	6	1	0	11	6
PROUDLOCK George	4	1	0	0	4	1
SADLER George	1	0	0	0	1	0
SMALL Sam	39	7	1	0	40	7
TAYLOR George	30	0	1	0	31	0
TRAVIS Don	1	0	0	0	1	0
WALKER Richard	34	0	1	0	35	0
WILSON Ron	1	0	0	0	1	0
WOOD John	33	10	0	0	33	10
WOODGATE Terry	41	5	1	1	42	6
WRIGHT Ken	7	1	0	0	7	1
own goal		1				1
Totals	**462**	**70**	**11**	**1**	**473**	**71**

goalkeeper Ernie Gregory, who went on to play in 406 games for the club.

There was an early exit from the FA Cup as Leicester City won 2–1 at the Boleyn Ground. Joe Payne was suffering from injuries and to replace him Frank Neary came from Millwall. He was an instant success, scoring seven goals in his first three games, which included a hat-trick against West Bromwich Albion. In April there was another burst of scoring from Neary as he scored twice in three successive games, culminating in a 4–0 home win over Southampton. The season ended with a 3–2 win at Newcastle and on the final day a 5–0 home defeat to Burnley. The inconsistent form saw the Hammers finish in twelfth spot in Division Two.

Football League - Division Two
Final Table 1946-47

		HOME					AWAY					
	P	W	D	L	F	A	W	D	L	F	A	Pts
Manchester City	42	17	3	1	49	14	9	7	5	29	21	62
Burnley	42	11	8	2	30	14	11	6	4	35	15	58
Birmingham City	42	17	2	2	51	11	8	3	10	23	22	55
Chesterfield	42	12	6	3	37	17	6	8	7	21	27	50
Newcastle United	42	11	4	6	60	32	8	6	7	35	30	48
Tottenham Hotspur	42	11	8	2	35	21	6	6	9	30	32	48
West Bromwich Albion	42	12	4	5	53	37	8	4	9	35	38	48
Coventry City	42	12	8	1	40	17	4	5	12	26	42	45
Leicester City	42	11	4	6	42	25	7	3	11	27	39	43
Barnsley	42	13	2	6	48	29	4	6	11	36	57	42
Nottingham Forest	42	13	5	3	47	20	2	5	14	22	54	40
West Ham United	**42**	**12**	**4**	**5**	**46**	**31**	**4**	**4**	**13**	**24**	**45**	**40**
Luton Town	42	13	4	4	50	29	3	3	15	21	44	39
Southampton	42	11	5	5	45	24	4	4	13	24	52	39
Fulham	42	12	4	5	40	25	3	5	13	23	49	39
Bradford Park Avenue	42	7	6	8	29	28	7	5	9	36	49	39
Bury	42	11	6	4	62	34	1	6	14	18	44	36
Millwall	42	7	7	7	30	30	7	1	13	26	49	36
Plymouth Argyle	42	11	3	7	45	34	3	2	16	34	62	33
Sheffield Wednesday	42	10	5	6	39	28	2	3	16	28	60	32
Swansea Town	42	9	1	11	36	40	2	6	13	19	43	29
Newport County	42	9	1	11	41	52	1	2	18	20	81	23

ERIC PARSONS

One of the fastest wingers in the game, Eric was spotted while playing for Worthing Boys at Upton Park.

He made his league debut at Leicester in January 1947 and soon became a first-team regular. Always looking for a goalscoring opportunity, in five seasons with West Ham he scored 34 league goals. After playing in 145 league games he was transferred in November 1950 to Chelsea for a fee of £23,000. While at Chelsea he gained two England B caps and a League Championship medal in 1955, when he was ever-present in the side. Eric spent six seasons with the Blues and after appearing in 158 league games he left to join Brentford on a free transfer in 1956. Despite breaking his leg he managed to play in 118 league games for the Bees before retiring in 1960. He passed away in Worthing in February 2011 aged 87.

Season **1946-47** Football League - Division Two
Match Details

Manager **Charlie Paynter**   Final League Position **12/22**

	Date		Competition	Venue	Opponents	Results		Attendance	Position	Scorers
1	Aug 31	Sat	Div 2	A	Plymouth Argyle	L	1-3	25,781	16	Wood
2	Sep 2	Mon	Div 2	H	Fulham	W	3-2	28,012	9	Macaulay 2, Small
3	Sep 7	Sat	Div 2	H	Leicester City	L	0-2	28,670	15	
4	Sep 9	Mon	Div 2	A	Fulham	L	2-3	19,908	18	Wood 2
5	Sep 14	Sat	Div 2	A	Chesterfield	L	1-3	14,173	21	Small
6	Sep 21	Sat	Div 2	H	Millwall	W	3-1	30,571	18	Dunn, Small, Fenton (og)
7	Sep 28	Sat	Div 2	A	Bradford Park Avenue	W	1-0	21,360	17	Wood
8	Oct 5	Sat	Div 2	H	Manchester City	W	1-0	33,007	13	Macaulay
9	Oct 12	Sat	Div 2	A	Burnley	L	1-2	22,233	15	Small
10	Oct 19	Sat	Div 2	H	Tottenham Hotspur	D	2-2	34,341	14	Bainbridge, Small
11	Oct 26	Sat	Div 2	A	Swansea Town	L	1-2	22,119	18	Bainbridge
12	Nov 2	Sat	Div 2	H	Newcastle United	L	0-2	32,617	18	
13	Nov 9	Sat	Div 2	A	West Bromwich Albion	W	3-2	23,284	16	Parker, Wood, Woodgate
14	Nov 16	Sat	Div 2	H	Birmingham City	L	0-4	24,719	18	
15	Nov 23	Sat	Div 2	A	Coventry City	L	1-2	19,436	18	Wright
16	Nov 30	Sat	Div 2	H	Nottingham Forest	D	2-2	14,652	20	Hall, Proudlock
17	Dec 7	Sat	Div 2	A	Southampton	L	2-4	17,305	21	Bainbridge, Payne
18	Dec 21	Sat	Div 2	A	Barnsley	W	2-1	11,109	19	Hall, Payne
19	Dec 25	Wed	Div 2	H	Luton Town	W	2-1	19,948	18	Payne, Woodgate
20	Dec 26	Thu	Div 2	A	Luton Town	L	1-2	22,320	18	Payne
21	Dec 28	Sat	Div 2	H	Plymouth Argyle	W	4-1	24,945	18	Bicknell, Payne, Small, Wood
22	Jan 1	Wed	Div 2	A	Sheffield Wednesday	D	1-1	31,852	18	Bainbridge
23	Jan 4	Sat	Div 2	A	Leicester City	L	0-4	27,613	18	
24	Jan 11	Sat	FAC 3	H	Leicester City	L	1-2	26,000		Woodgate
25	Jan 18	Sat	Div 2	H	Chesterfield	W	5-0	23,876	18	Wood 2, Hall, Payne, Small
26	Jan 25	Sat	Div 2	A	Millwall	D	0-0	22,244	18	
27	Feb 1	Sat	Div 2	H	Bradford Park Avenue	D	1-1	16,593	18	Bainbridge
28	Feb 8	Sat	Div 2	H	Newport County	W	3-0	12,447	14	Neary 2, Woodgate
29	Mar 1	Sat	Div 2	H	Swansea Town	W	3-0	20,624	13	Neary 2, Hall
30	Mar 15	Sat	Div 2	H	West Bromwich Albion	W	3-2	23,928	12	Neary 3
31	Mar 22	Sat	Div 2	A	Birmingham City	L	0-3	29,937	13	
32	Mar 29	Sat	Div 2	H	Coventry City	L	1-2	18,813	13	Neary
33	Apr 4	Fri	Div 2	A	Bury	L	0-4	15,266	16	
34	Apr 5	Sat	Div 2	A	Nottingham Forest	L	3-4	22,888	16	Neary 2, Parsons
35	Apr 7	Mon	Div 2	H	Bury	D	3-3	22,525	16	Neary 2, Bainbridge
36	Apr 12	Sat	Div 2	H	Southampton	W	4-0	21,095	14	Neary 2, Parsons, Wood
37	Apr 19	Sat	Div 2	A	Newport County	D	1-1	12,793	13	Bainbridge
38	Apr 26	Sat	Div 2	H	Barnsley	W	4-0	16,275	10	Parsons 2, Bainbridge, Woodgate
39	May 3	Sat	Div 2	H	Sheffield Wednesday	W	2-1	20,977	10	Neary, Woodgate
40	May 17	Sat	Div 2	A	Tottenham Hotspur	D	0-0	37,503	11	
41	May 24	Sat	Div 2	A	Manchester City	L	0-2	33,771	11	
42	May 26	Mon	Div 2	A	Newcastle United	W	3-2	30,112	11	Bainbridge, Hall, Wood
43	May 31	Sat	Div 2	H	Burnley	L	0-5	20,198	12	

Team Line-Ups

ATWELL Reg	BAINBRIDGE Ken	BANNER Arthur	BICKNELL Charlie	CATER Ron	CORBETT Norman	DEVLIN Ernie	DUNN Richard	FORDE Steve	GREGORY Ernie	HALL Almeric	MACAULAY Archibald	MEDHURST Harry	NEARY Frank	PARKER Derek	PARSONS Eric	PAYNE Joe	PROUDLOCK George	SADLER George	SMALL Sam	TAYLOR George	TRAVIS Don	WALKER Richard	WILSON Ron	WOOD John	WOODGATE Terry	WRIGHT Ken	
6		2	3	4						8	10	1							9			5		11	7		1
6		2	3	4						8	10	1							9			5		11	7		2
		3	2	4						8	10	1							6			5		11	7	9	3
6		3	2	4	8												10		9	1		5		11	7		4
6		3	2	4	8												10		9	1		5		11	7		5
	11		2	3	6	8								4					9	1		5		10	7		6
	11		2	3	6	8								4					9	1		5		10	7		7
	11		2	3	6	9					8			4						1		5		10	7		8
	11		2	3	6						8			4					9	1		5		10	7		9
	11		2	3	6						8			4					9	1		5		10	7		10
	11		2	3	6						8			4					9	1		5		10	7		11
	11	3	2		6						8			4					9	1		5		10	7		12
	11	3	2		6				9				8	4						1		5		10	7		13
	11		2		6			3	9				8	4						1		5		10	7		14
	11		2	4				3	9					6					8	1		5			7	10	15
	11	5	2	4				3	9									8	6	1					7	10	16
	11	2	4				8		9									3	6	1		5			7	10	17
	11	2	4					3	8									9	6	1		5			7	10	18
	11	2	4					3	8									9	6	1		5			7	10	19
	11	2	4				8	3										9	6	1		5		10	7		20
	11	2	4					3	1									9	8			5	6	10	7		21
	11	2	4				8	3										9	6	1		5		10	7		22
	11	2	4					3								8		9	6	1		5		10	7		23
	11		4	2				3		10						8		9	6	1		5			7		24
	11	5	4	2				3								8		9	6	1				10	7		25
	11	5	4	2				3								8		9	6	1				10	7		26
	11	5	4	2				3								8		9		1			6	10	7		27
	11	5	4	2				3					9		8					1			6	10	7		28
	11		4	2				3					9		8				6	1		5		10	7		29
	11		4	2				3					9		8				6	1		5		10	7		30
	11		4	2				3					9		8				6	1		5		10	7		31
	11	5	4	2				3					9		8				6	1				10	7		32
	11		4	2				3		10			9		8				6	1		5			7		33
	11		4	2				3		10			9		8				6	1		5			7		34
	11		4	2				3		8			9		7		10		6	1		5					35
	11	5	4	2				3	1				9		8				6					10	7		36
	11	5	4	2				3	1				9		8				6					10	7		37
	11	5	4	2				3	1				9		8				6					10	7		38
	11	5	4	2				3	1	10			9		8				6						7		39
			4	2		3			1				9		8				6			5		10	7	11	40
	11		4	2		3			1						8				6		9	5		10	7		41
	11	3	4	2					1	9					8				6			5		10	7		42
		3	4	2					1	10			9		8				6			5		11	7		43

1947-48
Story of the season

The Hammers found themselves **losing 3–0 after 30 minutes** at Bradford Park Avenue on the opening day, **and were finally beaten 4–1.**

Two tough home and away clashes with Millw: followed, which both ended 1–1. It was a memorable deb: for left-winger Ken Tucker as he scored a hat-trick in t: 4–0 home win against Chesterfield. The following week Newcastle there were 55,767 to see the Hammers narrow lose 1–0, after which there was an unbeaten run of sev: games. West Ham were sixth in the league when they fac: Sheffield Wednesday in two Christmas encounters. Th Yorkshire club proved too strong, winning 5–3 at home ar beating the Hammers 4–1 in the return at Upton Park.

The FA Cup brought an away tie with Blackburn Rove: where the teams drew 0–0. The Lancashire side won t:

Appearances & Goals 1947-48

	League		FA Cup		Total	
	Starts	Goals	Starts	Goals	Starts	Goal
ARMSTRONG Eric	1	0	0	0	1	0
BAINBRIDGE Ken	4	0	0	0	4	0
BANNER Arthur	5	0	0	0	5	0
CATER Ron	7	0	1	0	8	0
CORBETT Norman	42	1	2	0	44	1
DEVLIN Ernie	1	0	0	0	1	0
DUNN Richard	4	1	0	0	4	1
FORDE Steve	42	1	2	0	44	1
GREGORY Ernie	42	0	2	0	44	0
HALL Almeric	9	3	1	0	10	3
MORONEY Tommy	36	2	2	0	38	2
NEARY Frank	3	0	0	0	3	0
PARKER Derek	2	0	0	0	2	0
PARSONS Eric	42	11	2	1	44	12
PROUDLOCK George	10	3	0	0	10	3
SMALL Sam	14	3	1	0	15	3
STEPHENS Bill	21	6	2	1	23	7
TRAVIS Don	4	0	0	0	4	0
TUCKER Ken	5	3	0	0	5	3
WADE Don	16	1	2	0	18	1
WALKER Richard	39	1	1	0	40	1
WILSON Ron	2	0	0	0	2	0
WOOD John	12	3	0	0	12	3
WOODGATE Terry	38	7	2	0	40	7
WRIGHT Ken	21	8	0	0	21	8
YEOMANSON Jack	40	0	2	0	42	0
own goal		1				1
Totals:	**462**	**55**	**22**	**2**	**484**	**57**

play 4–2 after extra time. On their travels there were
xcellent 1–0 victories for West Ham at Coventry City and
 league leaders Birmingham City. But at home both West
romwich Albion and Newcastle United won 2–0 to leave
e Hammers in eighth place. The Easter fixtures gave the
ammers a double over Cardiff City, where Bill Stephens
ored a hat-trick in the 3–0 win at Ninian Park. On Easter
Ionday he scored again in the 4–2 win at the Boleyn
round. In April it was a disaster at Chesterfield, with the
ome side scoring three goals in the final six minutes to give
nem a 6–0 victory. The season ended with a run of three
ndefeated games to leave the Hammers in sixth place with
 mostly settled side. Four players – goalkeeper Ernie
regory, defenders Steve Forde and Norman Corbett,
ogether with forward Eric Parsons – were ever-present.

ootball League - Division Two
inal Table 1947-48

		HOME					AWAY					
	P	W	D	L	F	A	W	D	L	F	A	Pts
rmingham City	42	12	7	2	34	13	10	8	3	21	11	59
ewcastle United	42	18	1	2	46	13	6	7	8	26	28	56
outhampton	42	15	3	3	53	23	6	7	8	18	30	52
heffield Wednesday	42	13	6	2	39	21	7	5	9	27	32	51
ardiff City	42	12	6	3	36	18	6	5	10	25	40	47
West Ham United	42	10	7	4	29	19	6	7	8	26	34	46
est Bromwich Albion	42	11	4	6	37	29	7	5	9	26	29	45
ottenham Hotspur	42	10	6	5	36	24	5	8	8	20	19	44
eicester City	42	10	5	6	36	29	6	6	9	24	28	43
oventry City	42	10	5	6	33	16	4	8	9	26	36	41
ulham	42	6	9	6	24	19	9	1	11	23	27	40
arnsley	42	10	5	6	31	22	5	5	11	31	42	40
uton Town	42	8	8	5	31	25	6	4	11	25	34	40
radford Park Avenue	42	11	3	7	45	30	5	5	11	23	42	40
rentford	42	10	6	5	31	26	3	8	10	13	35	40
hesterfield	42	8	4	9	32	26	8	3	10	22	29	39
lymouth Argyle	42	8	9	4	27	22	1	11	9	13	36	38
eeds United	42	12	5	4	44	20	2	3	16	18	52	36
ottingham Forest	42	10	5	6	32	23	2	6	13	22	37	35
ury	42	6	8	7	27	28	3	8	10	31	40	34
oncaster Rovers	42	7	8	6	23	20	2	3	16	17	46	29
illwalll	42	7	7	7	27	28	2	4	15	17	46	29

TOMMY MORONEY

Wing-half Moroney was a member of the successful Cork United team of the 1940s where he won several League of Ireland titles.

He also played rugby union for Cork Constitution, helping them to win the Munster Cup on three occasions. He moved to West Ham in 1947, making his debut in September against Millwall. Tommy was a reliable defender and went on to play in 148 league games, scoring eight goals. Between 1948 and 1953 he made 12 appearances for the Republic of Ireland. He scored on his debut against Spain in May 1948, and was in the Irish side that beat England 2–0 in September 1949. In 1953 he returned to Cork, where he finished his career playing for Evergreen United. In 1961 he became manager for Cork Hibernians, staying in that post for three years. Tommy died in Ireland in May 1981.

Season **1947-48** Football League - Division Two
Match Details

Manager **Charlie Paynter**   Final League Position **6/22**

	Date		Competition	Venue	Opponents	Results		Attendance	Position	Scorers
1	Aug 23	Sat	Div 2	A	Bradford Park Avenue	L	1-4	14,523	19	Walker
2	Aug 25	Mon	Div 2	H	Millwall	D	1-1	25,741	15	Woodgate
3	Aug 30	Sat	Div 2	H	Nottingham Forest	W	2-1	19,416	13	Parsons, Hutchinson (og)
4	Sep 1	Mon	Div 2	A	Millwall	D	1-1	15,961	13	Small
5	Sep 6	Sat	Div 2	A	Doncaster Rovers	L	0-1	21,198	17	
6	Sep 8	Mon	Div 2	H	Tottenham Hotspur	D	1-1	25,732	15	Parsons
7	Sep 13	Sat	Div 2	H	Southampton	W	2-0	20,709	14	Hall, Wood
8	Sep 15	Mon	Div 2	A	Tottenham Hotspur	D	2-2	33,415	11	Parsons, Wood
9	Sep 20	Sat	Div 2	A	Bury	W	2-1	17,488	8	Proudlock, Wood
10	Sep 27	Sat	Div 2	H	Coventry City	W	1-0	27,087	6	Proudlock
11	Oct 4	Sat	Div 2	H	Chesterfield	W	4-0	25,888	5	Tucker 3, Proudlock
12	Oct 11	Sat	Div 2	A	Newcastle United	L	0-1	55,767	7	
13	Oct 18	Sat	Div 2	H	Birmingham City	D	0-0	32,228	7	
14	Oct 25	Sat	Div 2	A	West Bromwich Albion	W	2-1	37,764	5	Wright 2
15	Nov 1	Sat	Div 2	H	Barnsley	W	2-1	27,877	5	Moroney, Small
16	Nov 8	Sat	Div 2	A	Plymouth Argyle	D	1-1	29,477	4	Parsons
17	Nov 15	Sat	Div 2	H	Luton Town	D	0-0	30,535	5	
18	Nov 22	Sat	Div 2	A	Brentford	D	1-1	24,105	5	Small
19	Nov 29	Sat	Div 2	H	Leicester City	D	1-1	22,860	5	Woodgate [pen]
20	Dec 6	Sat	Div 2	A	Leeds United	L	1-2	21,866	6	Wright
21	Dec 13	Sat	Div 2	H	Fulham	W	3-0	27,332	6	Moroney, Parsons, Wright
22	Dec 20	Sat	Div 2	H	Bradford Park Avenue	D	0-0	24,412	6	
23	Dec 26	Fri	Div 2	A	Sheffield Wednesday	L	3-5	37,557	7	Corbett, Parsons, Woodgate
24	Dec 27	Sat	Div 2	H	Sheffield Wednesday	L	1-4	28,480	8	Stephens
25	Jan 3	Sat	Div 2	A	Nottingham Forest	L	1-2	26,141	10	Woodgate
26	Jan 10	Sat	FAC 3	A	Blackburn Rovers	D	0-0	32,500		
27	Jan 17	Sat	FAC 3 Rep	H	Blackburn Rovers	L	2-4	30,000		Parsons, Stephens
28	Jan 24	Sat	Div 2	H	Doncaster Rovers	W	2-1	17,082	9	Parsons 2
29	Jan 31	Sat	Div 2	A	Southampton	L	1-3	20,039	9	Wright
30	Feb 7	Sat	Div 2	H	Bury	W	2-0	19,247	8	Forde, Woodgate
31	Feb 14	Sat	Div 2	A	Coventry City	W	1-0	24,851	7	Wright
32	Feb 28	Sat	Div 2	H	Newcastle United	L	0-2	33,788	8	
33	Mar 6	Sat	Div 2	A	Birmingham City	W	1-0	43,709	8	Dunn
34	Mar 13	Sat	Div 2	H	West Bromwich Albion	L	0-2	25,170	8	
35	Mar 20	Sat	Div 2	A	Barnsley	D	1-1	18,905	8	Parsons
36	Mar 26	Fri	Div 2	A	Cardiff City	W	3-0	41,700	7	Stephens 3
37	Mar 27	Sat	Div 2	H	Plymouth Argyle	D	1-1	22,102	7	Stephens
38	Mar 29	Mon	Div 2	H	Cardiff City	W	4-2	31,667	6	Wright 2, Parsons, Stephens
39	Apr 3	Sat	Div 2	A	Luton Town	D	0-0	15,059	7	
40	Apr 7	Wed	Div 2	A	Chesterfield	L	0-6	11,914	7	
41	Apr 10	Sat	Div 2	H	Brentford	L	0-1	21,471	7	
42	Apr 17	Sat	Div 2	A	Leicester City	W	3-1	25,156	6	Hall, Wade, Woodgate
43	Apr 24	Sat	Div 2	H	Leeds United	W	2-1	13,549	6	Parsons, Woodgate
44	May 1	Sat	Div 2	A	Fulham	D	1-1	15,798	6	Hall

Team Line-Ups

ARMSTRONG Eric	BAINBRIDGE Ken	BANNER Arthur	CATER Ron	CORBETT Norman	DEVLIN Ernie	DUNN Richard	FORDE Steve	GREGORY Ernie	HALL Almeric	MORONEY Tommy	NEARY Frank	PARKER Derek	PARSONS Eric	PROUDLOCK George	SMALL Sam	STEPHENS Bill	TRAVIS Don	TUCKER Ken	WADE Don	WALKER Richard	WILSON Ron	WOOD John	WOODGATE Terry	WRIGHT Ken	YEOMANSON Jack	
	11	5		4			3	1			9		8							6			7	10	2	1
	11	5		4			3	1			9		8							6		10	7		2	2
			4	6			3	1	10				8	9						5	11		7		2	3
				4			3	1	8	6			7	10	9					5	11				2	4
				4			3	1	8	6			7	10	9					5	11				2	5
				4			3	1	9	6			8	10						5	11		7		2	6
				4			3	1	8	6	9		7							5		10		11	2	7
				4			3	1		6		7	8	10		9				5	11				2	8
				4			3	1		6			8	10	9					5	11		7		2	9
				4			3	1		6			8	10	9					5	11		7		2	10
				4			3	1		6			8	10	9				11	5			7		2	11
				4			3	1		6			8	10	9				11	5			7		2	12
				4			3	1		6			8	10	9					5			7	11	2	13
				4			3	1		6			8	9					11	5			7	10	2	14
				4			3	1		6			8	9					11	5			7	10	2	15
				4			3	1		6			8				9			5	11		7	10	2	16
				4			3	1		6			8				9			5		11	7	10	2	17
				4			3	1	10	6			8		9				11	5			7		2	18
				4			3	1		6			8			10				5	9		7	11	2	19
		5		4			3	1					8							6	9	11	7	10	2	20
				4			3	1		6			8			9		11		5			7	10	2	21
				4			3	1		6			8			9			11	5			7	10	2	22
		5		4			3	1		6			8			9			11				7	10	2	23
		5		4			3	1		10			8		6	9			11				7		2	24
			4		2		3	1		6			8		10	9			11	5			7			25
				4			3	1	9	6			8			10			11	5			7		2	26
			4	5			3	1		6			8		9	10			11				7		2	27
6			4	5		8	3	1					7				9		10			11			2	28
				4			3	1		6			8			9			10	5			7	11	2	29
				4			3	1		6			8			9			11	5			7	10	2	30
				4			3	1		6			8			9			11	5			7	10	2	31
			6	4			3	1					8			9			11	5			7	10	2	32
				4		10	3	1		6			8			9			11	5			7		2	33
				4		8	3	1		6			7	10		9				5		11			2	34
				4			3	1	10	6			8			9				5			7	11	2	35
				4			3	1		6			8			9			11	5			7	10	2	36
			2	4		11	3	1		6		10	8			9				5			7			37
			2	4			3	1		6			8			9				5			7	11	10	38
			2	4			3	1		6			8			9				5			7	11	10	39
			2	4			3	1		6			8			9			11	5			7		10	40
				4			3	1		6			8			9			10	5			7	11	2	41
				4			3	1	10	6			8			9			11	5			7		2	42
	11			4			3	1		6			8			9			10	5			7		2	43
	11			4			3	1	10	6			8			9				5			7		2	44

1948-49
Story of the season

The opening home game with Lincoln City ended 2–2, with **the luckless Bill Stephens breaking his leg**, after which he never played again.

There was only one victory in the first seven games b form began to improve in September. Successive hor games saw Plymouth Argyle beaten 3–0 followed by a 1 win against London rivals Tottenham, where Almer H scored the solitary goal. After six successive away gam without a goal, Ken Wright scored at Queens Park Range The one goal was not enough as the Hammers lost 2– The team fared better on their travels in November, winni 3–1 at both Bradford Park Avenue and Barnsley. T Christmas period brought a double over Leeds United, wi Ken Wright scoring twice in both games.

Appearances & Goals 1948-49

	League		FA Cup		Total	
	Starts	Goals	Starts	Goals	Starts	Goa
BAINBRIDGE Ken	16	2	0	0	16	2
CARROLL Johnny	5	0	0	0	5	0
CATER Ron	18	0	0	0	18	0
CHAPMAN Eddie	7	3	0	0	7	3
CORBETT Norman	39	1	1	0	40	1
DEVLIN Ernie	20	0	0	0	20	0
DICK George	14	1	1	0	15	1
FORDE Steve	31	0	1	0	32	0
GREGORY Ernie	27	0	1	0	28	0
HALL Almeric	17	3	0	0	17	3
JACKMAN Derek	1	0	0	0	1	0
McGOWAN Danny	15	3	0	0	15	3
MORONEY Tommy	36	0	1	0	37	0
PARSONS Eric	42	9	1	0	43	9
ROBINSON Bill	17	10	0	0	17	10
STEPHENS Bill	1	0	0	0	1	0
TAYLOR George	15	0	0	0	15	0
TUCKER Ken	2	0	0	0	2	0
WADE Don	8	0	1	1	9	1
WALKER Richard	40	1	1	0	41	1
WOOD John	3	0	0	0	3	0
WOODGATE Terry	38	9	1	0	39	9
WRIGHT Ken	21	11	1	0	22	11
YEOMANSON Jack	29	1	1	0	30	1
own goal		2				2
Totals:	**462**	**56**	**11**	**1**	**473**	**5**

For the third season running the Hammers were knocked out of the FA Cup at the first attempt. This time it was Luton Town who won 3–1 at their Kenilworth Road ground. To increase the goal tally, centre-forward Bill Robinson was signed from Charlton and promptly scored on his debut at West Bromwich Albion. The home faithful were treated to some good displays, with seven successive home wins including a 4–1 victory against Leicester City, where Robinson scored a hat-trick. After such a good home record it was a shock when the final home game with Nottingham Forest was lost 5–0. Winger Eric Parsons was ever-present as the campaign ended with West Ham finishing in seventh place.

DANNY MCGOWAN

Danny signed for West Ham in 1948 from the League of Ireland side Shelbourne.

A skilful inside-forward, he scored on his debut against Lincoln City. He completed six seasons at West Ham, playing in 83 games and scoring eight goals before joining Southern League Chelmsford City in 1954. While at West Ham he gained three Republic of Ireland caps, playing against Portugal, Sweden and Spain. At Chelmsford he played in 24 league games for one season as the Essex club struggled, finishing second from bottom. He then finished his playing career in the Kent League with Folkestone Town before spending 22 years working for the London Electricity Board. He died in April 1994 aged 69.

Football League - Division Two
Final Table 1948-49

		HOME					AWAY					
	P	W	D	L	F	A	W	D	L	F	A	Pts
Fulham	42	16	4	1	52	14	8	5	8	25	23	57
West Bromwich Albion	42	16	3	2	47	16	8	5	8	22	23	56
Southampton	42	16	4	1	48	10	7	5	9	21	26	55
Cardiff City	42	14	4	3	45	21	5	9	7	17	26	51
Tottenham Hotspur	42	14	4	3	50	18	3	12	6	22	26	50
Chesterfield	42	9	7	5	24	18	6	10	5	27	27	47
West Ham United	42	13	5	3	38	23	5	5	11	18	35	46
Sheffield Wednesday	42	12	6	3	36	17	3	7	11	27	39	43
Barnsley	42	10	7	4	40	18	4	5	12	22	43	40
Luton Town	42	11	6	4	32	16	3	6	12	23	41	40
Grimsby Town	42	10	5	6	44	28	5	5	11	28	48	40
Bury	42	12	5	4	41	23	5	1	15	26	53	40
Queens Park Rangers	42	11	4	6	31	26	3	7	11	13	36	39
Blackburn Rovers	42	12	5	4	41	23	3	3	15	12	40	38
Leeds United	42	11	6	4	36	21	1	7	13	19	42	37
Coventry City	42	12	3	6	35	20	3	4	14	20	44	37
Bradford Park Avenue	42	8	8	5	37	26	5	3	13	28	52	37
Brentford	42	7	10	4	28	21	4	4	13	14	32	36
Leicester City	42	6	10	5	41	38	4	6	11	21	41	36
Plymouth Argyle	42	11	4	6	33	25	1	8	12	16	39	36
Nottingham Forest	42	9	6	6	22	14	5	1	15	28	40	35
Lincoln City	42	6	7	8	31	35	2	5	14	22	56	28

Season **1948-49** Football League - Division Two
Match Details

Manager **Charlie Paynter**   Final League Position **7/22**

	Date		Competition	Venue	Opponents	Results		Attendance	Position	Scorers
1	Aug 21	Sat	Div 2	H	Lincoln City	D	2-2	31,079	12	McGowan, Wright
2	Aug 23	Mon	Div 2	A	Sheffield Wednesday	L	0-3	34,342	15	
3	Aug 28	Sat	Div 2	A	Chesterfield	D	0-0	16,489	20	
4	Aug 30	Mon	Div 2	H	Sheffield Wednesday	D	2-2	24,607	16	Bainbridge, Parsons
5	Sep 4	Sat	Div 2	H	West Bromwich Albion	W	1-0	28,065	11	Hall
6	Sep 6	Mon	Div 2	A	Coventry City	L	0-1	16,515	12	.
7	Sep 11	Sat	Div 2	A	Bury	L	0-2	23,754	20	
8	Sep 13	Mon	Div 2	H	Coventry City	D	2-2	14,400	17	Chapman, Cox (og)
9	Sep 18	Sat	Div 2	H	Plymouth Argyle	W	3-0	22,256	16	Chapman, Wright, Yeomanson
10	Sep 25	Sat	Div 2	H	Tottenham Hotspur	W	1-0	38,132	13	Hall
11	Oct 2	Sat	Div 2	A	Brentford	D	0-0	31,369	13	
12	Oct 9	Sat	Div 2	A	Blackburn Rovers	D	0-0	24,037	12	
13	Oct 16	Sat	Div 2	H	Cardiff City	W	3-1	29,433	8	Chapman, Parsons, Wright
14	Oct 23	Sat	Div 2	A	Queens Park Rangers	L	1-2	27,950	11	Wright
15	Oct 30	Sat	Div 2	H	Luton Town	L	0-1	28,132	12	
16	Nov 6	Sat	Div 2	A	Bradford Park Avenue	W	3-2	15,913	12	Hall, Parsons, Woodgate [pen]
17	Nov 13	Sat	Div 2	H	Southampton	D	1-1	34,538	11	Woodgate
18	Nov 20	Sat	Div 2	A	Barnsley	W	3-2	20,359	8	Walker, Woodgate, Wright
19	Dec 4	Sat	Div 2	A	Nottingham Forest	L	0-3	23,218	13	
20	Dec 11	Sat	Div 2	H	Fulham	W	1-0	22,689	11	Wright
21	Dec 18	Sat	Div 2	A	Lincoln City	L	3-4	15,609	13	Woodgate 2 [1 pen], Parsons
22	Dec 25	Sat	Div 2	H	Leeds United	W	3-2	20,660	12	Wright 2, Corbett
23	Dec 27	Mon	Div 2	A	Leeds United	W	3-1	32,577	9	Wright 2, Dick
24	Jan 1	Sat	Div 2	H	Chesterfield	L	1-2	16,946	11	Woodgate [pen]
25	Jan 8	Sat	FAC 3	A	Luton Town	L	1-3	21,629		Wade
26	Jan 15	Sat	Div 2	A	West Bromwich Albion	L	1-2	33,100	12	Robinson
27	Jan 22	Sat	Div 2	H	Bury	W	2-1	21,700	10	Parsons, Robinson
28	Feb 5	Sat	Div 2	A	Plymouth Argyle	L	0-2	18,481	12	
29	Feb 12	Sat	Div 2	H	Grimsby Town	W	1-0	14,578	10	Robinson
30	Feb 19	Sat	Div 2	A	Tottenham Hotspur	D	1-1	62,980	8	Woodgate
31	Mar 5	Sat	Div 2	H	Blackburn Rovers	W	2-1	18,245	8	Parsons, Wright
32	Mar 12	Sat	Div 2	A	Cardiff City	L	0-4	28,271	8	
33	Mar 19	Sat	Div 2	H	Queens Park Rangers	W	2-0	25,039	8	Robinson, Woodgate
34	Mar 26	Sat	Div 2	A	Luton Town	W	1-0	15,587	7	Robinson
35	Apr 2	Sat	Div 2	H	Bradford Park Avenue	W	4-1	18,645	6	Parsons 2, McGowan, Horsman (og)
36	Apr 9	Sat	Div 2	A	Southampton	W	1-0	25,644	6	Robinson
37	Apr 15	Fri	Div 2	H	Leicester City	W	4-1	32,896	6	Robinson 3 [1 pen], Woodgate
38	Apr 16	Sat	Div 2	H	Barnsley	W	2-0	20,482	6	McGowan, Parsons
39	Apr 18	Mon	Div 2	A	Leicester City	D	1-1	30,410	6	Robinson
40	Apr 23	Sat	Div 2	A	Grimsby Town	L	0-3	15,803	6	
41	Apr 25	Mon	Div 2	H	Brentford	D	1-1	15,553	6	Bainbridge
42	Apr 30	Sat	Div 2	H	Nottingham Forest	L	0-5	12,349	6	
43	May 7	Sat	Div 2	A	Fulham	L	0-2	41,133	7	

Team Line-Ups

BAINBRIDGE Ken	CARROLL Johnny	CATER Ron	CHAPMAN Eddie	CORBETT Norman	DEVLIN Ernie	DICK George	FORDE Steve	GREGORY Ernie	HALL Almeric	JACKMAN Derek	McGOWAN Danny	MORONEY Tommy	PARSONS Eric	ROBINSON Bill	STEPHENS Bill	TAYLOR George	TUCKER Ken	WADE Don	WALKER Richard	WOOD John	WOODGATE Terry	WRIGHT Ken	YEOMANSON Jack	
				4	3			1			10	6	7		9				5	8		11	2	1
				4	3			1	9		10	6	7						5	8		11	2	2
11				4	3			1	9		10	6	7						5	8			2	3
11	9			4	3			1			10	6	8						5		7		2	4
11	9	6		4	3			1	8			10	7						5				2	5
11	9	6		4	3			1				10	8						5		7		2	6
	9	6		4	3			1	8			10	7						5		11		2	7
	9	3	8	4				1	10			6	7						5		11		2	8
		3	8	4				1	10			6	7						5		11	9	2	9
			8	4	3			1	10			6	7						5		11	9	2	10
			8	4			3	1	10			6	7						5		11	9	2	11
		4	8	5			3	1	10			6	7								11	9	2	12
			8	4			3	1	10			6	7						5		11	9	2	13
		4	8				3	1	10			6	7						5		11	9	2	14
				4		10	3	1	8			6	7						5		11	9	2	15
				4		10	3	1	8			6	7						5		11	9	2	16
				4		10	3	1	8			6	7						5		11	9	2	17
				4		10	3	1	8			6	7						5		11	9	2	18
		4					3	1	8			6	7					10	5		11	9	2	19
				4			3	1	8			6	7					10	5		11	9	2	20
		4		5		8	3	1				6	7					10			11	9	2	21
				4		8	3					6	7				1	10	5		11	9	2	22
				4		10	3					6	8			1		11	5		7	9	2	23
				4		10	3					6	8			1		11	5		7	9	2	24
				4		9	3	1				6	8					10	5		7	11	2	25
				4		8	3	1				6	7	9				10	5		11		2	26
				4		8	3	1			10	6	7	9					5		11		2	27
				4		10	3	1				6	8	9				11	5		7		2	28
				4	2	10	3	1				6	8	9			11		5		7			29
	6			4	2	10	3	1					8	9			11		5		7			30
	6			4	2		3	1		10			8	7					5		11	9		31
11	6			4	2	10	3						8			1			5		7	9		32
11	6			4	2		3						8	9		1			5		7	10		33
11	6			4	2		3				10		8	9		1			5		7			34
11		4		3	2						10	6	8	9		1			5		7			35
11				4	2		3				10	6	8	9		1			5		7			36
11				4	2		3				10	6	8	9		1			5		7			37
11				4	2		3				10	6	8	9		1			5		7			38
11				4	2		3				10	6	8	9		1			5		7			39
11	4				2		3				10	6	8	9		1			5		7			40
11	4						3				10	6	8	9		1			5		7		2	41
11	6			4			3				10		8	9		1			5		7		2	42
11				4	2		3				10	6	8	9		1			5		7			43

1949-50
Story of the season

An **excellent start to the campaign** elevated West Ham to second in the table. In the 2–1 home win against Barnsley winger **Ken Bainbridge scored after only nine seconds.**

Up until the end of September there had only been on defeat but this all changed after Preston won 3–0 at th Boleyn Ground. A run of six games without a win pushe the team down to 10th spot. Early in the season winger Bainbridge and Parsons were scoring, but now the tean relied on centre-forward Bill Robinson to score. Inside forward Don Wade stepped up and scored in both th home wins over Hull City and Swansea Town.

In January the home FA Cup tie with Ipswich brought a 5– victory. Everton in the next round proved more formidab opponents as they won 2–1 at Goodison Park. On their wa by train to Chesterfield in February, a freight train blocke

Appearances & Goals 1949-50

	League		FA Cup		Total	
	Starts	Goals	Starts	Goals	Starts	Goals
BAINBRIDGE Ken	25	5	0	0	25	5
BARRETT Jim Jnr.	3	0	0	0	3	0
CATER Ron	4	0	1	0	5	0
CORBETT Norman	12	0	0	0	12	0
DEVLIN Ernie	28	0	2	0	30	0
FORDE Steve	27	0	0	0	27	0
GAZZARD Gerry	38	4	2	1	40	5
GREGORY Ernie	42	0	2	0	44	0
JACKMAN Derek	3	0	0	0	3	0
KEARNS Fred	8	0	0	0	8	0
McGOWAN Danny	37	2	2	1	39	3
MORONEY Tommy	21	0	0	0	21	0
PARKER Derek	32	2	2	0	34	2
PARSONS Eric	38	7	2	0	40	7
ROBINSON Bill	40	23	2	1	42	24
TUCKER Ken	2	0	0	0	2	0
WADE Don	12	4	1	1	13	5
WALKER Richard	39	0	2	0	41	0
WOODGATE Terry	29	4	2	2	31	6
WRIGHT Ken	2	0	0	0	2	0
YEOMANSON Jack	20	0	2	0	22	0
own goal		2				2
Totals:	**462**	**53**	**22**	**6**	**484**	**59**

he line and the Hammers did not arrive until 4.25 pm; by that time it was snowing and most of the spectators had gone home. The dispirited West Ham team lost 1–0 before a meagre crowd of 3,036. Two more home wins followed, including a decent 4–0 victory against Bury in March. However, this proved to be the last win of the season as the team slumped, without a victory in the remaining nine games. It had been a disappointing campaign and by finishing in nineteenth place the side had narrowly missed relegation.

Football League - Division Two Final Table 1949-50

	P	HOME					AWAY					Pts
		W	D	L	F	A	W	D	L	F	A	
Tottenham Hotspur	42	15	3	3	51	15	12	4	5	30	20	61
Sheffield Wednesday	42	12	7	2	46	23	6	9	6	21	25	52
Sheffield United	42	9	10	2	36	19	10	4	7	32	30	52
Southampton	42	13	4	4	44	25	6	10	5	20	23	52
Leeds United	42	11	8	2	33	16	6	5	10	21	29	47
Preston North End	42	12	5	4	37	21	6	4	11	23	28	45
Hull City	42	11	8	2	39	25	6	3	12	25	47	45
Swansea Town	42	11	3	7	34	18	6	6	9	19	31	43
Brentford	42	11	5	5	21	12	4	8	9	23	37	43
Cardiff City	42	13	3	5	28	14	3	7	11	13	30	42
Grimsby Town	42	13	5	3	53	25	3	3	15	21	48	40
Coventry City	42	8	6	7	32	24	5	7	9	23	31	39
Barnsley	42	11	6	4	45	28	2	7	12	19	39	39
Chesterfield	42	12	3	6	28	16	3	6	12	15	31	39
Leicester City	42	8	9	4	30	25	4	6	11	25	40	39
Blackburn Rovers	42	10	5	6	30	15	4	5	12	25	45	38
Luton Town	42	8	9	4	28	22	2	9	10	13	29	38
Bury	42	10	8	3	37	19	4	1	16	23	46	37
West Ham United	**42**	**8**	**7**	**6**	**30**	**25**	**4**	**5**	**12**	**23**	**36**	**36**
Queens Park Rangers	42	6	5	10	21	30	5	7	9	19	27	34
Plymouth Argyle	42	6	6	9	19	24	2	10	9	25	41	32
Bradford Park Avenue	42	7	6	8	34	34	3	5	13	17	43	31

DEREK PARKER

A popular wing-half, he joined West Ham in October 1944 from Grays Athletic.

He appeared briefly for the club in wartime, before gaining a regular place in the early 1950s. His league debut was against Millwall in 1946 and he went on to play in a total of 207 games spread over ten seasons. In 1951 he played in four games for the FA XI who were touring Australia. He played his last game for the Hammers in December 1956 when he scored in the 3–3 draw at Bury.

Three months later he joined his home-town club Colchester United in the Third Division and spent four seasons with the Essex club, playing in 137 games before going into non-league football with Stowmarket. Derek passed away in April 2011 aged 84.

Season **1949-50** Football League - Division Two
Match Details

Manager **Charlie Paynter**   Final League Position **19/22**

	Date		Competition	Venue	Opponents	Results		Attendance	Position	Scorers
1	Aug 20	Sat	Div 2	A	Luton Town	D	2-2	17,003	14	Robinson, Parsons
2	Aug 22	Mon	Div 2	H	Leeds United	W	3-1	24,728	4	Robinson 2, McGowan
3	Aug 27	Sat	Div 2	H	Barnsley	W	2-1	27,541	3	Bainbridge, Gazzard
4	Aug 31	Wed	Div 2	A	Leeds United	D	2-2	29,732	5	Bainbridge, Robinson
5	Sep 3	Sat	Div 2	A	Plymouth Argyle	W	3-0	22,401	2	Gazzard, Robinson, Parsons
6	Sep 5	Mon	Div 2	H	Southampton	L	1-2	25,498	2	Robinson [pen]
7	Sep 10	Sat	Div 2	A	Sheffield United	D	0-0	21,901	5	
8	Sep 17	Sat	Div 2	H	Grimsby Town	W	4-3	28,194	4	Bainbridge 2, Robinson 2
9	Sep 24	Sat	Div 2	A	Queens Park Rangers	W	1-0	24,578	3	Robinson
10	Oct 1	Sat	Div 2	H	Preston North End	L	0-3	36,653	4	
11	Oct 8	Sat	Div 2	H	Chesterfield	D	1-1	25,869	6	Parsons
12	Oct 15	Sat	Div 2	A	Bradford Park Avenue	L	1-2	13,863	7	Robinson [pen]
13	Oct 22	Sat	Div 2	H	Leicester City	D	2-2	22,466	8	Bainbridge, Parsons
14	Oct 29	Sat	Div 2	A	Bury	L	1-3	16,399	9	Gazzard
15	Nov 5	Sat	Div 2	H	Tottenham Hotspur	L	0-1	31,734	12	
16	Nov 12	Sat	Div 2	A	Cardiff City	W	1-0	21,644	10	Robinson
17	Nov 19	Sat	Div 2	H	Blackburn Rovers	L	0-2	19,687	13	
18	Nov 26	Sat	Div 2	A	Brentford	W	2-0	21,887	8	Robinson 2
19	Dec 3	Sat	Div 2	H	Hull City	W	2-1	29,421	6	Robinson, Wade
20	Dec 10	Sat	Div 2	A	Sheffield Wednesday	L	1-2	26,415	8	Wade
21	Dec 17	Sat	Div 2	H	Luton Town	D	0-0	16,445	9	
22	Dec 24	Sat	Div 2	A	Barnsley	D	1-1	17,377	8	Parsons
23	Dec 26	Mon	Div 2	H	Swansea Town	W	3-0	24,398	8	Parsons, Wade, Weston (og)
24	Dec 27	Tue	Div 2	A	Swansea Town	L	0-1	25,721	8	
25	Dec 31	Sat	Div 2	H	Plymouth Argyle	D	2-2	18,602	8	Robinson [pen], Wade
26	Jan 7	Sat	FAC 3	H	Ipswich Town	W	5-1	25,000		Woodgate 2, Gazzard, Wade, Robinson
27	Jan 14	Sat	Div 2	H	Sheffield United	D	0-0	22,389	8	
28	Jan 21	Sat	Div 2	A	Grimsby Town	L	0-2	17,067	9	
29	Jan 28	Sat	FAC 4	H	Everton	L	1-2	26,800		McGowan
30	Feb 4	Sat	Div 2	H	Queens Park Rangers	W	1-0	25,440	8	Robinson [pen]
31	Feb 18	Sat	Div 2	A	Preston North End	L	1-2	26,381	10	Waters (og)
32	Feb 25	Sat	Div 2	A	Chesterfield	L	0-1	3,036	12	
33	Mar 4	Sat	Div 2	H	Bradford Park Avenue	W	1-0	17,587	10	Parker
34	Mar 11	Sat	Div 2	A	Leicester City	L	1-2	29,705	11	Robinson
35	Mar 18	Sat	Div 2	H	Bury	W	4-0	15,835	9	Gazzard, Parker, Parsons, Woodgate
36	Mar 25	Sat	Div 2	A	Tottenham Hotspur	L	1-4	51,124	13	Robinson
37	Apr 1	Sat	Div 2	H	Brentford	D	2-2	18,826	13	Robinson 2 [2 pen]
38	Apr 8	Sat	Div 2	A	Hull City	D	2-2	31,049	13	McGowan, Robinson
39	Apr 10	Mon	Div 2	H	Coventry City	L	0-1	11,110	13	
40	Apr 11	Tue	Div 2	A	Coventry City	L	1-5	26,645	14	Woodgate
41	Apr 15	Sat	Div 2	H	Cardiff City	L	0-1	14,109	17	
42	Apr 22	Sat	Div 2	A	Blackburn Rovers	L	0-2	17,375	18	
43	Apr 29	Sat	Div 2	H	Sheffield Wednesday	D	2-2	10,361	18	Woodgate 2
44	May 6	Sat	Div 2	A	Southampton	L	2-3	24,778	19	Robinson 2

Team Line-Ups

BAINBRIDGE Ken	BARRETT Jim Jnr.	CATER Ron	CORBETT Norman	DEVLIN Ernie	FORDE Steve	GAZZARD Gerry	GREGORY Ernie	JACKMAN Derek	KEARNS Fred	McGOWAN Danny	MORONEY Tommy	PARKER Derek	PARSONS Eric	ROBINSON Bill	TUCKER Ken	WADE Don	WALKER Richard	WOODGATE Terry	WRIGHT Ken	YEOMANSON Jack	
11			4	2	3	8	1			10	6		7	9			5				1
11			4	2	3	8	1			10	6		7	9			5				2
11			4	2	3	8	1			10	6		7	9			5				3
11			4	2	3	8	1			10	6		7	9			5				4
11			4	2	3	8	1			10	6		7	9			5				5
11			4	2	3	8	1			10	6		7	9			5				6
11			4	2	3	10	1				6		8	9			5	7			7
11				2	3	8	1			10	6	4	7	9			5				8
11				2	3	8	1			10	6	4	7	9			5				9
11				2	3	8	1			10	6	4	7	9			5				10
11		6		2		8	1		3	10		4	7	9			5				11
11				2		10	1		3		6	4	8	9			5	7			12
11				2		10	1		3		6	4	8				5	7			13
11		6		2		10	1		3	9		4	8				5	7			14
11				2		8	1		3	10	6	4	7				5		9		15
11				2		8	1	10	3	6		4	7	9			5				16
11				2		8	1	10	3	6		4	7	9			5				17
				2	3	8	1	10		6		4	7	9			5	11			18
				2	3	8	1			6		4	7	9		10	5	11			19
				2		8	1			6		4	7	9		10		11	5	3	20
				2	3	8	1			6		4	7	9		10	5	11			21
				2		8	1			6		4	7	9		10	5	11		3	22
		3		2		8	1			6		4	7	9		10	5	11			23
				2		8	1		3	6		4	7	9		10	5	11			24
				2		8	1			6		4	7	9		10	5	11		3	25
				2		8	1			6		4	7	9		10	5	11		3	26
				2		8	1			6		4	7	9		10	5	11		3	27
		6		2		8	1			10		4	7	9			5	11		3	28
	10			2		8	1			6		4	7	9			5	11		3	29
				2		8	1			6		4	10	9		11	5	7		3	30
					3	10	1			6		4	8	9		11	5	7		2	31
					3	10	1			6		4	8	9		11	5	7		2	32
		6			3	8	1			10		4		9		11	5	7		2	33
11			5		3	8	1			10	6	4		9				7		2	34
11					3	10	1			6		4	8	9			5	7		2	35
11					3	10	1			6		4	8	9			5	7		2	36
11					3	10	1			6		4	8	9			5	7		2	37
11					3		1			10	6	4	8	9			5	7		2	38
11					3		1			10	6	4	8	9			5	7		2	39
11			5		3	10	1			4	6		8	9				7		2	40
			4		3		1			10	6		8	9	11		5	7		2	41
	8				3	10	1				6	4	7	9			5	11		2	42
11	8	4			3		1			10	6			9			5	7		2	43
	8				3	10	1				6	4		9	11		5	7		2	44

1950-51
Story of the season

Before the season got under way **manager Charlie Paynter retired** and **Ted Fenton took over.** Charlie had served the club for 50 years as trainer, secretary and manager.

After just a minute of the opening game, West Ham were leading Hull City 1–0 courtesy of an own goal by Jensen. The teams served up a treat for the spectators in the 3–3 draw. Following on from this there was a good 3–1 win at Blackburn Rovers, with Bill Robinson scoring twice. Also claiming a brace was Gerry Gazzard in the 3–0 home victory over Southampton. Against Sheffield United at the Boleyn Bill Robinson grabbed a hat-trick, but the Yorkshire side ran out 5–3 winners. It became the same old story after home wins against Coventry City (3–2) and Preston

Appearances & Goals 1950-51

	League		FA Cup		Other*		Total	
	Starts	Goals	Starts	Goals	Starts	Goals	Starts	Goal
ALLISON Malcolm	10	0	0	0	3	0	13	0
BARRETT Jim Jnr.	22	4	2	1	1	0	25	5
BETTS Eric	3	1	0	0	0	0	3	1
DEVLIN Ernie	13	0	0	0	1	0	14	0
FOAN Albert	5	0	0	0	0	0	5	0
FORDE Steve	32	0	2	0	2	0	36	0
GAZZARD Gerry	41	13	2	1	4	3	47	17
GREGORY Ernie	30	0	2	0	1	0	33	0
HOOPER Harry	11	3	0	0	3	2	14	5
JACKMAN Derek	4	0	0	0	1	0	5	0
JOHNS Stan	6	2	0	0	1	0	7	2
KEARNS Fred	6	0	1	0	1	0	8	0
KINSELL Harry	16	1	1	0	2	0	19	1
McGOWAN Danny	7	1	0	0	2	0	9	1
MORONEY Tommy	25	0	0	0	3	1	28	1
NELSON Bill	0	0	0	0	1	0	1	0
NIBLETT Vic	0	0	0	0	1	0	1	0
O'FARRELL Frank	18	0	2	0	2	0	22	0
PARKER Derek	38	1	2	0	2	0	42	1
PARSONS Eric	11	3	0	0	0	0	11	3
ROBINSON Bill	40	26	2	0	4	3	46	29
SOUTHREN Tommy	17	0	2	0	1	0	20	0
TAYLOR George	12	0	0	0	3	0	15	0
TUCKER Ken	3	0	0	0	0	0	3	0
WALKER Richard	33	3	2	0	0	0	35	3
WOODGATE Terry	42	12	2	0	4	0	48	12
WRIGHT George	0	0	0	0	1	0	1	0
YEOMANSON Jack	17	0	0	0	0	0	17	0
own goal		1						1
TOTALS	**462**	**71**	**22**	**2**	**44**	**9**	**528**	**82**

* Other = Essex Professional Cup

North End (2–0) there were away defeats at Notts County (4–1) and Birmingham City (3–1). On Christmas Day winger Terry Woodgate was the hero when scoring a hat-trick in the 3–1 home win against Leeds United.

The FA Cup saw a narrow 2–1 home win against Cardiff City, but there was no joy in the next round as the Hammers lost 1–0 away at Stoke City. Robinson then went on a scoring spree, scoring nine goals in seven games, but in that spell the only victory was the 4–2 home win against Barnsley. As the season came to a close there was one notable win as the Hammers won 1–0 away to champions elect Preston North End. A mid-table finish of thirteenth was achieved, being an improvement from the previous season. During the campaign Frank O'Farrell, who had been at the club since 1948, made his debut and Malcolm Allison was signed – both were to have an impact in the years to come.

Football League - Division Two Final Table 1950-51

	P	HOME					AWAY					Pts
	P	W	D	L	F	A	W	D	L	F	A	Pts
Preston North End	42	16	3	2	53	18	10	2	9	38	31	57
Manchester City	42	12	6	3	53	25	7	8	6	36	36	52
Cardiff City	42	13	7	1	36	20	4	9	8	17	25	50
Birmingham City	42	12	6	3	37	20	8	3	10	27	33	49
Leeds United	42	14	4	3	36	17	6	4	11	27	38	48
Blackburn Rovers	42	13	3	5	39	27	6	5	10	26	39	46
Coventry City	42	15	3	3	51	25	4	4	13	24	34	45
Sheffield United	42	11	4	6	44	27	5	8	8	28	35	44
Brentford	42	13	3	5	44	25	5	5	11	31	49	44
Hull City	42	12	5	4	47	28	4	6	11	27	42	43
Doncaster Rovers	42	9	6	6	37	32	6	7	8	27	36	43
Southampton	42	10	9	2	38	27	5	4	12	28	46	43
West Ham United	42	10	5	6	44	33	6	5	10	24	36	42
Leicester City	42	10	4	7	42	28	5	7	9	26	30	41
Barnsley	42	9	5	7	42	22	6	5	10	32	46	40
Queens Park Rangers	42	13	5	3	47	25	2	5	14	24	57	40
Notts County	42	7	7	7	37	34	6	6	9	24	26	39
Swansea Town	42	14	1	6	34	25	2	3	16	20	52	36
Luton Town	42	7	9	5	34	23	2	5	14	23	47	32
Bury	42	9	4	8	33	27	3	4	14	27	59	32
Chesterfield	42	7	7	7	30	28	2	5	14	14	41	30
Grimsby Town	42	6	8	7	37	38	2	4	15	24	57	28

HARRY HOOPER

Harry was a fast right-winger who signed for West Ham in 1951 and made his debut in February of that year against Barnsley at the Boleyn Ground.

By 1954 he was a regular in the side and was earning acclaim around the country. He was selected five times for the England B team, played twice for the England under-23 team and also made Football League XI appearances. After 130 appearances he was transferred to Wolverhampton Wanderers in 1956, a move which caused supporter unrest at Upton Park. He only played 39 league games for the Wolves before joining Birmingham City in 1957. He did better with the Blues, where he stayed for four seasons, playing in 119 games and scoring 42 goals. In September 1960 he was transferred to Sunderland, where he played a further 65 league games before going into non-league football with Kettering in 1963. Harry, now aged 81, is enjoying his retirement at his home in Kettering.

Season **1950-51** Football League - Division Two
Match Details

Manager **Ted Fenton**   Final League Position **13/22**

	Date		Competition	Venue	Opponents	Results		Attendance	Position	Scorers
1	Aug 19	Sat	Div 2	H	Hull City	D	3-3	30,056	12	Gazzard, Robinson, Jensen (og)
2	Aug 24	Thu	Div 2	H	Luton Town	W	2-1	20,560	7	Betts, Woodgate
3	Aug 26	Sat	Div 2	A	Doncaster Rovers	L	0-3	22,804	13	
4	Aug 30	Wed	Div 2	A	Luton Town	D	1-1	12,366	14	Gazzard
5	Sep 2	Sat	Div 2	H	Brentford	L	1-2	21,246	15	Parsons
6	Sep 4	Mon	Div 2	A	Cardiff City	L	1-2	32,292	16	Johns
7	Sep 9	Sat	Div 2	A	Blackburn Rovers	W	3-1	25,323	12	Robinson 2, Johns
8	Sep 16	Sat	Div 2	H	Southampton	W	3-0	23,559	11	Gazzard 2, Robinson
9	Sep 23	Sat	Div 2	A	Barnsley	W	2-1	25,679	10	Robinson, Woodgate
10	Sep 28	Thu	EPC 1*	H	Colchester United	W	2-1			Gazzard, Robinson
11	Sep 30	Sat	Div 2	H	Sheffield United	L	3-5	25,130	13	Robinson 3 [1 pen]
12	Oct 7	Sat	Div 2	H	Queens Park Rangers	W	4-1	26,375	10	Parsons 2, Robinson, Woodgate
13	Oct 14	Sat	Div 2	A	Bury	L	0-3	15,542	11	
14	Oct 21	Sat	Div 2	H	Leicester City	D	0-0	23,330	12	
15	Oct 28	Sat	Div 2	A	Chesterfield	W	2-1	11,197	9	Barrett, Woodgate
16	Nov 4	Sat	Div 2	H	Coventry City	W	3-2	26,044	8	Gazzard 2, Parker
17	Nov 11	Sat	Div 2	A	Manchester City	L	0-2	41,473	10	
18	Nov 18	Sat	Div 2	H	Preston North End	W	2-0	26,360	8	Gazzard, Robinson
19	Nov 25	Sat	Div 2	A	Notts County	L	1-4	27,073	11	Woodgate
20	Dec 2	Sat	Div 2	H	Grimsby Town	W	2-1	18,518	10	Barrett, Robinson
21	Dec 9	Sat	Div 2	A	Birmingham City	L	1-3	18,180	10	Robinson
22	Dec 16	Sat	Div 2	A	Hull City	W	2-1	20,623	10	Robinson, Woodgate
23	Dec 23	Sat	Div 2	H	Doncaster Rovers	D	0-0	16,186	9	
24	Dec 25	Mon	Div 2	H	Leeds United	W	3-1	19,519	9	Woodgate 3
25	Dec 26	Tue	Div 2	A	Leeds United	L	0-2	33,162	10	
26	Dec 30	Sat	Div 2	A	Brentford	D	1-1	19,291	9	Robinson
27	Jan 6	Sat	FAC 3	H	Cardiff City	W	2-1	26,000		Barrett, Gazzard
28	Jan 13	Sat	Div 2	H	Blackburn Rovers	L	2-3	22,667	13	Robinson 2 [1 pen]
29	Jan 20	Sat	Div 2	A	Southampton	D	2-2	21,167	11	Gazzard, Robinson
30	Jan 27	Sat	FAC 4	A	Stoke City	L	0-1	48,500		
31	Feb 3	Sat	Div 2	H	Barnsley	W	4-2	16,781	10	Gazzard 2, Robinson 2
32	Feb 17	Sat	Div 2	A	Sheffield United	D	1-1	19,384	8	Robinson
33	Feb 24	Sat	Div 2	A	Queens Park Rangers	D	3-3	21,444	8	Woodgate 2, McGowan
34	Mar 3	Sat	Div 2	H	Bury	L	2-3	19,652	13	Robinson 2
35	Mar 5	Mon	EPC SF*	A	Leyton Orient	D	0-0			
36	Mar 10	Sat	Div 2	A	Leicester City	L	0-1	22,779	14	
37	Mar 12	Mon	EPC SF Rep*	H	Leyton Orient	W	6-1			Gazzard 2, Hooper 2, Parker, Robinson
38	Mar 17	Sat	Div 2	H	Chesterfield	W	2-0	15,878	11	Gazzard, Robinson
39	Mar 23	Fri	Div 2	H	Swansea Town	D	1-1	25,385	10	Hooper
40	Mar 24	Sat	Div 2	A	Coventry City	L	0-1	21,894	12	
41	Mar 26	Mon	Div 2	A	Swansea Town	L	2-3	16,240	15	Hooper, Robinson
42	Mar 31	Sat	Div 2	H	Manchester City	L	2-4	21,533	16	Barrett, Woodgate
43	Apr 7	Sat	Div 2	A	Preston North End	W	1-0	32,043	13	Barrett
44	Apr 14	Sat	Div 2	H	Notts County	W	4-2	23,226	13	Robinson 2, Gazzard, Hooper
45	Apr 21	Sat	Div 2	A	Grimsby Town	W	1-0	10,674	10	Gazzard
46	Apr 28	Sat	Div 2	H	Birmingham City	L	1-2	12,396	12	Kinsell [pen]
47	May 5	Sat	Div 2	H	Cardiff City	D	0-0	17,942	13	
48	May 7	Mon	EPC F*	H	Southend United	W	2-0	6,000		Robinson, Moroney

* Essex Professional Cup

Team Line-Ups

ALLISON Malcolm	BARRETT Jim Jnr.	BETTS Eric	DEVLIN Ernie	FOAN Albert	FORDE Steve	GAZZARD Gerry	GREGORY Ernie	HOOPER Harry	JACKMAN Derek	JOHNS Stan	KEARNS Fred	KINSELL Harry	McGOWAN Danny	MORONEY Tommy	NELSON Bill	NIBLETT Vic	O'FARRELL Frank	PARKER Derek	PARSONS Eric	ROBINSON Bill	SOUTHREN Tommy	TAYLOR George	TUCKER Ken	WALKER Richard	WOODGATE Terry	WRIGHT George	YEOMANSON Jack	
		11	2	10		8	1		6									4		9				5	7	3		1
		11	2	10		8	1							6				4		9				5	7	3		2
		11	2			10	1							6				4	8	9				5	7	3		3
			2			10	1		6									4	8	9			11	5	7	3		4
			2			10	1		6									4	8	9			11	5	7	3		5
			2	10			1				8			6				4	7	9				5	11	3		6
			2		3	10	1				8			6				4	7	9				5	11			7
			2		3	10	1				8			6				4	7	9				5	11			8
			2		3	10	1				8			6				4	7	9				5	11			9
					3	10	1				8				2	5	6	4		9	7			5	11			10
			2		3	10	1				8			6				4		9	7			5	11			11
	8				3	10	1							6				4	7	9				5	11	2		12
			8		3	10	1							6				4		9	7			5	11	2		13
					3	10	1				8			6				4		9	7			5	11	2		14
8					3	10	1							6				4		9	7			5	11	2		15
8					3	10	1							6				4	7	9				5	11	2		16
8					3	10	1							6				4	7	9				5	11	2		17
8			2		3	10	1							6				4		9	7			5	11			18
8			2		3	10	1										6	4	7	9				5	11			19
8			2		3	10	1										6	4		9	7			5	11			20
8					3	10	1										6	4		9	7			5	11	2		21
8					3	10	1					2		6				4		9	7			5	11			22
8					3	10	1					2		6				4		9	7			5	11			23
8						10	1					2		6				4		9	7			5	11	3		24
			8			10						2		6				4		9		1	11	5	7	3		25
8						10						2					6	4		9	7	1		5	11	3		26
8					3	10	1					2					6	4		9	7			5	11			27
8						10	1					2	3				6	4		9	7			5	11			28
8			2			10	1					3					6	4		9	7			5	11			29
8					3	10	1					2					6	4		9	7			5	11			30
			2			10	1	7			3		8				6	4		9				5	11			31
			2			10	1				3		8				6	4		9	7			5	11			32
			2			10	1				3		8				6	4		9	7			5	11			33
			2			10	1				3		8				6	4		9	7			5	11			34
5						10		7	4	2	3		8				6			9		1			11			35
			2			10					3		8				6	4		9	7	1		5	11			36
5						10		7			3		8				6	4		9		1			11	2		37
5			2			10		7			3		8				6	4		9		1			11			38
5	8		2			10		7	9		3						6	4				1			11			39
5	8		2			10		7			3						6	4		9		1		9	11			40
5	8		2			10		7			3		8				6	4		9		1			11			41
5			2			10	1	7			3		4				6			9					11	3		42
5	8		2			10		7			3						6			9		1			11			43
5	8		2			10		7			3		4				6			9		1			11			44
5	8		2			10		7			3		4				6			9		1			11			45
5	8		2			10		7			3		4				6			9		1			11			46
5	8		2			10		7			3		4				6			9		1			11			47
5	8		2		3	10		7					4				6			9		1			11			48

1951-52
Story of the season

Goalkeeper **Ernie Gregory was injured** in the opening-day defeat at Queens Park Rangers and was **forced to miss** the next 14 games.

George Taylor took his place and had a torrid time Bury in the 4–0 defeat and at Sheffield United as the hom side scored six, with the Hammers' solitary goal comin from Doug Bing. Gregory returned to the side in Novembe and kept two clean sheets, a 0–0 draw at Nottingham Fore and a 1–0 home win against Brentford. For the visit o Everton, West Ham were in seventeenth place; althoug they did not win, the 3–3 draw was exciting to watch for th crowd of 20,141. The city of Sheffield was not to be spoke about in West Ham territory as after losing 6–1 to Unite the visit of Sheffield Wednesday brought a 6–0 defeat.

Appearances & Goals 1951-52

	League		FA Cup		Other*		Total	
	Starts	Goals	Starts	Goals	Starts	Goals	Starts	Goal
ALLISON Malcolm	38	0	3	0	3	1	44	1
ANDREWS Jimmy	23	2	3	1	2	1	28	4
BARRETT Jim Jnr.	23	9	0	0	2	1	25	10
BING Doug	10	3	0	0	0	0	10	3
BOND John	2	0	0	0	0	0	2	0
DEVLIN Ernie	5	0	0	0	2	0	7	0
FOAN Albert	3	0	0	0	0	0	3	0
FORDE Steve	7	0	0	0	0	0	7	0
GAZZARD Gerry	31	11	3	1	2	0	36	12
GREGORY Ernie	28	0	3	0	2	0	33	0
GREGORY John	9	3	0	0	1	0	10	3
HAWKINS Bert	32	15	3	0	2	0	37	15
HOOPER Harry	2	0	0	0	1	0	3	0
KEARNS Fred	3	1	0	0	0	0	3	1
KINSELL Harry	32	1	3	0	1	0	36	1
McGOWAN Danny	9	1	0	0	2	0	11	1
MORONEY Tommy	12	0	0	0	2	0	14	0
O'FARRELL Frank	41	2	3	1	0	0	44	3
PARKER Derek	30	3	3	0	3	0	36	3
ROBINSON Bill	4	1	0	0	0	0	4	1
SOUTHREN Tommy	11	0	0	0	0	0	11	0
STROUD Roy	1	0	0	0	0	0	1	0
TAYLOR George	14	0	0	0	1	0	15	0
TUCKER Ken	7	5	3	0	1	1	11	6
WALKER Richard	4	0	0	0	0	0	4	0
WILLIAMS Harry	5	1	0	0	1	2	6	3
WOODGATE Terry	38	8	3	1	2	0	43	9
WRIGHT George	38	0	3	0	3	0	44	0
own goal		1						1
TOTALS	**462**	**67**	**33**	**4**	**33**	**6**	**528**	**77**

* Other = Essex Professional Cup

week later there was an immediate response as a hat-trick from Bert Hawkins brought a 4–2 home win over Queens Park Rangers. On Christmas Day Luton Town were beaten 3–0, but the return with them on Boxing Day at Kenilworth Road saw the Hammers lose 6–1.

First Division Blackpool were the visitors in the FA Cup and an attendance of 38,600 saw West Ham win 2–1. It was an encouraging result and a week later the Hammers got their revenge on Sheffield United by beating them 5–1, helped by a hat-trick from Ken Tucker. The next round of the FA Cup brought Sheffield United back again to Upton Park but on this occasion they escaped with a 0–0 draw. In the replay, despite goals from Woodgate and Gazzard, the Hammers went out 4–2. The remainder of the campaign saw West Ham win the majority of their home games but fail on their travels, with the last away win being at Coventry in February. A mid-table place of twelfth was one place higher than the previous season.

Football League - Division Two
Final Table 1951-52

	P	HOME					AWAY					Pts
		W	D	L	F	A	W	D	L	F	A	
Sheffield Wednesday	42	14	4	3	54	23	7	7	7	46	43	53
Cardiff City	42	18	2	1	52	15	2	9	10	20	39	51
Birmingham City	42	11	6	4	36	21	10	3	8	31	35	51
Nottingham Forest	42	12	6	3	41	22	6	7	8	36	40	49
Leicester City	42	12	6	3	48	24	7	3	11	30	40	47
Leeds United	42	13	7	1	35	15	5	4	12	24	42	47
Everton	42	12	5	4	42	25	5	5	11	22	33	44
Luton Town	42	9	7	5	46	35	7	5	9	31	43	44
Rotherham United	42	11	4	6	40	25	6	4	11	33	46	42
Brentford	42	11	7	3	34	20	4	5	12	20	35	42
Sheffield United	42	13	2	6	57	28	5	3	13	33	48	41
West Ham United	**42**	**13**	**5**	**3**	**48**	**29**	**2**	**6**	**13**	**19**	**48**	**41**
Southampton	42	11	6	4	40	25	4	5	12	21	48	41
Blackburn Rovers	42	11	3	7	35	30	6	3	12	19	33	40
Notts County	42	11	5	5	45	27	5	2	14	26	41	39
Doncaster Rovers	42	9	4	8	29	28	4	8	9	26	32	38
Bury	42	13	2	6	43	22	2	5	14	24	47	37
Hull City	42	11	5	5	44	23	2	6	13	16	47	37
Swansea Town	42	10	4	7	45	26	2	8	11	27	50	36
Barnsley	42	8	7	6	39	33	3	7	11	20	39	36
Coventry City	42	9	5	7	36	33	5	1	15	23	49	34
Queens Park Rangers	42	8	8	5	35	35	3	4	14	17	46	34

ROY STROUD

A centre-forward, he began his career as an amateur with Hendon.

He played for Hendon for 15 seasons from 1939 and including the war years he made 426 appearances, scoring an impressive 212 goals. The England selectors noted his fine form and he was awarded 11 international amateur caps. He joined West Ham in 1952 and made his debut in April at Notts County. He was with the Hammers until 1957 but injuries severely limited his playing time. After playing in only 13 games and scoring four goals he moved on to Chelmsford City in the Southern League. With City he managed 48 goals in 68 games, but a broken leg suffered at Yiewsley (renamed Hillingdon Borough in the 1960s) in November 1958 ended his playing career. He later worked in the grocery business.

Roy died aged 90 in June 2015.

Season **1951-52** Football League - Division Two
Match Details
Manager **Ted Fenton**   Final League Position **12/22**

	Date		Competition	Venue	Opponents	Results		Attendance	Position	Scorers
1	Aug 18	Sat	Div 2	A	Queens Park Rangers	L	0-2	19,541	22	
2	Aug 23	Thu	Div 2	H	Bury	D	1-1	16,341	20	Robinson
3	Aug 25	Sat	Div 2	H	Blackburn Rovers	W	3-1	19,208	13	Barrett 2, Gazzard
4	Aug 29	Wed	Div 2	A	Bury	L	0-4	10,442	19	
5	Sep 1	Sat	Div 2	A	Hull City	D	1-1	33,444	17	Hawkins
6	Sep 6	Thu	Div 2	H	Swansea Town	D	2-2	16,640	16	Barrett, Bing
7	Sep 8	Sat	Div 2	H	Barnsley	W	2-1	20,235	14	Hawkins 2
8	Sep 13	Thu	Div 2	A	Swansea Town	L	1-2	16,135	15	Barrett
9	Sep 15	Sat	Div 2	A	Sheffield United	L	1-6	30,202	19	Bing
10	Sep 22	Sat	Div 2	H	Leeds United	W	2-0	19,464	16	Hawkins, Woodgate [pen]
11	Sep 29	Sat	Div 2	H	Coventry City	W	3-1	20,317	10	Hawkins, McGowan, Parker
12	Oct 6	Sat	Div 2	A	Rotherham United	L	1-2	19,998	14	Hawkins
13	Oct 13	Sat	Div 2	H	Cardiff City	D	1-1	24,103	14	Hawkins
14	Oct 20	Sat	Div 2	A	Birmingham City	L	1-2	20,295	17	Woodgate
15	Oct 27	Sat	Div 2	H	Leicester City	L	2-3	20,739	18	Bing, Woodgate
16	Nov 3	Sat	Div 2	A	Nottingham Forest	D	0-0	20,743	17	
17	Nov 10	Sat	Div 2	H	Brentford	W	1-0	26,288	15	Hawkins
18	Nov 17	Sat	Div 2	A	Doncaster Rovers	L	1-4	18,956	17	Gregory
19	Nov 24	Sat	Div 2	H	Everton	D	3-3	20,141	17	Gazzard, Kinsell, Woodgate
20	Dec 1	Sat	Div 2	A	Southampton	W	2-1	17,473	15	Hawkins, Williams
21	Dec 8	Sat	Div 2	H	Sheffield Wednesday	L	0-6	17,798	18	
22	Dec 15	Sat	Div 2	H	Queens Park Rangers	W	4-2	17,549	17	Hawkins 3, Woodgate
23	Dec 22	Sat	Div 2	A	Blackburn Rovers	L	1-3	19,617	17	O'Farrell
24	Dec 25	Tue	Div 2	H	Luton Town	W	3-0	20,403	15	Gazzard, Gregory, Hawkins
25	Dec 26	Wed	Div 2	A	Luton Town	L	1-6	19,476	16	Gregory
26	Dec 29	Sat	Div 2	H	Hull City	W	2-0	19,631	15	Parker, Tucker
27	Jan 5	Sat	Div 2	A	Barnsley	D	1-1	16,267	15	Tucker
28	Jan 12	Sat	FAC 3	H	Blackpool	W	2-1	38,600		Andrews, O'Farrell
29	Jan 19	Sat	Div 2	H	Sheffield United	W	5-1	21,063	13	Tucker 3 [1 pen], Gazzard 2
30	Jan 26	Sat	Div 2	A	Leeds United	L	1-3	32,297	15	Gazzard
31	Feb 2	Sat	FAC 4	H	Sheffield United	D	0-0	35,053		
32	Feb 6	Wed	FAC 4 Rep	A	Sheffield United	L	2-4	39,073		Woodgate, Hawkins
33	Feb 9	Sat	Div 2	A	Coventry City	W	2-1	19,487	13	Barrett, Hawkins
34	Feb 16	Sat	Div 2	H	Rotherham United	W	2-1	19,357	12	Hawkins, Woodgate
35	Mar 1	Sat	Div 2	A	Cardiff City	D	1-1	29,495	13	Montgomery (og)
36	Mar 8	Sat	Div 2	H	Birmingham City	L	0-1	24,011	13	
37	Mar 12	Wed	EPC 1*	H	Southend United	W	2-1			Allison, Andrews
38	Mar 15	Sat	Div 2	A	Leicester City	L	1-3	30,038	15	Andrews
39	Mar 22	Sat	Div 2	H	Nottingham Forest	W	3-1	23,129	14	Barrett, Gazzard, O'Farrell
40	Apr 3	Thu	EPC SF*	H	Chelmsford City	W	3-0			Williams 2 [1 pen], Tucker
41	Apr 5	Sat	Div 2	H	Doncaster Rovers	D	3-3	18,140	14	Andrews, Barrett, Gazzard
42	Apr 11	Fri	Div 2	H	Notts County	W	2-1	22,859	13	Gazzard 2
43	Apr 12	Sat	Div 2	A	Everton	L	0-2	36,498	14	
44	Apr 14	Mon	Div 2	A	Notts County	L	0-1	16,306	15	
45	Apr 19	Sat	Div 2	H	Southampton	W	4-0	18,119	13	Woodgate 2, Barrett, Kearns
46	Apr 21	Mon	Div 2	A	Brentford	D	1-1	12,563	11	Parker
47	Apr 26	Sat	Div 2	A	Sheffield Wednesday	D	2-2	44,051	12	Barrett, Gazzard
48	May 5	Mon	EPC F*	A	Colchester United	L	1-3			Barrett

* Essex Professional Cup

eam Line-Ups

ALLISON Malcolm	ANDREWS Jimmy	BARRETT Jim Jnr.	BING Doug	BOND John	DEVLIN Ernie	FOAN Albert	FORDE Steve	GAZZARD Gerry	GREGORY Ernie	GREGORY John	HAWKINS Bert	HOOPER Harry	KEARNS Fred	KINSELL Harry	McGOWAN Danny	MORONEY Tommy	O'FARRELL Frank	PARKER Derek	ROBINSON Bill	SOUTHREN Tommy	STROUD Roy	TAYLOR George	TUCKER Ken	WALKER Richard	WILLIAMS Harry	WOODGATE Terry	WRIGHT George	
5	8						2	10	1					3			6	4	9	7						11		1
5	8						2	10						3			6	4	9	7		1				11		2
5	8						2	10						3			6	4	9	7		1				11		3
5	8						2	10						3			6	4	9	7		1				11		4
5	8	7						10			9			3		4	6					1				11	2	5
5	8	7						10			9			3		4	6					1				11	2	6
5	8	7						10			9			3		4	6					1				11	2	7
5	8	7				10					9			3		4	6					1				11	2	8
5	8	7									9			3	10	4	6					1				11	2	9
5	8	7	3								9					4	6					1				11	2	10
5			3								9				10	4	6	8			7	1				11	2	11
5		7									9			3	10	4	6					1			8	11	2	12
5		7									9			3	10	4	6	8				1				11	2	13
5		7						10				8	9	3			6	4				1				11	2	14
5		7				10						8	9	3		6		4				1				11	2	15
5						10			1			8	9				6	4			7					11	2	16
5	8							10	1				9	3			6	4			7					11	2	17
5	8							10	1				9	3			6	4			7					11	2	18
5	11	8						10	1		9						6	4								7	2	19
5	11	8		3				10	1		9						6	4								7	2	20
5	11			3				10	1		9						6	4							8	7	2	21
	11							10	1		9						6	4						5	8	7	2	22
	11			3				10	1		9		7				6	4						5	8		2	23
	11			3				10	1			8	9				6	4						5		7	2	24
	11			3				10	1			8	9				6	4						5		7	2	25
5	10			3				8	1		9						6	4						11		7	2	26
5	10							8	1		9			3			6	4						11		7	2	27
5	10							8	1		9			3			6	4						11		7	2	28
5	10							8	1		9			3			6	4						11		7	2	29
5	10							8	1		9		7	3			6	4								11	2	30
5	10							8	1		9			3			6	4						11		7	2	31
5	10							8	1		9			3			6	4						11		7	2	32
5	8		3					10	1		9					4	6							11		7	2	33
5	10							8	1		9			3			6	4						11		7	2	34
5	10							8	1		9			3			6	4						11		7	2	35
5	10							8	1		9			3			6	4						11		7	2	36
9	11	8			3				1					5	10	7	6	4									2	37
5	11	8						10	1		9			3	4		6									7	2	38
5	11	8						10	1		9			3	4		6				7						2	39
5				3						10	9						6	4				1		11	8	7	2	40
5	11	8						10	1					3	4	9	6				7						2	41
5	11	8						10	1		9			3	4		6				7						2	42
5	11	8						10	1		9			3			6	4								7	2	43
5	11	8		3				10	1								6	4					9			7	2	44
5	11	8						10	1				9	3			6	4								7	2	45
5	11	8						10	1				9	3			6	4								7	2	46
5	11	8						10	1					3		9	6	4								7	2	47
5	11	8						10	1					3	6	9		4								7	2	48

1952-53
Story of the season

The match programme, priced at three old pence (about 1½p), was advertising season tickets at £5 and £7 respectively. **There was a distinct lack of goals in the opening games** – only three were scored in the first seven fixtures.

At home there was an improvement as after Leiceste City were beaten 4–1 what followed was a series of three goal wins against Nottingham Forest, Brentford an Swansea Town. With the side in mid-table the visit o Lincoln City in December brought a 5–1 victory, bot Albert Foan and John Gregory scoring twice.

Appearances & Goals 1952-53

	League		FA Cup		Other*		Total	
	Starts	Goals	Starts	Goals	Starts	Goals	Starts	Goal
ALLISON Malcolm	39	2	1	0	1	0	41	2
ANDREWS Jimmy	23	5	0	0	0	0	23	5
ARMSTRONG Eric	0	0	0	0	1	0	1	0
BARRETT Jim Jnr.	26	9	0	0	0	0	26	9
BING Doug	2	0	0	0	1	0	3	0
BOND John	14	0	1	0	1	0	16	0
BROWN Ken	3	0	0	0	1	0	4	0
CANTWELL Noel	4	0	0	0	1	0	5	0
CHISWICK Peter	0	0	0	0	1	0	1	0
DEVLIN Ernie	1	0	0	0	2	0	3	0
DIXON Tommy	6	4	0	0	1	0	7	4
FOAN Albert	13	3	1	0	1	0	15	3
GAZZARD Gerry	8	0	0	0	1	0	9	0
GREGORY Ernie	42	0	1	0	0	0	43	0
GREGORY John	15	3	1	0	1	0	17	3
GUNNING Harry	1	0	0	0	1	0	2	0
HAWKINS Bert	2	1	0	0	0	0	2	1
HOOPER Harry	12	4	0	0	0	0	12	4
KEARNS Fred	21	10	1	1	1	1	23	12
KINSELL Harry	25	0	0	0	0	0	25	0
McGOWAN Danny	5	1	0	0	1	0	6	1
MORONEY Tommy	18	6	0	0	2	3	20	9
O'FARRELL Frank	41	1	1	0	0	0	42	1
PARKER Derek	39	0	1	0	0	0	40	0
PETCHEY George	2	0	0	0	1	0	3	0
SEXTON Dave	3	1	0	0	0	0	3	1
SOUTHREN Tommy	12	1	0	0	1	0	13	1
TAYLOR George	0	0	0	0	1	0	1	0
TUCKER Ken	15	3	1	0	1	0	17	3
WALKER Richard	1	0	0	0	0	0	1	0
WOODGATE Terry	29	3	1	0	0	0	30	3
WRIGHT George	40	0	1	0	0	0	41	0
own goal		1						1
TOTALS	**462**	**58**	**11**	**1**	**22**	**4**	**495**	**63**

* Other = Essex Professional Cup

he FA Cup attracted a healthy attendance of 35,150 to the oleyn Ground for the visit of West Bromwich Albion. he First Division side proved too strong for the Hammers they won 4–1. Fred Kearns grabbed a hat-trick in the 3–2 ome win against Bury, after which there was a run of ven games without a win. Again the team were consistent, a good 4–1 win at Brentford being followed a 1–3 home reverse to Doncaster Rovers. At Easter ulham won 2–1 at Upton Park but the Hammers won the turn at Fulham 3–2. The big event of the season was the rst ever floodlit match at Upton Park, which took place on April 1953. It was a friendly match against Tottenham otspur, and in a keenly fought match goals from Jim arrett and Tommy Dixon gave West Ham a 2–1 victory. he campaign ended with the Hammers finishing in a ther disappointing fourteenth place.

ootball League - Division Two
inal Table 1952-53

	P	HOME					AWAY					Pts
		W	D	L	F	A	W	D	L	F	A	
heffield United	42	15	3	3	60	27	10	7	4	37	28	60
uddersfield Town	42	14	4	3	51	14	10	6	5	33	19	58
uton Town	42	15	1	5	53	17	7	7	7	31	32	52
lymouth Argyle	42	12	5	4	37	24	8	4	9	28	36	49
eicester City	42	13	6	2	55	29	5	6	10	34	45	48
irmingham City	42	11	3	7	44	38	8	7	6	27	28	48
ottingham Forest	42	11	5	5	46	32	7	3	11	31	35	44
ulham	42	14	1	6	52	28	3	9	9	29	43	44
lackburn Rovers	42	12	4	5	40	20	6	4	11	28	45	44
eeds United	42	13	4	4	42	24	1	11	9	29	39	43
wansea Town	42	10	9	2	45	26	5	3	13	33	55	42
otherham United	42	9	7	5	41	30	7	2	12	34	44	41
oncaster Rovers	42	9	9	3	26	17	3	7	11	32	47	40
West Ham United	**42**	**9**	**5**	**7**	**38**	**28**	**4**	**8**	**9**	**20**	**32**	**39**
incoln City	42	9	9	3	41	26	2	8	11	23	45	39
verton	42	9	8	4	38	23	3	6	12	33	52	38
rentford	42	8	8	5	38	29	5	3	13	21	47	37
ull City	42	11	6	4	36	19	3	2	16	21	50	36
otts County	42	11	5	5	41	31	3	3	15	19	57	36
ury	42	10	6	5	33	30	3	3	15	20	51	35
outhampton	42	5	7	9	45	44	5	6	10	23	41	33
arnsley	42	4	4	13	31	46	1	4	16	16	62	18

HARRY KINSELL

A tough left-back who captained West Ham occasionally, Kinsell signed for West Bromwich Albion in 1938 just before the war broke out.

During the war he was a guest player for many clubs including Blackpool, Grimsby, Mansfield, Middlesbrough and Southport. As the hostilities ended he played in three Victory Internationals for England against Switzerland, Ireland and Wales. He played for the Albion for two seasons after the war, making 83 league appearances before joining Bolton Wanderers in 1949. A year with the Lancashire club saw him play in 17 league games and this was followed with a short spell at Reading, where he figured in 12 matches. Harry joined West Ham in 1951 and made his debut against Blackburn Rovers in a 3–2 home defeat. After establishing himself in the side he went on to make a total of 105 appearances spread over five seasons. He finished his playing career in non-league football with Bedford Town. Harry died in the West Midlands in August 2000 aged 79.

Season **1952-53** Football League - Division Two
Match Details
Manager **Ted Fenton**   Final League Position **14/22**

	Date		Competition	Venue	Opponents	Results		Attendance	Position	Scorers
1	Aug 23	Sat	Div 2	H	Southampton	W	1-0	25,535	9	Barrett
2	Aug 25	Mon	Div 2	A	Hull City	L	0-1	35,964	6	
3	Aug 30	Sat	Div 2	A	Bury	D	1-1	13,863	12	Andrews
4	Sep 1	Mon	Div 2	H	Hull City	D	0-0	19,726	10	
5	Sep 6	Sat	Div 2	H	Birmingham City	L	1-2	23,903	15	Moroney
6	Sep 8	Mon	Div 2	A	Leicester City	D	0-0	23,382	13	
7	Sep 13	Sat	Div 2	A	Luton Town	D	0-0	16,009	16	
8	Sep 15	Mon	Div 2	H	Leicester City	W	4-1	15,492	10	Barrett 2, Kearns, Woodgate
9	Sep 20	Sat	Div 2	H	Leeds United	D	2-2	22,437	9	Moroney 2
10	Sep 27	Sat	Div 2	A	Plymouth Argyle	D	1-1	28,792	11	Barrett
11	Oct 4	Sat	Div 2	H	Rotherham United	L	2-4	21,895	13	Andrews, Selkirk (og)
12	Oct 11	Sat	Div 2	A	Blackburn Rovers	L	0-3	22,545	18	
13	Oct 18	Sat	Div 2	H	Nottingham Forest	W	3-2	21,444	14	Allison [pen], O'Farrell, Southren
14	Oct 25	Sat	Div 2	A	Everton	L	0-2	38,323	17	
15	Nov 1	Sat	Div 2	H	Brentford	W	3-1	23,263	15	Hawkins, McGowan, Tucker
16	Nov 8	Sat	Div 2	A	Doncaster Rovers	D	1-1	10,612	13	Tucker
17	Nov 13	Thu	EPC 1*	A	Colchester United	W	3-2			Moroney 3
18	Nov 15	Sat	Div 2	H	Swansea Town	W	3-0	18,600	10	Gregory, Kearns, Tucker
19	Nov 22	Sat	Div 2	A	Huddersfield Town	W	1-0	22,267	10	Kearns
20	Nov 29	Sat	Div 2	H	Sheffield United	D	1-1	22,687	10	Woodgate
21	Dec 6	Sat	Div 2	A	Barnsley	L	0-2	8,977	10	
22	Dec 13	Sat	Div 2	H	Lincoln City	W	5-1	14,436	10	Foan 2, Gregory 2, Kearns
23	Dec 20	Sat	Div 2	A	Southampton	W	2-1	12,284	8	Kearns, Woodgate
24	Dec 25	Thu	Div 2	H	Notts County	D	2-2	23,614	7	Foan, Kearns
25	Dec 27	Sat	Div 2	A	Notts County	D	1-1	24,189	9	Allison
26	Jan 3	Sat	Div 2	H	Bury	W	3-2	18,278	8	Kearns 3
27	Jan 10	Sat	FAC 3	H	West Bromwich Albion	L	1-4	35,150		Kearns
28	Jan 17	Sat	Div 2	A	Birmingham City	L	0-2	21,723	8	
29	Jan 24	Sat	Div 2	H	Luton Town	L	0-1	23,667	10	
30	Feb 7	Sat	Div 2	A	Leeds United	L	2-3	17,680	11	Barrett, Kearns
31	Feb 18	Wed	Div 2	H	Plymouth Argyle	L	0-1	8,340	12	
32	Feb 21	Sat	Div 2	A	Rotherham United	D	1-1	14,861	12	Andrews [pen]
33	Feb 28	Sat	Div 2	H	Blackburn Rovers	D	0-0	19,542	12	
34	Mar 7	Sat	Div 2	A	Nottingham Forest	D	0-0	18,088	12	
35	Mar 14	Sat	Div 2	H	Everton	W	3-1	19,022	11	Andrews, Hooper, Moroney
36	Mar 21	Sat	Div 2	A	Brentford	W	4-1	18,117	10	Hooper 2, Moroney 2
37	Mar 28	Sat	Div 2	H	Doncaster Rovers	L	1-3	13,435	10	Barrett
38	Apr 3	Fri	Div 2	H	Fulham	L	1-2	24,592	11	Barrett
39	Apr 4	Sat	Div 2	A	Swansea Town	L	1-4	17,944	13	Barrett
40	Apr 6	Mon	Div 2	A	Fulham	W	3-2	19,270	12	Dixon 2, Sexton
41	Apr 11	Sat	Div 2	H	Huddersfield Town	L	0-1	22,801	13	
42	Apr 18	Sat	Div 2	A	Sheffield United	L	1-3	32,403	14	Dixon
43	Apr 23	Thu	EPC SF*	H	Leyton Orient**	D	1-1			Kearns
44	Apr 25	Sat	Div 2	H	Barnsley	W	3-1	13,038	13	Andrews, Dixon, Hooper
45	May 1	Fri	Div 2	A	Lincoln City	L	1-3	14,285	14	Barrett

* Essex Professional Cup   ** Leyton Orient won on toss of coin

eam Line-Ups

	ANDREWS Jimmy	ARMSTRONG Eric	BARRETT Jim Jnr.	BING Doug	BOND John	BROWN Ken	CANTWELL Noel	CHISWICK Peter	DEVLIN Ernie	DIXON Tommy	FOAN Albert	GAZZARD Gerry	GREGORY Ernie	GREGORY John	GUNNING Harry	HAWKINS Bert	HOOPER Harry	KEARNS Fred	KINSELL Harry	McGOWAN Danny	MORONEY Tommy	O'FARRELL Frank	PARKER Derek	PETCHEY George	SEXTON Dave	SOUTHREN Tommy	TAYLOR George	TUCKER Ken	WALKER Richard	WOODGATE Terry	WRIGHT George	#
	11	8										10	1						3		9	6	4							7	2	1
	11	8										10	1						3		9	6	4							7	2	2
	11	8										10	1						3		9	6	4							7	2	3
	11	8											1						3		9	6	4	10						7	2	4
		8											1						3		9	6	4	10				11		7	2	5
		8	3										1			10					9	6	4					11		7	2	6
		8	3										1			10					9	6	4					11		7	2	7
	11	8	3										1					9			10	6	4							7	2	8
	11	8	3										1					9			10	6	4								2	9
	11	8	3										1					9			10	6	4			7					2	10
	11	8	3										1					9			10	6	4		7						2	11
	11	8	3										1					9			10	6	4		7						2	12
	11	8											1					9	3		10	6	4		7						2	13
	11	8									10		1						3		9	6	4		7						2	14
											10		1		9				3	8		6	4					11		7	2	15
											10		1		9				3	8		6	4					11		7	2	16
5		4		3	2	9									11							6	8			10				7	1	17
											10		1	8							9	6	4					11		7	2	18
											10		1	8					3		9	6	4					11		7	2	19
											10		1	8					3		9	6	4					11		7	2	20
			3								10		1	8							9	6	4					11		7	2	21
											10		1	8					3		9	6	4					11		7	2	22
											10		1	8					3		9	6	4					11		7	2	23
											10		1	8					3		9	6	4					11		7	2	24
			3								10		1	8							9	6	4					11		7	2	25
			3								10		1	8							9	6	4					11		7	2	26
			3								10		1	8							9	6	4					11		7	2	27
	11		3									10	1	8							9	6	4							7	2	28
	11		3								10		1	8							9	6	4							7	2	29
5		8	3								10		1	8			11				9	6	4							7	2	30
5		8									10		1				11		3		9	6	4						5	7	2	31
	10	8			2	5							1	8			11		3		9	6	4							7		32
9	10					5							1	8					3			6	4					11		7		33
	10	8				5							1				11		3		9	6	4		7						2	34
	10	8											1				11		3		9	6	4							7	2	35
	10	8											1				11		3		9	6	4							7	2	36
	11	8									10		1						3		9	6	4							7	2	37
		8											1				11		3		9	6	4	10	7						2	38
		8								9			1				11		3			6	4	10	7						2	39
5	10		3		2					9			1				11			4		6		8		7						40
5	10	8	3							9			1				11		3			6	4		7						2	41
5		8	6				3			9	10		1				11						4		7						2	42
	6		3	5			1	2			7	10		8							9		4						11			43
5	10	8	3							9			1				11			4		6			7						2	44
5	10	8	7				3			9			1				11			4		6									2	45

1953-54
Story of the season

It was a **whirlwind start to the season with nine goals** in two home games. Lincoln City were beaten 5–0 and **a hat-trick from Fred Kearns** came in the 4–1 victory over Leicester City.

There was a shock in the next game at Rotherham as t Yorkshire side won 5–0, but in the return game wi Rotherham six days later the Hammers got their revenge winning 3–0, with Dave Sexton scoring all three. Agair Swansea Town at home Tommy Dixon became the thi player to score a hat-trick that season as the Welsh cl were beaten 4–1. After ten games only one had been lo but this was followed by four successive defeats as t Hammers slipped to eighth. Inside-forward Johnny Di

Appearances & Goals 1953-54

	League		FA Cup		Other*		Total	
	Starts	Goals	Starts	Goals	Starts	Goals	Starts	Goa
ALLISON Malcolm	42	0	3	0	0	0	45	0
ANDREWS Jimmy	31	6	2	0	0	0	33	6
ARNOTT John	4	2	0	0	0	0	4	2
BARRETT Jim Jnr.	9	1	0	0	0	0	9	1
BING Doug	12	0	3	0	1	0	16	0
BOND John	18	0	3	0	1	0	22	0
CANTWELL Noel	23	0	0	0	0	0	23	0
CHISWICK Peter	15	0	0	0	1	0	16	0
COOPER Fred	0	0	0	0	1	0	1	0
DICK John	39	13	3	0	0	0	42	13
DIXON Tommy	29	17	3	2	0	0	32	19
FOAN Albert	4	0	0	0	1	0	5	0
GAZZARD Gerry	1	0	0	0	0	0	1	0
GREGORY Ernie	27	0	3	0	0	0	30	0
HOOPER Harry	23	6	3	2	1	1	27	9
KEARNS Fred	5	3	0	0	1	0	6	3
KINSELL Harry	10	0	0	0	1	0	11	0
MALCOLM Andy	14	0	3	0	1	0	18	0
MATTHEWS George	0	0	0	0	1	0	1	0
McGOWAN Danny	8	0	0	0	0	0	8	0
MUSGROVE Malcolm	4	0	0	0	0	0	4	0
O'FARRELL Frank	22	0	0	0	0	0	22	0
PARKER Derek	28	1	0	0	0	0	28	1
SEXTON Dave	31	12	3	2	0	0	34	14
SOUTHREN Tommy	24	2	0	0	0	0	24	2
STROUD Roy	4	2	0	0	0	0	4	2
TUCKER Ken	2	0	1	0	0	0	3	0
WOODGATE Terry	0	0	0	0	1	0	1	0
WRIGHT George	33	0	3	0	0	0	36	0
own goal		1						1
TOTALS	**462**	**66**	**33**	**6**	**11**	**1**	**506**	**73**

* Other = Essex Professional Cup

d been signed to score goals and he obliged with a hat-
ck in the 5–0 rout of Bury. He was again on target in the
-1 win at Lincoln City and he scored the only goal in the
n against Luton Town on Christmas Day.

rst Division Huddersfield Town were the visitors in the
A Cup and left after being thrashed 4–0. Blackpool in the
xt round were stronger and after a 1–1 draw in London
e Lancashire side won the replay 3–1. In a remarkable
me at Fulham, West Ham were losing 3–0 just before
lf-time. In an amazing comeback, Dick scored twice with
rther goals from Dixon and Sexton giving the Hammers
4–3 victory. After Leeds United were beaten 5–2 at home
ere were only three more wins in the remaining 14 games
the season. Skipper Malcolm Allison was the only ever-
esent as once again a mid-table place (thirteenth) was
hieved.

ootball League - Division Two
inal Table 1953-54

	P	HOME					AWAY					Pts
		W	D	L	F	A	W	D	L	F	A	
icester City	42	15	4	2	63	23	8	6	7	34	37	56
erton	42	13	6	2	55	27	7	10	4	37	31	56
ackburn Rovers	42	15	4	2	54	16	8	5	8	32	34	55
ottingham Forest	42	15	5	1	61	27	5	7	9	25	32	52
otherham United	42	13	4	4	51	26	8	3	10	29	41	49
ton Town	42	11	7	3	36	23	7	5	9	28	36	48
rmingham City	42	12	6	3	49	18	6	5	10	29	40	47
lham	42	12	3	6	62	39	5	7	9	36	46	44
istol Rovers	42	10	7	4	32	19	4	9	8	32	39	44
eds United	42	12	5	4	56	30	3	8	10	33	51	43
oke City	42	8	8	5	43	28	4	9	8	28	32	41
oncaster Rovers	42	9	5	7	32	28	7	4	10	27	35	41
est Ham United	42	11	6	4	44	20	4	3	14	23	49	39
otts County	42	8	6	7	26	29	5	7	9	28	45	39
ull City	42	14	1	6	47	22	2	5	14	17	44	38
ncoln City	42	11	6	4	46	23	3	3	15	19	60	37
ury	42	9	7	5	39	32	2	7	12	15	40	36
erby County	42	9	5	7	38	35	3	6	12	26	47	35
ymouth Argyle	42	6	12	3	38	31	3	4	14	27	51	34
wansea Town	42	11	5	5	34	25	2	3	16	24	57	34
entford	42	9	5	7	25	26	1	6	14	15	52	31
ldham Athletic	42	6	7	8	26	31	2	2	17	14	58	25

JOHNNY DICK

The Scottish inside-forward was on national
service in Colchester when West ham
manager Ted Fenton signed him in July 1953.

He made his debut in the 5–0 home win
against Lincoln City on the opening day of the
1953–54 season. In that first season he scored
13 league goals and was chosen to play for
the Scotland B side against England at Roker
Park. He was in the West Ham side that
became Second Division champions in
season 1957–58, where his partnership with
Vic Keeble yielded 40 league goals. In scoring
27 goals the following season he became the
first West Ham player to represent Scotland
when he was selected for the game against
England at Wembley. Dick had ten seasons at
Upton Park, making 351 appearances and
scoring 166 goals. In September 1962 he was
transferred to Brentford and his 23 goals that
season brought him a Fourth Division
Championship medal. He moved on to play
for Gravesend in 1965 after 72 games for the
Bees, and was back at West Ham in the early
1970s running the junior team. He later had
employment with the Inner London Education
Authority. John passed away in September
2000.

Season **1953-54** Football League - Division Two
Match Details

Manager **Ted Fenton**   Final League Position **13/22**

	Date		Competition	Venue	Opponents	Results		Attendance	Position	Scorers
1	Aug 19	Wed	Div 2	H	Lincoln City	W	5-0	17,045	4	Sexton 2, Andrews, Dixon, Parker
2	Aug 22	Sat	Div 2	H	Leicester City	W	4-1	22,157	1	Kearns 3, Andrews
3	Aug 24	Mon	Div 2	A	Rotherham United	L	0-5	12,895	5	
4	Aug 29	Sat	Div 2	A	Stoke City	D	1-1	20,746	5	Dixon
5	Aug 31	Mon	Div 2	H	Rotherham United	W	3-0	22,089	2	Sexton 3 [1 pen]
6	Sep 5	Sat	Div 2	H	Fulham	W	3-1	30,103	3	Andrews 2, Dixon
7	Sep 10	Thu	Div 2	A	Swansea Town	D	1-1	21,015	3	Southren
8	Sep 12	Sat	Div 2	A	Bristol Rovers	D	2-2	28,740	4	Dixon, Sexton
9	Sep 14	Mon	Div 2	H	Swansea Town	W	4-1	22,383	3	Dixon 3, Sexton
10	Sep 19	Sat	Div 2	A	Leeds United	W	2-1	28,635	2	Dixon, Hooper
11	Sep 26	Sat	Div 2	H	Birmingham City	L	1-2	36,091	3	Newman (og)
12	Oct 3	Sat	Div 2	A	Nottingham Forest	L	0-4	23,167	7	
13	Oct 10	Sat	Div 2	H	Brentford	L	0-1	24,934	8	
14	Oct 17	Sat	Div 2	A	Derby County	L	1-2	17,689	11	Dick
15	Oct 22	Sat	EPC 1*	A	Colchester United	L	1-5			Hooper
16	Oct 24	Mon	Div 2	H	Blackburn Rovers	W	2-1	22,814	7	Gazzard, Southren
17	Oct 31	Sat	Div 2	A	Doncaster Rovers	L	0-2	15,118	8	
18	Nov 7	Sat	Div 2	H	Bury	W	5-0	19,697	7	Dick 3, Sexton, Stroud
19	Nov 14	Sat	Div 2	A	Oldham Athletic	L	1-3	12,228	9	Stroud
20	Nov 21	Sat	Div 2	H	Everton	D	1-1	24,515	9	Sexton [pen]
21	Nov 28	Sat	Div 2	A	Hull City	L	1-2	21,620	11	Sexton
22	Dec 5	Sat	Div 2	H	Notts County	L	1-2	16,236	13	Dick
23	Dec 12	Sat	Div 2	A	Lincoln City	W	2-1	12,886	10	Dick, Dixon
24	Dec 19	Sat	Div 2	A	Leicester City	L	1-2	23,076	12	Dixon
25	Dec 25	Fri	Div 2	H	Luton Town	W	1-0	19,721	9	Dick
26	Dec 26	Sat	Div 2	A	Luton Town	L	1-3	20,133	10	Dixon
27	Jan 9	Sat	FAC 3	H	Huddersfield Town	W	4-0	25,250		Hooper 2, Dixon, Sexton
28	Jan 16	Sat	Div 2	A	Fulham	W	4-3	30,458	12	Dick 2, Dixon, Sexton
29	Jan 23	Sat	Div 2	H	Bristol Rovers	D	1-1	21,265	12	Hooper
30	Jan 30	Sat	FAC 4	H	Blackpool	D	1-1	37,000		Dixon
31	Feb 3	Wed	FAC 4 Rep	A	Blackpool	L	1-3	27,120		Sexton
32	Feb 6	Sat	Div 2	H	Leeds United	W	5-2	15,585	10	Dixon 2, Andrews, Dick, Hooper [pen]
33	Feb 13	Sat	Div 2	A	Birmingham City	L	0-2	22,716	12	
34	Feb 20	Sat	Div 2	H	Nottingham Forest	D	1-1	20,400	12	Dick
35	Feb 27	Sat	Div 2	A	Brentford	L	1-3	16,458	12	Sexton
36	Mar 6	Sat	Div 2	H	Derby County	D	0-0	18,592	13	
37	Mar 13	Sat	Div 2	A	Blackburn Rovers	L	1-4	25,294	13	Andrews
38	Mar 20	Sat	Div 2	H	Doncaster Rovers	W	2-1	14,655	13	Dick, Hooper
39	Mar 27	Sat	Div 2	A	Everton	W	2-1	41,653	12	Barrett, Dixon
40	Apr 3	Sat	Div 2	H	Hull City	W	1-0	13,467	11	Hooper [pen]
41	Apr 10	Sat	Div 2	A	Bury	L	0-2	13,370	13	
42	Apr 12	Mon	Div 2	H	Stoke City	D	2-2	10,449	13	Dick, Hooper
43	Apr 16	Fri	Div 2	H	Plymouth Argyle	D	2-2	16,465	11	Arnott 2
44	Apr 17	Sat	Div 2	H	Oldham Athletic	L	0-1	13,221	12	
45	Apr 19	Mon	Div 2	A	Plymouth Argyle	L	1-2	21,203	13	Dixon
46	Apr 24	Sat	Div 2	A	Notts County	L	1-3	9,971	13	Dixon

* Essex Professional Cup

eam Line-Ups

ANDREWS Jimmy	ARNOTT John	BARRETT Jim Jnr.	BING Doug	BOND John	CANTWELL Noel	CHISWICK Peter	COOPER Fred	DICK John	DIXON Tommy	FOAN Albert	GAZZARD Gerry	GREGORY Ernie	HOOPER Harry	KEARNS Fred	KINSELL Harry	MALCOLM Andy	MATTHEWS George	McGOWAN Danny	MUSGROVE Malcolm	O'FARRELL Frank	PARKER Derek	SEXTON Dave	SOUTHREN Tommy	STROUD Roy	TUCKER Ken	WOODGATE Terry	WRIGHT George	
11					3			10	9			1								6	4	8	7				2	1
11					3			10				1		9						6	4	8	7				2	2
11					3			10				1		9						6	4	8	7				2	3
11					3			10	9			1								6	4	8	7				2	4
11					3			10				1								6	4	8	7				2	5
11					3			10	9			1								6	4	8	7				2	6
11					3			10				1								6	4	8	7				2	7
					3			10	9			1	11							6	4	8	7				2	8
					3			10				1	11							6	4	8	7				2	9
					3			10	9			1	11							6	4	8	7				2	10
					3			10	9			1	11							6	4	8	7				2	11
			6		3			10	9			1	11								4	8	7				2	12
11					3				9	10		1								6	4	8	7				2	13
11					3			10	9			1								6	4	8	7				2	14
		6		2		1	5			10			7	9	3	4	8									11		15
11					3				9		10	1								6	4	8	7				2	16
11					3			10	9			1								6	4	8	7				2	17
11					3			10				1								6	4	8	7	9			2	18
11					3			10				1								6	4	8	7	9			2	19
11					3			10				1								6	4	8	7	9			2	20
								10				1			3					6		8	7	9	11		2	21
					3			10				1		9		4				6		8	7		11		2	22
11			6		3			10	9			1				4						8	7				2	23
11			6		3			10	9			1				4						8	7				2	24
11			6		3			10	9			1				4						8	7				2	25
11			6		3			10	9	8		1	7			4											2	26
11			6		3			10	9			1	7			4						8					2	27
11			6		3			10	9			1	7			4						8					2	28
11			6		3			10	9			1	7			4						8					2	29
			6		3			10	9			1	7			4						8			11		2	30
11			6		3			10	9			1	7			4						8					2	31
11	8		6		3		1	10	9				7								4						2	32
11	8				3		1	10	9				7							6	4						2	33
11	8		6	2	3		1	10	9				7			4												34
				2	3		1	10	9				7			4			11	6		8						35
			6	2	3		1		9	10			7			4			11			8						36
11				2	3		1	10					7	9		4				6		8						37
11							1	10					7	9	3					6	4	8					2	38
11	8						1	10	9				7		3					6	4						2	39
11	8						1	10	9				7		3					6	4						2	40
11	9		6				1	10					7		3	4						8					2	41
11	9	8	6	2			1	10					7		3	4												42
11	9	8		2			1	10					7		3	4		6										43
11	9	8		2			1	10					7		3	4		6										44
				2			1	10	9	8			7		3			6	11		4							45
	8			2			1	10	9				7		3	4		6	11									46

Back at the Boleyn for the first home game it was
improved performance as Notts County were beaten 3-
Two days later, however, in the return with Blackburn t
Rovers again won 5–2 to shock the home faithful. Afte
decent 2–1 win at Liverpool it was the Hammers' turn

1954-55
Story of the season

It was a **very unhappy start** to the season as **the Hammers crashed 5–2** away at both Swansea Town and Blackburn Rovers.

Appearances & Goals 1954-55

	League		FA Cup		Other*		Total	
	Starts	Goals	Starts	Goals	Starts	Goals	Starts	Goals
ALLISON Malcolm	25	0	2	0	0	0	27	0
ANDREWS Jimmy	21	6	1	0	0	0	22	6
ARNOTT John	2	0	0	0	0	0	2	0
BARRETT Jim Jnr.	2	1	0	0	1	0	3	1
BENNETT Leslie	19	2	2	1	0	0	21	3
BING Doug	5	0	1	0	1	0	7	0
BLACKBURN Alan	2	0	2	0	0	0	4	0
BOND John	25	1	1	0	0	0	26	1
BROWN Ken	23	0	0	0	0	0	23	0
CANTWELL Noel	17	0	2	0	1	0	20	0
CHISWICK Peter	4	0	0	0	0	0	4	0
DARE Billy	13	2	0	0	0	0	13	2
DICK John	39	26	2	0	0	0	41	26
DIXON Tommy	4	0	0	0	1	2	5	2
FOAN Albert	19	2	0	0	0	0	19	2
GREGORY Ernie	0	0	0	0	1	0	1	0
HALLAS Geoff	3	0	0	0	0	0	3	0
HOOPER Harry	41	11	2	2	0	0	43	13
KINSELL Harry	18	0	0	0	0	0	18	0
MALCOLM Andy	38	0	2	0	0	0	40	0
MOORE Brian	1	0	0	0	0	0	1	0
MUSGROVE Malcolm	21	8	1	0	0	0	22	8
NELSON Andy	0	0	0	0	1	0	1	0
NELSON Bill	2	0	0	0	0	0	2	0
NOAKES Alf	0	0	0	0	1	0	1	0
O'FARRELL Frank	28	1	1	0	0	0	29	1
PARKER Derek	7	0	0	0	1	1	8	1
SEXTON Dave	25	12	0	0	0	0	25	12
STROUD Roy	1	0	0	0	0	0	1	0
TAYLOR George	38	0	2	0	0	0	40	0
TUCKER Ken	0	0	0	0	1	0	1	0
WRAGG Doug	0	0	0	0	1	0	1	0
WRIGHT George	19	0	1	0	1	0	21	0
own goal		2						2
TOTALS	**462**	**74**	**22**	**3**	**11**	**3**	**495**	**80**

* Other = Essex Professional Cup

...n 5–2 as Bristol Rovers lost at the Boleyn. At home Port ...le, Nottingham Forest and Stoke City were beaten ...thout conceding a goal, but at Middlesbrough the side ...re heavily beaten, losing 6–0. Back at the Boleyn in ...ecember there were two exciting games with Bury and ...ansea which both ended 3–3.

...New Year's Day trip to Notts County ended in a 5–1 ...feat and a week later it was more gloom as Port Vale ...ocked the Hammers out of the FA Cup after a replay. ...ere was a quick change in fortunes as a hat-trick from ...hn Dick inspired a 4–2 victory at Bristol Rovers, which ...as followed by a hat-trick from Dave Sexton in the 6–1 ...me win over Plymouth Argyle. During March and early ...ril there were six successive wins as the Hammers, now ...fourth spot, pushed for promotion. It was a huge ...sappointment when the seven remaining games did not ...ld a single victory, resulting in an eighth-place finish.

...otball League - Division Two
...nal Table 1954-55

	P	HOME					AWAY					Pts
		W	D	L	F	A	W	D	L	F	A	
...rmingham City	42	14	4	3	56	22	8	6	7	36	25	54
...on Town	42	18	2	1	55	18	5	6	10	33	35	54
...therham United	42	17	1	3	59	22	8	3	10	35	42	54
...eds United	42	14	4	3	43	19	9	3	9	27	34	53
...oke City	42	12	5	4	38	17	9	5	7	31	29	52
...ackburn Rovers	42	14	4	3	73	31	8	2	11	41	48	50
...tts County	42	14	3	4	46	27	7	3	11	28	44	48
...est Ham United	42	12	4	5	46	28	6	6	9	28	42	46
...stol Rovers	42	15	4	2	52	23	4	3	14	23	47	45
...ansea Town	42	15	3	3	58	28	2	6	13	28	55	43
...verpool	42	11	7	3	55	37	5	3	13	37	59	42
...ddlesbrough	42	13	1	7	48	31	5	5	11	25	51	42
...ry	42	10	5	6	44	35	5	6	10	33	37	41
...lham	42	10	5	6	46	29	4	6	11	30	50	39
...ottingham Forest	42	8	4	9	29	29	8	3	10	29	33	39
...ncoln City	42	8	6	7	39	35	5	4	12	29	44	36
...rt Vale	42	10	6	5	31	21	2	5	14	17	50	35
...oncaster Rovers	42	10	5	6	35	34	4	2	15	23	61	35
...ll City	42	7	5	9	30	35	5	5	11	14	34	34
...ymouth Argyle	42	10	4	7	29	26	2	3	16	28	56	31
...swich Town	42	10	3	8	37	28	1	3	17	20	64	28
...erby County	42	6	6	9	39	34	1	3	17	14	48	23

KEN BROWN

Ken is one of the nicest men in soccer, he always has a smile on his face and is a genuine good guy liked by all who have been fortunate enough to be in his company.

He signed for West Ham in 1952 and made his debut at Rotherham in February 1953. He didn't become a regular in the side until the 1957–58 season, when he played in 41 league games as the Hammers became Second Division champions. Back in the First Division the following year he was ever-present and his good form earned him an England cap against Northern Ireland at Wembley. With the Hammers he won winners medals in the 1964 FA Cup final and the 1965 European Cup Winners' Cup. The club awarded him a deserved testimonial match against a Select XI in May 1967. Over 15 seasons he gave the club good service, playing in a total of 455 games before joining Torquay United in 1968. He played in one campaign for the Devon club appearing in 42 league games before going into management with Norwich City.

He led the East Anglian club to victory in the 1985 League Cup final, and after being dismissed by them in 1987 he became the manager at Plymouth Argyle until 1991. He later managed a leisure centre in Norwich and now, in his eighties, is enjoying happy retirement living in East Anglia.

Season **1954-55** Football League - Division Two
Match Details

Manager **Ted Fenton**   Final League Position **8/22**

	Date		Competition	Venue	Opponents	Results		Attendance	Position	Scorers
1	Aug 21	Sat	Div 2	A	Swansea Town	L	2-5	25,329	18	Dick 2
2	Aug 23	Mon	Div 2	A	Blackburn Rovers	L	2-5	26,813	20	Andrews 2
3	Aug 28	Sat	Div 2	H	Notts County	W	3-0	19,638	19	Andrews, Dick, Hooper
4	Aug 30	Mon	Div 2	H	Blackburn Rovers	L	2-5	17,699	19	Sexton 2
5	Sep 4	Sat	Div 2	A	Liverpool	W	2-1	37,592	18	Hooper, Sexton
6	Sep 6	Mon	Div 2	H	Hull City	D	1-1	17,615	14	Hooper
7	Sep 11	Sat	Div 2	H	Bristol Rovers	W	5-2	22,225	11	Andrews, Dick, Hooper, O'Farrell, Sexton
8	Sep 13	Mon	Div 2	A	Hull City	W	1-0	25,851	7	Bond
9	Sep 18	Sat	Div 2	A	Plymouth Argyle	D	1-1	18,771	10	Sexton
10	Sep 25	Sat	Div 2	H	Port Vale	W	2-0	25,155	9	Dick, Sexton
11	Oct 2	Sat	Div 2	A	Doncaster Rovers	L	1-2	13,841	10	Sexton
12	Oct 9	Sat	Div 2	H	Nottingham Forest	W	2-0	25,203	9	Foan, Hooper
13	Oct 16	Sat	Div 2	A	Leeds United	L	1-2	21,074	10	Dick
14	Oct 23	Sat	Div 2	H	Stoke City	W	3-0	27,005	8	Dick 2, Sexton
15	Oct 30	Sat	Div 2	A	Middlesbrough	L	0-6	25,601	9	
16	Nov 6	Sat	Div 2	H	Birmingham City	D	2-2	25,366	11	Dick, Hooper
17	Nov 11	Thu	EPC SF*	A	Colchester United	W	3-2			Dixon 2, Parker
18	Nov 13	Sat	Div 2	A	Ipswich Town	W	3-0	18,648	9	Andrews, Dick, Sexton
19	Nov 20	Sat	Div 2	H	Luton Town	W	2-1	23,034	8	Dick, Dunne (og)
20	Nov 27	Sat	Div 2	A	Rotherham United	D	2-2	13,501	8	Dick 2
21	Dec 4	Sat	Div 2	H	Bury	D	3-3	18,092	8	Musgrove 2, Dick
22	Dec 11	Sat	Div 2	A	Lincoln City	L	1-2	11,100	8	Dick
23	Dec 18	Sat	Div 2	H	Swansea Town	D	3-3	15,230	9	Barrett, Hooper [pen], Thomas (og)
24	Dec 25	Sat	Div 2	H	Derby County	W	1-0	23,545	7	Dick
25	Dec 27	Mon	Div 2	A	Derby County	D	0-0	20,475	8	
26	Jan 1	Sat	Div 2	A	Notts County	L	1-5	20,290	9	Hooper [pen]
27	Jan 8	Sat	FAC 3	H	Port Vale	D	2-2	21,000		Bennett, Hooper
28	Jan 10	Mon	FAC 3 Rep	A	Port Vale	L	1-3	12,410		Hooper
29	Jan 22	Sat	Div 2	A	Bristol Rovers	W	4-2	24,787	8	Dick 3, Hooper
30	Feb 5	Sat	Div 2	H	Plymouth Argyle	W	6-1	18,154	7	Sexton 3, Dick 2, Bennett
31	Feb 12	Sat	Div 2	A	Port Vale	D	1-1	12,621	7	Hooper [pen]
32	Feb 24	Tue	Div 2	H	Doncaster Rovers	L	0-1	4,373	7	
33	Mar 5	Sat	Div 2	H	Leeds United	W	2-1	19,664	7	Bennett, Foan
34	Mar 12	Sat	Div 2	A	Stoke City	W	2-0	20,500	6	Musgrove 2
35	Mar 19	Sat	Div 2	H	Middlesbrough	W	2-1	22,313	5	Dare, Musgrove
36	Mar 26	Sat	Div 2	A	Birmingham City	W	2-1	9,132	4	Dick, Musgrove
37	Apr 2	Sat	Div 2	H	Ipswich Town	W	4-0	24,023	4	Dare, Dick, Hooper, Musgrove
38	Apr 8	Fri	Div 2	H	Fulham	W	2-1	34,238	3	Dick, Musgrove
39	Apr 9	Sat	Div 2	A	Luton Town	L	0-2	27,148	5	
40	Apr 11	Mon	Div 2	A	Fulham	D	0-0	21,616	6	
41	Apr 16	Sat	Div 2	H	Rotherham United	L	1-2	24,056	7	Dick
42	Apr 23	Sat	Div 2	A	Bury	L	1-4	8,746	7	Dick
43	Apr 26	Tue	Div 2	H	Liverpool	L	0-3	9,448	7	
44	Apr 30	Sat	Div 2	H	Lincoln City	L	0-1	10,201	9	
45	May 2	Mon	Div 2	A	Nottingham Forest	D	1-1	5,825	8	Andrews

Team Line-Ups

ALLISON Malcolm	ANDREWS Jimmy	ARNOTT John	BARRETT Jim Jnr.	BENNETT Leslie	BING Doug	BLACKBURN Alan	BOND John	BROWN Ken	CANTWELL Noel	CHISWICK Peter	DARE Billy	DICK John	DIXON Tommy	FOAN Albert	GREGORY Ernie	HALLAS Geoff	HOOPER Harry	KINSELL Harry	MALCOLM Andy	MOORE Brian	MUSGROVE Malcolm	NELSON Andy	NELSON Bill	NOAKES Alf	O'FARRELL Frank	PARKER Derek	SEXTON Dave	STROUD Roy	TAYLOR George	TUCKER Ken	WRAGG Doug	WRIGHT George	#
	11				6		2	3	1			10					7									4	8	9				1	1
	11				6		2	3	1				9	10			7									4	8					2	2
	11	9			6		3	5	1			10					7									4	8				2		3
	11	9			6		3	5	1			10					7									4	8				2		4
	11						2	5				10		8			7		4			3			6		9					1	5
	11						2	5				10		8			7		4			3			6		9					1	6
	11						2	5				10		8			7	3	4						6		9					1	7
	11						2	5				10		8			7	3	4						6		9					1	8
	11						2	5				10		8			7	3	4						6		9					1	9
	11						2	5				10		8			7	3	4						6		9					1	10
	11						2	5				10		8			7	3	4						6		9					1	11
	11						2	5				10		8			7	3	4						6		9					1	12
	11						2	5				10		8			7	3	4						6		9					1	13
	11						2	5				10		8			7	3	4						6		9					1	14
	11						2	5				10		8			7	3	4						6		9					1	15
	11						2	5				10		8			7	3	4						6		9					1	16
		8		4						3			9		1					5	6				10			11		7	2		17
	11						2	5				10		8			7	3	4						6		9					1	18
	11						2	5				10		8			7	3	4						6		9					1	19
							2	5				10		8			7	3	4		11						9					1	20
							2	5				10		8			7	3	4		11						9					1	21
		8					2	5				10	9				7	3	4		11											1	22
		8					2	5				10	9				7	3	4		11											1	23
			8				2	5				10	9				7	3	4		11											1	24
	11		8			9	2	5	3			10					7		4													1	25
	11		8		6	9	2	5				10					7	3	4													1	26
	11		8		6	9	2		3			10					7		4													1	27
		8				9			3			10					7		4		11				6				1			2	28
		8							3			10					7		4		11				6		9		1			2	29
		8							3			10					7		4		11				6		9		1			2	30
		8							3			10					7		4		11				6		9		1			2	31
		8							3			10					7		4		11				6		9		1			2	32
		8							3			10	9				7		4		11				6				1			2	33
		8							3		9	10					7		4		11				6				1			2	34
		8							3		9	10					7		4		11				6				1			2	35
		8							3		9	10					7		4		11				6				1			2	36
		8							3		9	10					7		4		11				6				1			2	37
		8							3		9	10					7		4		11				6				1			2	38
		8							3		9	10					7		4		11				6				1			2	39
		8							3		9	10					7		4		11				6				1			2	40
		8							3		9	10					7		4		11				6				1			2	41
		8							3		9	10					7		4		11				6				1			2	42
		10				9			3								7		4		11				6	8			1			2	43
		8							3		9	10					7		4		11				6				1			2	44
	11								3		9	10					7		4	8					6				1			2	45

Winger Harry Hooper scored twice and this was note
by the England selectors, who awarded him two caps th
season at under-23 level. October proved to be a goo
month, with 14 goals being scored in three home game
First Barnsley were beaten 4–0, then another 4–0 w
against Plymouth Argyle saw Ken Tucker score a hat-tric

1955-56
Story of the season

The **first win of the season** did not come until 3 September when **Notts County were beaten 6–1** at home.

Appearances & Goals 1955-56

	League		FA Cup		Other*		Total	
	Starts	Goals	Starts	Goals	Starts	Goals	Starts	Goa
ALLISON Malcolm	40	3	6	0	1	0	47	3
ANDREWS Jimmy	16	2	0	0	1	0	17	2
BENNETT Leslie	7	1	0	0	2	0	9	1
BLACKBURN Alan	6	2	0	0	2	2	8	4
BOND John	34	1	6	0	4	0	44	1
BROWN Ken	2	0	0	0	1	0	3	0
CANTWELL Noel	40	0	6	0	2	0	48	0
COOPER Fred	0	0	0	0	2	0	2	0
DARE Billy	40	18	6	4	3	3	49	25
DICK John	35	8	6	6	4	1	45	15
FOAN Albert	5	1	6	3	2	0	13	4
GREGORY Ernie	36	0	6	0	4	0	46	0
GRICE Mike	2	0	0	0	2	1	4	1
HALLAS Geoff	0	0	0	0	1	0	1	0
HOOPER Harry	30	15	6	1	1	0	37	16
JOHNSTONE Robert	0	0	0	0	1	0	1	0
LANSDOWNE Bill	2	0	0	0	1	0	3	0
LAWRENCE Tommy	0	0	0	0	1	0	1	0
MALCOLM Andy	22	0	6	0	1	0	29	0
MATTHEWS George	9	1	0	0	0	0	9	1
MOORE Brian	8	1	0	0	1	1	9	2
MUSGROVE Malcolm	8	0	1	0	1	0	10	0
NELSON Andy	0	0	0	0	3	0	3	0
O'FARRELL Frank	40	1	6	0	1	1	47	2
PARKER Derek	8	0	0	0	3	1	11	1
SEXTON Dave	15	2	0	0	2	0	17	2
SMITH Roy	2	0	0	0	1	0	3	0
STROUD Roy	2	0	0	0	1	0	3	0
TAYLOR George	6	0	0	0	1	0	7	0
TUCKER Ken	37	14	5	0	2	3	44	17
WRAGG Doug	0	0	0	0	2	0	2	0
WRIGHT George	10	0	0	0	1	0	11	0
own goal		4						4
TOTALS	462	74	66	14	55	13	583	10

* Other = Essex Professional Cup and Southern Floodlight Cup

nally Harry Hooper scored three times in the 6–1 rout of
oncaster Rovers. After this match the team went eight
mes without winning and slumped to nineteenth in the
ague table.

5–1 win over Swansea Town put the team in good spirits
r the visit of First Division Preston North End in the FA
up. Losing 2–1 at half-time, the Hammers fought back
ith a splendid hat-trick from Albert Foan and eventually
on 5–2. Cardiff City were beaten 2–1 at home in the next
und with the fifth-round opponents being Blackburn
overs. Following a goalless draw at home the teams met
gain at Ewood Park, with West Ham winning 3–2. A huge
owd of 69,111 turned up to see the quarter-final tie at
ottenham Hotspur. An exciting match saw the Hammers
ce into a 3–1 lead with a hat-trick from Johnny Dick. The
urs fought back to draw level at full-time and it was the

North London side that won 2–1 in the replay. Only five
more league games were won, leaving the Hammers to
finish in sixteenth place. In March, to the fury of the
supporters, Harry Hooper was sold to Wolverhampton
Wanderers, and as the season came to a close Dave Sexton
was transferred to Leyton Orient.

BILL LANSDOWNE

After finishing his national service this wing-half signed for West Ham in 1955 and made his debut against Lincoln City in April 1956.

After Frank O'Farrell left for Preston Bill became a regular in the team and won a Second Division League Championship medal in season 1957–58. After being promoted to the First Division there was fierce competition for the left-half position and a youngster called Bobby Moore took his place. Bill continued to play in the reserve side with the odd appearance in the first team. After 60 appearances he retired as a player in 1965 and took on a coaching role with the junior side at Upton Park. A year later he joined Eastbourne United as manager of the non-league side. He continued in this role for two years before rejoining West Ham, first as manager to the youth side and later the reserves. He left the club in 1979 and set up a family business making curtains. Today Bill, aged 79, is in happy retirement living in Barkingside, Essex.

ootball League - Division Two Final Table 1955-56

		HOME					AWAY					
	P	W	D	L	F	A	W	D	L	F	A	Pts
heffield Wednesday	42	13	5	3	60	28	8	8	5	41	34	55
eeds United	42	17	3	1	51	18	6	3	12	29	42	52
verpool	42	14	3	4	52	25	7	3	11	33	38	48
ackburn Rovers	42	13	4	4	55	29	8	2	11	29	36	48
eicester City	42	15	3	3	63	23	6	3	12	31	55	48
istol Rovers	42	13	3	5	53	33	8	3	10	31	37	48
ottingham Forest	42	9	5	7	30	26	10	4	7	38	37	47
ncoln City	42	14	5	2	49	17	4	5	12	30	48	46
ulham	42	15	2	4	59	27	5	4	12	30	52	46
wansea Town	42	14	4	3	49	23	6	2	13	34	58	46
istol City	42	14	4	3	49	20	5	3	13	31	44	45
ort Vale	42	12	4	5	38	21	4	9	8	22	37	45
oke City	42	13	2	6	47	27	7	2	12	24	35	44
iddlesbrough	42	11	4	6	46	31	5	4	12	30	47	40
ury	42	9	5	7	44	39	7	3	11	42	51	40
est Ham United	**42**	**12**	**4**	**5**	**52**	**27**	**2**	**7**	**12**	**22**	**42**	**39**
oncaster Rovers	42	11	5	5	45	30	1	6	14	24	66	35
arnsley	42	10	5	6	33	35	1	7	13	14	49	34
otherham United	42	7	5	9	29	34	5	4	12	27	41	33
otts County	42	8	5	8	39	37	3	4	14	16	45	31
ymouth Argyle	42	7	6	8	33	25	3	2	16	21	62	28
ull City	42	6	4	11	32	45	4	2	15	21	52	26

Season 1955-56 Football League - Division Two
Match Details
Manager **Ted Fenton**   Final League Position **16/22**

	Date		Competition	Venue	Opponents	Results		Attendance	Position	Scorers
1	Aug 20	Sat	Div 2	H	Rotherham United	D	1-1	18,952	13	Dare
2	Aug 22	Mon	Div 2	A	Port Vale	L	1-2	19,259	14	Allison [pen]
3	Aug 27	Sat	Div 2	A	Swansea Town	L	2-4	19,960	19	Bennett, Dare
4	Aug 29	Mon	Div 2	H	Port Vale	L	0-2	13,052	21	
5	Aug 31	Wed	EPC F*	A	Southend United	D	3-3			Blackburn, Moore, Tucker
6	Sep 3	Sat	Div 2	H	Notts County	W	6-1	16,710	18	Dare 2, Hooper 2, Dick, O'Farrell
7	Sep 6	Tue	Div 2	A	Bristol City	L	1-3	25,993	18	Tucker
8	Sep 10	Sat	Div 2	A	Leeds United	D	3-3	21,855	19	Tucker 2, Dare
9	Sep 17	Sat	Div 2	H	Fulham	W	2-1	25,738	17	Hooper 2
10	Sep 24	Sat	Div 2	A	Bury	D	1-1	10,217	16	Tucker
11	Oct 1	Sat	Div 2	H	Barnsley	W	4-0	20,863	14	Dare 2, Hooper [pen], Jackson (og)
12	Oct 8	Sat	Div 2	H	Plymouth Argyle	W	4-0	19,669	12	Tucker 3, Allison
13	Oct 10	Mon	SFC 1**	H	Crystal Palace	W	3-0	6,000		Tucker, O'Farrell, Dare
14	Oct 15	Sat	Div 2	A	Liverpool	L	1-3	32,187	15	Hooper
15	Oct 22	Sat	Div 2	H	Doncaster Rovers	W	6-1	13,303	12	Hooper 3, Andrews, Dare, Taylor
16	Oct 29	Sat	Div 2	A	Lincoln City	D	1-1	11,078	11	Dare
17	Nov 5	Sat	Div 2	H	Blackburn Rovers	L	2-3	22,990	14	Dare, Hooper [pen]
18	Nov 12	Sat	Div 2	A	Hull City	L	1-3	24,050	15	Tucker
19	Nov 19	Sat	Div 2	H	Nottingham Forest	L	1-2	17,121	17	Hooper
20	Nov 26	Sat	Div 2	A	Sheffield Wednesday	D	1-1	20,767	17	Tucker
21	Dec 3	Sat	Div 2	H	Leicester City	L	1-3	17,577	19	Tucker
22	Dec 5	Mon	EPC SF	H	Southend United	L	2-3			Blackburn, Parker
23	Dec 10	Sat	Div 2	A	Bristol Rovers	D	1-1	20,710	19	Dick
24	Dec 17	Sat	Div 2	A	Rotherham United	L	2-3	10,293	19	Hooper, Moore
25	Dec 24	Sat	Div 2	H	Swansea Town	W	5-1	15,857	19	Bond, Dare, Dick, Hooper [pen], Tucker
26	Dec 26	Mon	Div 2	A	Middlesbrough	L	0-2	22,001	19	
27	Dec 27	Tue	Div 2	H	Middlesbrough	W	1-0	21,522	19	Bilcliff (og)
28	Dec 31	Sat	Div 2	A	Notts County	W	1-0	18,708	19	Dare
29	Jan 7	Sat	FAC 3	H	Preston North End	W	5-2	29,000		Foan 3, Dare 2
30	Jan 14	Sat	Div 2	H	Leeds United	D	1-1	20,000	18	Foan
31	Jan 21	Sat	Div 2	A	Fulham	L	1-3	24,322	19	Dare
32	Jan 28	Sat	FAC 4	H	Cardiff City	W	2-1	35,500		Dare, Dick
33	Feb 11	Sat	Div 2	A	Barnsley	D	1-1	8,432	19	Dare
34	Feb 18	Sat	FAC 5	H	Blackburn Rovers	D	0-0	28,000		
35	Feb 23	Thu	FAC 5 Rep	A	Blackburn Rovers	W	3-2	29,300		Dick 2, Hooper
36	Feb 25	Sat	Div 2	H	Liverpool	W	2-0	18,798	17	Molyneux (og), Twentyman (og)
37	Mar 3	Sat	FAC QF	A	Tottenham Hotspur	D	3-3	69,111		Dick 3
38	Mar 8	Thu	FAC QF Rep	H	Tottenham Hotspur	L	1-2	36,000		Dare
39	Mar 10	Sat	Div 2	H	Bristol Rovers	W	2-1	19,790	16	Hooper [pen], Tucker
40	Mar 17	Sat	Div 2	A	Blackburn Rovers	L	1-4	21,581	16	Matthews
41	Mar 19	Mon	Div 2	H	Bury	W	3-2	14,285	16	Dare, Dick, Hooper [pen]
42	Mar 24	Sat	Div 2	H	Hull City	D	1-1	12,718	16	Allison
43	Mar 26	Mon	Div 2	A	Doncaster Rovers	L	1-2	6,272	16	Dick
44	Mar 30	Fri	Div 2	H	Stoke City	W	2-0	17,883	15	Dare, Tucker
45	Mar 31	Sat	Div 2	A	Plymouth Argyle	W	1-0	18,667	14	Andrews
46	Apr 2	Mon	Div 2	A	Stoke City	L	0-3	17,285	14	
47	Apr 4	Wed	SFC SF**	A	Reading	W	3-1	5,000		Dare, Grice, Dick
48	Apr 7	Sat	Div 2	H	Sheffield Wednesday	D	3-3	17,549	14	Dick 2, Dare
49	Apr 14	Sat	Div 2	A	Leicester City	L	1-2	17,432	15	Blackburn
50	Apr 18	Wed	Div 2	A	Nottingham Forest	D	0-0	15,739	15	
51	Apr 21	Sat	Div 2	H	Lincoln City	L	2-4	13,347	16	Dare, Dick
52	Apr 23	Mon	SFC F**	H	Aldershot	W	2-1	5,000		Tucker, Dare
53	Apr 28	Sat	Div 2	H	Bristol City	W	3-0	13,534	16	Sexton 2, Blackburn

* Essex Professional Cup Final 1954-55 deferred from last season, trophy shared   ** Southern Floodlight Cup

Team Line-Ups

ALLISON Malcolm	ANDREWS Jimmy	BENNETT Leslie	BLACKBURN Alan	BOND John	BROWN Ken	CANTWELL Noel	COOPER Fred	DARE Billy	DICK John	FOAN Albert	GREGORY Ernie	GRICE Mike	HALLAS Geoff	HOOPER Harry	JOHNSTONE Robert	LANSDOWNE Bill	LAWRENCE Tommy	MALCOLM Andy	MATTHEWS George	MOORE Brian	MUSGROVE Malcolm	NELSON Andy	O'FARRELL Frank	PARKER Derek	SEXTON Dave	SMITH Roy	STROUD Roy	TAYLOR George	TUCKER Ken	WRAGG Doug	WRIGHT George	Game
		8				3		9	10									4			11		6				7	1			2	1
						3		9	10									4	8		11		6				7	1			2	2
		8				3		9	10					7				4			11		6					1			2	3
8						3		9	10					7				4			11		6					1			2	4
			9	2						10	1	3			6					8			5		4		7		11			5
		8				3		9	10					7				4					6					1	11		2	6
		8				3		9	10					7				4					6					1	11		2	7
10		8				3		9			1			7									6		4				11		2	8
		8				3		9	10		1			7									6		4				11		2	9
				2		3		9	10		1			7					8				6		4				11			10
8				2		3		9	10		1			7									6		4				11			11
8				2		3		9	10		1			7									6		4				11			12
8				2		3		9	10		1			7				4					6						11			13
8				2		3		9	10		1			7									6		4				11			14
8				2		3		9	10		1			7									6		4				11			15
8		10		2		3		9			1			7									6		4				11			16
8				2	5	3		9	10		1			7									6						11			17
8				2		3		9	10		1			7									6		4				11			18
10				2		3		9			1			7						8			6		4				11			19
10						3		9			1			7						8			6		4				11		2	20
10				2		3		9			1			7				4		8			6						11			21
		8	11		5	3			10								9					7	6		4			1			2	22
			9	2		3			10		1			7				4	8				6						11			23
			9	2		3			10		1			7				4	8				6						11			24
				2		3		9	10		1			7				4	8				6						11			25
				2		3		9	10		1			7				4	8				6						11			26
				2		3		9	10		1			7				4					6			8			11			27
				2		3		9	10	8	1			7				4					6						11			28
				2		3		9	10	8	1			7				4					6						11			29
				2		3		9	10	8	1			7				4					6						11			30
						3		9	10	8	1			7				4					6						11		2	31
				2		3		9	10	8	1			7				4					6						11			32
				2		3		9	10	8	1			7				4			11		6									33
				2		3		9	10	8	1			7				4			11		6									34
				2		3		9	10	8	1			7				4					6						11			35
8				2		3		9	10	8	1			7				4					6						11			36
				2		3		9	10	8	1			7				4					6						11			37
				2		3		9	10	8	1			7				4					6						11			38
				2		3		9	10		1			7				4					6			8			11			39
				2		3		9	10		1			7				4	8				6						11			40
				2		3		9	10		1			7				4	8				6						11			41
				2		3	7	9	10		1							4	8				6						11			42
				2		3		9	10		1							4	8	7			6						11			43
		10		2		3	7	9											8				6		4				11			44
8				2		3		9	10		1											7	6		4				11			45
				2		3		9	10		1	7											6		4		10		11			46
	4			2		3		9	10	8	1	7										5	6						11			47
			9	2		3	7		10		1								8				6		4				11			48
			9	2		3	7		10		1								8				6		4				11			49
			9	2		3	7		10		1								8				6		4				11			50
			9	2		3	8		10		1	7					6	4											11			51
				2		3		9	10		1	7					6					5			4		8			11		52
			9	2	5	3		7			1						6								4		8	10		11		53

After **Barnsley were beaten** 2–0 at home the tre▮
continued with home defeats to Huddersfield Town a▮
Grimsby Town. Fortunes changed in November: aft▮
Stoke City were beaten 1–0 at the Boleyn, the team went ▮
a run of nine consecutive home wins, which put the side ▮
fifth place in the table.

1956-57
Story of the season

It was a **strange start to the season** as after eight games the team were **unbeaten away** but had not **won a home game.**

Appearances & Goals 1956-57

	League		FA Cup		Other*		Total	
	Starts	Goals	Starts	Goals	Starts	Goals	Starts	Goal▮
ALLISON Malcolm	39	4	2	0	2	0	43	4
BLACKBURN Alan	6	1	0	0	1	0	7	1
BOND John	30	1	2	0	4	1	36	2
BROWN Ken	5	0	0	0	2	0	7	0
CANTWELL Noel	39	1	2	0	2	0	43	1
COOPER Fred	2	0	0	0	1	0	3	0
DARE Billy	30	9	2	1	3	2	35	1▮
DICK John	36	8	2	1	3	4	41	1▮
FENN George	0	0	0	0	1	0	1	0
FOAN Albert	4	0	0	0	0	0	4	0
GREGORY Ernie	29	0	0	0	4	0	33	0
GRICE Mike	11	1	0	0	3	0	14	1
JOHNSTONE Robert	2	0	0	0	0	0	2	0
LANSDOWNE Bill	26	1	2	0	3	0	31	1
LEWIS Eddie	24	9	2	1	1	0	27	1▮
MALCOLM Andy	37	0	2	0	3	0	42	0
MATTHEWS George	0	0	0	0	1	0	1	▮
MORLEY John	0	0	0	0	2	0	2	0
MUSGROVE Malcolm	39	8	2	1	3	1	44	1▮
NELSON Andy	0	0	0	0	1	0	1	0
NEWMAN Mick	4	0	0	0	0	0	4	
O'FARRELL Frank	7	1	0	0	0	0	7	
OBENEY Harry	1	0	0	0	0	0	1	
PARKER Derek	5	1	0	0	1	0	6	
PYKE Malcolm	2	0	0	0	0	0	2	
SMITH John	29	4	2	2	3	0	34	
SMITH Roy	4	1	0	0	2	0	6	
STROUD Roy	5	2	0	0	1	0	6	
TUCKER Ken	10	6	0	0	3	0	13	
WRAGG Doug	10	0	0	0	1	0	11	
WRIGHT George	13	0	0	0	3	0	16	
WYLLIE Robinson	13	0	2	0	1	0	16	
own goal		1						
TOTALS	**462**	**59**	**22**	**6**	**55**	**8**	**539**	▮

* Other = Essex Professional Cup and Southern Floodlight Cup

Grimsby Town were the visitors in the FA Cup and in an exciting game the Hammers won 5–3, with two goals from John Smith. There were 55,245 inside the ground at Everton for the next round, which saw West Ham narrowly lose 2–1 to the First Division side. Manager Ted Fenton was now putting together a good side. Ernie Gregory was reliable in goal, full-backs John Bond and Noel Cantwell were strong and rugged, and skipper and centre-half Malcolm Allison was a rock in defence. In the forward line flying winger Malcolm Musgrove was on hand to lay on chances for inside-forward Johnny Dick. There was a shock at Huddersfield in February as in snowy conditions the Hammers slumped to a 6–2 defeat. In the aftermath of this defeat only three wins were achieved in the remaining twelve games, which included a 5–3 defeat at Leicester City and a 4–1 reverse at Notts County. It was a disappointing end to the season, which gave a final placing of eighth.

Football League - Division Two
Final Table 1956-57

	P	HOME					AWAY					Pts
		W	D	L	F	A	W	D	L	F	A	
Leicester City	42	14	5	2	68	36	11	6	4	41	31	61
Nottingham Forest	42	13	4	4	50	29	9	6	6	44	26	54
Liverpool	42	16	1	4	53	26	5	10	6	29	28	53
Blackburn Rovers	42	12	6	3	49	32	9	4	8	34	43	52
Stoke City	42	16	2	3	64	18	4	6	11	19	40	48
Middlesbrough	42	12	5	4	51	29	7	5	9	33	31	48
Sheffield United	42	11	6	4	45	28	8	2	11	42	48	46
West Ham United	42	12	4	5	31	24	7	4	10	28	39	46
Bristol Rovers	42	12	5	4	47	19	6	4	11	34	48	45
Swansea Town	42	12	3	6	53	34	7	4	10	37	56	45
Fulham	42	13	1	7	53	32	6	3	12	31	44	42
Huddersfield Town	42	10	3	8	33	27	8	3	10	35	47	42
Bristol City	42	13	2	6	49	32	3	7	11	25	47	41
Doncaster Rovers	42	12	5	4	51	21	3	5	13	26	56	40
Leyton Orient	42	7	8	6	34	38	8	2	11	32	46	40
Grimsby Town	42	12	4	5	41	26	5	1	15	20	36	39
Rotherham United	42	9	7	5	37	26	4	4	13	37	49	37
Lincoln City	42	9	4	8	34	27	5	2	14	20	53	34
Barnsley	42	8	7	6	39	35	4	3	14	20	54	34
Notts County	42	7	6	8	34	32	2	6	13	24	54	30
Bury	42	5	3	13	37	47	3	6	12	23	49	25
Port Vale	42	7	4	10	31	42	1	2	18	26	59	22

JOHN SMITH

While playing for East London boys Smith was spotted by West Ham and in 1955 he joined the ground staff.

Playing at left-half, he made his debut at Port Vale in September 1956 and was soon an established member of the team. The following season he managed 32 league appearances and scored 11 goals as West Ham became Second Division champions. The Hammers were back in the First Division and his fine form saw him gain an England under-23 cap against France in November 1959. In March 1960 he played his last game for the club at Blackpool and it was a memorable one because he had to take over in goal when Brian Rhodes was injured. He had played 130 games, scoring 22 goals for the Hammers, before he joined Tottenham in an exchange deal that brought Dave Dunmore to Upton Park. At Tottenham he struggled and in four years played in only 21 games. Over the next seven years he became a journeyman, playing for Coventry City, Leyton Orient, Torquay, Swindon Town and finally Walsall. He retired from playing in 1972; during his career he had made 385 league appearances, scoring 43 goals. He later became the manager at both Walsall and Dundalk in Ireland. In 1988 John tragically died at the early age of 49.

Season **1956-57** Football League - Division Two
Match Details

Manager **Ted Fenton**   Final League Position **8/22**

	Date		Competition	Venue	Opponents	Results		Attendance	Position	Scorers
1	Aug 18	Sat	Div 2	A	Fulham	W	4-1	25,809	3	Dare 2, Grice, Tucker
2	Aug 20	Mon	Div 2	H	Blackburn Rovers	L	1-3	19,727	6	Tucker
3	Aug 25	Sat	Div 2	H	Swansea Town	L	1-2	17,067	13	Tucker
4	Aug 27	Mon	Div 2	A	Blackburn Rovers	W	2-0	15,003	8	Blackburn, Dick
5	Sep 1	Sat	Div 2	A	Lincoln City	W	2-0	13,131	4	Stroud 2
6	Sep 3	Mon	Div 2	H	Liverpool	D	1-1	25,671	4	O'Farrell
7	Sep 8	Sat	Div 2	H	Rotherham United	D	1-1	19,448	5	Dare
8	Sep 15	Sat	Div 2	A	Port Vale	D	0-0	17,582	9	
9	Sep 22	Sat	Div 2	H	Barnsley	W	2-0	19,412	6	Dare, Dick
10	Sep 29	Sat	Div 2	A	Sheffield United	L	0-1	23,529	9	
11	Oct 2	Tue	SFC 1**	H	Leyton Orient	W	4-1	14,500		Dick 3, Musgrove
12	Oct 6	Sat	Div 2	A	Leyton Orient	W	2-1	24,685	8	Musgrove, Willemse (og)
13	Oct 13	Sat	Div 2	H	Hudddersfield	L	0-2	22,643	10	
14	Oct 20	Sat	Div 2	A	Bristol Rovers	D	1-1	24,404	10	Dick
15	Oct 27	Sat	Div 2	H	Grimsby Town	L	0-1	17,579	11	
16	Nov 3	Sat	Div 2	A	Doncaster Rovers	L	0-3	13,071	14	
17	Nov 10	Sat	Div 2	H	Stoke City	W	1-0	17,668	12	Tucker [pen]
18	Nov 12	Mon	SFC 2	H	Arsenal	D	1-1	14,000		Dick
19	Nov 17	Sat	Div 2	A	Middlesbrough	L	1-3	31,513	13	Tucker
20	Nov 24	Sat	Div 2	H	Leicester City	W	2-1	19,789	13	Lewis, Tucker
21	Nov 26	Mon	EPC 1*	H	Chelmsford City	W	3-1	2,000		Dare 2, Bond [pen]
22	Dec 1	Sat	Div 2	A	Bury	D	3-3	8,757	11	Dick, Musgrove, Parker
23	Dec 4	Tue	SFC 2 Rep**	A	Arsenal	L	2-3	14,156		Musgrove 2
24	Dec 8	Sat	Div 2	H	Notts County	W	2-1	14,875	10	Dick, Smith R.
25	Dec 15	Sat	Div 2	H	Fulham	W	2-1	18,119	10	Bond, Musgrove
26	Dec 22	Sat	Div 2	A	Swansea Town	L	1-3	12,091	11	Lewis
27	Dec 25	Tue	Div 2	H	Nottingham Forest	W	2-1	16,300	10	Lewis, Musgrove
28	Dec 29	Sat	Div 2	H	Lincoln City	W	2-1	16,790	11	Dare 2
29	Jan 5	Sat	FAC 3	H	Grimsby Town	W	5-3	24,500		Smith J. 2, Dick, Lewis, Musgrove
30	Jan 12	Sat	Div 2	A	Rotherham United	W	1-0	11,090	9	Musgrove
31	Jan 19	Sat	Div 2	H	Port Vale	W	2-1	17,229	7	Dick, Smith J.
32	Jan 26	Sat	FAC 4	A	Everton	L	1-2	55,245		Dare
33	Feb 2	Sat	Div 2	A	Barnsley	W	2-1	15,931	6	Dare, Dick
34	Feb 9	Sat	Div 2	H	Sheffield United	W	3-2	22,130	5	Cantwell, Lewis, Smith J.
35	Feb 16	Sat	Div 2	H	Leyton Orient	W	2-1	36,318	5	Lansdowne, Lewis
36	Feb 23	Sat	Div 2	A	Huddersfield Town	L	2-6	5,878	5	Lewis, Smith J.
37	Feb 25	Mon	EPC SF*	H	Leyton Orient	L	0-2	6,500		
38	Mar 2	Sat	Div 2	H	Bristol Rovers	L	1-2	22,354	6	Lewis
39	Mar 9	Sat	Div 2	A	Grimsby Town	L	1-2	14,026	7	Allison [pen]
40	Mar 16	Sat	Div 2	H	Doncaster Rovers	D	1-1	15,336	8	Lewis [pen]
41	Mar 23	Sat	Div 2	A	Stoke City	W	1-0	19,794	8	Musgrove
42	Mar 30	Sat	Div 2	H	Middlesbrough	D	1-1	15,166	7	Allison
43	Apr 6	Sat	Div 2	A	Leicester City	L	3-5	33,338	10	Musgrove 2, Allison [pen]
44	Apr 13	Sat	Div 2	H	Bury	W	1-0	9,043	8	Dare
45	Apr 15	Mon	Div 2	A	Nottingham Forest	L	0-3	24,251	8	
46	Apr 19	Fri	Div 2	A	Bristol City	D	1-1	24,731	7	Allison
47	Apr 20	Sat	Div 2	A	Notts County	L	1-4	17,803	10	Smith J.
48	Apr 22	Mon	Div 2	H	Bristol City	W	3-1	9,343	8	Dare, Dick, Lewis
49	Apr 27	Sat	Div 2	A	Liverpool	L	0-1	36,236	8	

* Essex Professional Cup   ** Southern Floodlight Cup

Team Line-Ups

ALLISON Malcolm	BLACKBURN Alan	BOND John	BROWN Ken	CANTWELL Noel	COOPER Fred	DARE Billy	DICK John	FENN George	FOAN Albert	GREGORY Ernie	GRICE Mike	JOHNSTONE Robert	LANSDOWNE Bill	LEWIS Eddie	MALCOLM Andy	MATTHEWS George	MORLEY John	MUSGROVE Malcolm	NELSON Andy	NEWMAN Mick	O'FARRELL Frank	OBENEY Harry	PARKER Derek	PYKE Malcolm	SMITH John	SMITH Roy	STROUD Roy	TUCKER Ken	WRAGG Doug	WRIGHT George	WYLLIE Robinson	
			5		3	9	10	8		1	7				4						6							11		2		1
			5		3	9	10	8		1	7				4						6							11		2		2
	9		5	3		7	10	8		1					4						6							11		2		3
5	9			3			10			1					4			11			6					8		7		2		4
5				3			10			1					4			11			6				9	8		7		2		5
5	9			3			10			1					4			11			6					8		7		2		6
5				3		9	10			1					4			11			6					8		7		2		7
5				3		9	10			1	7		6		4			11								8				2		8
5				3		9	10			1	7		6		4			11								8				2		9
5				3		9	10			1	7		6		4			11								8				2		10
		3	5			9	10			1	7		6		4			11								8				2		11
5				3		9	10			1			6		4			11								8		7		2		12
5				3		9	10			1	7		6		4			11								8				2		13
5	9	2		3			10			1			6					11					4			8		7				14
5	9	2		3			10	8		1			6					11					4					7				15
5		2		3		9	10			1					4			11					6			8		7				16
5		2		3		9	10			1			6		4			7								8		11				17
5		2		3		10	9			1			6		4			7								8		11				18
5		2		3			10			1			6		4			7								8		11	9			19
5				3			10						6	9	4			7								8		11		2	1	20
	10	3			7					1	11					8	6			5			4						9	2		21
5		2		3			10						6	9	4			7								8		11			1	22
5		2		3			10						6	9	4			7							8			11			1	23
5		2		3			10						6	9	4			7							8			11			1	24
5		2		3			10						6	9	4			7							8			11			1	25
5		2		3			10						6	9	4			7							8			11			1	26
5		2		3		7	10						6	9	4			11								8					1	27
5		2		3		7	10						6	9	4			11								8					1	28
5		2		3		9	10						6	7	4			11								8					1	29
5		2		3		7	10						6		4			11								8	9				1	30
5		2		3		9	10						6	7	4			11								8					1	31
5		2		3		9	10						6	7	4			11								8					1	32
5		2		3		7	10						6	9	4			11								8					1	33
5		2		3		7	10						6	9	4			11								8					1	34
5		2		3		7	10						6	9	4			11								8					1	35
5		2		3		7	10						6	9	4			11								8					1	36
			5		3			9		1	7						6						4		10	8		11		2		37
5		2		3		7	10			1			6	9	4			11								8						38
5	10	2		3		7				1			6	9	4			11								8						39
5		2		3		8				1	7			9	4			11		10			6									40
5		2		3		9				1	7			10	4			11		8			6									41
5		2		3		9				1	7			10	4			11		8			6									42
5		2		3		9				1	7			10	4			11		8			6									43
5		2		3		9	10			1	7			8	4			11					6									44
5		2		3		9				1			6	10	4			11								8			7			45
5		2		3		9	11			1			6	10	4			7								8						46
5		2		3			11			1			6	9	4			7					8			10						47
		2	5	3		7	10			1				9				11					4			8						48
		2	5	3		7	10			1				9				11					4			8						49

1957-58
Story of the season

It was a **moderate beginning** to the campaign with just **three wins** in the **first ten games.**

Billy Dare was on form, scoring a hat-trick at Bristo Rovers in the 3–2 victory, and two more against Fulham a home as the Cottagers were beaten by the same score. I October there was a fine 3–0 win at leaders Charlto Athletic and more good news followed when days late West Ham signed centre-forward Vic Keeble from Newcastle. Keeble scored on his debut in the 1–1 hom draw with Doncaster Rovers and soon set up a usefu partnership with Johnny Dick. The team were now startin to put together an unbeaten run as Huddersfield Town los

Appearances & Goals 1957-58

	League		FA Cup		Other*		Total	
	Starts	Goals	Starts	Goals	Starts	Goals	Starts	Goals
ALLISON Malcolm	5	1	0	0	0	0	5	1
BLACKBURN Alan	1	0	0	0	0	0	1	0
BOND John	41	8	3	1	2	0	46	9
BROWN Ken	41	0	3	0	4	0	48	0
CANTWELL Noel	33	4	2	0	3	0	38	4
COOPER Fred	2	0	0	0	2	0	4	0
DARE Billy	26	14	0	0	1	0	27	14
DICK John	41	21	3	2	4	3	48	26
FENN George	0	0	0	0	2	0	2	0
GREGORY Ernie	37	0	3	0	3	0	43	0
GRICE Mike	29	2	3	1	2	0	34	3
HAYWARD Terry	0	0	0	0	1	0	1	0
KEEBLE Vic	29	19	3	4	1	1	33	24
KIRKUP Joe	0	0	0	0	1	0	1	0
LANSDOWNE Bill	17	2	1	0	2	0	20	2
LEWIS Eddie	7	3	3	2	2	1	12	6
MALCOLM Andy	42	3	3	0	2	0	47	3
MORLEY John	0	0	0	0	2	0	2	0
MUSGROVE Malcolm	39	9	3	0	4	1	46	10
NELSON Andy	3	0	0	0	1	0	4	0
NEVILLE Billy	3	0	0	0	2	1	5	1
NEWMAN Mick	3	2	0	0	2	1	5	3
PYKE Malcolm	15	0	2	0	4	0	21	0
RHODES Brian	5	0	0	0	1	0	6	0
SMILLIE Andy	0	0	0	0	1	1	1	1
SMITH John	32	11	0	0	1	1	33	12
WRAGG Doug	3	0	0	0	3	0	6	0
WRIGHT George	8	0	1	0	1	0	10	0
WYLLIE Robinson	0	0	0	0	1	0	1	0
own goal		2						2
TOTALS	**462**	**101**	**33**	**10**	**55**	**10**	**550**	**12**

* Other = Essex Professional Cup and Southern Floodlight Cup

–2 at the Boleyn and a Vic Keeble hat-trick helped the Hammers beat Stoke City 5–0 at home. At Lincoln City in December Keeble and Dick both scored twice in the 6–1 victory. After a run of 13 games undefeated the Hammers were finally beaten 2–1 by Ipswich Town on Boxing Day at Portman Road. Two days later Bristol Rovers faced the backlash as West Ham thrashed them 6–1 at home, with John Smith claiming a hat-trick.

First Division Blackpool were the visitors in the FA Cup and, bang in form, Hammers sent them home beaten 5–1 with a hat-trick from Vic Keeble. The next round brought Third Division Stockport County to Upton Park. The Cheshire club put up a brave fight, finally losing 3–2 to put West Ham through to the fifth round where they faced Fulham at home. In an exciting tie it was the Cottagers who went through, winning 3–2. Returning to the league, after Swansea were beaten 6–2 at home there was a good 4–1 win at neighbours Leyton Orient. Now favourites for

promotion, the Hammers stormed to victory at home to Rotherham United, winning 8–0 with Johnny Dick scoring four. Fellow promotion candidates Charlton and Liverpool both drew at Upton Park before the final day brought a trip to Middlesbrough. Dick, Keeble and Musgrove were the scorers in a 3–1 win and West Ham were Second Division champions. They had scored 101 league goals and would be returning to the First Division after an absence of 25 years.

VIC KEEBLE

Vic began his career at Colchester United, playing at centre-forward in the Southern League.

He had instant success as on his debut at Bedford he scored a hat-trick in a 5–1 win. Vic had three seasons playing in the Southern League, where he scored 55 goals in his 68 appearances. In 1950 Colchester were elected to the Football League and in March 1951 he became the first Colchester player to score a hat-trick at that level.

Newcastle United were alerted to his goalscoring abilities and in February 1952 they signed him for £15,000. His progress was limited as he spent long periods away doing his national service, but by 1955 he was at his peak as the Geordies went on to win the FA Cup when beating Manchester City 3–1. After 120 appearances for Newcastle he came back south in 1957 to join West Ham for a fee of £10,000. He set up a partnership with John Dick which yielded 40 goals as the Hammers became Second Division champions. The following season in the First Division brought a haul of 20 goals for Vic, including four goals in the 6–3 victory against Blackburn Rovers. In 1960, after 80 appearances and 49 goals, he retired due to back trouble.

Football League - Division Two Final Table 1957-58

		HOME					AWAY					
	P	W	D	L	F	A	W	D	L	F	A	Pts
West Ham United	42	12	8	1	56	25	11	3	7	45	29	57
Blackburn Rovers	42	13	7	1	50	18	9	5	7	43	39	56
Charlton Athletic	42	15	3	3	65	33	9	4	8	42	36	55
Liverpool	42	17	3	1	50	13	5	7	9	29	41	54
Fulham	42	13	5	3	53	24	7	7	7	44	35	52
Sheffield United	42	12	5	4	38	22	9	5	7	37	28	52
Middlesbrough	42	13	3	5	52	29	6	4	11	31	45	45
Ipswich Town	42	13	4	4	45	29	3	8	10	23	40	44
Huddersfield Town	42	9	8	4	28	24	5	8	8	35	42	44
Bristol Rovers	42	12	5	4	52	31	5	3	13	33	49	42
Stoke City	42	9	4	8	49	36	9	2	10	26	37	42
Leyton Orient	42	14	2	5	53	27	4	3	14	24	52	41
Grimsby Town	42	13	4	4	54	30	4	2	15	32	53	40
Barnsley	42	10	6	5	40	25	4	6	11	30	49	40
Cardiff City	42	10	5	6	44	31	4	4	13	19	46	37
Derby County	42	11	3	7	37	36	3	5	13	23	45	36
Bristol City	42	9	5	7	35	31	4	4	13	28	57	35
Rotherham United	42	8	3	10	38	44	6	2	13	27	57	33
Swansea Town	42	8	3	10	48	45	3	6	12	24	54	31
Lincoln City	42	6	6	9	33	35	5	3	13	22	47	31
Notts County	42	9	3	9	24	31	3	3	15	20	49	30
Doncaster Rovers	42	7	5	9	34	40	1	6	14	22	48	27

Season **1957-58** Football League - Division Two
Match Details

Manager **Ted Fenton**   Final League Position **1/22 Promoted as Champions to Division 1**

	Date		Competition	Venue	Opponents	Results		Attendance	Position	Scorers
1	Aug 24	Sat	Div 2	H	Lincoln City	D	2-2	18,907	12	Dare, Allison [pen]
2	Aug 26	Mon	Div 2	A	Blackburn Rovers	L	1-2	18,845	13	Dare
3	Aug 31	Sat	Div 2	A	Bristol Rovers	W	3-2	26,110	13	Dare 3
4	Sep 2	Mon	Div 2	H	Blackburn Rovers	D	1-1	24,009	9	Dare
5	Sep 7	Sat	Div 2	H	Derby County	W	2-1	18,955	10	Cantwell, Smith
6	Sep 9	Mon	Div 2	H	Sheffield United	L	0-3	21,746	13	
7	Sep 14	Sat	Div 2	A	Swansea Town	L	2-3	19,352	16	Dare, Smith
8	Sep 16	Mon	Div 2	A	Sheffield United	L	1-2	7,710	16	Dare
9	Sep 21	Sat	Div 2	H	Fulham	W	3-2	23,855	16	Dare 2, Cantwell
10	Sep 23	Mon	SFC 1**	H	Leyton Orient	W	1-0	10,000		Dick
11	Sep 28	Sat	Div 2	A	Barnsley	L	0-1	12,182	17	
12	Oct 5	Sat	Div 2	H	Leyton Orient	W	3-2	25,990	15	Lansdowne, Lewis, Smith
13	Oct 12	Sat	Div 2	A	Charlton Athletic	W	3-0	30,437	11	Dare, Musgrove, Smith
14	Oct 19	Sat	Div 2	H	Doncaster Rovers	D	1-1	20,216	12	Keeble
15	Oct 26	Sat	Div 2	A	Rotherham United	W	2-1	8,971	8	Bond [pen], Dick
16	Nov 2	Sat	Div 2	H	Huddersfield Town	W	5-2	21,525	8	Musgrove 2, Cantwell, Dick, Keeble
17	Nov 9	Sat	Div 2	A	Grimsby Town	W	2-1	12,088	8	Dick, Smith
18	Nov 16	Sat	Div 2	H	Stoke City	W	5-0	23,171	4	Keeble 3, Dare, Dick
19	Nov 23	Sat	Div 2	A	Bristol City	D	1-1	22,305	5	Dick
20	Nov 30	Sat	Div 2	H	Cardiff City	D	1-1	23,954	4	Dick
21	Dec 7	Sat	Div 2	A	Liverpool	D	1-1	34,030	5	Dick
22	Dec 14	Sat	Div 2	H	Middlesbrough	W	2-1	20,737	3	Bond [pen], Musgrove
23	Dec 21	Sat	Div 2	A	Lincoln City	W	6-1	8,384	3	Dick 2, Keeble 2, Musgrove, Newman
24	Dec 25	Wed	Div 2	H	Ipswich Town	D	1-1	25,515	3	Newman
25	Dec 26	Thu	Div 2	A	Ipswich Town	L	1-2	21,899	4	Bond
26	Dec 28	Sat	Div 2	H	Bristol Rovers	W	6-1	28,095	3	Smith 3, Keeble 2, Dick
27	Jan 4	Sat	FAC 3	H	Blackpool	W	5-1	34,000		Keeble 3, Dick 2
28	Jan 11	Sat	Div 2	A	Derby County	W	3-2	21,564	2	Bond [pen], Dick, Musgrove
29	Jan 13	Mon	SFC 2	H	Reading	D	3-3	5,000		Dick, Keeble, Smith
30	Jan 18	Sat	Div 2	H	Swansea Town	W	6-2	27,277	1	Keeble 2, Bond [pen], Cantwell, Dick, Lansdowne
31	Jan 25	Sat	FAC 4	H	Stockport County	W	3-2	36,000		Lewis 2, Keeble
32	Jan 29	Wed	SFC 2 Rep	A	Reading	L	3-5	13,000		Dick, Musgrove, Neville
33	Feb 1	Sat	Div 2	A	Fulham	D	2-2	42,195	2	Lewis, Musgrove
34	Feb 8	Sat	Div 2	H	Barnsley	D	1-1	27,182	1	Lewis [pen]
35	Feb 15	Sat	FAC 5	H	Fulham	L	2-3	37,500		Bond [pen], Grice
36	Feb 20	Thu	Div 2	A	Leyton Orient	W	4-1	25,284	1	Dare, Dick, Keeble, Smith
37	Feb 22	Sat	Div 2	H	Bristol City	W	3-2	22,795	1	Dare, Keeble, Malcolm
38	Mar 1	Sat	Div 2	A	Doncaster Rovers	W	2-1	12,411	1	Keeble, Smith
39	Mar 8	Sat	Div 2	H	Rotherham United	W	8-0	25,040	1	Dick 4, Keeble 2, Smith 2
40	Mar 10	Mon	EPC SF*	H	Southend United	W	2-1	3,000		Newman, Smillie
41	Mar 15	Sat	Div 2	A	Huddersfield Town	L	1-3	19,093	1	Grice
42	Mar 22	Sat	Div 2	H	Grimsby Town	W	2-0	25,152	1	Musgrove, Richardson (og)
43	Mar 29	Sat	Div 2	A	Stoke City	W	4-1	14,517	1	Keeble 2, Dick, Grice
44	Apr 4	Fri	Div 2	H	Notts County	W	3-1	29,866	1	Bond 2 [2 pens], Cruickshank (og)
45	Apr 5	Sat	Div 2	H	Charlton Athletic	D	0-0	30,208	1	
46	Apr 8	Tue	Div 2	A	Notts County	L	0-1	18,317	1	
47	Apr 12	Sat	Div 2	A	Cardiff City	W	3-0	17,596	1	Dick 2, Malcolm
48	Apr 19	Sat	Div 2	H	Liverpool	D	1-1	37,734	1	Bond
49	Apr 26	Sat	Div 2	A	Middlesbrough	W	3-1	30,526	1	Dick, Keeble, Musgrove
50	May 2	Fri	EPC F	A	Chelmsford City	L	1-5	4,235		Lewis

* Essex Professional Cup ** Southern Floodlight Cup

Team Line-Ups

ALLISON Malcolm	BLACKBURN Alan	BOND John	BROWN Ken	CANTWELL Noel	COOPER Fred	DARE Billy	DICK John	FENN George	GREGORY Ernie	GRICE Mike	HAYWARD Terry	KEEBLE Vic	KIRKUP Joe	LANSDOWNE Bill	LEWIS Eddie	MALCOLM Andy	MORLEY John	MUSGROVE Malcolm	NELSON Andy	NEVILLE Billy	NEWMAN Mick	PYKE Malcolm	RHODES Brian	SMILLIE Andy	SMITH John	WRAGG Doug	WRIGHT George	WYLLIE Robinson	No.
6		2	5	3		9	10		1	7						4		11							8				1
6		2	5	3		9	10		1	7						4		11							8				2
6		2	5	3		9	10		1	7						4		11							8				3
		2	5	3		9	10			7						4		11				6	1		8				4
		2	5	3		9	10			7						4		11				6	1		8				5
	10	2	5	3		9				7					8	4		11				6	1						6
6		2	5	3		9	10			7						4		11					1		8				7
6		2	5	3		8	10			7						4		11	9				1						8
		2	5	3		8	10		1							4		11	9			6				7			9
		2	5	3		8	10		1							4		11	9			6				7			10
		2	5	3		8	10		1					6		4		11	9							7			11
		2	5		3	7	10		1					6	9	4		11							8				12
		2	5	3		9	10		1	7				6		4		11							8				13
		2	5	3		8	10		1	7		9		6		4		11											14
		2	5	3		7	10		1			9		6		4		11							8				15
		2	5	3		7	10		1			9		6		4		11							8				16
		2	5	3		7	10		1			9		6		4		11							8				17
		2	5	3		7	10		1			9		6		4		11							8				18
		2	5	3		7	10		1			9		6		4		11							8				19
		2	5	3		7	10		1			9		6		4		11							8				20
		2	5	3		7	10		1			9		6		4		11							8				21
		2	5	3		7	10		1			9		6		4		11	8										22
		2	5	3		7	10		1			9				4		11	8						6				23
		2	5		3	7	10		1			9				4		11	8						6				24
		2	5				10		1	7		9			8	4		11							6		3		25
		2	5				10		1	7		9				4		11				6			8		3		26
		2	5				10		1	7		9			8	4		11				6					3		27
		2	5				10		1	7		9				4		11				6			8		3		28
			5	3			10		1	7		9				4		11				6			8		2		29
		2	5	3			10		1	7		9		6		4		11							8				30
		2	5	3			10		1	7		9		6	8	4		11											31
		2	5	3			10	9	1	7				6				11	8			4							32
		2	5	3			10		1	7		9			8	4		11				6							33
			5	3		9	10		1	7					8	4		11				6					2		34
		2	5	3			10		1	7		9			8	4		11				6							35
		2	5	3		7	10		1	11		9				4						6			8				36
		2	5	3		7	10		1	11		9				4						6			8				37
		2					10		1	7		9		6		4		11		5					8		3		38
		2	5				10		1	7		9		6		4		11							8		3		39
			5	3				7					2		9		6		10	4	1	8				11			40
		2	5				10		1	11		9		6		4									8	7	3		41
		2	5				10		1	7		9		6		4		11							8		3		42
		2	5	3			10		1	7		9				4		11				6			8				43
		2	5	3			10		1	7		9				4		11				6			8				44
		2	5	3			10		1	7		9				4		11				6			8				45
		2	5	3			10		1	7		9				4		11				6			8				46
		2	5	3			10		1	7		9			8	4		11	6										47
		2	5	3			10		1	7		9			8	4		11				6							48
		2	5	3			10		1	7		9				4		11	6						8				49
				3			10						2	6	9	4		11		5	8						7	1	50

1958-59
Story of the season

There were **40,740 inside Fratton Park** as the Hammers **kicked off the new season** against Portsmouth.

Roared on by 7,000 fans, goals from Dick and Keeble gave West Ham a 2–1 win. Two days later the gates were closed at Upton Park as the Hammers welcomed league champions Wolverhampton Wanderers. It was an exciting tussle, with the Hammers winning 2–0. Now enjoying life back in the First Division, Aston Villa were crushed 7–2 in the next home game. The euphoria was then forgotten with three away games ending in defeats at Luton, Nottingham Forest and Manchester United, the team conceding four goals in each match. The home game with Manchester United attracted great excitement as the Hammers raced into a three-goal lead before two goals from United made the contest more even. The 3–2 victory saw the debut of

Appearances & Goals 1958-59

	League		FA Cup		Other*		Total	
	Starts	Goals	Starts	Goals	Starts	Goals	Starts	Goals
BOND John	42	7	1	0	4	2	47	9
BROWN Ken	42	0	1	0	4	0	47	0
CANTWELL Noel	42	3	1	0	1	0	44	3
CARTWRIGHT Johnny	0	0	0	0	1	0	1	0
DARE Billy	2	1	0	0	1	0	3	1
DICK John	41	27	1	0	2	2	44	29
DWYER Noel	10	0	0	0	1	0	11	0
GREGORY Ernie	32	0	1	0	1	0	34	0
GRICE Mike	42	6	1	0	4	1	47	7
HILLS David	0	0	0	0	1	1	1	1
HURST Geoff	0	0	0	0	1	0	1	0
KEEBLE Vic	32	20	1	0	2	1	35	21
KIRKUP Joe	11	0	0	0	2	0	13	0
LANSDOWNE Bill	6	1	0	0	1	0	7	1
LYALL John	0	0	0	0	1	0	1	0
MALCOLM Andy	42	0	1	0	2	0	45	0
MOORE Bobby	5	0	0	0	1	0	6	0
MUSGROVE Malcolm	40	7	1	0	3	3	44	10
NELSON Andy	12	1	0	0	2	0	14	1
OBENEY Harry	6	3	0	0	2	0	8	3
PYKE Malcolm	0	0	0	0	1	0	1	0
RHODES Brian	0	0	0	0	2	0	2	0
SMILLIE Andy	4	0	1	0	0	0	5	0
SMITH John	36	4	1	0	2	0	39	4
WOOSNAM Phil	13	2	0	0	1	1	14	3
WRAGG Doug	2	0	0	0	1	0	3	0
own goal		3				1		4
TOTALS	**462**	**85**	**11**	**0**	**44**	**12**	**517**	**97**

* Other = Essex Professional Cup and Southern Floodlight Cup

17-year-old Bobby Moore, who was destined for greater achievements.

After Blackburn Rovers were beaten 6–3 at home there followed a period of six games without a win. This all changed during the Christmas period as Portsmouth were thrashed 6–0 at home and on Christmas Day rivals Tottenham were beaten 2–1. In the return with Tottenham on Boxing Day the Hammers triumphed again, winning 4–1.

West Ham were back at White Hart Lane to face Tottenham in the FA Cup, but on this occasion they lost 2–0. There were further away defeats but at home the goals were flowing, Johnny Dick scoring twice against Nottingham Forest in a 5–3 thriller and going one better to score a hat-trick in the 3–1 victory against West Bromwich Albion. As

an experiment, full-back John Bond was moved to centre-forward and this brought success as he scored twice against Bolton Wanderers in the 4–3 home win. The final home game against Manchester City saw Dick and Grice score two apiece in a 5–1 win. It had been an excellent campaign and it was a fine achievement to finish in sixth place.

PHIL WOOSNAM

As an amateur the Welsh inside-forward played one game for Manchester City back in 1953.

His career took off at Leyton Orient, who he joined in 1954. He was at the Orient for five seasons, playing in 112 games and scoring 19 goals. While there he gained his first Welsh cap, playing against England in October 1958. A fee of £30,000 took him to West Ham in November 1958, where he made his debut against Arsenal. With the Hammers he flourished, setting up many goals for Dick and Keeble. During his time at Upton Park he was selected for Wales on 15 occasions. Phil made 147 appearances for West Ham over five seasons and his move to Aston Villa in November 1962 seemed premature.

He became a favourite with the Villa fans, playing in 125 matches over four seasons. He retired as a player in 1966 and went to America as coach to the Atlanta Chiefs; later he was appointed head coach to the US national team. In 1969 he became commissioner of the NASL and president of the US Soccer Federation. He set about raising the profile of the game and did more to establish soccer in the US than any other person. He was living in Georgia when he died in July 2013 aged 80.

Football League - Division One Final Table 1958-59

	P	W	D	L	F	A	W	D	L	F	A	Pts
Wolverhampton Wanderers	42	15	3	3	68	19	13	2	6	42	30	61
Manchester United	42	14	4	3	58	27	10	3	8	45	39	55
Arsenal	42	14	3	4	53	29	7	5	9	35	39	50
Bolton Wanderers	42	14	3	4	56	30	6	7	8	23	36	50
West Bromwich Albion	42	8	7	6	41	33	10	6	5	47	35	49
West Ham United	42	15	3	3	59	29	6	3	12	26	41	48
Burnley	42	11	4	6	41	29	8	6	7	40	41	48
Blackpool	42	12	7	2	39	13	6	4	11	27	36	47
Birmingham City	42	14	1	6	54	35	6	5	10	30	33	46
Blackburn Rovers	42	12	3	6	48	28	5	7	9	28	42	44
Newcastle United	42	11	3	7	40	29	6	4	11	40	51	41
Preston North End	42	9	3	9	40	39	8	4	9	30	38	41
Nottingham Forest	42	9	4	8	37	32	8	2	11	34	42	40
Chelsea	42	13	2	6	52	37	5	2	14	25	61	40
Leeds United	42	8	7	6	28	27	7	2	12	29	47	39
Everton	42	11	3	7	39	38	6	1	14	32	49	38
Luton Town	42	11	6	4	50	26	1	7	13	18	45	37
Tottenham Hotspur	42	10	3	8	56	42	3	7	11	29	53	36
Leicester City	42	7	6	8	34	36	4	4	13	33	62	32
Manchester City	42	8	7	6	40	32	3	2	16	24	63	31
Aston Villa	42	8	5	8	31	33	3	3	15	27	54	30
Portsmouth	42	5	4	12	38	47	1	5	15	26	65	21

Season **1958-59** Football League - Division One
Match Details

Manager **Ted Fenton**   Final League Position **6/22**

	Date		Competition	Venue	Opponents	Results		Attendance	Position	Scorers
1	Aug 23	Sat	Div 1	A	Portsmouth	W	2-1	40,470	5	Dick, Keeble
2	Aug 25	Mon	Div 1	H	Wolverhampton Wanderers	W	2-0	37,487	2	Dick, Smith
3	Aug 30	Sat	Div 1	H	Aston Villa	W	7-2	30,263	2	Dick 2, Keeble 2, Musgrove 2, Lansdowne
4	Sep 3	Wed	Div 1	A	Wolverhampton Wanderers	D	1-1	53,317	2	Grice
5	Sep 6	Sat	Div 1	A	Luton Town	L	1-4	25,715	7	Keeble
6	Sep 8	Mon	Div 1	H	Manchester United	W	3-2	35,672	1	Dick, Musgrove, Smith
7	Sep 13	Sat	Div 1	A	Nottingham Forest	L	0-4	30,307	5	
8	Sep 17	Wed	Div 1	A	Manchester United	L	1-4	53,276	11	Bond
9	Sep 20	Sat	Div 1	H	Chelsea	W	4-2	31,127	8	Dick, Grice, Keeble, Smith
10	Sep 27	Sat	Div 1	A	Blackpool	L	0-2	32,662	11	
11	Oct 4	Sat	Div 1	H	Blackburn Rovers	W	6-3	25,280	6	Keeble 4, Cantwell, Woods (og)
12	Oct 11	Sat	Div 1	H	Birmingham City	L	1-2	29,139	11	Musgrove
13	Oct 18	Sat	Div 1	A	West Bromwich Albion	L	1-2	36,878	12	Keeble
14	Oct 25	Sat	Div 1	H	Burnley	W	1-0	29,387	8	Nelson
15	Oct 27	Mon	SFC 1**	H	Charlton Athletic	W	5-1	8,500		Musgrove 3, Dick 2
16	Nov 1	Sat	Div 1	A	Bolton Wanderers	W	2-0	31,067	8	Dick, Grice
17	Nov 8	Sat	Div 1	H	Arsenal	D	0-0	37,871	9	
18	Nov 15	Sat	Div 1	A	Everton	D	2-2	40,819	9	Bond [pen], Dick
19	Nov 22	Sat	Div 1	H	Leicester City	L	0-3	23,244	11	
20	Nov 29	Sat	Div 1	A	Preston North End	L	1-2	19,438	12	Dick
21	Dec 6	Sat	Div 1	H	Leeds United	L	2-3	22,022	12	Dick, Keeble
22	Dec 13	Sat	Div 1	A	Manchester City	L	1-3	22,250	14	Dick
23	Dec 15	Mon	SFC 2**	H	Fulham	W	3-1	4,500		Bond [pen], Keeble, Woosnam
24	Dec 20	Sat	Div 1	H	Portsmouth	W	6-0	21,316	12	Keeble 2, Dick, Musgrove, Smith Woosnam
25	Dec 25	Thu	Div 1	H	Tottenham Hotspur	W	2-1	26,178	10	Dick, Keeble
26	Dec 26	Fri	Div 1	A	Tottenham Hotspur	W	4-1	43,817	10	Bond, Dick, Keeble, Henry (og)
27	Jan 3	Sat	Div 1	A	Aston Villa	W	2-1	29,334	10	Cantwell, Dugdale (og)
28	Jan 10	Sat	FAC 3	A	Tottenham Hotspur	L	0-2	56,252		
29	Jan 31	Sat	Div 1	H	Nottingham Forest	W	5-3	26,769	9	Dick 2, Keeble 2, Woosnam
30	Feb 7	Sat	Div 1	A	Chelsea	L	2-3	52,698	9	Keeble 2
31	Feb 16	Mon	Div 1	H	Blackpool	W	1-0	28,417	9	Dick
32	Feb 21	Sat	Div 1	A	Blackburn Rovers	W	2-1	17,613	7	Keeble, Musgrove
33	Feb 28	Sat	Div 1	A	Birmingham City	L	0-3	19,910	7	
34	Mar 7	Sat	Div 1	H	West Bromwich Albion	W	3-1	29,510	6	Dick 3
35	Mar 14	Sat	Div 1	A	Burnley	L	0-1	17,311	6	
36	Mar 21	Sat	Div 1	H	Bolton Wanderers	W	4-3	27,722	7	Bond 2, Dick, Obeney
37	Mar 27	Fri	Div 1	H	Newcastle United	W	3-0	34,619	5	Dick, Musgrove, Obeney
38	Mar 28	Sat	Div 1	A	Arsenal	W	2-1	52,291	4	Dick 2
39	Mar 30	Mon	Div 1	A	Newcastle United	L	1-3	20,911	6	Obeney
40	Apr 4	Sat	Div 1	H	Everton	W	3-2	28,266	4	Bond, Dick, Grice
41	Apr 6	Mon	SFC 3**	H	Arsenal	L	0-2	15,681		
42	Apr 8	Wed	EPC SF*	H	Colchester United	W	4-3	2,200		Bond, Grice, Hills, (og)
43	Apr 11	Sat	Div 1	A	Leicester City	D	1-1	23,725	6	Bond
44	Apr 13	Mon	Div 1	H	Luton Town	D	0-0	26,784	4	
45	Apr 18	Sat	Div 1	H	Preston North End	D	1-1	21,129	6	Dare
46	Apr 20	Mon	Div 1	H	Manchester City	W	5-1	23,516	3	Dick 2, Grice 2, Cantwell
47	Apr 25	Sat	Div 1	A	Leeds United	L	0-1	11,257	6	

* Essex Pro Cup Final deferred to 1959-60 season ** Southern Floodlight Cup

Team Line-Ups

BOND John	BROWN Ken	CANTWELL Noel	CARTWRIGHT Johnny	DARE Billy	DICK John	DWYER Noel	GREGORY Ernie	GRICE Mike	HILLS David	HURST Geoff	KEEBLE Vic	KIRKUP Joe	LANSDOWNE Bill	LYALL John	MALCOLM Andy	MOORE Bobby	MUSGROVE Malcolm	NELSON Andy	OBENEY Harry	PYKE Malcolm	RHODES Brian	SMILLIE Andy	SMITH John	WOOSNAM Phil	WRAGG Doug	WRAGG Doug	
2	5	3			10		1	7			9		6		4		11						8				1
2	5	3			10		1	7			9		6		4		11						8				2
2	5	3			10		1	7			9		6		4		11						8				3
2	5	3			10		1	7			9		6		4		11						8				4
2	5	3			10		1	7			9		6		4		11						8				5
2	5	3			10		1	7			9				4	6	11						8				6
2	5	3			10		1	7			9				4	6	11						8				7
2	5	3			10		1	11			9		6		4		11						8		7		8
2	5	3			10		1	11			9				4					6			8		7	7	9
2	5	3			10		1	7			9				4		11	6					8			7	10
2	5	3			10		1	7			9				4		11	6					8			7	11
2	5	3			10		1	7			9				4		11	6					8				12
2	5	3			10		1	7			9				4		11	6					8				13
2	5	3			10		1	7			9				4		11	6					8				14
2	5	3	8		10		1	7			9				4		11	6									15
2	5	3			10		1	7			9				4		11	6					8				16
2	5	3			10		1	7			9				4		11	6						8			17
2	5	3			10		1	7			9				4		11	6						8			18
2	5	3			10		1	7			9				4		11	6						8			19
2	5	3			10		1	7			9				4		11	6						8			20
2	5	3			10		1	7			9				4		11	6						8			21
2	5	6			10		1	7			9	2			4		11							8			22
3	5				10			7		6	9	2					11				1	4		8			23
2	5	3			10		1	7			9				4		11						6	8			24
2	5	3			10		1	7			9				4		11						6	8			25
2	5	3			10		1	7			9				4		11					8	6				26
2	5	3			10		1	7			9				4		11					8	6				27
2	5	3			10		1	7			9				4		11					8	6				28
2	5	3			10		1	7			9				4		11						6	8			29
2	5	3			10		1	7			9				4		11						6	8			30
2	5	3			10		1	7			9				4		11						6	8			31
2	5	3			10		1	7			9				4		11						6	8			32
2	5	3			10		1	7			9				4		11					8	6				33
2	5	3			10		1	7			9				4		11						6	8			34
2	5	3	9		10		1	7							4	6	11							8			35
9	5	3			10	1		7				2			4		11	8					6				36
9	5	3			10	1		7				2			4		11	8					6				37
9	5	3			10	1		7				2			4		11	8					6				38
9	5	3			10	1		7				2			4		11	8					6				39
9	5	3			10	1		7				2			4		11	8					6			11	40
9	5					1		7				2		10	4	6	11	3	8						7		41
2	5			9				11	10				6						8	4	1		3	7			42
8	5	3				1		7			9	2			4		11					10	6				43
9	5	3			10	1		7				2			4		11	8					6				44
8	5	3	9		10	1		7				2			4		11						6				45
3	5	9			10	1		7				2			4	6	11						8				46
3	5	9			10	1		7				2			4	6	11						8			7	47

1959-60
Story of the season

Another season started well, with a **3-0 home win** over Leicester City followed by a draw at Preston and a **fine 3–1 victory** at Burnley.

Then after an exciting 2–2 draw at Tottenham the Hammers slumped to a 5–1 defeat at Bolton Wanderers. There were 54,349 inside Stamford Bridge to see the Hammers bounce back with a 4–2 victory over Chelsea. A week later Phil Woosnam, in sparkling form, inspired the team to a 4–1 home win against West Bromwich Albion. After Manchester City were beaten 4–1 at the Boleyn, a trip to Arsenal brought a 3–1 victory and put the Hammers top of the table. The following home game brought a visit from

Appearances & Goals 1959-60

	League		FA Cup		Other*		Total	
	Starts	Goals	Starts	Goals	Starts	Goals	Starts	Goals
BOND John	35	7	2	0	4	1	41	8
BOVINGTON Eddie	1	0	0	0	0	0	1	0
BOYCE Ron	0	0	0	0	1	0	1	0
BRETT Ron	7	2	0	0	1	1	8	3
BROWN Ken	40	0	2	0	6	0	48	0
CANTWELL Noel	40	3	2	0	5	1	47	4
CARTWRIGHT Johnny	3	0	0	0	2	3	5	3
CRIPPS Harry	0	0	0	0	1	0	1	0
DICK John	24	11	1	1	3	1	28	13
DUNMORE Dave	9	2	0	0	2	0	11	2
DWYER Noel	26	0	2	0	4	0	32	0
GREGORY Ernie	1	0	0	0	0	0	1	0
GRICE Mike	34	5	2	0	4	1	40	6
HURST Geoff	3	0	0	0	2	0	5	0
KEEBLE Vic	15	6	0	0	1	0	16	6
KIRKUP Joe	16	0	0	0	2	0	18	0
LANSDOWNE Bill	1	0	0	0	0	0	1	0
LYALL John	2	0	0	0	0	0	2	0
MALCOLM Andy	40	0	2	0	6	0	48	0
MOORE Bobby	13	0	0	0	2	0	15	0
MUSGROVE Malcolm	41	15	2	1	6	4	49	20
OBENEY Harry	9	5	2	0	2	4	13	9
RHODES Brian	15	0	0	0	2	0	17	0
SCOTT Tony	4	1	0	0	0	0	4	1
SMILLIE Andy	13	3	1	0	2	1	16	4
SMITH John	28	1	2	0	2	0	32	1
WOODLEY Derek	3	2	0	0	2	0	5	2
WOOSNAM Phil	38	11	2	0	3	1	43	12
WRAGG Doug	1	0	0	0	1	2	2	2
own goal		1				1		2
TOTALS	**462**	**75**	**22**	**2**	**66**	**21**	**550**	**98**

* Other = Essex Professional Cup and Southern Floodlight Cup

league champions Wolverhampton Wanderers. A sell-out crowd roared as Johnny Dick gave the Hammers a 3–0 lead with a stunning hat-trick. Wolves fought back with two goals but the Hammers held on to win 3–2.

League leaders West Ham were then totally shocked away to Sheffield Wednesday as the Yorkshire team won 7–0. The Hammers never recovered from this setback and a fortnight later lost 6–2 at Blackburn Rovers. The New Year brought further misery as Burnley won 5–2 at the Boleyn followed by Second Division Huddersfield Town winning 5–1 in the FA Cup.

In February there was some cheer as John Bond scored a hat-trick in the 4–2 home win against Chelsea, but the next home game brought a 5–3 defeat to Newcastle. By April the team were falling fast in the table and suffered a 5–0 defeat at Wolves and a 5–3 beating at Manchester United. The season ended with a placing of fourteenth, a huge disappointment after topping the table in November.

JOE KIRKUP

A signing-on fee of £10 brought right-back Kirkup to West Ham in 1957.

In that first season he won an England youth cap playing against Ireland and was in the Hammers youth team that reached the final of the FA Youth Cup, losing to Manchester United. Joe progressed through the reserve team and finally made his debut in December 1958 against Manchester City at Maine Road. He became a regular in the side until October 1963 when he lost his place to John Bond.

The following season he was brought back into the side and gained European honours when West Ham won the European Cup Winners' Cup in May 1965. He was transferred to Chelsea in 1966, where he spent two seasons with the Blues and won a FA Cup runners-up medal as an unused substitute against Tottenham in 1967. In February 1968 Joe moved on to Southampton, playing in 169 matches over six seasons. After retiring as a player he worked at a machine company, ran a pub in Hampshire and a sports shop in Surrey, and took over a newsagents in Ewell. In 2002 he moved to France but has since returned to England to enjoy retirement.

Football League - Division One Final Table 1959-60

	P	HOME					AWAY					Pts
		W	D	L	F	A	W	D	L	F	A	
Burnley	42	15	2	4	52	28	9	5	7	33	33	55
Wolverhampton Wanderers	42	15	3	3	63	28	9	3	9	43	39	54
Tottenham Hotspur	42	10	6	5	43	24	11	5	5	43	26	53
West Bromwich Albion	42	12	4	5	48	25	7	7	7	35	32	49
Sheffield Wednesday	42	12	7	2	48	20	7	4	10	32	39	49
Bolton Wanderers	42	12	5	4	37	27	8	3	10	22	24	48
Manchester United	42	13	3	5	53	30	6	4	11	49	50	45
Newcastle United	42	10	5	6	42	32	8	3	10	40	46	44
Preston North End	42	10	6	5	43	34	6	6	9	36	42	44
Fulham	42	12	4	5	42	28	5	6	10	31	52	44
Blackpool	42	9	6	6	32	32	6	4	11	27	39	40
Leicester City	42	8	6	7	38	32	5	7	9	28	43	39
Arsenal	42	9	5	7	39	38	6	4	11	29	42	39
West Ham United	42	12	3	6	47	33	4	3	14	28	58	38
Everton	42	13	3	5	50	20	0	8	13	23	58	37
Manchester City	42	11	2	8	47	34	6	1	14	31	50	37
Blackburn Rovers	42	12	3	6	38	29	4	2	15	22	41	37
Chelsea	42	7	5	9	44	50	7	4	10	32	41	37
Birmingham City	42	9	5	7	37	36	4	5	12	26	44	36
Nottingham Forest	42	8	6	7	30	28	5	3	13	20	46	35
Leeds United	42	7	5	9	37	46	5	5	11	28	46	34
Luton Town	42	6	5	10	25	29	3	7	11	25	44	30

Season 1959-60 Football League - Division One
Match Details

Manager **Ted Fenton**   Final League Position **14/22**

	Date		Competition	Venue	Opponents	Results		Attendance	Position	Scorers
1	Aug 22	Sat	Div 1	H	Leicester City	W	3-0	27,996	8	Grice, Keeble, Smith
2	Aug 25	Tue	Div 1	A	Preston North End	D	1-1	29,489	2	Musgrove
3	Aug 29	Sat	Div 1	A	Burnley	W	3-1	26,756	2	Grice, Smillie, Woosnam
4	Aug 31	Mon	Div 1	H	Preston North End	W	2-1	31,916	2	Keeble, Smillie
5	Sep 5	Sat	Div 1	H	Leeds United	L	1-2	27,777	4	Keeble
6	Sep 9	Wed	Div 1	A	Tottenham Hotspur	D	2-2	58,909	3	Keeble, Musgrove
7	Sep 12	Sat	Div 1	A	Bolton Wanderers	L	1-5	24,240	7	Keeble
8	Sep 14	Mon	Div 1	H	Tottenham Hotspur	L	1-2	36,831	7	Bond [pen]
9	Sep 19	Sat	Div 1	A	Chelsea	W	4-2	54,349	7	Dick 2, Musgrove, Woosnam
10	Sep 21	Mon	EPC F*	H	Leyton Orient	W	4-1			Brett, Cantwell, Dick, Lea (og)
11	Sep 26	Sat	Div 1	H	West Bromwich Albion	W	4-1	29,957	6	Musgrove 2, Grice, Woosnam
12	Oct 3	Sat	Div 1	A	Newcastle United	D	0-0	41,924	5	
13	Oct 10	Sat	Div 1	H	Luton Town	W	3-1	23,266	3	Woodley 2, Keeble
14	Oct 13	Tue	SFC 1**	H	Millwall	W	3-1	8,250		Wragg 2, Musgrove
15	Oct 17	Sat	Div 1	A	Everton	W	1-0	30,563	3	Musgrove
16	Oct 24	Sat	Div 1	H	Blackpool	W	1-0	32,374	2	Musgrove
17	Oct 26	Mon	SFC 2	H	Reading	W	6-1	5,400		Obeney 4, Grice, Smillie
18	Oct 31	Sat	Div 1	A	Fulham	L	0-1	44,858	3	
19	Nov 7	Sat	Div 1	H	Manchester City	W	4-1	25,243	2	Cantwell [pen], Musgrove, Obeney, McTavish (og)
20	Nov 14	Sat	Div 1	A	Arsenal	W	3-1	49,583	1	Dick, Musgrove, Obeney
21	Nov 21	Sat	Div 1	H	Wolverhampton Wanderers	W	3-2	37,941	1	Dick 3
22	Nov 28	Sat	Div 1	A	Sheffield Wednesday	L	0-7	36,899	3	
23	Dec 5	Sat	Div 1	H	Nottingham Forest	W	4-1	25,765	3	Obeney 2, Woosnam 2
24	Dec 7	Mon	SFC 3	H	Leyton Orient	W	4-3	8,606		Musgrove 2, Bond, Woosnam
25	Dec 12	Sat	Div 1	A	Blackburn Rovers	L	2-6	22,261	4	Dick, Woosnam
26	Dec 19	Sat	Div 1	A	Leicester City	L	1-2	17,316	6	Obeney
27	Dec 26	Sat	Div 1	A	Birmingham City	L	0-2	29,745	7	
28	Dec 28	Mon	Div 1	H	Birmingham City	W	3-1	26,154	5	Musgrove 2, Brett
29	Jan 2	Sat	Div 1	H	Burnley	L	2-5	25,752	6	Cantwell [pen], Woosnam
30	Jan 9	Sat	FAC 3	A	Huddersfield Town	D	1-1	40,526		Dick
31	Jan 13	Wed	FAC 3 Rep	H	Huddersfield Town	L	1-5	22,605		Musgrove
32	Jan 16	Sat	Div 1	A	Leeds United	L	0-3	15,284	8	
33	Jan 23	Sat	Div 1	H	Bolton Wanderers	L	1-2	21,155	10	Dick
34	Feb 6	Sat	Div 1	H	Chelsea	W	4-2	29,655	8	Bond 3 [1 pen], Dick
35	Feb 20	Sat	Div 1	H	Newcastle United	L	3-5	27,073	11	Woosnam 2, Dick
36	Feb 27	Sat	Div 1	A	Nottingham Forest	L	1-3	26,465	12	Musgrove
37	Mar 5	Sat	Div 1	H	Everton	D	2-2	25,029	10	Bond, Dick
38	Mar 9	Wed	Div 1	A	West Bromwich Albion	L	2-3	12,113	10	Bond [pen], Grice
39	Mar 12	Sat	Div 1	A	Blackpool	L	2-3	14,515	11	Bond, Brett
40	Mar 19	Sat	Div 1	H	Blackburn Rovers	W	2-1	25,921	11	Musgrove, Woosnam
41	Mar 30	Wed	Div 1	A	Manchester City	L	1-3	29,572	12	Musgrove
42	Apr 2	Sat	Div 1	H	Arsenal	D	0-0	28,818	12	
43	Apr 5	Tue	SFC SF	A	Arsenal	W	3-1	8,000		Cartwright 2, Musgrove
44	Apr 11	Mon	Div 1	A	Wolverhampton Wanderers	L	0-5	48,086	13	
45	Apr 15	Fri	Div 1	H	Manchester United	W	2-1	34,969	12	Grice, Musgrove
46	Apr 16	Sat	Div 1	H	Fulham	L	1-2	34,085	13	Smillie
47	Apr 18	Mon	Div 1	A	Manchester United	L	3-5	34,505	14	Cantwell [pen], Dunmore, Scott
48	Apr 23	Sat	Div 1	A	Luton Town	L	1-3	11,404	16	Dunmore
49	Apr 27	Wed	SFC F	A	Coventry City	L	1-2	16,921		Cartwright
50	Apr 30	Sat	Div 1	H	Sheffield Wednesday	D	1-1	21,964	14	Woosnam

* Essex Pro Cup Final 1958-59 deferred from last season ** Southern Floodlight Cup

eam Line-Ups

BOND John	BOVINGTON Eddie	BOYCE Ron	BRETT Ron	BROWN Ken	CANTWELL Noel	CARTWRIGHT Johnny	CRIPPS Harry	DICK John	DUNMORE Dave	DWYER Noel	GREGORY Ernie	GRICE Mike	HURST Geoff	KEEBLE Vic	KIRKUP Joe	LANSDOWNE Bill	LYALL John	MALCOLM Andy	MOORE Bobby	MUSGROVE Malcolm	OBENEY Harry	RHODES Brian	SCOTT Tony	SMILLIE Andy	SMITH John	WOODLEY Derek	WOOSNAM Phil	WRAGG Doug	
2				5	3			10		1		7		9				4		11					6		8		1
2				5	3			10		1		7		9				4		11					6		8		2
2				5	3					1		7		9				4		11				10	6		8		3
2				5	3					1		7		9				4		11				10	6		8		4
2				5	3						1	7		9				4		11				10	6		8		5
2				5	3					1		7		9				4		11				10	6		8		6
2				5	3					1		7		9				4		11				10	6		8		7
2			10	5	3					1		11		9				4							6		8	7	8
2				5	3			10		1		7		9				4		11					6		8		9
2			9	5	3			10		1			6			2		4		11						7	8		10
2				5	3			10		1		7		9				4		11					6		8		11
2				5	3			10		1		7		9				4		11					6		8		12
2				5	3			10		1				9				4		11					6	7	8		13
2	6			5			3	10		1				9				4		11							8	7	14
2				5	3	8				1		7		9				4	6	11				10					15
2				5	9			10		1		7				3		4		11					6		8		16
				5	3					1		7				2		4		11	9			10	6		8		17
				5	3			10		1		7		9		2		4		11					6		8		18
				5	3			10		1		7				2		4		11	9				6		8		19
				5	3			10		1		7				2		4		11	9				6		8		20
2				5	3			10				7						4		11	9	1			6		8		21
2				5	3			10		1		7						4		11	9				6		8		22
2				5	3			10		1		7						4		11	9				6		8		23
2				5	3			10		1		7						4		11	9				6		8		24
2				5	3			10		1		7						4		11	9				6		8		25
2				5	3			10		1		7						4		11	9				6		8		26
			9	5	3			10		1						2		4		11					6	7	8		27
			9	5	3			10		1						2		4		11			8		6	7			28
				5	3			10		1		7				2		4		11	9				6		8		29
2				5	3			10		1		7						4		11	9				6		8		30
2				5	3					1		7						4		11	9			10	6		8		31
2				5	3									9				4	6	7	10	1			8		11		32
3				5	9			10		1		7				2		4		11					6		8		33
		9		5				10		1						2	3	4	6	11			7				8		34
		9		5	3			10		1						2		4		11			7		6		8		35
		9		5	10								6			2	3	4		11		1	7				8		36
		9		5	3			10				7				2		4	6	11		1					8		37
		9		5	3			10				7				2		4	6	11		1					8		38
		9	10	5	3							7				2		4		11		1			6		8		39
2			10	5	3				9			7	6					4		11							8		40
3			10	5					9			7	6			2		4		11							8		41
2				5	3			10	9			7						4	6	11		1					8		42
2				5	3	8			9			7	10					4	6	11		1							43
2				5	3				9			7						4	6	11		1		10			8		44
2				5	3				9			7						4	6	11		1		10			8		45
2				5	3				9			7						4	6	11		1		10			8		46
	4	10			3	8			9							2		5		11		1	7	6					47
2					3	8			9			7				5		4	6	11		1		10					48
2				5	3	8			9			7						4	6	11		1		10					49
2				5	3				9			7						4	6	11		1		10			8		50

1960-61
Story of the season

The first few weeks of the season fell into a **familiar pattern** of **winning at home** but **losing away.**

A 4–2 defeat at Wolverhampton was followed by a goo 5–2 home win against Aston Villa. The trend continue with a 2–1 win over Manchester United at Upton Park b a 6–1 defeat in the return a fortnight later. A ne competition, the Football League Cup, was born and t Hammers beat Charlton 3–1 at home in the inaugu match. The next round brought a trip to Fourth Divisi Darlington and again a poor display in away games saw t Hammers beaten 3–2.

At home the goals were flowing as winger Mike Gri scored twice against Blackburn Rovers in a 4–3 win and hat-trick from Malcolm Musgrove came in a 5–2 victo

Appearances & Goals 1960-61

	League		FA Cup		League Cup		Total	
	Starts	Goals	Starts	Goals	Starts	Goals	Starts	Goa
BEESLEY Mick	2	1	0	0	0	0	2	1
BOND John	34	4	1	0	2	0	37	4
BOYCE Ron	3	0	0	0	0	0	3	0
BRETT Ron	5	2	1	0	0	0	6	2
BROWN Ken	42	0	2	0	2	0	46	0
CANTWELL Noel	10	0	0	0	0	0	10	0
CARTWRIGHT Johnny	1	0	0	0	1	0	2	0
DICK John	34	16	2	1	2	2	38	19
DUNMORE Dave	27	14	1	1	2	1	30	16
GRICE Mike	24	4	1	0	1	0	26	4
HURST Geoff	6	0	0	0	0	0	6	0
KIRKUP Joe	20	1	1	0	0	0	21	1
LYALL John	21	0	2	0	2	0	25	0
MALCOLM Andy	40	1	2	0	2	0	44	1
MOORE Bobby	38	1	2	0	2	1	42	2
MUSGROVE Malcolm	40	17	2	0	2	1	44	18
OBENEY Harry	9	4	0	0	0	0	9	4
RHODES Brian	36	0	2	0	2	0	40	0
SCOTT Tony	12	1	0	0	0	0	12	1
SEALEY Alan	6	1	0	0	0	0	6	1
SHEARING Peter	6	0	0	0	0	0	6	0
SMILLIE Andy	3	0	1	0	0	0	4	0
WOODLEY Derek	5	1	0	0	1	0	6	1
WOOSNAM Phil	38	6	2	0	1	0	41	6
own goal		3						3
TOTALS	**462**	**77**	**22**	**2**	**22**	**5**	**506**	**8**

ainst Preston North End. London rivals Arsenal were
ext to face the home onslaught and Dave Dunmore scored
hat-trick in a 6–0 win. Now in fine form, the Hammers
on their first away game when beating Manchester City
-1 at Maine Road. In an amazing game at Newcastle, West
am were leading 5–2 with eleven minutes remaining only
concede three goals and end up drawing 5–5.

oke City were the visitors in the FA Cup and after drawing
-2 they won the replay 1–0 at their Victoria Ground. The
vay results were dreadful, with heavy defeats at Blackpool
–0), Preston (4–0) and Blackburn (4–1). Finally, following
5–1 defeat at Leicester City, manager Ted Fenton was
lieved of his duties and Ron Greenwood became the new
anager. The Hammers finished sixteenth in the league,
ith only one away win on their travels.

ootball League - Division One
inal Table 1960-61

	P	HOME					AWAY					Pts
		W	D	L	F	A	W	D	L	F	A	
ttenham Hotspur	42	15	3	3	65	28	16	1	4	50	27	66
effield Wednesday	42	15	4	2	45	17	8	8	5	33	30	58
olverhampton Wanderers	42	17	2	2	61	32	8	5	8	42	43	57
urnley	42	11	4	6	58	40	11	3	7	44	37	51
erton	42	13	4	4	47	23	9	2	10	40	46	50
icester City	42	12	4	5	54	31	6	5	10	33	39	45
anchester United	42	14	5	2	58	20	4	4	13	30	56	45
ackburn Rovers	42	12	3	6	48	34	3	10	8	29	42	43
ston Villa	42	13	3	5	48	28	4	6	11	30	49	43
est Bromwich Albion	42	10	3	8	43	32	8	2	11	24	39	41
rsenal	42	12	3	6	44	35	3	8	10	33	50	41
helsea	42	10	5	6	61	48	5	2	14	37	52	37
anchester City	42	10	5	6	41	30	3	6	12	38	60	37
ottingham Forest	42	8	7	6	34	33	6	2	13	28	45	37
ardiff City	42	11	5	5	34	26	2	6	13	26	59	37
West Ham United	42	12	4	5	53	31	1	6	14	24	57	36
ulham	42	8	8	5	39	39	6	0	15	33	56	36
olton Wanderers	42	9	5	7	38	29	3	6	12	20	44	35
irmingham City	42	10	4	7	35	31	4	2	15	27	53	34
lackpool	42	9	3	9	44	34	3	6	12	24	39	33
ewcastle United	42	7	7	7	51	49	4	3	14	35	60	32
reston North End	42	7	6	8	28	25	3	4	14	15	46	30

RONNIE BOYCE

Ronnie played for England schoolboys and England youth before joining the ground staff at West Ham in 1959.

Playing at wing-half, he made his debut against Preston North End in a 5–2 home win in October 1960. By 1962–63 he was a regular member of the side and a perfect replacement for Phil Woosnam. Not known as a goalscorer, he gained a place in West Ham history when scoring two goals against Manchester United in the FA Cup semi-final in 1964, and he also scored the winning goal in that year's FA Cup Final against Preston North End. A year later he was back at Wembley as the Hammers won the European Cup Winners' Cup against TSV Munich. He did the simple things efficiently and quickly and was invaluable to the team. Ron was awarded a testimonial in November 1972 when Manchester United provided the opposition. He retired as a player in December 1972 after appearing in 339 games in the claret and blue. He then took up a coaching role with the club and later became chief scout. Ron is now enjoying his retirement living in Norfolk.

Season **1960-61** Football League - Division One
Match Details

Manager **Ted Fenton** (to March 14); **Ron Greenwood** (from April 11) Final League Position **16/22**
Following Fenton's departure team selection for 7 games was a board decision taken upon the advice of the coaches

	Date		Competition	Venue	Opponents	Results		Attendance	Position	Scorers
1	Aug 20	Sat	Div 1	A	Wolverhampton Wanderers	L	2-4	37,266	19	Dick, Woosnam
2	Aug 22	Mon	Div 1	H	Aston Villa	W	5-2	28,959	6	Bond, Dick, Dunmore, Musgrove, Woosnam
3	Aug 27	Sat	Div 1	H	Bolton Wanderers	W	2-1	24,283	8	Dick, Musgrove
4	Aug 29	Mon	Div 1	A	Aston Villa	L	1-2	32,098	10	Dunmore
5	Sep 3	Sat	Div 1	A	Sheffield Wednesday	L	0-1	26,359	12	
6	Sep 5	Mon	Div 1	H	Manchester United	W	2-1	30,506	9	Brett, Musgrove
7	Sep 10	Sat	Div 1	A	Chelsea	L	2-3	37,873	12	Dunmore, Grice
8	Sep 14	Wed	Div 1	A	Manchester United	L	1-6	33,288	16	Brett
9	Sep 17	Sat	Div 1	H	Blackpool	D	3-3	23,521	14	Bond, Musgrove, Woodley
10	Sep 24	Sat	Div 1	A	Everton	L	1-4	46,291	16	Beesley
11	Sep 26	Mon	FLC 1	H	Charlton Athletic	W	3-1	12,496		Dick, Moore, Musgrove
12	Oct 1	Sat	Div 1	H	Blackburn Rovers	W	3-2	17,519	15	Dick 2, Woosnam
13	Oct 8	Sat	Div 1	H	Birmingham City	W	4-3	15,954	12	Grice 2, Dunmore, Musgrove
14	Oct 15	Sat	Div 1	A	West Bromwich Albion	L	0-1	22,009	15	
15	Oct 22	Sat	Div 1	H	Preston North End	W	5-2	16,295	12	Musgrove 3, Bond [pen], Dick
16	Oct 24	Mon	FLC 2	A	Darlington	L	2-3	16,911		Dick, Dunmore
17	Oct 29	Sat	Div 1	A	Fulham	D	1-1	20,949	10	Dunmore
18	Nov 5	Sat	Div 1	H	Arsenal	W	6-0	29,275	10	Dunmore 3, Dick, Malcolm, Woosnam
19	Nov 12	Sat	Div 1	A	Manchester City	W	2-1	33,751	9	Dunmore, Grice
20	Nov 19	Sat	Div 1	H	Nottingham Forest	L	2-4	21,047	11	Dunmore, Palmer (og)
21	Dec 3	Sat	Div 1	H	Cardiff City	W	2-0	13,967	9	Dunmore, Musgrove
22	Dec 10	Sat	Div 1	A	Newcastle United	D	5-5	20,106	8	Bond [pen], Dick, Dunmore, Musgrove, McMichael (og)
23	Dec 17	Sat	Div 1	H	Wolverhampton Wanderers	W	5-0	22,336	7	Dunmore 2, Dick, Moore, Musgrove
24	Dec 24	Sat	Div 1	A	Tottenham Hotspur	L	0-2	54,930	7	
25	Dec 26	Mon	Div 1	H	Tottenham Hotspur	L	0-3	34,351	8	
26	Dec 31	Sat	Div 1	A	Bolton Wanderers	L	1-3	15,931	10	Musgrove
27	Jan 7	Sat	FAC 3	H	Stoke City	D	2-2	21,545		Dick, Dunmore
28	Jan 11	Wed	FAC 3 Rep	A	Stoke City	L	0-1	28,914		
29	Jan 14	Sat	Div 1	H	Sheffield Wednesday	D	1-1	20,650	11	Dick
30	Jan 21	Sat	Div 1	H	Chelsea	W	3-1	21,829	9	Dick, Obeney, Woosnam
31	Feb 4	Sat	Div 1	A	Blackpool	L	0-3	9,947	11	
32	Feb 11	Sat	Div 1	H	Everton	W	4-0	22,322	9	Obeney 2, Dick, Musgrove
33	Feb 25	Sat	Div 1	A	Birmingham City	L	2-4	16,856	13	Musgrove, Scott
34	Mar 4	Sat	Div 1	H	West Bromwich Albion	L	1-2	21,607	13	Dick
35	Mar 11	Sat	Div 1	A	Preston North End	L	0-4	12,084	13	
36	Mar 18	Sat	Div 1	H	Fulham	L	1-2	18,742	14	Obeney
37	Mar 20	Mon	Div 1	A	Blackburn Rovers	L	1-4	13,953	14	Woods (og)
38	Mar 25	Sat	Div 1	A	Arsenal	D	0-0	27,505	16	
39	Mar 31	Fri	Div 1	H	Leicester City	W	1-0	22,010	15	Dick
40	Apr 1	Sat	Div 1	H	Newcastle United	D	1-1	18,997	15	Musgrove
41	Apr 3	Mon	Div 1	A	Leicester City	L	1-5	23,776	16	Kirkup
42	Apr 8	Sat	Div 1	A	Nottingham Forest	D	1-1	23,083	16	Dick
43	Apr 15	Sat	Div 1	H	Manchester City	D	1-1	17,982	15	Sealey
44	Apr 18	Tue	Div 1	A	Burnley	D	2-2	11,609	14	Musgrove 2
45	Apr 22	Sat	Div 1	A	Cardiff City	D	1-1	9,549	13	Dick
46	Apr 29	Sat	Div 1	H	Burnley	L	1-2	18,759	16	Woosnam

eam Line-Ups

BEESLEY Mick	BOND John	BOYCE Ron	BRETT Ron	BROWN Ken	CANTWELL Noel	CARTWRIGHT Johnny	DICK John	DUNMORE Dave	GRICE Mike	HURST Geoff	KIRKUP Joe	LYALL John	MALCOLM Andy	MOORE Bobby	MUSGROVE Malcolm	OBENEY Harry	RHODES Brian	SCOTT Tony	SEALEY Alan	SHEARING Peter	SMILLIE Andy	WOODLEY Derek	WOOSNAM Phil	
	2			5	3		10	9	7				4	6	11		1						8	1
	2			5	3		10	9	7				4	6	11		1						8	2
	2			5	3		10	9	7				4	6	11		1						8	3
	2			5	3			9	7	4				6	11		1				10		8	4
	2			5	3		10	9	7				4	6	11					1			8	5
	2	10		5	3			9	7				4	6	11					1			8	6
	2	10		5	3			9	7				4	6	11					1			8	7
	2	10		5	3			9					4	6	11					1		7	8	8
	9			5	3		10				2		4	6	11					1		7	8	9
10	2			5	3			9					4	6	11					1		7	8	10
	2			5		8	10	9				3	4	6	11		1					7		11
	2			5			10	9	7			3	4	6	11		1						8	12
	2			5			10	9	7			3	4	6	11		1						8	13
	2			5			10	9	7			3	4	6	11		1						8	14
	2	8		5			10	9	7			3	4	6	11		1							15
	2			5			10	9	7			3	4	6	11		1						8	16
	2			5			10	9	11			3	4	6			1					7	8	17
	2			5			10	9	11			3	4	6			1					7	8	18
	2			5			10	9	7			3	4	6	11		1						8	19
	3			5			10	9	7		2		4	6	11		1						8	20
	2			5			10	9	7			3	4	6	11		1						8	21
	2			5			10	9	7			3	4	6	11		1						8	22
	2			5			10	9	7			3	4	6	11		1						8	23
	2			5			10	9	7			3	4	6	11		1						8	24
	2			5			10	9	7			3	4	6	11		1						8	25
	2			5			10	9			6	3	4		11		1				7		8	26
	2			5			10	9				3	4	6	11		1				7		8	27
			9	5			10				2	3	4	6	11		1						8	28
				5			10	9			2	3	4	6	11		1	7					8	29
				5			10				2	3	4	6	11	9	1	7					8	30
				5				10			2	3	4	6	11	9	1	7					8	31
				5			10				2	3	4	6	11	9	1	7					8	32
				5			10				2	3	4	6	11	9	1	7					8	33
	3			5			10	9			2		4	6	11		1	7					8	34
	3		7	5			10				2		4	6	11	9	1						8	35
	3			5			10		7		2		4	6	11	9	1						8	36
9	3			5					7		2		4	6	11		1				10		8	37
	3			5			10		7	4	2			6	11	9	1						8	38
	3			5			10		7		2		4	6	11	9	1						8	39
	3		7	5		8	10			6	2		4		11	9	1							40
	3	8		5			10			6	2		4		11		1	7	9					41
	3			5			10				2		4	6	11		1	7	9				8	42
	3			5			10				2		4	6	11		1	7	9					43
		8		5			10				2	3	4	6	11		1	7	9					44
				5			10				2	3	4	6	11		1	7	9				8	45
				5			10			6	2	3	4		11		1	7	9				8	46

At White Hart Lane the teams drew 2–2 and in an exciti
game at the Boleyn Ground the Hammers won 2–1. T
dismal away form of the last campaign was forgotten w
good wins at Aston Villa (4–2) and Sheffield United (4–
After 12 games the left-wing pairing of Dick and Musgro
had scored 15 goals between them.

Plymouth Argyle were narrowly beaten 3–2 in the Leag
Cup at home but the Hammers bowed out in the ne
round after losing 3–1 at home to Aston Villa. Losing 3
at half-time away to Manchester City, West Ham staged
remarkable comeback to win 5–3. Bobby Moore was se
off in the closing seconds of this match for the first a
only time in his West Ham career. The away form continu
to improve as following a decent 2–2 draw at Arsenal the
was a 2–1 win at Manchester United, where Johnny Di

1961-62
Story of the season

The **early fixtures** paired **West Ham with two games** against the **League Champions Tottenham Hotspur.**

Appearances & Goals 1961-62

	League		FA Cup		League Cup		Total	
	Starts	Goals	Starts	Goals	Starts	Goals	Starts	Goals
BOND John	37	2	1	0	2	0	40	2
BOVINGTON Eddie	7	0	0	0	0	0	7	0
BOYCE Ron	4	1	0	0	0	0	4	1
BROWN Ken	38	0	1	0	2	0	41	0
BURKETT Jack	1	0	0	0	0	0	1	0
BYRNE Johnny	11	1	0	0	0	0	11	1
CRAWFORD Ian	20	5	1	0	1	2	22	7
DICK John	35	23	1	0	2	0	38	23
DICKIE Alan	2	0	0	0	0	0	2	0
HURST Geoff	24	1	1	0	2	0	27	1
KIRKUP Joe	41	1	1	0	2	0	44	1
LANSDOWNE Bill	4	1	0	0	0	0	4	1
LESLIE Lawrie	37	0	1	0	1	0	39	0
LYALL John	4	0	0	0	0	0	4	0
MALCOLM Andy	8	0	0	0	0	0	8	0
MOORE Bobby	41	3	1	0	2	0	44	3
MUSGROVE Malcolm	35	13	1	0	1	1	37	14
PETERS Martin	5	0	0	0	0	0	5	0
RHODES Brian	3	0	0	0	1	0	4	0
SCOTT Tony	22	4	0	0	2	0	24	4
SEALEY Alan	32	11	0	0	2	0	34	11
TINDALL Ron	13	3	1	0	0	0	14	3
WOODLEY Derek	4	0	0	0	0	0	4	0
WOOSNAM Phil	34	6	1	0	2	1	37	7
own goal		1						1
TOTALS	**462**	**76**	**11**	**0**	**22**	**4**	**495**	**80**

ored twice. At home against Wolverhampton Wanderers usgrove scored after 14 seconds and Bobby Moore added o more in the 4–2 victory.

he FA Cup brought a shock as the Hammers crashed out, sing 3–0 away to Plymouth Argyle. February brought a -0 win at Chelsea followed by a 2–2 draw at home to ampions-elect Ipswich Town. A disastrous March saw est Ham crash 6–0 at Burnley and 4–0 at home to anchester City, where new signing Johnny Byrne made his ome debut. During the Easter period the spotlight was on e goalkeepers. Against Arsenal goalkeeper Lawrie Leslie is injured and was replaced by defender John Lyall in the -3 home draw, while at Cardiff City keeper Brian Rhodes d to retire injured and in his place came midfielder Martin eters, who played well despite the 3–0 defeat. The season ded with a 4–2 home win over Fulham, which gave West am a respectable eighth place in the league table.

ootball League - Division One
inal Table 1961-62

	P	HOME					AWAY					Pts
		W	D	L	F	A	W	D	L	F	A	
swich Town	42	17	2	2	58	28	7	6	8	35	39	56
rnley	42	14	4	3	57	26	7	7	7	44	41	53
tenham Hotspur	42	14	4	3	59	34	7	6	8	29	35	52
erton	42	17	2	2	64	21	3	9	9	24	33	51
effield United	42	13	5	3	37	23	6	4	11	24	46	47
effield Wednesday	42	14	4	3	47	23	6	2	13	25	35	46
ton Villa	42	13	5	3	45	20	5	3	13	20	36	44
est Ham United	42	11	6	4	49	37	6	4	11	27	45	44
est Bromwich Albion	42	10	7	4	50	23	5	6	10	33	44	43
senal	42	9	6	6	39	31	7	5	9	32	41	43
lton Wanderers	42	11	7	3	35	22	5	3	13	27	44	42
anchester City	42	11	3	7	46	38	6	4	11	32	43	41
ackpool	42	10	4	7	41	30	5	7	9	29	45	41
icester City	42	12	2	7	38	27	5	4	12	34	44	40
anchester United	42	10	3	8	44	31	5	6	10	28	44	39
ackburn Rovers	42	10	6	5	33	22	4	5	12	17	36	39
rmingham City	42	9	6	6	37	35	5	4	12	28	46	38
olverhampton Wanderers	42	8	7	6	38	34	5	3	13	35	52	36
ottingham Forest	42	12	4	5	39	23	1	6	14	24	56	36
lham	42	8	3	10	38	34	5	4	12	28	40	33
ardiff City	42	6	9	6	30	33	3	5	13	20	48	32
elsea	42	7	7	7	34	29	2	3	16	29	65	28

JOHNNY BYRNE

Nicknamed 'Budgie' because of his non stop chatter he started out on the ground staff at Crystal Palace in 1956 and in the next five seasons totalled 259 appearances scoring 101 goals.

While at Palace he won an England full cap when playing against Northern Ireland in November 1961. In March 1962 West Ham smashed the British record transfer fee when they signed Byrne for £65,000. He formed an exciting partnership with Geoff Hurst, the big target man feeding off the skilful smaller partner. Byrne's finest season was the 1963-64 campaign when he scored 33 goals in 45 league and cup games. As the season came to a close he won a FA Cup Winners medal as West Ham beat Preston North End at Wembley. Four days later he scored both goals as England beat Uruguay 2-1. In April 1965 when playing for England against Scotland he damaged a cartilage in his knee. The injury kept him out of West Ham's finest triumph the following month when they won the European Cup Winners Cup after beating TSV Munich 2-0 at Wembley. In November 1966 West Ham slaughtered Leeds United 7-0 in a League Cup tie at Upton Park. Although Byrne did not get on the score sheet he had a hand in every goal and his performance that night was perfection. In 1967 he was sold back to Crystal Palace but with continued knee problems he struggled and after 36 appearances he joined Fulham, The Cottagers were then relegated twice in two seasons and after playing in only 19 games his playing career came to an end. Johnny then emigrated to South Africa where he became manager of Durban City and later Hellenic. Byrne died aged 60 in October 1999 following a heart attack.

Season **1961-62** Football League - Division One
Match Details

Manager **Ron Greenwood**   Final League Position **8/22**

	Date		Competition	Venue	Opponents	Results		Attendance	Position	Scorers
1	Aug 19	Sat	Div 1	H	Manchester United	D	1-1	32,628	12	Dick
2	Aug 23	Wed	Div 1	A	Tottenham Hotspur	D	2-2	50,434	14	Musgrove, Woosnam
3	Aug 26	Sat	Div 1	A	Wolverhampton Wanderers	L	2-3	25,471	14	Musgrove, Sealey
4	Aug 28	Mon	Div 1	H	Tottenham Hotspur	W	2-1	36,274	9	Scott, Sealey
5	Sep 2	Sat	Div 1	H	Nottingham Forest	W	3-2	23,795	7	Musgrove, Scott, Sealey
6	Sep 4	Mon	Div 1	A	Blackpool	L	0-2	19,838	7	
7	Sep 9	Sat	Div 1	A	Aston Villa	W	4-2	31,836	7	Dick 2, Scott, Sealey
8	Sep 11	Mon	FLC 1	H	Plymouth Argyle	W	3-2	12,178		Crawford 2, Woosnam
9	Sep 16	Sat	Div 1	H	Chelsea	W	2-1	27,530	5	Dick, Musgrove
10	Sep 18	Mon	Div 1	H	Blackpool	D	2-2	25,925	4	Boyce, Musgrove
11	Sep 23	Sat	Div 1	A	Sheffield United	W	4-1	21,034	3	Dick 2, Musgrove, Sealey
12	Sep 30	Sat	Div 1	H	Leicester City	W	4-1	26,746	2	Dick 2, Sealey, Woosnam
13	Oct 7	Sat	Div 1	A	Ipswich Town	L	2-4	28,059	3	Musgrove, Sealey
14	Oct 9	Mon	FLC 2	H	Aston Villa	L	1-3	17,735		Musgrove
15	Oct 14	Sat	Div 1	H	Burnley	W	2-1	32,238	2	Crawford, Dick
16	Oct 21	Sat	Div 1	A	Fulham	L	0-2	32,375	2	
17	Oct 28	Sat	Div 1	H	Sheffield Wednesday	L	2-3	26,453	6	Bond [pen], Dick
18	Nov 4	Sat	Div 1	A	Manchester City	W	5-3	18,839	4	Dick 2, Sealey 2, Musgrove
19	Nov 11	Sat	Div 1	H	West Bromwich Albion	D	3-3	18,213	3	Bond [pen], Musgrove, Sealey
20	Nov 18	Sat	Div 1	A	Birmingham City	L	0-4	20,682	5	
21	Nov 25	Sat	Div 1	H	Everton	W	3-1	27,100	4	Dick 2, Crawford
22	Dec 2	Sat	Div 1	A	Arsenal	D	2-2	47,205	6	Tindall 2
23	Dec 9	Sat	Div 1	H	Bolton Wanderers	W	1-0	19,492	5	Woosnam
24	Dec 16	Sat	Div 1	A	Manchester United	W	2-1	29,472	4	Dick 2
25	Dec 18	Mon	Div 1	H	Wolverhampton Wanderers	W	4-2	21,261	2	Moore 2, Hurst, Musgrove
26	Dec 26	Tue	Div 1	H	Blackburn Rovers	L	2-3	22,280	5	Dick, Tindall
27	Jan 6	Sat	FAC 3	A	Plymouth Argyle	L	0-3	26,915		
28	Jan 13	Sat	Div 1	A	Nottingham Forest	L	0-3	20,537	5	
29	Jan 20	Sat	Div 1	H	Aston Villa	W	2-0	20,284	5	Dick, Woosnam
30	Feb 3	Sat	Div 1	A	Chelsea	W	1-0	34,259	4	Moore
31	Feb 10	Sat	Div 1	H	Sheffield United	L	1-2	21,829	5	Woosnam
32	Feb 17	Sat	Div 1	A	Leicester City	D	2-2	21,312	4	Dick, Woosnam
33	Feb 24	Sat	Div 1	H	Ipswich Town	D	2-2	27,763	4	Dick, Kirkup
34	Mar 3	Sat	Div 1	A	Burnley	L	0-6	24,379	5	
35	Mar 17	Sat	Div 1	A	Sheffield Wednesday	D	0-0	30,404	5	
36	Mar 24	Sat	Div 1	H	Manchester City	L	0-4	25,808	6	
37	Mar 28	Wed	Div 1	A	Blackburn Rovers	L	0-1	8,876	6	
38	Mar 31	Sat	Div 1	A	West Bromwich Albion	W	1-0	16,937	6	Musgrove
39	Apr 6	Fri	Div 1	H	Birmingham City	D	2-2	22,668	6	Musgrove 2
40	Apr 14	Sat	Div 1	A	Everton	L	0-3	35,108	7	
41	Apr 20	Fri	Div 1	H	Cardiff City	W	4-1	25,459	6	Byrne, Crawford, Sealey, Baker (og)
42	Apr 21	Sat	Div 1	H	Arsenal	D	3-3	31,912	6	Dick, Lansdowne, Scott
43	Apr 23	Mon	Div 1	A	Cardiff City	L	0-3	11,274	7	
44	Apr 28	Sat	Div 1	A	Bolton Wanderers	L	0-1	17,333	11	
45	Apr 30	Mon	Div 1	H	Fulham	W	4-2	24,737	8	Crawford 2, Dick 2

eam Line-Ups

BOND John	BOVINGTON Eddie	BOYCE Ron	BROWN Ken	BURKETT Jack	BYRNE Johnny	CRAWFORD Ian	DICK John	DICKIE Alan	HURST Geoff	KIRKUP Joe	LANSDOWNE Bill	LESLIE Lawrie	LYALL John	MALCOLM Andy	MOORE Bobby	MUSGROVE Malcolm	PETERS Martin	RHODES Brian	SCOTT Tony	SEALEY Alan	TINDALL Ron	WOODLEY Derek	WOOSNAM Phil	
3			5				10			2		1		4	6	11			7	9			8	1
3			5				10			2		1		4	6	11			7	9			8	2
3			5				10			2		1		4	6	11			7	9			8	3
3			5				10			2		1		4	6	11			7	9			8	4
3			5				10			2		1		4	6	11			7	9			8	5
3		8	5				10		4	2		1			6	11				9			7	6
3			5			11	10		4	2		1			6				7	9			8	7
3			5			11	10		4	2					6			1	7	9			8	8
3			5				10		4	2		1			6	11			7	9			8	9
3		8	5				10		4	2					6	11		1	7	9			8	10
3			5				10		4	2					6	11		1	7	9			8	11
3			5				10		4	2		1			6	11			7	9			8	12
3			5				10		4	2		1			6	11			7	9			8	13
3			5				10		4	2		1			6	11			7	9			8	14
3		8	5			7	10			2		1		4	6	11				9				15
3			5			7	10			2		1		4	6	11				9			8	16
3			5			7	10			2		1		4	6	11				9			8	17
3			5			7	10		4	2		1			6	11				9			8	18
3			5			7	10		4	2		1			6	11				9			8	19
3			5			7	10		4	2		1			6	11				9			8	20
3			5			7	10		4	2		1			6	11					9		8	21
3			5			7	10		4	2		1			6	11					9		8	22
3	6		5			7	10		4	2		1				11				9			8	23
3			5			7	10		4	2		1			6	11					9		8	24
3			5			7	10		4	2		1			6	11					9		8	25
3			5			7	10		4	2		1			6	11					9		8	26
3			5			7	10		4	2		1			6	11					9		8	27
3			5			7	10		4	2		1			6	11					9		8	28
3	4		5				10			2		1			6	11			7	9			8	29
3	4		5							2		1			6	11			7	9	10		8	30
3	4		5				10			2		1			6	11			7	9			8	31
3	4		5				10			2		1			6	11			7	9			8	32
3	4	8	5				10			2		1			6	11			7	9				33
	4		5				10			2		1	3		6	11			7	9			8	34
3			5		9	11			4	2		1			6				7		10		8	35
3			5		9				4	2		1			6	11					10	7	8	36
3			5		9				4	2		1			6	11					10	7	8	37
3			5		9				4	2		1			6	11					10	7	8	38
3			5		8				4	2		1			6	11				9	10	7		39
3			5		9		10		4	2		1			6	11					8	7		40
					8	11	10			2	5	1	3		6		4		7	9				41
					8	11	10			2	5	1	3		6		4		7	9				42
2			5		10	11			4						6	7	3	1		9			8	43
					8	11	10	1		2	5		3		6		4		7	9				44
				3	8	11	10	1		2	5				6		4		7	9				45

1962-63
Story of the season

A **poor start to the season** saw home defeats by 4–1 to Wolverhampton Wanderers and 6–1 to Tottenham Hotspur. The Hammers were now **bottom of the table** and for the Liverpool game manager **Ron Greenwood** moved wing-half **Geoff Hurst** to the **forward line.**

This move was the start of Hurst becoming one of t[he] world's deadliest strikers. Although he did not score in t[he] 1–0 win, Hurst looked a natural. The following Saturd[ay] away to Manchester City the Hammers beat their fello[w] strugglers 6–1. Now in improved form, Blackburn Rove[rs] were beaten 4–0 at Ewood Park followed by a 5-[1] demolition of Birmingham City, where Johnny Byr[ne] scored twice.

Byrne was on hand with a hat-trick in the League Cup [as] Plymouth Argyle were beaten 6–0 at home, but the trip [to] Rotherham in the next round brought a 3–1 defeat. Thre[e] forwards were transferred out, with Johnny Dick leaving f[or]

Appearances & Goals 1962-63

	League		FA Cup		League Cup		Total	
	Starts	Goals	Starts	Goals	Starts	Goals	Starts	Goa[ls]
BOND John	14	0	0	0	2	0	16	0
BOVINGTON Eddie	10	0	4	0	1	0	15	0
BOYCE Ron	27	3	5	2	1	0	33	5
BRABROOK Peter	29	7	5	0	0	0	34	7
BRITT Martin	1	0	0	0	0	0	1	0
BROWN Ken	40	2	5	0	2	0	47	2
BURKETT Jack	38	0	5	0	2	0	45	0
BYRNE Johnny	30	9	5	2	2	3	37	14
CHARLES John	1	0	0	0	0	0	1	0
CRAWFORD Ian	5	0	0	0	0	0	5	0
DEAR Brian	3	0	0	0	0	0	3	0
DICK John	2	0	0	0	0	0	2	0
DICKIE Alan	2	0	0	0	0	0	2	0
HURST Geoff	27	13	0	0	2	2	29	15
KIRKUP Joe	27	1	5	0	0	0	32	1
LANSDOWNE Bill	1	0	0	0	0	0	1	0
LESLIE Lawrie	20	0	0	0	2	0	22	0
LYALL John	4	0	0	0	0	0	4	0
MOORE Bobby	41	3	5	0	1	0	47	3
MUSGROVE Malcolm	15	7	0	0	2	1	17	8
PETERS Martin	36	8	1	0	2	1	39	9
RHODES Brian	2	0	0	0	0	0	2	0
SCOTT Tony	27	10	5	0	2	0	34	10
SEALEY Alan	26	6	5	0	0	0	31	6
SISSONS John	1	0	0	0	0	0	1	0
STANDEN Jim	18	0	5	0	0	0	23	0
WOOSNAM Phil	15	1	0	0	1	0	16	1
own goal		3						3
TOTALS	**462**	**73**	**55**	**4**	**22**	**7**	**539**	**84**

entford, Phil Woosnam joining Aston Villa and Malcolm
usgrove moving on to Leyton Orient. In late December
ere was excitement and goals as the Hammers drew 4–4
 Tottenham and won 4–3 at Nottingham Forest, where
nger Peter Brabrook scored twice.

he 'big freeze' then hit the country, with postponements
roughout January and February. On a snow-covered pitch
est Ham beat Fulham 2–1 in a FA Cup replay following a
alless draw. In March West Ham progressed in the FA
up with 1–0 home wins over Swansea Town and Everton.
he quarter-final saw the Hammers travel to Liverpool,
here a late goal put them out 1–0. The team were now in
d-table and Nottingham Forest were beaten 4–1 at home.
he scorers in this match were Hurst (2), Moore and Peters.
me three years later this trio would become World Cup
roes. On the final day of the season Manchester City
ere relegated after the Hammers beat them 6–1 and
ined a twelfth place finish in the league.

ootball League - Division One
inal Table 1962-63

		HOME					AWAY					
	P	W	D	L	F	A	W	D	L	F	A	Pts
erton	42	14	7	0	48	17	11	4	6	36	25	61
enham Hotspur	42	14	6	1	72	28	9	3	9	39	34	55
rnley	42	14	4	3	41	17	8	6	7	37	40	54
cester City	42	14	6	1	53	23	6	6	9	26	30	52
lverhampton Wanderers	42	11	6	4	51	25	9	4	8	42	40	50
effield Wednesday	42	10	5	6	38	26	9	5	7	39	37	48
senal	42	11	4	6	44	33	7	6	8	42	44	46
erpool	42	13	3	5	45	22	4	7	10	26	37	44
ttingham Forest	42	12	4	5	39	28	5	6	10	28	41	44
effield United	42	11	7	3	33	20	5	5	11	25	40	44
ackburn Rovers	42	11	4	6	55	34	4	8	9	24	37	42
est Ham United	42	8	6	7	39	34	6	6	9	34	35	40
ackpool	42	8	7	6	34	27	5	7	9	24	37	40
est Bromwich Albion	42	11	1	9	40	37	5	6	10	31	42	39
ton Villa	42	12	2	7	38	23	3	6	12	24	45	38
lham	42	8	6	7	28	30	6	4	11	22	41	38
swich Town	42	5	8	8	34	39	7	3	11	25	39	35
lton Wanderers	42	13	3	5	35	18	2	2	17	20	57	35
anchester United	42	6	6	9	36	38	6	4	11	31	43	34
rmingham City	42	6	8	7	40	40	4	5	12	23	50	33
anchester City	42	7	5	9	30	45	3	6	12	28	57	31
yton Orient	42	4	5	12	22	37	2	4	15	15	44	21

SIR GEOFF HURST

At his peak he was one of the best centre-forwards in the world and is the only player to score a hat-trick in a World Cup Final.

Ron Greenwood's decision in 1962 to switch his position from wing-half to striker was a masterstroke. Geoff was a near-post goalscorer who also selfishly ran and provided for others. Club success came his way when he won medals with West Ham when they won the FA Cup in 1964 and a year later the European Cup Winners' Cup. A runners-up medal was gained in 1966 when the Hammers reached the League Cup final, losing to West Bromwich Albion.

In season 1965–66 he scored a total of 40 goals in league and cup for the Hammers and won his first England cap in February 1966 against West Germany. Later that year the World Cup Finals began and Hurst was brought into the side in the quarter-final, scoring the goal in the 1–0 win against Argentina. After beating Portugal in the semi-final, worldwide acclaim came his way when he scored a hat-trick in the final against West Germany.

Playing against Sunderland in October 1968 he scored six goals in the 8–0 home win. After making 499 appearances and scoring 248 goals for West Ham he joined Stoke City in August 1972. He was with the Potters for three seasons, playing in 108 league games, before ending his playing career at West Bromwich Albion in 1976. He later played for Seattle Sounders and became manager at Telford United and Chelsea. He then spent many years working in insurance and nowadays is involved with supporting charities and other media work. He was knighted in 1998.

Season **1962-63** Football League - Division One
Match Details

Manager **Ron Greenwood**   Final League Position **12/22**

	Date		Competition	Venue	Opponents	Results		Attendance	Position	Scorers
1	Aug 18	Sat	Div 1	A	Aston Villa	L	1-3	37,657	20	Byrne
2	Aug 20	Mon	Div 1	H	Wolverhampton Wanderers	L	1-4	30,002	20	Musgrove
3	Aug 25	Sat	Div 1	H	Tottenham Hotspur	L	1-6	32,527	22	Woosnam
4	Aug 29	Wed	Div 1	A	Wolverhampton Wanderers	D	0-0	36,844	22	
5	Sep 1	Sat	Div 1	A	Leyton Orient	L	0-2	23,918	22	
6	Sep 3	Mon	Div 1	H	Liverpool	W	1-0	22,258	20	Scott
7	Sep 8	Sat	Div 1	A	Manchester City	W	6-1	24,069	19	Musgrove 2, Byrne, Hurst, Peters, Scott
8	Sep 12	Wed	Div 1	A	Liverpool	L	1-2	39,261	19	Byrne
9	Sep 14	Fri	Div 1	H	Blackpool	D	2-2	24,695	18	Musgrove, Scott
10	Sep 22	Sat	Div 1	A	Blackburn Rovers	W	4-0	15,545	15	Byrne, Hurst, Musgrove, Peters
11	Sep 26	Wed	FLC 2	H	Plymouth Argyle	W	6-0	9,714		Byrne 3 [1 pen], Hurst, Musgrove, Peters
12	Sep 29	Sat	Div 1	H	Sheffield United	D	1-1	22,800	13	Scott
13	Oct 6	Sat	Div 1	H	Birmingham City	W	5-0	21,150	11	Byrne 2, Brown, Hurst, Musgrove
14	Oct 13	Sat	Div 1	A	Arsenal	D	1-1	49,597	10	Scott
15	Oct 16	Tue	FLC 3	A	Rotherham United	L	1-3	11,581		Hurst
16	Oct 22	Mon	Div 1	H	Burnley	D	1-1	34,612	10	Hurst
17	Oct 27	Sat	Div 1	A	Manchester United	L	1-3	29,419	12	Musgrove
18	Nov 3	Sat	Div 1	H	Bolton Wanderers	L	1-2	19,885	16	Moore
19	Nov 10	Sat	Div 1	A	Leicester City	L	0-2	21,064	17	
20	Nov 17	Sat	Div 1	H	Fulham	D	2-2	17,668	19	Hurst, Peters [pen]
21	Nov 24	Sat	Div 1	A	Sheffield Wednesday	W	3-1	21,762	18	Brabrook, Peters [pen], Scott
22	Dec 1	Sat	Div 1	H	West Bromwich Albion	D	2-2	20,769	16	Hurst, Moore
23	Dec 8	Sat	Div 1	A	Everton	D	1-1	38,701	17	Brabrook
24	Dec 15	Sat	Div 1	H	Aston Villa	D	1-1	21,529	14	Peters
25	Dec 22	Sat	Div 1	A	Tottenham Hotspur	D	4-4	44,650	14	Boyce, Kirkup, Peters, Scott
26	Dec 29	Sat	Div 1	A	Nottingham Forest	W	4-3	18,660	11	Brabrook 2, Byrne, McKinlay (og)
27	Feb 4	Mon	FAC 3	H	Fulham	D	0-0	21,000		
28	Feb 16	Sat	Div 1	A	Sheffield United	W	2-0	18,176	10	Boyce, Sealey
29	Feb 20	Wed	FAC 3 Rep	A	Fulham	W	2-1	20,000		Boyce, Byrne [pen]
30	Mar 2	Sat	Div 1	H	Arsenal	L	0-4	31,967	12	
31	Mar 4	Mon	FAC 4	H	Swansea Town	W	1-0	25,924		Boyce
32	Mar 9	Sat	Div 1	A	Burnley	D	1-1	17,197	10	Byrne
33	Mar 16	Sat	FAC 5	H	Everton	W	1-0	31,770		Byrne [pen]
34	Mar 18	Mon	Div 1	H	Manchester United	W	3-1	28,950	10	Brown, Sealey, Brennan (og)
35	Mar 23	Sat	Div 1	A	Bolton Wanderers	L	0-3	19,177	11	
36	Mar 30	Sat	FAC QF	A	Liverpool	L	0-1	49,036		
37	Apr 2	Tue	Div 1	H	Sheffield Wednesday	W	2-0	20,048	12	Byrne [pen], Hurst
38	Apr 6	Sat	Div 1	A	Fulham	L	0-2	26,871	13	
39	Apr 12	Fri	Div 1	H	Ipswich Town	L	1-3	23,170	14	Scott
40	Apr 13	Sat	Div 1	H	Leicester City	W	2-0	25,689	13	Sealey 2
41	Apr 15	Mon	Div 1	A	Ipswich Town	W	3-2	21,988	11	Brabrook, Hurst, Peters
42	Apr 20	Sat	Div 1	A	West Bromwich Albion	L	0-1	10,315	12	
43	Apr 22	Mon	Div 1	H	Nottingham Forest	W	4-1	18,179	10	Hurst 2 [1 pen], Moore, Peters
44	Apr 27	Sat	Div 1	H	Everton	L	1-2	28,391	11	Meagan (og)
45	May 1	Wed	Div 1	A	Birmingham City	L	2-3	14,410	14	Hurst, Scott
46	May 4	Sat	Div 1	H	Blackburn Rovers	L	0-1	18,898	14	
47	May 11	Sat	Div 1	H	Leyton Orient	W	2-0	16,745	14	Brabrook, Scott
48	May 13	Mon	Div 1	A	Blackpool	D	0-0	12,434	13	
49	May 18	Sat	Div 1	H	Manchester City	W	6-1	16,602	12	Hurst 2, Sealey 2, Boyce, Brabrook

Team Line-Ups

	BOVINGTON Eddie	BOYCE Ron	BRABROOK Peter	BRITT Martin	BROWN Ken	BURKETT Jack	BYRNE Johnny	CHARLES John	CRAWFORD Ian	DEAR Brian	DICK John	DICKIE Alan	HURST Geoff	KIRKUP Joe	LANSDOWNE Bill	LESLIE Lawrie	LYALL John	MOORE Bobby	MUSGROVE Malcolm	PETERS Martin	RHODES Brian	SCOTT Tony	SEALEY Alan	SISSONS John	STANDEN Jim	WOOSNAM Phil	
		8					9	7			10		4	2	5	1		6	11	3							1
					5		9	7			10			2		1	3	6	11	4						8	2
					5		10	7						2		1	3	6	11	4			9			8	3
					5	3	10		11	7				2		1		6		4			9			8	4
					5	3	10		11	7				2		1		6		4			9			8	5
					5	3	9						10			1		6	11	4		7				8	6
					5	3	9						10			1		6	11	4		7				8	7
					5	3	9						10			1		6	11	4		7				8	8
					5	3	9						10			1		6	11	4		7				8	9
					5	3	9						10			1		6	11	4		7				8	10
		8			5	3	9						10			1		6	11	4		7					11
					5	3	9						10			1		6	11	4		7				8	12
					5	3	9						10			1		6	11	4		7				8	13
					5	3	9						10			1		6	11	4		7				8	14
	4				5	3	9						10					6	11			7				8	15
			7		5	3	9						10			1		6	11	4						8	16
			7		5	2	10									1	3	6	11	4			9			8	17
			7		5	3	9						10			1		6	11	4						8	18
		8	7		5	3	9					1	10					6	11	4							19
		8	7		5	3						1	10	2				6		4			11	9			20
		8	7		5	3							10	2				6		4			11	9	1		21
		8	7		5	3							10	2				6		4			11	9	1		22
		8	7		5	3	10							2				6		4			11	9	1		23
		8	7		5	3	10							2				6		4			11	9	1		24
		8	7		5	3								2				6		4			11	9	1		25
		8	7		5	3								2				6		4			11	9	1		26
	4	8	7		5	3	10							2				6					11	9	1		27
	4	8	7		5	3	10							2				6					11	9	1		28
	4	8	7		5	3	10											6					11	9	1		29
	4	8	7		5	3	10											6					11	9	1		30
	4	8	7		5	3	10											6					11	9	1		31
	4	8	7		5	3	10											6					11	9	1		32
		8	7		5	3	10											6					11	9	1		33
	4	8	7		5	3							10	2				6			1		11	9			34
	4	8	7		5	3							10	2				6			1		11	9			35
		8	7		5	3	10							2				6		4			11	9	1		36
		8	7		5	3	10						9	2				6		4			11		1		37
	4	8	7		5	3	10							2						6			11	9	1		38
		8	7		5	3	10						9	2				6		4		11			1		39
	4	8	11		5	3							9	2				6		10			7		1		40
	4	8	11		5	3							9	2				6		10			7		1		41
	4	8	11		5	3							9	2				6		10			7		1		42
		8	11		5	3							10	2				6		4		7	9		1		43
		8	11		5	3	9						10	2				6		4			7		1		44
		8	11		5	3							10	2				6		4		7	9		1		45
		8	11	9							6			2		1	3	5		4			7	10			46
2		8	7		5	3	10									1		6		4			11	9			47
2		8	7		5	3	11						10			1		6		4			9				48
2	4	8	7		5	3				11			10			1		6					9				49

1963-64
Story of the season

Fresh from **winning the International Soccer League in America,** the Hammers won two and drew two of their first four games to top the table. Two home defeats were to follow before **West Ham won 2–1 at Liverpool,** a victory that has not happened since.

The League Cup saw West Ham knock out neighbou Leyton Orient and Aston Villa to progress to the fou round. After a further six games without a league win t Hammers beat champions Everton 4–2 at home a followed this up with a 1–0 win at Manchester Unite Swindon Town were the next opponents in the League C and following an exciting 3–3 away draw West Ham w the replay 4–1. The next round brought a quarter-final cla with Fourth Division Workington, where Johnny Byr scored a hat-trick in a 6–0 win.

On Boxing Day the home crowd were shocked as visito Blackburn Rovers crushed West Ham 8–2. Two days lat with just one change to the side, the Hammers travelled Blackburn and in a remarkable turnaround won 3–1. A 3 home win in the FA Cup against Charlton Athletic w followed in the next round with a 3–0 victory agair neighbours Leyton Orient.

Appearances & Goals 1963-64

	League		FA Cup		League Cup		Total	
	Starts	Goals	Starts	Goals	Starts	Goals	Starts	Goa
BENNETT Peter	1	0	0	0	0	0	1	0
BICKLES Dave	2	0	0	0	1	0	3	0
BOND John	26	0	7	0	6	1	39	1
BOVINGTON Eddie	22	0	7	0	3	0	32	0
BOYCE Ron	41	6	7	3	7	2	55	1
BRABROOK Peter	38	8	7	2	6	2	51	1
BRITT Martin	9	3	0	0	2	1	11	4
BROWN Ken	36	0	7	0	6	0	49	0
BURKETT Jack	40	1	7	0	7	0	54	1
BYRNE Johnny	33	24	7	4	5	5	45	3
CHARLES John	0	0	0	0	2	0	2	0
DEAR Brian	3	0	0	0	0	0	3	0
DICKIE Alan	3	0	0	0	0	0	3	0
HUGO Roger	3	2	0	0	0	0	3	2
HURST Geoff	37	14	7	7	6	5	50	26
KIRKUP Joe	18	0	0	0	1	0	19	0
MOORE Bobby	37	2	7	0	6	0	50	2
PETERS Martin	32	3	0	0	4	0	36	3
SCOTT Tony	10	0	0	0	3	3	13	3
SEALEY Alan	18	2	0	0	4	1	22	3
SISSONS John	14	3	7	3	1	0	22	6
STANDEN Jim	39	0	7	0	7	0	53	0
own goal		1						1
TOTALS	**462**	**69**	**77**	**19**	**77**	**20**	**616**	**10**

ack to the League Cup, and in the first leg of the semi-
nal at Filbert Street the Hammers lost 4–3 to Leicester
ity. Geoff Hurst scored twice in that game and two more
West Ham knocked Swindon Town out of the FA Cup
ter winning 3–1 at the County Ground. February proved
be a good month, with home wins against Tottenham
–0) and Sheffield Wednesday (4–3), where Johnny Byrne
ored a hat-trick.

tough match in the quarter-final of the FA Cup saw
urnley beaten 3–2 at Upton Park to give a semi-final
iring with Manchester United. The game at Hillsborough
as Bobby Moore's finest performance as he inspired the
ammers to a 3–1 victory. The second leg of the League
up semi-final with Leicester was lost 2–0, a 6–3 aggregate
efeat, in what was West Ham's fourteenth cup tie of the
eason.

eading up to the FA Cup final the league form suffered a
tle, but the last home game brought a 5–0 victory against

Birmingham City. A thrilling game took place with Second
Division Preston North End in the Wembley final. The
Hammers were twice behind and the score stood at 2–2
with a minute remaining. Then Ronnie Boyce headed home
the winner to the delight of the delirious West Ham fans.
The Hammers were FA Cup winners for the first time in
their history.

JOHN SISSONS

**The England youth international winger
signed for West Ham in October 1962 and
made his debut against Blackburn Rovers in
May 1963.**

He was a rare talent, combining a brilliant left
foot, with a burst of speed. The following
season he established himself in the side and
played in every round as the Hammers won
the FA Cup. Playing against Preston North
End in the final he was at the time the
youngest player to have scored in an FA Cup
final. John played a big part in the European
campaign the following season when West
Ham won the European Cup Winners' Cup.
International honours followed as over the
next few years he gained ten England
under-23 caps.

Sissons never made the most of his talent at
Upton Park and after 265 appearances he left
in August 1970 to join Sheffield Wednesday. A
further 115 league games were played in
Owls colours, before in December 1973 he
was signed by former team-mate John Bond
at Norwich City. He only spent a short time
with the Norfolk side before returning to
London to join Chelsea. The Londoners were
facing relegation and he never settled there,
playing in only 10 games. He then went to
play in the USA for a year before immigrating
to South Africa where he still lives.

ootball League - Division One
inal Table 1963-64

	P	HOME					AWAY					Pts
		W	D	L	F	A	W	D	L	F	A	
verpool	42	16	0	5	60	18	10	5	6	32	27	57
anchester United	42	15	3	3	54	19	8	4	9	36	43	53
verton	42	14	4	3	53	26	7	6	8	31	38	52
ottenham Hotspur	42	13	3	5	54	31	9	4	8	43	50	51
helsea	42	12	3	6	36	24	8	7	6	36	32	50
heffield Wednesday	42	15	3	3	50	24	4	8	9	34	43	49
lackburn Rovers	42	10	4	7	44	28	8	6	7	45	37	46
rsenal	42	10	7	4	56	37	7	4	10	34	45	45
urnley	42	14	3	4	46	23	3	7	11	25	41	44
est Bromwich Albion	42	9	6	6	43	35	7	5	9	27	26	43
eicester City	42	9	4	8	33	27	7	7	7	28	31	43
heffield United	42	10	6	5	35	22	6	5	10	26	42	43
ottingham Forest	42	9	5	7	34	24	7	4	10	30	44	41
est Ham United	**42**	**8**	**7**	**6**	**45**	**38**	**6**	**5**	**10**	**24**	**36**	**40**
ulham	42	11	8	2	45	23	2	5	14	13	42	39
olverhampton Wanderers	42	6	9	6	36	34	6	6	9	34	46	39
toke City	42	9	6	6	49	33	5	4	12	28	45	38
lackpool	42	8	6	7	26	29	5	3	13	26	44	35
ston Villa	42	8	6	7	35	29	3	6	12	27	42	34
irmingham City	42	7	7	7	33	32	4	0	17	21	60	29
olton Wanderers	42	6	5	10	30	35	4	3	14	18	45	28
oswich Town	42	9	3	9	38	45	0	4	17	18	76	25

Season **1963-64** Football League - Division One
Match Details

Manager **Ron Greenwood**   Final League Position **14/22**

	Date		Competition	Venue	Opponents	Results		Attendance	Position	Scorers
1	Aug 24	Sat	Div 1	A	Chelsea	D	0-0	46,298		
2	Aug 26	Mon	Div 1	H	Blackpool	W	3-1	25,533	2	Boyce, Brabrook, Peters
3	Aug 30	Fri	Div 1	H	Ipswich Town	D	2-2	27,599	2	Boyce, Byrne
4	Sep 2	Mon	Div 1	A	Blackpool	W	1-0	18,407	1	Byrne [pen]
5	Sep 7	Sat	Div 1	H	Sheffield United	L	2-3	23,837	5	Boyce, Byrne
6	Sep 9	Mon	Div 1	H	Nottingham Forest	L	0-2	26,282	9	
7	Sep 14	Sat	Div 1	A	Liverpool	W	2-1	45,497	9	Hurst, Peters
8	Sep 17	Tue	Div 1	A	Nottingham Forest	L	1-3	25,741	10	Byrne
9	Sep 21	Sat	Div 1	H	Aston Villa	L	0-1	20,346	13	
10	Sep 25	W	FLC 2	H	Leyton Orient	W	2-1	11,920		Byrne, Scott
11	Sep 28	Sat	Div 1	A	Tottenham Hotspur	L	0-3	51,667	15	
12	Oct 5	Sat	Div 1	H	Wolverhampton Wanderers	D	1-1	21,409	18	Byrne
13	Oct 7	Mon	Div 1	H	Burnley	D	1-1	21,372	14	Sealey
14	Oct 12	Sat	Div 1	A	Sheffield Wednesday	L	0-3	22,810	16	
15	Oct 16	Wed	FLC 3	A	Aston Villa	W	2-0	11,194		Bond, Britt
16	Oct 19	Sat	Div 1	H	Everton	W	4-2	25,163	14	Brabrook 2, Boyce, Hurst
17	Oct 26	Sat	Div 1	A	Manchester United	W	1-0	46,333	13	Britt
18	Nov 2	Sat	Div 1	H	West Bromwich Albion	W	4-2	22,882	13	Hurst 2 [1 pen], Brabrook, Simpson (og)
19	Nov 9	Sat	Div 1	A	Arsenal	D	3-3	52,852	13	Byrne 2, Peters
20	Nov 16	Sat	Div 1	H	Leicester City	D	2-2	23,073	13	Britt, Hurst
21	Nov 19	Sat	FLC 4	A	Swindon Town	D	3-3	12,050		Boyce, Brabrook, Hurst
22	Nov 23	Sat	Div 1	A	Bolton Wanderers	D	1-1	11,041	12	Hurst
23	Nov 25	Mon	FLC 4 Rep	H	Swindon Town	W	4-1	15,754		Hurst, Brabrook, Byrne, Scott
24	Nov 30	Sat	Div 1	H	Fulham	D	1-1	23,175	13	Moore
25	Dec 7	Sat	Div 1	A	Birmingham City	L	1-2	15,483	14	Britt
26	Dec 14	Sat	Div 1	H	Chelsea	D	2-2	21,950	13	Byrne 2
27	Dec 16	Mon	FLC 5	H	Workington	W	6-0	10,160		Byrne 3, Boyce, Hurst, Scott
28	Dec 20	Fri	Div 1	A	Ipswich Town	L	2-3	11,730	13	Brabrook, Byrne [pen]
29	Dec 26	Thu	Div 1	H	Blackburn Rovers	L	2-8	20,500	16	Byrne 2
30	Dec 28	Sat	Div 1	A	Blackburn Rovers	W	3-1	28,990	16	Byrne 2, Hurst
31	Jan 4	Sat	FAC 3	H	Charlton Athletic	W	3-0	34,155		Brabrook, Hurst, Sissons
32	Jan 11	Sat	Div 1	A	Sheffield United	L	1-2	18,733	17	Sissons
33	Jan 18	Sat	Div 1	H	Liverpool	W	1-0	25,546	15	Byrne
34	Jan 25	Sat	FAC 4	A	Leyton Orient	D	1-1	34,345		Brabrook
35	Jan 29	Wed	FAC 4 Rep	H	Leyton Orient	W	3-0	35,383		Hurst 2, Byrne
36	Feb 1	Sat	Div 1	A	Aston Villa	D	2-2	16,721	15	Hurst 2
37	Feb 5	Wed	FLC SF:1	A	Leicester City	L	3-4	14,087		Hurst 2, Sealey,
38	Feb 8	Sat	Div 1	H	Tottenham Hotspur	W	4-0	36,838	14	Boyce, Byrne, Hurst Sissons
39	Feb 15	Sat	FAC 5	A	Swindon Town	W	3-1	28,582		Hurst 2, Byrne
40	Feb 17	Mon	Div 1	A	Wolverhampton Wanderers	W	2-0	14,455	14	Byrne, Hurst
41	Feb 22	Sat	Div 1	H	Sheffield Wednesday	W	4-3	24,578	14	Byrne 3 [1 pen], Hurst
42	Feb 29	Sat	FAC QF	H	Burnley	W	3-2	36,651		Byrne 2, Sissons
43	Mar 3	Tue	Div 1	A	Burnley	L	1-3	14,428	14	Byrne
44	Mar 7	Sat	Div 1	H	Manchester United	L	0-2	27,177	14	
45	Mar 14	Sat	FAC SF	N*	Manchester United	W	3-1	65,000		Boyce 2, Hurst
46	Mar 18	Wed	Div 1	A	Leicester City	D	2-2	11,908	15	Burkett, Hugo
47	Mar 21	Sat	Div 1	H	Arsenal	D	1-1	28,170	15	Hurst
48	Mar 23	Mon	FLC SF:2	H	Leicester City	L	0-2	27,329		
49	Mar 27	Fri	Div 1	H	Stoke City	W	4-1	29,484	13	Boyce, Brabrook. Byrne, Moore
50	Mar 28	Sat	Div 1	A	West Bromwich Albion	W	1-0	15,444	12	Hugo
51	Mar 31	Tue	Div 1	A	Stoke City	L	0-3	25,008	13	
52	Apr 4	Sat	Div 1	H	Bolton Wanderers	L	2-3	19,398	14	Byrne, Sealey
53	Apr 11	Sat	Div 1	A	Fulham	L	0-2	22,020	15	
54	Apr 17	Fri	Div 1	H	Birmingham City	W	5-0	22,106	14	Brabrook 2, Byrne, Hurst, Sissons
55	Apr 25	Sat	Div 1	A	Everton	L	0-2	33,090	14	
56	May 2	Sat	FAC F	N**	Preston North End	W	3-2	100,000		Boyce, Hurst, Sissons

N* Played at Hillsborough, Sheffield   N** Played at Wembley Stadium, London

Team Line-Ups

BENNETT Peter	BICKLES Dave	BOND John	BOVINGTON Eddie	BOYCE Ron	BRABROOK Peter	BRITT Martin	BROWN Ken	BURKETT Jack	BYRNE Johnny	CHARLES John	DEAR Brian	DICKIE Alan	HUGO Roger	HURST Geoff	KIRKUP Joe	MOORE Bobby	PETERS Martin	SCOTT Tony	SEALEY Alan	SISSONS John	STANDEN Jim	
				8	7		5	3	9					10	2	6	4	11			1	1
				8	7		5	3	9					10	2	6	4	11			1	2
				8	7		5	3	9					10	2	6	4	11			1	3
				8	7		5	3	9					10	2	6	4	11			1	4
				8	7		5	3	9					10	2	6	4	11			1	5
				8	7		5	3	9					11	2	6	4		10		1	6
	5			8	7			3	9		11			10	2	6	4				1	7
	5			8	7			3	9		11			10	2	6	4				1	8
			4	8	7			3	9		11			10	2	5	6				1	9
	5		4	8				3	10						2	6	9	11	7		1	10
			4	8			5	3	10						2	6	9	11	7		1	11
			4	8			5	3	10						2	6	9	11	7		1	12
			4	8			5	3	10						2	6	9	11	7		1	13
			4	8	7		5	3							2	6		11	9	10	1	14
	2			8	11	9	5	3						10		6	4		7		1	15
	2			8	11	9	5	3						10		6	4		7		1	16
	2			8	11	9	5	3						10		6	4		7		1	17
	2			8	11	9	5	3						10		6	4		7		1	18
	2			8	11		5	3	9					10		6	4		7		1	19
	2			8	11	9	5	3						10		6	4		7		1	20
	2			8	11	9	5	3	6					10			4		7		1	21
	2			8	11	9	5	3						10		6	4		7		1	22
	2			8	11		5	3	9	4				10		6		7			1	23
	2			8	11	9	5	3	7					10		6					1	24
	2			8	7	9	5	3	11					10		6	4				1	25
	2			8	11		5	3	9					10		6	4	7			1	26
	2		4	8	7		5	3	9					10		6		11			1	27
	2			8	7		5	3	9					10		6	4			11	1	28
	2			8	7		5	3	9					10		6	4			11	1	29
	2		4	8	7		5	3	9					10		6				11	1	30
	2		4	8	7		5	3	9					10		6				11	1	31
	2		4	8	7		5	3	9					10		6				11	1	32
	2		4	8	7		5	3	9					10		6				11	1	33
	2		4	8	7		5	3	9					10		6				11	1	34
	2		4	8	7		5	3	9					10		6				11	1	35
	2		4	8	7		5	3	9					10		6				11	1	36
	2			8	11		5	3	9					10		6	4		7		1	37
	2		4	8	7		5	3	9					10		6				11	1	38
	2		4	8	7		5	3	9					10		6				11	1	39
	3		4	8	7				9					10	2	6	5			11	1	40
	2		4	8	7		5	3	9					10		6				11	1	41
	2		4	8	7		5	3	9					10		6				11	1	42
			4	8	11			3	9					10	2	6	5		7		1	43
	2		4	8	7		5	3						10		6				11	1	44
	2		4	8	7		5	3	9					10		6				11	1	45
	2		4	8	11		5	3					10	9		6			7		1	46
	2		4	8	7		5	3	9					10		6				11	1	47
	2		4	8	7		5	3	9					10		6				11	1	48
	2		4	8	7		5	3	9					10		6			11			49
				8	7		5	3	9			1	10		2	6	4		11			50
	3		4	8			5		9			1	11	10	2	6			7			51
	2		4		7			3	9					10		6	5		11		1	52
	2		4	8	7	9	5	3						10		6				11	1	53
			4	8	7		5	3	9					10	2	6				11	1	54
	2		4	8	7	9	5	3						10		6				11	1	55
	2		4	8	7		5	3	9					10		6				11	1	56

1964-65
Story of the season

The annual **Charity Shield** match was played at Anfield, where West Ham and Liverpool **shared the trophy** after a 2–2 draw.

After winning 2–1 at Fulham on the opening day there was a good attendance of 37,298 at Upton Park for the visit of Manchester United. The FA Cup was paraded around the pitch beforehand and this set the mood for the Hammers to win 3–1. The big London derby at home to Tottenham was won 3–2, with Johnny Byrne scoring all three goals. Now playing in the European Cup Winners' Cup, the team travelled to Belgium where they won 1–0; in the return at Upton Park it finished 1–1.

The League Cup brought a dismal 4–1 defeat at Sunderland but in November West Ham were the pride of London, winning 3–0 at both Arsenal and Chelsea. European tie beckoned and after beating Sparta Prague 2–0 at home the Hammers progressed on aggregate, having lost 2–1 in Czechoslovakia. The FA Cup began with a thrilling tie at home against Birmingham City – the Hammers were losing 2–0 but fought back to win 4–2. The next round brought a disappointing 1–0 home defeat against Chelsea.

Back in Europe, bustling inside-forward Brian Dear scored in the 2–1 win at Lausanne and netted two more in a 4–3 victory in the return leg with the Swiss team.

Appearances & Goals 1964-65

	League		FA Cup		League Cup		Europe		Other		Total	
	Starts	Goals	Starts	Goals	Starts	Goals	Starts	Goals	Starts	Goals	Starts	Goals
BENNETT Peter	1	0	0	0	0	0	0	0	0	0	1	0
BICKLES Dave	2	0	0	0	0	0	0	0	0	0	2	0
BOND John	29	1	2	0	1	0	4	1	1	0	37	2
BOVINGTON Eddie	33	0	2	0	1	0	4	0	1	0	41	0
BOYCE Ron	41	4	2	0	1	0	9	1	1	0	54	5
BRABROOK Peter	22	3	0	0	1	1	1	0	1	0	25	4
BROWN Ken	33	1	2	0	1	0	9	0	1	0	46	1
BURKETT Jack	24	0	0	0	1	0	5	0	1	0	31	0
BYRNE Johnny	34	25	2	1	1	0	7	3	1	1	45	30
CHARLES John	1	0	0	0	0	0	0	0	0	0	1	0
DAWKINS Trevor	1	0	0	0	0	0	0	0	0	0	1	0
DEAR Brian	10	10	0	0	0	0	5	4	0	0	15	14
DICKIE Alan	0	0	0	0	0	0	1	0	0	0	1	0
HURST Geoff	42	17	1	2	1	0	9	0	1	1	54	20
KIRKUP Joe	15	2	1	0	0	0	5	0	0	0	21	2
MOORE Bobby	28	1	0	0	0	0	7	0	1	0	36	1
PETERS Martin	35	5	2	0	1	0	9	1	0	0	47	6
PRESLAND Eddie	4	1	0	0	0	0	0	0	0	0	4	1
SCOTT Tony	6	0	2	0	0	0	0	0	0	0	8	0
SEALEY Alan	21	2	2	0	0	0	7	3	0	0	30	5
SISSONS John	38	8	2	1	1	0	9	2	1	0	51	11
STANDEN Jim	42	0	2	0	1	0	8	0	1	0	54	0
own goal		2								1		
Totals	**462**	**82**	**22**	**4**	**11**	**1**	**99**	**16**	**11**	**2**	**605**	**105**

* Other = Charity Shield

he semi-final with Real Zaragoza ended 2–1 in the
ammers favour and after drawing 1–1 in Spain they were
ow in the final, where they would meet the German side
SV Munich at Wembley.

rian Dear was on form – against West Bromwich Albion
home he scored five goals in 20 minutes as the Hammers
on 6–1. The league campaign ended with a 2–1 win
gainst Blackpool, which ensured a respectable ninth-place
nish. Three weeks later a 100,000-strong crowd at
embley witnessed one of the greatest club matches in
urope. An exciting match saw West Ham win the Cup
inners' Cup after beating TSV Munich 2–0, with two
oals from Alan Sealey. Captain Bobby Moore collected the
ophy as the Hammers anthem 'Bubbles' rang round the
adium.

ALAN SEALEY

**Sealey began his career at Leyton Orient in
1960 but only played four games for them
before being transferred to West Ham in
March 1961.**

In April he made his debut at Leicester, where
the Hammers suffered a 5–1 defeat. Alan
became a frequent member of the Hammers
attack, playing at centre-forward before
manager Ron Greenwood switched him to the
wing. He came to the fore in the European
campaign in 1965; after scoring in an earlier
round he became a hero when scoring the
two goals in the Cup Winners' Cup Final
against TSV Munich.

In July of that year a freak training-ground
incident saw him suffer a broken leg as he fell
over a wooden bench. This virtually ended his
West Ham career and after 128 appearances
he joined Plymouth Argyle in November 1967.
Playing in just four games for the Devon club
he then continued playing for non-league
sides Romford and Bedford Town. After
retiring he worked with his family in the
bookmaking business but sadly passed away
at the early age of 53 in February 1996. His
nephew Les Sealey made a handful of
appearances for the Hammers at the end of
the century.

ootball League - Division One
inal Table 1964-65

	P	HOME					AWAY					Pts
		W	D	L	F	A	W	D	L	F	A	
anchester United	42	16	4	1	52	13	10	5	6	37	26	61
eds United	42	16	3	2	53	23	10	6	5	30	29	61
elsea	42	15	2	4	48	19	9	6	6	41	35	56
erton	42	9	10	2	37	22	8	5	8	32	38	49
ttingham Forest	42	10	7	4	45	33	7	6	8	26	34	47
ttenham Hotspur	42	18	3	0	65	20	1	4	16	22	51	45
verpool	42	12	5	4	42	33	5	5	11	25	40	44
effield Wednesday	42	13	5	3	37	15	3	6	12	20	40	43
est Ham United	**42**	**14**	**2**	**5**	**48**	**25**	**5**	**2**	**14**	**34**	**46**	**42**
ackburn Rovers	42	12	2	7	46	33	4	8	9	37	46	42
oke City	42	11	4	6	40	27	5	6	10	27	39	42
rnley	42	9	9	3	39	26	7	1	13	31	44	42
senal	42	11	5	5	42	31	6	2	13	27	44	41
est Bromwich Albion	42	10	5	6	45	25	3	8	10	25	40	39
nderland	42	12	6	3	45	26	2	3	16	19	48	37
ton Villa	42	14	1	6	36	24	2	4	15	21	58	37
ackpool	42	9	7	5	41	28	3	4	14	26	50	35
cester City	42	9	6	6	43	36	2	7	12	26	49	35
effield United	42	7	5	9	30	29	5	6	10	20	35	35
ham	42	10	5	6	44	32	1	7	13	16	46	34
lverhampton Wanderers	42	8	2	11	33	36	5	2	14	26	53	30
rmingham City	42	6	8	7	36	40	2	3	16	28	56	27

Season **1964-65** Football League - Division One
Match Details

Manager **Ron Greenwood**   Final League Position **9/22**

	Date		Competition	Venue	Opponents		Results	Attendance	Position	Scorers
1	Aug 15	Sat	C Shield	A	Liverpool	D	2-2	38,858		Byrne, Hurst
2	Aug 22	Sat	Div 1	A	Fulham	W	2-1	31,218	2	Byrne, Sissons
3	Aug 24	Mon	Div 1	H	Manchester United	W	3-1	37,298	1	Byrne, Hurst, Sissons
4	Aug 28	Fri	Div 1	H	Nottingham Forest	L	2-3	26,852	3	Byrne [pen], Sissons
5	Sep 2	Wed	Div 1	A	Manchester United	L	1-3	45,415	14	Stiles (og)
6	Sep 5	Sat	Div 1	A	Stoke City	L	1-3	26,886	17	Byrne
7	Sep 7	Mon	Div 1	H	Wolverhampton Wanderers	W	5-0	26,879	10	Hurst 2, Byrne [pen], Moore, Sissons
8	Sep 12	Sat	Div 1	H	Tottenham Hotspur	W	3-2	36,730	9	Byrne 3
9	Sep 14	Mon	Div 1	A	Wolverhampton Wanderers	L	3-4	19,405	9	Brabrook, Byrne [pen], Harris (og)
10	Sep 19	Sat	Div 1	A	Burnley	L	2-3	13,541	13	Boyce, Byrne
11	Sep 23	Wed	ECWC 1:1	A	La Gantoise (Belguim)	W	1-0	18,000		Boyce
12	Sep 26	Sat	Div 1	H	Sheffield United	W	3-1	22,526	12	Byrne 2 [1 pen], Sissons
13	Sep 30	Wed	FLC 2	A	Sunderland	L	1-4	22,382		Brabrook
14	Oct 3	Sat	Div 1	A	Everton	D	1-1	45,430	12	Byrne
15	Oct 7	Wed	ECWC 1:2	H	La Gantoise (Belguim)	D	1-1	24,000		Byrne
16	Oct 10	Sat	Div 1	H	Aston Villa	W	3-0	20,703	8	Boyce, Byrne, Peters
17	Oct 17	Sat	Div 1	A	Liverpool	D	2-2	36,029	11	Hurst 2
18	Oct 24	Sat	Div 1	H	Sheffield Wednesday	L	1-2	22,795	14	Brabrook
19	Oct 31	Sat	Div 1	A	Blackpool	W	2-1	14,383	12	Brabrook, Hurst
20	Nov 7	Sat	Div 1	H	Blackburn Rovers	D	1-1	22,725	12	Sissons
21	Nov 14	Sat	Div 1	A	Arsenal	W	3-0	36,026	7	Byrne, Hurst, Peters
22	Nov 21	Sat	Div 1	H	Leeds United	W	3-1	28,163	6	Byrne, Kirkup, Peters
23	Nov 25	Wed	ECWC 2:1	H	Spartak Prague (Czechoslovakia)	W	2-0	27,590		Bond, Sealey
24	Nov 28	Sat	Div 1	A	Chelsea	W	3-0	44,204	6	Hurst, Peters, Sealey
25	Dec 5	Sat	Div 1	H	Leicester City	D	0-0	20,515	6	
26	Dec 9	Wed	ECWC 2:2	A	Spartak Prague (Czechoslovakia)	L	1-2	45,000		Sissons
27	Dec 12	Sat	Div 1	H	Fulham	W	2-0	21,985	4	Byrne 2
28	Dec 19	Sat	Div 1	A	Nottingham Forest	L	2-3	20,009	5	Byrne, Hurst
29	Dec 26	Sat	Div 1	A	Birmingham City	L	1-2	23,324	7	Hurst
30	Dec 28	Mon	Div 1	H	Birmingham City	W	2-1	23,855	5	Byrne [pen], Kirkup
31	Jan 2	Sat	Div 1	H	Stoke City	L	0-1	23,913	7	
32	Jan 9	Sat	FAC 3	H	Birmingham City	W	4-2	31,056		Hurst 2, Byrne, Sissons
33	Jan 16	Sat	Div 1	A	Tottenham Hotspur	L	2-3	50,054	7	Byrne, Sissons
34	Jan 23	Sat	Div 1	H	Burnley	W	3-2	25,490	5	Bond, Boyce, Byrne
35	Jan 30	Sat	FAC 4	H	Chelsea	L	0-1	37,000		
36	Feb 6	Sat	Div 1	A	Sheffield United	L	1-2	16,264	7	Sealey
37	Feb 13	Sat	Div 1	H	Everton	L	0-1	25,163	10	
38	Feb 20	Sat	Div 1	A	Sunderland	L	2-3	32,885	11	Byrne, Hurst
39	Feb 27	Sat	Div 1	H	Liverpool	W	2-1	25,780	9	Hurst, Presland
40	Mar 6	Sat	Div 1	A	Sheffield Wednesday	L	0-2	14,136	10	
41	Mar 13	Sat	Div 1	H	Sunderland	L	2-3	23,218	12	Dear 2
42	Mar 16	Tue	ECWC 3:1	A	Lausanne Sports (Switzerland)	W	2-1	20,000		Byrne, Dear
43	Mar 20	Sat	Div 1	A	Blackburn Rovers	L	0-4	8,990	13	
44	Mar 23	Tue	ECWC 3:2	H	Lausanne Sports (Switzerland)	W	4-3	31,780		Dear 2, Peters, Tacchella (og)
45	Mar 27	Sat	Div 1	H	Arsenal	W	2-1	24,665	11	Byrne [pen], Hurst
46	Mar 31	Wed	Div 1	A	Aston Villa	W	3-2	19,966	9	Byrne, Dear, Hurst
47	Apr 3	Sat	Div 1	A	Leeds United	L	1-2	41,918	10	Dear
48	Apr 7	Wed	ECWC SF:1	H	Real Zaragoza (Spain)	W	2-1	35,086		Byrne, Dear
49	Apr 12	Mon	Div 1	H	Chelsea	W	3-2	33,288	9	Hurst 2, Sissons
50	Apr 16	Fri	Div 1	H	West Bromwich Albion	W	6-1	27,710	7	Dear 5, Peters
51	Apr 17	Sat	Div 1	A	Leicester City	L	0-1	15,888	8	
52	Apr 19	Mon	Div 1	A	West Bromwich Albion	L	2-4	13,713	10	Boyce, Hurst
53	Apr 23	Fri	Div 1	H	Blackpool	W	2-1	22,762	9	Brown, Dear
54	Apr 28	Fri	ECWC SF:2	A	Real Zaragoza (Spain)	D	1-1	28,000		Sissons
55	May 19	Wed	ECWC F	N*	TSV Munchen 1860 (Germany)	W	2-0	97,974		Sealey 2

C Shield = Charity Shield   * Played at Wembley Stadium, London

Team Line-Ups

BENNETT Peter	BICKLES Dave	BOND John	BOVINGTON Eddie	BOYCE Ron	BRABROOK Peter	BROWN Ken	BURKETT Jack	BYRNE Johnny	CHARLES John	DAWKINS Trevor	DEAR Brian	DICKIE Alan	HURST Geoff	KIRKUP Joe	MOORE Bobby	PETERS Martin	PRESLAND Eddie	SCOTT Tony	SEALEY Alan	SISSONS John	STANDEN Jim	
		2	4	8	7	5	3	9					10		6					11	1	1
		2	4	8	7	5	3	9					10		6					11	1	2
		2	4	8	7	5	3	9					10		6					11	1	3
		2	4	8	7	5	3	9					10		6					11	1	4
		2	4	8	7	5	3	9					10		6					11	1	5
		2	4	8	7	5	3	9					10		6					11	1	6
		2	4	8			3	9					10		6	5			7	11	1	7
		2	4	8			3	9					10		6	5			7	11	1	8
		2	4	8	11		3	9					10		6	5			7		1	9
		2	4	8			3	9					10		6	5			7	11	1	10
		2	4	8		5		9					10		6	3			7	11	1	11
		2	4	8	7	5		9					10		6	3				11	1	12
		2	4	8	7	5	3	9					10		6					11	1	13
		2	4	8	7	5	3	9					10			6				11	1	14
		2	4	8	7	5		9				1	10		6	3				11		15
		2	4	8	7	5		9					10		6	3				11	1	16
		2	4	8	7	5		9					10		6	3				11	1	17
		2	4	8	7	5		9					10		6	3				11	1	18
		2	4	8	7	5							9		6	3	11			10	1	19
		2	4	8	7	5	3	9					10		6					11	1	20
		2	4	8		5	3	9					10		6				7	11	1	21
			4	8		5	3	9					10	2	6				7	11	1	22
		2	4	8		5	3	9					10		6				7	11	1	23
		2	4	8		5	3	9					10		6				7	11	1	24
		2	4	8		5	3	9					10		6				7	11	1	25
		2	4	8		5	3	9					10		6				7	11	1	26
		2	4	8	7	5	3	9					10		6					11	1	27
		2	4	8	7	5	3	9					10		6					11	1	28
		2	4	8	7	5	3	9					10		6					11	1	29
			4	6		5		9					8	2		3		11	7	10	1	30
		3	4	8	7	5		9					10	2	6					11	1	31
		2	4	6		5		9					8			3		11	7	10	1	32
		2	4	6		5		9					8			3	11	7		10	1	33
		2	4	6		5		9					8			3		11	7	10	1	34
			4	8		5		9						2	6			11	7	10	1	35
		3	4	8		5		9					10	2	6				7	11	1	36
		2	4	8		5		9					10		6	3			7	11	1	37
		2	4	8		5		9					10		6	3			7	11	1	38
			4	8	7			9					10	2	5	6	3			11	1	39
			4	8	7			9					10	2	5	6	3			11	1	40
			4	8	7						10		9	2	5	6	3			11	1	41
			4			5		9			10		8	2	6	3			7	11	1	42
				8		5			4		10		9	2	6	3		11	7		1	43
			4			5		9			10		8	2	6	3			7	11	1	44
			4			5		9			10		8	2	6	3			7	11	1	45
	5						3	9			10		8	2	6	4			7	11	1	46
				11		5	3	9			10		8	2	6	4			7		1	47
				7		5	3	9			8		10	2	6	4				11	1	48
				8		5	3				10		9	2	6	4			7	11	1	49
	5			8	7		3				10		9	2	6	4				11	1	50
		2		8		5	3				10		9		6	4		11	7		1	51
7				8		5				4	10		9	2	6	3				11	1	52
			4		8	5	3				10		9	2	6				7	11	1	53
				8		5	3				10		9	2	6	4			7	11	1	54
				8		5	3				10		9	2	6	4			7	11	1	55

1965-66
Story of the season

The new season commenced with Sealey, Byrne and Dear all injured. A **3–0 defeat** at West Bromwich Albion on **the opening day paved the way for some dismal early performances** as the team conceded five goals in three successive games against Sheffield United, Liverpool and Leicester City.

By mid-October, after another 5–0 defeat at Nottingham Forest, th Hammers were third from bottom.

There was some joy in the League Cup as West Ham disposed c Bristol Rovers, Mansfield and Rotherham United, while the Europea journey in defence of the Cup Winners' Cup began with West Ha defeating Olympiakos 6–2 on aggregate. Results improved with leagu victories against Everton (3–0) and Newcastle (4–3), Geoff Hur scoring a hat-trick in the latter game. The League Cup saw Grimsb Town knocked out and this brought a semi-final clash with Cardi City. The Bluebirds were no match for the marauding Hammers, wh won 10–3 over two legs. Oldham Athletic were beaten in the FA Cu but in the fourth round, following a replay, Blackburn Rove triumphed 4–1.

March was a busy month: in the league Aston Villa and Blackbur suffered four-goal defeats while in Europe the Hammers be

Appearances & Goals 1965-66

	League			FA Cup			League Cup			Europe			Total		
	Starts	Subs	Goals	Starts	Subs	Goals	Starts	Subs	Goals	Starts	Subs	Goals	Starts	Subs	Goals
BENNETT Peter	7	1	1	0	0	0	2	0	0	0	0	0	9	1	
BICKLES Dave	12	1	0	0	0	0	0	0	0	0	0	0	12	1	
BLOOMFIELD Jimmy	9	1	0	2	0	1	0	0	0	2	0	0	13	1	
BOVINGTON Eddie	31	0	0	4	0	0	9	0	1	4	0	0	48	0	
BOYCE Ron	16	0	2	1	0	0	2	0	0	4	0	0	23	0	
BRABROOK Peter	32	0	8	4	0	1	8	0	2	6	0	1	50	0	
BRITT Martin	10	0	3	0	0	0	4	0	0	0	0	0	14	0	
BROWN Ken	23	0	1	3	0	0	9	0	0	6	0	0	41	0	
BURKETT Jack	19	0	2	4	0	0	4	0	0	2	0	0	29	0	
BURNETT Dennis	24	0	0	4	0	1	6	0	2	2	0	0	36	0	
BYRNE Johnny	23	0	9	3	0	0	6	0	5	5	0	3	37	0	
CHARLES John	25	0	0	0	0	0	7	0	1	4	0	0	36	0	
DAWKINS Trevor	2	0	0	0	0	0	0	0	0	0	0	0	2	0	
DEAR Brian	7	0	1	1	0	0	1	0	0	1	0	0	10	0	
DICKIE Alan	5	0	0	0	0	0	2	0	0	0	0	0	7	0	
HURST Geoff	39	0	23	4	0	4	10	0	11	6	0	2	59	0	
KIRKUP Joe	17	0	1	0	0	0	4	0	0	2	0	0	23	0	
MOORE Bobby	37	0	0	4	0	0	9	0	2	6	0	0	56	0	
PETERS Martin	40	0	11	4	0	0	10	0	3	6	0	3	60	0	
PRESLAND Eddie	2	0	0	0	0	0	0	0	0	0	0	0	2	0	
REDKNAPP Harry	7	0	1	0	0	0	0	0	0	0	0	0	7	0	
SCOTT Tony	2	0	0	0	0	0	0	0	0	0	0	0	2	0	
SISSONS John	36	0	5	2	0	1	9	0	1	4	0	1	51	0	
STANDEN Jim	37	0	0	4	0	0	8	0	0	6	0	0	55	0	
own goal			2												
Totals	462	3	70	44	0	8	110	0	28	66	0	10	682	3	1

Magdeburg 2–1 on aggregate. The League Cup final with West Bromwich Albion, a two-legged affair back then, saw West Ham gain a 2–1 advantage in the first leg at Upton Park, but the Midlands side recovered to win 4–1 in the second leg to lift the cup.

In the Cup Winners' Cup the German side Borussia Dortmund proved to be tough opposition as they won both legs of the semi-final and went through on a 5–2 aggregate. To round off the season to the delight of the home support, Arsenal, Tottenham and Manchester United were all beaten at Upton Park to give a twelfth place finish. It had been a hectic campaign, as in addition to the 42 league games there had been an extra 20 cup ties.

In July 1966 England won the World Cup and all West Ham supporters were proud that Bobby Moore captained the side, Geoff Hurst scored a hat-trick and the other goal came from Martin Peters in the 4–2 victory against West Germany.

Football League - Division One
Final Table 1965-66

	P	HOME					AWAY					Pts
		W	D	L	F	A	W	D	L	F	A	
Liverpool	42	17	2	2	52	15	9	7	5	27	19	61
Leeds United	42	14	4	3	49	15	9	5	7	30	23	55
Burnley	42	15	3	3	45	20	9	4	8	34	27	55
Manchester United	42	12	8	1	50	20	6	7	8	34	39	51
Chelsea	42	11	4	6	30	21	11	3	7	35	32	51
West Bromwich Albion	42	11	6	4	58	34	8	6	7	33	35	50
Leicester City	42	12	4	5	40	28	9	3	9	40	37	49
Tottenham Hotspur	42	11	6	4	55	37	5	6	10	20	29	44
Sheffield United	42	11	6	4	37	25	5	5	11	19	34	43
Stoke City	42	12	6	3	42	22	3	6	12	23	42	42
Everton	42	12	6	3	39	19	3	5	13	17	43	41
West Ham United	42	12	5	4	46	33	3	4	14	24	50	39
Blackpool	42	9	5	7	36	29	5	4	12	19	36	37
Arsenal	42	8	8	5	36	31	4	5	12	26	44	37
Newcastle United	42	10	5	6	26	20	4	4	13	24	43	37
Aston Villa	42	10	3	8	39	34	5	3	13	30	46	36
Sheffield Wednesday	42	11	6	4	35	18	3	2	16	21	48	36
Nottingham Forest	42	11	3	7	31	26	3	5	13	25	46	36
Sunderland	42	13	2	6	36	28	1	6	14	15	44	36
Fulham	42	9	4	8	34	37	5	3	13	33	48	35
Northampton Town	42	8	6	7	31	32	2	7	12	24	60	33
Blackburn Rovers	42	6	1	14	30	36	2	3	16	27	52	20

BOBBY MOORE

Captain of both West Ham and England, Bobby was one of the finest defenders in the world. He was calm and composed in every situation and led by example. As a 17-year-old he made his West Ham debut against Manchester United in September 1958, and by that time had gained 18 England Youth international caps. He led West Ham in 1964 when they won the FA Cup, after which he was named as Footballer of the Year. A year later he was back at Wembley as the Hammers won the European Cup Winners' Cup.

Then in July 1966, at the pinnacle of his career, he captained England when they beat West Germany to win the World Cup. He had earlier gained eight England under-23 caps and after making his full England debut against Peru in 1962 he went on to play in 108 internationals. In January 1967, in the wake of his World Cup triumph, he was awarded the OBE in the New Year's Honours List. In a glittering career spanning 15 seasons Bobby made a total of 642 appearances for West Ham.

He then joined Fulham, and in 1975 he inspired them to reach the FA Cup final, where he played against his former West Ham team-mates. After 150 games for the West London club he played his final game at Blackburn Rovers in May 1977.

Going into management first in Hong Kong coaching Eastern Athletic. Returning to England, he had spells as manager at Oxford City and Southend United before working for the Sunday Sport newspaper and later as a reporter for the Capitol Gold radio station. On 24 February 1993 the football world was shocked to hear that he had passed away aged 51.

Season **1965-66** Football League - Division One
Match Details

Manager **Ron Greenwood**   Final League Position **12/22**

#	Date		Competition	Venue	Opponents	Results		Attendance	Position	Scorers
1	Aug 21	Sat	Div 1	A	West Bromwich Albion	L	0-3	19,956	20	
2	Aug 23	Mon	Div 1	H	Sunderland	D	1-1	34,795	15	Peters
3	Aug 28	Sat	Div 1	H	Leeds United	W	2-1	27,995	14	Hurst, Peters
4	Sep 1	Wed	Div 1	A	Sunderland	L	1-2	48,626	17	Hurst
5	Sep 4	Sat	Div 1	A	Sheffield United	L	3-5	15,796	18	Byrne, Hurst, Kirkup
6	Sep 6	Mon	Div 1	H	Liverpool	L	1-5	32,144	20	Peters
7	Sep 11	Sat	Div 1	H	Leicester City	L	2-5	21,492	20	Hurst 2 [1 pen]
8	Sep 15	Wed	Div 1	A	Liverpool	D	1-1	44,553	20	Hurst
9	Sep 18	Sat	Div 1	A	Blackburn Rovers	W	2-1	10,178	18	Peters 2
10	Sep 21	Tue	FLC 2	A	Bristol Rovers	D	3-3	18,354		Hurst 2, Byrne
11	Sep 25	Sat	Div 1	H	Blackpool	D	1-1	20,740	18	Hurst
12	Sep 29	Wed	FLC 2 Rep	H	Bristol Rovers	W	3-2	13,160		Byrne 2, Hurst
13	Oct 2	Sat	Div 1	A	Fulham	L	0-3	22,310	19	
14	Oct 9	Sat	Div 1	A	Nottingham Forest	L	0-5	19,262	20	
15	Oct 13	Wed	FLC 3	H	Mansfield Town	W	4-0	11,590		Hurst 2, Brabrook, Burnett
16	Oct 16	Sat	Div 1	H	Sheffield Wednesday	W	4-2	20,828	20	Britt 2, Peters, Sissons
17	Oct 23	Sat	Div 1	A	Northampton Town	L	1-2	15,367	20	Brown
18	Oct 30	Sat	Div 1	H	Stoke City	D	0-0	21,545	19	
19	Nov 3	Wed	FLC 4	A	Rotherham United	W	2-1	13,902		Hurst, Moore
20	Nov 6	Sat	Div 1	A	Burnley	L	1-3	17,100	21	Britt
21	Nov 13	Sat	Div 1	H	Chelsea	W	2-1	31,553	20	Brabrook, Peters
22	Nov 17	Wed	FLC 5	A	Grimsby Town	D	2-2	16,281		Charles, Hurst
23	Nov 20	Sat	Div 1	A	Arsenal	L	2-3	35,855	20	Hurst, Peters
24	Nov 24	Wed	ECWC 2:1	H	Olympiakos (Greece)	W	4-0	27,270		Hurst 2, Brabrook, Byrne
25	Nov 27	Sat	Div 1	H	Everton	W	3-0	21,971	19	Sissons 2, Brabrook
26	Dec 1	Wed	ECWC 2:2	A	Olympiakos (Greece)	D	2-2	40,000		Peters 2
27	Dec 4	Sat	Div 1	A	Manchester United	D	0-0	33,172	17	
28	Dec 11	Sat	Div 1	H	Newcastle United	W	4-3	23,758	17	Hurst 3, Brabrook
29	Dec 15	Wed	FLC 5 Rep	H	Grimsby Town	W	1-0	17,500		Hurst
30	Dec 18	Sat	Div 1	A	Sheffield Wednesday	D	0-0	12,175	17	
31	Dec 20	Mon	FLC SF:1	H	Cardiff City	W	5-2	19,900		Bovington, Brabrook, Byrne, Hurst, Sissons
32	Jan 1	Sat	Div 1	H	Nottingham Forest	L	0-3	25,131	17	
33	Jan 8	Sat	Div 1	A	Newcastle United	L	1-2	31,754	17	Byrne
34	Jan 11	Tue	Div 1	A	Everton	D	2-2	29,915	17	Hurst, Peters
35	Jan 15	Sat	Div 1	H	Northampton Town	D	1-1	20,745	17	Hurst [pen]
36	Jan 22	Sat	FA 3	A	Oldham Athletic	D	2-2	25,035		Burnett, Hurst
37	Jan 24	Mon	FA 3 Rep	H	Oldham Athletic	W	2-1	35,330		Brabrook, Hurst
38	Jan 29	Sat	Div 1	H	West Bromwich Albion	W	4-0	25,518	17	Hurst 2 [1 pen], Peters, Sissons
39	Feb 2	Wed	FLC SF:2	A	Cardiff City	W	5-1	14,315		Hurst 2, Peters 2, Burnett
40	Feb 5	Sat	Div 1	A	Leeds United	L	0-5	33,112	18	
41	Feb 7	Mon	Div 1	A	Aston Villa	W	2-1	13,450	15	Hurst, Sissons
42	Feb 12	Sat	FAC 4	H	Blackburn Rovers	D	3-3	32,350		Bloomfield, Hurst, Sissons
43	Feb 16	Wed	FAC 4 Rep	A	Blackburn Rovers	L	1-4	25,547		Hurst
44	Feb 19	Sat	Div 1	H	Sheffield United	W	4-0	21,238	14	Brabrook, Hurst, Peters, Matthewson (og)
45	Mar 2	Wed	ECWC 3:1	H	FC Magdeburg (East Germany)	W	1-0	30,620		Byrne
46	Mar 5	Sat	Div 1	H	Aston Villa	W	4-2	22,074	14	Brabrook, Burkett, Byrne, Hurst
47	Mar 9	Wed	FLC F:1	H	West Bromwich Albion	W	2-1	28,341		Byrne, Moore
48	Mar 12	Sat	Div 1	H	Blackburn Rovers	W	4-1	18,686	13	Brabrook, Burkett, Dear, Hurst
49	Mar 16	Wed	ECWC 3:2	A	FC Magdeburg (East Germany)	D	1-1	35,000		Sisons
50	Mar 19	Sat	Div 1	A	Blackpool	L	1-2	10,559	13	Boyce
51	Mar 23	Wed	FLC F:2	A	West Bromwich Albion	L	1-4	31,925		Peters
52	Mar 26	Sat	Div 1	H	Fulham	L	1-3	18,992	13	Hurst
53	Apr 2	Sat	Div 1	H	Burnley	D	1-1	17,665	12	Brabrook
54	Apr 5	Tue	ECWC SF:1	H	Borussia Dortmund (West Germany)	L	1-2	28,130		Peters
55	Apr 8	Fri	Div 1	A	Tottenham Hotspur	W	4-1	50,635	12	Boyce, Byrne, Hurst, Redknapp
56	Apr 9	Sat	Div 1	A	Chelsea	L	2-6	35,958	12	Bennett, Harris (og)
57	Apr 13	Wed	ECWC SF:2	A	Borussia Dortmund (West Germany)	L	1-3	34,000		Byrne
58	Apr 16	Sat	Div 1	H	Arsenal	W	2-1	26,023	12	Brabrook, Byrne [pen]
59	Apr 25	Mon	Div 1	H	Tottenham Hotspur	W	2-0	32,232	12	Byrne 2 [2 pen]
60	Apr 30	Sat	Div 1	H	Manchester United	W	3-2	36,423	11	Hurst 2, Byrne [pen]
61	May 7	Sat	Div 1	A	Stoke City	L	0-1	15,672	12	
62	May 9	Mon	Div 1	A	Leicester City	L	1-2	16,066	12	Byrne

Team Line-Ups

BENNETT Peter	BICKLES Dave	BLOOMFIELD Jimmy	BOVINGTON Eddie	BOYCE Ron	BRABROOK Peter	BRITT Martin	BROWN Ken	BURKETT Jack	BURNETT Dennis	BYRNE Johnny	CHARLES John	DAWKINS Trevor	DEAR Brian	DICKIE Alan	HURST Geoff	KIRKUP Joe	MOORE Bobby	PETERS Martin	PRESLAND Eddie	REDKNAPP Harry	SCOTT Tony	SISSONS John	STANDEN Jim	
10			5	8	7			3							9	2	6	4				11	1	1
	5			8				3		9				1	10	2	6	4		7		11	1	2
a	5		4					3/a		9					10	2	6	8		7		11	1	3
	5		4							9					10	2	6	8	3	7		11	1	4
	5		4		7					9					10	2	6	8				11	1	5
	5			8	7			3		9					10	2	6	4			11		1	6
			4				5	3							9	2	6	8		7	11	10	1	7
7			4	10				3			5			1	9	2	6	8				11		8
7			4	10				3			5			1	9	2	6	8				11		9
7			4					3		10	5			1	9	2	6	8				11		10
7			4					3		9	5			1	10	2	6	8				11		11
7			4				5	3		10	6			1	9	2		8				11		12
7		8	6				5		2	9	3			1	10			4				11		13
10	a	8	5		11						3/a				9	2	6	4		7			1	14
			4		7	9	5		2		3				10		6	8				11	1	15
			4		7	9	5		2		3				10		6	8				11	1	16
		8			7	9	5		2		3				10		6	4				11	1	17
			4		7	9	5		2		3				10		6	8				11	1	18
			4		7	9	5		2		3				10		6	8				11	1	19
			4		7	9	5		2		3				10		6	8				11	1	20
			4		7	9	5		2		3				10		6	8				11	1	21
			4		7	9	5		2		3				10		6	8				11	1	22
	a		4		7	9	5		2/a		3				10		6	8				11	1	23
			4		7		5			9	3				10	2	6	8				11	1	24
			4		7		5			9	3				10	2	6	8				11	1	25
			4		7		5			9	3				10	2	6	8				11	1	26
			4		7		5			9	3				10	2	6	8				11	1	27
			4		7		5			9	3				10		6	8				11	1	28
			4		7		5			9	3				10	2	6	8				11	1	29
			4		7		5			9	3				10	2	6	8				11	1	30
			4		7		5			9	3				10	2	6	8				11	1	31
			4		7		5			9	3				10	2	6	8				11	1	32
			4		7		5			9	3				10		6	8				11	1	33
			4		7	9	5	3	2				11		10		6	8					1	34
			4		7	9	5	3	2				11		10		6	8					1	35
			4		7		5	3	2	9			11		10		6	8					1	36
			4		7		5	3	2	9					10		6	8				11	1	37
			4		7	9	5	3	2						10		6	8				11	1	38
			4		7	9	5	3	2						10		6	8				11	1	39
			4		7	9	5	3	2						10		6	8				11	1	40
		10	4		7		5	3	2						9		6	8				11	1	41
		10	4		7		5	3	2						9		6	8				11	1	42
		10	4	5	7			3	2	11					9		6	8					1	43
				8	7		5	3	2	9					10		6	4				11	1	44
				8	7		5	3	2	9					10		6	4				11	1	45
			6	8	7		5	3	2	9			11		10			4					1	46
				8	7		5	3	2	9			11		10			4					1	47
		8	4		7		5	3	2		2		10		9		6					11	1	48
			4	8	7		5	3	2						9		6	10				11	1	49
		8		10				3	2	9			7				6	4				11	1	50
			4	8	7		5		2	9					10		6	3				11	1	51
		8	5	10	7			3	2	9							6	4				11	1	52
		8		5	11				2	9	3	4	10				6			7			1	53
		8		5	7			2		9	3		11		10		6	4					1	54
	5		4	8					2	9	3				10		6			7		11	1	55
9	5	8			7			3	2			4	10				6					11	1	56
	11	2		8	7		5			9	3				10		6	4					1	57
	5			8	7				2	9	3				10		6	4				11	1	58
	5			8	7				2	9	3				10		6	4				11	1	59
	5			8	7				2	9	3				10		6	4				11	1	60
	5			8	7				2	9	3				10		6	4				11	1	61
	5		4	8	7				2	9	3				10		6					11	1	62

1966-67
Story of the season

West Ham's **World Cup winning trio** of **Moore, Hurst** and **Peters** received a **tremendous reception** on the opening day but Chelsea spoilt the day with a 2–1 win.

There was great entertainment at Leicester, the home team winning 5–4 after both Brabrook and Hurst had scored twice for the Hammers. Byrne and Hurst were in sparkling form as West Ham had four-goal away wins at Manchester City and Sunderland.

Tottenham, playing in their first ever League Cup tie, were beaten 1–0 at Upton Park and this was followed up in the next round with a fine 3–1 win at Arsenal. Within the space of a week in November the Hammers scored an amazing 17 goals. Fulham were crushed 6–1 at home, with Geoff Hurst scoring four goals; two days later the mighty Leeds United were humbled 7–0 in the League Cup, where both

Appearances & Goals 1966-67

	League			FA Cup			League Cup			Total		
	Starts	Subs	Goals	Starts	Subs	Goals	Starts	Subs	Goals	Starts	Subs	Goals
ANDREW George	2	0	0	0	0	0	0	0	0	2	0	0
BENNETT Peter	7	1	1	0	0	0	1	0	0	8	1	1
BICKLES Dave	8	0	0	2	0	0	0	0	0	10	0	0
BOVINGTON Eddie	28	0	1	2	0	0	4	0	0	34	0	1
BOYCE Ron	37	0	4	1	0	0	5	0	0	43	0	4
BRABROOK Peter	32	0	5	1	0	0	5	0	0	38	0	5
BROWN Ken	18	0	0	0	0	0	6	0	0	24	0	0
BURKETT Jack	11	1	1	2	0	0	2	0	0	15	1	1
BURNETT Dennis	24	2	0	0	0	0	4	0	0	28	2	0
BYRNE Johnny	25	0	11	1	0	0	5	0	2	31	0	13
CHARLES John	31	0	1	0	0	0	4	0	0	35	0	1
DAWKINS Trevor	2	1	0	0	0	0	0	0	0	2	1	0
DEAR Brian	4	1	3	2	0	0	0	0	0	6	1	3
EADIE Doug	2	0	0	0	0	0	0	0	0	2	0	0
HARTLEY Trevor	2	0	0	0	0	0	0	0	0	2	0	0
HEFFER Paul	9	0	0	0	0	0	0	0	0	9	0	0
HOWE Bobby	0	1	0	0	0	0	0	0	0	0	1	0
HURST Geoff	41	0	29	2	0	3	6	0	9	49	0	41
KITCHENER Bill	8	0	0	0	0	0	0	0	0	8	0	0
MACKLEWORTH Colin	3	0	0	0	0	0	0	0	0	3	0	0
MOORE Bobby	40	0	2	2	0	0	6	0	0	48	0	2
PETERS Martin	41	0	14	2	0	0	6	0	2	49	0	16
REDKNAPP Harry	10	2	1	0	0	0	0	0	0	10	2	1
SEALEY Alan	4	0	0	1	0	0	0	0	0	5	0	0
SISSONS John	34	1	7	2	0	0	6	0	3	42	1	10
STANDEN Jim	39	0	0	2	0	0	6	0	0	47	0	0
Totals	**462**	**10**	**80**	**22**	**0**	**4**	**66**	**0**	**16**	**550**	**10**	**100**

issons and Hurst grabbed hat-tricks; finally, a trip to Tottenham gave the Hammers a 4–3 victory. A 3–1 win at Blackpool in the League Cup was followed by another goal glut of 13 goals in three games as an amazing game at Chelsea ended all square at 5–5 and during the Christmas period Blackpool were beaten 4–1 away and 4–0 at home. Going into the New Year there was a dramatic change of fortune. The FA Cup saw the Hammers crash out after losing 3–1 at Swindon Town, while the League Cup semi-final was won by West Bromwich Albion on a 6–2 aggregate. In the league West Ham lost 6–2 at Southampton and 4–0 at Everton. There were three narrow wins in March, but the remaining eight games did not bring a solitary victory, and included a 6–1 home defeat to Manchester United. The alarming slump from Christmas was disappointing, and resulted in a sixteenth placed finish.

Football League - Division One
Final Table 1966-67

	P	HOME					AWAY					Pts
		W	D	L	F	A	W	D	L	F	A	
Manchester United	42	17	4	0	51	13	7	8	6	33	32	60
Nottingham Forest	42	16	4	1	41	13	7	6	8	23	28	56
Tottenham Hotspur	42	15	3	3	44	21	9	5	7	27	27	56
Leeds United	42	15	4	2	41	17	7	7	7	21	25	55
Liverpool	42	12	7	2	36	17	7	6	8	28	30	51
Everton	42	11	4	6	39	22	8	6	7	26	24	48
Arsenal	42	11	6	4	32	20	5	8	8	26	27	46
Leicester City	42	12	4	5	47	28	6	4	11	31	43	44
Chelsea	42	7	9	5	33	29	8	5	8	34	33	44
Sheffield United	42	11	5	5	34	22	5	5	11	18	37	42
Sheffield Wednesday	42	9	7	5	39	19	5	6	10	17	28	41
Stoke City	42	11	5	5	40	21	6	2	13	23	37	41
West Bromwich Albion	42	11	1	9	40	28	5	6	10	37	45	39
Burnley	42	11	4	6	43	28	4	5	12	23	48	39
Manchester City	42	8	9	4	27	25	4	6	11	16	27	39
West Ham United	42	8	6	7	40	31	6	2	13	40	53	36
Sunderland	42	12	3	6	39	26	2	5	14	19	46	36
Fulham	42	8	7	6	49	34	3	5	13	22	49	34
Southampton	42	10	3	8	49	41	4	3	14	25	51	34
Newcastle United	42	9	5	7	24	27	3	4	14	15	54	33
Aston Villa	42	7	5	9	30	33	4	2	15	24	52	29
Blackpool	42	1	5	15	18	36	5	4	12	23	40	21

DENNIS BURNETT

A full-back who made his West Ham debut at Craven Cottage against Fulham in October 1965, Burnett was a capable defender who won a runners-up medal when West Ham lost to West Bromwich Albion in the League Cup final in April 1966.

He will always be remembered for the amazing goal he scored at Oldham in the FA Cup in January 1966. The ball was cleared by Burnett some 80 yards from the Oldham goal and bounced over the goalkeeper into the net.

He made 66 appearances for the Hammers before joining Millwall in August 1967 for a fee of £15,000. During the 1971–72 season he took over the captaincy, and between 1967 and 1973 he missed only three games. He joined Hull City in October 1973 and played 46 matches for the Tigers, scoring two goals. He later returned to Millwall on loan to play in a further six games for them. In all Dennis played in an impressive 293 games for the Lions. In September 1975 he was transferred to Brighton, for whom he made 44 appearances for the Third Division club. He later played for St Louis Stars in the North American Soccer League and in Ireland with Shamrock Rovers.

Going into management, he spent three seasons in Norway until 1981 as manager of SK Haugar. He now enjoys his retirement living on the south coast in Sussex.

Season **1966-67** Football League - Division One
Match Details

Manager **Ron Greenwood**   Final League Position **16/22**

	Date		Competition	Venue	Opponents	Results		Attendance	Position	Scorers
1	Aug 20	Sat	Div 1	H	Chelsea	L	1-2	36,122	17	Byrne
2	Aug 23	Mon	Div 1	A	Arsenal	L	1-2	40,614	48	Byrne
3	Aug 27	Sat	Div 1	A	Leicester City	L	4-5	26,850	20	Brabrook 2, Hurst 2
4	Aug 29	Mon	Div 1	H	Arsenal	D	2-2	34,964	18	Brabrook, Moore
5	Sep 3	Sat	Div 1	H	Liverpool	D	1-1	32,951	19	Hurst
6	Sep 7	Wed	Div 1	A	Manchester City	W	4-1	31,989	17	Hurst 2, Boyce, Sissons
7	Sep 10	Sat	Div 1	A	Stoke City	D	1-1	27,299	19	Hurst
8	Sep 14	Wed	FLC 2	H	Tottenham Hotspur	W	1-0	34,000		Hurst
9	Sep 17	Sat	Div 1	A	Sheffield Wednesday	W	2-0	28,600	14	Boyce, Byrne
10	Sep 24	Sat	Div 1	H	Southampton	D	2-2	32,375	14	Hurst, Peters
11	Oct 1	Sat	Div 1	A	Sunderland	W	4-2	29,227	12	Byrne 2 [1 pen], Hurst, Peters
12	Oct 5	Wed	FLC 3	A	Arsenal	W	3-1	33,647		Hurst 2, Peters
13	Oct 8	Sat	Div 1	H	Everton	L	2-3	32,789	14	Hurst, Peters
14	Oct 15	Sat	Div 1	A	Fulham	L	2-4	34,826	15	Byrne, Hurst
15	Oct 26	Wed	Div 1	H	Nottingham Forest	W	3-1	22,982	12	Hurst 2, Bovington
16	Oct 29	Sat	Div 1	A	Sheffield United	L	1-3	20,579	14	Peters
17	Nov 5	Sat	Div 1	H	Fulham	W	6-1	22,272	13	Hurst 4, Peters 2
18	Nov 7	Mon	FLC 4	H	Leeds United	W	7-0	27,474		Hurst 3, Sissons 3, Peters 1
19	Nov 12	Sat	Div 1	A	Tottenham Hotspur	W	4-3	57,157	11	Brabrook, Byrne, Hurst, Sissons
20	Nov 19	Sat	Div 1	H	Newcastle United	W	3-0	31,240	8	Byrne [pen], Hurst, Peters
21	Nov 26	Sat	Div 1	A	Leeds United	L	1-2	37,382	11	Hurst
22	Dec 3	Sat	Div 1	H	West Bromwich Albion	W	3-0	22,961	10	Dear, Peters [pen], Redknapp
23	Dec 7	Wed	FLC 5	A	Blackpool	W	3-1	15,831		Hurst 2, Byrne
24	Dec 10	Sat	Div 1	A	Burnley	L	2-4	19,512	11	Hurst 2
25	Dec 17	Sat	Div 1	A	Chelsea	D	5-5	47,805	11	Sissons 2, Brabrook, Byrne, Peters
26	Dec 26	Mon	Div 1	A	Blackpool	W	4-1	26,901	11	Byrne, Dear, Hurst, Sissons
27	Dec 27	Tue	Div 1	H	Blackpool	W	4-0	29,417	7	Byrne, Hurst, Moore, Peters
28	Dec 31	Sat	Div 1	H	Leicester City	L	0-1	34,168	10	
29	Jan 7	Sat	Div 1	A	Liverpool	L	0-2	48,518	11	
30	Jan 14	Sat	Div 1	H	Stoke City	D	1-1	33,293	11	Hurst
31	Jan 18	Wed	FLC SF:1	A	West Bromwich Albion	L	0-4	29,796		
32	Jan 21	Sat	Div 1	H	Sheffield Wednesday	W	3-0	29,255	9	Dear, Hurst [pen], Sissons
33	Jan 28	Sat	FAC 3	H	Swindon Town	D	3-3	37,400		Hurst 3
34	Jan 31	Tue	FAC 3 Rep	A	Swindon Town	L	1-3	25,789		Sissons
35	Feb 4	Sat	Div 1	A	Southampton	L	2-6	30,123	11	Burkett, Hurst
36	Feb 8	Wed	FLC SF:2	H	West Bromwich Albion	D	2-2	35,790		Byrne, Hurst
37	Feb 11	Sat	Div 1	H	Sunderland	D	2-2	27,963	11	Byrne, Hurst
38	Feb 25	Sat	Div 1	A	Everton	L	0-4	42,504	13	
39	Mar 18	Sat	Div 1	A	Nottingham Forest	L	0-1	31,426	14	
40	Mar 24	Fri	Div 1	H	Aston Villa	W	2-1	28,715	14	Boyce, Peters
41	Mar 25	Sat	Div 1	H	Burnley	W	3-2	24,425	11	Peters 2, Sissons
42	Mar 28	Tue	Div 1	A	Aston Villa	W	2-0	22,011	10	Hurst 2
43	Apr 1	Sat	Div 1	A	Manchester United	L	0-3	61,308	11	
44	Apr 4	Tue	Div 1	H	Sheffield United	L	0-2	22,008	12	
45	Apr 22	Sat	Div 1	H	Leeds United	L	0-1	25,429	14	
46	Apr 26	Wed	Div 1	A	Newcastle United	L	0-1	38,863	14	
47	Apr 29	Sat	Div 1	A	West Bromwich Albion	L	1-3	23,006	14	Bennett
48	May 6	Sat	Div 1	H	Manchester United	L	1-6	38,424	17	Charles
49	May 9	Tue	Div 1	H	Tottenham Hotspur	L	0-2	35,758	17	
50	May 13	Sat	Div 1	H	Manchester City	D	1-1	17,186	16	Peters

Team Line-Ups

ANDREW George	BENNETT Peter	BICKLES Dave	BOVINGTON Eddie	BOYCE Ron	BRABROOK Peter	BROWN Ken	BURKETT Jack	BURNETT Dennis	BYRNE Johnny	CHARLES John	DAWKINS Trevor	DEAR Brian	EADIE Doug	HARTLEY Trevor	HEFFER Paul	HOWE Bobby	HURST Geoff	KITCHENER Bill	MACKLEWORTH Colin	MOORE Bobby	PETERS Martin	REDKNAPP Harry	SEALEY Alan	SISSONS John	STANDEN Jim	
			6	8	7			2	9	3							10			5	4			11	1	1
			6	8	7			2	9	3							10			5	4			11	1	2
			6	8	7			2	9	3							10			5	4			11	1	3
			6	8	7			2	9	3							10			5	4			11	1	4
	a	5/a		8	7			2	9	3							10			6	4			11	1	5
				8	7	5		2	9	3							10			6	4			11	1	6
				8	7	5		2	9	3	a						10			6	4/a			11	1	7
	9			8	7	5		2		3							10			6	4			11	1	8
				8	7	5		2	9	3							10			6	4			11	1	9
				8	7/a			2	9	3						a	10			6	4			11	1	10
				8	7	5		2	9	3							10			6	4			11	1	11
				8	7	5		2	9	3							10			6	4			11	1	12
				8	7	5		2	9	3							10			6	4			11	1	13
		5		8	7			2	9	3							10			6	4			11	1	14
	9		4	8	7	5	3	2									10			6	11				1	15
	9		4	8	7	5	3/a	2									10			6	11			a	1	16
			2	8	7	5			9	3							10			6	4			11	1	17
			2	8	7	5			9	3							10			6	4			11	1	18
			2	8	7	5			9	3							10			6	4			11	1	19
			2	8	7	5/a		a	9	3							10			6	4			11	1	20
		5	2	8	7				9	3							10			6	4			11	1	21
		5	4	8				2		3		9								6	10	7	11		1	22
			4		7	5		2	9	3							8			6	10			11	1	23
		5	4	8				2	9	3							10			6	7			11	1	24
			2	8	7	5		a	9	3/a							10			6	4			11	1	25
			2	8		5	3		9			7					10			6	4			11	1	26
			2		7	5	3		9			8					10	1		6	4			11		27
				8	7	5	a	2	9	3/a							10			6	4			11	1	28
				8	7	5	3	2	9								10			6	4			11	1	29
				8	7	5	3	2	9								10			6	4			11	1	30
			4		7	5	3	2	9								10			6	8			11	1	31
		5	2		7					3/a	a	9					10			6	4		8	11	1	32
		5	2	8						3		7					10			6	4		9	11	1	33
		5	2	8						3		9		7			10			6	4			11	1	34
			2	8	7	5				3		9					10			6	4			11	1	35
			2	8	7	5				3		9					10			6	4			11	1	36
5			6	8			3	2	9		4						10				11	7			1	37
5	8		3	6	9			2			4						10					7		11	1	38
	9/a			8	7					2					5		10	3		6	4	a		11	1	39
				8	11					2					5		9	3		6	4	7		10	1	40
			4	8						2					5		10	3		6	9	7		11	1	41
			4	8	7					2							10	3		6	9	a		11/a	1	42
			4	8	11					2							10	3		6	9	7			1	43
			4	8						2							10	3	1	6	9	7		11		44
	9		6	8	7					2							10	3		5	4			11	1	45
				8	11		3			2							9			6	4	7		10	1	46
	8		11				3			2		9			5		10			6	4	7			1	47
	8		9					2		3					5		10		1	6	4	7		11		48
		5	4	8				2		3		11					9			6		7	10		1	49
		5		8						2		11	9				10	3		6	4		7		1	50

1967-68
Story of the season

There were **three signings made to strengthen the defence.** Centre-half **John Cushley** arrived from Celtic, and also from Scotland came goalkeeper **Bobby Ferguson**, at £65,000 a record fee for a British goalkeeper. **Most significantly,** right-back **Billy Bonds was signed** from Charlton for £50,000.

During his time at Upton Park he was to become legend and his signing was one of the shrewdest bargains i West Ham's history.

The new boys took time to settle, with only one win in th first six games, which included a 5–1 defeat at Tottenham Results improved with a 5–1 victory at Sunderland followe by another 5–1 win at Walsall in the League Cup. Ther were still defensive worries as after leading 3–0 against Stoke City at home there was a complete collapse, Stok scoring four goals in seven minutes to win 4–3.

Geoff Hurst scored all four goals as Bolton Wanderer were beaten 4–1 in the League Cup, but the Hammer bowed out in the next round after losing 2–0 at Huddersfiel Town. By late December the team were in nineteenth plac but the Christmas period brought three welcome victories

Appearances & Goals 1967-68

	League			FA Cup			League Cup			Total		
	Starts	Subs	Goals	Starts	Subs	Goals	Starts	Subs	Goals	Starts	Subs	Goals
BENNETT Peter	2	1	0	2	0	0	0	0	0	4	1	0
BONDS Billy	37	0	1	3	0	0	2	0	0	42	0	1
BOVINGTON Eddie	6	0	0	0	0	0	0	0	0	6	0	0
BOYCE Ron	38	0	0	1	0	0	3	0	0	42	0	0
BRABROOK Peter	14	0	2	0	0	0	3	0	1	17	0	3
BROOKING Trevor	24	1	9	3	0	0	0	0	0	27	1	9
BURKETT Jack	8	0	0	0	0	0	1	0	0	9	0	0
CHARLES John	19	1	0	0	0	0	3	0	0	22	1	0
CUSHLEY John	27	0	0	3	0	0	3	0	0	33	0	0
DEAR Brian	25	1	14	3	0	2	1	0	0	29	1	16
FERGUSON Bobby	39	0	0	3	0	0	2	0	0	44	0	0
HEFFER Paul	1	0	0	0	0	0	0	0	0	1	0	0
HOWE Bobby	2	0	0	0	0	0	0	0	0	2	0	0
HURST Geoff	38	0	19	3	0	1	3	0	5	44	0	25
KITCHENER Bill	3	0	0	0	0	0	1	0	0	4	0	0
LAMPARD Frank	19	0	0	3	0	0	0	0	0	22	0	0
MOORE Bobby	40	0	4	3	0	0	3	0	0	46	0	4
PETERS Martin	40	0	14	3	0	2	3	0	2	46	0	18
REDKNAPP Harry	28	0	2	0	0	0	2	1	0	30	1	2
SISSONS John	37	0	8	3	0	2	2	0	0	42	0	10
STANDEN Jim	3	0	0	0	0	0	1	0	0	4	0	0
STEPHENSON Alan	12	0	0	0	0	0	0	0	0	12	0	0
own goal											1	1
Totals	462	4	73	33	0	7	33	1	9	528	5	8

After Tottenham were beaten 2–1 at home there were back-to-back 4–2 victories against Leicester City, which saw Brian Dear score a hat-trick at home and two more in the away game.

The FA Cup trail started well with a 3–1 win at Burnley and followed up with a 3–0 victory at Stoke City. In between these ties had been a 7–2 demolition of Fulham at Upton Park. In the fifth-round home tie with Sheffield United the Hammers played poorly and lost 2–1.

After a run of five league games without a win a young Trevor Brooking scored a hat-trick in the home game with Newcastle United where the Hammers scored five without reply. There were mixed results in the remaining games of the season, which saw the Hammers finish in a mid-table position of twelfth. With three World Cup winners in the side, the supporters expected a better showing.

Football League - Division One Final Table 1967-68

		HOME					AWAY					
	P	W	D	L	F	A	W	D	L	F	A	Pts
Manchester City	42	17	2	2	52	16	9	4	8	34	27	58
Manchester United	42	15	2	4	49	21	9	6	6	40	34	56
Liverpool	42	17	2	2	51	17	5	9	7	20	23	55
Leeds United	42	17	3	1	49	14	5	6	10	22	27	53
Everton	42	18	1	2	43	13	5	5	11	24	27	52
Chelsea	42	11	7	3	34	25	7	5	9	28	43	48
Tottenham Hotspur	42	11	7	3	44	20	8	2	11	26	39	47
West Bromwich Albion	42	12	4	5	45	25	5	8	8	30	37	46
Arsenal	42	12	6	3	37	23	5	4	12	23	33	44
Newcastle United	42	12	7	2	38	20	1	8	12	16	47	41
Nottingham Forest	42	11	6	4	34	22	3	5	13	18	42	39
West Ham United	**42**	**8**	**5**	**8**	**43**	**30**	**6**	**5**	**10**	**30**	**39**	**38**
Leicester City	42	7	7	7	37	34	6	5	10	27	35	38
Burnley	42	12	7	2	38	16	2	3	16	26	55	38
Sunderland	42	8	7	6	28	28	5	4	12	23	33	37
Southampton	42	9	8	4	37	31	4	3	14	29	52	37
Wolverhampton Wanderers	42	10	4	7	45	36	4	4	13	21	39	36
Stoke City	42	10	3	8	30	29	4	4	13	20	44	35
Sheffield Wednesday	42	6	10	5	32	24	5	2	14	19	39	34
Coventry City	42	8	5	8	32	32	1	10	10	19	39	33
Sheffield United	42	7	4	10	25	31	4	6	11	24	39	32
Fulham	42	6	4	11	27	41	4	3	14	29	57	27

BILLY BONDS

After playing 95 league games for Charlton Athletic, Bonds signed for West Ham in May 1967 for a fee of £50,000, a transfer which turned out to be West Ham's best ever.

The wing-half had ferocity and fight, and the sight of him marauding through opposition defences was a pleasing sight for the Hammers supporters. He was capped twice at under-23 level for England against Wales and the Netherlands in 1968. In season 1973/74 he fought almost a one-man rear guard against relegation, scoring a hat-trick against Chelsea and ending the campaign as leading scorer.

When Bobby Moore left in 1974 he was the natural choice for captain and he led West Ham when they won the FA Cup in 1975 and 1980. Bonds also won runners-up medals in the European Cup Winners' Cup in 1976 and the League Cup in 1981. He relinquished the captaincy to Alvin Martin in 1984 but was still a valuable member of the squad, passing on his experience and enthusiasm to all around him.

In recognition of his contribution to football he was awarded a richly deserved MBE in January 1988. Billy played his last game for the club at Southampton in April 1988 to end a Hammers playing career that had spanned 20 seasons and an amazing 793 appearances. He was then appointed youth team coach and was ideally placed to take over the manager's role in February 1990. Bonds was a popular choice as manager and he led West Ham to promotion in 1991 and 1993. He resigned in 1994, had a spell with Queens Park Rangers as youth team coach and was the manager at Millwall for the 1997/98 season.

Season **1967-68** Football League - Division One
Match Details

Manager **Ron Greenwood**   Final League Position **12/22**

	Date		Competition	Venue	Opponents	Results		Attendance	Position	Scorers
1	Aug 19	Sat	Div 1	H	Sheffield Wednesday	L	2-3	29,609	15	Hurst, Peters
2	Aug 21	Mon	Div 1	H	Burnley	W	4-2	30,414	6	Hurst 2, Peters, Redknapp
3	Aug 26	Sat	Div 1	A	Tottenham Hotspur	L	1-5	55,831	15	Sissons
4	Aug 29	Tue	Div 1	A	Burnley	D	3-3	16,625	14	Moore, Peters, Hurst
5	Sep 2	Sat	Div 1	H	Manchester United	L	1-3	36,562	20	Peters
6	Sep 5	Tue	Div 1	A	Everton	L	0-2	46,762	21	
7	Sep 9	Sat	Div 1	A	Sunderland	W	5-1	39,772	16	Hurst 2, Moore, Peters, Redknapp
8	Sep 13	Wed	FLC 2	A	Walsall	W	5-1	17,755		Peters 2, Brabrook, Hurst [pen], Evans (og)
9	Sep 16	Sat	Div 1	H	Wolverhampton Wanderers	L	1-2	30,752	20	Hurst
10	Sep 23	Sat	Div 1	A	Fulham	W	3-0	29,234	16	Hurst, Moore, Sissons
11	Sep 30	Sat	Div 1	H	Leeds United	D	0-0	29,760	15	
12	Oct 7	Sat	Div 1	H	Stoke City	L	3-4	24,469	17	Hurst 2, Peters
13	Oct 11	Wed	FLC 3	H	Bolton Wanderers	W	4-1	20,510		Hurst 4 [1 pen]
14	Oct 14	Sat	Div 1	A	Liverpool	L	1-3	46,951	19	Peters
15	Oct 23	Mon	Div 1	H	Southampton	L	0-1	32,541	19	
16	Oct 28	Sat	Div 1	A	Chelsea	W	3-1	40,303	18	Dear, Hurst, Peters
17	Nov 1	Wed	FLC 4	A	Huddersfield Town	L	0-2	17,729		
18	Nov 11	Sat	Div 1	A	Newcastle United	L	0-1	32,869	19	
19	Nov 18	Sat	Div 1	H	Manchester City	L	2-3	25,495	20	Hurst, Peters
20	Nov 25	Sat	Div 1	A	Arsenal	D	0-0	42,029	20	
21	Dec 2	Sat	Div 1	H	Sheffield United	W	3-0	22,711	20	Sissons 2, Brabrook
22	Dec 8	Fri	Div 1	A	Coventry City	D	1-1	28,077	19	Hurst
23	Dec 11	Mon	Div 1	H	West Bromwich Albion	L	2-3	19,018	19	Brabrook, Hurst [pen]
24	Dec 16	Sat	Div 1	A	Sheffield Wednesday	L	1-4	23,590	19	Dear
25	Dec 23	Sat	Div 1	H	Tottenham Hotspur	W	2-1	32,122	19	Bonds, Dear
26	Dec 26	Tue	Div 1	H	Leicester City	W	4-2	26,539	17	Dear 3, Brooking
27	Dec 30	Sat	Div 1	A	Leicester City	W	4-2	24,589	14	Dear 2, Brooking, Sissons
28	Jan 6	Sat	Div 1	A	Manchester United	L	1-3	59,516	15	Brooking
29	Jan 20	Sat	Div 1	A	Wolverhampton Wanderers	W	2-1	32,273	16	Dear, Hurst
30	Jan 27	Sat	FAC 3	A	Burnley	W	3-1	23,452		Peters 2, Dear
31	Feb 3	Sat	Div 1	H	Fulham	W	7-2	31,248	16	Brooking 2, Hurst 2, Dear, Moore, Peters
32	Feb 10	Sat	Div 1	A	Leeds United	L	1-2	41,814	16	Dear
33	Feb 17	Sat	FAC 4	A	Stoke City	W	3-0	36,704		Sissons 2, Hurst
34	Feb 26	Mon	Div 1	A	Stoke City	L	0-2	16,093	16	
35	Mar 9	Sat	FAC 5	H	Sheffield United	L	1-2	38,440		Dear
36	Mar 16	Sat	Div 1	A	Southampton	D	0-0	27,734	18	
37	Mar 23	Sat	Div 1	H	Chelsea	L	0-1	36,301	19	
38	Mar 29	Fri	Div 1	H	Arsenal	D	1-1	34,077	18	Brooking
39	Apr 6	Sat	Div 1	H	Newcastle United	W	5-0	27,681	17	Brooking 3, Sissons 2
40	Apr 12	Fri	Div 1	H	Nottingham Forest	W	3-0	36,589	15	Dear 2, Sissons
41	Apr 13	Sat	Div 1	A	Manchester City	L	0-3	38,755	15	
42	Apr 16	Tue	Div 1	A	Nottingham Forest	D	1-1	22,189	15	Peters
43	Apr 20	Sat	Div 1	H	Liverpool	W	1-0	33,164	15	Peters
44	Apr 24	Wed	Div 1	H	Sunderland	D	1-1	29,153	12	Dear
45	Apr 27	Sat	Div 1	A	Sheffield United	W	2-1	19,530	11	Hurst 2
46	May 1	Wed	Div 1	A	West Bromwich Albion	L	1-3	25,686	12	Peters
47	May 4	Sat	Div 1	H	Coventry City	D	0-0	30,181	12	
48	May 11	Sat	Div 1	H	Everton	D	1-1	28,319	12	Peters

Team Line-Ups

BENNETT Peter	BONDS Billy	BOVINGTON Eddie	BOYCE Ron	BRABROOK Peter	BROOKING Trevor	BURKETT Jack	CHARLES John	CUSHLEY John	DEAR Brian	FERGUSON Bobby	HEFFER Paul	HOWE Bobby	HURST Geoff	KITCHENER Bill	LAMPARD Frank	MOORE Bobby	PETERS Martin	REDKNAPP Harry	SISSONS John	STANDEN Jim	STEPHENSON Alan	#
	2	4	10				3	5		1			9			6	8	7	11			1
	2		10				3	5	8	1			9			6	4	7	11			2
	2		8				3	5	10	1			9			6	4	7	11			3
	2		10		8		3	5		1			9			6	4	7	11			4
	2/a		10		a		3	5	8	1			9			6	4	7	11			5
			10		8		2	5		1			9	3		6	4	7	11			6
			10	11	8		2	5					9	3		6	4	7		1		7
			8		9		2	5					10	3		6	4	7	11	1		8
			8		9		2	5					10	3		6	4	7	11	1		9
		2	8	9			3	5		1			10			6	4	7	11			10
	2	4	8	11			3	5		1			9			6	10	7				11
	2		8	9			3	5		1			10			6	4	7	11			12
	2		8	9			3	5		1			10			6	4	7	11			13
	2		8	9			3	5		1			10			6	4	7	11			14
	2	8		9			3	5		1			10			6	4	7	11			15
	2		8	9		7	3	5	11	1			10			6	4					16
	2		8/a	9		7	3	5	11	1			10			6	4	a				17
	2		10	7	8	3	4	5		1			9				6		11			18
			8	9		3		5		1			10		2	6	4	7	11			19
	2		10	8		3		5		1			9			6	4	7	11			20
	2		8	9		3						5	10			6	4	7	11	1		21
	5		8	9		3	2			1			10			6	4	7	11			22
a	5		8	9		3	2			1			10/a			6	4	7	11			23
	4	6	8		9	3	2	5	7	1			10									24
	2		8		9			5	7	1			10		3	6	4		11			25
	2		8		9			5	7	1			10		3	6	4		11			26
	2		8		9			5	7	1			10		3	6	4		11			27
	2		8	11	9			5	7	1			10		3	6	4					28
	2		8		9			5	7	1			10		3	6	4		11			29
	2		8		9			5	7	1			10		3	6	4		11			30
	2		8		9			5	7	1			10		3	6	4		11			31
8	2				9			5	7	1			10		3	6	4		11			32
8	2				9			5	7	1			10		3	6	4		11			33
8	2				9			5	7	1			10		3	6	4		11			34
8	2				9			5	7	1			10			6	4		11			35
	2		8		9				7	1			10		3	6	4		11		5	36
	2		8		9				7	1			10		3	6	4		11		5	37
	2		8		9				10	1					3	6	4	7	11		5	38
	2		8		9				10	1					3	6	4	7	11		5	39
	2		8		9				10	1					3	6	4	7	11		5	40
	2		8		9/a	a			10	1			11		3	6	4	7			5	41
	2		8		9				10	1			9		3	6	4	7	11		5	42
	2		8						9	1			10		3	6	4	7	11		5	43
	2		8		4				9	1			10		3	6		7	11		5	44
	2		8		9				a	1			10		3/a	6	4	7	11		5	45
	2		8		9	3		5	7	1			10			6	4		11			46
	2		8						9	1		3	10			6	4	7	11		5	47
	2		8		9				10	1		3				6	4	7	11		5	48

1968-69
Story of the season

There were no additions to the squad but Brabrook left for Orient and Burkett was transferred to Charlton. **An excellent beginning to the campaign** saw only **one defeat** in the **opening 12 games.**

Martin Peters had scored nine goals in these game including a hat-trick in the 5–0 home win against Burnle Another hat-trick was recorded to Geoff Hurst as th Hammers crushed Fulham 7–2 at home in the League Cu In the following round West Ham struggled as after goalless draw Coventry City won the replay 3–2. Octob brought West Ham's biggest win for years as Sunderlar were thrashed 8–0 at the Boleyn Ground, where in-for Geoff Hurst scored six goals. The home London derl with Queens Park Rangers saw Harry Redknapp volley th winning goal in a thrilling 4–3 victory.

Appearances & Goals 1968-69

	League			FA Cup			League Cup			Total		
	Starts	Subs	Goals	Starts	Subs	Goals	Starts	Subs	Goals	Starts	Subs	Goals
BENNETT Peter	1	0	0	0	0	0	0	0	0	1	0	
BONDS Billy	42	0	1	3	0	0	2	0	0	47	0	
BOYCE Ron	37	2	0	2	1	0	3	0	0	42	3	
BROOKING Trevor	29	3	7	2	0	0	3	0	1	34	3	
CHARLES John	35	0	0	1	0	0	3	0	0	39	0	
CROSS Roger	0	1	0	0	0	0	0	0	0	0	1	
CUSHLEY John	9	0	0	1	0	0	1	0	0	11	0	
DEAR Brian	11	0	5	0	0	0	1	0	0	12	0	
DEATH Stephen	1	0	0	0	0	0	0	0	0	1	0	0
FERGUSON Bobby	39	0	0	3	0	0	3	0	0	45	0	0
GROTIER Peter	2	0	0	0	0	0	0	0	0	2	0	0
HARTLEY Trevor	2	1	0	0	0	0	0	0	0	2	1	0
HEFFER Paul	0	0	0	1	0	0	0	0	0	1	0	0
HOLLAND Pat	1	0	0	0	0	0	0	0	0	1	0	0
HOWE Bobby	13	0	0	1	0	0	1	0	0	15	0	0
HURST Geoff	42	0	25	3	0	2	3	0	4	48	0	3
LAMPARD Frank	1	0	0	0	0	0	0	0	0	1	0	0
LINDSAY Jimmy	5	1	0	3	0	0	0	0	0	8	1	0
MILLER Keith	0	1	0	0	0	0	0	0	0	0	1	0
MOORE Bobby	41	0	2	3	0	0	3	0	0	47	0	2
PETERS Martin	42	0	19	3	0	3	3	0	2	48	0	2
REDKNAPP Harry	36	0	2	3	0	0	3	0	1	42	0	3
SISSONS John	31	1	4	1	0	0	2	0	1	34	1	5
STEPHENSON Alan	42	0	0	3	0	0	2	0	0	47	0	0
own goal			1									1
Totals	**462**	**10**	**66**	**33**	**1**	**5**	**33**	**0**	**9**	**528**	**11**	**8**

he new East Stand was opened for the visit of Bristol City
the FA Cup, and Peters scored twice in the 3–2 victory.
fter a 2–0 win at Huddersfield in the next round the
ammers travelled to Third Division Mansfield Town. In a
orror showing West Ham were dumped out of the Cup
ter losing 3–0. The league form was better as the team
oved into sixth place after beating Coventry City 5–2 at
ome and being unbeaten for seven games. In a
sappointing end to the season, however, there were no
ctories in the last nine games, with only four goals being
ored, and a final placing of eighth.

ootball League - Division One
inal Table 1968-69

	P	HOME					AWAY					Pts
		W	D	L	F	A	W	D	L	F	A	
eds United	42	18	3	0	41	9	9	10	2	25	17	67
verpool	42	16	4	1	36	10	9	7	5	27	14	61
erton	42	14	5	2	43	10	7	10	4	34	26	57
senal	42	12	6	3	31	12	10	6	5	25	15	56
nelsea	42	11	7	3	40	24	9	3	9	33	29	50
ttenham Hotspur	42	10	8	3	39	22	4	9	8	22	29	45
outhampton	42	13	5	3	41	21	3	8	10	16	27	45
est Ham United	**42**	**10**	**8**	**3**	**47**	**22**	**3**	**10**	**8**	**19**	**28**	**44**
ewcastle United	42	12	7	2	40	20	3	7	11	21	35	44
est Bromwich Albion	42	11	7	3	43	26	5	4	12	21	41	43
anchester United	42	13	5	3	38	18	2	7	12	19	35	42
swich Town	42	10	4	7	32	26	5	7	9	27	34	41
anchester City	42	13	6	2	49	20	2	4	15	15	35	40
urnley	42	11	6	4	36	25	4	3	14	19	57	39
heffield Wednesday	42	7	9	5	27	26	3	7	11	14	28	36
olverhampton Wanderers	42	7	10	4	26	22	3	5	13	15	36	35
underland	42	10	6	5	28	18	1	6	14	15	49	34
ottingham Forest	42	6	6	9	17	22	4	7	10	28	35	33
oke City	42	9	7	5	24	24	0	8	13	16	39	33
oventry City	42	8	6	7	32	22	2	5	14	14	42	31
eicester City	42	8	8	5	27	24	1	4	16	12	44	30
ueens Park Rangers	42	4	7	10	20	33	0	3	18	19	62	18

SIR TREVOR BROOKING

He joined West Ham as an apprentice in July
1965 and after playing six times for England
Youth he made his Hammers debut at
Burnley in August 1967. Trevor was an
elegant midfielder with an abundance of
skill. Capped once at under-23 level, he won
47 full England caps. Most memorable was
the World Cup qualifying game in Hungary in
1981 when his two goals sealed a 3–1 victory
and gained England a place in the finals.

At club level he won runners-up medals in the
1976 European Cup Winners' Cup and the
1981 League Cup Final. He was in the West
Ham side that won the FA Cup in 1975 when
beating Fulham 2–0, and scored the winning
goal in the 1980 final as the Hammers beat
Arsenal 1–0. A year later he won a Second
Division Championship medal when scoring
10 goals in 36 league appearances that
season.

Trevor decided to retire at the top and it was an
emotional evening against Everton in May
1984. One of the all-time greats, he had an
amazing career spanning 17 seasons, during
which he scored 102 goals in 634 appearances
for West Ham.

During 2003 he had two spells as caretaker
manager for West Ham where he was in
charge for 14 games, losing only once. From
2003 to July 2014 he was the FA director of
football development.

Trevor was awarded the MBE in 1981, the CBE
in 1999 and was knighted in 2004. In 2009 West
Ham announced that the Centenary Stand
would be renamed the Sir Trevor Brooking
Stand.

Season **1968-69** Football League - Division One
Match Details

Manager **Ron Greenwood**   Final League Position **8/22**

	Date		Competition	Venue	Opponents	Results		Attendance	Position	Scorers
1	Aug 10	Sat	Div 1	A	Newcastle United	D	1-1	37,307	12	Dear
2	Aug 14	Wed	Div 1	A	Stoke City	W	2-0	22,256	4	Peters, Sissons
3	Aug 17	Sat	Div 1	H	Nottingham Forest	W	1-0	31,114	2	Hurst
4	Aug 19	Mon	Div 1	H	Everton	L	1-4	34,895	3	Peters
5	Aug 24	Sat	Div 1	A	Coventry City	W	2-1	33,575	5	Brooking, Peters
6	Aug 26	Mon	Div 1	H	Burnley	W	5-0	28,340	1	Brooking 2, Hurst 2, Peters
7	Aug 31	Sat	Div 1	H	West Bromwich Albion	W	4-0	29,908	3	Peters 3, Redknapp
8	Sep 4	Wed	FLC 2	H	Bolton Wanderers	W	7-2	24,737		Hurst 3 [1 pen], Brooking, Peters, Redknapp, Sissons
9	Sep 7	Sat	Div 1	A	Manchester United	D	1-1	63,274	3	Hurst
10	Sep 14	Sat	Div 1	H	Tottenham Hotspur	D	2-2	35,802	4	Hurst, Peters
11	Sep 21	Sat	Div 1	A	Chelsea	D	1-1	58,062	5	Peters
12	Sep 25	Wed	FLC 3	H	Coventry City	D	0-0	27,598		
13	Sep 28	Sat	Div 1	H	Sheffield Wednesday	D	1-1	31,182	4	Hurst
14	Oct 1	Tue	FLC 3 Rep	A	Coventry City	L	2-3	25,988		Hurst, Peters
15	Oct 5	Sat	Div 1	H	Southampton	D	0-0	29,558	6	
16	Oct 8	Tue	Div 1	A	Burnley	L	1-3	13,799	6	Brooking
17	Oct 12	Sat	Div 1	A	Leeds United	L	0-2	40,686	6	
18	Oct 19	Sat	Div 1	H	Sunderland	W	8-0	24,903	6	Hurst 6, Brooking, Moore
19	Oct 26	Sat	Div 1	A	Arsenal	D	0-0	59,533	6	
20	Nov 2	Sat	Div 1	H	Queens Park Rangers	W	4-3	36,008	6	Hurst, Moore, Peters, Redknapp
21	Nov 9	Sat	Div 1	A	Wolverhampton Wanderers	L	0-2	29,740	7	
22	Nov 16	Sat	Div 1	H	Leicester City	W	4-0	26,328	5	Dear 2, Peters, Woollett (og)
23	Nov 23	Sat	Div 1	A	Ipswich Town	D	2-2	28,996	5	Hurst 2 [1 pen]
24	Nov 30	Sat	Div 1	H	Manchester City	W	2-1	33,082	5	Hurst, Peters
25	Dec 7	Sat	Div 1	A	Liverpool	L	0-2	48,632	5	
26	Dec 14	Sat	Div 1	H	Leeds United	D	1-1	24,418	5	Peters
27	Dec 21	Sat	Div 1	A	Sunderland	L	1-2	23,094	6	Hurst
28	Dec 26	Thu	Div 1	A	Southampton	D	2-2	27,465	6	Hurst 2 [1 pen]
29	Jan 4	Sat	FAC 3	H	Bristol City	W	3-2	32,526		Peters 2, Hurst
30	Jan 11	Sat	Div 1	A	Queens Park Rangers	D	1-1	28,645	6	Dear
31	Jan 25	Sat	FAC 4	A	Huddersfield Town	W	2-0	30,992		Hurst, Peters
32	Feb 1	Sat	Div 1	A	Leicester City	D	1-1	31,002	6	Dear
33	Feb 22	Sat	Div 1	H	Liverpool	D	1-1	36,498	7	Sissons
34	Feb 26	Wed	FAC 5	A	Mansfield Town	L	0-3	21,117		
35	Mar 1	Sat	Div 1	H	Newcastle United	W	3-1	26,336	5	Brooking, Hurst, Peters
36	Mar 8	Sat	Div 1	A	Nottingham Forest	W	1-0	24,303	6	Hurst
37	Mar 14	Fri	Div 1	H	Coventry City	W	5-2	29,053	6	Hurst 2 [2 pens], Bonds, Peters, Sissons
38	Mar 21	Fri	Div 1	H	Ipswich Town	L	1-3	32,574	6	Hurst
39	Mar 24	Mon	Div 1	H	Wolverhampton Wanderers	W	3-1	25,221	6	Peters 2, Brooking
40	Mar 29	Sat	Div 1	H	Manchester United	D	0-0	41,546	6	
41	Apr 1	Tue	Div 1	A	Everton	L	0-1	36,738	6	
42	Apr 5	Sat	Div 1	A	Sheffield Wednesday	D	1-1	24,090	6	Hurst
43	Apr 8	Tue	Div 1	H	Stoke City	D	0-0	26,577	6	
44	Apr 12	Sat	Div 1	H	Chelsea	D	0-0	32,332	6	
45	Apr 14	Mon	Div 1	A	West Bromwich Albion	L	1-3	19,780	6	Peters
46	Apr 19	Sat	Div 1	A	Tottenham Hotspur	L	0-1	50,970	7	
47	Apr 21	Mon	Div 1	H	Arsenal	L	1-2	34,941	7	Sissons
48	Apr 30	Wed	Div 1	A	Manchester City	D	1-1	31,846	8	Peters

Team Line-Ups

BENNETT Peter	BONDS Billy	BOYCE Ron	BROOKING Trevor	CHARLES John	CROSS Roger	CUSHLEY John	DEAR Brian	DEATH Stephen	FERGUSON Bobby	GROTIER Peter	HARTLEY Trevor	HEFFER Paul	HOLLAND Pat	HOWE Bobby	HURST Geoff	LAMPARD Frank	LINDSAY Jimmy	MILLER Keith	MOORE Bobby	PETERS Martin	REDKNAPP Harry	SISSONS John	STEPHENSON Alan	
	2	8	11	3/a			9		1						10				6	4	7	a	5	1
	2	8		3			9		1						10				6	4	7	11	5	2
	2	8		3			9		1						10				6	4	7	11	5	3
	2	8	a	3			9/a		1						10				6	4	7	11	5	4
	2	8	9	3					1						10				6	4	7	11	5	5
	2	8	9	3	a				1						10				6	4	7	11/a	5	6
	2	8	9	3					1						10				6	4	7	11	5	7
	2	8	9	3					1						10				6	4	7	11	5	8
	2	8	9	3					1						10				6	4	7	11	5	9
	2	8	9	3					1						10				6	4	7	11	5	10
	2	8	9						1					3	10				6	4	7	11	5	11
	2	8	9	3					1						10				6	4	7	11	5	12
	2	8	9	3					1						10				6	4	7	11	5	13
		8	9	3		5	11		1					2	10				6	4	7			14
	2	8	9	3					1						10				6	4	7	11	5	15
	2	8	9/a	3					1						10		a		6	4	7	11	5	16
	2	8	9	3					1						10				6	4	7	11	5	17
	2	8	9	3					1						10				6	4	7	11	5	18
	2	8	9	3					1		a				10				6	4	7	11/a	5	19
	2	8	9	3					1		11				10				6	4	7		5	20
	2	8	9	3					1		11				10				6	4	7		5	21
	2	8		3	4		9		1						10				6	7		11	5	22
	2	8		3	4		9		1						10		a		6	7		11/a	5	23
	2	8		3	4		9		1						10				6	11	7		5	24
	2	8		3	4		9		1						10				6	11	7		5	25
	2	8		3	4		9		1						10				6	11	7		5	26
	2	8		3	4				1						9	10			6	11	7		5	27
	2	8		3	4				1						9	10			6	11	7		5	28
	2	8		3	4				1						9	10			6	11	7		5	29
	2	a	9	3/a	6		11		1						10	8				4	7		5	30
	3	11	9						1			2			10	8			6	4	7		5	31
	2		9	3			11		1						10	8			6	4	7		5	32
	2	a	9	3/a					1						10	8			6	4	7	11	5	33
	2	a	9						1					3	10	8/a			6	4	7	11	5	34
	2	8	9						1					3	10				6	4	7	11	5	35
	2	8	9						1					3	10				6	4	7	11	5	36
	2	8	9						1					3	10				6	4	7	11	5	37
	2	8	9						1					3	10				6	4	7	11	5	38
7	8	9	2						1					3	10				6	4		11	5	39
7	8	9	2						1					3	10				6	4		11	5	40
8/a	9	a		3					1					2	10				6	4	7	11	5	41
	2	8	9	3					1						10				6	4	7	11	5	42
	8		9	3					1					2	10				6	4	7	11	5	43
7	2	8		3					1					4	9				6	10		11	5	44
	2	8	9	3					1					4	10				6	11	7		5	45
	2	8	a	3/a						1				4	9				6	10	7	11	5	46
	2	8				4				1			7	3	9				6	10		11	5	47
	2	8	9					1							10	3			6	4	7	11	5	48

1969-70
Story of the season

Two successive home wins heralded the new season but **five defeats** and **two draws** in the next seven games left West Ham near the bottom of the table.

The League Cup tie at home to Halifax Town saw t[he] Yorkshire team beaten 4–2, only for the Hammers to b[e] out in the next round, losing 1–0 at Nottingham Fore[st]. Clyde Best, the 18-year-old from Bermuda, scored tw[ice] against Burnley and again two days later against Stoke Ci[ty]. Results away from home were poor, with no wins in t[he] first 11 away games, but to the delight of supporters t[he] first away win came in the 2–0 victory at London riv[als] Tottenham in December.

Appearances & Goals 1969-70

	League			FA Cup			League Cup			Total	
	Starts	Subs	Goals	Starts	Subs	Goals	Starts	Subs	Goals	Starts	Subs
BENNETT Peter	11	1	0	0	0	0	0	0	0	11	1
BEST Clyde	24	0	5	1	0	0	1	0	1	26	0
BONDS Billy	42	0	3	1	0	0	2	0	0	45	0
BOYCE Ron	18	2	1	1	0	0	1	0	0	20	2
BROOKING Trevor	20	1	4	0	0	0	2	0	0	22	1
CHARLES John	5	0	0	0	0	0	0	0	0	5	0
CROSS Roger	5	1	1	0	0	0	1	0	0	6	1
CUSHLEY John	2	0	0	0	0	0	0	0	0	2	0
EUSTACE Peter	14	0	2	0	0	0	0	0	0	14	0
FERGUSON Bobby	30	0	0	1	0	0	2	0	0	33	0
GREAVES Jimmy	6	0	4	0	0	0	0	0	0	6	0
GROTIER Peter	12	0	0	0	0	0	0	0	0	12	0
HEFFER Paul	0	1	0	0	0	0	0	0	0	0	1
HOLLAND Pat	8	0	1	0	0	0	0	0	0	8	0
HOWE Bobby	32	1	1	1	0	0	0	0	0	33	1
HURST Geoff	38	1	16	1	0	0	2	0	2	41	1
LAMPARD Frank	30	0	0	1	0	0	2	0	1	33	0
LINDSAY Jimmy	17	0	2	0	0	0	1	0	0	18	0
LLEWELLYN David	0	2	0	0	0	0	0	0	0	0	2
MILLER Keith	1	1	0	0	0	0	0	0	0	1	1
MOORE Bobby	40	0	0	1	0	0	2	0	0	43	0
PETERS Martin	31	0	7	1	0	0	2	0	0	34	0
REDKNAPP Harry	23	0	1	0	1	0	2	0	0	25	1
SISSONS John	19	1	2	1	0	0	0	0	0	20	1
STEPHENSON Alan	34	0	0	1	0	1	2	0	0	37	0
own goal			1								
Totals	**462**	**12**	**51**	**11**	**1**	**1**	**22**	**0**	**4**	**495**	**13**

trip to Middlesbrough in the FA Cup brought another
ay defeat (2–1). Peter Eustace was signed from Sheffield
ednesday and made his debut against them in a 3–2
ctory at Hillsborough. The Hammers struggled
roughout February, dropping to seventeenth. A goalscorer
s needed and one arrived when a swap deal was arranged
th Tottenham in March, as Martin Peters joined Spurs
d legendary Jimmy Greaves came to Upton Park.

reaves made his debut at Manchester City and scored
ice in the Hammers 5–1 victory. The acquisition of
reaves sparked a late revival, with just one defeat in the
maining five games helping the team to seventeenth place.

ootball League - Division One
inal Table 1969-70

	P	HOME					AWAY					Pts
		W	D	L	F	A	W	D	L	F	A	
erton	42	17	3	1	46	19	12	5	4	26	15	66
eds United	42	15	4	2	50	19	6	11	4	34	30	57
elsea	42	13	7	1	36	18	8	6	7	34	32	55
rby County	42	15	3	3	45	14	7	6	8	19	23	53
erpool	42	10	7	4	34	20	10	4	7	31	22	51
ventry City	42	9	6	6	35	28	10	5	6	23	20	49
wcastle United	42	14	2	5	42	16	3	11	7	15	19	47
anchester United	42	8	9	4	37	27	6	8	7	29	34	45
oke City	42	10	7	4	31	23	5	8	8	25	29	45
anchester City	42	8	6	7	25	22	8	5	8	30	26	43
ttenham Hotspur	42	11	2	8	27	21	6	7	8	27	34	43
senal	42	7	10	4	29	23	5	8	8	22	26	42
olverhampton Wanderers	42	8	8	5	30	23	4	8	9	25	34	40
urnley	42	7	7	7	33	29	5	8	8	23	32	39
ottingham Forest	42	8	9	4	28	28	2	9	10	22	43	38
est Bromwich Albion	42	10	6	5	39	25	4	3	14	19	41	37
est Ham United	**42**	**8**	**8**	**5**	**28**	**21**	**4**	**4**	**13**	**23**	**39**	**36**
swich Town	42	9	5	7	23	20	1	6	14	17	43	31
outhampton	42	3	12	6	24	27	3	5	13	22	40	29
ystal Palace	42	5	6	10	20	36	1	9	11	14	32	27
underland	42	4	11	6	17	24	2	3	16	13	44	26
heffield Wednesday	42	6	5	10	23	27	2	4	15	17	44	25

CLYDE BEST

As an 18-year-old Best came over from Bermuda to join West Ham in 1968.

He made his first-team debut against Arsenal at home in August 1969 and the big centre-forward scored his first goals for the club in October, netting twice against Burnley. By 1970 he was an established member of the squad and was popular with the supporters. In November of that year he was involved in two exciting 3–3 draws. First was a home league match with Wolverhampton Wanderers, where he scored twice, and then he played in Bobby Moore's testimonial against Celtic. The Hammers were losing 3–2 when he scored the equaliser six minutes from time. The campaign of 1971–72 was his best season: he played in all 56 league and cup games, scoring 23 goals. The following season he was again ever-present and against Leeds United in April he was called upon to play in goal when Bobby Ferguson went off injured. He was now becoming a cult hero, and the fans looked upon him as a gentle giant. In February 1976, after 218 games and scoring 58 goals, he left to join Feyenoord in Holland for two seasons before going to the USA to play in the North American Soccer League. He then qualified as a coach and between 1997 and 2000 he was manager of the Bermuda national team. In January 2006 he was awarded an MBE for services to football and the community of Bermuda.

Season **1969-70** Football League - Division One
Match Details

Manager **Ron Greenwood**   Final League Position **17/22**

	Date		Competition	Venue	Opponents	Results		Attendance	Position	Scorers
1	Aug 9	Sat	Div 1	H	Newcastle United	W	1-0	33,323	7	Hurst
2	Aug 11	Mon	Div 1	H	Chelsea	W	2-0	39,003	1	Hurst, Peters
3	Aug 16	Sat	Div 1	H	Stoke City	L	1-2	23,362	8	Lindsay
4	Aug 20	Wed	Div 1	A	Chelsea	D	0-0	43,347	7	
5	Aug 23	Sat	Div 1	H	West Bromwich Albion	L	1-3	29,156	10	Hurst
6	Aug 25	Mon	Div 1	H	Arsenal	D	1-1	39,590	9	Cross
7	Aug 30	Sat	Div 1	A	Nottingham Forest	L	0-1	27,097	13	
8	Sep 3	Wed	FLC 2	H	Halifax Town	W	4-2	20,717		Hurst 2, Best, Lampard
9	Sep 6	Sat	Div 1	H	Tottenham Hotspur	L	0-1	40,561	17	
10	Sep 13	Sat	Div 1	A	Everton	L	0-2	49,052	20	
11	Sep 20	Sat	Div 1	H	Sheffield Wednesday	W	3-0	23,487	15	Hurst, Redknapp, Branfoot (og)
12	Sep 23	Tue	FLC 3	A	Nottingham Forest	L	0-1	20,939		
13	Sep 27	Sat	Div 1	A	Manchester United	L	2-5	58,579	17	Hurst 2
14	Oct 4	Sat	Div 1	H	Burnley	W	3-1	26,445	15	Best 2, Brooking
15	Oct 6	Mon	Div 1	H	Stoke City	D	3-3	27,128	14	Best, Brooking, Sissons
16	Oct 11	Sat	Div 1	A	Coventry City	D	2-2	34,279	15	Brooking, Sissons
17	Oct 18	Sat	Div 1	A	Wolverhampton Wanderers	L	0-1	28,762	16	
18	Oct 25	Sat	Div 1	H	Sunderland	D	1-1	29,191	16	Peters
19	Nov 1	Sat	Div 1	A	Southampton	D	1-1	26,894	16	Brooking
20	Nov 8	Sat	Div 1	H	Crystal Palace	W	2-1	31,515	14	Best, Hurst
21	Nov 15	Sat	Div 1	A	Liverpool	L	0-2	39,168	14	
22	Nov 22	Sat	Div 1	H	Derby County	W	3-0	32,485	14	Hurst 2, Peters
23	Nov 29	Sat	Div 1	A	Ipswich Town	L	0-1	17,454	15	
24	Dec 6	Sat	Div 1	H	Manchester City	L	0-4	27,485	16	
25	Dec 13	Sat	Div 1	H	Everton	L	0-1	26,689	17	
26	Dec 17	Wed	Div 1	A	Leeds United	L	1-4	30,699	17	Hurst
27	Dec 20	Sat	Div 1	A	Tottenham Hotspur	W	2-0	28,375	15	Hurst, Peters
28	Dec 26	Fri	Div 1	A	West Bromwich Albion	L	1-3	32,246	16	Peters
29	Dec 27	Sat	Div 1	H	Nottingham Forest	D	1-1	31,829	16	Bonds
30	Jan 3	Sat	FAC 3	A	Middlesbrough	L	1-2	31,295		Stephenson
31	Jan 10	Sat	Div 1	A	Sheffield Wednesday	W	3-2	28,097	16	Peters 2, Hurst [pen]
32	Jan 17	Sat	Div 1	H	Manchester United	D	0-0	41,643	16	
33	Jan 31	Sat	Div 1	A	Burnley	L	2-3	14,494	16	Eustace, Lindsay
34	Feb 11	Wed	Div 1	H	Coventry City	L	1-2	22,723	17	Hurst [pen]
35	Feb 21	Sat	Div 1	A	Sunderland	W	1-0	16,900	17	Hurst
36	Feb 28	Sat	Div 1	H	Southampton	D	0-0	27,092	17	
37	Mar 2	Mon	Div 1	A	Newcastle United	L	1-4	27,726	17	Eustace
38	Mar 7	Sat	Div 1	A	Derby County	L	0-3	35,615	17	
39	Mar 14	Sat	Div 1	H	Ipswich Town	D	0-0	20,934	17	
40	Mar 21	Sat	Div 1	A	Manchester City	W	5-1	28,353	17	Greaves 2, Hurst 2, Boyce
41	Mar 24	Tue	Div 1	A	Crystal Palace	D	0-0	34,808	17	
42	Mar 28	Sat	Div 1	H	Liverpool	W	1-0	38,239	17	Holland
43	Mar 31	Tue	Div 1	H	Wolverhampton Wanderers	W	3-0	26,386	17	Bonds, Greaves, Howe
44	Apr 2	Thu	Div 1	H	Leeds United	D	2-2	26,228	15	Best, Bonds
45	Apr 4	Sat	Div 1	A	Arsenal	L	1-2	36,212	17	Greaves

eam Line-Ups

	BEST Clyde	BONDS Billy	BOYCE Ron	BROOKING Trevor	CHARLES John	CROSS Roger	CUSHLEY John	EUSTACE Peter	FERGUSON Bobby	GREAVES Jimmy	GROTIER Peter	HEFFER Paul	HOLLAND Pat	HOWE Bobby	HURST Geoff	LAMPARD Frank	LINDSAY Jimmy	LLEWELLYN David	MILLER Keith	MOORE Bobby	PETERS Martin	REDKNAPP Harry	SISSONS John	STEPHENSON Alan	
		2	8	3					1						10					6	4	7	11	5	1
		2	6	3					1						10		8			5	4	7	11		2
		2	6	3					1						10		8			5	4	7	11		3
		2	6			7			1						10	3	8			5	4		11		4
		2	8	3					1						10		7			6	4		11	5	5
	7	2	8	9		11			1					a	10	3/a				6	4			5	6
	7	2	8	9		11/a			1						10	3			a	6	4			5	7
	11	2		9					1						10	3	8			6	4	7		5	8
	7/a	2	a	9					1					4	10	3				6	8		11	5	9
		2	8	9		11			1				7		10	3				6	4			5	10
		2	4	8		10			1						9	3				6	11	7		5	11
		2	4	8		10			1						9	3				6	11	7		5	12
	9	2							1					4	10	3	8			6	11	7		5	13
	11	2		9					1					4	10/a	3	8			6		7	a	5	14
	11	2	6	9		a			1					4		3/a	8					7	10	5	15
	11	2		9					1					4		3	8			6		7	10	5	16
	11	2		9					1					4/a	a	3	8			6		7	10	5	17
	11	2		9					1					4	10	3				6	8	7		5	18
	7	2		9					1					4	10	3				6	8		11	5	19
	11	2		9					1					4	10	3				6	8	7		5	20
	11	2	8	9					1					4	10	3				6		7		5	21
	11	2		9					1					4	10	3				6	8	7		5	22
	11	2		9					1					4	10	3				6	8	7		5	23
	11	2		9					1					4	10	3				6	8	7		5	24
	11	2	9	a					1					4	10	3				6	8	7		5/a	25
		2	6	9					1					4	10	3				5		7	11		26
		2	6	9					1					4	10	3				5	8	7	11		27
		2	6						1					4	8	3				5	11	7	10		28
a	11	2	6	10/a					1					4	9	3				5	8	7			29
	9/a	2	7						1					4	10	3				6	8	a	11	5	30
	11	2						10	1				7		3	9	8			6	4			5	31
	11	2						10	1				7		3	9	8			6	4			5	32
	11	2						10	1			a	7/a		3	9	8			6	4			5	33
	11	2		7				9	1						3	10	8			6	4			5	34
		2						10	1						3	9	8			6	4	7	11	5	35
		2						10	1						3	9	8			6	4	7	11	5	36
		2						10	1						3	9	8			6	4	7	11	5	37
	7	2					4	10	1					11	9	3				6	8			5	38
	7/a	2	a				4	10	1					11	9	3				6	8			5	39
		2	4					8/a		10	1		7	11	9	3			a	6				5	40
		2	4/a							10	1		7	11	9	3			a	6				5	41
		2						8		10	1		7	11	9	3				6				5	42
		2						8		10	1		7	11	9	3				6				5	43
	9	2			3			4		10	1						8			6	5	7	11		44
	4	2						8		10	1		7		9	3				6			11	5	45

1970-71
Story of the season

A **tough start** saw three London derbies, which all ended in draws. After **10 games the team were still without a win** and twentieth. The **League Cup brought some relief** with a narrow 1–0 home win against Hull City, but the journey ended with a 3–1 defeat at Coventry City.

Finally a league win arrived when Burnley were beat 3–1 at home, with Geoff Hurst grabbing a hat-trick. T following home game with Tottenham brought a reco attendance of 42,322, a figure which stands today. No signing centre-half Tommy Taylor made his debut and t Hammers twice came from behind to draw 2–2. It was great night for Bobby Moore as Celtic were the opponer in his testimonial match. This was England versus Scotlar an ear-shattering game that provided great entertainmer The Scots were leading 3–2 just six minutes from tir when Clyde Best equalised to give a final 3–3 scoreline.

Appearances & Goals 1970-71

	League			FA Cup			League Cup			Total	
	Starts	Subs	Goals	Starts	Subs	Goals	Starts	Subs	Goals	Starts	Subs
AYRIS Johnny	6	1	0	1	0	0	1	0	0	8	1
BENNETT Peter	8	0	1	0	0	0	0	0	0	8	0
BEST Clyde	20	2	5	1	0	0	2	0	0	23	2
BONDS Billy	37	0	0	1	0	0	2	0	0	40	0
BOYCE Ron	13	0	0	0	0	0	0	0	0	13	0
BROOKING Trevor	17	2	2	0	0	0	1	0	0	18	2
DEAR Brian	4	0	0	0	1	0	0	0	0	4	1
EUSTACE Peter	25	2	4	1	0	0	2	0	1	28	2
FERGUSON Bobby	23	0	0	1	0	0	0	0	0	24	0
GREAVES Jimmy	30	2	9	1	0	0	1	0	0	32	2
GROTIER Peter	19	0	0	0	0	0	2	0	0	21	0
HEFFER Paul	1	2	0	0	0	0	0	0	0	1	2
HOLLAND Pat	2	1	0	0	0	0	0	0	0	2	1
HOWE Bobby	20	1	3	1	0	0	1	0	0	22	1
HURST Geoff	39	0	15	0	0	0	2	0	1	41	0
LAMPARD Frank	41	0	1	1	0	0	2	0	0	44	0
LINDSAY Jimmy	14	2	0	1	0	0	1	0	0	16	2
LLEWELLYN David	1	1	0	0	0	0	0	0	0	1	1
McDOWELL John	25	0	0	0	0	0	0	0	0	25	0
MOORE Bobby	38	1	2	1	0	0	2	0	0	41	1
REDKNAPP Harry	20	1	0	0	0	0	1	0	0	21	1
ROBSON Bryan	14	0	3	0	0	0	0	0	0	14	0
STEPHENSON Alan	15	1	0	0	0	0	2	0	0	17	1
TAYLOR Tommy	30	0	1	1	0	0	0	0	0	31	0
own goal			1								
Totals	462	19	47	11	1	0	22	0	2	495	20

erby County in December Jimmy Greaves, playing in his ▮0th league game, scored in the 4–2 victory. A poor run of ▮sults followed, including a 4–0 FA Cup defeat at Blackpool ▮d a 4–1 home loss to Derby.

▮ February the Hammers snapped up goalscorer Bryan ▮op' Robson from Newcastle, who scored on his debut in ▮e 2–0 win against Nottingham Forest. It was a big boost ▮ the team in signing Robson and he was again on target in ▮ccessive home wins over Manchester United and West ▮omwich Albion. Relegation was avoided after finishing ▮ird from bottom.

▮ootball League - Division One ▮inal Table 1970-71

TOMMY TAYLOR

As a 15-year-old Taylor was in the first team at Leyton Orient as he displayed a maturity beyond his years.

He was with Orient for seven seasons and won a Third Division Championship medal in 1970. After playing in 256 games at centre-half he joined West Ham in October 1970 for a fee of £78,000. He went straight into the side for his debut against Tottenham before a record crowd at the Boleyn of 42,322. He was in the team that won the FA Cup in 1975 against Fulham and he also gained a runners-up medal in 1976 in the European Cup Winners' Cup. International honours followed as in his time with the Hammers he gained 13 England under-23 caps.

Tommy played for nine seasons at Upton Park, appearing in 396 games and scoring eight goals. He then re-joined Leyton Orient in May 1978, where he was appointed club captain and made a further 131 appearances before having a spell in Belgium with Beerschot in season 1982–83. After returning to England he spent two years as a youth team coach at Charlton before moving to New Zealand for three years, where he managed Hamilton FC. Returning to England once more he then went on a managerial journey that has seen him in charge at 12 clubs. Starting with Margate in 1991, he has managed Cambridge United, Leyton Orient, Darlington, Farnborough, King's Lynn, Peterborough, Boston United, the Grenada national team, Belper, Kemi Kings (Finland) and finally he is currently with IF Floya in Norway's Third Division.

	P	HOME					AWAY					Pts
		W	D	L	F	A	W	D	L	F	A	
▮senal	42	18	3	0	41	6	11	4	6	30	23	65
▮eds United	42	16	2	3	40	12	11	8	2	32	18	64
▮ttenham Hotspur	42	11	5	5	33	19	8	9	4	21	14	52
▮olverhampton Wanderers	42	13	3	5	33	22	9	5	7	31	32	52
▮verpool	42	11	10	0	30	10	6	7	8	12	14	51
▮helsea	42	12	6	3	34	21	6	9	6	18	21	51
▮outhampton	42	12	5	4	35	15	5	7	9	21	29	46
▮anchester United	42	9	6	6	29	24	7	5	9	36	42	43
▮erby County	42	9	5	7	32	26	7	5	9	24	28	42
▮oventry City	42	12	4	5	24	12	4	6	11	13	26	42
▮anchester City	42	7	9	5	30	22	5	8	8	17	20	41
▮ewcastle United	42	9	9	3	27	16	5	4	12	17	30	41
▮oke City	42	10	7	4	28	11	2	6	13	16	37	37
▮erton	42	10	7	4	32	16	2	6	13	22	44	37
▮ddersfield Town	42	7	8	6	19	16	4	6	11	21	33	36
▮ottingham Forest	42	9	4	8	29	26	5	4	12	13	35	36
▮est Bromwich Albion	42	9	8	4	34	25	1	7	13	24	50	35
▮ystal Palace	42	9	5	7	24	24	3	6	12	15	33	35
▮swich Town	42	9	4	8	28	22	3	6	12	14	26	34
▮est Ham United	**42**	**6**	**8**	**7**	**28**	**30**	**4**	**6**	**11**	**19**	**30**	**34**
▮rnley	42	4	8	9	20	31	3	5	13	9	32	27
▮ackpool	42	3	9	9	22	31	1	6	14	12	35	23

Season 1970-71 Football League - Division One
Match Details

Manager **Ron Greenwood**   Final League Position **20/22**

	Date		Competition	Venue	Opponents	Results		Attendance	Position	Scorers
1	Aug 15	Sat	Div 1	A	Tottenham Hotspur	D	2-2	53,640	12	Bennett, Greaves
2	Aug 17	Mon	Div 1	H	Arsenal	D	0-0	39,903	5	
3	Aug 22	Sat	Div 1	H	Chelsea	D	2-2	39,240	13	Howe, Hurst
4	Aug 26	Wed	Div 1	A	Leeds United	L	0-3	42,677	16	
5	Aug 29	Sat	Div 1	A	Manchester United	D	1-1	50,676	15	Hurst
6	Aug 31	Mon	Div 1	H	Southampton	D	1-1	26,213	14	Hurst [pen]
7	Sep 5	Sat	Div 1	H	Everton	L	1-2	29,171	18	Moore
8	Sep 9	Wed	FLC 2	H	Hull City	W	1-0	19,160		Eustace
9	Sep 12	Sat	Div 1	A	West Bromwich Albion	L	1-2	24,606	19	Howe
10	Sep 19	Sat	Div 1	H	Newcastle United	L	0-2	25,841	20	
11	Sep 26	Sat	Div 1	A	Huddersfield Town	D	1-1	20,885	20	Hurst [pen]
12	Oct 3	Sat	Div 1	H	Burnley	W	3-1	23,295	18	Hurst 3
13	Oct 6	Tue	FLC 3	A	Coventry City	L	1-3	19,362		Hurst
14	Oct 10	Sat	Div 1	A	Stoke City	L	1-2	23,035	19	Greaves
15	Oct 17	Sat	Div 1	H	Tottenham Hotspur	D	2-2	42,322	20	Eustace, Hurst
16	Oct 24	Sat	Div 1	A	Crystal Palace	D	1-1	41,396	20	Howe
17	Oct 31	Sat	Div 1	H	Blackpool	W	2-1	26,239	16	Eustace, Greaves
18	Nov 7	Sat	Div 1	A	Ipswich Town	L	1-2	22,993	17	Hurst
19	Nov 14	Sat	Div 1	H	Wolverhampton Wanderers	D	3-3	23,978	18	Best 2, Moore
20	Nov 21	Sat	Div 1	A	Manchester City	L	0-2	28,485	19	
21	Nov 28	Sat	Div 1	H	Coventry City	L	1-2	22,800	19	Best
22	Dec 5	Sat	Div 1	A	Derby County	W	4-2	30,806	19	Best 2, Brooking, Greaves
23	Dec 12	Sat	Div 1	H	Liverpool	L	1-2	27,459	19	Greaves
24	Dec 19	Sat	Div 1	A	Chelsea	L	1-2	42,075	19	Lampard
25	Jan 2	Sat	FAC 3	A	Blackpool	L	0-4	21,814		
26	Jan 9	Sat	Div 1	A	Arsenal	L	0-2	49,057	19	
27	Jan16	Sat	Div 1	H	Leeds United	L	2-3	34,407	20	Brooking, Eusatce
28	Feb 6	Sat	Div 1	H	Derby County	L	1-4	26,606	20	Eustace
29	Feb 9	Tue	Div 1	A	Coventry City	W	1-0	25,083	20	Greaves
30	Feb 16	Tue	Div 1	A	Liverpool	L	0-1	38,032	20	
31	Feb 20	Sat	Div 1	H	Manchester City	D	0-0	30,168	20	
32	Feb 24	Wed	Div 1	H	Nottingham Forest	W	2-0	35,601	20	Hurst, Robson
33	Feb 27	Sat	Div 1	A	Blackpool	D	1-1	15,689	19	Hurst [pen]
34	Mar 6	Sat	Div 1	H	Crystal Palace	D	0-0	26,157	19	
35	Mar 13	Sat	Div 1	A	Wolverhampton Wanderers	L	0-2	25,166	20	
36	Mar 20	Sat	Div 1	H	Ipswich Town	D	2-2	25,957	20	Greaves 2
37	Mar 30	Tue	Div 1	A	Everton	W	1-0	29,094	20	Kendall (og)
38	Apr 3	Sat	Div 1	H	Manchester United	W	2-1	38,507	20	Hurst, Robson
39	Apr 9	Fri	Div 1	H	West Bromwich Albion	W	2-1	34,981	19	Greaves, Robson
40	Apr 10	Sat	Div 1	A	Nottingham Forest	L	0-1	20,032	19	
41	Apr 13	Tue	Div 1	A	Burnley	L	0-1	15,841	20	
42	Apr 17	Sat	Div 1	H	Stoke City	W	1-0	26,269	20	Hurst
43	Apr 24	Sat	Div 1	A	Newcastle United	D	1-1	22,790	20	Hurst
44	Apr 27	Tue	Div 1	A	Southampton	W	2-1	19,935	17	Hurst, Taylor
45	May 1	Sat	Div 1	H	Huddersfield Town	L	0-1	24,983	20	

eam Line-Ups

	BENNETT Peter	BEST Clyde	BONDS Billy	BOYCE Ron	BROOKING Trevor	DEAR Brian	EUSTACE Peter	FERGUSON Bobby	GREAVES Jimmy	GROTIER Peter	HEFFER Paul	HOLLAND Pat	HOWE Bobby	HURST Geoff	LAMPARD Frank	LINDSAY Jimmy	LLEWELLYN David	McDOWELL John	MOORE Bobby	REDKNAPP Harry	ROBSON Bryan	STEPHENSON Alan	TAYLOR Tommy	
	4	7	2		8				10	1			11	9	3				6			5		1
	4	7	2		8				10	1			11	9	3				6			5		2
	4	7	2		8				10	1			11	9	3				6			5		3
	4	7	2		8				10	1			11	9	3				6			5		4
	4	7	2		8				10	1			11	9	3				6			5		5
	4/a	7	2		8		a		10	1			11	9	3				6			5		6
		7/a	2		8		4		1	1			11	9	3				6	a		5		7
		8	2				4		10	1			11	9	3				6	7		5		8
	4	9	2		7		8		10	1			11		3				6			5		9
	4	11	2		a		8		10	1				9	3				6	7/a		5		10
		7	2	4	8		10			1			11	9	3				6			5		11
7		10	2	4/a	8		5			1	a		11	9	3				6					12
7		8	2		10		11			1				9	3	4			6			5		13
		8	2	7/a	10		a		11	1				9	3	4			6			5		14
7			2			11	4		10	1				9	3	8			6				5	15
			2			11	4		10	1			7	9	3	8			6				5	16
7						11	4/a		10	1	a			9	3	8		2	6				5	17
		10					6			1	4/a	a	11	9	3	8		2		7			5	18
7		9					4			1			11	10	3	8		2	6				5	19
		11					4	1	9			7	a	10	3	8/a		2	6				5	20
		9					4	1	11			7	8	10	3			2	6				5	21
		9	2		8		4	1	11					10	3	7			6				5	22
a		9	2		8		4	1	11					10	3	7/a			6				5	23
7		a	2		8	9	4	1	11						3	10			6				5	24
/a		9	2			a	4	1	10				11		3	8			6				5	25
		9/a	4		10		11	1					6		3	8	a	2		7			5	26
			4		10		11			1			6	9	3	8		2		7			5	27
			4		10		11			1			6/a	9	3	8		2	a	7			5	28
			4	8			11	1	10/a					9	3	a		2	6	7			5	29
			4	8			11	1	10					9	3			2	6	7			5	30
			4	8			11	1	10					9	3			2	6	7			5	31
			4				11/a	1	10					9	3	a		2	6	7	8		5	32
			4	8			10/a	1	a					9	3			2	6	7	11		5	33
			4	8				1	11					9	3			2	6	7	10		5	34
			4	10			11	1	a					9	3			2	6	7/a	8		5	35
7		a	4	8				1	11					9	3			2	6		10		5	36
			4	8				1	11					9	3			2	6	7	10		5	37
			4	8				1	11					9	3			2	6	7	10		5	38
			4	8/a	a			1	11					9	3			2	6	7	10		5	39
			4					1	11					9	3/a	8		2	6	7	10	a	5	40
		11	4				8	1					3	9				2	6	7	10		5	41
			8					1	11					9	3			2	6	7	10	4	5	42
			8					1					11	9	3			2	6	7	10	4	5	43
			8					1					11	9	3		7	2	6		10	4	5	44
			8					1	11					9	3			2	6	7	10	4	5	45

1971-72
Story of the season

Another poor start saw the Hammers with **no wins** and **no goals from the opening four games.**

It was a vast improvement when the next 11 games o● yielded one defeat at Manchester United. Clyde Best v● the player in form as he scored twice against both Coven● City and Chelsea. Following a 1–1 home draw with Card● City in the League Cup, the Hammers won the replay 2-● with both goals being scored by Geoff Hurst. Leeds Unit● were the next opponents in the League Cup, which s● Clyde Best score the winner in a 1–0 win at Elland Ro● Despite losing four league games during November, t● League Cup journey progressed with a 2–1 home win ov● Liverpool and a 5–0 thrashing of Sheffield United, whi● saw Bryan Robson score a hat-trick. At Southampton ● December West Ham were leading 3–0 only to draw 3–3● The League Cup semi-final with Stoke City became a sa● played out over four games. The first leg at Stoke was w● 2–1, with goals from Best and Hurst. There was drama ●

Appearances & Goals 1971-72

	League			FA Cup			League Cup			Total	
	Starts	Subs	Goals	Starts	Subs	Goals	Starts	Subs	Goals	Starts	Subs
AYRIS Johnny	11	1	0	0	0	0	1	0	0	12	1
BEST Clyde	42	0	17	4	0	2	10	0	4	56	0
BONDS Billy	42	0	3	4	0	0	10	0	2	56	0
BOYCE Ron	0	1	0	0	0	0	0	0	0	0	1
BROOKING Trevor	40	0	6	4	0	0	10	0	1	54	0
CHARLES Clive	4	0	0	0	0	0	0	0	0	4	0
COKER Adewunmi	5	0	2	0	0	0	0	0	0	5	0
DURRELL Joe	5	1	0	0	0	0	0	0	0	5	1
EUSTACE Peter	2	0	0	0	1	0	0	1	0	2	2
FERGUSON Bobby	36	0	0	4	0	0	10	0	0	50	0
GROTIER Peter	6	0	0	0	0	0	0	0	0	6	0
HEFFER Paul	0	1	0	0	1	0	0	0	0	0	2
HOLLAND Pat	4	0	0	0	0	0	0	0	0	4	0
HOWE Bobby	1	4	0	0	0	0	0	2	0	1	6
HURST Geoff	34	0	8	4	0	4	10	0	4	48	0
LAMPARD Frank	39	0	1	4	0	0	10	0	0	53	0
LLEWELLYN David	1	1	0	0	0	0	0	0	0	1	1
LOCK Kevin	1	2	0	0	0	0	0	0	0	1	2
McDOWELL John	40	0	0	4	0	0	10	0	0	54	0
MOORE Bobby	40	0	1	4	0	0	10	0	0	54	0
REDKNAPP Harry	22	0	0	4	0	0	9	0	0	35	0
ROBSON Bryan	42	0	9	4	0	1	10	0	4	56	0
STEPHENSON Alan	3	1	0	0	0	0	0	0	0	3	1
TAYLOR Tommy	42	0	0	4	0	0	10	0	0	56	0
Totals	**462**	**12**	**47**	**44**	**2**	**7**	**110**	**3**	**15**	**616**	**17**	●

e second leg as, with Stoke winning 1–0 with just four
inutes left, Hurst stepped up to take a penalty – if he
ored the Hammers would be at Wembley.

nfortunately for the Hammers Gordon Banks made a
onder save and the tie went to a replay at Hillsborough.
hat game resulted in a 0–0 stalemate, which meant a
cond replay at Old Trafford. This next tie, for twists,
rns, upheavals and sheer football drama, was one of the
eat cup ties of the 1970s. On 13 minutes goalkeeper
obby Ferguson went off for lengthy treatment, to be
placed in goal by Bobby Moore. Later Stoke were awarded
penalty, which Moore saved, but the ball rebounded to
ike Bernard who scored for Stoke. The Hammers ten
en then rallied, with goals from Bonds and Brooking
tting them 2–1 ahead. Ferguson, still concussed, then
turned to play in goal, only to concede goals from Dobing
d Conroy, which saw Stoke reach the cup final.

After beating Luton Town in the FA Cup the next round
brought a trip to non-league Hereford United. It was a
tense 0–0 affair; the replay, however, saw Geoff Hurst score
a hat-trick as the gallant non-leaguers lost 3–1. Cup hopes
were dashed at Huddersfield Town as the Yorkshire side
knocked the Hammers out 4–2. After their cup exertions
the league form fell away, with the team winning just four
of their final 16 fixtures to leave them in a disappointing
fourteenth.

KEVIN LOCK

**Graduating through the youth team and the
reserves, Lock made his first-team debut
after coming on as a substitute at Sheffield
United in February 1972.**

Playing as a central defender, he had the
unenviable task of taking over from Bobby
Moore after he had left for Fulham. Kevin was
ever-present in 1974–75 and played in the FA
Cup final when the Hammers beat Fulham
2–0. The following season he was on the
bench as West Ham lost to Anderlecht in the
European Cup Winners' Cup final.

While at West Ham he gained four England
under-23 caps and came close to a full cap
when named as a substitute against Portugal
in 1975. He played in 161 games for the
Hammers, after which he was transferred to
Fulham for a fee of £60,000 in 1978. He played
211 games for the Cottagers before he
finished his playing career at Southend
United, appearing in 10 games in 1985. He
later had coaching jobs at Millwall and
Chelsea, and was assistant manager at
Brentford. After leaving the football scene he
was a licensee and now currently works as an
usher at Essex Magistrates' Court.

Football League - Division One Final Table 1971-72

		HOME					AWAY					
	P	W	D	L	F	A	W	D	L	F	A	Pts
erby County	42	16	4	1	43	10	8	6	7	26	23	58
eds United	42	17	4	0	54	10	7	5	9	19	21	57
verpool	42	17	3	1	48	16	7	6	8	16	14	57
anchester City	42	16	3	2	48	15	7	8	6	29	30	57
senal	42	15	2	4	36	13	7	6	8	22	27	52
ttenham Hotspur	42	16	3	2	45	13	3	10	8	18	29	51
helsea	42	12	7	2	41	20	6	5	10	17	29	48
anchester United	42	13	2	6	39	26	6	8	7	30	35	48
olverhampton Wanderers	42	10	7	4	35	23	8	4	9	30	34	47
heffield United	42	10	8	3	39	26	7	4	10	22	34	46
ewcastle United	42	10	6	5	30	18	5	5	11	19	34	41
icester City	42	9	6	6	18	11	4	7	10	23	35	39
swich Town	42	7	8	6	19	19	4	8	9	20	34	38
est Ham United	**42**	**10**	**6**	**5**	**31**	**19**	**2**	**6**	**13**	**16**	**32**	**36**
verton	42	8	9	4	28	17	1	9	11	9	31	36
est Bromwich Albion	42	6	7	8	22	23	6	4	11	20	31	35
oke City	42	6	10	5	26	25	4	5	12	13	31	35
oventry City	42	7	10	4	27	23	2	5	14	17	44	33
outhampton	42	8	5	8	31	28	4	2	15	21	52	31
rystal Palace	42	4	8	9	26	31	4	5	12	13	34	29
ottingham Forest	42	6	4	11	25	29	2	5	14	22	52	25
uddersfield Town	42	4	7	10	12	22	2	6	13	15	37	25

Season **1971-72** Football League - Division One
Match Details

Manager **Ron Greenwood**   Final League Position **14/22**

	Date		Competition	Venue	Opponents		Results	Attendance	Position	Scorers
1	Aug 14	Sat	Div 1	H	West Bromwich Albion	L	0-1	27,420	22	
2	Aug 18	Wed	Div 1	A	Derby County	L	0-2	30,783	22	
3	Aug 21	Sat	Div 1	A	Nottingham Forest	L	0-1	17,185	22	
4	Aug 23	Mon	Div 1	H	Ipswich Town	D	0-0	25,714	22	
5	Aug 28	Sat	Div 1	H	Everton	W	1-0	26,878	21	Best
6	Aug 30	Mon	Div 1	H	Coventry City	W	4-0	28,176	10	Best 2, Hurst, Robson
7	Sep 4	Sat	Div 1	A	Newcastle United	D	2-2	31,972	12	Hurst, Robson
8	Sep 8	Wed	FLC 2	H	Cardiff City	D	1-1	24,420		Bonds
9	Sep 11	Sat	Div 1	H	Chelsea	W	2-1	36,866	9	Best 2
10	Sep 18	Sat	Div 1	A	Manchester United	L	2-4	52,731	12	Best, Brooking
11	Sep 22	Wed	FLC 2 Rep	H	Cardiff City	W	2-1	30,100		Hurst 2
12	Sep 25	Sat	Div 1	H	Stoke City	W	2-1	29,193	10	Best, Moore
13	Oct 2	Sat	Div 1	A	Leeds United	D	0-0	30,942	10	
14	Oct 6	Wed	FLC 3	H	Leeds United	D	0-0	35,890		
15	Oct 9	Sat	Div 1	H	Leicester City	D	1-1	31,060	12	Hurst
16	Oct 16	Sat	Div 1	A	West Bromwich Albion	D	0-0	20,620	11	
17	Oct 20	Wed	FLC 3 Rep	A	Leeds United	W	1-0	26,504		Best
18	Oct 23	Sat	Div 1	H	Wolverhampton Wanderers	W	1-0	33,883	9	Best
19	Oct 27	Wed	FLC 4	H	Liverpool	W	2-1	40,878		Hurst, Robson
20	Oct 30	Sat	Div 1	A	Crystal Palace	W	3-0	41,540	9	Best, Bonds, Coker
21	Nov 6	Sat	Div 1	H	Sheffield United	L	1-2	36,593	10	Robson
22	Nov 13	Sat	Div 1	A	Huddersfield Town	L	0-1	14,177	10	
23	Nov 17	Wed	FLC 5	H	Sheffield United	W	5-0	36,834		Robson 3, Best 2
24	Nov 20	Sat	Div 1	H	Manchester City	L	0-2	33,694	13	
25	Nov 27	Sat	Div 1	A	Liverpool	L	0-1	43,399	13	
26	Dec 4	Sat	Div 1	H	Arsenal	D	0-0	35,155	13	
27	Dec 8	Wed	FLC SF:1	A	Stoke City	W	2-1	36,400		Best, Hurst [pen]
28	Dec 11	Sat	Div 1	A	Southampton	D	3-3	20,506	12	Best, Bonds, Brooking
29	Dec 15	Wed	FLC SF:2	H	Stoke City	L	0-1	38,771		
30	Dec 18	Sat	Div 1	H	Newcastle United	L	0-1	21,991	13	
31	Dec 27	Mon	Div 1	A	Tottenham Hotspur	W	1-0	53,868	12	Best
32	Jan 1	Sat	Div 1	H	Manchester United	W	3-0	41,892	11	Best, Hurst [pen], Robson
33	Jan 5	Wed	FLC SF Rep	N*	Stoke City	D	0-0	46,196		
34	Jan 8	Sat	Div 1	A	Everton	L	1-2	38,482	12	Hurst [pen]
35	Jan 15	Sat	FAC 3	H	Luton Town	W	2-1	32,099		Best, Hurst
36	Jan 22	Sat	Div 1	H	Derby County	D	3-3	31,045	12	Brooking, Lampard, Robson
37	Jan 26	Wed	FLC SF 2 Rep	N**	Stoke City	L	2-3	49,247		Bonds, Brooking
38	Jan 29	Sat	Div 1	A	Ipswich Town	L	0-1	22,757	13	
39	Feb 9	Wed	FAC 4	A	Hereford United	D	0-0	15,000		
40	Feb 12	Sat	Div 1	A	Wolverhampton Wanderers	L	0-1	28,852	15	
41	Feb 14	Mon	FAC 4 Rep	H	Hereford United	W	3-1	42,271		Hurst 3
42	Feb 19	Sat	Div 1	H	Crystal Palace	D	1-1	28,209	13	Best
43	Feb 26	Sat	FAC 5	A	Huddersfield Town	L	2-4	27,080		Best, Robson
44	Feb 29	Wed	Div 1	A	Sheffield United	L	0-3	24,034	14	
45	Mar 4	Sat	Div 1	H	Huddersfield Town	W	3-0	18,521	12	Best 2, Robson
46	Mar 11	Sat	Div 1	A	Leicester City	L	0-2	23,339	14	
47	Mar 18	Sat	Div 1	H	Nottingham Forest	W	4-2	20,960	12	Robson 2, Brooking, Hurst
48	Mar 21	Tue	Div 1	A	Coventry City	D	1-1	18,703	12	Best
49	Mar 25	Sat	Div 1	A	Chelsea	L	1-3	45,137	12	Best
50	Mar 31	Fri	Div 1	H	Leeds United	D	2-2	41,003	12	Bonds, Hurst
51	Apr 1	Sat	Div 1	H	Tottenham Hotspur	W	2-0	30,763	11	Brooking, Coker
52	Apr 4	Tue	Div 1	A	Stoke City	D	0-0	24,628	12	
53	Apr 8	Sat	Div 1	A	Manchester City	L	1-3	38,488	14	Hurst
54	Apr 15	Sat	Div 1	H	Liverpool	L	0-2	32,660	14	
55	Apr 22	Sat	Div 1	A	Arsenal	L	1-2	45,215	15	Brooking
56	May 1	Mon	Div 1	H	Southampton	W	1-0	18,421	14	Robson

* Played at Hillsborough, Sheffield ** Played at Old Trafford, Manchester

eam Line-Ups

AYRIS Johnny	BEST Clyde	BONDS Billy	BOYCE Ron	BROOKING Trevor	CHARLES Clive	COKER Adewunmi	DURRELL Joe	EUSTACE Peter	FERGUSON Bobby	GROTIER Peter	HEFFER Paul	HOLLAND Pat	HOWE Bobby	HURST Geoff	LAMPARD Frank	LLEWELLYN David	LOCK Kevin	McDOWELL John	MOORE Bobby	REDKNAPP Harry	ROBSON Bryan	STEPHENSON Alan	TAYLOR Tommy	#
7	8	4							1					9	3			2	6		11	5	10	1
7	8	4							1				a	9	3			2	6		11	5	10	2
7	9	4		10					1			11			3			2	6		8		5	3
7	8	4		10					1				a	9	3			2	6		11		5	4
7	8	4		10					1					9	3			2	6		11		5	5
7	8	4		10					1					9	3			2	6		11		5	6
7	8	4		10					1					9	3			2	6		11		5	7
7	8	4		10					1					9	3			2	6		11		5	8
7	8	4		10					1				a	9	3			2	6		11		5	9
	8	4		10					1					9	3			2	6	7	11		5	10
	8	4		10					1					9	3			2	6	7	11		5	11
	8	4		10			7		1					9	3			2	6		11		5	12
	8	4		10					1					9	3			2	6	7	11		5	13
	8	4		10					1					9	3			2	6	7	11		5	14
	8	4		10					1					9	3			2	6	7	11		5	15
	8	4		10					1					9	3			2	6	7	11		5	16
	8	4		10					1					9	3			2	6	7	11		5	17
	8	4		10/a			7		1				a	9	3			2	6		11		5	18
	8	4		10					1				a	9/a	3			2	6	7	11		5	19
	8	4		10	9					1					3			2	6	7	11		5	20
a	8	4		10					1					9	3			2/a	6	7	11		5	21
	8	4		10	9				1						3			2	6	7	11		5	22
	8	4		10					1				a	9/a	3			2	6	7	11		5	23
	8	2		10	9/a	a	4		1						3				6	7	11		5	24
	8	4		10					1					9	3			2	6	7	11		5	25
	8	4		10					1					9	3			2	6	7	11		5	26
	8	4		10					1					9	3			2	6	7	11		5	27
	8	4		10/a					1					9	3		a	2	6	7	11		5	28
	8	4		10					1					9	3			2	6	7	11		5	29
	8	4		10					1					9	3			2	6		11		5	30
	8	4		10					1					9	3			2	6	7	11		5	31
	8	4		10					1					9	3			2	6	7	11		5	32
	8	4		10					1					9	3			2	6	7	11		5	33
	8	4		10					1					9	3			2	6	7	11		5	34
	8	4		10				a	1					9	3			2	6/a	7	11		5	35
	8	4		10					1					9	3			2	6	7	11		5	36
	8	4		10				a	1					9	3			2	6	7/a	11		5	37
	8	4		10						1				9	3			2	6	7	11		5	38
	8	4		10					1					9	3			2	6	7	11		5	39
	8	4		10					1					9	3/a			2	6		11	a	5	40
	8	4		10					1					9	3			2	6	7	11		5	41
	8	4		10			7		1				a	9	3			2/a	6		11		5	42
	8	4		10					1				a	9/a	3			2	6	7	11		5	43
	8	4		10			7		1						3	9/a	a	2	6		11		5	44
	8	4		10					1					9	3			2	6	7	11		5	45
	8	4		10					1					9	3			2	6	7	11		5	46
	8	4		10			7		1					9	3			2	6		11		5	47
	8	4		10	3		7		1					9				2	6		11		5	48
	8	4		10			7		1					9	3			2	6		11		5	49
	8	4		10						1				9	3			2	6	7	11		5	50
a	8	4		10	3	9			1								a	2	6		11		5	51
	8	4		10						1				9	3			2	6	7	11		5	52
	8	4		10						1				9	3			2	6	7	11		5	53
	8	4		10					1					9	3			2	6	7	11		5	54
	8	4		10	3	9	7		1								6	2			11		5	55
	8	4	a	10/a	3		7						9					2			11	5	6	56

1972-73
Story of the season

There were **various departures at this time,** among them Eustace, Redknapp and Stephenson, but **the big shock came when Geoff Hurst was transferred** to Stoke City for a fee of £80,000.

It was a decent start to the season with just three loss in the first nine games. At home Coventry City were beat 5–2 and Norwich City 4–0. Bryan Robson was the man form, scoring eight goals in those nine games.

The League Cup began with a narrow 2–1 home victo against Bristol City but the next round was a disaster as t Hammers were humbled 2–1 away to Fourth Divisic Stockport County. After a 2–2 draw in November wi Wolves the team had moved up to fifth place, but the ne nine games only yielded two wins. Robson was still on t mark, scoring twice against both Stoke City and Tottenha

After winning 1–0 at Port Vale in the FA Cup, a trip to H City in the fourth round brought a 1–0 defeat. In Mar centre-forward Ted MacDougall was signed for £150,0

Appearances & Goals 1972-73

	League			FA Cup			League Cup			Total	
	Starts	Subs	Goals	Starts	Subs	Goals	Starts	Subs	Goals	Starts	Subs
AYRIS Johnny	13	2	1	0	0	0	0	0	0	13	2
BEST Clyde	41	1	7	2	0	0	2	0	2	45	1
BONDS Billy	39	0	3	2	0	0	2	0	0	43	0
BOYCE Ron	0	2	0	0	0	0	0	0	0	0	2
BROOKING Trevor	40	0	11	2	0	0	2	0	0	44	0
CHARLES Clive	7	3	0	0	0	0	0	0	0	7	3
COKER Adewunmi	4	0	1	0	0	0	0	0	0	4	0
FERGUSON Bobby	31	0	0	2	0	0	0	0	0	33	0
GROTIER Peter	11	0	0	0	0	0	2	0	0	13	0
HOLLAND Pat	30	2	1	2	0	1	2	0	0	34	2
LAMPARD Frank	38	0	0	2	0	0	2	0	0	42	0
LOCK Kevin	14	4	1	0	1	0	0	0	0	14	5
LUTTON Bertie	4	2	1	0	0	0	0	0	0	4	2
MacDOUGALL Ted	10	0	4	0	0	0	0	0	0	10	0
McDOWELL John	38	0	2	2	0	0	2	0	1	42	0
MOORE Bobby	42	0	3	2	0	0	2	0	0	46	0
ROBSON Bryan	42	0	28	2	0	0	2	0	0	46	0
TAYLOR Tommy	37	0	3	2	0	0	2	0	0	41	0
TYLER Dudley	21	0	1	2	0	0	2	0	0	25	0
Totals	**462**	**16**	**67**	**22**	**1**	**1**	**22**	**0**	**3**	**506**	**17**

om Manchester United, and his four goals in his first five
pearances helped the team to a nine-game unbeaten run.
ryan Robson scored a hat-trick against Southampton to
ke his tally of goals to 28, which made him the league's
p scorer. There had been poor performances in the cups
t a sixth-place finish in the league was the highest placing
nce 1959.

BRYAN ROBSON

'Pop' was a prolific goalscorer, scoring a career total of 265 league goals in his 674 appearances.

Although he gained two England under-23 caps it is a mystery as to why he was never chosen to play for the full England team. He began his career at Newcastle United in 1962 and in nine seasons on Tyneside he made 244 appearances, scoring 97 goals. While with Newcastle he won a Second Division Championship medal and a European Fairs Cup medal. In February 1971 West Ham paid a club record fee of £120,000 for his services and he scored on his debut against Nottingham Forest in a 2–0 win at Upton Park. A move to Sunderland in 1975 saw him win another Second Division Championship medal before West Ham bought him back for £80,000 in in October 1976. He stayed with the Hammers for a further three seasons before again joining Sunderland. After 52 league appearances for the Wearsiders he then had spells at Chelsea and Carlisle United, where he ended his playing career in 1985. He later coached at Carlisle, Manchester United, Sunderland and Leeds United.

ootball League - Division One
inal Table 1972-73

| | | | HOME | | | | AWAY | | | | | |
	P	W	D	L	F	A	W	D	L	F	A	Pts
erpool	42	17	3	1	45	19	8	7	6	27	23	60
senal	42	14	5	2	31	14	9	6	6	26	29	57
eds United	42	15	4	2	45	13	6	7	8	26	32	53
swich Town	42	10	7	4	34	20	7	7	7	21	25	48
lverhampton Wanderers	42	13	3	5	43	23	5	8	8	23	31	47
est Ham United	42	12	5	4	45	25	5	7	9	22	28	46
rby County	42	15	3	3	43	18	4	5	12	13	36	46
tenham Hotspur	42	10	5	6	33	23	6	8	7	25	25	45
wcastle United	42	12	6	3	35	19	4	7	10	25	32	45
mingham City	42	11	7	3	39	22	4	5	12	14	32	42
anchester City	42	12	4	5	36	20	3	7	11	21	40	41
elsea	42	9	6	6	30	22	4	8	9	19	29	40
uthampton	42	8	11	2	26	17	3	7	11	21	35	40
effield United	42	11	4	6	28	18	4	6	11	23	41	40
oke City	42	11	8	2	38	17	3	2	16	23	39	38
cester City	42	7	9	5	23	18	3	8	10	17	28	37
erton	42	9	5	7	27	21	4	6	11	14	28	37
anchester United	42	9	7	5	24	19	3	6	12	20	41	37
ventry City	42	9	5	7	27	24	4	4	13	13	31	35
rwich City	42	7	9	5	22	19	4	1	16	14	44	32
ystal Palace	42	7	7	7	25	21	2	5	14	16	37	30
est Bromwich Albion	42	8	7	6	25	24	1	3	17	13	38	28

Season **1972-73** Football League - Division One
Match Details

Manager **Ron Greenwood**   Final League Position **6/22**

	Date		Competition	Venue	Opponents	Results		Attendance	Position	Scorers
1	Aug 12	Sat	Div 1	A	West Bromwich Albion	D	0-0	22,234	14	
2	Aug 14	Mon	Div 1	H	Coventry City	W	1-0	27,498	1	Best
3	Aug 19	Sat	Div 1	H	Leicester City	W	5-2	25,490	5	Robson 2, Coker, Moore, Tyler
4	Aug 22	Tue	Div 1	A	Wolverhampton Wanderers	L	0-3	21,958	5	
5	Aug 26	Sat	Div 1	A	Liverpool	L	2-3	50,491	12	Robson 2
6	Aug 29	Tue	Div 1	A	Arsenal	L	0-1	43,802	14	
7	Sep 2	Sat	Div 1	H	Manchester United	D	2-2	31,939	12	Robson 2
8	Sep 6	Wed	FLC 2	H	Bristol City	W	2-1	17,688		Best, McDowell
9	Sep 9	Sat	Div 1	A	Chelsea	W	3-1	34,392	11	Bonds, Moore, Tyler
10	Sep 16	Sat	Div 1	H	Norwich City	W	4-0	28,058	9	Robson 2 [1 pen], Brooking, Taylor T.
11	Sep 23	Sat	Div 1	A	Tottenham Hotspur	L	0-1	51,291	12	
12	Sep 30	Sat	Div 1	H	Birmingham City	W	2-0	26,482	11	Best, Bonds
13	Oct 4	Wed	FLC 3	A	Stockport County	L	1-2	13,410		Best
14	Oct 7	Sat	Div 1	A	Ipswich Town	D	1-1	22,218	10	Best
15	Oct 14	Sat	Div 1	H	Sheffield United	W	3-1	25,379	7	Robson 2, Brooking
16	Oct 21	Sat	Div 1	A	Manchester City	L	3-4	31,052	10	Ayris, Best, Moore
17	Oct 28	Sat	Div 1	H	Crystal Palace	W	4-0	28,894	8	Brooking 2, McDowell, Robson
18	Nov 4	Sat	Div 1	H	Wolverhampton Wanderers	D	2-2	29,524	6	Brooking, Robson
19	Nov 11	Sat	Div 1	A	Coventry City	L	1-3	27,172	9	McDowell
20	Nov 18	Sat	Div 1	H	Derby County	L	1-2	28,154	11	Robson
21	Nov 25	Sat	Div 1	A	Everton	W	2-1	27,558	8	Best, Brooking
22	Dec 2	Sat	Div 1	H	Newcastle United	D	1-1	23,785	7	Brooking
23	Dec 9	Sat	Div 1	A	Leeds United	L	0-1	30,270	9	
24	Dec 16	Sat	Div 1	H	Stoke City	W	3-2	23,269	7	Robson 2, Best
25	Dec 23	Sat	Div 1	A	Southampton	D	0-0	19,429	8	
26	Dec 26	Tue	Div 1	H	Tottenham Hotspur	D	2-2	37,397	8	Robson 2 [1 pen]
27	Dec 30	Sat	Div 1	A	Leicester City	L	1-2	19,341	10	Brooking
28	Jan 6	Sat	Div 1	H	Liverpool	L	0-1	34,480	12	
29	Jan 13	Sat	FAC 3	A	Port Vale	W	1-0	20,619		Holland
30	Jan 20	Sat	Div 1	A	Manchester United	D	2-2	50,878	8	Best, Robson
31	Jan 27	Sat	Div 1	H	Chelsea	W	3-1	35,336	7	Robson 2, Taylor T.
32	Feb 3	Sat	FAC 4	A	Hull City	L	0-1	32,290		
33	Feb 10	Sat	Div 1	A	Norwich City	W	1-0	32,286	7	Robson
34	Feb 17	Sat	Div 1	H	West Bromwich Albion	W	2-1	26,079	7	Bonds, Robson
35	Feb 24	Sat	Div 1	A	Stoke City	L	0-2	21,885	7	
36	Mar 2	Fri	Div 1	H	Ipswich Town	L	0-1	37,004	7	
37	Mar 10	Sat	Div 1	A	Sheffield United	D	0-0	24,024	9	
38	Mar 17	Sat	Div 1	H	Manchester City	W	2-1	30,156	7	MacDougall, Robson
39	Mar 24	Sat	Div 1	A	Crystal Palace	W	3-1	36,865	7	Brooking, MacDougall, Robson
40	Mar 31	Sat	Div 1	H	Everton	W	2-0	25,531	7	Lock, Robson
41	Apr 7	Sat	Div 1	A	Newcastle United	W	2-1	24,075	5	MacDougall 2
42	Apr 14	Sat	Div 1	H	Leeds United	D	1-1	38,804	5	Holland
43	Apr 20	Fri	Div 1	H	Southampton	W	4-3	33,039	5	Robson 3, Brooking
44	Apr 21	Sat	Div 1	A	Derby County	D	1-1	28,727	5	Lutton
45	Apr 23	Mon	Div 1	A	Birmingham City	D	0-0	36,942	5	
46	Apr 28	Sat	Div 1	H	Arsenal	L	1-2	37,366	6	Brooking

Team Line-Ups

AYRIS Johnny	BEST Clyde	BONDS Billy	BOYCE Ron	BROOKING Trevor	CHARLES Clive	COKER Adewunmi	FERGUSON Bobby	GROTIER Peter	HOLLAND Pat	LAMPARD Frank	LOCK Kevin	LUTTON Bertie	MacDOUGALL Ted	McDOWELL John	MOORE Bobby	ROBSON Bryan	TAYLOR Tommy	TYLER Dudley	
	8	4		10		9	1			3				2	6	11	5	7	1
	8	4		10		9	1			3				2	6	11	5	7	2
	8	4		10		9	1			3				2	6	11	5	7	3
	8	4		10		9	1			3				2	6	11	5	7	4
	8	4		10			1		9	3				2	6	11	5	7	5
	8	4		10				1	9	3	a			2	6	11/a	5	7	6
	8	4		10				1	9	3				2	6	11	5	7	7
	8	4		10				1	9	3				2	6	11	5	7	8
	8	4		10				1	9	3				2	6	11	5	7	9
	8	4		10				1	9	3				2	6	11	5	7	10
	8	4		10	a			1	9	3				2/a	6	11	5	7	11
	8	4		10	2			1	9	3					6	11	5	7	12
	8	4		10				1	9	3				2	6	11	5	7	13
	8	4		10	3			1	9	2					6	11	5	7	14
	8	4		10				1	9	3				2	6	11	5	7	15
7	8	4		10				1	9	3				2	6	11	5		16
7	8			10	4		1		9	3				2	6	11	5		17
a	8			10			1		9	3		4		2	6	11	5	7/a	18
	8	4		10			1		9	3				2	6	11	5	7	19
8/a	a	4		10	2		1		9	3					6	11	5	7	20
	8	4		10			1		9	3/a	a			2	6	11	5	7	21
7	8	4		10			1		9		3			2	6	11	5		22
7/a	8	4	a	10	3		1		9					2	6	11	5		23
7	8	4		10			1		9	3				2	6	11	5		24
7	8	4		10			1		9	3	a			2/a	6	11	5		25
	8	4		10			1		9	3	7			2	6	11	5		26
7	8	4	a	10/a			1		9	3				2	6	11	5		27
7	8				a		1		9	3	4/a			2	6	11	5	10	28
	8	4		10	a		1		9	3/a				2	6	11	5	7	29
7	8	4			3		1		9					2	6	11	5	10	30
	8	4		10			1		9	3				2	6	11	5	7	31
	8	4		10			1		9	3	a			2	6	11	5	7/a	32
7	8	4		10			1			3			9	2	6	11	5		33
7	8	4		10			1		9	3				2	6	11	5		34
7/a	8	4		10			1		9	3	a			2	6	11	5		35
	8	4		10			1		9	3				2	6	11	5	7	36
	7	4		10			1			3	8		9	2	6	11	5		37
	7	4		10			1		a	3/a	8		9	2	6	11	5		38
	7	4		10			1			3	8		9	2	6	11	5		39
	8	4/a		10			1		a	3	7		9	2	6	11	5		40
	7	4		10			1			3	8		9	2	6	11	5		41
	7	4		10			1/a		8	3	5	a	9	2	6	11			42
	7	4		10				1	8	3	5	a	9	2/a	6	11			43
	7	4		10	2		1			3	5	8	9		6	11			44
	7	4		10			1			3	5	8	9	2	6	11			45
a	7/a	4		10			1			3	5	8	9	2	6	11			46

1973-74
Story of the season

It was a **wretched beginning** to the campaign as **the Hammers were winless after 11 games** and sat second to bottom in the league.

Young goalkeeper Mervyn Day was brought into the side and th team won their first game at Coventry City in October. The Leagu Cup brought no joy as Liverpool won 1–0 at Anfield in a replay. It too a further seven games before a second league win came whe Manchester City were beaten 2–1 at home in December.

New signings arrived when manager Ron Greenwood bought strike Bobby Gould, midfielder Graham Paddon and defender Mic McGiven. The new players helped, as there were two 4–2 victorie against Chelsea and Norwich City. This improvement was no maintained in the FA Cup, however, as Third Division Herefor United won 2–1 in the replay following a 2–2 draw at Upton Park.

Appearances & Goals 1973-74

	League			FA Cup			League Cup			Other*			Total		
	Starts	Subs	Goals	Starts	Subs	Goals	Starts	Subs	Goals	Starts	Subs	Goals	Starts	Subs	Goals
AYRIS Johnny	5	0	0	0	0	0	1	0	0	1	0	0	7	0	
BEST Clyde	34	0	12	2	0	1	2	0	0	0	0	0	38	0	
BONDS Billy	40	0	13	2	0	0	1	0	0	1	0	0	44	0	
BROOKING Trevor	38	0	6	0	0	0	2	0	0	1	0	0	41	0	
CHARLES Clive	1	0	0	0	0	0	0	0	0	0	0	0	1	0	
COKER Adewunmi	0	1	0	1	0	0	0	0	0	0	0	0	1	1	
COLEMAN Keith	31	2	0	1	0	0	2	0	0	0	0	0	34	2	
DAY Mervyn	33	0	0	2	0	0	2	0	0	0	0	0	37	0	
FERGUSON Bobby	9	0	0	0	0	0	0	0	0	1	0	0	10	0	
GOULD Bobby	11	1	4	1	0	0	0	0	0	0	0	0	12	1	
HOLLAND Pat	20	3	2	1	1	1	0	2	0	1	0	0	22	6	
LAMPARD Frank	42	0	2	2	0	0	2	0	0	1	0	0	47	0	
LOCK Kevin	9	2	0	0	0	0	2	0	0	0	1	0	11	3	
LUTTON Bertie	4	2	0	1	0	0	0	0	0	0	0	0	5	2	
MacDOUGALL Ted	14	0	1	0	0	0	1	0	1	1	0	1	16	0	
McDOWELL John	33	0	2	1	0	0	2	0	0	1	0	0	37	0	
McGIVEN Mick	21	0	0	2	0	0	0	0	0	0	0	0	23	0	
MOORE Bobby	22	0	0	1	0	0	1	0	0	1	0	0	25	0	
PADDON Graham	24	0	4	2	0	0	0	0	0	0	0	0	26	0	
ROBSON Bryan	22	0	7	0	0	0	1	0	1	1	0	0	24	0	
TAYLOR Tommy	40	0	0	2	0	0	2	0	0	1	0	0	45	0	
TYLER Dudley	8	0	0	0	0	0	1	0	0	0	1	0	9	1	
WOOLER Alan	1	1	0	1	0	0	0	0	0	0	0	0	2	1	
own goal			2												
Totals	**462**	**12**	**55**	**22**	**1**	**2**	**22**	**2**	**2**	**11**	**2**	**1**	**517**	**17**	

* Other = Watney Invitation Cup

gnificant event took place when Bobby Moore moved cross London to sign for Fulham. It was the end of an era he had played 642 games for the club.

spired by skipper Billy Bonds there was a 10-game nbeaten run that raised morale. Bonds was waging a one-an crusade against relegation, with a hat-trick against helsea in a 3–0 victory. Further wins against Leeds United d Southampton found the Hammers virtually safe and a nal day 2–2 home draw with Liverpool gave an eighteenth ace finish.

ootball League - Division One
inal Table 1973-74

	P	HOME					AWAY					Pts
		W	D	L	F	A	W	D	L	F	A	
eds United	42	12	8	1	38	18	12	6	3	28	13	62
verpool	42	18	2	1	34	11	4	11	6	18	20	57
rby County	42	13	7	1	40	16	4	7	10	12	26	48
swich Town	42	10	7	4	38	21	8	4	9	29	37	47
oke City	42	13	6	2	39	15	2	10	9	15	27	46
urnley	42	10	9	2	29	16	6	5	10	27	37	46
erton	42	12	7	2	29	14	4	5	12	21	34	44
eens Park Rangers	42	8	10	3	30	17	5	7	9	26	35	43
icester City	42	10	7	4	35	17	3	9	9	16	24	42
senal	42	9	7	5	23	16	5	7	9	26	35	42
ttenham Hotspur	42	9	4	8	26	27	5	10	6	19	23	42
lverhampton Wanderers	42	11	6	4	30	18	2	9	10	19	31	41
effield United	42	7	7	7	25	22	7	5	9	19	27	40
anchester City	42	10	7	4	25	17	4	5	12	14	29	40
wcastle United	42	9	6	6	28	21	4	6	11	21	27	38
oventry City	42	10	5	6	25	18	4	5	12	18	36	38
elsea	42	9	4	8	36	29	3	9	9	20	31	37
est Ham United	42	7	7	7	36	32	4	8	9	19	28	37
rmingham City	42	10	7	4	30	21	2	6	13	22	43	37
uthampton	42	8	10	3	30	20	3	4	14	17	48	36
anchester United	42	7	7	7	23	20	3	5	13	15	28	32
rwich City	42	6	9	6	25	27	1	6	14	12	35	29

MERVYN DAY

Goalkeeper Day joined West Ham as an apprentice in July 1971, and by August 1973 he was making his first-team debut in the 3–3 home draw with Ipswich Town.

He soon established himself as the first-choice keeper and from November 1973 he went on to play in 108 consecutive league games. In 1975 he won an FA Cup winners' medal and was named as the PFA Young Player of the Year. The following season he gained a runners-up medal when the Hammers lost to Anderlecht in the European Cup Winners' Cup Final.

Mervyn played 233 games for West Ham before transferring to Leyton Orient in July 1979 for a fee of £100,000. He captained Orient in 1982 and was the substitute goalkeeper for the England B side in 1979 against New Zealand. He played 170 league games for Orient before moving on in 1983 to play in 33 games for Aston Villa. His next club was Leeds United, where he spent eight seasons playing in 227 league games.

Towards the end of his time with the Yorkshire club he had short spells on loan at Luton Town and Sheffield United. His final club was Carlisle United, where he played in 16 league games in season 1993/94. After retiring as a player he managed Carlisle for two seasons before spending many years as coach at Charlton Athletic.

In December 2006 he was back at West Ham as assistant manager, a position he held until September 2008. He has since held scouting jobs at Leeds and Brighton and is currently the head of recruitment at West Bromwich Albion.

Season **1973-74** Football League - Division One
Match Details

Manager **Ron Greenwood**   Final League Position **18/22**

	Date		Competition	Venue	Opponents	Results		Attendance	Position	Scorers
1	Aug 11	Sat	WIC*	A	Bristol Rovers	D	1-1	19,974		MacDougall
2	Aug 25	Sat	Div 1	H	Newcastle United	L	1-2	28,169	14	Robson
3	Aug 27	Mon	Div 1	H	Ipswich Town	D	3-3	23,335	14	Best, Bonds, Brooking
4	Sep 1	Sat	Div 1	A	Norwich City	D	2-2	25,378	14	Best, Robson
5	Sep 4	Tue	Div 1	A	Queens Park Rangers	D	0-0	28,360	14	
6	Sep 8	Sat	Div 1	H	Tottenham Hotspur	L	0-1	30,888	17	
7	Sep 10	Mon	Div 1	H	Queens Park Rangers	L	2-3	26,042	17	Robson, Bonds [pen]
8	Sep 15	Sat	Div 1	A	Manchester United	L	1-3	44,757	21	Bonds [pen]
9	Sep 22	Sat	Div 1	H	Leicester City	D	1-1	23,567	21	Robson
10	Sep 29	Sat	Div 1	A	Stoke City	L	0-2	16,397	21	
11	Oct 6	Sat	Div 1	H	Burnley	L	0-1	23,604	21	
12	Oct 8	Mon	FLC 2	H	Liverpool	D	2-2	25,840		MacDougall, Robson
13	Oct 13	Sat	Div 1	A	Everton	L	0-1	34,708	22	
14	Oct 20	Sat	Div 1	A	Coventry City	W	1-0	21,141	21	McDowell
15	Oct 27	Sat	Div 1	H	Derby County	D	0-0	31,237	21	
16	Oct 29	Mon	FLC 2 Rep	A	Liverpool	L	0-1	26,002		
17	Nov 3	Sat	Div 1	A	Leeds United	L	1-4	35,869	21	MacDougall
18	Nov 10	Sat	Div 1	H	Sheffield United	D	2-2	21,245	21	Bonds, Brooking
19	Nov 17	Sat	Div 1	A	Wolverhampton Wanderers	D	0-0	19,587	21	
20	Nov 24	Sat	Div 1	H	Arsenal	L	1-3	28,287	21	Bonds
21	Dec 1	Sat	Div 1	A	Liverpool	L	0-1	34,857	22	
22	Dec 8	Sat	Div 1	H	Manchester City	W	2-1	20,790	20	Brooking, Doyle (og)
23	Dec 15	Sat	Div 1	A	Birmingham City	L	1-3	23,767	22	Gould
24	Dec 22	Sat	Div 1	H	Stoke City	L	0-2	16,513	22	
25	Dec 26	Wed	Div 1	A	Chelsea	W	4-2	26,982	21	Best 2, Gould, Lampard
26	Dec 29	Sat	Div 1	A	Tottenham Hotspur	L	0-2	33,176	21	
27	Jan 1	Tue	Div 1	H	Norwich City	W	4-2	32,259	21	Paddon 2, Brooking, Gould
28	Jan 5	Sat	FAC 3	H	Hereford United	D	1-1	23,087		Holland
29	Jan 9	Wed	FAC 3 Rep	A	Hereford United	L	1-2	17,423		Best
30	Jan 12	Sat	Div 1	H	Manchester United	W	2-1	34,147	19	Bonds, Holland
31	Jan 19	Sat	Div 1	A	Newcastle United	D	1-1	27,217	19	Holland
32	Feb 2	Sat	Div 1	H	Birmingham City	D	0-0	27,948	19	
33	Feb 5	Tue	Div 1	A	Ipswich Town	W	3-1	25,734	19	Best, McDowell, Mills (og)
34	Feb 9	Sat	Div 1	A	Leicester City	W	1-0	27,032	19	Best
35	Feb 16	Sat	Div 1	H	Everton	W	4-3	29,374	19	Best 2, Bonds, Paddon
36	Feb 23	Sat	Div 1	A	Burnley	D	1-1	18,258	19	Paddon
37	Mar 2	Sat	Div 1	H	Chelsea	W	3-0	34,143	16	Bonds 3
38	Mar 9	Sat	Div 1	A	Derby County	D	1-1	24,683	16	Bonds
39	Mar 16	Sat	Div 1	H	Coventry City	L	2-3	26,502	18	Bonds 2 [1 pen]
40	Mar 23	Sat	Div 1	A	Sheffield United	L	0-1	19,467	19	
41	Mar 30	Sat	Div 1	H	Leeds United	W	3-1	38,416	18	Best, Brooking, Robson
42	Apr 6	Sat	Div 1	A	Arsenal	D	0-0	37,865	18	
43	Apr 12	Fri	Div 1	H	Southampton	W	4-1	34,163	16	Best 2, Robson 2
44	Apr 13	Sat	Div 1	H	Wolverhampton Wanderers	D	0-0	29,488	17	
45	Apr 15	Mon	Div 1	A	Southampton	D	1-1	26,515	14	Best
46	Apr 20	Sat	Div 1	A	Manchester City	L	1-2	29,700	18	Gould
47	Apr 27	Sat	Div 1	H	Liverpool	D	2-2	36,160	18	Brooking, Lampard

* Watney Invitation Cup - lost 4-5 on penalties

Team Line-Ups

AYRIS Johnny	BEST Clyde	BONDS Billy	BROOKING Trevor	CHARLES Clive	COKER Adewunmi	COLEMAN Keith	DAY Mervyn	FERGUSON Bobby	GOULD Bobby	HOLLAND Pat	LAMPARD Frank	LOCK Kevin	LUTTON Bertie	MacDOUGALL Ted	McDOWELL John	McGIVEN Mick	MOORE Bobby	PADDON Graham	ROBSON Bryan	TAYLOR Tommy	TYLER Dudley	WOOLER Alan	#
/b		4	10					1		8	3	a		9	2/a		6		11	5	b		1
	7	4	10	3				1	a		2	8		9			6		11	5			2
	7	4	10				1			8	2	3		9			6		11	5			3
	7	4	10					1		8	2	3		9			6		11	5			4
9	7	4	10					1		8	2	3					6		11	5			5
	7	4	10					1	a		3	8		9/a	2		6		11	5			6
		4	10					1			3	8	9		2		6		11	5	7		7
		4	10					1		8	3	6	a	9	2				11	5	7/a		8
		4	10	a				1			3	8		9/a	2		6		11	5	7		9
		4	10					1			3	8		9	2		6		11	5	7		10
		4	10			2	1			8	3	a	7/a	9	5		6		11				11
7	8		10			4	1				a	3	6/a	9	2				11	5			12
7	8	4	10			2	1				3			9			6		11	5			13
9		4	10			2	1				3		a		8		6		11/a	5	7		14
9		4	10			2	1				3		11		8		6			5	7		15
9		4	10			2	1				a	3	11/a		8		6			5	7		16
9		4	10			2	1				3				8	11	6			5	7		17
		4	10			2	1				3				8	11	6	9		5	7		18
	7	4	10			2	1				3			9	8		6		11	5			19
		4	10			2	1		7		3			9	8		6		11	5			20
		4	10			2	1		7	11	3			9	8	5	6						21
7	11	4	10/a			a	1		9		3				2		6		8	5			22
7	11	4				10	1		9		3				2		6		8	5			23
/a	11		10				1		9	4	3				2		6		8	5		a	24
	11		10			2	1		9		3				4	7	6		8	5			25
	11	4				10/a	1		9	a	3				2	7	6		8	5			26
	11	4	10/a			a	1		9		3				2	7	6		8	5			27
	11	4		10			1		9	a	3				2	7	6/a		8	5			28
	11	4				2	1		10		3			9				7	8	5		6	29
	11	4				2	1		10		3			9				7	8	5		6	30
	11	4	6			2	1		9/a	10	3			a				7	8	5			31
	11	4	10			2	1			7	3			9			6		8	5			32
	11	4	10			2	1			7	3			9			6		8	5			33
	11	4	10			2	1			7	3			9			6		8	5			34
	11	4	10			2	1			7	3			9			6		8	5			35
	11	4	10			2	1			7	3			9			6		8	5			36
	11	4	10			2	1			7	3			9			6		8	5			37
	11	4	10			2	1			7	3			9			6		8	5			38
	11	4	10			2	1			7	3						6	8	9	5			39
	11	4	10			2	1			7	3						6	8	9	5			40
	11	4	10			2	1				3					7	6	8	9	5			41
	11	4	10			2	1				3					7	6	8	9	5			42
	11	4	10			2	1				3					7	6	8	9	5			43
	11	4	10			2	1				3					7	6	8	9	5			44
	11	4	10			2	1				3		a			7	6/a	8	9	5			45
	11	4	10			2	1		9	6	3							7	8	5			46
	11	4	10			2	1		9	7	3						6		8	5			47

1974-75
Story of the season

After a 4–0 opening-day defeat at Manchester City **the Hammers only won one game in the first seven matches** and were bottom of the league. **This led to a managerial change** and long-standing coach and former player **John Lyall became the team manager** under the guidance of Ron Greenwood.

Lyall was a member of the Hammers team that reached the F Youth Cup final in 1957. He went on to play in 35 games for the cl before injury cut short his playing career in 1963. New signings we made when forwards Billy Jennings and Keith Robson were boug and this had an immediate effect as both scored on their debuts. In the league Leicester City were thrashed 6–2 at home, and there w a fine 5–3 win at Burnley. The League Cup replay at Upton Park again Tranmere Rovers saw Bobby Gould scoring a hat-trick in the 6–0 wi Fulham and Bobby Moore were waiting in the next round at Crav Cottage, where the Hammers were 2–1 losers.

The promising league form continued with three successive wins November, including a 5–2 home win over Wolverhampton Wandere Following the 1–1 draw with Tottenham on Boxing Day the Hamme were in fifth place – quite a turnaround from being bottom September. There was a surprise signing when young centre-forwa Alan Taylor was signed for £45,000 from Fourth Division Rochdale.

The FA Cup brought a 2–1 win at Southampton and a 2–1 hom victory against Swindon Town. It was a London derby in the fif

Appearances & Goals 1974-75

	League			FA Cup			League Cup			Other*			Total		
	Starts	Subs	Goals	Starts	Subs	Goals	Starts	Subs	Goals	Starts	Subs	Goals	Starts	Subs	
AYRIS Johnny	2	4	0	0	0	0	3	0	1	0	2	0	5	6	
BEST Clyde	12	3	0	2	0	0	1	0	0	3	0	0	18	3	
BONDS Billy	31	0	7	8	0	0	3	0	2	3	0	2	45	0	
BROOKING Trevor	36	0	3	8	0	1	3	0	1	3	0	0	50	0	
COLEMAN Keith	27	2	0	1	0	0	1	0	0	3	0	0	32	2	
CURBISHLEY Alan	1	1	0	0	0	0	0	0	0	0	0	0	1	1	
DAY Mervyn	42	0	0	8	0	0	3	0	0	3	0	0	56	0	
GOULD Bobby	31	3	9	3	0	1	2	0	3	3	0	0	39	3	
HOLLAND Pat	18	4	4	4	3	2	1	1	0	2	1	0	25	9	
JENNINGS Billy	32	0	13	8	0	1	0	0	0	0	0	0	40	0	
LAMPARD Frank	40	0	4	8	0	1	3	0	0	3	0	0	54	0	
LOCK Kevin	41	1	0	8	0	0	3	0	0	0	0	0	52	1	
McDOWELL John	33	1	1	8	0	0	2	0	0	3	0	0	46	1	
McGIVEN Mick	0	0	0	0	0	0	0	0	0	1	0	0	1	0	
PADDON Graham	40	0	4	8	0	0	3	0	0	3	0	0	54	0	
ROBSON Keith	25	0	10	3	0	1	2	0	0	0	0	0	30	0	
TAYLOR Alan	11	3	2	4	0	6	0	0	0	0	0	0	15	3	
TAYLOR Tommy	39	0	0	7	0	0	3	0	0	3	0	0	52	0	
WOOLER Alan	1	0	0	0	0	0	0	0	0	0	0	0	1	0	
own goal			1												
Totals	462	22	58	88	3	13	33	1	7	33	3	2	616	29	

* Other = Texaco Cup

ound as Queens Park Rangers lost 2–0 at Upton Park. ollowing two league defeats the FA Cup quarter-final tie at lighbury with Arsenal saw Alan Taylor score twice in a 2–0 ictory. League form was suffering, but the FA Cup brought elief as another two goals from Taylor gave West Ham a –1 win in the semi-final replay against Ipswich Town. The eague season ended with a 1–0 home win against Arsenal nd the team finished in thirteenth spot.

he FA Cup final with Fulham proved to be an emotional ay as Bobby Moore faced his old team-mates. Star of the how again was Alan Taylor, with another brace of goals in he 2–0 victory. It was a fairy-tale season for young Taylor hat started with obscurity at Rochdale and ended with lory at Wembley.

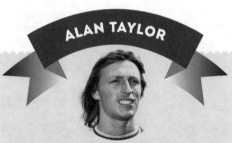

ALAN TAYLOR

Taylor became a household name in 1975 when his goals swept West Ham to Wembley.

He joined Rochdale from Morecambe in May 1973 and after 55 league games for the Spotland club he joined the Hammers in November 1974. A month later he made his debut against Leeds United. He won an FA Cup winners' medal in 1975 and a year later he was in the side that lost to Anderlecht in the European Cup Winners' Cup final. Alan played for five seasons at Upton Park, making 121 appearances and scoring 36 goals. In 1979 he moved to Norwich City and played in 24 games before going to Canada to join Vancouver Whitecaps. Returning to England in 1980, he had spells at Cambridge City, Hull City, Burnley and Bury. After retiring as a player he ran a newspaper shop for many years in Norwich. These days Alan is often seen at Upton Park working as a match-day host and giving visitors a tour of the ground.

ootball League - Division One inal Table 1974-75

	P	HOME					AWAY					Pts
		W	D	L	F	A	W	D	L	F	A	
erby County	42	14	4	3	41	18	7	7	7	26	31	53
verpool	42	14	5	2	44	17	6	6	9	16	22	51
oswich Town	42	17	2	2	47	14	6	3	12	19	30	51
verton	42	10	9	2	33	19	6	9	6	23	23	50
toke City	42	12	7	2	40	18	5	8	8	24	30	49
heffield United	42	12	7	2	35	20	6	6	9	23	31	49
liddlesbrough	42	11	7	3	33	14	7	5	9	21	26	48
lanchester City	42	16	3	2	40	15	2	7	12	14	39	46
eeds United	42	10	8	3	34	20	6	5	10	23	29	45
urnley	42	11	6	4	40	29	6	5	10	28	38	45
ueens Park Rangers	42	10	4	7	25	17	6	6	9	29	37	42
/olverhampton Wanderers	42	12	5	4	43	21	2	6	13	14	33	39
West Ham United	42	10	6	5	38	22	3	7	11	20	37	39
oventry City	42	8	9	4	31	27	4	6	11	20	35	39
ewcastle United	42	12	4	5	39	23	3	5	13	20	49	39
rsenal	42	10	6	5	31	16	3	5	13	16	33	37
irmingham City	42	10	4	7	34	28	4	5	12	19	33	37
eicester City	42	8	7	6	25	17	4	5	12	21	43	36
ottenham Hotspur	42	8	4	9	29	27	5	4	12	23	36	34
uton Town	42	8	6	7	27	26	3	5	13	20	39	33
helsea	42	4	9	8	22	31	5	6	10	20	41	33
arlisle United	42	8	2	11	22	21	4	3	14	21	38	29

Season **1974-75** Football League - Division One
Match Details

Manager **John Lyall**   Final League Position **13/22**

	Date		Competition	Venue	Opponents	Results		Attendance	Position	Scorers
1	Aug 3	Sat	TexC-Gp	H	Orient	W	1-0	16,338		Bonds
2	Aug 7	Wed	TexC-Gp	H	Luton Town	L	1-2	14,508		Bonds [pen]
3	Aug 10	Sat	TexC-Gp	A	Southampton	L	0-2	11,364		
4	Aug 17	Sat	Div 1	A	Manchester City	L	0-4	30,240	22	
5	Aug 19	Mon	Div 1	H	Luton Town	W	2-0	23,182	4	Bonds, Lampard
6	Aug 24	Sat	Div 1	H	Everton	L	2-3	22,486	16	Bonds [pen], McDowell
7	Aug 28	Wed	Div 1	A	Luton Town	D	0-0	16,931	16	
8	Aug 31	Sat	Div 1	A	Newcastle United	L	0-2	30,782	18	
9	Sep 7	Sat	Div 1	H	Sheffield United	L	1-2	20,977	21	Jennings
10	Sep 11	Wed	FLC 2	A	Tranmere Rovers	D	0-0	8,638		
11	Sep 14	Sat	Div 1	A	Tottenham Hotspur	L	1-2	27,959	22	Lampard
12	Sep 18	Wed	FLC 2 Rep	H	Tranmere Rovers	W	6-0	15,854		Gould 3 [1 pen], Bonds 2 [1 pen], Ayris
13	Sep 21	Sat	Div 1	H	Leicester City	W	6-2	21,377	19	Gould 2, Jennings 2, Bonds, Robson
14	Sep 25	Wed	Div 1	H	Birmingham City	W	3-0	25,495	13	Jennings, Paddon, Robson
15	Sep 28	Sat	Div 1	A	Burnley	W	5-3	17,644	12	Robson 2, Bonds, Brooking, Jennings
16	Oct 5	Sat	Div 1	H	Derby County	D	2-2	32,938	12	Bonds, Robson
17	Oct 8	Tue	FLC 3	A	Fulham	L	1-2	29,611		Brooking
18	Oct 12	Sat	Div 1	A	Coventry City	D	1-1	22,556	12	Gould
19	Oct 15	Tue	Div 1	A	Everton	D	1-1	31,882	12	Gould
20	Oct 19	Sat	Div 1	H	Ipswich Town	W	1-0	33,543	10	Jennings
21	Oct 26	Sat	Div 1	A	Arsenal	L	0-3	41,184	11	
22	Nov 2	Sat	Div 1	H	Middlesbrough	W	3-0	28,915	10	Paddon, Robson, Boam (og)
23	Nov 9	Sat	Div 1	A	Carlisle United	W	1-0	14,141	9	Lampard
24	Nov 16	Sat	Div 1	H	Wolverhampton Wanderers	W	5-2	31,708	7	Bonds [pen], Brooking, Gould, Jennings, Lampard
25	Nov 23	Sat	Div 1	A	Liverpool	D	1-1	46,346	6	Robson
26	Nov 30	Sat	Div 1	A	Queens Park Rangers	W	2-0	28,357	6	Jennings, Paddon
27	Dec 7	Sat	Div 1	H	Leeds United	W	2-1	39,562	5	Jennings, Gould
28	Dec 14	Sat	Div 1	H	Manchester City	D	0-0	33,479	6	
29	Dec 21	Sat	Div 1	A	Chelsea	D	1-1	34,969	5	Gould
30	Dec 26	Thur	Div 1	H	Tottenham Hotspur	D	1-1	37,682	5	Robson
31	Dec 28	Sat	Div 1	A	Stoke City	L	1-2	33,498	6	Holland
32	Jan 4	Sat	FAC 3	A	Southampton	W	2-1	24,615		Gould, Lampard
33	Jan 11	Sat	Div 1	A	Leeds United	L	1-2	40,099	9	Robson
34	Jan 18	Sat	Div 1	H	Queens Park Rangers	D	2-2	28,762	10	Bonds [pen], Jennings
35	Jan 25	Sat	FAC 4	H	Swindon Town	D	1-1	35,679		Jennings
36	Jan 28	Tue	FAC 4 Rep	A	Swindon Town	W	2-1	27,749		Brooking, Holland
37	Feb 1	Sat	Div 1	H	Carlisle United	W	2-0	26,910	6	Holland, Jennings
38	Feb 8	Sat	Div 1	A	Middlesbrough	D	0-0	29,179	7	
39	Feb 15	Sat	FAC 5	H	Queens Park Rangers	W	2-1	39,193		Holland Robson
40	Feb 19	Wed	Div 1	H	Liverpool	D	0-0	40,256	6	
41	Feb 22	Sat	Div 1	A	Wolverhampton Wanderers	L	1-3	24,794	9	Gould
42	Feb 28	Fri	Div 1	H	Newcastle United	L	0-1	32,753	10	
43	Mar 8	Sat	FAC QF	A	Arsenal	W	2-0	56,742		Taylor A. 2
44	Mar 15	Sat	Div 1	H	Burnley	W	2-1	28,830	12	Robson, Taylor A.
45	Mar 18	Tue	Div 1	A	Birmingham City	D	1-1	34,000	11	Taylor A.
46	Mar 22	Sat	Div 1	A	Sheffield United	L	2-3	25,527	12	Gould, Jennings
47	Mar 28	Fri	Div 1	H	Stoke City	D	2-2	29,811	12	Brooking, Jennings
48	Mar 29	Sat	Div 1	H	Chelsea	L	0-1	31,025	12	
49	Apr 1	Tue	Div 1	A	Leicester City	L	0-3	30,408	12	
50	Apr 5	Sat	FAC SF	N*	Ipswich Town	D	0-0	58,000		
51	Apr 9	Wed	FAC SF Rep	N**	Ipswich Town	W	2-1	45,344		Taylor A. 2
52	Apr 12	Sat	Div 1	A	Derby County	L	0-1	31,536	13	
53	Apr 19	Sat	Div 1	H	Coventry City	L	1-2	27,431	14	Holland
54	Apr 26	Sat	Div 1	A	Ipswich Town	L	1-4	31,642	16	Holland
55	Apr 28	Mon	Div 1	H	Arsenal	W	1-0	30,195	13	Paddon
56	May 3	Sat	FAC F	N***	Fulham	W	2-0	100,000		Taylor A. 2

TexC-Gp = Texaco Cup - Southern Group   * Played at Villa Park, Birmingham   ** Played at Stamford Bridge, London   *** Played at Wembley Stadium, London

Team Line-Ups

AYRIS Johnny	BEST Clyde	BONDS Billy	BROOKING Trevor	COLEMAN Keith	CURBISHLEY Alan	DAY Mervyn	GOULD Bobby	HOLLAND Pat	JENNINGS Billy	LAMPARD Frank	LOCK Kevin	McDOWELL John	McGIVEN Mick	PADDON Graham	ROBSON Keith	TAYLOR Alan	TAYLOR Tommy	WOOLER Alan	
a	9	4	10	2		1	11/a	6		3		7		8			5		1
	11	4	10	2		1	9	a		3		7/a	6	8			5		2
a	11	4	10	2/a		1	9	7		3		6		8			5		3
	11	4	10	2/a		1	9	7		3	a	6		8			5		4
9	11	4	10			1		7		3	6	2		8			5		5
	11	4		2		1	9	7		3	6	10		8			5		6
	11	4		2		1	9	7		3	6	10		8			5		7
a	11	4		2		1	9/a	7		3	6	10		8			5		8
7	11	4				1		10	9	3	6	2		8			5		9
7	11	4	10			1		9		3	6	2		8			5		10
	11	4	10			1		7	9	3	6	2		8			5		11
7		4	10			1	9			3	6	2		8	11		5		12
		4	10			1	9	a	7/a	3	6	2		8	11		5		13
		4	10			1	9		7	3	6	2		8	11		5		14
		4	10			1	9		7	3	6	2		8	11		5		15
		4	10			1	9	a	7	3	6	2/a		8	11		5		16
7/a		4	10	2		1	9	a		3	6			8	11		5		17
		4	10	2		1	9		7	3	6			8	11		5		18
		4	10	2		1	9		7	3	6			8	11		5		19
		4	10	2		1	9		7	3	6			8	11		5		20
		4	10	a		1	9		7	3	6	2/a		8	11		5		21
		4	10	2		1	9		7	3	6			8	11		5		22
		4	10	2		1	9		7	3	6			8	11		5		23
		4	10	2		1	9		7	3	6			8	11		5		24
		4	10	2		1	9		7	3	6			8	11		5		25
		4/a	10	2		1	9	a	7	3	6			8	11		5		26
		4		2		1	9		7/a	3	6	10		8	11	a	5		27
		4	10	2		1	9		7/a	3	6	a		8	11		5		28
	a	4/a	10	2		1	9			3	6	7		8	11		5		29
			10	2		1	9		7/a	3	6	4		8	11	a	5		30
a	11			2		1	9	4		3	6	10		8		7/a	5		31
		4	10	2		1	9/a	a	7	3	6	5		8	11				32
	9	4	10	2		1		7		3	6	5		8	11				33
a		4	10	2/a		1			7	3	6	9		8	11		5		34
	9	4	10			1		11	7	3	6	2		8			5		35
	9	4	10			1		11	7	3	6	2		8			5		36
	a	4	10/a			1		11	7	3	6	2		8	9		5		37
	9	4/a	10	a		1		11	7	3	6	2		8			5		38
		4	10			1		11	7	3	6	2		8	9		5		39
		4	10			1		11	7	3	6	2		8	9		5		40
			10	2/a		1	a	11	7	3	6	4		8	9		5		41
			10			1	9	11/a	7	3	6	2		8	4	a	5		42
		4	10			1			7	3	6	2		8	11	9	5		43
		4/a	10			1	a		7	3	6	2		8	11	9	5		44
			10	2		1	7			3	6	4		8	11	9	5		45
			10	2		1	11		7	3	6	4		8		9	5		46
a			10	2		1	11		7	3/a	6	4		8		9	5		47
a			10	2	4	1	11		7/a		6	3		8		9	5		48
	7		10	2		1	11	4			6	3				9	5	8	49
		4	10			1	11/a	a	7	3	6	2		8		9	5		50
		4	10			1	11	a	7/a	3	6	2		8		9	5		51
		4	10			1	11	a	7	3	6	2		8		9/a	5		52
			10	2	a	1	11	4	7	3	6	5		8/a		9			53
	8		10	2		1	11	4	7	3	6	5				9			54
		4	10			1	a	11	7/a	3	6	2		8		9	5		55
		4	10			1		11	7	3	6	2		8		9	5		56

1975-76
Story of the season

Returning to Wembley for the annual **Charity Shield** game, West Ham lost 2–0 to League Champions Derby County.

In the league Alan Taylor scored five goals in the first three games with the Hammers going on an unbeaten run of nine games. There had been a remarkable comeback at Leicester: after losing 3–0 at half-time West Ham scored three second-half goals to draw 3–3.

Progress was made in the League Cup with victories over Bristol City and Darlington. The European campaign began with a 5–2 aggregate win against Finnish part timers Lahden Reipas in the European Cup Winners' Cup. A gruelling trip to Russia came next, where the Hammers drew 1–1 with Ararat Yerevan; on their return they beat Manchester United 2–1 and won 5–1 at Birmingham City. The home leg with Ararat saw West Ham sweep into the last eight by winning 3–1 with scintillating display of attacking football. A setback came when following a replay Tottenham beat West Ham 2–0 in the League Cup.

December was a poor month with four defeats, and morale was low when Liverpool won 2–0 at Upton Park in the FA Cup. There were n

Appearances & Goals 1975-76

	League			FA Cup			League Cup			Europe			Other*			Total		
	Starts	Subs	Goals	Starts	Subs	Goals	Starts	Subs	Goals	Starts	Subs	Goals	Starts	Subs	Goals	Starts	Subs	Goals
AYRIS Johnny	3	6	0	0	0	0	0	1	0	1	0	0	0	0	0	4	7	0
BEST Clyde	5	2	1	0	0	0	2	0	1	0	0	0	0	0	0	7	2	2
BONDS Billy	17	1	1	0	0	0	5	0	1	10	0	2	0	0	0	32	1	4
BROOKING Trevor	34	0	5	1	0	0	4	0	1	9	0	3	1	0	0	49	0	9
COLEMAN Keith	26	0	0	1	0	0	1	0	0	6	2	0	0	1	0	34	3	0
CURBISHLEY Alan	12	2	2	1	0	0	0	0	0	1	2	0	0	0	0	14	4	2
DAY Mervyn	41	0	0	1	0	0	5	0	0	11	0	0	1	0	0	59	0	0
FERGUSON Bobby	1	0	0	0	0	0	0	0	0	0	0	0	0	0	0	1	0	0
GOULD Bobby	4	1	2	0	0	0	0	0	0	1	0	0	1	0	0	6	1	2
HOLLAND Pat	35	0	2	1	0	0	5	0	0	9	0	2	1	0	0	51	0	4
JENNINGS Billy	26	4	11	1	0	0	1	2	0	6	3	3	1	0	0	35	9	14
LAMPARD Frank	37	0	3	1	0	0	4	0	0	11	0	1	1	0	0	54	0	4
LOCK Kevin	26	0	0	1	0	0	5	0	0	6	0	0	1	0	0	39	0	0
McDOWELL John	36	1	0	0	0	0	5	0	0	9	0	0	1	0	0	51	1	0
McGIVEN Mick	6	1	0	1	0	0	0	0	0	1	1	0	0	0	0	8	2	0
ORHAN Yilmaz	5	0	0	0	0	0	0	0	0	0	0	0	0	0	0	5	0	0
PADDON Graham	39	0	2	1	0	0	5	0	1	11	0	2	1	0	0	57	0	5
PIKE Geoff	0	3	0	0	0	0	0	0	0	0	0	0	0	0	0	0	3	0
ROBSON Keith	33	1	3	0	0	0	4	0	1	10	0	4	0	1	0	47	2	8
TAYLOR Alan	33	2	13	1	0	0	4	0	1	8	1	3	1	0	0	47	3	17
TAYLOR Tommy	42	0	2	0	0	0	5	0	0	11	0	0	1	0	0	59	0	2
WOOLER Alan	1	0	0	0	0	0	0	0	0	0	0	0	0	0	0	1	0	0
own goal			1															1
Totals	462	24	48	11	0	0	55	3	6	121	9	20	11	2	0	660	38	74

* Other = Charity Shield Europe = European Cup Winners Cup and Anglo-Italian Cup

ins in February as the Hammers slid down the table to
ghteenth. Europe beckoned again in March and after
sing 4–2 to Den Haag in Holland the home leg brought a
–1 win, the Hammers progressing by virtue of the away-
oal rule. After a 6–1 defeat at Arsenal the Hammers
avelled to Eintracht Frankfurt where they lost 2–1 in the
mi-final. Their league form had lacked commitment but
e Hammers rose to the occasion in the home leg and two
oals from Trevor Brooking sent the Germans home,
eaten 3–1.

he league season ended with the Hammers finishing
ghteenth, without a win in 16 league matches. The Cup
inners' Cup final saw West Ham travel to Brussels where
ey would meet the Belgian side Anderlecht. It was a
arvellous match full of skill and passion, but two late
oals from Anderlecht gave them a 4–2 victory.

BILLY JENNINGS

Manager John Lyall paid Watford a fee of £110,000 for this striker in September 1974.

He scored on his debut against Sheffield United and his 13 league goals made him top scorer that season. He was ever-present when the Hammers won the FA Cup in 1975 after beating Fulham 2–0 at Wembley. That victory put the Hammers back in Europe, and after being four goals down to Den Haag his two second-half goals kept the team in with a chance for the second leg. West Ham went on to reach the final, where he won a runners-up medal in the defeat to Anderlecht.

Billy played in a total of 124 games for West Ham, scoring 39 goals before leaving for Leyton Orient in August 1979. In three seasons for Orient he scored 21 league goals in 67 games. Finally he had a short spell at Luton Town, playing two games in 1982. After retiring as a player he later ran a wine bar and a restaurant and since then he has been a successful football agent.

ootball League - Division One inal Table 1975-76

		HOME					AWAY					
	P	W	D	L	F	A	W	D	L	F	A	Pts
iverpool	42	14	5	2	41	21	9	9	3	25	10	60
ueens Park Rangers	42	17	4	0	42	13	7	7	7	25	20	59
anchester United	42	16	4	1	40	13	7	6	8	28	29	56
erby County	42	15	3	3	45	30	6	8	7	30	28	53
eeds United	42	13	3	5	37	19	8	6	7	28	27	51
oswich Town	42	11	6	4	36	23	5	8	8	18	25	46
eicester City	42	9	9	3	29	24	4	10	7	19	27	45
anchester City	42	14	5	2	46	18	2	6	13	18	28	43
ottenham Hotspur	42	6	10	5	33	32	8	5	8	30	31	43
lorwich City	42	10	5	6	33	26	6	5	10	25	32	42
verton	42	10	7	4	37	24	5	5	11	23	42	42
toke City	42	8	5	8	25	24	7	6	8	23	26	41
iddlesbrough	42	9	7	5	23	11	6	3	12	23	34	40
oventry City	42	6	9	6	22	22	7	5	9	25	35	40
ewcastle United	42	11	4	6	51	26	4	5	12	20	36	39
ston Villa	42	11	8	2	32	17	0	9	12	19	42	39
rsenal	42	11	4	6	33	19	2	6	13	14	34	36
West Ham United	42	10	5	6	26	23	3	5	13	22	48	36
irmingham City	42	11	5	5	36	26	2	2	17	21	49	33
olverhampton Wanderers	42	7	6	8	27	25	3	4	14	24	43	30
urnley	42	6	6	9	23	26	3	4	14	20	40	28
heffield United	42	4	7	10	19	32	2	3	16	14	50	22

Season 1975-76 Football League - Division One
Match Details

Manager **John Lyall**   Final League Position **18/22**

	Date		Competition	Venue	Opponents	Results		Attendance	Position	Scorers
1	Aug 9	Sat	C Shield	N*	Derby County	L	0-2	59,000		
2	Aug 16	Sat	Div 1	A	Stoke City	W	2-1	24,237	3	Gould, Taylor A.
3	Aug 19	Tue	Div 1	A	Liverpool	D	2-2	40,564	5	Taylor A. 2
4	Aug 23	Sat	Div 1	H	Burnley	W	3-2	28,048	6	Taylor A. 2, Paddon
5	Aug 25	Mon	Div 1	H	Tottenham Hotspur	W	1-0	36,567	1	Robson
6	Aug 30	Sat	Div 1	A	Queens Park Rangers	D	1-1	28,408	2	Jennings
7	Sep 3	Wed	AIC	A	AC Fiorentina (Italy)	L	0-1	35,000		
8	Sep 6	Sat	Div 1	H	Manchester City	W	1-0	29,752	2	Lampard
9	Sep 9	Tue	FLC 2	H	Bristol City	D	0-0	19,837		
10	Sep 13	Sat	Div 1	A	Leicester City	D	3-3	21,413	2	Bonds, Holland, Lampard
11	Sep 17	Wed	ECWC 1:1	A	Lahden Reipas (Finland)	D	2-2	4,587		Bonds, Brooking
12	Sep 20	Sat	Div 1	H	Sheffield United	W	2-0	28,744	2	Best, Taylor T.
13	Sep 24	Wed	FLC 2 Rep	A	Bristol City	W	3-1	19,634		Best, Brooking, Taylor A.
14	Sep 27	Sat	Div 1	A	Wolverhampton Wanderers	W	1-0	18,455	2	Paddon
15	Oct 1	Wed	ECWC 1:2	H	Lahden Reipas (Finland)	W	3-0	24,131		Holland, Jennings, Robson
16	Oct 4	Sat	Div 1	H	Everton	L	0-1	31,985	3	
17	Oct 8	Wed	FLC 3	H	Darlington	W	3-0	19,844		Bonds [pen], Paddon, Robson
18	Oct 11	Sat	Div 1	H	Newcastle United	W	2-1	30,828	3	Curbishley, Taylor A.
19	Oct 18	Sat	Div 1	A	Middlesbrough	L	0-3	25,831	3	
20	Oct 22	Wed	ECWC 2:1	A	Ararat Erevan (U.S.S.R.)	D	1-1	66,662		Taylor A.
21	Oct 25	Sat	Div 1	H	Manchester United	W	2-1	38,528	3	Gould, Taylor A.
22	Nov 1	Sat	Div 1	A	Birmingham City	W	5-1	28,474	2	Taylor A. 2, Brooking, Lampard, Pendrey (og)
23	Nov 5	Wed	ECWC 2:2	H	Ararat Erevan (U.S.S.R.)	W	3-1	30,399		Paddon, Robson, Taylor A.
24	Nov 8	Sat	Div 1	H	Coventry City	D	1-1	29,501	1	Robson
25	Nov 12	Wed	FLC 4	A	Tottenham Hotspur	D	0-0	49,125		
26	Nov 15	Sat	Div 1	A	Derby County	L	1-2	31,172	5	Brooking
27	Nov 22	Sat	Div 1	H	Middlesbrough	W	2-1	26,944	4	Holland, Jennings
28	Nov 24	Mon	FLC 4 Rep	H	Tottenham Hotspur	L	0-2	38,443		
29	Nov 29	Sat	Div 1	H	Arsenal	W	1-0	31,012	3	Taylor A.
30	Dec 6	Sat	Div 1	A	Norwich City	L	0-1	26,581	6	
31	Dec 10	Wed	AIC	H	AC Fiorentina (Italy)	L	0-1	14,699		
32	Dec 13	Sat	Div 1	A	Burnley	L	0-2	14,942	7	
33	Dec 20	Sat	Div 1	H	Stoke City	W	3-1	21,135	6	Jennings 3
34	Dec 26	Fri	Div 1	A	Aston Villa	L	1-4	51,250	6	Jennings
35	Dec 27	Sat	Div 1	H	Ipswich Town	L	1-2	33,052	6	Taylor T. [pen]
36	Jan 3	Sat	FAC 3	H	Liverpool	L	0-2	32,363		
37	Jan 10	Sat	Div 1	H	Leicester City	D	1-1	24,615	6	Taylor A.
38	Jan 17	Sat	Div 1	A	Manchester City	L	0-3	32,147	8	
39	Jan 24	Sat	Div 1	H	Queens Park Rangers	W	1-0	26,437	6	Taylor A.
40	Jan 31	Sat	Div 1	H	Liverpool	L	0-4	26,741	6	
41	Feb 7	Sat	Div 1	A	Tottenham Hotspur	D	1-1	32,832	6	Brooking
42	Feb 14	Sat	Div 1	A	Coventry City	L	0-2	16,156	6	
43	Feb 21	Sat	Div 1	H	Derby County	L	1-2	24,941	9	Brooking
44	Feb 23	Mon	Div 1	H	Leeds United	D	1-1	28,025	7	Taylor A.
45	Feb 28	Sat	Div 1	A	Manchester United	L	0-4	57,220	9	
46	Mar 3	Wed	ECWC 3:1	A	FC Den Haag (Holland)	L	2-4	26,000		Jennings 2
47	Mar 6	Sat	Div 1	H	Birmingham City	L	1-2	19,863	12	Curbishley
48	Mar 9	Tue	Div 1	A	Leeds United	D	1-1	28,451	8	Jennings
49	Mar 13	Sat	Div 1	A	Newcastle United	L	1-2	32,868	11	Jennings
50	Mar 17	Wed	ECWC 3:2	H	FC Den Haag (Holland)	W	3-1	29,829		Bonds [pen], Lampard, Taylor A.
51	Mar 20	Sat	Div 1	A	Arsenal	L	1-6	34,011	12	Jennings
52	Mar 27	Sat	Div 1	H	Norwich City	L	0-1	20,628	12	
53	Mar 31	Wed	ECWC SF:1	A	Eintracht Frankfurt (West Germany)	L	1-2	55,000		Paddon
54	Apr 3	Sat	Div 1	H	Wolverhampton Wanderers	D	0-0	16,769	13	
55	Apr 10	Sat	Div 1	A	Sheffield United	L	2-3	18,786	16	Jennings 2
56	Apr 14	Wed	ECWC SF:2	H	Eintracht Frankfurt (West Germany)	W	3-1	39,202		Brooking 2, Robson
57	Apr 17	Sat	Div 1	H	Aston Villa	D	2-2	21,642	17	Brooking, Robson
58	Apr 19	Mon	Div 1	A	Ipswich Town	L	0-4	28,181	18	
59	Apr 24	Sat	Div 1	A	Everton	L	0-2	26,101	18	
60	May 5	Wed	ECWC F	N**	Anderlecht (Belgium)	L	2-4	51,296		Holland, Robson

AIC = Anglo-Italian Cup * Played at Wembley Stadium, London ** Played at Stade du Heysel, Brussels, Belgium

eam Line-Ups

AYRIS Johnny	BEST Clyde	BONDS Billy	BROOKING Trevor	COLEMAN Keith	CURBISHLEY Alan	DAY Mervyn	FERGUSON Bobby	GOULD Bobby	HOLLAND Pat	JENNINGS Billy	LAMPARD Frank	LOCK Kevin	McDOWELL John	McGIVEN Mick	ORHAN Yilmaz	PADDON Graham	PIKE Geoff	ROBSON Keith	TAYLOR Alan	TAYLOR Tommy	WOOLER Alan	
			10	b		1		11/a	4	9/b	3	6	2			8		a	7	5		1
			10			1		9	4		3	6	2			8		11	7	5		2
			10			1		9/a	4	a	3	6	2			8		11	7	5		3
a			10			1			4	9/a	3	6	2			8		11	7	5		4
			10			1			4	9	3	6	2			8		11	7	5		5
			10			1			4	9	3	6	2			8		11	7	5		6
		4	10			1		9/a		a	3	6	2			8		11	7	5		7
		a	10			1			4	9	3	6	2			8		11	7/a	5		8
		4	10			1			7/a	9	3	6	2			8		11		5		9
		4	10			1			7	9	3	6	2			8		11		5		10
		4	10			1			9	a	3	6	2			8		11/a	7	5		11
	a	4	10			1			11		3	6	2			8			7/a	5		12
	9	4	10			1			11		3	6	2			8			7	5		13
	9	4	10			1			11		3	6	2			8			7	5		14
		4	10			1				9	3	6	2			8		11	7/a	5		15
9/a		4	10			1			11		3	6	2			8		7	a	5		16
9		4				1			11	a	3	6/a	2			8		10	7	5		17
9		4		6	10	1			11		3		2			8			7	5		18
9		4	10	6	a	1			11		3/a		2			8			7	5		19
		4		6		1		9	10		3		2			8		11	7	5		20
			10	6		1		9	4		3		2			8		11	7	5		21
		4	10	6		1				9	3		2			8		11	7	5		22
		4	10	6		1				9	3		2			8		11	7	5		23
		4/a	10	6		1			a	9	3		2			8		11	7	5		24
		4	10	6		1				9	3		2			8		11	7	5		25
a			10	6		1		8/a		9	3	4	2			8		11	7	5		26
				6		1			4	9	3		2			8		11	7	5		27
		4	10/a			1				9	3		2			8		11	7	5		28
				4		1			9	10	3		2			8		11	7	5		29
			10	4		1			9		3		2			8		11	7	5		30
1/b			10	a		1			4	9	3	6	2/a			8			7	5		31
a			10	2	4/a	1			9	11	3	6				8			7	5		32
				2		1			9	10	3	6	4			8		11	7	5		33
				2		1			9	10	3	6	4			8		11	7	5		34
			9	2/a	a	1			4	10	3	6				8			7	5		35
			9	2	11	1			4	10	3	6		5		8			7			36
	8		9		11	1			4	10	3	6	2						7	5		37
	a		10		11	1			4	9	3	6	2			8			7/a	5		38
			9	6		1			4	10	3		2		11	8			7	5		39
			10	6		1			4	9/a	3		2		11	8		a	7	5		40
			10	2		1			4	9	3			6		8		11	7	5		41
			10			1			4	9	3		2	6		8		11	7	5		42
			10	2		1			4	a	3		7	6	9/a	8		11		5		43
			10			1			4/a	a	3		2	6		8		11	7	5		44
		4	10		9	1				a	3		2	6		8		11	7/a	5		45
		4	10	a	10	1				9	3		2/a	6		8		11	7	5		46
7/a		4		2	9	1					3				10/a	8	a	11	6	5	6	47
7		4		2	10	1				9	3					8	a	11	6	5		48
7		4		2	10	1				9	3			a		8		11	6	5		49
		4	10	2	b	1				9	3			6		8/b		11	7	5/a		50
		4	10	2/a	8	1				9	3		a	6				11	7	5		51
		4		2	8	1				9	3			6				10	7	5		52
		4	10	2		1			7	9	3		6			8		11		5		53
a			10	2		1			7	9	3	6/a	4			8		11		5		54
a		4	10	2		1			7	9	3		6			8		11/a		5		55
		4	10	2		1			7	9	3		6			8		11		5		56
a			10	2		1			7	9	3	4/a		6		8		11		5		57
7		2	10	4		1					3		6		9/a	8		a	11	5		58
		4	10	2		1			7	9	3		6			8		11/a	a	5		59
		4	10	2		1			7	9	3/a		6			8		11	a	5		60

1976-77
Story of the season

There was an **opening-day shocker** as the **Hammers lost 4–0** away at Aston Villa.

Following on from that was a 1–0 home win again[st] Queens Park Rangers, which raised hopes. However, the[re] were no victories in the next 10 games as the team slumpe[d] to the bottom of the league. The League Cup brough[t] victories against Barnsley and Charlton, but another cu[p] run ended as Queens Park Rangers triumphed 2–0 at th[e] Boleyn Ground.

A home thriller with Tottenham ended 5–3 to West Ha[m] and the first away win came with a fine 2–0 victory [at] Manchester United. There were three new signings mad[e] with midfielders Alan Devonshire and Anton Otulakows[ki] joined by veteran forward John Radford. Bolton Wanderer[s] were the visitors in the FA Cup and were beaten 2–1, whic[h]

Appearances & Goals 1976-77

	League			FA Cup			League Cup			Total		
	Starts	Subs	Goals	Starts	Subs	Goals	Starts	Subs	Goals	Starts	Subs	Goals
AYRIS Johnny	1	2	0	0	0	0	0	0	0	1	2	
BONDS Billy	41	0	3	2	0	0	3	0	0	46	0	
BROOKING Trevor	42	0	4	2	0	0	3	0	0	47	0	
COLEMAN Keith	12	1	0	0	0	0	2	0	0	14	1	
CURBISHLEY Alan	8	2	1	1	0	0	1	0	0	10	2	
DAY Mervyn	42	0	0	2	0	0	3	0	0	47	0	
DEVONSHIRE Alan	27	1	0	0	0	0	1	0	0	28	1	
GREEN Bill	22	0	0	2	0	0	2	0	0	26	0	
HOLLAND Pat	6	0	0	0	0	0	1	0	2	7	0	
JENNINGS Billy	27	4	9	2	0	1	2	0	0	31	4	
LAMPARD Frank	36	0	1	2	0	0	1	0	0	39	0	
LOCK Kevin	25	1	0	2	0	0	2	0	0	29	1	
McGIVEN Mick	15	1	0	0	0	0	2	0	0	17	1	
ORHAN Yilmaz	1	2	0	0	0	0	1	0	0	2	2	
OTULAKOWSKI Anton	10	2	0	0	0	0	0	0	0	10	2	
PADDON Graham	12	0	1	0	0	0	3	0	1	15	0	
PIKE Geoff	20	0	6	1	0	1	0	0	0	21	0	
RADFORD John	18	0	0	1	0	0	0	0	0	19	0	
ROBSON Bryan	30	0	14	2	0	0	0	0	0	32	0	
ROBSON Keith	7	2	0	0	0	0	1	0	0	8	2	
TAYLOR Alan	24	1	5	1	0	0	2	0	1	27	1	
TAYLOR Tommy	36	0	0	2	0	0	3	0	0	41	0	
own goal			2									2
Totals	**462**	**19**	**46**	**22**	**0**	**2**	**33**	**0**	**4**	**517**	**19**	**5[2]**

t up a trip to Aston Villa where the home side won 3–0.

February there were three successive wins, moving the le up to eighteenth place, but a week later fellow relegation ndidates Sunderland beat the Hammers 6–0 at Roker rk. In the remaining 13 games there was only one defeat th three wins and nine draws, and on the last day of the ason the supporters went away happy after seeing the 4–2 in over Manchester United which ensured seventeenth ace and First Division survival.

ootball League - Division One inal Table 1976-77

	P	HOME					AWAY					Pts
	P	W	D	L	F	A	W	D	L	F	A	Pts
verpool	42	18	3	0	47	11	5	8	8	15	22	57
anchester City	42	15	5	1	38	13	6	9	6	22	21	56
swich Town	42	15	4	2	41	11	7	4	10	25	28	52
ton Villa	42	17	3	1	55	17	5	4	12	21	33	51
wcastle United	42	14	6	1	40	15	4	7	10	24	34	49
anchester United	42	12	6	3	41	22	6	5	10	30	40	47
est Bromwich Albion	42	10	6	5	38	22	6	7	8	24	34	45
senal	42	11	6	4	37	20	5	5	11	27	39	43
erton	42	9	7	5	35	24	5	7	9	27	40	42
eds United	42	8	8	5	28	26	7	4	10	20	25	42
icester City	42	8	9	4	30	28	4	9	8	17	32	42
iddlesbrough	42	11	6	4	25	14	3	7	11	15	31	41
rmingham City	42	10	6	5	38	25	3	6	12	25	36	38
ueens Park Rangers	42	10	7	4	31	21	3	5	13	16	31	38
erby County	42	9	9	3	36	18	0	10	11	14	37	37
orwich City	42	12	4	5	30	23	2	5	14	17	41	37
est Ham United	42	9	6	6	28	23	2	8	11	18	42	36
istol City	42	8	7	6	25	19	3	6	12	13	29	35
oventry City	42	7	9	5	34	26	3	6	12	14	33	35
underland	42	9	5	7	29	16	2	7	12	17	38	34
oke City	42	9	8	4	21	16	1	6	14	7	35	34
ttenham Hotspur	42	9	7	5	26	20	3	2	16	22	52	33

ALAN DEVONSHIRE

A bargain fee of just £5,000 in October 1976 saw the midfielder move to West Ham from Southall.

After making his debut in a League Cup tie against Queens Park Rangers he soon became a first-team regular. In 1980 he played an outstanding part in West Ham's FA Cup success. In the semi-final he scored a brilliant individual goal against Everton and it was his surging run and cross in the final that led to Brooking scoring the winning goal against Arsenal. In 1981 he won a Second Division Championship medal and a year later was in the side that lost to Liverpool in the League Cup final.

International honours came his way and after making his England debut against Northern Ireland in May 1980 he went on to gain eight full caps. There was heartbreak in January 1984 as he snapped ligaments in his right knee during the FA Cup tie with Wigan Athletic. It was a devastating blow, as it was 19 months before he was able to return to the side. His comeback coincided with West Ham's best ever season of 1985–86: he created many goals for Cottee and McAvennie as the Hammers finished third in the First Division.

Playing against Queens Park Rangers in August 1988 he suffered an Achilles tendon injury, which meant another year on the sidelines. Upon his return he made infrequent appearances and was given a free transfer to Watford in May 1990. Alan had spent 14 seasons at Upton Park, scoring 32 goals in 446 appearances. He spent two years at Watford, before retiring in 1992.

Season **1976-77** Football League - Division One
Match Details

Manager **John Lyall**   Final League Position **17/22**

	Date		Competition	Venue	Opponents	Results		Attendance	Position	Scorers
1	Aug 21	Sat	Div 1	A	Aston Villa	L	0-4	39,012	22	
2	Aug 23	Mon	Div 1	H	Queens Park Rangers	W	1-0	31,885	7	Paddon
3	Aug 28	Sat	Div 1	H	Leicester City	D	0-0	24,960	17	
4	Sep 1	Wed	FLC 2	H	Barnsley	W	3-0	17,889		Holland 2, Paddon
5	Sep 4	Sat	Div 1	A	Stoke City	L	1-2	19,131	20	Taylor A.
6	Sep 11	Sat	Div 1	H	Arsenal	L	0-2	31,965	21	
7	Sep 18	Sat	Div 1	A	Bristol City	D	1-1	28,535	20	Taylor A.
8	Sep 21	Tue	FLC 3	A	Charlton Athletic	W	1-0	34,000		Taylor A.
9	Sep 25	Sat	Div 1	H	Sunderland	D	1-1	24,319	20	Jennings
10	Oct 2	Sat	Div 1	A	Manchester City	L	2-4	37,795	21	Taylor A. Doyle (og)
11	Oct 6	Wed	Div 1	H	Leeds United	L	1-3	21,909	21	Jennings
12	Oct 16	Sat	Div 1	H	Ipswich Town	L	0-2	24,534	21	
13	Oct 23	Sat	Div 1	A	Everton	L	2-3	23,163	21	Bonds, McNaught (og)
14	Oct 27	Wed	FLC 4	H	Queens Park Rangers	L	0-2	24,565		
15	Oct 30	Sat	Div 1	A	West Bromwich Albion	L	0-3	20,396	22	
16	Nov 6	Sat	Div 1	H	Tottenham Hotspur	W	5-3	28,997	21	Bonds, Brooking, Curbishley, Jennings, Robson B
17	Nov 10	Wed	Div 1	A	Norwich City	L	0-1	24,092	22	
18	Nov 20	Sat	Div 1	H	Newcastle United	L	1-2	21,324	22	Robson B.
19	Nov 27	Sat	Div 1	A	Manchester United	W	2-0	55,366	22	Brooking, Jennings
20	Dec 4	Wed	Div 1	H	Middlesbrough	L	0-1	20,453	22	
21	Dec 18	Sat	Div 1	H	Liverpool	W	2-0	24,175	21	Brooking, Jennings
22	Dec 27	Mon	Div 1	A	Birmingham City	D	0-0	39,978	21	
23	Jan 1	Sat	Div 1	A	Tottenham Hotspur	L	1-2	44,972	21	Brooking
24	Jan 3	Mon	Div 1	H	West Bromwich Albion	D	0-0	25,236	21	
25	Jan 8	Sat	FAC 3	H	Bolton Wanderers	W	2-1	24,147		Jennings, Pike
26	Jan 22	Sat	Div 1	H	Aston Villa	L	0-1	27,577	21	
27	Jan 29	Sat	FAC 4	A	Aston Villa	L	0-3	46,954		
28	Feb 5	Sat	Div 1	A	Leicester City	L	0-2	16,201	21	
29	Feb 12	Sat	Div 1	H	Stoke City	W	1-0	20,106	21	Robson B.
30	Feb 19	Sat	Div 1	A	Arsenal	W	3-2	38,221	20	Taylor A. 2, Jennings
31	Feb 26	Sat	Div 1	H	Bristol City	W	2-0	29,713	18	Bonds [pen], Jennings
32	Mar 5	Sat	Div 1	A	Sunderland	L	0-6	35,357	20	
33	Mar 12	Sat	Div 1	H	Manchester City	W	1-0	24,974	18	Robson B.
34	Mar 22	Tue	Div 1	A	Ipswich Town	L	1-4	27,287	22	Robson B. [pen]
35	Apr 2	Sat	Div 1	H	Everton	D	2-2	22,518	22	Robson B. 2 [1 pen]
36	Apr 4	Mon	Div 1	A	Queens Park Rangers	D	1-1	24,930	22	Robson B.
37	Apr 8	Fri	Div 1	H	Birmingham City	D	2-2	28,167	21	Jennings, Pike
38	Apr 9	Sat	Div 1	A	Coventry City	D	1-1	15,755	21	Ronbson B.
39	Apr 11	Mon	Div 1	H	Norwich City	W	1-0	27,084	20	Pike
40	Apr 16	Sat	Div 1	A	Newcastle United	L	0-3	30,967	21	
41	Apr 20	Wed	Div 1	A	Derby County	D	1-1	21,380	21	Pike [pen]
42	Apr 26	Tue	Div 1	A	Leeds United	D	1-1	16,891	21	Robson B.
43	Apr 29	Fri	Div 1	A	Middlesbrough	D	1-1	16,360	19	Robson B.
44	May 4	Wed	Div 1	H	Coventry City	W	2-0	25,461	18	Pike [pen], Robson B.
45	May 7	Sat	Div 1	H	Derby County	D	2-2	32,079	19	Jennings, Pike
46	May 14	Sat	Div 1	A	Liverpool	D	0-0	54,341	19	
47	May 16	Mon	Div 1	H	Manchester United	W	4-2	29,904	17	Robson B. 2, Lampard, Pike

eam Line-Ups

ATKINS Johnny	BONDS Billy	BROOKING Trevor	COLEMAN Keith	CURBISHLEY Alan	DAY Mervyn	DEVONSHIRE Alan	GREEN Bill	HOLLAND Pat	JENNINGS Billy	LAMPARD Frank	LOCK Kevin	McGIVEN Mick	ORHAN Yilmaz	OTULAKOWSKI Anton	PADDON Graham	PIKE Geoff	RADFORD John	ROBSON Bryan	ROBSON Keith	TAYLOR Alan	TAYLOR Tommy	
	6	10	2	11	1		5	9		3					8					7	4	1
	6	10	2	11	1		5	4		3					8					9	7	2
	6	10	2		1		5	4	11	3					8					9	7	3
	6	10	2		1		5	4	11	3					8					9	7	4
	6	10	2		1		5	11	a	3		4			8					9	7/a	5
	4	10	2/a		1		5	11		3		6	a		8					9	7	6
	4	10	2		1		5	11	7	3/a		a			8					9	6	7
	4	10	2		1		5	7	11	3					8					9	6	8
	4	10	2		1		5	7		3	11				8					9	6	9
a	4	10	2		1		5	7		3	11/a				8					9	6	10
1	4	10	2		1		5	7		3					8					9	6	11
a	4	10	2		1		5	7		3					8			11		9/a	6	12
	2	10		4	1		5/a			3		a		7	8		9	11			6	13
	2	10		4	1	9				3	5			7	8			11			6	14
	2	10		4	1	7				3	5	a			8		9	11/a			6	15
	2	10		4	1	7		9		3	5				8			11			6	16
	2	10	a	4	1	7		9		3	5/a				8			11			6/a	17
	2	10		4	1	7		9		3	5				8			11	a		6/a	18
	6	10			1	7		9		3	2			4	8			11			5	19
	6	10	a		1	7		9/a		3	2			4	8			11			5	20
	6	10			1			9		3	2			4	8			11	7		5	21
	6	10			1			9		3	2			4	8			11	7		5	22
	6	10			1			9		3	2		a	4	8/a			11	7		5	23
	6	10			1			9		3	2			4	8			11	7		5	24
	6	10		7	1			9		3	2			4	8			11			5	25
	6	10		7	1	a		9		3	2			4	8/a			11			5	26
	6	10			1			9		3	2			4	8			11	7		5	27
	2	10			1	9	5			3		6		4			8	11		7		28
	2	10			1	9	5			3		6		4			8	11/a	a	7		29
	2	10			1	9	5	11		3		6		4			8			7		30
	2	10			1	9	5	11		3		6		4			8			7		31
	2	10			1	9	5	11		3		6		4			8			7		32
	2	10	a		1	9	5/a	11		3		6		4		7	8					33
	2	10			1	9		11		3		6		4		7	8				5	34
	2	10			1	9		11		3		6		4		7	8				5	35
	2	10			1	9/a		11		3		6	a	4		7	8				5	36
	2	10	3		1	9/a		11				6		4		7	8			a	5	37
	2	10			1	9		11		3		6		4		7	8				5	38
	2	10			1	9				3		6		4		7	8	11			5	39
	2	10			1	9		a		3		6		4		7	8	11/a			5	40
	2/a	10			1	9		a		3		6		4		7	8	11			5	41
	2	10			1	9				3		6		4		7	8	11			5	42
	2	10			1	9		7		3		6		4			8	11			5	43
	2	10			1	9				3		6		4		7	8	11			5	44
	2	10			1	9		a		3		6/a		4		7	8	11			5	45
	2	10			1	9		7		3		6		4			8	11			5	46
	2	10			1	9				3		6		4		7	8	11			5	47

1977-78
Story of the season

The first three games brought three defeats and **even at this early stage there was a threat of relegation.** Morale was even lower following a 5–0 defeat at Nottingham Forest in the League Cup.

There was a surprise 3–2 win at Newcastle United bu[t] would be a further nine games before another victo[ry] Striker Derek Hales had been signed from Derby Cou[nty] and he scored twice against Ipswich Town in the 2–0 aw[ay] win in October. The home form improved with success[ive] wins against Manchester United, Birmingham City a[nd] Leicester City, and to add to the firepower centre-forwa[rd] David Cross was bought from West Bromwich Albion.

The New Year began with a 1–0 win against Watford in t[he] FA Cup but progress was halted in the fourth round with

Appearances & Goals 1977-78

	League			FA Cup			League Cup			Total	
	Starts	Subs	Goals	Starts	Subs	Goals	Starts	Subs	Goals	Starts	Subs
BONDS Billy	29	0	1	3	0	1	0	0	0	32	0
BROOKING Trevor	37	0	4	2	0	0	0	0	0	39	0
BRUSH Paul	23	1	0	0	0	0	1	0	0	24	1
CROSS David	21	0	9	3	0	0	0	0	0	24	0
CURBISHLEY Alan	31	1	1	3	0	0	1	0	0	35	1
DAY Mervyn	23	0	0	0	0	0	1	0	0	24	0
DEVONSHIRE Alan	32	2	3	3	0	0	1	0	0	36	2
FERGUSON Bobby	19	0	0	3	0	0	0	0	0	22	0
GREEN Bill	13	0	1	0	0	0	1	0	0	14	0
HALES Derek	23	1	10	3	0	0	0	0	0	26	1
HOLLAND Pat	18	3	3	1	0	0	0	0	0	19	3
JENNINGS Billy	2	0	1	0	0	0	0	0	0	2	0
LAMPARD Frank	40	0	0	3	0	0	1	0	0	44	0
LOCK Kevin	6	0	1	0	0	0	1	0	0	7	0
MARTIN Alvin	5	2	1	0	0	0	0	0	0	5	2
McDOWELL John	12	2	1	3	0	0	0	0	0	15	2
McGIVEN Mick	4	0	0	0	0	0	0	0	0	4	0
OTULAKOWSKI Anton	0	5	0	0	0	0	0	0	0	0	5
PIKE Geoff	25	3	2	0	1	0	1	0	0	26	4
RADFORD John	10	0	0	0	0	0	1	0	0	11	0
ROBSON Bryan	37	0	9	3	0	2	1	0	0	41	0
TAYLOR Alan	10	1	2	0	1	0	1	0	0	11	2
TAYLOR Tommy	42	0	2	3	0	0	0	0	0	45	0
own goal			1								
Totals	462	21	52	33	2	3	11	0	0	506	23

astrous replay at Queens Park Rangers that ended in a
1 defeat. Poor results during February and early March,
ding with a 4–1 loss at Aston Villa, left the Hammers
entieth. At Easter the team gave their supporters a
mmer of hope as David Cross scored a hat-trick in the
0 win against Ipswich Town, and the following day there
s a 3–1 home victory over Chelsea. After a further four
ns in April the Hammers looked set to repeat their
udini act and avoid relegation.

ey needed to win their final game of the season at home
Liverpool. Before a season's best crowd of 37,448 the
erseysiders cruised to a 2–0 victory and the Hammers'
-year stay in the First Division was over.

ootball League - Division One
nal Table 1977-78

		HOME					AWAY					
	P	W	D	L	F	A	W	D	L	F	A	Pts
ttingham Forest	42	15	6	0	37	8	10	8	3	32	16	64
erpool	42	15	4	2	37	11	9	5	7	28	23	57
rton	42	14	4	3	47	22	8	7	6	29	23	55
nchester City	42	14	4	3	46	21	6	8	7	28	30	52
enal	42	14	5	2	38	12	7	5	9	22	25	52
st Bromwich Albion	42	13	5	3	35	18	5	9	7	27	35	50
ventry City	42	13	5	3	48	23	5	7	9	27	39	48
on Villa	42	11	4	6	33	18	7	6	8	24	24	46
ds United	42	12	4	5	39	21	6	6	9	24	32	46
nchester United	42	9	6	6	32	23	7	4	10	35	40	42
mingham City	42	8	5	8	32	30	8	4	9	23	30	41
by County	42	10	7	4	37	24	4	6	11	17	35	41
wich City	42	10	8	3	28	20	1	10	10	24	46	40
ddlesbrough	42	8	8	5	25	19	4	7	10	17	35	39
lverhampton Wanderers	42	7	8	6	30	27	5	4	12	21	37	36
elsea	42	7	11	3	28	20	4	3	14	18	49	36
stol City	42	9	6	6	37	26	2	7	12	12	27	35
wich Town	42	10	5	6	32	24	1	8	12	15	37	35
eens Park Rangers	42	8	8	5	27	26	1	7	13	20	38	33
st Ham United	42	8	6	7	31	28	4	2	15	21	41	32
wcastle United	42	4	6	11	26	37	2	4	15	16	41	22
cester City	42	4	7	10	16	32	1	5	15	10	38	22

ALVIN MARTIN

Martin signed for West Ham as an apprentice in 1974 and went on to become one of the Hammers' greatest defenders.

After making his debut against Aston Villa in March 1978 he became a regular in the side and set up a successful partnership with midfielder Billy Bonds. He was a rock in defence when West Ham won the FA Cup in 1980 and the following season he only missed one game as the Hammers became Second Division champions. In May 1981 he won the first of 17 England caps when playing against Brazil at Wembley. He remained a member of the England squad until 1986.

In 1984 he was made club captain and his pairing with Tony Gale was one of the best in the country. Alvin was the backbone of West Ham's best ever season in 1985–86 when they were challenging for the title but eventually finished third. In that campaign he scored a unique hat-trick when scoring against three different goalkeepers in the 8–1 demolition of Newcastle United. In 1996, after a wonderful career spanning 19 seasons at Upton Park, he left to join Leyton Orient. After 586 games for the Hammers he was given a marvellous reception as he left the pitch in his final game against Sheffield Wednesday.

He spent a season with the Orient, playing in 19 games where his experience was invaluable. After retiring as a player he became the manager at Southend United until 1999 and is presently a popular presenter on various football radio shows.

Season **1977-78** Football League - Division One
Match Details

Manager **John Lyall**   Final League Position **20/22 Relegated to Division 2**

	Date		Competition	Venue	Opponents	Results		Attendance	Position	Scorers
1	Aug 20	Sat	Div 1	H	Norwich City	L	1-3	28,178	20	Robson [pen]
2	Aug 24	Wed	Div 1	A	Leicester City	L	0-1	18,310	21	
3	Aug 27	Sat	Div 1	H	Manchester City	L	0-1	25,278	21	
4	Aug 30	Tue	FLC 2	A	Nottingham Forest	L	0-5	18,224		
5	Sep 3	Sat	Div 1	A	Newcastle United	W	3-2	26,942	18	Jennings, Taylor A., Robson
6	Sep 10	Sat	Div 1	H	Queens Park Rangers	D	2-2	26,922	17	Holland, Lock
7	Sep 17	Sat	Div 1	A	Bristol City	L	2-3	21,344	20	Pike, Robson
8	Sep 24	Sat	Div 1	H	Everton	D	1-1	25,296	17	Dobson (og)
9	Oct 1	Sat	Div 1	A	Arsenal	L	0-3	41,245	20	
10	Oct 3	Mon	Div 1	H	Middlesbrough	L	0-2	26,508	20	
11	Oct 8	Sat	Div 1	H	Nottingham Forest	D	0-0	26,128	20	
12	Oct 15	Sat	Div 1	A	Wolverhampton Wanderers	D	2-2	19,360	20	Pike, Robson
13	Oct 22	Sat	Div 1	H	Aston Villa	D	2-2	26,599	20	Hales, Taylor T.
14	Oct 29	Sat	Div 1	A	Ipswich Town	W	2-0	27,330	19	Hales 2
15	Nov 5	Sat	Div 1	A	Coventry City	L	0-1	23,268	19	
16	Nov 12	Sat	Div 1	H	West Bromwich Albion	D	3-3	23,601	20	Devonshire 2, Robson [pen]
17	Nov 19	Sat	Div 1	A	Derby County	L	1-2	23,273	20	Bonds
18	Nov 26	Sat	Div 1	H	Leeds United	L	0-1	26,853	20	
19	Dec 3	Sat	Div 1	A	Liverpool	L	0-2	39,659	20	
20	Dec 10	Sat	Div 1	H	Manchester United	W	2-1	20,242	20	Brooking, Hales
21	Dec 17	Sat	Div 1	A	West Bromwich Albion	L	0-1	18,896	21	
22	Dec 26	Mon	Div 1	H	Birmingham City	W	1-0	25,572	19	Curbishley
23	Dec 27	Tue	Div 1	A	Chelsea	L	1-2	44,093	19	Robson
24	Dec 31	Sat	Div 1	H	Leicester City	W	3-2	25,355	19	Cross, Hales, McDowell
25	Jan 2	Mon	Div 1	A	Norwich City	D	2-2	29,168	19	Devonshire, Hales
26	Jan 7	Sat	FAC 3	H	Watford	W	1-0	36,745		Robson
27	Jan 14	Sat	Div 1	A	Manchester City	L	2-3	43,627	19	Brooking, Cross
28	Jan 21	Sat	Div 1	H	Newcastle United	W	1-0	25,461	19	Hales
29	Jan 28	Sat	FAC 4	H	Queens Park Rangers	D	1-1	35,566		Bonds
30	Jan 31	Tue	FAC 4 Rep	A	Queens Park Rangers	L	1-6	24,057		Robson
31	Feb 11	Sat	Div 1	H	Bristol City	L	1-2	19,934	19	Robson
32	Feb 18	Sat	Div 1	A	Everton	L	1-2	33,826	19	Hales
33	Feb 25	Sat	Div 1	H	Arsenal	D	2-2	31,585	19	Cross, Taylor A.
34	Mar 4	Sat	Div 1	A	Nottingham Forest	L	0-2	33,924	19	
35	Mar 11	Sat	Div 1	H	Wolverhampton Wanderers	L	1-2	23,525	20	Hales
36	Mar 14	Tue	Div 1	A	Queens Park Rangers	L	0-1	20,394	20	
37	Mar 18	Sat	Div 1	A	Aston Villa	L	1-4	28,275	20	Brooking
38	Mar 24	Fri	Div 1	H	Ipswich Town	W	3-0	23,867	20	Cross 3
39	Mar 25	Sat	Div 1	H	Chelsea	W	3-1	24,987	19	Brooking, Green, Holland
40	Mar 28	Tue	Div 1	A	Birmingham City	L	0-3	23,554	19	
41	Apr 1	Sat	Div 1	H	Coventry City	W	2-1	19,260	19	Holland, Taylor T.
42	Apr 8	Sat	Div 1	A	Leeds United	W	2-1	22,953	18	Hales, Martin
43	Apr 15	Sat	Div 1	H	Derby County	W	3-0	25,424	17	Robson 2, Cross
44	Apr 22	Sat	Div 1	A	Manchester United	L	0-3	54,089	19	
45	Apr 25	Tue	Div 1	A	Middlesbrough	W	2-1	13,247	17	Cross 2
46	Apr 29	Sat	Div 1	H	Liverpool	L	0-2	37,448	20	

eam Line-Ups

BROOKING Trevor	BRUSH Paul	CROSS David	CURBISHLEY Alan	DAY Mervyn	DEVONSHIRE Alan	FERGUSON Bobby	GREEN Bill	HALES Derek	HOLLAND Pat	JENNINGS Billy	LAMPARD Frank	LOCK Kevin	MARTIN Alvin	McDOWELL John	McGIVEN Mick	OTULAKOWSKI Anton	PIKE Geoff	RADFORD John	ROBSON Bryan	TAYLOR Alan	TAYLOR Tommy	
10	2			1	11						3	6					4	9	8	7	5	1
	2		10	1	11/a						3	6				a	4	9	8	7	5	2
	3		10	1	11						2	6				a	4	9	8	7/a	5	3
	3		10	1	11		5				2	6					4	9	8	7		4
	3		10	1	11				4	9	2	6							8	7	5	5
	3		10	1	11				4	9/a	2	6				a	7		8		5	6
10	3		9	1	11/a				4		2	6				a			8	7	5	7
10	3		9	1	11				4		2				6				8	7	5	8
10	3		9/a	1	11				4		2			6		a			8	7	5	9
10	3			1	a			9/a	4		2			6			11		8	7	5	10
10	3		4	1	7						2				6		11	9	8		5	11
10	3			1	7			11			2						6	9	8		5	12
10	3			1	7			11			2						6	9	8		5	13
10	3			1	7			11			2						6	9	8		5	14
10	3			1	7			11			2						6	9	8		5	15
10	3		9	1	7			11			2						6		8		5	16
10	3			1	7			11			2						6	9	8		5	17
10	3		a	1	7			11			2						6	9/a	8		5	18
10	3		9	1	7			11	a		2						6		8		5/a	19
10	3		9	1	7			11			2/a				a		6		8		5	20
10	3	9		1	7			11						2			6		8		5	21
10		9	11	1	7						3			2			6		8		5	22
10		9	11	1	7						3			2			6		8		5	23
10		9	6		7	1		11			3			2					8		5	24
10	2	9	6		7	1		11			3								8		5	25
10		9	6/a		7	1		11			3			2		a			8		5	26
10		9	6		7	1		11			3			2					8		5	27
		9	6		7/a	1		11	a		3			2			8			10	5	28
10		9	6		7	1		11			3			2					8		5	29
		9	6		7/a	1		11		10	3			2					8	a	5	30
10		9		1	7		6	11/a			3			2					8	a	5	31
10		9			7	1	6	11			3			a			4		8		5	32
10		9	4		7	1	6				3			2/a		a			8	11	5	33
10		9	4		7	1	6/a	11	a		3			2					8		5	34
10		9	4		7	1		11	8		3			2/a		a					5	35
10		9	6		7	1			8		3			2			11				5	36
10		9	4		7/a	1		11	8		3		a	2							5	37
10		9	4			1	6	11	8		3						7				5	38
10		9	4			1	6		8		3						7		11		5	39
10		9	4			1	6/a	a	8		3						7		11		5	40
10			4			1	6	9	8		3		a				7/a		11		5	41
10	3		7			1	6	9	8			4							11		5	42
10	3	9	7/a			1	6		8		2	4				a			11		5	43
10	a	9	7			1	6		8		3		4/a						11		5	44
10		9	7			1	6		8		3		4						11		5	45
10		9	7		a	1	6		8		3		4						11		5/a	46

1978-79
Story of the season

It was a **whirlwind start to life in the Second Division** as the Hammers beat Notts County 5–2 at home and followed this up with a smart 3–0 win at Newcastle United.

Joy turned to gloom, however, with two home defeats four days: Third Division Swindon Town dumped W Ham out of the League Cup, winning 2–1, and then Fulha won 1–0 in the league. Bryan Robson then scored six go in three successive home games, which included a hat-tri in the 3–0 win against local rivals Millwall.

Inspired by Bonds and Brooking in midfield and t goalscoring abilities of Cross and Robson, the Hamme moved up to third spot after beating Cambridge Unit 5–0 at home in December. An upset on Boxing Day sa

Appearances & Goals 1978-79

	League			FA Cup			League Cup			Total		
	Starts	Subs	Goals	Starts	Subs	Goals	Starts	Subs	Goals	Starts	Subs	
BONDS Billy	39	0	4	1	0	0	1	0	0	41	0	
BRIGNULL Phil	0	1	0	0	0	0	0	0	0	0	1	
BROOKING Trevor	21	0	2	1	0	0	0	0	0	22	0	
BRUSH Paul	42	0	0	1	0	0	1	0	0	44	0	
CROSS David	40	0	18	1	0	0	1	0	0	42	0	
CURBISHLEY Alan	26	1	1	0	0	0	1	0	0	27	1	
DAY Mervyn	13	0	0	1	0	0	0	0	0	14	0	
DEVONSHIRE Alan	41	0	5	1	0	0	1	0	0	43	0	
FERGUSON Bobby	11	0	0	0	0	0	1	0	0	12	0	
HOLLAND Pat	39	0	3	0	0	0	1	0	0	40	0	
JENNINGS Billy	2	2	0	0	0	0	0	0	0	2	2	
LAMPARD Frank	28	1	3	1	0	0	1	0	0	30	1	
LANSDOWNE Billy Jnr	0	1	0	0	0	0	0	0	0	0	1	
MARTIN Alvin	22	0	1	1	0	0	0	0	0	23	0	
McDOWELL John	26	2	2	1	0	0	0	0	0	27	2	
MORGAN Nicky	2	0	0	0	0	0	0	0	0	2	0	
PARKES Phil	18	0	0	0	0	0	0	0	0	18	0	
PIKE Geoff	10	4	1	0	0	0	0	1	0	10	5	
ROBSON Bryan	40	0	24	1	0	1	1	0	1	42	0	
TAYLOR Alan	10	3	3	1	0	0	1	0	0	12	3	
TAYLOR Tommy	32	0	0	0	0	0	1	0	0	33	0	
own goal			3									
Totals	**462**	**15**	**70**	**11**	**0**	**1**	**11**	**1**	**1**	**484**	**16**	

e Orient win 2–0 at Upton Park, but days later Blackburn
overs were beaten 4–0 at home. Hopes of a run in the FA
up were dashed as Fourth Division Newport County won
1 at Somerton Park.

he football world were staggered in February when West
am paid a world record fee of £565,000 for goalkeeper
il Parkes from Queens Park Rangers. Apart from the 5–0
rashing of Newcastle United in March, the goals had
ied up, with a spell of just one goal in four games. With
st one win against Burnley in the last seven games the
ammers missed out on promotion and finished fifth.

PAUL BRUSH

A very dependable left-back who made his
debut against Norwich City in August 1977,
Brush was ever-present the following
season as the Hammers fought for
promotion to the First Division.

In 1980 West Ham reached the FA Cup final
and he played in every round, but unluckily
missed out on the final when named as
substitute. He did get to play at Wembley the
following year when he played in the annual
Charity Shield game against Liverpool.

After playing in 184 games for the Hammers
he left to join Crystal Palace in August 1985,
where he spent three seasons and made 53
appearances. Moving on to Southend United,
he played 92 games for them before going
into non-league football in 1989 with Enfield
and later Heybridge Swifts.

After retiring as a player he was appointed in
1994 as youth team coach at Leyton Orient
and later in 2001 he became their manager.
After leaving Orient in 2003 he was assistant
manager at both Southend United and
Lincoln City. In June 2012 he was installed at
Tottenham as their development coach.

ootball League - Division Two
inal Table 1978-79

	P	HOME					AWAY					Pts
		W	D	L	F	A	W	D	L	F	A	
ystal Palace	42	12	7	2	30	11	7	12	2	21	13	57
ghton and Hove Albion	42	16	3	2	44	11	7	7	7	28	28	56
oke City	42	11	7	3	35	15	9	9	3	23	16	56
nderland	42	13	3	5	39	19	9	8	4	31	25	55
est Ham United	42	12	7	2	46	15	6	7	8	24	24	50
tts County	42	8	10	3	23	15	6	6	9	25	45	44
eston North End	42	7	11	3	36	23	5	7	9	23	34	42
wcastle United	42	13	3	5	35	24	4	5	12	16	31	42
rdiff City	42	12	5	4	34	23	4	5	12	22	47	42
ham	42	10	7	4	35	19	3	8	10	15	28	41
yton Orient	42	11	5	5	32	18	4	5	12	19	33	40
mbridge United	42	7	10	4	22	15	5	6	10	22	37	40
rnley	42	11	6	4	31	22	3	6	12	20	40	40
dham Athletic	42	10	7	4	36	23	3	6	12	16	38	39
rexham	42	10	6	5	31	16	2	8	11	14	26	38
stol Rovers	42	10	6	5	34	23	4	4	13	14	37	38
icester City	42	7	8	6	28	23	3	9	9	15	29	37
ton Town	42	11	5	5	46	24	2	5	14	14	33	36
arlton Athletic	42	6	8	7	28	28	5	5	11	32	41	35
effield United	42	9	6	6	34	24	2	6	13	18	45	34
llwall	42	7	4	10	22	29	4	6	11	20	32	32
ackburn Rovers	42	5	8	8	24	29	5	2	14	17	43	30

Season **1978-79** Football League - Division Two
Match Details
Manager **John Lyall**   Final League Position **5/22**

#	Date		Competition	Venue	Opponents	Results		Attendance	Position	Scorers
1	Aug 19	Sat	Div 2	H	Notts County	W	5-2	25,387	2	Cross 3, Devonshire, Blockley (og)
2	Aug 23	Wed	Div 2	A	Newcastle United	W	3-0	27,167	1	Cross, Devonshire, Robson
3	Aug 26	Sat	Div 2	A	Crystal Palace	D	1-1	32,814	2	Taylor A.
4	Aug 30	Wed	FLC 2	H	Swindon Town	L	1-2	19,672		Robson
5	Sep 2	Sat	Div 2	H	Fulham	L	0-1	25,869	4	
6	Sep 9	Sat	Div 2	A	Burnley	L	2-3	12,392	7	Cross 2
7	Sep 16	Sat	Div 2	H	Bristol Rovers	W	2-0	22,189	4	Brooking, Robson
8	Sep 23	Sat	Div 2	H	Sheffield United	W	2-0	24,361	3	Robson 2 [2 pens]
9	Sep 30	Sat	Div 2	A	Sunderland	L	1-2	23,676	6	Cross
10	Oct 7	Sat	Div 2	H	Millwall	W	3-0	22,210	4	Robson 3 [1 pen]
11	Oct 14	Sat	Div 2	A	Oldham Athletic	D	2-2	9,191	3	Robson 2
12	Oct 21	Sat	Div 2	H	Stoke City	D	1-1	27,855	5	Brooking
13	Oct 28	Sat	Div 2	A	Brighton & Hove Albion	W	2-1	33,028	4	Robson 2
14	Nov 4	Sat	Div 2	H	Preston North End	W	3-1	23,572	2	Cross, Devonshire, Lampard
15	Nov 11	Sat	Div 2	A	Notts County	L	0-1	11,002	4	
16	Nov 18	Sat	Div 2	H	Crystal Palace	D	1-1	31,245	3	Bonds
17	Nov 21	Tue	Div 2	A	Fulham	D	0-0	26,556	3	
18	Nov 25	Sat	Div 2	A	Leicester City	W	2-1	16,149	3	Cross 2
19	Dec 2	Sat	Div 2	H	Cambridge United	W	5-0	21,379	3	Robson 2, Bonds, Curbishley, Taylor A.
20	Dec 9	Sat	Div 2	A	Wrexham	L	3-4	15,587	3	Cross, Lampard, Robson
21	Dec 16	Sat	Div 2	H	Charlton Athletic	W	2-0	23,833	3	Cross, Robson
22	Dec 26	Tue	Div 2	H	Orient	L	0-2	29,220	4	
23	Dec 30	Sat	Div 2	H	Blackburn Rovers	W	4-0	21,269	4	Cross, Robson, Taylor A., Curtis (og)
24	Jan 9	Tue	FAC 3	A	Newport County	L	1-2	14,124		Robson
25	Jan 20	Sat	Div 2	A	Bristol Rovers	W	1-0	12,418	4	Robson
26	Feb 10	Sat	Div 2	H	Sunderland	D	3-3	24,998	4	Cross 2, Robson
27	Feb 24	Sat	Div 2	H	Oldham Athletic	W	3-0	26,052	4	Holland, Martin, Robson
28	Feb 26	Mon	Div 2	A	Luton Town	W	4-1	14,205	3	Cross 2, Devonshire, Robson
29	Mar 3	Sat	Div 2	A	Stoke City	L	0-2	24,912	4	
30	Mar 10	Sat	Div 2	H	Brighton & Hove Albion	D	0-0	35,802	5	
31	Mar 17	Sat	Div 2	A	Preston North End	D	0-0	15,380	5	
32	Mar 24	Sat	Div 2	H	Newcastle United	W	5-0	24,650	5	McDowell 2, Devonshire, Lampard, Robson
33	Mar 31	Sat	Div 2	H	Leicester City	D	1-1	23,992	5	Robson
34	Apr 2	Mon	Div 2	A	Sheffield United	L	0-3	17,720	5	
35	Apr 7	Sat	Div 2	A	Cambridge United	D	0-0	11,406	5	
36	Apr 9	Mon	Div 2	H	Luton Town	W	1-0	25,398	5	Carr (og)
37	Apr 14	Sat	Div 2	A	Orient	W	2-0	17,517	5	Holland, Pike
38	Apr 16	Mon	Div 2	H	Cardiff City	D	1-1	29,058	5	Holland
39	Apr 21	Sat	Div 2	A	Charlton Athletic	D	0-0	22,816	5	
40	Apr 24	Tue	Div 2	H	Burnley	W	3-1	24,139	5	Bonds, Cross, Robson
41	Apr 28	Sat	Div 2	H	Wrexham	D	1-1	28,865	5	Bonds
42	May 5	Sat	Div 2	A	Blackburn Rovers	L	0-1	7,585	5	
43	May 11	Fri	Div 2	A	Cardiff City	D	0-0	13,124	5	
44	May 14	Mon	Div 2	A	Millwall	L	1-2	11,968	5	Robson

eam Line-Ups

	BRIGNULL Phil	BROOKING Trevor	BRUSH Paul	CROSS David	CURBISHLEY Alan	DAY Mervyn	DEVONSHIRE Alan	FERGUSON Bobby	HOLLAND Pat	JENNINGS Billy	LAMPARD Frank	LANSDOWNE Billy Jnr	MARTIN Alvin	McDOWELL John	MORGAN Nicky	PARKES Phil	PIKE Geoff	ROBSON Bryan	TAYLOR Alan	TAYLOR Tommy	
		10	3	9	7		8	1	4		2							11		5	1
		10/a	3	9	7		8	1	4		2							11	a	5	2
			3	9	7		8	1	4		2							11	10	5	3
			3	9	7		8	1	4		2						a	11	10/a	5	4
			3	9	7			1	4		2			a			8	11	10/a	5	5
			3	9	7		8	1	4		2		10					11		5	6
		10	3	9	7		8	1	4		2							11		5	7
		10	3		7		8	1	4	9	2/a						a	11		5	8
		10	3	9	7		8	1	4					2				11		5	9
		10	3	9	7		8	1	4		2							11		5	10
		10	3	9	7/a		8	1	4		2			a				11		5	11
		10	3	9	7		8	1	4					2				11		5	12
		10	3	9	7	1	8		4					2				11		5	13
		10	3	9	7	1	8		4		2							11		5	14
		10	3	9	7	1	8		4		2							11		5	15
		10	3	9	7	1	8		4/a		2							11	a	5	16
			3	9	7	1	8		4		2							11	10	5	17
			3	9		1	8		4		2						7	11	10	5	18
			3	9	7	1	8		4		2							11	10	5	19
			3	9	7	1	8		4		2		6					11	10	5	20
			3	9	7	1	8		4/a		2			6			a	11	10	5	21
			3	9	7/a	1	8			a	2			6			4	11	10	5	22
		10	3	9		1	8				2		5	6				11	7		23
		10	3	9		1	8				2		5	6				11	7		24
		10	3	9	4	1	8						5	2				11	7		25
		10	3	9	4	1	8		7	a				2				11/a		5	26
		10	3	9	4		8		7				5	2		1		11			27
		10	3	9	4		8		7				5	2		1		11			28
		10	3	9	4		8		7				5	2		1		11			29
			3	9	4		8		7		2		5	10		1		11			30
		10	3	9			8		7		2		5	4		1		11			31
		10/a	3	9			8		7		2		5	4		1	a	11			32
			3	9	a		8		7		2		5	4/a		1	10	11			33
			3	9			8		7		2		5	4		1	10	11			34
4			3	9			8		7		2/a		5	10		1	a	11		6	35
4			3				8		7				5	2	9	1	10	11		6	36
4			3	9			8		7				5	2		1	10	11		6	37
4			3	9			8		7				5	2		1	10	11		6	38
4			3	9			8		7	11/a	a		5	2		1	10			6	39
4			3	9			8		7				5	2		1	10	11		6	40
4			3	9			8		7		2	a	5	2		1	10/a	11		6	41
4			3	9			8		7		2		5	10/a		1		11	a	6	42
4	a		3	9			8		7		2		5	10/a	11	1				6	43
4		10	3	9			8		7		2		5			1		11		6	44

1979-80
Story of the season

A player exodus saw **Bryan Robson, Mervyn Day** and **Tommy Taylor all leave,** while new signings were full-back Ray Stewart and winger Jimmy Neighbour.

It was a poor start to the season, with just two wins seven games leaving the side in nineteenth place. Barnsl and Southend United were beaten in the League Cup, wi young Billy Lansdowne claiming a hat-trick in the 5- Southend win. November was a good month as all thr Welsh clubs, Cardiff, Swansea and Wrexham, were beate at home without conceding a goal, and after a replay We Ham beat Sunderland 2–1 in the League Cup. The tea was struggling on their travels with 3–0 defeats Shrewsbury and in a League Cup replay at Nottingha Forest.

On New Year's Day there was a good 4–0 win at neighbou Orient and the FA Cup trail started with a 2–1 home w against West Bromwich Albion. Orient were next in the F Cup and the Hammers advanced, winning 3–2. Durin February the three league wins moved the team to withi point of the leaders and, now in top form, Swansea we

Appearances & Goals 1979-80

	League			FA Cup			League Cup			Total		
	Starts	Subs	Goals	Starts	Subs	Goals	Starts	Subs	Goals	Starts	Subs	
ALLEN Paul	31	0	2	7	1	1	7	0	0	45	1	
BANTON Dale	2	2	0	0	0	0	1	0	0	3	2	
BONDS Billy	34	0	1	5	0	0	9	0	0	48	0	
BROOKING Trevor	37	0	3	7	0	2	8	0	1	52	0	
BRUSH Paul	27	0	0	6	0	0	4	0	0	37	0	
CROSS David	38	1	12	5	0	1	9	0	5	52	1	
DEVONSHIRE Alan	34	0	5	8	0	1	7	0	0	49	0	
FERGUSON Bobby	2	0	0	0	0	0	1	0	0	3	0	
HOLLAND Pat	21	5	4	1	0	0	8	0	1	30	5	
LAMPARD Frank	35	1	0	7	0	1	6	0	0	48	1	
LANSDOWNE Billy Jnr	5	3	1	0	0	0	4	1	3	9	4	
MARTIN Alvin	40	0	2	7	0	0	8	0	1	55	0	
MORGAN Nicky	4	2	1	0	0	0	1	0	0	5	2	
NEIGHBOUR Jimmy	22	1	1	4	0	0	0	0	0	26	1	
PARKES Phil	40	0	0	8	0	0	8	0	0	56	0	
PEARSON Stuart	24	1	5	8	0	2	3	0	1	35	1	
PIKE Geoff	27	4	5	7	1	1	6	0	1	40	5	
SMITH Mark	1	0	0	0	0	0	1	0	0	2	0	
STEWART Ray	38	0	10	8	0	3	8	0	1	54	0	
own goal			2			1						
Totals	**462**	**20**	**54**	**88**	**2**	**13**	**99**	**1**	**14**	**649**	**23**	

ocked out of the FA Cup following a 2–0 home win. Just
e win in March saw the team drop down to eighth in the
gue, but the FA Cup brought a 1–0 victory against Aston
lla thanks to a goal from Ray Stewart in the last minute.
vo home defeats in April brought the promotion dream
 an end as the Hammers looked for FA Cup success.
verton were the opponents in the semi-final and following
–1 draw West Ham won the replay 3–1 at Elland Road.
ne FA Cup final was an all-London affair as the Hammers
ced cup-holders and favourites Arsenal. On 13 minutes
evor Brooking scored with a rare headed goal and for the
mainder of the match the Hammers sat back, marshalled
 Bonds and Martin, and held out to win 1–0 .

ne final league match at Sunderland had to be delayed
itil after the cup final. A tired Hammers team lost 2–0,
iich ensured the Wearsiders promotion and left West
im in seventh place.

ootball League - Division Two
inal Table 1979-80

	P	HOME					AWAY					Pts
		W	D	L	F	A	W	D	L	F	A	
cester City	42	12	5	4	32	19	9	8	4	26	19	55
nderland	42	16	5	0	47	13	5	7	9	22	29	54
mingham City	42	14	5	2	37	16	7	6	8	21	22	53
elsea	42	14	3	4	34	16	9	4	8	32	36	53
eens Park Rangers	42	10	9	2	46	25	8	4	9	29	28	49
on Town	42	9	10	2	36	17	7	7	7	30	28	49
est Ham United	42	13	2	6	37	21	7	5	9	17	22	47
mbridge United	42	11	6	4	40	23	3	10	8	21	30	44
wcastle United	42	13	6	2	35	19	2	8	11	18	30	44
ston North End	42	8	10	3	30	23	4	9	8	26	29	43
lham Athletic	42	12	5	4	30	21	4	6	11	19	32	43
ansea City	42	13	1	7	31	20	4	8	9	17	33	43
ewsbury Town	42	12	3	6	41	23	6	2	13	19	30	41
ton Orient	42	7	9	5	29	31	5	8	8	19	23	41
diff City	42	11	4	6	21	16	5	4	12	20	32	40
exham	42	13	2	6	26	15	3	4	14	14	34	38
tts County	42	4	11	6	24	22	7	4	10	27	30	37
tford	42	9	6	6	27	18	3	7	11	12	28	37
stol Rovers	42	9	8	4	33	23	2	5	14	17	41	35
ham	42	6	4	11	19	28	5	3	13	23	46	29
rnley	42	5	9	7	19	23	1	6	14	20	50	27
arlton Athletic	42	6	6	9	25	31	0	4	17	14	47	22

PAUL ALLEN

This midfield dynamo signed apprentice forms for West Ham in 1978 and aged just 17 he made his debut against Burnley in September 1979.

He won a record 23 England youth caps and skippered England when they won the UEFA under-18 tournament in 1980.

In May 1980 he became the youngest player to play in a Wembley FA Cup final when he played in the side that beat Arsenal 1–0. He was still young enough to win an FA Youth Cup medal in 1981 when the Hammers beat Tottenham Hotspur in the final. By 1985 he was one of the best midfielders in the country and after 196 games for West Ham his fine form saw Tottenham pay £400,000 to take him to White Hart Lane. He played in both the 1987 and 1991 FA Cup finals for Spurs and made a total of 377 appearances for them.

In 1993 another big fee of £550,000 saw him move to Southampton, where in two seasons he played 49 games for the Saints. While at the Dell in season 1994–95 he was loaned out to Luton Town and Stoke City. Then followed a two-year spell at Swindon Town where he made 45 appearances before moving on in July 1997 to play 17 times for Bristol City. In the following campaign, under the management of his old captain Billy Bonds, he played 34 games for Millwall. He finished his playing career on a massive total of 742 appearances, scoring 43 goals.

Since giving up playing he has been working for the PFA alongside his old Hammers team-mate Bobby Barnes.

Season **1979-80** Football League - Division Two
Match Details
Manager **John Lyall**   Final League Position **7/22**

	Date		Competition	Venue	Opponents	Results		Attendance	Position	Scorers
1	Aug 18	Sat	Div 2	A	Wrexham	L	0-1	13,036	17	
2	Aug 20	Mon	Div 2	H	Chelsea	L	0-1	31,627	20	
3	Aug 25	Sat	Div 2	H	Oldham Athletic	W	1-0	18,319	15	Holland
4	Aug 28	Tue	FLC 2:1	H	Barnsley	W	3-1	12,320		Brooking, Pearson, Cross
5	Sep 1	Sat	Div 2	A	Watford	L	0-2	23,329	21	
6	Sep 4	Tue	FLC 2:2	A	Barnsley	W	2-0	15,898		Cross 2
7	Sep 8	Sat	Div 2	A	Preston North End	D	1-1	10,460	19	Cross
8	Sep 15	Sat	Div 2	H	Sunderland	W	2-0	24,021	17	Pearson, Cross
9	Sep 22	Sat	Div 2	A	Queens Park Rangers	L	0-3	24,692	19	
10	Sep 25	Tue	FLC 3	H	Southend United	D	1-1	19,658		Cross
11	Sep 29	Sat	Div 2	H	Burnley	W	2-1	18,327	16	Lansdowne, Stewart [pen]
12	Oct 1	Mon	FLC 3 Rep	A	Southend United	D	0-0	22,497		
13	Oct 6	Sat	Div 2	H	Newcastle United	D	1-1	23,206	16	Cross
14	Oct 8	Mon	FLC 3 : 2 Rep	H	Southend United	W	5-1	19,718		Lansdowne 3, Holland, Stewart [pen]
15	Oct 13	Sat	Div 2	A	Leicester City	W	2-1	22,472	14	Cross, Martin
16	Oct 20	Sat	Div 2	H	Luton Town	L	1-2	25,049	16	Allen
17	Oct 27	Sat	Div 2	A	Notts County	W	1-0	12,256	14	Holland
18	Oct 31	Wed	FLC 4	A	Sunderland	D	1-1	30,302		Pike
19	Nov 3	Sat	Div 2	H	Wrexham	W	1-0	20,595	14	Pike
20	Nov 5	Mon	FLC 4 Rep	H	Sunderland	W	2-1	24,454		Cross, Martin
21	Nov 10	Sat	Div 2	A	Fulham	W	2-1	16,478	11	Cross, Stewart [pen]
22	Nov 14	Wed	Div 2	A	Chelsea	L	1-2	31,573	11	Holland
23	Nov 17	Sat	Div 2	H	Swansea City	W	2-0	21,210	8	Brooking, Cross
24	Nov 24	Sat	Div 2	H	Cardiff City	W	3-0	20,292	7	Stewart 2 [2 pen], Cross
25	Dec 1	Sat	Div 2	A	Charlton Athletic	L	0-1	19,021	7	
26	Dec 4	Tue	FLC 5	H	Nottingham Forest	D	0-0	35,856		
27	Dec 8	Sat	Div 2	H	Bristol Rovers	W	2-1	17,763	7	Cross 2
28	Dec 12	Wed	FLC 5 Rep	A	Nottingham Forest	L	0-3	25,462		
29	Dec 15	Sat	Div 2	A	Shrewsbury Town	L	0-3	8,512	9	
30	Dec 21	Fri	Div 2	H	Cambridge United	W	3-1	11,721	8	Neighbour, Pearson, Stewart
31	Jan 1	Tue	Div 2	A	Orient	W	4-0	23,883	8	Pearson 2, Devonshire, Pike
32	Jan 5	Sat	FAC 3	A	West Bromwich Albion	D	1-1	20,572		Pearson
33	Jan 8	Tue	FAC 3 Rep	H	West Bromwich Albion	W	2-1	30,689		Brooking, Pike
34	Jan 12	Sat	Div 2	H	Watford	D	1-1	23,553	7	Bonds
35	Jan 19	Sat	Div 2	H	Preston North End	W	2-0	17,603	6	Allen, Stewart [pen]
36	Jan 26	Sat	FAC 4	A	Orient	W	3-2	21,521		Stewart 2 [1 pen], Gray (og)
37	Feb 9	Sat	Div 2	H	Queens Park Rangers	D	2-2	26,037	7	Pearson, Hazell (og)
38	Feb 16	Sat	FAC 5	H	Swansea City	W	2-0	30,497		Allen, Cross
39	Feb 19	Tue	Div 2	A	Burnley	W	1-0	9,030	5	Devonshire
40	Feb 23	Sat	Div 2	H	Leicester City	W	3-1	27,762	6	Cross, Holland, Pike
41	Mar 1	Sat	Div 2	A	Luton Town	D	1-1	20,040	5	Stewart
42	Mar 8	Sat	FAC QF	H	Aston Villa	W	1-0	36,393		Stewart [pen]
43	Mar 11	Tue	Div 2	H	Notts County	L	1-2	24,894	8	Pike
44	Mar 15	Sat	Div 2	A	Newcastle United	D	0-0	25,474	8	
45	Mar 22	Sat	Div 2	H	Fulham	L	2-3	30,030	8	Devonshire, Stewart [pen]
46	Mar 29	Sat	Div 2	A	Swansea City	L	1-2	13,455	8	Devonshire
47	Apr 1	Tue	Div 2	A	Cambridge United	L	0-2	8,863	8	
48	Apr 5	Sat	Div 2	H	Orient	W	2-0	22,066	8	Brooking, Gray (og)
49	Apr 7	Mon	Div 2	A	Birmingham City	D	0-0	28,377	8	
50	Apr 12	Sat	FAC SF	N*	Everton	D	1-1	47,685		Pearson
51	Apr 16	Wed	FAC SF Rep	N**	Everton	W	2-1	40,720		Devonshire, Lampard
52	Apr 19	Sat	Div 2	A	Cardiff City	W	1-0	12,051	8	Stewart
53	Apr 22	Tue	Div 2	H	Birmingham City	L	1-2	36,167	8	Martin
54	Apr 26	Sat	Div 2	H	Shrewsbury Town	L	1-3	19,765	9	Brooking
55	Apr 29	Tue	Div 2	A	Oldham Athletic	D	0-0	8,214	7	
56	May 3	Sat	Div 2	A	Bristol Rovers	W	2-0	9,824	7	Cross, Devonshire
57	May 5	Mon	Div 2	H	Charlton Athletic	W	4-1	19,314	7	Cross, Morgan, Pike, Stewart [pen]
58	May 10	Sat	FAC F	N***	Arsenal	W	1-0	100,000		Brooking
59	May 12	Mon	Div 2	A	Sunderland	L	0-2	47,129	7	

N* Played at Villa Park, Birmingham   N** Played at Elland Road, Leeds   N*** played at Wembley Stadium, London

eam Line-Ups

ALLEN Paul	BANTON Dale	BONDS Billy	BROOKING Trevor	BRUSH Paul	CROSS David	DEVONSHIRE Alan	FERGUSON Bobby	HOLLAND Pat	LAMPARD Frank	LANSDOWNE Billy Jnr	MARTIN Alvin	MORGAN Nicky	NEIGHBOUR Jimmy	PARKES Phil	PEARSON Stuart	PIKE Geoff	SMITH Mark	STEWART Ray	
		6	10	3	9	8		7	2		5			1	11	4			1
	a	4	10	3	9	11		6	2		5			1	8/a	7			2
		4	10	3	9	11		6	2		5	8		1		7			3
		4	10	3	9	11		6	2		5			1	8	7			4
		4	10	3	9	11		6	2	a	5			1	8/a	7			5
	8	4	10	3	9			6	2				11	1		7	5		6
	8	4	10	3	9			6	2				11	1		7	5		7
		4	10	3	9	11			2		5		7	1	8			6	8
		4	10	3	9	11		a	2		5		7	1		8/a		6	9
7		4	10	3	9	11		6			5							2	10
6		4	10	3	9	11				8	5		7	1				2	11
7		4	10	3	9	11				8	5			1				2	12
6		4	10	3	9	11		a		8	5		7/a	1				2	13
7		4	10		9			6			5			1		11	3	2	14
7		4	10		9			6	3	8	5		11	1				2	15
7		4			9			6	3	8	5		11	1		10		2	16
7		4	10		9			6	3		5		11	1		8		2	17
7		4	10/a		9	11		6	3		5			1		8		2	18
7		4			9	10/a		6	3	a	5		11	1		8		2	19
7		4			9	10	1	6	3	11	5					8		2	20
7		4			9	10	1	6	3		5		11			8		2	21
7/a		4	10		9	8	1	6	3	a	5		11					2	22
7		4	10		9	8		6		11	5			1			3	2	23
7		4	10		9	11		6	3		5			1	8			2	24
7		4	10		9	11		6/a	3		5		a	1	8			2	25
7		4	10		9	11		6	3		5			1	8			2	26
6		4	10		9	11			3		5		7	1	8			2	27
7		4	10		9	11			3		5			1	8	6		2	28
7		4	10		9				3		5		11	1	8	6		2	29
7		4	10		9/a	6			3		5		11	1	8	a		2	30
7		4	10			6			3		5		11	1	8	9		2	31
7		4	10			6			3		5		11	1	8	9		2	32
7			10	4		6			3		5		11	1	8	9		2	33
7			10			6			3		5		11	1	8	9		2	34
7	a	4		3		6			2		5		11	1	8	9		10	35
7	a	4		2		6			3		5		11	1	8	9		10	36
7			10	3	9	6			2		5			1	8	11		4	37
a			10	3	9	6			2		5		7	1	8/a	11		4	38
7			10	3	9	6			2		5		8	1		11		4	39
			10	3	9	6			2		5			1		11		4	40
7			10	3	9	6		8/a	2		5			1	a	11		4	41
7			10	3	9	6			2		5			1	8	11		4	42
7			10	3	9	6			2/a	a	5			1	8	11		4	43
7			10	3	9	6			2	a	5			1	8	11/a		4	44
7			10	3/a	9	6		11	2		5			1	8	a		4	45
/a		4	10	3	a	6		11			5			1	8	9		2	46
		4	10	3	9	6		11	2		5			1	8			7	47
		4	10	3	9	6		11	2/a		5			1	8	12		7	48
7		4	10	3	9	6		11			5			1	8			2	49
7		4	10	3	9	8		11			5			1	8/a	a		2	50
7		5	10	3	9	6			2					1	8	11		4	51
7		5	10	3	9	6			2					1	8	11		4	52
/a		4	10	3	9	6			2		5			1	8	a		11	53
7			10	3	9/a				2		5	a	6	1	8	11		4	54
6		4	10	3	9				2		5	a	7	1		8/a		11	55
7		4			9	6			2		5	8	11	1		10		3	56
6		4	10	3	9/a				a	a	5	11	7	1		8		2	57
7		4	10	3	9	6			3		5			1	8	11		2	58
7		4	10	3	9	6		a			5		7	1	8/a	11		2	59

1980-81
Story of the season

After a narrow 1–0 defeat against Liverpool in the **Charity Shield at Wembley** the Hammers were disappointed to lose the opening league game at home to Luton Town.

With Brooking providing the service, strikers Goddard and Cro[ss] began scoring freely as the Hammers went on an unbeaten league ru[n] of 15 games. In that period both Burnley and Charlton were beaten [in] the League Cup.

In Europe the Spanish side Castilla were beaten 6–4 on aggregate, b[ut] there were crowd disturbances during the first leg in Spain and We[st] Ham had to play the home leg behind closed doors. There were defea[ts] at Luton and Derby County but the team were still top of the league[.] The Hammers marched into the League Cup semi-final after victori[es] over Barnsley and Tottenham Hotspur, and in the Cup Winners' C[up] they knocked out the Romanian side Poli Timisoara on a 4–1 aggrega[te.] Despite the shock of a 3–0 loss to Queens Park Rangers on Boxi[ng] Day, the Hammers were still on course for promotion.

In the FA Cup after two draws with Wrexham the Welsh side fina[lly] won 1–0 in the second replay. But in the league there was no stoppi[ng] the Hammers, with Brooking and Devonshire brilliant in midfield. [At] home the team were formidable, beating Preston 5–0 and Chelsea 4[–0.] Leading 2–0 at Coventry City in the League Cup semi-final first leg, t[he]

Appearances & Goals 1980-81

	League			FA Cup			League Cup			Europe			Other*			Total	
	Starts	Subs	Goals	Starts	Subs	Goals	Starts	Subs	Goals	Starts	Subs	Goals	Starts	Subs	Goals	Starts	Subs
ALLEN Paul	1	2	1	1	0	0	1	2	0	1	1	0	1	0	0	5	5
BARNES Bobby	1	5	1	0	0	0	1	0	0	0	1	0	0	0	0	2	6
BONDS Billy	41	0	0	3	0	0	8	0	1	6	0	1	1	0	0	59	0
BROOKING Trevor	36	0	10	3	0	0	7	0	0	4	1	0	1	0	0	51	1
BRUSH Paul	8	3	0	1	0	0	3	0	0	1	3	0	1	0	0	14	6
CROSS David	41	0	22	3	0	0	9	0	5	6	0	6	1	0	0	60	0
DEVONSHIRE Alan	39	0	6	3	0	0	9	0	0	4	0	0	1	0	0	56	0
GODDARD Paul	37	0	17	3	0	0	9	0	4	6	0	2	0	0	0	55	0
HOLLAND Pat	25	0	3	2	0	0	4	0	0	3	0	0	1	0	0	35	0
LAMPARD Frank	38	1	1	2	0	0	8	0	0	6	0	0	0	0	0	54	1
MARTIN Alvin	41	0	1	3	0	0	9	0	1	6	0	0	1	0	0	60	0
MORGAN Nicky	5	1	1	0	0	0	0	0	0	1	2	0	0	1	0	6	4
NEIGHBOUR Jimmy	22	2	2	0	1	0	4	0	1	4	0	0	0	0	0	30	3
PARKES Phil	42	0	0	3	0	0	9	0	0	6	0	0	1	0	0	61	0
PEARSON Stuart	2	3	0	0	0	0	0	2	0	0	1	1	0	0	0	2	6
PIKE Geoff	42	0	6	3	0	0	9	0	1	6	0	1	1	0	0	61	0
STEWART Ray	41	0	5	3	0	1	9	0	2	6	0	1	1	0	0	60	0
own goal			3									2					
Totals	**462**	**17**	**79**	**33**	**1**	**1**	**99**	**4**	**17**	**66**	**9**	**12**	**11**	**1**	**0**	**671**	**32**

* Other = Charity Shield Europe = European Cup Winners Cup

ammers collapsed to lose 3–2. But there was late drama in
e second leg as Jimmy Neighbour scored a late goal to put
e Hammers through on a 4–3 aggregate. West Ham
ntested the League Cup Final with Liverpool and after a
-1 draw at Wembley it was the Reds who took the cup after
nning 2–1 in the replay at Villa Park.

e Russian side Dinamo Tbilisi put on a great show at
ton Park, winning 4–1 in the Cup Winners Cup; the
ammers restored some pride in winning 1–0 in the away
, but bowed out on a 4–2 aggregate score. The team had
t lost a league game since Boxing Day and after the 2–0
n at Bristol Rovers in April they were promoted. Five
ore games were won and West Ham were declared Second
vision Champions with a record 66 points.

ootball League - Division Two
inal Table 1980-81

	P	HOME					AWAY					Pts
		W	D	L	F	A	W	D	L	F	A	
est Ham United	42	19	1	1	53	12	9	9	3	26	17	66
ts County	42	10	8	3	26	15	8	9	4	23	23	53
ansea City	42	12	5	4	39	19	6	9	6	25	25	50
ckburn Rovers	42	12	8	1	28	7	4	10	7	14	22	50
on Town	42	10	6	5	35	23	8	6	7	26	23	48
by County	42	9	8	4	34	26	6	7	8	23	26	45
msby Town	42	10	8	3	21	10	5	7	9	23	32	45
eens Park Rangers	42	11	7	3	36	12	4	6	11	20	34	43
tford	42	13	5	3	34	18	3	6	12	16	27	43
effield Wednesday	42	14	4	3	38	14	3	4	14	15	37	42
wcastle United	42	11	7	3	22	13	3	7	11	8	32	42
elsea	42	8	6	7	27	15	6	6	9	19	26	40
mbridge United	42	13	1	7	36	23	4	5	12	17	42	40
ewsbury Town	42	9	7	5	33	22	2	10	9	13	25	39
ham Athletic	42	7	9	5	19	16	5	6	10	20	32	39
exham	42	5	8	8	22	24	7	6	8	21	21	38
ton Orient	42	9	8	4	34	20	4	4	13	18	36	38
ton Wanderers	42	10	5	6	40	27	4	5	12	21	39	38
diff City	42	7	7	7	23	24	5	5	11	21	36	36
ston North End	42	8	7	6	28	26	3	7	11	13	36	36
stol City	42	6	10	5	19	15	1	6	14	10	36	30
stol Rovers	42	4	9	8	21	24	1	4	16	13	41	23

PAUL GODDARD

After scoring 23 league goals for Queens Park Rangers, the striker was signed by West Ham for a club record fee of £800,000 in August 1980.

In his first season his 17 goals were vital as the Hammers became Second Division champions. He also played a key role in the League Cup that season, scoring in both the semi-final and final. A dislocated shoulder suffered against Birmingham City in 1985 forced him to miss the rest of the season and upon his return he found his first-team chances restricted.

After scoring 71 goals in 213 appearances for the Hammers he signed for Newcastle United in November 1986 for a fee of £415,000. He spent two seasons in the North-east before transferring to Derby County in August 1988. However, he was soon on the move again as in December 1989 he came back to London to play for Millwall. After 20 league games for the Lions he was given a free transfer and joined Ipswich Town. Paul played 72 league games for the Suffolk side and was in the side that won promotion to the new Premier League in 1992. In 1994 he was appointed as first-team coach at Portman Road and later took charge of the youth team. He then became assistant manager at West Ham in 2001, but following Alan Pardew's arrival he left the club in January 2004. While playing for West Ham he gained eight England under-21 caps and one full cap when playing against Iceland in 1982. Since 2005 he has been employed by the Stellar Group as a football agent for the Anglian region.

Season **1980-81** Football League - Division One

Match Details

Manager **John Lyall**   Final League Position **1/22 Promoted as Champions to Division 1**

	Date		Competition	Venue	Opponents	Results		Attendance	Position	Scorers
1	Aug 9	Sat	C Shield	N*	Liverpool	L	0-1	90,000		
2	Aug 16	Sat	Div 2	H	Luton Town	L	1-2	28,033	19	Stewart [pen]
3	Aug 19	Tue	Div 2	A	Bristol City	D	1-1	14,001	17	Cross
4	Aug 23	Sat	Div 2	A	Preston North End	D	0-0	9,306	17	
5	Aug 26	Tue	FLC 2:1	A	Burnley	W	2-0	6,818		Cross, Goddard
6	Aug 30	Sat	Div 2	H	Notts County	W	4-0	21,769	7	Goddard 2, Cross, Stewart [pen]
7	Sep 2	Tue	FLC 2:2	H	Burnley	W	4-0	15,216		Goddard, Pike, Stewart [pen], Wood (og)
8	Sep 6	Sat	Div 2	A	Chelsea	W	1-0	32,669	4	Wilkins (og)
9	Sep 13	Sat	Div 2	H	Shrewsbury Town	W	3-0	22,339	3	Cross, Goddard, King (og)
10	Sep 17	Wed	ECWC 1:1	A	Castilla (Spain)	L	1-3	40,000		Cross
11	Sep 20	Sat	Div 2	H	Watford	W	3-2	24,288	2	Barnes, Brooking, Cross
12	Sep 23	Tue	FLC 3	A	Charlton Athletic	W	2-1	17,884		Cross 2
13	Sep 27	Sat	Div 2	A	Cambridge United	W	2-1	8,591	2	Cross, Goddard
14	Oct 1	Wed	ECWC 1:2 (*)	H	Castilla (Spain)	W	5-1	262		Cross 3, Goddard, Pike
15	Oct 4	Sat	Div 2	A	Newcastle United	D	0-0	24,866	3	
16	Oct 7	Tue	Div 2	H	Cardiff City	W	1-0	20,402	2	Neighbour
17	Oct 11	Sat	Div 2	H	Blackburn Rovers	W	2-0	32,402	1	Cross 2
18	Oct 18	Sat	Div 2	A	Oldham Athletic	W	0-0	8,444	2	
19	Oct 22	Wed	ECWC 2:1	H	Politechnic Timisoara	W	4-0	27,157		Bonds, Cross, Goddard, Stewart [pen]
20	Oct 25	Sat	Div 2	H	Bolton Wanderers	W	2-1	25,277	2	Pike, Walsh (og)
21	Oct 28	Tue	FLC 4	H	Barnsley	W	2-1	21,548		Cross, Martin
22	Nov 1	Sat	Div 2	A	Bristol Rovers	W	1-0	6,353	2	Goddard
23	Nov 5	Wed	ECWC 2:2	A	Politechnic Timisoara	L	0-1	25,000		
24	Nov 8	Sat	Div 2	H	Grimsby Town	W	2-1	25,468	2	Cross 2
25	Nov 11	Tue	Div 2	H	Bristol City	W	5-0	25,210	1	Goddard 2, Brooking, Cross, Martin
26	Nov 15	Sat	Div 2	A	Luton Town	L	2-3	17,031	1	Brooking 2
27	Nov 22	Sat	Div 2	H	Swansea City	W	2-0	27,376	1	Cross, Goddard
28	Nov 26	Wed	Div 2	A	Derby County	L	0-2	18,446	1	
29	Nov 29	Sat	Div 2	A	Wrexham	D	2-2	8,941	1	Devonshire, Goddard
30	Dec 2	Sat	FLC 5	H	Tottenham Hotspur	W	1-0	36,003		Cross
31	Dec 6	Sat	Div 2	H	Sheffield Wednesday	W	2-1	30,480	1	Brooking, Holland
32	Dec 13	Sat	Div 2	A	Blackburn Rovers	D	0-0	13,279	1	
33	Dec 20	Sat	Div 2	H	Derby County	W	3-1	24,671	1	Brooking, Cross, Goddard
34	Dec 26	Fri	Div 2	A	Queens Park Rangers	L	0-3	23,811	1	
35	Dec 27	Sat	Div 2	H	Orient	W	2-1	34,408	1	Allen, Holland
36	Jan 3	Sat	FAC 3	H	Wrexham	D	1-1	30,137		Stewart [pen]
37	Jan 6	Tue	FAC 3 Rep	A	Wrexham	D	0-0	13,643		
38	Jan 10	Sat	Div 2	A	Swansea City	W	3-1	22,160	1	Brooking, Cross, Pike
39	Jan 17	Sat	Div 2	H	Notts County	D	1-1	13,745	1	Holland
40	Jan 19	Mon	FAC 3 2 Rep	A	Wrexham	L	0-1	14,615		
41	Jan 27	Tue	FLC SF:1	A	Coventry City	L	2-3	35,468		Bonds, Thompson (og)
42	Jan 31	Sat	Div 2	H	Preston North End	W	5-0	26,398	1	Devonshire 2, Goddard, Lampard, Pike
43	Feb 7	Sat	Div 2	A	Shrewsbury Town	W	2-0	9,303	1	Cross, Devonshire
44	Feb 10	Tue	FLC SF:2	H	Coventry City	W	2-0	36,551		Goddard, Neighbour
45	Feb 14	Sat	Div 2	H	Chelsea	W	4-0	35,247	1	Brooking 2, Cross, Devonshire
46	Feb 21	Sat	Div 2	H	Cambridge United	W	4-2	36,032	1	Stewart 2 [1 pen], Devonshire, Goddard
47	Feb 28	Sat	Div 2	A	Watford	W	2-1	20,776	1	Cross 2
48	Mar 4	Wed	ECWC 3:1	H	Dinamo Tbilisi	L	1-4	34,957		Cross
49	Mar 7	Sat	Div 2	H	Newcastle United	W	1-0	27,174	1	Cross
50	Mar 14	Sat	FLC F	N*	Liverpool	D	1-1	100,000	1	Stewart [pen]
51	Mar 18	Wed	ECWC 3:2	A	Dinamo Tbilisi	W	1-0	80,000		Pearson
52	Mar 21	Sat	Div 2	H	Oldham Athletic	D	1-1	24,416	1	Goddard
53	Mar 28	Sat	Div 2	A	Bolton Wanderers	D	1-1	13,271	1	Brooking
54	Apr 1	Wed	FLC F Rep	N**	Liverpool	L	1-2	36,693		Goddard
55	Apr 4	Sat	Div 2	H	Bristol Rovers	W	2-0	23,444	1	Goddard, Pike
56	Apr 11	Sat	Div 2	A	Grimsby Town	W	5-1	17,924	1	Cross 4, Pike
57	Apr 18	Sat	Div 2	A	Orient	W	2-0	14,592	1	Neighbour, Pike
58	Apr 21	Tue	Div 2	H	Queens Park Rangers	W	3-0	24,599	1	Goddard 3
59	May 2	Sat	Div 2	H	Wrexham	W	1-0	30,515	1	Stewart [pen]
60	May 6	Wed	Div 2	A	Cardiff City	D	0-0	10,535	1	
61	May 8	Fri	Div 2	A	Sheffield Wednesday	W	1-0	21,319	1	Morgan

C Shield = Charity Shield * Played at Wembley Stadium, London ** Played at Villa Park, Birmingham (*) Played behind closed doors following crowd disorder in Spain – Official attendance 262

Team Line-Ups

ALLEN Paul	BARNES Bobby	BONDS Billy	BROOKING Trevor	BRUSH Paul	CROSS David	DEVONSHIRE Alan	GODDARD Paul	HOLLAND Pat	LAMPARD Frank	MARTIN Alvin	MORGAN Nicky	NEIGHBOUR Jimmy	PARKES Phil	PEARSON Stuart	PIKE Geoff	STEWART Ray	
7		4	10	3	9	6	8			5	a		1		11/a	2	1
		4	10	3	9	6	8/a	7	a	5			1		11	2	2
		4	10	3	9	6	8	7		5			1		11	2	3
			10	3	9	6	8	7	2	5			1		11	4	4
		4	10		9	6	8	7	3	5			1		11	2	5
		4	10		9	6	8	7	3	5			1		11	2	6
a		4	10		9	6	8	7/a	3	5			1		11	2	7
		4	10		9	6	8	7	3	5			1		11	2	8
		4	10		9	6	8		3	5	a	7/a	1		11	2	9
	b	4	10	a	9	6/a	8		3	5	7/b		1		11	2	10
	7	4	10		9	6	8		3	5			1		11	2	11
	7	4		10	9	6	8		3	5			1		11	2	12
		4	10		9	6	8	7	3	5			1		11	2	13
		4	10	a	9	6	8/b	7/a	3	5	b		1		11	2	14
		4		a	9	6	8/a	7	3	5		10	1		11	2	15
		4			9	6		7	3	5	8	10	1		11	2	16
		4			9	6	8	7	3	5		10	1		11	2	17
	a	4			9	6/a		7	3	5	8	10	1		11	2	18
		4			9	6	8/a	7	3	5	a	10	1		11	2	19
		4		3	9	6	8	7		5		10	1		11	2	20
a			4		9	6	8	7	3/a	5		10	1		11	2	21
		4		a	9	6/a	8	7	3	5		10	1		11	2	22
6		4	b	a	9		8	7	3	5		10/b	1		11	2/a	23
		4	10	2	9		8	7	3	5		6	1		11		24
		4	10		9	6	8	7	3	5			1		11	2	25
		4	10		9	6	8	7	3	5			1		11	2	26
		4	10		9	6/a	8	7	3	5		a	1		11	2	27
		4	10		9	6	8	7	3	5			1		11	2	28
		4	10		9	6	8	7	3	5			1		11	2	29
		4	10		9	6	8	7	3	5			1		11	2	30
		4	10		9	6	8	7	3	5			1		11	2	31
		4	10		9	6	8	7	3	5			1		11	2	32
		4	10		9	6	8	7	3	5			1		11	2	33
		4	10		9/a	6	8	7	3	5		a	1		11	2	34
a		4	10			6	8	7	3/a	5	9		1		11	2	35
		4	10		9	6	8	7	3	5			1		11	2	36
		4	10		9	6	8	7	3	5			1		11	2	37
		4	10		9	6	8	7	3	5			1		11	2	38
a		4	10	3	9	6	8	7/a		5			1		11	2	39
7/a		4	10	3	9	6	8			5		a	1		11	2	40
7		4	10	3	9	6	8			5			1		11	2	41
		4	10		9	6	8		3	5		7	1		11	2	42
	a	4	10		9	6	8/a		3	5		7	1		11	2	43
		4	10		9	6	8		3	5		7	1		11	2	44
		4	10		9	6	8		3	5		7	1		11	2	45
		4	10		9	6	8		3	5		7	1		11	2	46
		4	10		9	6	8		3	5		7	1		11	2	47
a		4	10		9	6/a	8		3	5		7	1		11	2	48
6/a		4	10		9		8		3	5		7	1	a	11	2	49
		4	10		9	6	8/a		3	5		7	1	a	11	2	50
		4	10	6	9		8/a		3	5		7	1	a	11	2	51
	a	4	10	6/a	9		8		3	5			1	7	11	2	52
		4	10		9	6	8		3	5/a		7	1	a	11	2	53
		4	10		9	6	8		3	5		7	1	a	11/a	2	54
		4	10	5	9	6	8		3			7	1		11	2	55
		4	10		9	6	8		3	5		7	1		11	2	56
	a	4	10		9	6			3	5		7	1	8/a	11	2	57
	a	4	10/a		9	6	8		3	5		7	1		11	2	58
		4	10		9	6	8/a		3	5		7	1	a	11	2	59
		4	10		9	6			3	5	8	7	1		11	2	60
		4	10	a	9	6			3	5/a	8	7	1		11	2	61

1981-82
Story of the season

The excitement of being back in the First Division was forgotten as West Ham and Brighton struggled to impress in their 1–1 draw on the opening day.

All this changed a few days later as the Hammer crushed rivals Tottenham 4–0 at White Hart Lane. It was personal triumph for centre-forward David Cross, wh scored all four goals. Another player in form was inside forward Paul Goddard, who scored twice against Stok City in the 3–2 home victory and then grabbed a hat-tric in the 4–2 home win over Southampton. Moving up to fift in the league, the Hammers went nine games unbeate before losing 3–2 at Aston Villa in October. Derby Count were beaten over two legs in the League Cup but in the nex round West Bromwich Albion went through, winning 1– in a second replay at Upton Park. Trevor Brooking was o target, scoring in the 5–2 win against Coventry City and week later netting twice in a thrilling 3–3 draw at Leed After the 2–1 home defeat against Arsenal in earl December there were no games for a month due to th snowy conditions.

Appearances & Goals 1981-82

	League			FA Cup			League Cup			Total		
	Starts	Subs	Goals	Starts	Subs	Goals	Starts	Subs	Goals	Starts	Subs	
ALLEN Paul	27	1	0	0	0	0	0	2	0	27	3	
BANTON Dale	0	1	0	0	0	0	0	0	0	0	1	
BARNES Bobby	1	2	0	0	0	0	0	0	0	1	2	
BONDS Billy	29	0	1	2	0	1	4	0	0	35	0	
BROOKING Trevor	34	0	8	2	0	0	5	0	1	41	0	
BRUSH Paul	10	3	0	0	0	0	1	0	0	11	3	
COWIE George	5	1	0	0	0	0	0	0	0	5	1	
CROSS David	38	0	16	2	0	1	5	0	2	45	0	
DEVONSHIRE Alan	35	0	1	1	0	0	5	0	0	41	0	
GODDARD Paul	38	1	15	2	0	0	5	0	2	45	1	
HOUGHTON Ray	0	1	0	0	0	0	0	0	0	0	1	
LA RONDE Everald	6	1	0	0	0	0	0	0	0	6	1	
LAMPARD Frank	27	1	0	2	0	0	5	0	0	34	1	
MARTIN Alvin	28	0	4	2	0	0	5	0	0	35	0	
McALISTER Tom	3	0	0	0	0	0	1	0	0	4	0	
NEIGHBOUR Jimmy	19	4	2	2	0	0	5	0	0	26	4	
ORR Neil	24	0	1	0	0	0	0	0	0	24	0	
PARKES Phil	39	0	0	2	0	0	4	0	0	45	0	
PEARSON Stuart	2	2	1	0	2	0	0	0	0	2	4	
PIKE Geoff	34	0	2	2	0	0	5	0	0	41	0	
STEWART Ray	42	0	10	2	0	0	5	0	3	49	0	
VAN der ELST Francois	21	1	5	1	0	0	0	0	0	22	1	
Totals	**462**	**19**	**66**	**22**	**2**	**2**	**55**	**2**	**8**	**539**	**23**	

verton were beaten 2–1 at home in the FA Cup, but a poor
–0 loss at Watford saw the Hammers go out of the
ompetition. There were two new signings: Belgian
ternational forward Francois Van Der Elst joined along
ith midfielder Neil Orr. Without a win in February the
ammers had slipped to fourteenth, but the return of Alan
evonshire, who had been out injured, sparked a revival,
ith only one defeat in nine games. In true West Ham
shion, however, the next nine games yielded just one
ctory. To add to the misery, Alvin Martin broke his
ollarbone at Coventry, an injury that forced him to miss
e World Cup finals.

FRANCOIS VAN DER ELST

Van der Elst was a star of the talented
Anderlecht side that made a unique
hat-trick of appearances in the final of the
European Cup Winners' Cup.

The first of these in 1976 was against West
Ham, where he scored twice in the Belgians'
4–2 victory in Brussels. He was on the losing
side against Hamburg in 1977 and a winner
the following year versus WAC Austria.
Francois made 243 league appearances in
nine seasons with Anderlecht before playing
one campaign for New York Cosmos in
season 1980–81. He was a regular in the
Belgian national side where he gained 44
caps.

In January 1982 West Ham bought him for a
fee of £400,000 and he made his debut that
month against Brighton. He was a popular
figure at Upton Park and in his two seasons
there he scored 19 goals in 70 games. When
his family failed to settle in England he
returned to Belgium in 1983, where he played
a further 57 league games for Lokeren. After
finishing his playing career he later ran a
snooker club in his home town of Opwijk.

ootball League - Division One
inal Table 1981-82

	P	HOME					AWAY					Pts
		W	D	L	F	A	W	D	L	F	A	
verpool	42	14	3	4	39	14	12	6	3	41	18	87
swich Town	42	17	1	3	47	25	9	4	8	28	28	83
anchester United	42	12	6	3	27	9	10	6	5	32	20	78
ttenham Hotspur	42	12	4	5	41	26	8	7	6	26	22	71
senal	42	13	5	3	27	15	7	6	8	21	22	71
vansea City	42	13	3	5	34	16	8	3	10	24	35	69
uthampton	42	15	2	4	49	30	4	7	10	23	37	66
erton	42	11	7	3	33	21	6	6	9	23	29	64
est Ham United	**42**	**9**	**10**	**2**	**42**	**29**	**5**	**6**	**10**	**24**	**28**	**58**
anchester City	42	9	7	5	32	23	6	6	9	17	27	58
ton Villa	42	9	6	6	28	24	6	6	9	27	29	57
ttingham Forest	42	7	7	7	19	20	8	5	8	23	28	57
ghton and Hove Albion	42	8	7	6	30	24	5	6	10	13	28	52
ventry City	42	9	4	8	31	24	4	7	10	25	38	50
tts County	42	8	5	8	32	33	5	3	13	29	36	47
rmingham City	42	8	6	7	29	25	2	8	11	24	36	44
est Bromwich Albion	42	6	6	9	24	25	5	5	11	22	32	44
oke City	42	9	2	10	27	28	3	6	12	17	35	44
nderland	42	6	5	10	19	26	5	6	10	19	32	44
eds United	42	6	11	4	23	20	4	1	16	16	41	42
lverhampton Wanderers	42	8	5	8	19	20	2	5	14	13	43	40
ddlesbrough	42	5	9	7	20	24	3	6	12	14	28	39

Season **1981-82** Football League - Division One
Match Details

Manager **John Lyall**   Final League Position **9/22**

	Date		Competition	Venue	Opponents	Results		Attendance	Position	Scorers
1	Aug 29	Sat	Div 1	H	Brighton & Hove Albion	D	1-1	30,468	13	Stewart [pen]
2	Sep 2	Wed	Div 1	A	Tottenham Hotspur	W	4-0	41,200	3	Cross 4
3	Sep 5	Sat	Div 1	A	Sunderland	W	2-0	28,347	1	Cross, Goddard
4	Sep 12	Sat	Div 1	H	Stoke City	W	3-2	28,774	1	Goddard 2, Stewart [pen]
5	Sep 19	Sat	Div 1	A	West Bromwich Albion	D	0-0	19,459	1	
6	Sep 22	Tue	Div 1	H	Southampton	W	4-2	34,026	1	Goddard 3, Pike
7	Sep 26	Sat	Div 1	H	Liverpool	D	1-1	30,802	2	Pike
8	Oct 3	Sat	Div 1	A	Birmingham City	D	2-2	22,290	2	Cross 2
9	Oct 7	Wed	FLC 2:1	A	Derby County	W	3-2	13,764		Brooking, Cross, Stewart [pen]
10	Oct 10	Sat	Div 1	H	Everton	D	1-1	31,608	4	Martin
11	Oct 17	Sat	Div 1	A	Aston Villa	L	2-3	32,064	5	Brooking, Cross
12	Oct 24	Sat	Div 1	A	Notts County	D	1-1	12,456	6	Brooking
13	Oct 27	Tue	FLC 2:2	H	Derby County	W	2-0	21,043		Goddard 2
14	Oct 31	Sat	Div 1	H	Middlesbrough	W	3-2	27,604	6	Goddard, Neighbour, Stewart [pen]
15	Nov 7	Sat	Div 1	A	Nottingham Forest	D	0-0	26,327	6	
16	Nov 10	Tue	FLC 3	H	West Bromwich Albion	D	2-2	24,168		Cross, Stewart [pen]
17	Nov 21	Sat	Div 1	H	Coventry City	W	5-2	26,065	5	Martin 2, Brooking, Neighbour, Stewart [pen]
18	Nov 24	Tue	FLC 3 Rep	A	West Bromwich Albion	D	1-1	15,869		Stewart [pen]
19	Nov 28	Sat	Div 1	A	Leeds United	D	3-3	25,637	6	Brooking 2, Cross
20	Dec 1	Tue	FLC 3 2 Rep	H	West Bromwich Albion	L	0-1	24,760		
21	Dec 5	Sat	Div 1	H	Arsenal	L	1-2	33,833	7	Pearson
22	Jan 2	Sat	FAC 3	H	Everton	W	2-1	24,431		Bonds, Cross
23	Jan 5	Tue	Div 1	A	Liverpool	L	0-3	28,427	12	
24	Jan 16	Sat	Div 1	A	Brighton & Hove Albion	L	0-1	22,591	12	
25	Jan 23	Sat	FAC 4	A	Watford	L	0-2	27,004		
26	Jan 27	Tue	Div 1	A	Manchester United	L	0-1	41,291	12	
27	Jan 30	Sat	Div 1	H	West Bromwich Albion	W	3-1	24,423	12	Cross 2, Goddard
28	Feb 2	Tue	Div 1	H	Manchester City	D	1-1	26,552	12	Bonds
29	Feb 6	Sat	Div 1	A	Stoke City	L	1-2	11,987	12	Van der Elst
30	Feb 13	Sat	Div 1	H	Birmingham City	D	2-2	22,512	12	Orr, Stewart [pen]
31	Feb 20	Sat	Div 1	A	Southampton	L	1-2	24,026	14	Stewart [pen]
32	Feb 27	Sat	Div 1	A	Everton	D	0-0	28,598	14	
33	Mar 2	Tue	Div 1	H	Ipswich Town	W	2-0	24,846	12	Devonshire, Van der Elst
34	Mar 6	Sat	Div 1	H	Aston Villa	D	2-2	26,894	12	Stewart [pen], Van der Elst
35	Mar 13	Sat	Div 1	H	Notts County	W	1-0	22,145	12	Stewart [pen]
36	Mar 20	Sat	Div 1	A	Middlesbrough	W	3-2	12,134	11	Goddard 2, Van der Elst
37	Mar 27	Sat	Div 1	H	Nottingham Forest	L	0-1	24,633	11	
38	Mar 30	Tue	Div 1	A	Swansea City	W	1-0	20,272	10	Van der Elst
39	Apr 3	Sat	Div 1	A	Manchester City	W	1-0	30,875	9	Goddard
40	Apr 6	Tue	Div 1	H	Wolverhampton Wanderers	W	3-1	20,651	8	Goddard 2, Martin
41	Apr 10	Sat	Div 1	H	Swansea City	D	1-1	26,566	8	Goddard
42	Apr 13	Tue	Div 1	A	Ipswich Town	L	2-3	29,050	8	Cross 2
43	Apr 17	Sat	Div 1	A	Coventry City	L	0-1	13,446	8	
44	Apr 24	Sat	Div 1	H	Leeds United	W	4-3	24,748	8	Brooking 2, Cross, Stewart [pen]
45	May 1	Sat	Div 1	A	Arsenal	L	0-2	34,977	9	
46	May 4	Tue	Div 1	H	Sunderland	D	1-1	17,130	9	Stewart [pen]
47	May 8	Sat	Div 1	H	Manchester United	D	1-1	26,337	10	Cross
48	May 10	Mon	Div 1	H	Tottenham Hotspur	D	2-2	27,667	9	Brooking, Goddard
49	May 15	Sat	Div 1	A	Wolverhampton Wanderers	L	1-2	13,283	9	Cross

Team Line-Ups

ALLEN Paul	BANTON Dale	BARNES Bobby	BONDS Billy	BROOKING Trevor	BRUSH Paul	COWIE George	CROSS David	DEVONSHIRE Alan	GODDARD Paul	HOUGHTON Ray	LA RONDE Everald	LAMPARD Frank	MARTIN Alvin	McALISTER Tom	NEIGHBOUR Jimmy	ORR Neil	PARKES Phil	PEARSON Stuart	PIKE Geoff	STEWART Ray	VAN der ELST Francois	
10			4				9	6	8			3	5		7		1		11	2		1
10			4				9	6	8			3	5		7		1		11	2		2
10			4				9	6	8/a			3	5		7		1	a	11	2		3
10			4				9	6	8			3	5		7		1		11	2		4
10			4				9	6	8			3	5		7		1		11	2		5
10			4				9	6	8			3	5		7		1		11	2		6
10			4				9	6	8			3	5		7		1		11	2		7
			4	10			9	6	8			3	5	1	7				11	2		8
			4	10			9	6	8			3	5	1	7				11	2		9
			4	10			9	6	8			3	5	1	7				11	2		10
			4	10	a		9	6	8			3	5	1	7/a				11	2		11
			4	10	7		9	6	8			3	5				1		11	2		12
			4	10			9	6	8			3	5		7		1		11	2		13
			4	10			9	6	8			3	5		7		1		11	2		14
4/a				10	a		9	6	8			3	5		7		1		11	2		15
				10	2		9	6	8			3	5		7		1		11	4		16
			4	10			9	6	8			3	5		7		1		11	2		17
a			4	10			9	6	8/a			3	5				1		11	2		18
a			4	10			9	6	8			3	5		7/a		1		11	2		19
a			4	10			9/a	6	8			3	5		7		1		11	2		20
11	a	7/a	4	10			9	6				3	5				1	8		2		21
			4	10			9	6	8/a			3	5		7		1	a	11	2		22
			4	10	a		9	6/a				3	5		7		1	8	11	2		23
			4	10			9	6/a	8			3	5		7		1		11	2	a	24
			4	10			9		8			3	5		7/a		1	a	11	2	6	25
			4	10	2		9	a				3/a	5			6	1		11	8	7	26
			4	10	3		9		8				5			6	1		11	2	7	27
			4	10	3/a		9		8				5			6	1	a	11	2	7	28
			4	10	3		9		8				5			6	1		11	2	7	29
			4	10	3/a		9		8			2			a	6	1		11	5	7	30
			4	10	3		9		8						7	5	1		11	2	6	31
6			4	10	3				8			a			7/a	5	1		11	2	9	32
7			4	10	3			6	8							5	1		11	2	9	33
7			4	10	3			6	8							5	1		11	2	9	34
7			4				9	6	8			3				5	1		11	2	10	35
7			4	10				6	8			3			a	5	1		11/a	2	9	36
1/a			4	10			9	6	8			3			a	5	1			2	7	37
1				10			9	6	8			3	5			4	1			2	7	38
1				10			9	6	8			3	5			4	1			2	7	39
1				10			9	6	8			3	5			4	1			2	7	40
1				10			9	6	8			3/a	5		a	4	1			2	7	41
3				10		a	9	6	8				5		11/a	4	1			2	7	42
1				10		3	9	6	8		a		5			4	1			2	7	43
4				10			9	6	8			3				5	1		11	2	7	44
4				10	8/a		9	6		a		3				5	1		11	2	7	45
4				10			9	6	8			3				5	1		11	2	7	46
4		a		10	7/a		9	6	8			3				5	1		11	2		47
4		a		10	7		9/a	6	8			3				5	1		11	2		48

1982-83
Story of the season

The **excitement** of being back in the **First Division was forgotten** as West Ham and Brighton struggled to impress in their 1–1 draw on the opening day.

Striker Sandy Clark was signed from Airdrie to replace the departed David Cross, who had gone to Manchester City. After an opening day defeat against Nottingham Forest the Hammers hit a purple patch with five successive wins, Sandy Clark scoring five goals. Included in the run was a 5–0 home thrashing of Birmingham City and decent 3–2 win at Arsenal. Stoke City were beaten in the League Cup but the Potters got their revenge days later winning 5–2 in the league game. Third Division Lincoln City were the next opponents in the League Cup and after a replay they were beaten 2–1 at the Boleyn Ground. The fourth-round League Cup tie saw a thrilling 3–3 draw at Notts County where Van Der Elst scored a hat-trick; back at the Boleyn the Hammers won 3–0 in the replay.

On New Year's Day 17-year-old Tony Cottee made his debut against Tottenham and scored the first goal in the

Appearances & Goals 1982-83

	League			FA Cup			League Cup			Total		
	Starts	Subs	Goals	Starts	Subs	Goals	Starts	Subs	Goals	Starts	Subs	Goals
ALLEN Paul	33	0	0	1	0	0	7	0	2	41	0	2
BARNES Bobby	0	0	0	0	0	0	0	1	0	0	1	0
BONDS Billy	34	0	3	1	0	0	4	0	0	39	0	3
BROOKING Trevor	1	0	0	0	0	0	0	0	0	1	0	0
BRUSH Paul	6	0	0	0	0	0	2	1	0	8	1	0
CLARK Alexander	26	0	7	1	0	0	7	0	3	34	0	10
COTTEE Tony	3	5	5	1	0	0	0	0	0	4	5	5
COWIE George	1	1	0	0	0	0	1	0	0	2	1	0
DEVONSHIRE Alan	39	0	3	1	0	0	6	0	0	46	0	3
DICKENS Alan	12	3	6	0	0	0	0	0	0	12	3	6
GALLAGHER Joe	8	1	0	1	0	0	1	0	0	10	1	0
GODDARD Paul	39	0	10	0	0	0	7	0	2	46	0	12
LAMPARD Frank	37	0	2	1	0	0	4	0	0	42	0	2
MARTIN Alvin	38	0	3	0	0	0	7	0	0	45	0	3
MORGAN Nicky	3	4	0	0	0	0	0	0	0	3	4	0
NEIGHBOUR Jimmy	3	0	0	0	0	0	2	1	0	5	1	0
ORR Neil	9	5	0	0	0	0	4	0	0	13	5	0
PARKES Phil	42	0	0	1	0	0	7	0	0	50	0	0
PIKE Geoff	40	0	6	1	0	0	7	0	0	48	0	6
STEWART Ray	39	0	8	1	0	0	6	0	3	46	0	11
SWINDLEHURST Dave	9	0	3	0	0	0	0	0	0	9	0	3
VAN der ELST Francois	40	0	9	1	0	0	5	1	3	46	0	12
own goal			3									
Totals	462	19	68	11	0	0	77	4	13	550	23	81

3–0 victory. An early exit from the FA Cup was made in the 2–0 defeat at Manchester United. Following on was four defeats, three in the league and a 2–1 loss in the League Cup at Liverpool.

With just one win in February and March the Hammers were plunging down the table. Sandy Clark was sold to Glasgow Rangers and Dave Swindlehurst was bought from Derby County. A revival began when Swindlehurst scored on his home debut in a 2–1 win over Watford. Trevor Brooking had been absent all season with a groin injury and 18-year-old Alan Dickens was drafted into the side and scored twice in the 5–1 victory at Swansea. Three straight wins in April saw hopes of a European place, but 2–0 defeats at both Manchester City and Everton put paid to that. Tony Cottee scored twice at Coventry as the Hammers won 4–2 on the final day of the season to finish in eighth place.

Football League - Division One
Final Table 1982-83

		HOME					AWAY					
	P	W	D	L	F	A	W	D	L	F	A	Pts
Liverpool	42	16	4	1	55	16	8	6	7	32	21	82
Watford	42	16	2	3	49	20	6	3	12	25	37	71
Manchester United	42	14	7	0	39	10	5	6	10	17	28	70
Tottenham Hotspur	42	15	4	2	50	15	5	5	11	15	35	69
Nottingham Forest	42	12	5	4	34	18	8	4	9	28	32	69
Aston Villa	42	17	2	2	47	15	4	3	14	15	35	68
Everton	42	13	6	2	43	19	5	4	12	23	29	64
West Ham United	42	13	3	5	41	23	7	1	13	27	39	64
Ipswich Town	42	11	3	7	39	23	4	10	7	25	27	58
Arsenal	42	11	6	4	36	19	5	4	12	22	37	58
West Bromwich Albion	42	11	5	5	35	20	4	7	10	16	29	57
Southampton	42	11	5	5	36	22	4	7	10	18	36	57
Stoke City	42	13	4	4	34	21	3	5	13	19	43	57
Norwich City	42	10	6	5	30	18	4	6	11	22	40	54
Notts County	42	12	4	5	37	25	3	3	15	18	46	52
Sunderland	42	7	10	4	30	22	5	4	12	18	39	50
Birmingham City	42	9	7	5	29	24	3	7	11	11	31	50
Luton Town	42	7	7	7	34	33	5	6	10	31	51	49
Coventry City	42	10	5	6	29	17	3	4	14	19	42	48
Manchester City	42	9	5	7	26	23	4	3	14	21	47	47
Swansea City	42	10	4	7	32	29	0	7	14	19	40	41
Brighton and Hove Albion	42	8	7	6	25	22	1	6	14	13	46	40

TONY COTTEE

On New Year's Day 1983, aged 17, he made his first-team debut and scored against Tottenham in the 3–0 win at Upton Park.

By the 1985/86 season he was a regular member of the side and had also been capped by England at under-21 level. He set up a partnership with Frank McAvennie and the pair scored 46 league goals as the Hammers finished in third place in the First Division. In September 1986 he won the first of seven England caps when coming on as a substitute against Sweden in Stockholm.

A British record fee of £2.05 million paid by Everton in August 1988 saw him join the Merseyside club, where he scored a hat-trick on his debut against Newcastle United. Tony spent six seasons with the Blues, scoring 72 goals in 184 league outings. West Ham manager Harry Redknapp brought him back to Upton Park in September 1994. He spent another three years with the Hammers and in his West Ham career he scored 145 goals in 335 appearances.

A move abroad came next when he signed for the Malaysian club Selangor, where he played 31 games in 1996/97. On returning to England he signed for Leicester City and won his first major honour as Leicester beat Tranmere Rovers in the 2000 League Cup final. While at Leicester he was loaned out to Birmingham City and later had spells at Norwich City and was player-manager at Barnet. Finally in 2001 he ended his playing career by making two substitute appearances for Millwall.

Season **1982-83** Football League - Division One
Match Details

Manager **John Lyall**   Final League Position **8/22**

	Date		Competition	Venue	Opponents	Results		Attendance	Position	Scorers
1	Aug 28	Sat	Div 1	H	Nottingham Forest	L	1-2	24,796	17	Stewart [pen]
2	Aug 31	Tue	Div 1	A	Luton Town	W	2-0	13,403	8	Bonds, Goddard
3	Sep 4	Sat	Div 1	A	Sunderland	L	0-1	19,239	14	
4	Sep 7	Tue	Div 1	H	Ipswich Town	D	1-1	21,963	14	Lampard
5	Sep 11	Sat	Div 1	H	Birmingham City	W	5-0	18,754	8	Clark, Goddard, Martin, Stewart [pen], Van der Elst
6	Sep 18	Sat	Div 1	A	West Bromwich Albion	W	2-1	15,204	6	Clark, Van der Elst
7	Sep 25	Sat	Div 1	H	Manchester City	W	4-1	23,833	4	Clark 2, Goddard, Van der Elst
8	Oct 2	Sat	Div 1	A	Arsenal	W	3-2	30,487	4	Goddard, Martin, Van der Elst
9	Oct 6	Wed	FLC 2:1	A	Stoke City	D	1-1	18,079		Stewart [pen]
10	Oct 9	Sat	Div 1	H	Liverpool	W	3-1	32,500	2	Clark, Martin, Pike,
11	Oct 16	Sat	Div 1	A	Southampton	L	0-3	19,840	2	
12	Oct 23	Sat	Div 1	A	Brighton & Hove Albion	L	1-3	20,493	5	Devonshire
13	Oct 26	Tue	FLC 2:2	H	Stoke City	W	2-1	18,270		Clark, Goddard
14	Oct 30	Sat	Div 1	H	Manchester United	W	3-1	31,684	2	Goddard, Pike, Stewart [pen]
15	Nov 6	Sat	Div 1	A	Stoke City	L	2-5	17,510	3	Pike, Stewart [pen]
16	Nov 10	Wed	FLC 3	A	Lincoln City	D	1-1	13,899		Goddard
17	Nov 13	Sat	Div 1	H	Norwich City	W	1-0	22,463	2	Clark
18	Nov 20	Sat	Div 1	A	Tottenham Hotspur	L	1-2	41,960	4	Van Der Elst
19	Nov 27	Sat	Div 1	H	Everton	W	2-0	21,424	5	Bonds, Stevens (og)
20	Nov 29	Mon	FLC 3 Rep	H	Lincoln City	W	2-1	13,686		Clark, Stewart
21	Dec 4	Sat	Div 1	A	Aston Villa	L	0-1	24,658	6	
22	Dec 7	Tue	FLC 4	A	Notts County	D	3-3	7,525		Van Der Elst 3
23	Dec 11	Sat	Div 1	H	Coventry City	L	0-3	19,321	7	
24	Dec 18	Sat	Div 1	A	Notts County	W	2-1	8,441	6	Dickens, Hunt (og)
25	Dec 21	Tue	FLC 4 Rep	H	Notts County	W	3-0	13,140		Allen, Clark, Stewart [pen]
26	Dec 27	Mon	Div 1	H	Swansea City	W	3-2	23,843	4	Goddard, Stewart [pen], Van der Elst
27	Dec 29	Wed	Div 1	A	Watford	L	1-2	24,870	5	Stewart [pen]
28	Jan 1	Sat	Div 1	H	Tottenham Hotspur	W	3-0	33,383	5	Cottee, Pike, Stewart [pen]
29	Jan 4	Tue	Div 1	H	Luton Town	L	2-3	21,435	5	Clark, Cottee
30	Jan 8	Sat	FAC 3	A	Manchester United	L	0-2	44,143		
31	Jan 15	Sat	Div 1	A	Nottingham Forest	L	0-1	17,031	6	
32	Jan 18	Tue	FLC 5	A	Liverpool	L	1-2	23,953		Allen
33	Jan 22	Sat	Div 1	H	West Bromwich Albion	L	0-1	19,887	6	
34	Feb 5	Sat	Div 1	A	Birmingham City	L	0-3	12,539	8	
35	Feb 26	Sat	Div 1	H	Southampton	D	1-1	19,626	12	Lampard
36	Mar 5	Sat	Div 1	H	Brighton & Hove Albion	W	2-1	16,850	10	Cottee, Dickens
37	Mar 12	Sat	Div 1	A	Liverpool	L	0-3	28,551	11	
38	Mar 19	Sat	Div 1	H	Stoke City	D	1-1	16,466	13	Bould (og)
39	Mar 22	Tue	Div 1	A	Manchester United	L	1-2	30,227	14	Devonshire
40	Mar 26	Sat	Div 1	A	Norwich City	D	1-1	17,639	14	Dickens
41	Apr 2	Sat	Div 1	H	Watford	W	2-1	22,647	12	Swindlehurst, Van der Elst
42	Apr 5	Tue	Div 1	A	Swansea City	W	5-1	13,282	10	Pike 2, Dickens 2, Devonshire
43	Apr 9	Sat	Div 1	H	Sunderland	W	2-1	20,053	7	Dickens, Goddard
44	Apr 16	Sat	Div 1	A	Manchester City	L	0-2	23,015	9	
45	Apr 23	Sat	Div 1	H	Aston Villa	W	2-0	21,822	9	Bonds, Swindlehurst
46	Apr 30	Sat	Div 1	A	Everton	L	0-2	16,353	10	
47	May 3	Tue	Div 1	A	Ipswich Town	W	2-1	18,817	8	Goddard, Stewart [pen]
48	May 7	Sat	Div 1	H	Notts County	W	2-0	17,534	8	Goddard, Van Der Elst
49	May 10	Tue	Div 1	H	Arsenal	L	1-3	28,920	8	Van Der Elst
50	May 14	Sat	Div 1	A	Coventry City	W	4-2	11,214	8	Cottee 2, Goddard, Swindlehurst

Team Line-Ups

ALLEN Paul	BANTON Dale	BARNES Bobby	BONDS Billy	BROOKING Trevor	BRUSH Paul	COWIE George	CROSS David	DEVONSHIRE Alan	GODDARD Paul	HOUGHTON Ray	LA RONDE Everald	LAMPARD Frank	MARTIN Alvin	McALISTER Tom	NEIGHBOUR Jimmy	ORR Neil	PARKES Phil	PEARSON Stuart	PIKE Geoff	STEWART Ray	VAN der ELST Francois	
10		4			9			6			8	3	5				1	11	2		7	1
10		4			9			6			8	3	5	a	11/a		1		2		7	2
10		4			9			6			8	3	5				1	11	2		7	3
10		4			9			6			8	3	5				1	11	2		7	4
10		4			9			6			8	3	5				1	11	2		7	5
10		4			9			6			8	3	5				1	11	2		7	6
10		4			9			6			8	3	5			a	1	11	2/a		7	7
10		4			9			6			8	3	5			a	1	11	2		7/a	8
10					9			6			8	3	5		7	4	1	11	2			9
10		4/a			9			6			8	3	5		7	a	1	11	2			10
10		4			9			6			8	3	5				1	11	2		7	11
10		4			9			6			8	3	5				1	11	2		7	12
10		4			9			6			8	3	5	a			1	11/a	2		7	13
10		4			9			6			8	3	5				1	11	2		7	14
10		4		3	9			6			8		5			a	1	11	2		7/a	15
10		4		3	9			6			8		5			7/a	1	11	2		a	16
10		4			9			6			8	3	5				1	11	2		7	17
10		4			9						8	3	5		6		1	11	2		7	18
10		4			9			6/a			8	3	5	a			1	11	2		7	19
10	a	4			9						8	3	5		6/a		1	11	2		7	20
10			6		9						8	3	5			4	1	11	2		7	21
10				a	9			6/a			8	3	5			4	1	11	2		7	22
10					9			6/a		5	8	3		a		4	1	11	2		7	23
10				3	9			6		5	8	2				4	1	11			7	24
10				3	9			6			8		5			4	1	11	2		7	25
10				3	9			6			8		5			4	1	11	2		7	26
10					9			6		4	8	3	5				1	11	2		7	27
10					9	8		6	4	3			5				1	11	2		7	28
10					9	8		6	4	3			5	a			1	11	2		7	29
10		4			9	8		6		5		3					1	11	2		7	30
10		4			9			6		a	8	3	5				1	11	2/a		7	31
10		4			9		2	6		3	8		5				1	11			7	32
10		4			9		a	6		3	8	2	5				1	11			7/a	33
10/a		4			9		11	6	a	3	8	2	5				1				7	34
10		4			9/a	a		6			8	3	5				1	11	2		7	35
10						9		6	a	4		3	5	8			1	11	2/a		7	36
10		4						6	10		9	3	5	8			1	11	2		7	37
10		4						6	10		8	3	5	9			1	11	2		7	38
10		4						6	a	10	8	3	5			9/a	1	11	2		7	39
		4						6	10		8	3	5			7	1	11	2	9		40
		4				a		6	10		8	3	5				1	11	2	9/a	7	41
		4						6	10		8	3	5			9	1	11	2		7	42
		4				a		6	10		8	3	5				1	11	2	9/a	7	43
9		4				a		6	10		8/a	3				5	1	11	2		7	44
		4						6	10		8	3/a	5		a		1	11	2	9	7	45
		4		3				6	10		8		5				1	11	2	9	7	46
		4						6	10		8	3	5				1	11	2	9	7	47
		4						6	10		8	3	5				1	11	2	9	7	48
		4	10					6			8	3	5				1	11	2	9	7	49
10		4				a		6			8	3				5	1	11/a	2	9	7	50

1983-84
Story of the season

West Ham's best ever start to a league season saw the first five games yield **five wins** and **15 goals.**

A London derby at Tottenham was won 2–0 and there wa a remarkable home game with Coventry City. The Hammer missed a penalty and were losing 0–2 when a burst o scoring saw West Ham score three goals in three minutes t demoralise the visitors. West Ham went on to win 5–2 wit a hat-trick from Dave Swindlehurst. There was only on win in the next six games but the League Cup brought a abundance of goals. Already leading 2–1 from the first le at Bury, the Lancashire side were crushed 10–0 at th Boleyn Ground with Tony Cottee scoring four. Durin November there were away wins at both Wolverhampto Wanderers and Sunderland and a home 1–0 victory again Brighton in the League Cup. Progress in that competitio was halted as Everton went through in a replay.

Supporters were cheered with a fine 4–1 victory ove Tottenham and a tough FA Cup match with Wigan wa won 1–0, but marred by a bad injury to Devonshire th

Appearances & Goals 1983-84

	League			FA Cup			League Cup			Total		
	Starts	Subs	Goals	Starts	Subs	Goals	Starts	Subs	Goals	Starts	Subs	Goals
ALLEN Paul	19	0	0	1	2	0	1	0	0	21	2	
BARNES Bobby	11	2	2	3	1	1	0	0	0	14	3	
BONDS Billy	27	0	0	0	1	0	2	0	0	29	1	
BROOKING Trevor	35	0	4	3	0	0	5	0	2	43	0	
BRUSH Paul	10	0	0	4	0	0	0	0	0	14	0	
COTTEE Tony	37	2	15	4	0	0	4	0	4	45	2	
DEVONSHIRE Alan	22	0	1	1	0	0	4	0	2	27	0	
DICKENS Alan	7	3	0	1	0	0	0	1	0	8	4	
DONALD Warren	1	1	0	0	0	0	0	0	0	1	1	
GODDARD Paul	3	2	1	0	0	0	1	0	1	4	2	
HILTON Paul	7	1	2	0	0	0	0	0	0	7	1	
LAMPARD Frank	17	1	0	3	0	0	3	0	0	23	1	
MARTIN Alvin	29	0	3	1	0	0	5	0	1	35	0	
ORR Neil	28	1	0	4	0	0	2	3	1	34	4	
PARKES Phil	42	0	0	4	0	0	5	0	0	51	0	
PIKE Geoff	27	1	2	2	0	1	5	0	1	34	1	
STEWART Ray	42	0	7	4	0	1	5	0	1	51	0	
SWINDLEHURST Dave	35	1	13	4	0	1	5	0	1	44	1	
WALFORD Steve	41	0	2	4	0	0	5	0	0	50	0	
WHITTON Steve	22	0	5	1	0	0	3	0	0	26	0	
own goal			3								1	
Totals	**462**	**15**	**60**	**44**	**4**	**4**	**55**	**4**	**15**	**561**	**23**	

aw him miss the rest of the season. An injury crisis then hit
ard as Allen, Bonds and Goddard were all in plaster and,
ollowing a car crash, Martin had six broken ribs and
Whitton a dislocated shoulder. The patched-up side did
vell, with three more league victories and a win over Crystal
Palace in the FA Cup. The Hammers FA Cup journey was
nded at Birmingham City where a poor display saw them
eaten 3–0, with a pitch invasion bringing shame to the
lub.

After this the team struggled; a 4–1 defeat at Leicester was
ollowed by a 6–0 drubbing at Liverpool. There were
reditable draws at Manchester United and Arsenal, but the
eason ended on a sad note with Trevor Brooking's last
ame for the club ending in a 1–0 home defeat against
Everton.

Manager John Lyall was hoping for a top-six finish but with
nly one win in the last 12 games the side finished ninth.

Canon League – Division One Final Table 1983-84

PAUL HILTON

A former England schoolboy international, the centre-half joined Bury in 1977 and made his league debut at Wrexham in August 1978.

Paul went on to score 39 goals in 148 league appearances for the Lancashire side, although 27 of those goals were scored in season 1979/80 when he played as a forward. He was in the Bury side beaten 10–0 by West Ham in the League Cup tie in 1983. Soon after that he was transferred to the Hammers for a fee of £100,000. He was used mainly as cover for first-team regulars Gale and Martin but did play in 75 games before injuries ended his career in October 1989. He was then appointed as the youth team coach at Upton Park and in May 1991 he was granted a testimonial match against Crystal Palace. He later had similar coaching roles at Ipswich and Gillingham before returning to West Ham as Assistant Academy Director. In 2011 he moved on to Stevenage Town as Head of Youth and in 2012 he became the assistant manager at Bishop's Stortford.

| | P | HOME | | | | | AWAY | | | | | Pts |
		W	D	L	F	A	W	D	L	F	A	
iverpool	42	14	5	2	50	12	8	9	4	23	20	80
outhampton	42	15	4	2	44	17	7	7	7	22	21	77
ottingham Forest	42	14	4	3	47	17	8	4	9	29	28	74
Manchester United	42	14	3	4	43	18	6	11	4	28	23	74
ueens Park Rangers	42	14	4	3	37	12	8	3	10	30	25	73
rsenal	42	10	5	6	41	29	8	4	9	33	31	63
verton	42	9	9	3	21	12	7	5	9	23	30	62
ottenham Hotspur	42	11	4	6	31	24	6	6	9	33	41	61
West Ham United	42	10	4	7	39	24	7	5	9	21	31	60
ston Villa	42	14	3	4	34	22	3	6	12	25	39	60
atford	42	9	7	5	36	31	7	2	12	32	46	57
swich Town	42	11	4	6	34	23	4	4	13	21	34	53
underland	42	8	9	4	26	18	5	4	12	16	35	52
orwich City	42	9	8	4	34	20	3	7	11	14	29	51
eicester City	42	11	5	5	40	30	2	7	12	25	38	51
uton Town	42	7	5	9	30	33	7	4	10	23	33	51
est Bromwich Albion	42	10	4	7	30	25	4	5	12	18	37	51
toke City	42	11	4	6	30	23	2	7	12	14	40	50
oventry City	42	8	5	8	33	33	5	6	10	24	44	50
rmingham City	42	7	7	7	19	18	5	5	11	20	32	48
otts County	42	6	7	8	31	36	4	4	13	19	36	41
olverhampton Wanderers	42	4	8	9	15	28	2	3	16	12	52	29

Season **1983-84** Canon League - Division One
Match Details
Manager **John Lyall**   Final League Position **9/22**

	Date		Competition	Venue	Opponents	Results		Attendance	Position	Scorers
1	Aug 27	Sat	Div 1	H	Birmingham City	W	4-0	19,729	2	Cottee 2, Martin, Swindlehurst
2	Aug 29	Mon	Div 1	A	Everton	W	1-0	20,999	1	Walford
3	Sep 3	Sat	Div 1	A	Tottenham Hotspur	W	2-0	38,042	1	Swindlehurst, Whitton
4	Sep 6	Tue	Div 1	H	Leicester City	W	3-1	22,131	1	Cottee, Swindlehurst, Walford
5	Sep 10	Sat	Div 1	H	Coventry City	W	5-2	23,077	1	Swindlehurst 3, Whitton 2
6	Sep 17	Sat	Div 1	A	West Bromwich Albion	L	0-1	15,113	1	
7	Sep 24	Sat	Div 1	H	Notts County	W	3-0	20,613	1	Brooking, Goddard, Stewart [pen]
8	Oct 1	Sat	Div 1	A	Stoke City	L	1-3	13,643	1	Stewart [pen]
9	Oct 4	Tue	FLC 2:1	A	Bury	W	2-1	8,050		Goddard, Orr
10	Oct 15	Sat	Div 1	H	Liverpool	L	1-3	32,535	2	Devonshire
11	Oct 22	Sat	Div 1	H	Norwich City	D	0-0	18,958	3	
12	Oct 25	Tue	FLC 2:2	H	Bury	W	10-0	10,896		Cottee 4, Brooking 2, Devonshire 2, Martin, Stewart [pen]
13	Oct 28	Fri	Div 1	A	Watford	D	0-0	14,559	2	
14	Nov 5	Sat	Div 1	H	Ipswich Town	W	2-1	20,682	3	Swindlehurst 2
15	Nov 8	Tue	FLC 3	H	Brighton & Hove Albion	W	1-0	17,082		Swindlehurst
16	Nov 12	Sat	Div 1	A	Wolverhampton Wanderers	W	3-0	12,062	2	Brooking, Cottee, Swindlehurst
17	Nov 19	Sat	Div 1	A	Sunderland	W	1-0	19,921	2	Swindlehurst
18	Nov 27	Sun	Div 1	H	Manchester United	D	1-1	23,355	2	Swindlehurst
19	Nov 30	Wed	FLC 4	H	Everton	D	2-2	19,702		Pike, Mountfield (og)
20	Dec 3	Sat	Div 1	A	Aston Villa	L	0-1	21,297	2	
21	Dec 6	Tue	FLC 4 Rep	A	Everton	L	0-2	21,609		
22	Dec 10	Sat	Div 1	H	Arsenal	W	3-1	25,118	2	Brooking, Pike, Whyte (og)
23	Dec 17	Sat	Div 1	A	Nottingham Forest	L	0-3	14,440	3	
24	Dec 26	Mon	Div 1	H	Southampton	L	0-1	22,221	5	
25	Dec 27	Tue	Div 1	A	Luton Town	W	1-0	16,343	4	Cottee
26	Dec 31	Sat	Div 1	H	Tottenham Hotspur	W	4-1	30,939	3	Brooking, Cottee, Martin, Stewart
27	Jan 2	Mon	Div 1	A	Notts County	D	2-2	8,667	3	Stewart [pen], Swindlehurst
28	Jan 7	Sat	FAC 3	H	Wigan Athletic	W	1-0	16,000		Stewart [pen]
29	Jan 14	Sat	Div 1	A	Birmingham City	L	0-3	10,334	3	
30	Jan 21	Sat	Div 1	H	West Bromwich Albion	W	1-0	17,213	3	Cottee
31	Jan 28	Sat	FAC 4	A	Crystal Palace	W	1-1	27,590		Swindlehurst
32	Jan 31	Tue	FAC 4 Rep	H	Crystal Palace	W	2-0	27,127		Barnes, Pike
33	Feb 4	Sat	Div 1	H	Stoke City	W	3-0	18,775	3	Barnes, Cottee, Stewart [pen]
34	Feb 7	Tue	Div 1	A	Queens Park Rangers	D	1-1	20,102	3	Cottee
35	Feb 11	Sat	Div 1	A	Coventry City	W	2-1	13,290	3	Cottee, Bamber (og)
36	Feb 18	Sat	FAC 5	A	Birmingham City	L	0-3	29,570		
37	Feb 21	Tue	Div 1	H	Watford	L	2-4	21,263	4	Barnes, Swindlehurst
38	Feb 25	Sat	Div 1	A	Norwich City	L	0-1	15,937	4	
39	Mar 3	Sat	Div 1	A	Ipswich Town	W	3-0	17,384	4	Cottee, Hilton, Butcher (og)
40	Mar 10	Sat	Div 1	H	Wolverhampton Wanderers	D	1-1	18,111	3	Cottee
41	Mar 17	Sat	Div 1	A	Leicester City	L	1-4	13,533	5	Stewart [pen]
42	Mar 31	Sat	Div 1	H	Queens Park Rangers	D	2-2	21,099	4	Cottee, Pike
43	Apr 7	Sat	Div 1	A	Liverpool	L	0-6	38,359	6	
44	Apr 14	Sat	Div 1	H	Sunderland	L	0-1	16,558	6	
45	Apr 17	Tue	Div 1	H	Luton Town	W	3-1	15,430	6	Cottee 2, Martin
46	Apr 21	Sat	Div 1	A	Southampton	L	0-2	20,846	6	
47	Apr 28	Sat	Div 1	A	Manchester United	D	0-0	44,124	7	
48	May 5	Sat	Div 1	H	Aston Villa	L	0-1	17,393	9	
49	May 7	Mon	Div 1	A	Arsenal	D	3-3	33,347	7	Whitton 2, Hilton
50	May 12	Sat	Div 1	H	Nottingham Forest	L	1-2	18,458	8	Stewart [pen]
51	May 14	Mon	Div 1	H	Everton	L	0-1	25,452	9	

Team Line-Ups

ALLEN Paul	BARNES Bobby	BONDS Billy	BROOKING Trevor	BRUSH Paul	COTTEE Tony	DEVONSHIRE Alan	DICKENS Alan	DONALD Warren	GODDARD Paul	HILTON Paul	LAMPARD Frank	MARTIN Alvin	ORR Neil	PARKES Phil	PIKE Geoff	STEWART Ray	SWINDLEHURST Dave	WALFORD Steve	WHITTON Steve	
		4	10/a		8	6						5	a	1	11	2	9	3	7	1
		4			8	6						5	10	1	11	2	9	3	7	2
		4	10		8	6						5		1	11	2	9	3	7	3
		4	10		8	6						5		1	11	2	9	3	7	4
		4	10		8	6						5		1	11	2	9	3	7	5
		4	10		8	6			a			5	7/a	1	11	2	9	3		6
		4	10		8	6		7				5		1	11	2	9	3		7
		4	10			6			8			5		1	11	2	9	3	7	8
		4	10			6			8			5	a	1	11	2	9	3/a	7	9
		4	10		a	6			8/a			5		1	11	2	9	3	7	10
		4	10		8	6	a					5		1	11	2	9	3	7/a	11
7	4/a		10		8	6						5	a	1	11	2	9	3		12
7		4	10		8	6						5	11	1		2	9	3		13
		4/a			8	6	10				a	5	7	1	11	2	9	3		14
			10		8	6					3	5	7	1	11	2	9	4		15
			10		8	6					3	5	7	1	11	2	9	4		16
			10		8	6					3	5		1	11	2	9	4	7	17
			10		8	6					3	5		1	11	2	9	4	7	18
			10	8/a		6					3	5	a	1	11	2	9	4	7	19
			10	a		6					3	5	8/a	1	11	2	9	4	7	20
			10	8/a			a				3	5	6	1	11	2	9	4	7	21
			10			6					3	5	8	1	11	2	9	4	7	22
			10			6	a				3	5	8	1	11/a	2	9	4	7	23
			10		8	6	11	a			3/a	5	7	1		2		4	9	24
	11		10	3	9	6						5	8	1		2		4	7	25
			10	3	8	6						5	11	1		2	9	4	7	26
			10	3	8	6						5	11	1		2	9	4	7	27
	a		10	3		6/a						5	11	1		2	9	4	7	28
	6		10	3	8							5	11	1		2	9	4	7	29
	7		10	6	8						3			1	11	2	9	4		30
a	7		10	6/a	8						3			1		2	9	4		31
a	7		10	6	8						3			1	11/a	2	9	4		32
10	7			6	8		11				3			1		2	9	4		33
10	7			6	8		11				3			1		2	9	4		34
10	7			6	8		11				3			1		2	9	4		35
10	7	a		6/a	8		11				3			1		2	9	4		36
10	7	4			8		11			5	3			1		2	9	6		37
10	7	4			8		11			6	3			1		2	9	5		38
11	7	4	10		8					6	3		7	1		2	9	5		39
11	7/a	4	10		8		a				3		6	1		2	9	5		40
7	a	4	10		8						3		6/a	1	11	2	9	5		41
7		4	10		8							5	6	1	11	2	9	3		42
7		4	10/a		8							5	6	1	11	2		3	9	43
7	a	4	10		8						3	5	6/a	1	11	2	9			44
7	6	4	10		8							5		1	11	2	9	3		45
7	6/a	4	10		8				a			5		1	11	2	9	3		46
7		4	10		8					6		5	9	1	11	2		3		47
7		4	10		8				a	6			5	1	11	2/a	9	3		48
7		4	10	3	8					6			9	1		2		5	11	49
7		4	10	3/a	8					6			9	1	a	2		5	11	50
7		4	10		8			6					3	1	11/a	2	a	5	9	51

1984-85
Story of the season

West Ham **kicked off the season** without injured goalkeeper Phil Parkes in a **drab 0–0 draw** at home to Ipswich Town.

At Southampton Paul Goddard scored twice and put the Hammers on the road to three successive wins. A bad 3-defeat at Chelsea caused a riot on the terraces and led to government inquiry into hooliganism. Leicester City we beaten 3–1 at home, which took the side up to fifth.

Third Division Bristol City were beaten 8–3 on aggrega in the League Cup but the Hammers bowed out in the ne round after losing 2–1 at home to Manchester City in replay. A 5–1 thrashing at Manchester United was followe by good victories at Stoke and home to Arsenal. Goalkeep Tom McAlister was proving an excellent deputy and Cotte and Goddard were looking sharp up front. Decemb proved to be a poor month, with injuries to Bonds ar Stewart and a run of five games without a win.

Appearances & Goals 1984-85

	League			FA Cup			League Cup			Total		
	Starts	Subs	Goals	Starts	Subs	Goals	Starts	Subs	Goals	Starts	Subs	
ALLEN Paul	38	0	3	5	0	2	4	0	0	47	0	
BARNES Bobby	18	2	2	2	0	0	1	1	0	21	3	
BONDS Billy	19	3	3	0	0	0	4	0	0	23	3	
BRUSH Paul	18	0	1	5	0	0	0	0	0	23	0	
CAMPBELL Greg	2	0	0	0	0	0	0	0	0	2	0	
COTTEE Tony	40	1	17	5	0	4	4	0	3	49	1	2
DEVONSHIRE Alan	0	0	0	2	0	0	0	0	0	2	0	
DICKENS Alan	24	1	2	4	0	2	1	1	0	29	2	
GALE Tony	36	1	0	0	0	0	3	0	0	39	1	
GODDARD Paul	38	2	9	5	0	3	3	0	2	46	2	
HILTON Paul	5	4	1	1	1	0	0	0	0	6	5	
LAMPARD Frank	1	0	0	0	0	0	0	0	0	1	0	
MARTIN Alvin	40	0	1	5	0	0	4	0	0	49	0	
McALISTER Tom	32	0	0	5	0	0	4	0	0	41	0	
McPHERSON Keith	1	0	0	0	0	0	0	0	0	1	0	
ORR Neil	17	3	0	4	0	0	1	1	0	22	4	
PARKES Phil	10	0	0	0	0	0	0	0	0	10	0	
PARRIS George	1	0	0	0	0	0	0	0	0	1	0	
PIKE Geoff	30	0	2	4	0	1	4	0	0	38	0	
POTTS Steve	1	0	0	0	0	0	0	0	0	1	0	
STEWART Ray	37	0	6	4	0	1	4	0	0	45	0	
SWINDLEHURST Dave	8	8	0	0	1	0	0	0	0	8	9	
WALFORD Steve	33	0	0	4	0	0	4	0	2	41	0	
WHITTON Steve	13	4	1	0	0	0	3	0	2	16	4	
own goal			3			1						
Totals	**462**	**29**	**51**	**55**	**2**	**14**	**44**	**3**	**9**	**561**	**34**	

e FA Cup began with a Goddard hat-trick in the 4–1
me win against Port Vale, after which the Arctic weather
ok over with no further fixtures during January. February
ought an FA Cup win over Norwich City and an exciting
-2 home draw with Manchester United that left the side in
irteenth spot. In March the fifth-round FA Cup tie with
imbledon saw Cottee score a hat-trick in a 5–1 replay
ctory, but days later the Hammers went out of the
mpetition after losing 4–2 at Manchester United. Their
igue form then suffered badly with a 5–0 reverse at
atford and a 5–1 defeat at West Bromwich Albion. The
ammers were in trouble and relegation was looming until
late goal from Barnes was enough to beat Norwich 1–0
d a Billy Bonds-inspired side beat Stoke City 5–1. Injuries
d poor home form summed up the campaign in which
est Ham finished sixteenth.

TOM McALISTER

The much-travelled goalkeeper gave service to seven league clubs and began his career at Sheffield United in 1970.

He soon established himself as first-team keeper until October 1973 when he broke his leg playing against Manchester City. The injury forced him out of action for two years until his return against Queens Park Rangers in October 1975. The following season the Blades were relegated and he joined Rotherham United, where he made 185 consecutive league and cup appearances before transferring to Blackpool in July 1979. He only played in 16 games for the Seasiders before moving on again to play once for Swindon Town; while there he made 13 appearances on loan at Bristol Rovers.

He then signed for West Ham on a free transfer in May 1981 and made his debut at Birmingham City in October of that year. Tom was an able deputy to Phil Parkes and enjoyed a good season in 1984–85 when he made 32 league appearances. The last of these was against QPR in April 1985 when he suffered a broken rib and a punctured lung. Returning after injury, he only missed one game in season 1987–88 as his Upton Park career was coming to an end. He was loaned out to Blackpool for a spell, playing in 20 league games before he retired in 1989.

anon League - Division One
inal Table 1984-85

	P	HOME					AWAY					Pts
		W	D	L	F	A	W	D	L	F	A	
erton	42	16	3	2	58	17	12	3	6	30	26	90
erpool	42	12	4	5	36	19	10	7	4	32	16	77
tenham Hotspur	42	11	3	7	46	31	12	5	4	32	20	77
nchester United	42	13	6	2	47	13	9	4	8	30	34	76
uthampton	42	13	4	4	29	18	6	7	8	27	29	68
elsea	42	13	3	5	38	20	5	9	7	25	28	66
senal	42	14	5	2	37	14	5	4	12	24	35	66
effield Wednesday	42	12	7	2	39	21	5	7	9	19	24	65
ttingham Forest	42	13	4	4	35	18	6	3	12	21	30	64
on Villa	42	10	7	4	34	20	5	4	12	26	40	56
tford	42	10	5	6	48	30	4	8	9	33	41	55
st Bromwich Albion	42	11	4	6	36	23	5	3	13	22	39	55
ton Town	42	12	5	4	40	22	3	4	14	17	39	54
wcastle United	42	11	4	6	33	26	2	9	10	22	44	52
cester City	42	10	4	7	39	25	5	2	14	26	48	51
est Ham United	**42**	**7**	**8**	**6**	**27**	**23**	**6**	**4**	**11**	**24**	**45**	**51**
wich Town	42	8	7	6	27	20	5	4	12	19	37	50
ventry City	42	11	3	7	29	22	4	2	15	18	42	50
eens Park Rangers	42	11	6	4	41	30	2	5	14	12	42	50
rwich City	42	9	6	6	28	24	4	4	13	18	40	49
nderland	42	7	6	8	20	26	3	4	14	20	36	40
oke City	42	3	3	15	18	41	0	5	16	6	50	17

Season **1984-85** Canon League - Division One
Match Details

Manager **John Lyall**   Final League Position **16/22**

	Date		Competition	Venue	Opponents	Results		Attendance	Position	Scorers
1	Aug 25	Sat	Div 1	H	Ipswich Town	D	0-0	19,032	15	
2	Aug 27	Mon	Div 1	A	Liverpool	L	0-3	32,633	17	
3	Sep 1	Sat	Div 1	A	Southampton	W	3-2	18,448	12	Goddard 2, Dickens
4	Sep 4	Tue	Div 1	H	Coventry City	W	3-1	14,949	5	Stewart 2 [2 pen], Cottee
5	Sep 8	Sat	Div 1	H	Watford	W	2-0	20,277	2	Barnes, Sinnott (og)
6	Sep 15	Sat	Div 1	A	Chelsea	L	0-3	32,411	6	
7	Sep 22	Sat	Div 1	H	Nottingham Forest	D	0-0	17,434	7	
8	Sep 25	Tue	FLC 2:1	A	Bristol City	D	2-2	15,894		Cottee, Walford
9	Sep 29	Sat	Div 1	A	Newcastle United	D	1-1	29,966	8	Allen
10	Oct 6	Sat	Div 1	H	Leicester City	W	3-1	15,306	5	Bonds, Cottee, Stewart [pen]
11	Oct 9	Tue	FLC 2:2	H	Bristol City	W	6-1	11,376		Cottee 2, Goddard 2, Walford, Whitton
12	Oct 13	Sat	Div 1	A	Manchester United	L	1-5	47,559	8	Goddard
13	Oct 20	Sat	Div 1	H	Stoke City	W	4-2	10,054	7	Allen, Cottee, Goddard, Berry (og)
14	Oct 27	Sat	Div 1	H	Arsenal	W	3-1	33,218	5	Cottee, Goddard, Pike
15	Oct 31	Wed	FLC 3	A	Manchester City	D	0-0	20,510		
16	Nov 3	Sat	Div 1	A	Aston Villa	D	0-0	15,709	5	
17	Nov 6	Tue	FLC 3 Rep	H	Manchester City	L	1-2	17,461		Whitton
18	Nov 10	Sat	Div 1	H	Everton	L	0-1	24,089	6	
19	Nov 17	Sat	Div 1	H	Sunderland	W	1-0	15,204	5	Cottee
20	Nov 24	Sat	Div 1	A	Luton Town	D	2-2	10,789	5	Martin, Whitton
21	Dec 1	Sat	Div 1	H	West Bromwich Albion	L	0-2	15,572	8	
22	Dec 8	Sat	Div 1	A	Norwich City	L	0-1	13,485	12	
23	Dec 15	Sat	Div 1	H	Sheffield Wednesday	D	0-0	14,896	12	
24	Dec 22	Sat	Div 1	H	Southampton	L	2-3	14,221	12	Cottee 2
25	Dec 26	Wed	Div 1	A	Tottenham Hotspur	D	2-2	37,186	12	Cottee, Goddard
26	Dec 29	Sat	Div 1	A	Coventry City	W	2-1	10,732	12	Cottee 2
27	Jan 1	Tue	Div 1	H	Queens Park Rangers	L	1-3	20,857	12	Brush
28	Jan 5	Sat	FAC 3	H	Port Vale	W	4-1	11,452		Goddard 3, Dickens
29	Feb 2	Sat	Div 1	H	Newcastle United	D	1-1	17,807	13	Allen
30	Feb 4	Mon	FAC 4	H	Norwich City	W	2-1	20,098		Pike, Stewart [pen]
31	Feb 23	Sat	Div 1	H	Aston Villa	L	1-2	14,855	15	Goddard
32	Mar 2	Sat	Div 1	A	Arsenal	L	1-2	25,818	16	Cottee
33	Mar 4	Mon	FAC 5	A	Wimbledon	D	1-1	13,500		Cottee
34	Mar 6	Wed	FAC 5 Rep	H	Wimbledon	W	5-1	20,258		Cottee 3, Allen, Dickens
35	Mar 9	Sat	FAC 6	A	Manchester United	L	2-4	46,769		Allen, Hogg (og)
36	Mar 15	Fri	Div 1	H	Manchester United	D	2-2	16,674	16	Stewart [pen], Duxbury (og)
37	Mar 23	Sat	Div 1	A	Leicester City	L	0-1	11,375	19	
38	Mar 30	Sat	Div 1	A	Nottingham Forest	W	2-1	13,560	16	Cottee, Goddard
39	Apr 2	Tue	Div 1	A	Watford	L	0-5	17,389	17	
40	Apr 6	Sat	Div 1	H	Tottenham Hotspur	D	1-1	24,435	17	Dickens
41	Apr 8	Mon	Div 1	A	Queens Park Rangers	L	2-4	16,085	17	Cottee 2
42	Apr 13	Sat	Div 1	H	Chelsea	D	1-1	19,003	17	Cottee
43	Apr 20	Sat	Div 1	A	Sunderland	W	1-0	15,622	17	Goddard
44	Apr 27	Sat	Div 1	H	Luton Town	D	0-0	17,303	19	
45	May 4	Sat	Div 1	A	West Bromwich Albion	L	1-5	8,834	19	Stewart [pen]
46	May 6	Mon	Div 1	H	Norwich City	W	1-0	16,233	18	Barnes
47	May 8	Wed	Div 1	A	Everton	L	0-3	32,606	18	
48	May 11	Sat	Div 1	A	Sheffield Wednesday	L	1-2	24,314	19	Cottee
49	May 14	Tue	Div 1	H	Stoke City	W	5-1	13,362	19	Bonds 2, Hilton, Pike, Stewart [pen]
50	May 17	Fri	Div 1	A	Ipswich Town	W	1-0	19,278	16	Cottee
51	May 20	Mon	Div 1	H	Liverpool	L	0-3	22,369	16	

eam Line-Ups

BARNES Bobby	BONDS Billy	BRUSH Paul	CAMPBELL Greg	COTTEE Tony	DEVONSHIRE Alan	DICKENS Alan	GALE Tony	GODDARD Paul	HILTON Paul	LAMPARD Frank	MARTIN Alvin	McALISTER Tom	McPHERSON Keith	ORR Neil	PARKES Phil	PARRIS George	PIKE Geoff	POTTS Steve	STEWART Ray	SWINDLEHURST Dave	WALFORD Steve	WHITTON Steve	
				8		10	6	9	a		5	1					11		2		3	7/a	1
7	8			a			6	9			5	1					11		2	10/a	3		2
7				9		10	6	8/a	a		5	1					11		2		3		3
7/a	a		8	9		10	6				5	1					11		2		3		4
7	a		8/a	9		10	6				5	1					11		2		3		5
7	8			9		10	6	a			5/a	1					11		2		3		6
7	5			9		10	6	8				1					11		2		3		7
	7			9		10	6	8			5	1					11		2		3		8
7	10			9			6	8			5	1					11		2		3		9
7/a	10			9			6	8			5	1					11		2		3	a	10
a	10/a			9			6	8			5	1					11		2		3	7	11
	10			9			6	8			5	1					11		2		3	7	12
	10			9			6	8			5	1		a			11/a		2		3	7	13
	10			9			6	8			5	1					11		2		3	7	14
8	10			9			6				5	1		a			11		2		3	7/a	15
	10			9			6/a	8			5	1		a			11		2		3	7	16
	10			9		a		8			5	1		6/a			11		2		3	7	17
	10			9		a	6/a	8			5	1					11		2		3	7	18
	10			9			6	8			5	1					11		2		3	7	19
	10			9			6	8			5	1					11		2	a	3/a	7	20
	10/a			9			6	8			5	1					11		2		3	7	21
				9		10	6	8	a		5	1					11/a		2		3	7	22
						10	4	6	8		5	1					11			9	3	7	23
						10	4/a	6	8		5	1		a			11			9	3	7	24
		3				10	4	6	a	8	5	1				7	11			9/a			25
		3				10	4	6	9	8/a	5	1				7	11					a	26
		3				10	4	6/a	9	8	5	1				7		11				a	27
8		3				10	4	9			5	1				7	11				6		28
8		3				10	4	9			5	1					11		2		6		29
8		3				10	4	9			5	1					11		2		6		30
8/a		3				10	4	9			5	1					11		2	a	6		31
		3				10	4	9			5	1		8			11		2		6		32
		3		10	6			9			5	1		8			11		2		4		33
		3		10	6	11		9/a	4		5	1		8					2		a		34
		3		10		6		9	a		5	1		8			11/a		2		4		35
		3		10		11/a		9	6		5	1		8					2	a	4		36
		3		10		11/a	6	9			5	1		8					2		4		37
8				10			6	9/a			5	1		3			11		2	a	4		38
8				10			6	9			5	1		3			11/a		2	a	4		39
8/a				10		11	6	9			5	1		3					2	a	4		40
a				10		11	6	9			5	1/a		3					2	8	4		41
		3		10		11	6	9			5				1				2	8	4		42
		3		10		11	6	9			5			4	1				2	8			43
	a	3		10		11	6	9			5			4	1				2	8/a			44
	4	3		10		11	6	9			5				1				2			8	45
a	8	3		10		11/a	6	9			5			4	1				2				46
11	8	3		10			6	9			5			4	1				2				47
11	8	3		10			6	9			5			4	1				2		7/a	a	48
7	8	3		10			6	9	a		5			4/a	1		11		2				49
7	8	3		10				9	6		5				1		11		2		4		50
7		3					a	9		6/a	5		4		1	8	11		2			10	51

1985-86
Story of the season

New signings were made with the acquisition of **winger Mark Ward** and **striker Frank McAvennie.**

It was a poor start with only one win in the first sev games but in that spell McAvennie scored six goals and up an exciting partnership with Tony Cottee. The Hamm then went 18 successive league games without defeat ur they lost 1–0 at Tottenham on Boxing Day. The r included a victory over champions Everton, five success away wins and four goals against Nottingham Forest, Ast Villa and West Bromwich Albion. Tony Gale and Alv Martin were strong at the back and Alan Devonshire w back to his best following his long injury lay-off.

In that period the League Cup brought a 6–2 aggregate v over Swansea City, with the Hammers going out after a 1 setback at Manchester United. West ham went into t New Year in third spot and then began their FA Cup r There was a lucky 1–0 win at Charlton followed by a thr match marathon with Ipswich Town. A late goal from To Cottee in the snow put the Hammers through to the fi round where the Hammers were paired with cup hold Manchester United. In a superb display at Old Traffo

Appearances & Goals 1985-86

	League			FA Cup			League Cup			Total	
	Starts	Subs	Goals	Starts	Subs	Goals	Starts	Subs	Goals	Starts	Subs
BARNES Bobby	0	1	0	0	0	0	0	0	0	0	1
CAMPBELL Greg	1	2	0	0	0	0	0	0	0	1	2
COTTEE Tony	41	1	20	7	0	4	3	0	2	51	1
DEVONSHIRE Alan	38	0	3	6	0	0	3	0	0	47	0
DICKENS Alan	40	1	4	7	0	0	3	0	0	50	1
GALE Tony	42	0	0	7	0	0	3	0	0	52	0
GODDARD Paul	1	5	1	0	1	0	0	0	0	1	6
HILTON Paul	2	0	0	0	0	0	0	0	0	2	0
MARTIN Alvin	40	0	4	7	0	0	3	0	0	50	0
McAVENNIE Frank	41	0	26	7	0	1	3	0	1	51	0
ORR Neil	33	3	2	1	1	0	3	0	0	37	4
PARKES Phil	42	0	0	7	0	0	3	0	0	52	0
PARRIS George	23	3	1	7	0	0	0	2	0	30	5
PIKE Geoff	10	0	0	5	0	1	0	0	0	15	0
POTTS Steve	0	1	0	0	0	0	0	0	0	0	1
STEWART Ray	39	0	6	6	0	1	3	0	3	48	0
WALFORD Steve	27	0	0	3	0	0	3	0	0	33	0
WARD Mark	42	0	3	7	0	0	3	0	0	52	0
own goal			4								
Totals	**462**	**17**	**74**	**77**	**2**	**7**	**33**	**2**	**6**	**572**	**21**

y won 1–0, but three days later a jaded display saw West
[Ha]m go out of the competition after losing 2–1 at Sheffield
[We]dnesday.

[Tw]o vital league games were then lost at Arsenal and Aston
[Vil]la, results that may have cost West Ham the title. At
[Lei]ster further victories over London rivals Tottenham and
[Ch]elsea were gained, the 4–0 win at Stamford Bridge being
[par]ticularly rewarding. With four home games to play in
[onl]y nine days the team needed some luck and determination.
[Fir]st Newcastle United were annihilated 8–1, then narrow
[1–]0 wins were gained against Coventry and Manchester
[Cit]y. The final home game of the season saw Ray Stewart
[sco]re a dramatic late penalty to give the Hammers a 2–1
[vic]tory against Ipswich Town. On the final Saturday of the
[sea]son West Ham won 3–2 at West Bromwich Albion to
[cli]nch third place in the table. This proved to be West Ham's
[be]st season and highest league placing in the top flight.

[C]anon League - Division One
[Fi]nal Table 1985-86

	P	HOME					AWAY					Pts
		W	D	L	F	A	W	D	L	F	A	
[Liv]erpool	42	16	4	1	58	14	10	6	5	31	23	88
[Eve]rton	42	16	3	2	54	18	10	5	6	33	23	86
[We]st Ham United	42	17	2	2	48	16	9	4	8	26	24	84
[Ma]nchester United	42	12	5	4	35	12	10	5	6	35	24	76
[She]ffield Wednesday	42	13	6	2	36	23	8	4	9	27	31	73
[Che]lsea	42	12	4	5	32	27	8	7	6	25	29	71
[Ars]enal	42	13	5	3	29	15	7	4	10	20	32	69
[Not]tingham Forest	42	11	5	5	38	25	8	6	7	31	28	68
[Luto]n Town	42	12	6	3	37	15	6	6	9	24	29	66
[Tott]enham Hotspur	42	12	2	7	47	25	7	6	8	27	27	65
[New]castle United	42	12	5	4	46	31	5	7	9	21	41	63
[Wat]ford	42	11	6	4	40	22	5	5	11	29	40	59
[Que]ens Park Rangers	42	12	3	6	33	20	3	4	14	20	44	52
[Sou]thampton	42	10	6	5	32	18	2	4	15	19	44	46
[Man]chester City	42	7	7	7	25	26	4	5	12	18	31	45
[Ast]on Villa	42	7	6	8	27	28	3	8	10	24	39	44
[Cov]entry City	42	6	5	10	31	35	5	5	11	17	36	43
[Oxf]ord United	42	7	7	7	34	27	3	5	13	28	53	42
[Leic]ester City	42	7	8	6	35	35	3	4	14	19	41	42
[Ipsw]ich Town	42	8	5	8	20	24	3	3	15	12	31	41
[Birm]ingham City	42	5	2	14	13	25	3	3	15	17	48	29
[We]st Bromwich Albion	42	3	8	10	21	36	1	4	16	14	53	24

FRANK MCAVENNIE

**The Scottish striker started out at St Mirren
in 1980 and went on to score 48 goals in a
total of 135 league appearances.**

West Ham manager John Lyall bought him for
£340,000 in July 1985 and he quickly set up a
prolific scoring partnership with Tony Cottee.
Their best season was 1985/86, where
between them they scored 46 league goals.
That year he was awarded his first of five
Scotland caps when he was selected to play
against Australia. In October 1987 he was
transferred for £750,000 to his boyhood idols
Celtic. He was with the Glasgow club for two
seasons and won winners' medals as Celtic
did the league and cup double in his first
season. In March 1989 he was sold back to
West Ham but this time was not as successful.
The Hammers were relegated in that
campaign and his first game playing in the
Second Division saw him suffer a broken leg
at Stoke City. In May 1992 he played his final
game for the club at home to Nottingham
Forest and said goodbye in style as he scored
a hat-trick in the 3–0 victory.

He then joined Aston Villa on a free transfer,
but only played three games before having
short spells at Cliftonville and Hong Kong
side South China. He then returned to Celtic
and played in a further 30 league games;
while there he was loaned out to Swindon
Town for seven games. Finally he had a spell
at Falkirk before signing again for St Mirren,
where he ended his career in 1995. From 2007
until 2012 he was a director at the football
agency Calcio Promotions.

Season **1985-86** Canon League - Division One
Match Details

Manager **John Lyall**   Final League Position **3/22**

	Date		Competition	Venue	Opponents	Results		Attendance	Position	Scorers
1	Aug 17	Sat	Div 1	A	Birmingham City	L	0-1	11,164	18	
2	Aug 20	Tue	Div 1	H	Queens Park Rangers	W	3-1	15,628	6	McAvennie 2, Dickens
3	Aug 24	Sat	Div 1	H	Luton Town	L	0-1	14,004	14	
4	Aug 26	Mon	Div 1	A	Manchester United	L	0-2	50,773	17	
5	Aug 31	Sat	Div 1	H	Liverpool	D	2-2	19,762	17	McAvennie 2
6	Sep 3	Tue	Div 1	A	Southampton	D	1-1	14,477	15	McAvennie
7	Sep 7	Sat	Div 1	A	Sheffield Wednesday	D	2-2	19,287	17	Cottee, McAvennie
8	Sep 14	Sat	Div 1	H	Leicester City	W	3-0	12,225	13	Cottee, Devonshire, McAvennie
9	Sep 21	Sat	Div 1	A	Manchester City	D	2-2	22,001	13	Cottee, McCarthy (og)
10	Sep 24	Tue	FLC 2:1	H	Swansea City	W	3-0	9,242		Cottee, McAvennie, Stewart [pen]
11	Sep 28	Sat	Div 1	H	Nottingham Forest	W	4-2	14,540	13	McAvennie 2, Cottee, Dickens
12	Oct 5	Sat	Div 1	A	Newcastle United	W	2-1	26,957	11	Cottee, McAvennie
13	Oct 8	Tue	FLC 2:2	A	Swansea City	W	3-2	3,584		Stewart 2 [2 pen], Cottee
14	Oct 12	Sat	Div 1	H	Arsenal	D	0-0	24,057	11	
15	Oct 19	Sat	Div 1	H	Aston Villa	W	4-1	15,034	7	Cottee 2, McAvennie 2
16	Oct 26	Sat	Div 1	A	Ipswich Town	W	1-0	16,917	7	Cottee
17	Oct 29	Tue	FLC 3	A	Manchester United	L	0-1	32,056		
18	Nov 2	Sat	Div 1	H	Everton	W	2-1	23,844	6	McAvennie 2
19	Nov 9	Sat	Div 1	A	Oxford United	W	2-1	13,140	5	Cottee, Ward
20	Nov 16	Sat	Div 1	H	Watford	W	2-1	21,490	4	McAvennie, Ward
21	Nov 23	Sat	Div 1	A	Coventry City	W	1-0	11,027	4	McAvennie
22	Nov 30	Sat	Div 1	H	West Bromwich Albion	W	4-0	16,325	3	Cottee, Devonshire, Orr, Parris
23	Dec 7	Sat	Div 1	A	Queens Park Rangers	W	1-0	20,002	3	McAvennie
24	Dec 14	Sat	Div 1	H	Birmingham City	W	2-0	17,481	3	McAvennie, Stewart [pen]
25	Dec 21	Sat	Div 1	A	Luton Town	D	0-0	14,599	3	
26	Dec 26	Thur	Div 1	A	Tottenham Hotspur	L	0-1	33,835	3	
27	Jan 5	Sun	FAC 3	A	Charlton Athletic	W	1-0	13,037		Cottee
28	Jan 11	Sat	Div 1	A	Leicester City	W	1-0	11,512	4	McAvennie
29	Jan 18	Sat	Div 1	A	Liverpool	L	1-3	41,056	3	Dickens
30	Jan 25	Sat	FAC 4	H	Ipswich Town	D	0-0	25,035		
31	Feb 2	Sun	Div 1	H	Manchester United	W	2-1	20,170	5	Cottee, Ward
32	Feb 4	Tue	FAC 4 Rep	A	Ipswich Town	D	1-1	25,384		Cottee
33	Feb 6	Thur	FAC 4 2 Rep	A	Ipswich Town	W	1-0	14,515		Cottee
34	Mar 5	Wed	FAC 5	H	Manchester United	D	1-1	26,441		McAvennie
35	Mar 9	Sun	FAC 5 Rep	A	Manchester United	W	2-0	30,441		Pike, Stewart [pen]
36	Mar 12	Wed	FAC 6	A	Sheffield Wednesday	L	1-2	35,522		Cottee
37	Mar 15	Sat	Div 1	A	Arsenal	L	0-1	31,235	7	
38	Mar 19	Wed	Div 1	A	Aston Villa	L	1-2	11,567	7	Hunt (og)
39	Mar 22	Sat	Div 1	H	Sheffield Wednesday	W	1-0	16,604	7	McAvennie
40	Mar 29	Sat	Div 1	A	Chelsea	W	4-0	29,935	6	Cottee 2, Devonshire, McAvennie
41	Mar 31	Mon	Div 1	H	Tottenham Hotspur	W	2-1	27,568	5	Cottee, McAvennie
42	Apr 2	Wed	Div 1	A	Nottingham Forest	L	1-2	17,498	5	Cottee
43	Apr 8	Tue	Div 1	H	Southampton	W	1-0	22,459	4	Martin
44	Apr 12	Sat	Div 1	H	Oxford United	W	3-1	23,956	5	McAvennie, Stewart [pen], Trewick (og)
45	Apr 15	Tue	Div 1	H	Chelsea	L	1-2	29,360	5	Cottee
46	Apr 19	Sat	Div 1	A	Watford	W	2-0	16,696	5	Cottee, McAvennie
47	Apr 21	Mon	Div 1	H	Newcastle United	W	8-1	24,734	3	Martin 3, Goddard, McAvennie, Orr, Stewart [pen], Roeder (og)
48	Apr 26	Sat	Div 1	A	Coventry City	W	1-0	27,251	4	Cottee
49	Apr 28	Mon	Div 1	H	Manchester City	W	1-0	27,153	3	Stewart [pen]
50	Apr 30	Wed	Div 1	H	Ipswich Town	W	2-1	31,121	2	Dickens, Stewart [pen]
51	May 3	Sat	Div 1	A	West Bromwich Albion	W	3-2	17,751	2	Cottee, McAvennie, Stewart [pen]
52	May 5	Mon	Div 1	A	Everton	L	1-3	39,712	3	Cottee

eam Line-Ups

	CAMPBELL Greg	COTTEE Tony	DEVONSHIRE Alan	DICKENS Alan	GALE Tony	GODDARD Paul	HILTON Paul	MARTIN Alvin	McAVENNIE Frank	ORR Neil	PARKES Phil	PARRIS George	PIKE Geoff	POTTS Steve	STEWART Ray	WALFORD Steve	WARD Mark	
		10	6	a	4	9/a		5	8	11	1				2	3	7	1
		10	6	9	4			5	8	11	1				2	3	7	2
	a	10/a	6	9	4			5	8	11	1				2	3	7	3
	a	10/a	6	9	4			5	8	11	1				2	3	7	4
		10	6	9	4			5	8	11	1				2	3	7	5
	10/a	a	6	9	4			5	8	11	1				2	3	7	6
a		10		9	4			5	8/a	11	1	6			2	3	7	7
		10	6	9	4			5	8	11	1				2	3	7	8
		10	6	9	4			5	8	11	1				2	3	7	9
		10	6	9	4			5	8	11	1				2	3	7	10
		10	6	9	4			5	8	11	1				2	3	7	11
		10	6	9	4			5	8	11	1				2	3	7	12
		10	6	9	4			5	8/a	11	1	a			2	3	7	13
		10	6	9/a	4			5	8	11	1	a			2	3	7	14
		10	6		4			5	8	11	1	9			2	3	7	15
		10	6/a	9	4			5	8	11	1	2		a		3	7	16
		10	6	9/a	4			5	8	11	1	a			2	3	7	17
		10	6	9	4			5	8	11	1	a			2	3/a	7	18
		10	6	9	4			5	8	11	1				2	3	7	19
		10	6	9	4			5	8	11	1				2	3	7	20
		10	6	9	4			5	8	11	1				2	3	7	21
		10	6	9	4			5		11	1	8			2	3	7	22
		10	6	9	4			5	8	11	1				2	3	7	23
		10	6	9	4			5	8	11	1	a			2	3/a	7	24
		10	6	9	4			5	8	11	1				2	3	7	25
		10	6	9	4			5	8	11	1				2	3	7	26
		10	6	9	4			5	8		1	11			2	3	7	27
		10	6	9	4			5	8		1	11			2	3	7	28
		10	6	9	4			5	8		1	11			2	3	7	29
		10	6	9	4	a		5	8		1	11			2	3/a	7	30
		10	6	9	4			5	8		1	2	11			3	7	31
		10	6	9	4			5	8	a	1	2	11			3/a	7	32
		10		9	4			5	8	6	1	3	11		2		7	33
		10	6	9	4			5	8		1	3	11		2		7	34
		10	6	9	4			5	8		1	3	11		2		7	35
		10	6	9	4			5	8		1	3	11		2		7	36
		10	6	9	4			5	8		1	3	11		2		7	37
		10/a		9	4	a		5	8	6	1	2	11			3	7	38
		10/a		9	4	a		5	8	6	1	3	11		2		7	39
		10	6/a	9	4		5		8	a	1	3	11		2		7	40
		10	6	9	4		5		8	a	1	3	11		2		7/a	41
		10		9	4			5	8	6	1	3	11		2		7	42
		10	6	9	4			5	8		1	3	11		2		7	43
		10	6	9	4			5	8		1	3	11		2		7	44
		10	6	9	4/a			5	8	a	1	3	11		2		7	45
		10	6	9	4			5	8	11	1	3			2		7	46
		10	6	9/a	4	a		5	8	11	1	3			2		7	47
		10	6	9	4			5	8	11	1	3			2		7	48
		10	6	9	4			5	8	11	1	3			2		7	49
		10	6	9	4	a		5	8	11/a	1	3			2		7	50
		10	6	9	4			5	8	11	1	3			2		7	51
		10	6	9/a	4	a		5	8	11	1	3			2		7	52

1986-87
Story of the season

There were **no new signings** to excite the fans but with **wins over Coventry and Manchester United** it had been a good start.

The visit of Liverpool brought warning signs as t Merseysiders won 5–2, but a week later Tony Cottee sco a hat-trick in the 3–2 victory at Queens Park Range Another Cottee hat-trick saw Preston North End knock out of the League Cup and this was followed in the ne round with a 3–2 win at Watford. At home to Chelsea t Hammers were losing 3–2 after an hour but in an exciti finish West Ham won 5–3 to move up to fourth place.

A penalty by Cottee gave West Ham a 1–0 victory ov Oxford United in the League Cup, which was followed by poor showing in the 4–0 defeat at Newcastle in the leag The team struggled throughout December and it was miserable Christmas for Hammers supporters after the 4 loss at Tottenham on Boxing Day.

Appearances & Goals 1986-87

	League			FA Cup			League Cup			Other*			Total	
	Starts	Subs	Goals	Starts	Subs	Goals	Starts	Subs	Goals	Starts	Subs	Goals	Starts	Subs
BONDS Billy	13	4	0	3	1	0	1	2	0	0	0	0	17	7
BRADY Liam	12	0	2	0	0	0	0	0	0	0	0	0	12	0
COTTEE Tony	42	0	22	5	0	1	6	0	5	1	0	1	54	0
DEVONSHIRE Alan	20	0	2	3	0	0	4	0	0	0	0	0	27	0
DICKENS Alan	31	5	3	1	1	0	4	0	2	1	0	0	37	6
DOLAN Eamonn	0	1	0	0	0	0	0	0	0	0	0	0	0	1
GALE Tony	32	0	2	4	0	1	4	0	0	1	0	0	41	0
GODDARD Paul	3	1	1	0	0	0	1	0	1	0	0	0	4	1
HILTON Paul	15	1	1	2	0	1	4	1	0	1	0	0	22	2
INCE Paul	7	3	1	1	1	0	0	0	0	1	0	0	9	4
KEEN Kevin	7	6	0	1	0	1	2	0	0	1	0	0	11	6
MARTIN Alvin	16	0	2	1	0	0	3	0	0	0	0	0	20	0
McALISTER Tom	9	0	0	0	0	0	0	0	0	0	0	0	9	0
McAVENNIE Frank	36	0	7	5	0	4	5	0	0	1	0	0	47	0
McQUEEN Tommy	9	0	0	0	0	0	0	0	0	0	0	0	9	0
ORR Neil	21	1	1	1	0	0	4	0	0	0	0	0	26	1
PARKES Phil	33	0	0	5	0	0	6	0	0	1	0	0	45	0
PARRIS George	35	1	2	5	0	1	6	0	0	1	0	0	47	1
PIKE Geoff	10	1	0	4	0	0	1	0	0	0	0	0	15	1
POTTS Steve	8	0	0	0	0	0	0	0	0	0	1	0	8	1
ROBSON Stewart	18	0	1	3	0	1	2	0	0	0	0	0	23	0
STEWART Ray	23	0	4	3	0	0	3	0	0	0	0	0	29	0
STRODDER Gary	12	0	0	0	0	0	0	0	0	0	0	0	12	0
WALFORD Steve	13	1	0	3	0	0	4	1	0	1	0	0	21	2
WARD Mark	37	0	1	5	0	0	6	0	2	1	0	0	49	0
Totals	**462**	**25**	**52**	**55**	**3**	**10**	**66**	**4**	**10**	**11**	**1**	**1**	**594**	**33**

* Other = Full Members' Cup

sults improved in January as Orient were beaten in the
Cup and there were league victories over Leicester City
d Coventry City. Disaster struck in the League Cup,
ugh, as after a 1–1 home draw with Tottenham the
mmers crashed out when losing 5–0 at White Hart Lane.
the FA Cup Sheffield United were beaten 4–0 at home
t the next round brought a 2–0 home loss to Sheffield
ednesday.

e squad was now hit with injuries and five successive
gue defeats brought a threat of relegation. There was
od news in March when midfielder Liam Brady was
ned from Ascoli, and he soon showed his wonderful skill
scoring against Arsenal in a 3–1 home win. Despite 4–0
ay defeats at Everton and Aston Villa the side managed
finish fifteenth.

LIAM BRADY

Liam was regarded as one of the Republic of Ireland's greatest ever players, winning 72 caps in an illustrious career.

He began as an apprentice at Arsenal in June 1971 and soon became one of their leading players throughout the 1970s. He gained two FA Cup winners' medals as the Gunners won the trophy in 1978 and 1979. He was at Highbury for eight seasons, scoring 67 goals in his 355 appearances. To the dismay of the Arsenal followers, in 1980 he moved to Italy to play for Juventus, where he was successful in winning two Serie A medals. He later played for Sampdoria, Internazionale and Ascoli and after seven years playing in Serie A he returned to England to sign for West Ham in 1987.

Although in the twilight of his career, he was still an accomplished player and the Upton Park faithful marvelled at his skill during his 115 outings and 10 goals in the claret and blue. After retiring as a player he had managerial spells at both Celtic and Brighton, which were both overshadowed by financial problems encountered by the clubs. In 1996 he rejoined Arsenal as the Head of Youth Development, a post he held until May 2014.

e Today League - Division One
nal Table 1986-87

| | P | HOME | | | | | AWAY | | | | | Pts |
		W	D	L	F	A	W	D	L	F	A	
rton	42	16	4	1	49	11	10	4	7	27	20	86
erpool	42	15	3	3	43	16	8	5	8	29	26	77
ttenham Hotspur	42	14	3	4	40	14	7	5	9	28	29	71
senal	42	12	5	4	31	12	8	5	8	27	23	70
wich City	42	9	10	2	27	20	8	7	6	26	31	68
mbledon	42	11	5	5	32	22	8	4	9	25	28	66
on Town	42	14	5	2	29	13	4	7	10	18	32	66
ttingham Forest	42	12	8	1	36	14	6	3	12	28	37	65
tford	42	12	5	4	38	20	6	4	11	29	34	63
ventry City	42	14	4	3	35	17	3	8	10	15	28	63
nchester United	42	13	3	5	38	18	1	11	9	14	27	56
uthampton	42	11	5	5	44	24	3	5	13	25	44	52
effield Wednesday	42	9	7	5	39	24	4	6	11	19	35	52
elsea	42	8	6	7	30	30	5	7	9	23	34	52
est Ham United	**42**	**10**	**4**	**7**	**33**	**28**	**4**	**6**	**11**	**19**	**39**	**52**
eens Park Rangers	42	9	7	5	31	27	4	4	13	17	37	50
wcastle United	42	10	4	7	33	29	2	7	12	14	36	47
ford United	42	8	8	5	30	25	3	5	13	14	44	46
arlton Athletic	42	7	7	7	26	22	4	4	13	19	33	44
cester City	42	9	7	5	39	24	2	2	17	15	52	42
anchester City	42	8	6	7	28	24	0	9	12	8	33	39
ton Villa	42	7	7	7	25	25	1	5	15	20	54	36

Season **1986-87** The Today League - Division On

Match Details

Manager **John Lyall**   Final League Position **15/22**

	Date		Competition	Venue	Opponents	Results		Attendance	Position	Scorers
1	Aug 23	Sat	Div 1	H	Coventry City	W	1-0	21,368	8	Gale
2	Aug 25	Mon	Div 1	A	Manchester United	W	3-2	43,306	1	McAvennie 2, Devonshire
3	Aug 30	Sat	Div 1	A	Oxford United	D	0-0	11,684	3	
4	Sep 2	Tue	Div 1	H	Nottingham Forest	L	1-2	21,305	6	McAvennie
5	Sep 6	Sat	Div 1	H	Liverpool	L	2-5	29,807	12	Cottee, Stewart [pen]
6	Sep 13	Sat	Div 1	A	Queens Park Rangers	W	3-2	16,257	6	Cottee 3
7	Sep 20	Sat	Div 1	H	Luton Town	W	2-0	19,133	4	Gale, Parris
8	Sep 23	Tue	FLC 2 : 1	A	Preston North End	D	1-1	13,153		Ward
9	Sep 27	Sat	Div 1	A	Sheffield Wednesday	D	2-2	25,715	7	Martin, Orr
10	Oct 4	Sat	Div 1	A	Watford	D	2-2	16,560	8	Dickens, McAvennie
11	Oct 7	Tue	FLC 2 : 2	H	Preston North End	W	4-1	12,742		Cottee 3, Dickens
12	Oct 11	Sat	Div 1	H	Chelsea	W	5-3	26,859	4	Cottee 2, Stewart 2 [2 pen], McAvennie
13	Oct 18	Sat	Div 1	A	Norwich City	D	1-1	22,776	5	Goddard
14	Oct 25	Sat	Div 1	H	Charlton Athletic	L	1-3	24,141	8	Cottee
15	Oct 29	Wed	FLC 3	A	Watford	W	3-2	17,253		Dickens, Goddard, Ward
16	Nov 2	Sun	Div 1	H	Everton	W	1-0	19,094	4	Dickens
17	Nov 8	Sat	Div 1	A	Arsenal	D	0-0	35,793	7	
18	Nov 15	Sat	Div 1	A	Wimbledon	W	1-0	10,342	5	Cottee
19	Nov 18	Tue	FLC 4	H	Oxford United	W	1-0	20,530		Cottee [pen]
20	Nov 22	Sat	Div 1	H	Aston Villa	D	1-1	21,959	4	Cottee
21	Nov 25	Tue	FMC 3	H	Chelsea	L	1-2	12,140		Cottee
22	Nov 30	Sun	Div 1	A	Newcastle United	L	0-4	23,151	7	
23	Dec 6	Sat	Div 1	H	Southampton	W	3-1	18,111	5	Cottee [pen], Devonshire, Ince
24	Dec 13	Sat	Div 1	A	Manchester City	L	1-3	19,067	6	Martin
25	Dec 20	Sat	Div 1	H	Queens Park Rangers	D	1-1	17,290	7	Cottee [pen]
26	Dec 26	Fri	Div 1	A	Tottenham Hotspur	L	0-4	39,019	9	
27	Dec 27	Sat	Div 1	H	Wimbledon	L	2-3	19,122	12	Cottee, Hilton
28	Jan 1	Thur	Div 1	H	Leicester City	W	4-1	16,625	8	Cottee 2, Dickens, McAvennie
29	Jan 3	Sat	Div 1	A	Liverpool	L	0-1	41,286	10	
30	Jan 10	Sat	FAC 3	A	Orient	D	1-1	19,225		Hilton
31	Jan 24	Sat	Div 1	A	Coventry City	W	3-1	14,170	9	Cottee 3
32	Jan 27	Tue	FLC 5	H	Tottenham Hotspur	D	1-1	29,477		Cottee
33	Jan 31	Sat	FAC 3 Rep	H	Orient	W	4-1	19,424		Cottee, Keen, McAvennie, Parris
34	Feb 2	Mon	FLC 5 Rep	A	Tottenham Hotspur	L	0-5	41,995		
35	Feb 7	Sat	Div 1	H	Oxford United	L	0-1	15,220	9	
36	Feb 9	Mon	FAC 4	H	Sheffield United	W	4-0	17,194		McAvennie 2, Gale, Robson
37	Feb 14	Sat	Div 1	A	Nottingham Forest	D	1-1	19,373	9	Stewart [pen]
38	Feb 21	Sat	FAC 5	A	Sheffield Wednesday	D	1-1	31,134		McAvennie
39	Feb 25	Wed	FAC 5 Rep	H	Sheffield Wednesday	L	0-2	30,257		
40	Feb 28	Sat	Div 1	A	Luton Town	L	1-2	11,101	13	Cottee
41	Mar 7	Sat	Div 1	A	Charlton Athletic	L	1-2	10,100	14	Robson
42	Mar 14	Sat	Div 1	H	Norwich City	L	0-2	21,531	14	
43	Mar 21	Sat	Div 1	A	Chelsea	L	0-1	25,386	15	
44	Mar 24	Tue	Div 1	H	Sheffield Wednesday	L	0-2	13,514	15	
45	Mar 28	Sat	Div 1	H	Watford	W	1-0	17,793	15	Parris
46	Apr 8	Wed	Div 1	H	Arsenal	W	3-1	26,174	14	Cottee 2 [1 pen], Brady
47	Apr 11	Sat	Div 1	A	Everton	L	0-4	35,746	14	
48	Apr 14	Tue	Div 1	H	Manchester United	D	0-0	23,486	14	
49	Apr 18	Sat	Div 1	A	Leicester City	L	0-2	10,434	14	
50	Apr 20	Mon	Div 1	H	Tottenham Hotspur	W	2-1	23,972	14	Cottee [pen], McAvennie
51	Apr 25	Sat	Div 1	A	Aston Villa	L	0-4	13,584	14	
52	May 2	Sat	Div 1	H	Newcastle United	D	1-1	17,844	15	Ward
53	May 4	Mon	Div 1	A	Southampton	L	0-1	16,810	16	
54	May 9	Sat	Div 1	H	Manchester City	W	2-0	18,413	15	Cottee, Brady

*FMC = Full Members Cup

eam Line-Ups

BRADY Liam	COTTEE Tony	DEVONSHIRE Alan	DICKENS Alan	DOLAN Eamonn	GALE Tony	GODDARD Paul	HILTON Paul	INCE Paul	KEEN Kevin	MARTIN Alvin	McALISTER Tom	McAVENNIE Frank	McQUEEN Tommy	ORR Neil	PARKES Phil	PARRIS George	PIKE Geoff	POTTS Steve	ROBSON Stewart	STEWART Ray	STRODDER Gary	WALFORD Steve	WARD Mark	
	10	6	9		4					5		8		11	1	3				2			7	1
	10	6	9				4			5		8		11	1	3				2			7	2
	10	6	9		4					5		8		11	1	3				2			7	3
	10	6/a	9		4	a				5		8		11	1	3				2			7	4
	10		9		4				a	5		8		11	1	3	6/a			2			7	5
	10		9		4		7			5		8		11	1	3				2		6	7	6
	10		9/a		4		7			5		8		11	1	3	a			2		6		7
	10				4					5		8		11	1	3	9			2		6	7	8
	10		9		4					5		8		11	1	3				2		6	7	9
	10		9		4/a		5		a			8		11	1	3				2		6	7	10
	10		9/a				5			4		8		11	1	3				2		6	7	11
	10		9		4		5		6			8/a		11	1	3				2			7	12
	10		9		4	8	5		6					11	1	3				2			7	13
	10	6/a	9		4	8	5		a					11	1	3				2			7	14
	10	6	9		4	8	5/a							11	1	3				2		a	7	15
	10	6	9		4	8	5							11	1	3				2			7	16
	10	6	9		4		5					8			1	3				2		11	7	17
	10	6	9		4		5					8		11	1	3				2		a	7	18
	10	6	9		4		5		11			8			1	3						2/a	7	19
	10	6	9		4		5		11/a			8			1	3						2	7	20
	10		9		4		5	6	11			8			1	3		a				2/a	7	21
	10	6	9/a		4		5	a				8		11	1	3				2			7	22
	10	6			4			9		5		8		11	1	3		2					7	23
	10	6	a		4			9		5		8		11/a	1	3		2					7	24
	10	6	9		4					5		8		11	1	3		2					7	25
	10	6	9				a			5		8		11	1	3		2				4/a	7	26
	10		a				4	6	9/a	5		8			1	3	11	2					7	27
	10	6	9				4			5		8			1	3	11					2	7	28
	10	6	9/a				4	a		5		8	7		1	3	11					2		29
	10						4	9		5		8			1	3	11					2	7	30
	10	6	9				4			5		8			1	3			11			2	7	31
	10	6	9				4			5		8			1	3			11			2	7	32
	10		9		4		5		6			8		11	1	3						2/a	7	33
	10	6			4		a			5		8		9	1	3/a			11				7	34
	10	6	9/a		4		5					8			1	3			11	2			7	35
	10	6/a			4				a			8			1	3	9		11/a		5		7	36
	10				4							8			1	3	9		11	2		6	7	37
	10				4							8			1	3	9		11	2		6	7	38
	10	6	a		4							8			1	3/a	9		11	2			7	39
	10	6			4		a					8			1		9		11	2		3/a	7	40
	10	6			4							8/a			1	a	9		11	2		3	7	41
7	10				5			8	a						1	3	9/a		11	2				42
6	10				4							8			1	3	9		11	2	5		7	43
6	10		9		4				a			8			1	3			11	2/a	5		7	44
6	10		a		4							8	3		1	9			11/a		5		7	45
6	10		8		4						1		3				9		11		5		7	46
6	10		8		4/a						1		3	a			9	7	11					47
6	10		9								1	8	3					2	11		5		7	48
6	10		a		4						1	8	3			9/a			11		5		7	49
9	10	6			4						1	8	3						11		5		7	50
9	10	6	a		4						1	8	3						11		5		7	51
	10		9					6	a		1	8	3/a					2	11		5		7	52
9	10							6			1	8	3					4	11		5		7	53
6	10			a				11	4		1	8	3					2	9		5		7/a	54

1987-88
Story of the season

An awful start saw **Queens Park Rangers win 3–0 at Upton Park** on the opening day.

The trend continued with only one win in the first [...] games leaving the club seventeenth, and the sombre moo[...] was not helped when striker Frank McAvennie was sold [...] Celtic. There was more gloom as Third Division Barnsl[...] won 5–2 at Upton Park in the League Cup, but resul[...] improved with 2–1 away wins at both Oxford United a[...] Watford. Billy Bonds was brought back into the team a[...] the side responded with home wins against Nottingha[...] Forest, Southampton and Newcastle.

Appearances & Goals 1987-88

	League			FA Cup			League Cup			Other*			Total	
	Starts	Subs	Goals	Starts	Subs	Goals	Starts	Subs	Goals	Starts	Subs	Goals	Starts	Subs
BONDS Billy	22	0	0	2	0	0	0	0	0	0	0	0	24	0
BRADY Liam	21	1	2	2	0	1	2	0	0	1	0	0	26	1
COTTEE Tony	40	0	13	2	0	2	2	0	0	0	0	0	44	0
DEVONSHIRE Alan	1	0	0	0	0	0	0	0	0	0	0	0	1	0
DICKENS Alan	25	3	3	1	0	0	0	1	0	1	0	1	27	4
DICKS Julian	8	0	0	0	0	0	0	0	0	0	0	0	8	0
DOLAN Eamonn	1	3	0	0	0	0	0	0	0	1	0	0	2	3
GALE Tony	17	1	0	2	0	0	0	0	0	0	0	0	19	1
HILTON Paul	9	5	3	1	1	0	0	1	0	1	0	0	11	7
INCE Paul	26	2	3	0	1	0	2	0	0	1	0	0	29	3
KEEN Kevin	19	4	1	0	0	0	1	0	1	0	1	0	20	5
MARTIN Alvin	15	0	0	0	0	0	2	0	0	1	0	0	18	0
McALISTER Tom	39	0	0	2	0	0	2	0	0	1	0	0	44	0
McAVENNIE Frank	8	0	0	0	0	0	1	0	0	0	0	0	9	0
McQUEEN Tommy	10	2	0	1	0	0	1	1	0	0	0	0	12	3
ORR Neil	1	0	0	0	0	0	0	0	0	0	0	0	1	0
PARKES Phil	1	0	0	0	0	0	0	0	0	0	0	0	1	0
PARRIS George	27	3	1	0	0	0	2	0	0	1	0	0	30	3
POTTS Steve	7	1	0	1	0	0	1	0	0	1	0	0	10	1
ROBSON Stewart	37	0	2	2	0	0	2	0	1	1	0	0	42	0
ROSENIOR Leroy	9	0	5	0	0	0	0	0	0	0	0	0	9	0
SLATER Stuart	0	2	0	0	0	0	0	0	0	0	0	0	0	2
STEWART Ray	33	0	4	2	0	0	0	0	0	0	0	0	35	0
STRODDER Gary	27	3	1	2	0	0	2	0	0	0	0	0	31	3
WARD Mark	37	0	1	2	0	0	2	0	0	1	0	0	42	0
own goal			1											
Totals	**440**	**30**	**40**	**22**	**2**	**3**	**22**	**3**	**2**	**11**	**1**	**1**	**495**	**36**

* Other = Simod Cup

Christmas there were defeats to fellow Londoners imbledon and Tottenham, and New Year's Day brought a d 4–1 defeat at Norwich City. The FA Cup saw some ief when fellow strugglers Charlton were beaten 2–0, but the fourth round Queens Park Rangers won 3–1 at ftus Road. In March striker Leroy Rosenior was signed om Fulham and became an instant hero as he scored on s debut in the 1–0 victory over Watford. Injuries were ing up, though, and relegation was looming until the me game with Chelsea saw the Hammers win 4–1 in an hilarating display, with two goals scored by Rosenior. It d been a disappointing season (sixteenth place) and it was ad day when Billy Bonds announced his retirement.

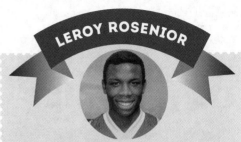

LEROY ROSENIOR

A striker who began his career at Fulham in 1982, scoring 15 goals in 54 league games, he moved to Queens Park Rangers in 1985 for £50,000.

At Rangers he scored 10 goals in a total of 47 games before returning to Fulham in 1987. Now playing in the Third Division, he scored 20 goals in 34 league games.

He signed for West Ham in March 1988 and scored on his debut against Watford. He added another four goals in the remaining games that ensured survival from relegation. Persistent knee injuries limited his outings and he was loaned out to Fulham and Charlton Athletic. With the signings of Trevor Morley and Jimmy Quinn the competition for places intensified, and he left to join Bristol City in March 1992.

At Ashton Gate he became a regular in the side and went on to score 12 goals in 51 league games. After a period as Bristol City's youth team coach he went into management, first at Gloucester City then Merthyr Tydfil, Torquay United and Brentford. Leroy now works in the media as a television pundit.

arclays League - Division One
inal Table 1987-88

	P	HOME					AWAY					Pts
		W	D	L	F	A	W	D	L	F	A	
erpool	40	15	5	0	49	9	11	7	2	38	15	90
anchester United	40	14	5	1	41	17	9	7	4	30	21	81
ttingham Forest	40	11	7	2	40	17	9	6	5	27	22	73
erton	40	14	4	2	34	11	5	9	6	19	16	70
eens Park Rangers	40	12	4	4	30	14	7	6	7	18	24	67
senal	40	11	4	5	35	16	7	8	5	23	23	66
mbledon	40	8	9	3	32	20	6	6	8	26	27	57
wcastle United	40	9	6	5	32	23	5	8	7	23	30	56
ton Town	40	11	6	3	40	21	3	5	12	17	37	53
ventry City	40	6	8	6	23	25	7	6	7	23	28	53
effield Wednesday	40	10	2	8	27	30	5	6	9	25	36	53
uthampton	40	6	8	6	27	26	6	6	8	22	27	50
tenham Hotspur	40	9	5	6	26	23	3	6	11	12	25	47
rwich City	40	7	5	8	26	26	5	4	11	14	26	45
rby County	40	6	7	7	18	17	4	6	10	17	28	43
est Ham United	40	6	9	5	23	21	3	6	11	17	31	42
arlton Athletic	40	7	7	6	23	21	2	8	10	15	31	42
elsea	40	7	11	2	24	17	2	4	14	26	51	42
rtsmouth	40	4	8	8	21	27	3	6	11	15	39	35
tford	40	4	5	11	15	24	3	6	11	12	27	32
ford United	40	5	7	8	24	34	1	6	13	20	46	31

Season **1987-88** Barclays League - Division One
Match Details

Manager **John Lyall**   Final League Position **16/22**

	Date		Competition	Venue	Opponents	Results		Attendance	Position	Scorers
1	Aug 15	Sat	Div 1	H	Queens Park Rangers	L	0-3	22,880	20	
2	Aug 22	Sat	Div 1	A	Luton Town	D	2-2	8,073	18	Brady, Stewart [pen]
3	Aug 29	Sat	Div 1	H	Norwich City	W	2-0	16,394	14	Cottee 2
4	Aug 31	Mon	Div 1	A	Portsmouth	L	1-2	16,104	14	Strodder
5	Sep 5	Sat	Div 1	H	Liverpool	D	1-1	29,865	15	Cottee
6	Sep 12	Sat	Div 1	A	Wimbledon	D	1-1	8,000	16	Cottee
7	Sep 19	Sat	Div 1	H	Tottenham Hotspur	L	0-1	27,750	18	
8	Sep 22	Tue	FLC 2:1	A	Barnsley	D	0-0	10,330		
9	Sep 26	Sat	Div 1	A	Arsenal	L	0-1	40,127	19	
10	Oct 3	Sat	Div 1	H	Derby County	D	1-1	17,226	17	Brady
11	Oct 6	Tue	FLC 2:2	H	Barnsley	L	2-5	12,403		Keen, Robson
12	Oct 10	Sat	Div 1	H	Charlton Athletic	D	1-1	15,757	17	Ince
13	Oct 17	Sat	Div 1	A	Oxford United	W	2-1	8,992	15	Cottee, Caton (og)
14	Oct 25	Sun	Div 1	H	Manchester United	D	1-1	19,863	15	Stewart [pen]
15	Oct 31	Sat	Div 1	A	Watford	W	2-1	14,225	14	Cottee, Dickens
16	Nov 7	Sat	Div 1	H	Sheffield Wednesday	L	0-1	16,277	15	
17	Nov 10	Tue	SimC 1*	H	Millwall	L	1-2	11,337		Dickens
18	Nov 14	Sat	Div 1	A	Everton	L	1-3	29,456	15	Hilton
19	Nov 21	Sat	Div 1	H	Nottingham Forest	W	3-2	17,216	13	Cottee 2, Stewart [pen]
20	Nov 28	Sat	Div 1	A	Coventry City	D	0-0	16,754	14	
21	Dec 5	Sat	Div 1	H	Southampton	W	2-1	14,975	11	Dickens, Keen
22	Dec 12	Sat	Div 1	A	Chelsea	D	1-1	22,850	12	Parris
23	Dec 19	Sat	Div 1	H	Newcastle United	W	2-1	18,675	9	Ince, Robson
24	Dec 26	Sat	Div 1	H	Wimbledon	L	1-2	18,605	10	Stewart [pen]
25	Dec 28	Mon	Div 1	A	Tottenham Hotspur	L	1-2	39,456	13	Hilton
26	Jan 1	Fri	Div 1	A	Norwich City	L	1-4	20,394	14	Cottee
27	Jan 2	Sat	Div 1	H	Luton Town	D	1-1	16,716	14	Ince
28	Jan 9	Sat	FAC 3	H	Charlton Athletic	W	2-0	22,043		Brady, Cottee
29	Jan 16	Sat	Div 1	A	Queens Park Rangers	W	1-0	14,909	12	Dickens
30	Jan 30	Sat	FAC 4	A	Queens Park Rangers	L	1-3	23,651		Cottee
31	Feb 6	Sat	Div 1	A	Liverpool	D	0-0	42,049	13	
32	Feb 13	Sat	Div 1	H	Portsmouth	D	1-1	18,639	13	Cottee
33	Feb 27	Sat	Div 1	A	Derby County	L	0-1	16,301	13	
34	Mar 5	Sat	Div 1	H	Oxford United	D	1-1	14,980	13	Ward
35	Mar 12	Sat	Div 1	A	Charlton Athletic	L	0-3	8,118	15	
36	Mar 19	Sat	Div 1	H	Watford	W	1-0	16,035	15	Rosenior
37	Mar 26	Sat	Div 1	A	Manchester United	L	1-3	37,269	15	Rosenior
38	Apr 2	Sat	Div 1	A	Sheffield Wednesday	L	1-2	18,435	15	Rosenior
39	Apr 4	Mon	Div 1	H	Everton	D	0-0	21,195	16	
40	Apr 12	Tue	Div 1	H	Arsenal	L	0-1	26,746	17	
41	Apr 20	Wed	Div 1	A	Nottingham Forest	D	0-0	15,775	17	
42	Apr 23	Sat	Div 1	H	Coventry City	D	1-1	17,733	17	Cottee
43	Apr 30	Sat	Div 1	A	Southampton	L	1-2	15,702	18	Cottee
44	May 2	Mon	Div 1	H	Chelsea	W	4-1	28,521	16	Rosenior 2, Cottee, Hilton
45	May 7	Sat	Div 1	A	Newcastle United	L	1-2	23,862	16	Robson

*SimC = Simod Cup

Team Line-Ups

BONDS Billy	BRADY Liam	COTTEE Tony	DEVONSHIRE Alan	DICKENS Alan	DICKS Julian	DOLAN Eamonn	GALE Tony	HILTON Paul	INCE Paul	KEEN Kevin	MARTIN Alvin	McALISTER Tom	McAVENNIE Frank	McQUEEN Tommy	ORR Neil	PARKES Phil	PARRIS George	POTTS Steve	ROBSON Stewart	ROSENIOR Leroy	SLATER Stuart	STEWART Ray	STRODDER Gary	WARD Mark	
9	10		6/a	a							5	1	8	3	4				11			2/b	b	7	1
6	10								9		5	1	8	3					11			2	4	7	2
6	10								9		5	1	8	3					11			2	4	7	3
6	10								9		5	1	8	3			a		11			2/a	4	7	4
6	10								9		5	1	8	3/a			a		11			2	4	7	5
6	10								9		5	1	8				3		11			2	4	7	6
6	10							a	9		5	1	8				3		11			2	4/a	7	7
6	10								9		5	1	8	a			3	2/a	11				4	7	8
6	10								9	7	5	1	8				3		11			2	4		9
6	10							a	9	7	5	1		3/a			8		11	b		2/b	4		10
6	10		a					b	9	8	5	1		3/b			2/a		11				4	7	11
6	10		8						9	4	5	1					3		11			2		7	12
6	10		4						9	7	5	1					3		11			2		8	13
6	10		8						9	4	5	1	11				3		11			2		7	14
6	10		8						9	4	5	1					3		11			2		7	15
6	10		8		a				9	4/a	5	1					3		11			2		7	16
6			8	10				4	9	a	5	1					3	2/a	11					7	17
6	10		8					4	9	b	5/b	1					3/a		11				a	7	18
	10		8					4	9	6		1					3		11			5		7	19
	10		8					4	9	6		1					3		11			5		7	20
	10		8						9	6		1					3		11			5	4	7	21
	10		8						9	6		1					3		11			5	4	7	22
7	10		8					a	9	6		1					3		11			5	4		23
b	10		8/b					a	9	6		1					3/a		11			5	a	7/a	24
8	10							4	9	6		1					3		11			5	a	7/a	25
	10		8			b	a	4	9/a	6/b		1					3		11			5		7	26
	10		8				9	a				1					3/a	6	11			5	4	7	27
8/a	10							6	9	a		1					3		11			2	5	7	28
8	10	9					6					1					3		11			2	5	7	29
8	10	9					6			a		1					3/a		11			2	5	7	30
8	10	9/a					6	3				1	a						11			2	5	7	31
8	10	9					6	3				1							11			2	5	7	32
8/a	10	9/b					6	3			a	1	b						11			2	5	7	33
	10			a			6		9/a	8		1					3		11			2	5	7	34
	10	9	8/a				6	a				1					3		11			2	5	7	35
	10			a			6			8		1						3	11/a	9		2	5	7	36
	10		11				6			8/a		1					a	3		9		2	5	7	37
	10			a	3		6					1					8	b	11	9		2	5/b	7	38
	10		8		3		6	a				1					4		11	9		2/a	5	7	39
	10				3		6	a								1	8	2/a	11	9			5	7	40
	10		8		3		6					1					2		11	9			5	7	41
	10		8		3		6	a	9/a	4/b		1					2		11	b			5	7	42
	10		8		3		6					1					11	2		9			5	7	43
	10		8		3		6				5	1					2	4	11	9				7	44
	10		8		3		6				5	1					2	4	11	9				7	45

1988-89
Story of the season

The Hammers were **in trouble from the start,** losing 4–0 at Southampton and 3–1 at home to Charlton.

Tony Cottee had been sold to Everton for a sum excess of £2 million, making him the most expensive pla in British football. New signings inside-forward Da Kelly and goalkeeper Alan McKnight found it difficul settle. Although West Ham slumped to 4–1 league def against Arsenal and Luton, their form in the League (was far better. Sunderland were beaten 5–1 on aggreg and the next round brought a 5–0 demolition of De County. The fourth-round home tie with Liverpool shoc the nation as the Hammers crushed the Reds 4–1, with I Ince scoring twice. But as the year ended there had c been three league victories and West Ham were bottom the table.

Appearances & Goals 1988-89

	League			FA Cup			League Cup			Other*			Tota	
	Starts	Subs	Goals	Starts	Subs	Goals	Starts	Subs	Goals	Starts	Subs	Goals	Starts	Subs
BRADY Liam	21	1	3	7	0	0	4	1	0	2	0	0	34	2
DEVONSHIRE Alan	14	6	0	7	0	0	4	0	0	0	0	0	25	6
DICKENS Alan	34	3	5	5	2	1	6	0	1	1	0	0	46	5
DICKS Julian	34	0	2	6	0	0	7	0	0	2	0	0	49	0
GALE Tony	31	0	0	5	0	0	6	0	1	2	0	0	44	0
HILTON Paul	9	2	0	0	1	0	2	0	0	1	1	0	12	4
INCE Paul	32	1	3	7	0	1	7	0	3	2	0	1	48	1
KEEN Kevin	16	8	3	0	5	0	1	1	1	2	0	0	19	14
KELLY David	21	4	6	6	0	0	6	1	4	1	0	1	34	5
MARTIN Alvin	27	0	1	5	0	0	5	0	2	1	0	0	38	0
McALISTER Tom	2	0	0	0	0	0	0	0	0	0	0	0	2	0
McAVENNIE Frank	8	1	0	0	0	0	0	0	0	0	0	0	8	1
McKNIGHT Allen	23	0	0	4	0	0	6	0	0	2	0	0	35	0
McQUEEN Tommy	0	2	0	0	0	0	0	0	0	0	0	0	0	2
PARKES Phil	13	0	0	3	0	0	1	0	0	0	0	0	17	0
PARRIS George	23	4	1	1	0	0	3	0	0	0	1	0	27	5
POTTS Steve	23	5	0	7	0	0	5	1	0	2	0	0	37	6
ROBSON Stewart	6	0	0	0	0	0	1	0	0	0	0	0	7	0
ROSENIOR Leroy	26	2	7	4	0	2	5	0	2	2	0	4	37	2
SLATER Stuart	16	2	1	3	0	1	1	0	0	0	0	0	20	2
STEWART Ray	5	1	2	2	0	0	1	0	1	0	0	0	8	1
STRODDER Gary	4	3	0	2	2	0	1	0	0	0	0	0	7	5
WARD Mark	30	0	2	3	0	0	5	1	0	2	0	0	40	1
own goal			1											1
Totals	**418**	**45**	**37**	**77**	**10**	**6**	**77**	**5**	**16**	**22**	**2**	**6**	**594**	**62**

* Other = Simod Cup

e New Year saw more league defeats but there was relief the cups. In the FA Cup Arsenal and Swindon Town re beaten and in the League Cup the Hammers marched o the semi-final after beating Aston Villa 2–1. Still they uggled in the league, and both cup runs finally ended as t Luton Town won 5–0 on aggregate in the League Cup ni-final and then Norwich went through in the FA Cup, ning the quarter-final 3–1 at Carrow Road.

ring April there were four successive home games and ly the final one against Millwall brought a victory. markably, the remaining seven games of the campaign ught five wins, but sadly the Hammers were relegated er losing 5–1 on the final day at Liverpool.

rclays League - Division One nal Table 1988-89

	P	HOME					AWAY					Pts
		W	D	L	F	A	W	D	L	F	A	
nal	38	10	6	3	35	19	12	4	3	38	17	76
rpool	38	11	5	3	33	11	11	5	3	32	17	76
ingham Forest	38	8	7	4	31	16	9	6	4	33	27	64
wich City	38	8	7	4	23	20	9	4	6	25	25	62
by County	38	9	3	7	23	18	8	4	7	17	20	58
enham Hotspur	38	8	6	5	31	24	7	6	6	29	22	57
entry City	38	9	4	6	28	23	5	9	5	19	19	55
ton	38	10	7	2	33	18	4	5	10	17	27	54
ens Park Rangers	38	9	5	5	23	16	5	6	8	20	21	53
wall	38	10	3	6	27	21	4	8	7	20	31	53
chester United	38	10	5	4	27	13	3	7	9	18	22	51
bledon	38	10	3	6	30	19	4	6	9	20	27	51
hampton	38	6	7	6	25	26	4	8	7	27	40	45
lton Athletic	38	6	7	6	25	24	4	5	10	19	34	42
field Wednesday	38	6	6	7	21	25	4	6	9	13	26	42
n Town	38	8	6	5	32	21	2	5	12	10	31	41
n Villa	38	7	6	6	25	22	2	7	10	20	34	40
dlesbrough	38	6	7	6	28	30	3	5	11	16	31	39
st Ham United	38	3	6	10	19	30	7	2	10	18	32	38
castle United	38	3	6	10	19	28	4	4	11	13	35	31

STUART SLATER

An exciting product of West Ham's youth system, sadly Stuart never fulfilled his huge potential.

He started as an apprentice in July 1985 and within two years was a regular member of the side. His close control and ball skills were a joy to watch. His finest game for West Ham came in the FA Cup against Everton in March 1991, where his penetrating runs and outstanding performance were capped by the winning goal.

In May 1991 he was awarded an England B cap against Switzerland at Walsall. In the summer of 1992 Glasgow giants Celtic bought him for a fee of £1.5 million, but the big-money signing did not like the intense scrutiny in Glasgow and missed the quiet life. So after 15 months and just three goals he returned to England to play for Ipswich Town, where he was reunited with his former manager John Lyall. When Town were relegated in his second season he left on a free transfer to Leicester City for a spell, before joining Watford where an Achilles tendon injury hampered his appearances. Stuart then went to Australia to play for Carlton in Melbourne but they went into liquidation and he returned home. In 2000 he went into non-league football and played for Forest Green Rovers, Aberystwyth Town and Weston-super-Mare before retiring as a player in 2009. He has since coached the youth academy at both West Ham and Chelmsford City.

Season **1988-89** Barclays League - Division One
Match Details

Manager **John Lyall**   Final League Position **19/20 Relegated to League Division 2**

	Date		Competition	Venue	Opponents	Results		Attendance	Position	Scorers
1	Aug 27	Sat	Div 1	A	Southampton	L	0-4	18,407	18	
2	Sep 3	Sat	Div 1	H	Charlton Athletic	L	1-3	19,566	20	Keen (pen)
3	Sep 10	Sat	Div 1	A	Wimbledon	W	1-0	8,326	13	Ward
4	Sep 17	Sat	Div 1	H	Aston Villa	D	2-2	19,186	13	Kelly, Mountfield (og)
5	Sep 24	Sat	Div 1	A	Manchester United	L	0-2	39,941	17	
6	Sep 27	Tue	FLC 2:1	A	Sunderland	W	3-0	13,691		Kelly 2, Rosenior
7	Oct 1	Sat	Div 1	H	Arsenal	L	1-4	27,658	20	Dickens
8	Oct 8	Sat	Div 1	A	Middlesbrough	L	0-1	19,591	20	
9	Oct 12	Wed	FLC 2:2	H	Sunderland	W	2-1	10,558		Dickens, Kelly
10	Oct 15	Sat	Div 1	A	Queens Park Rangers	L	1-2	14,566	20	Kelly
11	Oct 22	Sat	Div 1	H	Newcastle United	W	2-0	17,765	19	Dickens, Stewart [pen]
12	Oct 29	Sat	Div 1	H	Liverpool	L	0-2	30,188	20	
13	Nov 1	Tue	FLC 3	H	Derby County	W	5-0	14,226		Martin 2, Keen, Rosenior, Stewart [pen]
14	Nov 5	Sat	Div 1	A	Coventry City	D	1-1	14,618	18	Kelly
15	Nov 9	Wed	SimC 1*	H	West Bromwich Albion	W	5-2	5,960		Rosenior 4, Kelly
16	Nov 12	Sat	Div 1	H	Nottingham Forest	D	3-3	21,583	18	Kelly 2, Rosenior
17	Nov 19	Sat	Div 1	A	Luton Town	L	1-4	9,308	19	Martin
18	Nov 22	Tue	SimC 2	A	Watford	D	1-1**	6,468		Ince
19	Nov 26	Sat	Div 1	H	Everton	L	0-1	22,176	19	
20	Nov 30	Wed	FLC 4	H	Liverpool	W	4-1	26,971		Ince 2, Gale, (og)
21	Dec 3	Sat	Div 1	A	Millwall	W	1-0	20,105	19	Ince
22	Dec 10	Sat	Div 1	H	Sheffield Wednesday	D	0-0	16,676	19	
23	Dec 17	Sat	Div 1	H	Tottenham Hotspur	L	0-2	28,365	20	
24	Dec 27	Tue	Div 1	A	Norwich City	L	1-2	17,491	20	Stewart [pen]
25	Dec 31	Sat	Div 1	A	Charlton Athletic	D	0-0	11,084	20	
26	Jan 2	Mon	Div 1	H	Wimbledon	L	1-2	18,346	20	Rosenior
27	Jan 8	Sun	FAC 3	H	Arsenal	D	2-2	22,017		Dickens, Bould (og)
28	Jan 11	Wed	FAC 3 Rep	A	Arsenal	W	1-0	44,124		Rosenior
29	Jan 14	Sat	Div 1	A	Derby County	W	2-1	16,793	19	Brady (pen), Kelly
30	Jan 18	Wed	FLC 5	H	Aston Villa	W	2-1	30,110		Ince, Kelly
31	Jan 21	Sat	Div 1	H	Manchester United	L	1-3	29,822	19	Brady [pen]
32	Jan 28	Sat	FAC 4	A	Swindon Town	D	0-0	18,627		
33	Feb 1	Wed	FAC 4 Rep	H	Swindon Town	W	1-0	24,723		Rosenior
34	Feb 4	Sat	Div 1	A	Arsenal	L	1-2	40,137	20	Dicks
35	Feb 12	Sun	FLC SF:1	H	Luton Town	L	0-3	24,602		
36	Feb 18	Sat	FAC 5	A	Charlton Athletic	W	1-0	18,785		Slater
37	Feb 25	Sat	Div 1	H	Queens Park Rangers	D	0-0	17,371	20	
38	Mar 1	Wed	FLC SF:2	A	Luton Town	L	0-2	12,020		
39	Mar 11	Sat	Div 1	A	Coventry City	D	1-1	15,205	20	Ince
40	Mar 18	Sat	FAC 6	H	Norwich City	D	0-0	29,119		
41	Mar 22	Wed	FAC 6 Rep	A	Norwich City	L	1-3	25,785		Ince
42	Mar 25	Sat	Div 1	A	Aston Villa	W	1-0	22,471	20	Ince
43	Mar 27	Mon	Div 1	H	Norwich City	L	0-2	27,265	20	
44	Apr 1	Sat	Div 1	A	Tottenham Hotspur	L	0-3	28,375	20	
45	Apr 8	Sat	Div 1	H	Derby County	D	1-1	16,560	20	Rosenior
46	Apr 11	Tue	Div 1	H	Middlesbrough	L	1-2	16,227	20	Keen
47	Apr 15	Sat	Div 1	H	Southampton	L	1-2	14,766	20	Brady [pen]
48	Apr 22	Sat	Div 1	H	Millwall	W	3-0	16,603	20	Dickens, Dicks, Parris
49	May 3	Wed	Div 1	A	Newcastle United	W	2-1	14,445	20	Keen, Ward
50	May 6	Sat	Div 1	H	Luton Town	W	1-0	18,686	19	Dickens
51	May 9	Tue	Div 1	A	Sheffield Wednesday	W	2-0	19,905	19	Dickens, Rosenior
52	May 13	Sat	Div 1	A	Everton	L	1-3	23,438	19	Slater
53	May 18	Thur	Div 1	A	Nottingham Forest	W	2-1	20,843	19	Rosenior 2
54	May 23	Tue	Div 1	A	Liverpool	L	1-5	41,855	19	Rosenior

*SimC = Simod Cup ** Lost 1-3 pens

eam Line-Ups

	DEVONSHIRE Alan	DICKENS Alan	DICKS Julian	GALE Tony	HILTON Paul	INCE Paul	KEEN Kevin	KELLY David	MARTIN Alvin	McALISTER Tom	McAVENNIE Frank	McKNIGHT Allen	McQUEEN Tommy	PARKES Phil	PARRIS George	POTTS Steve	ROBSON Stewart	ROSENIOR Leroy	SLATER Stuart	STEWART Ray	STRODDER Gary	WARD Mark	
	b		3	4/a	a	6		10	5	1					8	2	11		9/b			7	1
	a	4	3		b	6/a		10	5	1					8	2/b	11		9			7	2
a		10	3		4	6		8/a	5			1				2	11	9				7	3
a		10	3			6		8	5			1				2	11	9			4/a	7	4
a		10	3		5	6		8				1				2	11	9			4/a	7	5
		10	3	4		6		8	5/a			1			a	2	11	9				7	6
a		10	3	4		6		8	5			1			2/b		11	9/a			b	7	7
6		10	3	4	5	11	a	8				1				2/a		9				7	8
6/a		10	3	4	5	11	a	8				1				2		9				7	9
6/a		10	3	4	5	11	a	8				1				2		9				7	10
6/a		10	3	4		11	a	8	5			1						9		2		7	11
6		10	3	4		11		8/a	5			1			a			9		2		7	12
		10	3	4	11	6		8/a	5			1				2		9				7	13
		10	3	4	11	6		8	5			1				2		9				7	14
'a			3	4	5	11	6	8				1			a	2		9				7	15
		10	3	4	11/b	6		8/a	5			1			b	2		9				7	16
		10/a	3	4	a	11	6/b		5			1			b	2		9				7	17
		10	3	4	a	11	6		5/a			1				2		9				7	18
a		10	3	4		11	6		5			1				2		9				7/a	19
6		10	3	4		11		8	5			1				2		9				7	20
6		10	3	4		11		8	5			1				2		9				7	21
6		10		4		11		8	5			1			3	2		9				7	22
6/a		10		4		11	a	8	5			1			3	2		9				7	23
6		10/b		4		11	b	8	5/a			1			3	2		9		a		7	24
		10	3	4		11		8	5			1			a	2		9		6			25
		10	3	4		11		8	5			1				2		9		6			26
6/a		10	3			11	a	8	5			1			4			9		2			27
b	6	10	3			11	b	8	5/a			1			4			9		2	a		28
	6	10		4		11	b	8				1			5			9		2/a	a		29
	6	10/a	3	4		11		8				1				2		9		5	a		30
	6/b		3	4		11	b	8/a	5			1				2		9		a	10		31
	6/a	a	3	4		11		8	5			1				2		9				7	32
	6	b	3	4		11		8/b	5/a			1				2		9		a		7	33
	6/a	8	3	4		11		a				1				2		9		5		7	34
	6	8	3	4		11		a	5			1				2		9				7	35
	6/a	8		4		11	a		5					1	3	2			9			7	36
	6	8/a	3	4		11			5					1	a	2			9			7	37
			3	4		11		6	5					1	8	2			9			7	38
	6	8	3	4		11	7		5					1		2			9				39
	6/a	8	3	4		11	a	7						1		2			9	5			40
	6/a	8	3	4	a	11	b	7/b						1		2			9	5			41
	6/a	a	3	4	5	11		8						1	2				9			7	42
	6		3	4	5	11		8						1	2			a	9			7	43
	a		3	4		11		8						1	2		6		9		5/a	7	44
b	6		3	4/a		11		8	5					1	2		a		9	b		7	45
	6		3		5	11		8						1	2		4		9			7	46
a	6/b				5	11	3	8					a	1	2		4		9	b		7	47
	6		3	4		11/a	10	8					a	1	2		5		9			7	48
	6		3	4		11	10	a	5		8/a			1	2				9			7	49
	6		3	4/a		11	10	b	5					1	2		a		9/b	8		7	50
	6		3	4/a		11	10		5					1	2		a		9	8		7	51
	6		3	4		11/a	10/b	b	5					1	2		a		9	8		7	52
'a	6		3	4			10		5			1			2		a		9	8		7	53
'a	6		3	4		11/b	b		5		a	1			2				9	8		7	54

1989-90
Story of the season

During the summer **the football world was shocked** when manager **John Lyall was sacked after 34 years' service** to be replaced by Swindon boss and former Manchester United player Lou Macari.

A further setback occurred when, in the opening game Stoke City, Frank McAvennie broke his leg and missed t remainder of the season. The players were struggling adjust to life in the Second Division and the team we lying tenth in the table.

Another League Cup adventure began when bc Birmingham City and Aston Villa were knocked out at t

Appearances & Goals 1989-90

	League			FA Cup			League Cup			Other*			Total	
	Starts	Subs	Goals	Starts	Subs	Goals	Starts	Subs	Goals	Starts	Subs	Goals	Starts	Subs
ALLEN Martin	39	0	9	1	0	0	6	0	2	2	0	0	48	0
BISHOP Ian	13	4	2	1	0	0	0	0	0	0	0	0	14	4
BRADY Liam	25	8	2	0	0	0	8	2	0	1	0	0	34	10
DEVONSHIRE Alan	3	4	0	0	0	0	0	3	0	1	0	0	4	7
DICKS Julian	40	0	9	1	0	0	9	0	4	2	0	1	52	0
DOLAN Eamonn	8	2	3	0	0	0	4	0	0	0	1	1	12	3
FASHANU Justin	2	0	0	0	0	0	0	1	0	0	0	0	2	1
FOSTER Colin	20	2	0	0	0	0	0	0	0	1	1	0	21	3
GALE Tony	36	0	1	1	0	0	7	0	0	1	0	0	45	0
INCE Paul	1	0	0	0	0	0	0	0	0	0	0	0	1	0
KEEN Kevin	43	1	10	1	0	0	10	0	1	2	0	2	56	1
KELLY David	8	8	1	0	0	0	5	2	1	1	1	1	14	11
KELLY Paul	0	1	0	0	0	0	0	0	0	0	0	0	0	1
MARTIN Alvin	31	0	0	1	0	0	10	0	1	1	0	1	43	0
McAVENNIE Frank	1	4	0	0	0	0	0	0	0	0	0	0	1	4
McQUEEN Tommy	5	2	0	0	0	0	1	2	0	0	0	0	6	4
MIKLOSKO Ludek	18	0	0	0	0	0	1	0	0	0	0	0	19	0
MILNE Ralph	0	0	0	0	0	0	0	1	0	0	0	0	0	1
MORLEY Trevor	18	1	10	1	0	0	0	0	0	0	0	0	19	1
PARKES Phil	22	0	0	1	0	0	9	0	0	2	0	0	34	0
PARRIS George	35	3	2	1	0	0	10	0	0	0	0	0	46	3
POTTS Steve	30	2	0	1	0	0	7	0	0	2	0	0	40	2
QUINN Jimmy	18	3	13	1	0	0	0	0	0	0	0	0	19	3
ROBSON Stewart	7	0	1	0	0	0	3	0	0	0	0	0	10	0
ROSENIOR Leroy	4	1	2	0	1	0	2	0	0	0	0	0	6	2
SLATER Stuart	40	0	7	0	0	0	9	1	2	2	0	2	51	1
STRODDER Gary	16	0	1	0	0	0	5	0	0	2	0	0	23	0
SUCKLING Perry	6	0	0	0	0	0	0	0	0	0	0	0	6	0
WARD Mark	17	2	5	0	0	0	4	0	0	2	0	0	23	2
own goal			2											
Totals	506	48	80	11	1	0	110	12	11	22	3	8	649	64

*Other = Zenith Data Systems Cup

...leyn Ground. League results improved with a 2–0 win at ...effield United followed by a 5–0 thrashing of Sunderland. ...e League Cup tie with Wimbledon was a stormy affair, ...th five bookings and one dismissal, but the Hammers ...re happy with the 1–0 victory. In December there was ...ly one goal scored in five games, prompting manager ...acari to buy two forwards, Trevor Morley and Jimmy ...uinn.

...e trip to Fourth Division Torquay United in the FA Cup ...s a disaster, with West Ham losing 1–0. In the League ...p it took two replays to beat Derby County but the team ...re now in the semi-finals for the second season running. ...March Lou Macari was found guilty by the FA for betting ...egularities while at former club Swindon Town. The ...ense media pressure was not the ideal preparation for the

League Cup semi-final at Oldham. The team gave a shameful display, losing 6–0, and by the end of that week Macari had resigned.

The appointment of Billy Bonds as manager was greeted with enthusiasm and the upsurge in spirits under Billy's leadership was remarkable. In the last 17 league games, 10 were won, three drawn, and only four were lost. The final memory of the season was Liam Brady scoring in his last competitive match in the 3–1 home victory against Wolverhampton Wanderers. The side finished in seventh place, but under Bonds they had shown greater consistency.

...rclays League - Division Two ...nal Table 1989-90

LUDEK MIKLOSKO

The big Czech goalkeeper was signed from Banik Ostrava in December 1989 and made his debut at Swindon Town in February 1990.

In his first full season with West Ham he kept 21 clean sheets, almost equalling the club record of 22 set by Phil Parkes. He was in the Czech side that played against England at Wembley in April 1990 and while at West Ham he gained a further 10 caps. From March 1992 until December 1995 he played in a total of 162 consecutive league games, the run only halted by a suspension following a red card at Everton. He was hugely popular with the fans but after nine seasons and 365 appearances he left to join Queens Park Rangers in October 1998. He went on to play in 65 games for the west London club before returning to Upton Park in 2001 as the goalkeeping coach, a role he maintained until 2010. He now works as a sports agent in the Czech Republic.

		HOME					AWAY					
	P	W	D	L	F	A	W	D	L	F	A	Pts
...ds United	46	16	6	1	46	18	8	7	8	33	34	85
...effield United	46	14	5	4	43	27	10	8	5	35	31	85
...wcastle United	46	17	4	2	51	26	5	10	8	29	29	80
...ndon Town	46	12	6	5	49	29	8	8	7	30	30	74
...ckburn Rovers	46	10	9	4	43	30	9	8	6	31	29	74
...derland	46	10	8	5	41	32	10	6	7	29	32	74
...st Ham United	**46**	**14**	**5**	**4**	**50**	**22**	**6**	**7**	**10**	**30**	**35**	**72**
...ham Athletic	46	15	7	1	50	23	4	7	12	20	34	71
...wich Town	46	13	7	3	38	22	6	5	12	29	44	69
...verhampton Wanderers	46	12	5	6	37	20	6	8	9	30	40	67
...t Vale	46	11	9	3	37	20	4	7	12	25	37	61
...tsmouth	46	9	8	6	40	34	6	8	9	22	31	61
...cester City	46	10	8	5	34	29	5	6	12	33	50	59
...l City	46	7	8	8	27	31	7	8	8	31	34	58
...ford	46	11	6	6	41	28	3	9	11	17	32	57
...mouth Argyle	46	9	8	6	30	23	5	5	13	28	40	55
...rd United	46	8	7	8	35	31	7	2	14	22	35	54
...hton and Hove Albion	46	10	6	7	28	27	5	3	15	28	45	54
...nsley	46	7	9	7	22	23	6	6	11	27	48	54
...st Bromwich Albion	46	6	8	9	35	37	6	7	10	32	34	51
...dlesbrough	46	10	3	10	33	29	3	8	12	19	34	50
...C Bournemouth	46	8	6	9	30	31	4	6	13	27	45	48
...dford City	46	9	6	8	26	24	0	8	15	18	44	41
...ke City	46	4	11	8	20	24	2	8	13	15	39	37

Season **1989-90** Barclays League - Division Two

Match Details

Manager **Lou Macari** (to Feb 20); Caretaker Manager **Ron Boyce** (Feb 18); Manager **Billy Bonds** (from Feb 2
Final League Position **7/24**

	Date		Competition	Venue	Opponents	Results		Attendance	Position	Scorers
1	Aug 19	Sat	Div 2	A	Stoke City	D	1-1	16,209	15	Keen
2	Aug 23	Wed	Div 2	H	Bradford City	W	2-0	19,881	3	Slater 2
3	Aug 26	Sat	Div 2	H	Plymouth Argyle	W	3-2	20,235	1	Allen, Keen, Kelly
4	Sep 2	Sat	Div 2	A	Hull City	D	1-1	9,235	1	Ward
5	Sep 9	Sat	Div 2	H	Swindon Town	D	1-1	21,469	3	Allen
6	Sep 16	Sat	Div 2	A	Brighton & Hove Albion	L	0-3	12,689	8	
7	Sep 19	Tue	FLC 2:1	A	Birmingham City	W	2-1	10,987		Allen, Slater
8	Sep 23	Sat	Div 2	H	Watford	W	1-0	21,525	5	Dicks [pen]
9	Sep 26	Tue	Div 2	A	Portsmouth	W	1-0	12,632	2	Rosenior
10	Sep 30	Sat	Div 2	H	West Bromwich Albion	L	2-3	19,842	7	Dolan, Parris
11	Oct 4	Wed	FLC 2:2	H	Birmingham City	D	1-1	12,187		Dicks
12	Oct 7	Sat	Div 2	H	Leeds United	L	0-1	23,539	10	
13	Oct 14	Sat	Div 2	A	Sheffield United	W	2-0	20,822	8	Ward 2 [1 pen]
14	Oct 18	Wed	Div 2	H	Sunderland	W	5-0	20,901	5	Dolan 2, Allen, Keen, Slater
15	Oct 21	SAt	Div 2	A	Port Vale	D	2-2	8,899	4	Keen, Slater
16	Oct 25	Wed	FLC 3	A	Aston Villa	D	0-0	20,989		
17	Oct 28	Sat	Div 2	H	Oxford United	W	3-2	19,177	4	Dicks, Parris, Slater
18	Nov 1	Wed	Div 2	A	AFC Bournemouth	D	1-1	9,970	5	Strodder
19	Nov 4	Sat	Div 2	A	Wolverhampton Wanderers	L	0-1	22,231	5	
20	Nov 8	Wed	FLC 3 Rep	H	Aston Villa	W	1-0	23,833		Dicks
21	Nov 11	Sat	Div 2	H	Newcastle United	D	0-0	25,892	7	
22	Nov 18	Sat	Div 2	H	Middlesbrough	W	2-0	18,720	5	Dicks [pen], Slater
23	Nov 22	Wed	FLC 4	H	Wimbledon	W	1-0	24,746		Allen
24	Nov 25	Sat	Div 2	A	Blackburn Rovers	L	4-5	10,238	7	Brady, Dicks [pen], Slater, Ward
25	Nov 29	Wed	ZDSC 2*	H	Plymouth Argyle	W	5-2	5,409		Keen, Dolan, Dicks, Martin, Slater
26	Dec 2	Sat	Div 2	H	Stoke City	D	0-0	17,704	7	
27	Dec 9	Sat	Div 2	A	Bradford City	L	1-2	9,257	7	Ward
28	Dec 16	Sat	Div 2	H	Oldham Athletic	L	0-2	14,960	8	
29	Dec 22	Fri	ZDSC QF	A	Chelsea	L	3-4	8,418		Keen, Slater, Kelly
30	Dec 26	Tue	Div 2	A	Ipswich Town	L	0-1	25,326	10	
31	Dec 30	Sat	Div 2	A	Leicester City	L	0-1	16,925	11	
32	Jan 1	Mon	Div 2	H	Barnsley	W	4-2	18,391	10	Keen 2, Allen, Dicks [pen]
33	Jan 6	Sat	FAC 3	A	Torquay United	L	0-1	5,342		
34	Jan 13	Sat	Div 2	A	Plymouth Argyle	D	1-1	11,671	10	Quinn
35	Jan 17	Wed	FLC 5	H	Derby County	D	1-1	25,035		Dicks
36	Jan 20	Sat	Div 2	H	Hull City	L	1-2	16,847	13	Morley
37	Jan 24	Wed	FLC 5 Rep	A	Derby County	D	0-0	22,510		
38	Jan 31	Wed	FLC 5 : 2 Rep	H	Derby County	W	2-1	25,166		Keen, Slater
39	Feb 10	Sat	Div 2	H	Brighton & Hove Albion	W	3-1	19,101	11	Quinn 2, Dicks
40	Feb 14	Wed	FLC SF:1	A	Oldham Athletic	L	0-6	19,263		
41	Feb 18	Sun	Div 2	A	Swindon Town	D	2-2	14,993	12	Quinn 2
42	Feb 24	Sat	Div 2	H	Blackburn Rovers	D	1-1	20,054	14	Quinn
43	Mar 3	Sat	Div 2	A	Middlesbrough	W	1-0	23,617	10	Allen
44	Mar 7	Wed	FLC SF:2	H	Oldham Athletic	W	3-0	15,431		Dicks [pen], Kelly, Martin
45	Mar 10	Sat	Div 2	H	Portsmouth	W	2-1	20,961	10	Allen, Dicks [pen]
46	Mar 13	Tue	Div 2	A	Watford	W	1-0	15,682	9	Morley
47	Mar 17	Sat	Div 2	A	Leeds United	L	2-3	40,494	10	Morley, Chapman (og)
48	Mar 21	Wed	Div 2	H	Sheffield United	W	5-0	21,629	9	Quinn 3 [1 pen], Allen, Morley
49	Mar 24	Sat	Div 2	A	Sunderland	L	3-4	13,925	10	Quinn 2, Morley
50	Mar 31	Sat	Div 2	H	Port Vale	D	2-2	20,507	10	Gale, Morley
51	Apr 4	Wed	Div 2	A	West Bromwich Albion	W	3-1	11,556	9	Bishop, Keen, Quinn
52	Apr 7	Sat	Div 2	A	Oxford United	W	2-0	8,369	8	Morley, Quinn
53	Apr 11	Wed	Div 2	H	AFC Bournemouth	W	4-1	20,202	8	Allen, Bishop, Dcks [pen], Miller (og)
54	Apr 14	Sat	Div 2	A	Barnsley	D	1-1	10,344	7	Morley
55	Apr 17	Tue	Div 2	A	Ipswich Town	W	2-0	25,178	7	Allen, Keen
56	Apr 21	Sat	Div 2	A	Oldham Athletic	L	0-3	12,170	7	
57	Apr 28	Sat	Div 2	A	Newcastle United	L	1-2	31,461	7	Dicks [pen]
58	May 2	Wed	Div 2	H	Leicester City	W	3-1	17,939	7	Keen, Morley, Rosenior
59	May 5	Sat	Div 2	H	Wolverhampton Wanderers	W	4-0	22,509	7	Brady, Keen, Morley, Robson

*ZDSC = Zenith Data Systems Cup

Team Line-Ups

ALLEN Martin	BISHOP Ian	BRADY Liam	DEVONSHIRE Alan	DICKS Julian	DOLAN Eamonn	FASHANU Justin	FOSTER Colin	GALE Tony	INCE Paul	KEEN Kevin	KELLY David	KELLY Paul	MARTIN Alvin	McAVENNIE Frank	McQUEEN Tommy	MIKLOSKO Ludek	MILNE Ralph	MORLEY Trevor	PARKES Phil	PARRIS George	POTTS Steve	QUINN Jimmy	ROBSON Stewart	ROSENIOR Leroy	SLATER Stuart	STRODDER Gary	SUCKLING Perry	WARD Mark	No.
		10						4	11	6	a		5	8/a					1	3	2				9			7	1
		10		3				4		6	8		5						1	11	2				9			7	2
9		10		3				4		6	8		5						1	11	2							7	3
9		10/a	a	3				4		6	8		5						1		2				11			7	4
9		10/a	a	3	b			4		6	8/b		5						1	11	2							7	5
9		10		3				4		6			5						1	11	2				8			7	6
9		a		3	10			4		6			5						1	11	2				8			7/a	7
7				3	9/a		10	4		6			5						1	11	2			a	8				8
7				3			10	4		6			5						1	11	2		9		8				9
7				3	a		10	4		6	9/a		5						1	11	2				8				10
7		b		3	9/a			4		6	a		5						1	11	2				8			10/b	11
7		a		3				4/a	10	6			5						1	11	2				8			9	12
				3			9		10	6			5						1	11	2				8	4		7	13
10		a		3/a			9			6			5						1	11	2				8	4		7	14
10				3			9			6			5						1	11	2				8	4		7	15
10		7/a		3			9			6	a		5						1	11	2				8	4			16
10		7		3			9			6			5						1	11	2				8	4			17
10		7		3			9			6/a			5						1	11	2				8	4		a	18
10		7		3			9/a	a		6/b			5						1	11	2				8	4		b	19
		7/a	a	3			9/b			6	b		5						1	11	2				8	4		10	20
		7		3			9			6			5						1	11	2				8	4		10	21
9		7		3				4		6			5						1	11	2				8			10	22
9		7	b	3	a					6/a			5						1	11/b	2				8	4		10	23
9		7	6	3		11							5						1		2				8	4		10	24
9		7		3	a	b				6	11/a		5						1		2				8	4		10/b	25
		7	6/a	3	11/b	a	9	b					5						1		2				8	4		10	26
11		7					9			6			5		3				1		2				8	4		10	27
11		7	a	3			9/a			6	b		5								2				8	4/b	1	10	28
11		7/a		3			9			6	a		5						1		2				8	4		10	29
10		7/a		3			9			6	b									a	2				8/b	4	1	10	30
7	8			3				6			10		5			9				11	2	7				4	1		31
11	8			3				6			9/a		5			10				4	2	7					1		32
11	8			3				9					5			10	1		4/a	2	7		a					33
	8	6/a	a	3									5			10			b	2	11	9/a	a			1		34
10		7		3				6					5				11	1	4	2			9/a	a				35
	8	7						6	11	b	a		5		3			10	2/a	9				4/b		1		36
		7/b	a					6	11	8			5		3	1	b		4			10/a	9	2				37
	8	7		3				6	11	8			5		a	1			4	2/a		10	9	2				38
8		7		3				6	11	9			5			1		4/a	a	2			10					39
		7	a	3				6	11	10			5			1		4	2			8	9/a					40
a		7		3				6	11/b				5			1		4	9	2			10/a					41
a		7/a		3				6	11	b			5			1		4	9	2/b			10					42
a		7/a		3				6	11				5			1	b		4	9/b			10					43
		7/a		3				6	11	10			5		a	1			4			9	2					44
b		7/a		3			5	6	10	11						1			4			a	9/b	2				45
		7		3			5	6	10							1	11		4			a	9/b	2				46
	7	a					5	6	10						3	1	11		4/a			9	2					47
	7						5	6	10						3	1	11		4			9	2					48
	7	a					5	6	10/a						3	1	11		4			9	2	5				49
	7	a		3			5	6	10/a	b						1			4	9/b			2					50
	7			3			5	6	10							1	11		4			9	2	5				51
	7			3			5	6	10/a	a						1	11		4			9	2					52
	11			3			5	6	10					a		1	11/a		4	b	b	9	2					53
	11			3			5	6	7							1	10		4			9	2					54
	7/b			3			5	6	10							1	11/a		4	b		9	2					55
	7			3			5	6	10							1	11/a		4			9	2					56
				3			5	6	10					a		1	11/b		b	4		9/a	2	7				57
		a		3			5	6	10/a							1	11			4		b	2	7	9			58
		a		3			5	6	10/a							1	11/b			4		b	2	7	9			59

1990-91
Story of the season

The Hammers were one of **the fanced teams for promotion** and by the end of September, after 1-1 draws at Newcastle and Sheffield Wednesday, they found themselves **unbeaten and in fourth place.**

Stoke City were beaten 5–1 on aggregate in the League Cup while in the league Hull City were thrashed 7–1 at home. In a stubborn defence, Colin Foster and Alvin Martin were proving to be a formidable partnership, and behind them goalkeeper Ludek Miklosko was in fine form. A late goal at Oxford United saw the Hammers beaten 1– in the League Cup.

Bad news came when skipper Julian Dicks was injured and ruled out for the season. By mid-December West Ham were league leaders and there were new signings with full backs Tim Breacker and Chris Hughton signing. A run o

Appearances & Goals 1990-91

	League			FA Cup			League Cup			Other*			Total		
	Starts	Subs	Goals	Starts	Subs	Goals	Starts	Subs	Goals	Starts	Subs	Goals	Starts	Subs	Goals
ALLEN Martin	28	12	3	2	0	0	3	0	2	1	0	0	34	12	
BISHOP Ian	40	0	4	5	1	2	3	0	0	0	0	0	48	1	
BREACKER Tim	23	1	1	6	0	0	0	0	0	0	0	0	29	1	
CARR Franz	1	2	0	0	0	0	0	0	0	0	0	0	1	2	
CLARKE Simon	0	1	0	0	0	0	0	0	0	0	0	0	0	1	
DICKS Julian	13	0	4	0	0	0	2	0	1	0	0	0	15	0	
DOWIE Iain	12	0	4	0	0	0	0	0	0	0	0	0	12	0	
FOSTER Colin	36	0	3	3	0	1	3	0	0	0	0	0	42	0	
GALE Tony	23	1	1	7	0	0	0	1	0	1	0	0	31	2	
HUGHTON Chris	32	0	0	7	0	0	0	0	0	0	0	0	39	0	
KEEN Kevin	36	4	0	6	1	0	3	0	1	1	0	1	46	5	
KELLY Paul	0	0	0	0	0	0	0	0	0	1	0	0	1	0	
LIVETT Simon	1	0	0	0	1	0	0	0	0	1	0	0	2	1	
MARTIN Alvin	20	0	1	0	0	0	3	0	0	0	0	0	23	0	
McAVENNIE Frank	24	10	10	3	1	1	0	1	0	0	0	0	27	12	1
McKNIGHT Allen	0	0	0	0	0	0	0	0	0	1	0	0	1	0	
MIKLOSKO Ludek	46	0	0	7	0	0	3	0	0	0	0	0	56	0	
MORLEY Trevor	38	0	12	6	0	4	3	0	1	1	0	0	48	0	1
PARRIS George	37	7	5	7	0	3	2	1	0	1	0	0	47	8	
POTTS Steve	36	1	1	7	0	0	2	0	0	1	0	0	46	1	
QUINN Jimmy	16	10	6	3	2	2	3	0	1	1	0	0	23	12	
ROBSON Stewart	0	1	0	1	0	0	0	0	0	0	0	0	1	1	
ROSENIOR Leroy	0	2	0	0	0	0	0	0	0	0	0	0	0	2	
RUSH Matthew	2	3	0	0	0	0	1	0	0	0	0	0	3	3	
SLATER Stuart	37	3	3	7	0	2	2	0	0	1	0	0	47	3	
STEWART Ray	5	0	0	0	1	0	0	0	0	0	0	0	5	1	
own goal			2												
Totals	**506**	**58**	**60**	**77**	**7**	**15**	**33**	**3**	**6**	**11**	**0**	**1**	**627**	**68**	

*Other = Zenith Data Systems Cup

1 undefeated league games came to an end following the –0 loss at Barnsley.

The FA Cup saw Fourth Division Aldershot force a replay, in which two goals from Trevor Morley helped the Hammers to a 6–1 victory. Morley scored two more in the next round as Luton Town were beaten 5–0 at the Boleyn Ground. During February rivals Millwall were beaten 3–1 in the league while in the FA Cup Crewe Alexandra were narrowly beaten 1–0 at home. March brought four league games without a win but there were joyous scenes at Upton Park as the Hammers marched into the FA Cup semi-final after beating Everton 2–1. The semi-final at Villa Park brought disappointment as 10-man Hammers were beaten –0 by Nottingham Forest after Tony Gale had been dismissed early in the game. The final home game proved to

be an anticlimax as West Ham lost 2–1 at home to Notts County, but at the final whistle news broke that Oldham had drawn, which meant West Ham were champions. As thousands celebrated on the pitch it was learned that Oldham had in fact scored from an injury-time penalty; the news was greeted with stunned silence. Still, it was no small consolation that by finishing second in the league the Hammers were promoted to the top flight.

TREVOR MORLEY

A bustling striker and target man who relished a physical battle, Morley began his soccer career with non-league Nuneaton Borough, where he won a Southern League Championship medal in 1982.

He then signed for Northampton Town in the summer of 1985 and helped the Cobblers win the Fourth Division title in 1986/87. After scoring 39 league goals in 107 appearances he joined Manchester City for a fee of £175,000 in January 1988. In three seasons at Maine Road he had 72 league outings, scoring 18 goals.

In December 1989 he was involved in a swap deal when along with Ian Bishop he joined West Ham, with Mark Ward joining City.

Morley's goals played a big part in the Hammers promotion campaigns in 1991 and 1993, where he was the top scorer. After an injury-plagued campaign in season 1994/95 he left to join Reading on a free transfer.

He had been a popular figure at Upton Park, scoring 69 goals in his 208 appearances. In his third game for the Royals he suffered a fractured skull at Portsmouth and had to have six steel plates inserted in his head. After a long lay-off he bravely returned until 1998, when he went to live in Norway.

Barclays League - Division Two
Final Table 1990-91

	P	HOME					AWAY					Pts
		W	D	L	F	A	W	D	L	F	A	
Oldham Athletic	46	17	5	1	55	21	8	8	7	28	32	88
West Ham United	46	15	6	2	41	18	9	9	5	19	16	87
Sheffield Wednesday	46	12	10	1	43	23	10	6	7	37	28	82
Notts County	46	14	4	5	45	28	9	7	7	31	27	80
Millwall	46	11	6	6	43	28	9	7	7	27	23	73
Brighton and Hove Albion	46	12	4	7	37	31	9	3	11	26	38	70
Middlesbrough	46	12	4	7	36	17	8	5	10	30	30	69
Barnsley	46	13	7	3	39	16	6	5	12	24	32	69
Bristol City	46	14	5	4	44	28	6	2	15	24	43	67
Oxford United	46	10	9	4	41	29	4	10	9	28	37	61
Newcastle United	46	8	10	5	24	22	6	7	10	25	34	59
Wolverhampton Wanderers	46	11	6	6	45	35	2	13	8	18	28	58
Bristol Rovers	46	11	7	5	29	20	4	6	13	27	39	58
Ipswich Town	46	9	8	6	32	28	4	10	9	28	40	57
Port Vale	46	10	4	9	32	24	5	8	10	24	40	57
Charlton Athletic	46	8	7	8	27	25	5	10	8	30	36	56
Portsmouth	46	10	6	7	34	27	4	5	14	24	43	53
Plymouth Argyle	46	10	10	3	36	20	2	7	14	18	48	53
Blackburn Rovers	46	8	6	9	26	27	6	4	13	25	39	52
Watford	46	5	8	10	24	32	7	7	9	21	27	51
Swindon Town	46	8	6	9	31	30	4	8	11	34	43	50
Leicester City	46	12	4	7	41	33	2	4	17	19	50	50
West Bromwich Albion	46	7	11	5	26	21	3	7	13	26	40	48
Hull City	46	6	10	7	35	32	4	5	14	22	53	45

Season **1990-91** Barclays League - Division Two
Match Details

Manager **Billy Bonds**   Final League Position **2/24 Promoted to League Division One**

	Date		Competition	Venue	Opponents	Results		Attendance	Position	Scorers
1	Aug 25	Sat	Div 2	A	Middlesbrough	D	0-0	20,680	14	
2	Aug 29	Wed	Div 2	H	Portsmouth	D	1-1	20,835	14	McAvennie
3	Sep 1	Sat	Div 2	H	Watford	W	1-0	19,872	7	Dicks [pen]
4	Sep 8	Sat	Div 2	A	Leicester City	W	2-1	14,605	4	Morley, James (og)
5	Sep 15	Sat	Div 2	H	Wolverhampton Wanderers	D	1-1	23,241	6	Martin
6	Sep 19	Wed	Div 2	H	Ipswich Town	W	3-1	18,764	3	Bishop, Morley, Quinn
7	Sep 22	Sat	Div 2	A	Newcastle United	D	1-1	25,462	3	Morley
8	Sep 26	Wed	FLC 2:1	H	Stoke City	W	3-0	15,870		Dicks [pen], Keen, Quinn
9	Sep 29	Sat	Div 2	A	Sheffield Wednesday	D	1-1	28,786	4	Dicks
10	Oct 3	Wed	Div 2	H	Oxford United	W	2-0	18,125	4	Foster, Morley
11	Oct 6	Sat	Div 2	H	Hull City	W	7-1	19,472	3	Dicks 2 [1 pen], Quinn 2, Morley, Parris, Potts
12	Oct 10	Wed	FLC 2:2	A	Stoke City	W	2-1	8,411		Allen 2
13	Oct 13	Sat	Div 2	A	Bristol City	D	1-1	16,838	3	McAvennie
14	Oct 20	Sat	Div 2	A	Swindon Town	W	1-0	13,658	3	McAvennie
15	Oct 24	Wed	Div 2	H	Blackburn Rovers	W	1-0	20,003	3	Bishop
16	Oct 27	Sat	Div 2	H	Charlton Athletic	W	2-1	24,019	2	Allen 2
17	Oct 31	Wed	FLC 3	A	Oxford United	L	1-2	7,528		Morley
18	Nov 3	Sat	Div 2	A	Notts County	W	1-0	10,781	2	Morley
19	Nov 10	Sat	Div 2	A	Millwall	D	1-1	20,591	2	McAvennie
20	Nov 17	Sat	Div 2	H	Brighton & Hove Albion	W	2-1	23,082	2	Foster, Slater
21	Nov 24	Sat	Div 2	A	Plymouth Argyle	W	1-0	11,490	1	McAvennie
22	Dec 1	Sat	Div 2	H	West Bromwich Albion	W	3-1	24,753	1	McAvennie, Morley, Parris
23	Dec 8	Sat	Div 2	A	Portsmouth	W	1-0	12,045	1	Morley
24	Dec 15	Sat	Div 2	H	Middlesbrough	D	0-0	23,705	1	
25	Dec 19	Wed	ZDSC 2*	A	Luton Town	L	1-5	5,759		Keen
26	Dec 22	Sat	Div 2	A	Barnsley	L	0-1	10,348	2	
27	Dec 26	Wed	Div 2	H	Oldham Athletic	W	2-0	24,950	1	Morley, Slater
28	Dec 29	Sat	Div 2	H	Port Vale	D	0-0	23,603	1	
29	Jan 1	Tue	Div 2	A	Bristol Rovers	W	1-0	7,932	1	Quinn
30	Jan 5	Sat	FAC 3**	A	Aldershot	D	0-0	22,929		
31	Jan 12	Sat	Div 2	A	Watford	W	1-0	17,172	1	Morley
32	Jan 16	Wed	FAC 3 Rep	H	Aldershot	W	6-1	21,484		Morley 2, Bishop, Parris, Quinn, Slater
33	Jan 19	Sat	Div 2	H	Leicester City	W	1-0	21,652	1	Parris
34	Jan 26	Sat	FAC 4	A	Luton Town	D	1-1	12,087		Parris
35	Jan 30	Wed	FAC 4 Rep	H	Luton Town	W	5-0	25,659		Morley 2, Bishop, McAvennie, Parris
36	Feb 2	Sat	Div 2	A	Wolverhampton Wanderers	L	1-2	19,454	1	McAvennie
37	Feb 16	Sat	FAC 5	H	Crewe Alexandra	W	1-0	25,298		Quinn
38	Feb 24	Sun	Div 2	H	Millwall	W	3-1	20,503	1	McAvennie 2, Morley
39	Mar 2	Sat	Div 2	A	West Bromwich Albion	D	0-0	16,089	1	
40	Mar 5	Tue	Div 2	H	Plymouth Argyle	D	2-2	18,933	1	Breacker, Marker (og)
41	Mar 11	Mon	FAC QF	H	Everton	W	2-1	28,162		Foster, Slater
42	Mar 13	Wed	Div 2	A	Oxford United	L	1-2	8,225	2	Quinn
43	Mar 16	Sat	Div 2	H	Sheffield Wednesday	L	1-3	26,182	2	Quinn
44	Mar 20	Wed	Div 2	H	Bristol City	W	1-0	22,951	2	Gale
45	Mar 23	Sat	Div 2	A	Hull City	D	0-0	9,558	2	
46	Mar 29	Fri	Div 2	A	Oldham Athletic	D	1-1	16,932	2	Bishop [pen]
47	Apr 1	Mon	Div 2	H	Barnsley	W	3-2	24,607	2	Dowie, Foster, McAvennie
48	Apr 6	Sat	Div 2	A	Port Vale	W	1-0	9,658	1	Bishop
49	Apr 10	Wed	Div 2	A	Brighton & Hove Albion	L	0-1	11,904	1	
50	Apr 14	Sun	FAC SF	N***	Nottingham Forest	L	0-4	40,041		
51	Apr 17	Wed	Div 2	A	Ipswich Town	W	1-0	20,451	1	Morley
52	Apr 20	Sat	Div 2	H	Swindon Town	W	2-0	26,109	1	Dowie, Parris
53	Apr 24	Wed	Div 2	H	Newcastle United	D	1-1	24,195	1	Dowie
54	Apr 27	Sat	Div 2	A	Blackburn Rovers	L	1-3	10,808	1	Dowie
55	May 4	Sat	Div 2	A	Charlton Athletic	D	1-1	16,139	1	Allen
56	May 8	Wed	Div 2	H	Bristol Rovers	W	1-0	23,054	1	Slater
57	May 11	Sat	Div 2	H	Notts County	L	1-2	26,551	2	Parris

*ZDSC = Zenith Data Systems Cup ** Away Cup-tie switched to Upton Park for safety reasons *** Villa Park, Birmingham

Team Line-Ups

ALLEN Martin	BISHOP Ian	BREACKER Tim	CARR Franz	CLARKE Simon	DICKS Julian	DOWIE Iain	FOSTER Colin	GALE Tony	HUGHTON Chris	KEEN Kevin	KELLY Paul	LIVETT Simon	MARTIN Alvin	McAVENNIE Frank	McKNIGHT Allen	MIKLOSKO Ludek	MORLEY Trevor	PARRIS George	POTTS Steve	QUINN Jimmy	ROBSON Stewart	ROSENIOR Leroy	RUSH Matthew	SLATER Stuart	STEWART Ray	
10	7				3		4			6			5	8		1	11		2					9		1
10	7				3		4			6			5	8		1	11		2					9		2
10/b	7				3		4			6			5	8		1	11/a	b	2	a				9		3
10	7				3		4			6			5	8/a		1	11	b	2	a				9/b		4
10	7				3		4			6		9/a	5	8		1	11	a	2							5
10	7				3		4			6			5	8/a		1	11	b	2/b					9		6
10/a	7				3		4			6			5			1	11	a	2	8/a				9/b		7
10	7				3		4			6			5			1	11	a	2	8				9		8
10	7				3		4			6			5/b	a		1	11	b	2	8/a				9		9
10	7				3		4			6			5			1	11	a	2	8				9/a		10
10	7				3		4			6/a			5	a		1	11	9	2	8/b			b			11
10	7				3		4		a	6/a			5	b		1	11	8	2	9/b						12
10	7				3		4						5	a		1	11	6	2	8				9/a		13
10	7	b			3/b		4	9					5	a		1	11	6	2	8/a						14
10	7	2			3/b		4	9					5	a		1	11	6		8/a				b		15
10	7	2					4		3				5	8		1	11	6					a	9/a		16
10	7						4		3				5			1	11	6		8			2	9		17
10	7	2					4		6	8			5			1	11	3						9		18
10/a	7	2					4		6	8			5	9		1	11	3					a			19
	7	2					4		6	10			5	8		1	11	3					9/a	a		20
	7	2					4		6	10			5	8		1	11	3						9		21
a	7	2					4		6	10/a			5	8		1	11	3						9		22
10	7	2					4		b	6			5/b	8/a		1	11	3		a				9		23
10		2							4	6		7		8		1	11/a	3	5	a				9		24
									4	10	2	6			1		11	3	5	8				9		25
10									4	6		7		8/a		1	11	3	5	a				9		26
10		2						5	4	6		7				1	11	3		8				9		27
10/a		2						5	4	6		7				1	11	3	a	8				9		28
		2						5	4	6		7				1	11	3	8	9				10		29
		2						5/a	4	6		7		a		1	11	3	10	9				8		30
		2	a					5/b	4	6		7				1	11	3	10	9/a	b			8		31
a		2							4	6		7				1	11	3	10	9		5/a		8		32
	5	2							4	6		7		a		1	11	3	10	9/a				8		33
	5	2							4	6		7/a		a		1	11	3	10					8		34
	5	2							4	6		7		8		1	11	3	10					9		35
	5	2							4	6		7		8		1	11	3/b	10				a	9/a		36
	5	2							4	6		7		8/a		1	11	3	10				a	9		37
	5	2							4/a	6		7		8		1	11	3	10					9		38
	5	2							4	6		7/a		8		1	11	3	10					9		39
	5	2							4	6/a		7		8		1		3	10	11				9		40
	7	2						5	4	6		a		8		1		3	10	11/a				9		41
	7	2/a	9/b					5	4	6				8		1		3	10	11				a		42
	7		b					5	4	6/a		10		8		1		3	2	11/b				9		43
	7							5	4	6		10		8		1		3	2	11/b		b		9/a		44
11	7		b			9		5	4	6		10/b		8/a		1		3	2			a				45
11	7					9		5	4	6						1	11	3	2					10		46
11	7					9		5	4	6/a		a				1	11	3	2					10		47
11	7					9		5	4	6						1	11	3	2					8		48
	7					9/a		5		6/b				8		1	11	3	2	a				11	4	49
10/a	7							5	4	6		10				1	11/b	3	2	b				8	a	50
a	7					9/a		5/b	4	6		10		a		1	11	3	2					8		51
	7					9		5	4	6		10/a				1	11	3	2					8	5	52
	7					9		5	4	6		10				1	11	3	2					8	5/a	53
	7					9		5	4	6				8		1	11/b	3	2	b				10/a	5	54
	7	4				9/a				6						1	11	3	2	a				10	5	55
10/a	7	2				9/b		5		6		b		a		1	11	3	4					8		56
10/a	7	4				9/a		5		6/b		b		a		1	11	3	2					8		57

1991-92
Story of the season

Manager Billy Bonds was given **restricted spending money** and was only able to **pay small fees** for defender Mitchell Thomas, full-back Kenny Brown and striker Mike Small.

On the evidence of the goalless draw with Luton Tow on the opening day it seemed likely that it was going to b a difficult campaign. By the end of September only tw league wins had been recorded, but it was encouraging th. Mike Small had scored seven goals.

Bradford City were beaten 5–1 on aggregate in the Leagu Cup and during October and early November fortune changed, with successive wins against Tottenham an Arsenal and a 2–0 away victory in the League Cup again Sheffield United. A slump in December, however, brough defeats at Everton, Aston Villa and Notts County, and last-minute penalty gave Norwich City a 2–1 win in th League Cup.

Appearances & Goals 1991-92

	League			FA Cup			League Cup			Other*			Total	
	Starts	Subs	Goals	Starts	Subs	Goals	Starts	Subs	Goals	Starts	Subs	Goals	Starts	Subs
ALLEN Clive	4	0	1	0	0	0	0	0	0	0	0	0	4	0
ALLEN Martin	14	5	0	2	0	2	1	1	0	1	0	0	18	6
ATTEVELD Ray	1	0	0	2	0	0	0	0	0	0	0	0	3	0
BISHOP Ian	41	0	1	3	0	0	4	0	0	3	0	1	51	0
BREACKER Tim	33	1	2	6	0	0	4	0	0	3	0	0	46	1
BROWN Kenny	25	2	3	4	0	0	1	0	0	1	0	0	31	2
CLARKE Simon	0	1	0	0	0	0	0	0	0	0	0	0	0	1
DICKS Julian	23	0	3	6	0	2	0	0	0	1	0	0	30	0
FOSTER Colin	24	0	0	5	0	1	2	0	0	1	0	0	32	0
GALE Tony	24	1	0	2	0	0	3	1	0	3	0	0	32	2
HUGHTON Chris	0	1	0	0	0	0	0	0	0	1	0	0	1	1
KEEN Kevin	20	9	0	5	0	0	2	0	1	3	0	0	30	9
MARTIN Alvin	7	0	0	0	0	0	0	0	0	0	0	0	7	0
MARTIN Dean	1	1	0	0	1	0	0	0	0	0	0	0	1	2
McAVENNIE Frank	16	4	6	4	0	0	2	1	1	3	0	3	25	5
MIKLOSKO Ludek	36	0	0	3	0	0	4	0	0	3	0	0	46	0
MORLEY Trevor	13	11	2	2	3	2	2	0	1	0	1	0	17	15
PARKS Tony	6	0	0	3	0	0	0	0	0	0	0	0	9	0
PARRIS George	20	1	0	0	0	0	4	0	1	2	0	1	26	1
POTTS Steve	34	0	0	5	0	0	3	0	0	2	0	0	44	0
ROSENIOR Leroy	5	4	1	0	0	0	0	0	0	0	0	0	5	4
RUSH Matthew	3	7	2	0	0	0	0	0	0	0	0	0	3	7
SLATER Stuart	41	0	0	6	0	0	4	0	0	2	0	0	53	0
SMALL Mike	37	3	13	4	1	1	4	0	4	2	0	0	47	4
THOMAS Mitchell	34	1	3	4	0	0	4	0	0	2	0	0	44	1
Totals	**462**	**52**	**37**	**66**	**5**	**8**	**44**	**3**	**8**	**33**	**1**	**5**	**605**	**61**

*Other = Zenith Data Systems Cup

the New Year the Hammers struggled in the FA Cup but
managed to knock out non-league Farnborough Town and
ourth Division Wrexham, both in replays. League form
mproved with successive 1–0 victories over Luton and
Oldham, but the Hammers went out of the FA Cup
ollowing a 3–2 home defeat by Sunderland. The team
lumped to the bottom of the league in March after going
our games without a goal. Striker Clive Allen was bought
rom Chelsea but arrived too late in the campaign to make
n impact. Despite beating Norwich City 4–0 and
Manchester United 1–0 there was no escape, and the
Hammers were relegated. The final home game against
Nottingham Forest saw Frank McAvennie make his last
ppearance for the club and he responded with a hat-trick
n the 3–0 victory.

uring the season, to finance ground improvements a
ond scheme was introduced to the anger of the supporters.

There were ugly scenes and protests during games, which
did not help matters on the pitch. In hindsight it was a bad
scheme, and the rift between supporters and the club took
years to heal.

MITCHELL THOMAS

The full-back started his career with Luton Town in 1982 and made his first-team debut in January 1983 at Upton Park against West Ham.

He spent four seasons with the Hatters, playing in 107 league games, and while there he was capped three times for England at under-21 level. In 1986 he moved on to Tottenham Hotspur and played for them in the 1987 FA Cup final where they lost to Coventry City.

After 157 league games for the Spurs he signed for West Ham in August 1991 for £500,000. His debut came against his old club Luton in a 0–0 draw on the opening day of the season. He had been bought to replace the injured Julian Dicks but when Dicks returned he lost his place in the side. He only played in 47 games for the Hammers before being transferred back to Luton in November 1993. He played a further 185 games for his home-town club before ending his playing career at Burnley, where he made 112 league and cup appearances for the Clarets before his retirement in 2002.

Barclays League - Division One Final Table 1991-92

		HOME					AWAY					
	P	W	D	L	F	A	W	D	L	F	A	Pts
Leeds United	42	13	8	0	38	13	9	8	4	36	24	82
Manchester United	42	12	7	2	34	13	9	8	4	29	20	78
Sheffield Wednesday	42	13	5	3	39	24	8	7	6	23	25	75
Arsenal	42	12	7	2	51	23	7	8	6	30	24	72
Manchester City	42	13	4	4	32	14	7	6	8	29	34	70
Liverpool	42	13	5	3	34	17	3	11	7	13	23	64
Aston Villa	42	13	3	5	31	16	4	6	11	17	28	60
Nottingham Forest	42	10	7	4	36	27	6	4	11	24	31	59
Sheffield United	42	9	6	6	29	23	7	3	11	36	40	57
Crystal Palace	42	7	8	6	24	25	7	7	7	29	36	57
Queens Park Rangers	42	6	10	5	25	21	6	8	7	23	26	54
Everton	42	8	8	5	28	19	5	6	10	24	32	53
Wimbledon	42	10	5	6	32	20	3	9	9	21	33	53
Chelsea	42	7	8	6	31	30	6	6	9	19	30	53
Tottenham Hotspur	42	7	3	11	33	35	8	4	9	25	28	52
Southampton	42	7	5	9	17	28	7	5	9	22	27	52
Oldham Athletic	42	11	5	5	46	36	3	4	14	17	31	51
Norwich City	42	8	6	7	29	28	3	6	12	18	35	45
Coventry City	42	6	7	8	18	15	5	4	12	17	29	44
Luton Town	42	10	7	4	25	17	0	5	16	14	54	42
Notts County	42	7	5	9	24	29	3	5	13	16	33	40
West Ham United	42	6	6	9	22	24	3	5	13	15	35	38

Season **1991-92** Barclays League - Division One
Match Details

Manager **Billy Bonds**   Final League Position **22/22**   **Relegated to League Division 1 (Formerly League Division**

	Date		Competition	Venue	Opponents	Results		Attendance	Position	Scorers
1	Aug 17	Sat	Div 1	H	Luton Town	D	0-0	25,079	14	
2	Aug 20	Tue	Div 1	A	Sheffield United	D	1-1	21,473	11	Small
3	Aug 24	Sat	Div 1	A	Wimbledon	L	0-2	10,081	18	
4	Aug 28	Wed	Div 1	H	Aston Villa	W	3-1	23,644	10	Brown, Rosenior, Small
5	Aug 31	Sat	Div 1	H	Notts County	L	0-2	20,093	16	
6	Sep 4	Wed	Div 1	A	Queens Park Rangers	D	0-0	16,616	17	
7	Sep 7	Sat	Div 1	H	Chelsea	D	1-1	18,897	17	Small
8	Sep 14	Sat	Div 1	A	Norwich City	L	1-2	15,348	18	Small
9	Sep 17	Tue	Div 1	A	Crystal Palace	W	3-2	21,363	16	Morley, Small, Thomas
10	Sep 21	Sat	Div 1	H	Manchester City	L	1-2	25,678	18	Brown
11	Sep 24	Tue	FLC 2:1	A	Bradford City	D	1-1	7,034		Small
12	Sep 28	Sat	Div 1	A	Nottingham Forest	D	2-2	25,613	18	Small 2 [1 pen]
13	Oct 5	Sat	Div 1	H	Coventry City	L	0-1	21,817	18	
14	Oct 9	Wed	FLC 2:2	H	Bradford City	W	4-0	17,232		Keen, Morley, Parris, Small
15	Oct 19	Sat	Div 1	A	Oldham Athletic	D	2-2	14,365	18	McAvennie, Small
16	Oct 22	Tue	ZDSC 2*	H	Cambridge United	W	2-1	7,812		Parris, McAvennie
17	Oct 26	Sat	Div 1	H	Tottenham Hotspur	W	2-1	23,990	17	Small, Thomas
18	Oct 29	Tue	FLC 3	A	Sheffield United	W	2-0	11,144		McAvennie, Small [pen]
19	Nov 2	Sat	Div 1	A	Arsenal	W	1-0	33,539	14	Small
20	Nov 17	Sun	Div 1	H	Liverpool	D	0-0	23,569	15	
21	Nov 23	Sat	Div 1	A	Manchester United	L	1-2	47,185	17	McAvennie
22	Nov 26	Tue	ZDSC 3	H	Brighton & Hove Albion	W	2-0	8,146		McAvennie 2
23	Nov 30	Sat	Div 1	H	Sheffield Wednesday	L	1-2	24,116	17	Breacker
24	Dec 4	Wed	FLC 4	A	Norwich City	L	1-2	16,325		Small
25	Dec 7	Sat	Div 1	A	Everton	L	0-4	21,513	18	
26	Dec 21	Sat	Div 1	H	Sheffield United	D	1-1	19,287	18	Dicks [pen]
27	Dec 26	Thur	Div 1	A	Aston Villa	L	1-3	31,959	19	McAvennie
28	Dec 28	Sat	Div 1	A	Notts County	L	0-3	11,128	21	
29	Jan 1	Wed	Div 1	H	Leeds United	L	1-3	21,766	21	Dicks [pen]
30	Jan 4	Sat	FAC 3**	A	Farnborough Town	D	1-1	23,449		Dicks
31	Jan 7	Tue	ZDSC SF	A	Southampton	L	1-2	6,861		Bishop
32	Jan 11	Sat	Div 1	H	Wimbledon	D	1-1	18,485	21	Morley
33	Jan 14	Tue	FAC 3 Rep	H	Farnborough Town	W	1-0	23,869		Morley
34	Jan 18	Sat	Div 1	A	Luton Town	W	1-0	11,088	20	Small
35	Jan 25	Sat	FAC 4	H	Wrexham	D	2-2	24,712		Dicks, Morley
36	Feb 1	Sat	Div 1	H	Oldham Athletic	W	1-0	19,012	20	Thomas
37	Feb 4	Tue	FAC 4 Rep	A	Wrexham	W	1-0	17,995		Foster
38	Feb 15	Sat	FAC 5	A	Sunderland	D	1-1	25,475		Small
39	Feb 22	Sat	Div 1	A	Sheffield Wednesday	L	1-2	26,150	21	Small
40	Feb 26	Wed	FAC 5 Rep	H	Sunderland	L	2-3	25,830		Allen 2
41	Feb 29	Sat	Div 1	H	Everton	L	0-2	20,976	21	
42	Mar 3	Tue	Div 1	A	Southampton	L	0-1	12,883	22	
43	Mar 11	Wed	Div 1	A	Liverpool	L	0-1	30,821	22	
44	Mar 14	Sat	Div 1	H	Arsenal	L	0-2	22,650	22	
45	Mar 21	Sat	Div 1	H	Queens Park Rangers	L	2-2	21,401	22	Breacker, Small
46	Mar 28	Sat	Div 1	A	Leeds United	D	0-0	31,101	22	
47	Apr 1	Wed	Div 1	A	Tottenham Hotspur	L	0-3	31,809	22	
48	Apr 4	Sat	Div 1	A	Chelsea	L	1-2	20,684	22	Allen C.
49	Apr 11	Sat	Div 1	H	Norwich City	W	4-0	16,896	22	Rush 2, Bishop, Dicks [pen]
50	Apr 14	Tue	Div 1	H	Southampton	L	0-1	18,298	22	
51	Apr 18	Sat	Div 1	A	Manchester City	L	0-2	25,601	22	
52	Apr 20	Mon	Div 1	H	Crystal Palace	L	0-2	17,710	22	
53	Apr 22	Wed	Div 1	H	Manchester United	W	1-0	24,197	22	Brown
54	Apr 25	Sat	Div 1	A	Coventry City	L	0-1	15,380	22	
55	May 2	Sat	Div 1	H	Nottingham Forest	W	3-0	20,629	22	McAvennie 3

*ZDSC = Zenith Data Systems Cup   ** Away Cup-tie switched to Upton Park for safety reasons

Team Line-Ups

Allen Clive	Allen Martin	Atteveld Ray	Bishop Ian	Breacker Tim	Brown Kenny	Clarke Simon	Dicks Julian	Foster Colin	Gale Tony	Hughton Chris	Keen Kevin	Martin Alvin	Martin Dean	McAvennie Frank	Miklosko Ludek	Morley Trevor	Parks Tony	Parris George	Potts Steve	Rosenior Leroy	Rush Matthew	Slater Stuart	Small Mike	Thomas Mitchell	#
	11		7/a	4	2			5			a				1			6		10		8	9	3	1
	11/b		7	4	2			5			b				1	a		6		10/a		8	9	3	2
	11/a		7	4	2			5							1	a		6		10	b	8/b	9	3	3
	11/a		7	4	2			5							1			6		10	a	8	9	3	4
			7	4	2			5		b				a	1			6		10/a	11/b	8	9	3	5
			7	4	2			5							1	11/b		6	10	b	a	8	9/a	3	6
			7	4	2			5							1	11		6	10			8	9	3	7
			7	4	2			5							1	11/b		6/a	10	b	a	8	9	3	8
			7	6	2			5							1	11		3	10			8	9	4	9
			7	4	2			5							1	11/a		6	10	a		8	9	3	10
			7	6	2			5	a						1	11/a		3	10			8	9	4	11
			7		2			5	4						1	11		6	10			8	9/a	3	12
	a		7		2			5	4		b				1	11/b		6	10			8	9	3/a	13
			7		2			5	4		10			a	1	11		6				8/a	9	3	14
	a		7		2				4		10			b	1	11/b		6	5			8/a	9	3	15
	11		7		2				4	3	10			8	1			6	5				9		16
	a		7		2				4		10/a			8	1			6	5			11	9	3	17
	a		7		2				4/a		10			8	1			6	5			11	9	3	18
			7		2				4		10			8	1			6	5			11	9	3	19
			7		2				4		10			8	1			6	5			11	9	3	20
	a		7		2				4		10/a			8	1			6	5			11	9	3	21
			7		2				4		10			8	1			6	5			11	9	3	22
	a		7		2				4		10/a			8	1			6	5			11	9	3	23
	10		7		2				4					8	1			6	5			11	9	3	24
	10		7		2				4		a			8	1			6/a	5			11	9	3	25
	10			2			3	6	4		a			8	1				5			11	9/a		26
			7	2			3		4		10			8	1	a		6	5			11	9/a		27
			7	2			3	6	4		10			8	1				5			11	9		28
			7	2			3		4		10			8	1	a			5			11	9/a	6	29
			7	2			3		4		10			8	1	a			5/a			11	9	6	30
			7	2	9		3	5	4		10/a			8	1	a						11		6	31
			7	2	9		3	5	4		10/b			8	1	a						11	b	6/a	32
			7	2	9		3	5	4					8	1	10						11		6	33
			7	2	9		3	5			a			8/b	1	10			4			11/a	b	6	34
				2	9		3	5			7			8/a	1	10			4			11	a	6	35
				2	9		3	5			7			8		10/a	1		4			11	a	6	36
				2	9		3	5			7		a	8/a		b	1		4			11	10/b	6	37
	10	6		2			3	5			7			8			1		4			11	9		38
	10	6	7	2		a	3	5						8/a			1		4			11	9		39
	10	6/a	7	2			3	5						8		a	1		4			11	9		40
	10		7	2/b			3	5						8		a	1		4		b	11/a	9	6	41
	10		7				3	5	4/b					8		a	1		2		b	11	9	6/a	42
	10		7	2			3		4					8	1				5			11	9	6	43
	10/b		7	2			3	5	4					8/a	1	a		6				11	9		44
	10		7/a	b	2		3	5	4					8	1			6/b				11	9	a	45
	10/b		7	4	2		3	5			b			a	1				6			11/a	9	8	46
			7	6/a	2/b		3	5	4		b			a	1	10						11	9	8	47
10			7	2			3	5	4		11/a			8	1	a			6				9		48
10			7	2			3				a	5			1				4		8	11	9/a	6	49
10			7	2			3				a	5			1			6	4		8/a	11	9		50
			7	2		a	3		6			5		8	1	10			4			11	9/a		51
10			7	2		a	3					5		8	1	9			4			11		6	52
			7		10		3		4			5		8	1				2			11	9	6	53
			7/b		10/a		3		4			5	b	8	1	a			2			11	9	6	54
	8		7				3	5	4				10	a	1				2			11	9	6/a	55

1992-93
Story of the season

Despite relegation, the Hammers found themselves in Division One as the advent of the Premier League led to **the restructure of the Football League.** Yet after the opening three games they were nineteenth in the table. **September brought three good victories,** which included a 5–1 win at Bristol City, and the **partnership of Clive Allen and Trevor Morley was beginning to blossom.**

Following a 0–0 home draw in the League Cup wit[h] Crewe Alexandra there was disappointment in the replay [as] the Hammers lost 2–0. In early October the team move[d] up to second spot after beating Sunderland 6–0 and Brist[ol] Rovers 4–0, but then came a setback when losing 2–1 [at] rivals Millwall. The good league form continued with fo[ur] successive home wins and away draws at Brentford an[d] Charlton.

In the New Year there was a decent 2–0 win at Derb[y] County, but it was marred by the sending-off of Julia[n] Dicks and an injury to Alvin Martin that forced him to mis[s] the rest of the season. In the FA Cup West Bromwic[h] Albion were beaten 2–0 away but the next round saw cu[p] hopes dashed when Barnsley won 4–1 at Oakwell.

Appearances & Goals 1992-93

	League			FA Cup			League Cup			Europe			Total		
	Starts	Subs	Goals	Starts	Subs	Goals	Starts	Subs	Goals	Starts	Subs	Goals	Starts	Subs	Goals
ALLEN Clive	25	2	14	1	0	1	2	0	0	6	0	3	34	2	
ALLEN Martin	33	1	4	2	0	0	2	0	0	6	0	0	43	1	
BANKS Steven	0	0	0	0	0	0	0	0	0	1	0	0	1	0	
BISHOP Ian	15	7	1	0	0	0	0	0	0	1	1	0	16	8	
BREACKER Tim	39	0	2	2	0	0	2	0	0	4	0	0	47	0	
BROWN Kenny	13	2	2	1	0	0	0	0	0	1	2	0	15	4	
BUNBURY Alex	2	2	0	0	1	0	0	0	0	1	0	0	3	3	
BUTLER Peter	39	0	2	2	0	0	2	0	0	1	0	0	44	0	
CLARKE Simon	0	1	0	0	0	0	0	0	0	0	0	0	0	1	
DICKS Julian	34	0	11	1	0	0	1	0	0	6	0	3	42	0	
FOSTER Colin	3	3	1	1	0	0	0	0	0	0	0	0	4	3	
GALE Tony	21	2	1	0	0	0	0	0	0	1	0	0	22	2	
HOLMES Matt	6	12	1	1	0	0	0	0	0	3	0	0	10	12	
JONES Steve	4	2	2	0	0	0	0	0	0	1	1	0	5	3	
KEEN Kevin	46	0	7	2	0	0	2	0	0	5	1	0	55	1	
MARTIN Alvin	23	0	1	1	0	0	2	0	0	6	0	0	32	0	
MIKLOSKO Ludek	46	0	0	2	0	0	2	0	0	5	0	0	55	0	
MORLEY Trevor	41	0	20	2	0	1	2	0	0	4	0	1	49	0	
PARRIS George	10	6	0	0	0	0	0	0	0	2	0	0	12	6	
POTTS Steve	46	0	0	2	0	0	2	0	0	6	0	0	56	0	
ROBSON Mark	41	3	8	2	0	1	2	0	0	4	1	0	49	4	
RUSH Matthew	0	0	0	0	0	0	0	0	0	2	1	0	2	1	
SMALL Mike	5	4	0	0	0	0	0	0	0	0	1	0	5	5	
SPEEDIE David	11	0	4	0	0	0	0	0	0	0	0	0	11	0	
THOMAS Mitchell	3	0	0	0	0	0	1	0	0	0	0	0	4	0	
Totals	**506**	**47**	**81**	**22**	**1**	**3**	**22**	**0**	**0**	**66**	**8**	**7**	**616**	**56**	**9**

n 24 February the whole nation was shocked and ddened to hear of the death of Bobby Moore. To all at pton Park he was a hero and England's finest captain. efore the home game with Wolverhampton Wanderers reaths were laid around the pitch and there was a one-inute silence before the kick-off. A crowd of 24,679 had me to pay their last respects and it was fitting that West am won 3–1.

ith Clive Allen injured, the Hammers signed striker David peedie on loan from Southampton. The veteran forward bliged with two goals in the 3–0 home win over Leicester ity. Following a 3–1 win at Swindon the Hammers needed beat Cambridge on the final day to ensure automatic romotion. The tension at that match was unbearable, but cond-half goals from Speedie and Allen sealed a 2–0 ctory and the Hammers were now in the Premier League. this campaign the Hammers had also participated in the

Anglo-Italian Cup and after finishing above Bristol Rovers and Southend United in the preliminary round they qualified for the international stage. They played against four Italian sides, with their only defeat coming against Cremonese, the eventual tournament winners.

MATT HOLMES

A midfielder who had close control and excellent ball skills, he began his career at Bournemouth in 1988 after his home-town club Luton Town told him he was too small to play.

On the South Coast he played for four seasons, appearing in 114 league games and scoring eight goals before being transferred to West Ham in August 1992. That first season he was used mainly as a substitute, but impressive performances saw him a regular in the side the following season. Matt's profile soared and champions Blackburn Rovers paid £1.2 million for his services in August 1995. His time at Ewood Park was blighted with injuries and he made only 12 appearances before the Lancashire side cut their losses and sold him to Charlton for £250,000 in July 1997.

Playing against Wolverhampton Wanderers in the FA Cup he suffered a bad tackle from defender Kevin Muscat. This virtually ended his career and after taking legal action he accepted an out-of-court settlement. He had to give up first-class soccer but played for a spell in non-league football with Dorchester Town. He now runs a coaching school and also works for Bournemouth running their youngsters' development centre.

arclays League - Division One*
inal Table 1992-93

		HOME					AWAY					
	P	W	D	L	F	A	W	D	L	F	A	Pts
ewcastle United	46	16	6	1	58	15	13	3	7	34	23	96
est Ham United	46	16	5	2	50	17	10	5	8	31	24	88
rtsmouth	46	19	2	2	48	9	7	8	8	32	37	88
anmere Rovers	46	15	4	4	48	24	8	6	9	24	32	79
vindon Town	46	15	5	3	41	23	6	8	9	33	36	76
icester City	46	14	5	4	43	24	8	5	10	28	40	76
lwall	46	14	6	3	46	21	4	10	9	19	32	70
rby County	46	11	2	10	40	33	8	7	8	28	24	66
msby Town	46	12	6	5	33	25	7	1	15	25	32	64
terborough United	46	7	11	5	30	26	9	3	11	25	37	62
lverhampton Wanderers	46	11	6	6	37	26	5	7	11	20	30	61
arlton Athletic	46	10	8	5	28	19	6	5	12	21	27	61
rnsley	46	12	4	7	29	19	5	5	13	27	41	60
ford United	46	8	7	8	29	21	6	7	10	24	35	56
istol City	46	10	7	6	29	25	4	7	12	20	42	56
atford	46	8	7	8	27	30	6	6	11	30	41	55
tts County	46	10	7	6	33	21	2	9	12	22	49	52
uthend United	46	9	8	6	33	22	4	5	14	21	42	52
rmingham City	46	10	4	9	30	32	3	8	12	20	40	51
on Town	46	6	13	4	26	26	4	8	11	22	36	51
nderland	46	9	6	8	34	28	4	5	14	16	36	50
entford	46	7	6	10	28	30	6	4	13	24	41	49
mbridge United	46	8	6	9	29	32	3	10	10	19	37	49
stol Rovers	46	6	6	11	30	42	4	5	14	25	45	41

rmerly Football Lague Division Two

Season **1992-93** Barclays League - Division One

Match Details

Manager **Billy Bonds**   Final League Position **2/24 Promoted to Premier League**

	Date		Competition	Venue	Opponents	Results		Attendance	Position	Scorers
1	Aug 16	Sun	Div 1	A	Barnsley	W	1-0	6,798	11	Allen C.
2	Aug 22	Sat	Div 1	H	Charlton Athletic	L	0-1	17,054	14	
3	Aug 29	Sat	Div 1	A	Newcastle United	L	0-2	29,891	18	
4	Sep 2	Wed	AIC Pre	H	Bristol Rovers	D	2-2	4,809		Dicks 2
5	Sep 5	Sat	Div 1	H	Watford	W	2-1	11,921	13	Allen C., Allen M.
6	Sep 12	Sat	Div 1	A	Peterborough United	W	3-1	10,807	7	Allen M., Keen, Morley
7	Sep 15	Tue	Div 1	A	Bristol City	W	5-1	14,094	5	Allen C. 2, Morley 2, Robson
8	Sep 20	Sun	Div 1	H	Derby County	D	1-1	11,493	5	Morley
9	Sep 23	Wed	FLC 2:1	H	Crewe Alexandra	D	0-0	6,981		
10	Sep 27	Sun	Div 1	A	Portsmouth	W	1-0	12,388	4	Allen C.
11	Sep 30	Wed	AIC Pre	A	Southend United	W	3-0	6,482		Dicks (pen), Holmes, Morley
12	Oct 4	Sun	Div 1	A	Wolverhampton Wanderers	D	0-0	14,391	7	
13	Oct 7	Wed	FLC 2:2	A	Crewe Alexandra	L	0-2	5,427		
14	Oct 11	Sun	Div 1	H	Sunderland	W	6-0	10,326	5	Robson 2, Allen M., Keen, Martin, Morley
15	Oct 17	Sat	Div 1	A	Bristol Rovers	W	4-0	6,182	2	Allen C., Dicks [pen], Keen, Morley
16	Oct 24	Sat	Div 1	H	Swindon Town	L	0-1	17,842	3	
17	Oct 31	Sat	Div 1	A	Cambridge United	L	1-2	7,209	4	Morley
18	Nov 3	Tue	Div 1	A	Grimsby Town	D	1-1	9,119	4	Morley
19	Nov 7	Sat	Div 1	H	Notts County	W	2-0	12,345	3	Allen C., Morley
20	Nov 11	Wed	AIC Grp	A	Cremonese	L	0-2	1,639		
21	Nov 15	Sun	Div 1	A	Millwall	L	1-2	12,445	5	Robson
22	Nov 21	Sat	Div 1	H	Oxford United	W	5-3	11,842	4	Dicks 2, Breacker, Allen C., Morley
23	Nov 24	Tue	AIC Grp	H	Reggiana	W	2-0	6,872		Allen C. 2
24	Nov 28	Sat	Div 1	H	Birmingham City	W	3-1	15,004	3	Allen C. 2, Morley
25	Dec 4	Fri	Div 1	A	Tranmere Rovers	L	2-5	11,782	3	Allen C., Morley
26	Dec 8	Tue	AIC Grp	A	Cosenza	W	1-0	800		Allen C.
27	Dec 12	Sat	Div 1	H	Southend United	W	2-0	15,874	3	Allen C., Morley
28	Dec 16	Wed	AIC Grp	H	Pisa SC	D	0-0	7,123		
29	Dec 20	Sun	Div 1	A	Brentford	D	0-0	11,912	3	
30	Dec 26	Sat	Div 1	A	Charlton Athletic	D	1-1	8,337	3	Dicks
31	Dec 28	Mon	Div 1	H	Luton Town	D	2-2	18,786	3	Breacker, Dicks [pen]
32	Jan 2	Sat	FAC 3	A	West Bromwich Albion	W	2-0	25,896		Allen C., Robson
33	Jan 10	Sun	Div 1	A	Derby County	W	2-0	13,737	2	Morley, Robson
34	Jan 16	Sat	Div 1	H	Portsmouth	W	2-0	18,127	2	Foster, Morley
35	Jan 24	Sun	FAC 4	A	Barnsley	L	1-4	13,716		Morley [pen]
36	Jan 27	Wed	Div 1	H	Bristol City	W	2-0	12,118	3	Morley, Robson
37	Jan 30	Sat	Div 1	A	Leicester City	W	2-1	18,838	2	Gale, Robson
38	Feb 6	Sat	Div 1	H	Barnsley	D	1-1	14,101	2	Jones
39	Feb 9	Tue	Div 1	H	Peterborough United	W	2-1	12,537	2	Butler, Jones
40	Feb 13	Sat	Div 1	A	Watford	W	2-1	13,115	2	Keen, Robson
41	Feb 21	Sun	Div 1	H	Newcastle United	D	0-0	24,159	2	
42	Feb 27	Sat	Div 1	A	Sunderland	D	0-0	19,068	2	
43	Mar 6	Sat	Div 1	H	Wolverhampton Wanderers	W	3-1	24,679	2	Dicks [pen], Holmes, Morley
44	Mar 9	Tue	Div 1	H	Grimsby Town	W	2-1	13,170	2	Dicks 2
45	Mar 13	Sat	Div 1	A	Notts County	L	0-1	10,272	2	
46	Mar 20	Sat	Div 1	H	Tranmere Rovers	W	2-0	16,369	2	Dicks 2 [1 pen]
47	Mar 23	Tue	Div 1	A	Oxford United	L	0-1	9,499	2	
48	Mar 28	Sun	Div 1	H	Millwall	D	2-2	15,723	2	Keen, Morley
49	Apr 3	Sat	Div 1	A	Birmingham City	W	2-1	19,053	2	Bshop, Brown
50	Apr 7	Wed	Div 1	A	Southend United	L	0-1	12,813	2	
51	Apr 11	Sun	Div 1	H	Leicester City	W	3-0	13,951	2	Speedie 2, Keen
52	Apr 13	Tue	Div 1	A	Luton Town	L	0-2	10,959	3	
53	Apr 17	Sat	Div 1	H	Brentford	W	4-0	16,522	3	Allen M., Butler, Keen, Morley
54	Apr 24	Sat	Div 1	H	Bristol Rovers	W	2-1	16,682	3	Dicks [pen], Speedie
55	May 2	Sun	Div 1	A	Swindon Town	W	3-1	16,508	2	Allen C., Brown, Morley
56	May 8	Sat	Div 1	H	Cambridge United	W	2-0	27,399	2	Allen C., Speedie

AIC Pre = Anglo-Italian Cup (Preliminary) AIC Grp = Anglo-Italian Cup (Group)

Team Line-Ups

ALLEN Clive	ALLEN Martin	BANKS Steven	BISHOP Ian	BREACKER Tim	BROWN Kenny	BUNBURY Alex	BUTLER Peter	CLARKE Simon	DICKS Julian	FOSTER Colin	GALE Tony	HOLMES Matt	JONES Steve	KEEN Kevin	MARTIN Alvin	MIKLOSKO Ludek	MORLEY Trevor	PARRIS George	POTTS Steve	ROBSON Mark	RUSH Matthew	SMALL Mike	SPEEDIE David	THOMAS Mitchell	
10/a			7	2			8		3		a			11	5	1		6/b	4	b		9			1
10			7/a	2			8		3					11	5	1		6	4	a		9			2
10	9		7	2			8		3			6/a		11	5	1			4			a			3
10	6	1					8		3		4			11	5		9	2		7/a	a				4
10/a	6			2			8		3					11	5	1	9	a	4	7/a					5
10/a	6			2			8							11	5	1	9		4	7		a		3	6
10	6			2			8							11	5	1	9		4	7/a		a		3	7
10	6			2			8							11	5	1	9		4	7/a		a		3	8
10	6			2			8							11/a	5	1	9		4	7		a		3	9
10	6			2			8		3			a		11	5	1	9		4	7/a					10
10	6			2					3			8		11	5	1	9		4	7					11
10/b	6			2			8		3		b	a		11	5	1	9		4	7/a					12
10	6			2			8		3					11	5	1	9		4	7					13
10	6			2			8		3					11	5	1	9		4	7					14
10	6			2			8							11	5	1	9		4	7					15
10	6			2			8							11	5	1	9	3	4	7					16
10	6			2			8							11	5	1	9	3	4	7					17
10	6			2			8					a		11	5	1	9	3	4	7/a					18
10	6			2	3		8							11	5	1	9		4	7					19
10	6			2	3							11		a	5	1	9	8/a	4	7					20
10				2	3	a	8							11/a	5	1	9	6	4	7					21
10				2		a	8		3					11/a	5	1	9	6	4	7					22
10	6		b	2		a			3			8		11	5/a	1	9		4	7/b					23
10			a	2					3	5		8		11/a		1	9	6	4	7					24
10	6/b		a	2					3	b				11	5	1	9	8/a	4	7					25
10	6			2		a			3				9	11/a	5	1	8		4	7/a	7				26
10	8		a	2					3					11	5	1	9	6/a	4	7					27
10/a	8			2		9			3				a	11/b	5	1	8		4	b	7				28
10	6		8	2		a			3					11	5	1	9		4	7/a					29
10	6		8/a	2		a			3					11	5	1	9		4	7					30
10	6			2			8		3					11	5	1	9		4	7					31
10	6			2			8		3					11	5	1	9		4	7					32
10	6			2			8		3			a		11	5/b	1	9	b	4	7/a					33
10/a	6			2			8		3	5		a		11		1	9	b	4	7/b					34
	6			2	3	a	8			5		10		11		1	9		4	7/a					35
	6			2	3	10/a	8			5		a		11		1	9	b	4	7/b					36
	6			2	3		8			5		10	b	11/b		1	9	a	4	7/a					37
	6			2			8		3	5		10		11		1	9		4	7					38
	6			2			8		3	5	a	10		11/a		1	9		4	7					39
	6		b	2			8		3	5	a	10/b		11		1	9		4	7/a					40
	6		10	2			8		3	5		a		11/a		1	9		4	7					41
	6		10/a	2			8		3	5		b		11		1	9	a	4	7/b					42
	6			2			8		3	5		a		11/a		1	9		4	7			10		43
	6		a	2			8		3	5				11		1	9		4	7			10/a		44
	6		a	2			8		3	5				11		1	9		4	7/a			10		45
	6			2			8		3	5		a		11		1	10		4	7/a		9			46
	6			2			8		3	5		7		11/a		1	10		4	a		9			47
	6			2	3		8			5				11		1	10		4	7		9			48
	6			2	3		8	b		5		a	10/b	11		1			4	7/a		9			49
	6			2			8		3	5				11		1	10		4	7		9			50
	6			2			8		3	5				11		1	10		4	7		9			51
7/a	6			2			8		3	5	a			11		1	10		4			9			52
	6			2			8		3	5				11		1	10		4	7		9			53
	6		a	2			8		3	5				11		1	10		4	7/a		9			54
a	6			2	b		8		3	5				11		1	10/b		4	7/a		9			55
b	6			2			8		3	5				11		1	10		4	7/a		9/b			56

1993-94
Story of the season

Playing in the **Premier League for the first time,** the Hammers started badly with **home defeats** against Wimbledon and Queens Park Rangers.

In September Julian Dicks joined Liverpool in a swap de which involved full-back David Burrows and midfield Mike Marsh coming to West Ham. To add some power the forwards, Lee Chapman was bought from Portsmou and the following day scored in the 2–0 win at Blackbu Rovers.

Third Division Chesterfield were beaten 7–1 on aggrega in the League Cup but the Hammers found it tougher in th next round, losing 2–1 at Nottingham Forest. There was good 3–1 home win against Manchester City and after aw wins at Wimbledon and Southampton the team moved in tenth place. Over the holiday period West Ham bounce back from a home defeat by Tottenham to win 1–0 Everton on New Year's Day.

Appearances & Goals 1993-94

	League			FA Cup			League Cup			Total	
	Starts	Subs	Goals	Starts	Subs	Goals	Starts	Subs	Goals	Starts	Subs
ALLEN Clive	7	0	2	1	2	0	0	0	0	8	2
ALLEN Martin	20	6	7	6	0	2	0	2	1	26	8
BISHOP Ian	36	0	1	6	0	1	3	0	0	45	0
BOERE Jeroen	0	4	0	0	0	0	0	1	1	0	5
BREACKER Tim	40	0	3	6	0	0	2	0	0	48	0
BROWN Kenny	6	3	0	2	1	0	0	0	0	8	4
BURROWS David	25	0	1	3	0	0	3	0	1	31	0
BUTLER Peter	26	0	1	1	0	0	2	0	0	29	0
CHAPMAN Lee	26	4	7	6	0	2	3	0	2	35	4
DICKS Julian	7	0	0	0	0	0	0	0	0	7	0
FOSTER Colin	5	0	0	0	0	0	0	0	0	5	0
GALE Tony	31	1	0	1	0	0	2	0	0	34	1
GORDON Dale	8	0	1	0	0	0	1	0	0	9	0
HOLMES Matt	33	1	3	4	0	0	3	0	0	40	1
JONES Steve	3	5	2	2	2	1	0	0	0	5	7
MARQUIS Paul	0	1	0	0	0	0	0	0	0	0	1
MARSH Mike	33	0	1	6	0	1	3	0	0	42	0
MARTIN Alvin	6	1	2	3	0	0	1	0	0	10	1
MIKLOSKO Ludek	42	0	0	6	0	0	3	0	0	51	0
MITCHELL Paul	0	1	0	0	0	0	0	0	0	0	1
MORLEY Trevor	39	3	13	3	1	0	3	0	3	45	4
POTTS Steve	41	0	0	6	0	0	3	0	0	50	0
ROBSON Mark	1	2	0	0	0	0	0	0	0	1	2
ROWLAND Keith	16	7	0	4	0	0	1	0	0	21	7
RUSH Matthew	9	1	1	0	0	0	0	0	0	9	1
WILLIAMSON Danny	2	1	1	0	0	0	0	0	0	2	1
own goal			1								
Totals	**462**	**41**	**47**	**66**	**6**	**7**	**33**	**3**	**8**	**561**	**50**

the FA Cup Marsh scored his first goal for the club when
atford were beaten 2–1 at home and in the next round
otts County were edged out in a replay with a late goal
om Chapman. Non-league Kidderminster Harriers were
rd to beat on their tiny ground in the fifth round, but
hapman came to the rescue with the only goal of the
me. There was an exciting match with league leaders
anchester United which finished 2–2, United equalising in
e last minute. Drawn at home to Luton Town in the FA
up it was a nervy 0–0 draw; the replay at Kenilworth Road
w West Ham lose 3–2 to end their chance of a semi-final
ace.

onfidence was low after the cup exit and there were
pressing defeats at Chelsea and Sheffield United.
oungsters Steve Jones and Matt Rush were brought into
e side to add some pace and Ipswich were beaten 2–1 at
me, followed by an excellent 4–1 win at Tottenham.
uring April Martin Allen was the man in form, scoring
ur goals in four games including a 2–0 win at Arsenal.

The final home game brought a 3–3 draw with Southampton
and a thirteenth-place finish. It also saw an end to terraces
at Upton Park after it was converted into an all-seater
stadium.

MIKE MARSH

Signed by Liverpool on a free transfer in 1987 from Kirkby Town, the midfielder soon impressed with his creative flair.

He established himself as a first-team regular in season 1991/92 and was an unused substitute in the 1992 FA Cup Final with Sunderland.

In September 1993 he was involved in the swap deal that took Dicks to Liverpool and along with David Burrows he signed for West Ham. He had good passing skills and deft touches and set up an understanding with Ian Bishop in midfield. After 61 games for the Hammers he was transferred to Coventry City for a fee of £450,000 in December 1994. He only made 19 league and cup appearances at Highfield Road before going abroad to Turkey to join Galatasaray. His time with them was a short one, playing in three games before returning home to join Southend United in September 1995. Mike managed to play 112 games for the Shrimpers but a persistent knee injury dogged his whole time there and he then went on a journey of non-league clubs.

Starting with Barrow he then moved on to Kidderminster Harriers, Southport, Boston United and Accrington Stanley, where he retired in June 2003.

A Carling Premiership
inal Table 1993-94

	P	W	D	L	F	A	W	D	L	F	A	Pts
			HOME					AWAY				
nchester United	42	14	6	1	39	13	13	5	3	41	25	92
ckburn Rovers	42	14	5	2	31	11	11	4	6	32	25	84
wcastle United	42	14	4	3	51	14	9	4	8	31	27	77
enal	42	10	8	3	25	15	8	9	4	28	13	71
ds United	42	13	6	2	37	18	5	10	6	28	21	70
mbledon	42	12	5	4	35	21	6	6	9	21	32	65
effield Wednesday	42	10	7	4	48	24	6	9	6	28	30	64
erpool	42	12	4	5	33	23	5	5	11	26	32	60
eens Park Rangers	42	8	7	6	32	29	8	5	8	30	32	60
on Villa	42	8	5	8	23	18	7	7	7	23	32	57
ventry City	42	9	7	5	23	17	5	7	9	20	28	56
wich City	42	4	9	8	26	29	8	8	5	39	32	53
est Ham United	42	6	7	8	26	31	7	6	8	21	27	52
elsea	42	11	5	5	31	20	2	7	12	18	33	51
tenham Hotspur	42	4	8	9	29	33	7	4	10	25	26	45
nchester City	42	6	10	5	24	22	3	8	10	14	27	45
erton	42	8	4	9	26	30	4	4	13	16	33	44
uthampton	42	9	2	10	30	31	3	5	13	19	35	43
wich Town	42	5	8	8	21	32	4	8	9	14	26	43
effield United	42	6	10	5	24	23	2	8	11	18	37	42
ham Athletic	42	5	8	8	24	33	4	5	12	18	35	40
ndon Town	42	4	7	10	25	45	1	8	12	22	55	30

Season **1993-94** FA Carling Premiership
Match Details

Manager **Billy Bonds**   Final League Position **13/22**

	Date		Competition	Venue	Opponents	Results		Attendance	Position	Scorers
1	Aug 14	Sat	Prem	H	Wimbledon	L	0-2	20,369	17	
2	Aug 17	Tue	Prem	A	Leeds United	L	0-1	34,588	22	
3	Aug 21	Sat	Prem	A	Coventry City	D	1-1	12,864	19	Gordon
4	Aug 25	Wed	Prem	H	Sheffield Wednesday	W	2-0	19,441	15	Allen C. 2
5	Aug 28	Sat	Prem	H	Queens Park Rangers	L	0-4	18,084	17	
6	Sep 1	Wed	Prem	A	Manchester United	L	0-3	44,613	19	
7	Sep 11	Wed	Prem	H	Swindon Town	D	0-0	15,777	19	
8	Sep 18	Wed	Prem	A	Blackburn Rovers	W	2-0	14,437	18	Chapman, Morley
9	Sep 22	Wed	FLC 2:1	H	Chesterfield	W	5-1	12,823		Chapman 2, Morley 2 [1 pen], Burrows
10	Sep 25	Sat	Prem	A	Newcastle United	L	0-2	34,179	18	
11	Oct 2	Sat	Prem	H	Chelsea	W	1-0	18,917	17	Morley
12	Oct 5	Tue	FLC 2:2	A	Chesterfield	W	2-0	4,890		Allen M., Boere
13	Oct 16	Sat	Prem	H	Aston Villa	D	0-0	20,416	17	
14	Oct 23	Sat	Prem	A	Norwich City	D	0-0	20,175	17	
15	Oct 27	Wed	FLC 3	A	Nottingham Forest	L	1-2	17,857		Morley
16	Nov 1	Mon	Prem	H	Manchester City	W	3-1	16,605	15	Burrows, Chapman, Holmes
17	Nov 6	Sat	Prem	A	Liverpool	L	0-2	42,254	15	
18	Nov 20	Sat	Prem	H	Oldham Athletic	W	2-0	17,211	14	Martin, Morley
19	Nov 24	Wed	Prem	H	Arsenal	D	0-0	20,279	14	
20	Nov 29	Mon	Prem	A	Southampton	W	2-0	13,258	10	Chapman, Morley
21	Dec 4	Sat	Prem	A	Wimbledon	W	2-1	10,903	10	Chapman 2
22	Dec 8	Wed	Prem	H	Leeds United	L	0-1	20,468	10	
23	Dec 11	Sat	Prem	H	Coventry City	W	3-2	17,243	9	Breacker, Butler, Morley [pen]
24	Dec 18	Sat	Prem	A	Sheffield Wednesday	L	0-5	26,350	11	
25	Dec 27	Mon	Prem	A	Ipswich Town	D	1-1	20,988	12	Chapman
26	Dec 28	Tue	Prem	H	Tottenham Hotspur	L	1-3	20,787	13	Holmes
27	Jan 1	Sat	Prem	A	Everton	W	1-0	19,602	11	Breacker
28	Jan 3	Mon	Prem	H	Sheffield United	D	0-0	20,365	11	
29	Jan 8	Sat	FAC 3	H	Watford	W	2-1	19,802		Allen M., Marsh
30	Jan 15	Sat	Prem	A	Aston Villa	L	1-3	28,869	11	Allen M.
31	Jan 24	Mon	Prem	H	Norwich City	D	3-3	20,738	11	Jones, Morley, Allen M.
32	Jan 29	Sat	FAC 4	A	Notts County	D	1-1	14,952		Jones
33	Feb 9	Wed	FAC 4 Rep	H	Notts County	W	1-0	23,373		Chapman
34	Feb 12	Sat	Prem	A	Manchester City	D	0-0	29,118	12	
35	Feb 19	Sat	FAC 5	A	Kidderminster Harriers	W	1-0	8,000		Chapman
36	Feb 26	Sat	Prem	H	Manchester United	D	2-2	28,832	12	Chapman, Morley
37	Mar 5	Sat	Prem	A	Swindon Town	D	1-1	15,929	13	Morley
38	Mar 14	Mon	FAC QF	H	Luton Town	D	0-0	27,331		
39	Mar 19	Sat	Prem	H	Newcastle United	L	2-4	23,132	14	Breacker, Martin
40	Mar 23	Wed	FAC QF Rep	A	Luton Town	L	2-3	13,166		Allen M., Bishop
41	Mar 26	Sat	Prem	A	Chelsea	L	0-2	19,545	15	
42	Mar 28	Mon	Prem	A	Sheffield United	L	2-3	13,646	15	Bishop, Holmes
43	Apr 2	Sat	Prem	H	Ipswich Town	W	2-1	18,307	14	Morley, Rush
44	Apr 4	Mon	Prem	A	Tottenham Hotspur	W	4-1	31,502	13	Morley 2 [1 pen], Jones, Marsh
45	Apr 9	Sat	Prem	H	Everton	L	0-1	20,243	13	
46	Apr 16	Sat	Prem	A	Oldham Athletic	W	2-1	11,669	13	Allen M., Morley
47	Apr 23	Sat	Prem	H	Liverpool	L	1-2	26,106	13	Allen M.
48	Apr 27	Wed	Prem	H	Blackburn Rovers	L	1-2	22,186	14	Allen M.
49	Apr 30	Sat	Prem	A	Arsenal	W	2-0	33,700	12	Allen M., Morley
50	May 3	Tue	Prem	A	Queens Park Rangers	D	0-0	10,850	13	
51	May 7	Sat	Prem	H	Southampton	D	3-3	26,952	13	Allen M., Williamson, Monkou (og)

Team Line-Ups

ALLEN Clive	ALLEN Martin	BISHOP Ian	BOERE Jeroen	BREACKER Tim	BROWN Kenny	BURROWS David	BUTLER Peter	CHAPMAN Lee	DICKS Julian	FOSTER Colin	GALE Tony	GORDON Dale	HOLMES Matt	JONES Steve	MARQUIS Paul	MARSH Mike	MARTIN Alvin	MIKLOSKO Ludek	MITCHELL Paul	MORLEY Trevor	POTTS Steve	ROBSON Mark	ROWLAND Keith	RUSH Matthew	WILLIAMSON Danny	
10	6			2			8		3		5	11	16/a					1		9	4		a			1
10/a	6			2			8		3	22	6	11						1		9	4/b	b	a			2
10	6			2			8		3	22		11						1		9	4		23			3
10	6			2			8		3	22		11/a	a					1		9	4		23			4
10	6			2			8		3	22								1		9	4	7	23			5
	6/a			2					3	22	a	11/b	16					1		9	4	b	23			6
	14			2					3		12	11/a	16	17				1		9	4		23	a		7
a	14			2		33		25			12	11	16			34/a		1		9			23			8
	14					33		25			12	11	16			34		1		9			23			9
a	14	b		15/a		33		25			12	11	16			34		1		9/b	4					10
a	14			2		33	8	25			12		16			34/a		1		9	4					11
a	14	b		2		33	8/a	25/b			12		16			34		1		9	4					12
	14			2		33	8	25			12		16			34		1		9	4					13
	14			2		33	8	25			12/a		16			34		1		9	4			a		14
a	14			2		33	8/a	25					16			34	18	1		9	4					15
	14			2		33	8	25					16/a			34	18	1		9	4			a		16
	14			2		33	8	25					16			34	18	1		9	4					17
	14			2		33	8	25					16			34	18	1		9	4					18
	14			2		33	8	25			12		16			34		1		9	4					19
6	14			2		33	8	25			12		16					1		9	4					20
6	14			2		33	8	25			12		16					1		9	4					21
	14	a		2		33	8	25			12		16			34		1		9/a	4					22
a	14/a			2		33	8	25			12		16			34		1		9	4					23
a	14/a	b		2		33	8	25			12		16/b			34		1		9	4					24
	14			2		33	8	25			12		16/a			34		1		9	4					25
	14			2		33	8	25			12		16/a	a		34		1		9	4					26
	14			2		33	8	25			12		16/a			34		1		9	4			a		27
	14			2		33	8	25			12			a		34		1		9/a	4		23			28
6	14			2	a	33/a		25			12		b			34		1		9/b	4		23			29
6	14			2				25			12		16	a		34		1		9/a	4		23			30
6	14			2	b			25/a			12/b		16	17		34		1		a	4		23			31
6	14			2	15			25					16	17		34		1			4		23			32
6	14			2	15			25					16	17/a		34		1			4		23			33
6	14			2	15			25					16			34/b		1	b		4		a			34
6	14			2	15			25					16			34	18	1			4		23			35
6	14			2		33		25					16			34	18	1		9	4					36
6	14			2		33		25					16/a			34	18	1		9	4			a		37
6	14			2		33		25/a					16			34	18	1		9	4					38
	14	a		2			8						16			34	18	1		9/a	4		23			39
6/a	14			2		33/b	8	25			12			a		34		1	b		4					40
a	14			2	b		8	25			12		16/a			34/b		1	a		4		23			41
	14			2	a		8				12		16			34		1		9	4		23	28		42
	14			2			8/a				12		16	a		34		1		9	4		23	28		43
	14			2							12		16	17		34	a	1		9	4		23/a	28		44
6	14			2	15	33					12		16			34		1		9				28		45
6	14/a			2		33					12		16			34		1		9	4			28		46
6	14			2	15						12		16/b			34		1	b	9	4			28/a		47
6	14			2	15	33/a					12					34		1		9	4			28	a	48
6	14			2	15	33/a					12					34		1		9	4			28/a	20	49
6	14/a			2	15						12					34		1		9	4			28/a	20	50
6	14/a			2		33					12					34		1		9	4			28	20	51

1994-95
Story of the season

There was a shock just before the season began as **manager Billy Bonds resigned** and assistant **Harry Redknapp was installed as the club's eighth manager.**

After a poor pre-season the Hammers found it tough, a after five games without a win and only one goal scored team were nineteenth. Midfielder Don Hutchison w signed for a club record fee of £1.5 million and for ex goal power former striker Tony Cottee was brought ba from Everton. Cottee scored on his home debut in the 1 win against Aston Villa and his homecoming inspir further victories in the London derbies against Chelsea a Crystal Palace. Further good news came when Julian Dic the fans' favourite, was transferred back to West Ham fro Liverpool.

In the League Cup Walsall were beaten 3–2 on aggrega

Appearances & Goals 1994-95

	League			FA Cup			League Cup			Total	
	Starts	Subs	Goals	Starts	Subs	Goals	Starts	Subs	Goals	Starts	Subs
ALLEN Martin	26	3	2	1	0	0	3	0	0	30	3
BISHOP Ian	31	0	1	2	0	0	3	0	0	36	0
BOERE Jeroen	15	5	6	2	0	0	1	0	0	18	5
BREACKER Tim	33	0	0	2	0	0	3	0	0	38	0
BROWN Kenny	8	1	0	0	1	1	1	1	0	9	3
BURROWS David	4	0	0	0	0	0	0	0	0	4	0
BUTLER Peter	5	0	0	0	0	0	0	0	0	5	0
CHAPMAN Lee	7	3	0	0	0	0	1	1	0	8	4
COTTEE Tony	31	0	13	2	0	1	3	0	1	36	0
DICKS Julian	29	0	5	2	0	0	2	0	0	33	0
HOLMES Matt	24	0	1	1	0	0	1	0	0	26	0
HUGHES Michael	15	2	2	2	0	0	0	0	0	17	2
HUTCHISON Don	22	1	9	0	1	0	3	0	2	25	2
JONES Steve	1	1	0	0	0	0	0	0	0	1	1
MARSH Mike	13	3	0	0	0	0	3	0	0	16	3
MARTIN Alvin	24	0	0	2	0	0	2	0	0	28	0
MIKLOSKO Ludek	42	0	0	2	0	0	4	0	0	48	0
MONCUR John	30	0	2	2	0	0	3	0	1	35	0
MORLEY Trevor	10	4	0	0	1	0	0	1	0	10	6
POTTS Steve	42	0	0	2	0	0	4	0	0	48	0
RIEPER Marc	17	4	1	0	0	0	0	0	0	17	4
ROWLAND Keith	11	1	0	0	0	0	2	0	0	13	1
RUSH Matthew	15	8	2	0	0	0	3	0	0	18	8
WEBSTER Simon	0	5	0	0	0	0	0	0	0	0	5
WHITBREAD Adrian	3	5	0	0	0	0	2	1	0	5	6
WILLIAMSON Danny	4	0	0	0	0	0	0	0	0	4	0
own goal									1		
Totals	462	46	44	22	3	2	44	4	5	528	53

ich set up a home tie with Chelsea where an inspired
play from goalkeeper Miklosko and a goal from
utchison saw the west London team beaten 1–0.
ovember was a poor month, with three 1–0 defeats in the
gue followed by a 3–1 home defeat to Bolton Wanderers
the League Cup. The big Dutchman Jeroen Boere was
ought in to partner Cottee and it was his two goals that
rned a 2–2 draw at Leeds United. Cottee was then on
get with a hat-trick in the 3–0 home win against
anchester City. Redknapp made two more signings when
ying midfielder Michael Hughes and the Danish defender
arc Rieper.

difficult FA Cup tie at Wycombe Wanderers was won 2–0
t the Hammers went out in the next round after losing
0 at Queens Park Rangers. By early March the team were
relegation trouble, but in an excellent run there were only
o defeats in the remaining 13 games. In that spell Arsenal
re beaten 1–0 at Highbury, there was a 2–0 win at Aston

Villa and a 2–0 home win over champions-elect Blackburn
Rovers. The final two home games brought a 3–0 win
against Liverpool and a 1–1 draw with Manchester United
that ended the Reds' title hopes.

MARC RIEPER

A central defender, he began his career with
the Danish side AGF Aarhus in 1988 and
while playing for them gained the first of his
61 Danish caps against Sweden in 1990.

At Aarhus he played in 85 league games up
to 1992 when he joined Brondby, where he
made 93 league appearances and won a cup
winners' medal in 1994.

In December 1994 West Ham manager Harry
Redknapp bought him for £1.5 million. After
making his debut at Leeds United he became
a regular and popular member of the side. He
was selected by Denmark to play in the Euro
96 finals in England, where he created a
record for his country when he won his 37th
consecutive cap. Marc played in a total of 101
games for the Hammers, scoring five goals,
before leaving in September 1997 to join
Scottish giants Celtic. He was successful in
his first season, being in the side that won the
Scottish League Cup and the League
Championship. A bad injury the following
season forced him to retire and after playing
in 37 league games he returned to Denmark.
He was assistant coach at Aarhus for a spell
until he resigned in 2002, but still remains a
director of the club. Marc now runs a hotel in
the town of Aarhus.

A Carling Premiership
inal Table 1994-95

	P	HOME					AWAY					Pts
	P	W	D	L	F	A	W	D	L	F	A	Pts
ckburn Rovers	42	17	2	2	54	21	10	6	5	26	18	89
nchester United	42	16	4	1	42	5	10	6	5	35	24	88
tingham Forest	42	12	6	3	36	18	10	5	6	36	25	77
erpool	42	13	5	3	38	13	8	6	7	27	24	74
ds United	42	13	5	3	35	15	7	8	6	24	23	73
wcastle United	42	14	6	1	46	20	6	6	9	21	27	72
kenham Hotspur	42	10	5	6	32	25	6	9	6	34	33	62
eens Park Rangers	42	11	3	7	36	26	6	6	9	25	33	60
mbledon	42	9	5	7	26	26	6	6	9	22	39	56
uthampton	42	8	9	4	33	27	4	9	8	28	36	54
elsea	42	7	7	7	25	22	6	8	7	25	33	54
enal	42	6	9	6	27	21	7	3	11	26	28	51
effield Wednesday	42	7	7	7	26	26	6	5	10	23	31	51
est Ham United	**42**	**9**	**6**	**6**	**28**	**19**	**4**	**5**	**12**	**16**	**29**	**50**
erton	42	8	9	4	31	23	3	8	10	13	28	50
ventry City	42	7	7	7	23	25	5	7	9	21	37	50
nchester City	42	8	7	6	37	28	4	6	11	16	36	49
on Villa	42	6	9	6	27	24	5	6	10	24	32	48
stal Palace	42	6	6	9	16	23	5	6	10	18	26	45
wich City	42	8	8	5	27	21	2	5	14	10	33	43
cester City	42	5	6	10	28	37	1	5	15	17	43	29
wich Town	42	5	3	13	24	34	2	3	16	12	59	27

Season **1994-95** FA Carling Premiership
Match Details

Manager **Harry Redknapp**   Final League Position **14/22**

	Date		Competition	Venue	Opponents	Results		Attendance	Position	Scorers
1	Aug 20	Sat	Prem	H	Leeds United	D	0-0	18,610	14	
2	Aug 24	Wed	Prem	A	Manchester City	L	0-3	19,150	18	
3	Aug 27	Sat	Prem	A	Norwich City	L	0-1	19,110	19	
4	Aug 31	Wed	Prem	H	Newcastle United	L	1-3	17,375	21	Hutchison [pen]
5	Sep 10	Sat	Prem	A	Liverpool	D	0-0	30,907	19	
6	Sep 17	Sat	Prem	H	Aston Villa	W	1-0	18,326	17	Cottee
7	Sep 20	Tue	FLC 2:1	A	Walsall	L	1-2	5,994		Ntamark (og)
8	Sep 25	Sun	Prem	H	Arsenal	L	0-2	18,495	19	
9	Oct 2	Sun	Prem	A	Chelsea	W	2-1	18,696	15	Allen M., Moncur
10	Oct 5	Wed	FLC 2:2	H	Walsall	W	2-0	13,553		Hutchison, Moncur
11	Oct 8	Sat	Prem	H	Crystal Palace	W	1-0	16,959	13	Hutchison
12	Oct 15	Sat	Prem	A	Manchester United	L	0-1	43,795	14	
13	Oct 22	Sat	Prem	H	Southampton	W	2-0	18,853	12	Allen M., Rush
14	Oct 26	Wed	FLC 3	H	Chelsea	W	1-0	18,815		Hutchison
15	Oct 29	Sat	Prem	A	Tottenham Hotspur	L	1-3	26,271	14	Rush
16	Nov 1	Tue	Prem	A	Everton	L	0-1	28,353	14	
17	Nov 5	Sat	Prem	H	Leicester City	W	1-0	18,780	14	Dicks [pen]
18	Nov 19	Sat	Prem	A	Sheffield Wednesday	L	0-1	25,300	17	
19	Nov 26	Sat	Prem	H	Coventry City	L	0-1	17,251	17	
20	Nov 30	Wed	FLC 4	H	Bolton Wanderers	L	1-3	18,190		Cottee
21	Dec 4	Sun	Prem	A	Queens Park Rangers	L	1-2	12,780	18	Boere
22	Dec 10	Sat	Prem	A	Leeds United	D	2-2	28,987	19	Boere 2
23	Dec 17	Sat	Prem	H	Manchester City	W	3-0	17,286	17	Cottee 3
24	Dec 26	Mon	Prem	H	Ipswich Town	D	1-1	20,562	18	Cottee
25	Dec 28	Wed	Prem	A	Wimbledon	L	0-1	11,212	18	
26	Dec 31	Sat	Prem	H	Nottingham Forest	W	3-1	20,644	16	Bishop, Cottee, Hughes
27	Jan 2	Mon	Prem	A	Blackburn Rovers	L	2-4	25,503	16	Cottee, Dicks
28	Jan 7	Sat	FAC 3	A	Wycombe Wanderers	W	2-0	9,007		Brown, Cottee
29	Jan 14	Sat	Prem	H	Tottenham Hotspur	L	1-2	24,578	19	Boere
30	Jan 23	Mon	Prem	H	Sheffield Wednesday	L	0-2	14,554	20	
31	Jan 28	Sat	FAC 4	A	Queens Park Rangers	L	0-1	17,694		
32	Feb 4	Sat	Prem	A	Leicester City	W	2-1	20,375	19	Cottee, Dicks [pen]
33	Feb 13	Mon	Prem	H	Everton	D	2-2	21,081	20	Cottee 2
34	Feb 18	Sat	Prem	A	Coventry City	L	0-2	17,563	20	
35	Feb 25	Sat	Prem	H	Chelsea	L	1-2	21,500	20	Hutchison
36	Mar 5	Sun	Prem	A	Arsenal	W	1-0	36,295	19	Hutchison
37	Mar 8	Wed	Prem	A	Newcastle United	L	0-2	34,595	19	
38	Mar 11	Sat	Prem	H	Norwich City	D	2-2	21,464	18	Cottee 2
39	Mar 15	Wed	Prem	A	Southampton	D	1-1	15,178	19	Hutchison
40	Mar 18	Sat	Prem	A	Aston Villa	W	2-0	28,682	18	Hutchison, Moncur
41	Apr 8	Sat	Prem	A	Nottingham Forest	D	1-1	28,361	20	Dicks
42	Apr 13	Thur	Prem	H	Wimbledon	W	3-0	21,084	17	Boere, Cottee, Dicks [pen]
43	Apr 17	Mon	Prem	A	Ipswich Town	D	1-1	18,882	18	Boere
44	Apr 30	Sun	Prem	H	Blackburn Rovers	W	2-0	24,202	16	Hutchison, Rieper
45	May 3	Wed	Prem	H	Queens Park Rangers	D	0-0	22,923	15	
46	May 6	Sat	Prem	A	Crystal Palace	L	0-1	18,224	16	
47	May 10	Wed	Prem	H	Liverpool	W	3-0	22,446	13	Hutchison 2, Holmes
48	May 14	Sun	Prem	H	Manchester United	D	1-1	24,783	14	Hughes

eam Line-Ups

BISHOP Ian	BOERE Jeroen	BREACKER Tim	BROWN Kenny	BURROWS David	BUTLER Peter	CHAPMAN Lee	COTTEE Tony	DICKS Julian	HOLMES Matt	HUGHES Michael	HUTCHISON Don	JONES Steve	MARSH Mike	MARTIN Alvin	MIKLOSKO Ludek	MONCUR John	MORLEY Trevor	POTTS Steve	RIEPER Marc	ROWLAND Keith	RUSH Matthew	WEBSTER Simon	WHITBREAD Adrian	WILLIAMSON Danny	
7		2	33	8	25				11/b				b	5	1		9	4/a					a		1
7		2	33	8/a	25/b				11				b	5	1		9	4					a		2
7		2	33		b					17			19/a	5	1	10		4		12/b			a		3
		2	33	8					11		26	a	19	5	1	10		4							4
		2		8			9						19	5	1	10		4		12	14				5
		2		8/a		a	9						19	5	1	10		4		12	14				6
		2				b	9				26		19	5	1	10		4		12	14/b		a		7
		2			25				11/a		26		19	5	1	10		4		12	a				8
		2			25						26		19	5	1	10		4		12	14				9
7		2	a		25						26		19		1	10/a		4		12			22		10
		2			25/a		9				26		19	5	1	10		4		12	a				11
		2					9				26		19	5	1	10		4		12	14				12
7		2			25		9	3					19	5	1			4			14				13
7		2					9	3			26		19	5	1			4			14				14
7/a						a	9	3			26		19	5	1			4		12	14		b		15
7					25		9	3			26		19	5	1			4			14		22		16
7		a					9/a	3			26			5	1	10	9	4			14		22		17
7			15				9	3				a		5	1	10	9	4			14				18
7/a			15				9	3	11				19		1	10	9	4			a		22		19
7	25		15				9	3	11/a						1	10	a	4			14		22		20
	25		15				9	3		17			6		1	10		4		12	14				21
7	25		15				9	3	11	a					1			4	8	12/a	14		22		22
7	25	2					9	3	11	17				5	1			4			14				23
7	25	2					9	3	11	17				5	1			4/a	a		14				24
7	25	2					9	3	11	17				5	1			4	8/a	a					25
7	25/a	2					9	3	11	17				5	1	10/b		4	b	a					26
7	25	2					9	3	11/a	17					1	10		4	8	a					27
7	25/b	2	a				9	3	11/a	17				5	1	10	b	4							28
7	25	2	15				9		11/b	17/a				5	1	10	b	4							29
7	25	2	15				9		11/a	17/b				5	1	10	b	4							30
7/a	25	2					9	3		17	a			5	1	10		4							31
a		2					9	3		17	26/a			5	1	10		4						20	32
a			15				9	3		17/a	26			5	1	10		4						20	33
a		2					9	3	11/a		26			5/b	1	10		4	b					20	34
7		2					9	3			26				1	10	9	4	8						35
7		2					9	3			26				1	10	9/a	4	8		a				36
7		2					9	3		17	26				1		a	4	8		14/a				37
7		2					9	3		a	26				1	10/a	9	4	8					20	38
7	a	2					9	3	11		26				1	10		4	8		14/a				39
7/a	b	2					9	3	11		26/b				1	10		4	8	a					40
7	25		15				9	3	11/a	17					1			4	8				a		41
7	25	2					9	3	11	17					1			4	8						42
7	25	2					9	3	11		a				1	10		4	8						43
7/a	25	2						3	11		26/b				1	10		4	8				a	b	44
7	25/b	2						3	11		26/a				1	10	a	4	8					b	45
7	25	2						3	11		26/a				1	10	a	4	8					b	46
7		2						3/a	11	17	26				1	10	9	4	8				a		47
7		2							11	17/b	26/a				1	10	9	4	8	12			b		48

1995-96
Story of the season

The opening day defeat at home to Leeds **set the pattern for the early-season games.** After further defeats to Arsenal and Chelsea **the Hammers were struggling in nineteenth place without a win.**

To add height and aggression to the forward line, Hammer Iain Dowie was bought from Crystal Palace, and further acquisitions were made when Australian winger Stan Lazaridis and Robbie Slater were bought to boost the squad.

Two goals from Julian Dicks against Everton saw the first league victory and in the League Cup Bristol Rovers were beaten 4–0 on aggregate, but the next round saw the

Appearances & Goals 1995-96

	League			FA Cup			League Cup			Total	
	Starts	Subs	Goals	Starts	Subs	Goals	Starts	Subs	Goals	Starts	Subs
ALLEN Martin	3	0	1	0	0	0	0	0	0	3	0
BILIC Slaven	13	0	0	0	0	0	0	0	0	13	0
BISHOP Ian	35	0	1	3	0	0	3	0	1	41	0
BOERE Jeroen	0	1	0	0	0	0	0	0	0	0	1
BOOGERS Marco	0	4	0	0	0	0	0	0	0	0	4
BREACKER Tim	19	3	0	0	0	0	2	0	0	21	3
BROWN Kenny	3	0	0	0	0	0	0	0	0	3	0
CARVALHO Dani	3	6	2	0	0	0	0	0	0	3	6
COTTEE Tony	30	3	10	3	0	0	3	0	2	36	3
DICKS Julian	34	0	10	3	0	0	3	0	1	40	0
DOWIE Iain	33	0	8	3	0	1	3	0	0	39	0
DUMITRESCU Ilie	2	1	0	0	0	0	0	0	0	2	1
FERDINAND Rio	0	1	0	0	0	0	0	0	0	0	1
FINN Neil	1	0	0	0	0	0	0	0	0	1	0
GORDON Dale	0	1	0	0	1	0	0	0	0	0	2
HARKES John	6	5	0	1	1	0	0	0	0	7	6
HUGHES Michael	28	0	0	3	0	1	2	0	0	33	0
HUTCHISON Don	8	4	2	0	0	0	0	0	0	8	4
LAMPARD Frank Jnr	0	2	0	0	0	0	0	0	0	0	2
LAZARIDIS Stan	2	2	0	0	1	0	1	0	0	3	3
MARTIN Alvin	10	4	0	1	0	0	2	0	0	13	4
MIKLOSKO Ludek	36	0	0	3	0	0	3	0	0	42	0
MONCUR John	19	1	0	1	0	1	3	0	1	23	1
POTTS Steve	34	0	0	3	0	0	3	0	0	40	0
RIEPER Marc	35	1	2	3	0	0	2	1	0	40	2
ROWLAND Keith	19	4	0	1	1	0	0	0	0	20	5
SEALEY Les	1	1	0	0	0	0	0	0	0	1	1
SLATER Robbie	16	6	2	1	0	0	3	0	0	20	6
WATSON Mark	0	1	0	0	0	0	0	0	0	0	1
WHITBREAD Adrian	0	2	0	1	0	0	0	0	0	1	2
WILLIAMSON Danny	28	1	4	3	0	0	0	1	0	31	2
own goal			1								
Totals	418	54	43	33	4	3	33	2	5	484	60

mmers bow out after losing 2–1 at Southampton. rrow home wins were recorded over Queens Park ngers and Southampton, but the away form was causing ncern, with three defeats and 11 goals conceded.

the FA Cup Southend United were beaten 2–0 at home the following round brought a shock as the Hammers mped to a 3–0 defeat at Grimsby Town. Manager dknapp then made some new signings, with three eigners joining the squad. The Romanian forward Ilie mitrescu was joined by Croatian defender Slaven Bilic d the Portuguese forward Dani. This had an effect, with e successive victories including wins at London rivals elsea and Tottenham. A top-ten place was the target, and headed goals from Dowie against Manchester City ped the cause. The team did, however, lack a quality ker, which was evident in defeats at Liverpool and ewcastle where no goals were scored. The last home me of the season against Sheffield Wednesday saw Alvin

Martin make his final appearance for the club, and the standing ovation he received was fully deserved.

STAN LAZARIDIS

The flying winger began his career as a teenager playing for the Western Australian Premier League team Floreat Athena.

After making 28 appearances in season 1991–92 he joined West Adelaide in the National Soccer League. His outstanding form saw him selected for the Australian national side and he went on to make 60 appearances for his country.

In 1995 West Ham went on a tour of Australia and he was in the Western Australian side that faced the Hammers. After impressing in that game he signed for West Ham in September 1995 and made his debut that month against Chelsea. Later that season he suffered a broken leg against Grimsby Town in the FA Cup, which forced him to miss the rest of the campaign. After returning to the side he became a regular member and was later converted to a capable wing-back. He played 86 games for the Hammers before West Ham accepted a bid of £1.5 million for him from Birmingham City in July 1999.
At St Andrews he settled in well and won a runners-up medal in the 2001 League Cup final against Liverpool, while the following season he gained promotion to the Premier League as the Blues were successful in winning the playoff final with Norwich City. After making 223 appearances for Birmingham he was released at the end of the 2005/06 season and returned to Australia. Back home he played 15 games for his home town club Perth Glory before retiring in 2008.

Carling Premiership
nal Table 1995-96

	P	HOME					AWAY					Pts
		W	D	L	F	A	W	D	L	F	A	
ckburn Rovers	42	17	2	2	54	21	10	6	5	26	18	89
nchester United	42	16	4	1	42	5	10	6	5	35	24	88
kingham Forest	42	12	6	3	36	18	10	5	6	36	25	77
erpool	42	13	5	3	38	13	8	6	7	27	24	74
ds United	42	13	5	3	35	15	7	8	6	24	23	73
wcastle United	42	14	6	1	46	20	6	6	9	21	27	72
enham Hotspur	42	10	5	6	32	25	6	9	6	34	33	62
eens Park Rangers	42	11	3	7	36	26	6	6	9	25	33	60
nbledon	42	9	5	7	26	26	6	6	9	22	39	56
thampton	42	8	9	4	33	27	4	9	8	28	36	54
lsea	42	7	7	7	25	22	6	8	7	25	33	54
enal	42	6	9	6	27	21	7	3	11	26	28	51
ffield Wednesday	42	7	7	7	26	26	6	5	10	23	31	51
st Ham United	42	9	6	6	28	19	4	5	12	16	29	50
rton	42	8	9	4	31	23	3	8	10	13	28	50
entry City	42	7	7	7	23	25	5	7	9	21	37	50
nchester City	42	7	7	6	37	28	4	6	11	16	36	49
on Villa	42	6	9	6	27	24	5	6	10	24	32	48
stal Palace	42	6	6	9	16	23	5	6	10	18	26	45
wich City	42	8	8	5	27	21	2	5	14	10	33	43
ester City	42	5	6	10	28	37	1	5	15	17	43	29
wich Town	42	5	3	13	24	34	2	3	16	12	59	27

Season **1995-96** FA Carling Premiership
Match Details

Manager **Harry Redknapp**   Final League Position **10/20**

	Date		Competition	Venue	Opponents	Results		Attendance	Position	Scorers
1	Aug 19	Sat	Prem	H	Leeds United	L	1-2	22,901	14	Williamson
2	Aug 23	Wed	Prem	A	Manchester United	L	1-2	31,966	18	Bruce (og)
3	Aug 26	Sat	Prem	A	Nottingham Forest	D	1-1	26,645	17	Allen M.
4	Aug 30	Wed	Prem	H	Tottenham Hotspur	D	1-1	23,516	17	Hutchison
5	Sep 11	Mon	Prem	H	Chelsea	L	1-3	19,228	19	Hutchison
6	Sep 16	Sat	Prem	A	Arsenal	L	0-1	38,065	19	
7	Sep 20	Wed	FLC 2:1	A	Bristol Rovers	W	1-0	7,103		Moncur
8	Sep 23	Sat	Prem	H	Everton	W	2-1	21,085	17	Dicks 2 [1 pen]
9	Oct 2	Mon	Prem	A	Southampton	D	0-0	13,568	16	
10	Oct 4	Wed	FLC 2:2	H	Bristol Rovers	W	3-0	15,375		Bishop, Cottee, Dicks [pen]
11	Oct 16	Mon	Prem	A	Wimbledon	W	1-0	9,411	13	Cottee
12	Oct 21	Sat	Prem	H	Blackburn Rovers	D	1-1	21,776	13	Dowie
13	Oct 25	Wed	FLC 3	A	Southampton	L	1-2	11,059		Cottee
14	Oct 28	Sat	Prem	A	Sheffield Wednesday	W	1-0	23,917	12	Dowie
15	Nov 4	Sat	Prem	H	Aston Villa	L	1-4	23,637	12	Dicks [pen]
16	Nov 18	Sat	Prem	A	Bolton Wanderers	W	3-0	19,047	11	Bishop, Cottee, Williamson
17	Nov 22	Wed	Prem	H	Liverpool	D	0-0	24,324	13	
18	Nov 25	Sat	Prem	H	Queens Park Rangers	W	1-0	21,504	10	Cottee
19	Dec 2	Sat	Prem	A	Blackburn Rovers	L	2-4	26,638	13	Dicks [pen], Slater
20	Dec 9	Sat	Prem	A	Everton	L	0-3	31,178	13	
21	Dec 16	Sat	Prem	H	Southampton	W	2-1	18,501	13	Cottee, Dowie
22	Dec 23	Sat	Prem	A	Middlesbrough	L	2-4	28,640	13	Cottee, Dicks
23	Jan 1	Mon	Prem	A	Manchester City	L	1-2	26,024	14	Dowie
24	Jan 6	Sat	FAC 3	H	Southend United	W	2-0	23,284		Hughes, Moncur
25	Jan 13	Sat	Prem	A	Leeds United	L	0-2	30,472	14	
26	Jan 22	Mon	Prem	H	Manchester United	L	0-1	24,197	16	
27	Jan 31	Wed	Prem	H	Coventry City	W	3-2	18,884	14	Cottee, Dowie, Rieper
28	Feb 3	Sat	Prem	H	Nottingham Forest	W	1-0	21,651	13	Slater
29	Feb 7	Wed	FAC 4	H	Grimsby Town	D	1-1	22,020		Dowie
30	Feb 12	Mon	Prem	A	Tottenham Hotspur	W	1-0	29,781	13	Dani
31	Feb 14	Wed	FAC 4 Rep	A	Grimsby Town	L	0-3	8,382		
32	Feb 17	Sat	Prem	A	Chelsea	W	2-1	25,252	12	Dicks, Williamson
33	Feb 21	Wed	Prem	H	Newcastle United	W	2-0	23,843	11	Cottee, Williamson
34	Feb 24	Sat	Prem	H	Arsenal	L	0-1	24,217	11	
35	Mar 2	Sat	Prem	A	Coventry City	D	2-2	17,448	11	Cottee, Rieper
36	Mar 9	Sat	Prem	H	Middlesbrough	W	2-0	23,850	11	Dicks [pen], Dowie
37	Mar 18	Mon	Prem	A	Newcastle United	L	0-3	36,331	11	
38	Mar 23	Sat	Prem	H	Manchester City	W	4-2	24,017	11	Dowie 2, Dani, Dicks
39	Apr 6	Sat	Prem	H	Wimbledon	D	1-1	20,462	10	Dicks
40	Apr 8	Mon	Prem	A	Liverpool	L	0-2	40,326	10	
41	Apr 13	Sat	Prem	H	Bolton Wanderers	W	1-0	23,086	10	Cottee
42	Apr 17	Wed	Prem	A	Aston Villa	D	1-1	26,768	10	Cottee
43	Apr 27	Sat	Prem	A	Queens Park Rangers	L	0-3	18,828	11	
44	May 5	Sun	Prem	H	Sheffield Wednesday	D	1-1	23,790	10	Dicks

Team Line-Ups

BILIC Slaven	BISHOP Ian	BOERE Jeroen	BOOGERS Marco	BREACKER Tim	BROWN Kenny	CARVALHO Dani	COTTEE Tony	DICKS Julian	DOWIE Iain	DUMITRESCU Ilie	FERDINAND Rio	FINN Neil	GORDON Dale	HARKES John	HUGHES Michael	HUTCHISON Don	LAMPARD Frank Jnr	LAZARIDIS Stan	MARTIN Alvin	MIKLOSKO Ludek	MONCUR John	POTTS Steve	RIEPER Marc	ROWLAND Keith	SEALEY Les	SLATER Robbie	WATSON Mark	WHITBREAD Adrian	WILLIAMSON Danny	#
	7		b	2			9	3							16			a		1	10	4	8	12/b					20/a	1
	7	a		2			9	3							16					1	10	4	8						20/a	2
	7			2			9/a	3							16			a		1	10	4	8		19					3
	7	a		2			9	3							16/a					1	10	4	8		19					4
	7/a			2			9	3		14					16			a		1	10	4	8		19					5
	7			2			9/a	3		14					16/b	b		a		1	10/c	4	8	c	19					6
	7			2			9	3		14/a								17	5	1	10	4	a		19/b			b		7
	7			2			9/b	3		14								17	5	1	10	4/a	8		19			b		8
	7			2		a	9	3		14					16			17/a	5	1	10	4		12	19					9
	7						9	3		14						24				1	10	4	8		19					10
	7						9	3		14						24			5	1		4	8		19					11
	7						9	3		14						24		a	5	1	10/a	4	8		19/a					12
	7						9	3		14						24			5	1		4	8		19					13
	7						9	3		14				b	24			a	5	1	10/a	4	8		19/b					14
	7		a				9	3		14					16/a	24			5	1		4	8		19/b					15
	7									14				25		24			5	1		4	8	12					20	16
	7						9			14				25		24			5	1		4	8	12					20	17
	7		a				9			14				25/b		24			5	1		4	8	12/a	b				20	18
	7/a	c		2			9/c	3		14				25/b		24		a		1		4	8		b				20	19
	7			2			9/a	3		14						24				1		4	8	a	19				20	20
	7		a				9	3		14						24			5/a	1	10/b	4	8		b				20	21
	7			2			9	3		14						24/b				1	10/a	4	8	a					20	22
	7							3		14		31		25		24		a			10	4	8	19					20/a	23
	7						9	3		14				25		24				1		4	8	12					20	24
	7						9	3		14						24				1	10	4	8	12/a	a				20	25
	7				15		9	3		14						24				1	10	4	8	a	19/a				20	26
	7				15		9/a	3		14						24				1	10/b	4	8					a	20	27
	7				15	b	9/b	3		14						24				1		4	8		19/a			a	20	28
	7						9	3		14						24	a/b			1		4	8	b	19/a		22		20	29
28	7				15/a	a		3		14					b	24/b				1		4	8	12					20	30
	7						9	3		14				a	b	24			5/a	1		4	8	12/b					20	31
28	7				15/a	a		3		14						24				1		4	8	12					20	32
28/a	7						9/b	3		14				b	a	24				1		4	8	12					20	33
	7					a	9	3		14				25		24				1		4	8	12					20	34
28	7						9/a	3		14						24				1		4	8	12					20	35
28	7			2			9/a	3		14	a					24				1		4		12					20	36
28	7/a				b	a		3		14			18/b			24				1		4	8	12		30			20	37
28	7			2		a		3		14			18/a			24				1			8	12					20	38
28	7			2	16			3		14						24/a				1			8	12/a	a				20	39
28	7			2		a		3		14						24/a				1			8	12	19				20	40
28	7			2			9	3		14						24/a				1	a		8	b	19/b				20	41
28	7			2		a	9	3		14										1	10	4/a	8	12					20	42
28				2			9	3								24				1	10/a	4	8	12				a	20	43
28				2			9/c	3		14/a	c					24	b	a		1		4	8	12/b					20	44

1996-97
Story of the season

The pre-season **new signings brought expectancy** of an exciting season. Central defender Richard Hall arrived for £1.9 million, a free transfer saw the Portuguese superstar Paulo Futre join from AC Milan and **a club record fee of £2.4 million was paid** for the Romanian international forward Florin Raducioiu.

Unfortunately there were many injuries in the pɪ season matches and the early league results were poor. Bc Romanian forwards, Dumitrescu and Raducioiu, we finding it difficult to adjust to the demands of the Prem League.

The League Cup brought a 2–1 aggregate victory ov Barnet and another signing was made with the acquisiti of forward Hugo Porfirio on loan from Sporting Lisbc Results improved, with league wins over Leicester City a Blackburn Rovers and a 4–1 home win in the League C

Appearances & Goals 1996-97

	League			FA Cup			League Cup			Total	
	Starts	Subs	Goals	Starts	Subs	Goals	Starts	Subs	Goals	Starts	Subs
BILIC Slaven	35	0	2	1	0	0	5	0	1	41	0
BISHOP Ian	26	3	1	2	0	0	5	0	0	33	3
BOWEN Mark	15	2	1	0	0	0	3	0	0	18	2
BOYLAN Lee	0	1	0	0	0	0	0	0	0	0	1
BREACKER Tim	22	4	0	2	0	0	3	0	0	27	4
COTTEE Tony	2	1	0	0	0	0	2	0	1	4	1
DICKS Julian	31	0	6	2	0	0	5	0	2	38	0
DOWIE Iain	18	5	0	0	0	0	5	0	2	23	5
DUMITRESCU Ilie	3	4	0	0	0	0	2	1	0	5	5
FERDINAND Rio	11	4	2	1	0	0	0	1	0	12	5
FUTRE Paulo	4	5	0	0	0	0	0	0	0	4	5
HALL Richard	7	0	0	0	0	0	0	0	0	7	0
HARTSON John	11	0	5	0	0	0	0	0	0	11	0
HUGHES Michael	31	2	3	2	0	0	4	0	0	37	2
JONES Steve	5	3	0	2	0	0	0	1	0	7	4
KITSON Paul	14	0	8	0	0	0	0	0	0	14	0
LAMPARD Frank Jnr	3	10	0	1	0	0	1	1	0	5	11
LAZARIDIS Stan	13	9	1	1	0	0	3	1	0	17	10
LOMAS Steve	7	0	0	0	0	0	0	0	0	7	0
MAUTONE Steve	1	0	0	0	0	0	2	0	0	3	0
MIKLOSKO Ludek	36	0	0	2	0	0	3	0	0	41	0
MONCUR John	26	1	2	1	0	0	4	0	0	31	1
NEWELL Mike	6	1	0	0	0	0	0	0	0	6	1
OMOYINMI Emmanuel	0	1	0	0	0	0	0	0	0	0	1
PORFIRIO Hugo	15	8	2	1	1	1	2	0	1	18	9
POTTS Steve	17	3	0	1	0	0	1	0	0	19	3
RADUCIOIU Florin	6	5	2	0	0	0	1	0	1	7	5
RIEPER Marc	26	2	1	1	0	0	4	0	0	31	2
ROWLAND Keith	11	4	1	0	0	0	0	0	0	11	4
SEALEY Les	1	1	0	0	0	0	0	0	0	1	1
SLATER Robbie	2	1	0	0	0	0	0	0	0	2	1
WILLIAMSON Danny	13	2	0	2	0	0	0	1	0	15	3
own goal			2								
Totals	418	82	39	22	1	1	55	6	8	495	89

inst Nottingham Forest. Dicks and Bilic were superb at
e heart of the defence but a striker was needed to convert
e chances. Centre-forward Iain Dowie had a night to
get in the League Cup at Stockport County – he headed
own goal and then broke his ankle in a tie which saw the
mmers beaten 2–1. During December and January there
s only one win and further misery came when Second
vision Wrexham knocked the Hammers out of the FA
p after winning 1–0 at Upton Park.

ow out of both cup competitions and eighteenth in the
gue, the fans were getting frustrated. Manager Harry
dknapp then signed two quality forwards in Paul Kitson
d John Hartson, and there was an immediate effect as
ttenham were beaten 4–3, Kitson scored twice against
elsea in a 3–2 win and two goals from Hartson at
ventry saw the Hammers win 3–1. The pair finally
cued West Ham from relegation when a hat-trick from
tson and two goals from Hartson gave West Ham a 5–1
me victory against Sheffield Wednesday. The season
ded with Slaven Bilic being sold to Everton for a decent

fee of £4.5 million; waiting to replace him was young Rio
Ferdinand – a star of the future.

JOHN HARTSON

The Welsh international striker started his career with Luton Town in 1992. With the Hatters he scored 11 goals in 54 outings before a fee of £2.5 million took him to Arsenal in January 1995.

He became a regular in the side and forged an exciting partnership with Ian Wright. His fine form led to his first cap for Wales and he went on to score 14 goals and represent his country on 51 occasions.

After scoring 17 goals in 70 appearances for the Gunners he was signed by West Ham in February 1997. The signing of Hartson together with strike partner Kitson saved the Hammers from relegation that season. The following campaign he could not stop scoring at first, having netted 19 goals before Christmas, but in the New Year he suffered a loss of form, scoring only a further three league goals., Manager Redknapp accepted a hefty fee of £7.5 million for him from Wimbledon in January 1999.. John had been a popular figure at Upton Park and he left after scoring 33 goals in 73 appearances.

His time with the Dons was beset with injuries and after two seasons he moved on to Coventry City for a short spell. In August 2001 his career took a turn for the better when he joined Celtic for a fee of £6 million. With the Glasgow giants he scored 109 goals in a total of 201 appearances. He returned to England in 2006 and had short spells with West Bromwich Albion and on loan at Norwich City.

Carling Premiership
nal Table 1996-97

	P	HOME					AWAY					Pts
		W	D	L	F	A	W	D	L	F	A	
achester United	38	12	5	2	38	17	9	7	3	38	27	75
wcastle United	38	13	3	3	54	20	6	8	5	19	20	68
enal	38	10	5	4	36	18	9	6	4	26	14	68
rpool	38	10	6	3	38	19	9	5	5	24	18	68
n Villa	38	11	5	3	27	13	6	5	8	20	21	61
lsea	38	9	8	2	33	22	7	3	9	25	33	59
ffield Wednesday	38	8	10	1	25	16	6	5	8	25	35	57
nbledon	38	9	6	4	28	21	6	5	8	21	25	56
ester City	38	7	5	7	22	26	5	6	8	24	28	47
enham Hotspur	38	8	4	7	19	17	5	3	11	25	34	46
ds United	38	7	7	5	15	13	4	6	9	13	25	46
by County	38	8	6	5	25	22	3	7	9	20	36	46
ckburn Rovers	38	8	4	7	28	23	1	11	7	14	20	42
st Ham United	38	7	6	6	27	25	3	6	10	12	23	42
rton	38	7	4	8	24	22	3	8	8	20	35	42
thampton	38	6	7	6	32	24	4	4	11	18	32	41
entry City	38	4	8	7	19	23	5	6	8	19	31	41
derland	38	7	6	6	20	18	3	4	12	15	35	40
ldlesbrough	38	8	5	6	34	25	2	7	10	17	35	39
ingham Forest	38	3	9	7	15	27	3	7	9	16	32	34

Season **1996-97** FA Carling Premiership
Match Details

Manager **Harry Redknapp**   Final League Position **14/20**

	Date		Competition	Venue	Opponents	Results		Attendance	Position	Scorers
1	Aug 17	Sat	Prem	A	Arsenal	L	0-2	38,056	16	
2	Aug 21	Wed	Prem	H	Coventry City	D	1-1	21,580	17	Rieper
3	Aug 24	Sat	Prem	H	Southampton	W	2-1	21,227	11	Hughes, Dicks [pen]
4	Sep 3	Tue	Prem	A	Middlesbrough	L	1-4	30,061	15	Hughes
5	Sep 8	Sun	Prem	A	Sunderland	D	0-0	18,581	16	
6	Sep 14	Sat	Prem	H	Wimbledon	L	0-2	21,924	17	
7	Sep 18	Wed	FLC 2:1	A	Barnet	D	1-1	3,849		Cottee
8	Sep 21	Sat	Prem	A	Nottingham Forest	W	2-0	23,352	13	Bowen, Hughes
9	Sep 25	Wed	FLC 2:2	H	Barnet	W	1-0	15,264		Bilic
10	Sep 29	Sun	Prem	H	Liverpool	L	1-3	25,064	15	Bilic
11	Oct 12	Sat	Prem	A	Everton	L	1-2	36,541	16	Dicks [pen]
12	Oct 19	Sat	Prem	H	Leicester City	W	1-0	22,285	13	Moncur
13	Oct 23	Wed	FLC 3	H	Nottingham Forest	W	4-1	19,402		Dowie 2, Dicks [pen], Porfirio
14	Oct 26	Sat	Prem	H	Blackburn Rovers	W	2-1	23,947	10	Porfirio, Berg (og)
15	Nov 2	Sat	Prem	A	Tottenham Hotspur	L	0-1	32,975	12	
16	Nov 16	Sat	Prem	A	Newcastle United	D	1-1	36,552	12	Rowland
17	Nov 23	Sat	Prem	H	Derby County	D	1-1	24,576	13	Bishop
18	Nov 27	Wed	FLC 4	H	Stockport County	D	1-1	20,061		Raducioiu
19	Nov 30	Sat	Prem	A	Sheffield Wednesday	D	0-0	22,321	13	
20	Dec 4	Wed	Prem	H	Aston Villa	L	0-2	19,105	15	
21	Dec 8	Sun	Prem	H	Manchester United	D	2-2	25,045	14	Raducioiu, Dicks [pen]
22	Dec 18	Wed	FLC 4 Rep	A	Stockport County	L	1-2	9,834		Dicks
23	Dec 21	Sat	Prem	A	Chelsea	L	1-3	27,012	15	Porfirio
24	Dec 28	Sat	Prem	H	Sunderland	W	2-0	24,077	16	Bilic, Raducioiu
25	Jan 1	Wed	Prem	H	Nottingham Forest	L	0-1	22,358	16	
26	Jan 4	Sat	FAC 3	A	Wrexham	D	1-1	9,747		Porfirio
27	Jan 11	Sat	Prem	A	Liverpool	D	0-0	40,102	17	
28	Jan 20	Mon	Prem	H	Leeds United	L	0-2	19,441	18	
29	Jan 25	Sat	FAC 3 Rep	H	Wrexham	L	0-1	16,763		
30	Jan 29	Wed	Prem	H	Arsenal	L	1-2	24,382	18	Rose (og)
31	Feb 1	Sat	Prem	A	Blackburn Rovers	L	1-2	21,994	18	Ferdinand
32	Feb 15	Sat	Prem	A	Derby County	L	0-1	18,057	18	
33	Feb 24	Mon	Prem	H	Tottenham Hotspur	W	4-3	23,998	17	Dicks 2 [1 pen], Hartson, Kitson
34	Mar 1	Sat	Prem	A	Leeds United	L	0-1	30,575	18	
35	Mar 12	Wed	Prem	H	Chelsea	W	3-2	24,502	17	Kitson 2, Dicks [pen]
36	Mar 15	Sat	Prem	A	Aston Villa	D	0-0	35,992	17	
37	Mar 18	Tue	Prem	A	Wimbledon	D	1-1	15,771	16	Lazaridis
38	Mar 22	Sat	Prem	A	Coventry City	W	3-1	22,290	15	Hartson 2, Ferdinand
39	Apr 9	Wed	Prem	H	Middlesbrough	D	0-0	23,988	16	
40	Apr 12	Sat	Prem	A	Southampton	L	0-2	15,245	17	
41	Apr 19	Sat	Prem	H	Everton	D	2-2	24,525	18	Kitson 2
42	Apr 23	Wed	Prem	H	Leicester City	W	1-0	20,327	16	Moncur
43	May 3	Sat	Prem	H	Sheffield Wednesday	W	5-1	24,960	15	Kitson 3, Hartson 2
44	May 6	Tue	Prem	H	Newcastle United	D	0-0	24,617	12	
45	May 11	Sun	Prem	A	Manchester United	L	0-2	55,249	14	

eam Line-Ups

	BISHOP Ian	BOWEN Mark	BOYLAN Lee	BREACKER Tim	COTTEE Tony	DICKS Julian	DOWIE Iain	DUMITRESCU Ilie	FERDINAND Rio	FUTRE Paulo	HALL Richard	HARTSON John	HUGHES Michael	JONES Steve	KITSON Paul	LAMPARD Frank Jnr	LAZARIDIS Stan	LOMAS Steve	MAUTONE Steve	MIKLOSKO Ludek	MONCUR John	NEWELL Mike	OMOYINMI Emmanuel	PORFIRIO Hugo	POTTS Steve	RADUCIOIU Florin	RIEPER Marc	ROWLAND Keith	SEALEY Les	SLATER Robbie	WILLIAMSON Danny	#
c				2		3	14		c				24	23		26/a	b			1							8	12/b		a	6	1
b				2/a		3	14			a			24	23/b			17			1							8			19	6	2
		20	a			3	14		c	10			24				17/c			1						b	8/b			19/a	6	3
		20		2		3	a	b		10			24			c	17/b			1					4/a	11/c					6	4
		20		2		3		18/b	c	10/c			24	a						1						11/a	8			b	6	5
		20	2/a		c	3	14	18/b		10/c			24							1	b						8				6	6
	7	20		2/a	9	3	14						24			b	a		30		16/b						8					7
	7/b	20	a		9/a	3	14						24			b	17		30		16						8					8
	7			2	9/a	3	14	18	b							a	17/b		30		16						8					9
	7	20/b		2	9/a	3	14	a					24							1	16					b	8					10
	7/b	20				3	14			b			24							1	16			13	4/a	a		12				11
	7	20/a	a			3	14						24			b	17			1	16			13		11/b	8					12
	7	20				3	14						24				17			1	16			13			8					13
	7	20/a	a			3	14		c				24			b	17			1	16/c			13/b			8					14
	7			2		3	14			a			24				17			1	16/a			13			8					15
	7			2		3	14			a			24								16				4	11/a		12				16
	7			2		3	14			a			24				17/a			1	16			13	4	11						17
	7			2		3	14			a			24	6			17/a			1					4	11						18
	7			2		3	14						24/a		7	a				1	16						8	12				19
	7	a		2/a		3	14						24			b				1	16					11	8	12/b				20
	7	20				3	14	18					24							1	16		a			b	8	12/b				21
	7	20				3	14/a	18					24							1	16			13			8			a		22
	7/a	20				3							24			a				1	16/c	19		13		b	8	12/b		c		23
	7	20				3							24			a				1	16/a	19/b		13		b	8				6	24
	7/a	20/c				3							24			b	a			1		19/b	c	13		11	8				6	25
	7			2		3							24	23						1	16			13	4		8				6	26
	7			2		3							24	23/a		a				1	16	c		13/c	b		8				6/b	27
	7			2		3							24	23			17/a			1		19		a			8				6	28
	7			2		3			27				24	23		26	17/a			1										a	6	29
				2		6							24	b		a				1	16/a	19		13			8	12/b			6	30
	7			2		3			b				24	23/b		a						19					8	12/a		21	6	31
	7			2		3			27			10			9	b				1				a	4		8/a	12/b			6	32
	7	20		2		3	a		27			10	24		9/a					1	16				4							33
	7/b	20/a	2/c			3	14		27				24		9	b				1	16			c						a		34
	7/b			2		3	14		27/a				24		9	c				1	16			a	4						b/c	35
	7			2		3			a			10			9	26/a	17			1	16				4							36
	7/a			2		3			27			10			9		a			1	16			b	4/b		8					37
	7/c			2/a		3	b		27/b			10			9					1	16			c	4		8			a		38
	7										5	10	24		9		17/a	11		1				a	4		8					39
	7/c			b							5	10	24		9		a	11		1				c	4		8/b	12/a				40
	a								27		5	10	24					11		1	16/a			13/b	4			b				41
	a								27		5	10	24		9/a			11		1	16/a			13/b	4		8			b		42
b	c								27		5	10			9		17/b	11/c		1	16			13				a				43
b									27		5	10	a		9		17	11		1	16/b			13/a	4							44
							14		27/a		5		a		9		17	11		1/b	16			13	4			b				45

1997-98
Story of the season

The first signing of the season was made when Israeli international midfielder **Eyal Berkovic was purchased for a fee of £1.75 million.** The first two games were won as the Hammers beat Barnsley 2–1 away and old rivals Tottenham 1–0 at home. **In September there were mixed results;** Newcastle won 1–0 at Upton Park followed by a poor 4–0 reverse at Arsenal.

Both Hartson and Berkovic were on target in the 2- home victory against Liverpool and in the League Cup hat-trick from Hartson saw Huddersfield Town beat 3–0.

There was a flurry of transfer activity as Danny Willia went to Everton in a swap for defender David Unswort Danish defender Marc Rieper went to Celtic, wh midfielder Michael Hughes joined Wimbledon. In th place West Ham signed defender Ian Pearce and wing Andy Impey.

In top form was John Hartson as he scored twice in the 3- League Cup win against Aston Villa. The away form w causing concern, with defeats at Leicester City, Chelsea a

Appearances & Goals 1997-98

	League			FA Cup			League Cup			Total	
	Starts	Subs	Goals	Starts	Subs	Goals	Starts	Subs	Goals	Starts	Subs
ABOU Samassi	12	7	5	3	2	0	1	1	1	16	10
ALVES Paulo	0	4	0	0	0	0	0	0	0	0	4
BERKOVIC Eyal	34	1	7	6	0	2	5	0	0	45	1
BISHOP Ian	3	0	0	0	0	0	0	1	0	3	1
BREACKER Tim	18	1	0	2	1	0	4	0	0	24	2
DOWIE Iain	7	5	0	0	1	0	2	1	0	9	7
FERDINAND Rio	35	0	0	6	0	0	5	0	0	46	0
FORREST Craig	13	0	0	4	0	0	3	0	0	20	0
HARTSON John	32	0	15	5	0	3	5	0	6	42	0
HODGES Lee	0	2	0	0	3	0	0	0	0	0	5
HUGHES Michael	2	3	0	0	0	0	1	0	0	3	3
IMPEY Andy	19	0	0	3	0	0	3	0	0	25	0
KITSON Paul	12	1	4	2	0	1	2	0	0	16	1
LAMA Bernard	12	0	0	2	0	0	0	0	0	14	0
LAMPARD Frank Jnr	27	4	4	6	0	1	5	0	4	38	4
LAZARIDIS Stan	27	1	2	6	0	0	1	0	0	34	1
LOMAS Steve	33	0	2	5	0	1	4	0	0	42	0
MEAN Scott	0	3	0	0	0	0	0	0	0	0	3
MIKLOSKO Ludek	13	0	0	0	0	0	2	0	0	15	0
MONCUR John	17	3	1	2	1	0	1	0	0	20	4
MOORE Ian	0	1	0	0	0	0	0	0	0	0	1
OMOYINMI Emmanuel	1	4	2	0	0	0	0	0	0	1	4
PEARCE Ian	30	0	1	6	0	1	3	0	0	39	0
POTTS Steve	14	9	0	4	1	0	3	1	0	21	11
RIEPER Marc	5	0	1	0	0	0	0	0	0	5	0
ROWLAND Keith	6	1	0	0	0	0	0	2	0	6	3
SINCLAIR Trevor	14	0	7	0	0	0	0	0	0	14	0
TERRIER David	0	1	0	0	0	0	0	0	0	0	1
UNSWORTH David	32	0	2	4	0	0	5	0	0	41	0
own goal			3								
Totals	418	51	56	66	9	9	55	6	11	539	66

eeds United. Young Frank Lampard scored a hat-trick as
alsall were knocked out of the League Cup 4–1 at Upton
ark.

riker Kitson was missing with a groin injury, which
rompted the purchase of French forward Samassi Abou.
itson returned from injury in December and scored the
inning goals in victories over Sheffield Wednesday,
oventry City and Wimbledon. The Yorkshire non-league
de Emley were the visitors in the FA Cup and were
arrowly beaten 2–1. Days later the Hammers went out of
e League Cup after losing 2–1 at home to Arsenal. At
me to Barnsley Abou scored twice as the Yorkshire side
ere crushed 6–0.

hen the Irish pair Rowland and Dowie joined Queens
rk Rangers in a swap deal for winger Trevor Sinclair, who
ored twice on his Hammers debut against Everton. An
-form West Ham side then won 2–1 at Manchester City in
e FA Cup and in the next round Blackburn Rovers were
ocked out following a tense penalty shoot-out at Ewood
rk. In March there were fine home wins against Chelsea

and Leeds but the FA Cup game at home to Arsenal saw the
Hammers this time lose on penalties.

A UEFA Cup place was looking likely until a 4–2 home
defeat by Southampton was followed by a 5–0 thrashing at
Liverpool. The final home game saw an exciting clash with
Leicester City, with the Hammers winning 4–3. Former
Hammer Tony Cottee was given a rousing welcome and
repaid the ovation by scoring twice. An eighth-place finish
was the Hammers highest finish in the Premier League.

TREVOR SINCLAIR

**He first made his breakthrough in 1990
when he joined Third Division side
Blackpool.**

Over four seasons at Bloomfield Road he
scored 15 goals in 112 league appearances.
A fee of £650,000 took him to Queens Park
Rangers in August 1993 . Trevor was at Loftus
Road for five seasons, scoring 16 goals in 167
league outings before transferring to West
Ham in January 1998.

He was an immediate hit, scoring seven goals
in his first 14 league games. His all-round
ability saw him gain his first full England cap
against Sweden in November 2001. He later
played for England in the 2002 World Cup
finals in Japan and while with West Ham
gained a total of 11 England caps. Following
West Ham's relegation in 2003 he left to join
Manchester City for a fee of £2.5 million. He
had been a popular figure at Upton Park,
having scored 38 goals in 206 appearances.
Having played in 82 league games for City he
was released at the end of the 2006/07 season

A Carling Premiership
inal Table 1997-98

	P	HOME					AWAY					Pts
		W	D	L	F	A	W	D	L	F	A	
senal	38	15	2	2	43	10	8	7	4	25	23	78
nchester United	38	13	4	2	42	9	10	4	5	31	17	77
erpool	38	13	2	4	42	16	5	9	5	26	26	65
elsea	38	13	2	4	37	14	7	1	11	34	29	63
eds United	38	9	5	5	31	21	8	3	8	26	25	59
ckburn Rovers	38	11	4	4	40	26	5	6	8	17	26	58
on Villa	38	9	3	7	26	24	8	3	8	23	24	57
est Ham United	**38**	**13**	**4**	**2**	**40**	**18**	**3**	**4**	**12**	**16**	**39**	**56**
rby County	38	12	3	4	33	18	4	4	11	19	31	55
cester City	38	6	10	3	21	15	7	4	8	30	26	53
ventry City	38	8	9	2	26	17	4	7	8	20	27	52
uthampton	38	10	1	8	28	23	4	5	10	22	32	48
effield Wednesday	38	9	5	5	30	26	3	3	13	22	41	44
tenham Hotspur	38	7	8	4	23	22	4	3	12	21	34	44
wcastle United	38	8	5	6	22	20	3	6	10	13	24	44
mbledon	38	5	6	8	18	25	5	8	6	16	21	44
erton	38	7	5	7	25	27	2	8	9	16	29	40
ton Wanderers	38	7	8	4	25	22	2	5	12	16	39	40
nsley	38	7	4	8	25	35	3	1	15	12	47	35
stal Palace	38	2	5	12	15	39	6	4	9	22	32	33

Season **1997-98** FA Carling Premiership
Match Details

Manager **Harry Redknapp**   Final League Position **8/20**

	Date		Competition	Venue	Opponents	Results		Attendance	Position	Scorers
1	Aug 9	Sat	Prem	A	Barnsley	W	2-1	18,667	4	Hartson, Lampard
2	Aug 13	Wed	Prem	H	Tottenham Hotspur	W	2-1	25,354	3	Berkovic, Hartson
3	Aug 23	Sat	Prem	A	Everton	L	1-2	34,356	7	Watson (og)
4	Aug 27	Wed	Prem	A	Coventry City	D	1-1	18,291	5	Kitson
5	Aug 30	Sat	Prem	H	Wimbledon	W	3-1	24,516	3	Berkovic, Hartson, Rieper
6	Sep 13	Sat	Prem	A	Manchester United	L	1-2	55,068	6	Hartson
7	Sep 16	Tue	FLC 2:1	A	Huddersfield Town	L	0-1	8,525		
8	Sep 20	Sat	Prem	H	Newcastle United	L	0-1	25,884	6	
9	Sep 24	Wed	Prem	A	Arsenal	L	0-4	38,012	10	
10	Sep 27	Sat	Prem	H	Liverpool	W	2-1	25,908	7	Berkovic, Hartson
11	Sep 29	Mon	FLC 2:2	H	Huddersfield Town	W	3-0	16,137		Hartson 3
12	Oct 4	Sat	Prem	A	Southampton	L	0-3	15,212	9	
13	Oct 15	Wed	FLC 3	H	Aston Villa	W	3-0	20,360		Hartson 2, Lampard
14	Oct 18	Sat	Prem	H	Bolton Wanderers	W	3-0	24,864	8	Hartson 2, Berkovic
15	Oct 27	Mon	Prem	A	Leicester City	L	1-2	20,201	11	Berkovic
16	Nov 9	Sun	Prem	A	Chelsea	L	1-2	33,256	14	Hartson [pen]
17	Nov 19	Wed	FLC 4	H	Walsall	W	4-1	17,463		Lampard 3, Hartson
18	Nov 23	Sun	Prem	A	Leeds United	L	1-3	29,447	15	Lampard
19	Nov 29	Sat	Prem	H	Aston Villa	W	2-1	24,976	12	Hartson 2
20	Dec 3	Wed	Prem	H	Crystal Palace	W	4-1	23,335	10	Berkovic, Hartson, Lomas, Unsworth
21	Dec 6	Sat	Prem	A	Derby County	L	0-2	29,300	10	
22	Dec 13	Sat	Prem	H	Sheffield Wednesday	W	1-0	24,344	10	Kitson
23	Dec 20	Sat	Prem	A	Blackburn Rovers	L	0-3	21,653	10	
24	Dec 26	Fri	Prem	H	Coventry City	W	1-0	22,477	8	Kitson
25	Dec 28	Sun	Prem	A	Wimbledon	W	2-1	22,087	8	Kitson, Kimble (og)
26	Jan 3	Sat	FAC 3	H	Emley	W	2-1	18,629		Hartson, Lampard
27	Jan 6	Tue	FLC 5	H	Arsenal	L	1-2	24,770		Abou
28	Jan 10	Sat	Prem	H	Barnsley	W	6-0	23,714	7	Abou 2, Hartson, Lampard, Lazaridis, Moncur
29	Jan 17	Sat	Prem	A	Tottenham Hotspur	L	0-1	30,284	8	
30	Jan 25	Sun	FAC 4	A	Manchester City	W	2-1	26,495		Berkovic, Lomas
31	Jan 31	Sat	Prem	H	Everton	D	2-2	25,905	8	Sinclair 2
32	Feb 7	Sat	Prem	A	Newcastle United	W	1-0	36,736	8	Lazaridis
33	Feb 14	Sat	FAC 5	H	Blackburn Rovers	D	2-2	25,729		Berkovic, Kitson
34	Feb 21	Sat	Prem	A	Bolton Wanderers	D	1-1	25,000	8	Sinclair
35	Feb 25	Wed	FAC 5 Rep	A	Blackburn Rovers	D	1-1*	21,972		Hartson
36	Mar 2	Mon	Prem	H	Arsenal	D	0-0	25,717	8	
37	Mar 8	Sun	FAC QF	A	Arsenal	D	1-1	38,077		Pearce
38	Mar 11	Wed	Prem	H	Manchester United	D	1-1	25,892	8	Sinclair
39	Mar 14	Sat	Prem	H	Chelsea	W	2-1	25,829	8	Sinclair, Unsworth
40	Mar 17	Tue	FAC QF Rep	H	Arsenal	D	1-1**	25,859		Hartson
41	Mar 30	Mon	Prem	H	Leeds United	W	3-0	24,107	7	Abou, Hartson, Pearce
42	Apr 4	Sat	Prem	A	Aston Villa	L	0-2	39,372	7	
43	Apr 11	Sat	Prem	H	Derby County	D	0-0	25,155	7	
44	Apr 13	Mon	Prem	A	Sheffield Wednesday	D	1-1	28,036	8	Berkovic
45	Apr 18	Sat	Prem	H	Blackburn Rovers	W	2-1	24,733	6	Hartson 2
46	Apr 25	Sat	Prem	H	Southampton	L	2-4	25,878	7	Lomas, Sinclair
47	May 2	Sat	Prem	A	Liverpool	L	0-5	44,414	10	
48	May 5	Tue	Prem	A	Crystal Palace	D	3-3	19,129	9	Omoyinmi 2, Curcic (og)
49	May 10	Sun	Prem	H	Leicester City	W	4-3	25,781	8	Abou 2, Lampard, Sinclair

* After extra time - won 5-4 on penalties (0-0 at 90 minutes)   ** After extra time - lost 3-4 on penalties (1-1 after 90 minutes)

eam Line-Ups

ABOU Samassi	ALVES Paulo	BERKOVIC Eyal	BISHOP Ian	BREACKER Tim	DOWIE Iain	FERDINAND Rio	FORREST Craig	HARTSON John	HODGES Lee	HUGHES Michael	IMPEY Andy	KITSON Paul	LAMA Bernard	LAMPARD Frank Jnr	LAZARIDIS Stan	LOMAS Steve	MEAN Scott	MIKLOSKO Ludek	MONCUR John	MOORE Ian	OMOYINMI Emmanuel	PEARCE Ian	POTTS Steve	RIEPER Marc	ROWLAND Keith	SINCLAIR Trevor	TERRIER David	UNSWORTH David	#
		29/b		2/a		15		10	24			9/c	b	a		11		1	16				4			8	c		1
		29		2	c	15		10/c	a			9/a	b		17	11		1	16/b				4			8			2
		29/b		2/c	c	15		10	a			9	b		17	11		1	16/a							8		6	3
		29		2	a	15		10				9/a			17	11		1	16							8		6	4
		29		2	14	15		10							17	11		1	16							8		6	5
		29		2		15		10	24			9		a		11		1	16/a				4					6	6
		29		2	a	15		10	24			9/a		18		11		1					4					6	7
		29/b		2/a	14	15		10	a					18	17	11		1				19	b					6	8
			7	2	14	15/a		10						18	17	11		1				19	a					6	9
		29		2	14	15		10			20			18		11		1				19						6	10
		29		2	14	15		10			20/a			18		11		1				19						6	11
		29	7	2	14/a	15		10			20					11		1			a	19						6	12
		29	b	2/a	14/b	15		10			20			18		11							4		a			6	13
		29			14	15	22	10						18		11			16				4	12				6	14
		29			14	15	22	10						18		11			16				4	12				6	15
		29				15	22	10			20			18		11			16/b			19	a	12				6/a	16
4		29		2		15	22	10						18		11			16			19						6	17
/b		29/a		2	b			10			20			18		11		1	a			19	4					6	18
/a	a	29		2		15		10								11		1				19	4	12				6	19
4	b	29		2		15	22	10/b							17/a	11			16			19				a		6	20
b		29		2/a		15		10						18	17/b	11		1	16			19						6	21
		29		a		15	22	10			20/a	9/b		18		11						19		12				6	22
		29				15	22	10			20	9/a		18		11						19		12				6	23
		29/a				15	22	10			20	9		18	17	11						19	a					6	24
				2		15	22	10			20	9		18	17	11						19						6	25
		29		2/a		15	22	10				9		18	17							19	4					6	26
		29				15	22	10			20	9/b		18	17							19/a	4		a			6	27
4	b	29/b				15	22	10			20/a			18	17				a			19	4					6	28
4		29/b		a		15	22	10	b					18	17/a				16			19	4					6	29
/b		29		a	b	15	22	10						18	17	11						19	4					6/a	30
		29		2		15	22	10			a			18	17	11						19	4			8/a			31
	a			2		15	22	10			20/b	9/a			17	11			16			19	b			8			32
		29		2/a		15	22	10		b	20	9/b		18	17	11						19	a						33
		29				15	22	10			20			18	17				16			19				8		6	34
		29/a				15	22	10			20			18	17	11			16			19						6	35
		29		2/a				10			20		32	18	17	11						19	a			8		6	36
4		29/a				15		a			20		32	18	17	11			16			19	4						37
4		29				15					20		32	18	17	11						19	4			8			38
4		29	7			15					20/a		32	18	17							19	a			8		6	39
4		29				15		10			a		32	18	17	11					b	19/b	4/a					6	40
/b		29/a				15		10					32		17		a		16		b	19	4			8		6	41
						15		10					32	18	17	11			16			19	4/a			8		6	42
		29/b				15		10			20/c		32	18	17	11					b	19/a	a			8		6	43
		29				15		10			20		32	18	17	11					a	19				8		6	
		29/a				15		10			20		32	18	17	11						19				8		6	
		29				15						9/b	32	18	17	11	b		16/c		c	19				8		6	44
	a	29									20	9	32	18	17	11	a					19				8		6	
		29/a				15							32	18	17	11	a				27	19				8		6	45

1998-99
Story of the season

A busy pre-season for transfers saw the Hammers purchase five new players: defenders **Javier Margas** and **Neil Ruddock**, experienced striker **Ian Wright,** midfielder **Marc Keller** and goalkeeper **Shaka Hislop.**

On the opening day Wright scored on his debut Sheffield Wednesday in the 1–0 victory. The goals we flowing in the home game with Wimbledon as goals fro Hartson and Wright gave the Hammers a 3–0 lead, bu there followed a complete collapse as they conceded fou goals to give Wimbledon victory. Three days later th Hammers bounced back as they knocked Liverpool off th top spot with a 2–1 home win.

A poor performance in the League Cup saw the Hamme lose 2–1 on aggregate to Third Division Northampto Town. Ian Wright scored twice at Newcastle in a 3–0 wi and three successive victories in November moved the sid up to second in the table. The away form got worse wit

Appearances & Goals 1998-99

	League			FA Cup			League Cup			Total		
	Starts	Subs	Goals	Starts	Subs	Goals	Starts	Subs	Goals	Starts	Subs	
ABOU Samassi	2	1	0	0	1	0	1	0	0	3	2	
BERKOVIC Eyal	28	2	3	1	1	0	1	0	0	30	3	
BREACKER Tim	2	1	0	1	0	0	0	1	0	3	2	
COLE Joe	2	6	0	0	1	0	0	0	0	2	7	
COYNE Chris	0	1	0	0	0	0	0	0	0	0	1	
DI CANIO Paolo	12	1	4	0	0	0	0	0	0	12	1	
DICKS Julian	9	0	0	2	0	1	1	0	0	12	0	
FERDINAND Rio	31	0	0	1	0	0	1	0	0	33	0	
FOE Marc-Vivien	13	0	0	0	0	0	0	0	0	13	0	
FORREST Craig	1	1	0	0	0	0	0	0	0	1	1	
HALL Richard	0	0	0	0	1	0	0	0	0	0	1	
HARTSON John	16	1	4	2	0	0	1	0	0	19	1	
HISLOP Shaka	37	0	0	2	0	0	2	0	0	41	0	
HODGES Lee	0	1	0	0	0	0	0	0	0	0	1	
HOLLIGAN Gavin	0	1	0	0	0	0	0	0	0	0	1	
IMPEY Andy	6	2	0	0	0	0	1	0	0	7	2	
KELLER Marc	17	4	5	0	0	0	1	0	0	18	4	
KITSON Paul	13	4	3	0	0	0	0	0	0	13	4	
LAMPARD Frank Jnr	38	0	5	1	0	0	2	0	1	41	0	
LAZARIDIS Stan	11	4	0	2	0	0	1	0	0	14	4	
LOMAS Steve	30	0	1	2	0	0	0	0	0	32	0	
MARGAS Javier	3	0	0	0	0	0	0	0	0	3	0	
MINTO Scott	14	1	0	0	0	0	0	0	0	14	1	
MONCUR John	6	8	0	0	0	0	1	0	0	7	8	
OMOYINMI Emmanuel	0	3	0	1	1	0	0	1	0	1	5	
PEARCE Ian	33	0	2	1	0	0	2	0	0	36	0	
POTTS Steve	11	8	0	1	0	0	2	0	0	14	8	
RUDDOCK Neil	27	0	2	2	0	0	1	0	0	30	0	
SINCLAIR Trevor	36	0	7	2	0	0	2	0	0	40	0	
WRIGHT Ian	20	2	9	1	0	0	2	0	0	23	2	
own goal			1									
Totals	418	52	46	22	5	1	22	2	1	462	59	

ve successive defeats, including a 1–0 loss in the FA Cup
Swansea City. More transfer activity saw Ludek Miklosko
d Tim Breacker join Queens Park Rangers, and John
artson was sold to Wimbledon for £7.5 million. With
nds at his disposal, manager Redknapp then bought
idfielder Marc-Vivien Foe together with Italian forward
olo Di Canio, who had recently served an 11-match ban
r pushing over referee Paul Alcock. The arrival of Di
anio caused great excitement as he brought a degree of
ill, showmanship, and awesome talent.

fter this there were shock defeats as both Sheffield
ednesday and Arsenal won 4–0 at Upton Park. Results
en improved and by the end of April, following a good
-1 win at Tottenham, the side were in seventh spot and
asing a European place. There was a setback in May as
e home game with Leeds saw Wright, Hislop and Lomas
l sent off, which resulted in a 5–1 defeat. The final home
me with Middlesbrough ended with a 4–0 victory and in
ishing fifth the Hammers qualified to play in the Intertoto
up, giving them a possible route to the UEFA Cup.

A Carling Premiership
inal Table 1998-99

	P	HOME					AWAY					Pts
		W	D	L	F	A	W	D	L	F	A	
anchester United	38	14	4	1	45	18	8	9	2	35	19	79
senal	38	14	5	0	34	5	8	7	4	25	12	78
elsea	38	12	6	1	29	13	8	9	2	28	17	75
eds United	38	12	5	2	32	9	6	8	5	30	25	67
est Ham United	38	11	3	5	32	26	5	6	8	14	27	57
ton Villa	38	10	3	6	33	28	5	7	7	18	18	55
verpool	38	10	5	4	44	24	5	4	10	24	25	54
rby County	38	8	7	4	22	19	5	6	8	18	26	52
ddlesbrough	38	7	9	3	25	18	5	6	8	23	36	51
cester City	38	7	6	6	25	25	5	7	7	15	21	49
tenham Hotspur	38	7	7	5	28	26	4	7	8	19	24	47
effield Wednesday	38	7	5	7	20	15	6	2	11	21	27	46
wcastle United	38	7	6	6	26	25	4	7	8	22	29	46
erton	38	6	8	5	22	12	5	2	12	20	35	43
ventry City	38	8	6	5	26	21	3	3	13	13	30	42
mbledon	38	7	7	5	22	21	3	5	11	18	42	42
uthampton	38	9	4	6	29	26	2	4	13	8	38	41
arlton Athletic	38	4	7	8	20	20	4	5	10	21	36	36
ackburn Rovers	38	6	5	8	21	24	1	9	9	17	28	35
ttingham Forest	38	3	7	9	18	31	4	2	13	17	38	30

MARC VIVIEN FOE

The Cameroon midfielder was affectionately
known as the Gentle Giant. In 1991 he
started his career with Cameroon's leading
club Canon Yaounde and he helped them
win the Cameroon Cup in 1993.

That same year he made his international
debut for his country against Mexico. His
performances in the 1994 World Cup finals
prompted interest from European clubs and
he signed for the French club Lens in August
1994; he was in their side when they won the
French title in 1998. After 85 league games for
the French team he became West Ham's
record signing when he arrived in January
1999 for a fee of £4.2 million. He was a
tremendous athlete and a key member of the
side but his time at Upton Park only lasted for
one season. He scored twice in 48 games for
West Ham before returning to France to play
for Lyon. Marc was in their side when they
won the French League Cup in 2001 and the
league title in 2002. For the 2002/03 season he
was loaned out to Manchester City, scoring
nine goals in 38 appearances. He had the
distinction of scoring the last ever goal at
Maine Road before the club moved to their
new stadium. In June 2003 he was chosen to
play for Cameroon in the Confederations Cup
and on 26 June he faced Colombia in Lyon. In
the 72nd minute he collapsed on the pitch
and tragically died shortly after. The football
world was shocked, and a minute's silence in
his memory was later held at the grounds of
West Ham and Manchester City. He was
posthumously decorated with the Commander
of the National Order of Valour.

Season **1998-99** FA Carling Premiership
Match Details

Manager **Harry Redknapp**   Final League Position **5/20**

	Date		Competition	Venue	Opponents	Results		Attendance	Position	Scorers
1	Aug 15	Sat	Prem	A	Sheffield Wednesday	W	1-0	30,236	4	Wright
2	Aug 22	Sat	Prem	H	Manchester United	D	0-0	25,912	7	
3	Aug 29	Sat	Prem	A	Coventry City	D	0-0	20,818	8	
4	Sep 9	Wed	Prem	H	Wimbledon	L	3-4	24,601	11	Wright 2, Hartson
5	Sep 12	Sat	Prem	H	Liverpool	W	2-1	26,010	8	Berkovic, Hartson
6	Sep 15	Tue	FLC 2:1	A	Northampton Town	L	0-2	7,254		
7	Sep 19	Sat	Prem	A	Nottingham Forest	D	0-0	26,463	7	
8	Sep 22	Tue	FLC 2:2	H	Northampton Town	W	1-0	25,435		Lampard
9	Sep 28	Mon	Prem	H	Southampton	W	1-0	23,153	4	Wright
10	Oct 3	Sat	Prem	A	Blackburn Rovers	L	0-3	25,213	9	
11	Oct 17	Sat	Prem	H	Aston Villa	D	0-0	26,002	8	
12	Oct 24	Sat	Prem	A	Charlton Athletic	L	2-4	20,043	14	Berkovic, Rufus (og)
13	Oct 31	Sat	Prem	A	Newcastle United	W	3-0	36,744	8	Wright 2, Sinclair
14	Nov 8	Sun	Prem	H	Chelsea	D	1-1	26,023	9	Ruddock
15	Nov 14	Sat	Prem	H	Leicester City	W	3-2	25,642	6	Kitson, Lampard, Lomas
16	Nov 22	Sun	Prem	A	Derby County	W	2-0	31,366	6	Hartson, Keller
17	Nov 28	Sat	Prem	H	Tottenham Hotspur	W	2-1	26,044	2	Sinclair 2
18	Dec 5	Sat	Prem	A	Leeds United	L	0-4	36,315	5	
19	Dec 12	Sat	Prem	A	Middlesbrough	L	0-1	34,623	7	
20	Dec 19	Sat	Prem	H	Everton	W	2-1	25,998	7	Keller, Sinclair
21	Dec 26	Sat	Prem	A	Arsenal	L	0-1	38,098	7	
22	Dec 28	Mon	Prem	H	Coventry City	W	2-0	25,662	6	Hartson, Wright
23	Jan 2	Sat	FAC 3	H	Swansea City	D	1-1	26,039		Dicks
24	Jan 10	Sun	Prem	A	Manchester United	L	1-4	55,180	8	Lampard
25	Jan 13	Wed	FAC 3 Rep	A	Swansea City	L	0-1	10,116		
26	Jan 16	Sat	Prem	H	Sheffield Wednesday	L	0-4	25,642	8	
27	Jan 30	Sat	Prem	A	Wimbledon	D	0-0	23,035	9	
28	Feb 6	Sat	Prem	H	Arsenal	L	0-4	26,042	9	
29	Feb 13	Sat	Prem	H	Nottingham Forest	W	2-1	25,458	8	Lampard, Pearce
30	Feb 20	Sat	Prem	A	Liverpool	D	2-2	44,511	8	Keller, Lampard [pen]
31	Feb 27	Sat	Prem	H	Blackburn Rovers	W	2-0	25,529	6	Pearce, Di Canio
32	Mar 6	Sat	Prem	A	Southampton	L	0-1	15,240	7	
33	Mar 13	Sat	Prem	A	Chelsea	W	1-0	34,765	7	Kitson
34	Mar 20	Sat	Prem	H	Newcastle United	W	2-0	25,997	5	Di Canio, Kitson
35	Apr 2	Fri	Prem	A	Aston Villa	D	0-0	36,813	5	
36	Apr 5	Mon	Prem	H	Charlton Athletic	L	0-1	26,041	5	
37	Apr 10	Sat	Prem	A	Leicester City	D	0-0	20,402	6	
38	Apr 17	Sat	Prem	H	Derby County	W	5-1	25,485	6	Berkovic, Di Canio, Ruddock, Sinclair, Wright
39	Apr 24	Sat	Prem	A	Tottenham Hotspur	W	2-1	36,089	6	Keller, Wright
40	May 1	Sat	Prem	H	Leeds United	L	1-5	25,997	6	Di Canio
41	May 8	Sat	Prem	A	Everton	L	0-6	40,029	6	
42	May 16	Sun	Prem	H	Middlesbrough	W	4-0	25,902	5	Sinclair 2, Keller, Lampard

Team Line-Ups

ABOU Samassi	BERKOVIC Eyal	BREACKER Tim	COLE Joe	COYNE Chris	DI CANIO Paolo	DICKS Julian	FERDINAND Rio	FOE Marc-Vivien	FORREST Craig	HALL Richard	HARTSON John	HISLOP Shaka	HODGES Lee	HOLLIGAN Gavin	IMPEY Andy	KELLER Marc	KITSON Paul	LAMPARD Frank Jnr	LAZARIDIS Stan	LOMAS Steve	MARGAS Javier	MINTO Scott	MONCUR John	OMOYINMI Emmanuel	PEARCE Ian	POTTS Steve	RUDDOCK Neil	SINCLAIR Trevor	WRIGHT Ian	
	29/a						15					12			20			18	17	11			a		19		6	8	14	1
	29/a						15				10	12			20			18	17	11					19		6	8		2
	29						15				10	12			20			18	17	11/a	30		a				6		14	3
	29/a										10	12				a		18	17		30		16		19		6	8	14	4
	29/a	a									10/b	12					b	18	17				16		19	4	6	8	14	5
	29	a									10	12						18	17				16		19	4	6/a	8	14	6
a	29						15					12			20	7		18					a		19	4		8	14	7
a	29					3	15					12			20	7		18					a		19	4		8	14	8
	29/a					3	15				10	12				7/b		18	a				b		19	c	6	8	14/c	9
						3	15/b				10	12	b		20	a		18					16		19	4/a		8	14	10
	29					3	15				10	12				a	b	18		11					19		6/a	8	14/b	11
	29/a					3	15				10	12					b	18		11			a		19		6	8	14/b	12
							15				b	12			20/a	7	9/b	18		11					19	a	6	8	14	13
	29/a						15					12				7	9	18		11					19	a	6	8	14	14
	29					3	15					12				7	9/a	18		11			a		19			8	14	15
	29						15				10	12				7	9	18		11					19	a	6	8		16
	29/a						15				10	12					9	18	17	11					19		6	8		17
											10	12				7		18	17/a	11	30		a		19			8	14	18
							15				10	12				7/a		18	17/b	11			a	b	19	4		8	14	19
	29					3	15				10	12				7		18		11					19			8	14	20
	29						15				10	12				7/a		18	a	11					19	4		8	14	21
	29/a					3	15				10	12						18	17	11			b		19			8	14/b	22
	29/a					3					10/b	12							17/c	11				c	19	4	6	8	14	23
	29	a					15				10	12						18	17	11					19	4	6	8/a		24
a		2/b				3	15			b	10	12						18	17	11				27/a			6	8		25
	29/b	a					15					12				7	b	18		11		20			19		6/a	8		26
		2	26/a		a	3	15	13				12					9	18				20	16				6			27
a		2/a			10	3	15	13				12					9	18				20					6	8		28
	29/a	a			10		15					12					9	18	17/b	11		b			19		6	8		29
	29		26/c				15	13				12		c			b	18	a	11		20/b			19/a	4		8		30
	29				10		15	13				12				7		18		11					19	4		8		31
	29				10		15	13/a				12				7	a	18		11					19		6	8		32
					10		15	13				12				7/a	9	18		11		20			19		6	8		33
					10		15	13				12					9	18		11		20			19		6	8		34
					10		15/a	13				12					9	18		11		20			19	a	6	8		35
a					10			13				12				7	9/a	18		11		20			19		6	8		36
	29				10/b							12					9/a	18		11		20	b		19	4	6	8	a	37
	29	b			10			13				12						18		11/b		20			19	4/a	6	8	a	38
	29						15					12				7		18	a	11		20	16		19			8	14/a	39
	29/c	a	b		10/b			13	c			12						18		11		20	16				6	8/a	14	40
	29				10		15	13				12				a		18		11		20					6	8	14/a	41
	29	a			10		15	13	22			12				7		18				20				4	6	8/a		42

1999-2000
Story of the season

Departures from the club saw Eyal Berkovic join Celtic, Stan Lazaridis move to Birmingham City and Julian Dicks retire from playing. **Harry Redknapp then bought striker Paolo Wanchope,** central defender **Igor Stimac** and full-back **Gary Charles.**

The new season started early in July as the Hammers were in the Intertoto Cup. The Finnish side Jokerit were beaten 2–1 on aggregate and this was followed up with a 2–0 aggregate win against Dutch side Heerenveen. The Hammers were now in the final, where they faced the French team Metz over two legs. There was disappointment in the home leg as Metz went back to France with a 1– lead, but in the return a stirring performance by the Hammers gave them a 3–1 victory and qualification for the UEFA Cup.

Appearances & Goals 1999-2000

	League			FA Cup			League Cup			Europe			Total	
	Starts	Subs	Goals	Starts	Subs	Goals	Starts	Subs	Goals	Starts	Subs	Goals	Starts	Subs
BYRNE Shaun	0	1	0	0	0	0	0	0	0	0	0	0	0	1
BYWATER Stephen	3	1	0	0	0	0	0	0	0	0	0	0	3	1
CARRICK Michael	4	4	1	0	0	0	0	0	0	0	1	0	4	5
CHARLES Gary	2	2	0	0	0	0	1	0	0	0	0	0	3	2
COLE Joe	17	5	1	1	0	0	2	1	1	2	3	0	22	9
DI CANIO Paolo	29	1	16	1	0	0	3	0	0	10	0	1	43	1
FERDINAND Rio	33	0	0	1	0	0	3	0	0	9	0	0	46	0
FEUER Ian	3	0	0	0	0	0	0	0	0	0	0	0	3	0
FOE Marc-Vivien	25	0	1	1	0	0	3	0	0	5	1	1	34	1
FORREST Craig	9	2	0	0	0	0	0	0	0	1	0	0	10	2
HISLOP Shaka	22	0	0	1	0	0	3	0	0	9	0	0	35	0
ILIC Sasa	1	0	0	0	0	0	0	0	0	0	0	0	1	0
JONES Rob	0	0	0	0	0	0	0	0	0	1	0	0	1	0
KANOUTE Frederic	8	0	2	0	0	0	0	0	0	0	0	0	8	0
KELLER Marc	19	4	0	0	0	0	2	1	1	6	1	0	27	6
KITSON Paul	4	6	0	0	1	0	0	2	1	3	5	2	7	14
LAMPARD Frank Jnr	34	0	7	1	0	0	3	0	2	10	0	4	48	0
LAZARIDIS Stan	0	0	0	0	0	0	0	0	0	0	1	0	0	1
LOMAS Steve	25	0	1	1	0	0	2	0	1	10	0	0	38	0
MARGAS Javier	15	3	1	0	0	0	1	0	0	2	1	0	18	4
MINTO Scott	15	3	0	1	0	0	1	0	0	5	0	0	22	3
MONCUR John	20	2	1	0	0	0	0	0	0	5	1	0	25	3
NEWTON Adam	0	2	0	0	0	0	0	0	0	0	1	0	0	3
PEARCE Ian	1	0	0	0	0	0	0	0	0	1	1	0	2	1
PEARCE Stuart	8	0	0	0	0	0	0	0	0	0	0	0	8	0
POTTS Steve	16	1	0	1	0	0	1	0	0	7	1	0	25	2
RUDDOCK Neil	12	3	0	1	0	0	2	1	0	5	1	1	20	5
SINCLAIR Trevor	36	0	7	1	0	0	2	1	0	10	0	1	49	1
STIMAC Igor	24	0	1	0	0	0	2	0	0	2	0	0	28	0
WANCHOPE Paulo	33	2	12	0	1	0	2	0	0	7	1	3	42	4
WRIGHT Ian	0	0	0	0	0	0	0	0	0	0	1	0	0	1
own goal			1											
Totals	**418**	**42**	**52**	**11**	**2**	**0**	**33**	**6**	**6**	**110**	**20**	**13**	**572**	**70**

the league there were five wins and a draw in the opening games and by mid-September they were in second place. Also in September the Croatian side Osijek were beaten home and away in the UEFA Cup. It was a busy month in October as Di Canio scored twice against Arsenal in a 2–1 win. The home League Cup game with Bournemouth was won 2–0 but there was no joy in Romania in the UEFA Cup as Steaua Bucharest won 2–0; the Hammers were knocked out after the home leg was drawn 0–0. The good league form continued with home wins against Sheffield Wednesday and Liverpool, and in the League Cup the Hammers progressed after a thrilling 3–2 win at Birmingham City. December proved to be a black month as West Ham gave an inept performance in losing 1–0 in the FA Cup at Tranmere Rovers – the FA's tinkering with tradition in holding the third round before Christmas has never been repeated. Days later in the League Cup, after a 2–2 draw they beat Aston Villa on penalties. However, it was later found that Manny Omoyinmi (who had come on as a substitute) was ineligible to play and the FA ordered the tie to be replayed, which the Villa won 3–1.

By early February the Hammers were in ninth place as they faced Bradford City at Upton Park. In an amazing game the Hammers were losing 4–2 after 50 minutes yet fought back to win 5–4. Another highlight came in the home game with Wimbledon when Di Canio scored a wonder goal that was later acclaimed as the Goal of the Season. A week later on April Fools' Day, after taking the lead the Hammers lost 7–1 at Manchester United. West Ham finished the season in ninth place, and had now achieved three top-ten placings in successive seasons.

PAULO WANCHOPE

The Costa Rican international striker came to England from his home-town club Herediano and signed for Derby County in March 1997.

He scored 20 goals in 83 appearances for the Rams before he was transferred to West Ham in July 1999. He was brilliant and erratic, and playing alongside Di Canio in the 1999/2000 season they gave great entertainment to the Hammers fans. He only played one season at Upton Park but his 15 goals were invaluable as West Ham finished in ninth spot. A fee of £3.65 million took him to Manchester City in August 2000, where he scored a hat-trick on his debut against Sunderland. He stayed with City for four years, scoring 27 goals in 64 league outings. Over the next three years he became an international nomad, playing in six different countries. Starting in Spain with Malaga he went on to play for Al Gharafa (Qatar), Herediano (Costa Rica), Rosario Central (Argentina), FC Tokyo (Japan) and finally Chicago Fire (USA). At international level he represented Costa Rica on 73 occasions, scoring 45 goals.

After retiring as a player in November 2007 he later managed Herediano for a spell. More recently he has been the head coach to the Costa Rican national team.

A Carling Premiership Final Table 1999-2000

		HOME					AWAY					
	P	W	D	L	F	A	W	D	L	F	A	Pts
Manchester United	38	15	4	0	59	16	13	3	3	38	29	91
Arsenal	38	14	3	2	42	17	8	4	7	31	26	73
Leeds United	38	12	2	5	29	18	9	4	6	29	25	69
Liverpool	38	11	4	4	28	13	8	6	5	23	17	67
Chelsea	38	12	5	2	35	12	6	6	7	18	22	65
Aston Villa	38	8	8	3	23	12	7	5	7	23	23	58
Sunderland	38	10	6	3	28	17	6	4	9	29	39	58
Leicester City	38	10	3	6	31	24	6	4	9	24	31	55
West Ham United	38	11	5	3	32	23	4	5	10	20	30	55
Tottenham Hotspur	38	10	3	6	40	26	5	5	9	17	23	53
Newcastle United	38	10	5	4	42	20	4	5	10	21	34	52
Middlesbrough	38	8	5	6	23	26	6	5	8	23	26	52
Everton	38	7	9	3	36	21	5	5	9	23	28	50
Coventry City	38	12	1	6	38	22	0	7	12	9	32	44
Southampton	38	8	4	7	26	22	4	4	11	19	40	44
Derby County	38	6	3	10	22	25	3	8	8	22	32	38
Bradford City	38	6	8	5	26	29	3	1	15	12	39	36
Wimbledon	38	6	7	6	30	28	1	5	13	16	46	33
Sheffield Wednesday	38	6	3	10	21	23	2	4	13	17	47	31
Watford	38	5	4	10	24	31	1	2	16	11	46	24

Season **1999-2000** FA Carling Premiership
Match Details

Manager **Harry Redknapp**   Final League Position **9/20**

	Date		Competition	Venue	Opponents	Results		Attendance	Position	Scorers
1	Jul 17	Sat	Toto 3:1	H	FC Jokerit (Finland)	W	1-0	11,908		Kitson
2	Jul 24	Sat	Toto 3:2	A	FC Jokerit (Finland)	D	1-1	7,667		Lampard
3	Jul 28	Wed	Toto SF:1	H	SC Heerenveen (Holland)	W	1-0	7,485		Lampard
4	Aug 4	Wed	Toto SF:2	A	SC Heerenveen (Holland)	W	1-0	13,500		Wanchope
5	Aug 7	Sat	Prem	H	Tottenham Hotspur	W	1-0	26,010	8	Lampard
6	Aug 10	Tue	Toto F:1	H	FC Metz (France)	L	0-1	25,372		
7	Aug 16	Mon	Prem	A	Aston Villa	D	2-2	26,250	9	Sinclair, Southgate (og)
8	Aug 21	Sat	Prem	H	Leicester City	W	2-1	23,631	7	Di Canio, Wanchope
9	Aug 24	Tue	Toto F:2	A	FC Metz (France)	W	3-1	19,599		Lampard, Sinclair, Wanchope
10	Aug 28	Sat	Prem	A	Bradford City	W	3-0	17,936	4	Di Canio, Sinclair, Wanchope
11	Sep 11	Sat	Prem	H	Watford	W	1-0	25,310	3	Di Canio
12	Sep 16	Thur	UEFA 1:1	H	NK Osijek (Croatia)	W	3-0	25,331		Di Canio, Lampard, Wanchope
13	Sep 18	Sat	Prem	A	Everton	L	0-1	35,154	8	
14	Sep 25	Sat	Prem	A	Coventry City	L	0-1	19,985	9	
15	Sep 30	Thur	UEFA 1:2	A	NK Osijek (Croatia)	W	3-1	15,000		Foe, Kitson, Ruddock
16	Oct 3	Sun	Prem	H	Arsenal	W	2-1	26,009	9	Di Canio 2
17	Oct 13	Wed	FLC 3	H	AFC Bournemouth	W	2-0	22,067		Keller, Lampard
18	Oct 17	Sun	Prem	A	Middlesbrough	L	0-2	31,822	10	
19	Oct 21	Thur	UEFA 2:1	A	Steaua Bucharest (Romania)	L	0-2	12,500		
20	Oct 24	Sun	Prem	H	Sunderland	D	1-1	26,022	11	Sinclair
21	Oct 27	Wed	Prem	A	Liverpool	L	0-1	44,012	12	
22	Oct 30	Sat	Prem	A	Leeds United	L	0-1	40,190	12	
23	Nov 4	Thur	UEFA 2:2	H	Steaua Bucharest (Romania)	D	0-0	24,514		
24	Nov 7	Sun	Prem	A	Chelsea	D	0-0	34,935	11	
25	Nov 21	Sun	Prem	H	Sheffield Wednesday	W	4-3	23,015	10	Di Canio [pen], Foe, Lampard, Wanchope
26	Nov 27	Sat	Prem	H	Liverpool	W	1-0	26,043	8	Sinclair
27	Nov 30	Tue	FLC 4	A	Birmingham City	W	3-2	17,728		Cole, Kitson, Lomas
28	Dec 6	Mon	Prem	A	Tottenham Hotspur	D	0-0	36,233	8	
29	Dec 11	Sat	FAC 3	A	Tranmere Rovers	L	0-1	13,629		
30	Dec 18	Sat	Prem	H	Manchester United	L	2-4	26,037	9	Di Canio 2
31	Dec 26	Sun	Prem	A	Wimbledon	D	2-2	21,180	11	Lampard, Sinclair
32	Dec 28	Tue	Prem	H	Derby County	D	1-1	24,998	10	Di Canio
33	Jan 3	Mon	Prem	A	Newcastle United	D	2-2	36,314	11	Lampard, Stimac
34	Jan 11	Tue	FLC QF	H	Aston Villa	L	1-3	25,592		Lampard
35	Jan 15	Sat	Prem	H	Aston Villa	D	1-1	24,237	11	Di Canio
36	Jan 22	Sat	Prem	A	Leicester City	W	3-1	19,019	8	Wanchope 2, Di Canio
37	Feb 5	Sat	Prem	A	Southampton	L	1-2	15,257	10	Lampard
38	Feb 12	Sat	Prem	H	Bradford City	W	5-4	25,417	9	Cole, Di Canio [pen], Lampard, Moncur, Sinclair
39	Feb 26	Sat	Prem	H	Everton	L	0-4	26,025	11	
40	Mar 4	Sat	Prem	A	Watford	W	2-1	18,619	10	Lomas, Wanchope
41	Mar 8	Wed	Prem	H	Southampton	W	2-0	23,484	6	Sinclair, Wanchope
42	Mar 11	Sat	Prem	A	Sheffield Wednesday	L	1-3	21,147	10	Lampard
43	Mar 18	Sat	Prem	H	Chelsea	D	0-0	26,041	9	
44	Mar 26	Sun	Prem	H	Wimbledon	W	2-1	22,438	8	Di Canio, Kanoute
45	Apr 1	Sat	Prem	A	Manchester United	L	1-7	61,611	8	Wanchope
46	Apr 12	Wed	Prem	H	Newcastle United	W	2-1	25,817	8	Wanchope 2
47	Apr 15	Sat	Prem	A	Derby County	W	2-1	31,202	8	Wanchope 2
48	Apr 22	Sat	Prem	H	Coventry City	W	5-0	24,719	8	Di Canio 2, Carrick, Kanoute, Margas
49	Apr 29	Sat	Prem	H	Middlesbrough	L	0-1	25,472	8	
50	May 2	Tue	Prem	A	Arsenal	L	1-2	38,093	8	Di Canio
51	May 6	Sat	Prem	A	Sunderland	L	0-1	41,684	9	
52	May 14	Sun	Prem	H	Leeds United	D	0-0	26,044	9	

Toto = Intertoto Cup

Team Line-Ups

BYWATER Stephen	CARRICK Michael	CHARLES Gary	COLE Joe	DI CANIO Paolo	FERDINAND Rio	FEUER Ian	FOE Marc-Vivien	FORREST Craig	HISLOP Shaka	ILIC Sasa	JONES Rob	KANOUTE Frederic	KELLER Marc	KITSON Paul	LAMPARD Frank Jnr	LAZARIDIS Stan	LOMAS Steve	MARGAS Javier	MINTO Scott	MONCUR John	NEWTON Adam	PEARCE Ian	PEARCE Stuart	POTTS Steve	RUDDOCK Neil	SINCLAIR Trevor	STIMAC Igor	WANCHOPE Paulo	WRIGHT Ian	#
			26	10	15			22					b	9	18		11		20						6	8/b	4/a		a	1
	c			10/b	15				1		2/a		7	9	18	b	11		20					a	6	8				2
				10/c	15				1				7/b	c	18		11		20	b	a				6/a	8	4	9		3
		a		10/a	15		13		1					b	18		11		20	16/b	19					8		9		4
		b		10/b	15		13		1						18				20		19/a		3			8	4	9		5
				10	15		13/a		1					a	18		11		20	16						8	4	9		6
				10	15		13		1				a	b	18		11		20/a	16/b			3			8	4	9		7
				10	15		13		1				7		18		11			16			3			8	4	9		8
		a		10/a	15		13		1				7		18		11			16						8	4	9		9
	a			10	15/a				1				7		18		11			16			3			8	4	9		10
	b			10					1				7		18		11		a	16/b		5	3/a			8	4	9		11
				10/a				b	1				7/a		18		11	30		16/b		5				8	4	9/a		12
				10					1				7		18		11	30		16		5				8	4	9		13
				10			13		1				7/a		18		11			16	a	5				8	4	9		14
				10/c	15/b		13		1				7	9	18		11				a	5			b	8/a	4	c		15
				10			13		1					a	18	b	11			16/b		5			6	8	4	9/a		16
			26	10	15		13		1				7	a	18										6	8	4	9/a		17
		a		10	15		b		1				7/a		18		11			16/b					6	8	4	9		18
		b		10/b	15		13		1						18		11		a	16					6	8	4/a	9		19
			26	10	15		13		1				7	b	18		11/c	30		c				a		8	4/a	9/b		20
			26	10	15				1				7	9	18		11								6	8	4	9		21
		a			15		13/a		1				7	9	18		11	30		16					6			9		22
			26	10	15		13		1				7/a	a	18		11	30							6	8		9		23
			26/a		15		13	22	1				7		18		11	30						a		8		9		24
			26	10	15		13		1				7		18											8	4	9		25
			26	10	15		13		1				7	a	18		11	30							6	8		9/a		26
	2/b	b		10	15		13		1				7	c	18		11	30/a							6	a		9/c		27
			26	10/c	15		13		1					9/a	18		11	30/b		a				b	6	8				28
			26	10/b	15		13		1				7		18		11		20						6	8	4/a	b		29
			26	10	15		13		1				7		18		11		20						6	8		9		30
			26	10	15		13		1						18			30	20						6	8		9		31
			26	10	15		13		1				a		18			30	20/a							8	4	9		32
	21		26		15		13		1				7/a		18				20						6	8	4			33
			26	10	15		13		1				b		18		11		20					a	6	8/b	4/a			34
			26	10	15		13		1				7		18		11	30								8	4	9		35
		b	26	10	15		a		1/a				7/c		18		11/b	30		c					6	8		9		36
	2		26		15			22							18		11	30/a	20	a						8	4	9		37
a	2/b	b	26	10	15				1/a						18		11		20	16					6	8				38
			26		15					28			7	9			11			16			3		6	8		9		39
					15		13	22							18		11		20	16			3			8	4	9		40
		b	26/b	10	15		13	22							18		11		a	16			3/a		6	8		9		41
		a		10	15		13	22							18		11			16/a					6	8	4	9		42
		c		10	15		13	22					a/b		18		11		20	16/c				b		8	4	9/a		43
				10	15		13	22				14	a		18		11		20	16/a						8	4	9		44
					15		13	22				14			18		11		20	16						8	4	9		45
		b	26	10	15		13	22				14	7/a		18				20	c					6/b		4/c		a	46
a	b		26/a	10	15	29	13								18			30	20							8	4/b	9		47
	21			10	15	29									18			30	20/a		a					8	4	9		48
				10	15	29	13					14	7		18			30								8	4	9		49
32	21			10			13					14	7							16		5				8	4	9		54
32	21			10	15		13					14								16						8	4	9		55
32				10	15		13					14						30		16				4		8	4	9		56

2000-01
Story of the season

Joining the Hammers were full-back **Nigel Winterburn** and striker **Davor Suker,** who both came from Arsenal.

The Hammers youth were making their mark as **Frank Lampard** and **Michael Carrick** were in the **England under-21** squad, with **Rio Ferdinand** chosen for the **senior England** team. And construction of the new **West Stand was under way**, the first step in the **£35 million redevelopment of the ground**.

The opening six games brought three defeats and thr[ee] draws and left West Ham firmly on the bottom of the tabl[e]. The Hammers progressed in the League Cup with victori[es] over Walsall and Blackburn Rovers and then went on a[n] impressive run of eight games without defeat that move[d] the side up to eighth. Included in that run were a 4–1 hom[e] win against Manchester City and victories at Leeds Unite[d] and Southampton. In November the fans were shocke[d] when West Ham accepted a bid of £18 million from Lee[ds] United for Rio Ferdinand. This prompted a spending spre[e] with Harry Redknapp buying Rigobert Song, Titi Cama[ra]

Appearances & Goals 2000-01

	League			FA Cup			League Cup			Total		
	Starts	Subs	Goals	Starts	Subs	Goals	Starts	Subs	Goals	Starts	Subs	
BASSILA Christian	0	3	0	0	1	0	0	0	0	0	4	
BYWATER Stephen	1	0	0	0	0	0	0	0	0	1	0	
CAMARA Titi	5	1	0	1	0	0	0	0	0	6	1	
CARRICK Michael	32	1	1	4	0	0	4	0	0	40	1	
CHARLES Gary	0	1	0	0	0	0	0	0	0	0	1	
COLE Joe	24	6	5	4	0	0	2	0	0	30	6	
DAILLY Christian	11	1	0	3	0	0	0	0	0	14	1	
DEFOE Jermain	0	1	0	0	0	0	0	1	1	0	2	
DI CANIO Paolo	31	0	9	3	0	1	3	0	1	37	0	
DIAWARA Kaba	6	5	0	0	0	0	0	0	0	6	5	
FERDINAND Rio	12	0	0	0	0	0	2	0	0	14	0	
FORREST Craig	3	1	0	0	0	0	0	0	0	3	1	
FOXE Hayden	3	2	0	0	0	0	0	0	0	3	2	
HISLOP Shaka	34	0	0	4	0	0	4	0	0	42	0	
KANOUTE Frederic	32	0	11	4	0	3	3	0	0	39	0	
KELLER Marc	0	0	0	0	0	0	1	0	0	1	0	
KITSON Paul	0	2	0	0	0	0	0	0	0	0	2	
LAMPARD Frank Jnr	30	0	7	4	0	1	3	0	1	37	0	
LOMAS Steve	20	0	1	0	0	0	3	0	1	23	0	
MARGAS Javier	3	0	0	0	0	0	1	0	0	4	0	
McCANN Grant	0	1	0	0	0	0	0	0	0	0	1	
MINTO Scott	1	0	0	0	0	0	0	0	0	1	0	
MONCUR John	6	10	0	0	0	0	0	1	0	6	11	
PEARCE Ian	13	2	1	0	1	0	1	0	0	14	3	
PEARCE Stuart	34	0	2	4	0	1	4	0	0	42	0	
POTTS Steve	2	6	0	0	0	0	2	1	0	4	7	
SCHEMMEL Sebastien	10	2	0	3	0	0	0	0	0	13	2	
SINCLAIR Trevor	19	0	3	1	0	0	3	0	0	23	0	
SOMA Ragnvald	2	2	0	0	1	0	0	0	0	2	3	
SONG Rigobert	18	1	0	1	0	0	1	0	0	20	1	
STIMAC Igor	19	0	0	2	0	0	3	0	0	24	0	
SUKER Davor	7	4	2	0	0	0	1	1	1	8	5	
TIHINEN Hannu	5	3	0	2	0	0	0	0	0	7	3	
TODOROV Svetoslav	2	6	1	0	1	1	0	0	0	2	7	
WINTERBURN Nigel	33	0	1	4	0	0	3	0	0	40	0	
own goal			1									
Totals	418	61	45	44	4	7	44	4	5	506	69	

gnvald Soma, Christian Dailly and Svetoslav Todorov for
ombined total of around £7.5 million. A poor showing
the League Cup gave Sheffield Wednesday a 2–1 victory
Upton Park, but after decent results in December
luding a 5–0 victory against Charlton Athletic the team
re in eighth place.

e FA Cup campaign began with a 3–2 win at Walsall,
lowed by an excellent 1–0 win at Manchester United in
e fourth round. The Hammers were roared on by 6,000
is at Sunderland in the fifth round and were delighted
h the 1–0 victory. The team was now battling against a
ppling injury list and London derbies against Arsenal and
elsea were lost before the team met Tottenham in the FA
p quarter-final. The game with Tottenham was played in
leluge at the Boleyn Ground and Spurs raced into a 3–1
d; Todorov pulled a goal back but despite a barnstorming
ish the Hammers were beaten 3–2. The lengthening
uries took their toll as the Hammers struggled through
ril but the final home game with Southampton was won
0 and the team were now safe from relegation.

Carling Premiership
nal Table 2000-01

	P	HOME					AWAY					Pts
		W	D	L	F	A	W	D	L	F	A	
nchester United	38	15	2	2	49	12	9	6	4	30	19	80
enal	38	15	3	1	45	13	5	7	7	18	25	70
erpool	38	13	4	2	40	14	7	5	7	31	25	69
ds United	38	11	3	5	36	21	9	5	5	28	22	68
wich Town	38	11	5	3	31	15	9	1	9	26	27	66
elsea	38	13	3	3	44	20	4	7	8	24	25	61
nderland	38	9	7	3	24	16	6	5	8	22	25	57
on Villa	38	8	8	3	27	20	5	7	7	19	23	54
arlton Athletic	38	11	5	3	31	19	3	5	11	19	38	52
uthampton	38	11	2	6	27	22	3	8	8	13	26	52
wcastle United	38	10	4	5	26	17	4	5	10	18	33	51
tenham Hotspur	38	11	6	2	31	16	2	4	13	16	38	49
cester City	38	10	4	5	28	23	4	2	13	11	28	48
ddlesbrough	38	4	7	8	18	23	5	8	6	26	21	42
st Ham United	**38**	**6**	**6**	**7**	**24**	**20**	**4**	**6**	**9**	**21**	**30**	**42**
erton	38	6	8	5	29	27	5	1	13	16	32	42
rby County	38	8	7	4	23	24	2	5	12	14	35	42
anchester City	38	4	3	12	20	31	4	7	8	21	34	34
ventry City	38	4	7	8	14	23	4	3	12	22	40	34
adford City	38	4	7	8	20	29	1	4	14	10	41	26

Days later there came shock news when it was announced
that following a meeting with the chairman Harry Redknapp
was no longer the manager, and together with assistant
manager Frank Lampard senior the pair parted company
with the club. The task of caretaker manager was given to
the club's coach Glenn Roeder, who was in charge for the
final league game at Middlesbrough.

IGOR STIMAC

**An experienced Croatian international
defender who began his career with Hajduk
Split in 1985, in seven seasons there he
made 64 league appearances, also playing
on loan at Dinamo Vinkovci.**

He went to Spain in 1992 and played in 62
league games for Cadiz before returning to
Hadjuk in 1994. After a further two seasons he
was transferred to Derby County for a fee of
£1.5 million in October 1995. He scored on his
debut at Tranmere Rovers and helped the
Rams as they won promotion to the Premier
League that season. The tough defender was
by now a key figure in the Croatian national
side and he went on to gain 53 caps for his
country.

After four seasons with the Rams a fee of
£600,000 brought him to West Ham in
September 1999. After making his debut in
the 1–0 victory against Watford he became an
indispensable member of the Hammers
rearguard as they competed in the UEFA Cup.
The following campaign was to be his last
and after appearing in a total of 52 games he
returned to Croatia to play 11 games for his
former club Hadjuk Split.

Season **2000-01** FA Carling Premiership
Match Details

Manager **Harry Redknapp** (to May 9); Caretaker Manager **Glenn Roeder** (last game of season)
Final League Position **15/20**

	Date		Competition	Venue	Opponents	Results		Attendance	Position	Scorers
1	Aug 19	Sat	Prem	A	Chelsea	L	2-4	34,914	14	Di Canio, Kanoute
2	Aug 23	Wed	Prem	H	Leicester City	L	0-1	25,195	20	
3	Aug 26	Sat	Prem	H	Manchester United	D	2-2	25,998	20	Di Canio [pen], Suker
4	Sep 5	Tue	Prem	A	Sunderland	D	1-1	45,285	20	Suker
5	Sep 11	Mon	Prem	A	Tottenham Hotspur	L	0-1	33,133	20	
6	Sep 17	Sun	Prem	H	Liverpool	D	1-1	25,998	20	Di Canio [pen]
7	Sep 19	Tue	FLC 2 : 1	A	Walsall	W	1-0	5,435		Defoe
8	Sep 23	Sat	Prem	A	Coventry City	W	3-0	20,132	18	Cole, Di Canio, Lampard
9	Sep 27	Wed	FLC 2 : 2	H	Walsall	D	1-1	11,963		Lomas
10	Sep 30	Sat	Prem	H	Bradford City	D	1-1	25,407	17	Cole
11	Oct 14	Sat	Prem	A	Ipswich Town	D	1-1	22,246	18	Di Canio
12	Oct 21	Sat	Prem	H	Arsenal	L	1-2	26,034	18	Pearce S.
13	Oct 28	Sat	Prem	H	Newcastle United	W	1-0	26,044	15	Kanoute
14	Oct 31	Tue	FLC 3	H	Blackburn Rovers	W	2-0	21,863		Di Canio, Suker
15	Nov 6	Mon	Prem	A	Derby County	D	0-0	24,621	15	
16	Nov 11	Sat	Prem	H	Manchester City	W	4-1	26,022	13	Di Canio [pen], Lomas, Pearce S., Sinclair
17	Nov 18	Sat	Prem	A	Leeds United	W	1-0	40,005	11	Winterburn
18	Nov 25	Sat	Prem	A	Southampton	W	3-2	15,232	9	Kanoute, Pearce S., Sinclair
19	Nov 29	Wed	FLC 4	H	Sheffield Wednesday	L	1-2	25,857		Lampard
20	Dec 2	Sat	Prem	H	Middlesbrough	W	1-0	25,459	6	Di Canio
21	Dec 9	Sat	Prem	H	Aston Villa	D	1-1	25,888	7	Carrick
22	Dec 16	Sat	Prem	A	Everton	D	1-1	31,246	8	Kanoute
23	Dec 23	Sat	Prem	A	Leicester City	L	1-2	21,524	10	Kanoute
24	Dec 26	Tue	Prem	H	Charlton Athletic	W	5-0	26,046	8	Kanoute 2, Lampard, Sinclair, Rufus (og)
25	Jan 1	Mon	Prem	A	Manchester United	L	1-3	67,603	10	Kanoute
26	Jan 6	Sat	FAC 3	A	Walsall	W	3-2	9,402		Kanoute 2, Lampard
27	Jan 13	Sat	Prem	H	Sunderland	L	0-2	26,014	11	
28	Jan 22	Sat	Prem	A	Charlton Athletic	D	1-1	20,043	11	Di Canio
29	Jan 28	Sun	FAC 4	A	Manchester United	W	1-0	67,029		Di Canio
30	Jan 31	Wed	Prem	H	Tottenham Hotspur	D	0-0	26,048	13	
31	Feb 3	Sat	Prem	A	Liverpool	L	0-3	44,045	14	
32	Feb 12	Mon	Prem	H	Coventry City	D	1-1	22,586	14	Cole
33	Feb 17	Sat	FAC 5	A	Sunderland	W	1-0	36,005		Kanoute
34	Feb 24	Sat	Prem	A	Bradford City	W	2-1	20,469	13	Lampard 2
35	Mar 3	Sat	Prem	A	Arsenal	L	0-3	38,076	13	
36	Mar 7	Wed	Prem	H	Chelsea	L	0-2	26,016	13	
37	Mar 11	Wed	FAC QF	H	Tottenham Hotspur	L	2-3	26,048		Pearce S., Todorov
38	Mar 17	Sat	Prem	H	Ipswich Town	L	0-1	26,046	14	
39	Mar 31	Sat	Prem	H	Everton	L	0-2	26,044	14	
40	Apr 7	Sat	Prem	A	Aston Villa	D	2-2	31,432	14	Kanoute, Lampard
41	Apr 14	Sat	Prem	H	Derby County	W	3-1	25,319	13	Cole, Kanoute, Lampard
42	Apr 16	Mon	Prem	A	Newcastle United	L	1-2	51,107	14	Lampard [pen]
43	Apr 21	Sat	Prem	H	Leeds United	L	0-2	26,041	14	
44	Apr 28	Sat	Prem	A	Manchester City	L	0-1	33,737	15	
45	May 5	Sat	Prem	H	Southampton	W	3-0	26,041	14	Cole, Di Canio, Kanoute
46	May 19	Sat	Prem	A	Middlesbrough	L	1-2	33,057	15	Todorov

eam Line-Ups

BYWATER Stephen	CAMARA Titi	CARRICK Michael	CHARLES Gary	COLE Joe	DAILLY Christian	DEFOE Jermain	DI CANIO Paolo	DIAWARA Kaba	FERDINAND Rio	FORREST Craig	FOXE Hayden	HISLOP Shaka	KANOUTE Frederic	KELLER Marc	KITSON Paul	LAMPARD Frank Jnr	LOMAS Steve	MARGAS Javier	McCANN Grant	MINTO Scott	MONCUR John	PEARCE Ian	PEARCE Stuart	POTTS Steve	SCHEMMEL Sebastien	SINCLAIR Trevor	SOMA Ragnvald	SONG Rigobert	STIMAC Igor	SUKER Davor	TIHINEN Hannu	TODOROV Svetoslav	WINTERBURN Nigel	
		21/a		a			10					1	14			18	11	30					3						5	9			17	1
		21	a	c			10		15			1	14/b	b			11	30/c					3						5	9/a			17	2
		21		26			10		15/a			1		b			11	30/b					3						5	9			17	3
		21		26			10					1				18	11				a		3			8			5	9/a			17	4
		21		26			10		15			1	14			18	11						3			8							17	5
		21		26			10					1	14				11						3			8							17	6
		21		26			a		15			1		7/a			11						3	4		8							17	7
		b		26			10	c	15/b			1	14/c			18	11						3	a		8/a			5				17	8
		21		26			10					1	14			18/a	11	30					3			a			5				17	9
		21		26			10		15			1	14				11						3			8			5				17	10
				26			10		15			1	14			18	11				a		3	b		8			5/b				17/a	11
				26			10		15			1	14			18	11					16/a	3			8			a				17	12
		21		26/b			10		15			1	14/c			18			c		19		3	a		8			b				17/a	13
		21					10		15			1	14/a			18				a	19		3	4		8				9				14
		21					10	b	15			1	14/a			18	11			a	19		3			8				9/b				15
		21					10/a		15			1	14			18	11				19		3	a		8							17	16
		21					10	25	15			1	14			18	11				19/a		3	a		8							17	17
		21					10	25				1	14			18/a	11				a		3			8			5				17	18
		21					10					1	14			18	11						3			8		15/a	5	a			17	19
		21					10	25				1	14			18/b					b		3	a		8		15	5/a				17	20
		21					10	25/a				1	14				11			a	19		3	4		8		15						21
		21					10					1	14			18	11				19		3			8		15					17	22
29		21					a					1	14			18	11				19/a		3			8		15					17	23
29/b		21			b		10/c					1	14			18	11				a		3			8/a		15				c	17	24
29/a		21					a					1	14			18	11					16/b	3			8		15				b	17	25
29/a		21		26								1	14			18	11						3			8		15				28	17	26
a				26			10				b	1/b	14			18	11						3			8		15				28/a	17	27
		21		26/a	7		10			22			14			18					a				30			15				28	17	28
		21		26/a	7		10/b					1	14			18					b		3		30	a						28	17	29
		21		26	7		10					1	14			18							3		30							28	17	30
29		21		26/b	7					22			14/c			18							3		30/a	b	a				c	28	17	31
		21		26	7		10			22			14			18							3		30							28	17	32
		21		26	7		10					1	14			18							3		30				5				17	33
32	29/b	21		26	7		10									18					a		3		30/a				5	b			17	34
					7						25/c	1				18						b	3/a		30		36	15	5/b	9	a	c	17	35
				26	7		10				b	1				18					19		3/a	4	a/b		36	15		9/c				36
		21		26	7		10					1	14			18							3		30/a				5		a		17	37
		21		26/a			10					1	14			18				b	19		3		30/b			15	a				17	38
		21		26			10				6	1	14			18							3					15	5				17	39
		21		a			10/b					1	14			18						16	3		30/a		b	15	5				17	40
		21		26			10					1	14			18					19	16						15	5				17	41
		21		26	a		c					1	14/b			18					19	16/c			30/a			15	5			b	17	42
		21		26	7/b		10			b	c	1	14/a			18					19	16/c							5	a			17	43
		21		26	7		10			b	25/c	1									19/b		3					15	5	c	a		17/a	44
		21		26	7		10				6	1	14										3		b			15	5/a		37/b			45
		21		26	7		b				6	1	14			a			20/a				3		30			15			37/b			46

2001-02
Story of the season

Glenn Roeder was **officially appointed as the club's manager** and he brought in former Hammers Paul Goddard as coach and Ludek Miklosko as goalkeeping coach.

After his father had been dismissed by West Ham unhappy Frank Lampard junior left to join Chelsea for a f of £11 million. Now with money to spend, Roeder boug midfielder Don Hutchison for £5 million and Cze defender Tomas Repka for £5.5 million, but it was not ur the fifth game of the season against Newcastle that t Hammers got their first win. They had also been beaten penalties in the League Cup tie at Reading. Worse was follow as the team crashed 5–0 at Everton and 7–1

Appearances & Goals 2001-02

	League			FA Cup			League Cup			Total	
	Starts	Subs	Goals	Starts	Subs	Goals	Starts	Subs	Goals	Starts	Subs
BYRNE Shaun	0	1	0	0	0	0	0	0	0	0	1
CAMARA Titi	0	1	0	0	0	0	0	0	0	0	1
CARRICK Michael	30	0	2	1	0	0	1	0	0	32	0
COLE Joe	29	1	0	3	0	1	0	0	0	32	1
COURTOIS Laurent	5	2	0	0	0	0	0	1	0	5	3
DAILLY Christian	38	0	0	3	0	0	1	0	0	42	0
DEFOE Jermain	14	21	10	2	1	4	1	0	0	17	22
DI CANIO Paolo	26	0	9	1	0	0	0	0	0	27	0
FOXE Hayden	4	2	0	0	1	0	0	0	0	4	3
GARCIA Richard	2	6	0	0	0	0	0	1	0	2	7
HISLOP Shaka	12	0	0	0	0	0	1	0	0	13	0
HUTCHISON Don	24	0	1	3	0	0	1	0	0	28	0
JAMES David	26	0	0	3	0	0	0	0	0	29	0
KANOUTE Frederic	27	0	11	1	0	1	0	0	0	28	0
KITSON Paul	3	4	3	2	0	0	0	0	0	5	4
LABANT Vladimir	7	5	0	0	2	0	0	0	0	7	7
LOMAS Steve	14	1	4	1	1	0	0	0	0	15	2
McCANN Grant	0	3	0	0	0	0	0	0	0	0	3
MINTO Scott	5	0	0	0	0	0	1	0	0	6	0
MONCUR John	7	12	0	1	0	0	1	0	0	9	12
PEARCE Ian	8	1	2	0	0	0	0	0	0	8	1
REPKA Tomas	31	0	0	3	0	0	0	0	0	34	0
SCHEMMEL Sebastien	35	0	1	3	0	0	1	0	0	39	0
SINCLAIR Trevor	34	0	5	2	0	0	1	0	0	37	0
SOMA Ragnvald	1	2	0	1	0	0	0	0	0	2	2
SONG Rigobert	5	0	0	0	0	0	1	0	0	6	0
TODOROV Svetoslav	2	4	0	0	1	0	1	0	0	3	5
WINTERBURN Nigel	29	2	0	3	0	0	0	0	0	32	2
Totals	**418**	**68**	**48**	**33**	**6**	**6**	**11**	**2**	**0**	**462**	**76**

ckburn Rovers. After this results improved with three
ccessive victories and a thrilling 4–4 draw at Charlton,
ere Paul Kitson grabbed a hat trick. On Boxing Day
rby County were beaten 4–0 at home, which left the
mmers in eleventh place.

enager Jermaine Defoe was beginning to score freely and
netted twice at Macclesfield in the FA Cup win. In the
xt round Chelsea proved to be tougher opponents and
er a 1–1 away draw the Hammers went out 3–2 in the
lay. There were seven home games remaining and six of
se were won, the only loss being a 5–3 defeat to
nchester United. Glen Roeder had done well in his first
son as manager, the team finishing in fifth place. As the
son came to a close Her Majesty the Queen officially
ened the new Dr Martens West Stand.

TOMAS REPKA

**The Czech defender began his career with
Banik Ostrava in 1991 where he made 77
league appearances before signing for
Sparta Prague in 1995.**

He stayed three seasons in the Czech capital,
playing in 82 league games before going to
Italy to join Fiorentina. He was by now a
mainstay in the Czech Republic international
side and he went on to play 46 times for his
country. Tomas was in Italy for three seasons,
having 89 league outings before coming to
England in September 2001 to sign for West
Ham. His introduction to the Premier League
was not good – he was sent off on his debut at
Middlesbrough and after serving a
suspension was sent off again at Blackburn
Rovers. He finally settled down and struck up
a formidable partnership with Christian Dailly
at the heart of the defence. Sadly he failed to
address his disciplinary problems and over
the next two seasons gained 29 yellow cards
and one more red. He was, however, a
favourite with the fans who loved his
no-nonsense approach.

After 182 games in the Hammers shirt he
returned to the Czech Republic in 2006 to sign
for his former club Sparta Prague. He spent
four seasons there, playing in 130 league
games until 2011. He later played for short
spells at Ceska Budejovice and Hvozdnice.

Barclaycard Premiership
nal Table 2001-02

		HOME					AWAY					
	P	W	D	L	F	A	W	D	L	F	A	Pts
enal	38	12	4	3	42	25	14	5	0	37	11	87
rpool	38	12	5	2	33	14	12	3	4	34	16	80
chester United	38	11	2	6	40	17	13	3	3	47	28	77
castle United	38	12	3	4	40	23	9	5	5	34	29	71
ds United	38	9	6	4	31	21	9	6	4	22	16	66
lsea	38	11	4	4	43	21	6	9	4	23	17	64
st Ham United	38	12	4	3	32	14	3	4	12	16	43	53
on Villa	38	8	7	4	22	17	4	7	8	24	30	50
enham Hotspur	38	10	4	5	32	24	4	4	11	17	29	50
ckburn Rovers	38	8	6	5	33	20	4	4	11	22	31	46
thampton	38	7	5	7	23	22	5	4	10	23	32	45
dlesbrough	38	7	5	7	23	26	5	4	10	12	21	45
nam	38	7	7	5	21	16	3	7	9	15	28	44
rlton Athletic	38	5	6	8	23	30	5	8	6	15	19	44
ton	38	8	4	7	26	23	3	6	10	19	34	43
on Wanderers	38	5	7	7	20	31	4	6	9	24	31	40
derland	38	7	7	5	18	16	3	3	13	11	35	40
wich Town	38	6	4	9	20	24	3	5	11	21	40	36
by County	38	5	4	10	20	26	3	2	14	13	37	30
ester City	38	3	7	9	15	34	2	6	11	15	30	28

Season **2001-02** FA Barclaycard Premiership
Match Details

Manager **Glenn Roeder**   Final League Position **7/20**

	Date		Competition	Venue	Opponents	Results		Attendance	Position	Scorers
1	Aug 18	Sat	Prem	A	Liverpool	L	1-2	43,935	12	Di Canio [pen]
2	Aug 25	Sat	Prem	H	Leeds United	D	0-0	24,517	17	
3	Sep 8	Sat	Prem	A	Derby County	D	0-0	27,802	17	
4	Sep 11	Tue	FLC 2	A	Reading	D	0-0*	21,173		
5	Sep 15	Sat	Prem	A	Middlesbrough	L	0-2	25,445	20	
6	Sep 23	Sun	Prem	H	Newcastle United	W	3-0	28,840	15	Di Canio, Hutchison, Kanoute
7	Sep 29	Sat	Prem	A	Everton	L	0-5	32,049	18	
8	Oct 14	Sun	Prem	A	Blackburn Rovers	L	1-7	22,712	19	Carrick
9	Oct 20	Sat	Prem	H	Southampton	W	2-0	25,842	15	Kanoute 2
10	Oct 24	Wed	Prem	H	Chelsea	W	2-1	26,520	14	Carrick, Kanoute
11	Oct 28	Sun	Prem	A	Ipswich Town	W	3-2	22,834	11	Defoe, Di Canio, Kanoute
12	Nov 3	Sat	Prem	H	Fulham	L	0-2	26,217	14	
13	Nov 19	Mon	Prem	A	Charlton Athletic	D	4-4	23,198	15	Kitson 3, Defoe
14	Nov 24	Sat	Prem	H	Tottenham Hotspur	L	0-1	32,780	15	
15	Dec 1	Sat	Prem	A	Sunderland	L	0-1	47,437	16	
16	Dec 5	Wed	Prem	H	Aston Villa	D	1-1	28,377	16	Defoe
17	Dec 8	Sat	Prem	A	Manchester United	W	1-0	67,582	16	Defoe
18	Dec 15	Sat	Prem	H	Arsenal	D	1-1	34,523	14	Kanoute
19	Dec 22	Sat	Prem	A	Leicester City	D	1-1	20,131	15	Di Canio [pen]
20	Dec 26	Wed	Prem	H	Derby County	W	4-0	31,397	11	Defoe, Di Canio, Schemmel, Sinclair
21	Dec 29	Sat	Prem	H	Liverpool	D	1-1	35,103	11	Sinclair
22	Jan 1	Tue	Prem	A	Leeds United	L	0-3	39,320	11	
23	Jan 6	Sun	FAC 3	A	Macclesfield Town	W	3-0	5,706		Defoe 2, Cole
24	Jan 12	Sat	Prem	H	Leicester City	W	1-0	34,698	11	Di Canio
25	Jan 20	Sun	Prem	A	Chelsea	L	1-5	40,035	12	Defoe
26	Jan 26	Sat	FAC 4	A	Chelsea	D	1-1	33,443		Kanoute
27	Jan 30	Wed	Prem	A	Southampton	L	0-2	31,879	14	
28	Feb 2	Sat	Prem	H	Blackburn Rovers	W	2-0	35,307	11	Sinclair, Kanoute
29	Feb 6	Wed	FAC 4 Rep	H	Chelsea	L	2-3	27,272		Defoe 2
30	Feb 9	Sat	Prem	A	Bolton Wanderers	L	0-1	24,342	12	
31	Feb 23	Sat	Prem	H	Middlesbrough	W	1-0	35,420	10	Kanoute
32	Mar 2	Sat	Prem	A	Aston Villa	L	1-2	37,341	13	Di Canio [pen]
33	Mar 6	Wed	Prem	H	Everton	W	1-0	29,883	10	Sinclair
34	Mar 16	Sat	Prem	H	Manchester United	L	3-5	35,281	10	Defoe, Kanoute, Lomas
35	Mar 30	Sat	Prem	H	Ipswich Town	W	3-1	33,871	10	Defoe, Di Canio, Lomas
36	Apr 1	Mon	Prem	A	Fulham	W	1-0	19,416	8	Kanoute
37	Apr 6	Sat	Prem	H	Charlton Athletic	W	2-0	32,389	7	Di Canio [pen], Kanoute
38	Apr 13	Sat	Prem	A	Tottenham Hotspur	D	1-1	36,083	7	Pearce
39	Apr 20	Sat	Prem	H	Sunderland	W	3-0	33,319	7	Defoe, Lomas, Sinclair
40	Apr 24	Wed	Prem	A	Arsenal	L	0-2	38,038	7	
41	Apr 27	Sat	Prem	A	Newcastle United	L	1-3	51,127	8	Defoe
42	May 11	Sat	Prem	H	Bolton Wanderers	W	2-1	35,546	7	Lomas, Pearce

* lost 5-6 on penalties after extra time

eam Line-Ups

CAMARA Titi	CARRICK Michael	COLE Joe	COURTOIS Laurent	DAILLY Christian	DEFOE Jermain	DI CANIO Paolo	FOXE Hayden	GARCIA Richard	HISLOP Shaka	HUTCHISON Don	JAMES David	KANOUTE Frederic	KITSON Paul	LABANT Vladimir	LOMAS Steve	McCANN Grant	MINTO Scott	MONCUR John	PEARCE Ian	REPKA Tomas	SCHEMMEL Sebastien	SINCLAIR Trevor	SOMA Ragnvald	SONG Rigobert	TODOROV Svetoslav	WINTERBURN Nigel	#
	21	26/c	c	7	b	10			17							a		16/b			30	8		15	18/b	3	1
	21	26		7	a	10			17							b		16/b			30	8		15	18/a	3	2
	21	26/a		7	c	10/c			17	4		14/b						a			30	8		15	b	3	3
	21	a		7	25			b	17	4							20	16/a			30	8		15	18/b		4
	21	26		7	a				17	4								16/b		2	30	8	c	15/a	b	3/c	5
	21	28/a		7	b	10			17	4		14/b						a		2	30	8				3	6
	21	28/b		7		10			17	4		14/c	c								30	8	a	15		3/a	7
	21			7/a		10	a		17	4		14					b	16/b		2	30	8		24			8
	21	28/a		7		10			17	4		14						a		2	30	8				3	9
	21	28/a		7	a	10			17	4		14/b	b							2	30	8				3	10
	21			7	a	10/a	6		17	4		14					20				30	8				3	11
	21	28/a		7	a	10	6		17	4		14								2	30	8				3	12
	21	b		7		10	6		17	4/b		12/a	c				20/c			2	30						13
		26		7	25					4	1	12			11/a		20	a		2	30	8					14
	21	26/a		7	25					4	1	12					20/b	a		2	30	8			b		15
	21	26		7	25	10				4	1									2	30	8				3	16
a	21	26		7	25/a	10				4	1									2	30	8				3	17
	21	26		7	a	10				4	1	14/a								2	30	8				3	18
	21	26		7	25/a	10				4	1							a		2	30	8				3	19
	21	26		7	a	10/b				4	1	14/a						b		2	30	8				3	20
	21	26		7	25					4	1	14								2	30	8				3	21
		26		7	25/a			b		4	1	14/b						16		2	30	8			a	3	22
		26		7	25		a			4/a	1	12						16		2	30	8				3	23
		26		7	a	10		b		4	1	14/a						16/b		2	30	8				3	24
	21	26	a	7	b	10				4	1	14/b								2	30	8/a				3	25
	21	26		7	a	10				4/b	1	14	c	b						2	30	24/b				3/c	26
	21/b	26		7	a	10				4/a	1	14			11			b	5	2	30						27
		26		7	b	10				4/a	1	14/b		a	11			c		2	30	8/c				3	28
		26		7	25					4/a	1	12/b		a	11					2	30	8			b	3	29
		26		7	25		6	33/a			1	14	a		11		20		5		30						30
		26		7	25			b		4/a	1	14	a		11/b	19		16		2						3	31
		26		7	25	10		33/a			1	a				19				2	30	8				3	32
		26		7	b	10		a			1	14/b				19			5	2	30/a	8				3	33
	21	26		7	a	10					1	14			11				5	2	30					3/a	34
	21	26		7	a	10/b					1	14/a			11				b	2	30	8				3	35
	21	26		7	c	10/b					1	14/c			11	b		a	5/a	2	30	8					36
	21	26/b		7	a	10/a					1	14			11				b	2	30	8				3	37
	21			7	25						1	14			11	19			5/a	2	30	8			a		38
	21	26		7	25/b			b			1	a			11	19				2	30/a	8				3	39
	21	26		7	b						1	14/b		a	11	19				2	30/a	8				3	40
	21	26		7	25			a			1	14			11	19			5/a	2		8/b			b		41
	21/a	26		7	25			b			1	14/b			11	19		a		2						3	42

2002-03
Story of the season

Departing the club during the summer were **Steve Potts, Paul Kitson, Shaka Hislop, Gary Charles** and **Craig Forrest.**

On a restricted budget, Roeder signed replacements free transfers: joining the Hammers were defender Ga Breen, striker Youseff Sofiane and midfielder Edoua Cisse. The team made a bad start, and after losing 4–0 Newcastle on the opening day they did not win a game ur late September when Di Canio scored twice in a 3–2 victo at Chelsea.

They laboured in the League Cup at Chesterfield, winni the tie on penalties, and went out in the next round with dismal 1–0 home defeat against Oldham Athletic. Only fi points were gained from the next nine games and by t end of December the side was in bottom place. Injuries strikers Di Canio and Kanoute in this period added to t plight and forced Roeder to purchase the experienc striker Les Ferdinand.

Appearances & Goals 2002-03

	League			FA Cup			League Cup			Total	
	Starts	Subs	Goals	Starts	Subs	Goals	Starts	Subs	Goals	Starts	Subs
BOWYER Lee	10	0	0	1	0	0	0	0	0	11	0
BREEN Gary	9	5	0	2	0	0	2	0	0	13	5
BREVETT Rufus	12	1	0	0	0	0	0	0	0	12	1
CAMARA Titi	0	4	0	0	1	0	1	0	0	1	5
CARRICK Michael	28	2	1	2	0	0	2	0	0	32	2
CISSE Edouard	18	7	0	2	0	0	1	0	0	21	7
COLE Joe	36	0	4	2	0	1	2	0	0	40	0
DAILLY Christian	23	3	0	1	1	0	1	0	0	25	4
DEFOE Jermain	29	9	8	2	0	2	2	0	1	33	9
DI CANIO Paolo	16	2	9	0	0	0	1	0	0	17	2
FERDINAND Les	12	2	2	0	0	0	0	0	0	12	2
GARCIA Richard	0	0	0	0	1	0	0	1	0	0	2
HUTCHISON Don	0	10	0	0	0	0	0	0	0	0	10
JAMES David	38	0	0	2	0	0	2	0	0	42	0
JOHNSON Glen	14	1	0	0	1	0	0	0	0	14	2
KANOUTE Frederic	12	5	5	0	0	0	0	0	0	12	5
LABANT Vladimir	0	1	0	0	0	0	0	0	0	0	1
LOMAS Steve	27	2	0	1	0	0	2	0	0	30	2
MINTO Scott	9	3	0	1	0	0	2	0	0	12	3
MONCUR John	0	7	0	0	0	0	0	0	0	0	7
PEARCE Ian	26	4	2	2	0	0	1	0	0	29	4
REPKA Tomas	32	0	0	0	1	0	1	0	0	33	1
SCHEMMEL Sebastien	15	1	0	1	0	0	1	1	0	17	2
SINCLAIR Trevor	36	2	8	2	0	0	1	0	0	39	2
WINTERBURN Nigel	16	2	0	1	0	0	0	1	0	17	2
own goal			3								
Totals	418	73	42	22	5	3	22	3	1	462	81

he FA Cup saw the Hammers struggle to beat Nottingham
orest 3–2 at home, after which they faced a daunting tie at
anchester United. The 9,000 fans who travelled were
dly let down as the Hammers slumped to a 6–0 defeat.
nally in late January West Ham won their first home
ague game when beating Blackburn Rovers 2–1. Despite
rther home wins against Tottenham and Sunderland, the
essure of avoiding relegation was intense. Following the
–0 victory against Middlesbrough manager Roeder
llapsed and was rushed to hospital with a brain tumour.
e underwent surgery and later recovered but would not
ke part in any further club matters that season. Club
gend Trevor Brooking then agreed to be in charge for the
al three games. There were 1–0 victories over Manchester
ty and Chelsea, but following the 2–2 draw at Birmingham
ty the club were relegated. The fans were left puzzled as
how a team with so many star names could end up facing
e in the Championship.

A Barclaycard Premiership
inal Table 2002-03

| | P | HOME | | | | | AWAY | | | | | |
		W	D	L	F	A	W	D	L	F	A	Pts
anchester United	38	16	2	1	42	12	9	6	4	32	22	83
senal	38	15	2	2	47	20	8	7	4	38	22	78
wcastle United	38	15	2	2	36	17	6	4	9	27	31	69
elsea	38	12	5	2	41	15	7	5	7	27	23	67
erpool	38	9	8	2	30	16	9	2	8	31	25	64
ckburn Rovers	38	9	7	3	24	15	7	5	7	28	28	60
erton	38	11	5	3	28	19	6	3	10	20	30	59
uthampton	38	9	8	2	25	16	4	5	10	18	30	52
nchester City	38	9	2	8	28	26	6	4	9	19	28	51
tenham Hotspur	38	9	4	6	30	29	5	4	10	21	33	50
ddlesbrough	38	10	7	2	36	21	3	3	13	12	23	49
arlton Athletic	38	8	3	8	26	30	6	4	9	19	26	49
rmingham City	38	8	5	6	25	23	5	4	10	16	26	48
ham	38	11	3	5	26	18	2	6	11	15	32	48
eds United	38	7	3	9	25	26	7	2	10	33	31	47
on Villa	38	11	2	6	25	14	1	7	11	17	33	45
ton Wanderers	38	7	8	4	27	24	3	6	10	14	27	44
est Ham United	38	5	7	7	21	24	5	5	9	21	35	42
st Bromwich Albion	38	3	5	11	17	34	3	3	13	12	31	26
nderland	38	3	2	14	11	31	1	5	13	10	34	19

GLEN JOHNSON

A product of the Hammers youth academy, the right-back was tipped for stardom at an early age.

He started season 2002–03 in the reserves and was later loaned to Millwall, playing eight games for them in the Championship. After making his debut at Charlton in January 2003 he was ever-present until the end of the season, playing in 16 games. The club were relegated in that campaign and the fans were furious when he was transferred to Chelsea for £6 million.

With the Blues he was successful and picked up winners' medals in 2005 when Chelsea won the Premier League and the Football League Cup. In November 2004 he won the first of his 54 England caps when being selected to play against Denmark. He went on loan to Portsmouth in 2006 and made the move permanent in August 2007. A year later he was in the side that won the 2008 FA Cup final. Glen spent three seasons playing at Fratton Park and after making 99 appearances was transferred to Liverpool in June 2009. He became a regular in the side and gained another winners' medal when Liverpool beat Cardiff City in the 2012 League Cup Final. After playing in 160 league games for Liverpool he left in July 2015 to join Stoke City.

Season **2002-03** FA Barclaycard Premiership
Match Details

Manager **Glenn Roeder** taken ill: (Caretaker Manager: **Trevor Brooking** for last three games)
Final League Position: **18/20 Relegated to Nationwide League Division 1**

	Date		Competition	Venue	Opponents	Results		Attendance	Position	Scorers
1	Aug 19	Mon	Prem	A	Newcastle United	L	0-4	51,072	20	
2	Aug 24	Sat	Prem	H	Arsenal	D	2-2	35,048	16	Cole, Kanoute
3	Aug 31	Sat	Prem	H	Charlton Athletic	L	0-2	32,424	19	
4	Sep 11	Wed	Prem	H	West Bromwich Albion	L	0-1	34,957	20	
5	Sep 15	Sun	Prem	A	Tottenham Hotspur	L	2-3	36,005	20	Sinclair, Kanoute
6	Sep 21	Sat	Prem	H	Manchester City	D	0-0	35,050	20	
7	Sep 28	Sat	Prem	A	Chelsea	W	3-2	38,929	20	Di Canio 2, Defoe
8	Oct 1	Tue	FLC 2	A	Chesterfield	D	1-1*	7,102		Defoe
9	Oct 5	Sat	Prem	H	Birmingham City	L	1-2	35,010	20	Cole
10	Oct 19	Sat	Prem	A	Sunderland	W	1-0	44,352	16	Sinclair
11	Oct 23	Wed	Prem	A	Fulham	W	1-0	15,858	14	Di Canio [pen]
12	Oct 27	Sun	Prem	H	Everton	L	0-1	34,117	15	
13	Nov 2	Sat	Prem	A	Liverpool	L	0-2	44,048	16	
14	Nov 6	Wed	FLC 3	H	Oldham Athletic	L	0-1	21,919		
15	Nov 10	Sun	Prem	H	Leeds United	L	3-4	33,297	18	Di Canio 2 [1 pen], Sinclair
16	Nov 17	Sun	Prem	H	Manchester United	D	1-1	35,049	19	Defoe
17	Nov 23	Sat	Prem	A	Aston Villa	L	1-4	33,279	20	Di Canio
18	Dec 2	Mon	Prem	H	Southampton	L	0-1	28,844	20	
19	Dec 7	Sat	Prem	A	Middlesrough	D	2-2	28,283	20	Cole, Pearce I.
20	Dec 14	Sat	Prem	A	Manchester United	L	0-3	67,555	20	
21	Dec 21	Sat	Prem	H	Bolton Wanderers	D	1-1	34,892	20	Pearce I.
22	Dec 26	Thur	Prem	H	Fulham	D	1-1	35,025	20	Sinclair [pen]
23	Dec 28	Sat	Prem	A	Blackburn Rovers	D	2-2	24,998	20	Defoe, Taylor (og)
24	Jan 4	Sat	FAC 3	H	Nottingham Forest	W	3-2	29,612		Defoe 2, Cole
25	Jan 11	Sat	Prem	H	Newcastle United	D	2-2	35,048	19	Cole, Defoe
26	Jan 19	Sun	Prem	A	Arsenal	L	1-3	38,053	20	Defoe
27	Jan 22	Wed	Prem	A	Charlton Athletic	L	2-4	26,340	20	Rufus (og), Fish (og)
28	Jan 26	Sun	FAC 4	A	Manchester United	L	0-6	67,181		
29	Jan 29	Wed	Prem	H	Blackburn Rovers	W	2-1	34,743	18	Di Canio [pen], Defoe
30	Feb 2	Sun	Prem	H	Liverpool	L	0-3	35,033	19	
31	Feb 8	Sat	Prem	A	Leeds United	L	0-1	40,126	19	
32	Feb 23	Sun	Prem	A	West Bromwich Albion	W	2-1	27,042	18	Sinclair 2
33	Mar 1	Sat	Prem	H	Tottenham Hotspur	W	2-0	35,049	18	Ferdinand L., Carrick M.
34	Mar 15	Sat	Prem	A	Everton	D	0-0	40,158	18	
35	Mar 22	Sat	Prem	H	Sunderland	W	2-0	35,033	17	Defoe, Kanoute
36	Apr 5	Sat	Prem	A	Southampton	D	1-1	31,941	18	Defoe
37	Apr 12	Sat	Prem	H	Aston Villa	D	2-2	35,029	18	Sinclair, Kanoute
38	Apr 19	Sat	Prem	A	Bolton Wanderers	L	0-1	27,160	18	
39	Apr 21	Mon	Prem	H	Middlesbrough	W	1-0	35,019	18	Sinclair
40	Apr 27	Sun	Prem	A	Manchester City	W	1-0	34,815	18	Kanoute
41	May 3	Sat	Prem	H	Chelsea	W	1-0	35,042	18	Di Canio
42	May 11	Sun	Prem	A	Birmingham City	D	2-2	29,505	18	Ferdinand L., Di Canio

* After extra time - won 5-4 on penalties (1-1 at 90 minutes)

eam Line-Ups

BREEN Gary	BREVETT Rufus	CAMARA Titi	CARRICK Michael	CISSE Edouard	COLE Joe	DAILLY Christian	DEFOE Jermain	DI CANIO Paolo	FERDINAND Les	GARCIA Richard	HUTCHISON Don	JAMES David	JOHNSON Glen	KANOUTE Frederic	LABANT Vladimir	LOMAS Steve	MINTO Scott	MONCUR John	PEARCE Ian	REPKA Tomas	SCHEMMEL Sebastien	SINCLAIR Trevor	WINTERBURN Nigel	
			6	25/b	26	7	9					1			a			b	19	2	30/a	8	3	1
a			6	25	26/b	7	9					1		14				b		2	30	8	3/a	2
		b	6	25/a	26	7	9					1		14		a				2	30	8	3/b	3
15			6/b	25	26	a	c	10/c				1		14		b				2	30	8	3/a	4
15			b	25	26	7	c	10/b				1		14/c		11			19	2/a		8	a	5
15			b	25/b	26/a		c	10/c				1		14		11	20	a		2	30	8		6
15			6	b	26		a	10/b				1		14/a		11	20			2	30	8		7
15			6		26		9	10				1				11	20			2	30	8		8
15		b	6		26/b		9	10				1				11	20	a		2	30/a	8		9
b			6	a	26	7	9	10				1				11	20		19/b	2		8/a		10
			6	25	26	7	9	10				1					20		19	2		8		11
		a	6	b	26	7	9	10				1				11/b	20/a		19	2		8		12
		a	6	25	26	7	9/a					1				11	20		19	2		8		13
15/a	29		6	25/c	26	7	9				c	1				11	20/b		19		b		a	14
			6	b	26	7	9	10				1				11/b			19	2/a	a	8	3	15
			6	25	26	7	9	10				1							19		30	8	3	16
			6	25	26	7	9	10				1							19		30	8	3	17
			6		26	7	9	10/a				1						a	19	2	30	8	3	18
a			6	25/b	26	7	9					1						b	19/a	2	30	8	3	19
a			6		26	7	9					1				11/b	20/a	b	19	2	30	8	3	20
			6		26	7	9				a	1				11			19/a	2	30	8	3	21
			6		26	7	9				a	1		14/b		11/a			b	2	30	8	3	22
15			6	25/b	26	7	a					1				11/a	c	b	19		30	8	3/c	23
15		b	6	25	26	7	9					1							19/b	a	30	8	3/a	24
15			6	25/c	26	7	9				c	1				11	a		b			8/b	3/a	25
15			6	25/b	26	7	9					1				11	a		19			8	3/a	26
15			6	25/b		7	9		22			1	b			11	20/a					8	a	27
15/a			6	25/c	26	a	9				c	1	b			11	20		19			8/b		28
			6		26		c	10/b	22/a			1	23	a		11			19	2		b	3/c	29
	a		6		26	7	b	10	22/c			1	23	c					19	2		8/b	3/a	30
	24/a		6/c		26		b	10/b			c	1	23	14		11			19	2		a		31
c	24		6				a	10/a	22/b		b	1	23			11			19	2		8		32
	24		6		26		9		22/a		a	1	23						19	2		8		33
	24		6	b	26/b	a	9		22/a			1	23			11			19	2		8		34
	24		6	b	26/b		9		22/c		a	1	23	c		11/a			19	2		8		35
	24			a	26		9		22/b			1	23	b		11/a			19	2		8		36
	24				26		9		a		b	1	23	14/b		11			19	2		8		37
	24			25/a	26		9		a			1	23	14		11			19	2		8		38
	24			25	26		9		22			1	23			11			19	2		8		39
	24			25/a	26	c	9		22/b		b	1	23	a		11			19/c	2		8		40
	24				26	7	9	a	22/a			1	23	14		11				2		8		41
	24/a				26/b	7	9	a	22		b	1	23	14		11				2		8		42

The players responded to Brooking's style and there wa only one defeat in the next 10 games, with the team no lying in fifth place. A hat-trick from Jermain Defoe gave th Hammers a 3–2 win in the League Cup at Cardiff City.

West Ham announced that their new manager was to b Reading's Alan Pardew; after a spell on 'gardening leave' h

2003-04
Story of the season

The **opening games saw a 2–1 victory** at Preston North End followed by a 3–1 home win against Rushden & Diamonds in the League Cup. The next away game brought a 1–0 defeat at Rotherham United, after which **Glen Roeder was sacked** and once again **Trevor Brooking was made caretaker manager**.

Appearances & Goals 2003-04

	League			FA Cup			League Cup			Other			Total	
	Starts	Subs	Goals	Starts	Subs	Goals	Starts	Subs	Goals	Starts	Subs	Goals	Starts	Subs
ALEXANDERSSON Niclas	5	3	0	0	0	0	0	0	0	0	0	0	5	3
BREVETT Rufus	2	0	0	0	0	0	1	0	0	0	0	0	3	0
BYRNE Shaun	0	0	0	0	0	0	0	1	0	0	0	0	0	1
BYWATER Stephen	17	0	0	3	0	0	0	0	0	3	0	0	23	0
CAROLE Sebastien	0	1	0	0	0	0	0	0	0	0	0	0	0	1
CARRICK Michael	34	1	1	4	0	0	1	0	0	3	0	0	42	1
COHEN Chris	1	6	0	0	0	0	0	0	0	0	0	0	1	6
CONNOLLY David	37	2	10	4	0	2	2	0	2	3	0	0	46	2
DAILLY Christian	43	0	2	3	1	0	3	0	0	3	0	1	52	1
DEANE Brian	9	17	6	3	0	1	0	0	0	0	3	0	12	20
DEFOE Jermain	19	0	11	0	0	0	3	0	4	0	0	0	22	0
ETHERINGTON Matthew	34	1	5	4	0	0	3	0	0	3	0	1	44	1
FERDINAND Anton	9	11	0	3	0	0	2	1	0	0	0	0	14	12
GARCIA Richard	2	5	0	0	0	0	0	3	0	0	0	0	2	8
HAREWOOD Marlon	28	0	13	4	0	1	0	0	0	3	0	0	35	0
HARLEY Jon	15	0	1	1	0	0	0	0	0	0	0	0	16	0
HORLOCK Kevin	23	4	1	4	0	0	2	0	0	0	0	0	29	4
HUTCHISON Don	10	14	4	0	1	0	1	0	0	0	1	0	11	16
JAMES David	27	0	0	1	0	0	3	0	0	0	0	0	31	0
KILGALLON Matthew	1	2	0	0	0	0	1	0	0	0	0	0	2	2
LEE Robert	12	4	0	0	1	0	2	0	0	0	0	0	14	5
LOMAS Steve	5	0	0	0	2	0	0	0	0	3	0	0	8	2
McANUFF Jobi	4	8	1	0	0	0	0	0	0	0	1	0	4	9
MELLOR Neil	8	8	2	0	3	0	1	1	0	0	0	0	9	12
MELVILLE Andy	11	3	0	0	0	0	0	0	0	3	0	0	14	3
MULLINS Hayden	27	0	0	4	0	1	0	0	0	3	0	0	34	0
NOBLE David	0	3	0	0	0	0	1	0	0	0	0	0	1	3
NOWLAND Adam	2	9	0	0	0	0	0	0	0	0	0	0	2	9
PEARCE Ian	24	0	1	1	0	0	1	0	0	0	0	0	26	0
QUINN Wayne	22	0	0	2	1	0	2	0	0	0	0	0	26	1
REO-COKER Nigel	13	2	2	0	0	0	0	0	0	0	3	0	13	5
REPKA Tomas	40	0	0	2	0	0	2	0	0	3	0	0	47	0
SOFIANE Youssef	0	1	0	0	0	0	1	0	0	0	0	0	1	1
SRNICEK Pavel	2	1	0	0	0	0	0	0	0	0	0	0	2	1
STOCKDALE Robbie	5	2	0	1	0	0	1	0	0	0	0	0	7	2
ZAMORA Bobby	15	2	5	0	0	0	0	0	0	3	0	0	18	2
own goal			2											
Totals	506	110	67	44	9	5	33	6	6	33	8	2	616	133

* Other = Play-off matches

s in charge for the home game with Nottingham Forest
October. Pardew's first signings were midfielder Hayden
ullins and veteran striker Brian Deane, who arrived in
:tober,.. A late goal in the League Cup gave Tottenham a
0 victory at White Hart Lane. Pardew's first 11 games in
arge saw only one defeat. This was at home to West
mwich Albion, where the Hammers were leading 3–0
er eighteen minutes but collapsed to lose 4–3.

e FA Cup began with away wins at Wigan and
olverhampton Wanderers but after a draw at Fulham they
nt out, losing 3–0 in the replay.. An eight-match unbeaten
was interrupted by a 2–0 defeat at Sunderland in March.
e team were now in fifth place and despite a very
appointing 4–1 defeat at Millwall they maintained their
omotion hopes to the season's end. In finishing fourth
y qualified for the playoffs, where they would meet
swich Town. In the first leg at Ipswich the Hammers lost

1–0 but in an emotional night in the return leg goals from
Etherington and Dailly gave West Ham a 2–0 victory and a
passage to the final in Cardiff. The final with Crystal Palace
turned out to be an anti-climax as the Hammers gave a
lacklustre performance and lost 1–0.

MATTHEW ETHERINGTON

As a 15-year-old this exciting left-winger made his debut for Peterborough United in May 1997.

After scoring six goals in 58 outings he moved on to Tottenham in 2000. He was not able to gain a regular place in the Spurs team and was loaned out to Bradford City in 2001, where he played in 13 league games. In August 2003, after 51 games for Tottenham, he joined West Ham and made his debut against Preston North End. He flourished at Upton Park and became very popular with the supporters, who voted him as 'Hammer of the Year' in his first season. In 2005 he scored a vital goal in the playoff semi-final with Ipswich and provided the cross for Zamora to score the winning goal in the final against Preston. He gained a losers' medal in the 2006 FA Cup final when the Hammers were beaten by Liverpool.

After six seasons at Upton Park, where he scored 17 goals in 189 appearances, he was transferred to Stoke City in 2009. Mattie had a successful career with the Potters, scoring 16 goals in 177 games. He gained another losers' medal when playing against Manchester City in the 2011 FA Cup final. A back injury was hampering his career and in May 2014 he was released by Stoke and retired.

ationwide League Division One nal Table 2003-04

	P	HOME					AWAY					Pts
		W	D	L	F	A	W	D	L	F	A	
wich City	46	18	3	2	44	15	10	7	6	35	24	94
st Bromwich Albion	46	14	5	4	34	16	11	6	6	30	26	86
aderland	46	13	8	2	33	15	9	5	9	29	30	79
st Ham United	46	12	7	4	42	20	7	10	6	25	25	74
wich Town	46	12	3	8	49	36	9	7	7	35	36	73
stal Palace	46	10	8	5	34	25	11	2	10	38	36	73
an Athletic	46	11	8	4	29	16	7	9	7	31	29	71
effield United	46	11	6	6	37	25	9	5	9	28	31	71
ding	46	11	6	6	29	25	9	4	10	26	32	70
lwall	46	11	8	4	28	15	7	7	9	27	33	69
ke City	46	11	7	5	35	24	7	5	11	23	31	66
ventry City	46	9	9	5	34	22	8	5	10	33	32	65
diff City	46	10	6	7	40	25	7	8	8	28	33	65
tingham Forest	46	8	9	6	33	25	7	6	10	28	33	60
ston North End	46	11	7	5	43	29	4	7	12	26	42	59
tford	46	9	8	6	31	28	6	4	13	23	40	57
herham United	46	8	8	7	31	27	5	7	11	22	34	54
we Alexandra	46	11	3	9	33	26	3	8	12	24	40	53
rnley	46	9	6	8	37	32	4	8	11	23	45	53
by County	46	11	5	7	39	33	2	8	13	14	34	52
ingham	46	10	1	12	28	34	4	8	11	20	33	51
lsall	46	8	7	8	29	31	5	5	13	16	34	51
dford City	46	6	3	14	23	35	4	3	16	15	34	36
mbledon	46	3	4	16	21	40	5	1	17	20	49	29

Season **2003-04** Nationwide League Division On

Match Details

Manager **Glenn Roeder** (to Aug 25); (Caretaker Manager: **Trevor Brooking** (Aug 26));
Manager: **Alan Pardew** (from October 20)   Final League Position **4/24**

	Date		Competition	Venue	Opponents	Results		Attendance	Position	Scorers
1	Aug 9	Sat	Champ	A	Preston North End	W	2-1	18,246	7	Connolly, Defoe
2	Aug 13	Wed	FLC 2	H	Rushden & Diamonds	W	3-1	13,715		Connolly 2, Defoe
3	Aug 16	Sat	Champ	H	Sheffield United	D	0-0	28,972	8	
4	Aug 23	Sat	Champ	A	Rotherham United	L	0-1	8,739	12	
5	Aug 26	Tue	Champ	H	Bradford City	W	1-0	30,370	10	Defoe
6	Aug 30	Sat	Champ	A	Ipswich Town	W	2-1	29,679	6	Connolly, Defoe
7	Sep 13	Sat	Champ	H	Reading	W	1-0	32,634	3	Dailly
8	Sep 16	Tue	Champ	A	Crewe Alexandra	W	3-0	9,575	2	Connolly 2, Etherington
9	Sep 20	Sat	Champ	A	Gillingham	L	0-2	11,418	4	
10	Sep 23	Tue	FLC 3	A	Cardiff City	W	3-2	10,724		Defoe 3 [1 pen]
11	Sep 28	Sun	Champ	H	Millwall	D	1-1	31,626	5	Connolly
12	Oct 1	Wed	Champ	H	Crystal Palace	W	3-0	31,861	4	Mellor 2, Defoe
13	Oct 4	Sat	Champ	A	Derby County	W	1-0	22,810	3	Hutchison
14	Oct 15	Wed	Champ	H	Norwich City	D	1-1	31,308	4	Edworthy (og)
15	Oct 18	Sat	Champ	H	Burnley	D	2-2	31,474	5	Connolly, Hutchison
16	Oct 22	Wed	Champ	H	Nottingham Forest	D	1-1	29,544	5	Defoe
17	Oct 25	Sat	Champ	A	Cardiff City	D	0-0	19,202	6	
18	Oct 29	Wed	FLC 4	A	Tottenham Hotspur	L	0-1	36,053		
19	Nov 1	Sat	Champ	A	Coventry City	D	1-1	19,126	6	Defoe
20	Nov 8	Sat	Champ	H	West Bromwich Albion	L	3-4	30,359	6	Deane 2, Defoe
21	Nov 22	Sat	Champ	A	Watford	D	0-0	20,950	9	
22	Nov 25	Tue	Champ	A	Wimbledon	D	1-1	8,118	9	Deane
23	Nov 29	Sat	Champ	H	Wigan Athletic	W	4-0	34,375	7	Harewood 2 [1 pen], Horlock, Jarrett (og)
24	Dec 6	Sat	Champ	A	West Bromwich Albion	D	1-1	26,194	8	Deane
25	Dec 9	Tue	Champ	H	Stoke City	L	0-1	24,365	9	
26	Dec 13	Sat	Champ	H	Sunderland	W	3-2	30,329	6	Defoe 2, Pearce I.
27	Dec 20	Sat	Champ	A	Walsall	D	1-1	9,272	6	Harewood
28	Dec 26	Fri	Champ	H	Ipswich Town	L	1-2	35,021	8	Defoe
29	Dec 28	Sun	Champ	A	Nottingham Forest	W	2-0	27,491	7	Defoe, Harewood
30	Jan 3	Sat	FAC 3	A	Wigan Athletic	W	2-1	11,793		Connolly, Mullins
31	Jan 10	Sat	Champ	H	Preston North End	L	1-2	28,777	8	Connolly
32	Jan 17	Sat	Champ	A	Sheffield United	D	3-3	22,787	8	Carrick, Harewood, Harley
33	Jan 25	Sun	FAC 4	A	Wolverhampton Wanderers	W	3-1	24,413		Connolly, Deane, Harewood
34	Jan 31	Sat	Champ	H	Rotherham United	W	2-1	34,483	7	Dailly, Deane
35	Feb 7	Sat	Champ	A	Bradford City	W	2-1	13,078	5	Harewood, Zamora
36	Feb 14	Sat	FAC 5	A	Fulham	D	0-0	14,705		
37	Feb 21	Sat	Champ	A	Norwich City	D	1-1	23,940	5	Harewood
38	Feb 24	Tue	FAC 5 Rep	H	Fulham	L	0-3	27,934		
39	Feb 28	Sat	Champ	H	Cardiff City	W	1-0	31,858	6	Zamora
40	Mar 2	Tue	Champ	A	Burnley	D	1-1	12,440	5	Connolly [pen]
41	Mar 6	Sat	Champ	H	Walsall	D	0-0	33,177	5	
42	Mar 9	Tue	Champ	H	Wimbledon	W	5-0	29,818	3	Etherington 3, Reo-Coker, Zamora
43	Mar 13	Sat	Champ	A	Sunderland	L	0-2	29,533	5	
44	Mar 17	Wed	Champ	H	Crewe Alexandra	W	4-2	31,158	3	Harewood 2, McAnuff, Reo-Coker
45	Mar 21	Sun	Champ	A	Millwall	L	1-4	14,055	5	Harewood [pen]
46	Mar 27	Sat	Competition	Venue	Gillingham	W	2-1	34,551	4	Etherington, Zamora
47	Apr 3	Sat	Champ	A	Reading	L	0-2	21,718	4	
48	Apr 10	Sat	Champ	H	Derby County	D	0-0	28,207	6	
49	Apr 12	Mon	Champ	A	Crystal Palace	L	0-1	23,977	8	
50	Apr 17	Sat	Champ	H	Coventry City	W	2-0	27,890	6	Connolly [pen], Zamora
51	Apr 24	Sat	Champ	A	Stoke City	W	2-0	18,227	5	Connolly, Harewood
52	May 1	Sat	Champ	H	Watford	W	4-0	34,685	3	Hutchison 2, Harewood 2 [1 pen]
53	May 9	Sun	Champ	A	Wigan Athletic	D	1-1	20,669	4	Deane
54	May 15	Sat	PO SF:1	A	Ipswich Town	L	0-1	28,435		
55	May 18	Tue	PO SF:2	H	Ipswich Town	W	2-0	34,002		Dailly, Etherington
56	May 29	Sat	PO F	N*	Crystal Palace	L	0-1	72,523		

* Millennium Stadium, Cardiff

eam Line-Ups

BREVETT Rufus	BYRNE Shaun	BYWATER Stephen	CAROLE Sebastien	CARRICK Michael	COHEN Chris	CONNOLLY David	DAILLY Christian	DEANE Brian	DEFOE Jermain	ETHERINGTON Matthew	FERDINAND Anton	GARCIA Richard	HAREWOOD Marlon	HARLEY Jon	HORLOCK Kevin	HUTCHISON Don	JAMES David	KILGALLON Matthew	LEE Robert	LOMAS Steve	McANUFF Jobi	MELLOR Neil	MELVILLE Andy	MULLINS Hayden	NOBLE David	NOWLAND Adam	PEARCE Ian	QUINN Wayne	REO-COKER Nigel	REPKA Tomas	SOFIANE Youssef	SRNICEK Pavel	STOCKDALE Robbie	ZAMORA Bobby	
3						a	7		9	12	15	21/a				4	1		5			33/a								2	b				1
3	b					8	7		9	12	15/a	a					1		5							28				2		18/b			2
3/a						8	7		9	12		a/b			16	4	1		5/c		b					c		19		2					3
					a	8/c	7		9	12	15/b	b			16	4/a	1		5		c							19		2					4
					6	8	7		9	12					16	a	1		5/a			33						19		2					5
					6	8	7		9	12					16	a	1	22				33/a						19		2					6
						8	7		9	12	15/a				16		1		5			33/b						19	14	2					7
						8	7		9	12/b	b				16	a	1		5		c							19	14/a	2					8
						8	7		9	12	a				16/b		1		5		b							19	14	2					9
						8	7		9	12	15	a			16		1		5			33/a						19	14	2					10
						8	7		9	12	b				16		1		5			33/a						19	14/b	2					11
						8	7		9	12	a				16	b	1		5/a			33/c						19	14/b	2					12
					6/b	8	7			12					16	a	1		b			33/a						19	14	2					13
					6		7			12/c	c	21/b			16/a	b	1		a			33						19	14	2					14
					6	8	7			12					b		1		5			a						19	14/a	2					15
					6	8/b	7		9	12	a					4	1		5/a		b		17						14	2					16
					6	8/a	7		9	12	c					4	1		b		a/c		17/b						14	2			20		17
					6		7		9	12	a	b			16/c	4	1	22	5/b		c								14	2			20/a		18
							7	29	9	12					16		1		5/a				17					19	14	2					19
					6		7	29	9	12						4	1		a				17					19	14/a	2					20
					6	8	7	29/a		a					16	4	1						17					19	14	2					21
					6	8	7	29/a		a					16	4	1						17					19	14	2					22
					6	8/a	7	29			b	c	10		16/c		1						17					19	14	2/b					23
					6	8	7	29/b					10		a	b	1						17					19	14	2			20/a		24
					6	8	7	29/b					10		a	b	1						17					19	14	2/a			20		25
				c		8	7	b	9	12/c			10/b		16	a	1						17					19	14/a	2					26
					6	8/a		b	9	12			10/b		16	a	1						17					19	14	2					27
					6	8/a			9	12					16/b	a	1				c		17					19	14/c	2	b				28
					6	8/a			9	12	b		10			a	1				c		17					19	14	2			20/b		29
					6	8		b		12			10/c		16/a		1				c		17					19	14	2/b			20		30
					6	8	7	a		12	b		10/c			4/a	1				c		17					19	14/b				20/c		31
		32			6	8	7	a		12/c	15		10/b	24	16/a					c	22		17							b					32
		32			6	8	7	29		12	15/a		10	24	16								17				a								33
		32			6	8	7	29/b		12			10/a	24	16						b		17				a		20	2					34
		32			6	8/c	7	29/a					10	24							26/b					c	17		20	2				a	35
		32			6	8/a	7			12	15		10		16					b	a		17							2					36
		32			6	8/a	7			12			10	24									17					a	20	2				25/b	37
		32			6	8	7/c	29/a		12	15		10		16/b					b	a		c				17		14						38
		32			6	8/b	7	b		12			10/a	24							c						17	a	20	2				25/c	39
		32			6	8/b	7			12/c			10	24							a						17	c	20	2				25	40
		32			6	8/c	7	c					10	24							b		a			19/b	17/a		20	2				25	41
		32			6/b	8	7			12	c		10	24/c						a	22							c	20/c	2				25/a	42
		32			6		7	b		12/a			10	24	a						26/b				22				20/c	2				25	43
		32		c	6	a	7	b					10	24	16						26/c				22				20/a	2				25/b	44
		32			6		7	a		12/b			10/c	24	16/a						c				22				20	2			b	25	45
		32			6	8/a	7	b		12			10	24											22			a	20/b	2				25	46
		32			6	8/b	7	b		12			10/a	24							c				22/c			a	20	2				25	47
				35/b	6	8	7	a					10/c	24						11	c						17		b	2		30		25/a	48
		b				8	7	c			15		10	24/b	16						26/a						17		20/c	2		30		a	49
		32		a		8	7	c			15		10/b		16					11	b				22	19/a	17							25/c	50
		32		a	6	8/b	7			12/a	15		10		b					11					22		17							25	51
		32		a	6		7			12/a	15		10			4				11	b				22		17							25/b	52
		32		a	6		7	b		12/c	15		10			4/a				11					22		17	c						25/b	53
		32			6	8	7	b		12/c			10/b							11	a				22		17	c		2				25/a	54
		32			6	8/b	7	a		12			10							11					22		17	b		2				25/a	55
		32			6	8/c	7	a		12			10/b		c					11					22		17	b		2				25/a	56

As the season began Michael Carrick was sold t
Tottenham for £2 million, the last of half a team of youn
England internationals who had been sold in the last 1
months. A moderate start saw the Hammers in fifth plac
by the end of September. There were home League Cu
victories against Southend United and Notts County, b
the cup trail ended with a narrow 1–0 defeat at Chelse
Leading up to Christmas the home form was good, b

2004-05
Story of the season

New signings included goalkeeper Jimmy Walker and **forwards Sergei Rebrov** and the experienced **Teddy Sheringham.**

Appearances & Goals 2004-05

	League			FA Cup			League Cup			Other			Total	
	Starts	Subs	Goals	Starts	Subs	Goals	Starts	Subs	Goals	Starts	Subs	Goals	Starts	Subs
BREVETT Rufus	10	0	1	0	0	0	3	0	0	0	0	0	13	0
BYWATER Stephen	36	0	0	2	0	0	0	0	0	0	1	0	38	1
CHADWICK Luke	22	10	1	3	0	0	1	0	0	0	0	0	26	10
COHEN Chris	1	10	0	0	1	0	1	1	0	0	0	0	2	12
DAILLY Christian	2	1	0	0	0	0	0	0	0	0	2	0	2	3
DAVENPORT Calum	10	0	0	0	0	0	0	0	0	0	0	0	10	0
ETHERINGTON Matthew	37	2	4	0	0	0	2	0	0	3	0	0	42	2
FERDINAND Anton	24	5	1	3	0	0	1	0	0	3	0	0	31	5
FLETCHER Carl	26	6	2	3	0	0	0	0	0	1	0	0	30	6
GARCIA Richard	0	1	0	0	0	0	0	0	0	0	0	0	0	1
HAREWOOD Marlon	45	0	17	3	0	2	3	0	2	3	0	1	54	0
HUTCHISON Don	2	3	0	0	0	0	0	1	0	0	0	0	2	4
LOMAS Steve	18	5	1	0	0	0	2	0	0	0	0	0	20	5
MACKAY Malky	17	1	2	3	0	0	1	0	0	0	0	0	21	1
McANUFF Jobi	0	1	0	0	0	0	0	0	0	0	0	0	0	1
McCLENAHAN Trent	0	2	0	0	0	0	1	0	0	0	0	0	1	2
MELVILLE Andy	3	0	0	0	0	0	0	1	0	0	0	0	3	1
MULLINS Hayden	32	5	1	2	1	0	2	0	0	3	0	0	39	6
NEWTON Shaun	11	0	0	0	0	0	0	0	0	2	1	0	13	1
NOBLE Mark	10	3	0	3	0	0	0	2	0	0	3	0	13	8
NOWLAND Adam	3	1	1	0	0	0	2	0	0	0	0	0	5	1
POWELL Chris	35	1	0	3	0	0	0	0	0	3	0	0	41	1
POWELL Darren	5	0	1	0	0	0	0	0	0	0	0	0	5	0
REBROV Sergei	12	14	1	1	1	0	2	1	1	0	1	0	15	17
REO-COKER Nigel	34	5	3	1	1	0	3	0	0	3	0	0	41	6
REPKA Tomas	42	0	0	3	0	0	3	0	0	3	0	0	51	0
SHERINGHAM Teddy	26	7	20	2	0	1	0	1	0	0	0	0	28	8
TARICCO Mauricio	1	0	0	0	0	0	0	0	0	0	0	0	1	0
WALKER James	10	0	0	1	0	0	3	0	0	3	0	0	17	0
WARD Elliott	10	1	0	0	0	0	1	0	0	3	0	0	14	1
WILLIAMS Gavin	7	3	1	0	0	0	0	0	0	0	0	0	7	3
ZAMORA Bobby	15	19	7	0	0	0	2	0	2	3	0	4	20	19
own goal			2											
Totals	506	106	66	33	4	3	33	7	5	33	8	5	605	125

* Other = Play-off matches

ere was concern in away games with a 4–1 defeat at rdiff City and a 1–0 loss to old rivals Millwall.

was a short FA Cup journey as following a 1–0 home win ainst Norwich City the Hammers were knocked out in e next round in a replay at Sheffield United. Marlon rewood and in particular Teddy Sheringham were oring freely and by the end of February the side was in th place. While automatic promotion seemed unlikely, ree successive wins in April gave hope of a playoff place d this was confirmed when Watford were beaten 2–1 on e final day of the season. For the playoff semi-final the ponents were once again Ipswich Town. The home leg v the Hammers lead 2–0 after eighteen minutes only for swich to draw level; the tie ended 2–2. In the second leg bby Zamora scored twice as West Ham won the tie 2–0.

The playoff final was again in Cardiff with the opponents being Preston North End. On this occasion the Hammers were determined to win and a goal from Zamora in the second half gave them a 1–0 victory and promotion to the Premier League.

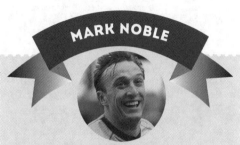

MARK NOBLE

Mark graduated through the Academy and as a 15-year-old he was playing in the West Ham reserve side.

Being a local lad he has great affection for the team, and is backed up by his family and friends who are all Hammers supporters. The midfielder showed early promise and has now been capped by England from under-16 level through to being captain of the under-21 side that played in the European Championships in 2009.

It was in August 2004 that he made his first-team debut against Southend United in the League Cup. Later that season he had a run of 10 games in the side and also came on as a substitute in the playoff final against Preston. To gain more experience in 2006 he was loaned out in spells to both Hull City and Ipswich Town. A popular figure at Upton Park, he is now the longest-serving player in the current squad and has twice won the 'Hammer of the Year' trophy. His appearance against Newcastle United in November 2014 was his 205th Premier League game, more than any other West Ham player. Claret and blue through and through is Mark, and the fans love him.

oca-Cola Championship nal Table 2004-05

	P		HOME					AWAY				Pts
		W	D	L	F	A	W	D	L	F	A	
nderland	46	16	4	3	45	21	13	3	7	31	20	94
gan Athletic	46	13	5	5	42	15	12	7	4	37	20	87
wich Town	46	17	3	3	53	26	7	10	6	32	30	85
by County	46	10	7	6	38	30	12	3	8	33	30	76
ston North End	46	14	7	2	44	22	7	5	11	23	36	75
st Ham United	46	12	5	6	36	24	9	5	9	30	32	73
ading	46	13	7	3	33	15	6	6	11	18	29	70
effield United	46	9	7	7	28	23	9	6	8	29	33	67
verhampton Wanderers	46	9	11	3	40	26	6	10	7	32	33	66
lwall	46	12	5	6	33	22	6	7	10	18	23	66
eens Park Rangers	46	10	7	6	32	26	7	4	12	22	32	62
ke City	46	11	2	10	22	18	6	8	9	14	20	61
nley	46	10	7	6	26	19	5	8	10	12	20	60
ds United	46	7	10	6	28	26	7	8	8	21	26	60
cester City	46	8	8	7	24	20	4	13	6	25	26	57
diff City	46	10	4	9	24	19	3	11	9	24	32	54
mouth Argyle	46	9	8	6	31	23	5	3	15	21	41	53
ford	46	5	10	8	25	25	7	6	10	27	34	52
ventry City	46	8	7	8	32	24	5	6	12	29	45	52
hton and Hove Albion	46	7	7	9	24	29	6	5	12	16	36	51
we Alexandra	46	6	8	9	37	38	6	6	11	29	48	50
ingham	46	10	6	7	22	23	2	8	13	23	43	50
ttingham Forest	46	7	10	6	26	28	2	7	14	16	38	44
herham United	46	2	7	14	17	34	3	7	13	18	35	29

Season **2004-05** Coca-Cola Championship
Match Details

Manager **Alan Pardew**   Final League Position **6/24 Promoted via Play-off Final to Barclays Premier League**

	Date		Competition	Venue	Opponents	Results		Attendance	Position	Scorers
1	Aug 7	Sat	Champ	A	Leicester City	D	0-0	30,231	17	
2	Aug 10	Tue	Champ	H	Reading	W	1-0	26,242	5	Sheringham
3	Aug 15	Sun	Champ	H	Wigan Athletic	L	1-3	23,271	15	Zamora
4	Aug 21	Sat	Champ	A	Crewe Alexandra	W	3-2	7,857	7	Sheringham 2, Brevett
5	Aug 24	Tue	FLC 2	H	Southend United	W	2-0	16,910		Harewood 2
6	Aug 28	Sat	Champ	H	Burnley	W	1-0	22,119	6	Nowland
7	Aug 30	Mon	Champ	A	Coventry City	L	1-2	17,404	7	Sheringham
8	Sep 11	Sat	Champ	A	Sheffield United	W	2-1	21,058	5	Harewood, Sheringham
9	Sep 14	Tue	Champ	H	Rotherham United	W	1-0	26,233	4	Etherington
10	Sep 18	Sat	Champ	H	Ipswich Town	D	1-1	28,812	5	MacKay
11	Sep 21	Tue	FLC 3	H	Notts County	W	3-2	11,111		Zamora 2, Rebrov
12	Sep 26	Sun	Champ	A	Nottingham Forest	L	1-2	25,615	6	Harewood
13	Sep 29	Wed	Champ	A	Derby County	D	1-1	23,112	6	Etherington
14	Oct 2	Sat	Champ	H	Wolverhampton Wanderers	W	1-0	29,585	5	Sheringham
15	Oct 16	Sat	Champ	A	Queens Park Rangers	L	0-1	18,363	6	
16	Oct 19	Tue	Champ	H	Stoke City	W	2-0	29,808	5	Harewood, Sheringham
17	Oct 23	Sat	Champ	H	Gillingham	W	3-1	25,247	4	Harewood, Mullins, Zamora
18	Oct 27	Wed	FLC 4	A	Chelsea	L	0-1	41,774		
19	Oct 30	Sat	Champ	A	Plymouth Argyle	D	1-1	20,220	6	Lomas
20	Nov 2	Tue	Champ	A	Cardiff City	L	1-4	14,222	6	Harewood [pen]
21	Nov 6	Sat	Champ	H	Queens Park Rangers	W	2-1	31,365	5	Harewood 2, [1 pen]
22	Nov 13	Sat	Champ	H	Brighton & Hove Albion	L	0-1	29,514	6	
23	Nov 21	Sun	Champ	A	Millwall	L	0-1	15,025	6	
24	Nov 27	Sat	Champ	H	Watford	W	3-2	24,541	6	Powell D., Rebrov, Reo-Coker
25	Dec 4	Sat	Champ	A	Sunderland	W	2-0	29,510	5	Harewood, Sheringham
26	Dec 10	Fri	Champ	H	Leeds United	D	1-1	30,684	5	Chadwick
27	Dec 18	Sat	Champ	A	Preston North End	L	1-2	13,451	6	Reo-Coker
28	Dec 26	Sun	Champ	H	Nottingham Forest	W	3-2	32,270	6	Sherringham 2, Etherington
29	Dec 28	Tue	Champ	A	Rotherham United	D	2-2	7,769	7	Harewood [pen], Sheringham [pen]
30	Jan 1	Sat	Champ	A	Ipswich Town	W	2-0	30,003	5	Etherington, Harewood
31	Jan 3	Mon	Champ	H	Sheffield United	L	0-2	27,424	6	
32	Jan 8	Sat	FAC 3	H	Norwich City	W	1-0	23,289		Harewood
33	Jan 15	Sat	Champ	A	Wolverhampton Wanderers	L	2-4	28,411	7	Zamora 2
34	Jan 23	Sun	Champ	H	Derby County	L	1-2	30,347	9	Fletcher
35	Jan 29	Sat	FAC 4	H	Sheffield United	D	1-1	19,444		Harewood
36	Feb 6	Sun	Champ	H	Cardiff City	W	1-0	23,716	7	Fletcher
37	Feb 13	Sun	FAC 4 Rep	A	Sheffield United	D	1-1*	15,067		Sheringham [pen]
38	Feb 19	Sat	Champ	H	Plymouth Argyle	W	5-0	25,490	6	Sheringham 2 [1 pen], Harewood [pen], Mackay, McCormick (o
39	Feb 22	Tue	Champ	A	Gillingham	W	1-0	9,510	5	Harewood
40	Feb 26	Sat	Champ	A	Leeds United	L	1-2	34,115	6	Williams
41	Mar 5	Sat	Champ	H	Preston North End	L	1-2	26,442	7	Zamora
42	Mar 12	Sat	Champ	A	Reading	L	1-3	22,268	7	Sheringham
43	Mar 15	Tue	Champ	H	Crewe Alexandra	D	1-1	26,593	7	Sheringham
44	Mar 18	Fri	Champ	H	Leicester City	D	2-2	22,031	7	Sheringham 2
45	Apr 2	Sat	Champ	A	Wigan Athletic	W	2-1	12,993	7	Harewood, Sheringham
46	Apr 5	Tue	Champ	A	Burnley	W	1-0	12,209	7	Sheringham
47	Apr 9	Sat	Champ	H	Coventry City	W	3-0	26,839	7	Sheringham [pen], Zamora, Shaw (og)
48	Apr 16	Sat	Champ	H	Millwall	D	1-1	28,221	7	Harewood
49	Apr 19	Tue	Champ	A	Stoke City	W	1-0	14,534	7	Zamora
50	Apr 23	Sat	Champ	A	Brighton & Hove Albion	D	2-2	6,819	6	Harewood, Reo-Coker
51	Apr 29	Fri	Champ	H	Sunderland	L	1-2	33,482	7	Harewood
52	May 8	Sun	Champ	A	Watford	W	2-1	19,673	6	Ferdinand A., Harewood [pen]
53	May 14	Sat	PO SF:1	H	Ipswich Town	D	2-2	33,723		Harewood, Zamora
54	May 18	Wed	PO SF:2	A	Ipswich Town	W	2-0	30,010		Zamora 2
55	May 30	Mon	PO F	A	Preston North End	W	1-0	70,275	6	Zamora

* After extra time - lost 1-3 on penalties (1-1 at 90 minutes)

eam Line-Ups

	BYWATER Stephen	CHADWICK Luke	COHEN Chris	DAILLY Christian	DAVENPORT Calum	ETHERINGTON Matthew	FERDINAND Anton	FLETCHER Carl	GARCIA Richard	HAREWOOD Marlon	HUTCHISON Don	LOMAS Steve	MACKAY Malky	McANUFF Jobi	McCLENAHAN Trent	MELVILLE Andy	MULLINS Hayden	NEWTON Shaun	NOBLE Mark	NOWLAND Adam	POWELL Chris	POWELL Darren	REBROV Sergei	REO-COKER Nigel	REPKA Tomas	SHERINGHAM Teddy	TARICCO Mauricio	WALKER James	WARD Elliott	WILLIAMS Gavin	ZAMORA Bobby	
	1		c	7		12				10/a				b		5	17						16/b	20	2	11/c				a		1
	1	c	14	7		12	a			10/b						5/a	17						16/c	20	2	11				b		2
c	1	b	c			12	15			10/a						5	17						16/b	20	2	11				a		3
	1	30	b			12/b	15			10					a		17/a			19				20	2	11						4
		30/a	14							10					28	a				19			16/b	20	2	b		23	22			5
	1	30/a	b			12	15			10		a					17			19				20	2	11/b						6
c	1	b				12	15		c	10		a								19/a			16/b	20	2	11						7
	1	30/a			26	12		6		10				c			17			a				20	2	11						8
	1	30/a			26	12/b		6		10			21				b				34		a	20	2	11						9
	1	30/b			26	12		6		10			21				a				34		b	20	2	11/a						10
		b				12/b				10		8	21		a		17						16	20	2/a			23			25	11
	1	30/a			26	12		6		10		a	21								34			20	2	11						12
	1	30			26	12		6		10							17				34			20	2	11/a					a	13
	1	30/b			26	12/a		6		10		a					17				34		b	20	2	c					25/c	14
	1	30/a	a				15			10	b	11					17				34		16	20	2						25/b	15
	1	30/b				12/a		b		10		11	21				17						c	20	2	a					25/c	16
	1	c	b			12/b		a		10		11	21				17						16	20/a	2						25/c	17
						12/c	15			10	b	11					17	a		19/a			c	20	2			23			25/b	18
	1				26	12		6		10	a	11					17							20	2						25/a	19
c	1	30/a			26	12		6		10	a	11					17/b				c		b		2						25	20
	1	30/a			26	12	b	6		10	4/b	11					17				34				2						a	21
	1	30/b			26	12/a		6		10	4/c	11					17				34	c	b		2						a	22
	1	9/b				12	a	6		10		11								19	34			20	2	9/a					b	23
	1	30				12/a		6		10		11								19	34		16		2						25	24
	1	30/b				12	15	6		10		11								19	34		16/a		2	a					b	25
	1	30/b				12	15	6		10		11								19	34				2							26
	1	30/a				12	15	6		10		11								19/b	34		b		2	11						27
	1	30/b				12	15/a			10		11	21				a				34			20	2	11				b		28
	1	a				12				10		11/a	21				17				34			20	2	11/b				35	b	29
	1					12/c	b	6		10			21			c	17				34		a	20/b	2					35	25/a	30
	1	b	c			12/b		6		10			21/c				17				34		a	20	2					35	25/a	31
		30/a	a				15	6		10			21				17		24		34		16		2			23				32
		30/b	b				15			10			21				17		24/a		34		16		2			23	a		25	33
		30						6									17		a		34		16/b	20	2	b		23		35/a		34
	1	30/a					15	6		10			21				17/b		24		34		b	a	2	11						35
	1	a					15	6		10			21				17		24/b		34		b	20	10						25/a	36
	1	30/a					15	6		10			21				a		24		34			20	2	11						37
	1						15	6		10		b	21				17/b		24/c		34		16/a	a	2	11					c	38
	1	b				12/a	15			10		11	21								34			20/c	2	a				c	25/b	39
	1	b				12/b	15/a	6		10		11	21				a					34/c			2	11				35	c	40
	1					12		6		10		11	21/b				17				34		b		2	11/a				35	a	41
	1	a				12		6/a		10		11	21				17/c	26	24		34		b							c	25/b	42
	1	a				12/a	15	6		10						c		26	24		34					11/c			22	35/b	b	43
	1	30/a					15	6		10								26	24		34		a/b	20		11			22		b	44
							15	a		10							17	26/a	24		34			20		11		23	22			45
		b					15			10/c							17/a	26	24/b		34			20	2	11		23	22		c	46
		a					15			10/b							17/a	26	24		34			20	2	11		23	22		b	47
						12	15			10								26/a	24		34			20	2	11		23	22		a	48
c						12	15	a		10/c							17/a	26			34			20	2/b	11		23	22		b	49
						12/b	15	b		10							17	26			34			20	2	11/a		23	22		a	50
						12/a	15			10							17	26/b	a		34		b	20	2			23	22		25	51
c						12/a	15			10							17	26/b	a		34		b	20/c	2			23	22		25	52
						12	15			10							17	26/b	a		34			20	2			23	22		25/a	53
a						12/c	15	6		10							17	b	c		34			20	2/a			23	22		25/b	54
c		a				12	15			10							17	26/b	b		34			20	2			23/c	22		25/a	55

2005-06
Story of the season

The team **impressed** in the opening day 3-1 victory over Blackburn Rovers. **A hat-trick from Marlon Harewood** gave the Hammers a 4–0 home win against Aston Villa and **two goals from Bobby Zamora** came in the 4–2 League Cup victory at Sheffield Wednesday. The League Cup trail ended with a disappointing 1–0 defeat away to Bolton Wanderers.

The team was inconsistent as following excellent away wins at Birmingham City and Everton there were home defeats to Newcastle United and Wigan. In January centre forward Dean Ashton was signed for a club record fee of £7 million. Bobby Zamora was on target in the FA Cup scoring in the 2–1 win at Norwich City and again in the 4– home win against Blackburn Rovers. The two cup wins added to the team's confidence, which brought four successive league wins that pushed the side up to eighth

Appearances & Goals 2005-06

	League			FA Cup			League Cup			Total		
	Starts	Subs	Goals	Starts	Subs	Goals	Starts	Subs	Goals	Starts	Subs	
ALIADIERE Jeremie	1	6	0	0	0	0	0	1	0	1	7	
ASHTON Dean	9	2	3	5	0	3	0	0	0	14	2	
BELLION David	2	6	0	0	0	0	1	1	1	3	7	
BENAYOUN Yossi	30	4	5	6	0	0	0	0	0	36	4	
BYWATER Stephen	0	1	0	0	0	0	0	0	0	0	1	
CARROLL Roy	19	0	0	0	0	0	0	0	0	19	0	
CLARKE Clive	2	0	0	0	0	0	1	0	0	3	0	
COHEN Chris	0	0	0	0	0	0	1	0	0	1	0	
COLLINS James	13	1	2	3	0	0	2	0	0	18	1	
DAILLY Christian	6	16	0	2	4	0	2	0	1	10	20	
EPHRAIM Hogan	0	0	0	0	0	0	0	1	0	0	1	
ETHERINGTON Matthew	33	0	2	7	0	1	0	0	0	40	0	
FERDINAND Anton	32	1	2	5	0	0	0	0	0	37	1	
FLETCHER Carl	6	6	1	1	3	0	0	1	0	7	10	
GABBIDON Daniel	31	1	0	7	0	0	0	0	0	38	1	
HAREWOOD Marlon	31	6	14	6	1	2	2	0	0	39	7	
HISLOP Shaka	16	0	0	7	0	0	2	0	0	25	0	
KATAN Yaniv	2	4	0	0	2	0	0	0	0	2	6	
KONCHESKY Paul	36	1	1	7	0	1	1	0	0	44	1	
MULLINS Hayden	35	0	0	6	0	1	1	0	0	42	0	
NEWTON Shaun	8	18	1	1	1	0	1	1	0	10	20	
NOBLE Mark	4	1	0	0	0	0	1	0	0	5	1	
REID Kyel	1	1	0	0	0	0	0	0	0	1	1	
REO-COKER Nigel	31	0	5	7	0	0	0	0	0	38	0	
REPKA Tomas	19	0	0	1	0	0	2	0	0	22	0	
SCALONI Lionel	13	0	0	3	1	0	0	0	0	16	1	
SHERINGHAM Teddy	15	11	6	1	3	1	1	0	0	17	14	
STOKES Tony	0	0	0	0	0	0	0	1	0	0	1	
WALKER James	3	0	0	0	0	0	0	0	0	3	0	
WARD Elliott	3	1	0	0	0	0	2	0	0	5	1	
WILLIAMS Gavin	0	0	0	0	0	0	1	0	0	1	0	
ZAMORA Bobby	17	17	6	2	5	2	1	0	2	20	22	
own goal			4			3						
Totals	**418**	**104**	**52**	**77**	**20**	**14**	**22**	**6**	**4**	**517**	**130**	

e table. A tough fifth-round FA Cup tie was in prospect as
e Hammers travelled to play Bolton Wanderers. The
ame was a frustrating goalless draw but the replay brought
2–1 victory, with Harewood grabbing the winner in extra
me. The quarter-final tie saw the Hammers travel to
Ianchester City, where Dean Ashton scored twice in a 2–1
ictory.

1 April all at West Ham were saddened to hear that former
anager John Lyall had passed away. He epitomised
verything the club stands for and holds dear. Leading up to
e semi-final the Hammers struggled in the league, but this
as forgotten when Marlon Harewood scored the winning
oal as Middlesbrough were beaten 1–0 at Villa Park to seal
place in the FA Cup final. The Hammers ended the league
eason in fine style as London rivals Tottenham were beaten
–1 at Upton Park.

he FA Cup final against Liverpool at the Millennium
tadium in Cardiff was one of the greatest finals ever. It
as a fantastic spectacle for English football seen by
illions around the world. The Hammers took a 2–0 lead,

with the Reds fighting back to equalise. In the second half
Paul Konchesky put West Ham in front again but in injury
time Gerrard equalised with an amazing shot from 30 yards.
Harewood hit the bar in extra time but no further scoring
meant a penalty shootout, which was won by Liverpool.
The Hammers fans were heartbroken but very proud of
their team.

DEAN ASHTON

He graduated through the youth
development policy at Crewe Alexandra
and as a 16-year-old made his first-team
debut in 2000.

He soon established himself in the side and
began to score goals on a regular basis. He
spent five seasons at Gresty Road and was
attracting attention from a number of clubs
and in January 2005 he joined Norwich City
for a £3 million fee. While at Crewe he had
scored 74 goals in 178 appearances. At
Norwich his seven goals that season were not
enough to save Norwich from relegation.

With the Canaries relegated, in January 2006
a fee of £7 million took him to West Ham. He
scored vital goals in that campaign as the
Hammers progressed to the FA Cup Final. In
August 2006 he suffered a broken ankle while
training with the England squad and was
forced to miss the whole of the 2006/07
season.. He started the 2008/09 season with
two goals in the opening day 2–1 victory
against Wigan, but a further injury to his
ankle saw him only start in a further four
games. In December 2009 he sadly
announced his retirement after failing to
recover from his long-term ankle injury.

arclays Premier League
inal Table 2005-06

	P	HOME					AWAY					Pts
		W	D	L	F	A	W	D	L	F	A	
helsea	38	18	1	0	47	9	11	3	5	25	13	91
anchester United	38	13	5	1	37	8	12	3	4	35	26	83
verpool	38	15	3	1	32	8	10	4	5	25	17	82
rsenal	38	14	3	2	48	13	6	4	9	20	18	67
ttenham Hotspur	38	12	5	2	31	16	6	6	7	22	22	65
lackburn Rovers	38	13	3	3	31	17	6	3	10	20	25	63
ewcastle United	38	11	5	3	28	15	6	2	11	19	27	58
olton Wanderers	38	11	5	3	29	13	4	6	9	20	28	56
est Ham United	38	9	3	7	30	25	7	4	8	22	30	55
igan Athletic	38	7	3	9	24	26	8	3	8	21	26	51
verton	38	8	4	7	22	22	6	4	9	12	27	50
lham	38	13	2	4	31	21	1	4	14	17	37	48
harlton Athletic	38	8	4	7	22	21	5	4	10	19	34	47
iddlesbrough	38	7	5	7	28	30	5	4	10	20	28	45
anchester City	38	9	2	8	26	20	4	2	13	17	28	43
ston Villa	38	6	6	7	20	20	4	6	9	22	35	42
ortsmouth	38	5	7	7	17	24	5	1	13	20	38	38
rmingham City	38	6	5	8	19	20	2	5	12	9	30	34
est Bromwich Albion	38	6	2	11	21	24	1	7	11	10	34	30
nderland	38	1	4	14	12	37	2	2	15	14	32	15

Season 2005-06 Barclays Premier League
Match Details

Manager **Alan Pardew**   Final League Position **9/24**

	Date		Competition	Venue	Opponents	Results		Attendance	Position	Scorers
1	Aug 13	Sat	Prem	H	Blackburn Rovers	W	3-1	33,305	2	Sheringham, Reo-Coker, Etherington
2	Aug 20	Sat	Prem	A	Newcastle United	D	0-0	51,620	4	
3	Aug 27	Sat	Prem	H	Bolton Wanderers	L	1-2	31,629	9	Sheringham [pen]
4	Sep 12	Mon	Prem	H	Aston Villa	W	4-0	29,582	7	Harewood 3, Benayoun
5	Sep 17	Sat	Prem	A	Fulham	W	2-1	21,907	4	Harewood, Warner (og)
6	Sep 20	Tue	FLC 2	A	Sheffield Wednesday	W	4-2	14,976		Zamora 2, Bellion, Dailly
7	Sep 24	Sat	Prem	H	Arsenal	D	0-0	34,742	4	
8	Oct 1	Sat	Prem	A	Sunderland	D	1-1	31,212	6	Benayoun
9	Oct 16	Sun	Prem	A	Manchester City	L	1-2	43,647	9	Zamora
10	Oct 23	Sun	Prem	H	Middlesbrough	W	2-1	34,612	9	Sheringham, Riggott (og)
11	Oct 26	Wed	FLC 3	A	Bolton Wanderers	L	0-1	10,926		
12	Oct 29	Sat	Prem	A	Liverpool	L	0-2	44,537	9	
13	Nov 5	Sat	Prem	H	West Bromwich Albion	W	1-0	34,325	8	Sheringham
14	Nov 20	Sun	Prem	A	Tottenham Hotspur	D	1-1	36,154	8	Ferdinand
15	Nov 27	Sun	Prem	H	Manchester United	L	1-2	34,755	9	Harewood
16	Dec 5	Mon	Prem	A	Birmingham City	W	2-1	24,010	9	Harewood, Zamora
17	Dec 10	Sat	Prem	A	Blackburn Rovers	L	2-3	20,370	9	Harewood, Zamora
18	Dec 14	Wed	Prem	A	Everton	W	2-1	35,704	7	Zamora, Weir (og)
19	Dec 17	Sat	Prem	H	Newcastle United	L	2-4	34,836	9	Harewood [pen], Solano (og)
20	Dec 26	Mon	Prem	A	Portsmouth	D	1-1	20,168	9	Collins
21	Dec 28	Wed	Prem	H	Wigan Athletic	L	0-2	34,131	9	
22	Dec 31	Sat	Prem	A	Charlton Athletic	L	0-2	25,952	10	
23	Jan 2	Mon	Prem	H	Chelsea	L	1-3	34,758	10	Harewood
24	Jan 7	Sat	FAC 3	A	Norwich City	W	2-1	23,968		Mullins, Zamora
25	Jan 14	Sat	Prem	A	Aston Villa	W	2-1	36,700	10	Harewood [pen], Zamora
26	Jan 23	Mon	Prem	H	Fulham	W	2-1	29,812	9	Benayoun, Ferdinand
27	Jan 28	Sat	FAC 4	H	Blackburn Rovers	W	4-2	23,700		Etherington, Sheringham [pen], Zamora, Khizanishvili (o
28	Feb 1	Wed	Prem	A	Arsenal	W	3-2	38,216	9	Etherington, Reo-Coker, Zamora
29	Feb 4	Sat	Prem	H	Sunderland	W	2-0	34,745	8	Ashton, Konchesky
30	Feb 13	Mon	Prem	H	Birmingham City	W	3-0	31,294	6	Harewood 2, Ashton
31	Feb 18	Sat	FAC 5	A	Bolton Wanderers	D	0-0	17,120		
32	Mar 4	Sat	Prem	H	Everton	D	2-2	34,866	8	Ashton, Harewood
33	Mar 11	Sat	Prem	A	Bolton Wanderers	L	1-4	24,461	9	Sheringham
34	Mar 15	Wed	FAC 5 Rep	H	Bolton Wanderers	W	2-1	24,685		Harewood, Jaaskelainen (og)
35	Mar 18	Sat	Prem	H	Portsmouth	L	2-4	34,837	10	Benayoun, Sheringham
36	Mar 20	Mon	FAC 6	A	Manchester City	W	2-1	39,357		Ashton 2
37	Mar 25	Sat	Prem	A	Wigan Athletic	W	2-1	18,736	9	Harewood, Reo-Coker
38	Mar 29	Wed	Prem	A	Manchester United	L	0-1	69,522	9	
39	Apr 2	Sun	Prem	H	Charlton Athletic	D	0-0	34,753	8	
40	Apr 9	Sun	Prem	A	Chelsea	L	1-4	41,919	9	Collins
41	Apr 15	Sat	Prem	H	Manchester City	W	1-0	34,305	7	Newton
42	Apr 17	Mon	Prem	A	Middlesbrough	L	0-2	27,658	9	
43	Apr 23	Sun	FAC SF	N	Middlesbrough	W	1-0	39,148		Harewood
44	Apr 26	Wed	Prem	H	Liverpool	L	1-2	34,852	10	Reo-Coker
45	May 1	Mon	Prem	A	West Bromwich Albion	W	1-0	24,462	9	Reo-Coker
46	May 7	Sun	Prem	H	Tottenham Hotspur	W	2-1	34,970	9	Benayoun, Fletcher
47	May 13	Sat	FAC F	N*	Liverpool (aet: 1-3 pens)	D	3-3	74,000		Ashton, Konchesky, Carragher (og)

*Played at Millnnium Stadium, Cardiff

Team Line-Ups

	ASHTON Dean	BELLION David	BENAYOUN Yossi	BYWATER Stephen	CARROLL Roy	CLARKE Clive	COHEN Chris	COLLINS James	DAILLY Christian	EPHRAIM Hogan	ETHERINGTON Matthew	FERDINAND Anton	FLETCHER Carl	GABBIDON Daniel	HAREWOOD Marlon	HISLOP Shaka	KATAN Yaniv	KONCHESKY Paul	MULLINS Hayden	NEWTON Shaun	NOBLE Mark	REID Kyel	REO-COKER Nigel	REPKA Tomas	SCALONI Lionel	SHERINGHAM Teddy	STOKES Tony	WALKER James	WARD Elliott	WILLIAMS Gavin	ZAMORA Bobby	
		15			1				7		11	5		4	10			3	17/b	a	b		20			8/a						1
		15/b			1					b	11	5		4	10/c			3	17	a			20	2		8/a				c		2
		15			1						11/a	5		4/c	10/b			3	17				20	2		8				c	b	3
		15			1				c		11/a	5		4	10/b			3	17/c	a			20	2		8					b	4
		15/b			1						11	5		4	10/c			3	17	a			20	2		b					25/a	5
	a					14	19	7	b						10/a	34				26	24			2/c			c	22	22	9/b	25	6
		15			1						11/b	5		4	10			3	17	b			20	2		8/a					a	7
		15			1				c		11/b	5		4	10			3	17	b			20	2/c		8/a					a	8
		15			1				a		11/c	5		4	10			3	17	c			20	2		8/a					b	9
		15/c							c		11/b	5		4	10	34		3	17	b			20	2		a					25/a	10
	21			30/a			19	7					c		10/c	34		3	17	a				2		8/b			22			11
	21/a	15						c			11/b	5		4	10	34		3	17				20	2/c		b						12
		15/c	b						a		11	5		4	10	34/b		3	17	c			20/a	2		8						13
	c	15									11/c	5		4	10/b	34		3	17	a	24			2/a		8					b	14
		15			1				a		11/c	5		4	10			3	17/b	c	24			2		8/a					b	15
	a	15/c			1				b		11	5		4	10			3	17	c	24/b			2							25/a	16
	b	15			1				a		11	5		4/a	10			3	17		24/b			2							25/c	17
		15			1			19	a		11/a	5	6		10			3	17	b				2							25/b	18
	a	15/a			1			19			11	5	6		10			3	17					2/b							25	19
					1			19	c		11	5	a	b/c	10			3	17/a	26			20	2/b							25	20
	21/b				1			19	7		11	5	6/a		10/c			3	17	b			20								a	21
'b	b	a						19	7/a		11	5			10			3	7	26			20									22
	b	15			1			19	7		11/b	5	6		10			3	17/a				20								a	23
								19	b		11/b	a		4	10	34	c	3	17/a	26			20	2							25/c	24
		a			1				c		11/c	5		4	10		b	3	17	26/a			20	2							25/b	25
		15/b			1				a		11/c	5		4	10		b	3	17	c			20	2							25/a	26
		15/c							7		11	5	c	4	a	34	b	3	17				20			8/a					25/b	27
b		15/a		30/c							11	5	c	4	10	34		3	17	a			20								25/b	28
9/c		15							c		11	5		4	b	34		3	17/b				20	2		a					25/a	29
9/c		15							a		11/b	5		4	10	34	b	3	17/a				20	2							c	30
9/b		15/c							c		11	5		4	10/a	34		3	17				20	2		b					a	31
9/b		15/a									11/c	5		4	10	34		3	17	c			20	2		b					a	32
		b							a		11	5		4		34		3	17	26/b				2		8			22/a		25	33
9/b		15							a		11/c	5		4	10	34		3	17				20/a	2		b					c	34
		a		30/a				7			5/c	c	4	b			18/b	3					20	2		8		23			25	35
9/c		15					19	7/a		11	b		4	10	34		3	17					20/b	a							c	36
9/b		15/c					19			11/a			4	10	34		3	17	c				20	2		b					a	37
9/c		15					19			11/b	a		4	10	34		3	17					20	2/a	c						b	38
9/a		15					19			11	5		4	10/c	34	c	3	17					20/b			a					b	39
9/b		15/a					19			11			4	10	34		3	17					20	2		a					b	40
9/c		15					19				b		4	a			3	17	26/b				20	2	c			23		25/a	41
	a						19					c	4	10	34	18/b	3	17	26				20	2/c	8					b	42
9/a		15					19			11/b	5		4	10	34		3	17	b				20								a	43
		15/b					19/a			11	5			a		b		17					20	2		8		23	22		25	44
9/a								7/c				6	4	b	34	c			26		35		20	2		a			22		25/b	45
		5/b										5	6	4	a	34		3		26	b		20	2		8/a					25	46
9/a		5							b		11/c	5	6/b	4	10	34		3					20	2	c						a	47

2006-07
Story of the season

After the opening day 3–1 win against Charlton **the side went on a dismal run of 11 games without a victory**. Included in that run was a 2–1 defeat in the League Cup to Third Division Chesterfield, **while in Europe the Hammers were beaten home and away by Palermo**.

In September the Hammers fans were delighted and shocked to learn that West Ham had purchased two Argentinian international players. Securing midfielder Javier Mascherano and forward Carlos Tevez was the biggest transfer coup in the club's history. The signing of Tevez, however, was to lead to controversy and repercussions that would haunt the club for many years. There were three successive home wins but away from home the team struggled to score. In November the board of West Ham accepted an £85 million takeover by an Iceland consortium headed by Eggert Magnusson. Following a 4– defeat at Bolton Wanderers in December manager Ala

Appearances & Goals 2006-07

	League			FA Cup			League Cup			Europe*			Total	
	Starts	Subs	Goals	Starts	Subs	Goals	Starts	Subs	Goals	Starts	Subs	Goals	Starts	Subs
BENAYOUN Yossi	25	4	3	1	0	0	0	0	0	1	1	0	27	5
BLANCO Kepa	1	7	1	0	0	0	0	0	0	0	0	0	1	7
BOA MORTE Luis	8	6	1	2	0	0	0	0	0	0	0	0	10	6
BOWYER Lee	18	2	0	0	0	0	0	0	0	2	0	0	20	2
CARROLL Roy	12	0	0	2	0	0	0	0	0	2	0	0	16	0
COLE Carlton	5	12	2	2	0	1	0	0	0	1	1	0	8	13
COLLINS James	16	0	0	0	0	0	0	0	0	1	0	0	17	0
DAILLY Christian	10	4	0	2	0	0	1	0	0	0	0	0	13	4
DAVENPORT Calum	5	1	0	0	0	0	0	0	0	0	0	0	5	1
ETHERINGTON Matthew	24	3	0	0	1	0	0	1	0	0	1	0	24	6
FERDINAND Anton	31	0	0	1	0	0	1	0	0	1	0	0	34	0
GABBIDON Daniel	18	0	0	1	0	0	1	0	0	2	0	0	22	0
GREEN Robert	26	0	0	0	0	0	1	0	0	0	0	0	27	0
HAREWOOD Marlon	19	13	3	0	0	0	1	0	1	1	1	0	21	14
KONCHESKY Paul	22	0	0	0	0	0	0	1	0	2	0	0	24	1
MASCHERANO Javier	3	2	0	0	0	0	0	0	0	2	0	0	5	2
McCARTNEY George	16	6	0	2	0	0	1	0	0	0	0	0	19	6
MEARS Tyrone	3	2	0	0	0	0	0	0	0	1	0	0	4	2
MULLINS Hayden	21	9	2	1	0	1	1	0	0	0	0	0	23	9
NEILL Lucas	11	0	0	1	0	0	0	0	0	0	0	0	12	0
NEWTON Shaun	0	3	0	1	1	0	0	0	0	0	0	0	1	4
NOBLE Mark	10	0	2	1	0	1	0	0	0	0	0	0	11	0
PANTSIL John	3	2	0	0	1	0	1	0	0	0	0	0	4	3
QUASHIE Nigel	7	0	0	1	0	0	0	0	0	0	0	0	8	0
REID Kyel	0	0	0	0	0	0	1	0	0	0	0	0	1	0
REO-COKER Nigel	35	0	1	1	0	0	1	0	0	2	0	0	39	0
SHERINGHAM Teddy	4	13	2	0	1	0	0	1	0	0	1	0	4	16
SPECTOR Jonathan	17	8	0	1	1	0	0	0	0	1	0	0	19	9
TEVEZ Carlos	19	7	7	1	0	0	0	0	0	2	0	0	22	7
UPSON Matthew	2	0	0	0	0	0	0	0	0	0	0	0	2	0
ZAMORA Bobby	27	5	11	1	1	0	1	0	0	1	1	0	30	7
Totals	**418**	**109**	**35**	**22**	**6**	**3**	**11**	**3**	**1**	**22**	**6**	**0**	**473**	**124**

* UEFA Cup

ardew was sacked and in his place former player Alan
urbishley was appointed. He brought with him former
oalkeeper Mervyn Day as assistant manager and days later
ey celebrated a 1–0 home win against Manchester United.

wo home defeats at Christmas led up to a New Year's Day
assacre at Reading as the home side won 6–0. . There was
3–0 FA Cup win against Brighton but the next round
rought a 1–0 home defeat to Watford. The team hit rock
ottom in February after losing 4–0 at relegation rivals
harlton. It seemed only a miraculous turnaround would
ve West Ham from relegation. In March goals from
amora and Tevez gave survival hopes a major boost with
ctories against Blackburn and Middlesbrough. Then,
llowing on from a magnificent 1–0 win at Arsenal, there
as a downturn with defeats at Sheffield United and at
ome to Chelsea. In April a Premier League Independent
ommission fined the club £5.5 million in respect of the
gning of Carlos Tevez. The club were told they broke rule
18, which relates to third-party influence. A resounding
–0 win at Wigan gave the Hammers hope and a week later,
spired by two goals from Tevez, Bolton Wanderers were

beaten 3–1. The Hammers were now out of the bottom
three but to escape relegation they needed to win at Old
Trafford against Manchester United on the final day of the
season. On a tense and emotional day the Hammers won
1–0 courtesy of a goal from Carlos Tevez, and the great
escape was achieved.

GEORGE McCARTNEY

**The Irish international full-back began his
career with Sunderland in May 1998 and
went on to play in 134 league games spread
over eight seasons.**

His consistent displays saw him gain his first
international cap for Northern Ireland when
playing against Iceland in September 2001.
He went on to play in 34 games for his
country. In season 2004/05 he was in the side
that won the Football League Championship
and was voted 'Player of the Season' by the
Sunderland fans.

The following season Sunderland were
relegated and he left to join West Ham. After
making his debut in October 2006 against
Chesterfield in the League Cup he went on to
play in 61 league games for the Hammers
before returning to Sunderland in September
2008. Initially he was a regular in the side but
after losing his place when injured he was
loaned out to Leeds United for a few months,
playing in 32 league games. He was then
loaned back to West Ham for the 2011/12
season and this was later made permanent.
George was in the Hammers side that beat
Blackpool in the 2012 playoff final and in his
second spell at Upton Park he played in a
total of 84 games before being released by
the club in May 2014.

arclays Premier League
inal Table 2006-07

		HOME					AWAY					
	P	W	D	L	F	A	W	D	L	F	A	Pts
anchester United	38	15	2	2	46	12	13	3	3	37	15	89
elsea	38	12	7	0	37	11	12	4	3	27	13	83
verpool	38	14	4	1	39	7	6	4	9	18	20	68
senal	38	12	6	1	43	16	7	5	7	20	19	68
ttenham Hotspur	38	12	3	4	34	22	5	6	8	23	32	60
erton	38	11	4	4	33	17	4	9	6	19	19	58
lton Wanderers	38	9	5	5	26	20	7	3	9	21	32	56
ading	38	11	2	6	29	20	5	5	9	23	27	55
rtsmouth	38	11	5	3	28	15	3	7	9	17	27	54
ackburn Rovers	38	9	3	7	31	25	6	4	9	21	29	52
ton Villa	38	7	8	4	20	14	4	9	6	23	27	50
ddlesbrough	38	10	3	6	31	24	2	7	10	13	25	46
wcastle United	38	7	7	5	23	20	4	3	12	15	27	43
anchester City	38	5	6	8	10	16	6	3	10	19	28	42
est Ham United	**38**	**8**	**2**	**9**	**24**	**26**	**4**	**3**	**12**	**11**	**33**	**41**
lham	38	7	7	5	18	18	1	8	10	20	42	39
gan Athletic	38	5	4	10	18	30	5	4	10	19	29	38
effield United	38	7	6	6	24	21	3	2	14	8	34	38
arlton Athletic	38	7	5	7	19	20	1	5	13	15	40	34
atford	38	3	9	7	19	25	2	4	13	10	34	28

Season **2006-07** Barclays Premier League
Match Details

Manager **Alan Pardew** (to December 11); Manager **Alan Curbishley** (from December 13)
Final League Position: **15/20**

	Date		Competition	Venue	Opponents	Results		Attendance	Position	Scorers
1	Aug 19	Sat	Prem	H	Charlton Athletic	W	3-1	34,937	2	Zamora 2, Cole
2	Aug 22	Tue	Prem	A	Watford	D	1-1	18,344	1	Zamora
3	Aug 26	Sat	Prem	A	Liverpool	L	1-2	43,965	4	Zamora
4	Sep 10	Sun	Prem	H	Aston Villa	D	1-1	34,576	8	Zamora
5	Sep 14	Thur	UEFA 1:1	H	Palermo (Italy)	L	0-1	32,222		
6	Sep 17	Sun	Prem	H	Newcastle United	L	0-2	34,938	11	
7	Sep 23	Sat	Prem	A	Manchester City	L	0-2	41,073	15	
8	Sep 28	Thur	UEFA 1:2	A	Palermo (Italy)	L	0-3	19,228		
9	Oct 1	Sun	Prem	H	Reading	L	0-1	34,872	16	
10	Oct 14	Sat	Prem	A	Portsmouth	L	0-2	20,142	18	
11	Oct 22	Sun	Prem	A	Tottenham Hotspur	L	0-1	36,162	19	
12	Oct 24	Tue	FLC 3	A	Chesterfield	L	1-2	7,787		Harewood
13	Oct 29	Sun	Prem	H	Blackburn Rovers	W	2-1	33,833	16	Mullins, Sheringham
14	Nov 5	Sun	Prem	H	Arsenal	W	1-0	34,969	15	Harewood
15	Nov 11	Sat	Prem	A	Middlesbrough	L	0-1	25,898	16	
16	Nov 18	Sat	Prem	A	Chelsea	L	0-1	41,916	16	
17	Nov 25	Sat	Prem	H	Sheffield United	W	1-0	34,454	15	Mullins
18	Dec 3	Sun	Prem	A	Everton	L	0-2	32,968	17	
19	Dec 6	Wed	Prem	H	Wigan Athletic	L	0-2	33,805	18	
20	Dec 9	Sat	Prem	A	Bolton Wanderers	L	0-4	22,283	18	
21	Dec 17	Sun	Prem	H	Manchester United	W	1-0	34,966	18	Reo-Coker
22	Dec 23	Sat	Prem	A	Fulham	D	0-0	22,452	18	
23	Dec 26	Tue	Prem	H	Portsmouth	L	1-2	34,913	18	Sheringham
24	Dec 30	Sat	Prem	H	Manchester City	L	0-1	34,574	18	
25	Jan 1	Mon	Prem	A	Reading	L	0-6	24,073	18	
26	Jan 6	Sat	FAC 3	H	Brighton & Hove Albion	W	3-0	32,874		Cole, Mullins, Noble
27	Jan 13	Sat	Prem	H	Fulham	D	3-3	34,977	18	Benayoun 2, Zamora
28	Jan 20	Sat	Prem	A	Newcastle United	D	2-2	52,095	18	Cole, Harewood
29	Jan 27	Sat	FAC 4	H	Watford	L	0-1	31,168		
30	Jan 30	Tue	Prem	H	Liverpool	L	1-2	34,966	18	Blanco
31	Feb 3	Sat	Prem	A	Aston Villa	L	0-1	41,202	18	
32	Feb 10	Sat	Prem	H	Watford	L	0-1	34,625	18	
33	Feb 24	Sat	Prem	A	Charlton Athletic	L	0-4	27,111	19	
34	Mar 4	Sun	Prem	H	Tottenham Hotspur	L	3-4	34,966	20	Noble, Tevez, Zamora
35	Mar 17	Sat	Prem	A	Blackburn Rovers	W	2-1	18,591	19	Tevez [pen], Zamora
36	Mar 31	Sat	Prem	H	Middlesbrough	W	2-0	34,977	19	Tevez, Zamora
37	Apr 7	Sat	Prem	A	Arsenal	W	1-0	60,098	19	Zamora
38	Apr 14	Sat	Prem	A	Sheffield United	L	0-3	31,593	19	
39	Apr 18	Wed	Prem	H	Chelsea	L	1-4	34,966	19	Tevez
40	Apr 21	Sat	Prem	H	Everton	W	1-0	34,945	19	Zamora
41	Apr 28	Sat	Prem	A	Wigan Athletic	W	3-0	24,726	18	Benayoun, Boa Morte, Harewood
42	May 5	Sat	Prem	H	Bolton Wanderers	W	3-1	34,404	17	Tevez 2, Noble
43	May 13	Sun	Prem	A	Manchester United	W	1-0	75,927	15	Tevez

Team Line-Ups

BENAYOUN Yossi	BLANCO Kepa	BOA MORTE Luis	BOWYER Lee	CARROLL Roy	COLE Carlton	COLLINS James	DAILLY Christian	DAVENPORT Calum	ETHERINGTON Matthew	FERDINAND Anton	GABBIDON Daniel	GREEN Robert	HAREWOOD Marlon	KONCHESKY Paul	MASCHERANO Javier	McCARTNEY George	MEARS Tyrone	MULLINS Hayden	NEILL Lucas	NEWTON Shaun	NOBLE Mark	PANTSIL John	QUASHIE Nigel	REID Kyel	REO-COKER Nigel	SHERINGHAM Teddy	SPECTOR Jonathan	TEVEZ Carlos	UPSON Matthew	ZAMORA Bobby	#
15		29	1	c						5	4		10/c	3			2/a	17					a		20	b				25/b	1
b		29	1		19					5	4/b		10/a	3				17					14		20	a				25/c	2
15		29	1	a						5	4		10/a	3/b			b	17					14		20/c		c			25	3
15		29/b	1	c					b	5	4		10/a	3			2	17							20			a		25/c	4
15		29/a	1	c					a	5	4		b	3	16		2								20			32/b		25/c	5
c		29	1						11	5	4		a	3	16/c		2/b	b							20			32/a		25	6
15			1	c				7	11	5/a			10/b	3	16			a							20		b			25/c	7
b		29	1		12/a	19					4		10/c	3	16/b			17							20	c	18	32		a	8
15			1		12/b			7	11		4		c	3				17							20/c	a	18	32/a		b	9
15/c			1	a					11	5	4		b	3	c			17							20	8/a	18			25/b	10
15/b		b					c			5	4	21	10/c	3	16/a			17					14		20			a		25	11
								7	b	5	4	21	10/a	c		6/c		17					14	28/b	20					25	12
15/b		b					c		11	5	4	21	a			6/c		17							20	8/a	18			25	13
15		29/c							11	5/a	4		b	3		a		17							20	c	18			25/b	14
15/b				b	19				11		4	21	10/a	3				17							20	8	18	a			15
		29/b							11/c	5	4	21	a	3		c		17							20	b	18	32		25/a	16
		29							11	5	4/a	21	c	3		a		17							20	b	18	32/b		25/c	17
		29/b			19				11	5		21	a	3		c		17							20	b	18/c	32		25/a	18
15/a		c			19				11/c	5/b		21	10	3		b		17							20	a	18	32			19
					19			7	11			21	10	3		6		17						b	20	a	18/b	32/a			20
b		29			19				11/c	5		21	10	3		c		17/b							20	a	18			25/a	21
a		29/a						7	11	5		21	10/c	3		c		17							20	b	18			25/b	22
15							c		11/b	5	4	21	10/a	3				17							20	a	18/c	b		25	23
15		29		b				7	11/a	5	4/c		10			c		17								8/b	18	a			24
15/c		29/a		c				7		5	4	21	10/b	3				17		a					20	b				25	25
15	13/c		1		12/b			7		5/a	4					6		17	c		24						a	32		b	26
15	13		1		12	19/a		7			4/c					6			c			33			20		a	32/b		b	27
15	13		1		12/a			7	a	5/b			10			6			3			33			20					b	28
	13/c		1		12			7	c							6			3/a	26/b	a	33			20	b	18			25	29
15	b	13	1		12/a			7	27				10/b			6						33			20		18			a	30
15	37/b	13/c	1		a				27	c			b			6						33			20		18		35/a	25	31
15	c					27			11	5		21	10			6			3/a			33/c			20		a	b		25/b	32
15	b				12/b			7	27	11/a	5	21	a			3		17/c	c			33						32			33
	b	29							11/c	5		21	10	3		3					24	33/b						32	35/a	c	34
	c	29			19				11	5		21	10/b			6			3	a	24/a				20			32/c		b	35
b	c	29			19				11	5		21				6			3	a	24				20/a			32/c		25/b	36
c	b	29			19				11	5		21				6/a			3		24				20		a	32/c		25/b	37
c	a	29/b			19				11/a	5		21				6			b	3	24/c				20			32		25	38
15	c	13	a		19							21				6			3		24				20/b		18	32/c		25/a	39
15	b		a		19				11/b	5		21				6			3		24				20			32		25/a	40
15	13				19					5		21	a			6		c	3		24				20/c	b		32/b		25/a	41
15	13/b				19					5		21	a			6		c	3		24				20/c	b		32		25/a	42
15	13				19					5		21	b			6/a		c	3		24				20		a	32/c		25/b	43

2007-08
Story of the season

After playing a huge part in the Hammers' survival **Carlos Tevez left to join Manchester United.** In his place **West Ham broke their transfer record** when paying Liverpool **£7.5 million** for striker **Craig Bellamy.**

Other quality signings were midfielders Scott Parker and Freddie Ljungberg and French international winger Julien Faubert. After the opening home defeat against Manchester City results improved with away wins at Birmingham City and Reading. Craig Bellamy scored twice in the 2–1 League Cup win at Bristol Rovers and further progress was made in that competition with a 1–0 home win against Plymouth Argyle. Lee Bowyer scored twice in the 5–0 demolition of Derby County and Carlton Cole scored an injury-time

Appearances & Goals 2007-08

	League			FA Cup			League Cup			Total		
	Starts	Subs	Goals	Starts	Subs	Goals	Starts	Subs	Goals	Starts	Subs	Goals
ASHTON Dean	20	11	10	2	0	0	2	0	1	24	11	11
BELLAMY Craig	7	1	2	0	0	0	1	0	2	8	1	4
BOA MORTE Luis	18	9	0	1	0	0	4	0	0	23	9	0
BOWYER Lee	12	3	4	1	1	0	2	1	0	15	5	4
CAMARA Henri	3	7	0	0	0	0	0	0	0	3	7	0
COLE Carlton	21	10	4	1	1	0	3	1	2	25	12	6
COLLINS James	2	1	0	0	0	0	1	1	0	3	2	0
COLLISON Jack	1	1	0	0	0	0	0	0	0	1	1	0
DYER Kieron	2	0	0	0	0	0	1	0	0	3	0	0
ETHERINGTON Matthew	15	3	3	2	0	0	1	0	0	18	3	3
FAUBERT Julien	4	3	0	0	1	0	0	0	0	4	4	0
FERDINAND Anton	22	3	2	2	0	0	2	0	0	26	3	2
GABBIDON Daniel	8	2	0	0	0	0	3	1	0	11	3	0
GREEN Robert	38	0	0	2	0	0	1	0	0	41	0	0
LJUNGBERG Fredrik	22	3	2	1	0	0	2	0	0	25	3	2
McCARTNEY George	38	0	1	2	0	0	4	0	0	44	0	1
MULLINS Hayden	32	2	0	1	0	0	4	0	0	37	2	0
NEILL Lucas	34	0	0	2	0	0	4	0	0	40	0	0
NOBLE Mark	25	6	3	2	0	0	1	2	0	28	8	3
PANTSIL John	4	10	0	1	0	0	0	2	0	5	12	0
PARKER Scott	17	1	1	0	0	0	2	0	0	19	1	1
REID Kyel	0	1	0	0	1	0	0	2	0	0	4	0
SEARS Freddie	1	6	1	0	0	0	0	0	0	1	6	1
SOLANO Nolberto	14	9	4	0	0	0	0	0	0	14	9	4
SPECTOR Jonathan	13	13	0	0	1	0	0	1	0	13	15	0
TOMKINS James	5	1	0	0	0	0	0	0	0	5	1	0
UPSON Matthew	29	0	1	2	0	0	2	0	0	33	0	1
WRIGHT Richard	0	0	0	0	0	0	3	0	0	3	0	0
ZAMORA Bobby	11	2	1	0	0	0	1	0	0	12	2	1
own goal			3						1			4
Totals	418	108	42	22	5	0	44	11	6	484	124	48

inner as the Hammers won 2–1 at Coventry City in the
eague Cup. In December Everton won twice at Upton
ark in the space of four days, a 2–1 League Cup win being
llowed by a 2–0 league victory. The year ended on a high
Manchester United were beaten 2–1 at home, captain
att Upson scoring a late winner.

here was an early FA Cup exit as after a 0–0 home draw
ith Manchester City the Hammers lost 1–0 in the replay.
he first week in March was a disaster, with embarrassing
-0 defeats against Chelsea, Liverpool and Tottenham. The
llowing home game against Blackburn Rovers saw
enager Freddie Sears make his debut and the youngster
bliged by scoring the winning goal in a 2–1 victory. The
ason ended with a 2–2 draw at home to Aston Villa,
hich gave a tenth place finish

arclays Premier League
inal Table 2007-08

	P	HOME					AWAY					Pts
		W	D	L	F	A	W	D	L	F	A	
anchester United	38	17	1	1	47	7	10	5	4	33	15	87
elsea	38	12	7	0	36	13	13	3	3	29	13	85
senal	38	14	5	0	37	11	10	6	3	37	20	83
verpool	38	12	6	1	43	13	9	7	3	24	15	76
erton	38	11	4	4	34	17	8	4	7	21	16	65
ton Villa	38	10	3	6	34	22	6	9	4	37	29	60
ackburn Rovers	38	8	7	4	26	19	7	6	6	24	29	58
rtsmouth	38	7	8	4	24	14	9	1	9	24	26	57
anchester City	38	11	4	4	28	20	4	6	9	17	33	55
est Ham United	**38**	**7**	**7**	**5**	**24**	**24**	**6**	**3**	**10**	**18**	**26**	**49**
ttenham Hotspur	38	8	5	6	46	34	3	8	8	20	27	46
wcastle United	38	8	5	6	25	26	3	5	11	20	39	43
ddlesbrough	38	7	5	7	27	23	3	7	9	16	30	42
gan Athletic	38	8	5	6	21	17	2	5	12	13	34	40
nderland	38	9	3	7	23	21	2	3	14	13	38	39
lton Wanderers	38	7	5	7	23	18	2	5	12	13	36	37
lham	38	5	5	9	22	31	3	7	9	16	29	36
ading	38	8	2	9	19	25	2	4	13	22	41	36
rmingham City	38	6	8	5	30	23	2	3	14	16	39	35
rby County	38	1	5	13	12	43	0	3	16	8	46	11

JULIEN FAUBERT

A pacey right-winger who can also play at right-back, he is a product of the Cannes academy.

Playing in the French Second Division from 2002 he played in 45 league games before being signed by Bordeaux in 2004. He spent four seasons there, playing in a total of 110 games including eight outings in the Champions League. He was also capped by France in August 2006 against Bosnia, and scored in the 2–1 victory. In July 2007 he was transferred to West Ham for a fee of £6 million but his full debut was delayed. Playing in a pre-season friendly he suffered a ruptured Achilles tendon and was out of action for six months. He finally made his debut against Fulham in January 2008 but further niggling injuries restricted his appearances to eight in that campaign. In January 2009 in a surprise move he was loaned out to Real Madrid but in five months there made only two appearances.

He returned to West Ham for the start of the 2009–10 season and settled down to become a regular member of the side. By 2011 he was now the first-choice right-back and played a part in the Hammers' promotion to the Premier League. In May 2012, after playing 119 games for West Ham, his contract expired and he joined the Turkish side Elazigspor for a spell, playing in 16 league games. He then joined his old club Bordeaux and is currently playing for them as well as international football for Martinique.

Season **2007-08** Barclays Premier League
Match Details

Manager **Alan Curbishley**   Final League Position: **10/20**

	Date		Competition	Venue	Opponents	Results		Attendance	Position	Scorers
1	Aug 11	Sat	Prem	H	Manchester City	L	0-2	34,921	20	
2	Aug 18	Sat	Prem	A	Birmingham City	W	1-0	24,961	15	Noble [pen]
3	Aug 25	Sat	Prem	H	Wigan Athletic	D	1-1	33,793	12	Bowyer
4	Aug 28	Tue	FLC 2	A	Bristol Rovers	W	2-1	10,831		Bellamy 2
5	Sep 1	Sat	Prem	A	Reading	W	3-0	23,533	8	Etherington 2, Bellamy
6	Sep 15	Sat	Prem	H	Middlesbrough	W	3-0	34,351	5	Ashton, Bowyer, Young (og)
7	Sep 23	Sun	Prem	A	Newcastle United	L	1-3	50,104	7	Ashton
8	Sep 26	Wed	FLC 3	H	Plymouth Argyle	W	1-0	25,774		Ashton
9	Sep 29	Sat	Prem	H	Arsenal	L	0-1	34,966	10	
10	Oct 6	Sat	Prem	A	Aston Villa	L	0-1	40,842	11	
11	Oct 21	Sun	Prem	H	Sunderland	W	3-1	34,913	10	Bellamy, Cole, Gordon (og)
12	Oct 27	Sat	Prem	A	Portsmouth	D	0-0	20,525	9	
13	Oct 30	Tue	FLC 4	A	Coventry City	W	2-1	23,968		Cole, Hall (og)
14	Nov 4	Sun	Prem	H	Bolton Wanderers	D	1-1	33,867	11	McCartney
15	Nov 10	Sat	Prem	A	Derby County	W	5-0	32,440	9	Bowyer 2, Etherington, Solano, Lewis (og)
16	Nov 25	Sun	Prem	H	Tottenham Hotspur	D	1-1	34,996	10	Cole
17	Dec 1	Sat	Prem	A	Chelsea	L	0-1	41,830	10	
18	Dec 9	Sun	Prem	A	Blackburn Rovers	W	1-0	20,870	10	Ashton
19	Dec 12	Wed	FLC 5	H	Everton	L	1-2	28,877		Cole
20	Dec 15	Sat	Prem	H	Everton	L	0-2	34,430	11	
21	Dec 22	Sat	Prem	A	Middlesbrough	W	2-1	26,007	10	Ashton, Parker
22	Dec 26	Wed	Prem	H	Reading	D	1-1	34,277	9	Solano
23	Dec 29	Sat	Prem	H	Manchester United	W	2-1	34,966	9	Ferdinand, Upson
24	Jan 1	Tue	Prem	A	Arsenal	L	0-2	60,102	10	
25	Jan 5	Sat	FAC 3	H	Manchester City	D	0-0	33,806		
26	Jan 12	Sat	Prem	H	Fulham	W	2-1	34,947	10	Ashton, Ferdinand
27	Jan 16	Wed	FAC 3 Rep	A	Manchester City	L	0-1	27,809		
28	Jan 20	Sun	Prem	A	Manchester City	D	1-1	39,042	10	Cole
29	Jan 30	Wed	Prem	H	Liverpool	W	1-0	34,977	10	Noble [pen]
30	Feb 2	Sat	Prem	A	Wigan Athletic	L	0-1	20,525	10	
31	Feb 9	Sat	Prem	H	Birmingham City	D	1-1	34,884	10	Ljungberg
32	Feb 23	Sat	Prem	A	Fulham	W	1-0	25,280	9	Solano
33	Mar 1	Sat	Prem	H	Chelsea	L	0-4	34,969	10	
34	Mar 5	wed	Prem	A	Liverpool	L	0-4	42,954	10	
35	Mar 9	Sun	Prem	A	Tottenham Hotspur	L	0-4	36,062	10	
36	Mar 15	Sat	Prem	H	Blackburn Rovers	W	2-1	34,006	10	Ashton, Sears
37	Mar 22	Sat	Prem	A	Everton	D	1-1	37,430	10	Ashton
38	Mar 29	Sat	Prem	A	Sunderland	L	1-2	45,690	10	Ljungberg
39	Apr 8	Tue	Prem	H	Portsmouth	L	0-1	33,629	10	
40	Apr 12	Sat	Prem	A	Bolton Wanderers	L	0-1	23,043	10	
41	Apr 19	Sat	Prem	H	Derby County	W	2-1	34,612	10	Cole, Zamora
42	Apr 26	Sat	Prem	H	Newcastle United	D	2-2	34,980	10	Ashton, Noble
43	May 3	Sat	Prem	A	Manchester United	L	1-4	76,013	10	Ashton
44	May 11	Sun	Prem	H	Aston Villa	D	2-2	34,969	10	Ashton, Solano

eam Line-Ups

ASHTON Dean	BELLAMY Craig	BOA MORTE Luis	BOWYER Lee	CAMARA Henri	COLE Carlton	COLLINS James	COLLISON Jack	DYER Kieron	ETHERINGTON Matthew	FAUBERT Julien	FERDINAND Anton	GABBIDON Daniel	GREEN Robert	LJUNGBERG Fredrik	McCARTNEY George	MULLINS Hayden	NEILL Lucas	NOBLE Mark	PANTSIL John	PARKER Scott	REID Kyel	SEARS Freddie	SOLANO Nolberto	SPECTOR Jonathan	TOMKINS James	UPSON Matthew	WRIGHT Richard	ZAMORA Bobby	
	10	13/b	29/a						b		5		1	7	3/c	a		16						18		6		25	1
	10							32	11		5	a	1		3	17		16						18/a		6		25	2
a	10/c	c	b					32	11		5		1		3	17/b	2	16								6		25/a	3
	10/c	13	29	c	b			32/a			5	4			3/b	17	2	a									21	25	4
a	10/c	c	29/b	a					11		5		1		3	17	2	16						b		6			5
c	10/a	b	29	a		19			11/b				1	c	3	17	2	16								6			6
			29	b	12/b				11/c		5		1	a	3	17/a	2	16						c		6			7
		13	b		12/a	19						4		7/b	3		2	c		8/c	a						21		8
		c	29/c	33							5/b	b	1	7	3	a	2	16		8/a						6			9
		c	29	33/a	a				11/c			4	1	7	3	17/b	2	b								6			10
	10	b	29		12/c				11/b		c	4	1		3	17	2	16/a					a			6			11
	10/b	13			12/c				b		c	4	1		3	17	2	16					15/a	a		6			12
		13	29		12				11		5/c	c			3	17/a	2	16/b	b					a		6	21		13
		13	29/c	b	12				11			4	1		3	17/a	2		c				15	a		6			14
		13	29/b		12	b			11			4	1		3/a		2		a				15	5		6			15
		13/b			12				11			4	1		3	17	2	16/a	a				15/c	c		6			16
		13			12				11/c			4	1	a	3	17	2			8/b			15/a	b		6			17
		13		c	12/c				11/a			4	1		3	17	2			8			15/b	b		6			18
		13/a			12/b							4	1	7	3	17	2		b	8	a					6			19
			a		12/a	19							1	7	3	17/c	2	b		8	c		15/b			6			20
			33/b										1	7	3	17	2	a	b	8			15/a	18		6			21
			a		12/a								1	7	3	17	2	b		8			15/b	18		6			22
					12						b		1	7/c	3	17	2	16	a	8/b			15/a	18		6			23
				c	12/b		a				5		1	7/a	3	17/c	2	16	14					18		6			24
		c			12				11/b		5		1		3	17/c	2/a	16	14		b			a		6			25
	a	b			12/a				11/b	c	5		1	7/c	3	17		16						18		6			26
		13/b	29		b				11	a	5		1	7/a	3		2	16								6			27
		13/a	29/b		12					a	5		1	7	3	17	2	16						b		6			28
		13/b	29/a		12/c				b		5		1	7	3	17	2	16						c		6			29
b		c			12/b				11/a		5		1	7	3	17	2	16/c						a		6			30
c			29	b	12/a				11/b	a	5		1	7	3	17	2							c		6			31
		13			12/b					20/a	5		1	7/c	3	17	2	16						a	c	6			32
		13/a			12/b					20/c	5		1	7	3	17	2	16						c		6		b	33
		13			12/c						5		1	7	3	17	2	16					15/b	a		6/a		c	34
					c						5		1	7/a	3	17	2	b	a	8/b				18				25	35
											5		1	7/c	3	17	2	a	c	8/a	b		15/b	18				25	36
		13/a									5		1	7/b	3	17	2	16		8/c	a	b	c		30				37
					12/b						5		1	7	3/a	17	2	16	a/c	8			b	18	c				38
		13			b						5		1		3	17/b	2	c		8	a		15/c	18				25/a	39
		13			b		39/b				5/a		1		3	17		a		8			c	18		6		25/c	40
	c				a					20/b			1	7/c	3		2	16	14	8		40/a	b		30			25	41
	a				b					20/c			1	7/a	3		2	16	14	8			c		30			25/b	42
		13/a			b								1		3	17/c	2	16	14	8			c	a	30			25	43
		13			b						5		1		3/a		2	16		8		c	15/c		30			25/b	44

2008-09
Story of the season

The league season started with **two goals from Dean Ashton** in the 2–1 home win against Wigan Athletic, and following on there were **two 4–1 home wins** against Blackburn Rovers and Macclesfield Town in the League Cup. The Cup trail would end in the next round when the Hammers lost 1–0 at Watford.

Manager Alan Curbishley was unhappy with the club' transfer policy and resigned; on 3 September it w announced that the former Chelsea legend Gianfran Zola was to be the new West Ham manager. Just prior Zola's first game against Newcastle United the Itali striker David Di Michele joined West Ham. He had excellent debut, scoring two goals in the 3–1 victory. Aft this came three successive home defeats to leave the si fourteenth. There was an improvement away from hom

Appearances & Goals 2008-09

	League			FA Cup			League Cup			Total		
	Starts	Subs	Goals	Starts	Subs	Goals	Starts	Subs	Goals	Starts	Subs	Goals
ASHTON Dean	4	0	2	0	0	0	1	0	0	5	0	
BEHRAMI Valon	24	0	1	2	0	1	1	0	0	27	0	
BELLAMY Craig	13	3	5	1	0	0	0	0	0	14	3	
BOA MORTE Luis	13	14	0	2	1	0	2	0	0	17	15	
BOWYER Lee	4	2	0	0	0	0	1	0	1	5	2	
COLE Carlton	26	1	10	4	0	1	0	1	1	30	2	
COLLINS James	17	1	0	3	0	0	0	0	0	20	1	
COLLISON Jack	16	4	3	3	1	0	0	0	0	19	5	
DAVENPORT Calum	7	0	1	0	0	0	1	0	0	8	0	
DI MICHELE David	22	8	4	2	1	0	1	0	0	25	9	
DYER Kieron	1	6	0	0	1	0	0	0	0	1	7	
ETHERINGTON Matthew	8	5	2	0	1	0	1	0	0	9	6	
FAUBERT Julien	15	5	0	2	0	0	2	0	0	19	5	
GREEN Robert	38	0	0	4	0	0	1	0	0	43	0	
HINES Zavon	0	0	0	0	0	0	0	1	0	0	1	
ILUNGA Herita	35	0	0	4	0	2	0	0	0	39	0	
KOVAC Radoslav	8	1	1	1	0	0	0	0	0	9	1	
LASTUVKA Jan	0	0	0	0	0	0	1	0	0	1	0	
LOPEZ Walter	0	5	0	0	0	0	1	0	0	1	5	
McCARTNEY George	0	1	0	0	0	0	1	0	0	1	1	
MULLINS Hayden	5	12	1	1	1	0	2	0	0	8	13	
NEILL Lucas	34	0	1	2	0	0	1	0	0	37	0	
NOBLE Mark	28	1	3	4	0	2	1	0	0	33	1	
NSEREKO Savio	1	9	0	0	1	0	0	0	0	1	10	
PARKER Scott	28	0	1	3	0	0	0	1	0	31	1	
PAYNE Josh	0	2	0	0	0	0	0	0	0	0	2	
REID Kyel	0	0	0	0	0	0	0	2	1	0	2	
SEARS Freddie	4	13	0	1	2	0	2	0	0	7	15	
SPECTOR Jonathan	4	5	0	0	0	0	0	0	0	4	5	
STANISLAS Junior	7	2	2	0	0	0	0	0	0	7	2	
TOMKINS James	11	1	1	3	0	0	0	0	0	14	1	
TRISTAN Diego	8	6	3	0	3	0	0	0	0	8	9	
UPSON Matthew	37	0	0	2	0	0	2	0	0	41	0	
own goal			1									
Totals	418	107	42	44	12	6	22	5	3	484	124	5

th a 1–0 win at Middlesbrough and a 0–0 draw at
verpool. The home form was still a concern with
ecember bringing two further defeats, but after a decent
1 win at Portsmouth the Hammers finally won at Upton
rk, beating Stoke City 2–1.

ogress was made in the FA Cup after beating Barnsley
0 at home and Hartlepool United 2–0 away. Czech
public defender Radoslav Kovak came on loan from
artak Moscow and made his first-team debut in the 2–0
Cup defeat at Middlesbrough. The team moved into
th place following 1–0 wins against Manchester City and
igan, and Scott Parker was in sparkling form with a string
man-of-the-match displays.

March an independent Football Association arbitration
nel was due to meet to discuss the compensation claim by
effield United that third-party rules had been broken
en West Ham signed Carlos Tevez. In fielding the player
was claimed that he had been instrumental in West Ham
ying in the top flight while Sheffield United were
egated. Days before the meeting was due, West Ham

agreed to settle the claim of £30 million by paying Sheffield
United in instalments.

The final home game saw Carlton Cole score in the 2–1
victory over Middlesbrough..

HERITA ILUNGA

**After playing in youth football with Rennes
Ilunga went to Spain to play for Espanyol.**

Playing as a left-back he had 19 league
games for the Espanyol B team in the Third
Division in season 2002/03. Moving back to
France in 2003 he spent four seasons playing
for St Etienne, where he made 136 league
appearances. By now he was a regular
member of the DR Congo international side
and he went on to play in 32 games for his
country. In the summer of 2007 he moved on
to Toulouse and was able to enjoy
participation in the Champions League and
the UEFA Cup. In the league Toulouse were
struggling and they narrowly avoided
relegation in 2008, which prompted him to
join West Ham.

He quickly established himself in the side and
scored goals in the FA Cup that season
against Barnsley and Middlesbrough. The
following season a few injuries hampered his
playing time and following the Hammers
relegation in 2011 he was loaned to
Doncaster Rovers, where he played in 15
league games for the Yorkshire side. In
January 2012, after making 73 appearances
for West Ham, his contract was terminated.
He then signed permanently for Doncaster
but only played in four games before
returning to France to sign for his first club
Rennes. A short spell with them saw him play
in three games before he joined US Creteil,
where he currently plays in League Two.

arclays Premier League
inal Table 2008-09

	P	HOME					AWAY					Pts
		W	D	L	F	A	W	D	L	F	A	
nchester United	38	16	2	1	43	13	12	4	3	25	11	90
erpool	38	12	7	0	41	13	13	4	2	36	14	86
elsea	38	11	6	2	33	12	14	2	3	35	12	83
senal	38	11	5	3	31	16	9	7	3	37	21	72
erton	38	8	6	5	31	20	9	6	4	24	17	63
on Villa	38	7	9	3	27	21	10	2	7	27	27	62
ham	38	11	3	5	28	16	3	8	8	11	18	53
tenham Hotspur	38	10	5	4	21	10	4	4	11	24	35	51
est Ham United	38	9	2	8	23	22	5	7	7	19	23	51
anchester City	38	13	0	6	40	18	2	5	12	18	32	50
gan Athletic	38	8	5	6	17	18	4	4	11	17	27	45
oke City	38	10	5	4	22	15	2	4	13	16	40	45
lton Wanderers	38	7	5	7	21	21	4	3	12	20	32	41
rtsmouth	38	8	5	8	26	29	2	8	9	12	28	41
ackburn Rovers	38	6	7	6	22	23	4	4	11	18	37	41
nderland	38	6	3	10	21	25	3	6	10	13	29	36
ll City	38	3	5	11	18	36	5	6	8	21	28	35
wcastle United	38	5	7	7	24	29	2	6	11	16	30	34
ddlesbrough	38	5	9	5	17	20	2	2	15	11	37	32
est Bromwich Albion	38	7	3	9	26	33	1	5	13	10	34	32

Season **2008-09** Barclays Premier League
Match Details

Manager **Alan Curbishley** (to September 2); Caretaker Manager **Kevin Keen** (September 13)
Manager **Gianfranco Zola** (from September 14)   Final League Position: **9/20**

	Date		Competition	Venue	Opponents	Results		Attendance	Position	Scorers
1	Aug 16	Sat	Prem	H	Wigan Athletic	W	2-1	32,758	5	Ashton 2
2	Aug 24	Sun	Prem	A	Manchester City	L	0-3	36,635	15	
3	Aug 27	Wed	FLC 2	H	Macclesfield Town	W	4-1*	10,055		Bowyer, Cole, Hines, Reid
4	Aug 30	Sat	Prem	H	Blackburn Rovers	W	4-1	32,905	4	Bellamy, Cole, Davenport, Samba (og)
5	Sep 13	Sat	Prem	A	West Bromwich Albion	L	2-3	26,213	7	Neill, Noble
6	Sep 20	Sat	Prem	H	Newcastle United	W	3-1	34,743	4	Di Michele 2, Etherington
7	Sep 23	Tue	FLC 3	A	Watford	L	0-1	12,914		
8	Sep 27	Sat	Prem	A	Fulham	W	2-1	23,926	5	Cole, Etherington
9	Oct 5	Sun	Prem	H	Bolton Wanderers	L	1-3	33,715	6	Cole
10	Oct 19	Sun	Prem	A	Hull City	L	0-1	24,896	8	
11	Oct 26	Sun	Prem	H	Arsenal	L	0-2	34,802	10	
12	Oct 29	Wed	Prem	A	Manchester United	L	0-2	75,397	11	
13	Nov 1	Sat	Prem	A	Middlesbrough	D	1-1	25,164	11	Mullins
14	Nov 8	Sat	Prem	H	Everton	L	1-3	33,961	13	Collison
15	Nov 15	Sat	Prem	H	Portsmouth	D	0-0	32,328	13	
16	Nov 23	Sun	Prem	A	Sunderland	W	1-0	35,222	13	Behrami
17	Dec 1	Mon	Prem	A	Liverpool	D	0-0	41,169	13	
18	Dec 8	Mon	Prem	H	Tottenham Hotspur	L	0-2	34,277	16	
19	Dec 14	Sun	Prem	A	Chelsea	D	1-1	41,675	16	Bellamy
20	Dec 20	Sat	Prem	H	Aston Villa	L	0-1	31,353	17	
21	Dec 26	Fri	Prem	A	Portsmouth	W	4-1	20,102	13	Bellamy 2, Cole, Collison
22	Dec 28	Sun	Prem	H	Stoke City	W	2-1	34,477	10	Cole, Tristan
23	Jan 3	Sat	FAC 3	H	Barnsley	W	3-0	28,869		Cole, Ilunga, Noble [pen]
24	Jan 10	Sat	Prem	A	Newcastle United	D	2-2	47,571	10	Bellamy, Cole
25	Jan 18	Sun	Prem	H	Fulham	W	3-1	31,818	8	Di Michelle, Noble [pen], Cole
26	Jan 24	Sat	FAC 4	A	Hartlepool United	W	2-0	6,849		Behrami, Noble [pen]
27	Jan 28	Wed	Prem	H	Hull City	W	2-0	34,340	8	Cole, Di Michele
28	Jan 31	Sat	Prem	A	Arsenal	D	0-0	60,109	8	
29	Feb 8	Sun	Prem	H	Manchester United	L	0-1	34,958	8	
30	Feb 14	Sat	FAC 5	H	Middlesbrough	D	1-1	33,658		Illunga
31	Feb 21	Sat	Prem	A	Bolton Wanderers	L	1-2	21,245	8	Parker
32	Feb 25	Wed	FAC 5 Rep	A	Middlesbrough	L	0-2	15,602		
33	Mar 1	Sun	Prem	H	Manchester City	W	1-0	34,562	7	Collison
34	Mar 4	Wed	Prem	A	Wigan Athletic	W	1-0	14,169	7	Cole
35	Mar 16	Mon	Prem	H	West Bromwich Albion	D	0-0	30,842	7	
36	Mar 21	Sat	Prem	A	Blackburn Rovers	D	1-1	21,672	7	Noble
37	Apr 4	Sat	Prem	H	Sunderland	W	2-0	34,761	7	Stanislas, Tomkins
38	Apr 11	Sat	Prem	A	Tottenham Hotspur	L	0-1	35,969	7	
39	Apr 18	Sat	Prem	A	Aston Villa	D	1-1	39,534	7	Tristan
40	Apr 25	Sat	Prem	H	Chelsea	L	0-1	34,749	8	
41	May 2	Sat	Prem	A	Stoke City	W	1-0	27,500	7	Tristan
42	May 9	Sat	Prem	H	Liverpool	L	0-3	34,951	9	
43	May 16	Sat	Prem	A	Everton	L	1-3	38,501	9	Kovac
44	May 24	Sun	Prem	H	Middlesbrough	W	2-1	34,007	9	Cole, Stanislas

* After extra time (1-1 after 90 minutes)

eam Line-Ups

BEHRAMI	BELLAMY	BOA MORTE	BOWYER	COLE	COLLINS	COLLISON	DAVENPORT	DI MICHELE	DYER	ETHERINGTON	FAUBERT	GREEN	HINES	ILUNGA	KOVAC	LASTUVKA	LOPEZ	McCARTNEY	MULLINS	NEILL	NOBLE	NSEREKO	PARKER	PAYNE	REID	SEARS	SPECTOR	STANISLAS	TOMKINS	TRISTAN	UPSON	#
10	13/b	29/a					b				5	1	7	3/c	a						16						18				6	1
10							32	11			5	1	a	3	17						16						18/a				6	2
10/c	c	b					32	11			5	1		3	17/b	2					16										6	3
10/c	13	29		c	b		32/a				5			3/b	17	2			4		a											4
10/c	c	29/b					a	11			5	1		3	17	2					16									b	6	5
10/a	b	29		a	19			11/b				1	c	3	17/a	2					16					c					6	6
		29		12/b	b			11/c			5	1	a	3	17/a	2					16					c					6	7
	13	b		12/a	19						7/b			3	17	2			4		c		8/c			a					6	8
	c	29/c	33	a					b		5/b	1	7	3	a	2					16		8/a								6	9
	c	29	33/a	a				11/c				1	7	3	17/b	2			4		b										6	10
10	b	29		12/c				11/b	c			1		3	17	2			4		16/a							a			6	11
10/b	13			12/c	b				c			1		3	17	2			4		16							15/a		a	6	12
	13	29		12				11	c		5/c			3	17/a	2			b		16/b							a			6	13
	13	29/c	b	12/b				11				1		3	17/a	2			4		c							15	a		6	14
	13	29/b		12	b			11	c		5/c			3/a		2										a		15	5		6	15
	13/b			12				11				1	a	3	17	2			4		16/a				a			15/c	c		6	16
	13			12				11/c				1		3	17	2			4				8/b					15/a	b		6	17
	13	c		12/c				11/a				1		3	17	2			4				8					15/b	b		6	18
	13/a			12/b								1	7	3	17	2	b		4				8			a		15/b			6	19
		a		12/a	19							1	7	3	17/c	2	b						8			c		15/b			6	20
		33/b										1	7	3	17	2	a		b				8					15/a	18		6	21
		a		12/a								1	7	3	17	2	b						8					15/b	18		6	22
				12						b		1	7/c	3	17/c	2	16	a					8/b					15/a	18		6	23
		c		12/b	a						5	1	7/a	3	17/c	2	16					14							18		6	24
	c			12	c			11/b			5	1	7/c	3	17	2/a	16					14			b					a	6	25
	a	b		12/a	c			11/b			5	1	7/c	3	17		16										18				6	26
	13/b	29		b				11	a		5	1	7/a	3		2	16														6	27
	13/a	29/b		12					a		5	1	7	3	17	2	16												b		6	28
	13/b	29/a		12/c			b				5	1	7	3	17	2	16												c		6	29
b	c			12/b				11/a			5	1	7	3	17	2	16/c												a		6	30
		29	b	12/a				11/b	a		5	1	7	3	17	2													c		6	31
	13			12/b				20/a			5	1	7/c	3	17	2	16										a		c		6	32
	13/a			12/b				20/c			5	1	7	3	17	2	16												c		6/a	33
	13			12/c							5	1	7	3	17	2	16											15/b	a		6/a	34
	13			c							5	1	7/a	3	17	2	b		a				8/b						18			35
											5	1	7/c	3	17	2	a	c					8/a			b		15/b	18			36
	13/a										5	1	7/b	3	17	2	16						8/c		a	b		c	18	30		37
				12/b							5	1	7	3/a	17	2	16	a/c					8			b	18			c		38
	13			b							5	1		3	17/b	2		c					8		a			15/c	18			39
	13			b		39/b					5/a	1		3	17		a						8			c			18		6	40
	c			a			b		20/b			1	7/c	3		2	16					14	8		40/a		b			30		41
	a			b					20/c			1	7/a	3		2	16					14	8				c			30		42
	13/a			b								1		3	17/c	2	16					14	8			c	a			30		43
	13			b							5	1		3/a		2	16				a		8			c		15/c		30		44

2009-10
Story of the season

Joining the club for the new campaign was the **Chilean international forward Luis Jiminez,** together with **Italian striker Alessandro Diamanti** and **Argentinian forward Guillermo Franco.**

An opening day 2–0 win at Wolverhampton Wander got the season off to a flying start and the League C began with a 3–1 home victory against local rivals Millw The tie was halted for ten minutes in the second half crowd trouble broke out, and on a night of shame violence continued after the match. Moving on to the n round, the Hammers were leading 1–0 at Bolton Wander only to concede a late equaliser and lose 3–1 after ex time. With no wins in the next nine games the team w

Appearances & Goals 2009-10

	League			FA Cup			League Cup			Total	
	Starts	Subs	Goals	Starts	Subs	Goals	Starts	Subs	Goals	Starts	Subs
BEHRAMI Valon	24	3	1	1	0	0	0	0	0	25	3
BOA MORTE Luis	1	0	1	0	0	0	0	0	0	1	0
COLE Carlton	26	4	10	0	0	0	1	1	0	27	5
COLLINS James	3	0	0	0	0	0	0	0	0	3	0
COLLISON Jack	19	3	2	0	0	0	1	0	0	20	3
DA COSTA Manuel	12	3	2	0	0	0	1	0	0	13	3
DAPRELA Fabio	4	3	0	1	0	0	0	0	0	5	3
DIAMANTI Alessandro	18	9	7	1	0	1	1	0	0	20	9
DYER Kieron	4	6	0	0	0	0	1	0	0	5	6
EDGAR Anthony	0	0	0	0	1	0	0	0	0	0	1
FAUBERT Julien	32	1	1	1	0	0	1	1	0	34	2
FRANCO Guillermo	16	7	5	0	0	0	0	0	0	16	7
GABBIDON Daniel	8	2	0	0	0	0	1	0	0	9	2
GREEN Robert	38	0	0	1	0	0	2	0	0	41	0
HINES Zavon	5	8	1	0	0	0	1	1	1	6	9
ILAN Araujo	6	5	4	0	0	0	0	0	0	6	5
ILUNGA Herita	16	0	0	0	0	0	1	0	1	17	0
JIMENEZ Luis	6	5	1	1	0	0	0	0	0	7	5
KOVAC Radoslav	27	4	2	1	0	0	2	0	0	30	4
KURUCZ Peter	0	1	0	0	0	0	0	0	0	0	1
McCARTHY Benni	2	3	0	0	0	0	0	0	0	2	3
MIDO Hossam	5	4	0	0	0	0	0	0	0	5	4
N'GALA Bondz	0	0	0	0	0	0	0	1	0	0	1
NOBLE Mark	25	2	2	0	0	0	1	0	0	26	2
NOUBLE Frank	3	5	0	1	0	0	0	1	0	4	6
PARKER Scott	30	1	2	0	0	0	2	0	0	32	1
PAYNE Josh	0	0	0	0	0	0	1	0	0	1	0
SEARS Freddie	0	1	0	0	1	0	0	0	0	0	2
SPECTOR Jonathan	22	5	0	0	0	0	2	0	0	24	5
SPENCE Jordan	0	1	0	0	0	0	0	0	0	0	1
STANISLAS Junior	11	15	2	1	0	0	1	0	2	13	15
TOMKINS James	22	1	0	1	0	0	2	0	0	25	1
UPSON Matthew	33	0	3	1	0	0	0	1	0	34	1
own goal			1								
Totals	**418**	**102**	**47**	**11**	**2**	**1**	**22**	**6**	**4**	**451**	**110**

uggling at the bottom. An improvement at home in ovember, however, brought victories against Aston Villa d Burnley. After that the next victory did not come until xing Day, when bottom club Portsmouth were beaten 0 at home.

the FA Cup, despite winning 1–0 at half-time the mmers went out after losing 2–1 at home to Arsenal. In uary lifetime West Ham supporters David Gold and vid Sullivan announced that they had bought the club. ey were both optimistic for their future plans for the club d supporters. Two new signings were made when strikers nni McCarthy and Mido were bought, but they both uggled for fitness. There was real pressure on the side as y slipped to home defeats against Wolverhampton anderers and Stoke City. Relegation was finally avoided lowing home wins against Sunderland and Wigan to give eventeenth place finish.

May West Ham announced that they had terminated anfraco Zola's contract and that his successor would be ram Grant.

rclays Premier League nal Table 2009-10

	P		HOME					AWAY				Pts
		W	D	L	F	A	W	D	L	F	A	
lsea	38	17	1	1	68	14	10	4	5	35	18	86
nchester United	38	16	1	2	52	12	11	3	5	34	16	85
enal	38	15	2	2	48	15	8	4	7	35	26	75
enham Hotspur	38	14	2	3	40	12	7	5	7	27	29	70
nchester City	38	12	4	3	41	20	6	9	4	32	25	67
on Villa	38	8	8	3	29	16	9	5	5	23	23	64
erpool	38	13	3	3	43	15	5	6	8	18	20	63
rton	38	11	6	2	35	21	5	7	7	25	28	61
mingham City	38	8	9	2	19	13	5	2	12	19	34	50
ckburn Rovers	38	10	6	3	28	18	3	5	11	13	37	50
ke City	38	7	6	6	24	21	4	8	7	10	27	47
ham	38	11	3	5	27	15	1	7	11	12	31	46
nderland	38	9	7	3	32	19	2	4	13	16	37	44
ton Wanderers	38	6	6	7	26	31	4	3	12	16	36	39
verhampton Wanderers	38	5	6	8	13	22	4	5	10	19	34	38
gan Athletic	38	6	7	6	19	24	3	2	14	18	55	36
est Ham United	38	7	5	7	30	29	1	6	12	17	37	35
nley	38	7	5	7	25	30	1	1	17	17	52	30
l City	38	6	6	7	22	29	0	6	13	12	46	30
tsmouth	38	5	3	11	24	32	2	4	13	10	34	19

ALESSANDRO DIAMANTI

An attacking midfielder known for his excellent set pieces and penalties, Diamanti's first club was Prato, where he spent five seasons from 1999 and played in 72 league games.

While there he went on loan to Empoli, Fucecchio and Fiorentina. In 2004 he played 26 league games for Albinoleffe before moving on to play for Livorno. He scored 24 league goals for Livorno but after their relegation to Serie B in 2009 he came to England to play for West Ham.

Making his debut in September at Wigan, he went on to play 30 games, scoring eight goals that season. He proved popular with the fans, being voted runner-up in the annual Hammer of the Year awards. In 2010 he returned to Italy to play for Brescia, appearing in 32 games in a season that saw Brescia relegated. His fine form saw him selected to play for Italy against Romania and he then went on to play in 17 games for his country. Once again he was on the move and this time he joined Bologna, making 83 league appearances over three seasons. In 2014 he was transferred to Guangzhou Evergrande where he helped them win the Chinese Super League. Diamante is currently on loan at his former club Fiorentina.

Season **2009-10** Barclays Premier League
Match Details

Manager **Gianfranco Zola**   Final League Position: **17/20**

	Date		Competition	Venue	Opponents	Results		Attendance	Position	Scorers
1	Aug 15	Sat	Prem	A	Wolverhampton Wanderers	W	2-0	28,674	4	Noble, Upson
2	Aug 23	Sun	Prem	H	Tottenham Hotspur	L	1-2	33,095	11	Cole
3	Aug 25	Tue	FLC 2	H	Millwall	W	3-1*	24,492		Stanislas 2 [1 pen], Hines
4	Aug 29	Sat	Prem	A	Blackburn Rovers	D	0-0	23,421	10	
5	Sep 12	Sat	Prem	A	Wigan Athletic	L	0-1	17,142	12	
6	Sep 19	Sat	Prem	H	Liverpool	D	2-2	34,658	14	Cole, Diamanti [pen]
7	Sep 22	Tue	FLC 3	A	Bolton Wanderers	L	1-3*	8,050		Ilunga
8	Sep 28	Mon	Prem	A	Manchester City	L	1-3	42,745	18	Cole
9	Oct 4	Sun	Prem	H	Fulham	D	2-2	32,612	19	Cole, Stanislas
10	Oct 17	Sat	Prem	A	Stoke City	L	1-2	27,026	19	Upson
11	Oct 25	Sun	Prem	H	Arsenal	D	2-2	34,442	19	Cole, Diamanti [pen]
12	Oct 31	Sat	Prem	A	Sunderland	D	2-2	39,033	19	Cole, Franco
13	Nov 4	Wed	Prem	H	Aston Villa	W	2-1	30,024	16	Hines, Noble [pen]
14	Nov 8	Sun	Prem	H	Everton	L	1-2	32,466	18	Stanislas
15	Nov 21	Sat	Prem	A	Hull City	D	3-3	24,909	17	Collison, Da Costa, Franco
16	Nov 28	Sat	Prem	H	Burnley	W	5-3	34,003	17	Cole [pen], Collison, Franco, Jimenez [pen], Stanis
17	Dec 5	Sat	Prem	H	Manchester United	L	0-4	34,980	17	
18	Dec 12	Sat	Prem	A	Birmingham City	L	0-1	28,203	18	
19	Dec 15	Tue	Prem	A	Bolton Wanderers	L	1-3	17,849	19	Diamanti
20	Dec 20	Sun	Prem	H	Chelsea	D	1-1	33,388	19	Diamanti [pen]
21	Dec 26	Sat	Prem	H	Portsmouth	W	2-0	33,686	17	Diamanti [pen], Kovac
22	Dec 28	Mon	Prem	A	Tottenham Hotspur	L	0-2	35,994	17	
23	Jan 3	Sun	FAC 3	H	Arsenal	L	1-2	25,549		Diamanti
24	Jan 17	Sun	Prem	A	Aston Villa	D	0-0	35,646	16	
25	Jan 26	Tue	Prem	A	Portsmouth	D	1-1	18,322	16	Upson
26	Jan 30	Sat	Prem	H	Blackburn Rovers	D	0-0	33,093	15	
27	Feb 6	Sat	Prem	A	Burnley	L	1-2	21,001	18	Ilan
28	Feb 10	Wed	Prem	H	Birmingham City	W	2-0	34,458	14	Cole, Diamanti
29	Feb 20	Sat	Prem	H	Hull City	W	3-0	33,971	13	Behrami, Cole, Faubert
30	Feb 23	Tue	Prem	A	Manchester United	L	0-3	73,797	13	
31	Mar 6	Sat	Prem	H	Bolton Wanderers	L	1-2	33,824	14	Diamanti
32	Mar 13	Sat	Prem	A	Chelsea	L	1-4	41,755	16	Parker
33	Mar 20	Sat	Prem	A	Arsenal	L	0-2	60,077	17	
34	Mar 23	Tue	Prem	H	Wolverhampton Wanderers	L	1-3	33,988	17	Franco
35	Mar 27	Sat	Prem	H	Stoke City	L	0-1	34,564	17	
36	Apr 4	Sun	Prem	A	Everton	D	2-2	37,451	17	Da Costa, Ilan
37	Apr 10	Sat	Prem	H	Sunderland	W	1-0	34,685	16	Ilan
38	Apr 19	Mon	Prem	A	Liverpool	L	0-3	37,697	17	
39	Apr 24	Sat	Prem	H	Wigan Athletic	W	3-2	33,057	17	Ilan, Kovac, Parker
40	May 2	Sun	Prem	A	Fulham	L	2-3	24,201	17	Cole, Franco
41	May 9	Sun	Prem	H	Manchester City	D	1-1	34,989	17	Boa Morte

* After extra time (1-1 after 90 minutes)

eam Line-Ups

BOA MORTE Luis	COLE Carlton	COLLINS James	COLLISON Jack	DA COSTA Manuel	DAPRELA Fabio	DIAMANTI Alessandro	DYER Kieron	EDGAR Anthony	FAUBERT Julien	FRANCO Guillermo	GABBIDON Daniel	GREEN Robert	HINES Zavon	ILAN Araujo	ILUNGA Herita	JIMENEZ Luis	KOVAC Radoslav	KURUCZ Peter	McCARTHY Benni	MIDO Hossam	N'GALA Bondz	NOBLE Mark	NOUBLE Frank	PARKER Scott	PAYNE Josh	SEARS Freddie	SPECTOR Jonathan	SPENCE Jordan	STANISLAS Junior	TOMKINS James	UPSON Matthew	
12/c	19	31					7/b		20			1			23/a	17						16	c	8		a			b		15	1
12	19	31/c							20			1	b			17/a	a					16	c	8/b			18		46		15	2
12/c		31							20		4	1	a				14/b						b	8	35/a		18		46	30	c	3
12	19	31/b			a				20			1				17/a	b					16		8			18		46		15	4
12						b			20		4	1	41				14/a					16/c	c	8					46/b	30	15	5
12						32/c	c		20	a		1	41		23		b					16		8						30	15/a	6
b			22/a			32	7/b			c		1	41/c		23		14			a		16		8			18			30		7
12			22			32			20			1	a		23	17/a	14/b					16		8					b	30		8
12						32			20			1	41/b		23	17						16		8/a					b	30	15	9
12		31/c				32/a			20	c		1	a		23		14/b					16							b	30	15	10
12		31				a				10/b		1	b		23		c					16/a		8			18			30	15	11
12		31				a				10/b		1	b		23		14					16					18			30	15	12
12/b		31	22						20	10/c		1	b		23/a		c					16		8			a				15	13
		31/a	22			b			20	10		1	41			17/b								8			18		a		15	14
12		31	22						20	10/b	4	1	a				b							8					46		15	15
12/a		31/c	22			c				10/b	4	1	a		23	b	14							8			18		46			16
		31					a		b	10	4	1/c	41/a		23		14/b	c						8			18		46	30		17
	b					32	a		20	10	4	1			23/c		14/a					16	c	8					46/b	30		18
		31/b	b			32	7/a		20	10	4	1			23		14							8					a	30		19
		31				32			20	10	4/a	1			23		14					16		8					a		15	20
		31				32/b			20	10/c		1			23	a	14					16/a	c	8						30	15	21
		31/c				32			20	10		1			23/b	a	14							8/a		b			c	30	15	22
				33		32	b		20			1				17	14						24/a			a			46/b	30		23
		31	c				a		20			1					14/b					16	24/c	8/a			18		b	30	15	24
a		31	b			32/c			20			1					14					16	24/a				18		c	30/b	15	25
a		31				32			20			1					14/a					16	24/c	b		c	18			30	15	26
12		31/b							20			1	c			17/a	a					16/c		8			18		b	30	15	27
12						32			20			1	b		23/a		14		11/b			c		8/c			a			30	15	28
12/b	c					32/c			20	10/a		1	a				14		b					8			18			30	15	29
12	b					32/c	c		20	10/a		1					14		a			16					18			30	15	30
12						32	a		20/a	10/b		1					14/c		b					8			18		c	30	15	31
a				33		c	7/b				4	1		9/c			14		11/a					8			18		b		15	32
a				33		32				10/a		1					14/b	c	11/c			b					18		46	30	15	33
12				33		32			20		c	1				17/c	14/b										a		b	30/a	15	34
12			22			a	7/a		20			1		b			c		11/c			16/b		8			18				15	35
12			22						20		b	1		a			14		11/a			16		8			18		46/b		15	36
12			22			b			20		a	1		9/b			14					16					18		46/a		15	37
12/b			22			c			20		a	1		9			14		b			16					18/c		46/a		15	38
12			22			b			20		a	1		9/a			14					16/b		8			18				15	39
12			22			a			20/a		b	1		9/b			14					16		8			18		c		15	40
13/b	12/a		22	33		32/c			20		a	1		9			14							8			c		b		15	41

2010-11
Story of the season

A **bad start** with four successive defeats sent the Hammers to the **bottom of the table.** There was relief in the League Cup with a narrow **1–0 home win over Oxford United** followed by a **2–1 victory at Sunderland**.

A further two new players arrived when Nigerian forward Victor Obinna was joined by Danish full-back Lars Jacobsen. **The first league victory** came in September with a **1–0 home win against rivals Tottenham Hotspur.**

There were away draws at Wolves and Birmingham the team were still struggling at the bottom. Progress made in the League Cup as Stoke City were beaten 3–1 the Boleyn Ground to set up a quarter-final home tie w Manchester United. It was a night to remember and v midfielder Jonathan Spector's finest hour. Spector sco twice and two more from Carlton Cole gave West Har stunning 4–0 victory. Going into the New Year the te

Appearances & Goals 2010-11

	League			FA Cup			League Cup			Total	
	Starts	Subs	Goals	Starts	Subs	Goals	Starts	Subs	Goals	Starts	Subs
BA Demba	10	2	7	1	0	0	0	0	0	11	2
BARRERA Pablo	6	8	0	2	1	0	4	0	0	12	9
BEHRAMI Valon	6	1	2	0	0	0	0	1	0	6	2
BEN-HAIM Tal	8	0	0	0	0	0	4	0	0	12	0
BOA MORTE Luis	19	3	0	1	1	0	4	0	0	24	4
BOFFIN Ruud	1	0	0	0	0	0	0	0	0	1	0
BRIDGE Wayne	15	0	0	2	0	0	1	0	0	18	0
COLE Carlton	21	14	5	2	0	2	3	3	4	26	17
COLLISON Jack	2	1	0	0	0	0	0	0	0	2	1
DA COSTA Manuel	14	2	1	1	0	0	2	0	1	17	2
DIAMANTI Alessandro	0	1	0	0	0	0	0	0	0	0	1
DYER Kieron	8	3	0	0	0	0	0	2	0	8	5
EDGAR Anthony	0	0	0	0	1	0	0	0	0	0	1
FAUBERT Julien	7	2	0	1	0	0	6	0	0	14	2
GABBIDON Daniel	24	2	0	1	0	0	0	0	0	25	2
GREEN Robert	37	0	0	4	0	0	3	0	0	44	0
HINES Zavon	4	5	0	1	2	0	1	2	0	6	9
HITZLSPERGER Thomas	11	0	2	2	0	1	0	0	0	13	0
ILUNGA Herita	10	1	0	1	0	0	0	0	0	11	1
JACOBSEN Lars	22	2	0	2	0	0	0	0	0	24	2
KEANE Robbie	5	4	2	0	1	0	0	0	0	5	5
KOVAC Radoslav	7	6	0	1	0	0	3	1	0	11	7
McCARTHY Benni	0	6	0	0	0	0	1	2	0	1	8
NOBLE Mark	25	1	4	4	0	0	3	2	1	32	3
NOUBLE Frank	0	2	0	1	1	0	0	0	0	1	3
O'NEIL Gary	7	1	0	0	0	0	0	1	0	7	2
OBINNA Victor	17	8	3	3	0	3	3	1	2	23	9
PARKER Scott	30	2	5	2	1	0	5	0	2	37	3
PIQUIONNE Frederic	26	8	6	2	2	2	3	0	1	31	10
REID Winston	3	4	0	3	0	1	1	1	0	7	5
SEARS Freddie	9	2	1	2	0	1	2	0	0	13	2
SPECTOR Jonathan	10	4	1	1	2	1	4	0	2	15	6
SPENCE Jordan	2	0	0	0	0	0	0	0	0	2	0
STANISLAS Junior	4	2	1	0	0	0	1	1	0	5	3
STECH Marek	0	0	0	0	0	0	3	0	0	3	0
TOMKINS James	18	1	1	3	0	0	6	0	0	27	1
UPSON Matthew	30	0	0	1	0	0	3	0	0	34	0
own goal			2								
Totals	**418**	**98**	**43**	**44**	**12**	**11**	**66**	**17**	**13**	**528**	**127**

re still in bottom place but managed to beat Barnsley 3–0
home in the FA Cup. A 5–0 defeat at Newcastle was not
od preparation for the next round of the FA Cup but the
m responded and Nottingham Forest were beaten 3–2,
h Victor Obinna scoring a hat-trick. The League Cup
ni-final paired the Hammers with Birmingham City and
st Ham won the home leg 2–1. New recruits in the
nsfer window were forwards Demba Ba and Robbie
ane, midfielder Gary O'Neil and full back Wayne Bridge.
e second leg of the League Cup semi-final was a huge
appointment, as after leading 1–0 at half-time the side
nceded three second-half goals and lost the tie 4–3 on
gregate.

ay to West Bromwich Albion the Hammers were losing
0 at half-time but in a spirited fightback two goals from
mba Ba and one from Carlton Cole earned them a 3–3
w. The new-found confidence was in evidence as Burnley
re beaten 5–1 at home in the FA Cup, and this was
lowed by league victories against Liverpool and Stoke
y. The FA Cup trail ended with a 2–1 defeat at Stoke in
quarter-final.

Five successive defeats followed and relegation seemed
inevitable. A trip to Wigan saw West Ham race into a 2–0
lead only to collapse to a 3–2 defeat, and this led to the
immediate sacking of manager Avram Grant. Relegation
was confirmed in a poor campaign that only yielded seven
league victories.

THOMAS HITZLSPERGER

The German midfielder began his career in 1999 with the Bayern Munich youth team.

In August 2000 he came to England and joined Aston Villa but only played in one game that season. The following year he was loaned out to Chesterfield, where he played five league games. Thomas spent five seasons at Villa Park, playing in 99 league games. While there he made his debut for Germany against Iran in 2004 and went on to play in 52 games for his country. He left on a free transfer in 2005 as he returned to Germany to join Stuttgart; he became a regular in the side and gained a championship medal when Stuttgart won the Bundesliga in 2007. After scoring 28 goals in 160 appearances he left and had a spell in 2010 playing six games for Lazio.

He then came to England in June 2010 to sign for West Ham but due to an injury he did not make his debut until February 2011 against Burnley in the FA Cup. He scored on his debut and as his nickname was 'Der Hammer' he soon became a favourite with the Hammers fans. He played in 13 matches that season but when West Ham were relegated he was released and signed for Wolfsburg. He played in only six games for the German side before having another spell in England, playing in nine games for Everton before retiring in September 2013.

rclays Premier League
nal Table 2010-11

	P	HOME					AWAY					Pts
		W	D	L	F	A	W	D	L	F	A	
nchester United	38	18	1	0	49	12	5	10	4	29	25	80
lsea	38	14	3	2	39	13	7	5	7	30	20	71
nchester City	38	13	4	2	34	12	8	4	7	26	21	71
enal	38	11	4	4	33	15	8	7	4	39	28	68
enham Hotspur	38	9	9	1	30	19	7	5	7	25	27	62
erpool	38	12	4	3	37	14	5	3	11	22	30	58
rton	38	9	7	3	31	23	4	8	7	20	22	54
ham	38	8	7	4	30	23	3	9	7	19	20	49
on Villa	38	8	7	4	26	19	4	5	10	22	40	48
derland	38	7	5	7	25	27	5	6	8	20	29	47
st Bromwich Albion	38	8	6	5	30	30	4	5	10	26	41	47
wcastle United	38	6	8	5	41	27	5	5	9	15	30	46
ke City	38	10	4	5	31	18	3	3	13	15	30	46
ton Wanderers	38	10	5	4	34	24	2	5	12	18	32	46
ckburn Rovers	38	7	7	5	22	16	4	3	12	24	43	43
gan Athletic	38	5	8	6	22	34	4	7	8	18	27	42
verhampton Wanderers	38	8	4	7	30	30	3	3	13	16	36	40
mingham City	38	6	8	5	19	22	2	7	10	18	36	39
ckpool	38	5	5	9	30	37	5	4	10	25	41	39
st Ham United	38	5	5	9	24	31	2	7	10	19	39	33

Season 2010-11 Barclays Premier League
Match Details

Manager **Avram Grant** (to May 15); Caretaker Manager **Kevin Keen** (May 22)
Final League Position **20/20 Relegated to npower Championship**

	Date		Competition	Venue	Opponents	Results		Attendance	Position	Scorers
1	Aug 14	Sat	Prem	A	Aston Villa	L	0-3	36,604	18	
2	Aug 21	Sat	Prem	H	Bolton Wanderers	L	1-3	32,533	19	Noble [pen]
3	Aug 24	Tue	FLC 2	H	Oxford United	W	1-0	20,902		Parker
4	Aug 28	Sat	Prem	A	Manchester United	L	0-3	75,061	20	
5	Sep 11	Sat	Prem	H	Chelsea	L	1-3	33,014	20	Parker
6	Sep 18	Sat	Prem	A	Stoke City	D	1-1	27,028	20	Parker
7	Sep 21	Tue	FLC 3	A	Sunderland	W	2-1	21,907		Obinna, Piquionne
8	Sep 25	Sat	Prem	H	Tottenham Hotspur	W	1-0	34,190	19	Piquionne
9	Oct 2	Sat	Prem	H	Fulham	D	1-1	34,589	20	Piquionne
10	Oct 16	Sat	Prem	A	Wolverhampton Wanderers	D	1-1	28,582	20	Noble [pen]
11	Oct 23	Sat	Prem	H	Newcastle United	L	1-2	34,486	20	Cole
12	Oct 27	Wed	FLC 4	H	Stoke City	W	3-1*	25,304		Da Costa, Obinna, Parker
13	Oct 30	Sat	Prem	A	Arsenal	L	0-1	60,086	20	
14	Nov 6	Sat	Prem	A	Birmingham City	D	2-2	26,474	20	Behrami, Piquionne
15	Nov 10	Wed	Prem	H	West Bromwich Albion	D	2-2	33,023	20	Parker, Piquionne [pen]
16	Nov 13	Sat	Prem	H	Blackpool	D	0-0	31,194	20	
17	Nov 20	Sat	Prem	A	Liverpool	L	0-3	43,024	20	
18	Nov 27	Sat	Prem	H	Wigan Athletic	W	3-1	34,178	20	Behrami, Obinna, Parker
19	Nov 30	Tue	FLC QF	H	Manchester United	W	4-0	33,551		Cole 2, Spector 2
20	Dec 5	Sun	Prem	A	Sunderland	L	0-1	36,940	20	
21	Dec 11	Sat	Prem	H	Manchester City	L	1-3	32,813	20	Tomkins
22	Dec 18	Sat	Prem	A	Blackburn Rovers	D	1-1	21,934	20	Stanislas
23	Dec 26	Sun	Prem	A	Fulham	W	3-1	25,332	19	Cole 2, Piquionne
24	Dec 28	Tue	Prem	H	Everton	D	1-1	33,422	19	Hibbert (og)
25	Jan 1	Sat	Prem	H	Wolverhampton Wanderers	W	2-0	33,500	15	Sears, Zubar (og)
26	Jan 5	Wed	Prem	A	Newcastle United	L	0-5	42,387	20	
27	Jan 8	Sat	FAC 3	H	Barnsley	W	2-0	24,881		Piquionne, Spector
28	Jan 11	Tue	FLC SF:1	H	Birmingham City	W	2-1	34,753		Cole, Noble
29	Jan 15	Sat	Prem	H	Arsenal	L	0-3	32,682	20	
30	Jan 22	Sat	Prem	A	Everton	D	2-2	34,179	20	Piquionne, Spector
31	Jan 26	Wed	FLC SF:2	A	Birmingham City	L	1-3	27,519		Cole
32	Jan 30	Sun	FAC 4	H	Nottingham Forest	W	3-2	29,287		Obinna 3 [1 pen]
33	Feb 2	Wed	Prem	A	Blackpool	W	3-1	15,095	18	Obinna 2, Keane
34	Feb 6	Sun	Prem	H	Birmingham City	L	0-1	32,927	20	
35	Feb 12	Sat	Prem	A	West Bromwich Albion	D	3-3	23,916	19	Ba 2, Cole
36	Feb 21	Mon	FAC 5	H	Burnley	W	5-1	24,488		Cole 2, Hitzlsperger, Reid, Sears
37	Feb 27	Sun	Prem	H	Liverpool	W	3-1	34,941	18	Ba, Cole, Parker
38	Mar 5	Sat	Prem	H	Stoke City	W	3-0	33,066	17	Ba, Da Costa, Hitzlsperger
39	Mar 13	Sun	FAC 6	A	Stoke City	L	1-2	24,550		Piquionne
40	Mar 19	Sat	Prem	A	Tottenham Hotspur	D	0-0	36,010	17	
41	Apr 2	Sat	Prem	H	Manchester United	L	2-4	34,546	18	Noble 2 [2 pens]
42	Apr 9	Sat	Prem	A	Bolton Wanderers	L	0-3	25,857	18	
43	Apr 16	Sat	Prem	H	Aston Villa	L	1-2	34,672	19	Keane
44	Apr 23	Sat	Prem	A	Chelsea	L	0-3	41,656	20	
45	May 1	Sun	Prem	H	Manchester City	L	1-2	44,511	20	Ba
46	May 7	Sat	Prem	H	Blackburn Rovers	D	1-1	33,789	20	Hitzlsperger
47	May 15	Sun	Prem	A	Wigan Athletic	L	2-3	22,043	20	Ba 2
48	May 22	Sun	Prem	H	Sunderland	L	0-3	32,792	20	

* After extra time (1-1 after 90 minutes)

eam Line-Ups

BARRERA Pablo	BEHRAMI Valon	BEN-HAIM Tal	BOA MORTE Luis	BOFFIN Ruud	BRIDGE Wayne	COLE Carlton	COLLISON Jack	DA COSTA Manuel	DIAMANTI Alessandro	DYER Kieron	EDGAR Anthony	FAUBERT Julien	GABBIDON Daniel	GREEN Robert	HINES Zavon	HITZLSPERGER Thomas	ILUNGA Herita	JACOBSEN Lars	KEANE Robbie	KOVAC Radoslav	McCARTHY Benni	NOBLE Mark	NOUBLE Frank	O'NEIL Gary	OBINNA Victor	PARKER Scott	PIQUIONNE Frederic	REID Winston	SEARS Freddie	SPECTOR Jonathan	SPENCE Jordan	STANISLAS Junior	STECH Marek	TOMKINS James	UPSON Matthew	ZAMORA Bobby	
a			13/a			9					c	20		1		23			14/b			16				8	b			2				5/c	15		1
12						9/c				7/b		20	4	1		23					b	16				8	30	a	c						15/a	c	2
12		3				a						20									b	16				8	30			19/b	18	25/a		29	5	b	3
a			13/c			9				7/b		20/a	4	1		23						16				8	b	c			18				15	b	4
	21/b	3	13/a			9								1		23	37					16			33	8		b							15	25/a	5
	21/a	b				9	22						4	1			37		a			16			33/b	8	30								15	25	6
12/c		3	13			b	22			a		20							14		c				33/a	8	30/b					29		5		a	7
a			13			b	22			7/a			4	1			37				c	16			33/c	8	30/b								15	a	8
12/a			13			a	22						4	1			37					16			33	8	30								15	b	9
		3	13			a	22			7/a			4	1			37					16			33	8	30									25/a	10
c	21/c					9	22						4	1		a	37				b	16			33	8	30/b								15/a		11
12	b	3	13/b			9	22					20							14/a	17/c	c		a			8						29		5			12
c	21/c		13			a	22			b			4	1		23	37					16			33/b	8	30/a										13
	21		13/a			9	a						4	1		23	37		b						33/c	8	30								15	b	14
12/c			13/a			9/b				7			4	1		23	37		a		c		b			8	30								15	b	15
a			13/b			b				7/a			4	1		23	37		c			16			33	8	30/c								15	25/a	16
a			13			9/b							4	1		23/c	37		14		b	16			33/a		30							c	15	25/c	17
12	21					b							4	1			37/a		c						33	8/c	30/b	a				25		5	15	25/b	18
12/b		3	13			9/c						20		1	b				14						33			a			18	c		5/a	15	25	19
	3/c		13/a			9				7/b	c		4	1		a									33	8		b			18			5	15	25	20
12/b		3				b				a		20		1	c										33	8	30/c				18	25/a		5	15	a	21
12/a		3	13		31	b				7/c			4								c					8	30				18/b	a		5	15		22
		3				9							4	1					14		a					8	30/a			19		25		5	15	a	23
			13			9						20		1	c	23/a			14						33/c	8	30/b			19	a			5	15	25/c	24
		3				9							4	1					14		a					8	30			19		25/a		5	15	25/b	25
a		3				9							4	1	c				14/b			16/c	b			8	30/a			19				5	15	25/a	26
12			13								c	20		1	26/c							16		24/b	33/a	a		b		2	18	c		5/a	15	25/b	27
a												20		1	b						c	16/c			33	8	30/a	2		19/b	18			5	15	25/b	28
b	a			36/c		9						20		1	26				14			16/a	c							19/b	18			5	15	25/a	29
			13	36								20		1	26/a							16				8	30	b	a/b		18			5	15	c	30
			13/b	36		9	a					20		1	26/a						c	16	b			8					18/c			5	15	a	31
12/c	a												4	1	c	23	37		14			16/a	b		33		30/b	2		19	a						32
	b			36								4/a		1			37	34/c	c			16		32	33/b	8	30	a								5	33
				36		b	a							1			37	34/c				16		32	33	8	30/b	2							15/a	c	34
			13/a	36		9	22							1			37					16		32/b		8	a	2		b						25	35
a				36		9/b								1	11/a		37					16				8	c	2		19	b			5		c	36
				36		b								1	11		37					16		32		8	30/a	a						5	15	a	37
				36		9/b	22				c			1	11							16	a	b		8/c	30							5	15	b	38
				36		9	22						c	1	11		b					16/c			33/b	8	30/a	a						5	15	b	39
				36		9/a	22							1	11		37					16		32	a	8									15	b	40
				36		9/a	22							1	11		37		b			16/b		32/c	c	8	a								15	25/a	41
				36		a	22							1	11		b	34				16				8/c	30/a	c						5	15/b	b	42
				36		9	22/a						a	1	11		37	34	b			16		32/c	33/b										15	a	43
				36		9/b	22						4	1	11		37		a			16/a			c			b		19/c	18					25	44
			13/c			b	a						4	1	11		37	34/b							c					19	18			5	15/a	25/b	45
			13/a	36		9	b						4	1	11		37/c		a						c					19/b	18						46
				36	b	10/c							4	1	26		11		c						a		30/b				18/a	27		5		25	47
			13/c	36		10							4	1	26/b		11		a			b			c		30			19		27		5/a		a	48

2011-12
Story of the season

Sam Allardyce was appointed as the new manager and his first signings were four of his old Bolton players, midfielders Kevin Nolan and Matt Taylor, together with defenders Joey O'Brien and Abdoulaye Faye. **The aim this season was to gain promotion at the first attempt,** so it was a shock to lose 1–0 in the opening home game against Cardiff City.

The side then bounced back with successive away w at Doncaster Rovers and Watford. The League Cup brou another setback when League Two side Aldershot came the Boleyn Ground and won 2–1.

There were further signings with the acquisition forwards John Carew, David Bentley and Sam Bald together with midfielder Henri Lansbury and full-back G Demel. Leaving West Ham – to the dismay of the fan: was Scott Parker, who joined rivals Tottenham Hotsp The side started to adjust to life in the Championship a the goals began to flow. A 4–1 win at Nottingham For

Appearances & Goals 2011-12

	League			FA Cup			League Cup			Other			Total	
	Starts	Subs	Goals	Starts	Subs	Goals	Starts	Subs	Goals	Starts	Subs	Goals	Starts	Subs
ALMUNIA Manuel	4	0	0	0	0	0	0	0	0	0	0	0	4	0
BALDOCK Sam	10	13	5	1	0	0	0	0	0	0	0	0	11	13
BARRERA Pablo	0	1	0	0	0	0	1	0	0	0	0	0	1	1
BENTLEY David	2	3	0	0	0	0	0	0	0	0	0	0	2	3
BOFFIN Ruud	0	0	0	1	0	0	1	0	0	0	0	0	2	0
CAREW John	7	12	2	0	0	0	1	0	0	0	0	0	9	12
COLE Carlton	28	12	14	0	0	0	0	0	0	3	0	1	31	12
COLLINS Danny	4	7	1	0	0	0	0	0	0	0	0	0	4	7
COLLISON Jack	26	5	4	1	0	0	0	0	0	3	0	2	30	5
DEMEL Guy	7	0	0	0	0	0	0	0	0	3	0	0	10	0
DIOP Papa Bouba	14	2	1	0	0	0	0	0	0	0	0	0	14	2
FAUBERT Julien	28	6	1	0	0	0	1	0	0	0	2	0	29	8
FAYE Abdoulaye	25	4	0	0	0	0	0	0	0	0	0	0	25	4
GREEN Robert	42	0	0	0	0	0	0	0	0	3	0	0	45	0
HALL Robert	0	3	0	0	1	0	0	0	0	0	0	0	0	4
ILUNGA Herita	4	0	0	0	0	0	0	1	0	0	0	0	4	1
LANSBURY Henri	13	9	1	1	0	0	0	0	0	0	1	0	14	10
MAYNARD Nicky	9	5	2	0	0	0	0	0	0	0	2	1	9	7
McCARTNEY George	36	2	1	1	0	0	1	0	0	0	3	0	38	5
McNAUGHTON Callum	0	0	0	0	0	0	1	0	0	0	0	0	1	0
MONTENEGRO Brian	0	0	0	0	1	0	0	0	0	0	0	0	0	1
MORRISON Ravel	0	1	0	0	0	0	0	0	0	0	0	0	0	1
NOBLE Mark	43	2	8	0	0	0	0	0	0	3	0	0	46	2
NOLAN Kevin	42	0	12	0	0	0	1	0	0	3	0	1	46	0
NOUBLE Frank	1	2	1	0	1	0	0	1	0	0	0	0	1	4
O'BRIEN Joey	27	5	1	1	0	0	0	0	0	0	0	0	28	5
O'NEIL Gary	9	7	2	1	0	0	0	0	0	3	0	0	13	7
PARKER Scott	4	0	1	0	0	0	0	0	0	0	0	0	4	0
PIQUIONNE Frederic	8	12	2	0	0	0	1	0	0	0	0	0	9	12
POTTS Daniel	3	0	0	1	0	0	0	0	0	0	0	0	4	0
REID Winston	27	1	3	1	0	0	1	0	0	3	0	0	32	1
SEARS Freddie	2	8	0	1	0	0	1	0	0	0	0	0	4	8
STANISLAS Junior	0	1	0	0	0	0	1	0	1	0	0	0	1	1
TAYLOR Matthew	26	2	1	0	0	0	0	1	0	3	0	0	29	3
TOMKINS James	42	2	4	0	0	0	0	0	0	3	0	0	45	2
VAZ TE Ricardo	13	2	10	0	0	0	0	0	0	3	0	2	16	2
own goal			4											
Totals	506	129	81	11	3	0	11	3	1	33	8	7	561	143

s followed by a 4–3 home victory against Portsmouth. ...n Baldock scored twice in the 4–0 thrashing of Blackpool ...the side moved into second place. The good form ...ntinued through November with four successive victories ...d despite three defeats in December the Hammers went ...o the New Year in second place.

...st Ham fielded a weakened side at Sheffield Wednesday ...the FA Cup and lost 1–0 to the League One side. Two ...re league games were won before the Hammers slumped ...their worst defeat of the season in losing 5–1 away to ...wich Town. This was a wake-up call, and the Hammers ...ponded by going on an 11-game unbeaten run, including ...tories against Millwall and Blackpool playing with ten ...n. Going into April the side were on top form, beating ...rnsley 4–0 away and Brighton 6–0 at home, where Vaz Te ...red a hat trick.

...ishing in third place, they qualified to play Cardiff City

in the playoffs. Two goals from Jack Collison at Cardiff saw the Hammers win 2–0 in the first leg. Back at home in the second leg the Hammers cruised to a 3–0 victory and now looked forward to the playoff final with Blackpool at Wembley. Promotion to the Premier League was achieved as goals from Cole and Vaz Te gave the Hammers a 2–1 win before their 40,000 delirious fans. The pride was back at West Ham as they prepared for a return to the big time.

JACK COLLISON

As a youth the Welsh midfielder had spells at Peterborough and Cambridge United before joining the youth academy at West Ham in 2005.

He continued with his development and was given his first-team debut at Arsenal in January 2008. Later in May he was awarded his first international cap when selected by Wales for their game in Iceland. While with the Hammers he represented his country on 17 occasions. In May 2009 at Wigan he dislocated his kneecap and was ruled out for six weeks. Throughout the 2009–10 season he was still having problems with his knee and in May 2010 it was announced that he undergone knee surgery and would be out of action for a considerable time. After being out for 14 months he returned for the 2011/12 season, where he helped the Hammers to qualify for the playoffs. In the playoff semi-final first leg against Cardiff City he scored both goals in the 2–0 victory and was on target again in the 3–0 home win in the second leg. The following season back in the Premier League he only played in 10 league games and as the season ended he was released by the club after scoring 12 goals in 118 appearances. As he searched for a new club he had loan spells at Bournemouth, Wigan, Ipswich and Queens Park Rangers. As of 2015, Jack has joined Peterborough.

...power Championship
...nal Table 2011-12

	P	W	D	L	F	A	W	D	L	F	A	Pts
			HOME					AWAY				
...ding	46	14	5	4	36	18	13	3	7	33	23	89
...thampton	46	16	4	3	49	18	10	6	7	36	28	88
...st Ham United	46	11	8	4	41	26	13	6	4	40	22	86
...ningham City	46	13	9	1	37	14	7	7	9	41	37	76
...ckpool	46	13	7	3	42	21	7	8	8	37	38	75
...diff City	46	11	7	5	37	29	8	11	4	29	24	75
...dlesbrough	46	8	10	5	22	21	10	6	7	30	30	70
...l City	46	12	4	7	28	22	7	7	9	19	22	68
...cester City	46	11	6	6	36	22	7	6	10	30	33	66
...hton and Hove Albion	46	11	8	4	36	21	6	7	10	16	31	66
...ford	46	10	6	7	32	33	6	10	7	24	31	64
...by County	46	11	4	8	28	23	7	6	10	22	35	64
...nley	46	7	9	7	33	27	10	2	11	28	31	62
...ds United	46	9	3	11	34	41	8	7	8	31	27	61
...wich Town	46	11	3	9	39	32	6	7	10	30	45	61
...lwall	46	7	7	9	27	30	8	5	10	28	27	57
...stal Palace	46	7	11	5	22	19	6	6	11	24	32	56
...erborough United	46	10	3	10	41	38	3	6	12	26	39	50
...tingham Forest	46	6	5	12	21	32	8	3	12	27	31	50
...stol City	46	7	6	10	26	32	5	7	11	18	36	49
...nsley	46	9	4	10	31	37	4	5	14	18	37	48
...tsmouth	46	10	5	8	30	24	3	6	14	20	35	40
...ventry City	46	8	7	8	28	26	1	6	16	13	39	40
...ncaster Rovers	46	4	8	11	22	35	4	4	15	21	45	36

Season **2011-12** npower Championship
Match Details

Manager **Sam Allardyce**   Final League Position **3/24 Promoted to Barclays Premier League via Play-**

	Date		Competition	Venue	Opponents	Results		Attendance	Position	Scorers
1	Aug 7	Sun	Champ	H	Cardiff City	L	0-1	25,680	22	
2	Aug 13	Sat	Champ	A	Doncaster Rovers	W	1-0	11,344	13	Nolan
3	Aug 16	Tue	Champ	A	Watford	W	4-0	14,747	3	Tomkins, O'Brien, Cole, Parker
4	Aug 21	Sun	Champ	H	Leeds United	D	2-2	28,252	7	Cole, Kisnorbo (og)
5	Aug 24	Wed	FLC 1	H	Aldershot Town	L	1-2	19,879		Stanislas
6	Aug 28	Sun	Champ	A	Nottingham Forest	W	4-1	21,379	5	Nolan, Cole, Reid, Chambers (og)
7	Sep 10	Sat	Champ	H	Portsmouth	W	4-3	33,465	4	Taylor, Lansbury, Noble [pen], Cole
8	Sep 17	Sat	Champ	A	Millwall	D	0-0	16,078	5	
9	Sep 24	Sat	Champ	H	Peterborough United	W	1-0	29,895	4	Noble [pen]
10	Sep 27	Tue	Champ	H	Ipswich Town	L	0-1	27,709	4	
11	Oct 1	Sat	Champ	A	Crystal Palace	D	2-2	20,074	4	Nolan, Carew
12	Oct 15	Sat	Champ	H	Blackpool	W	4-0	31,448	2	Carew, Baldock 2, Collison
13	Oct 18	Tue	Champ	A	Southampton	L	0-1	32,152	2	
14	Oct 24	Mon	Champ	A	Brighton & Hove Albion	W	1-0	20,686	2	Nolan
15	Oct 29	Sat	Champ	H	Leicester City	W	3-2	30,410	2	Baldock 2, Faubert
16	Nov 1	Tue	Champ	H	Bristol City	D	0-0	27,980	2	
17	Nov 5	Sat	Champ	A	Hull City	W	2-0	21,756	2	Baldock, Collison
18	Nov 19	Sat	Champ	A	Coventry City	W	2-1	20,524	2	Cole, Piquionne
19	Nov 26	Sat	Champ	H	Derby County	W	3-1	27,864	2	Cole, Nolan, Noble [pen]
20	Nov 29	Tue	Champ	A	Middlesbrough	W	2-0	18,457	2	Piquionne, Cole
21	Dec 3	Sat	Champ	H	Burnley	L	1-2	26,274	2	Nolan
22	Dec 10	Sat	Champ	A	Reading	L	0-3	24,026	2	
23	Dec 17	Sat	Champ	H	Barnsley	W	1-0	34,749	2	Diop
24	Dec 26	Mon	Champ	A	Birmingham City	D	1-1	20,214	2	Cole
25	Dec 31	Sat	Champ	A	Derby County	L	1-2	28,067	3	Nouble
26	Jan 2	Mon	Champ	H	Coventry City	W	1-0	34,936	2	Nolan
27	Jan 8	Sun	FAC 3	A	Sheffield Wednesday	L	0-1	17,916		
28	Jan 14	Sat	Champ	A	Portsmouth	W	1-0	18,492	2	Noble [pen]
29	Jan 21	Sat	Champ	H	Nottingham Forest	W	2-1	31,718	1	Noble [2 pen]
30	Jan 31	Tue	Champ	A	Ipswich Town	L	1-5	22,185	1	Collison
31	Feb 4	Sat	Champ	H	Millwall	W	2-1	27,774	1	Cole, Reid
32	Feb 14	Tue	Champ	H	Southampton	D	1-1	32,875	1	Noble [pen]
33	Feb 21	Tue	Champ	A	Blackpool	W	4-1	13,043	1	Tomkins, Maynard, O'Neil, Vaz Te
34	Feb 25	Sat	Champ	H	Crystal Palace	D	0-0	34,900	2	
35	Mar 4	Sun	Champ	A	Cardiff City	W	2-0	23,872	2	Nolan, McCartney
36	Mar 7	Wed	Champ	H	Watford	D	1-1	31,674	2	Vaz Te
37	Mar 10	Sat	Champ	H	Doncaster Rovers	D	1-1	34,650	2	Nolan
38	Mar 17	Sat	Champ	A	Leeds United	D	1-1	33,366	3	Collins
39	Mar 20	Tue	Champ	H	Middlesbrough	D	1-1	27,250	3	Faye
40	Mar 24	Sat	Champ	A	Burnley	D	2-2	15,246	3	Nolan, Tomkins
41	Mar 27	Tue	Champ	A	Peterborough United	W	2-0	13,517	3	Vaz Te, O'Neil
42	Mar 31	Sat	Champ	H	Reading	L	2-4	33,350	3	Cole, Vaz Te
43	Apr 6	Fri	Champ	A	Barnsley	W	4-0	11,151	3	Nolan, Maynard, Noble, Vaz Te
44	Apr 9	Mon	Champ	H	Birmingham City	D	3-3	31,045	3	Vaz Te 2 [1 pen], Cole
45	Apr 14	Sat	Champ	H	Brighton & Hove Albion	W	6-0	32,339	3	Vaz Te 3, Nolan, Cole, Dicker (og)
46	Apr 17	Tue	Champ	A	Bristol City	D	1-1	16,669	3	Tomkins
47	Apr 23	Mon	Champ	A	Leicester City	W	2-1	23,172	3	Reid, Collison
48	Apr 28	Sat	Champ	H	Hull City	W	2-1	35,000	3	Cole 2
49	May 3	Thur	PO SF:1	A	Cardiff City	W	2-0	23,029		Collison 2
50	May 7	Mon	PO SF:2	H	Cardiff City	W	3-0	34,682		Nolan, Vaz Te, Maynard
51	May 19	Sat	PO F	N*	Blackpool	W	2-1	78,523		Cole, Vaz Te

* Played at Wembley Stadium, London

eam Line-Ups

BALDOCK Sam	BARRERA Pablo	BENTLEY David	BOFFIN Ruud	CAREW John	COLE Carlton	COLLINS Danny	COLLISON Jack	DEMEL Guy	DIOP Papa Bouba	FAUBERT Julien	FAYE Abdoulaye	GREEN Robert	HALL Robert	ILUNGA Herita	LANSBURY Henri	MAYNARD Nicky	McCARTNEY George	McNAUGHTON Callum	MONTENEGRO Brian	MORRISON Ravel	NOBLE Mark	NOLAN Kevin	NOUBLE Frank	O'BRIEN Joey	O'NEIL Gary	PARKER Scott	PIQUIONNE Frederic	POTTS Daniel	REID Winston	SEARS Freddie	STANISLAS Junior	TAYLOR Matthew	TOMKINS James	VAZ TE Ricardo	No.
c					b		a					1	23								16/a	4		17		8	30/b		2		19/c	14	5		1
					a		10/b					1	23/c								16	4		17		8	30/a		2	b	c	14	5		2
					9/b		10/c		c	a		1	23								16	4		17		8	b		2			14	5/a		3
			b		9/b		10/a			a		1	23								16/c	4		17		8	c		2			14	5		4
12/b		31		11/a						18				a			3	37				4		c			30/c		2	19	25	b	5		5
					9/a		10/b			18	b	1					3				16	4		17			a		2			14	5		6
	a				9/b					18/a		1			22		3				16	4		17			b		2			14	5		7
c	b				9					18	15	1			22/c		3				16	4		17			a					14/b	5/a		8
	b				9/a	a				18/b	15	1			22		3				16	4		17					2			14/c	c		9
7	8/c				9/a	a			b	c	15	1			22/b		3				16/c	4		17									5		10
b	8/c			a	9/b		10/a		21	18	15				22		3					4				c							5		11
7						11/c	10		21	18	a						3				c	4							2	b		14/b	5/a		12
7						11/c			21/b	18	15				22		3				b	4		c	a				2			14/a			13
c						11/b	10		21/a	18/c	15						3				16	4		17			b		2	a		14			14
7/c						11/a	10			18	15/b	1					3				16	4		17			a		2	c		b			15
7/b						b			c	18	a	1					3				16	4		17			30		2/a		19/c		5		16
7/c						10/a	a	10	21/b	18	15	1					3				16	4		17	c		b						5		17
7/c						10/a	a	10	21/b	18	15	1					3				16	4		17	c		b						5		18
7/a			b		9/b		10/a			18/c	15	1					3				16	4		17			a					c	5		19
	a							20/b	21	18	15	1					3				16	4		b			30/a					14	5		20
	a				9		10			18	15	1					3				16	4		17/a			b					14/b	5		21
					c	b	10	20/a	21/b	18	15	1					3				16	4		a			30/c						5		22
				11/a	9				21	18/b		1			b						16	4					30	48		a			5		23
			b		9/b				21	18/c		1			a						16	4		17			30/a	48					5		24
b						a			21/c			1		c	22						16		24	17	32/a		30/b	48	2				5		25
7/a					9/b		10		21	18		1					3				16	4		a	b				2				5		26
7		31		11/a			10							b	22		3				c	a		17	32/c			48	2	19/b					27
					9		10		21	18/a		1			a		3				16	4		17					2				5		28
7/b					9/c		10		21/a	18		1	b		a		3				16	4			c				2				5		29
a					9/c		10			18		1	b		22		3				16/a	4			c				2			14/b	5		30
					9/c		10/a			18/b	15	1					3				16	4		17			b		2		a		5	c	31
					9/b		10/a			18	15	1			b		a				16			17	c				2			14	5	12/c	32
						c	10			18/a	15/b	1			a	8/c	3				16			17			b		2				5	12	33
c						a	10			18/a	15	1				8/c	3				16			17			b		2				5	12/b	34
						a	10				15	1			22/b	8/a	3				16	4		17			b						5	12	35
a					9					18	15	1			b	8/a	3				16	4		17/b								14/c	5	c	36
a					9	c	10				15	1			22/b		3				16	4/c		b								14	5	12/a	37
					b	25	10/c				15	1				8/b	3		c		16	4		17			a		2			14	5/a		38
c				a	9/a	25	b				15	1				8/b	3				16/c	4		17								14/b	5		39
a				c	9/a	25	10/c					1			b		3				16	4		17	32							14/b	5		40
					9	b			a		15/b	1				c	3				16	4		17/a	32/c							14		12	41
b					9/c	a				18	15	1				c	3				16/a	4			32							14/b		12	42
						a		20/a	c			1			b	8	3				16/c	4			32/b							14		12	43
c					9	a					15	1			b	8/b	3/a				16/c	4			32								5	12	44
c					9	b	a	20/b				1				8					16	4			32/a				2			14	5	12/c	45
					a	25/a	c	20/b	b			1			22	8/c					16	4							2			14	5	12/b	46
					9/b	b	10/c	20/a	a			1			c						16	4			32				2			14	5	12	47
a					9/a			20							22		b		c		16	4/c			32				2			14	5	12/b	48
					9		10/c	20/b				1			c	a					16	4			32				2			14	5	12/a	49
					9/c		10/a	20				1			a	c	b				16	4/b			32				2			14	5	12	51
					9		10	20/b	b			1			a						16	4			32/a				2			14	5	12	52

2012-13
Story of the season

Now back in the Premier League, **the squad was strengthened with the purchase of five new players.** Experienced goalkeeper Jussi Jaaskelainen was joined by French defender Alou Diarra. In midfield came the Senegal international Mohamed Diame and to complete the signings there was Malian forward Modibo Maiga and winger Matt Jarvis.

Aston Villa were beaten 1–0 at home on the opening da followed by a 3–0 reverse at Swansea City. The League Cu began with a 2–0 home win over Crewe Alexandra but poor showing in the next round saw Wigan win 4–1 Upton Park. Another two signings were made when strik Andy Carroll came from Liverpool on loan and midfielde Yossi Benayoun arrived from Chelsea for a second spell the club. During October and November there were mixe results, leaving the side in mid-table. The opening game

Appearances & Goals 2012-13

	League			FA Cup			League Cup			Total		
	Starts	Subs	Goals	Starts	Subs	Goals	Starts	Subs	Goals	Starts	Subs	
BENAYOUN Yossi	4	2	0	0	0	0	0	0	0	4	2	
CARROLL Andy	22	2	7	0	0	0	0	0	0	22	2	
CHAMAKH Marouane	2	1	0	0	0	0	0	0	0	2	1	
COLE Carlton	14	13	2	2	0	0	0	0	0	16	13	
COLE Joe	7	4	2	1	0	0	0	0	0	8	4	
COLLINS James	29	0	0	1	0	2	0	0	0	30	0	
COLLISON Jack	5	12	2	1	1	0	0	0	0	6	13	
DEMEL Guy	28	3	0	1	0	0	0	0	0	29	3	
DIAME Mohamed	31	2	3	1	0	0	0	0	0	32	2	
DIARRA Alou	1	2	0	2	0	0	1	0	0	4	2	
FANIMO Matthias	0	0	0	0	0	0	0	2	0	0	2	
HALL Robert	0	1	0	0	0	0	1	1	0	1	2	
HENDERSON Stephen	0	0	0	0	0	0	2	0	0	2	0	
JAASKELAINEN Jussi	38	0	0	2	0	0	0	0	0	40	0	
JARVIS Matthew	29	3	2	0	1	0	1	0	0	30	4	
LEE Elliot	0	0	0	0	1	0	0	0	0	0	1	
MAIGA Modibo	2	15	2	0	0	0	2	0	2	4	15	
MAYNARD Nicky	0	0	0	0	0	0	1	0	1	1	0	
McCARTNEY George	9	3	0	0	0	0	1	0	0	10	3	
MONCUR George	0	0	0	0	0	0	0	1	0	0	1	
NOBLE Mark	25	3	4	0	1	0	1	0	0	26	4	
NOLAN Kevin	35	0	10	1	1	0	1	0	0	37	1	
O'BRIEN Joey	32	1	2	0	0	0	1	0	0	33	1	
O'NEIL Gary	17	7	1	1	0	0	2	0	0	20	7	
POGATETZ Emanuel	1	5	0	0	0	0	0	0	0	1	5	
POTTS Daniel	1	1	0	2	0	0	2	0	0	5	1	
REID Winston	36	0	1	1	0	0	0	0	0	37	0	
SPENCE Jordan	0	4	0	1	0	0	2	0	0	3	4	
TAYLOR Matthew	14	14	1	1	1	0	1	1	0	16	16	
TOMBIDES Dylan	0	0	0	0	0	0	0	1	0	0	1	
TOMKINS James	18	8	1	2	0	0	1	0	0	21	8	
VAZ TE Ricardo	18	6	3	2	0	0	2	0	0	22	6	
own goal			2									
Totals	**418**	**112**	**45**	**22**	**6**	**2**	**22**	**6**	**3**	**462**	**124**	

ecember saw the Hammers put on a great second-half
splay as Chelsea were beaten 3–1 at home, but no other
n was recorded that month.

ter a 1–1 home draw with Manchester United in the FA
p the Hammers narrowly lost 1–0 in the replay. During
e transfer window West Ham snapped up former
vourite Joe Cole, which pleased the fans. In the league the
ammers were struggling after away defeats at Arsenal and
elsea as they dropped to thirteenth. They put on a
irited display at home to Tottenham but the Spurs won
2 after scoring in the last minute. March proved a better
onth, with a 1–0 victory at Stoke City and an excellent 3–1
me win over West Brom. Against the Albion Andy
rroll scored twice, showing his outstanding all-round
ility. Three draws and a 2–0 home win against Wigan in
ril saw the Hammers move up to tenth.

n the final day of the season club captain Kevin Nolan
ored a hat-trick in the 4–2 home win against Reading. In
eir first season back in the Premier League, all at Upton
rk were pleased with the tenth place finish.

rclays Premier League
inal Table 2012-13

ANDY CARROLL

He began his career at Newcastle United in 2006 and at the age of 17 made his debut in the UEFA Cup against Palermo.

Before establishing himself in the first team he spent six months on loan at Preston North End, playing in 11 league games. Back with Newcastle he continued to score goals on a regular basis and his 17 league goals in 2010 helped the Magpies to achieve promotion to the Premier League. He gained his first England international cap when selected to play against France at Wembley in 2010.

After scoring 33 goals in 91 appearances for Newcastle he left in January 2011 to join Liverpool. The fee of £35 million made him the most expensive British footballer of all time. In 2012 he won a League Cup winners' medal as Liverpool beat Cardiff in the final. That same year he scored in the FA Cup final in the 2–1 defeat to Chelsea. Carroll played in three seasons at Anfield, scoring 11 goals in 58 appearances, before coming to London to sign on loan for West Ham. He had an immediate effect, setting up two goals in the 3–0 home win against Fulham. In May 2013 the loan was made permanent for a club record fee of £15 million. In a pre-season tour prior to the 2014/15 season he suffered an ankle ligament injury which prevented him playing in the first 11 league games. After returning from injury he scored five goals in the next 14 league games. In February 2015 at Southampton he was injured again that forced him to miss the remainder of the campaign.

	P	HOME					AWAY					Pts
		W	D	L	F	A	W	D	L	F	A	
nchester United	38	16	0	3	45	19	12	5	2	41	24	89
nchester City	38	14	3	2	41	15	9	6	4	25	19	78
elsea	38	12	5	2	41	16	10	4	5	34	23	75
enal	38	11	5	3	47	23	10	5	4	25	14	73
tenham Hotspur	38	11	5	3	29	18	10	4	5	37	28	72
erton	38	12	6	1	33	17	4	9	6	22	23	63
erpool	38	9	6	4	33	16	7	7	5	38	27	61
st Bromwich Albion	38	9	4	6	32	25	5	3	11	21	32	49
ansea City	38	6	8	5	28	26	5	5	9	19	25	46
st Ham United	**38**	**9**	**6**	**4**	**34**	**22**	**3**	**4**	**12**	**11**	**31**	**46**
wich City	38	8	7	4	25	20	2	7	10	16	38	44
ham	38	7	3	9	28	30	4	7	8	22	30	43
ke City	38	7	7	5	21	22	2	8	9	13	23	42
uthampton	38	6	7	6	26	24	3	7	9	23	36	41
on Villa	38	5	5	9	23	28	5	6	8	24	41	41
wcastle United	38	9	1	9	24	31	2	7	10	21	37	41
nderland	38	5	8	6	20	19	4	4	11	21	35	39
gan Athletic	38	4	6	9	26	39	5	3	11	21	34	36
ading	38	4	8	7	23	33	2	2	15	20	40	28
eens Park Rangers	38	2	8	9	13	28	2	5	12	17	32	25

Season **2012-13** Barclays Premier League
Match Details

Manager **Sam Allardyce**   Final League Position: **10/20**

	Date		Competition	Venue	Opponents	Results		Attendance	Position	Scorers
1	Aug 18	Sat	Prem	H	Aston Villa	W	1-0	34,172	5	Nolan
2	Aug 25	Sat	Prem	A	Swansea City	L	0-3	20,424	10	
3	Aug 28	Tue	FLC 2	H	Crewe Alexandra	W	2-0	18,053		Maiga, Maynard
4	Sep 1	Sat	Prem	H	Fulham	W	3-0	33,458	6	Nolan, Reid, Taylor
5	Sep 15	Sat	Prem	A	Norwich City	D	0-0	26,806	7	
6	Sep 22	Sat	Prem	H	Sunderland	D	1-1	33,052	8	Nolan
7	Sep 25	Tue	FLC 3	H	Wigan Athletic	L	1-4	25,934		Maiga
8	Oct 1	Mon	Prem	A	Queens Park Rangers	W	2-1	17,363	7	Jarvis, Vaz Te
9	Oct 6	Sat	Prem	H	Arsenal	L	1-3	34,974	8	Diame
10	Oct 20	Sat	Prem	H	Southampton	W	4-1	34,925	6	Noble 2 [1 pen], Maiga, Nolan
11	Oct 27	Sat	Prem	A	Wigan Athletic	L	1-2	19,090	9	Tomkins
12	Nov 3	Sat	Prem	H	Manchester City	D	0-0	35,005	8	
13	Nov 11	Sun	Prem	A	Newcastle United	W	1-0	51,855	6	Nolan
14	Nov 19	Mon	Prem	H	Stoke City	D	1-1	35,005	7	O'Brien
15	Nov 25	Sun	Prem	A	Tottenham Hotspur	L	1-3	36,043	8	Carroll
16	Nov 28	Wed	Prem	A	Manchester United	L	0-1	75,572	10	
17	Dec 1	Sat	Prem	H	Chelsea	W	3-1	35,005	8	Cole, Diame, Maiga
18	Dec 9	Sun	Prem	H	Liverpool	L	2-3	35,005	11	Noble [pen], Gerrard (og)
19	Dec 16	Sun	Prem	A	West Bromwich Albion	D	0-0	24,186	11	
20	Dec 22	Sat	Prem	H	Everton	L	1-2	35,005	12	Cole C.
21	Dec 29	Sat	Prem	A	Reading	L	0-1	24,183	12	
22	Jan 1	Tue	Prem	H	Norwich City	W	2-1	35,005	11	Noble [pen], O'Brien
23	Jan 5	Sat	FAC 3	H	Manchester United	D	2-2	35,005		Collins 2
24	Jan 12	Sat	Prem	A	Sunderland	L	0-3	39,918	11	
25	Jan 16	Wed	FAC 3 Rep	A	Manchester United	L	0-1	71,081		
26	Jan 19	Sat	Prem	H	Queens Park Rangers	D	1-1	34,962	12	Cole J.
27	Jan 23	Wed	Prem	A	Arsenal	L	1-5	60,081	12	Collison
28	Jan 30	Wed	Prem	A	Fulham	L	1-3	24,791	13	Nolan
29	Feb 2	Sat	Prem	H	Swansea City	W	1-0	34,962	11	Carroll
30	Feb 10	Sun	Prem	A	Aston Villa	L	1-2	30,503	11	Westwood (og)
31	Feb 25	Mon	Prem	H	Tottenham Hotspur	L	2-3	35,005	14	Carroll [pen], Cole J.
32	Mar 2	Sat	Prem	A	Stoke City	W	1-0	22,690	12	Collison
33	Mar 17	Sun	Prem	A	Chelsea	L	0-2	41,639	14	
34	Mar 30	Sat	Prem	H	West Bromwich Albion	W	3-1	34,966	11	Carroll 2, O'Neil
35	Apr 7	Sun	Prem	A	Liverpool	D	0-0	45,007	12	
36	Apr 13	Sat	Prem	A	Southampton	D	1-1	31,984	12	Carroll
37	Apr 17	Wed	Prem	H	Manchester United	D	2-2	34,692	11	Diame, Vaz Te
38	Apr 20	Sat	Prem	H	Wigan Athletic	W	2-0	34,544	10	Jarvis, Nolan
39	Apr 27	Sat	Prem	A	Manchester City	L	1-2	47,189	10	Carroll
40	May 4	Sat	Prem	H	Newcastle United	D	0-0	34,962	10	
41	May 12	Sun	Prem	A	Everton	L	0-2	39,475	10	
42	May 19	Sun	Prem	H	Reading	W	4-2	34,973	10	Nolan 3, Vaz Te

Team Line-Ups

CARROLL Andy	CHAMAKH Marouane	COLE Carlton	COLE Joe	COLLINS James	COLLISON Jack	DEMEL Guy	DIAME Mohamed	DIARRA Alou	FANIMO Matthias	HALL Robert	HENDERSON Stephen	JAASKELAINEN Jussi	JARVIS Matthew	LEE Elliot	MAIGA Modibo	MAYNARD Nicky	McCARTNEY George	MONCUR George	NOBLE Mark	NOLAN Kevin	O'BRIEN Joey	O'NEIL Gary	POGATETZ Emanuel	POTTS Daniel	REID Winston	SPENCE Jordan	TAYLOR Matthew	TOMBIDES Dylan	TOMKINS James	VAZ TE Ricardo	
		9/c		19		20	21					1		c			3/a		16	4/b	a				2		14		b	12	1
		9/b		19		20	21/c	c				1	7	b			3		16	4					2				5/a	a	2
							a	23	46	b	13		7		11		3	8	c	4/c	17	32	33			27	14/a		5	12/b	3
8/b	b			19/a		20/c	21	c				1							16	4	17				2		14		a	12	4
		9/b		19		20	21					1	a				b		16	4	17				2		14/a			12/c	5
		9/c		19		20	21					1	b				c		16	4	17				2		14/a			12/b	6
							a	23	46		13		7		11		3		16/b			32/c	33			27	b	c	5	12/a	7
c		9/c		19		20	21					1	7	b					16	4	17/b				2/a	a				12	8
8		c		19		20/b	21/c					1	7				3		16	4					2	a			b	12/a	9
8/b				19			21/a					1	7	b			3		16	4	a				2	c			5/c		10
8	b			19			21/c					1	7	a			3		16/b	4	c				2				5		11
8/b	b			19/c			21/a					1	7	b			3		16	4	17	a			2	c			5		12
8					c		21					1	7/a	b			3/c		16	4	17	a			2				5		13
8/b	b	a					21					1			11/c		3		16	4	17/a	32			2	c			5		14
8		c					21					1	a		11/a		3		16	4/c	17	32/b			2	b			5		15
8/a	a			19		20	21/c					1	7/b				b			4	17	c			2		14		5		16
		9/c		19		20	a					1	7	c					16	4	17	32/a			2	b			5/b		17
		9		19		20/a	21/b					1	7	c	a				16	4	17				2		14/c		b		18
		9		19		20/b						1	7/a		a				16	4	17	32			2		14		b		19
		9		19	c							1	7/c		a				16	4	17/b	32/a			2	b	14		5		20
		9		19	a							1	7		c				16/c	4	17	32/b			2		14/a		5	b	21
		9		19	10	20						1	7/c	b					16		17/a	a			2	c	14		5	12/b	22
		9	26/c	19	10	20		23/b				1	a	b						4			33			c			5	12/a	23
c		9/c	26	19/a	10/b	20		23				1	7							4			33		2	a	b				24
		9/b	a				21/a	23				1		c			b					32	33		2	27	14		5	12/c	25
	29/a	a	26			20	21					1	7						16	4/b	17				2				5	b	26
		9			10/b	20	c	a				1							16	4	17	b			2/a		14		5	12/c	27
c	29/a	a	26/c			20/b						1	7						16	4	17				2	b			5		28
8			a				21/b					1	7/a						16	4/c	17	b	c		2		14		5	12	29
8		c	26			a	21					1							16/c	4	17/a	18			2		14/b		5	b	30
8			26	19	c	20/b	21/c					1	7							4/a	17	32	b		2	a					31
8			26/b	19	a	20	21					1	7/c								17	32			2		14/a		b		32
8		c		19/b	10	20	21/a					1	7								17	32			2	a	b			12/c	33
8				19	c	20/b	21/c					1	7		b					4/a	17	32			2	a				12	34
		9		19	a	20	21					1	7							4/b	17	32	c			b			5/c	12/a	35
8				19	a	20	21					1	7/a							4	17	32	b		2	c			5/b	12/c	36
8				19	b	20	21/b					1	7		a					4/c	17	32/a			2	c				12	37
8	b			19	c	20	21/c					1	7		a					4	17	32/a			2					12/b	38
8	b			19	a	20	21					1	7							4/c	17/b	32			2	c				12/a	39
8	c			19	a	20/b	21					1	7/c							4	17	32			2	b				12/a	40
8	a	b		19	10/b	20	21/a					1	7						c	4	17	32/c			2						41
8			26/a	19	a	20	21					1	b						16	4	17/c				2	c				12/b	42

2013-14
Story of the season

A good start was achieved with a **2–0 home win against Cardiff City,** followed up with a **2–1 home League Cup victory over Cheltenham Town.**
The mood dampened with **successive home defeats** to Stoke City and Everton and two goalless away draws.

Cardiff City were beaten 3–2 at home in the League Cup and, , rivals Tottenham Hotspur were beaten 3–0 in the league at White Hart Lane.

A tricky League Cup tie at Burnley saw the Hammers wi 2–0, but in the league they were struggling. After losing 3– at Norwich City in November the next eight games onl

Appearances & Goals 2013-14

	League			FA Cup			League Cup			Total		
	Starts	Subs	Goals	Starts	Subs	Goals	Starts	Subs	Goals	Starts	Subs	Goals
ADRIAN del CASTILLO	20	0	0	1	0	0	5	0	0	26	0	
ARMERO Pablo	3	2	0	0	0	0	0	0	0	3	2	
BORRIELLO Marco	0	2	0	0	0	0	0	0	0	0	2	
BURKE Reece	0	0	0	0	0	0	0	1	0	0	1	
CARROLL Andy	12	3	2	0	0	0	1	0	0	13	3	
CHAMBERS Leo	0	0	0	0	0	0	3	0	0	3	0	
COLE Carlton	9	17	6	0	0	0	2	2	0	11	19	
COLE Joe	6	14	3	0	0	0	5	0	0	11	14	
COLLINS James	22	2	1	0	0	0	2	0	0	24	2	
COLLISON Jack	6	4	0	0	0	0	3	2	1	9	6	
DEMEL Guy	30	2	1	0	0	0	1	0	0	31	2	
DIAME Mohamed	29	6	4	0	0	0	3	3	0	32	9	
DIARRA Alou	1	2	0	1	0	0	3	1	0	5	3	
DOWNING Stewart	29	3	1	1	0	0	1	3	0	31	6	
DRIVER Callum	0	0	0	1	0	0	0	0	0	1	0	
FANIMO Matthias	0	0	0	0	1	0	0	0	0	0	1	
JAASKELAINEN Jussi	18	0	0	0	0	0	1	0	0	19	0	
JARVIS Matthew	23	9	2	1	0	0	2	0	2	26	9	
JOHNSON Roger	2	2	0	0	0	0	2	0	0	4	2	
LEE Elliot	0	1	0	0	0	0	0	0	0	0	1	
LLETGET Sebastian	0	0	0	1	0	0	0	0	0	1	0	
MAIGA Modibo	11	3	1	1	0	0	3	1	1	15	4	
McCARTNEY George	20	2	0	0	0	0	4	0	0	24	2	
MONCUR George	0	0	0	1	0	0	0	0	0	1	0	
MORRISON Ravel	12	4	3	1	0	0	3	1	2	16	5	
NOBLE Mark	38	0	3	0	0	0	1	0	0	39	0	
NOCERINO Antonio	2	8	0	0	0	0	0	0	0	2	8	
NOLAN Kevin	33	0	7	0	0	0	1	1	0	34	1	
O'BRIEN Joey	13	4	0	0	0	0	3	0	0	16	4	
PETRIC Mladen	0	3	0	0	0	0	0	1	0	0	4	
POTTS Daniel	0	0	0	1	0	0	1	0	0	2	0	
RAT Razvan	11	4	0	0	0	0	3	2	0	14	6	
REID Winston	18	4	1	0	0	0	0	0	0	18	4	
RUDDOCK Pelly	0	0	0	0	0	0	1	0	0	1	0	
TAYLOR Matthew	16	4	0	0	0	0	6	0	1	22	4	
TOMKINS James	31	0	0	0	0	0	4	0	0	35	0	
TURGOTT Blair	0	0	0	0	1	0	0	0	0	0	1	
VAZ TE Ricardo	3	5	2	0	0	0	2	0	2	5	5	
WHITEHEAD Danny	0	0	0	1	0	0	0	0	0	1	0	
own goal						3						
Totals	418	110	40	11	2	0	66	18	9	495	130	

fielded one victory, the 3–0 home win against Fulham. There was joy, however, in the League Cup as another trip to Tottenham gave the Hammers a 2–1 victory and a place in the semi–finals.. Injuries to central defenders Collins and Tomkins and full-back Demel were causing concern..A weakened team was fielded at Nottingham Forest in the FA Cup as Sam Allardyce gave debuts to no fewer than five youth team players, which in hindsight was a disaster. The Hammers were overrun by the more experienced Forest side, who won 5–0.

A few days later came the trip to Manchester City in the League Cup semi-final first leg. A dispirited, weakened West Ham side were thrashed 6–0 by an in-form City team. The second leg at the Boleyn Ground was a formality, with City winning 3–0 to give them a record 9–0 aggregate victory. Alarm bells were ringing as the Hammers were in the bottom three at the end of January.

February, however, turned out to be a defining month as all four games were won.. Next came home wins against Norwich City and Southampton that lifted the side up to

tenth but April, with four defeats, was poor. The final home game was against Tottenham which brought a 2–0 victory. A finish of thirteenth was achieved in a campaign that had an unusual number of injuries to key players.

STEWART DOWNING

Downing began his career at Middlesbrough, where he made his debut at Ipswich Town in April 2002.

Initially he only played in a few games and in 2003 he was loaned out to Sunderland, where he made seven appearances. Back at Boro, the 2004/05 season saw him make 48 appearances playing as a left-winger. He was in the side that reached the UEFA Cup final where Middlesbrough lost 4–0 to Seville. In that season he gained the first of 35 England caps when coming on as a substitute against the Netherlands at Villa Park.

In 2008/09 Middlesbrough were relegated and Downing moved on to play for Aston Villa. In eight seasons at Boro he scored 22 goals in a total of 234 appearances. He spent two seasons at Villa Park, playing in 79 games, before Liverpool paid a fee of around £20 million for him in July 2011. In his first campaign he won a League Cup medal when Liverpool beat Cardiff City at Wembley. He was named as man of the match and was awarded the Alan Hardaker Trophy.

Downing scored seven goals in 91 outings before signing for West Ham in August 2013 for a fee reported to be £5 million. He made his debut on the opening day of the 2013/14 season when coming on as a substitute against Cardiff City at the Boleyn Ground. He became a regular in the side for two seasons playing in 79 games before joining Middlesborough in July 2015.

Barclays Premier League Final Table 2013-14

	P	HOME					AWAY					Pts
		W	D	L	F	A	W	D	L	F	A	
Manchester City	38	17	1	1	63	13	10	4	5	39	24	86
Liverpool	38	16	1	2	53	18	10	5	4	48	32	84
Chelsea	38	15	3	1	43	11	10	4	5	28	16	82
Arsenal	38	13	5	1	36	11	11	2	6	32	30	79
Everton	38	13	3	3	38	19	8	6	5	23	20	72
Tottenham Hotspur	38	11	3	5	30	23	10	3	6	25	28	69
Manchester United	38	9	3	7	29	21	10	4	5	35	22	64
Southampton	38	8	6	5	32	23	7	5	7	22	23	56
Stoke City	38	10	6	3	27	17	3	5	11	18	35	50
Newcastle United	38	8	3	8	23	28	7	1	11	20	31	49
Crystal Palace	38	8	5	6	18	23	5	3	11	15	25	45
Swansea City	38	6	5	8	33	26	5	4	10	21	28	42
West Ham United	**38**	**7**	**3**	**9**	**25**	**26**	**4**	**4**	**11**	**15**	**25**	**40**
Sunderland	38	5	3	11	21	27	5	5	9	20	33	38
Aston Villa	38	6	3	10	22	29	4	5	10	17	32	38
Hull City	38	7	4	8	20	21	3	3	13	18	32	37
West Bromwich Albion	38	4	9	6	24	27	3	6	10	19	32	36
Norwich City	38	6	6	7	17	18	2	3	14	11	44	33
Fulham	38	5	3	11	24	38	4	2	13	16	47	32
Cardiff City	38	5	5	9	20	35	2	4	13	12	39	30

Season **2013-14** Barclays Premier League
Match Details

Manager **Sam Allardyce**   Final League Position **12/20**

	Date		Competition	Venue	Opponents	Results		Attendance	Position	Scorers
1	Aug 17	Sat	Prem	H	Cardiif City	W	2-0	34,977	3	Cole J., Nolan
2	Aug 24	Sat	Prem	A	Newcastle United	D	0-0	49,622	3	
3	Aug 27	Tue	FLC 2	H	Cheltenham Town	W	2-1	23,440		Morrison, Vaz Te
4	Aug 31	Sat	Prem	H	Stoke City	L	0-1	34,946	7	
5	Sep 15	Sun	Prem	A	Southampton	D	0-0	28,794	10	
6	Sep 21	Sat	Prem	H	Everton	L	2-3	34,952	14	Morrison, Noble [pen]
7	Sep 24	Tue	FLC 3	H	Cardiff City	W	3-2	18,611		Jarvis, Morrison, Vaz Te
8	Sep 28	Sat	Prem	A	Hull City	L	0-1	24,291	17	
9	Oct 6	Sun	Prem	A	Tottenham Hotspur	W	3-0	35,977	13	Morrison, Reid, Vaz Te
10	Oct 19	Sat	Prem	H	Manchester City	L	1-3	34,507	14	Vaz Te
11	Oct 27	Sun	Prem	A	Swansea City	D	0-0	20,455	15	
12	Oct 29	Tue	FLC 4	A	Burnley	W	2-0	14,376		Collison [pen], Taylor [pen]
13	Nov 2	Sat	Prem	H	Aston Villa	D	0-0	34,977	14	
14	Nov 9	Sat	Prem	A	Norwich City	L	1-3	26,824	15	Morrison
15	Nov 23	Sat	Prem	H	Chelsea	L	0-3	34,977	17	
16	Nov 30	Sat	Prem	H	Fulham	W	3-0	34,946	15	Cole C., Cole J., Diame
17	Dec 3	Tue	Prem	A	Crystal Palace	L	0-1	23,891	15	
18	Dec 7	Sat	Prem	A	Liverpool	L	1-4	44,781	17	Skrtel (og)
19	Dec 14	Sat	Prem	H	Sunderland	D	0-0	31,843	17	
20	Dec 18	Wed	FLC QF	A	Tottenham Hotspur	W	2-1	34,080		Jarvis, Maiga
21	Dec 21	Sat	Prem	A	Manchester United	L	1-3	75,350	17	Cole C.
22	Dec 26	Thur	Prem	H	Arsenal	L	1-3	34,977	19	Cole C.
23	Dec 28	Sat	Prem	H	West Bromwich Albion	D	3-3	34,946	19	Cole J., Maiga, Nolan
24	Jan 1	Wed	Prem	A	Fulham	L	1-2	25,335	19	Diame
25	Jan 5	Sun	FAC 3	A	Nottingham Forest	L	0-5	14,397		
26	Jan 8	Wed	LC SF : 1	A	Manchester City	L	0-6	30,381		
27	Jan 11	Sat	Prem	A	Cardiff City	W	2-0	27,750	17	Cole C., Noble
28	Jan 18	Sat	Prem	H	Newcastle United	L	1-3	33,343	18	Cole C.
29	Jan 21	Tue	LC SF : 2	H	Manchester City	L	0-3	14,390		
30	Jan 29	Wed	Prem	A	Chelsea	D	0-0	41,376	18	
31	Feb 1	Sat	Prem	H	Swansea City	W	2-0	31,848	18	Nolan 2
32	Feb 8	Sat	Prem	A	Aston Villa	W	2-0	36,261	15	Nolan 2
33	Feb 11	Tue	Prem	H	Norwich City	W	2-0	31,153	10	Collins, Diame
34	Feb 22	Sat	Prem	H	Southampton	W	3-1	33,148	10	Cole C., Jarvis, Nolan
35	Mar 1	Sat	Prem	A	Everton	L	0-1	38,286	10	
36	Mar 15	Sat	Prem	A	Stoke City	L	1-3	27,015	12	Carroll
37	Mar 22	Sat	Prem	H	Manchester United	L	0-2	34,237	14	
38	Mar 26	Wed	Prem	H	Hull City	W	2-1	31,033	11	Noble [pen], Chester (og)
39	Mar 31	Mon	Prem	A	Sunderland	W	2-1	37,396	11	Carroll, Diame
40	Apr 6	Sun	Prem	H	Liverpool	L	1-2	34,977	11	Demel
41	Apr 15	Tue	Prem	A	Arsenal	L	1-3	59,977	11	Jarvis
42	Apr 19	Sat	Prem	H	Crystal Palace	L	0-1	34,977	12	
43	Apr 26	Sat	Prem	A	West Bromwich Albion	L	0-1	26,541	14	
44	May 3	Sat	Prem	H	Tottenham Hotspur	W	2-0	34,977	12	Downing, Kane (og)
45	May 11	Sun	Prem	A	Manchester City	L	0-2	47,300	12	

eam Line-Ups

ARMERO Pablo	BORRIELLO Marco	BURKE Reece	CARROLL Andy	CHAMBERS Leo	COLE Carlton	COLE Joe	COLLINS James	COLLISON Jack	DEMEL Guy	DIAME Mohamed	DIARRA Alou	DOWNING Stewart	DRIVER Callum	FANIMO Matthias	JAASKELAINEN Jussi	JARVIS Matthew	JOHNSON Roger	LEE Elliot	LLETGET Sebastian	MAIGA Modibo	McCARTNEY George	MONCUR George	MORRISON Ravel	NOBLE Mark	NOCERINO Antonio	NOLAN Kevin	O'BRIEN Joey	PETRIC Mladen	POTTS Daniel	RAT Razvan	REID Winston	RUDDOCK Pelly	TAYLOR Matthew	TOMKINS James	TURGOTT Blair	VAZ TE Ricardo	WHITEHEAD Danny	No.
					26/c		19	20	21/b	b	a				22	7/a				11				16		4	17				2					c		1
					a		19	20	21/b	23/a					22	7		c		11			b	16		4	17				2							2
		37			26/b	10					a	18/a	b								3		15							8			14	5		12		3
						b	19	20	21/c	23/a					22	7		c		11			a	16/b		4	17				2							4
							19	20/a	21						22	7				11/b			15/c	16		4	17	a		8	2					c	b	5
							19		21						22	7/b				11/a			15	16		4/c	17	a		8	2					c	b	6
		37	9			10	19	b								7				11/a	3/c		15/b			a	c						14	5		12		7
									21/b	b					22	7/c				11/a			15	16		4	17	a		8	2			5		c		8
					b	a		20	21/a	23					22								15	16/c		4	c			8	2			5		12/b		9
								20/a	21	23					22	b							15	16		4/c	a	c		8	2			5		12/b		10
					b	c		20	21/b	23					22	a							15/c	16		4				8	2			5		12/a		11
		37	9		24/a			b	21/b	a	6									11	c						17		33				14	5/c				12
					a	10/a	b	20	c	23					22	7/b							15	16		4				8/c	2			5				13
			b		26/a	10/b	19	20	a	23					22	c							15	16/c						8				5				14
					26/b	10/a	19	20	b	23					22	c					a		15	16		4/c	17							5				15
					c	a	19	20	21	23					22	7/a				11/c	3		b	16		4/b								5				16
					24/b	a	19	21	21?	23					22	b					c		15	16		4/a	17			8/c				5				17
					a		19	20	21	23/a					22	7/c				11	3			16		4	b						c	5/b				18
			c		26/c	a	19	20/b	21						22	7/a				11	3		15	16			b						5				19
				24/a	26/b	10	19	b				18/c				7				a	3		c				17			8			14					20
					b		19/c	a	20? 21							7/b				11	3		15	16			c						14/a	5				21
				24	26		19/a	b	21							7					3			16		4/c	17/b			a				5		c		22
				24/b	26/c	c	a	21?							22	7				b	3			16		4	17			8				5/a				23
					c	10	20	21/b	18	b					22					11/c	3			16/a		4	17			a			14					24
	b											18/b	23/c	41	a	7		35		11	34/a		15		27											c	31	25
			a	26				20	21	23	b							28		11/a	3		16/b				17/c			c			14					26
			b	24/b	c	10/c		20/a	c	23						7		28		a	16?			16						8			14	5				27
			b	24	c	10/a	19	21/b	21/b	23						7/c		28		a				16						8			14					28
			9/a	a	26/b	c	19?	21/c	21/c	18	b	18			22			28					15			4				8			14	5				29
			9/b	b	19?		19	20	21/a	23	a					a								16	c	4/c	17						14	5				30
			9	a			19	20		23						7/a					3			16	c	4/c				b			14/b	5				31
a				24/a			19	20		23						7/c					3			16	b	4/b				c			14	5				32
a				24/a			19	20	b	23						7/b					3			16	c	4							14/c	5				33
				24			19	20	a	23						7/a					3			16		4/b				b			14	5				34
a				24/a			19	20/c	b	23						7/b					3			16		4				c			14	5				35
c			9/c	b	a?		a	20	21	23/a											3			16	47/b	4					2			5				36
			9	b			19	20	21/a	23						a					3			16	c	4/b							14/c	5				37
			9	b			19/a	20	21/b	23						a					3			16		4							14	5				38
a			9					20	21/b	23						b					3/a			16	c	4/c					2		14	5				39
8			9	c				20	21/c	23						b					3			16	a	4/a					2		14/b	5				40
8			9/c	c	a			20	21	23/a						7/b								16	47						2			5	b			41
8			9	a	b?			b	21	23/b						7/a					3			16	c	4/c					2			5				42
			9	c	b	a		20	21	23/b						7/c					3			16		4					2			5/a				43
			9/a	a				20	21	23						b					3			16		4/b					2		14	5				44
			9/b	b	c				21/c	23						a					3			16		4/a	17				2		14	5				45

2014-15
Story of the season

Youthful additions were added to the squad and **nine new players were signed.** Full backs Aaron Cresswell and on loan Carl Jenkinson; midfielders Cheikhou Kouyate, Diego Poyet, Morgan Amalfitano and on loan Alex Song; and forwards Enner Valencia, Mauro Zarate, and Diafra Sakho.

The opening home game with Tottenham was disappointing as the Hammers missed a penalty and conceded an injury time goal, gifting Spurs a 1-0 victory.

There was a fine 3-1 win at Crystal Palace but this was followed by home defeats to Sheffield United in the League Cup and Southampton in the league. A big improvement then took place as after beating Liverpool 3-1 at home in September there were three successive wins in October which included a 2-1 home victory against champions Manchester City. The side were fifth in the table and Diafra Sakho had scored in six successive games. All the new boys had settled in and were playing well and there was renewed

Appearances & Goals 2014-15

	League			FA Cup			League Cup			Total		
	Starts	Subs	Goals	Starts	Subs	Goals	Starts	Subs	Goals	Starts	Subs	Goals
ADRIAN del CASTILLO	38	0	0	4	0	0	0	0	0	42	0	0
AMALFITANO Morgan	14	10	3	1	3	0	0	0	0	15	13	3
BURKE Reece	4	1	0	0	0	0	1	0	0	5	1	0
CARROLL Andy	12	2	5	2	0	0	0	0	0	14	2	5
COLE Carlton	8	15	2	0	3	1	0	0	0	8	18	3
COLLINS James	21	6	0	2	0	1	0	0	0	23	6	1
CRESSWELL Aaron	38	0	2	4	0	0	0	0	0	42	0	2
DEMEL Guy	3	3	0	0	1	0	1	0	0	4	4	0
DIAME Mohamed	0	3	0	0	0	0	1	0	0	1	3	0
DOWNING Stewart	37	0	6	4	0	0	0	1	0	41	1	6
JAASKELAINEN Jussi	0	1	0	0	0	0	1	0	0	1	1	0
JARVIS Matthew	4	7	0	2	0	0	0	0	0	6	7	0
JENKINSON Carl	29	3	0	4	0	0	0	0	0	33	3	0
KOUYATE Cheikhou	30	1	4	1	0	0	0	0	0	31	1	4
LEE Elliot	0	1	0	0	0	0	0	0	0	0	1	0
MORRISON Ravel	0	1	0	0	0	0	1	0	0	1	1	0
NENE	0	8	0	0	0	0	0	0	0	0	8	0
NOBLE Mark	27	1	2	4	0	0	0	1	0	31	2	2
NOLAN Kevin	19	10	1	3	1	0	0	0	0	22	11	1
O'BRIEN Joey	6	3	0	0	2	0	0	0	0	6	5	0
POTTS Daniel	0	0	0	0	0	0	1	0	0	1	0	0
POYET Diego	1	2	0	0	1	0	1	0	0	2	3	0
REID Winston	29	1	1	2	0	0	1	0	0	32	1	1
SAKHO Diafra	20	3	10	1	1	1	1	0	1	22	4	
SONG Alex	25	3	0	3	0	0	0	0	0	28	3	0
TOMKINS James	20	2	1	3	0	0	0	0	0	23	2	1
VALENCIA Enner	25	7	4	4	0	1	1	0	0	30	7	
VAZ TE Ricardo	3	1	0	0	0	0	1	0	0	4	1	0
ZARATE Mauro	5	1	2	0	0	0	0	1	0	5	3	2
Own goals:												
Totals	418	97	43	44	12	4	11	3	1	473	112	

optimism amongst the fans. A narrow 2-1 loss at Everton was the only defeat in the next eight games with Newcastle, Swansea and Leicester all being beaten at the Boleyn Ground

By Christmas the team were lying in fourth spot and dreaming of a Champions League place. There was a setback with two London Derby defeats to Chelsea and Arsenal before the Hammers were paired with Everton in the FA Cup. At Goodison Park a late Everton goal forced a replay with the teams drawing 1-1. There was excitement in the replay as after extra time the score was 2-2 and a penalty shootout followed. It was tense as the score reached 8-8 when Adrian the Hammers goalkeeper stepped up to score the winner. Next up in the cup was a trip to Bristol City where the League One side were narrowly beaten 1-0 with a goal from Sakho.

In February a last minute goal by Manchester United earned them a 1-1 draw at Upton Park and days later the Hammers gained a creditable 0-0 draw at Southampton where an injury to Andy Carroll forced him to miss the rest of the season. The Fifth Round of the FA Cup was a disaster as a poor display at West Bromwich Albion saw the home team triumph winning 4-0. To the delight of the fans the Hammers were leading 2-0 at Tottenham but a last minute penalty brought Spurs a 2-2 draw. Three successive defeats followed as the side slid down to tenth place in the table. There were only two 1-0 home wins against Sunderland and Burnley in the remaining nine games. After being fourth at Christmas it was disappointing to finish the season in twelfth place. Shortly after the game ending at Newcastle on the final day the club announced that they would not be renewing manager Sam Allardyce's contract.

Barclays Premier League Final Table 2014-15

| | P | HOME | | | | | AWAY | | | | | Pts |
		W	D	L	F	A	W	D	L	F	A	
Chelsea	38	15	4	0	36	9	11	5	3	37	23	87
Manchester City	38	14	3	2	44	14	10	4	5	39	24	79
Arsenal	38	12	5	2	41	14	10	4	5	30	22	75
Manchester United	38	14	2	3	41	15	6	8	5	21	22	70
Tottenham Hotspur	38	10	3	6	31	24	9	4	6	27	29	64
Liverpool	38	10	5	4	30	20	8	3	8	22	28	62
Southampton	38	11	4	4	37	13	7	2	10	17	20	60
Swansea City	38	9	5	5	27	22	7	3	9	19	27	56
Stoke City	38	10	3	6	32	22	5	6	8	16	23	54
Crystal Palace	38	6	3	10	21	27	7	6	6	26	24	48
Everton	38	7	7	5	27	21	5	4	10	21	29	47
West Ham United	**38**	**9**	**4**	**6**	**25**	**18**	**3**	**7**	**9**	**19**	**29**	**47**
West Bromwich Albion	38	7	4	8	24	26	4	7	8	14	25	44
Leicester City	38	7	5	7	28	22	4	3	12	18	33	41
Newcastle United	38	7	5	7	26	27	3	4	12	14	36	39
Sunderland	38	4	8	7	16	27	3	9	7	15	26	38
Aston Villa	38	5	6	8	18	25	5	2	12	13	32	38
Hull City	38	5	5	9	19	24	3	6	10	14	27	35
Burnley	38	4	7	8	14	21	3	5	11	14	32	33
Queens Park Rangers	38	6	5	8	23	24	2	1	16	19	49	30

AARON CRESSWELL

The talented left back grew up in Merseyside supporting Liverpool.

Aged twelve he joined the Academy at Liverpool where he spent three years before being released in 2005. He then joined Tranmere Rovers and made his debut against MK Dons in November 2008. He spent three seasons with the Rovers playing in 80 games and scoring six goals. He had attracted the attention of a host of clubs, but it was Ipswich Town who gained his signature in 2011. With the Blues he was a model of consistency and was chosen as their Player of the Year in 2012 and the following season he was named in the PFA Championship Team of the Year.

Aaron made a total of 138 appearances scoring seven goals for Ipswich before joining West Ham in 2014. He had an outstanding first season with the Hammers being ever present throughout the campaign, making 42 appearances and scoring two goals. His fine displays saw him named as the fans' Hammer of the Year and the Players Player of the Year.

Season **2014-15** Barclays Premier League
Match Details

Manager **Sam Allardyce**   Final League Position **12/20**

	Date		Competition	Venue	Opponents	Results		Attendance	Position	Scorers
1	Aug 16	Sat	Prem	H	Tottenham Hotspur	L	0-1	34,977	20	
2	Aug 23	Sat	Prem	A	Crystal Palace	W	3-1	24,242	6	Cole, Downing, Zarate
3	Aug 26	Tue	FLC 2*	H	Sheffield United	D	1-1	28,930		Sakho
4	Aug 30	Sat	Prem	H	Southampton	L	1-3	34,907	10	Noble
5	Sep 15	Mon	Prem	A	Hull City	D	2-2	21,275	13	Valencia, Sakho
6	Sep 20	Sat	Prem	H	Liverpool	W	3-1	34,977	8	Amalfitano, Reid, Sakho
7	Sep 27	Sat	Prem	A	Manchester United	L	1-2	75,317	11	Sakho
8	Oct 5	Sun	Prem	H	Queens Park Rangers	W	2-0	34,907	7	Sakho, Onuoha (og)
9	Oct 18	Sat	Prem	A	Burnley	W	3-1	18,936	4	Cole, Sakho, Valencia
10	Oct 25	Sat	Prem	H	Manchester City	W	2-1	34,977	4	Amalfitano, Sakho
11	Nov 1	Sat	Prem	A	Stoke City	D	2-2	27,174	5	Downing, Valencia
12	Nov 8	Sat	Prem	H	Aston Villa	D	0-0	34,857	4	
13	Nov 22	Sat	Prem	A	Everton	L	1-2	39,182	6	Zarate
14	Nov 29	Sat	Prem	H	Newcastle United	W	1-0	34,977	5	Cresswell
15	Dec 2	Tue	Prem	A	West Bromwich Albion	W	2-1	23,975	5	Nolan, Tomkins
16	Dec 7	Sun	Prem	H	Swansea City	W	3-1	34,125	3	Carroll 2, Sakho
17	Dec 13	Sat	Prem	A	Sunderland	D	1-1	41,694	4	Downing
18	Dec 20	Sat	Prem	H	Leicester City	W	2-0	34,977	4	Carroll, Downing
19	Dec 26	Fri	Prem	A	Chelsea	L	0-2	41,589	5	
20	Dec 28	Sun	Prem	H	Arsenal	L	1-2	34,977	6	Kouyate
21	Jan 1	Thur	Prem	H	West Bromwich Albion	D	1-1	34,914	7	Sakho
22	Jan 6	Tue	FAC 3	A	Everton	D	1-1	22,236		Collins
23	Jan 10	Sat	Prem	A	Swansea City	D	1-1	20,745	7	Carroll
24	Jan 13	Tue	FAC 3 Rep	H	Everton	D	2-2**	25,301		Cole, Valencia
25	Jan 18	Sun	Prem	H	Hull City	W	3-0	34,914	7	Amalfitano, Carroll, Downing
26	Jan 25	Sun	FAC 4	A	Bristol City	W	1-0	12,682		Sakho
27	Jan 31	Sat	Prem	A	Liverpool	L	0-2	44,718	8	
28	Feb 8	Sun	Prem	H	Manchester United	D	1-1	34,499	8	Kouyate
29	Feb 11	Wed	Prem	A	Southampton	D	0-0	31,241	8	
30	Feb 14	Sat	FAC 5	A	West Bromwich Albion	L	0-4	19,956		
31	Feb 22	Sun	Prem	A	Tottenham Hotspur	D	2-2	35,837	8	Kouyate, Sakho
32	Feb 28	Sat	Prem	H	Crystal Palace	L	1-3	34,857	9	Valencia
33	Mar 4	Wed	Prem	H	Chelsea	L	0-1	34,927	10	
34	Mar 14	Sat	Prem	A	Arsenal	L	0-3	60,002	10	
35	Mar 21	Sat	Prem	H	Sunderland	W	1-0	34,914	9	Sakho
36	Apr 4	Sat	Prem	A	Leicester City	L	1-2	31,863	9	Kouyate
37	Apr 11	Sat	Prem	H	Stoke City	D	1-1	34,946	9	Cresswell
38	Apr 19	Sun	Prem	A	Manchester City	L	0-2	45,041	10	
39	Apr 25	Sat	Prem	A	Queens Park Rangers	D	0-0	18,036	11	
40	May 2	Sat	Prem	H	Burnley	W	1-0	34,946	9	Noble [pen]
41	May 9	Sat	Prem	A	Aston Villa	L	0-1	34,946	10	
42	May 16	Sat	Prem	H	Everton	L	1-2	34,977	11	Downing
43	May 24	Sun	Prem	A	Newcastle United	L	0-2	52,094	12	

* 1-1 (aet lost 4-5 pens)   * *Won 9-8 penalties - (2-2 after extra time, 1-1 after 90 minutes)

Team Line-Ups

ADRIAN del CASTILLO	AMALFITANO Morgan	BURKE Reece	CARROLL Andy	COLE Carlton	COLLINS James	CRESSWELL Aaron	DEMEL Guy	DIAME Mohamed	DOWNING Stewart	JAASKELAINEN Jussi	JARVIS Matthew	JENKINSON Carl	KOUYATE Cheikhou	LEE Elliot	MORRISON Ravel	NENE	NOBLE Mark	NOLAN Kevin	O'BRIEN Joey	POTTS Daniel	POYET Diego	REID Winston	SAKHO Diafra	SONG Alex	TOMKINS James	VALENCIA Enner	VAZ TE Ricardo	ZARATE Mauro	No.
3				24/c	19	3	a	b	11				8				16		17/a			2				c	12/b		1
3				24/a		3		c	11/c				8				16				b	2	a		5		12	10/b	2
		32					20	21	a	22					14/c		16			33	23	2	15/a			31	12/b	b	3
3				24/c		3	b		11				8		a		16		17			2			5	c	12/b	10/a	4
3	c					3	20/b		11		b		8				16					2	15/c	a	5	31		10/a	5
3	b		c			3	20/a		11		a		8				16					2	15	30/b	5	31/c			6
3	21/a		a			3	20/b		11		b						c				23/c	2	15	30	5	31			7
3	21					3			11		b	18					a					2	15	30	5	31/b		10/a	8
3	21		a		19	3			11			18					16		b			2	15	30/b		31/a			9
3	21/a		b		19	3			11			18	a				16		c			2	15/c	30		31/b			10
3	21/b		b		19	3			11			18	8				16/c		c			2/a		30	a	31			11
3	c		b		19	3			11			18	8/a				16/c		a			2	15	30		31/b			12
3	21/c		9	24/a	19	3			b			18					16/b	4				2			5		c	a	13
3	21		9		19	3			11		7/a	18	8/b				16					b			5	a			14
3	21/a		9/b	c	a	3			11			18	8					4				2			5	b		10/c	15
3			9	c		3			11			18/b	8/c					4	b			2	a	30	5	31/a			16
3			9			3			11			18	8					4/a				2	15	30	5	a			17
3	a		9		a	3			11			18	8					4/c				2	15/b	30	5/a	b			18
3	c		9/a		19	3			11/c			18	8				16/b	4				2	a		b	31			19
3	21		9			3	b		11				8/c				c		17/b			2	15/a	30	5	a			20
3	21/a		9/c	c	19	3			11		a	18	8									2	15/b	30		b			21
3	21/c		a		19	3			11		7/b	18					16	4	c		b	2				31/a			22
3	a		9		19	3			11			18					16	4/b	b			2			5	31/a			23
3	b		9	c	19/c	3			11		7/b	18					16					a		30/a	5	31			24
3	b		9		19/a	3			11			18					16/b	4	c				a	30	5/c	31			25
3	a		9			3	c		11			18					16	4/c				2	b	30/a	5	31/b			26
3	21/a		9/b	b	19/c	3	c		11				a					4	17			2		30		31			27
3						3			11		a	18					16	4					15	30	5	31/a			28
3	21		b	24/c		3			11	c	a	18	8										15/b	30	5	31			29
3	a		b			3			11			18	8				16	4/a	c				15/b	30/c	5	31			30
3			a/c		c	3			11			18	8				16/a					2	15	30	5	31/b			31
3						3			11			18	8			a	16					2	15	30/b	5	31			32
3	a					3			11			18	8/b			b	16	4				2/a	15		5	31			33
3	a				19	3			11		7/a		8			b	16/b	4	17				15	30					34
3	a				19	3			11		7/a	18	8			b	16	4/b	c				15/c	30					35
3	a		b			3			11			18	8			c	16	4/a				2	15/b	30/c					36
3	c		a		19	3			11			18	8				16		b			2	15/a	30/b		31/c			37
3				24/b	19	3			11		a	18	8				16		b			2		30/a		31			38
3		32	a		19	3			11		7/a	18	8				16	4								31			39
3	21	32	b		19	3			11			18	8			a	16	4/a								31/b			40
3	21/a	32	c		19	3			11			18	8			a	16/c	4/b							b	31			41
3	a			24/b	19/a	3			11			18	8			b	16					2		30		31			41
3	a	32/b		24		3			11			18	8/c				c	4				2		30	b	31/a			43

PART TWO

CAREER RECORDS

THAMES IRONWORKS
WEST HAM UNITED

Career Records
Thames Ironworks

Player	London League Apps	London League Goals	Southern League Apps	Southern League Goals	FA Cup Apps	FA Cup Goals	London Senior Cup Apps	London Senior Cup Goals	Essex Senior Cup Apps	Essex Senior Cup Goals	Test Match Apps	Test Match Goals	Total Apps	Total Goals
ADAMS F.	0	0	8	2	5	0	0	0	0	0	0	0	13	2
ALLAN Robert	0	0	21	1	0	0	0	0	0	0	1	0	22	1
ATKINSON W.	0	0	2	2	0	0	0	0	0	0	0	0	2	2
BARNES T.	1	0	0	0	0	0	0	0	1	0	0	0	2	0
BIGDEN James	0	0	11	0	2	0	0	0	0	0	0	0	13	0
BIRD Richard	9	0	1	0	1	0	7	1	0	0	0	0	18	1
BONE J.	1	1	0	0	0	0	0	0	0	0	0	0	1	1
BRADSHAW Thomas	0	0	5	0	7	2	0	0	0	0	0	0	12	2
BRETT Frank	0	0	1	0	0	0	0	0	0	0	0	0	1	0
BULLER	0	0	1	0	0	0	0	0	0	0	0	0	1	0
BUTTERWORTH H.	6	4	0	0	0	0	0	0	0	0	0	0	6	4
CARNELLY Albert	0	0	27	8	6	6	0	0	0	0	1	0	34	14
CHALKLEY Frederick	9	0	0	0	3	0	5	0	1	0	0	0	18	0
CHAPMAN William	1	0	0	0	0	0	0	0	0	0	0	0	1	0
CHARSLEY A.J.	1	0	0	0	0	0	1	0	0	0	0	0	2	0
CHISHOLM Simon	15	0	16	1	5	2	2	0	0	0	1	0	39	3
COBB R.	0	0	2	0	3	0	0	0	0	0	0	0	5	0
COOPER T.	2	2	0	0	0	0	1	1	0	0	0	0	3	3
CORBETT Fred	0	0	3	0	0	0	0	0	0	0	0	0	3	0
COWIE Andrew	2	1	0	0	0	0	0	0	0	0	0	0	2	1
COX Francis	1	0	0	0	0	0	0	0	0	0	0	0	1	0
CRAIG Charles	0	0	17	0	4	0	0	0	0	0	1	0	22	0
DANDRIDGE Frank	11	0	0	0	4	0	6	1	0	0	0	0	21	1
DARBY Arthur	0	0	0	0	1	0	2	0	0	0	0	0	3	0
DAVIE Peter	3	0	0	0	1	0	4	0	0	0	0	0	8	0
DENHAM	1	0	0	0	0	0	0	0	0	0	0	0	1	0
DOVE Charles	20	1	30	3	10	0	8	2	1	0	1	0	70	6
DUFF Alex	4	0	0	0	0	0	5	0	0	0	0	0	9	0
DUNN Thomas	0	0	33	0	7	0	0	0	0	0	2	0	42	0
EDWARDS A.	12	6	0	0	3	0	2	0	0	0	0	0	17	6
FITZJOHN J.	1	0	0	0	0	0	0	0	0	0	0	0	1	0
FOSS L.	2	0	1	0	0	0	0	0	0	0	0	0	3	0
FREEMAN Thomas	0	0	0	0	1	0	0	0	0	0	0	0	1	0
FRENCH Barnabas	0	0	0	0	1	0	0	0	0	0	0	0	1	0
FURNELL David	11	0	0	0	3	0	2	0	0	0	0	0	16	0
GENTLE	0	0	1	0	1	0	0	0	0	0	0	0	2	0
GILLIES	11	1	0	0	1	0	0	0	0	0	0	0	12	1
GILMORE Henry	0	0	5	1	0	0	0	0	0	0	0	0	5	1
GRAHAM Hugh	3	0	0	0	0	0	1	0	0	0	0	0	4	0
GRESHAM George	25	13	14	4	7	1	8	5	0	0	1	0	55	23
HATTON Edward	5	4	0	0	4	1	0	0	0	0	0	0	9	5
HAY Sam	0	0	6	2	1	0	0	0	0	0	0	0	7	2
HEATH Robert	6	0	0	0	0	0	0	0	0	0	0	0	6	0
HENDERSON R.	0	0	9	8	0	0	0	0	0	0	1	0	10	8
HICKMAN William	2	0	0	0	0	0	2	0	1	0	0	0	5	0
HIRD Henry	12	5	20	3	7	1	0	0	0	0	0	0	39	9
HITCH Alf	0	0	3	0	2	0	0	0	0	0	0	0	5	0
HOLSTOCK Albert	1	0	0	0	1	0	0	0	0	0	0	0	2	0
HOUNSELL Robert	10	8	2	1	0	0	1	1	0	0	0	0	13	10

ayer	London League		Southern League		FA Cup		London Senior Cup		Essex Senior Cup		Test Match		Total	
	Apps	Goals	Apps	Goals	Apps	Goals	Apps	Goals	Apps	Goals	Apps	Goals	Apps	Goals
RST Joseph	1	0	0	0	0	0	0	0	0	0	0	0	1	0
NES W.	0	0	2	0	0	0	0	0	0	0	0	0	2	0
NES	1	0	0	0	0	0	0	0	0	0	0	0	1	0
YCE William	0	0	27	8	7	7	0	0	0	0	1	3	35	18
NG Syd	0	0	16	0	7	0	0	0	0	0	0	0	23	0
ONARD Patrick	0	0	11	8	0	0	0	0	0	0	1	0	12	8
DSAY Jamie	0	0	0	0	1	0	0	0	0	0	0	0	1	0
OYD David	0	0	12	13	3	0	0	0	0	0	1	1	16	14
ARJERAM Arthur	0	0	8	0	0	0	0	0	0	0	0	0	8	0
CEACHRANE Roderick	0	0	51	1	10	3	0	0	0	0	2	0	63	4
EWAN L.	0	0	8	2	0	0	0	0	0	0	0	0	8	2
cKAY Kenny	0	0	28	8	7	5	0	0	0	0	1	0	36	13
cMANUS Peter	0	0	10	0	4	1	0	0	0	0	1	0	15	1
LLS Percy	1	0	0	0	0	0	1	0	0	0	0	0	2	0
OORE Thomas	0	0	49	0	10	0	0	0	0	0	2	0	61	0
ORRISON John	8	1	0	0	1	0	9	2	0	0	0	0	18	3
ORTON William	6	0	0	0	0	0	3	0	1	0	0	0	10	0
EIL George	15	1	2	0	1	0	2	0	0	0	0	0	20	1
CHOLS Albert	1	0	0	0	1	0	0	0	0	0	0	0	2	0
DER	0	0	0	0	2	0	0	0	0	0	0	0	2	0
IVANT A.	3	0	0	0	0	0	0	0	0	0	0	0	3	0
KSPRING Arthur	3	0	0	0	0	0	0	0	0	0	0	0	3	0
ARKS Walter	0	0	1	0	0	0	0	0	0	0	0	0	1	0
EAD Charles	3	2	0	0	0	0	1	0	0	0	0	0	4	2
EID George	0	0	6	1	0	0	0	0	0	0	0	0	6	1
EID Jimmy	16	10	15	9	4	2	1	0	0	0	0	0	36	21
EYNOLDS J.	0	0	13	5	0	0	0	0	0	0	1	0	14	5
DGES Victor	0	0	0	0	0	0	1	0	0	0	0	0	1	0
OFF J.	2	0	0	0	0	0	0	0	0	0	0	0	2	0
OSSITER H.	3	0	0	0	0	0	6	1	0	0	0	0	10	1
AGE George	1	1	0	0	1	0	1	0	1	0	0	0	4	1
OUTHWOOD	0	0	0	0	1	0	0	0	0	0	0	0	1	0
TARES Colin	0	0	0	0	0	0	5	1	1	0	0	0	6	1
TEVENSON Robert	3	0	0	0	1	0	4	3	1	1	0	0	9	4
TEWART Johnny	0	0	0	0	1	0	0	0	0	0	0	0	2	0
TEWART William	0	0	16	0	0	0	0	0	0	0	1	1	17	1
UNDERLAND H.	0	0	1	0	0	0	0	0	0	0	0	0	1	0
AYLOR Frank	0	0	14	1	0	0	0	0	0	0	1	0	15	1
AYLOR William	11	0	0	0	1	0	1	0	1	0	0	0	14	0
RANTER Walter	18	0	21	0	5	0	6	0	0	0	1	0	51	0
LL Henry	0	0	0	0	1	0	0	0	0	0	0	0	1	0
URNER	0	0	4	0	0	0	0	0	0	0	0	0	4	0
WALKER Len	0	0	7	0	0	0	0	0	0	0	0	0	7	0
ATSON John	0	0	0	0	1	0	0	0	0	0	0	0	1	0
ENHAM	0	0	1	1	0	0	0	0	0	0	0	0	1	1
ILLIAMS A.	1	0	0	0	1	0	0	0	0	0	0	0	2	0
OODCOCK A.	1	0	0	0	0	0	0	0	0	0	0	0	1	0
OODS John	0	0	0	0	1	0	0	0	0	0	0	0	1	0
OODS W.	0	0	0	0	0	0	1	0	1	0	0	0	2	0

Career Records
West Ham United

Player	Date of Birth	Career	League				Premier League			
			Apps	Starts	Subs	Goals	Apps	Starts	Subs	Goal
Samassi ABOU	4 April 1973	1997/98 - 1998/99	0	0	0	0	22	14	8	5
William ADAMS	3 November 1902	1936/37	3	3	0	1	0	0	0	0
ADRIAN del Castillo	3 January 1987	2013/14 -	0	0	0	0	58	58	0	0
Niclas ALEXANDERSSON	29 December 1971	2003/04	8	5	3	0	0	0	0	0
Jeremie ALIADIERE	29 March 1983	2005/06	0	0	0	0	7	1	6	0
Robert ALLAN	1876	1900/01 - 1902/03	52	52	0	1	0	0	0	0
Clive ALLEN	20 May 1961	1991/92 - 1993/94	31	29	2	17	7	7	0	0
Martin ALLEN	18 August 1965	1989/90 - 1995/96	132	114	18	16	58	49	9	10
Paul ALLEN	28 August 1962	1979/80 - 1984/85	152	149	3	6	0	0	0	0
Percy ALLEN	2 July 1895	1919/20 - 1922/23	80	80	0	5	0	0	0	0
Robert ALLEN	3 November 1902	1919/20	1	1	0	1	0	0	0	0
Malcolm ALLISON	5 September 1927	1950/51 - 1957/58	238	238	0	10	0	0	0	0
Tommy ALLISON	1875	1903/04 - 1908/09	156	156	0	7	0	0	0	0
Manuel ALMUNIA	19 May 1977	2011/12	4	4	0	0	0	0	0	0
Paulo ALVES	10 December 1969	1997/98	0	0	0	0	4	0	4	0
Morgan AMALFITANO	20 March 1985	2014/15 -	0	0	0	0	24	14	10	3
Charles AMBLER	1868	1901/02	1	1	0	0	0	0	0	0
Edward ANDERSON	17 July 1911	1933/34 - 1934/35	26	26	0	0	0	0	0	0
George ANDREW	24 November 1945	1966/67	2	2	0	0	0	0	0	0
Jimmy ANDREWS	1 February 1927	1951/52 - 1955/56	114	114	0	21	0	0	0	0
Pablo ARMERO	2 November 1986	2013/14	0	0	0	0	5	3	2	0
Eric ARMSTRONG	25 May 1921	1947/48 - 1952/53	1	1	0	0	0	0	0	0
John ARNOTT	6 September 1932	1953/54 - 1954/55	6	6	0	2	0	0	0	0
Dean ASHTON	24 November 1983	2005/06 - 2008/09	0	0	0	0	46	33	13	15
Herbert ASHTON	23 May 1885	1908/09 - 1914/15	224	224	0	22	0	0	0	0
William ASKEW	22 May 1888	1912/13 - 1914/15	104	104	0	2	0	0	0	0
C. ATKINS	Unknown	1908/09	2	2	0	1	0	0	0	0
Ray ATTEVELD	8 September 1966	1991/92	1	1	0	0	0	0	0	0
Reg ATTWELL	23 March 1920	1937/38	5	5	0	0	0	0	0	0
Johnny AYRIS	8 January 1953	1970/71 - 1976/77	57	41	16	1	0	0	0	0
Demba BA	25 May 1985	2010/11	0	0	0	0	12	10	2	7
Daniel BAILEY	26 June 1893	1912/13 - 1920/21	84	84	0	22	0	0	0	0
David BAILLIE	6 June 1905	1925/26 - 1928/29	16	16	0	0	0	0	0	0
Ken BAINBRIDGE	15 January 1921	1945/46 - 1949/50	80	80	0	16	0	0	0	0
Sam BALDOCK	15 March 1989	2011/12	23	10	13	5	0	0	0	0
John BALL	29 September 1899	1929/30	15	15	0	9	0	0	0	0
Tommy BAMLETT	31 May 1882	1904/05	18	18	0	0	0	0	0	0
Steven BANKS	9 February 1972	1992/93	0	0	0	0	0	0	0	0
Arthur BANNER	28 June 1918	1938/39 - 1947/48	27	27	0	0	0	0	0	0
Dale BANTON	15 May 1961	1979/80 - 1981/82	5	2	3	0	0	0	0	0
Bobby BARNES	17 December 1962	1980/81 - 1985/86	43	31	12	5	0	0	0	0
William BARNES	20 May 1879	1902/03 - 1903/04	49	49	0	5	0	0	0	0
Pablo BARRERA	21 June 1987	2010/11 - 2011/12	1	0	1	0	14	6	8	0

	FA Cup				League Cup				Europe				Other				Total		
Apps	Starts	Subs	Goals	Apps	Starts	Subs	Goals	Apps	Starts	Subs	Goals	Apps	Starts	Subs	Goals	Apps	Starts	Subs	Goals
6	3	3	0	3	2	1	1	0	0	0	0	0	0	0	0	31	19	12	6
0	0	0	0	0	0	0	0	0	0	0	0	0	0	0	0	3	3	0	1
5	5	0	0	5	5	0	0	0	0	0	0	0	0	0	0	68	68	0	0
0	0	0	0	0	0	0	0	0	0	0	0	0	0	0	0	8	5	3	0
0	0	0	0	1	0	1	0	0	0	0	0	0	0	0	0	8	1	7	0
5	5	0	0	0	0	0	0	0	0	0	0	0	0	0	0	57	57	0	1
4	2	2	1	2	2	0	0	0	0	0	0	6	6	0	3	50	46	4	21
14	14	0	4	18	15	3	5	0	0	0	0	10	10	0	0	232	202	30	35
18	15	3	3	24	20	4	2	2	1	1	0	1	1	0	0	197	186	11	11
6	6	0	0	0	0	0	0	0	0	0	0	0	0	0	0	86	86	0	5
0	0	0	0	0	0	0	0	0	0	0	0	0	0	0	0	1	1	0	1
17	17	0	0	0	0	0	0	0	0	0	0	10	10	0	1	265	265	0	11
9	9	0	0	0	0	0	0	0	0	0	0	0	0	0	0	165	165	0	7
0	0	0	0	0	0	0	0	0	0	0	0	0	0	0	0	4	4	0	0
0	0	0	0	0	0	0	0	0	0	0	0	0	0	0	0	4	0	4	0
4	1	3	0	0	0	0	0	0	0	0	0	0	0	0	0	28	15	13	3
1	1	0	0	0	0	0	0	0	0	0	0	0	0	0	0	2	2	0	0
2	2	0	0	0	0	0	0	0	0	0	0	0	0	0	0	28	28	0	0
0	0	0	0	0	0	0	0	0	0	0	0	0	0	0	0	2	2	0	0
6	6	0	1	0	0	0	0	0	0	0	0	3	3	0	1	123	123	0	23
0	0	0	0	0	0	0	0	0	0	0	0	0	0	0	0	5	3	2	0
0	0	0	0	0	0	0	0	0	0	0	0	1	1	0	0	2	2	0	0
0	0	0	0	0	0	0	0	0	0	0	0	0	0	0	0	6	6	0	2
7	7	0	3	3	3	0	1	0	0	0	0	0	0	0	0	56	43	13	19
25	25	0	2	0	0	0	0	0	0	0	0	0	0	0	0	249	249	0	24
8	8	0	0	0	0	0	0	0	0	0	0	0	0	0	0	112	112	0	2
0	0	0	0	0	0	0	0	0	0	0	0	0	0	0	0	2	2	0	1
2	2	0	0	0	0	0	0	0	0	0	0	0	0	0	0	3	3	0	0
0	0	0	0	0	0	0	0	0	0	0	0	0	0	0	0	5	5	0	0
1	1	0	0	7	6	1	1	0	0	0	0	4	2	2	0	69	50	19	2
1	1	0	0	0	0	0	0	0	0	0	0	0	0	0	0	13	11	2	7
7	7	0	4	0	0	0	0	0	0	0	0	0	0	0	0	91	91	0	26
1	1	0	0	0	0	0	0	0	0	0	0	0	0	0	0	17	17	0	0
4	4	0	1	0	0	0	0	0	0	0	0	0	0	0	0	84	84	0	17
1	1	0	0	0	0	0	0	0	0	0	0	0	0	0	0	24	11	13	5
0	0	0	0	0	0	0	0	0	0	0	0	0	0	0	0	15	15	0	9
1	1	0	0	0	0	0	0	0	0	0	0	0	0	0	0	19	19	0	0
0	0	0	0	0	0	0	0	0	0	0	0	1	1	0	0	1	1	0	0
0	0	0	0	0	0	0	0	0	0	0	0	0	0	0	0	27	27	0	0
0	0	0	0	1	1	0	0	0	0	0	0	0	0	0	0	6	3	3	0
6	5	1	1	4	2	2	0	1	0	1	0	0	0	0	0	54	38	16	6
5	5	0	0	0	0	0	0	0	0	0	0	0	0	0	0	54	54	0	5
3	2	1	0	5	5	0	0	0	0	0	0	0	0	0	0	23	13	10	0

Player	Date of Birth	Career	League				Premier League			
			Apps	Starts	Subs	Goals	Apps	Starts	Subs	Goal
Jim BARRETT Jnr.	5 November 1930	1949/50 - 1955/56	85	85	0	24	0	0	0	0
Jim BARRETT Snr.	19 January 1907	1924/25 - 1938/39	442	442	0	49	0	0	0	0
Christian BASSILA	5 October 1977	2000/01	0	0	0	0	3	0	3	0
Robert BEALE	Unknown	1913/14	1	1	0	0	0	0	0	0
Mick BEESLEY	10 June 1942	1960/61	2	2	0	1	0	0	0	0
Valon BEHRAMI	19 April 1985	2008/09 - 2010/11	0	0	0	0	58	54	4	4
George BELL	1889	1911/12	2	2	0	0	0	0	0	0
Richard BELL	Unknown	1938/39	1	1	0	1	0	0	0	0
Craig BELLAMY	13 July 1979	2007/08 - 2008/09	0	0	0	0	24	20	4	7
David BELLION	27 November 182	2005/06	0	0	0	0	8	2	6	0
Yossi BENAYOUN	5 May 1980	2005/06 - 2006/07 and 2012/13	0	0	0	0	69	59	10	8
Tal BEN-HAIM	31 March 1982	2010/11	0	0	0	0	8	8	0	0
Leslie BENNETT	10 January 1918	1954/55 - 1955/56	26	26	0	3	0	0	0	0
Peter BENNETT	24 June 1946	1963/64 - 1970/71	42	38	4	3	0	0	0	0
David BENTLEY	27 August 1984	2011/12	5	2	3	0	0	0	0	0
Eyal BERKOVIC	2 April 1972	1997/98 - 1998/99	0	0	0	0	65	62	3	10
Clyde BEST	24 February 1951	1969/70 - 1975/76	186	178	8	47	0	0	0	0
Eric BETTS	27 July 1925	1950/51	3	3	0	1	0	0	0	0
Dave BICKLES	6 April 1944	1963/64 - 1966/67	25	24	1	0	0	0	0	0
Charlie BICKNELL	6 November 1905	1935/36 - 1946/47	137	137	0	1	0	0	0	0
James BIGDEN	25 February 1880	1901/02 - 1903/04	91	91	0	3	0	0	0	0
William BIGGAR	16 October 1874	1902/03	8	8	0	0	0	0	0	0
Horace BIGGIN	1897	1919/20	2	2	0	0	0	0	0	0
Slaven BILIC	11 September 1968	1995/96 - 1996/97	0	0	0	0	48	48	0	2
Doug BING	27 October 1928	1951/52 - 1954/55	29	29	0	3	0	0	0	0
Frank BIRCHENOUGH	1898	1919/20	1	1	0	0	0	0	0	0
Alexander BIRNIE	11 January 1884	1903/04	1	1	0	0	0	0	0	0
Ian BISHOP	29 May 1965	1989/90 - 1997/98	120	109	11	8	134	131	3	4
Syd BISHOP	10 February 1900	1920/21 - 1926/27	159	159	0	10	0	0	0	0
Robert BLACK	17 July 1915	1936/37 - 1937/38	2	2	0	0	0	0	0	0
Alan BLACKBURN	4 August 1935	1954/55 - 1957/58	15	15	0	3	0	0	0	0
Fred BLACKBURN	1879	1905/06 - 1912/13	218	218	0	24	0	0	0	0
John BLACKWOOD	1877	1904/05	4	4	0	1	0	0	0	0
Kepa BLANCO	13 January 1984	2006/07	0	0	0	0	8	1	7	0
Jimmy BLOOMFIELD	15 February 1934	1965/66	10	9	1	0	0	0	0	0
Vincent BLORE	25 February 1907	1935/36	9	9	0	0	0	0	0	0
James BLYTH	Unknown	1906/07	3	3	0	0	0	0	0	0
Joe BLYTHE	1877	1902/03 - 1903/04	52	52	0	0	0	0	0	0
Luis BOA MORTE	4 August 1977	2006/07 - 2010/11	0	0	0	0	91	59	32	2
Jeroen BOERE	18 November 1967	1993/94 - 1995/96	0	0	0	0	25	15	10	6
Ruud BOFFIN	5 November 1987	2010/11 - 2011/12	0	0	0	0	1	1	0	0
John BOND	17 December 1932	1951/52 - 1964/65	381	381	0	32	0	0	0	0
Billy BONDS	17 September 1946	1967/68 - 1987/88	663	655	8	48	0	0	0	0
Marco BOOGERS	12 January 1967	1995/96	0	0	0	0	4	0	4	0
Marco BORRIELLO	18 June 1982	2013/14	0	0	0	0	2	0	2	0
Stanley BOURNE	1888	1906/07 - 1911/12	13	13	0	0	0	0	0	0
William BOURNE	1890	1913/14	1	1	0	0	0	0	0	0
Eddie BOVINGTON	23 April 1941	1959/60 - 1967/68	138	138	0	1	0	0	0	0

FA Cup				League Cup				Europe				Other				Total			
pps	Starts	Subs	Goals	Apps	Starts	Subs	Goals	Apps	Starts	Subs	Goals	Apps	Starts	Subs	Goals	Apps	Starts	Subs	Goals
2	2	0	1	0	0	0	0	0	0	0	0	4	4	0	1	91	91	0	26
25	25	0	4	0	0	0	0	0	0	0	0	0	0	0	0	467	467	0	53
1	0	1	0	0	0	0	0	0	0	0	0	0	0	0	0	4	0	4	0
0	0	0	0	0	0	0	0	0	0	0	0	0	0	0	0	1	1	0	0
0	0	0	0	0	0	0	0	0	0	0	0	0	0	0	0	2	2	0	1
3	3	0	1	2	1	1	0	0	0	0	0	0	0	0	0	63	58	5	5
0	0	0	0	0	0	0	0	0	0	0	0	0	0	0	0	2	2	0	0
0	0	0	0	0	0	0	0	0	0	0	0	0	0	0	0	1	1	0	1
1	1	0	0	1	1	0	2	0	0	0	0	0	0	0	0	26	22	4	9
0	0	0	0	2	1	1	1	0	0	0	0	0	0	0	0	10	3	7	1
7	7	0	0	0	0	0	0	2	1	1	0	0	0	0	0	78	67	11	8
4	4	0	0	0	0	0	0	0	0	0	0	0	0	0	0	12	12	0	0
2	2	0	1	0	0	0	0	0	0	0	0	2	2	0	0	30	30	0	4
2	2	0	0	3	3	0	0	0	0	0	0	0	0	0	0	47	43	4	3
0	0	0	0	0	0	0	0	0	0	0	0	0	0	0	0	5	2	3	0
8	7	1	2	6	6	0	0	0	0	0	0	0	0	0	0	79	75	4	12
12	12	0	3	20	20	0	8	0	0	0	0	3	3	0	0	221	213	8	58
0	0	0	0	0	0	0	0	0	0	0	0	0	0	0	0	3	3	0	1
2	2	0	0	1	1	0	0	0	0	0	0	0	0	0	0	28	27	1	0
12	12	0	0	0	0	0	0	0	0	0	0	0	0	0	0	149	149	0	1
5	5	0	0	0	0	0	0	0	0	0	0	0	0	0	0	96	96	0	3
0	0	0	0	0	0	0	0	0	0	0	0	0	0	0	0	8	8	0	0
0	0	0	0	0	0	0	0	0	0	0	0	0	0	0	0	2	2	0	0
1	1	0	0	5	5	0	1	0	0	0	0	0	0	0	0	54	54	0	3
4	4	0	0	0	0	0	0	0	0	0	0	3	3	0	0	36	36	0	3
0	0	0	0	0	0	0	0	0	0	0	0	0	0	0	0	1	1	0	0
1	1	0	0	0	0	0	0	0	0	0	0	0	0	0	0	2	2	0	0
23	22	1	3	22	21	1	1	0	0	0	0	5	4	1	1	304	287	17	17
13	13	0	0	0	0	0	0	0	0	0	0	0	0	0	0	172	172	0	10
0	0	0	0	0	0	0	0	0	0	0	0	0	0	0	0	2	2	0	0
2	2	0	0	0	0	0	0	0	0	0	0	3	3	0	2	20	20	0	5
20	20	0	4	0	0	0	0	0	0	0	0	0	0	0	0	238	238	0	28
0	0	0	0	0	0	0	0	0	0	0	0	0	0	0	0	4	4	0	1
0	0	0	0	0	0	0	0	0	0	0	0	0	0	0	0	8	1	7	0
2	2	0	1	0	0	0	0	2	2	0	0	0	0	0	0	14	13	1	1
0	0	0	0	0	0	0	0	0	0	0	0	0	0	0	0	9	9	0	0
0	0	0	0	0	0	0	0	0	0	0	0	0	0	0	0	3	3	0	0
5	5	0	0	0	0	0	0	0	0	0	0	0	0	0	0	57	57	0	0
8	6	2	0	10	10	0	0	0	0	0	0	0	0	0	0	109	75	34	2
2	2	0	0	2	1	1	1	0	0	0	0	0	0	0	0	29	18	11	7
1	1	0	0	1	1	0	0	0	0	0	0	0	0	0	0	3	3	0	0
30	30	0	1	13	13	0	1	4	4	0	1	21	21	0	4	449	449	0	39
48	46	2	2	67	65	2	6	15	15	0	3	6	6	0	2	799	787	12	61
0	0	0	0	0	0	0	0	0	0	0	0	0	0	0	0	4	0	4	0
0	0	0	0	0	0	0	0	0	0	0	0	0	0	0	0	2	0	2	0
3	3	0	0	0	0	0	0	0	0	0	0	0	0	0	0	16	16	0	0
0	0	0	0	0	0	0	0	0	0	0	0	0	0	0	0	1	1	0	0
19	19	0	0	18	18	0	1	8	8	0	0	1	1	0	0	184	184	0	2

Player	Date of Birth	Career	League				Premier League			
			Apps	Starts	Subs	Goals	Apps	Starts	Subs	Goal
Mark BOWEN	7 December 1963	1996/97	0	0	0	0	17	15	2	1
Lee BOWYER	3 January 1977	2002/03 and 2006/07 - 2008/09	0	0	0	0	51	44	7	4
Ron BOYCE	6 January 1943	1959/60 - 1972/73	282	275	7	21	0	0	0	0
Lee BOYLAN	2 September 1978	1996/97	0	0	0	0	1	0	1	0
Peter BRABROOK	8 November 1937	1962/63 - 1967/68	167	167	0	33	0	0	0	0
T. BRADFORD	Unknown	1911/12	1	1	0	0	0	0	0	0
Harry BRADSHAW	8 August 1896	1919/20 - 1920/21	14	14	0	0	0	0	0	0
Liam BRADY	13 February 1956	1986/87 - 1989/90	89	79	10	9	0	0	0	0
Thomas BRANDON	28 May 1893	1913/14 - 1914/15	33	33	0	0	0	0	0	0
Tim BREACKER	2 July 1965	1990/91 - 1998/99	97	95	2	5	143	134	9	3
Gary BREEN	12 December 1973	2002/03	0	0	0	0	14	9	5	0
Ron BRETT	4 September 1937	1959/60 - 1960/61	12	12	0	4	0	0	0	0
Rufus BREVETT	24 September 1969	2002/03 - 2004/05	12	12	0	1	13	12	1	0
Wayne BRIDGE	5 August 1980	2010/11	0	0	0	0	15	15	0	0
William BRIDGEMAN	24 December 1883	1903/04 - 1905/06	72	72	0	19	0	0	0	0
Phil BRIGNULL	2 October 1960	1978/79	1	0	1	0	0	0	0	0
Martin BRITT	17 January 1946	1962/63 - 1965/66	20	20	0	6	0	0	0	0
Trevor BROOKING	2 October 1948	1967/68 - 1983/84	528	521	7	88	0	0	0	0
Ken BROWN	16 February 1932	1952/53 - 1966/67	386	386	0	4	0	0	0	0
Kenny BROWN	11 July 1967	1991/92 - 1995/96	42	38	6	5	21	17	4	0
William BROWN	Unknown	1907/08 - 1908/09	20	20	0	4	0	0	0	0
William BROWN	22 August 1900	1920/21 - 1923/24	60	60	0	15	0	0	0	0
Fred BRUNTON	1880	1904/05	1	1	0	0	0	0	0	0
Paul BRUSH	22 February 1958	1977/78 - 1984/85	151	144	7	1	0	0	0	0
Alex BUNBURY	18 June 1967	1992/93	4	2	2	0	0	0	0	0
Dick BURGESS	23 October 1986	1922/23	2	2	0	0	0	0	0	0
Reece BURKE	2 September 1996	2013/14 -	0	0	0	0	5	4	1	0
Jack BURKETT	21 August 1942	1961/62 - 1966/67	142	141	1	4	0	0	0	0
Dennis BURNETT	27 September 1944	1965/66 - 1966/67	50	48	2	0	0	0	0	0
Frank BURRILL	31 August 1892	1911/12 - 1913/14	17	17	0	2	0	0	0	0
David BURROWS	25 October 1968	1993/94 - 1994/95	0	0	0	0	29	29	0	1
Frank BURTON	1891	1912/13 - 1920/21	114	114	0	6	0	0	0	0
John BURTON	31 July 1885	1908/09	15	15	0	3	0	0	0	0
Stanley BURTON	3 December 1912	1938/39	1	1	0	0	0	0	0	0
Robert BUSH	10 July 1879	1902/03 - 1905/06	20	20	0	1	0	0	0	0
James BUTCHART	1882	1903/04	3	3	0	0	0	0	0	0
George BUTCHER	25 October 1890	1909/10 - 1920/21	96	96	0	17	0	0	0	0
Peter BUTLER	27 August 1966	1992/93 - 1994/95	39	39	0	2	31	31	0	1
Johnny BYRNE	13 May 1939	1961/62 - 1966/67	156	156	0	79	0	0	0	0
Shaun BYRNE	21 January 1981	1999/00 - 2003/04	0	0	0	0	2	0	2	0
Stephen BYWATER	7 June 1981	1999/00 - 2005/06	53	53	0	0	6	4	2	0
Albert CADWELL	1 November 1900	1923/24 - 1932/33	272	272	0	1	0	0	0	0
Thomas CALDWELL	1885	1909/10 - 1911/12	84	84	0	12	0	0	0	0
John CALLADINE	Unknown	1920/21	1	1	0	0	0	0	0	0
Henri CAMARA	10 May 1977	2007/08	0	0	0	0	10	3	7	0
Titi CAMARA	17 November 1972	2000/01 - 2002/03	0	0	0	0	11	5	6	0
Greg CAMPBELL	13 July 1965	1984/85 - 1985/86	5	3	2	0	0	0	0	0
John CAMPBELL	1877	1902/03	18	18	0	1	0	0	0	0

Apps	Starts	Subs	Goals	Apps	Starts	Subs	Goals	Apps	Starts	Subs	Goals	Apps	Starts	Subs	Goals	Apps	Starts	Subs	Goals
	FA Cup				League Cup				Europe				Other				Total		
0	0	0	0	3	3	0	0	0	0	0	0	0	0	0	0	20	18	2	1
3	2	1	0	4	3	1	1	2	2	0	0	0	0	0	0	60	51	9	5
21	20	1	5	23	23	0	2	13	13	0	1	2	2	0	0	341	333	8	29
0	0	0	0	0	0	0	0	0	0	0	0	0	0	0	0	1	0	1	0
17	17	0	3	23	23	0	6	7	7	0	1	1	1	0	0	215	215	0	43
0	0	0	0	0	0	0	0	0	0	0	0	0	0	0	0	1	1	0	0
1	1	0	0	0	0	0	0	0	0	0	0	0	0	0	0	15	15	0	0
9	9	0	1	17	14	3	0	0	0	0	0	4	4	0	0	119	106	13	10
3	3	0	0	0	0	0	0	0	0	0	0	0	0	0	0	36	36	0	0
28	27	1	0	21	20	1	0	0	0	0	0	7	7	0	0	296	283	13	8
2	2	0	0	2	2	0	0	0	0	0	0	0	0	0	0	18	13	5	0
1	1	0	0	0	0	0	0	0	0	0	0	1	1	0	1	14	14	0	5
0	0	0	0	4	4	0	0	0	0	0	0	0	0	0	0	29	28	1	1
2	2	0	0	1	1	0	0	0	0	0	0	0	0	0	0	18	18	0	0
3	3	0	1	0	0	0	0	0	0	0	0	0	0	0	0	75	75	0	20
0	0	0	0	0	0	0	0	0	0	0	0	0	0	0	0	1	0	1	0
0	0	0	0	6	6	0	1	0	0	0	0	0	0	0	0	26	26	0	7
40	40	0	3	55	55	0	8	12	11	1	3	8	8	0	0	643	635	8	102
26	26	0	0	28	28	0	0	15	15	0	0	19	19	0	0	474	474	0	4
9	7	0	1	3	2	1	0	0	0	0	0	4	2	2	0	79	66	13	6
0	0	0	0	0	0	0	0	0	0	0	0	0	0	0	0	20	20	0	4
11	11	0	5	0	0	0	0	0	0	0	0	0	0	0	0	71	71	0	20
0	0	0	0	0	0	0	0	0	0	0	0	0	0	0	0	1	1	0	0
17	17	0	0	13	12	1	0	4	1	3	0	1	1	0	0	186	175	11	1
1	0	1	0	0	0	0	0	0	0	0	0	1	1	0	0	6	3	3	0
0	0	0	0	0	0	0	0	0	0	0	0	0	0	0	0	2	2	0	0
1	0	1	0	1	1	0	0	0	0	0	0	0	0	0	0	7	5	2	0
18	18	0	0	17	17	0	0	7	7	0	0	1	1	0	0	185	184	1	4
4	4	0	1	10	10	0	2	2	2	0	0	0	0	0	0	66	64	2	3
0	0	0	0	0	0	0	0	0	0	0	0	0	0	0	0	17	17	0	2
3	3	0	0	3	3	0	1	0	0	0	0	0	0	0	0	35	35	0	2
11	11	0	0	0	0	0	0	0	0	0	0	0	0	0	0	125	125	0	6
4	4	0	0	0	0	0	0	0	0	0	0	0	0	0	0	19	19	0	3
0	0	0	0	0	0	0	0	0	0	0	0	0	0	0	0	1	1	0	0
1	1	0	0	0	0	0	0	0	0	0	0	0	0	0	0	21	21	0	1
Apps	Starts	Subs	Goals	Apps	Starts	Subs	Goals	Apps	Starts	Subs	Goals	Apps	Starts	Subs	Goals	3	3	0	0
13	13	0	5	0	0	0	0	0	0	0	0	0	0	0	0	109	109	0	22
3	3	0	0	4	4	0	0	0	0	0	0	1	1	0	0	78	78	0	3
18	18	0	7	19	19	0	15	12	12	0	6	1	1	0	1	206	206	0	108
1	0	1	0	0	0	0	0	0	0	0	0	0	0	0	0	3	0	3	0
5	5	0	0	0	0	0	0	0	0	0	0	4	3	1	0	68	65	3	0
25	25	0	0	0	0	0	0	0	0	0	0	0	0	0	0	297	297	0	1
12	12	0	1	0	0	0	0	0	0	0	0	0	0	0	0	96	96	0	13
0	0	0	0	0	0	0	0	0	0	0	0	0	0	0	0	1	1	0	0
0	0	0	0	0	0	0	0	0	0	0	0	0	0	0	0	10	3	7	0
2	1	1	0	1	1	0	0	0	0	0	0	0	0	0	0	14	7	7	0
0	0	0	0	0	0	0	0	0	0	0	0	0	0	0	0	5	3	2	0
0	0	0	0	0	0	0	0	0	0	0	0	0	0	0	0	18	18	0	1

Player	Date of Birth	Career	League				Premier League			
			Apps	Starts	Subs	Goals	Apps	Starts	Subs	Goa
John CAMPBELL	12 May 1901	1923/24 - 1927/28	28	28	0	11	0	0	0	0
Frank CANNON	8 November 1884	1909/10	3	3	0	1	0	0	0	0
Noel CANTWELL	28 February 1932	1952/53 - 1960/61	248	248	0	11	0	0	0	0
John CAREW	5 September 1979	2011/12	19	7	12	2	0	0	0	0
Sebastien CAROLE	8 September 1982	2003/04	1	0	1	0	0	0	0	0
Franz CARR	24 September 1966	1990/91	3	1	2	0	0	0	0	0
James CARR	19 December 1893	1914/15	9	9	0	1	0	0	0	0
Christopher CARRICK	8 October 1882	1904/05	18	18	0	6	0	0	0	0
Michael CARRICK	28 July 1981	1999/00 - 2003/04	35	34	1	1	101	94	7	5
Andy CARROLL	6 January 1989	2012/13 -	0	0	0	0	53	46	7	14
Johnny CARROLL	11 May 1923	1948/49	5	5	0	0	0	0	0	0
Roy CARROLL	30 September 1977	2005/06 - 2006/07	0	0	0	0	31	31	0	0
George CARTER	19 October 1900	1919/20 - 1926/27	136	136	0	1	0	0	0	0
Henry CARTER	16 September 1892	1912/13 - 1913/14	10	10	0	0	0	0	0	0
Johnny CARTWRIGHT	5 November 1940	1956/57 - 1960/61	4	4	0	0	0	0	0	0
Jack CASEY	1888	1912/13 - 1914/15	74	74	0	12	0	0	0	0
Ron CATER	2 February 1922	1945/46 - 1949/50	63	63	0	0	0	0	0	0
Harold CATON	1891	1912/13 - 1914/15	10	10	0	0	0	0	0	0
Luke CHADWICK	18 November 1980	2004/05	32	22	10	1	0	0	0	0
Alfred CHALKLEY	16 August 1904	1931/32 - 1936/37	188	188	0	1	0	0	0	0
George CHALKLEY	1883	1908/09	7	7	0	0	0	0	0	0
Marouane CHAMAKH	10 January 1984	2012/13	0	0	0	0	3	2	1	0
Leo CHAMBERS	5 August 1995	2013/14 -	0	0	0	0	0	0	0	0
Eddie CHAPMAN	3 August 1923	1948/49	7	7	0	3	0	0	0	0
Lee CHAPMAN	5 February 1959	1993/94 - 1994/95	0	0	0	0	40	33	7	7
Clive CHARLES	3 October 1951	1971/72 - 1973/74	14	12	2	0	0	0	0	0
Gary CHARLES	13 April 1970	1999/00 - 2000/01	0	0	0	0	5	2	3	0
John CHARLES	20 September 1944	1962/63 - 1969/70	118	117	1	1	0	0	0	0
William CHARLTON	10 October 1900	1922/23	8	8	0	0	0	0	0	0
Peter CHISWICK	19 September 1929	1953/54 - 1954/55	19	19	0	0	0	0	0	0
William CHURCH	Unknown	1903/04	2	2	0	0	0	0	0	0
Edouard CISSE	30 March 1978	2002/03	0	0	0	0	25	18	7	0
Alexander CLARK	28 October 1956	1982/83	26	26	0	7	0	0	0	0
Clive CLARKE	14 January 1980	2005/06	0	0	0	0	2	2	0	0
David CLARKE	21 May 1878	1906/07 - 1908/09	17	17	0	0	0	0	0	0
Simon CLARKE	23 September 1971	1990/91 - 1992/93	3	0	3	0	0	0	0	0
Joe COCKROFT	20 June 1911	1932/33 - 1938/39	251	251	0	3	0	0	0	0
Chris COHEN	5 March 1987	2003/04 - 2005/06	18	2	16	0	0	0	0	0
Adewunmi COKER	19 May 1954	1971/72 - 1973/74	10	9	1	3	0	0	0	0
Carlton COLE	12 November 1983	2006/07 - 2014/15	40	28	12	14	216	130	86	41
Joe COLE	8 November 1981	1998/99 - 2002/03 and 2012/13 - 2013/14	0	0	0	0	157	121	36	15
Keith COLEMAN	24 May 1951	1973/74 - 1976/77	101	96	5	0	0	0	0	0
Danny COLLINS	6 August 1980	2011/12	11	4	7	1	0	0	0	0
James COLLINS	23 August 1983	2005/06 - 2009/10 and 2012/13 -	0	0	0	0	134	123	11	3
Jimmy COLLINS	28 September 1903	1923/24 - 1935/36	311	311	0	3	0	0	0	0
Jack COLLISON	2 October 1988	2007/08 - 2013/14	31	26	5	4	74	49	25	7
David CONNOLLY	6 June 1977	2003/04	39	37	2	10	0	0	0	0
Herman CONWAY	11 October 1908	1934/35 - 1938/39	122	122	0	0	0	0	0	0

FA Cup				League Cup				Europe				Other				Total			
Apps	Starts	Subs	Goals	Apps	Starts	Subs	Goals	Apps	Starts	Subs	Goals	Apps	Starts	Subs	Goals	Apps	Starts	Subs	Goals
1	1	0	0	0	0	0	0	0	0	0	0	0	0	0	0	29	29	0	11
1	1	0	0	0	0	0	0	0	0	0	0	0	0	0	0	4	4	0	1
15	15	0	0	0	0	0	0	0	0	0	0	15	15	0	1	278	278	0	12
1	1	0	0	1	1	0	0	0	0	0	0	0	0	0	0	21	9	12	2
0	0	0	0	0	0	0	0	0	0	0	0	0	0	0	0	1	0	1	0
0	0	0	0	0	0	0	0	0	0	0	0	0	0	0	0	3	1	2	0
0	0	0	0	0	0	0	0	0	0	0	0	0	0	0	0	9	9	0	1
0	0	0	0	0	0	0	0	0	0	0	0	0	0	0	0	18	18	0	6
11	11	0	0	8	8	0	0	1	0	1	0	3	3	0	0	159	150	9	6
2	2	0	0	1	1	0	0	0	0	0	0	0	0	0	0	56	49	7	14
0	0	0	0	0	0	0	0	0	0	0	0	0	0	0	0	5	5	0	0
2	2	0	0	0	0	0	0	2	2	0	0	0	0	0	0	35	35	0	0
19	19	0	0	0	0	0	0	0	0	0	0	0	0	0	0	155	155	0	1
0	0	0	0	0	0	0	0	0	0	0	0	0	0	0	0	10	10	0	0
0	0	0	0	1	1	0	0	0	0	0	0	3	3	0	3	8	8	0	3
9	9	0	1	0	0	0	0	0	0	0	0	0	0	0	0	83	83	0	13
7	7	0	0	0	0	0	0	0	0	0	0	0	0	0	0	70	70	0	0
0	0	0	0	0	0	0	0	0	0	0	0	0	0	0	0	10	10	0	0
3	3	0	0	1	1	0	0	0	0	0	0	0	0	0	0	36	26	10	1
14	14	0	0	0	0	0	0	0	0	0	0	0	0	0	0	202	202	0	1
4	4	0	0	0	0	0	0	0	0	0	0	0	0	0	0	11	11	0	0
0	0	0	0	0	0	0	0	0	0	0	0	0	0	0	0	3	2	1	0
0	0	0	0	3	3	0	0	0	0	0	0	0	0	0	0	3	3	0	0
0	0	0	0	0	0	0	0	0	0	0	0	0	0	0	0	7	7	0	3
6	6	0	2	5	4	1	2	0	0	0	0	0	0	0	0	51	43	8	11
1	0	1	0	0	0	0	0	0	0	0	0	0	0	0	0	15	12	3	0
0	0	0	0	1	1	0	0	0	0	0	0	0	0	0	0	6	3	3	0
1	1	0	0	19	19	0	1	4	4	0	0	0	0	0	0	142	141	1	2
0	0	0	0	0	0	0	0	0	0	0	0	0	0	0	0	8	8	0	0
0	0	0	0	0	0	0	0	0	0	0	0	2	2	0	0	21	21	0	0
0	0	0	0	0	0	0	0	0	0	0	0	0	0	0	0	2	2	0	0
2	2	0	0	1	1	0	0	0	0	0	0	0	0	0	0	28	21	7	0
1	1	0	0	7	7	0	3	0	0	0	0	0	0	0	0	34	34	0	10
0	0	0	0	1	1	0	0	0	0	0	0	0	0	0	0	3	3	0	0
0	0	0	0	0	0	0	0	0	0	0	0	0	0	0	0	17	17	0	0
0	0	0	0	0	0	0	0	0	0	0	0	0	0	0	0	3	0	3	0
12	12	0	0	0	0	0	0	0	0	0	0	0	0	0	0	263	263	0	3
1	0	1	0	3	2	1	0	0	0	0	0	0	0	0	0	22	4	18	0
1	1	0	0	0	0	0	0	0	0	0	0	0	0	0	0	11	10	1	3
15	11	4	5	17	9	8	7	2	1	1	0	3	3	0	1	293	182	111	68
12	11	1	2	12	11	1	1	5	2	3	0	0	0	0	0	186	145	41	18
3	3	0	0	6	6	0	0	7	6	1	0	5	3	2	0	122	114	8	0
0	0	0	0	0	0	0	0	0	0	0	0	0	0	0	0	11	4	7	1
9	9	0	3	6	5	1	0	1	1	0	0	0	0	0	0	150	138	12	6
25	25	0	0	0	0	0	0	0	0	0	0	0	0	0	0	336	336	0	3
7	5	2	0	6	4	2	1	0	0	0	0	3	3	0	2	121	87	34	14
4	4	0	2	2	2	0	2	0	0	0	0	3	3	0	0	48	46	2	14
5	5	0	0	0	0	0	0	0	0	0	0	0	0	0	0	127	127	0	0

Player	Date of Birth	Career	League				Premier League			
			Apps	Starts	Subs	Goals	Apps	Starts	Subs	Goal
Lawrence CONWELL	26 September 1909	1935/36 - 1936/37	8	8	0	1	0	0	0	0
Fred COOPER	18 November 1934	1956/57 - 1957/58	4	4	0	0	0	0	0	0
William COPE	25 November 1884	1914/15 - 1921/22	137	137	0	0	0	0	0	0
David CORBETT	1 February 1910	1936/37	4	4	0	0	0	0	0	0
Fred CORBETT	1879	1900/01 - 1901/02	33	33	0	13	0	0	0	0
Norman CORBETT	23 June 1919	1936/37 - 1949/50	166	166	0	3	0	0	0	0
John COSHALL	21 January 1901	1928/29	2	2	0	0	0	0	0	0
Frank COSTELLO	1884	1908/09	12	12	0	3	0	0	0	0
Tony COTTEE	11 July 1965	1982/83 - 1987-88 and 1994/95 - 1996/97	212	203	9	92	67	63	4	23
Charles COTTON	January 1881	1903/04 - 1905/06	18	18	0	0	0	0	0	0
Laurent COURTOIS	11 September 1978	2001/02	0	0	0	0	7	5	2	0
Herbert COWELL	Unknown	1920/21	1	1	0	0	0	0	0	0
George COWIE	6 May 1961	1981/82 - 1982/83	8	6	2	0	0	0	0	0
Peter COWPER	1 September 1902	1924/25	2	2	0	0	0	0	0	0
Charlie COX	31 July 1905	1927/28 - 1931/32	89	89	0	0	0	0	0	0
Chris COYNE	20 December 1978	1998/99	0	0	0	0	1	0	1	0
Charles CRAIG	11 July 1874	1900/01 - 1901/02	53	53	0	0	0	0	0	0
Ian CRAWFORD	14 July 1934	1961/62 - 1962/63	25	25	0	5	0	0	0	0
Aaron CRESSWELL	15 December 1989	2014/15 -	0	0	0	0	38	38	0	2
Harry CRIPPS	29 April 1941	1959/60	0	0	0	0	0	0	0	0
David CROSS	8 December 1950	1977/78 - 1981/82	179	178	1	77	0	0	0	0
Roger CROSS	20 October 1948	1968/69 - 1969/70	7	5	2	1	0	0	0	0
Charles CROSSLEY	17 December 1891	1922/23	15	15	0	1	0	0	0	0
George CROWTHER	1892	1920/21	3	3	0	0	0	0	0	0
James CUMMING	1890	1919/20 - 1920/21	15	15	0	0	0	0	0	0
Alan CURBISHLEY	8 November 1954	1974/75 - 1978/79	85	78	7	5	0	0	0	0
Frank CURTIS	1890	1909/10 - 1910/11	6	6	0	4	0	0	0	0
John CUSHLEY	21 January 1943	1967/68 - 1969/70	38	38	0	0	0	0	0	0
Manuel Da COSTA	6 May 1986	2009/10 - 2010/11	0	0	0	0	31	26	5	3
Dani Da Cruz CARVALHO	2 November 1976	1995/96	0	0	0	0	9	3	6	2
Christian DAILLY	23 October 1973	2000/01 - 2006/07	46	45	1	2	112	88	24	0
Fabio DAPRELA	19 February 1991	2009/10	0	0	0	0	7	4	3	0
Billy DARE	14 February 1927	1954/55 - 1958/59	111	111	0	44	0	0	0	0
Calum DAVENPORT	1 January 1983	2004/05 and 2006/07 - 2008/09	10	10	0	0	13	12	1	1
Alexander DAVIDSON	27 September 1878	1902/03	9	9	0	2	0	0	0	0
Trevor DAWKINS	7 October 1945	1964/65 - 1966/67	6	5	1	0	0	0	0	0
Charles DAWSON	1886	1908/09 - 1909/10	6	6	0	0	0	0	0	0
Harold DAWSON	18 March 1888	1911/12 - 1912/13	22	22	0	3	0	0	0	0
Mervyn DAY	26 June 1955	1973/74 - 1978/79	194	194	0	0	0	0	0	0
Richard DEACON	26 May 1911	1932/33	3	3	0	0	0	0	0	0
Brian DEANE	7 February 1968	2003/04	26	9	17	6	0	0	0	0
Brian DEAR	18 September 1943	1962/63 - 1968/69 and 1970/71	69	67	2	33	0	0	0	0
Stephen DEATH	19 September 1949	1968/69	1	1	0	0	0	0	0	0
Jermain DEFOE	7 October 1982	2000/01 - 2003/04	19	19	0	11	74	43	31	18
Fred DELL	10 December 1915	1936/37 - 1937/38	4	4	0	0	0	0	0	0
Guy DEMEL	13 June 1981	2011/12 - 2014/15	7	7	0	0	69	61	8	1
Albert DENYER	9 April 1893	1912/13 - 1913/14	46	46	0	17	0	0	0	0
Frank DENYER	1890	1913/14	2	2	0	0	0	0	0	0

	FA Cup				League Cup				Europe				Other				Total			
ps	Starts	Subs	Goals	Apps	Starts	Subs	Goals	Apps	Starts	Subs	Goals	Apps	Starts	Subs	Goals	Apps	Starts	Subs	Goals
0	0	0	0	0	0	0	0	0	0	0	0	0	0	0	0	8	8	0	1
0	0	0	0	0	0	0	0	0	0	0	0	6	6	0	0	10	10	0	0
0	10	0	0	0	0	0	0	0	0	0	0	0	0	0	0	147	147	0	0
0	0	0	0	0	0	0	0	0	0	0	0	0	0	0	0	4	4	0	0
2	2	0	2	0	0	0	0	0	0	0	0	0	0	0	0	35	35	0	15
8	8	0	0	0	0	0	0	0	0	0	0	0	0	0	0	174	174	0	3
0	0	0	0	0	0	0	0	0	0	0	0	0	0	0	0	2	2	0	0
0	0	0	0	0	0	0	0	0	0	0	0	0	0	0	0	12	12	0	3
29	29	0	12	27	27	0	18	0	0	0	0	1	1	0	1	336	323	13	146
1	1	0	0	0	0	0	0	0	0	0	0	0	0	0	0	19	19	0	0
0	0	0	0	1	0	1	0	0	0	0	0	0	0	0	0	8	5	3	0
0	0	0	0	0	0	0	0	0	0	0	0	0	0	0	0	1	1	0	0
1	1	0	0	0	0	0	0	0	0	0	0	0	0	0	0	9	7	2	0
0	0	0	0	0	0	0	0	0	0	0	0	0	0	0	0	2	2	0	0
8	8	0	0	0	0	0	0	0	0	0	0	0	0	0	0	97	97	0	0
0	0	0	0	0	0	0	0	0	0	0	0	0	0	0	0	1	0	1	0
7	7	0	0	0	0	0	0	0	0	0	0	0	0	0	0	60	60	0	0
1	1	0	0	1	1	0	2	0	0	0	0	0	0	0	0	27	27	0	7
4	4	0	0	0	0	0	0	0	0	0	0	0	0	0	0	42	42	0	2
0	0	0	0	0	0	0	0	0	0	0	0	1	1	0	0	1	1	0	0
14	14	0	2	24	24	0	12	6	6	0	6	1	1	0	0	224	223	1	97
0	0	0	0	1	1	0	0	0	0	0	0	0	0	0	0	8	6	2	1
1	1	0	0	0	0	0	0	0	0	0	0	0	0	0	0	16	16	0	1
0	0	0	0	0	0	0	0	0	0	0	0	0	0	0	0	3	3	0	0
0	0	0	0	0	0	0	0	0	0	0	0	0	0	0	0	15	15	0	0
5	5	0	0	3	3	0	0	2	1	1	0	1	0	1	0	96	87	9	5
0	0	0	0	0	0	0	0	0	0	0	0	0	0	0	0	6	6	0	4
4	4	0	0	4	4	0	0	0	0	0	0	0	0	0	0	46	46	0	0
1	1	0	0	3	3	0	1	0	0	0	0	0	0	0	0	35	30	5	4
0	0	0	0	0	0	0	0	0	0	0	0	0	0	0	0	9	3	6	2
20	14	6	0	8	8	0	1	0	0	0	0	5	3	2	1	191	158	33	4
1	1	0	0	0	0	0	0	0	0	0	0	0	0	0	0	8	5	3	0
8	8	0	5	0	0	0	0	0	0	0	0	8	8	0	5	127	127	0	54
0	0	0	0	1	1	0	0	0	0	0	0	0	0	0	0	24	23	1	1
0	0	0	0	0	0	0	0	0	0	0	0	0	0	0	0	9	9	0	2
0	0	0	0	0	0	0	0	0	0	0	0	0	0	0	0	6	5	1	0
0	0	0	0	0	0	0	0	0	0	0	0	0	0	0	0	6	6	0	0
0	0	0	0	0	0	0	0	0	0	0	0	0	0	0	0	22	22	0	3
14	14	0	0	14	14	0	0	9	9	0	0	6	6	0	0	237	237	0	0
0	0	0	0	0	0	0	0	0	0	0	0	0	0	0	0	3	3	0	0
3	3	0	1	0	0	0	0	0	0	0	0	3	0	3	0	32	12	20	7
7	6	1	2	3	3	0	0	6	6	0	4	0	0	0	0	85	82	3	39
0	0	0	0	0	0	0	0	0	0	0	0	0	0	0	0	1	1	0	0
5	4	1	6	7	6	1	6	0	0	0	0	0	0	0	0	105	72	33	41
0	0	0	0	0	0	0	0	0	0	0	0	0	0	0	0	4	4	0	0
2	1	1	0	2	2	0	0	0	0	0	0	3	3	0	0	83	74	9	1
4	4	0	1	0	0	0	0	0	0	0	0	0	0	0	0	50	50	0	18
0	0	0	0	0	0	0	0	0	0	0	0	0	0	0	0	2	2	0	0

Player	Date of Birth	Career	League				Premier League			
			Apps	Starts	Subs	Goals	Apps	Starts	Subs	Goal
Ernie DEVLIN	6 March 1920	1946/47 - 1952/53	70	70	0	0	0	0	0	0
Alan DEVONSHIRE	13 April 1956	1976/77 - 1989/90	358	345	13	29	0	0	0	0
Paolo DI CANIO	9 July 1968	1998/99 - 2002/03	0	0	0	0	118	114	4	47
David Di MICHELE	6 January 1976	2008/09	0	0	0	0	30	22	8	4
Alessandro DIAMANTI	2 May 1983	2009/10 - 2010/11	0	0	0	0	28	18	10	7
Mohamed DIAME	14 June 1987	2012/13 - 2014/15	0	0	0	0	71	60	11	7
Alou DIARRA	15 July 1981	2012/13 - 2013/14	0	0	0	0	6	2	4	0
Kaba DIAWARA	16 December 1975	2000/01	0	0	0	0	11	6	5	0
George DICK	12 June 1921	1948/49	14	14	0	1	0	0	0	0
John DICK	19 March 1930	1953/54 - 1962/63	326	326	0	153	0	0	0	0
Alan DICKENS	3 September 1964	1982/83 - 1988/89	192	173	19	23	0	0	0	0
Alan DICKIE	30 January 1944	1961/62 - 1965/66	12	12	0	0	0	0	0	0
Julian DICKS	8 August 1968	1987/88 - 1993/94 and 1994/95 - 1998/99	152	152	0	29	110	110	0	21
Papa Bouba DIOP	28 January 1978	2011/12	16	14	2	1	0	0	0	0
Robert DIXON	30 August 1901	1928/29 - 1932/33	65	65	0	0	0	0	0	0
Tommy DIXON	8 June 1929	1952/53 - 1954/55	39	39	0	21	0	0	0	0
Eamonn DOLAN	20 September 1967	1986/87 - 1989/90	15	9	6	3	0	0	0	0
Warren DONALD	7 October 1964	1983/84	2	1	1	0	0	0	0	0
Charles DOVE	8 April 1977	1900/01	13	13	0	0	0	0	0	0
James DOW	25 April 1873	1902/03	13	13	0	0	0	0	0	0
John DOWEN	31 October 1914	1935/36	1	1	0	0	0	0	0	0
Iain DOWIE	9 January 1965	1990/91 - 1991/92 and 1995/96 - 1997/98	12	12	0	4	68	58	10	8
Stewart DOWNING	22 July 1984	2013/14 -	0	0	0	0	69	66	3	7
John DOWSEY	1 May 1905	1926/27	1	1	0	0	0	0	0	0
Callum DRIVER	23 October 1992	2013/14	0	0	0	0	0	0	0	0
Ilie DUMITRESCU	6 January 1969	1995/96 - 1996/97	0	0	0	0	10	5	5	0
Dave DUNMORE	18 February 1934	1959/60 - 1960/61	36	36	0	16	0	0	0	0
Richard DUNN	23 December 1919	1946/47 - 1947/48	11	11	0	2	0	0	0	0
Joe DURRELL	15 March 1953	1971/72	6	5	1	0	0	0	0	0
Noel DWYER	30 October 1934	1958/59 - 1959/60	36	36	0	0	0	0	0	0
James DYER	24 August 1880	1908/09	3	3	0	0	0	0	0	0
Kieron DYER	29 December 1978	2007/08 - 2010/11	0	0	0	0	30	15	15	0
Doug EADIE	22 September 1946	1966/67	2	2	0	0	0	0	0	0
Alfred EARL	19 March 1903	1925/26 - 1932/33	191	191	0	0	0	0	0	0
Arthur EARL	Unknown	1903/04	1	1	0	0	0	0	0	0
Stanley EARLE	6 September 1897	1924/25 - 1931/32	258	258	0	56	0	0	0	0
George EASTMAN	7 April 1903	1924/25 - 1925/26	2	2	0	0	0	0	0	0
Henry EASTWOOD	1887	1908/09	6	6	0	0	0	0	0	0
George ECCLES	1872	1902/03 - 1903/04	59	59	0	0	0	0	0	0
Anthony EDGAR	30 September 1990	2009/10 - 2010/11	0	0	0	0	0	0	0	0
William EDWARDS	1896	1922/23 - 1925/26	37	37	0	3	0	0	0	0
Ernest ENGLAND	3 February 1901	1930/31	5	5	0	0	0	0	0	0
Hogan EPHRAIM	31 March 1988	2005/06	0	0	0	0	0	0	0	0
Matthew ETHERINGTON	14 August 1981	2003/04 - 2008/09	74	71	3	9	91	80	11	7
Cliff ETTE	17 June 1910	1933/34	1	1	0	1	0	0	0	0
Peter EUSTACE	31 July 1944	1969/70 - 1971/72	43	41	2	6	0	0	0	0
Arthur EVANS	8 July 1906	1930/31	1	1	0	0	0	0	0	0
Roger EVANS	17 November 1879	1902/03	1	1	0	0	0	0	0	0

...ps	\<FA Cup\> Starts	Subs	Goals	\<League Cup\> Apps	Starts	Subs	Goals	\<Europe\> Apps	Starts	Subs	Goals	\<Other\> Apps	Starts	Subs	Goals	\<Total\> Apps	Starts	Subs	Goals
2	2	0	0	0	0	0	0	0	0	0	0	5	5	0	0	77	77	0	0
6	36	0	1	48	45	3	2	4	4	0	0	2	2	0	0	448	432	16	32
5	5	0	1	7	7	0	1	4	4	0	1	6	6	0	0	140	136	4	50
3	2	1	0	1	1	0	0	0	0	0	0	0	0	0	0	34	25	9	4
1	1	0	1	1	1	0	0	0	0	0	0	0	0	0	0	30	20	10	8
1	1	0	0	7	4	3	0	0	0	0	0	0	0	0	0	79	65	14	7
3	3	0	0	5	4	1	0	0	0	0	0	0	0	0	0	14	9	5	0
0	0	0	0	0	0	0	0	0	0	0	0	0	0	0	0	11	6	5	0
1	1	0	0	0	0	0	0	0	0	0	0	0	0	0	0	15	15	0	1
21	21	0	11	4	4	0	2	0	0	0	0	16	16	0	11	367	367	0	177
22	19	3	3	17	14	3	3	0	0	0	0	3	3	0	1	234	209	25	30
0	0	0	0	2	2	0	0	1	1	0	0	0	0	0	0	15	15	0	0
23	23	0	3	30	30	0	8	0	0	0	0	11	11	0	4	326	326	0	65
0	0	0	0	0	0	0	0	0	0	0	0	0	0	0	0	16	14	2	1
3	3	0	0	0	0	0	0	0	0	0	0	0	0	0	0	68	68	0	0
3	3	0	2	0	0	0	0	0	0	0	0	2	2	0	2	44	44	0	25
0	0	0	0	4	4	0	0	0	0	0	0	2	1	1	1	21	14	7	4
0	0	0	0	0	0	0	0	0	0	0	0	0	0	0	0	2	1	1	0
3	3	0	0	0	0	0	0	0	0	0	0	0	0	0	0	16	16	0	0
1	1	0	0	0	0	0	0	0	0	0	0	0	0	0	0	14	14	0	0
0	0	0	0	0	0	0	0	0	0	0	0	0	0	0	0	1	1	0	0
4	3	1	1	11	10	1	2	0	0	0	0	0	0	0	0	95	83	12	15
5	5	0	0	5	1	4	0	0	0	0	0	0	0	0	0	79	72	7	7
0	0	0	0	0	0	0	0	0	0	0	0	0	0	0	0	1	1	0	0
1	0	0	0	0	0	0	0	0	0	0	0	0	0	0	0	1	0	0	0
0	0	0	0	3	2	1	0	0	0	0	0	0	0	0	0	13	7	6	0
1	1	0	1	2	2	0	1	0	0	0	0	2	2	0	0	41	41	0	18
0	0	0	0	0	0	0	0	0	0	0	0	0	0	0	0	11	11	0	2
0	0	0	0	0	0	0	0	0	0	0	0	0	0	0	0	6	5	1	0
2	2	0	0	0	0	0	0	0	0	0	0	5	5	0	0	43	43	0	0
0	0	0	0	0	0	0	0	0	0	0	0	0	0	0	0	3	3	0	0
1	0	1	0	4	2	2	0	0	0	0	0	0	0	0	0	35	17	18	0
0	0	0	0	0	0	0	0	0	0	0	0	0	0	0	0	2	2	0	0
15	15	0	0	0	0	0	0	0	0	0	0	0	0	0	0	206	206	0	0
0	0	0	0	0	0	0	0	0	0	0	0	0	0	0	0	1	1	0	0
15	15	0	2	0	0	0	0	0	0	0	0	0	0	0	0	273	273	0	58
0	0	0	0	0	0	0	0	0	0	0	0	0	0	0	0	2	2	0	0
0	0	0	0	0	0	0	0	0	0	0	0	0	0	0	0	6	6	0	0
5	5	0	0	0	0	0	0	0	0	0	0	0	0	0	0	64	64	0	0
2	0	2	0	0	0	0	0	0	0	0	0	0	0	0	0	2	0	2	0
2	2	0	0	0	0	0	0	0	0	0	0	0	0	0	0	39	39	0	3
0	0	0	0	0	0	0	0	0	0	0	0	0	0	0	0	5	5	0	0
0	0	0	0	1	0	1	0	0	0	0	0	0	0	0	0	1	0	1	0
15	13	2	1	8	7	1	0	1	0	1	0	6	6	0	1	195	177	18	18
0	0	0	0	0	0	0	0	0	0	0	0	0	0	0	0	1	1	0	1
2	1	1	0	3	2	1	1	0	0	0	0	0	0	0	0	48	44	4	7
0	0	0	0	0	0	0	0	0	0	0	0	0	0	0	0	1	1	0	0
0	0	0	0	0	0	0	0	0	0	0	0	0	0	0	0	1	1	0	0

Player	Date of Birth	Career	League				Premier League			
			Apps	Starts	Subs	Goals	Apps	Starts	Subs	Goa
Aubrey FAIR	1881	1901/02 - 1906/07	31	31	0	1	0	0	0	0
Robert FAIRMAN	1883	1909/10 - 1911/12	91	91	0	0	0	0	0	0
Matthias FANIMO	28 January 1994	2012/13 - 2014/15	0	0	0	0	0	0	0	0
John FARRELL	1873	1902/03	20	20	0	3	0	0	0	0
Justin FASHANU	19 February 1961	1989/90	2	2	0	0	0	0	0	0
Julien FAUBERT	1 August 1983	2007/08 - 2011/12	34	28	6	1	69	58	11	1
Abdoulaye FAYE	26 February 1978	2011/12	29	25	4	0	0	0	0	0
Arthur FEATHERSTONE	1885	1905/06 - 1907/08	24	24	0	1	0	0	0	0
George FENN	January 1939	1956/57 - 1957/58	0	0	0	0	0	0	0	0
Benny FENTON	28 October 1918	1937/38 - 1937/38	21	21	0	9	0	0	0	0
Edward FENTON	7 November 1914	1932/33 - 1945/46	163	163	0	18	0	0	0	0
Frederick FENTON	16 November 1879	1900/01	14	14	0	2	0	0	0	0
Alfred FENWICK	26 March 1891	1914/15 - 1919/20	21	21	0	1	0	0	0	0
Anton FERDINAND	18 February 1985	2003/04 - 2007/08	49	33	16	1	89	85	4	4
Les FERDINAND	8 December 1966	2002/03	0	0	0	0	14	12	2	2
Rio FERDINAND	7 November 1978	1995/96 - 2000/01	0	0	0	0	127	122	5	2
Bobby FERGUSON	1 March 1945	1967/68 - 1979/80	240	240	0	0	0	0	0	0
Ian FEUER	20 May 1971	1999/00	0	0	0	0	3	3	0	0
Neil FINN	29 December 1978	1995/96	0	0	0	0	1	1	0	0
Albert FLETCHER	30 December 1898	1922/23 - 1923/24	8	8	0	1	0	0	0	0
Carl FLETCHER	7 April 1980	2004/05 - 2005/06	32	26	6	2	12	6	6	1
Jack FLETCHER	Unknown	1904/05	25	25	0	7	0	0	0	0
Jack FLYNN	4 October 1875	1904/05	20	20	0	3	0	0	0	0
Albert FOAN	30 October 1923	1950/51 - 1956/57	53	53	0	6	0	0	0	0
Marc-Vivien FOE	1 May 1975	1998/99 - 1999/00	0	0	0	0	38	38	0	1
William FORD	14 April 1881	1905/06	7	7	0	1	0	0	0	0
Steve FORDE	29 August 1914	1937/38 - 1951/52	170	170	0	1	0	0	0	0
George FOREMAN	1 March 1914	1938/39 - 1945/46	6	6	0	1	0	0	0	0
John FOREMAN	13 November 1913	1934/35 - 1936/37	49	49	0	7	0	0	0	0
Craig FORREST	20 September 1967	1997/98 - 2000/01	0	0	0	0	30	26	4	0
Harry FORSTER	1884	1912/13 - 1913/14	40	40	0	0	0	0	0	0
Colin FOSTER	16 July 1964	1989/90 - 1993/94	88	83	5	4	5	5	0	0
Jack FOSTER	19 November 1877	1908/09	15	15	0	9	0	0	0	0
Joseph FOXALL	8 October 1914	1934/35 - 1938/39	106	106	0	37	0	0	0	0
Hayden FOXE	23 June 1977	2000/01 - 2001/02	0	0	0	0	11	7	4	0
Guillermo FRANCO	3 November 1976	2009/10	0	0	0	0	23	16	7	5
Alf FROST	1888	1910/11 - 1911/12	4	4	0	0	0	0	0	0
James FROST	1880	1907/08 - 1908/09	20	20	0	4	0	0	0	0
Arthur FRYATT	17 April 1905	1930/31 - 1932/33	3	3	0	0	0	0	0	0
Paulo FUTRE	28 February 1966	1996/97	0	0	0	0	9	4	5	0
Daniel GABBIDON	8 August 1979	2005/06 - 2010/11	0	0	0	0	96	89	7	0
Tony GALE	19 November 1959	1984/85 - 1993/94	268	262	6	5	32	31	1	0
Tommy GALL	5 May 1906	1934/35	1	1	0	0	0	0	0	0
Joe GALLAGHER	11 January 1955	1982/83	9	8	1	0	0	0	0	0
Frederick GAMBLE	29 May 1905	1930/31	2	2	0	2	0	0	0	0
Richard GARCIA	4 September 1981	2001/02 - 2004/05	8	2	6	0	8	2	6	0
David GARDNER	31 March 1873	1904/05 - 1906/07	77	77	0	0	0	0	0	0
William GATLAND	6 July 1898	1920/21	1	1	0	0	0	0	0	0

	FA Cup				League Cup				Europe				Other				Total			
ps	Starts	Subs	Goals	Apps	Starts	Subs	Goals	Apps	Starts	Subs	Goals	Apps	Starts	Subs	Goals	Apps	Starts	Subs	Goals
2	2	0	0	0	0	0	0	0	0	0	0	0	0	0	0	33	33	0	1
2	12	0	0	0	0	0	0	0	0	0	0	0	0	0	0	103	103	0	0
1	0	1	0	2	0	2	0	0	0	0	0	0	0	0	0	3	0	3	0
1	1	0	0	0	0	0	0	0	0	0	0	0	0	0	0	21	21	0	3
	0	0	0	3	0	1	0	0	0	0	0	0	0	0	0	5	2	1	0
5	4	1	0	11	10	1	0	0	0	0	0	2	0	2	0	121	100	21	2
	0	0	0	0	0	0	0	0	0	0	0	0	0	0	0	29	25	4	0
1	1	0	0	0	0	0	0	0	0	0	0	0	0	0	0	25	25	0	1
	0	0	0	0	0	0	0	0	0	0	0	3	3	0	0	3	3	0	0
1	1	0	0	0	0	0	0	0	0	0	0	0	0	0	0	22	22	0	9
3	13	0	0	0	0	0	0	0	0	0	0	0	0	0	0	176	176	0	18
5	5	0	1	0	0	0	0	0	0	0	0	0	0	0	0	19	19	0	3
2	2	0	0	0	0	0	0	0	0	0	0	0	0	0	0	23	23	0	1
4	14	0	0	7	6	1	0	1	1	0	0	3	3	0	0	163	142	21	5
	0	0	0	0	0	0	0	0	0	0	0	0	0	0	0	14	12	2	2
9	9	0	0	12	11	1	0	9	9	0	0	0	0	0	0	157	151	6	2
7	17	0	0	19	19	0	0	0	0	0	0	1	1	0	0	277	277	0	0
	0	0	0	0	0	0	0	0	0	0	0	0	0	0	0	3	3	0	0
	0	0	0	0	0	0	0	0	0	0	0	0	0	0	0	1	1	0	0
	0	0	0	0	0	0	0	0	0	0	0	0	0	0	0	8	8	0	1
7	4	3	0	1	0	1	0	0	0	0	0	1	1	0	0	53	37	16	3
1	1	0	0	0	0	0	0	0	0	0	0	0	0	0	0	26	26	0	7
1	1	0	1	0	0	0	0	0	0	0	0	0	0	0	0	21	21	0	4
7	7	0	3	0	0	0	0	0	0	0	0	4	4	0	0	64	64	0	9
1	1	0	0	3	3	0	0	6	5	1	1	0	0	0	0	48	47	1	2
0	0	0	0	0	0	0	0	0	0	0	0	0	0	0	0	7	7	0	1
6	6	0	0	0	0	0	0	0	0	0	0	2	2	0	0	178	178	0	1
3	3	0	1	0	0	0	0	0	0	0	0	0	0	0	0	9	9	0	2
2	2	0	0	0	0	0	0	0	0	0	0	0	0	0	0	51	51	0	7
4	4	0	0	3	3	0	0	1	1	0	0	0	0	0	0	38	34	4	0
4	4	0	0	0	0	0	0	0	0	0	0	0	0	0	0	44	44	0	0
9	9	0	2	5	5	0	0	0	0	0	0	3	2	1	0	110	104	6	6
0	0	0	0	0	0	0	0	0	0	0	0	0	0	0	0	15	15	0	9
7	7	0	5	0	0	0	0	0	0	0	0	0	0	0	0	113	113	0	42
1	0	1	0	0	0	0	0	0	0	0	0	0	0	0	0	12	7	5	0
0	0	0	0	0	0	0	0	0	0	0	0	0	0	0	0	23	16	7	5
0	0	0	0	0	0	0	0	0	0	0	0	0	0	0	0	4	4	0	0
5	5	0	0	0	0	0	0	0	0	0	0	0	0	0	0	25	25	0	4
0	0	0	0	0	0	0	0	0	0	0	0	0	0	0	0	3	3	0	0
0	0	0	0	0	0	0	0	0	0	0	0	0	0	0	0	9	4	5	0
9	9	0	0	6	5	1	0	2	2	0	0	0	0	0	0	113	105	8	0
29	29	0	1	30	28	2	1	0	0	0	0	9	9	0	0	368	359	9	7
0	0	0	0	0	0	0	0	0	0	0	0	0	0	0	0	1	1	0	0
1	1	0	0	1	1	0	0	0	0	0	0	0	0	0	0	11	10	1	0
0	0	0	0	0	0	0	0	0	0	0	0	0	0	0	0	2	2	0	2
1	0	1	0	5	0	5	0	0	0	0	0	0	0	0	0	22	4	18	0
3	3	0	0	0	0	0	0	0	0	0	0	0	0	0	0	80	80	0	0
0	0	0	0	0	0	0	0	0	0	0	0	0	0	0	0	1	1	0	0

Player	Date of Birth	Career	League				Premier League			
			Apps	Starts	Subs	Goals	Apps	Starts	Subs	Goals
James GAULT	Unknown	1907/08 - 1908/09	47	47	0	0	0	0	0	0
Gerry GAZZARD	15 March 1925	1949/50 - 1953/54	119	119	0	29	0	0	0	0
John GEGGUS	1890	1909/10 - 1911/12	31	31	0	0	0	0	0	0
Vivian GIBBINS	10 August 1901	1923/24 - 1931/32	129	129	0	58	0	0	0	0
Victor GLOVER	1883	1911/12	29	29	0	0	0	0	0	0
James GODDARD	Unknown	1913/14	1	1	0	0	0	0	0	0
Paul GODDARD	12 October 1959	1980/81 - 1986/87	170	159	11	54	0	0	0	0
Reg GOODACRE	24 July 1908	1930/31 - 1932/33	20	20	0	0	0	0	0	0
Dale GORDON	9 January 1967	1993/94 - 1995/96	0	0	0	0	9	8	1	1
Reg GORE	1 August 1913	1938/39	5	5	0	1	0	0	0	0
Bobby GOULD	12 June 1946	1973/74 - 1975/76	51	46	5	15	0	0	0	0
Len GOULDEN	16 July 1912	1932/33 - 1938/39	239	239	0	52	0	0	0	0
William GRASSAM	20 November 1878	1900/01 - 1902/03 and 1905/06 - 1908/9	169	169	0	65	0	0	0	0
Jimmy GREAVES	20 February 1940	1969/70 - 1970/71	38	36	2	13	0	0	0	0
Bill GREEN	22 December 1950	1976/77 - 1977/78	35	35	0	1	0	0	0	0
Robert GREEN	18 January 1980	2006/07 - 2011/12	42	42	0	0	177	177	0	0
Tommy GREEN	25 November 1893	1919/20	3	3	0	0	0	0	0	0
Tommy GREEN	27 May 1913	1936/37 - 1938/39	40	40	0	6	0	0	0	0
Ernie GREGORY	10 November 1921	1946/47 - 1959/60	382	382	0	0	0	0	0	0
John GREGORY	24 September 1926	1951/52 - 1952/53	24	24	0	6	0	0	0	0
Mike GRICE	3 November 1931	1955/56 - 1960/61	142	142	0	18	0	0	0	0
Frederick GRIFFITHS	13 September 1873	1902/03 - 1903/04	48	48	0	0	0	0	0	0
Peter GROTIER	18 October 1950	1968/69 - 1972/73	50	50	0	0	0	0	0	0
William GUEST	8 February 1914	1936/37	3	3	0	1	0	0	0	0
Harry GUNNING	8 February 1932	1952/53	1	1	0	0	0	0	0	0
John GURKIN	9 September 1895	1921/22	1	1	0	0	0	0	0	0
Derek HALES	15 December 1955	1977/78	24	23	1	10	0	0	0	0
Almeric HALL	12 November 1912	1945/46 - 1948/49	50	50	0	11	0	0	0	0
Richard HALL	14 March 1972	1996/97 - 1998/99	0	0	0	0	7	7	0	0
Robert HALL	20 October 1993	2011/12 - 2012/13	4	0	4	0	0	0	0	0
Geoff HALLAS	8 December 1930	1954/55	3	3	0	0	0	0	0	0
John HAMILTON	1880	1904/05	5	5	0	0	0	0	0	0
Sidney HAMMOND	1883	1904/05 - 1907/08	32	32	0	0	0	0	0	0
Tommy HAMPSON	30 May 1897	1920/21 - 1924/25	70	70	0	0	0	0	0	0
Marlon HAREWOOD	25 August 1979	2003/04 - 2006/07	73	73	0	30	69	50	19	17
John HARKES	8 March 1967	1995/96	0	0	0	0	11	6	5	0
Jon HARLEY	26 September 1979	2003/04	15	15	0	1	0	0	0	0
Jim HARRIS	7 March 1907	1930/31 - 1931/32	7	7	0	1	0	0	0	0
Fred HARRISON	2 July 1880	1910/11 - 1912/13	54	54	0	19	0	0	0	0
Joseph HART	1899	1920/21	1	1	0	0	0	0	0	0
Trevor HARTLEY	16 March 1947	1966/67 - 1968/69	5	4	1	0	0	0	0	0
John HARTSON	5 April 1975	1996/97 - 1998/99	0	0	0	0	60	59	1	24
Alfred HARWOOD	16 April 1879	1907/08 - 1908/09	12	12	0	0	0	0	0	0
Bert HAWKINS	29 September 1923	1951/52 - 1952/53	34	34	0	16	0	0	0	0
Vincent HAYNES	1887	1909/10	15	15	0	5	0	0	0	0
Terry HAYWARD	Unknown	1957/58	0	0	0	0	0	0	0	0
Jack HEBDEN	12 November 1901	1920/21 - 1927/28	110	110	0	0	0	0	0	0
Paul HEFFER	21 December 1947	1966/67 - 1971/72	15	11	4	0	0	0	0	0

	FA Cup				League Cup				Europe				Other				Total		
Apps	Starts	Subs	Goals	Apps	Starts	Subs	Goals	Apps	Starts	Subs	Goals	Apps	Starts	Subs	Goals	Apps	Starts	Subs	Goals
2	2	0	0	0	0	0	0	0	0	0	0	0	0	0	0	49	49	0	0
7	7	0	3	0	0	0	0	0	0	0	0	7	7	0	3	133	133	0	35
0	0	0	0	0	0	0	0	0	0	0	0	0	0	0	0	31	31	0	0
9	9	0	5	0	0	0	0	0	0	0	0	0	0	0	0	138	138	0	63
5	5	0	0	0	0	0	0	0	0	0	0	0	0	0	0	34	34	0	0
0	0	0	0	0	0	0	0	0	0	0	0	0	0	0	0	1	1	0	0
11	10	1	3	26	26	0	12	6	6	0	2	0	0	0	0	213	201	12	71
0	0	0	0	0	0	0	0	0	0	0	0	0	0	0	0	20	20	0	0
1	0	1	0	1	1	0	0	0	0	0	0	0	0	0	0	11	9	2	1
0	0	0	0	0	0	0	0	0	0	0	0	0	0	0	0	5	5	0	1
4	4	0	1	2	2	0	3	1	1	0	0	4	4	0	0	62	57	5	19
14	14	0	1	0	0	0	0	0	0	0	0	0	0	0	0	253	253	0	53
10	10	0	3	0	0	0	0	0	0	0	0	0	0	0	0	179	179	0	68
1	1	0	0	1	1	0	0	0	0	0	0	0	0	0	0	40	38	2	13
2	2	0	0	3	3	0	0	0	0	0	0	0	0	0	0	40	40	0	1
11	11	0	0	8	8	0	0	0	0	0	0	3	3	0	0	241	241	0	0
0	0	0	0	0	0	0	0	0	0	0	0	0	0	0	0	3	3	0	0
4	4	0	0	0	0	0	0	0	0	0	0	0	0	0	0	44	44	0	6
24	24	0	0	0	0	0	0	0	0	0	0	16	16	0	0	422	422	0	0
1	1	0	0	0	0	0	0	0	0	0	0	2	2	0	0	27	27	0	6
7	7	0	1	1	1	0	0	0	0	0	0	15	15	0	3	165	165	0	22
4	4	0	0	0	0	0	0	0	0	0	0	0	0	0	0	52	52	0	0
0	0	0	0	4	4	0	0	0	0	0	0	0	0	0	0	54	54	0	0
0	0	0	0	0	0	0	0	0	0	0	0	0	0	0	0	3	3	0	1
0	0	0	0	0	0	0	0	0	0	0	0	1	1	0	0	2	2	0	0
0	0	0	0	0	0	0	0	0	0	0	0	0	0	0	0	1	1	0	0
3	3	0	0	0	0	0	0	0	0	0	0	0	0	0	0	27	26	1	10
6	6	0	3	0	0	0	0	0	0	0	0	0	0	0	0	56	56	0	14
1	0	1	0	0	0	0	0	0	0	0	0	0	0	0	0	8	7	1	0
1	0	1	0	2	1	1	0	0	0	0	0	0	0	0	0	7	1	6	0
0	0	0	0	0	0	0	0	0	0	0	0	1	1	0	0	4	4	0	0
0	0	0	0	0	0	0	0	0	0	0	0	0	0	0	0	5	5	0	0
2	2	0	0	0	0	0	0	0	0	0	0	0	0	0	0	34	34	0	0
9	9	0	0	0	0	0	0	0	0	0	0	0	0	0	0	79	79	0	0
14	13	1	5	6	6	0	3	2	1	1	0	6	6	0	1	170	149	21	56
2	1	1	0	0	0	0	0	0	0	0	0	0	0	0	0	13	7	6	0
1	1	0	0	0	0	0	0	0	0	0	0	0	0	0	0	16	16	0	1
0	0	0	0	0	0	0	0	0	0	0	0	0	0	0	0	7	7	0	1
8	8	0	4	0	0	0	0	0	0	0	0	0	0	0	0	62	62	0	23
0	0	0	0	0	0	0	0	0	0	0	0	0	0	0	0	1	1	0	0
0	0	0	0	0	0	0	0	0	0	0	0	0	0	0	0	5	4	1	0
7	7	0	3	6	6	0	6	0	0	0	0	0	0	0	0	73	72	1	33
0	0	0	0	0	0	0	0	0	0	0	0	0	0	0	0	12	12	0	0
3	3	0	0	0	0	0	0	0	0	0	0	2	2	0	0	39	39	0	16
0	0	0	0	0	0	0	0	0	0	0	0	0	0	0	0	15	15	0	5
0	0	0	0	0	0	0	0	0	0	0	0	1	1	0	0	1	1	0	0
6	6	0	0	0	0	0	0	0	0	0	0	0	0	0	0	116	116	0	0
2	1	1	0	0	0	0	0	0	0	0	0	0	0	0	0	17	12	5	0

Player	Date of Birth	Career	League				Premier League			
			Apps	Starts	Subs	Goals	Apps	Starts	Subs	Goal
Stephen HENDERSON	2 May 1988	2012/13 - 2013/14	0	0	0	0	0	0	0	0
William HENDERSON	5 January 1900	1921/22 - 1927/28	162	162	0	0	0	0	0	0
David HILLS	9 April 1940	1958/59	0	0	0	0	0	0	0	0
George HILSDON	10 August 1885	1904/05 - 1905/06 and 1912/13 - 1914/15	85	85	0	31	0	0	0	0
Jack HILSDON	12 October 1876	1903/04	1	1	0	0	0	0	0	0
Paul HILTON	8 October 1959	1983/84 - 1988/89	60	47	13	7	0	0	0	0
Harry HINDLE	17 July 1883	1905/06	3	3	0	0	0	0	0	0
Zavon HINES	27 December 1988	2008/09 - 2010/11	0	0	0	0	22	9	13	1
Shaka HISLOP	22 February 1969	1998/99 - 2001/02 and 2005/06	0	0	0	0	121	121	0	0
J. HITCHENS	Unknown	1901/02	1	1	0	0	0	0	0	0
Thomas HITZLSPERGER	5 April 1982	2010/11	0	0	0	0	11	11	0	2
Harry HODGES	17 May 1897	1923/24	2	2	0	1	0	0	0	0
Lee HODGES	2 March 1978	1997/98 - 1998/99	0	0	0	0	3	0	3	0
Tommy HODGSON	19 January 1903	1921/22 - 1929/30	87	87	0	0	0	0	0	0
Pat HOLLAND	13 September 1950	1968/69 - 1980/81	245	227	18	23	0	0	0	0
Gavin HOLLIGAN	13 June 1980	1998/99	0	0	0	0	1	0	1	0
Jim HOLMES	27 December 1908	1936/37	2	2	0	0	0	0	0	0
Matt HOLMES	1 August 1969	1992/93 - 1994/95	18	6	12	1	58	57	1	4
Harry HOOPER	14 June 1933	1950/51 - 1955/56	119	119	0	39	0	0	0	0
George HORLER	10 February 1895	1922/23 - 1927/28	47	47	0	0	0	0	0	0
Kevin HORLOCK	1 November 1972	2003/04	27	23	4	1	0	0	0	0
George HORN	1884	1906/07 - 1907/08	8	8	0	0	0	0	0	0
Ray HOUGHTON	9 January 1962	1981/82	1	0	1	0	0	0	0	0
Bobby HOWE	22 December 1945	1966/67 - 1971/72	75	68	7	4	0	0	0	0
Cliff HUBBARD	1911	1938/39	1	1	0	1	0	0	0	0
Edward HUFTON	25 November 1892	1919/20 - 1931/32	371	371	0	0	0	0	0	0
Joseph HUGHES	1891	1911/12 - 1914/15	90	90	0	0	0	0	0	0
Michael HUGHES	2 August 1971	1994/95 - 1997/98	0	0	0	0	83	76	7	5
Chris HUGHTON	11 December 1958	1990/91 - 1991/92	33	32	1	0	0	0	0	0
Roger HUGO	6 September 1942	1963/64	3	3	0	2	0	0	0	0
Archie HULL	8 August 1902	1926/27 - 1928/29	2	2	0	0	0	0	0	0
Fergus HUNT	1875	1900/01 - 1901/02	42	42	0	9	0	0	0	0
Geoff HURST	8 December 1941	1958/59 - 1971/72	411	410	1	180	0	0	0	0
Don HUTCHISON	9 May 1971	1994/95 - 1995/97 and 2001/02 - 2004/05	29	12	17	4	69	54	15	12
Araujo ILAN	18 September 1980	2009/10	0	0	0	0	11	6	5	4
Sasa ILIC	18 July 1972	1999/00	0	0	0	0	1	1	0	0
Herita ILUNGA	25 February 1982	2008/09 - 2011/12	4	4	0	0	62	61	1	0
Andy IMPEY	30 September 1971	1997/98 - 1998/99	0	0	0	0	27	25	2	0
Paul INCE	21 October 1967	1986/87 - 1989/90	72	66	6	7	0	0	0	0
William INGHAM	1886	1903/04	2	2	0	0	0	0	0	0
Tommy INNS	30 January 1911	1933/34	4	4	0	0	0	0	0	0
George IRVINE	1889	1912/13 - 1913/14	21	21	0	0	0	0	0	0
Jussi JAASKELAINEN	19 April 1975	2012/13 - 2014/15	0	0	0	0	57	56	1	0
Derek JACKMAN	20 August 1927	1948/49 - 1950/51	8	8	0	0	0	0	0	0
James JACKSON	15 September 1875	1905/06	24	24	0	0	0	0	0	0
Thomas JACKSON	1896	1921/22	3	3	0	1	0	0	0	0
William JACKSON	15 July 1902	1927/28	2	2	0	0	0	0	0	0
Lars JACOBSEN	20 September 1979	2010/11	0	0	0	0	24	22	2	0

FA Cup				League Cup				Europe				Other				Total			
Apps	Starts	Subs	Goals	Apps	Starts	Subs	Goals	Apps	Starts	Subs	Goals	Apps	Starts	Subs	Goals	Apps	Starts	Subs	Goals
0	0	0	0	2	2	0	0	0	0	0	0	0	0	0	0	2	2	0	0
21	21	0	1	0	0	0	0	0	0	0	0	0	0	0	0	183	183	0	1
0	0	0	0	0	0	0	0	0	0	0	0	1	1	0	0	1	1	0	0
7	7	0	4	0	0	0	0	0	0	0	0	0	0	0	0	92	92	0	35
0	0	0	0	0	0	0	0	0	0	0	0	0	0	0	0	1	1	0	0
7	4	3	1	8	6	2	0	0	0	0	0	4	3	1	0	79	60	19	8
0	0	0	0	0	0	0	0	0	0	0	0	0	0	0	0	3	3	0	0
3	1	2	0	6	2	4	2	0	0	0	0	0	0	0	0	31	12	19	3
14	14	0	0	12	12	0	0	9	9	0	0	0	0	0	0	156	156	0	0
1	1	0	0	0	0	0	0	0	0	0	0	0	0	0	0	2	2	0	0
2	2	0	1	0	0	0	0	0	0	0	0	0	0	0	0	13	13	0	3
0	0	0	0	0	0	0	0	0	0	0	0	0	0	0	0	2	2	0	1
3	0	3	0	0	0	0	0	0	0	0	0	0	0	0	0	6	0	6	0
5	5	0	0	0	0	0	0	0	0	0	0	0	0	0	0	92	92	0	0
16	12	4	4	25	22	3	3	10	10	0	2	8	7	1	0	304	278	26	32
0	0	0	0	0	0	0	0	0	0	0	0	0	0	0	0	1	0	1	0
0	0	0	0	0	0	0	0	0	0	0	0	0	0	0	0	2	2	0	0
6	6	0	0	4	4	0	0	0	0	0	0	3	3	0	1	89	76	13	6
11	11	0	5	0	0	0	0	0	0	0	0	6	6	0	3	136	136	0	47
5	5	0	0	0	0	0	0	0	0	0	0	0	0	0	0	52	52	0	0
4	4	0	0	2	2	0	0	0	0	0	0	0	0	0	0	33	29	4	1
1	1	0	0	0	0	0	0	0	0	0	0	0	0	0	0	9	9	0	0
0	0	0	0	0	0	0	0	0	0	0	0	0	0	0	0	1	0	1	0
3	3	0	0	4	2	2	0	0	0	0	0	0	0	0	0	82	73	9	4
0	0	0	0	0	0	0	0	0	0	0	0	0	0	0	0	1	1	0	1
31	31	0	0	0	0	0	0	0	0	0	0	0	0	0	0	402	402	0	0
15	15	0	0	0	0	0	0	0	0	0	0	0	0	0	0	105	105	0	0
7	7	0	1	7	7	0	0	0	0	0	0	0	0	0	0	97	90	7	6
7	7	0	0	0	0	0	0	0	0	0	0	1	1	0	0	41	40	1	0
0	0	0	0	0	0	0	0	0	0	0	0	0	0	0	0	3	3	0	2
0	0	0	0	0	0	0	0	0	0	0	0	0	0	0	0	2	2	0	0
6	6	0	1	0	0	0	0	0	0	0	0	0	0	0	0	48	48	0	10
26	26	0	23	47	47	0	43	15	15	0	2	4	4	0	1	503	502	1	249
5	3	2	0	6	5	1	2	0	0	0	0	1	0	1	0	110	74	36	18
0	0	0	0	0	0	0	0	0	0	0	0	0	0	0	0	11	6	5	4
0	0	0	0	0	0	0	0	0	0	0	0	0	0	0	0	1	1	0	0
5	5	0	2	2	1	1	1	0	0	0	0	0	0	0	0	73	71	2	3
3	3	0	0	4	4	0	0	0	0	0	0	0	0	0	0	34	32	2	0
10	8	2	1	9	9	0	3	0	0	0	0	4	4	0	1	95	87	8	12
0	0	0	0	0	0	0	0	0	0	0	0	0	0	0	0	2	2	0	0
0	0	0	0	0	0	0	0	0	0	0	0	0	0	0	0	4	4	0	0
0	0	0	0	0	0	0	0	0	0	0	0	0	0	0	0	21	21	0	0
2	2	0	0	2	2	0	0	0	0	0	0	0	0	0	0	61	60	1	0
0	0	0	0	0	0	0	0	0	0	0	0	1	1	0	0	9	9	0	0
0	0	0	0	0	0	0	0	0	0	0	0	0	0	0	0	24	24	0	0
0	0	0	0	0	0	0	0	0	0	0	0	0	0	0	0	3	3	0	1
0	0	0	0	0	0	0	0	0	0	0	0	0	0	0	0	2	2	0	0
2	2	0	0	0	0	0	0	0	0	0	0	0	0	0	0	26	24	2	0

Player	Date of Birth	Career	League				Premier League			
			Apps	Starts	Subs	Goals	Apps	Starts	Subs	Goal
David JAMES	1 August 1970	2001/02 - 2003/04	27	27	0	0	64	64	0	0
Wilf JAMES	19 February 1904	1929/30 - 1931/32	40	40	0	7	0	0	0	0
William JAMES	1892	1920/21 - 1921/22	54	54	0	7	0	0	0	0
Len JARVIS	1884	1903/04 - 1908/09	133	133	0	5	0	0	0	0
Matthew JARVIS	22 May 1986	2012/13 -	0	0	0	0	75	56	19	4
Carl JENKINSON	8 February 1992	2014/15 -	0	0	0	0	32	29	3	0
William JENKINSON	1874	1901/02	19	19	0	2	0	0	0	0
Billy JENNINGS	20 February 1952	1974/75 - 1979/80	99	89	10	34	0	0	0	0
Samuel JENNINGS	18 December 1898	1924/25	9	9	0	3	0	0	0	0
Luis JIMENEZ	17 June 1984	2009/10	0	0	0	0	11	6	5	1
Stan JOHNS	28 June 1924	1950/51	6	6	0	2	0	0	0	0
Glen JOHNSON	23 August 1984	2002/03	0	0	0	0	15	14	1	0
Joseph JOHNSON	23 June 1899	1926/27 - 1927/28	15	15	0	7	0	0	0	0
Roger JOHNSON	28 April 1983	2013/14	0	0	0	0	4	2	2	0
William JOHNSON	Unknown	1919/20	2	2	0	0	0	0	0	0
William JOHNSON	9 November 1909	1932/33	5	5	0	0	0	0	0	0
Robert JOHNSTONE	19 November 1934	1955/56 - 1956/57	2	2	0	0	0	0	0	0
Rob JONES	5 November 1971	1999/00	0	0	0	0	0	0	0	0
Steve JONES	17 March 1970	1992/93 - 1994/95 and 1996/97	6	4	2	2	18	9	9	2
William JONES	1876	1901/02	15	15	0	0	0	0	0	0
William KAINE	27 June 1900	1924/25	7	7	0	0	0	0	0	0
Alex KANE	22 January 1900	1925/26 - 1926/27	2	2	0	0	0	0	0	0
Frederic KANOUTE	2 September 1977	1999/00 - 2002/03	0	0	0	0	84	79	5	29
Yaniv KATAN	27 January 1981	2005/06	0	0	0	0	6	2	4	0
George KAY	21 September 1891	1919/20 - 1925/26	237	237	0	15	0	0	0	0
Albert KAYE	6 May 1875	1900/01	14	14	0	2	0	0	0	0
Robbie KEANE	8 July 1980	2010/11	0	0	0	0	9	5	4	2
Fred KEARNS	8 November 1927	1949/50 - 1953/54	43	43	0	14	0	0	0	0
Vic KEEBLE	25 June 1930	1957/58 - 1959/60	76	76	0	45	0	0	0	0
Kevin KEEN	25 February 1967	1986/87 - 1992/93	219	187	32	21	0	0	0	0
Marc KELLER	14 January 1968	1998/99 - 2000/01	0	0	0	0	44	36	8	5
David KELLY	25 November 1965	1988/89 - 1989/90	41	29	12	7	0	0	0	0
Paul KELLY	12 October 1969	1989/90 - 1990/91	1	0	1	0	0	0	0	0
William KELLY	27 March 1880	1900/01 - 1902/03	33	33	0	0	0	0	0	0
Fred KEMP	1887	1906/07 - 1907/08	10	10	0	0	0	0	0	0
William KENNEDY	21 November 1890	1910/11 - 1911/12	21	21	0	10	0	0	0	0
Matthew KILGALLON	8 January 1984	2003/04	3	1	2	0	0	0	0	0
Syd KING	August 1873	1900/01 - 1902/03	59	59	0	0	0	0	0	0
Matthew KINGSLEY	1875	1904/05	29	29	0	0	0	0	0	0
Harry KINSELL	3 May 1921	1950/51 - 1954/55	101	101	0	2	0	0	0	0
William KIRBY	21 June 1882	1903/04	33	33	0	10	0	0	0	0
Jack KIRKALDIE	2 August 1917	1936/37 - 1938/39	11	11	0	1	0	0	0	0
Joe KIRKUP	17 December 1939	1957/58 - 1965/66	165	165	0	6	0	0	0	0
George KITCHEN	6 May 1876	1905/06 - 1910/11	184	184	0	5	0	0	0	0
Bill KITCHENER	3 November 1946	1966/67 - 1967/68	11	11	0	0	0	0	0	0
Paul KITSON	9 January 1971	1996/97 - 2001/02	0	0	0	0	63	46	17	18
Paul KONCHESKY	15 May 1981	2005/06 - 2006/07	0	0	0	0	59	58	1	1
Cheikhou KOUYATE	21 December 1989	2014/15 -	0	0	0	0	31	30	1	4

	FA Cup				League Cup				Europe				Other				Total		
Apps	Starts	Subs	Goals	Apps	Starts	Subs	Goals	Apps	Starts	Subs	Goals	Apps	Starts	Subs	Goals	Apps	Starts	Subs	Goals
6	6	0	0	5	5	0	0	0	0	0	0	0	0	0	0	102	102	0	0
1	1	0	0	0	0	0	0	0	0	0	0	0	0	0	0	41	41	0	7
3	3	0	0	0	0	0	0	0	0	0	0	0	0	0	0	57	57	0	7
7	7	0	0	0	0	0	0	0	0	0	0	0	0	0	0	140	140	0	5
4	3	1	0	3	3	0	2	0	0	0	0	0	0	0	0	82	62	20	6
4	4	0	0	0	0	0	0	0	0	0	0	0	0	0	0	36	33	3	0
0	0	0	0	0	0	0	0	0	0	0	0	0	0	0	0	19	19	0	2
11	11	0	2	5	3	2	0	7	5	2	3	3	2	1	0	125	110	15	39
0	0	0	0	0	0	0	0	0	0	0	0	0	0	0	0	9	9	0	3
1	1	0	0	0	0	0	0	0	0	0	0	0	0	0	0	12	7	5	1
0	0	0	0	0	0	0	0	0	0	0	0	1	1	0	0	7	7	0	2
1	0	1	0	0	0	0	0	0	0	0	0	0	0	0	0	16	14	2	0
0	0	0	0	0	0	0	0	0	0	0	0	0	0	0	0	15	15	0	7
0	0	0	0	2	2	0	0	0	0	0	0	0	0	0	0	6	4	2	0
0	0	0	0	0	0	0	0	0	0	0	0	0	0	0	0	2	2	0	0
0	0	0	0	0	0	0	0	0	0	0	0	0	0	0	0	5	5	0	0
0	0	0	0	0	0	0	0	0	0	0	0	1	1	0	0	3	3	0	0
0	0	0	0	0	0	0	0	1	1	0	0	0	0	0	0	1	1	0	0
6	4	2	1	1	0	1	0	0	0	0	0	2	1	1	0	33	18	15	5
0	0	0	0	0	0	0	0	0	0	0	0	0	0	0	0	15	15	0	0
0	0	0	0	0	0	0	0	0	0	0	0	0	0	0	0	7	7	0	0
0	0	0	0	0	0	0	0	0	0	0	0	0	0	0	0	2	2	0	0
5	5	0	4	3	3	0	0	0	0	0	0	0	0	0	0	92	87	5	33
2	0	2	0	0	0	0	0	0	0	0	0	0	0	0	0	8	2	6	0
22	22	0	2	0	0	0	0	0	0	0	0	0	0	0	0	259	259	0	17
6	6	0	3	0	0	0	0	0	0	0	0	0	0	0	0	20	20	0	5
1	0	1	0	0	0	0	0	0	0	0	0	0	0	0	0	10	5	5	2
2	2	0	1	0	0	0	0	0	0	0	0	3	3	0	1	48	48	0	16
4	4	0	4	0	0	0	0	0	0	0	0	4	4	0	2	84	84	0	51
21	15	6	1	22	21	1	5	0	0	0	0	16	14	2	3	278	237	41	30
0	0	0	0	6	5	1	1	7	6	1	0	0	0	0	0	57	47	10	6
6	6	0	0	14	11	3	5	0	0	0	0	3	2	1	2	64	48	16	14
0	0	0	0	0	0	0	0	0	0	0	0	1	1	0	0	2	1	1	0
4	4	0	0	0	0	0	0	0	0	0	0	0	0	0	0	37	37	0	0
0	0	0	0	0	0	0	0	0	0	0	0	0	0	0	0	10	10	0	0
2	2	0	0	0	0	0	0	0	0	0	0	0	0	0	0	23	23	0	10
0	0	0	0	1	1	0	0	0	0	0	0	0	0	0	0	4	2	2	0
7	7	0	0	0	0	0	0	0	0	0	0	0	0	0	0	66	66	0	0
1	1	0	0	0	0	0	0	0	0	0	0	0	0	0	0	30	30	0	0
4	4	0	0	0	0	0	0	0	0	0	0	4	4	0	0	109	109	0	2
3	3	0	1	0	0	0	0	0	0	0	0	0	0	0	0	36	36	0	11
1	1	0	0	0	0	0	0	0	0	0	0	0	0	0	0	12	12	0	1
8	8	0	0	7	7	0	0	7	7	0	0	5	5	0	0	192	192	0	6
21	21	0	1	0	0	0	0	0	0	0	0	0	0	0	0	205	205	0	6
0	0	0	0	1	1	0	0	0	0	0	0	0	0	0	0	12	12	0	0
5	4	1	1	4	2	2	1	8	3	5	2	0	0	0	0	80	55	25	22
7	7	0	1	2	1	1	0	2	2	0	0	0	0	0	0	70	68	2	2
1	1	0	0	0	0	0	0	0	0	0	0	0	0	0	0	32	31	1	4

Player	Date of Birth	Career	League				Premier League			
			Apps	Starts	Subs	Goals	Apps	Starts	Subs	Goa
Radoslav KOVAC	27 November 1979	2008/09 - 2010/11	0	0	0	0	53	42	11	3
Peter KURUCZ	30 May 1988	2009/10	0	0	0	0	1	0	1	0
Peter KYLE	21 December 1878	1901/02	1	1	0	0	0	0	0	0
Everald LA RONDE	24 January 1963	1981/82	7	6	1	0	0	0	0	0
Vladimir LABANT	8 June 1974	2001/02 - 2002/03	0	0	0	0	13	7	6	0
Bernard LAMA	7 April 1963	1997/98	0	0	0	0	12	12	0	0
Frank LAMPARD Jnr.	20 June 1978	1995/96 - 2000/01	0	0	0	0	148	132	16	23
Frank LAMPARD Snr	20 September 1948	1967/68 - 1984/85	551	546	5	18	0	0	0	0
Jack LANDELLS	20 November 1904	1933/34	21	21	0	4	0	0	0	0
Harry LANE	23 October 1894	1919/20 - 1920/21	19	19	0	0	0	0	0	0
Henri LANSBURY	12 October 1990	2011/12	22	13	9	1	0	0	0	0
Bill LANSDOWNE Snr.	9 November 1935	1955/56 - 1962/63	57	57	0	5	0	0	0	0
Billy LANSDOWNE Jnr.	28 April 1959	1978/79 - 1979/80	9	5	4	1	0	0	0	0
Jan LASTUVKA	7 July 1982	2008/09	0	0	0	0	0	0	0	0
William LAVERY	1885	1909/10 - 1910/11	17	17	0	0	0	0	0	0
Tommy LAWRENCE	Unknown	1955/56	0	0	0	0	0	0	0	0
Stan LAZARIDIS	16 August 1972	1995/96 - 1999/00	0	0	0	0	69	53	16	3
Alfred LEAFE	1891	1913/14 - 1921/22	94	94	0	40	0	0	0	0
Alf LEE	1892	1919/20 - 1921/22	26	26	0	0	0	0	0	0
Elliot LEE	16 December 1994	2012/13 -	0	0	0	0	2	0	2	0
Robert LEE	1 February 1966	2003/04	16	12	4	0	0	0	0	0
Thomas LEE	Unknown	1907/08	6	6	0	0	0	0	0	0
Lawrie LESLIE	17 March 1935	1961/62 - 1962/63	57	57	0	0	0	0	0	0
Eddie LEWIS	3 January 1935	1956/57 - 1957/58	31	31	0	12	0	0	0	0
Harry LEWIS	25 October 1910	1935/36	4	4	0	4	0	0	0	0
David LINDSAY	Unknown	1906/07 - 1907/08	51	51	0	4	0	0	0	0
Jimmy LINDSAY	12 July 1949	1968/69 - 1970/71	39	36	3	2	0	0	0	0
William LINWARD	8 February 1879	1901/02 - 1902/03	40	40	0	3	0	0	0	0
Simon LIVETT	8 January 1969	1990/91 - 1991/92	1	1	0	0	0	0	0	0
Fredrik LJUNGBERG	16 April 1977	2007/08	0	0	0	0	25	22	3	2
Sebastian LLETGET	3 September 1992	2013/14	0	0	0	0	0	0	0	0
David LLEWELYN	9 August 1949	1969/70 - 1971/72	6	2	4	0	0	0	0	0
Kevin LOCK	27 December 1953	1971/72 - 1977/78	132	122	10	2	0	0	0	0
Steve LOMAS	18 January 1974	1996/97 - 2004/05	28	23	5	1	159	156	3	9
Thomas LONSDALE	21 December 1882	1913/14	21	21	0	0	0	0	0	0
Walter LOPEZ	15 October 1985	2008/09	0	0	0	0	5	0	5	0
James LOUGHLIN	9 October 1904	1927/28	10	10	0	4	0	0	0	0
Bertie LUTTON	13 July 1950	1972/73 - 1973/74	12	8	4	1	0	0	0	0
John LYALL	24 February 1940	1958/59 - 1962/63	31	31	0	0	0	0	0	0
Herbert LYON	18 May 1875	1903/04	29	29	0	4	0	0	0	0
Archibald MACAULAY	30 July 1915	1937/38 - 1946/47	83	83	0	29	0	0	0	0
Ted MacDOUGALL	8 January 1947	1972/73 - 1973/74	24	24	0	5	0	0	0	0
Malky MACKAY	19 February 1972	2004/05	18	17	1	2	0	0	0	0
Jack MACKESY	13 October 1890	1911/12 - 1922/23	20	20	0	2	0	0	0	0
Charles MACKIE	21 April 1882	1905/06	10	10	0	3	0	0	0	0
Colin MACKLEWORTH	24 March 1947	1966/67	3	3	0	0	0	0	0	0
Modibo MAIGA	3 September 1987	2012/13 -	0	0	0	0	31	13	18	3
Andy MALCOLM	4 May 1933	1953/54 - 1961/62	283	283	0	4	0	0	0	0

FA Cup				League Cup				Europe				Other				Total			
Apps	Starts	Subs	Goals	Apps	Starts	Subs	Goals	Apps	Starts	Subs	Goals	Apps	Starts	Subs	Goals	Apps	Starts	Subs	Goals
3	3	0	0	6	5	1	0	0	0	0	0	0	0	0	0	62	50	12	3
0	0	0	0	0	0	0	0	0	0	0	0	0	0	0	0	1	0	1	0
2	2	0	0	0	0	0	0	0	0	0	0	0	0	0	0	3	3	0	0
0	0	0	0	0	0	0	0	0	0	0	0	0	0	0	0	7	6	1	0
2	0	2	0	0	0	0	0	0	0	0	0	0	0	0	0	15	7	8	0
2	2	0	0	0	0	0	0	0	0	0	0	0	0	0	0	14	14	0	0
13	13	0	2	15	14	1	8	10	10	0	4	0	0	0	0	186	169	17	37
43	43	0	2	54	54	0	1	15	15	0	1	7	7	0	0	670	665	5	22
1	1	0	0	0	0	0	0	0	0	0	0	0	0	0	0	22	22	0	4
0	0	0	0	0	0	0	0	0	0	0	0	0	0	0	0	19	19	0	0
1	1	0	0	0	0	0	0	0	0	0	0	1	0	1	0	24	14	10	1
3	3	0	0	0	0	0	0	0	0	0	0	7	7	0	0	67	67	0	5
0	0	0	0	5	4	1	3	0	0	0	0	0	0	0	0	14	9	5	4
0	0	0	0	1	1	0	0	0	0	0	0	0	0	0	0	1	1	0	0
2	2	0	0	0	0	0	0	0	0	0	0	0	0	0	0	19	19	0	0
0	0	0	0	0	0	0	0	0	0	0	0	1	1	0	0	1	1	0	0
10	9	1	0	7	6	1	0	1	0	1	0	0	0	0	0	87	68	19	3
7	7	0	4	0	0	0	0	0	0	0	0	0	0	0	0	101	101	0	44
2	2	0	0	0	0	0	0	0	0	0	0	0	0	0	0	28	28	0	0
1	0	1	0	0	0	0	0	0	0	0	0	0	0	0	0	3	0	3	0
1	0	1	0	2	2	0	0	0	0	0	0	0	0	0	0	19	14	5	0
0	0	0	0	0	0	0	0	0	0	0	0	0	0	0	0	6	6	0	0
1	1	0	0	3	3	0	0	0	0	0	0	0	0	0	0	61	61	0	0
5	5	0	3	0	0	0	0	0	0	0	0	3	3	0	1	39	39	0	16
0	0	0	0	0	0	0	0	0	0	0	0	0	0	0	0	4	4	0	4
2	2	0	0	0	0	0	0	0	0	0	0	0	0	0	0	53	53	0	4
4	4	0	0	2	2	0	0	0	0	0	0	0	0	0	0	45	42	3	2
2	2	0	1	0	0	0	0	0	0	0	0	0	0	0	0	42	42	0	4
1	0	1	0	0	0	0	0	0	0	0	0	1	1	0	0	3	2	1	0
1	1	0	0	2	2	0	0	0	0	0	0	0	0	0	0	28	25	3	2
1	1	0	0	0	0	0	0	0	0	0	0	0	0	0	0	1	1	0	0
0	0	0	0	0	0	0	0	0	0	0	0	0	0	0	0	6	2	4	0
12	11	1	0	13	13	0	0	4	4	0	0	4	3	1	0	165	153	12	2
13	10	3	1	13	13	0	2	10	10	0	0	3	3	0	0	226	215	11	13
0	0	0	0	0	0	0	0	0	0	0	0	0	0	0	0	21	21	0	0
0	0	0	0	1	1	0	0	0	0	0	0	0	0	0	0	6	1	5	0
0	0	0	0	0	0	0	0	0	0	0	0	0	0	0	0	10	10	0	4
1	1	0	0	0	0	0	0	0	0	0	0	0	0	0	0	13	9	4	1
2	2	0	0	2	2	0	0	0	0	0	0	1	1	0	0	36	36	0	0
4	4	0	5	0	0	0	0	0	0	0	0	0	0	0	0	33	33	0	9
7	7	0	2	0	0	0	0	0	0	0	0	0	0	0	0	90	90	0	31
0	0	0	0	1	1	0	1	0	0	0	0	1	1	0	1	26	26	0	7
3	3	0	0	1	1	0	0	0	0	0	0	0	0	0	0	22	21	1	2
0	0	0	0	0	0	0	0	0	0	0	0	0	0	0	0	20	20	0	2
0	0	0	0	0	0	0	0	0	0	0	0	0	0	0	0	10	10	0	3
0	0	0	0	0	0	0	0	0	0	0	0	0	0	0	0	3	3	0	0
1	1	0	0	6	5	1	3	0	0	0	0	0	0	0	0	38	19	19	6
21	21	0	0	2	2	0	0	0	0	0	0	15	15	0	0	321	321	0	4

Player	Date of Birth	Career	League				Premier League			
			Apps	Starts	Subs	Goals	Apps	Starts	Subs	Goals
David MANGNALL	21 September 1905	1934/35 - 1935/36	35	35	0	29	0	0	0	0
Percy MAPLEY	24 November 1882	1903/04	13	13	0	0	0	0	0	0
Javier MARGAS	10 May 1969	1998/99 - 2000/01	0	0	0	0	24	21	3	1
Paul MARQUIS	29 August 1972	1993/94	0	0	0	0	1	0	1	0
Mike MARSH	21 July 1969	1993/94 - 1994/95	0	0	0	0	49	46	3	1
James MARSHALL	3 January 1908	1934/35 - 1936/37	57	57	0	13	0	0	0	0
Alvin MARTIN	29 July 1958	1977/78 - 1995/96	424	422	2	25	45	40	5	2
Dean MARTIN	31 August 1972	1991/92	2	1	1	0	0	0	0	0
Tudor MARTIN	20 April 1904	1936/37	11	11	0	7	0	0	0	0
Javier MASCHERANO	8 June 1984	2006/07	0	0	0	0	5	3	2	0
Frederick MASSEY	2 November 1883	1909/10 - 1911/12	38	38	0	0	0	0	0	0
George MATTHEWS	25 February 1936	1955/56 - 1956/57	9	9	0	1	0	0	0	0
Steve MAUTONE	10 August 1970	1996/97	0	0	0	0	1	1	0	0
Nicky MAYNARD	11 December 1986	2011/12 - 2012/13	14	9	5	2	0	0	0	0
Tom McALISTER	10 December 1952	1981/82 - 1988/89	85	85	0	0	0	0	0	0
Jobi McANUFF	9 November 1981	2003/04 - 2004/05	13	4	9	1	0	0	0	0
Tommy McATEER	8 August 1878	1902/03	13	13	0	0	0	0	0	0
Frank McAVENNIE	22 November 1960	1985/86 - 1987/88 and 1988/89 - 1991/92	153	134	19	49	0	0	0	0
Grant McCANN	15 April 1980	2000/01 - 2001/02	0	0	0	0	4	0	4	0
Benni McCARTHY	11 December 1977	2009/10 - 2010/11	0	0	0	0	11	2	9	0
Alex McCARTNEY	14 November 1879	1905/06	6	6	0	0	0	0	0	0
George McCARTNEY	29 April 1981	2006/07 - 2008/09 and 2011/12 - 2013/14	38	36	2	1	95	83	12	1
William McCARTNEY	Unknown	1904/05	28	28	0	3	0	0	0	0
Trent McCLENAHAN	4 February 1985	2004/05	2	0	2	0	0	0	0	0
James McCRAE	2 September 1894	1919/20 - 1920/21	50	50	0	0	0	0	0	0
Alex McDONALD	12 April 1878	1901/02	4	4	0	2	0	0	0	0
John McDOWELL	7 September 1951	1970/71 - 1978/79	249	243	6	8	0	0	0	0
Roderick McEACHRANE	3 February 1877	1900/01 - 1901/02	53	53	0	5	0	0	0	0
Robert McGEORGE	29 February 1876	1901/02	0	0	0	0	0	0	0	0
Mick McGIVEN	7 February 1951	1973/74 - 1977/78	48	46	2	0	0	0	0	0
Danny McGOWAN	8 November 1924	1948/49 - 1953/54	81	81	0	8	0	0	0	0
Allen McKNIGHT	27 January 1964	1988/89 - 1990/91	23	23	0	0	0	0	0	0
Pat McMAHON	26 October 1908	1932/33 - 1933/34	16	16	0	0	0	0	0	0
Callum McNAUGHTON	25 October 1991	2011/12	0	0	0	0	0	0	0	0
Keith McPHERSON	11 September 1963	1984/85	1	1	0	0	0	0	0	0
Tommy McQUEEN	25 April 1963	1986/87 - 1989/90	30	24	6	0	0	0	0	0
Scott MEAN	13 December 1973	1997/98	0	0	0	0	3	0	3	0
Tyrone MEARS	18 February 1983	2006/07	0	0	0	0	5	3	2	0
Harry MEDHURST	5 February 1916	1938/39 - 1946/47	24	24	0	0	0	0	0	0
Neil MELLOR	4 November 1982	2003/04	16	8	8	2	0	0	0	0
Andy MELVILLE	29 November 1968	2003/04 - 2004/05	17	14	3	0	0	0	0	0
Frederick MERCER	1882	1903/04	7	7	0	1	0	0	0	0
Hossam MIDO	23 February 1983	2009/10	0	0	0	0	9	5	4	0
Walter MIECZNIKOWSKI	22 April 1877	1902/03	3	3	0	0	0	0	0	0
Joe MEILLEAR	3 July 1890	1910/11 - 1911/12	3	3	0	0	0	0	0	0
Ludek MIKLOSKO	9 December 1961	1989/90 - 1997/98	146	146	0	0	169	169	0	0
Keith MILLER	26 January 1948	1968/69 - 1969/70	3	1	2	0	0	0	0	0
Walter MILLER	1882	1908/09	11	11	0	5	0	0	0	0

FA Cup				League Cup				Europe				Other				Total			
Apps	Starts	Subs	Goals	Apps	Starts	Subs	Goals	Apps	Starts	Subs	Goals	Apps	Starts	Subs	Goals	Apps	Starts	Subs	Goals
2	2	0	1	0	0	0	0	0	0	0	0	0	0	0	0	37	37	0	30
4	4	0	0	0	0	0	0	0	0	0	0	0	0	0	0	17	17	0	0
0	0	0	0	2	2	0	0	3	2	1	0	0	0	0	0	29	25	4	1
0	0	0	0	0	0	0	0	0	0	0	0	0	0	0	0	1	0	1	0
6	6	0	1	6	6	0	0	0	0	0	0	0	0	0	0	61	58	3	2
2	2	0	0	0	0	0	0	0	0	0	0	0	0	0	0	59	59	0	13
40	40	0	0	71	71	0	6	6	6	0	0	10	10	0	1	596	589	7	34
1	0	1	0	0	0	0	0	0	0	0	0	0	0	0	0	3	1	2	0
0	0	0	0	0	0	0	0	0	0	0	0	0	0	0	0	11	11	0	7
0	0	0	0	0	0	0	0	2	2	0	0	0	0	0	0	7	5	2	0
3	3	0	0	0	0	0	0	0	0	0	0	0	0	0	0	41	41	0	0
0	0	0	0	0	0	0	0	0	0	0	0	2	2	0	0	11	11	0	1
0	0	0	0	2	2	0	0	0	0	0	0	0	0	0	0	3	3	0	0
0	0	0	0	1	1	0	1	0	0	0	0	2	0	2	1	17	10	7	4
7	7	0	0	7	7	0	0	0	0	0	0	1	1	0	0	100	100	0	0
0	0	0	0	0	0	0	0	0	0	0	0	1	0	1	0	14	4	10	1
0	0	0	0	0	0	0	0	0	0	0	0	0	0	0	0	13	13	0	0
20	19	1	6	13	11	2	2	0	0	0	0	4	4	0	3	190	168	22	60
0	0	0	0	0	0	0	0	0	0	0	0	0	0	0	0	4	0	4	0
0	0	0	0	3	1	2	0	0	0	0	0	0	0	0	0	14	3	11	0
0	0	0	0	0	0	0	0	0	0	0	0	0	0	0	0	6	6	0	0
5	5	0	0	12	12	0	0	0	0	0	0	3	0	3	0	153	136	17	2
1	1	0	0	0	0	0	0	0	0	0	0	0	0	0	0	29	29	0	3
0	0	0	0	1	1	0	0	0	0	0	0	0	0	0	0	3	1	2	0
4	4	0	0	0	0	0	0	0	0	0	0	0	0	0	0	54	54	0	0
0	0	0	0	0	0	0	0	0	0	0	0	0	0	0	0	4	4	0	2
19	19	0	0	21	21	0	1	7	7	0	0	7	7	0	0	303	297	6	9
7	7	0	0	0	0	0	0	0	0	0	0	0	0	0	0	60	60	0	5
2	2	0	0	0	0	0	0	0	0	0	0	0	0	0	0	2	2	0	0
3	3	0	0	2	2	0	0	2	1	1	0	1	1	0	0	56	53	3	0
2	2	0	1	0	0	0	0	0	0	0	0	5	5	0	0	88	88	0	9
4	4	0	0	6	6	0	0	0	0	0	0	3	3	0	0	36	36	0	0
1	1	0	0	0	0	0	0	0	0	0	0	0	0	0	0	17	17	0	0
0	0	0	0	1	1	0	0	0	0	0	0	0	0	0	0	1	1	0	0
0	0	0	0	0	0	0	0	0	0	0	0	0	0	0	0	1	1	0	0
1	1	0	0	5	2	3	0	0	0	0	0	0	0	0	0	36	27	9	0
0	0	0	0	0	0	0	0	0	0	0	0	0	0	0	0	3	0	3	30
0	0	0	0	0	0	0	0	1	1	0	0	0	0	0	0	6	4	2	0
9	9	0	0	0	0	0	0	0	0	0	0	0	0	0	0	33	33	0	0
3	0	3	0	2	1	1	0	0	0	0	0	0	0	0	0	21	9	12	2
0	0	0	0	1	0	1	0	0	0	0	0	3	3	0	0	21	17	4	0
0	0	0	0	0	0	0	0	0	0	0	0	0	0	0	0	7	7	0	1
0	0	0	0	0	0	0	0	0	0	0	0	0	0	0	0	9	5	4	0
0	0	0	0	0	0	0	0	0	0	0	0	0	0	0	0	3	3	0	0
1	1	0	0	0	0	0	0	0	0	0	0	0	0	0	0	4	4	0	0
25	25	0	0	25	25	0	0	0	0	0	0	8	8	0	0	373	373	0	0
0	0	0	0	0	0	0	0	0	0	0	0	0	0	0	0	3	1	2	0
6	6	0	1	0	0	0	0	0	0	0	0	0	0	0	0	17	17	0	6

Player	Date of Birth	Career	League				Premier League			
			Apps	Starts	Subs	Goals	Apps	Starts	Subs	Goals
Hugh MILLS	9 March 1909	1932/33 - 1934/35	21	21	0	16	0	0	0	0
Ralph MILNE	13 May 1961	1989/90	1	0	1	0	0	0	0	0
Frederick MILNES	26 January 1878	1904/05	2	2	0	0	0	0	0	0
Scott MINTO	6 August 1971	1998/99 - 2002/03	0	0	0	0	51	44	7	0
Paul MITCHELL	20 October 1971	1993/94	0	0	0	0	1	0	1	0
George MONCUR	18 August 1993	2012/13 - 2013/14	0	0	0	0	0	0	0	0
John MONCUR	22 September 1966	1994/95 - 2002/03	0	0	0	0	175	131	44	6
Hughie MONTEITH	14 August 1874	1900/01 - 1901/02	53	53	0	0	0	0	0	0
Brian MONTENEGRO	18 June 1993	2011/12	0	0	0	0	0	0	0	0
Bobby MOORE	12 April 1941	1958/59 - 1973/74	544	543	1	24	0	0	0	0
Brian MOORE	29 Decemebr 1933	1954/55 - 1955/56	9	9	0	1	0	0	0	0
Ian MOORE	26 August 1976	1997/98	0	0	0	0	1	0	1	0
Thomas MOORE	1875	1900/01	4	4	0	0	0	0	0	0
William MOORE	6 October 1894	1922/23 - 1928/29	181	181	0	42	0	0	0	0
Nicky MORGAN	30 October 1959	1978/79 - 1982/83	21	14	7	2	0	0	0	0
John MORLEY	1934	1956/57 - 1957/58	0	0	0	0	0	0	0	0
Trevor MORLEY	20 March 1961	1989/90 - 1994/95	122	110	12	44	56	49	7	13
Tommy MORONEY	10 November 1923	1947/48 - 1952/53	148	148	0	8	0	0	0	0
Robert MORRIS	Unknown	1919/20	3	3	0	0	0	0	0	0
Jack MORRISON	1875	1911/12	15	15	0	1	0	0	0	0
Ravel MORRISON	2 February 1993	2011/12 - 2014/15	18	12	6	3	0	0	0	0
John MORTON	26 February 1914	1931/32 - 1938/39	258	258	0	54	0	0	0	0
James MOYES	Unknown	1919/20	2	2	0	1	0	0	0	0
Hayden MULLINS	27 March 1979	2003/04 - 2008/09	64	59	5	1	116	93	23	3
Frank MURRAY	Unknown	1919/20	2	2	0	0	0	0	0	0
Joe MUSGRAVE	29 February 1908	1930/31 - 1935/36	36	36	0	1	0	0	0	0
Malcolm MUSGROVE	8 July 1933	1953/54 - 1962/63	282	282	0	84	0	0	0	0
Bondz N'GALA	13 September 1989	2009/10	0	0	0	0	0	0	0	0
Frank NEARY	6 March 1921	1946/47 - 1947/48	17	17	0	15	0	0	0	0
Jimmy NEIGHBOUR	15 November 1950	1979/80 - 1982/83	73	66	7	5	0	0	0	0
George NEIL	11 November 1874	1900/01	1	1	0	0	0	0	0	0
Lucas NEILL	9 March 1978	2006/07 - 2008/09	0	0	0	0	79	79	0	1
Andy NELSON	5 July 1935	1954/55 - 1958/59	15	15	0	1	0	0	0	0
Bill NELSON	20 September 1929	1950/51 - 1954/55	2	2	0	0	0	0	0	0
NENE	19 July 1981	2014/15	0	0	0	0	8	0	8	0
Billy NEVILLE	15 May 1935	1957/58	3	3	0	0	0	0	0	0
Mike NEWELL	27 January 1965	1996/97	0	0	0	0	7	6	1	0
Mick NEWMAN	2 April 1932	1956/57 - 1957/58	7	7	0	2	0	0	0	0
Adam NEWTON	4 December 1980	1999/00	0	0	0	0	2	0	2	0
Shaun NEWTON	20 August 1975	2004/05 - 2006/07	11	11	0	0	29	8	21	1
Vic NIBLETT	Unknown	1950/51	0	0	0	0	0	0	0	0
Alf NOAKES	Unknown	1954/55	0	0	0	0	0	0	0	0
David NOBLE	2 February 1982	2003/04	3	0	3	0	0	0	0	0
Mark NOBLE	8 May 1987	2004/05 -	58	53	5	8	222	207	15	23
Antonia NOCERINO	9 April 1985	2013/14	0	0	0	0	10	2	8	0
Kevin NOLAN	24 June 1982	2011/12 -	42	42	0	12	97	87	10	18
Cyril NORRINGTON	3 June 1901	1927/28 - 1928/29	27	27	0	0	0	0	0	0
Fred NORRIS	14 August 1903	1928/29 - 1932/33	65	65	0	6	0	0	0	0

FA Cup				League Cup				Europe				Other				Total			
Apps	Starts	Subs	Goals	Apps	Starts	Subs	Goals	Apps	Starts	Subs	Goals	Apps	Starts	Subs	Goals	Apps	Starts	Subs	Goals
2	2	0	1	0	0	0	0	0	0	0	0	0	0	0	0	23	23	0	17
0	0	0	0	0	0	0	0	0	0	0	0	0	0	0	0	1	0	1	0
2	2	0	0	0	0	0	0	0	0	0	0	0	0	0	0	4	4	0	0
2	2	0	0	4	4	0	0	5	5	0	0	0	0	0	0	62	55	7	0
0	0	0	0	0	0	0	0	0	0	0	0	0	0	0	0	1	0	1	0
1	1	0	0	1	0	1	0	0	0	0	0	0	0	0	0	2	1	1	0
8	7	1	1	14	13	1	2	6	5	1	0	0	0	0	0	203	156	47	9
7	7	0	0	0	0	0	0	0	0	0	0	0	0	0	0	60	60	0	0
1	0	1	0	0	0	0	0	0	0	0	0	0	0	0	0	1	0	1	0
36	36	0	0	49	49	0	3	13	13	0	0	5	5	0	0	647	646	1	27
0	0	0	0	0	0	0	0	0	0	0	0	1	1	0	1	10	10	0	2
0	0	0	0	0	0	0	0	0	0	0	0	0	0	0	0	1	0	1	0
0	0	0	0	0	0	0	0	0	0	0	0	0	0	0	0	4	4	0	0
21	21	0	6	0	0	0	0	0	0	0	0	0	0	0	0	202	202	0	48
0	0	0	0	1	1	0	0	3	1	2	0	1	0	1	0	26	16	10	2
0	0	0	0	0	0	0	0	0	0	0	0	4	4	0	0	4	4	0	0
19	14	5	7	11	10	1	5	0	0	0	0	6	5	1	1	214	188	26	70
3	3	0	0	0	0	0	0	0	0	0	0	7	7	0	4	158	158	0	12
0	0	0	0	0	0	0	0	0	0	0	0	0	0	0	0	3	3	0	0
0	0	0	0	0	0	0	0	0	0	0	0	0	0	0	0	15	15	0	1
1	1	0	0	5	4	1	2	0	0	0	0	0	0	0	0	24	17	7	5
17	17	0	3	0	0	0	0	0	0	0	0	0	0	0	0	275	275	0	57
0	0	0	0	0	0	0	0	0	0	0	0	0	0	0	0	2	2	0	1
17	15	2	3	10	10	0	0	0	0	0	0	6	6	0	0	213	183	30	7
0	0	0	0	0	0	0	0	0	0	0	0	0	0	0	0	2	2	0	0
4	4	0	1	0	0	0	0	0	0	0	0	0	0	0	0	40	40	0	2
13	13	0	2	5	5	0	3	0	0	0	0	17	17	0	9	317	317	0	98
0	0	0	0	1	0	1	0	0	0	0	0	0	0	0	0	1	0	1	0
0	0	0	0	0	0	0	0	0	0	0	0	0	0	0	0	17	17	0	15
7	6	1	0	12	11	1	1	4	4	0	0	0	0	0	0	96	87	9	6
0	0	0	0	0	0	0	0	0	0	0	0	0	0	0	0	1	1	0	0
5	5	0	0	5	5	0	0	0	0	0	0	0	0	0	0	89	89	0	1
0	0	0	0	0	0	0	0	0	0	0	0	8	8	0	0	23	23	0	1
0	0	0	0	0	0	0	0	0	0	0	0	1	1	0	0	3	3	0	0
0	0	0	0	0	0	0	0	0	0	0	0	0	0	0	0	8	0	8	0
0	0	0	0	0	0	0	0	0	0	0	0	2	2	0	1	5	5	0	1
0	0	0	0	0	0	0	0	0	0	0	0	0	0	0	0	7	6	1	0
0	0	0	0	0	0	0	0	0	0	0	0	2	2	0	1	9	9	0	3
0	0	0	0	0	0	0	0	1	0	1	0	0	0	0	0	3	0	3	0
4	2	2	0	2	1	1	0	0	0	0	0	3	2	1	0	49	24	25	1
0	0	0	0	0	0	0	0	0	0	0	0	1	1	0	0	1	1	0	0
0	0	0	0	0	0	0	0	0	0	0	0	1	1	0	0	1	1	0	0
0	0	0	0	1	1	0	0	0	0	0	0	0	0	0	0	4	1	3	0
19	18	1	3	16	9	7	1	0	0	0	0	6	3	3	0	321	290	31	35
0	0	0	0	0	0	0	0	0	0	0	0	0	0	0	0	10	2	8	0
6	4	2	0	4	3	1	0	0	0	0	0	3	3	0	1	152	139	13	31
0	0	0	0	0	0	0	0	0	0	0	0	0	0	0	0	27	27	0	0
0	0	0	0	0	0	0	0	0	0	0	0	0	0	0	0	65	65	0	6

Player	Date of Birth	Career	League				Premier League			
			Apps	Starts	Subs	Goals	Apps	Starts	Subs	Goal
Frank NOUBLE	24 September 1991	2009/10 - 2011/12	3	1	2	1	10	3	7	0
Adam NOWLAND	6 July 1981	2003/04 - 2004/05	15	5	10	0	0	0	0	0
Savio NSEREKO	27 July 1989	2008/09 - 2009/10	0	0	0	0	10	1	9	0
Joey O'BRIEN	17 February 1986	2011/12 -	32	27	5	1	59	51	8	2
Frank O'FARRELL	9 October 1927	1950/51 - 1956/57	197	197	0	6	0	0	0	0
Gary O'NEIL	18 May 1983	2010/11 - 2012/13	16	9	7	2	32	24	8	1
William OAKES	16 June 1881	1903/04	14	14	0	0	0	0	0	0
Harry OBENEY	9 March 1938	1956/57 - 1960/61	25	25	0	12	0	0	0	0
Victor OBINNA	25 March 1987	2010/11	0	0	0	0	25	17	8	3
Emmanuel OMOYINMI	28 December 1977	1996/97 - 1999/00	0	0	0	0	9	1	8	2
Yilmaz ORHAN	13 March 1955	1975/76 - 1976/77	8	6	2	0	0	0	0	0
Neil ORR	13 May 1959	1981/82 - 1987/88	146	133	13	4	0	0	0	0
Anton OTULAKOWSKI	29 January 1956	1976/77 - 1977/78	17	10	7	0	0	0	0	0
Graham PADDON	24 August 1950	1973/74 - 1976/77	115	115	0	11	0	0	0	0
James PALMER	Unknown	1919/20 - 1920/21	13	13	0	1	0	0	0	0
John PANTSIL	15 June 1981	2006/07 - 2007/08	0	0	0	0	19	7	12	0
Derek PARKER	23 June 1926	1946/47 - 1956/57	199	199	0	9	0	0	0	0
Reginald PARKER	17 February 1913	1935/36	2	2	0	0	0	0	0	0
Scott PARKER	13 October 1980	2007/08 - 2011/12	4	4	0	1	109	105	4	9
Phil PARKES	8 August 1950	1978/79 - 1989/90	344	344	0	0	0	0	0	0
Harry PARKINSON	Unknown	1902/03	2	2	0	0	0	0	0	0
Tony PARKS	26 January 1963	1991/92	6	6	0	0	0	0	0	0
George PARRIS	11 September 1964	1984/85 - 1992/93	239	211	28	12	0	0	0	0
Eric PARSONS	9 November 1923	1946/47 - 1950/51	145	145	0	34	0	0	0	0
Joe PAYNE	17 January 1914	1946/47	10	10	0	6	0	0	0	0
John PAYNE	1908	1926/27 - 1928/29	4	4	0	1	0	0	0	0
Josh PAYNE	25 November 1990	2008/09 - 2009/10	0	0	0	0	2	0	2	0
Ian PEARCE	7 May 1974	1997/98 - 2003/04	24	24	0	1	118	111	7	8
Stuart PEARCE	24 April 1962	1999/00 - 2000/01	0	0	0	0	42	42	0	2
Stuart PEARSON	21 June 1949	1979/80 - 1981/82	34	28	6	6	0	0	0	0
George PETCHEY	24 June 1931	1952/53	2	2	0	0	0	0	0	0
Martin PETERS	8 November 1943	1961/62 - 1969/70	302	302	0	81	0	0	0	0
Mladen PETRIC	1 January 1981	2013/14	0	0	0	0	3	0	3	0
Wilf PHILLIPS	11 February 1900	1931/32	21	21	0	3	0	0	0	0
Cecil PHIPPS	25 October 1896	1919/20	1	1	0	0	0	0	0	0
Frank PIERCY	1879	1904/05 - 1911/12	214	214	0	7	0	0	0	0
Geoff PIKE	28 September 1956	1975/76 - 1986/87	291	275	16	32	0	0	0	0
A. PINDER	Unknown	1900/01 - 1901/02	1	1	0	0	0	0	0	0
Frederic PIQUIONNE	8 December 1978	2010/11 - 2011/12	20	8	12	2	34	26	8	6
Emanuel POGATEZ	16 January 1983	2012/13	0	0	0	0	6	1	5	0
Walter POLLARD	26 September 1906	1929/30 - 1932/33	37	37	0	3	0	0	0	0
Hugo PORFIRIO	28 September 1973	1996/97	0	0	0	0	23	15	8	2
Daniel POTTS	13 April 1994	2011/12 - 2014/15	3	3	0	0	2	1	1	0
Steve POTTS	7 May 1967	1984/85 - 2000/01	195	185	10	1	204	177	27	0
Chris POWELL	8 September 1969	2004/05	36	35	1	0	0	0	0	0
Darren POWELL	10 March 1976	2004/05	5	5	0	1	0	0	0	0
Diego POYET	8 April 1995	2014/15 -	0	0	0	0	3	1	2	0
Eddie PRESLAND	27 March 1943	1964/65 - 1965/66	6	6	0	1	0	0	0	0

FA Cup				League Cup				Europe				Other				Total			
Apps	Starts	Subs	Goals	Apps	Starts	Subs	Goals	Apps	Starts	Subs	Goals	Apps	Starts	Subs	Goals	Apps	Starts	Subs	Goals
4	2	2	0	2	0	2	0	0	0	0	0	0	0	0	0	19	6	13	1
0	0	0	0	2	2	0	0	0	0	0	0	0	0	0	0	17	7	10	0
1	0	1	0	0	0	0	0	0	0	0	0	0	0	0	0	11	1	10	0
3	1	2	0	4	4	0	0	0	0	0	0	0	0	0	0	98	83	15	3
13	13	0	1	0	0	0	0	0	0	0	0	3	3	0	1	213	213	0	8
2	2	0	0	3	2	1	0	0	0	0	0	3	3	0	0	56	40	16	3
0	0	0	0	0	0	0	0	0	0	0	0	0	0	0	0	14	14	0	0
2	2	0	0	0	0	0	0	0	0	0	0	4	4	0	4	31	31	0	16
3	3	0	3	4	3	1	2	0	0	0	0	0	0	0	0	32	23	9	8
2	1	1	0	1	0	1	0	0	0	0	0	0	0	0	0	12	2	10	2
0	0	0	0	1	1	0	0	0	0	0	0	0	0	0	0	9	7	2	0
11	10	1	0	18	14	4	1	0	0	0	0	0	0	0	0	175	157	18	5
0	0	0	0	0	0	0	0	0	0	0	0	0	0	0	0	17	10	7	0
11	11	0	0	11	11	0	2	9	9	0	2	6	6	0	0	152	152	0	15
0	0	0	0	0	0	0	0	0	0	0	0	0	0	0	0	13	13	0	1
2	1	1	0	3	1	2	0	0	0	0	0	0	0	0	0	24	9	15	0
8	8	0	0	0	0	0	0	0	0	0	0	10	10	0	3	217	217	0	12
0	0	0	0	0	0	0	0	0	0	0	0	0	0	0	0	2	2	0	0
6	5	1	0	10	9	1	2	0	0	0	0	0	0	0	0	129	123	6	12
34	34	0	0	52	52	0	0	6	6	0	0	4	4	0	0	440	440	0	0
0	0	0	0	0	0	0	0	0	0	0	0	0	0	0	0	2	2	0	0
3	3	0	0	0	0	0	0	0	0	0	0	0	0	0	0	9	9	0	0
21	21	0	4	30	27	3	1	0	0	0	0	8	7	1	1	298	266	32	18
6	6	0	1	0	0	0	0	0	0	0	0	0	0	0	0	151	151	0	35
1	1	0	0	0	0	0	0	0	0	0	0	0	0	0	0	11	11	0	6
0	0	0	0	0	0	0	0	0	0	0	0	0	0	0	0	4	4	0	1
0	0	0	0	1	1	0	0	0	0	0	0	0	0	0	0	3	1	2	0
11	10	1	1	8	8	0	0	0	0	0	0	2	1	1	0	163	154	9	10
4	4	0	1	4	4	0	0	0	0	0	0	0	0	0	0	50	50	0	3
10	8	2	2	5	3	2	1	1	0	1	1	0	0	0	0	50	39	11	10
0	0	0	0	0	0	0	0	0	0	0	0	1	1	0	0	3	3	0	0
16	16	0	5	31	31	0	10	15	15	0	4	0	0	0	0	364	364	0	100
0	0	0	0	1	0	1	0	0	0	0	0	0	0	0	0	4	0	4	0
2	2	0	0	0	0	0	0	0	0	0	0	0	0	0	0	23	23	0	3
0	0	0	0	0	0	0	0	0	0	0	0	0	0	0	0	1	1	0	0
17	17	0	0	0	0	0	0	0	0	0	0	0	0	0	0	231	231	0	7
31	29	2	5	39	38	1	3	6	6	0	1	1	1	0	0	368	349	19	41
1	1	0	0	0	0	0	0	0	0	0	0	0	0	0	0	2	2	0	0
4	2	2	2	4	4	0	1	0	0	0	0	0	0	0	0	62	40	22	11
0	0	0	0	0	0	0	0	0	0	0	0	0	0	0	0	6	1	5	0
6	6	0	2	0	0	0	0	0	0	0	0	0	0	0	0	43	43	0	5
2	1	1	1	2	2	0	1	0	0	0	0	0	0	0	0	27	18	9	4
4	4	0	0	4	4	0	0	0	0	0	0	0	0	0	0	13	12	1	0
42	41	1	0	42	39	3	0	8	7	1	0	15	14	1	0	506	463	43	1
3	3	0	0	0	0	0	0	0	0	0	0	3	3	0	0	42	41	1	0
0	0	0	0	0	0	0	0	0	0	0	0	0	0	0	0	5	5	0	1
1	0	1	0	1	1	0	0	0	0	0	0	0	0	0	0	5	2	3	0
0	0	0	0	0	0	0	0	0	0	0	0	0	0	0	0	6	6	0	1

Player	Date of Birth	Career	League				Premier League			
			Apps	Starts	Subs	Goals	Apps	Starts	Subs	Goals
Norman PROCTER	11 May 1896	1923/24	7	7	0	1	0	0	0	0
George PROUDLOCK	19 September 1919	1938/39 - 1947/48	18	18	0	5	0	0	0	0
Richard PUDAN	1881	1900/01 - 1901/02	7	7	0	0	0	0	0	0
Syd PUDDEFOOT	17 October 1894	1912/13 - 1921/22 and 1931/32 - 1932/33	180	180	0	95	0	0	0	0
Malcolm PYKE	6 March 1938	1956/57 - 1958/59	17	17	0	0	0	0	0	0
Nigel QUASHIE	20 July 1978	2006/07	0	0	0	0	7	7	0	0
Jimmy QUINN	18 November 1959	1989/90 - 1990/91	47	34	13	19	0	0	0	0
Wayne QUINN	19 November 1976	2003/04	22	22	0	0	0	0	0	0
John RADFORD	22 February 1947	1976/77 - 1977/78	28	28	0	0	0	0	0	0
Florin RADUCIOIU	17 March 1970	1996/97	0	0	0	0	11	6	5	2
Luke RAISBECK	2 September 1878	1900/01	2	2	0	0	0	0	0	0
Tommy RANDALL	1886	1906/07 - 1914/15	189	189	0	9	0	0	0	0
Razvan RAT	26 May 1981	2013/14	0	0	0	0	15	11	4	0
George RATCLIFFE	1874	1900/01 - 1901/02	41	41	0	14	0	0	0	0
Sergei REBROV	3 June 1974	2004/05	26	12	14	1	0	0	0	0
Harry REDKNAPP	2 March 1947	1965/66 - 1971/72	149	146	3	7	0	0	0	0
Frank REDWARD	1889	1910/11 - 1911/12	7	7	0	0	0	0	0	0
George REDWOOD	26 April 1885	1911/12	3	3	0	0	0	0	0	0
James REID	20 February 1879	1900/01	13	13	0	5	0	0	0	0
Kyel REID	26 November 1987	2005/06 - 2008/09	0	0	0	0	3	1	2	0
Winston REID	3 July 1988	2010/11 -	28	27	1	3	95	86	9	3
Nigel REO-COKER	14 May 1984	2003/04 - 2006/07	54	47	7	5	66	66	0	6
Tomas REPKA	2 January 1974	2001/02 - 2005/06	82	82	0	0	82	82	0	0
Brian RHODES	23 October 1937	1957/58 - 1962/63	61	61	0	0	0	0	0	0
Dick RICHARDS	14 January 1892	1922/23 - 1923/24	43	43	0	5	0	0	0	0
Frank RICHARDSON	29 January 1897	1923/24	10	10	0	2	0	0	0	0
Marc RIEPER	5 May 1968	1994/95 - 1997/98	0	0	0	0	90	83	7	5
Bill ROBERTS	3 March 1914	1937/38	1	1	0	0	0	0	0	0
Vivian ROBERTS	Unknown	1919/20	1	1	0	0	0	0	0	0
ROBERTSON	Unknown	1907/08	1	1	0	0	0	0	0	0
Bill ROBINSON	4 April 1919	1948/49 - 1951/52	101	101	0	60	0	0	0	0
Leslie ROBINSON	2 May 1898	1920/21 - 1923/24	19	19	0	2	0	0	0	0
Bryan ROBSON	11 November 1945	1970/71 - 1973/74 and 1976/77 - 1978/79	227	227	0	94	0	0	0	0
George ROBSON	17 June 1905	1927/28 - 1930/31	17	17	0	2	0	0	0	0
Keith ROBSON	15 November 1953	1974/75 - 1976/77	68	65	3	13	0	0	0	0
Mark ROBSON	22 May 1969	1992/93 - 1993/94	44	41	3	8	3	1	2	0
Stewart ROBSON	6 November 1964	1986/87 - 1990/91	69	68	1	4	0	0	0	0
William ROBSON	1906	1933/34	3	3	0	0	0	0	0	0
Leroy ROSENIOR	24 August 1964	1987/88 - 1991/92	53	44	9	15	0	0	0	0
James ROTHWELL	1883	1910/11 - 1913/14	87	87	0	4	0	0	0	0
Keith ROWLAND	1 September 1971	1993/94 - 1997/98	0	0	0	0	80	63	17	1
Neil RUDDOCK	9 May 1968	1998/99 - 1999/00	0	0	0	0	42	39	3	2
Pelly RUDDOCK	17 July 1993	2013/14	0	0	0	0	0	0	0	0
James RUFFELL	11 August 1900	1921/22 - 1936/37	505	505	0	159	0	0	0	0
Matthew RUSH	6 August 1971	1990/91 - 1994/95	15	5	10	2	33	24	9	3
John RUSSELL	1880	1904/05	16	16	0	0	0	0	0	0
Jack RUTHERFORD	6 November 1908	1933/34	33	33	0	0	0	0	0	0
George SADLER	7 May 1915	1946/47	1	1	0	0	0	0	0	0

FA Cup				League Cup				Europe				Other				Total			
Apps	Starts	Subs	Goals	Apps	Starts	Subs	Goals	Apps	Starts	Subs	Goals	Apps	Starts	Subs	Goals	Apps	Starts	Subs	Goals
0	0	0	0	0	0	0	0	0	0	0	0	0	0	0	0	7	7	0	1
0	0	0	0	0	0	0	0	0	0	0	0	0	0	0	0	18	18	0	5
2	2	0	0	0	0	0	0	0	0	0	0	0	0	0	0	9	9	0	0
14	14	0	12	0	0	0	0	0	0	0	0	0	0	0	0	194	194	0	107
2	2	0	0	0	0	0	0	0	0	0	0	5	5	0	0	24	24	0	0
1	1	0	0	0	0	0	0	0	0	0	0	0	0	0	0	8	8	0	0
6	4	2	2	3	3	0	1	0	0	0	0	1	1	0	0	57	42	15	22
3	2	1	0	2	2	0	0	0	0	0	0	0	0	0	0	27	26	1	0
1	1	0	0	1	1	0	0	0	0	0	0	0	0	0	0	30	30	0	0
0	0	0	0	1	1	0	1	0	0	0	0	0	0	0	0	12	7	5	3
2	2	0	0	0	0	0	0	0	0	0	0	0	0	0	0	4	4	0	0
16	16	0	1	0	0	0	0	0	0	0	0	0	0	0	0	205	205	0	10
0	0	0	0	5	3	2	0	0	0	0	0	0	0	0	0	20	14	6	0
2	2	0	0	0	0	0	0	0	0	0	0	0	0	0	0	43	43	0	14
2	1	1	0	3	2	1	1	0	0	0	0	1	0	1	0	32	15	17	2
8	7	1	0	18	17	1	1	0	0	0	0	0	0	0	0	175	170	5	8
3	3	0	0	0	0	0	0	0	0	0	0	0	0	0	0	10	10	0	0
0	0	0	0	0	0	0	0	0	0	0	0	0	0	0	0	3	3	0	0
6	6	0	0	0	0	0	0	0	0	0	0	0	0	0	0	19	19	0	5
1	0	1	0	5	1	4	1	0	0	0	0	0	0	0	0	9	2	7	1
7	7	0	1	4	3	1	0	0	0	0	0	3	3	0	0	137	126	11	7
10	9	1	0	4	4	0	0	2	2	0	0	6	3	3	0	142	131	11	11
10	9	1	0	8	8	0	0	0	0	0	0	6	6	0	0	188	187	1	0
2	2	0	0	3	3	0	0	0	0	0	0	5	5	0	0	71	71	0	0
10	10	0	1	0	0	0	0	0	0	0	0	0	0	0	0	53	53	0	6
1	1	0	0	0	0	0	0	0	0	0	0	0	0	0	0	11	11	0	2
4	4	0	0	7	6	1	0	0	0	0	0	0	0	0	0	101	93	8	5
0	0	0	0	0	0	0	0	0	0	0	0	0	0	0	0	1	1	0	0
0	0	0	0	0	0	0	0	0	0	0	0	0	0	0	0	1	1	0	0
0	0	0	0	0	0	0	0	0	0	0	0	0	0	0	0	1	1	0	0
4	4	0	1	0	0	0	0	0	0	0	0	4	4	0	3	109	109	0	64
0	0	0	0	0	0	0	0	0	0	0	0	0	0	0	0	19	19	0	2
12	12	0	4	15	15	0	6	0	0	0	0	1	1	0	0	255	255	0	104
1	1	0	0	0	0	0	0	0	0	0	0	0	0	0	0	18	18	0	2
3	3	0	1	7	7	0	1	9	9	0	4	2	1	1	0	89	85	4	19
2	2	0	1	2	2	0	0	0	0	0	0	5	4	1	0	56	50	6	9
6	6	0	1	8	8	0	1	0	0	0	0	1	1	0	0	84	83	1	6
0	0	0	0	0	0	0	0	0	0	0	0	0	0	0	0	3	3	0	0
5	4	1	2	7	7	0	2	0	0	0	0	2	2	0	4	67	57	10	23
11	11	0	0	0	0	0	0	0	0	0	0	0	0	0	0	98	98	0	4
6	5	1	0	5	3	2	0	0	0	0	0	0	0	0	0	91	71	20	1
3	3	0	0	4	3	1	0	6	5	1	1	0	0	0	0	55	50	5	3
0	0	0	0	1	1	0	0	0	0	0	0	0	0	0	0	1	1	0	0
43	43	0	7	0	0	0	0	0	0	0	0	0	0	0	0	548	548	0	166
0	0	0	0	4	4	0	0	0	0	0	0	3	2	1	0	55	35	20	5
1	1	0	0	0	0	0	0	0	0	0	0	0	0	0	0	17	17	0	0
2	2	0	0	0	0	0	0	0	0	0	0	0	0	0	0	35	35	0	0
0	0	0	0	0	0	0	0	0	0	0	0	0	0	0	0	1	1	0	0

Player	Date of Birth	Career	League				Premier League			
			Apps	Starts	Subs	Goals	Apps	Starts	Subs	Goals
Diafra SAKHO	24 December 1989	2014/15 -	0	0	0	0	23	20	3	10
Charles SATTERTHWAITE	1877	1903/04	32	32	0	13	0	0	0	0
Lionel SCALONI	16 May 1978	2005/06	0	0	0	0	13	13	0	0
Albert SCANES	19 December 1887	1909/10	3	3	0	3	0	0	0	0
Sebastien SCHEMMEL	2 June 1975	2000/01 - 2002/03	0	0	0	0	63	60	3	1
Tony SCOTT	1 April 1941	1959/60 - 1965/66	83	83	0	16	0	0	0	0
Alan SEALEY	22 April 1942	1960/61 - 1966/67	107	107	0	22	0	0	0	0
Les SEALEY	29 September 1957	1995/96 - 1996/97	0	0	0	0	4	2	2	0
Freddie SEARS	27 November 1989	2007/08 - 2011/12	10	2	8	0	36	14	22	2
Dave SEXTON	6 April 1930	1952/53 - 1955/56	74	74	0	27	0	0	0	0
Danny SHEA	6 November 1887	1907/08 - 1912/13 and 1920/21	195	195	0	112	0	0	0	0
Peter SHEARING	26 August 1938	1960/61	6	6	0	0	0	0	0	0
Teddy SHERINGHAM	2 April 1966	2004/05 - 2006/07	33	26	7	20	43	19	24	8
Danny SHONE	24 May 1899	1928/29	12	12	0	5	0	0	0	0
Frederick SHREEVE	17 December 1882	1908/09 - 1910/11	65	65	0	4	0	0	0	0
William SILOR	11 November 1885	1909/10	6	6	0	0	0	0	0	0
Charles SIMMONS	9 September 1878	1904/05	34	34	0	8	0	0	0	0
Jim SIMMONS	27 June 1892	1920/21 - 1921/22	27	27	0	1	0	0	0	0
Peter SIMPSON	13 November 1904	1935/36 - 1936/37	32	32	0	12	0	0	0	0
Trevor SINCLAIR	2 March 1973	1997/98 - 2002/03	0	0	0	0	177	175	2	37
John SISSONS	30 September 1945	1962/63 - 1969/70	213	210	3	37	0	0	0	0
Robbie SLATER	22 November 1964	1995/96 - 1996/97	0	0	0	0	25	18	7	2
Stuart SLATER	27 March 1969	1987/88 - 1991/92	141	134	7	11	0	0	0	0
Matthew SMAILES	25 March 1899	1928/29	7	7	0	0	0	0	0	0
Mike SMALL	2 March 1962	1991/92 - 1992/93	49	42	7	13	0	0	0	0
Sam SMALL	15 May 1912	1936/37 - 1947/48	108	108	0	40	0	0	0	0
Andy SMILLIE	15 March 1941	1958/59 - 1960/61	20	20	0	3	0	0	0	0
David SMITH	7 June 1897	1919/20	1	1	0	0	0	0	0	0
Harold SMITH	10 March 1904	1927/28	1	1	0	0	0	0	0	0
John SMITH	4 January 1939	1956/57 - 1959/60	125	125	0	20	0	0	0	0
Mark SMITH	10 October 1961	1979/80	1	1	0	0	0	0	0	0
Roy SMITH	19 March 1936	1955/56 - 1956/57	6	6	0	1	0	0	0	0
Sidney SMITH	Unknown	1904/05	2	2	0	1	0	0	0	0
Stephen SMITH	27 March 1896	1919/20 - 1921/22	27	27	0	0	0	0	0	0
William SMITH	29 September 1901	1927/28 - 1928/29	2	2	0	0	0	0	0	0
Edgar SMITHURST	5 November 1895	1919/20 - 1920/21	3	3	0	0	0	0	0	0
Youssef SOFIANE	8 July 1984	2003/04	1	0	1	0	0	0	0	0
Nolberto SOLANO	12 December 1974	2007/08	0	0	0	0	23	14	9	4
Ragnvald SOMA	10 November 1979	2000/01 - 2001/02	0	0	0	0	7	3	4	0
Alex SONG	9 September 1987	2014/15	0	0	0	0	28	25	3	0
Rigobert SONG	1 July 1976	2000/01 - 2001/02	0	0	0	0	24	23	1	0
Tommy SOUTHREN	1 August 1927	1950/51 - 1953/54	64	64	0	3	0	0	0	0
George SPEAK	7 November 1890	1914/15	13	13	0	0	0	0	0	0
Jonathan SPECTOR	1 March 1986	2006/07 - 2010/11	0	0	0	0	101	66	35	1
David SPEEDIE	20 February 1960	1992/93	11	11	0	4	0	0	0	0
Jordan SPENCE	24 May 1990	2009/10 - 2013/14	0	0	0	0	7	2	5	0
Pavel SRNICEK	10 March 1968	2003/04	3	2	1	0	0	0	0	0
Wally St PIER	8 October 1904	1929/30 - 1932/33	24	24	0	0	0	0	0	0

FA Cup				League Cup				Europe				Other				Total			
Apps	Starts	Subs	Goals	Apps	Starts	Subs	Goals	Apps	Starts	Subs	Goals	Apps	Starts	Subs	Goals	Apps	Starts	Subs	Goals
2	1	1	1	1	1	0	1	0	0	0	0	0	0	0	0	26	22	4	12
4	4	0	5	0	0	0	0	0	0	0	0	0	0	0	0	36	36	0	18
4	3	1	0	0	0	0	0	0	0	0	0	0	0	0	0	17	16	1	0
0	0	0	0	0	0	0	0	0	0	0	0	0	0	0	0	3	3	0	3
7	7	0	0	3	2	1	0	0	0	0	0	0	0	0	0	73	69	4	1
7	7	0	0	7	7	0	3	0	0	0	0	0	0	0	0	97	97	0	19
8	8	0	0	6	6	0	1	7	7	0	3	0	0	0	0	128	128	0	26
0	0	0	0	0	0	0	0	0	0	0	0	0	0	0	0	4	2	2	0
7	4	3	1	5	5	0	0	0	0	0	0	0	0	0	0	58	25	33	3
3	3	0	2	0	0	0	0	0	0	0	0	2	2	0	0	79	79	0	29
22	22	0	10	0	0	0	0	0	0	0	0	0	0	0	0	217	217	0	122
0	0	0	0	0	0	0	0	0	0	0	0	0	0	0	0	6	6	0	0
7	3	4	2	3	1	2	0	1	0	1	0	0	0	0	0	87	49	38	30
0	0	0	0	0	0	0	0	0	0	0	0	0	0	0	0	12	12	0	5
10	10	0	0	0	0	0	0	0	0	0	0	0	0	0	0	75	75	0	4
0	0	0	0	0	0	0	0	0	0	0	0	0	0	0	0	6	6	0	0
1	1	0	0	0	0	0	0	0	0	0	0	0	0	0	0	35	35	0	8
0	0	0	0	0	0	0	0	0	0	0	0	0	0	0	0	27	27	0	1
4	4	0	0	0	0	0	0	0	0	0	0	0	0	0	0	36	36	0	12
8	8	0	0	10	9	1	0	10	10	0	1	0	0	0	0	205	202	3	38
18	18	0	8	21	21	0	5	13	13	0	3	1	1	0	0	266	263	3	53
1	1	0	0	3	3	0	0	0	0	0	0	0	0	0	0	29	22	7	2
16	16	0	3	17	16	1	2	0	0	0	0	5	5	0	2	179	171	8	18
3	3	0	0	0	0	0	0	0	0	0	0	0	0	0	0	10	10	0	0
5	4	1	1	5	4	1	4	0	0	0	0	2	2	0	0	61	52	9	18
10	10	0	0	0	0	0	0	0	0	0	0	0	0	0	0	118	118	0	40
3	3	0	0	0	0	0	0	0	0	0	0	3	3	0	2	26	26	0	5
0	0	0	0	0	0	0	0	0	0	0	0	0	0	0	0	1	1	0	0
0	0	0	0	0	0	0	0	0	0	0	0	0	0	0	0	1	1	0	0
5	5	0	2	0	0	0	0	0	0	0	0	8	8	0	1	138	138	0	23
0	0	0	0	1	1	0	0	0	0	0	0	0	0	0	0	2	2	0	0
0	0	0	0	0	0	0	0	0	0	0	0	3	3	0	0	9	9	0	1
0	0	0	0	0	0	0	0	0	0	0	0	0	0	0	0	2	2	0	1
4	4	0	1	0	0	0	0	0	0	0	0	0	0	0	0	31	31	0	1
0	0	0	0	0	0	0	0	0	0	0	0	0	0	0	0	2	2	0	0
0	0	0	0	0	0	0	0	0	0	0	0	0	0	0	0	3	3	0	0
0	0	0	0	1	1	0	0	0	0	0	0	0	0	0	0	2	1	1	0
0	0	0	0	0	0	0	0	0	0	0	0	0	0	0	0	23	14	9	4
2	1	1	0	0	0	0	0	0	0	0	0	0	0	0	0	9	4	5	0
3	3	0	0	0	0	0	0	0	0	0	0	0	0	0	0	31	28	3	0
1	1	0	0	2	2	0	0	0	0	0	0	0	0	0	0	27	26	1	0
2	2	0	0	0	0	0	0	0	0	0	0	2	2	0	0	68	68	0	3
0	0	0	0	0	0	0	0	0	0	0	0	0	0	0	0	13	13	0	0
6	2	4	1	7	6	1	2	1	1	0	0	0	0	0	0	115	75	40	4
0	0	0	0	0	0	0	0	0	0	0	0	0	0	0	0	11	11	0	4
1	1	0	0	2	2	0	0	0	0	0	0	0	0	0	0	10	5	5	0
0	0	0	0	0	0	0	0	0	0	0	0	0	0	0	0	3	2	1	0
0	0	0	0	0	0	0	0	0	0	0	0	0	0	0	0	24	24	0	0

Player	Date of Birth	Career	League				Premier League			
			Apps	Starts	Subs	Goals	Apps	Starts	Subs	Goal
Arthur STALLARD	1 September 1892	1913/14 - 1914/15	13	13	0	8	0	0	0	0
Jim STANDEN	30 May 1935	1962/63 - 1967/68	178	178	0	0	0	0	0	0
Junior STANISLAS	26 November 1989	2008/09 - 2011/12	1	0	1	0	41	22	19	5
Thomas STANLEY	Unknown	1919/20	1	1	0	0	0	0	0	0
Harry STAPLEY	29 April 1883	1905/06 - 1907/08	71	71	0	39	0	0	0	0
Marek STECH	28 January 1990	2010/11	0	0	0	0	0	0	0	0
Bill STEPHENS	13 September 1919	1947/48 - 1948/49	22	22	0	6	0	0	0	0
Alan STEPHENSON	26 September 1944	1967/68 - 1971/72	108	106	2	0	0	0	0	0
Ray STEWART	7 September 1959	1979/80 - 1990/91	345	344	1	62	0	0	0	0
Igor STIMAC	6 September 1967	1999/00 - 2000/01	0	0	0	0	43	43	0	1
Robbie STOCKDALE	30 November 1979	2003/04	7	5	2	0	0	0	0	0
Tony STOKES	7 January 1987	2005/06	0	0	0	0	0	0	0	0
Gary STRODDER	1 April 1965	1986/87 - 1989/90	65	59	6	2	0	0	0	0
Roy STROUD	16 March 1925	1951/52 - 1956/57	13	13	0	4	0	0	0	0
Perry SUCKLING	12 October 1965	1989/90	6	6	0	0	0	0	0	0
Sidney SUGDEN	30 October 1880	1902/03	1	1	0	0	0	0	0	0
Davor SUKER	1 January 1968	2000/01	0	0	0	0	11	7	4	2
Dave SWINDLEHURST	6 January 1956	1982/83 - 1984/85	61	52	9	16	0	0	0	0
Mauricio TARICCO	10 March 1973	2004/05	1	1	0	0	0	0	0	0
Isaac TATE	28 July 1906	1927/28 - 1928/29	14	14	0	0	0	0	0	0
Alan TAYLOR	14 November 1953	1974/75 - 1978/79	98	88	10	25	0	0	0	0
Archie TAYLOR	25 November 1879	1907/08 - 1908/09	60	60	0	0	0	0	0	0
Frank TAYLOR	Unknown	1900/01 - 1901/02	12	12	0	4	0	0	0	0
George TAYLOR	21 March 1920	1946/47 - 1955/56	115	115	0	0	0	0	0	0
Matthew TAYLOR	27 November 1981	2011/12	28	26	2	1	48	30	18	1
Tommy TAYLOR	26 September 1951	1970/71 - 1978/79	340	340	0	8	0	0	0	0
William TAYLOR	1885	1906/07	4	4	0	0	0	0	0	0
David TERRIER	4 August 1973	1997/98	0	0	0	0	1	0	1	0
Carlos TEVEZ	5 February 1984	2006/07	0	0	0	0	26	19	7	7
William THIRLAWAY	1 October 1896	1921/22 - 1923/24	36	36	0	2	0	0	0	0
Mitchell THOMAS	2 October 1964	1991/92 - 1992/93	38	37	1	3	0	0	0	0
Alec THOMPSON	Unknown	1903/04	9	9	0	1	0	0	0	0
Percy THORPE	18 July 1899	1933/34	3	3	0	0	0	0	0	0
Hannu TIHINEN	1 July 1976	2000/01	0	0	0	0	8	5	3	0
Ron TINDALL	23 September 1935	1961/62	13	13	0	3	0	0	0	0
Tommy TIPPETT	10 July 1904	1933/34 - 1935/36	27	27	0	10	0	0	0	0
Alfred TIRRELL	7 February 1892	1913/14 - 1919/20	8	8	0	0	0	0	0	0
Patrick TIRRELL	1885	1908/09	13	13	0	1	0	0	0	0
Svetoslav TODOROV	30 August 1978	2000/01 - 2001/02	0	0	0	0	14	4	10	1
Dylan TOMBIDES	8 March 1994	2012/13	0	0	0	0	0	0	0	0
James TOMKINS	29 March 1989	2007/08 -	44	42	2	4	139	125	14	4
Arthur TONNER	10 March 1909	1935/36	1	1	0	0	0	0	0	0
Walter TRANTER	September 1874	1900/01	4	4	0	0	0	0	0	0
Don TRAVIS	21 January 1924	1946/47	5	5	0	0	0	0	0	0
Jack TRESADERN	26 September 1890	1913/14 - 1924/25	150	150	0	5	0	0	0	0
Diego TRISTAN	5 January 1976	2008/09	0	0	0	0	14	8	6	3
Ken TUCKER	2 October 1925	1947/48 - 1956/57	83	83	0	31	0	0	0	0
Blair TURGOTT	22 May 1994	2013/14 - 2014/15	0	0	0	0	0	0	0	0

pps	Starts	Subs	Goals	Apps	Starts	Subs	Goals	Apps	Starts	Subs	Goals	Apps	Starts	Subs	Goals	Apps	Starts	Subs	Goals
	FA Cup				League Cup				Europe				Other				Total		
0	0	0	0	0	0	0	0	0	0	0	0	0	0	0	0	13	13	0	8
20	20	0	0	23	23	0	0	14	14	0	0	1	1	0	0	236	236	0	0
1	1	0	0	4	3	1	3	0	0	0	0	0	0	0	0	47	26	21	8
0	0	0	0	0	0	0	0	0	0	0	0	0	0	0	0	1	1	0	0
4	4	0	2	0	0	0	0	0	0	0	0	0	0	0	0	75	75	0	41
0	0	0	0	3	3	0	0	0	0	0	0	0	0	0	0	3	3	0	0
2	2	0	1	0	0	0	0	0	0	0	0	0	0	0	0	24	24	0	7
4	4	0	1	6	6	0	0	0	0	0	0	0	0	0	0	118	116	2	1
36	35	1	7	44	44	0	14	6	6	0	1	1	1	0	0	432	430	2	84
2	2	0	0	5	5	0	0	2	2	0	0	0	0	0	0	52	52	0	1
1	1	0	0	1	1	0	0	0	0	0	0	0	0	0	0	9	7	2	0
0	0	0	0	1	0	1	0	0	0	0	0	0	0	0	0	1	0	1	0
6	4	2	0	8	8	0	0	0	0	0	0	2	2	0	0	81	73	8	2
0	0	0	0	0	0	0	0	0	0	0	0	2	2	0	0	15	15	0	4
0	0	0	0	0	0	0	0	0	0	0	0	0	0	0	0	6	6	0	0
0	0	0	0	0	0	0	0	0	0	0	0	0	0	0	0	1	1	0	0
0	0	0	0	2	1	1	1	0	0	0	0	0	0	0	0	13	8	5	3
5	4	1	1	5	5	0	1	0	0	0	0	0	0	0	0	71	61	10	18
0	0	0	0	0	0	0	0	0	0	0	0	0	0	0	0	1	1	0	0
0	0	0	0	0	0	0	0	0	0	0	0	0	0	0	0	14	14	0	0
8	7	1	6	8	8	0	2	7	6	1	3	3	3	0	0	124	112	12	36
7	7	0	0	0	0	0	0	0	0	0	0	0	0	0	0	67	67	0	0
1	1	0	1	0	0	0	0	0	0	0	0	0	0	0	0	13	13	0	5
3	3	0	0	0	0	0	0	0	0	0	0	6	6	0	0	124	124	0	0
2	1	1	0	9	7	2	1	0	0	0	0	3	3	0	0	90	67	23	3
21	21	0	0	26	26	0	0	9	9	0	0	7	7	0	0	403	403	0	8
0	0	0	0	0	0	0	0	0	0	0	0	0	0	0	0	4	4	0	0
0	0	0	0	0	0	0	0	0	0	0	0	0	0	0	0	1	0	1	0
1	1	0	0	0	0	0	0	2	2	0	0	0	0	0	0	29	22	7	7
3	3	0	0	0	0	0	0	0	0	0	0	0	0	0	0	39	39	0	2
4	4	0	0	5	5	0	0	0	0	0	0	2	2	0	0	49	48	1	3
0	0	0	0	0	0	0	0	0	0	0	0	0	0	0	0	9	9	0	1
0	0	0	0	0	0	0	0	0	0	0	0	0	0	0	0	3	3	0	0
2	2	0	0	0	0	0	0	0	0	0	0	0	0	0	0	10	7	3	0
1	1	0	0	0	0	0	0	0	0	0	0	0	0	0	0	14	14	0	3
1	1	0	0	0	0	0	0	0	0	0	0	0	0	0	0	28	28	0	10
0	0	0	0	0	0	0	0	0	0	0	0	0	0	0	0	8	8	0	0
4	4	0	0	0	0	0	0	0	0	0	0	0	0	0	0	17	17	0	1
2	0	2	1	1	1	0	0	0	0	0	0	0	0	0	0	17	5	12	2
0	0	0	0	1	0	1	0	0	0	0	0	0	0	0	0	1	0	1	0
12	12	0	0	13	13	0	0	0	0	0	0	3	3	0	0	211	195	16	8
0	0	0	0	0	0	0	0	0	0	0	0	0	0	0	0	1	1	0	0
2	2	0	0	0	0	0	0	0	0	0	0	0	0	0	0	6	6	0	0
0	0	0	0	0	0	0	0	0	0	0	0	0	0	0	0	5	5	0	0
16	16	0	0	0	0	0	0	0	0	0	0	0	0	0	0	166	166	0	5
3	0	3	0	0	0	0	0	0	0	0	0	0	0	0	0	17	8	9	3
10	10	0	0	0	0	0	0	0	0	0	0	9	9	0	4	102	102	0	35
1	0	1	0	0	0	0	0	0	0	0	0	0	0	0	0	1	0	1	0

Player	Date of Birth	Career	League				Premier League			
			Apps	Starts	Subs	Goals	Apps	Starts	Subs	Goal
Charlie TURNER	1911	1937/38 - 1938/39	11	11	0	0	0	0	0	0
Cyril TURNER	Unknown	1919/20 - 1921/22	7	7	0	1	0	0	0	0
Dudley TYLER	21 September 1944	1972/73 - 1973/74	29	29	0	1	0	0	0	0
David UNSWORTH	16 October 1973	1997/98	0	0	0	0	32	32	0	2
Matthew UPSON	18 April 1979	2006/07 - 2010/11	0	0	0	0	131	131	0	4
Enner VALENCIA	4 November 1989	2014/15 -	0	0	0	0	32	25	7	4
Francois VAN der ELST	1 December 1954	1981/82 - 1982/83	62	61	1	14	0	0	0	0
Ricardo VAZ TE	1 October 1986	2011/12 - 2014/15	15	13	2	10	36	24	12	5
Don WADE	5 June 1926	1947/48 - 1949/50	36	36	0	5	0	0	0	0
Reg WADE	5 August 1907	1929/30 - 1931/32	32	32	0	0	0	0	0	0
William WADE	22 March 1901	1929/30 - 1931/32	16	16	0	0	0	0	0	0
David WAGGOTT	1878	1908/09 - 1909/10	10	10	0	3	0	0	0	0
Edward WAGSTAFF	2 March 1885	1909/10	3	3	0	0	0	0	0	0
George WALDEN	1893	1911/12	2	2	0	0	0	0	0	0
Steve WALFORD	5 January 1958	1983/84 - 1986/87	115	114	1	2	0	0	0	0
Albert WALKER	4 February 1910	1932/33 - 1937/38	162	162	0	0	0	0	0	0
Charlie WALKER	14 May 1911	1936/37 - 1938-39	110	110	0	0	0	0	0	0
James WALKER	9 July 1973	2004/05 - 2005/06	10	10	0	0	3	3	0	0
Len WALKER	Unknown	1900/01	1	1	0	0	0	0	0	0
Richard WALKER	22 July 1913	1934/35 - 1952/53	292	292	0	2	0	0	0	0
James WALLACE	Unknown	1901/02 - 1902/03	17	17	0	3	0	0	0	0
Fred WALLBANKS	14 May 1908	1934/35	0	0	0	0	0	0	0	0
Paulo WANCHOPE	31 July 1976	1999/00	0	0	0	0	35	33	2	12
Elliott WARD	19 January 1985	2004/05 - 2005/06	11	10	1	0	4	3	1	0
Mark WARD	10 October 1962	1985/86 - 1989/90	165	163	2	12	0	0	0	0
Tommy WARD	1879	1901/02	0	0	0	0	0	0	0	0
George WATSON	4 December 1905	1932/33 - 1934/35	33	33	0	0	0	0	0	0
Lionel WATSON	27 May 1882	1905/06	76	76	0	26	0	0	0	0
Mark WATSON	28 December 1973	1995/96	0	0	0	0	1	0	1	0
Victor WATSON	10 November 1897	1920/21 - 1934/35	462	462	0	298	0	0	0	0
Ernest WATTS	11 April 1872	1903/04	25	25	0	1	0	0	0	0
William WAUGH	25 July 1898	1921/22	6	6	0	0	0	0	0	0
Robert WEALE	9 November 1903	1925/26	3	3	0	0	0	0	0	0
Arthur WEARE	21 September 1912	1936/37 - 1937/38	57	57	0	0	0	0	0	0
George WEBB	4 May 1887	1908/09 - 1911/12	52	52	0	23	0	0	0	0
Joseph WEBSTER	1886	1914/15 - 1919/20	19	19	0	0	0	0	0	0
Simon WEBSTER	20 January 1964	1994/95	0	0	0	0	5	0	5	0
Anthony WELDON	12 November 1900	1931/32	20	20	0	3	0	0	0	0
Adrian WHITBREAD	22 October 1971	1994/95 - 1995/96	0	0	0	0	10	3	7	0
Danny WHITEHEAD	23 October 1993	2013/14	0	0	0	0	0	0	0	0
Robert WHITEMAN	1885	1909/10 - 1914/15	136	136	0	3	0	0	0	0
Steve WHITTON	4 December 1960	1983/84 - 1984/85	39	35	4	6	0	0	0	0
William WILDMAN	5 March 1880	1906/07 - 1907/08	39	39	0	0	0	0	0	0
Henry WILKINSON	1883	1905/06	13	13	0	2	0	0	0	0
Gavin WILLIAMS	20 July 1980	2004/05 - 2005/06	10	7	3	1	0	0	0	0
Harry WILLIAMS	24 February 1929	1951/52	5	5	0	1	0	0	0	0
Rod WILLIAMS	2 December 1909	1937/38	9	9	0	5	0	0	0	0
William WILLIAMS	27 September 1905	1921/22 - 1926/27	35	35	0	8	0	0	0	0

	FA Cup				League Cup				Europe				Other				Total			
pps	**Starts**	**Subs**	**Goals**	**Apps**	**Starts**	**Subs**	**Goals**	**Apps**	**Starts**	**Subs**	**Goals**	**Apps**	**Starts**	**Subs**	**Goals**	**Apps**	**Starts**	**Subs**	**Goals**
0	0	0	0	0	0	0	0	0	0	0	0	0	0	0	0	11	11	0	0
0	0	0	0	0	0	0	0	0	0	0	0	0	0	0	0	7	7	0	1
2	2	0	0	3	3	0	0	0	0	0	0	1	0	1	0	35	34	1	1
4	4	0	0	5	5	0	0	0	0	0	0	0	0	0	0	41	41	0	2
6	6	0	0	8	7	1	0	0	0	0	0	0	0	0	0	145	144	1	4
4	4	0	1	1	1	0	0	0	0	0	0	0	0	0	0	37	30	7	5
2	2	0	0	6	5	1	3	0	0	0	0	0	0	0	0	70	68	2	17
2	2	0	0	5	5	0	2	0	0	0	0	3	3	0	2	61	47	14	19
4	4	0	2	0	0	0	0	0	0	0	0	0	0	0	0	40	40	0	7
1	1	0	0	0	0	0	0	0	0	0	0	0	0	0	0	33	33	0	0
0	0	0	0	0	0	0	0	0	0	0	0	0	0	0	0	16	16	0	0
1	1	0	0	0	0	0	0	0	0	0	0	0	0	0	0	11	11	0	3
0	0	0	0	0	0	0	0	0	0	0	0	0	0	0	0	3	3	0	0
0	0	0	0	0	0	0	0	0	0	0	0	0	0	0	0	2	2	0	0
14	14	0	0	17	16	1	2	0	0	0	0	1	1	0	0	147	145	2	4
12	12	0	0	0	0	0	0	0	0	0	0	0	0	0	0	174	174	0	0
8	8	0	0	0	0	0	0	0	0	0	0	0	0	0	0	118	118	0	0
1	1	0	0	3	3	0	0	0	0	0	0	3	3	0	0	20	20	0	0
0	0	0	0	0	0	0	0	0	0	0	0	0	0	0	0	1	1	0	0
19	19	0	0	0	0	0	0	0	0	0	0	0	0	0	0	311	311	0	2
1	1	0	0	0	0	0	0	0	0	0	0	0	0	0	0	18	18	0	3
1	1	0	0	0	0	0	0	0	0	0	0	0	0	0	0	1	1	0	0
1	0	1	0	2	2	0	0	8	7	1	3	0	0	0	0	46	42	4	15
0	0	0	0	3	3	0	0	0	0	0	0	3	3	0	0	21	19	2	0
17	17	0	0	21	20	1	2	0	0	0	0	6	6	0	0	209	206	3	14
1	1	0	0	0	0	0	0	0	0	0	0	0	0	0	0	1	1	0	0
5	5	0	0	0	0	0	0	0	0	0	0	0	0	0	0	38	38	0	0
4	4	0	1	0	0	0	0	0	0	0	0	0	0	0	0	80	80	0	27
0	0	0	0	0	0	0	0	0	0	0	0	0	0	0	0	1	0	1	0
43	43	0	28	0	0	0	0	0	0	0	0	0	0	0	0	505	505	0	326
4	4	0	1	0	0	0	0	0	0	0	0	0	0	0	0	29	29	0	2
1	1	0	0	0	0	0	0	0	0	0	0	0	0	0	0	7	7	0	0
0	0	0	0	0	0	0	0	0	0	0	0	0	0	0	0	3	3	0	0
2	2	0	0	0	0	0	0	0	0	0	0	0	0	0	0	59	59	0	0
10	10	0	9	0	0	0	0	0	0	0	0	0	0	0	0	62	62	0	32
0	0	0	0	0	0	0	0	0	0	0	0	0	0	0	0	19	19	0	0
0	0	0	0	0	0	0	0	0	0	0	0	0	0	0	0	5	0	5	0
2	2	0	1	0	0	0	0	0	0	0	0	0	0	0	0	22	22	0	4
1	1	0	0	3	2	1	0	0	0	0	0	0	0	0	0	14	6	8	0
1	1	0	0	0	0	0	0	0	0	0	0	0	0	0	0	1	1	0	0
10	10	0	0	0	0	0	0	0	0	0	0	0	0	0	0	146	146	0	3
1	1	0	0	6	6	0	2	0	0	0	0	0	0	0	0	46	42	4	8
2	2	0	0	0	0	0	0	0	0	0	0	0	0	0	0	41	41	0	0
1	1	0	0	0	0	0	0	0	0	0	0	0	0	0	0	14	14	0	2
0	0	0	0	1	1	0	0	0	0	0	0	0	0	0	0	11	8	3	1
0	0	0	0	0	0	0	0	0	0	0	0	1	1	0	2	6	6	0	3
1	1	0	0	0	0	0	0	0	0	0	0	0	0	0	0	10	10	0	5
9	9	0	1	0	0	0	0	0	0	0	0	0	0	0	0	44	44	0	9

Player	Date of Birth	Career	League				Premier League			
			Apps	Starts	Subs	Goals	Apps	Starts	Subs	Goal
Danny WILLIAMSON	5 December 1973	1993/94 - 1996/97	0	0	0	0	51	47	4	5
Arthur WILSON	6 October 1908	1932/33 - 1933/34	29	29	0	14	0	0	0	0
Ron WILSON	10 September 1924	1946/47 - 1947/48	3	3	0	0	0	0	0	0
Nigel WINTERBURN	11 December 1963	2000/01 - 2002/03	0	0	0	0	82	78	4	1
Arthur WINTERHALDER	1884	1905/06 - 1906/07	18	18	0	6	0	0	0	0
Herbert WINTERHALDER	1879	1905/06	4	4	0	0	0	0	0	0
Jim WOOD	Unknown	1929/30 - 1934/35	63	63	0	14	0	0	0	0
John WOOD	23 October 1919	1937/38 - 1948/49	58	58	0	13	0	0	0	0
Dan WOODARDS	18 November 1886	1906/07 - 1920/21	125	125	0	3	0	0	0	0
John WOODBURN	Unknown	1919/20	4	4	0	0	0	0	0	0
Terry WOODGATE	11 December 1919	1938/39 - 1953/54	259	259	0	48	0	0	0	0
Derek WOODLEY	2 March 1942	1958/59 - 1961/62	12	12	0	3	0	0	0	0
Alan WOOLER	17 August 1953	1973/74 - 1975/76	4	3	1	0	0	0	0	0
Phil WOOSNAM	22 December 1932	1958/59 - 1962/63	138	138	0	26	0	0	0	0
Doug WRAGG	12 September 1934	1954/55 - 1959/60	16	16	0	0	0	0	0	0
George WRIGHT	19 March 1930	1950/51 - 1957/58	161	161	0	0	0	0	0	0
Ian WRIGHT	3 November 1963	1998/99 - 1999/00	0	0	0	0	22	20	2	9
Ken WRIGHT	16 May 1922	1946/47 - 1949/50	51	51	0	20	0	0	0	0
Percy WRIGHT	6 June 1890	1914/15	10	10	0	1	0	0	0	0
Richard WRIGHT	5 November 1977	2007/08	0	0	0	0	0	0	0	0
Robinson WYLLIE	4 April 1929	1956/57 - 1957/58	13	13	0	0	0	0	0	0
William YENSON	1883	1901/02 - 1902/03 and 1908/09	50	50	0	0	0	0	0	0
Jack YEOMANSON	3 March 1920	1947/48 - 1950/51	106	106	0	1	0	0	0	0
Tommy YEWS	28 February 1902	1923/24 - 1930/31	332	332	0	46	0	0	0	0
Jack YOUNG	1895	1919/20 - 1925/26	124	124	0	3	0	0	0	0
Len YOUNG	23 December 1911	1933/34 - 1937/38	12	12	0	0	0	0	0	0
Robert YOUNG	7 September 1886	1907/08 - 1908/09	42	42	0	1	0	0	0	0
Bobby ZAMORA	16 January 1981	2003/04 - 2007/08	51	30	21	12	79	55	24	18
Mauro ZARATE	18 March 1989	2014/15 -	0	0	0	0	7	5	2	2

	FA Cup				League Cup				Europe				Other				Total			
Apps	Starts	Subs	Goals	Apps	Starts	Subs	Goals	Apps	Starts	Subs	Goals	Apps	Starts	Subs	Goals	Apps	Starts	Subs	Goals
5	5	0	0	2	0	2	0	0	0	0	0	0	0	0	0	58	52	6	5
6	6	0	2	0	0	0	0	0	0	0	0	0	0	0	0	35	35	0	16
0	0	0	0	0	0	0	0	0	0	0	0	0	0	0	0	3	3	0	0
8	8	0	0	4	3	1	0	0	0	0	0	0	0	0	0	94	89	5	1
2	2	0	1	0	0	0	0	0	0	0	0	0	0	0	0	20	20	0	7
0	0	0	0	0	0	0	0	0	0	0	0	0	0	0	0	4	4	0	0
1	1	0	0	0	0	0	0	0	0	0	0	0	0	0	0	64	64	0	14
4	4	0	2	0	0	0	0	0	0	0	0	0	0	0	0	62	62	0	15
14	14	0	0	0	0	0	0	0	0	0	0	0	0	0	0	139	139	0	3
0	0	0	0	0	0	0	0	0	0	0	0	0	0	0	0	4	4	0	0
16	16	0	4	0	0	0	0	0	0	0	0	7	7	0	0	282	282	0	52
0	0	0	0	1	1	0	0	0	0	0	0	2	2	0	0	15	15	0	3
1	1	0	0	0	0	0	0	0	0	0	0	0	0	0	0	5	4	1	0
5	5	0	0	4	4	0	1	0	0	0	0	4	4	0	2	151	151	0	29
0	0	0	0	0	0	0	0	0	0	0	0	8	8	0	2	24	24	0	2
9	9	0	0	0	0	0	0	0	0	0	0	10	10	0	0	180	180	0	0
1	1	0	0	2	2	0	0	1	0	1	0	0	0	0	0	26	23	3	9
1	1	0	0	0	0	0	0	0	0	0	0	0	0	0	0	52	52	0	20
0	0	0	0	0	0	0	0	0	0	0	0	0	0	0	0	10	10	0	1
0	0	0	0	3	3	0	0	0	0	0	0	0	0	0	0	3	3	0	0
2	2	0	0	0	0	0	0	0	0	0	0	2	2	0	0	17	17	0	0
7	7	0	0	0	0	0	0	0	0	0	0	0	0	0	0	57	57	0	0
5	5	0	0	0	0	0	0	0	0	0	0	0	0	0	0	111	111	0	1
29	29	0	5	0	0	0	0	0	0	0	0	0	0	0	0	361	361	0	51
14	14	0	0	0	0	0	0	0	0	0	0	0	0	0	0	138	138	0	3
0	0	0	0	0	0	0	0	0	0	0	0	0	0	0	0	12	12	0	0
2	2	0	0	0	0	0	0	0	0	0	0	0	0	0	0	44	44	0	1
9	3	6	2	5	5	0	4	2	1	1	0	6	6	0	4	152	100	52	40
0	0	0	0	1	0	1	0	0	0	0	0	0	0	0	0	8	5	3	2

PART THREE

AT A GLANCE
SEASON BY SEASON

MOST APPEARANCES
MOST SUB APPEARANCES
MOST GOALS
MOST CLEAN SHEETS
SQUAD NUMBERS
MANAGERS RECORDS
HIGH/LOW ATTENDANCES
BIGGEST WINS/DRAWS/DEFEATS
RECORD IN ALL COMPETITIONS
RECORD AGAINST OTHER CLUBS

At a glance
Season by season

SEASON	DIV	P	HOME					AWAY					Pts	LGE POS	FAC	LC	OTHER COMPETITIONS
			W	D	L	F	A	W	D	L	F	A					
2014-15	P	38	9	4	6	25	18	3	7	9	27	49	47	12	5	2	
2013-14	P	38	7	3	9	25	26	4	4	11	15	25	40	13	3	SF	
2012-13	P	38	9	6	4	34	22	3	4	12	11	31	46	10	3	3	
2011-12	Ch	46	11	8	4	41	26	13	6	4	40	22	86	3(Q)	3	1	POC-W
2010-11	P	38	5	5	9	24	31	2	7	10	19	39	33	20(R)	QF	SF	
2009-10	P	38	7	5	7	30	29	1	6	12	17	37	35	17	3	3	
2008-09	P	38	9	2	8	23	22	5	7	7	19	23	51	9	5	3	
2007-08	P	38	7	7	5	24	24	6	3	10	18	26	49	10	3	5	
2006-07	P	38	8	2	9	24	26	4	3	12	11	33	41	15	4	2	UEFA 1
2005-06	P	38	9	3	7	30	25	7	4	8	22	30	55	9	RU	3	
2004-05	Ch	46	12	5	6	36	24	9	5	9	30	32	73	6(Q)	4	4	POC-W
2003-04	Ch	46	12	7	4	42	20	7	10	6	25	25	74	4	5	4	POC-RU
2002-03	P	38	5	7	7	21	24	5	5	9	21	35	42	18(R)	4	3	
2001-02	P	38	12	4	3	32	14	3	4	12	16	43	53	7	4	2	
2000-01	P	38	6	6	7	24	20	4	6	9	21	30	42	15	QF	4	
1999-00	P	38	11	5	3	32	23	4	5	10	20	30	55	9	3	5	TOTO-W, UEFA 2
1998-99	P	38	11	3	5	32	26	5	6	8	14	27	57	5	3	2	
1997-98	P	38	13	4	2	40	18	3	4	12	16	39	56	8	QF	5	
1996-97	P	38	7	6	6	27	25	3	6	10	12	23	42	14	3	4	
1995-96	P	38	9	5	5	25	21	5	4	10	18	31	51	10	4	3	
1994-95	P	42	9	6	6	28	19	4	5	12	16	29	50	14	4	4	
1993-94	P	42	6	7	8	26	31	7	6	8	21	27	52	13	QF	3	
1992-93	D1	46	16	5	2	50	17	10	5	8	31	24	88	2(P)	4	2	AIC-Gp
1991-92	D1	42	6	6	9	22	24	3	5	13	15	35	38	22(R)	5	4	ZDSC-SF
1990-91	D2	46	15	6	2	41	18	9	9	5	19	16	87	2(P)	SF	3	ZDSC-2
1989-90	D2	46	14	5	4	50	22	6	7	10	30	35	72	7	3	SF	ZDSC-3
1988-89	D1	38	3	6	10	19	30	7	2	10	18	32	38	19(R)	QF	SF	SimC-2
1987-88	D1	40	6	9	5	23	21	3	6	11	17	31	42	16	4	2	SimC-1
1986-87	D1	42	10	4	7	33	28	4	6	11	19	39	52	15	5	4	FMC-3
1985-86	D1	42	17	2	2	48	16	9	4	8	26	24	84	3	QF	3	
1984-85	D1	42	7	8	6	27	23	6	4	11	24	45	51	16	QF	3	
1983-84	D1	42	10	4	7	39	24	7	5	9	21	31	60	9	5	4	
1982-83	D1	42	13	3	5	41	23	7	1	13	27	39	64	8	3	5	
1981-82	D1	42	9	10	2	42	29	5	6	10	24	28	58	9	4	3	
1980-81	D2	42	19	1	1	53	12	9	9	3	26	17	66	1(P)	3	RU	CS-RU, ECWC-3
1979-80	D2	42	13	2	6	37	21	7	5	9	17	22	47	7	W	5	
1978-79	D2	42	12	7	2	46	15	6	7	8	24	24	50	5	3	2	
1977-78	D1	42	8	6	7	31	28	4	2	15	21	41	32	20(R)	4	2	
1976-77	D1	42	9	6	6	28	23	2	8	11	18	42	36	17	4	4	
1975-76	D1	42	10	5	6	26	23	3	5	13	22	48	36	18	3	4	AIC-RU, CS-RU, ECWC-RU
1974-75	D1	42	10	6	5	38	22	3	7	11	20	37	39	13	W	3	TexC-Gp
1973-74	D1	42	7	7	7	36	32	4	8	9	19	28	37	18	3	2	
1972-73	D1	42	12	5	4	45	25	5	7	9	22	28	46	6	4	3	
1971-72	D1	42	10	6	5	31	19	2	6	13	16	32	36	14	5	SF	

		TOP SCORER				
LEAGUE	**PLAYER**	**ALL**	**PLAYER**	**AVG LEAGUE ATT**	**SEASON**
10	Diafra Sakho	12	Diafra Sakho	34,871	2014-15
7	Kevin Nolan	7	Kevin Nolan	33,986	2013-14
10	Kevin Nolan	10	Kevin Nolan	34,720	2012-13
14	Carlton Cole	15	Carlton Cole	30,923	2011-12
7	Demba Ba	11	Carlton Cole	33,492	2010-11
10	Carlton Cole	10	Carlton Cole	33,683	2009-10
10	Carlton Cole	12	Carlton Cole	33,700	2008-09
10	Dean Ashton	11	Dean Ashton	34,603	2007-08
11	Bobby Zamora	11	Bobby Zamora	34,719	2006-07
15	Marlon Harewood	17	Marlon Harewood	33,743	2005-06
17	Teddy Sheringham	22	Marlon Harewood	27,403	2004-05
13	Marlon Harewood	15	Jermain Defoe	31,167	2003-04
9	Paolo Di Canio	11	Jermain Defoe	34,406	2002-03
11	Frederic Kanoute	14	Jermain Defoe	31,570	2001-02
11	Frederic Kanoute	14	Frederic Kanoute	25,697	2000-01
16	Paolo Di Canio	18	Paolo Di Canio	25,093	1999-00
9	Ian Wright	9	Ian Wright	25,639	1998-99
15	John Hartson	24	John Hartson	24,967	1997-98
8	Paul Kitson	8	Paul Kitson, Julian Dicks	23,242	1996-97
10	Tony Cottee, Julian Dicks	12	Tony Cottee	22,340	1995-96
13	Tony Cottee	15	Tony Cottee	20,084	1994-95
13	Trevor Morley	16	Trevor Morley	20,593	1993-94
20	Trevor Morley	22	Trevor Morley	16,001	1992-93
13	Mike Small	18	Mike Small	21,342	1991-92
12	Trevor Morley	17	Trevor Morley	22,572	1990-91
13	Jimmy Quinn	14	Julian Dicks	20,311	1989-90
7	Leroy Rosenior	15	Leroy Rosenior	20,738	1988-89
13	Tony Cottee	15	Tony Cottee	19,802	1987-88
22	Tony Cottee	29	Tony Cottee	20,608	1986-87
26	Frank McAvennie	28	Frank McAvennie	21,179	1985-86
17	Tony Cottee	24	Tony Cottee	18,433	1984-85
15	Tony Cottee	19	Tony Cottee	21,386	1983-84
10	Paul Goddard	12	Paul Goddard, Francois Van der Elst	22,819	1982-83
16	David Cross	20	David Cross	26,585	1981-82
22	David Cross	33	David Cross	27,140	1980-81
12	David Cross	19	David Cross	22,825	1979-80
24	Bryan Robson	26	Bryan Robson	25,778	1978-79
10	Derek Hales	11	Bryan Robson	25,620	1977-78
14	Bryan Robson	14	Bryan Robson	26,064	1976-77
13	Alan Taylor	17	Alan Taylor	27,417	1975-76
13	Billy Jennings	14	Billy Jennings	29,872	1974-75
13	Billy Bonds	13	Clyde Best, Billy Bonds	28,394	1973-74
28	Bryan Robson	28	Bryan Robson	30,174	1972-73
17	Clyde Best	23	Clyde Best	30,005	1971-72

SEASON	DIV	P	HOME					AWAY					Pts	LGE POS	FAC	LC	OTHER COMPETITIONS
			W	D	L	F	A	W	D	L	F	A					
1970-71	D1	42	6	8	7	28	30	4	6	11	19	30	34	20	3	3	
1969-70	D1	42	8	8	5	28	21	4	4	13	23	39	36	17	3	3	
1968-69	D1	42	10	8	3	47	22	3	10	8	19	28	44	8	5	3	
1967-68	D1	42	8	5	8	43	30	6	5	10	30	39	38	12	5	4	
1966-67	D1	42	8	6	7	40	31	6	2	13	40	53	36	16	3	SF	
1965-66	D1	42	12	5	4	46	33	3	4	14	24	50	39	12	4	RU	ECWC-SF
1964-65	D1	42	14	2	5	48	25	5	2	14	34	46	42	9	4	2	CS-W*, ECWC-W
1963-64	D1	42	8	7	6	45	38	6	5	10	24	36	40	14	W	SF	
1962-63	D1	42	8	6	7	39	34	6	6	9	34	35	40	12	QF	3	
1961-62	D1	42	11	6	4	49	37	6	4	11	27	45	44	8	3	2	
1960-61	D1	42	12	4	5	53	31	1	6	14	24	57	36	16	3	2	
1959-60	D1	42	12	3	6	47	33	4	3	14	28	58	38	14	3		SFC-RU
1958-59	D1	42	15	3	3	59	29	6	3	12	26	41	48	6	3		SFC-3, EPC-W
1957-58	D2	42	12	8	1	56	25	11	3	7	45	29	57	1(P)	5		SFC-2, EPC-RU
1956-57	D2	42	12	4	5	31	24	7	4	10	28	39	46	8	4		SFC-2, EPC-SF
1955-56	D2	42	12	4	5	52	27	2	7	12	22	42	39	16	QF		SFC-W, EPC-SF
1954-55	D2	42	12	4	5	46	28	6	6	9	28	42	46	8	3		EPC-W
1953-54	D2	42	11	6	4	44	20	4	3	14	23	49	39	13	4		EPC-1
1952-53	D2	42	9	5	7	38	28	4	8	9	20	32	39	14	3		EPC-SF
1951-52	D2	42	13	5	3	48	29	2	6	13	19	48	41	12	4		EPC-RU
1950-51	D2	42	10	5	6	44	33	6	5	10	24	36	42	13	4		EPC-W
1949-50	D2	42	8	7	6	30	25	4	5	12	23	36	36	19	4		
1948-49	D2	42	13	5	3	38	23	5	5	11	18	35	46	7	3		
1947-48	D2	42	10	7	4	29	19	6	7	8	26	34	46	6	4		
1946-47	D2	42	12	4	5	46	31	4	4	13	24	45	40	12	3		
1945-46															4		Only the FA Cup was contested
1938-39	D2	42	10	5	6	36	21	7	5	9	34	31	44	11	5		
1937-38	D2	42	13	5	3	34	16	1	9	11	19	36	42	9	3		
1936-37	D2	42	14	5	2	47	18	5	6	10	26	37	49	6	3		
1935-36	D2	42	13	5	3	51	23	9	3	9	39	45	52	4	3		
1934-35	D2	42	18	1	2	46	17	8	3	10	34	46	56	3	3		
1933-34	D2	42	13	3	5	51	28	4	8	9	27	42	45	7	4		
1932-33	D2	42	12	6	3	56	31	1	3	17	19	62	35	20	SF		
1931-32	D1	42	9	5	7	35	37	3	2	16	27	70	31	22(R)	4		
1930-31	D1	42	11	3	7	56	44	3	5	13	23	50	36	18	3		
1929-30	D1	42	14	2	5	51	26	5	3	13	35	53	43	7	QF		
1928-29	D1	42	11	6	4	55	31	4	3	14	31	65	39	17	QF		
1927-28	D1	42	9	7	5	48	34	5	4	12	33	54	39	17	4		
1926-27	D1	42	9	6	6	50	36	10	2	9	36	34	46	6	4		
1925-26	D1	42	14	2	5	45	27	1	5	15	18	49	37	18	3		
1924-25	D1	42	12	7	2	37	12	3	5	13	25	48	42	13	3		
1923-24	D1	42	10	6	5	26	17	3	9	9	14	26	41	13	2		
1922-23	D2	42	9	8	4	21	11	11	3	7	42	27	51	2(P)	RU		
1921-22	D2	42	15	3	3	39	13	5	5	11	13	26	48	4	1		
1920-21	D2	42	13	5	3	38	11	6	5	10	13	19	48	5	1		
1919-20	D2	42	14	3	4	34	14	5	6	10	13	26	47	7	3		
1914-15	S1	38	14	4	1	42	18	4	5	10	16	29	45	4	1		

		TOP SCORER				
EAGUE	**PLAYER**	**ALL**	**PLAYER**	**AVG LEAGUE ATT**	**SEASON**
15	Geoff Hurst	16	Geoff Hurst	30,005	1970-71
16	Geoff Hurst	18	Geoff Hurst	30,530	1969-70
25	Geoff Hurst	31	Geoff Hurst	30,982	1968-69
19	Geoff Hurst	25	Geoff Hurst	29,843	1967-68
29	Geoff Hurst	41	Geoff Hurst	29,271	1966-67
23	Geoff Hurst	40	Geoff Hurst	24,836	1965-66
25	Johnny Byrne	30	Johnny Byrne	25,858	1964-65
24	Johnny Byrne	33	Johnny Byrne	24,951	1963-64
13	Geoff Hurst	15	Geoff Hurst	23,644	1962-63
23	John Dick	23	John Dick	25,733	1961-62
17	Macolm Musgrove	19	John Dick	21,948	1960-61
15	Macolm Musgrove	20	Macolm Musgrove	28,554	1959-60
27	John Dick	29	John Dick	28,368	1958-59
21	John Dick	26	John Dick	24,854	1957-58
9	Billy Dare, Eddie Lewis	13	John Dick	18,667	1956-57
18	Billy Dare	25	Billy Dare	17,679	1955-56
26	John Dick	26	John Dick	20,299	1954-55
17	Tommy Dixon	19	Tommy Dixon	20,090	1953-54
10	Fred Kearns	11	Fred Kearns	19,797	1952-53
15	Bert Hawkins	15	Bert Hawkins	20,264	1951-52
26	Bill Robinson	26	Bill Robinson	21,540	1950-51
23	Bill Robinson	24	Bill Robinson	22,233	1949-50
11	Ken Wright	11	Ken Wright	23,354	1948-49
11	Eric Parsons	12	Eric Parsons	24,875	1947-48
15	Frank Neary	15	Frank Neary	23,278	1946-47
		3	Alemeric Hall		1945-46
14	Joseph Foxall	19	Joseph Foxall	20,135	1938-39
10	Joseph Foxall, Archibald Macauley	10	Joseph Foxall, Archibald Macauley	23,004	1937-38
15	Len Goulden	15	Len Goulden	20,704	1936-37
23	Davd Mangnall	24	Davd Mangnall	25,468	1935-36
20	James Ruffell	20	James Ruffell	23,734	1934-35
26	Victor Watson	29	Victor Watson	18,464	1933-34
24	Victor Watson	28	Victor Watson	16,244	1932-33
23	Victor Watson	25	Victor Watson	19,239	1931-32
18	Vivian Gibbins	19	Vivian Gibbins	18,505	1930-31
42	Victor Watson	50	Victor Watson	20,127	1929-30
29	Victor Watson	30	Victor Watson	19,989	1928-29
18	James Ruffell	19	James Ruffell	21,419	1927-28
34	Victor Watson	37	Victor Watson	18,136	1926-27
20	Victor Watson	20	Victor Watson	20,040	1925-26
22	Victor Watson	23	Victor Watson	20,667	1924-25
9	William Moore	10	William Moore	22,095	1923-24
22	Victor Watson	27	Victor Watson	19,048	1922-23
14	Syd Puddefoot	14	Syd Puddefoot	19,952	1921-22
29	Syd Puddefoot	29	Syd Puddefoot	20,190	1920-21
21	Syd Puddefoot	26	Syd Puddefoot	20,048	1919-20
18	Syd Puddefoot	18	Syd Puddefoot	8,032	1914-15

SEASON	DIV	P	HOME					AWAY					Pts	LGE POS	FAC	LC	OTHER COMPETITIONS
			W	D	L	F	A	W	D	L	F	A					
1913-14	S1	38	9	7	3	39	22	6	5	8	22	38	42	6	3		
1912-13	S1	38	11	6	2	39	15	7	6	6	27	31	48	3	2		
1911-12	S1	38	10	3	6	40	27	3	4	12	24	42	33	13	3		
1910-11	S1	38	12	6	1	44	17	5	5	9	19	29	45	5	4		
1909-10	S1	42	10	7	4	43	23	5	8	8	26	33	45	9	3		
1908-09	S1	40	16	1	3	43	13	0	3	17	13	47	36	17	3		
1907-08	S1	38	9	6	4	27	16	6	4	9	20	32	40	10	2		
1906-07	S1	38	12	5	2	39	12	3	9	7	21	29	44	5	2		
1905-06	S1	34	12	2	3	30	9	2	3	12	12	30	33	11	1		
1904-05	S1	34	9	3	5	30	15	3	5	9	18	27	32	11	Q6		
1903-04	S1	34	8	4	5	26	14	2	3	12	13	30	27	12	1		
1902-03	S1	30	8	5	2	25	14	1	5	9	10	35	28	10	1		
1901-02	S1	30	10	2	3	27	13	7	4	4	18	15	40	4	Q4		
1900-01	S1	28	10	2	2	28	10	4	3	7	12	18	33	6	1		
1899-00	S1	28	6	4	4	19	13	2	1	11	11	32	21	14	Q5		
1898-99	S2	22	11	0	0	39	6	8	1	2	25	10	39	1	Q2		
1897-98	LL	16	8	0	0	31	7	4	3	1	16	8	27	1	Q3		
1896-97	LL	12	4	1	1	11	9	3	1	2	6	8	16	2	Q1		

AIC = Anglo-Italian Cup

AIC-Gp = Anglo-Italian group stage

CS = Charity Shield

CS-W* = Shared trophy

EPC = Essex Professional Cup

POC = Play-Off Championship

SFC = Southern Floodlight Cup

TexC-Gp = Texaco Cup Group match

TOTO = Intertoto Cup

UEFA = UEFA Cup

	TOP SCORER					
EAGUE	**PLAYER**	**ALL**	**PLAYER**	**AVG LEAGUE ATT**	**SEASON**
20	Alfred Leafe	21	Alfred Leafe	11,789	1913-14
15	Danny Shea	17	George Hilsdon	10,368	1912-13
24	Danny Shea	24	Danny Shea	9,526	1911-12
25	Danny Shea	28	Danny Shea	10,579	1910-11
28	Danny Shea	31	Danny Shea	8,762	1909-10
16	Danny Shea	20	Danny Shea	7,550	1908-09
10	Harry Stapley	10	Harry Stapley	8,684	1907-08
20	Harry Stapley	22	Harry Stapley	8,921	1906-07
9	Harry Stapley	9	Harry Stapley	8,471	1905-06
11	William Bridgeman	11	William Bridgeman	7,618	1904-05
13	Charles Satterthwaite	18	Charles Satterthwaite	5,338	1903-04
19	William Grassam	19	William Grassam	4,887	1902-03
10	William Grassam, George Ratcliffe	10	William Grassam, George Ratcliffe	5,367	1901-02
12	William Grassam	15	William Grassam	3,536	1900-01
8	A. Carnelly, W. Joyce, K. McKay	18	William Joyce	x	1899-00
12	David Lloyd	13	David Lloyd	x	1898-99
12	George Gresham	13	George Gresham	x	1897-98
4	Butterworth H.	5	George Gressham	x	1896-97

Most appearances All competitions

#	Player	Total Apps	Starts	Subs	Goals	League Apps	Starts	Subs	Goals	FA Cup Apps	Starts	Subs	Goals	League Cup Apps	Starts	Subs	Goals	Europe Apps	Starts	Subs	Goals	Other Apps	Starts	Subs	Goals
1	Billy BONDS	799	787	12	61	663	655	8	48	48	46	2	2	67	65	2	6	15	15	0	3	6	6	0	2
2	Frank LAMPARD Snr	670	665	5	22	551	546	5	18	43	43	0	2	54	54	0	1	15	15	0	1	7	7	0	0
3	Bobby MOORE	647	646	1	27	544	543	1	24	36	36	0	0	49	49	0	3	13	13	0	0	5	5	0	0
4	Trevor BROOKING	643	635	8	102	528	521	7	88	40	40	0	3	55	55	0	8	12	11	1	3	8	8	0	0
5	Alvin MARTIN	596	589	7	34	469	462	7	27	40	40	0	0	71	71	0	6	6	6	0	0	10	10	0	1
6	James RUFFELL	548	548	0	166	505	505	0	159	43	43	0	7	0	0	0	0	0	0	0	0	0	0	0	0
7	Steve POTTS	506	463	43	1	399	362	37	1	42	41	1	0	42	39	3	0	8	7	1	0	15	14	1	0
8	Victor WATSON	505	505	0	326	462	462	0	298	43	43	0	28	0	0	0	0	0	0	0	0	0	0	0	0
9	Geoff HURST	503	502	1	249	411	410	1	180	26	26	0	23	47	47	0	43	15	15	0	2	4	4	0	1
10	Ken BROWN	474	474	0	4	386	386	0	4	26	26	0	0	28	28	0	0	15	15	0	0	19	19	0	0
11	Jim BARRETT Snr.	467	467	0	53	442	442	0	49	25	25	0	4	0	0	0	0	0	0	0	0	0	0	0	0
12	John BOND	449	449	0	39	381	381	0	32	30	30	0	1	13	13	0	1	4	4	0	1	21	21	0	4
13	Alan DEVONSHIRE	448	432	16	32	358	345	13	29	36	36	0	1	48	45	3	2	4	4	0	0	2	2	0	0
14	Phil PARKES	440	440	0	0	344	344	0	0	34	34	0	0	52	52	0	0	6	6	0	0	4	4	0	0
15	Ray STEWART	432	430	2	84	345	344	1	62	36	35	1	7	44	44	0	14	6	6	0	1	1	1	0	0
16	Ernie GREGORY	422	422	0	0	382	382	0	0	24	24	0	0	0	0	0	0	0	0	0	0	16	16	0	0
17	Tommy TAYLOR	403	403	0	8	340	340	0	8	21	21	0	0	26	26	0	0	9	9	0	0	7	7	0	0
18	Edward HUFTON	402	402	0	0	371	371	0	0	31	31	0	0	0	0	0	0	0	0	0	0	0	0	0	0
19	Ludek MIKLOSKO	373	373	0	0	315	315	0	0	25	25	0	0	25	25	0	0	0	0	0	0	8	8	0	0
20	Tony GALE	368	359	9	7	300	293	7	5	29	29	0	1	30	28	2	1	0	0	0	0	9	9	0	0
21	Geoff PIKE	368	349	19	41	291	275	16	32	31	29	2	5	39	38	1	3	6	6	0	1	1	1	0	0
22	John DICK	367	367	0	177	326	326	0	153	21	21	0	11	4	4	0	2	0	0	0	0	16	16	0	1
23	Martin PETERS	364	364	0	100	302	302	0	81	16	16	0	5	31	31	0	10	15	15	0	4	0	0	0	0
24	Tommy YEWS	361	361	0	51	332	332	0	46	29	29	0	5	0	0	0	0	0	0	0	0	0	0	0	0
25	Ron BOYCE	341	333	8	29	282	275	7	21	21	20	1	5	23	23	0	2	13	13	0	1	2	2	0	0
26	Jimmy COLLINS	336	336	0	3	311	311	0	3	25	25	0	0	0	0	0	0	0	0	0	0	0	0	0	0
27	Tony COTTEE	336	323	13	146	279	266	13	115	29	29	0	12	27	27	0	18	0	0	0	0	1	1	0	1
28	Julian DICKS	326	326	0	65	262	262	0	50	23	23	0	3	30	30	0	8	0	0	0	0	11	11	0	4
29	Andy MALCOLM	321	321	0	4	283	283	0	4	21	21	0	0	2	2	0	0	0	0	0	0	15	15	0	0
30	Mark NOBLE	321	290	31	35	280	260	20	31	19	18	1	3	16	9	7	1	0	0	0	0	6	3	3	0
31	Malcolm MUSGROVE	317	317	0	98	282	282	0	84	13	13	0	2	5	5	0	0	0	0	0	0	17	17	0	9
32	Richard WALKER	311	311	0	2	292	292	0	2	19	19	0	0	0	0	0	0	0	0	0	0	0	0	0	0
33	Ian BISHOP	304	287	17	17	254	240	14	12	23	22	1	3	22	21	1	1	0	0	0	0	5	4	1	1
34	Pat HOLLAND	304	278	26	32	245	227	18	23	16	12	4	4	25	22	3	3	10	10	0	2	8	7	1	0
35	John McDOWELL	303	297	6	9	249	243	6	8	19	19	0	0	21	21	0	0	7	7	0	0	7	7	0	0
36	George PARRIS	298	266	32	18	239	211	28	12	21	21	0	4	30	27	3	1	0	0	0	0	8	7	1	0
37	Albert CADWELL	297	297	0	1	272	272	0	1	25	25	0	0	0	0	0	0	0	0	0	0	0	0	0	0
38	Tim BREACKER	296	283	13	8	240	229	11	8	28	27	1	0	21	20	1	0	0	0	0	0	7	7	0	0
39	Carlton COLE	293	182	111	68	256	158	98	55	15	11	4	5	17	9	8	7	2	1	1	0	3	3	0	1
40	Terry WOODGATE	282	282	0	52	259	259	0	48	16	16	0	4	0	0	0	0	0	0	0	0	7	7	0	0
41	Noel CANTWELL	278	278	0	12	248	248	0	11	15	15	0	0	0	0	0	0	0	0	0	0	15	15	0	1
42	Kevin KEEN	278	237	41	30	219	187	32	21	21	15	6	1	22	21	1	5	0	0	0	0	16	14	2	3
43	Bobby FERGUSON	277	277	0	0	240	240	0	0	17	17	0	0	19	19	0	0	0	0	0	0	1	1	0	0
44	John MORTON	275	275	0	57	258	258	0	54	17	17	0	3	0	0	0	0	0	0	0	0	0	0	0	0
45	Stanley EARLE	273	273	0	58	258	258	0	56	15	15	0	2	0	0	0	0	0	0	0	0	0	0	0	0
46	John SISSONS	266	263	3	53	213	210	3	37	18	18	0	8	21	21	0	3	13	13	0	3	1	1	0	2
47	Malcolm ALLISON	265	265	0	11	238	238	0	10	17	17	0	0	0	0	0	0	0	0	0	0	10	10	0	1
48	Joe COCKROFT	263	263	0	3	251	251	0	3	12	12	0	0	0	0	0	0	0	0	0	0	0	0	0	0
49	George KAY	259	259	0	17	237	237	0	15	22	22	0	2	0	0	0	0	0	0	0	0	0	0	0	0
50	Bryan ROBSON	255	255	0	104	227	227	0	94	12	12	0	4	15	15	0	6	0	0	0	0	1	1	0	0

		Total				League				FA Cup				League Cup				Europe				Other		
		Apps	Starts	Subs	Goals	Apps	Starts	Subs	Goals	Apps	Starts	Subs	Goals	Apps	Starts	Subs	Goals	Apps	Starts	Subs	Goals	Apps	Starts	Subs	Goals
51	Len GOULDEN	253	253	0	53	239	239	0	52	14	14	0	1	0	0	0	0	0	0	0	0	0	0	0	0
52	Herbert ASHTON	249	249	0	24	224	224	0	22	25	25	0	2	0	0	0	0	0	0	0	0	0	0	0	0
53	Robert GREEN	241	241	0	0	219	219	0	0	11	11	0	0	8	8	0	0	0	0	0	0	3	3	0	0
54	Fred BLACKBURN	238	238	0	28	218	218	0	24	20	20	0	4	0	0	0	0	0	0	0	0	0	0	0	0
55	Mervyn DAY	237	237	0	0	194	194	0	0	14	14	0	0	14	14	0	0	9	9	0	0	6	6	0	0
56	Jim STANDEN	236	236	0	0	178	178	0	0	20	20	0	0	23	23	0	0	14	14	0	0	1	1	0	0
57	Alan DICKENS	234	209	25	30	192	173	19	23	22	19	3	3	17	14	3	3	0	0	0	0	3	3	0	1
58	Martin ALLEN	232	202	30	35	190	163	27	26	14	14	0	4	18	15	3	5	0	0	0	0	10	10	0	0
59	Frank PIERCY	231	231	0	7	214	214	0	7	17	17	0	0	0	0	0	0	0	0	0	0	0	0	0	0
60	Steve LOMAS	226	215	11	13	187	179	8	10	13	10	3	1	13	13	0	2	10	10	0	0	3	3	0	0
61	David CROSS	224	223	1	97	179	178	1	77	14	14	0	2	24	24	0	12	6	6	0	6	1	1	0	0
62	Clyde BEST	221	213	8	58	186	178	8	47	12	12	0	3	20	20	0	8	0	0	0	0	3	3	0	0
63	Derek PARKER	217	217	0	12	199	199	0	9	8	8	0	0	0	0	0	0	0	0	0	0	10	10	0	3
64	Danny SHEA	217	217	0	122	195	195	0	112	22	22	0	10	0	0	0	0	0	0	0	0	0	0	0	0
65	Peter BRABROOK	215	215	0	43	167	167	0	33	17	17	0	3	23	23	0	6	7	7	0	1	1	1	0	0
66	Trevor MORLEY	214	188	26	70	178	159	19	57	19	14	5	7	11	10	1	5	0	0	0	0	6	5	1	1
67	Paul GODDARD	213	201	12	71	170	159	11	54	11	10	1	3	26	26	0	12	6	6	0	2	0	0	0	0
68	Hayden MULLINS	213	183	30	7	180	152	28	4	17	15	2	3	10	10	0	0	0	0	0	0	6	6	0	0
69	Frank O'FARRELL	213	213	0	8	197	197	0	6	13	13	0	1	0	0	0	0	0	0	0	0	3	3	0	1
70	James TOMKINS	211	195	16	8	183	167	16	8	12	12	0	0	13	13	0	0	0	0	0	0	3	3	0	0
71	Mark WARD	209	206	3	14	165	163	2	12	17	17	0	0	21	20	1	2	0	0	0	0	6	6	0	0
72	Johnny BYRNE	206	206	0	108	156	156	0	79	18	18	0	7	19	19	0	15	12	12	0	6	1	1	0	1
73	Alfred EARL	206	206	0	0	191	191	0	0	15	15	0	0	0	0	0	0	0	0	0	0	0	0	0	0
74	George KITCHEN	205	205	0	6	184	184	0	5	21	21	0	1	0	0	0	0	0	0	0	0	0	0	0	0
75	Tommy RANDALL	205	205	0	10	189	189	0	9	16	16	0	1	0	0	0	0	0	0	0	0	0	0	0	0
76	Trevor SINCLAIR	205	202	3	38	177	175	2	37	8	8	0	0	10	9	1	0	10	10	0	1	0	0	0	0
77	John MONCUR	203	156	47	9	175	131	44	6	8	7	1	1	14	13	1	2	6	5	1	0	0	0	0	0
78	Alfred CHALKLEY	202	202	0	1	188	188	0	1	14	14	0	0	0	0	0	0	0	0	0	0	0	0	0	0
79	William MOORE	202	202	0	48	181	181	0	42	21	21	0	6	0	0	0	0	0	0	0	0	0	0	0	0
80	Paul ALLEN	197	186	11	11	152	149	3	6	18	15	3	3	24	20	4	2	2	1	1	0	1	1	0	0
81	Matthew ETHERINGTON	195	177	18	18	165	151	14	16	15	13	2	1	8	7	1	0	1	0	1	0	6	6	0	1
82	Syd PUDDEFOOT	194	194	0	107	180	180	0	95	14	14	0	12	0	0	0	0	0	0	0	0	0	0	0	0
83	Joe KIRKUP	192	192	0	6	165	165	0	6	8	8	0	0	7	7	0	0	7	7	0	0	5	5	0	0
84	Christian DAILLY	191	158	33	4	158	133	25	2	20	14	6	0	8	8	0	0	0	0	0	0	5	3	2	1
85	Frank McAVENNIE	190	168	22	60	153	134	19	49	20	19	1	6	13	11	2	2	0	0	0	0	4	4	0	3
86	Tomas REPKA	188	187	1	0	164	164	0	0	10	9	1	0	8	8	0	0	0	0	0	0	6	6	0	0
87	Paul BRUSH	186	175	11	1	151	144	7	1	17	17	0	0	13	12	1	0	4	1	3	0	1	1	0	0
88	Joe COLE	186	145	41	18	157	121	36	15	12	11	1	2	12	11	1	1	5	2	3	0	0	0	0	0
89	Frank LAMPARD Jnr.	186	169	17	37	148	132	16	23	13	13	0	2	15	14	1	8	10	10	0	4	0	0	0	0
90	Jack BURKETT	185	184	1	4	142	141	1	4	18	18	0	0	17	17	0	0	7	7	0	0	1	1	0	0
91	Eddie BOVINGTON	184	184	0	2	138	138	0	1	19	19	0	0	18	18	0	1	8	8	0	0	1	1	0	0
92	William HENDERSON	183	183	0	1	162	162	0	0	21	21	0	1	0	0	0	0	0	0	0	0	0	0	0	0
93	George WRIGHT	180	180	0	0	161	161	0	0	9	9	0	0	0	0	0	0	0	0	0	0	10	10	0	0
94	William GRASSAM	179	179	0	68	169	169	0	65	10	10	0	3	0	0	0	0	0	0	0	0	0	0	0	0
95	Stuart SLATER	179	171	8	18	141	134	7	11	16	16	0	3	17	16	1	2	0	0	0	0	5	5	0	2
96	Steve FORDE	178	178	0	1	170	170	0	1	6	6	0	0	0	0	0	0	0	0	0	0	2	2	0	0
97	Edward FENTON	176	176	0	18	163	163	0	18	13	13	0	0	0	0	0	0	0	0	0	0	0	0	0	0
98	Neil ORR	175	157	18	5	146	133	13	4	11	10	1	0	18	14	4	1	0	0	0	0	0	0	0	0
99	Harry REDKNAPP	175	170	5	8	149	146	3	7	8	7	1	0	18	17	1	1	0	0	0	0	0	0	0	0
100	Norman CORBETT	174	174	0	3	166	166	0	3	8	8	0	0	0	0	0	0	0	0	0	0	0	0	0	0

Most appearances League

#	Name	Apps	Starts	Subs	Goals
1	Billy BONDS	663	655	8	48
2	Frank LAMPARD Snr	551	546	5	18
3	Bobby MOORE	544	543	1	24
4	Trevor BROOKING	528	521	7	88
5	James RUFFELL	505	505	0	159
6	Victor WATSON	462	462	0	298
7	Jim BARRETT Snr.	442	442	0	49
8	Alvin MARTIN	424	422	2	25
9	Geoff HURST	411	410	1	180
10	Ken BROWN	386	386	0	4
11	Ernie GREGORY	382	382	0	0
12	John BOND	381	381	0	32
13	Edward HUFTON	371	371	0	0
14	Alan DEVONSHIRE	358	345	13	29
15	Ray STEWART	345	344	1	62
16	Phil PARKES	344	344	0	0
17	Tommy TAYLOR	340	340	0	8
18	Tommy YEWS	332	332	0	46
19	John DICK	326	326	0	153
20	Jimmy COLLINS	311	311	0	3
21	Martin PETERS	302	302	0	81
22	Richard WALKER	292	292	0	2
23	Geoff PIKE	291	275	16	32
24	Andy MALCOLM	283	283	0	4
25	Ron BOYCE	282	275	7	21
26	Malcolm MUSGROVE	282	282	0	84
27	Albert CADWELL	272	272	0	1
28	Tony GALE	268	262	6	5
29	Terry WOODGATE	259	259	0	48
30	Stanley EARLE	258	258	0	56
31	John MORTON	258	258	0	5
32	Joe COCKROFT	251	251	0	3
33	John McDOWELL	249	243	6	
34	Noel CANTWELL	248	248	0	1
35	Pat HOLLAND	245	227	18	2
36	Bobby FERGUSON	240	240	0	0
37	Len GOULDEN	239	239	0	5
38	George PARRIS	239	211	28	1
39	Malcolm ALLISON	238	238	0	1
40	George KAY	237	237	0	1
41	Bryan ROBSON	227	227	0	9
42	Herbert ASHTON	224	224	0	2
43	Kevin KEEN	219	187	32	2
44	Fred BLACKBURN	218	218	0	2
45	Frank PIERCY	214	214	0	

Most appearances Premier League

#	Name	Apps	Starts	Subs	Goals
1	Mark NOBLE	222	207	15	23
2	Carlton COLE	216	130	86	41
3	Steve POTTS	204	177	27	0
4	Robert GREEN	177	177	0	0
5	Trevor SINCLAIR	177	175	2	37
6	John MONCUR	175	131	44	6
7	Ludek MIKLOSKO	169	169	0	0
8	Steve LOMAS	159	156	3	9
9	Joe COLE	157	121	36	15
10	Frank LAMPARD Jnr.	148	132	16	23
11	Tim BREACKER	143	134	9	3
12	James TOMKINS	139	125	14	4
13	Ian BISHOP	134	131	3	4
14	James COLLINS	134	123	11	3
15	Matthew UPSON	131	131	0	4
16	Rio FERDINAND	127	122	5	2
17	Shaka HISLOP	121	121	0	0
18	Paolo DI CANIO	118	114	4	47
19	Ian PEARCE	118	111	7	8
20	Hayden MULLINS	116	93	23	3
21	Christian DAILLY	112	88	24	0
22	Julian DICKS	110	110	0	21
23	Scott PARKER	109	105	4	9
24	Michael CARRICK	101	94	7	5
25	Jonathan SPECTOR	101	66	35	1
26	Kevin NOLAN	97	87	10	18
27	Daniel GABBIDON	96	89	7	0
28	George McCARTNEY	95	83	12	1
29	Winston REID	95	86	9	3
30	Luis BOA MORTE	91	59	32	2
31	Matthew ETHERINGTON	91	80	11	
32	Marc RIEPER	90	83	7	
33	Anton FERDINAND	89	85	4	
34	Frederic KANOUTE	84	79	5	2
35	Michael HUGHES	83	76	7	
36	Tomas REPKA	82	82	0	
37	Nigel WINTERBURN	82	78	4	
38	Keith ROWLAND	80	63	17	
39	Lucas NEILL	79	79	0	
40	Bobby ZAMORA	79	55	24	1
41	Matthew JARVIS	75	56	19	
42	Jack COLLISON	74	49	25	
43	Jermain DEFOE	74	43	31	1
44	Yossi BENAYOUN	69	59	10	
45	Guy DEMEL	69	61	8	

Most appearances FA Cup

#	Name	Apps	Starts	Subs	Goals
1	Billy BONDS	48	46	2	2
2	Frank LAMPARD Snr	43	43	0	0
3	James RUFFELL	43	43	0	7
4	Victor WATSON	43	43	0	28
5	Steve POTTS	42	41	1	0
6	Trevor BROOKING	40	40	0	3
7	Alvin MARTIN	40	40	0	0
8	Alan DEVONSHIRE	36	36	0	1
9	Bobby MOORE	36	36	0	0
10	Ray STEWART	36	35	1	7
11	Phil PARKES	34	34	0	0
12	Edward HUFTON	31	31	0	0
13	Geoff PIKE	31	29	2	5
14	John BOND	30	30	0	1
15	Tony COTTEE	29	29	0	12
16	Tony GALE	29	29	0	1
17	Tommy YEWS	29	29	0	5
18	Tim BREACKER	28	27	1	0
19	Ken BROWN	26	26	0	0
20	Geoff HURST	26	26	0	23
21	Herbert ASHTON	25	25	0	2
22	Jim BARRETT Snr.	25	25	0	4
23	Albert CADWELL	25	25	0	0
24	Jimmy COLLINS	25	25	0	0
25	Ludek MIKLOSKO	25	25	0	0
26	Ernie GREGORY	24	24	0	0
27	Ian BISHOP	23	22	1	3
28	Julian DICKS	23	23	0	3
29	Alan DICKENS	22	19	3	3
30	George KAY	22	22	0	2
31	Danny SHEA	22	22	0	
32	Ron BOYCE	21	20	1	
33	John DICK	21	21	0	1
34	William HENDERSON	21	21	0	
35	Kevin KEEN	21	15	6	
36	George KITCHEN	21	21	0	
37	Andy MALCOLM	21	21	0	
38	William MOORE	21	21	0	
39	George PARRIS	21	21	0	
40	Tommy TAYLOR	21	21	0	
41	Fred BLACKBURN	20	20	0	
42	Christian DAILLY	20	14	6	
43	Frank McAVENNIE	20	19	1	
44	Jim STANDEN	20	20	0	
45	Eddie BOVINGTON	19	19	0	

Most appearances League Cup

		Apps	Starts	Subs	Goals			Apps	Starts	Subs	Goals			Apps	Starts	Subs	Goals
1	Alvin MARTIN	71	71	0	6	16	Ken BROWN	28	28	0	0	31	John SISSONS	21	21	0	5
2	Billy BONDS	67	65	2	6	17	Tony COTTEE	27	27	0	18	32	Mark WARD	21	20	1	2
3	Trevor BROOKING	55	55	0	8	18	Paul GODDARD	26	26	0	12	33	Clyde BEST	20	20	0	8
4	Frank LAMPARD Snr	54	54	0	1	19	Tommy TAYLOR	26	26	0	0	34	Johnny BYRNE	19	19	0	15
5	Phil PARKES	52	52	0	0	20	Pat HOLLAND	25	22	3	3	35	John CHARLES	19	19	0	1
6	Bobby MOORE	49	49	0	3	21	Ludek MIKLOSKO	25	25	0	0	36	Bobby FERGUSON	19	19	0	0
7	Alan DEVONSHIRE	48	45	3	2	22	Paul ALLEN	24	20	4	2	37	Martin ALLEN	18	15	3	5
8	Geoff HURST	47	47	0	43	23	David CROSS	24	24	0	12	38	Eddie BOVINGTON	18	18	0	1
9	Ray STEWART	44	44	0	14	24	Ron BOYCE	23	23	0	2	39	Neil ORR	18	14	4	1
10	Steve POTTS	42	39	3	0	25	Peter BRABROOK	23	23	0	6	40	Harry REDKNAPP	18	17	1	1
11	Geoff PIKE	39	38	1	3	26	Jim STANDEN	23	23	0	0	41	Liam BRADY	17	14	3	0
12	Martin PETERS	31	31	0	10	27	Ian BISHOP	22	21	1	1	42	Jack BURKETT	17	17	0	0
13	Julian DICKS	30	30	0	8	28	Kevin KEEN	22	21	1	5	43	Carlton COLE	17	9	8	7
14	Tony GALE	30	28	2	1	29	Tim BREACKER	21	20	1	0	44	Alan DICKENS	17	14	3	3
15	George PARRIS	30	27	3	1	30	John McDOWELL	21	21	0	1	45	Stuart SLATER	17	16	1	2

Most appearances Europe

		Apps	Starts	Subs	Goals			Apps	Starts	Subs	Goals			Apps	Starts	Subs	Goals
1	Billy BONDS	15	15	0	3	16	Mervyn DAY	9	9	0	0	31	Joe KIRKUP	7	7	0	0
2	Ken BROWN	15	15	0	0	17	Rio FERDINAND	9	9	0	0	32	John McDOWELL	7	7	0	0
3	Geoff HURST	15	15	0	2	18	Shaka HISLOP	9	9	0	0	33	Alan SEALEY	7	7	0	3
4	Frank LAMPARD Snr	15	15	0	1	19	Graham PADDON	9	9	0	2	34	Alan TAYLOR	7	6	1	3
5	Martin PETERS	15	15	0	4	20	Keith ROBSON	9	9	0	4	35	David CROSS	6	6	0	6
6	Jim STANDEN	14	14	0	0	21	Tommy TAYLOR	9	9	0	0	36	Brian DEAR	6	6	0	4
7	Ron BOYCE	13	13	0	1	22	Eddie BOVINGTON	8	8	0	0	37	Marc-Vivien FOE	6	5	1	1
8	Bobby MOORE	13	13	0	0	23	Paul KITSON	8	3	5	2	38	Paul GODDARD	6	6	0	2
9	John SISSONS	13	13	0	3	24	Steve POTTS	8	7	1	0	39	Alvin MARTIN	6	6	0	0
10	Trevor BROOKING	12	11	1	3	25	Paulo WANCHOPE	8	7	1	3	40	John MONCUR	6	5	1	0
11	Johnny BYRNE	12	12	0	6	26	Peter BRABROOK	7	7	0	1	41	Phil PARKES	6	6	0	0
12	Pat HOLLAND	10	10	0	2	27	Jack BURKETT	7	7	0	0	42	Geoff PIKE	6	6	0	1
13	Frank LAMPARD Jnr.	10	10	0	4	28	Keith COLEMAN	7	6	1	0	43	Neil RUDDOCK	6	5	1	1
14	Steve LOMAS	10	10	0	0	29	Billy JENNINGS	7	5	2	3	44	Ray STEWART	6	6	0	1
15	Trevor SINCLAIR	10	10	0	1	30	Marc KELLER	7	6	1	0	45	Joe COLE	5	2	3	0

Most sub appearances All competitions

#	Player	Apps	#	Player	Apps	#	Player	Apps	#	Player	Apps
1	Carlton COLE	111	16	Mark NOBLE	31	31	Brian DEANE	20	46	Ian BISHOP	17
2	Bobby ZAMORA	52	17	Martin ALLEN	30	32	Matthew JARVIS	20	47	Frank LAMPARD Jnr.	17
3	John MONCUR	47	18	Hayden MULLINS	30	33	Keith ROWLAND	20	48	George McCARTNEY	17
4	Steve POTTS	43	19	Pat HOLLAND	26	34	Matthew RUSH	20	49	Sergei REBROV	17
5	Joe COLE	41	20	Trevor MORLEY	26	35	Johnny AYRIS	19	50	Bobby BARNES	16
6	Kevin KEEN	41	21	Alan DICKENS	25	36	Paul HILTON	19	51	Alan DEVONSHIRE	16
7	Jonathan SPECTOR	40	22	Paul KITSON	25	37	Zavon HINES	19	52	Carl FLETCHER	16
8	Teddy SHERINGHAM	38	23	Shaun NEWTON	25	38	Stan LAZARIDIS	19	53	David KELLY	16
9	Don HUTCHISON	36	24	Matthew TAYLOR	23	39	Modibo MAIGA	19	54	Gary O'NEIL	16
10	Luis BOA MORTE	34	25	Frank McAVENNIE	22	40	Geoff PIKE	19	55	James TOMKINS	16
11	Jack COLLISON	34	26	Frederic PIQUIONNE	22	41	Chris COHEN	18	56	Billy JENNINGS	15
12	Christian DAILLY	33	27	Julien FAUBERT	21	42	Kieron DYER	18	57	Steve JONES	15
13	Jermain DEFOE	33	28	Anton FERDINAND	21	43	Matthew ETHERINGTON	18	58	Joey O'BRIEN	15
14	Freddie SEARS	33	29	Marlon HAREWOOD	21	44	Richard GARCIA	18	59	John PANTSIL	15
15	George PARRIS	32	30	Junior STANISLAS	21	45	Neil ORR	18	60	Jimmy QUINN	15

Most sub appearances League

#	Player	Apps	#	Player	Apps	#	Player	Apps	#	Player	Apps
1	Kevin KEEN	32	16	Alan DEVONSHIRE	13	31	Luke CHADWICK	10	46	Freddie SEARS	8
2	George PARRIS	28	17	Paul HILTON	13	32	Billy JENNINGS	10	47	Ron BOYCE	7
3	Bobby ZAMORA	21	18	Neil ORR	13	33	Kevin LOCK	10	48	Trevor BROOKING	7
4	Alan DICKENS	19	19	Jimmy QUINN	13	34	Adam NOWLAND	10	49	Paul BRUSH	7
5	Frank McAVENNIE	19	20	Bobby BARNES	12	35	Steve POTTS	10	50	Danny COLLINS	7
6	Martin ALLEN	18	21	John CAREW	12	36	Matthew RUSH	10	51	Alan CURBISHLEY	7
7	Pat HOLLAND	18	22	Carlton COLE	12	37	Alan TAYLOR	10	52	Bobby HOWE	7
8	Brian DEANE	17	23	Matt HOLMES	12	38	Tony COTTEE	9	53	Nicky MORGAN	7
9	Don HUTCHISON	17	24	David KELLY	12	39	Henri LANSBURY	9	54	Jimmy NEIGHBOUR	7
10	Johnny AYRIS	16	25	Trevor MORLEY	12	40	Jobi McANUFF	9	55	Gary O'NEIL	7
11	Chris COHEN	16	26	Frederic PIQUIONNE	12	41	Leroy ROSENIOR	9	56	Anton OTULAKOWSKI	7
12	Anton FERDINAND	16	27	Ian BISHOP	11	42	Dave SWINDLEHURST	9	57	Nigel REO-COKER	7
13	Geoff PIKE	16	28	Mohamed DIAME	11	43	Clyde BEST	8	58	Teddy SHERINGHAM	7
14	Sergei REBROV	14	29	Paul GODDARD	11	44	Billy BONDS	8	59	Stuart SLATER	7
15	Sam BALDOCK	13	30	Liam BRADY	10	45	Neil MELLOR	8	60	Mike SMALL	7

Most sub appearances Premier League

#	Player	Apps	#	Player	Apps	#	Player	Apps	#	Player	Apps
1	Carlton COLE	86	16	Matthew JARVIS	19	31	John PANTSIL	12	46	Steve JONES	9
2	John MONCUR	44	17	Junior STANISLAS	19	32	Ricardo VAZ TE	12	47	Benni McCARTHY	9
3	Joe COLE	36	18	Modibo MAIGA	18	33	James COLLINS	11	48	Savio NSEREKO	9
4	Jonathan SPECTOR	35	19	Matthew TAYLOR	18	34	Matthew ETHERINGTON	11	49	Winston REID	9
5	Luis BOA MORTE	32	20	Paul KITSON	17	35	Julien FAUBERT	11	50	Matthew RUSH	9
6	Jermain DEFOE	31	21	Keith ROWLAND	17	36	Radoslav KOVAC	11	51	Nolberto SOLANO	9
7	Steve POTTS	27	22	Frank LAMPARD Jnr.	16	37	Morgan AMALFITANO	10	52	Samassi ABOU	8
8	Jack COLLISON	25	23	Stan LAZARIDIS	16	38	Yossi BENAYOUN	10	53	Pablo BARRERA	8
9	Christian DAILLY	24	24	Kieron DYER	15	39	Jeroen BOERE	10	54	Guy DEMEL	8
10	Teddy SHERINGHAM	24	25	Don HUTCHISON	15	40	Alessandro DIAMANTI	10	55	David Di MICHELE	8
11	Bobby ZAMORA	24	26	Mark NOBLE	15	41	Iain DOWIE	10	56	Marc KELLER	8
12	Hayden MULLINS	23	27	James TOMKINS	14	42	Kevin NOLAN	10	57	NENE	8
13	Freddie SEARS	22	28	Dean ASHTON	13	43	Svetoslav TODOROV	10	58	Antonia NOCERINO	8
14	Shaun NEWTON	21	29	Zavon HINES	13	44	Martin ALLEN	9	59	Joey O'BRIEN	8
15	Marlon HAREWOOD	19	30	George McCARTNEY	12	45	Tim BREACKER	9	60	Gary O'NEIL	8

Most sub appearances FA Cup

		Apps			Apps			Apps			Apps
1	Christian DAILLY	6	12	Alan DICKENS	3	23	Jack COLLISON	2	34	Kevin NOLAN	2
2	Kevin KEEN	6	13	Carl FLETCHER	3	24	Anthony EDGAR	2	35	Frank NOUBLE	2
3	Bobby ZAMORA	6	14	Paul HILTON	3	25	Matthew ETHERINGTON	2	36	Joey O'BRIEN	2
4	Trevor MORLEY	5	15	Lee HODGES	3	26	Zavon HINES	2	37	Stuart PEARSON	2
5	Carlton COLE	4	16	Steve LOMAS	3	27	Don HUTCHISON	2	38	Geoff PIKE	2
6	Pat HOLLAND	4	17	Neil MELLOR	3	28	Paul INCE	2	39	Frederic PIQUIONNE	2
7	Teddy SHERINGHAM	4	18	Freddie SEARS	3	29	Steve JONES	2	40	Jimmy QUINN	2
8	Jonathan SPECTOR	4	19	Diego TRISTAN	3	30	Yaniv KATAN	2	41	Gary STRODDER	2
9	Samassi ABOU	3	20	Clive ALLEN	2	31	Vladimir LABANT	2	42	Svetoslav TODOROV	2
10	Paul ALLEN	3	21	Luis BOA MORTE	2	32	Hayden MULLINS	2			
11	Morgan AMALFITANO	3	22	Billy BONDS	2	33	Shaun NEWTON	2			

Most sub appearances League Cup

		Apps			Apps			Apps			Apps
1	Carlton COLE	8	11	Alan DEVONSHIRE	3	21	Jack COLLISON	2	31	Frank NOUBLE	2
2	Mark NOBLE	7	12	Mohamed DIAME	3	22	Kieron DYER	2	32	John PANTSIL	2
3	Richard GARCIA	5	13	Alan DICKENS	3	23	Matthias FANIMO	2	33	Stuart PEARSON	2
4	Paul ALLEN	4	14	Pat HOLLAND	3	24	Tony GALE	2	34	Razvan RAT	2
5	Stewart DOWNING	4	15	David KELLY	3	25	Paul HILTON	2	35	Keith ROWLAND	2
6	Zavon HINES	4	16	Tommy McQUEEN	3	26	Bobby HOWE	2	36	Teddy SHERINGHAM	2
7	Neil ORR	4	17	George PARRIS	3	27	Billy JENNINGS	2	37	Matthew TAYLOR	2
8	Kyel REID	4	18	Steve POTTS	3	28	Paul KITSON	2	38	Danny WILLIAMSON	2
9	Martin ALLEN	3	19	Bobby BARNES	2	29	Frank McAVENNIE	2			
10	Liam BRADY	3	20	Billy BONDS	2	30	Benni McCARTHY	2			

Most sub appearances Europe

		Apps			Apps			Apps			Apps
1	Paul KITSON	5	9	Trevor BROOKING	1	17	Marc KELLER	1	25	Neil RUDDOCK	1
2	Paul BRUSH	3	10	Michael CARRICK	1	18	Stan LAZARIDIS	1	26	Teddy SHERINGHAM	1
3	Joe COLE	3	11	Carlton COLE	1	19	Javier MARGAS	1	27	Alan TAYLOR	1
4	Billy JENNINGS	2	12	Keith COLEMAN	1	20	Mick McGIVEN	1	28	Paulo WANCHOPE	1
5	Nicky MORGAN	2	13	Alan CURBISHLEY	1	21	John MONCUR	1	29	Ian WRIGHT	1
6	Paul ALLEN	1	14	Matthew ETHERINGTON	1	22	Adam NEWTON	1	30	Bobby ZAMORA	1
7	Bobby BARNES	1	15	Marc-Vivien FOE	1	23	Stuart PEARSON	1			
8	Yossi BENAYOUN	1	16	Marlon HAREWOOD	1	24	Steve POTTS	1			

Most goals All competitions

		Total			League			FA Cup			League Cup			Europe			Other		
		Starts	Subs	Goals	Starts	Subs	Goals	Starts	Subs	Goals	Starts	Subs	Goals	Starts	Subs	Goals	Starts	Subs	Goals
1	Victor WATSON	505	0	326	462	0	298	43	0	28	0	0	0	0	0	0	0	0	0
2	Geoff HURST	502	1	249	410	1	180	26	0	23	47	0	43	15	0	2	4	0	1
3	John DICK	367	0	177	326	0	153	21	0	11	4	0	2	0	0	0	16	0	11
4	James RUFFELL	548	0	166	505	0	159	43	0	7	0	0	0	0	0	0	0	0	0
5	Tony COTTEE	323	13	146	266	13	115	29	0	12	27	0	18	0	0	0	1	0	1
6	Danny SHEA	217	0	122	195	0	112	22	0	10	0	0	0	0	0	0	0	0	0
7	Johnny BYRNE	206	0	108	156	0	79	18	0	7	19	0	15	12	0	6	1	0	1
8	Syd PUDDEFOOT	194	0	107	180	0	95	14	0	12	0	0	0	0	0	0	0	0	0
9	Bryan ROBSON	255	0	104	227	0	94	12	0	4	15	0	6	0	0	0	1	0	0
10	Trevor BROOKING	635	8	102	521	7	88	40	0	3	55	0	8	11	1	3	8	0	0
11	Martin PETERS	364	0	100	302	0	81	16	0	5	31	0	10	15	0	4	0	0	0
12	Malcolm MUSGROVE	317	0	98	282	0	84	13	0	2	5	0	3	0	0	0	17	0	9
13	David CROSS	223	1	97	178	1	77	14	0	2	24	0	12	6	0	6	1	0	0
14	Ray STEWART	430	2	84	344	1	62	35	1	7	44	0	14	6	0	1	1	0	0
15	Paul GODDARD	201	12	71	159	11	54	10	1	3	26	0	12	6	0	2	0	0	0
16	Trevor MORLEY	188	26	70	159	19	57	14	5	7	10	1	5	0	0	0	5	1	1
17	Carlton COLE	182	111	68	158	98	55	11	4	5	9	8	7	1	1	0	3	0	1
18	William GRASSAM	179	0	68	169	0	65	10	0	3	0	0	0	0	0	0	0	0	0
19	Julian DICKS	326	0	65	262	0	50	23	0	3	30	0	8	0	0	0	11	0	4
20	Bill ROBINSON	109	0	64	101	0	60	4	0	1	0	0	0	0	0	0	4	0	3
21	Vivian GIBBINS	138	0	63	129	0	58	9	0	5	0	0	0	0	0	0	0	0	0
22	Billy BONDS	787	12	61	655	8	48	46	2	2	65	2	6	15	0	3	6	0	2
23	Frank McAVENNIE	168	22	60	134	19	49	19	1	6	11	2	2	0	0	0	4	0	3
24	Clyde BEST	213	8	58	178	8	47	12	0	3	20	0	8	0	0	0	3	0	0
25	Stanley EARLE	273	0	58	258	0	56	15	0	2	0	0	0	0	0	0	0	0	0
26	John MORTON	275	0	57	258	0	54	17	0	3	0	0	0	0	0	0	0	0	0
27	Marlon HAREWOOD	149	21	56	123	19	47	13	1	5	6	0	3	1	1	0	6	0	1
28	Billy DARE	127	0	54	111	0	44	8	0	5	0	0	0	0	0	0	8	0	5
29	Jim BARRETT Snr.	467	0	53	442	0	49	25	0	4	0	0	0	0	0	0	0	0	0
30	Len GOULDEN	253	0	53	239	0	52	14	0	1	0	0	0	0	0	0	0	0	0
31	John SISSONS	263	3	53	210	3	37	18	0	8	21	0	5	13	0	3	1	0	0
32	Terry WOODGATE	282	0	52	259	0	48	16	0	4	0	0	0	0	0	0	7	0	0
33	Vic KEEBLE	84	0	51	76	0	45	4	0	4	0	0	0	0	0	0	4	0	2
34	Tommy YEWS	361	0	51	332	0	46	29	0	5	0	0	0	0	0	0	0	0	0
35	Paolo DI CANIO	136	4	50	114	4	47	5	0	1	7	0	1	4	0	1	6	0	0
36	William MOORE	202	0	48	181	0	42	21	0	6	0	0	0	0	0	0	0	0	0
37	Harry HOOPER	136	0	47	119	0	39	11	0	5	0	0	0	0	0	0	6	0	3
38	Alfred LEAFE	101	0	44	94	0	40	7	0	4	0	0	0	0	0	0	0	0	0
39	Peter BRABROOK	215	0	43	167	0	33	17	0	3	23	0	6	7	0	1	1	0	0
40	Joseph FOXALL	113	0	42	106	0	37	7	0	5	0	0	0	0	0	0	0	0	0
41	Jermain DEFOE	72	33	41	62	31	29	4	1	6	6	1	6	0	0	0	0	0	0
42	Geoff PIKE	349	19	41	275	16	32	29	2	5	38	1	3	6	0	1	1	0	0
43	Harry STAPLEY	75	0	41	71	0	39	4	0	2	0	0	0	0	0	0	0	0	0
44	Sam SMALL	118	0	40	108	0	40	10	0	0	0	0	0	0	0	0	0	0	0
45	Bobby ZAMORA	100	52	40	85	45	30	3	6	2	5	0	4	1	1	0	6	0	4
46	John BOND	449	0	39	381	0	32	30	0	1	13	0	1	4	0	1	21	0	4
47	Brian DEAR	82	3	39	67	2	33	6	1	2	3	0	0	6	0	4	0	0	0
48	Billy JENNINGS	110	15	39	89	10	34	11	0	2	3	2	0	5	2	3	2	1	0
49	Trevor SINCLAIR	202	3	38	175	2	37	8	0	0	9	1	0	10	0	1	0	0	0
50	Frank LAMPARD Jnr.	169	17	37	132	16	23	13	0	2	14	1	8	10	0	4	0	0	0

		Total			League			FA Cup			League Cup			Europe			Other		
		Starts	Subs	Goals	Starts	Subs	Goals	Starts	Subs	Goals	Starts	Subs	Goals	Starts	Subs	Goals	Starts	Subs	Goals
51	Alan TAYLOR	112	12	36	88	10	25	7	1	6	8	0	2	6	1	3	3	0	0
52	Martin ALLEN	202	30	35	163	27	26	14	0	4	15	3	5	0	0	0	10	0	0
53	Gerry GAZZARD	133	0	35	119	0	29	7	0	3	0	0	0	0	0	0	7	0	3
54	George HILSDON	92	0	35	85	0	31	7	0	4	0	0	0	0	0	0	0	0	0
55	Mark NOBLE	290	31	35	260	20	31	18	1	3	9	7	1	0	0	0	3	3	0
56	Eric PARSONS	151	0	35	145	0	34	6	0	1	0	0	0	0	0	0	0	0	0
57	Ken TUCKER	102	0	35	83	0	31	10	0	0	0	0	0	0	0	0	9	0	4
58	Alvin MARTIN	589	7	34	462	7	27	40	0	0	71	0	6	6	0	0	10	0	1
59	John HARTSON	72	1	33	59	1	24	7	0	3	6	0	6	0	0	0	0	0	0
60	Frederic KANOUTE	87	5	33	79	5	29	5	0	4	3	0	0	0	0	0	0	0	0
61	Alan DEVONSHIRE	432	16	32	345	13	29	36	0	1	45	3	2	4	0	0	2	0	0
62	Pat HOLLAND	278	26	32	227	18	23	12	4	4	22	3	3	10	0	2	7	1	0
63	George WEBB	62	0	32	52	0	23	10	0	9	0	0	0	0	0	0	0	0	0
64	Archibald MACAULAY	90	0	31	83	0	29	7	0	2	0	0	0	0	0	0	0	0	0
65	Kevin NOLAN	139	13	31	129	10	30	4	2	0	3	1	0	0	0	0	3	0	1
66	Alan DICKENS	209	25	30	173	19	23	19	3	3	14	3	3	0	0	0	3	0	1
67	Kevin KEEN	237	41	30	187	32	21	15	6	1	21	1	5	0	0	0	14	2	3
68	David MANGNALL	37	0	30	35	0	29	2	0	1	0	0	0	0	0	0	0	0	0
69	Teddy SHERINGHAM	49	38	30	45	31	28	3	4	2	1	2	0	0	1	0	0	0	0
70	Ron BOYCE	333	8	29	275	7	21	20	1	5	23	0	2	13	0	1	2	0	0
71	Dave SEXTON	79	0	29	74	0	27	3	0	2	0	0	0	0	0	0	2	0	0
72	Phil WOOSNAM	151	0	29	138	0	26	5	0	1	4	0	0	0	0	0	4	0	2
73	Fred BLACKBURN	238	0	28	218	0	24	20	0	4	0	0	0	0	0	0	0	0	0
74	Bobby MOORE	646	1	27	543	1	24	36	0	0	49	0	3	13	0	0	5	0	0
75	Lionel WATSON	80	0	27	76	0	26	4	0	1	0	0	0	0	0	0	0	0	0
76	Daniel BAILEY	91	0	26	84	0	22	7	0	4	0	0	0	0	0	0	0	0	0
77	Jim BARRETT Jnr.	91	0	26	85	0	24	2	0	1	0	0	0	0	0	0	4	0	1
78	Alan SEALEY	128	0	26	107	0	22	8	0	0	6	0	1	7	0	3	0	0	0
79	Tommy DIXON	44	0	25	39	0	21	3	0	2	0	0	0	0	0	0	2	0	2
80	Herbert ASHTON	249	0	24	224	0	22	25	0	2	0	0	0	0	0	0	0	0	0
81	Jimmy ANDREWS	123	0	23	114	0	21	6	0	1	0	0	0	0	0	0	3	0	1
82	Fred HARRISON	62	0	23	54	0	19	8	0	4	0	0	0	0	0	0	0	0	0
83	Leroy ROSENIOR	57	10	23	44	9	15	4	1	2	7	0	2	0	0	0	2	0	4
84	John SMITH	138	0	23	125	0	20	5	0	2	0	0	0	0	0	0	8	0	1
85	George BUTCHER	109	0	22	96	0	17	13	0	5	0	0	0	0	0	0	0	0	0
86	Mike GRICE	165	0	22	142	0	18	7	0	1	1	0	0	0	0	0	15	0	3
87	Paul KITSON	55	25	22	46	17	18	4	1	1	2	2	1	3	5	2	0	0	0
88	Frank LAMPARD Snr	665	5	22	546	5	18	43	0	2	54	0	1	15	0	1	7	0	0
89	Jimmy QUINN	42	15	22	34	13	19	4	2	2	3	0	1	0	0	0	1	0	0
90	Clive ALLEN	46	4	21	36	2	17	2	2	1	2	0	0	0	0	0	6	0	3
91	William BRIDGEMAN	75	0	20	72	0	19	3	0	1	0	0	0	0	0	0	0	0	0
92	William BROWN	71	0	20	60	0	15	11	0	5	0	0	0	0	0	0	0	0	0
93	Ken WRIGHT	52	0	20	51	0	20	1	0	0	0	0	0	0	0	0	0	0	0
94	Dean ASHTON	43	13	19	33	13	15	7	0	3	3	0	1	0	0	0	0	0	0
95	Bobby GOULD	57	5	19	46	5	15	4	0	1	2	0	3	1	0	0	4	0	0
96	Keith ROBSON	85	4	19	65	3	13	3	0	1	7	0	1	9	1	4	1	1	0
97	Tony SCOTT	97	0	19	83	0	16	7	0	0	7	0	3	0	0	0	0	0	0
98	Ricardo VAZ TE	47	14	19	37	14	15	2	0	0	5	0	2	0	0	0	3	0	2
99	Joe COLE	145	41	18	121	36	15	11	1	2	11	1	1	2	3	0	0	0	0
100	Albert DENYER	50	0	18	46	0	17	4	0	1	0	0	0	0	0	0	0	0	0

Most goals League

#	Name	Goals	Starts	Sub	#	Name	Goals	Starts	Sub	#	Name	Goals	Starts	Sub
1	Victor WATSON	298	462	0	18	Stanley EARLE	56	258	0	35	Harry STAPLEY	39	71	0
2	Geoff HURST	180	410	1	19	Paul GODDARD	54	159	11	36	Joseph FOXALL	37	106	0
3	James RUFFELL	159	505	0	20	John MORTON	54	258	0	37	John SISSONS	37	210	3
4	John DICK	153	326	0	21	Len GOULDEN	52	239	0	38	Billy JENNINGS	34	89	10
5	Danny SHEA	112	195	0	22	Jim BARRETT Snr.	49	442	0	39	Eric PARSONS	34	145	0
6	Syd PUDDEFOOT	95	180	0	23	Frank McAVENNIE	49	134	19	40	Peter BRABROOK	33	167	0
7	Bryan ROBSON	94	227	0	24	Billy BONDS	48	655	8	41	Brian DEAR	33	67	2
8	Tony COTTEE	92	203	9	25	Terry WOODGATE	48	259	0	42	John BOND	32	381	0
9	Trevor BROOKING	88	521	7	26	Clyde BEST	47	178	8	43	Geoff PIKE	32	275	16
10	Malcolm MUSGROVE	84	282	0	27	Tommy YEWS	46	332	0	44	George HILSDON	31	85	0
11	Martin PETERS	81	302	0	28	Vic KEEBLE	45	76	0	45	Ken TUCKER	31	83	0
12	Johnny BYRNE	79	156	0	29	Billy DARE	44	111	0	46	Marlon HAREWOOD	30	73	0
13	David CROSS	77	178	1	30	Trevor MORLEY	44	110	12	47	Alan DEVONSHIRE	29	345	13
14	William GRASSAM	65	169	0	31	William MOORE	42	181	0	48	Julian DICKS	29	152	0
15	Ray STEWART	62	344	1	32	Alfred LEAFE	40	94	0	49	Gerry GAZZARD	29	119	0
16	Bill ROBINSON	60	101	0	33	Sam SMALL	40	108	0	50	Archibald MACAULAY	29	83	0
17	Vivian GIBBINS	58	129	0	34	Harry HOOPER	39	119	0	51	David MANGNALL	29	35	0

Most goals Premier League

#	Name	Goals	Starts	Sub	#	Name	Goals	Starts	Sub	#	Name	Goals	Starts	Sub
1	Paolo DI CANIO	47	114	4	18	Trevor MORLEY	13	49	7	35	Alessandro DIAMANTI	7	18	10
2	Carlton COLE	41	130	86	19	Don HUTCHISON	12	54	15	36	Stewart DOWNING	7	66	3
3	Trevor SINCLAIR	37	175	2	20	Paulo WANCHOPE	12	33	2	37	Matthew ETHERINGTON	7	80	11
4	Frederic KANOUTE	29	79	5	21	Martin ALLEN	10	49	9	38	Carlos TEVEZ	7	19	7
5	John HARTSON	24	59	1	22	Eyal BERKOVIC	10	62	3	39	Jeroen BOERE	6	15	10
6	Tony COTTEE	23	63	4	23	Diafra SAKHO	10	20	3	40	John MONCUR	6	131	44
7	Frank LAMPARD Jnr.	23	132	16	24	Steve LOMAS	9	156	3	41	Frederic PIQUIONNE	6	26	8
8	Mark NOBLE	23	207	15	25	Scott PARKER	9	105	4	42	Nigel REO-COKER	6	66	0
9	Julian DICKS	21	110	0	26	Ian WRIGHT	9	20	2	43	Samassi ABOU	5	14	8
10	Jermain DEFOE	18	43	31	27	Yossi BENAYOUN	8	59	10	44	Michael CARRICK	5	94	7
11	Paul KITSON	18	46	17	28	Iain DOWIE	8	58	10	45	Guillermo FRANCO	5	16	7
12	Kevin NOLAN	18	87	10	29	Ian PEARCE	8	111	7	46	Michael HUGHES	5	76	7
13	Bobby ZAMORA	18	55	24	30	Teddy SHERINGHAM	8	19	24	47	Marc KELLER	5	36	8
14	Marlon HAREWOOD	17	50	19	31	Demba BA	7	10	2	48	Marc RIEPER	5	83	7
15	Dean ASHTON	15	33	13	32	Craig BELLAMY	7	20	4	49	Junior STANISLAS	5	22	19
16	Joe COLE	15	121	36	33	Lee CHAPMAN	7	33	7	50	Ricardo VAZ TE	5	24	12
17	Andy CARROLL	14	46	7	34	Jack COLLISON	7	49	25	51	Danny WILLIAMSON	5	47	4

Most goals FA Cup

#	Name	Goals	Starts	Sub	#	Name	Goals	Starts	Sub	#	Name	Goals	Starts	Sub
1	Victor WATSON	28	43	0	11	James RUFFELL	7	43	0	21	Billy DARE	5	8	0
2	Geoff HURST	23	26	0	12	Ray STEWART	7	35	1	22	Joseph FOXALL	5	7	0
3	Tony COTTEE	12	29	0	13	Jermain DEFOE	6	4	1	23	Vivian GIBBINS	5	9	0
4	Syd PUDDEFOOT	12	14	0	14	Frank McAVENNIE	6	19	1	24	Marlon HAREWOOD	5	13	1
5	John DICK	11	21	0	15	William MOORE	6	21	0	25	Harry HOOPER	5	11	0
6	Danny SHEA	10	22	0	16	Alan TAYLOR	6	7	1	26	Herbert LYON	5	4	0
7	George WEBB	9	10	0	17	Ron BOYCE	5	20	1	27	Martin PETERS	5	16	0
8	John SISSONS	8	18	0	18	William BROWN	5	11	0	28	Geoff PIKE	5	29	2
9	Johnny BYRNE	7	18	0	19	George BUTCHER	5	13	0	29	Charles SATTERTHWAITE	5	4	0
10	Trevor MORLEY	7	14	5	20	Carlton COLE	5	11	4	30	Tommy YEWS	5	29	0

Most goals League Cup

#	Player	Goals	Starts	Sub	#	Player	Golas	Starts	Sub	#	Player	Goals	Starts	Sub
1	Geoff HURST	43	47	0	14	Peter BRABROOK	6	23	0	27	Alan DICKENS	3	14	3
2	Tony COTTEE	18	27	0	15	Jermain DEFOE	6	6	1	28	Bobby GOULD	3	2	0
3	Johnny BYRNE	15	19	0	16	John HARTSON	6	6	0	29	Marlon HAREWOOD	3	6	0
4	Ray STEWART	14	44	0	17	Alvin MARTIN	6	71	0	30	Pat HOLLAND	3	22	3
5	David CROSS	12	24	0	18	Bryan ROBSON	6	15	0	31	Paul INCE	3	9	0
6	Paul GODDARD	12	26	0	19	Martin ALLEN	5	15	3	32	Billy LANSDOWNE Jnr.	3	4	1
7	Martin PETERS	10	31	0	20	Kevin KEEN	5	21	1	33	Modibo MAIGA	3	5	1
8	Clyde BEST	8	20	0	21	David KELLY	5	11	3	34	Bobby MOORE	3	49	0
9	Trevor BROOKING	8	55	0	22	Trevor MORLEY	5	10	1	35	Malcolm MUSGROVE	3	5	0
10	Julian DICKS	8	30	0	23	John SISSONS	5	21	0	36	Geoff PIKE	3	38	1
11	Frank LAMPARD Jnr.	8	14	1	24	Mike SMALL	4	4	1	37	Tony SCOTT	3	7	0
12	Carlton COLE	7	9	8	25	Bobby ZAMORA	4	5	0	38	Junior STANISLAS	3	3	1
13	Billy BONDS	6	65	2	26	Alexander CLARK	3	7	0	39	Francois VAN der ELST	3	5	1

Most goals Europe

#	Player	Goals	Starts	Sub	#	Player	Golas	Starts	Sub	#	Player	Goals	Starts	Sub
1	Johnny BYRNE	6	12	0	11	John SISSONS	3	13	0	21	Peter BRABROOK	1	7	0
2	David CROSS	6	6	0	12	Alan TAYLOR	3	6	1	22	Paolo DI CANIO	1	4	0
3	Brian DEAR	4	6	0	13	Paulo WANCHOPE	3	7	1	23	Marc-Vivien FOE	1	5	1
4	Frank LAMPARD Jnr.	4	10	0	14	Paul GODDARD	2	6	0	24	Frank LAMPARD Snr	1	15	0
5	Martin PETERS	4	15	0	15	Pat HOLLAND	2	10	0	25	Stuart PEARSON	1	0	1
6	Keith ROBSON	4	9	0	16	Geoff HURST	2	15	0	26	Geoff PIKE	1	6	0
7	Billy BONDS	3	15	0	17	Paul KITSON	2	3	.5	27	Neil RUDDOCK	1	5	1
8	Trevor BROOKING	3	11	1	18	Graham PADDON	2	9	0	28	Trevor SINCLAIR	1	10	0
9	Billy JENNINGS	3	5	2	19	John BOND	1	4	0	29	Ray STEWART	1	6	0
10	Alan SEALEY	3	7	0	20	Ron BOYCE	1	13	0					

Most clean sheets All competitions

		Total			League			FA Cup			League Cup			Europe			Other			
		CS	Starts	Sub	CS	Starts	Sub	CS	Starts	Sub	CS	Starts	Sub	CS	Starts	Sub	CS	Starts	Sub	Conceded
1	Phil PARKES	146	440	0	114	344	0	13	34	0	17	52	0	2	6	0	0	4	0	506
2	Ludek MIKLOSKO	126	373	0	100	315	0	11	25	0	10	25	0	0	0	0	5	8	0	425
3	Edward HUFTON	113	402	0	103	371	0	10	31	0	0	0	0	0	0	0	0	0	0	606
4	Ernie GREGORY	87	406	0	83	382	0	4	24	0	0	0	0	0	0	0	0	0	0	613
5	Bobby FERGUSON	70	276	0	60	240	0	5	17	0	5	19	0	0	0	0	0	0	0	381
6	George KITCHEN	67	205	0	61	184	0	6	21	0	0	0	0	0	0	0	0	0	0	230
7	Robert GREEN	62	241	0	55	219	0	4	11	0	1	8	0	0	0	0	2	3	0	339
8	Mervyn DAY	58	234	0	47	194	0	3	14	0	7	14	0	1	9	0	0	3	0	339
9	Shaka HISLOP	49.67	157	0	36.67	121	0	4	14	0	5	13	0	4	9	0	0	0	0	209
10	Jim STANDEN	45	236	0	29	178	0	5	20	0	6	23	0	5	14	0	0	1	0	408
11	Tommy HAMPSON	32	79	0	28	70	0	4	9	0	0	0	0	0	0	0	0	0	0	90
12	Herman CONWAY	30	127	0	30	122	0	0	5	0	0	0	0	0	0	0	0	0	0	192
13	David JAMES	29	102	0	28	91	0	1	6	0	0	5	0	0	0	0	0	0	0	135
14	Hughie MONTEITH	26	60	0	25	53	0	1	7	0	0	0	0	0	0	0	0	0	0	55
15	George TAYLOR	25	118	0	25	115	0	0	3	0	0	0	0	0	0	0	0	0	0	195
16	Joseph HUGHES	23	105	0	21	90	0	2	15	0	0	0	0	0	0	0	0	0	0	157
17	Arthur WEARE	22	59	0	21	57	0	1	2	0	0	0	0	0	0	0	0	0	0	68
18	Stephen BYWATER	20.36	65	3	19.33	57	2	1	5	0	0	0	0	0	0	0	0.3	3	1	74
19	Jussi JAASKELAINEN	19.32	60	1	19.32	56	1	0	2	0	0	2	0	0	0	0	0	0	0	84
20	Tom McALISTER	18	100	0	15	85	0	1	7	0	2	7	0	0	0	0	0	1	0	156
21	Thomas MOORE	18	41	0	11	31	0	7	10	0	0	0	0	0	0	0	0	0	0	58
22	Adrian del CASTILLO	16.68	68	0	14.68	57	0	1	5	0	1	5	0	0	0	0	0	0	0	96
23	Frederick GRIFFITHS	15	52	0	13	48	0	2	4	0	0	0	0	0	0	0	0	0	0	59
24	Peter GROTIER	13	54	0	12	50	0	0	0	0	1	4	0	0	0	0	0	0	0	79
25	Lawrie LESLIE	12	61	0	11	57	0	0	1	0	1	3	0	0	0	0	0	0	0	112
26	Craig FORREST	11	34	4	9	26	4	0	4	0	1	3	0	1	1	0	0	0	0	41
27	Harry MEDHURST	11	36	0	9	27	0	2	9	0	0	0	0	0	0	0	0	0	0	40
28	Allen McKNIGHT	10	36	0	5	23	0	3	4	0	2	6	0	0	0	0	0	3	0	56
29	Robert DIXON	9	68	0	9	65	0	0	3	0	0	0	0	0	0	0	0	0	0	138
30	John GEGGUS	9	31	0	9	31	0	0	0	0	0	0	0	0	0	0	0	0	0	55
31	Matthew KINGSLEY	9	30	0	9	29	0	0	1	0	0	0	0	0	0	0	0	0	0	41
32	Charles COTTON	8	19	0	7	18	0	1	1	0	0	0	0	0	0	0	0	0	0	22
33	James WALKER	7.97	20	0	6	13	0	1	1	0	1	3	0	0	0	0	0.97	3	0	24
34	Brian RHODES	7	66	0	7	61	0	0	2	0	0	3	0	0	0	0	0	0	0	136
35	George WATSON	7	38	0	4	33	0	3	5	0	0	0	0	0	0	0	0	0	0	80
36	Jack RUTHERFORD	7	35	0	7	33	0	0	2	0	0	0	0	0	0	0	0	0	0	52
37	Noel DWYER	6	38	0	6	36	0	0	2	0	0	0	0	0	0	0	0	0	0	71
38	Joseph WEBSTER	5	19	0	5	19	0	0	0	0	0	0	0	0	0	0	0	0	0	27
39	Roy CARROLL	4	35	0	3	31	0	1	2	0	0	0	0	0	2	0	0	0	0	53
40	Thomas LONSDALE	4	21	0	4	21	0	0	0	0	0	0	0	0	0	0	0	0	0	32

Adrian del Castillo was replaced by Jussi Jaaskelainen in the 61st minute in a Premier League match against Southampton on 11 February 2015 which ended 0-0. Adrian hadn't conceded a goal when he went off so he has been credited with 68% of a clean sheet. Likewise Jaaskelainen has been credited with the remaining 32% of a clean sheet.

Shaka Hislop was forced off with an injury after an hour play in the Premier League 1-0 win against West Bromwich Albion on 5 November 2005. Hislop is credited with 67% of a clean sheets, Stephen Bywater his replacement has been cedited with the remaining 33% of a clean sheet.

James Walker was replaced by Stephen Bywater after he was stretched off in the 87th minute in the Play-off Final against Preston North End on 30 May 2005 which ended 1-0 to West Ham United. Walker h been credited with 97% of a clean sheet, Bywater credited with the remaining 3% of a clean sheet.

Most clean sheets
League

		Total		
		CS	Starts	Sub
1	Phil PARKES	114	344	0
2	Ludek MIKLOSKO	53	146	0
3	Edward HUFTON	103	371	0
4	Ernie GREGORY	83	382	0
5	Bobby FERGUSON	60	240	0
6	George KITCHEN	61	184	0
7	Mervyn DAY	47	194	0
8	Jim STANDEN	29	178	0
9	Tommy HAMPSON	28	70	0
10	Herman CONWAY	30	122	0
11	Hughie MONTEITH	25	53	0
12	George TAYLOR	25	115	0
13	Joseph HUGHES	21	90	0
14	Arthur WEARE	21	57	0
15	Stephen BYWATER	18	53	0
16	Robert GREEN	15	42	0
17	Tom McALISTER	15	85	0
18	Thomas MOORE	11	31	0
19	Frederick GRIFFITHS	13	48	0
20	Peter GROTIER	12	50	0
21	Lawrie LESLIE	11	57	0

Most clean sheets
Premier League

		Total		
		CS	Starts	Sub
1	Ludek MIKLOSKO	47	169	0
2	Robert GREEN	40	177	0
3	Shaka HISLOP	36.67	121	0
4	David JAMES	28	91	0
5	Jussi JAASKELAINEN	19.32	56	1
6	Adrian del CASTILLO	14.68	57	0
7	Craig FORREST	9	26	4
8	James WALKER	6	13	0
9	Bernard LAMA	3	12	0
10	Roy CARROLL	3	31	0
11	Tony PARKS	2	6	0
12	Manuel ALMUNIA	2	4	0
13	Stephen BYWATER	1.33	6	2
14	Steve MAUTONE	1	1	0

Most clean sheets
Best seasons – League

Total	Season
29	1980-1981
25	1990-1991
23	1992-1993
22	1922-1923
21	1979-1980
20	1921-1922, 1985-1986
19	1971-1972, 1989-1990, 2003-2004, 2011-2012
18	1919-1920, 1923-1924, 1978-1979, 1993-1994, 2004-2005
17	1920-1921, 1974-1975, 1983-1984, 1988-1989
15	1900-1901, 1924-1925, 1991-1992, 2001-2002, 2013-2014

Most clean sheets
Best seasons – Premier League

Total	Season
18	1993-1994
17	1998-1999
16	1994-1995, 1999-2000
15	2001-2002, 2013-2014
14	1995-1996
12	2000-2001, 2008-2009, 2012-2013
11	1996-1997, 2005-2006
10	1997-1998, 2006-2007, 2007-2008, 2014-2015
9	2002-2003
8	2009-2010, 2010-2011

Squad numbers

SHIRT	1993/94	1994/95	1995/96	1996/97
1	Ludek Miklosko	Ludek Miklosko	Ludek Miklosko	Ludek Miklosko
2	Tim Breacker	Tim Breacker	Tim Breacker	Tim Breacker
3	Julian Dicks	Julian Dicks	Julian Dicks	Julian Dicks
4	Steve Potts	Steve Potts	Steve Potts	Steve Potts
5		Alvin Martin	Alvin Martin	Richard Hall
6	Martin Allen	Martin Allen	Martin Allen	Danny Williamson
7	Mark Robson	Ian Bishop	Ian Bishop	Ian Bishop
8	Peter Butler	Peter Butler / Marc Rieper	Marc Rieper	Marc Rieper
9	Trevor Morley	Trevor Morley / Tony Cottee	Tony Cottee	Tony Cottee / Paul Kitson
10	Clive Allen	John Moncur	John Moncur	Paulo Futre / John Hartson
11	Dale Gordon	Matt Holmes	Marco Boogers	Florin Raducioiu / Steve Lomas
12	Tony Gale	Keith Rowland	Keith Rowland	Keith Rowland
13				Hugo Porfirio
14	Ian Bishop	Matthew Rush	Iain Dowie	Iain Dowie
15	Kenny Brown	Kenny Brown	Kenny Brown	
16	Matt Holmes		Don Hutchison / Dani Carvalho	John Moncur
17	Steve Jones	Steve Jones / Michael Hughes	Stan Lazaridis	Stan Lazaridis
18	Alvin Martin	Simon Webster	Frank Lampard / Ilie Dumitrescu	Ilie Dumitrescu
19		Mike Marsh	Robbie Slater	Robbie Slater / Mike Newell
20	Danny Williamson	Danny Williamson	Danny Williamson	Mark Bowen
21				Les Sealey
22	Colin Foster	Adrian Whitbread	Adrian Whitbread	
23	Keith Rowland		Dale Gordon	Steve Jones
24	Paul Mitchell		Michael Hughes	Michael Hughes
25	Lee Chapman	Lee Chapman / Jeroen Boere	Jeroen Boere / John Harkes	
26		Don Hutchison		Frank Lampard
27			Rio Ferdinand	Rio Ferdinand
28	Matthew Rush		Slaven Bilic	Slaven Bilic
29				Emmanuel Omoyinmi
30			Les Sealey	Steve Mautone
31			Neil Finn	
32				
33	David Burrows	David Burrows		Lee Boylan
34	Mike Marsh			
35	Jeroen Boere			
36				
37				
38				
39				
40				
41				
42				
43				
44				
45				
46				
47				
48				
60	Paul Marquis		Mark Watson	

1997-98	1998-99	1999-00	2000-01	SHIRT
Ludek Miklosko		Shaka Hislop	Shaka Hislop	1
Tim Breacker	Tim Breacker	Rob Jones / Gary Charles	Gary Charles	2
	Julian Dicks	Stuart Pearce	Stuart Pearce	3
Steve Potts	Steve Potts	Steve Potts	Steve Potts	4
	Richard Hall	Igor Stimac	Igor Stimac	5
David Unsworth	Neil Ruddock	Neil Ruddock	Hayden Foxe	6
Ian Bishop	Marc Keller	Marc Keller	Marc Keller / Christian Dailly	7
Marc Rieper / Trevor Sinclair	Trevor Sinclair	Trevor Sinclair	Trevor Sinclair	8
Paul Kitson	Paul Kitson	Paul Kitson	Davor Suker	9
John Hartson	John Hartson / Paolo Di Canio	Paolo Di Canio	Paolo Di Canio	10
Steve Lomas	Steve Lomas	Steve Lomas	Steve Lomas	11
Keith Rowland	Shaka Hislop	Paulo Wanchope	Paul Kitson	12
David Terrier	Marc Vivien-Foe	Marc Vivien-Foe		13
Iain Dowie	Ian Wright	Ian Wright / Frederic Kanoute	Frederic Kanoute	14
Rio Ferdinand	Rio Ferdinand	Rio Ferdinand	Rio Ferdinand / Rigobert Song	15
John Moncur	John Moncur	John Moncur	John Moncur	16
Stan Lazaridis	Stan Lazaridis	Stan Lazaridis	Nigel Winterburn	17
Frank Lampard	Frank Lampard	Frank Lampard	Frank Lampard	18
Ian Pearce	Ian Pearce	Ian Pearce	Ian Pearce	19
Andy Impey	Andy Impey / Scott Minto	Scott Minto	Scott Minto	20
		Michael Carrick	Michael Carrick	21
Craig Forrest	Craig Forrest	Craig Forrest	Craig Forrest	22
Scott Mean				23
Michael Hughes / Samassi Abou	Samassi Abou		Christian Bassila	24
Lee Hodges	Lee Hodges		Kaba Diawara	25
Ian Moore	Joe Cole	Joe Cole	Joe Cole	26
Emmanuel Omoyinmi	Emmanuel Omoyinmi			27
	Chris Coyne	Sasa Ilic	Hannu Tihinen	28
Eyal Berkovic	Eyal Berkovic	Ian Feuer	Titi Camara	29
Paulo Alves	Javier Margas	Javier Margas	Javier Margas / Sebastien Schemmel	30
				31
Bernard Lama		Stephen Bywater	Stephen Bywater	32
				33
			Grant McCann	34
			Jermain Defoe	35
			Ragnvald Soma	36
		Shaun Byrne	Svetoslav Todorov	37
		Adam Newton		38
				39
	Gavin Holligan			40
				41
				42
				43
				44
				45
				46
				47
				48
				60

SHIRT	2001-02	2002-03	2003-04	2004-05
1	David James	David James	David James	Stephen Bywater
2	Tomas Repka	Tomas Repka	Tomas Repka	Tomas Repka
3	Nigel Winterburn	Nigel Winterburn	Rufus Brevett	Rufus Brevett
4	Don Hutchison	Don Hutchison	Don Hutchison	Don Hutchison
5	Vladimir Labant	Vladimir Labant / Lee Bowyer	Robert Lee	Andy Melville
6	Hayden Foxe	Michael Carrick	Michael Carrick	Carl Fletcher
7	Christian Dailly	Christian Dailly	Christian Dailly	Christian Dailly
8	Trevor Sinclair	Trevor Sinclair	David Connolly	Teddy Sheringham
9		Jermain Defoe	Jermain Defoe	Jobi McAnuff / Mauricio Taricco
10	Paolo Di Canio	Paolo Di Canio	Marlon Harewood	Marlon Harewood
11	Steve Lomas	Steve Lomas	Steve Lomas	Steve Lomas
12	Paul Kitson		Matthew Etherington	Matthew Etherington
13				
14	Frederic Kanoute	Frederic Kanoute	Wayne Quinn	Chris Cohen
15	Rigobert Song	Gary Breen	Anton Ferdinand	Anton Ferdinand
16	John Moncur	John Moncur	Kevin Horlock	Sergei Rebrov
17	Shaka Hislop		Hayden Mullins	Hayden Mullins
18	Svetoslav Todorov		Youssef Sofiane	
19	Ian Pearce	Ian Pearce	Ian Pearce / Adam Nowland	Adam Nowland / Darren Powell
20	Scott Minto	Scott Minto	Niclas Alexandersson / Robbie Stockdale / Nigel Reo-Coker	Nigel Reo-Coker
21	Michael Carrick	Richard Garcia	Richard Garcia	Richard Garcia / Malky Mackay
22		Les Ferdinand	Matthew Kilgallon / Andy Melville	Elliott Ward
23		Glen Johnson	Sebastien Carole	James Walker
24	Ragnvald Soma	Rufus Brevett	Jon Harley	Mark Noble
25	Jermain Defoe	Edouard Cisse	Bobby Zamora	Bobby Zamora
26	Joe Cole	Joe Cole	Jobi McAnuff	Calum Davenport / Shaun Newton
27	Shaun Byrne		Shaun Byrne	
28	Laurent Courtois		David Noble	Trent McClenahan
29	Titi Camara	Titi Camara	Brian Deane	
30	Sebastien Schemmel	Sebastien Schemmel	Pavel Srnicek	Luke Chadwick
31				
32			Stephen Bywater	
33	Richard Garcia		Neil Mellor	
34	Grant McCann			Chris Powell
35			Chris Cohen	Gavin Williams
36				
37				
38				
39				
40				
41				
42				
43				
44				
45				
46				
47				
48				
60				

2005-06	2006-07	2007-08	2008-09	SHIRT
Roy Carroll	Roy Carroll	Robert Green	Robert Green	1
Tomas Repka / Lionel Scaloni	Tyrone Mears	Lucas Neill	Lucas Neill	2
Paul Konchesky	Paul Konchesky / Lucas Neill	George McCartney	George McCartney / Herita Ilunga	3
Daniel Gabbidon	Daniel Gabbidon	Daniel Gabbidon		4
Anton Ferdinand	Anton Ferdinand	Anton Ferdinand	Walter Lopez	5
Carl Fletcher	George McCartney	Matthew Upson		6
Christian Dailly	Christian Dailly	Fredrik. Ljungberg	Kieron Dyer	7
Teddy Sheringham	Teddy Sheringham	Scott Parker	Scott Parker	8
Dean Ashton		Dean Ashton	Dean Ashton	9
Marlon Harewood	Marlon Harewood	Craig Bellamy	Craig Bellamy / Savio Nsereko	10
Matthew Etherington	Matthew Etherington	Matthew Etherington	Matthew Etherington	11
	Carlton Cole	Carlton Cole	Carlton Cole	12
Stephen Bywater	Luis Boa Morte	Luis Boa Morte	Luis Boa Morte	13
Chris Cohen	John Paintsil	John Paintsil	Radoslav Kovac	14
Yossi Benayoun	Yossi Benayoun	Nolberto Solano	Matthew Upson	15
Gavin Williams	Javier Mascherano	Mark Noble	Mark Noble	16
Hayden Mullins	Hayden Mullins	Hayden Mullins	Hayden Mullins	17
Yaniv Katan	Jonathan Spector	Jonathan Spector	Jonathan Spector	18
James Collins	James Collins	James Collins	James Collins	19
Nigel Reo-Coker	Nigel Reo-Coker	Julien Faubert	Julien Faubert	20
David Bellion	Robert Green	Richard Wright	Valon Behrami	21
Elliott Ward				22
James Walker				23
Mark Noble	Mark Noble		Jan Lastuvka	24
Bobby Zamora	Bobby Zamora	Bobby Zamora	Diego Tristan	25
Shaun Newton	Shaun Newton			26
	Calum Davenport		Calum Davenport	27
	Kyel Reid	Kyel Reid	Kyel Reid	28
Hogan Ephraim	Lee Bowyer	Lee Bowyer	Lee Bowyer	29
Clive Clarke		James Tomkins	James Tomkins	30
Tony Stokes			Jack Collison	31
	Carlos Tevez	Kieron Dyer	David Di Michele	32
	Nigel Quashie	Henri Camara	Freddie Sears	33
Shaka Hislop				34
Kyel Reid	Matthew Upson		Josh Payne	35
				36
	Kepa Blanco			37
				38
Jeremie Aliadiere		Jack Collison		39
		Freddie Sears		40
			Zavon Hines	41
				42
				43
				44
				45
			Junior Stanislas	46
				47
				48
				60

SHIRT	2009-10	2010-11	2011-12	2012-13
1	Robert Green	Robert Green	Robert Green	
2		Winston Reid	Winston Reid	Winston Reid
3		Tal Ben-Haim	George McCartney	George McCartney
4	Daniel Gabbidon	Daniel Gabbidon	Kevin Nolan	Kevin Nolan
5		James Tomkins	James Tomkins	James Tomkins
6				
7	Kieron Dyer	Kieron Dyer	Sam Baldock	Matthew Jarvis
8	Scott Parker	Scott Parker	Scott Parker / David Bentley / Nicky Maynard	Nicky Maynard / Andy Carroll
9	Araujo Ilan	Carlton Cole	Carlton Cole	Carlton Cole
10	Guillermo Franco	Jack Collison	Jack Collison	Jack Collison
11	Hossam Mido	Thomas Hitzlsperger	John Carew	Modibo Maiga
12	Carlton Cole	Pablo Barrera	Pablo Barrera / Ricardo Vaz Te	Ricardo Vaz Te
13	Luis Boa Morte	Luis Boa Morte	Manuel Almunia	Stephen Henderson
14	Radoslav Kovac	Radoslav Kovac	Matthew Taylor	Matthew Taylor
15	Matthew Upson	Matthew Upson	Abdoulaye Faye	Yossi Benayoun
16	Mark Noble	Mark Noble	Mark Noble	Mark Noble
17	Luis Jimenez / Benni McCarthy	Benni McCarthy	Joey O'Brien	Joey O'Brien
18	Jonathan Spector	Jonathan Spector	Julien Faubert	Emanuel Pogatetz
19	James Collins / Freddie Sears	Freddie Sears	Freddie Sears	James Collins
20	Julien Faubert	Julien Faubert	Guy Demel	Guy Demel
21	Valon Behrami	Valon Behrami / Demba Ba	Papa Bouba Diop	Mohamed Diame
22	Manuel Da Costa	Manuel Da Costa	Henri Lansbury	Jussi Jaaskelainen
23	Herita Ilunga	Herita Ilunga	Herita Ilunga / Ravel Morrison	Alou Diarra
24	Frank Nouble	Frank Nouble	Frank Nouble	
25		Junior Stanislas	Junior Stanislas / Danny Collins	
26		Zavon Hines	Brian Montenegro	Joe Cole
27		Jordon Spence		Jordon Spence
28	Peter Kurucz			
29		Marek Stech		Marouane Chamakh
30	James Tomkins	Frederic Piquionne	Frederic Piquionne	
31	Jack Collison	Ruud Boffin	Ruud Boffin	
32	Alessandro Diamanti	Alessandro Diamanti / Gary O'Neil	Gary O'Neil	Gary O'Neil
33	Fabio Daprela	Victor Obinna		Daniel Potts
34		Robbie Keane		
35	Josh Payne			
36	Anthony Edgar	Wayne Bridge		
37		Lars Jacobsen	Callum McNaughton	
38				
39				Dylan Tombides
40		Anthony Edgar		Matthias Fanimo
41	Zavon Hines			
42	Jordon Spence			
43				
44	Bondz N'Gala			George Moncur
45				
46	Junior Stanislas		Robert Hall	Robert Hall
47				Elliot Lee
48			Daniel Potts	
60				

2013-14	2014-15	SHIRT
		1
Winston Reid	Winston Reid	2
George McCartney	Aaron Cresswell	3
Kevin Nolan	Kevin Nolan	4
James Tomkins	James Tomkins	5
		6
Matthew Jarvis	Matthew Jarvis	7
Razvan Rat / Pablo Armero	Cheikhou Kouyate	8
Andy Carroll	Andy Carroll	9
Jack Collison	Mauro Zarate	10
Modibo Maiga	Stewart Downing	11
Ricardo Vaz Te	Ricardo Vaz Te / Nene	12
Adrian Del Castillo	Adrian Del Castillo	13
Matthew Taylor	Ravel Morrison	14
Ravel Morrison	Diafra Sakho	15
Mark Noble	Mark Noble	16
Joey O'Brien	Joey O'Brien	17
Alou Diarra	Carl Jenkinson	18
James Collins	James Collins	19
Guy Demel	Guy Demel	20
Mohamed Diame	Mohamed Diame / Morgan Amalfitano	21
Jussi Jaaskelainen	Jussi Jaaskelainen	22
Stewart Downing	Diego Poyet	23
Carlton Cole	Carlton Cole	24
		25
Joe Cole		26
Daniel Potts		27
Roger Johnson		28
		29
Mladen Petric	Alexandre Song	30
Danny Whitehead	Enner Valencia	31
Elliot Lee	Reece Burke	32
Pelly Ruddock	Daniel Potts	33
George Moncur		34
Sebastian Lletget		35
Blair Turgott	Elliot Lee	36
Leo Chambers		37
		38
		39
Matthias Fanimo		40
Callum Driver		41
		42
		43
Reece Burke		44
		45
Marco Borriello		46
Antonio Nocerino		47
		48
		60

Manager records All managers

Committee
September 1900 - April 1902

	Pld	W	D	L	F	A
League	58	31	11	16	85	56
FAC	8	4	2	2	12	8
Total	**66**	**35**	**13**	**18**	**97**	**64**

Syd King
September 1902 - October 1932

	Pld	W	D	L	F	A
League	1038	403	246	389	1586	1543
FAC	86	36	24	26	144	108
Total	**1124**	**439**	**270**	**415**	**1730**	**1651**

Charlie Paynter
November 1932 - May 1950

	Pld	W	D	L	F	A
League	450	188	109	153	733	665
FAC	30	10	7	13	44	45
Total	**480**	**198**	**116**	**166**	**777**	**710**

Ted Fenton
August 1950 - March 1961

	Pld	W	D	L	F	A
League	451	182	99	170	794	761
FAC	27	9	7	11	50	52
LC	2	1	0	1	5	4
Other	36	22	5	9	90	62
Total	**516**	**214**	**111**	**191**	**939**	**879**

Board Members
March - April 1961

	Pld	W	D	L	F	A
League	7	1	3	3	6	13
Total	**7**	**1**	**3**	**3**	**6**	**13**

Ron Greenwood
April 1961 - April 1974

	Pld	W	D	L	F	A
League	550	182	151	217	861	872
FAC	37	18	7	12	62	55
LC	52	28	9	15	120	76
Europe	15	8	4	3	26	17
Other	2	0	2	0	3	3
Total	**656**	**236**	**173**	**247**	**1072**	**1023**

John Lyall
August 1974 - May 1989

	Pld	W	D	L	F	A
League	624	238	156	230	855	838
FAC	59	29	17	13	79	62
LC	70	34	19	17	128	81
Europe	17	7	2	8	32	27
Other	9	2	1	6	10	14
Total	**779**	**310**	**195**	**274**	**1104**	**1022**

Lou Macari
July 1989 - February 1990

	Pld	W	D	L	F	A
League	28	10	8	10	41	35
FAC	1	0	0	1	0	1
LC	9	4	4	1	8	10
Other	2	1	0	1	8	6
Total	**40**	**15**	**12**	**13**	**57**	**52**

Ron Boyce (Caretaker)
February 1990

	Pld	W	D	L	F	A
League	1	0	1	0	2	2
Total	**1**	**0**	**1**	**0**	**2**	**2**

Billy Bonds
February 1990 - May 1994

	Pld	W	D	L	F	A
League	193	82	52	59	262	212
FAC	21	10	7	4	33	23
LC	13	7	2	4	25	11
Europe	4	2	1	1	3	2
Other	6	3	1	2	11	10
Total	**237**	**104**	**63**	**70**	**334**	**258**

Harry Redknapp
August 1994 - May 2001

	Pld	W	D	L	F	A
League	269	94	71	104	324	359
FAC	20	7	7	6	23	22
LC	26	14	3	9	41	26
Europe	10	6	2	2	13	6
Total	**325**	**121**	**83**	**121**	**401**	**413**

Glenn Roeder
May 2001 - August 2003

	Pld	W	D	L	F	A
League	77	24	20	33	89	118
FAC	5	2	1	2	9	12
LC	4	1	2	1	4	3
Total	**86**	**27**	**23**	**36**	**102**	**133**

Trevor Brooking (2 spells as Caretaker Manager)
April May 2003 and August - October 2003

	Pld	W	D	L	F	A
League	13	8	4	1	19	9
LC	1	1	0	0	3	2
Total	**14**	**9**	**4**	**1**	**22**	**11**

Alan Pardew
October 2003 - December 2006

	Pld	W	D	L	F	A
League	134	53	32	49	178	171
FAC	14	8	5	1	22	15
LC	7	3	0	4	10	9
Europe	2	0	0	2	0	4
Other	6	3	1	2	7	4
Total	**163**	**67**	**38**	**58**	**217**	**203**

Alan Curbishley
December 2006 - September 2008

	Pld	W	D	L	F	A
League	62	23	13	26	73	90
FAC	4	1	1	2	3	2
LC	5	4	0	1	10	5
Total	**71**	**28**	**14**	**29**	**86**	**97**

Kevin Keen (2 spells as Caretaker Manager)
September 2008 and May 2011

	Pld	W	D	L	F	A
League	2	0	0	2	2	6
Total	2	0	0	2	2	6

Gianfranco Zola
September 2008 - May 2010

	Pld	W	D	L	F	A
League	72	20	20	32	81	103
FAC	5	2	1	2	7	5
LC	3	1	0	2	4	5
Total	80	23	21	36	92	113

Avram Grant
June 2010 - May 2011

	Pld	W	D	L	F	A
League	37	7	12	18	43	67
FAC	4	3	0	1	11	5
LC	6	5	0	1	13	6
Total	47	15	12	20	67	78

Sam Allardyce
June 2011 - May 2015

	Pld	W	D	L	F	A
League	160	59	42	59	210	199
FAC	8	1	3	4	6	16
LC	10	5	1	4	14	20
Other	3	3	0	0	7	1
Total	181	68	46	67	237	236

Manager ranking

s difficult to realistically rank a football club's managers through history given that there are many factors outside the top man's control. Some managers inherited poor teams; e club may have had to battle with limited finances during a manager's reign; his team may have played poorly but won trophies or attractively but lost games. Ultimately, owever a manager is judged on results and so this ranking is based on results.

e percentage figure in the final column is based on 2 points for a win, 1 point for a draw, the points are then divided by the total number that were available in all competitve mes in his time at the helm.

Rank	Manager	Reign	Pld	W	D	L	F	A	%
1	Trevor Brooking (Caretaker)	April - May and August - October 2003	14	9	4	1	22	11	78.5
2	Committee	September 1900 - April 1902	66	35	13	18	97	64	62.8
3	Billy Bonds	February 1990 - May 1994	237	104	63	70	334	258	57.1
4	Charlie Paynter	August 1932 - May 1950	480	198	116	166	777	710	53.3
5	Alan Pardew	October 2003 - December 2006	163	67	38	58	217	203	52.7
6	Lou Macari	July 1989 - February 1990	40	15	12	13	57	52	52.5
7	John Lyall	August 1974 - May 1989	779	310	195	274	1104	1022	52.3
8	Ted Fenton	August 1950 - March 1961	516	214	111	191	939	879	52.2
9	Syd King	September 1902 - May 1932	1124	439	270	415	1730	1651	51.0
10	Sam Allardyce	June 2011 - May 2015	181	68	46	67	237	236	50.2
11	Harry Redknapp	August 1994 - May 2001	325	121	83	121	401	413	50.0
12	Ron Boyce (Caretaker)	February 1990	1	0	1	0	2	2	50.0
13	Alan Curbishley	December 2006 - September 2008	71	28	14	29	86	97	49.2
14	Ron Greenwood	April 1961 - April 1974	656	236	173	247	1072	1023	49.1
15	Glenn Roeder	May 2001 - August 2003	86	27	23	36	102	133	44.7
16	Avram Grant	June 2010 - May 2011	47	15	12	20	67	78	44.6
17	Gianfranco Zola	September 2008 - May 2010	80	23	21	36	92	113	41.8
18	Board Members (Caretaker)	March - April 1961	7	1	3	3	6	13	35.7
19	Kevin Keen (Caretaker)	September 2008 and May 2011	2	0	0	2	2	6	0.0

High and low attendances
Highest attendances

ALL COMPETITIONS – ALL VENUES

Date		Competition	Venue	Opponents	Results		Attendance	Scorers
Apr 28	1923	FAC F	N	Bolton Wanderers	L	0-2	126,047	(at Wembley)
May 2	1964	FAC F	N	Preston North End	W	3-2	100,000	Boyce, Hurst, Sissons (at Wembley)
May 3	1975	FAC F	N	Fulham	W	2-0	100,000	Taylor A. 2 (at Wembley)
May 10	1980	FAC F	N	Arsenal	W	1-0	100,000	Brooking (at Wembley)
Mar 14	1981	FAC F	N	Liverpool	D	1-1	100,000	Stewart [pen] (at Wembley)
May 19	1965	ECWC F	N	TSV Munchen 1860	W	2-0	97,974	Sealey 2 (at Wembley)
Aug 9	1980	C Shield	N	Liverpool	L	0-1	90,000	(at Wembley)
Mar 18	1981	ECWC QF:2	A	Dinamo Tbilisi	W	1-0	80,000	Pearson (agg 2-4)
May 19	2012	PO F	N	Blackpool	W	2-1	78,523	Cole C., Vaz Te (at Wembley)
May 3	2008	Prem	A	Manchester United	L	1-4	76,013	Ashton

ALL COMPETITIONS – HOME

Date		Competition	Venue	Opponents	Results		Attendance	Scorers
Jan 8	1927	FAC 3	H	Tottenham Hotspur	W	3-2	44,417	Watson 3
Jan 21	1938	FAC 4	H	Tottenham Hotspur	D	3-3	42,716	Foxall 2, Macaulay [pen]
Oct 17	1970	Div 1	H	Tottenham Hotspur	D	2-2	42,322	Eustace, Hurst
Jan 16	1937	Div 2	H	Bolton Wanderers	D	0-0	42,300	
Feb 14	1972	FAC 4 Rep	H	Hereford United	W	3-1	42,271	Hurst 3
Jan 26	1929	FAC 4	H	Corinthians	W	3-0	42,000	Earle, Watson, Yews
Jan 11	1936	FAC 3	H	Luton Town	D	2-2	42,000	Mangnall, Ruffell
Jan 1	1972	Div 1	H	Manchester United	W	3-0	41,892	Best, Hurst [pen], Robson
Jan 17	1970	Div 1	H	Manchester United	D	0-0	41,643	
Mar 29	1969	Div 1	H	Manchester United	D	0-0	41,546	

ALL COMPETITIONS – AWAY

Date		Competition	Venue	Opponents	Results		Attendance	Scorers
May 3	2008	Prem	A	Manchester United	L	1-4	76,013	Ashton
May 13	2007	Prem	A	Manchester United	W	1-0	75,927	Tevez
Nov 28	2012	Prem	A	Manchester United	L	0-1	75,572	
Oct 29	2008	Prem	A	Manchester United	L	0-2	75,397	
Dec 21	2013	Prem	A	Manchester United	L	1-3	75,350	Cole C.
Sep 27	2014	Prem	A	Manchester United	L	1-2	75,317	Sakho
Aug 28	2010	Prem	A	Manchester United	L	0-3	75,061	
Feb 23	2010	Prem	A	Manchester United	L	0-3	73,797	
Jan 16	2013	FAC 3	A	Manchester United	L	0-1	71,081	
Mar 29	2006	Prem	A	Manchester United	L	0-1	69,522	

AGUE – HOME

Date		Competition	Venue	Opponents	Results		Attendance	Scorers
ct 17	1970	Div 1	H	Tottenham Hotspur	D	2-2	42,322	Eustace, Hurst
n 1	1972	Div 1	H	Manchester United	W	3-0	41,892	Best, Hurst [pen], Robson
n 17	1970	Div 1	H	Manchester United	D	0-0	41,643	
ar 29	1969	Div 1	H	Manchester United	D	0-0	41,546	
r 18	1936	Div 2	H	Charlton Athletic	L	1-3	41,254	Simpson
ar 31	1972	Div 1	H	Leeds United	D	2-2	41,003	Bonds, Hurst
ep 6	1969	Div 1	H	Tottenham Hotspur	L	0-1	40,561	
ov 13	1937	Div 2	H	Coventry City	D	0-0	40,547	
eb 19	1975	Div 1	H	Liverpool	D	0-0	40,256	
ov 9	1935	Div 2	H	Tottenham Hotspur	D	2-2	40,245	Mangnall, Ruffell

AGUE – AWAY

Date		Competition	Venue	Opponents	Results		Attendance	Scorers
ec 27	1920	Div 2	A	Birmingham	L	1-2	65,000	Puddefoot
ep 7	1968	Div 1	A	Manchester United	D	1-1	63,274	Hurst
eb 19	1949	Div 2	A	Tottenham Hotspur	D	1-1	62,980	Woodgate
r 1	1967	Div 1	A	Manchester United	L	0-3	61,308	
ct 26	1968	Div 1	A	Arsenal	D	0-0	59,533	
an 6	1968	Div 1	A	Manchester United	L	1-3	59,516	Brooking
ep 9	1959	Div 1	A	Tottenham Hotspur	D	2-2	58,909	Keeble, Musgrove
ep 27	1969	Div 1	A	Manchester United	L	2-5	58,579	Hurst 2
ep 21	1968	Div 1	A	Chelsea	D	1-1	58,062	Peters
ar 14	1936	Div 2	A	Tottenham Hotspur	W	3-1	57,417	Goulden, Marshall, Simpson

REMIER LEAGUE – HOME

Date		Competition	Venue	Opponents	Results		Attendance	Scorers
eb 23	2002	Prem	H	Middlesbrough	W	1-0	35,420	Kanoute
eb 2	2002	Prem	H	Blackburn Rovers	W	2-0	35,307	Kanoute, Sinclair
ar 16	2002	Prem	H	Manchester United	L	3-5	35,281	Defoe, Kanoute, Lomas
ec 29	2001	Prem	H	Liverpool	D	1-1	35,103	Sinclair
ep 21	2002	Prem	H	Manchester City	D	0-0	35,050	
ov 17	2002	Prem	H	Manchester United	D	1-1	35,049	Defoe
ar 1	2003	Prem	H	Tottenham Hotspur	W	2-0	35,049	Ferdinand L., Carrick
ug 24	2002	Prem	H	Arsenal	D	2-2	35,048	Cole, Kanoute
an 11	2003	Prem	H	Newcastle United	D	2-2	35,048	Cole, Defoe
May 3	2003	Prem	H	Chelsea	W	1-0	35,042	Di Canio

REMIER LEAGUE – AWAY

Date		Competition	Venue	Opponents	Results		Attendance	Scorers
May 3	2008	Prem	A	Manchester United	L	1-4	76,013	Ashton
May 13	2007	Prem	A	Manchester United	W	1-0	75,927	Tevez
ov 28	2012	Prem	A	Manchester United	L	0-1	75,572	
ct 29	2008	Prem	A	Manchester United	L	0-2	75,397	
ec 21	2013	Prem	A	Manchester United	L	1-3	75,350	Cole C.
ug 28	2010	Prem	A	Manchester United	L	0-3	75,061	
eb 23	2010	Prem	A	Manchester United	L	0-3	73,797	
ar 29	2006	Prem	A	Manchester United	L	0-1	69,522	
an 1	2001	Prem	A	Manchester United	L	1-3	67,603	Kanoute
ec 8	2001	Prem	A	Manchester United	W	1-0	67,582	Defoe

FA CUP - ALL VENUES

Date		Competition	Venue	Opponents	Results		Attendance	Scorers
Apr 28	1923	FAC F	N	Bolton Wanderers	L	0-2	126,047	(at Wembley)
May 2	1964	FAC F	N	Preston North End	W	3-2	100,000	Boyce, Hurst, Sissons (at Wembley)
May 3	1975	FAC F	N	Fulham	W	2-0	100,000	Taylor A. 2 (at Wembley)
May 10	1980	FAC F	N	Arsenal	W	1-0	100,000	Brooking (at Wembley)
May 13	2006	FAC F	N	Liverpool	D	3-3	74,000	Ashton, Konchesky, Carragher (og) (at Millennium Stadium)
Jan 16	2013	FAC 3 Rep	A	Manchester United	L	0-1	71,081	
Mar 3	1956	FAC 6	A	Tottenham Hotspur	D	3-3	69,111	Dick 3
Jan 26	2003	FAC 4	A	Manchester United	L	0-6	67,181	
Jan 28	2001	FAC 4	A	Manchester United	W	1-0	67,029	Di Canio
Jan 26	1946	FAC 4	A	Chelsea	L	0-2	65,000	

FA CUP – HOME

Date		Competition	Venue	Opponents	Results		Attendance	Scorers
Jan 8	1927	FAC 3	H	Tottenham Hotspur	W	3-2	44,417	Watson 3
Mar 4	1933	FAC 6	H	Birmingham City	W	4-0	44,232	Pollard, Wilson, Morton, Barkas (og)
Jan 21	1939	FAC 4	H	Tottenham Hotspur	D	3-3	42,716	Foxall 2, Macaulay [pen]
Jan 16	1937	FAC 3	H	Bolton Wanderers	D	0-0	42,300	
Feb 14	1972	FAC 4 Rep	H	Hereford United	W	3-1	42,271	Hurst 3
Jan 26	1929	FAC 4	H	Corinthians	W	3-0	42,000	Earle, Watson, Yews
Jan 11	1936	FAC 3	H	Luton Town	D	2-2	42,000	Mangnall, Ruffell
Mar 1	1930	FAC 6	H	Arsenal	L	0-3	40,492	
Jan 29	1927	FAC 4	H	Brentford	D	1-1	40,000	Ruffell
Feb 15	1975	FAC 5	H	Queens Park Rangers	W	2-1	39,193	Holland, Robson

FA CUP – AWAY

Date		Competition	Venue	Opponents	Results		Attendance	Scorers
Jan 16	2013	FAC 3 Rep	A	Manchester United	L	0-1	71,081	
Mar 3	1956	FAC 6	A	Tottenham Hotspur	D	3-3	69,111	Dick 3
Jan 26	2003	FAC 4	A	Manchester United	L	0-6	67,181	
Jan 28	2001	FAC 4	A	Manchester United	W	1-0	67,029	Di Canio
Jan 26	1946	FAC 4	A	Chelsea	L	0-2	65,000	
Mar 8	1975	FAC 6	A	Arsenal	W	2-0	56,742	Taylor A. 2
Jan 10	1959	FAC 3	A	Tottenham Hotspur	L	0-2	56,252	
Jan 26	1957	FAC 4	A	Everton	L	1-2	55,245	Dare
Jan 27	1934	FAC 4	A	Tottenham Hotspur	L	1-4	51,747	Watson
Jan 30	1939	FAC 4 Rep	A	Tottenham Hotspur	D	1-1	50,798	Foxall

EAGUE CUP – ALL VENUES

Date		Competition	Venue	Opponents	Results		Attendance	Scorers
Mar 14	1981	FLC F	N	Liverpool	D	1-1	100,000	Stewart [pen] (at Wembley)
Jan 26	1972	FLC SF 2 Rep	N	Stoke City	L	2-3	49,247	Bonds, Brooking (at Old Trafford)
Nov 12	1975	FLC 4	A	Tottenham Hotspur	D	0-0	49,125	
Jan 5	1972	LC SF Rep	N	Stoke City	D	0-0	46,196	(at Hillsborough)
Feb 2	1987	FLC 5 Rep	A	Tottenham Hotspur	L	0-5	41,995	
Oct 27	2004	FLC 3	A	Chelsea	L	0-1	41,774	
Oct 27	1971	FLC 4	H	Liverpool	W	2-1	40,878	Hurst, Robson
Dec 15	1971	FLC SF:2	H	Stoke City	L	0-1	38,771	(agg 2-2)
Nov 24	1975	FLC 4 Rep	H	Tottenham Hotspur	L	0-2	38,443	
Nov 17	1971	FLC 5 Rep	H	Sheffield United	W	5-0	36,834	Robson 3, Best 2

EAGUE CUP – HOME

Date		Competition	Venue	Opponents	Results		Attendance	Scorers
Oct 27	1971	FLC 4	H	Liverpool	W	2-1	40,878	Hurst, Robson
Dec 15	1971	FLC SF:2	H	Stoke City	L	0-1	38,771	(agg 2-2)
Nov 24	1975	FLC 4 Rep	H	Tottenham Hotspur	L	0-2	38,443	
Nov 17	1971	FLC 5 Rep	H	Sheffield United	W	5-0	36,834	Robson 3, Best 2
Feb 10	1981	LC SF:2	H	Coventry City	W	2-0	36,551	Goddard, Neighbour (agg 4-3)
Dec 2	1980	FLC 5	H	Tottenham Hotspur	W	1-0	36,003	Cross
Oct 6	1971	FLC 3	H	Leeds United	D	0-0	35,890	
Dec 4	1979	FLC 5	H	Nottingham Forest	D	0-0	35,856	
Feb 8	1967	FLC SF:2	H	West Bromwich Albion	D	2-2	35,790	Byrne, Hurst (agg 2-6)
Jan 11	2011	FLC SF:1	H	Birmingham City	W	2-1	34,753	Cole, Noble

EAGUE CUP – AWAY

Date		Competition	Venue	Opponents	Results		Attendance	Scorers
Nov 12	1975	FLC 4	A	Tottenham Hotspur	D	0-0	49,125	
Feb 2	1987	FLC 5 Rep	A	Tottenham Hotspur	L	0-5	41,995	
Oct 27	2004	FLC 3	A	Chelsea	L	0-1	41,774	
Apr 1	1981	FLC Final Rep	N	Liverpool	L	1-2	36,693	Goddard (at Villa Park)
Dec 8	1971	FLC SF:1	A	Stoke City	W	2-1	36,400	Best, Hurst [pen]
Oct 29	2003	FLC 3	A	Tottenham Hotspur	L	0-1	36,053	(aet) 0-0 at 90 mins
Jan 27	1981	FLC SF:1	A	Coventry City	L	2-3	35,468	Bonds, Thompson (og)
Dec 18	2013	FLC QF	A	Tottenham Hotspur	W	2-1	34,080	Jarvis, Maiga
Sep 21	1976	FLC 3	A	Charlton Athletic	W	1-0	34,000	Taylor A.
Oct 5	1966	FLC 3	A	Arsenal	W	3-1	33,647	Hurst 2, Peters

EUROPE - ALL VENUES

Date		Competition	Venue	Opponents	Results		Attendance	Scorers
May 19	1965	ECWC Final	N	TSV Munchen 1860	W	2-0	97,974	Sealey 2 (at Wembley)
Mar 18	1981	ECWC QF:2	A	Dinamo Tbilisi	W	1-0	80,000	Pearson (agg 2-4)
Oct 22	1975	ECWC 2:1	A	Ararat Erevan	D	1-1	66,662	Taylor A.
Mar 31	1976	ECWC SF:1	A	Eintracht Frankfurt	L	1-2	55,000	Paddon
May 5	1976	ECWC Final	N	Anderlecht	L	2-4	51,296	Holland, Robson (at Stade Du Heysel, Brussels)
Dec 9	1964	ECWC 1:2	A	Spartak Prague	L	1-2	45,000	Sissons (agg 3-2)
Dec 1	1965	ECWC 1:2	A	Olympiakos	D	2-2	40,000	Peters 2 (agg 6-2)
Sep 17	1980	ECWC 1:1	A	Castilla	L	1-3	40,000	Cross
Apr 14	1976	ECWC SF:2	H	Eintracht Frankfurt	W	3-1	39,202	Brooking 2, Robson (agg 4-3)
Apr 7	1965	ECWC SF:1	H	Real Zaragoza	W	2-1	35,086	Byrne, Dear

EUROPE – HOME

Date		Competition	Venue	Opponents	Results		Attendance	Scorers
Apr 14	1976	ECWC SF:2	H	Eintracht Frankfurt	W	3-1	39,202	Brooking 2, Robson (agg 4-3)
Apr 7	1965	ECWC SF:1	H	Real Zaragoza	W	2-1	35,086	Byrne, Dear
Mar 4	1981	ECWC QF:1	H	Dinamo Tbilisi	L	1-4	34,957	Cross
Sep 14	2006	UEFA 1:1	H	Palermo	L	0-1	32,222	
Mar 23	1965	ECWC 2:2	H	Lausanne Sports	W	4-3	31,780	Dear 2, Peters, Tacchella (og) (agg 6-4)
Mar 2	1966	ECWC 2:1	H	FC Magdeburg	W	1-0	30,620	Byrne
Nov 5	1975	ECWC 2:2	H	Ararat Erevan	W	3-1	30,399	Paddon, Robson, Taylor A. (agg 4-2)
Mar 17	1976	ECWC 3:2	H	Den Haag	W	3-1	29,829	Bonds [pen], Lampard, Taylor A. (agg 5-5 won on away goals
Apr 5	1966	ECWC SF:1	H	Borussia Dortmund	L	1-2	28,130	Peters
Nov 25	1964	ECWC 1:1	H	Spartak Prague	W	2-0	27,590	Bond, Sealey

EUROPE – AWAY

Date		Competition	Venue	Opponents	Results		Attendance	Scorers
Mar 18	1981	ECWC QF:2	A	Dinamo Tbilisi	W	1-0	80,000	Pearson (agg 2-4)
Oct 22	1975	ECWC 2:1	A	Ararat Erevan	D	1-1	66,662	Taylor A.
Mar 31	1976	ECWC SF:1	A	Eintracht Frankfurt	L	1-2	55,000	Paddon
Dec 9	1964	ECWC 1:2	A	Spartak Prague	L	1-2	45,000	Sissons (agg 3-2)
Dec 1	1965	ECWC 1:2	A	Olmpiakos	D	2-2	40,000	Peters 2 (agg 6-2)
Sep 17	1980	ECWC 1:1	A	Castilla	L	1-3	40,000	Cross
Mar 16	1966	ECWC 2:2	A	FC Magdeburg	D	1-1	35,000	Sissons (agg 2-1)
Sep 3	1975	AIC:1	A	Fiorentina	L	0-1	35,000	
Apr 13	1966	ECWC SF:2	A	Borussia Dortmund	L	1-3	34,000	Byrne (agg 2-5)
Apr 28	1965	ECWC SF:2	A	Real Zaragoza	D	1-1	28,000	Sissons (agg 3-1)

Notes:

AIC = Anglo-Italian Cup

C Shield = Charity Shield

ECWC = European Cup Winners Cup

PO Final = Play-Off Final

Lowest attendances before 1919

SOUTHERN LEAGUE - HOME

Date		Competition	Venue	Opponents	Results		Attendance	Scorers
Jan 30	1904	SL Div 1	H	Wellingborough Town	W	4-1	250	Kirby 2, Thompson, Satterthwaite
Mar 28	1903	SL Div 1	H	Luton Town	W	4-1	800	Grassam 2, Bigden, Farrell
Feb 9	1901	SL Div 1	H	Luton Town	W	2-0	1,000	Corbett, Taylor
Mar 30	1901	SL Div 1	H	Kettering Town	D	1-1	1,000	Taylor
Mar 23	1903	SL Div 1	H	New Brompton	D	1-1	1,000	Farrell
Sep 7	1903	SL Div 1	H	Kettering Town	W	4-1	1,000	Lyon 2, Allison, Bigden
Feb 25	1905	SL Div 1	H	Southampton	W	2-1	1,500	Hilsdon, McCartney
Sep 1	1900	SL Div 1	H	Gravesend United	W	7-0	2,000	Grassam 4, Reid 2, Hunt
Apr 20	1901	SL Div 1	H	New Brompton	W	2-0	2,000	Ratcliffe, Taylor
Sep 30	1901	SL Div 1	H	Wellingborough Town	W	4-2	2,000	Corbett 3, Grassam

SOUTHERN LEAGUE - AWAY

Date		Competition	Venue	Opponents	Results		Attendance	Scorers
Mar 3	1902	SL Div 1	A	Brentford	W	2-0	500	Hunt, Jenkinson
Dec 15	1900	SL Div 1	A	Gravesend United	D	0-0	1,000	
Mar 23	1901	SL Div 1	A	Kettering Town	W	1-0	1,000	Grassam
Apr 10	1901	SL Div 1	A	Reading	L	1-3	1,000	Grassam
Mar 29	1902	SL Div 1	A	Swindon Town	W	1-0	1,000	Ratcliffe
Sep 7	1903	SL Div 1	A	Northampton Town	W	3-1	1,000	Allison, Kirby, Mercer
Mar 2	1904	SL Div 1	A	Reading	L	0-1	1,000	
Apr 9	1904	SL Div 1	A	Kettering Town	W	1-0	1,000	Bridgeman
Apr 17	1904	SL Div 1	A	Fulham	W	3-0	1,000	Allison, Hilsdon, Simmons
Apr 25	1905	SL Div 1	A	Watford	W	3-0	1,000	Piercy, Simmons, Smith

FA CUP - HOME

Date		Competition	Venue	Opponents	Results		Attendance	Scorers
Nov 16	1901	FAC Q	H	Grays United	L	1-2	2,000	Linward
Nov 3	1900	FAC 3Q	H	Olympic	W	1-0	3,000	Fenton
Nov 21	1900	FAC 4Q	H	New Brompton	W	4-1	4,000	Kaye 2, Corbett, Hunt
Oct 31	1903	FAC Q	H	Brighton & Hove Albion	W	4-0	5,000	Lyon 2, Satterthwaite, Watts
Jan 5	1901	FAC Sup	H	Liverpool	L	0-1	6,000	
Dec 10	1904	FAC Q	H	Brighton & Hove Albion	L	1-2	6,000	Flynn
Jan 20	1910	FAC 1R	H	Carlisle United	W	5-0	7,000	Blackburn 2, Randall, Shea, Webb
Jan 11	1908	FAC 1	H	Rotherham County	W	1-0	9,500	Blackburn
Dec 8	1900	FAC 5Q	H	Clapton	D	1-1	10,000	Kaye
Feb 8	1912	FAC 2R	H	Middlesbrough	W	2-1	10,000	Ashton, Harrison

FA CUP - HOME

Date		Competition	Venue	Opponents	Results		Attendance	Scorers
Nov 17	1900	FAC 4Q	A	New Brompton	D	1-1	1,200	Corbett
Nov 2	1901	FAC Q	A	Leyton	W	1-0	2,000	Taylor
Dec 13	1902	FAC Int	A	Lincoln City	L	0-2	3,000	
Nov 14	1903	FAC Q	A	Clapton Orient	W	3-0	4,500	Lyon 2, Satterthwaite
Dec 12	1900	FAC 5QR	A	Clapton	W	3-2	5,000	Grassam 3
Nov 28	1903	FAC Q	A	Chatham	W	5-0	5,000	Satterthwaite 3, Kirby, Lyon
Feb 3	1912	FAC 2	A	Middlesbrough	D	1-1	12,300	Harrison
Feb 28	1912	FAC 3R	A	Swindon Town	L	0-4	13,328	
Jan 16	1909	FAC 1	A	Queens Park Rangers	D	0-0	17,000	
Feb 5	1910	FAC 2	A	Wolverhampton Wanderers	W	5-1	17,000	Webb 3, Shea 2

Lowest attendances post 1919

ALL COMPETITIONS – HOME

Date		Competition	Venue	Opponents	Results		Attendance	Scorers
Oct 1	1980	ECWC 1:2	H	Castilla	W	5-1	262	Cross 3, Goddard, Pike (agg 6-4) Played behind closed doors
Nov 26	1956	EPC 1	H	Chelmsford City	W	3-1	2,000	Bond [pen], Dare 2
Apr 8	1959	EPC SF	H	Colchester United	W	4-3	2,200	Bond, Grice, Hills, (og)
Mar 10	1958	EPC SF	H	Southend United	W	2-1	3,000	Newman, Smillie
Feb 24	1955	Div 2	H	Doncaster Rovers	L	0-1	4,373	
Dec 15	1958	SFC 2	H	Fulham	W	3-1	4,500	Bond [pen], Keeble, Woosnam
Sep 2	1992	AIC	H	Bristol Rovers	D	2-2	4,809	Dicks 2
Apr 2	1925	Div 1	H	Nottingham Forest	D	0-0	5,000	
Apr 23	1956	SFC F	H	Aldershot	W	2-1	5,000	Tucker, Dare
Jan 13	1958	SFC 2	H	Reading	D	3-3	5,000	Dick, Keeble, Smith

ALL COMPETITIONS – AWAY

Date		Competition	Venue	Opponents	Results		Attendance	Scorers
Dec 8	1992	AIC	A	Cosenza	W	1-0	800	Allen C.
Nov 11	1992	AIC	A	Cremonese	L	0-2	1,639	
Feb 25	1950	Div 2	A	Chesterfield	L	0-1	3,036	
Oct 8	1985	FLC 2:2	A	Swansea City	W	3-2	3,584	Stewart 2 [2 pen], Cottee (agg 6-2)
Sep 18	1996	FLC 2:1	A	Barnet	D	1-1	3,849	Cottee
Jan 30	1933	Div 2	A	Millwall	L	0-1	4,063	
Mar 22	1926	Div 1	A	Notts County	D	1-1	4,278	Ruffell
May 5	1934	Div 2	A	Notts County	W	2-1	4,436	Tippett 2
Sep 17	1975	ECWC 1:1	A	Reipas Lahden	D	2-2	4,587	Bonds, Brooking
Dec 4	1937	Div 2	A	Bury	L	3-4	4,724	Foxall 2, Williams

LEAGUE – HOME

Date		Competition	Venue	Opponents	Results		Attendance	Scorers
Feb 24	1955	Div 2	H	Doncaster Rovers	L	0-1	4,373	
Apr 2	1925	Div 1	H	Nottingham Forest	D	0-0	5,000	
Mar 12	1928	Div 1	H	Leicester City	W	4-0	6,211	Watson 3, Yews
Dec 19	1931	Div 1	H	Sunderland	D	2-2	6,505	Watson, Barrett [pen]
Mar 20	1933	Div 2	H	Bradford Park Avenue	W	2-1	7,258	Wilson 2
Nov 13	1926	Div 1	H	Aston Villa	W	5-1	7,647	Watson 3, Earle, Yews
Jan 1	1921	Div 2	H	Coventry City	W	7-0	8,000	Puddefoot 4, Leafe 2, Bishop
Feb 18	1953	Div 2	H	Plymouth Argyle	L	0-1	8,340	
Mar 16	1931	Div 1	H	Birmingham City	L	1-2	8,521	Watson
Mar 4	1929	Div 1	H	Leicester City	W	2-1	8,603	Earle, Ruffell

LEAGUE – AWAY

Date		Competition	Venue	Opponents	Results		Attendance	Scorers
Feb 25	1950	Div 2	A	Chesterfield	L	0-1	3,036	
Jan 30	1933	Div 2	A	Millwall	L	0-1	4,063	
Mar 22	1926	Div 1	A	Notts County	D	1-1	4,278	Ruffell
May 5	1934	Div 2	A	Notts County	W	2-1	4,436	Tippett 2
Dec 4	1937	Div 2	A	Bury	L	3-4	4,724	Foxall 2, Williams
Feb 11	1920	Div 2	A	Bury	L	0-1	5,000	
Apr 26	1920	Div 2	A	Stockport County	L	0-1	5,000	
Jan 19	1924	Div 1	A	Blackburn Rovers	D	0-0	5,000	
Mar 28	1936	Div 2	A	Hull City	W	3-2	5,038	Goulden, Ruffell, Simpson
Mar 10	1934	Div 2	A	Lincoln City	W	2-0	5,213	Ruffell, Wood

EMIER LEAGUE - HOME

Date		Competition	Venue	Opponents	Results		Attendance	Scorers
23	1995	Prem	H	Sheffield Wednesday	L	0-2	14,554	
p 11	1993	Prem	H	Swindon Town	D	0-0	15,777	
v 1	1993	Prem	H	Manchester City	W	3-1	16,605	Burrows, Chapman, Holmes
t 8	1994	Prem	H	Crystal Palace	W	1-0	16,959	Hutchison
v 20	1993	Prem	H	Oldham Athletic	W	2-0	17,211	Martin, Morley
c 11	1993	Prem	H	Coventry City	W	3-2	17,243	Breacker, Butler, Morley [pen]
v 26	1994	Prem	H	Coventry City	L	0-1	17,251	
c 17	1994	Prem	H	Manchester City	W	3-0	17,286	Cottee 3
g 31	1994	Prem	H	Newcastle United	L	1-3	17,375	Hutchison [pen]
g 28	1993	Prem	H	Queens Park Rangers	L	0-4	18,084	

EMIER LEAGUE - AWAY

Date		Competition	Venue	Opponents	Results		Attendance	Scorers
t 16	1995	Prem	A	Wimbledon	W	1-0	9,411	Cottee
ay 3	1994	Prem	A	Queens Park Rangers	D	0-0	10,850	
ec 4	1993	Prem	A	Wimbledon	W	2-1	10,903	Chapman 2
ec 28	1994	Prem	A	Wimbledon	L	0-1	11,212	
r 16	1994	Prem	A	Oldham Athletic	W	2-1	11,669	Allen M., Morley
ec 4	1994	Prem	A	Queens Park Rangers	L	1-2	12,780	Boere
ug 21	1993	Prem	A	Coventry City	D	1-1	12,864	Gordon
ov 29	1993	Prem	A	Southampton	D	0-0	13,568	
ar 28	1994	Prem	A	Sheffield United	L	2-3	13,646	Bishop, Holmes
ar 4	2009	Prem	A	Wigan Athletic	W	1-0	14,376	Cole

CUP - HOME

Date		Competition	Venue	Opponents	Results		Attendance	Scorers
n 5	1985	FAC 3	H	Port Vale	W	4-1	11,452	Goddard 3, Dickens
n 7	1984	FAC 3	H	Wigan Athletic	W	1-0	16,000	Stewart [pen]
n 25	1997	FAC 3 Rep	H	Wrexham	L	0-1	16,763	
eb 9	1987	FAC 4	H	Sheffield United	W	4-0	17,194	McAvennie 2, Gale, Robson
n 3	1998	FAC 3	H	Emley	W	2-1	18,629	Hartson, Lampard
an 31	1987	FAC 3 Rep	H	Leyton Orient	W	4-1	19,424	Cottee, Keen, McAvennie, Parris
an 8	1994	FAC 3	H	Watford	W	2-1	19,802	Allen M., Marsh
an 11	1922	FAC 1 Rep	H	Swansea Town	D	1-1	20,000	Watson
eb 7	1923	FAC 2 Rep	H	Brighton & Hove Albion	W	1-0	20,000	Moore
eb 4	1985	FAC 4	H	Norwich City	W	2-1	20,098	Pike, Stewart [pen]

CUP - AWAY

Date		Competition	Venue	Opponents	Results		Attendance	Scorers
an 6	1990	FAC 3	A	Torquay United	L	0-1	5,342	
an 6	2002	FAC 3	A	Macclesfield Town	W	3-0	5,706	Defoe 2, Cole
an 24	2009	FAC 4	A	Hartlepool	W	2-0	6,849	Behrami, Noble [pen]
eb 19	1994	FAC 5	A	Kidderminster Harriers	W	1-0	8,000	Chapman
an 16	1922	FAC 2 Rep	A	Swansea Town	L	0-1	8,976	
an 7	1995	FAC 3	A	Wycombe Wanderers	W	2-0	9,007	Brown, Cottee
an 6	2001	FAC 3	A	Walsall	W	3-2	9,402	Kanoute 2, Lampard
an 4	1997	FAC 3	A	Wrexham	D	1-1	9,747	Porfirio
an 13	1999	FAC 3 Rep	A	Swansea City	L	0-1	10,116	
an 31	1925	FAC 2	A	Nottingham Forest	W	2-0	10,590	Ruffell, Yews

LEAGUE CUP – HOME

Date		Competition	Venue	Opponents	Results		Attendance	Scorers
Sep 23	1992	FLC 2:1	H	Crewe Alexandra	D	0-0	6,981	
Sep 24	1985	FLC 2:1	H	Swansea City	W	3-0	9,282	Cottee, McAvennie, Stewart [pen]
Sep 26	1962	FLC 2	H	Plymouth Argyle	W	6-0	9,714	Byrne 3 [1 pen], Hurst, Musgrove, Peters
Aug 27	2008	FLC 3	H	Macclesfield Town	W	4-1	10,055	Bowyer, Cole, Hines, Reid
Dec 16	1963	FLC 5	H	Workington	W	6-0	10,160	Byrne 3, Boyce, Hurst, Scott
Oct 12	1988	FLC 2:2	H	Sunderland	W	2-1	10,558	Dickens, Kelly (agg 5-1)
Oct 25	1983	FLC 2:2	H	Bury	W	10-0	10,896	Cottee 4, Brooking 2, Devonshire 2, Martin, Stewart [pen] (agg 12-1)
Sep 21	2004	FLC 2	H	Notts County	W	3-2	11,111	Zamora 2, Rebrov
Oct 9	1984	FLC 2:2	H	Bristol City	W	6-1	11,376	Cottee 2, Goddard 2, Walford, Whitton (agg 8-3)
Oct 13	1965	FLC 3	H	Mansfield Town	W	4-0	11,590	Hurst 2, Brabrook, Burnett

LEAGUE CUP – AWAY

Date		Competition	Venue	Opponents	Results		Attendance	Scorers
Oct 8	1985	FLC 2:2	A	Swansea City	W	3-2	3,584	Stewart 2 [2 pens], Cottee (agg 6-2)
Sep 18	1996	FLC 2:1	A	Barnet	D	1-1	3,849	Cottee
Oct 5	1993	FLC 2:2	A	Chesterfield	W	2-0	4,890	Allen M., Boere (agg 7-1)
Oct 7	1992	FLC 2:2	A	Crewe Alexandra	L	0-2	5,427	(agg 0-2)
Sep 19	2000	FLC 2:1	A	Walsall	W	1-0	5,435	Defoe
Sep 20	1994	FLC 2:1	A	Walsall	L	1-2	5,994	Ntamark (og)
Aug 26	1980	FLC 2:1	A	Burnley	W	2-0	6,818	Cross, Goddard
Sep 24	1991	FLC 2:1	A	Bradford City	D	1-1	7,034	Small
Oct 01	2002	FLC 2	A	Chesterfield	D	1-1	7,102	Defoe (aet: 5-4 pens)
Sep 20	1995	FLC 2:1	A	Bristol Rovers	D	1-1	7,103	Moncur

EUROPE – HOME

Date		Competition	Venue	Opponents	Results		Attendance	Scorers
Oct 1	1980	ECWC 1:2	H	Castilla	W	5-1	262	Cross 3, Goddard, Pike (agg 6-4) Played behind closed doors
Nov 24	1992	AIC	H	Reggiana	W	2-0	6,872	Allan C. 2
Dec 16	1992	AIC	H	Pisa SC	D	0-0	7,123	
Jul 28	1999	Toto SF:1	H	SC Heerenveen	W	1-0	7,485	Lampard
Jul 17	1999	Toto 3:1	H	FC Jokerit	W	1-0	11,908	Kitson
Dec 10	1975	AIC:2	H	Fiorentina	L	0-1	14,699	(agg 0-2)
Oct 7	1964	ECWC Pre:2	H	La Gantoise	D	1-1	24,000	Byrne (agg 2-1)
Oct 1	1975	ECWC 1:2	H	Reipas Lahden	W	3-0	24,131	Holland, Jennings, Robson (agg 5-2)
Nov 4	1999	UEFA 2:2	H	Steaua Bucharest	D	0-0	24,514	(agg 0-2)
Sep 16	1999	UEFA 1:1	H	NK Osijek	W	3-0	25,331	Di Canio, Lampard, Wanchope

EUROPE – AWAY

Date		Competition	Venue	Opponents	Results		Attendance	Scorers
Dec 8	1992	AIC	A	Cosenza	W	1-0	800	Allen C.
Nov 11	1992	AIC	A	Cremonese	L	0-2	1,639	
Sep 17	1975	ECWC 1:1	A	Reipas Lahden	D	2-2	4,587	Bonds, Brooking
Jul 24	1999	Toto 3:2	A	FC Jokerit	D	1-1	7,667	Lampard (agg 2-1)
Oct 21	1999	UEFA 2:1	A	Steaua Bucharest	L	0-2	12,500	
Aug 4	1999	UEFA SF:2	A	SC Heerenveen	W	1-0	13,500	Wanchope (agg 2-1)
Sep 30	1999	UEFA 1:2	A	NK Osijek	W	3-1	15,000	Foe, Kitson, Ruddock (agg 6-1)
Sep 23	1964	ECWC Pre:1	A	La Gantoise	W	1-0	18,000	Boyce
Sep 28	2006	UEFA 1:2	A	Palermo	L	0-3	19,228	
Aug 24	1999	Toto F:2	A	FC Metz	W	3-1	19,599	Lampard, Sinclair, Wanchope (agg 3-2)

Notes:

AIC = Anglo-Italian Cup   ECWC = European Cup Winners Cup   EPC = Essex Professional Cup   SFC = Southern Floodlight Cup   Toto = Intertoto Cup

Biggest wins/draws/defeats
Most goals scored

Date	Competition	Venue	Opponents	Results		Attendance	Scorers
Oct 25 1983	League Cup 2nd round 2 leg	H	Bury	W	10-0	10,896	Cottee 4, Brooking 2, Devonshire 2, Martin, Stewart [pen]
Mar 08 1958	2nd Division	H	Rotherham United	W	8-0	25,040	Dick 4, Keeble 2, Smith 2
Oct 19 1968	1st Division	H	Sunderland	W	8-0	24,903	Hurst 6, Brooking, Moore
Jan 10 1914	FA Cup 1st round	H	Chesterfield	W	8-1	16,000	Puddefoot 5, Ashton, Bailey, Leafe
Apr 21 1986	1st Division	H	Newcastle United	W	8-1	24,734	Martin 3, Goddard, McAvennie, Orr, Stewart [pen], Roeder (og)
Feb 09 1929	1st Division	H	Leeds United	W	8-2	18,055	Watson 6, Gibbins, Yews
Oct 28 1899	FA Cup Q3	A	Dartford	W	7-0	1,200	Carnelly 2, McKay 2, Bradshaw, Joyce, McEachrane
Sep 01 1900	Southern League 1st Division	H	Gravesend United	W	7-0	2,000	Grassam 4, Reid 2, Hunt
Jan 01 1921	2nd Division	H	Coventry City	W	7-0	8,000	Puddefoot 4, Leafe 2, Bishop
Mar 07 1927	1st Division	H	Arsenal	W	7-0	11,764	Watson 3, Johnson, Ruffell, Parker (og), John (og)
Sep 01 1930	1st Division	H	Liverpool	W	7-0	11,682	Watson 4, Earle 2, James
Nov 07 1966	League Cup 4th round	H	Leeds United	W	7-0	27,474	Hurst 3, Sissons 3, Peters
Oct 06 1990	2nd Division	H	Hull City	W	7-1	19,472	Dicks 2 [1 pen], Quinn 2, Morley, Parris, Potts
Aug 30 1958	1st Division	H	Aston Villa	W	7-2	30,263	Dick 2, Keeble 2, Musgrove 2, Lansdowne
Feb 03 1968	1st Division	H	Fulham	W	7-2	31,248	Brooking 2, Hurst 2, Dear, Moore, Peters
Sep 04 1968	League Cup 2nd round	H	Bolton Wanderers	W	7-2	24,737	Hurst 3 [1 pen], Brooking, Peters, Redknapp, Sissons
Nov 26 1932	2nd Division	H	Charlton Athletic	W	7-3	18,347	Watson 2, Wilson, 2, Barrett, Morton, Yews
Oct 21 1911	Southern League 1st Division	H	Brentford	W	7-4	10,000	Kennedy 3, Shea 3, Harrison
Sep 23 1899	FA Cup Pre	H	Royal Engineers	W	6-0	1,000	Joyce 3, McEachrane, McKay, Reid
Dec 31 1910	Southern League 1st Division	A	Southend United	W	6-0	3,000	Shea 4, Caldwell, Kennedy
Jan 31 1920	FA Cup 2nd round	H	Bury	W	6-0	27,000	Puddefoot 3, Bailey, Butcher, Smith S.
Feb 15 1923	2nd Division	A	Leicester City	W	6-0	12,000	Moore 3, Richards, Ruffell, Tresadern
Feb 13 1926	1st Division	H	Bolton Wanderers	W	6-0	24,062	Gibbins 2, Ruffell 2, Watson 2
Sep 23 1933	2nd Division	H	Preston North End	W	6-0	15,738	Watson 3, Goulden, Morton, Tippett
Feb 01 1936	2nd Division	H	Bury	W	6-0	26,204	Lewis 3, Cockroft, Morton, Simpson
Jan 05 1946	FA Cup 3rd round 1 leg	H	Arsenal	W	6-0	35,000	Hall 2, Wood 2, Bainbridge, Foreman
Dec 20 1958	1st Division	H	Portsmouth	W	6-0	21,316	Keeble 2, Dick, Musgrove, Smith Woosnam
Nov 05 1960	1st Division	H	Arsenal	W	6-0	29,275	Dunmore 3, Dick, Malcolm, Woosnam
Sep 26 1962	League Cup 2nd round	H	Plymouth Argyle	W	6-0	9,714	Byrne 3 [1 pen], Hurst, Musgrove, Peters
Dec 16 1963	League Cup 5th round	H	Workington	W	6-0	10,160	Byrne 3, Boyce, Hurst, Scott
Sep 18 1974	League Cup 2nd round Replay	H	Tranmere Rovers	W	6-0	15,854	Gould 3 [1 pen], Bonds 2 [1 pen], Ayris
Oct 11 1992	1st Division	H	Sunderland	W	6-0	10,326	Robson 2, Allen M., Keen, Martin, Morley
Jan 10 1998	Premier League	H	Barnsley	W	6-0	23,714	Abou 2, Hartson, Lampard, Lazaridis, Moncur
Apr 14 2012	Championship	H	Brighton and Hove Albion	W	6-0	32,339	Vaz Te 3, Nolan, Cole, Dicker (og)
Feb 10 1906	Southern League 1st Division	H	Norwich City	W	6-1	6,000	Stapley 2, Watson 2, Grassam, Kitchen [pen]
Jan 03 1914	Southern League 1st Division	H	Bristol Rovers	W	6-1	14,000	Puddefoot 3, Bailey, Casey, Leafe
Sep 24 1938	2nd Division	H	Tranmere Rovers	W	6-1	20,549	Macaulay 3, Cockroft, Corbett, Foxall
Feb 05 1955	2nd Division	H	Plymouth Argyle	W	6-1	18,154	Sexton 3, Dick 2, Bennett
Sep 03 1955	2nd Division	H	Notts County	W	6-1	16,710	Dare 2, Hooper 2, Dick, O'Farrell
Oct 22 1955	2nd Division	H	Doncaster Rovers	W	6-1	13,303	Hooper 3, Andrews, Dare, Taylor
Dec 21 1957	2nd Division	A	Lincoln City	W	6-1	8,384	Dick 2, Keeble 2, Musgrove, Newman
Dec 28 1957	2nd Division	H	Bristol Rovers	W	6-1	28,095	Smith 3, Keeble 2, Dick
Sep 08 1962	1st Division	A	Manchester City	W	6-1	24,069	Musgrove 2, Byrne, Hurst, Peters, Scott
May 18 1963	1st Division	H	Manchester City	W	6-1	16,602	Hurst 2, Sealey 2, Boyce, Brabrook
Apr 16 1965	1st Division	H	West Bromwich Albion	W	6-1	27,710	Dear 5, Peters
Nov 05 1966	1st Division	H	Fulham	W	6-1	22,272	Hurst 4, Peters 2
Oct 09 1984	League Cup 2nd round 2 leg	H	Bristol City	W	6-1	11,376	Cottee 2, Goddard 2, Walford, Whitton
Jan 16 1991	FA Cup 3rd round Replay	H	Aldershot	W	6-1	21,484	Morley 2, Bishop, Parris, Quinn, Slater
Jan 28 1905	Southern League 1st Division	H	Luton Town	W	6-2	5,000	Carrick 3, Bridgeman 2, Simmons
Mar 23 1912	Southern League 1st Division	H	Bristol Rovers	W	6-2	4,000	Harrison 2, Shea 2, Dawson, Woodards
Apr 14 1925	1st Division	H	Sheffield United	W	6-2	12,000	Ruffell 2, Watson 2, Earle, Moore

Date	Competition	Venue	Opponents	Results		Attendance	Scorers
Mar 11 1939	2nd Division	A	Norwich City	W	6-2	15,027	Small 3, Foxall 2, Morton
Jan 18 1958	2nd Division	H	Swansea City	W	6-2	27,277	Keeble 2, Bond [pen], Cantwell, Dick, Lansdowne
Sep 21 1974	1st Division	H	Leicester City	W	6-2	21,377	Gould 2, Jennings 2, Bonds, Robson
Oct 04 1958	1st Division	H	Blackburn Rovers	W	6-3	25,280	Keeble 4, Cantwell, Woods (og)
Nov 28 1903	FA Cup Q5	A	Chatham	W	5-0	5,000	Satterthwaite 3, Kirby, Lyon
Feb 13 1904	Southern League 1st Division	H	Brighton and Hove Albion	W	5-0	3,000	Satterthwaite 4, Lyon
Oct 04 1909	Southern League 1st Division	H	Bristol Rovers	W	5-0	4,000	Caldwell 3, Shea, Webb
Jan 08 1910	Southern League 1st Division	H	Norwich City	W	5-0	6,000	Cadwell 2, Shea, Cannon
Jan 20 1910	FA Cup 1st round Replay	H	Carlisle United	W	5-0	7,000	Blackburn 2, Randall, Shea, Webb
Sep 23 1911	Southern League 1st Division	H	Reading	W	5-0	10,000	Piercy, Rothwell [pen], Shea, Webb, Whiteman
Dec 25 1912	Southern League 1st Division	H	Stoke City	W	5-0	8,000	Shea 2, Ashton, Askew, Denyer
Nov 27 1920	2nd Division	H	Stockport County	W	5-0	20,000	Leafe 3, Puddefoot 2
Jan 12 1924	FA Cup 1st round	H	Aberdare Athletic	W	5-0	23,000	Brown 2, Henderson, Moore, Williams
Jan 21 1933	2nd Division	H	Port Vale	W	5-0	13,908	Watson 2, Wilson 2, Barrett
Sep 13 1937	2nd Division	H	Chesterfield	W	5-0	15,010	Goulden 2, Small 2, Morton
Feb 18 1939	2nd Division	H	Nottingham Forest	W	5-0	15,472	Fenton B. 2, Foxall, Goulden, Macaulay
Jan 18 1947	2nd Division	H	Chesterfield	W	5-0	23,876	Wood 2, Hall, Payne, Small
Aug 19 1953	2nd Division	H	Lincoln City	W	5-0	17,045	Sexton 2, Andrews, Dixon, Parker
Nov 07 1953	2nd Division	H	Bury	W	5-0	19,697	Dick 3, Sexton, Stroud
Nov 16 1957	2nd Division	H	Stoke City	W	5-0	23,171	Keeble 3, Dare, Dick
Dec 17 1960	1st Division	H	Wolverhampton Wanderers	W	5-0	22,336	Dunmore 2, Dick, Moore, Musgrove
Oct 06 1962	1st Division	H	Birmingham City	W	5-0	21,150	Byrne 2, Brown, Hurst, Musgrove
Apr 17 1964	1st Division	H	Birmingham City	W	5-0	22,106	Brabrook 2, Byrne, Hurst, Sissons
Sep 07 1964	1st Division	H	Wolverhampton Wanderers	W	5-0	26,879	Hurst 2, Byrne [pen], Moore, Sissons
Apr 06 1968	1st Division	H	Newcastle United	W	5-0	27,681	Brooking 3, Sissons 2
Aug 26 1968	1st Division	H	Burnley	W	5-0	28,340	Brooking 2, Hurst 2, Peters
Nov 17 1971	League Cup 5th round	H	Sheffield United	W	5-0	36,834	Robson 3, Best 2
Dec 02 1978	2nd Division	H	Cambridge United	W	5-0	21,379	Robson 2, Bonds, Curbishley, Taylor A.
Mar 24 1979	2nd Division	H	Newcastle United	W	5-0	24,650	McDowell 2, Devonshire, Lampard, Robson
Nov 11 1980	2nd Division	H	Bristol City	W	5-0	25,210	Goddard 2, Brooking, Cross, Martin
Jan 31 1981	2nd Division	H	Preston North End	W	5-0	26,398	Devonshire 2, Goddard, Lampard, Pike
Sep 11 1982	1st Division	H	Birmingham City	W	5-0	18,754	Clark, Goddard, Martin, Stewart [pen], Van der Elst
Nov 01 1988	League Cup 3rd round	H	Derby County	W	5-0	14,226	Martin 2, Keen, Rosenior, Stewart [pen]
Oct 18 1989	2nd Division	H	Sunderland	W	5-0	20,901	Dolan 2, Allen, Keen, Slater
Mar 21 1990	2nd Division	H	Sheffield United	W	5-0	21,629	Quinn 3 [1 pen], Allen, Morley
Jan 30 1991	FA Cup 4th round Replay	H	Luton Town	W	5-0	25,659	Morley 2, Bishop, McAvennie, Parris
Apr 22 2000	Premier League	H	Coventry City	W	5-0	24,719	Di Canio 2, Carrick, Kanoute, Margas
Dec 26 2000	Premier League	H	Charlton Athletic	W	5-0	26,046	Kanoute 2, Lampard, Sinclair, Rufus (og)
Mar 09 2004	1st Division	H	Wimbledon	W	5-0	29,818	Etherington 3, Reo-Coker, Zamora
Feb 19 2005	Championship	H	Plymouth Argyle	W	5-0	25,490	Sheringham 2 [1 pen], Harewood [pen], Mackay, McCormick (og)
Nov 10 2007	Premier League	A	Derby County	W	5-0	32,440	Bowyer 2, Etherington, Solano, Lewis (og)
Apr 15 1905	Southern League 1st Division	H	Northampton Town	W	5-1	7,000	Carrick 2, Simmons 2, Bridgeman
Sep 22 1906	Southern League 1st Division	H	Luton Town	W	5-1	13,000	Watson 3, Lindsay, Stapley
Nov 06 1909	Southern League 1st Division	H	Croydon Common	W	5-1	10,000	Shea 2 [2 pens], Ashton, Caldwell, Whiteman
Feb 05 1910	FA Cup 2nd round	A	Wolverhampton Wanderers	W	5-1	17,000	Webb 3, Shea 2
Oct 11 1913	Southern League 1st Division	H	Southampton	W	5-1	6,000	Hilsdon 2, Ashton, Burton, Casey
Apr 02 1920	2nd Division	H	Nottingham Forest	W	5-1	20,000	Puddefoot 4, Bailey
Mar 31 1923	2nd Division	A	Crystal Palace	W	5-1	16,000	Watson 4, Brown
Nov 13 1926	1st Division	H	Aston Villa	W	5-1	7,647	Watson 3, Earle, Yews
Apr 02 1927	1st Division	A	Aston Villa	W	5-1	22,413	Watson 2, Earle, Johnson, Ruffell
Mar 24 1928	1st Division	A	Cardiff City	W	5-1	14,529	Earle 2, Watson 2, Yews

Biggest wins/draws/defeats
Most goals conceded

Date	Competition	Venue	Opponents	Results		Attendance	Scorers
Oct 10 1896	FA Cup 1Q	A	Sheppey United	L	0-8	Unknown	
Dec 26 1963	1st Division	H	Blackburn Rovers	L	2-8	20,500	Byrne 2
Nov 04 1899	Southern League 1st Division	A	Tottenham Hotspur	L	0-7	7,000	
Sep 01 1919	2nd Division	A	Barnsley	L	0-7	6,000	
Oct 22 1927	1st Division	A	Everton	L	0-7	20,151	
Nov 28 1959	1st Division	A	Sheffield Wednesday	L	0-7	36,899	
Oct 24 1925	1st Division	A	West Bromwich Albion	L	1-7	18,014	Ruffell
Apr 01 2000	Premier League	A	Manchester United	L	1-7	61,611	Wanchope
Oct 14 2001	Premier League	A	Blackburn Rovers	L	1-7	22,712	Carrick
Apr 02 1932	1st Division	A	Blackpool	L	2-7	13,092	Morton, Watson
Dec 20 1902	Southern League 1st Division	A	Reading	L	0-6	4,000	
Apr 13 1903	Southern League 1st Division	A	Southampton	L	0-6	6,000	
Feb 27 1909	Southern League 1st Division	A	Northampton Town	L	0-6	5,000	
Apr 01 1914	Southern League 1st Division	A	Watford	L	0-6	4,000	
Dec 08 1928	1st Division	A	Derby County	L	0-6	15,284	
Apr 13 1929	1st Division	A	The Wednesday	L	0-6	22,596	
Sep 07 1931	1st Division	A	Sheffield United	L	0-6	11,055	
Oct 08 1932	2nd Division	A	Lincoln City	L	0-6	9,887	
Apr 07 1948	2nd Division	A	Chesterfield	L	0-6	11,914	
Dec 08 1951	2nd Division	H	Sheffield Wednesday	L	0-6	17,798	
Oct 30 1954	2nd Division	A	Middlesbrough	L	0-6	25,601	
Mar 03 1962	1st Division	A	Burnley	L	0-6	24,379	
Mar 05 1977	1st Division	A	Sunderland	L	0-6	35,357	
Apr 07 1984	1st Division	A	Liverpool	L	0-6	38,359	
Feb 14 1990	League Cup SF 1 leg	A	Oldham Athletic	L	0-6	19,263	
May 08 1999	Premier League	A	Everton	L	0-6	40,029	
Jan 26 2003	FA Cup 4th round	A	Manchester United	L	0-6	67,181	
Jan 01 2007	Premier League	A	Reading	L	0-6	24,073	
Jan 08 2014	League Cup SF 1 leg	A	Manchester City	L	0-6	30,381	
Mar 03 1906	Southern League 1st Division	A	Reading	L	1-6	5,000	Watson
Dec 30 1911	Southern League 1st Division	H	Crystal Palace	L	1-6	8,000	Shea
Sep 06 1930	1st Division	A	Aston Villa	L	1-6	35,897	Watson
Dec 20 1930	1st Division	A	Sunderland	L	1-6	20,846	Gibbins
Mar 28 1932	1st Division	A	Sheffield Wednesday	L	1-6	14,848	Watson
Apr 16 1932	1st Division	A	Everton	L	1-6	26,997	Cresswell (og)
Feb 11 1933	2nd Division	A	Bury	L	1-6	7,516	Barrett
Sep 15 1951	2nd Division	A	Sheffield United	L	1-6	30,202	Bing
Dec 26 1951	2nd Division	A	Luton Town	L	1-6	19,476	Gregory
Sep 14 1960	1st Division	A	Manchester United	L	1-6	33,288	Brett
Aug 25 1962	1st Division	H	Tottenham Hotspur	L	1-6	32,527	Woosnam
May 06 1967	1st Division	H	Manchester United	L	1-6	38,424	Charles
Mar 20 1976	1st Division	A	Arsenal	L	1-6	34,011	jennings
Jan 31 1978	FA Cup 4th round Replay	A	Queens Park Rangers	L	1-6	24,057	Robson
Jan 18 1913	Southern League 1st Division	A	Merthyr Town	L	2-6	4,000	Butcher 2
Dec 26 1927	1st Division	A	Sheffield United	L	2-6	23,591	Gibbins, Yews
Feb 23 1957	2nd Division	A	Huddersfield Town	L	2-6	5,878	Lewis, Smith J.
Dec 12 1959	1st Division	A	Blackburn Rovers	L	2-6	22,261	Dick, Woosnam
Apr 09 1966	1st Division	A	Chelsea	L	2-6	35,958	Bennett, Harris (og)
Feb 04 1967	1st Division	A	Southampton	L	2-6	30,123	Burkett, Hurst

Date	Competition	Venue	Opponents	Results		Attendance	Scorers
ec 12 1908	Southern League 1st Division	A	Norwich City	L	3-6	4,500	Burton 2, Grassam
r 30 1927	1st Division	A	Leeds United	L	3-6	10,997	Watson 2, Johnson
t 12 1895	FA Cup	A	Chatham	L	0-5	3,000	
r 30 1910	Southern League 1st Division	A	Swindon Town	L	0-5	4,000	
b 01 1913	FA Cup 2nd round	A	Aston Villa	L	0-5	50,000	
ov 29 1924	1st Division	A	Bolton Wanderers	L	0-5	25,977	
n 09 1926	FA Cup 3rd round	A	Tottenham Hotspur	L	0-5	49,800	
ep 15 1928	1st Division	A	Leicester City	L	0-5	24,652	
ov 07 1936	2nd Division	A	Fulham	L	0-5	22,281	
ay 31 1947	2nd Division	H	Burnley	L	0-5	20,198	
r 30 1949	2nd Division	H	Nottingham Forest	L	0-5	12,349	
ug 24 1953	2nd Division	A	Rotherham United	L	0-5	12,895	
r 11 1960	1st Division	A	Wolverhampton Wanderers	L	0-5	48,086	
ct 09 1965	1st Division	A	Nottingham Forest	L	0-5	19,262	
eb 05 1966	1st Division	A	Leeds United	L	0-5	33,112	
ug 30 1977	League Cup 2nd round	A	Nottingham Forest	L	0-5	18,224	
r 02 1985	1st Division	A	Watford	L	0-5	17,389	
eb 02 1987	League Cup 5th round Replay	A	Tottenham Hotspur	L	0-5	41,995	
ec 18 1993	Premier League	A	Sheffield Wednesday	L	0-5	26,350	
ay 02 1998	Premier League	A	Liverpool	L	0-5	44,414	
ep 29 2001	Premier League	A	Everton	L	0-5	32,049	
n 05 2011	Premier League	A	Newcastle United	L	0-5	42,387	
an 05 2014	FA Cup 3rd round	A	Nottingham Forest	L	0-5	14,397	
ep 27 1902	Southern League 1st Division	A	Wellingborough Town	L	1-5	4,000	Grassam
ar 09 1912	Southern League 1st Division	A	Millwall	L	1-5	28,400	Harrison
ov 23 1912	Southern League 1st Division	A	Brentford	L	1-5	7,000	Shea
eb 25 1914	FA Cup 3rd round Replay	A	Liverpool	L	1-5	45,000	Puddefoot
r 25 1914	Southern League 1st Division	A	Portsmouth	L	1-5	8,000	Bailey
ov 17 1923	1st Division	A	Burnley	L	1-5	9,000	Moore
ep 11 1926	1st Division	H	Blackburn Rovers	L	1-5	20,680	Watson
ct 31 1931	1st Division	A	Derby County	L	1-5	10,424	Watson
ov 07 1931	1st Division	H	West Bromwich Albion	L	1-5	20,685	Ruffell
ep 07 1932	2nd Division	A	Bradford City	L	1-5	17,137	Watson
ec 30 1933	2nd Division	A	Bolton Wanderers	L	1-5	9,551	Mills
r 11 1950	2nd Division	A	Coventry City	L	1-5	26,645	Woodgate
an 01 1955	2nd Division	A	Notts County	L	1-5	20,290	Hooper [pen]
ep 12 1959	1st Division	A	Bolton Wanderers	L	1-5	24,240	Keeble
an 13 1960	FA Cup 3rd round Replay	H	Huddersfield Town	L	1-5	22,605	Musgrove
pr 03 1961	1st Division	A	Leicester City	L	1-5	23,776	Kirkup
ep 06 1965	1st Division	H	Liverpool	L	1-5	32,144	Peters
ug 26 1967	1st Division	A	Tottenham Hotspur	L	1-5	55,831	Sissons
ct 13 1984	1st Division	A	Manchester United	L	1-5	47,559	Goddard
ay 04 1985	1st Division	A	West Bromwich Albion	L	1-5	8,834	Stewart [pen]
ay 23 1989	1st Division	A	Liverpool	L	1-5	41,855	Rosenior
ec 19 1990	Zenith Data Systems Cup 2nd round	A	Luton Town	L	1-5	5,759	Keen
ay 01 1999	Premier League	H	Leeds United	L	1-5	25,997	Di Canio
an 20 2002	Premier League	A	Chelsea	L	1-5	40,035	Defoe
an 31 2012	Championship	A	Ipswich Town	L	1-5	22,185	Collison
an 23 2013	Premier League	A	Arsenal	L	1-5	60,081	Collison

Biggest wins/draws/defeats
Biggest scoring draws

Date	Competition	Venue	Opponents	Results		Attendance	Scorers
Jan 03 1931	1st Division	H	Aston Villa	D	5-5	18,810	Gibbins 2, Barrett, Harris, Yews
Dec 10 1960	1st Division	A	Newcastle United	D	5-5	20,106	Bond [pen], Dick, Dunmore, Musgrove, McMichael (og)
Dec 17 1966	1st Division	A	Chelsea	D	5-5	47,805	Sissons 2, Brabrook, Byrne, Peters
Mar 26 1927	1st Division	H	Bolton Wanderers	D	4-4	17,752	Ruffell 2, Earle, Watson
Oct 29 1932	2nd Division	H	Burnley	D	4-4	12,009	Watson 3, Morton
Aug 30 1933	2nd Division	A	Plymouth Argyle	D	4-4	24,312	Barrett [pen], Goulden, Landells, Mills
Dec 22 1962	1st Division	A	Tottenham Hotspur	D	4-4	44,650	Boyce, Kirkup, Peters, Scott
Nov 19 2001	Premier League	A	Charlton Athletic	D	4-4	23,198	Kitson 3, Defoe
Feb 04 1905	Southern League 1st Division	A	Swindon Town	D	3-3	3,000	Bridgeman, Fletcher, Piercy
Apr 16 1910	Southern League 1st Division	A	Queens Park Rangers	D	3-3	7,000	Curtis, Shea, Waggott
Sep 03 1910	Southern League 1st Division	H	Southend United	D	3-3	15,000	Ashton, Blackburn, Webb
Oct 14 1911	Southern League 1st Division	A	Exeter City	D	3-3	8,000	Shea 2, Webb
Aug 28 1926	1st Division	H	Leicester City	D	3-3	20,615	Earle, Ruffell, Watson
May 07 1927	1st Division	H	Liverpool	D	3-3	10,225	Barrett, Collins, Johnson
Apr 28 1928	1st Division	H	Birmingham	D	3-3	17,917	Barrett 2, Loughlin
Sep 03 1928	1st Division	A	Burnley	D	3-3	17,719	Watson 2, Yews
Dec 15 1928	1st Division	H	Sunderland	D	3-3	16,206	Ruffell 2, Robson
Dec 29 1928	1st Division	A	Sheffield United	D	3-3	21,547	Ruffell, Watson, Yews
Mar 09 1929	1st Division	H	Blackburn Rovers	D	3-3	24,379	Yews 2, Watson
Aug 31 1929	1st Division	A	Blackburn Rovers	D	3-3	21,817	Ball, Watson, Jones (og)
Sep 27 1930	1st Division	H	Sheffield Wednesday	D	3-3	26,487	Gibbins, James, Ruffell
Nov 02 1935	2nd Division	A	Newcastle United	D	3-3	22,873	Mangnall 2, Ruffell
Oct 10 1936	2nd Division	A	Norwich City	D	3-3	16,350	Barrett, Cockroft, Martin
Mar 13 1937	2nd Division	H	Fulham	D	3-3	29,405	Goulden, Morton, Small
Sep 18 1937	2nd Division	A	Southampton	D	3-3	19,478	Small 2, Foxall
Dec 28 1937	2nd Division	H	Norwich City	D	3-3	17,087	Barrett, Green, Williams,
Jan 21 1939	FA Cup 4th round	H	Tottenham Hotspur	D	3-3	42,716	Foxall 2, Macaulay [pen]
Apr 07 1947	2nd Division	H	Bury	D	3-3	22,525	Neary 2, Bainbridge
Aug 19 1950	2nd Division	H	Hull City	D	3-3	30,056	Gazzard, Robinson, Jensen (og)
Feb 24 1951	2nd Division	A	Queens Park Rangers	D	3-3	21,444	Woodgate 2, McGowan
Nov 24 1951	2nd Division	H	Everton	D	3-3	20,141	Gazzard, Kinsell, Woodgate
Apr 05 1952	2nd Division	H	Doncaster Rovers	D	3-3	18,140	Andrews, Barrett, Gazzard
Dec 04 1954	2nd Division	H	Bury	D	3-3	18,092	Musgrove 2, Dick
Dec 18 1954	2nd Division	H	Swansea Town	D	3-3	15,230	Barrett, Hooper [pen], Thomas (og)
Sep 10 1955	2nd Division	A	Leeds United	D	3-3	21,855	Tucker 2, Dare
Mar 03 1956	FA Cup 6th round	A	Tottenham Hotspur	D	3-3	69,111	Dick 3
Apr 07 1956	2nd Division	H	Sheffield Wednesday	D	3-3	17,549	Dick 2, Dare
Dec 01 1956	2nd Division	A	Bury	D	3-3	8,757	Dick, Musgrove, Parker
Sep 17 1960	1st Division	H	Blackpool	D	3-3	23,521	Bond, Musgrove, Woodley
Nov 11 1961	1st Division	H	West Bromwich Albion	D	3-3	18,213	Bond [pen], Musgrove, Sealey
Apr 21 1962	1st Division	H	Arsenal	D	3-3	31,912	Dick, Lansdowne, Scott
Nov 09 1963	1st Division	A	Arsenal	D	3-3	52,852	Byrne 2, Peters
Nov 19 1963	League Cup 4th round	A	Swindon Town	D	3-3	12,050	Boyce, Brabrook, Hurst
Sep 21 1965	League Cup 2nd round	A	Bristol Rovers	D	3-3	18,354	Hurst 2, Byrne
Feb 12 1966	FA Cup 4th round	H	Blackburn Rovers	D	3-3	32,350	Bloomfield, Hurst, Sissons
Jan 28 1967	FA Cup 3rd round	H	Swindon Town	D	3-3	37,400	Hurst 3
Aug 29 1967	1st Division	A	Burnley	D	3-3	16,625	Moore, Peters, Hurst
Oct 06 1969	1st Division	H	Stoke City	D	3-3	27,128	Best, Brooking, Sissons
Nov 14 1970	1st Division	H	Wolverhampton Wanderers	D	3-3	23,978	Best 2, Moore
Dec 11 1971	1st Division	A	Southampton	D	3-3	20,506	Best, Bonds, Brooking
Jan 22 1972	1st Division	H	Derby County	D	3-3	31,045	Brooking, Lampard, Robson

Record in all competitions

	Home						Away						Neutral Grounds						Total					
	Pld	W	D	L	F	A	Pld	W	D	L	F	A	Pld	W	D	L	F	A	Pld	W	D	L	F	A
Division 1	818	394	213	211	1554	1065	818	181	185	452	954	1590	0	0	0	0	0	0	1636	575	398	663	2508	2655
Premier League	384	168	94	122	551	462	384	81	103	200	353	636	0	0	0	0	0	0	768	249	197	322	904	1098
Top Flight Total	1202	562	307	333	2105	1527	1202	262	288	652	1307	2226	0	0	0	0	0	0	2404	824	595	985	3412	3753

	Home						Away						Neutral Grounds						Total					
	Pld	W	D	L	F	A	Pld	W	D	L	F	A	Pld	W	D	L	F	A	Pld	W	D	L	F	A
Division 2	592	351	134	107	1182	603	592	160	156	276	695	978	0	0	0	0	0	0	1184	511	290	383	1877	1581
Championship	69	35	20	14	119	70	69	29	21	19	95	79	0	0	0	0	0	0	138	64	41	33	214	149
Play-off	3	2	1	0	7	2	3	2	0	1	4	1	3	2	0	1	3	2	9	6	1	2	14	5
Southern League	294	177	67	50	580	257	294	68	74	152	307	507	0	0	0	0	0	0	588	245	141	202	887	764
London League	14	12	1	1	42	16	14	7	4	3	22	16	0	0	0	0	0	0	28	19	5	4	64	32
League Total	972	577	223	172	1930	948	972	266	255	451	1123	1581	3	2	0	1	3	2	1947	845	478	624	3056	2531

	Home						Away						Neutral Grounds						Total					
	Pld	W	D	L	F	A	Pld	W	D	L	F	A	Pld	W	D	L	F	A	Pld	W	D	L	F	A
FA Cup	166	92	44	30	336	182	159	44	44	71	170	252	19	12	3	4	31	21	344	148	91	105	537	455
League Cup	111	75	17	19	256	103	93	33	21	39	125	149	4	0	2	2	4	6	208	108	40	60	385	258
Charity Shield	0	0	0	0	0	0	1	0	1	0	2	2	2	0	0	2	0	3	3	0	1	2	2	5
Cup Total	277	167	61	49	592	285	253	77	66	110	297	403	25	12	5	8	35	30	555	256	132	167	924	718

	Home						Away						Neutral Grounds						Total					
	Pld	W	D	L	F	A	Pld	W	D	L	F	A	Pld	W	D	L	F	A	Pld	W	D	L	F	A
European Cup Winners Cup	14	11	1	2	37	15	14	3	5	6	17	23	2	1	0	1	4	4	30	15	6	9	58	42
Anglo-Italian Cup	4	1	2	1	4	3	4	2	0	2	4	3	0	0	0	0	0	0	8	3	2	3	8	6
Intertoto Cup	3	2	0	1	2	1	3	2	1	0	5	2	0	0	0	0	0	0	6	4	1	1	7	3
UEFA Cup	2	1	1	0	3	0	2	1	0	1	3	3	0	0	0	0	0	0	4	2	1	1	6	3
Europe Total	23	15	4	4	46	19	23	8	6	9	29	31	2	1	0	1	4	4	48	24	10	14	79	54

	Home						Away						Neutral Grounds						Total					
	Pld	W	D	L	F	A	Pld	W	D	L	F	A	Pld	W	D	L	F	A	Pld	W	D	L	F	A
Essex Professional Cup	12	9	1	2	31	15	7	2	2	3	12	20	0	0	0	0	0	0	19	11	3	5	43	35
Southern Floodlight Cup	11	8	2	1	30	14	6	3	0	3	17	13	0	0	0	0	0	0	17	11	2	4	47	27
All Members Cup	6	4	0	2	16	9	4	0	1	3	6	12	0	0	0	0	0	0	10	4	1	5	22	21
Watney Cup	0	0	0	0	0	0	1	0	1	0	1	1	0	0	0	0	0	0	1	0	1	0	1	1
Texaco Cup	2	1	0	1	2	2	1	0	0	1	0	2	0	0	0	0	0	0	3	1	0	2	2	4
Minor Cup Total	31	22	3	6	79	40	19	5	4	10	36	48	0	0	0	0	0	0	50	27	7	16	115	88
Total	2505	1343	598	564	4752	2819	2469	618	619	1232	2792	4289	30	15	5	10	42	36	5004	1976	1222	1806	7586	7144

Record against other clubs
League Meetings Only

	Home							Away							Total						
	Pld	W	D	L	F	A	%	Pld	W	D	L	F	A	%	Pld	W	D	L	F	A	%
AFC Bournemouth	1	1	0	0	4	1	100.00%	1	0	1	0	1	1	50.00%	2	1	1	0	5	2	75.00%
Arsenal	57	14	19	24	70	88	41.23%	57	13	13	31	58	102	34.21%	114	27	32	55	128	190	37.72%
Aston Villa	49	22	19	8	95	57	64.29%	49	12	11	26	57	91	35.71%	98	34	30	34	152	148	50.00%
Barnsley	23	18	4	1	57	19	86.96%	23	8	9	6	26	29	54.35%	46	26	13	7	83	48	70.65%
Birmingham	11	3	3	5	17	18	40.91%	11	4	2	5	14	17	45.45%	22	7	5	10	31	35	43.18%
Birmingham City	32	14	8	10	63	38	56.25%	32	6	8	18	30	58	31.25%	64	20	16	28	93	96	43.75%
Blackburn Rovers	48	26	8	14	94	77	62.50%	48	12	8	28	60	102	33.33%	96	38	16	42	154	179	47.92%
Blackpool	22	13	7	2	41	21	75.00%	22	6	4	12	29	42	36.36%	44	19	11	14	70	63	55.68%
Bolton Wanderers	28	15	4	9	61	43	60.71%	28	3	4	21	21	67	17.86%	56	18	8	30	82	110	39.29%
Bradford City	10	5	2	3	19	15	60.00%	10	5	1	4	16	16	55.00%	20	10	3	7	35	31	57.50%
Bradford Park Avenue	12	8	2	2	16	8	75.00%	12	4	1	7	13	21	37.50%	24	12	3	9	29	29	56.25%
Brentford	10	5	2	3	17	10	60.00%	10	2	5	3	12	15	45.00%	20	7	7	6	29	25	52.50%
Brighton and Hove Albion	7	4	2	1	14	5	71.43%	7	2	1	4	6	11	35.71%	14	6	3	5	20	16	53.57%
Bristol City	12	10	1	1	26	5	87.50%	12	2	7	3	15	14	45.83%	24	12	8	4	41	19	66.67%
Bristol Rovers	10	8	1	1	24	9	85.00%	10	7	3	0	20	8	85.00%	20	15	4	1	44	17	85.00%
Burnley	38	23	7	8	71	48	69.74%	38	5	10	23	53	88	26.32%	76	28	17	31	124	136	48.03%
Bury	27	14	6	7	58	32	62.96%	27	6	5	16	35	63	31.48%	54	20	11	23	93	95	47.22%
Cambridge United	4	4	0	0	14	3	100.00%	4	1	1	2	3	5	37.50%	8	5	1	2	17	8	68.75%
Cardiff City	22	12	8	2	36	16	72.73%	22	9	6	7	27	23	54.55%	44	21	14	9	63	39	63.64%
Carlisle United	1	1	0	0	2	0	100.00%	1	1	0	0	1	0	100.00%	2	2	0	0	3	0	100.00%
Charlton Athletic	16	7	3	6	29	20	53.13%	16	1	7	8	18	32	28.13%	32	8	10	14	47	52	40.63%
Chelsea	46	23	8	15	80	64	58.70%	46	12	10	24	61	84	36.96%	92	35	18	39	141	148	47.83%
Chesterfield	9	5	3	1	23	6	72.22%	9	2	2	5	5	14	33.33%	18	7	5	6	28	20	52.78%
Clapton Orient	4	2	0	2	3	3	50.00%	4	2	1	1	3	1	62.50%	8	4	1	3	6	4	56.25%
Coventry City	44	27	8	9	90	40	70.45%	44	15	15	14	48	51	51.14%	88	42	23	23	138	91	60.80%
Crewe Alexandra	2	1	1	0	5	3	75.00%	2	2	0	0	6	2	100.00%	4	3	1	0	11	5	87.50%
Crystal Palace	14	6	5	3	20	11	60.71%	14	6	5	3	26	16	60.71%	28	12	10	6	46	27	60.71%
Derby County	34	13	15	6	57	37	60.29%	34	9	8	17	39	56	38.24%	68	22	23	23	96	93	49.26%
Doncaster Rovers	12	4	5	3	19	15	54.17%	12	4	1	7	13	20	37.50%	24	8	6	10	32	35	45.83%
Everton	59	22	14	23	89	86	49.15%	59	10	11	38	46	119	26.27%	118	32	25	61	135	205	37.71%
Fulham	41	23	10	8	83	48	68.29%	41	14	8	19	53	71	43.90%	82	37	18	27	136	119	56.10%
Gillingham	2	2	0	0	5	2	100.00%	2	1	0	1	1	2	50.00%	4	3	0	1	6	4	75.00%
Grimsby Town	13	11	0	2	30	15	84.62%	13	4	3	6	16	21	42.31%	26	15	3	8	46	36	63.46%
Huddersfield Town	15	5	4	6	26	23	46.67%	15	2	2	11	13	36	20.00%	30	7	6	17	39	59	33.33%
Hull City	21	13	6	2	44	18	76.19%	21	4	9	8	22	30	40.48%	42	17	15	10	66	48	58.33%
Ipswich Town	29	10	11	8	41	33	53.45%	29	12	5	12	43	47	50.00%	58	22	16	20	84	80	51.72%
Leeds United	49	18	17	14	85	69	54.08%	49	6	10	33	49	105	22.45%	98	24	27	47	134	174	38.27%
Leicester City	60	36	14	10	127	72	71.67%	60	15	15	30	73	102	37.50%	120	51	29	40	200	174	54.58%
Leyton Orient	6	5	0	1	11	6	83.33%	6	5	0	1	14	4	83.33%	12	10	0	2	25	10	83.33%
Lincoln City	10	4	4	2	23	13	60.00%	10	5	1	4	22	19	55.00%	20	9	5	6	45	32	57.50%
Liverpool	57	20	15	22	75	81	48.25%	57	3	15	39	30	110	18.42%	114	23	30	61	105	191	33.33%
Luton Town	26	11	8	7	29	19	57.69%	26	6	10	10	30	43	42.31%	52	17	18	17	59	62	50.00%
Manchester City	46	25	9	12	79	50	64.13%	46	9	5	32	58	98	25.00%	92	34	14	44	137	148	44.57%
Manchester United	59	25	19	15	94	85	58.47%	59	12	6	41	58	137	25.42%	118	37	25	56	152	222	41.95%
Middlesbrough	29	17	5	7	46	29	67.24%	29	7	7	15	29	51	36.21%	58	24	12	22	75	80	51.72%
Millwall	12	6	6	0	23	9	75.00%	12	2	5	5	10	14	37.50%	24	8	11	5	33	23	56.25%
Newcastle United	61	30	15	16	104	68	61.48%	61	9	20	32	63	117	31.15%	122	39	35	48	167	185	46.31%

	Home							Away							Total						
	Pld	W	D	L	F	A	%	Pld	W	D	L	F	A	%	Pld	W	D	L	F	A	%
wport County	1	1	0	0	3	0	100.00%	1	0	1	0	1	1	50.00%	2	1	1	0	4	1	75.00%
rthampton Town	1	0	1	0	1	1	50.00%	1	0	0	1	1	2	0.00%	2	0	1	1	2	3	25.00%
rwich City	22	13	5	4	41	23	70.45%	22	3	9	10	28	35	34.09%	44	16	14	14	69	58	52.27%
ttingham Forest	52	32	9	11	113	72	70.19%	52	9	16	27	43	79	32.69%	104	41	25	38	156	151	51.44%
ts County	26	17	3	6	59	27	71.15%	26	6	8	12	23	42	38.46%	52	23	11	18	82	69	54.81%
dham Athletic	11	7	1	3	18	10	68.18%	11	2	5	4	13	20	40.91%	22	9	6	7	31	30	54.55%
ford United	6	4	1	1	14	8	75.00%	6	3	1	2	7	5	58.33%	12	7	2	3	21	13	66.67%
erborough United	2	2	0	0	3	1	100.00%	2	2	0	0	5	1	100.00%	4	4	0	0	8	2	100.00%
rmouth Argyle	18	10	6	2	48	21	72.22%	18	4	7	7	20	28	41.67%	36	14	13	9	68	49	56.94%
t Vale	13	8	4	1	26	8	76.92%	13	4	5	4	16	18	50.00%	26	12	9	5	42	26	63.46%
tsmouth	16	8	3	5	31	21	59.38%	16	6	3	7	15	21	46.88%	32	14	6	12	46	42	53.13%
ston North End	14	9	2	3	33	14	71.43%	14	2	4	8	13	25	28.57%	28	11	6	11	46	39	50.00%
een's Park Rangers	25	13	8	4	43	32	68.00%	25	6	9	10	22	33	42.00%	50	19	17	14	65	65	55.00%
ading	6	3	1	2	9	8	58.33%	6	1	0	5	4	15	16.67%	12	4	1	7	13	23	37.50%
therham United	13	8	2	3	29	13	69.23%	13	4	4	5	15	21	46.15%	26	12	6	8	44	34	57.69%
effield United	39	18	10	11	73	46	58.97%	39	9	8	22	53	86	33.33%	78	27	18	33	126	132	46.15%
effield Wednesday	43	17	12	14	73	69	53.49%	43	10	11	22	46	82	36.05%	86	27	23	36	119	151	44.77%
rewsbury Town	2	1	0	1	4	3	50.00%	2	1	0	1	2	3	50.00%	4	2	0	2	6	6	50.00%
uth Shields	4	3	1	0	5	2	87.50%	4	0	2	2	0	4	25.00%	8	3	3	2	5	6	56.25%
uthampton	46	25	11	10	84	45	66.30%	46	10	16	20	56	78	39.13%	92	35	27	30	140	123	52.72%
uthend United	1	1	0	0	2	0	100.00%	1	0	0	1	0	1	0.00%	2	1	0	1	2	1	50.00%
ockport County	4	3	0	1	9	1	75.00%	4	0	1	3	1	5	12.50%	8	3	1	4	10	6	43.75%
oke City	37	18	12	7	64	34	64.86%	37	10	7	20	38	56	36.49%	74	28	19	27	102	90	50.68%
nderland	39	17	13	9	74	46	60.26%	39	11	8	20	45	67	38.46%	78	28	21	29	119	113	49.36%
ansea City	24	18	5	1	64	21	85.42%	24	4	6	14	32	46	29.17%	48	22	11	15	96	67	57.29%
indon Town	4	1	2	1	3	2	50.00%	4	2	2	0	7	4	75.00%	8	3	4	1	10	6	62.50%
ttenham Hotspur	62	27	15	20	92	84	55.65%	62	15	16	31	82	109	37.10%	124	42	31	51	174	193	46.37%
nmere Rovers	2	2	0	0	8	1	100.00%	2	0	1	1	4	7	25.00%	4	2	1	1	12	8	62.50%
alsall	1	0	1	0	0	0	50.00%	1	0	1	0	1	1	50.00%	2	0	2	0	1	1	50.00%
atford	16	12	2	2	27	14	81.25%	16	9	4	3	22	17	68.75%	32	21	6	5	49	31	75.00%
st Bromwich Albion	41	21	8	12	84	57	60.98%	41	11	8	22	46	75	36.59%	82	32	16	34	130	132	48.78%
gan Athletic	9	5	1	3	16	12	61.11%	9	4	1	4	12	10	50.00%	18	9	2	7	28	22	55.56%
mbledon	12	4	2	6	22	19	41.67%	12	5	5	2	12	10	62.50%	24	9	7	8	34	29	52.08%
lverhampton Wanderers	29	18	7	4	64	28	74.14%	29	8	7	14	34	45	39.66%	58	26	14	18	98	73	56.90%
exham	3	2	1	0	3	1	83.33%	3	0	1	2	5	7	16.67%	6	2	2	2	8	8	50.00%

igure is based on 2pts for a win, 1pt for a draw and is the number of points won divided by the total number of points available)

PART FOUR

MISCELLANEOUS

DEBUT SCORERS

OWN GOALS SCORED BY
WEST HAM PLAYERS

HAT TRICKS

SENDING OFFS

EVER PRESENTS IN THE LEAGUE

YOUNGEST/OLDEST DEBUTANTS

PENALTIES

Miscellaneous
Debut scorers

Player	Date		Competition	Venue	Opponents	Result		No. Goal
William GRASSAM	Sep 1	1900	SL Div 1	H	Gravesend United	W	7-0	4
Fergus HUNT	Sep 1	1900	SL Div 1	H	Gravesend United	W	7-0	1
James REID	Sep 1	1900	SL Div 1	H	Gravesend United	W	7-0	2
George RATCLIFFE	Sep 1	1900	SL Div 1	H	Reading	W	1-0	1
Alex McDONALD	Dec 21	1901	SL Div 1	H	Bristol Rovers	W	2-0	2
William BARNES	Sep 6	1902	SL Div 1	H	Reading	D	1-1	1
Robert BUSH	Apr 15	1903	SL Div 1	H	Kettering Town	D	1-1	1
William KIRBY	Sep 5	1903	SL Div 1	A	Millwall	L	2-4	1
Charles SATTERTHWAITE	Sep 5	1903	SL Div 1	A	Millwall	L	2-4	1
Tommy ALLISON	Sep 7	1903	SL Div 1	H	Kettering Town	W	4-1	1
Jack FLYNN	Sep 1	1904	SL Div 1	H	Millwall	W	3-0	1
John BLACKWOOD	Dec 26	1904	SL Div 1	A	Portsmouth	L	1-4	1
George HILSDON	Feb 11	1905	SL Div 1	H	New Brompton	W	2-0	1
George KITCHEN	Sep 2	1905	SL Div 1	H	Swindon Town	W	1-0	1
Harry STAPLEY	Dec 23	1905	SL Div 1	H	Portsmouth	W	1-0	1
Tommy RANDALL	Apr 27	1907	SL Div 1	H	Fulham	W	4-1	1
Jack FOSTER	Sep 1	1908	SL Div 1	H	Queens Park Rangers	W	2-0	1
Frederick SHREEVE	Oct 24	1908	SL Div 1	H	Northampton Town	W	2-1	1
C. ATKINS	Mar 20	1909	SL Div 1	H	Southend United	W	4-0	1
George WEBB	Apr 9	1909	SL Div 1	H	Leyton	W	1-0	1
George BUTCHER	Mar 2	1910	SL Div 1	A	Watford	L	1-2	1
Albert SCANES	Mar 28	1910	SL Div 1	A	Crystal Palace	W	4-2	2
William KENNEDY	Nov 5	1910	SL Div 1	H	Brighton & Hove Albion	W	3-1	1
Fred HARRISON	Apr 14	1911	SL Div 1	H	Southampton	W	4-1	1
Jack MACKESY	Apr 22	1912	SL Div 1	A	Swindon Town	L	1-3	1
Alfred LEAFE	Sep 6	1913	SL Div 1	H	Swindon Town	L	2-3	2
Arthur STALLARD	Apr 14	1914	SL Div 1	H	Millwall	W	3-2	1
James MOYES	Aug 30	1919	Div 2	H	Lincoln City	D	1-1	1
Robert ALLEN	Nov 1	1919	Div 2	H	Birmingham	L	1-2	1
Syd BISHOP	Dec 25	1920	Div 2	H	Birmingham	D	1-1	1
William JAMES	Jan 22	1921	Div 2	H	Clapton Orient	W	1-0	1
Thomas JACKSON	Sep 3	1921	Div 2	H	Stoke City	W	3-0	1
William WILLIAMS	May 6	1922	Div 2	A	Blackpool	L	1-3	1
Harry HODGES	Sep 10	1923	Div 2	A	Arsenal	L	1-4	1
Samuel JENNINGS	Aug 30	1924	Div 1	H	Preston North End	W	1-0	1
Joseph JOHNSON	Feb 5	1927	Div 1	H	Huddersfield Town	W	3-2	1
James LOUGHLIN	Sep 3	1927	Div 1	H	Huddersfield Town	W	4-2	1
Danny SHONE	Aug 25	1928	Div 1	H	Sheffield United	W	4-0	1
John BALL	Aug 31	1929	Div 1	A	Blackburn Rovers	D	3-3	1
Frederick GAMBLE	Apr 4	1931	Div 1	A	Leicester City	D	1-1	1
Wilf PHILLIPS	Nov 28	1931	Div 1	A	Blackburn Rovers	W	4-2	1
Cliff ETTE	Feb 3	1934	Div 2	H	Preston North End	L	1-3	1
James MARSHALL	Mar 16	1935	Div 2	A	Port Vale	D	2-2	1
David MANGNALL	Mar 16	1935	Div 2	A	Port Vale	D	2-2	1
Tudor MARTIN	Sep 9	1936	Div 2	A	Newcastle United	L	3-5	3
William ADAMS	Nov 21	1936	Div 2	A	Southampton	W	2-0	1
Sam SMALL	Jan 23	1937	Div 2	H	Bury	W	5-1	2

ayer	Date		Competition	Venue	Opponents	Result		No. Goals
eorge PROUDLOCK	Mar 27	1939	Div 2	A	Millwall	W	2-0	1
g GORE	Apr 11	1939	Div 2	A	Bradford Park Avenue	W	2-1	1
chard BELL	Apr 15	1939	Div 2	H	West Bromwich Albion	W	2-1	1
iff HUBBARD	May 6	1939	Div 2	H	Manchester City	W	2-1	1
meric HALL	Jan 5	1946	FAC 3:1	H	Arsenal	W	6-0	2
n BAINBRIDGE	Jan 5	1946	FAC 3:1	H	Arsenal	W	6-0	1
e PAYNE	Dec 7	1946	Div 2	A	Southampton	L	2-4	1
ank NEARY	Feb 8	1947	Div 2	H	Newport County	W	3-0	2
n TUCKER	Oct 4	1947	Div 2	H	Chesterfield	W	4-0	3
anny McGOWAN	Aug 21	1948	Div 2	H	Lincoln City	D	2-2	1
ldie CHAPMAN	Sep 13	1948	Div 2	H	Coventry City	D	2-2	1
l ROBINSON	Jan 15	1949	Div 2	A	West Bromwich Albion	L	1-2	1
an JOHNS	Sep 4	1950	Div 2	A	Cardiff City	L	1-2	1
ert HAWKINS	Sep 1	1951	Div 2	A	Hull City	D	1-1	1
ldie LEWIS	Nov 24	1956	Div 2	H	Leicester City	W	2-1	1
c KEEBLE	Oct 19	1957	Div 2	H	Doncaster Rovers	D	1-1	1
ick BEESLEY	Sep 24	1960	Div 1	A	Everton	L	1-4	1
ger HUGO	Mar 18	1964	Div 1	A	Leicester City	D	2-2	1
ldie PRESLAND	Feb 27	1965	Div 1	H	Liverpool	W	2-1	1
mmy GREAVES	Mar 21	1970	Div 1	A	Manchester City	W	5-1	2
yan ROBSON	Feb 24	1971	Div 1	H	Nottingham Forest	W	2-0	1
ewunmi COKER	Oct 30	1971	Div 1	A	Crystal Palace	W	3-0	1
ly JENNINGS	Sep 7	1974	Div 1	H	Sheffield United	L	1-2	1
an DICKENS	Dec 18	1982	Div 1	A	Notts County	W	2-1	1
ny COTTEE	Jan 1	1983	Div 1	H	Tottenham Hotspur	W	3-0	1
roy ROSENIOR	Mar 19	1988	Div 1	H	Watford	W	1-0	1
artin ALLEN	Aug 26	1989	Div 1	H	Plymouth Argyle	W	3-2	1
ive ALLEN	Apr 4	1992	Div 1	A	Chelsea	L	1-2	1
e CHAPMAN	Sep 18	1993	Prem	A	Blackburn Rovers	W	2-0	1
n HUTCHISON	Aug 31	1994	Prem	H	Newcastle United	L	1-3	1 [Pen]
evor SINCLAIR	Jan 31	1998	Prem	H	Everton	D	2-2	2
n WRIGHT	Aug 15	1998	Prem	A	Sheffield Wednesday	W	1-0	1
ederic KANOUTE	Mar 26	2000	Prem	H	Wimbledon	W	2-1	1
rmain DEFOE	Sep 19	2000	FLC 2:1	A	Walsall	W	1-0	1
avid CONNOLLY	Aug 9	2003	Champ	A	Preston North End	W	2-1	1
n HARLEY	Jan 17	2004	Champ	A	Sheffield United	D	3-3	1
bby ZAMORA	Feb 7	2004	Champ	A	Bradford City	W	2-1	1
avid BELLION	Sep 20	2005	FLC 2	A	Sheffield Wednesday	W	4-2	1
arlton COLE	Aug 19	2006	Prem	H	Charlton Athletic	W	3-1	1
epa BLANCO	Jan 30	2007	Prem	H	Liverpool	L	1-2	1
eddie SEARS	Mar 15	2008	Prem	H	Blackburn Rovers	W	2-1	1
von HINES	Aug 27	2008	FLC 2	H	Macclesfield Town	W	4-1	1
aujo ILAN	Feb 6	2010	Prem	A	Burnley	L	1-2	1
bbie KEANE	Feb 2	2011	Champ	A	Blackpool	W	3-1	1
omas HITZLSPERGER	Feb 21	2011	FAC 5	H	Burnley	W	5-1	1
enri LANSBURY	Sep 10	2011	Champ	H	Portsmouth	W	4-3	1

Miscellaneous
Own goals scored by West Ham United players

Player	Date	Competition	Venue	Opponents	Result	
John BOND	Dec 06 1958	First Division	H	Leeds United	L	2-3
Bobby MOORE	Apr 18 1961	First Division	A	Burnley	D	2-2
John BOND	Oct 09 1961	League Cup 2	H	Aston Villa	L	1-3
John LYALL	Aug 25 1962	First Division	H	Tottenham Hotspur	L	1-6
Ken BROWN	Sep 09 1963	First Division	A	Tottenham Hotspur	L	0-3
Martin PETERS	Oct 10 1964	European Cup Winners Cup	H	La Gantoise	D	1-1
John CHARLES	Oct 02 1965	First Division	A	Fulham	L	0-3
Ken BROWN	Oct 16 1965	First Division	H	Sheffield Wednesday	W	4-2
Eddie BOVINGTON	Dec 01 1965	European Cup Winners Cup	A	Olympiakos	D	2-2
Eddie BOVINGTON	Jan 01 1966	First Division	H	Nottingham Forest	L	0-3
Dennis BURNETT	Oct 15 1966	First Division	A	Fulham	L	2-4
Dennis BURNETT	Oct 29 1966	First Division	A	Sheffield United	L	1-3
Jack BURKETT	Apr 26 1967	First Division	A	Newcastle United	L	0-1
Bobby MOORE	Sep 09 1967	First Division	A	Sunderland	W	5-1
Frank LAMPARD	Aug 08 1969	First Division	H	Arsenal	D	1-1
Billy BONDS	Nov 11 1969	First Division	H	Crystal Palace	W	2-1
Bobby FERGUSON	Aug 26 1972	First Division	A	Liverpool	L	2-3
Frank LAMPARD	Sep 23 1972	First Division	A	Tottenham Hotspur	L	0-1
Tommy TAYLOR	Oct 14 1972	First Division	H	Sheffield United	W	3-1
Billy JENNINGS	Apr 09 1975	FA Cup SF Rep	N	Ipswich Town	W	2-1
Tommy TAYLOR	Mar 22 1977	First Division	A	Ipswich Town	L	1-4
Mick McGIVEN	May 07 1977	First Division	H	Derby County	D	2-2
Kevin LOCK	Sep 10 1977	First Division	H	Queens Park Rangers	D	2-2
Ray STEWART	Oct 07 1981	League Cup 2:1	A	Derby County	W	3-2
Alexander CLARK	Nov 29 1982	League Cup 3 Rep	H	Lincoln City	W	2-1
Geoff PIKE	Mar 12 1983	First Division	A	Liverpool	L	0-3
Tom McALISTER	Dec 22 1984	First Division	H	Southampton	L	2-3
Steve WALFORD	Feb 23 1985	First Division	H	Aston Villa	L	1-2
Ray STEWART	Aug 15 1987	First Division	H	Queens Park Rangers	L	0-3
Julian DICKS	May 07 1988	First Division	A	Newcastle United	L	1-2
Stewart ROBSON	Sep 03 1988	First Division	H	Charlton Athletic	L	1-3
Alvin MARTIN	Oct 21 1989	Second Division	A	Port Vale	D	2-2
Tim BREACKER	Oct 19 1991	First Division	A	Oldham Athletic	D	2-2
Mitchell THOMAS	Sep 20 1992	League Division One	H	Derby County	D	1-1
Alvin MARTIN	Nov 06 1993	Premier League	A	Liverpool	L	0-2
Mike MARSH	Dec 18 1993	Premier League	A	Sheffield Wednesday	L	0-5
Steve POTTS	Aug 31 1994	Premier League	H	Newcastle United	L	1-3
Steve POTTS	Sep 20 1994	League Cup 2:1	A	Walsall	L	1-2
Adrian WHITBREAD	Nov 30 1994	League Cup 4	H	Bolton Wanderers	L	1-3
Ian BISHOP	Dec 16 1995	Premier League	H	Southampton	W	2-1
Ian DOWIE	Dec 18 1996	League Cup 4 Rep	A	Stockport County	L	1-2
Marc RIEPER	Mar 22 1997	Premier League	A	Coventry City	W	3-1
Rio FERDINAND	Nov 09 1997	Premier League	A	Chelsea	L	1-2
Ludek MIKLOSKO	Dec 12 1997	Premier League	A	Derby County	L	0-2
Frank LAMPARD	Nov 14 1998	Premier League	H	Leicester City	W	3-2
Gary CHARLES	Feb 05 2000	Premier League	A	Southampton	L	1-2
Rio FERDINAND	Oct 21 2000	Premier League	H	Arsenal	L	1-2

Player	Date	Competition	Venue	Opponents	Result	
Chistian DAILLY	Feb 12 2001	Premier League	H	Coventry City	D	1-1
Ian PEARCE	Apr 28 2001	Premier League	A	Manchester City	L	0-1
Don HUTCHISON	Sep 29 2001	Premier League	A	Everton	L	0-5
Grant McCANN	Oct 14 2001	Premier League	A	Blackburn Rovers	L	1-7
Sebastien SCHEMMEL	Dec 14 2002	Premier League	A	Manchester United	L	0-3
Hayden MULLINS	Dec 06 2003	Premier League	A	West Bromwich Albion	D	1-1
Tomas REPKA	Jan 31 2004	Championship	H	Rotherham United	W	2-1
Wayne QUINN	Jan 03 2004	FA Cup 3	A	Wigan Athletic	W	2-1
Chistian DAILLY	Mar 21 2004	Championship	A	Millwall	L	1-4
Tomas REPKA	Jan 03 2005	Championship	H	Sheffield United	L	0-2
James WALKER	May 15 2005	Play-off 1:1	H	Ipswich Town	D	2-2
Jonathan SPECTOR	Dec 06 2006	Premier League	H	Wigan Athletic	L	0-2
Anton FERDINAND	Jan 01 2007	Premier League	A	Reading	L	0-6
Hayden MULLINS	Sep 23 2007	League Cup 3	A	Watford	L	0-1
George McCARTNEY	Apr 26 2008	Premier League	H	Newcastle United	D	2-2
Lucus NEILL	Dec 20 2008	Premier League	H	Aston Villa	L	0-1
Hayden MULLINS	Sep 23 2008	League Cup 3	A	Watford	L	0-1
Julian FAUBERT	Oct 26 2008	Premier League	H	Arsenal	L	0-2
Lucas NEILL	Dec 20 2008	Premier League	H	Aston Villa	L	0-1
Robert GREEN	Apr 19 2010	Premier League	A	Liverpool	L	0-3
Carlton COLE	May 02 2010	Premier League	A	Fulham	L	2-3
Matthew UPSON	Aug 21 2010	Premier League	H	Bolton Wanderers	L	1-3
Winston REID	Feb 12 2011	Premier League	A	West Bromwich Albion	D	3-3
Joey O'BRIEN	Jan 30 2013	Premier League	A	Fulham	L	1-3
Guy DEMEL	Dec 07 2013	Premier League	A	Liverpool	L	1-4
Winston REID	Aug 26 2014	League Cup 2	H	Sheffield United	D	1-1
Mark NOBLE	Jan 10 2015	Premier League	A	Swansea City	D	1-1
James COLLINS	Apr 19 2015	Premier League	A	Manchester City	L	0-2

Miscellaneous
Hat tricks

Goals	Player	Date	Competition	Venue	Opponents	Result	
6	Vic WATSON	Feb 09 1929	Div 1	H	Leeds United	W	8-2
6	Geoff HURST	Oct 19 1968	Div 1	H	Sunderland	W	8-0
5	Brian DEAR	Apr 16 1965	Div 1	H	West Bromwich Albion	W	6-1
5	Syd PUDDEFOOT	Jan 10 1914	FA Cup	H	Chesterfield	W	8-1
4	William GRASSAM	Sep 01 1900	SL Div 1	H	Gravesend United	W	7-0
4	Danny SHEA	Dec 28 1908	SL Div 1	H	Plymouth Argyle	W	4-0
4	Danny SHEA	Dec 31 1910	SL Div 1	A	Southend United	W	6-0
4	Syd PUDDEFOOT	Apr 02 1920	Div 2	H	Nottingham Forest	W	5-1
4	Syd PUDDEFOOT	Nov 13 1920	Div 2	H	Sheffield Wednesday	W	4-0
4	Syd PUDDEFOOT	Jan 01 1921	Div 2	H	Coventry City	W	7-0
4	Vic WATSON	Mar 31 1923	Div 2	A	Crystal Palace	W	5-1
4	Vic WATSON	Jan 25 1930	FA Cup	H	Leeds United	W	4-1
4	Vic WATSON	Sep 01 1930	Div 1	H	Liverpool	W	7-0
4	Johnny DICK	Mar 08 1958	Div 2	H	Rotherham United	W	8-0
4	Vic KEEBLE	Oct 04 1958	Div 1	H	Blackburn Rovers	W	6-3
4	Geoff HURST	Nov 05 1966	Div 1	H	Fulham	W	6-1
4	Geoff HURST	Oct 11 1967	FL Cup	H	Bolton Wanderers	W	4-1
4	David CROSS	Apr 11 1981	Div 2	A	Grimsby Town	W	5-1
4	David CROSS	Sep 02 1981	Div 1	A	Tottenham Hotspur	W	4-0
4	Tony COTTEE	Oct 25 1983	FL Cup	H	Bury	W	10-0
4	Leroy ROSENIOR	Nov 09 1988	Simod Cup	H	West Bromwich Albion	W	5-2
3	William GRASSAM	Dec 12 1900	FA Cup	A	Clapton	W	3-2
3	Fred CORBETT	Sep 30 1901	SL Div 1	H	Wellingborough Town	W	4-2
3	Charles SATTERTHWAITE	Nov 28 1903	FA Cup	A	Chatham	W	5-0
3	Jack FLETCHER	Oct 22 1904	SL Div 1	H	Wellingborough Town	W	4-0
3	Christopher CARRICK	Jan 28 1905	SL Div 1	H	Luton Town	W	6-2
3	Lionel WATSON	Sep 22 1906	SL Div 1	H	Luton Town	W	5-1
3	William GRASSAM	Oct 27 1906	SL Div 1	A	Portsmouth	L	3-4
3	Lionel WATSON	Dec 22 1906	SL Div 1	A	Fulham	W	4-1
3	Arthur WINTERHALDER	Dec 29 1906	SL Div 1	H	Tottenham Hotspur	W	4-2
3	Jack FOSTER	Oct 10 1908	SL Div 1	H	Portsmouth	W	3-1
3	Danny SHEA	Mar 08 1909	SL Div 1	H	Swindon Town	W	4-2
3	Danny SHEA	Sep 11 1909	SL Div 1	H	Brentford	W	3-2
3	Thomas CALDWELL	Oct 04 1909	SL Div 1	H	Bristol Rovers	W	5-0
3	George WEBB	Feb 05 1910	FA Cup	A	Wolverhampton Wanderers	W	5-1
3	George WEBB	Feb 04 1911	FA Cup	H	Preston North End	W	3-0
3	George WEBB	Mar 18 1911	SL Div 1	H	Exeter City	W	4-1
3	Danny SHEA	Oct 21 1911	SL Div 1	H	Brentford	W	7-4
3	William KENNEDY	Oct 21 1911	SL Div 1	H	Brentford	W	7-4
3	Danny SHEA	Apr 05 1912	SL Div 1	H	Norwich City	W	4-0
3	Alfred LEAFE	Nov 01 1913	SL Div 1	A	Coventry City	W	4-2
3	Syd PUDDEFOOT	Jan 03 1914	SL Div 1	H	Bristol Rovers	W	6-1
3	Syd PUDDEFOOT	Jan 02 1915	SL Div 1	H	Exeter City	W	4-1
3	Syd PUDDEFOOT	Jan 31 1920	FA Cup	H	Bury	W	6-0
3	Syd PUDDEFOOT	Feb 07 1920	Div 2	H	Port Vale	W	3-1
3	Alfred LEAFE	Nov 27 1920	Div 2	H	Stockport County	W	5-0
3	Syd PUDDEFOOT	Feb 05 1921	Div 2	H	Leeds United	W	3-0

Goals	Player	Date	Competition	Venue	Opponents	Result	
3	Vic WATSON	Dec 30 1922	Div 2	A	Coventry City	W	3-1
3	William MOORE	Feb 15 1923	Div 2	A	Leicester City	W	6-0
3	Stanley EARLE	Dec 25 1925	Div 1	H	Aston Villa	W	5-2
3	Vic WATSON	Nov 13 1926	Div 1	H	Aston Villa	W	5-1
3	Vic WATSON	Jan 08 1927	FA Cup	H	Tottenham Hotspur	W	3-2
3	Vic WATSON	Mar 07 1927	Div 1	H	Arsenal	W	7-0
3	VIVIAN GIBBINS	Dec 24 1927	Div 1	H	Newcastle United	W	5-2
3	Vic WATSON	Mar 12 1928	Div 1	H	Leicester City	W	4-0
3	Vivian GIBBINS	Apr 10 1929	Div 1	A	Everton	W	4-0
3	Vic WATSON	Dec 21 1929	Div 1	H	Aston Villa	W	5-2
3	Vic WATSON	Mar 22 1930	Div 1	H	Leeds United	W	3-0
3	Vic WATSON	Apr 26 1930	Div 1	A	Aston Villa	W	3-2
3	Vivian GIBBINS	Oct 11 1930	Div 1	H	Manchester United	W	5-1
3	James RUFFELL	Feb 07 1931	Div 1	H	Grimsby Town	L	3-4
3	James RUFFELL	Dec 05 1931	Div 1	H	Everton	W	4-2
3	Fred NORRIS	Oct 15 1932	Div 2	H	Oldham Athletic	W	5-2
3	Vic WATSON	Oct 29 1932	Div 2	H	Burnley	D	4-4
3	Vic WATSON	Sep 23 1933	Div 2	H	Preston North End	W	6-0
3	Vic WATSON	Oct 28 1933	Div 2	H	Lincoln City	W	4-1
3	Edward FENTON	Mar 17 1934	Div 2	H	Bury	W	3-1
3	Vic WATSON	Mar 31 1934	Div 2	H	Fulham	W	5-1
3	Vic WATSON	Dec 01 1934	Div 2	H	Notts County	W	4-0
3	David MANGNALL	Sep 07 1935	Div 2	H	Nottingham Forest	W	5-2
3	David MANGNALL	Dec 28 1935	Div 2	H	Norwich City	W	3-2
3	Harry LEWIS	Feb 01 1936	Div 2	H	Bury	W	6-0
3	Tudor MARTIN	Sep 09 1936	Div 2	A	Newcastle United	W	5-3
3	Archibald MACAULAY	Sep 24 1938	Div 2	H	Tranmere Rovers	W	6-1
3	Sam SMALL	Mar 11 1939	Div 2	A	Norwich City	W	6-2
3	Frank NEARY	Mar 15 1947	Div 2	H	West Bromwich Albion	W	3-2
3	Ken TUCKER	Oct 04 1947	Div 2	H	Chesterfield	W	4-0
3	Bill STEPHENS	Mar 26 1948	Div 2	A	Cardiff City	W	3-0
3	Bill ROBINSON	Apr 15 1949	Div 2	H	Leicester City	W	4-1
3	Bill ROBINSON	Sep 30 1950	Div 2	H	Sheffield United	L	3-5
3	Terry WOODGATE	Dec 25 1950	Div 2	H	Leeds United	W	3-1
3	Bert HAWKINS	Dec 15 1951	Div 2	H	Queens Park Rangers	W	4-2
3	Ken TUCKER	Jan 19 1952	Div 2	H	Sheffield United	W	5-1
3	Fred KEARNS	Jan 03 1953	Div 2	H	Bury	W	3-2
3	Fred KEARNS	Aug 22 1953	Div 2	H	Leicester City	W	4-1
3	Dave SEXTON	Aug 31 1953	Div 2	H	Rotherham United	W	3-0
3	Tommy DIXON	Sep 14 1953	Div 2	H	Swansea Town	W	4-1
3	John DICK	Nov 07 1953	Div 2	H	Bury	W	5-0
3	John DICK	Jan 22 1955	Div 2	A	Bristol Rovers	W	4-2
3	Dave SEXTON	Feb 05 1955	Div 2	H	Plymouth Argyle	W	6-1
3	Ken TUCKER	Oct 08 1955	Div 2	H	Plymouth Argyle	W	4-0
3	Harry HOOPER	Oct 22 1955	Div 2	H	Doncaster Rovers	W	6-1
3	Albert FOAN	Jan 07 1956	FA Cup	H	Preston North End	W	5-2
3	John DICK	Mar 03 1956	FA Cup	H	Tottenham Hotspur	D	3-3
3	Billy DARE	Aug 31 1957	Div 2	A	Bristol Rovers	W	3-2
3	Vic KEEBLE	Nov 16 1957	Div 2	H	Stoke City	W	5-0
3	John SMITH	Dec 28 1957	Div 2	H	Bristol Rovers	W	6-1
3	Vic KEEBLE	Jan 04 1958	FA Cup	H	Blackpool	W	5-1

Goals	Player	Date	Competition	Venue	Opponents	Result	
3	John DICK	Mar 07 1959	Div 1	H	West Bromwich Albion	W	3-1
3	John DICK	Nov 21 1959	Div 1	H	Wolverhampton Wanderers	W	3-2
3	John BOND	Feb 06 1960	Div 1	H	Chelsea	W	4-2
3	Malcolm MUSGROVE	Oct 22 1960	Div 1	H	Preston North End	W	5-2
3	Dave DUNMORE	Nov 05 1960	Div 1	H	Arsenal	W	6-0
3	Johnny BYRNE	Sep 26 1962	FL Cup	H	Plymouth Argyle	W	6-0
3	Johnny BYRNE	Dec 16 1963	FL Cup	H	Workington	W	6-0
3	Johnny BYRNE	Feb 22 1964	Div 1	H	Sheffield Wednesday	W	4-3
3	Johnny BYRNE	Sep 12 1964	Div 1	H	Tottenham Hotspur	W	3-2
3	Geoff HURST	Dec 11 1965	Div 1	H	Newcastle United	W	4-3
3	John SISSONS	Nov 07 1966	FL Cup	H	Leeds United	W	7-0
3	Geoff HURST	Nov 07 1966	FL Cup	H	Leeds United	W	7-0
3	Geoff HURST	Jan 28 1967	FA Cup	H	Swindon Town	D	3-3
3	BRIAN DEAR	Dec 26 1967	Div 1	H	Leicester City	W	4-2
3	Trevor BROOKING	Apr 06 1968	Div 1	H	Newcastle United	W	5-0
3	Martin PETERS	Aug 31 1968	Div 1	H	West Bromwich Albion	W	4-0
3	Geoff HURST	Sep 04 1968	FL Cup	H	Bolton Wanderers	W	7-2
3	Geoff HURST	Oct 03 1970	Div 1	H	Burnley	W	3-1
3	Bryan ROBSON	Nov 17 1971	FL Cup	H	Sheffield United	W	5-0
3	Geoff HURST	Feb 14 1972	FA Cup	H	Hereford United	W	3-1
3	Bryan ROBSON	Apr 20 1973	Div 1	H	Southampton	W	4-3
3	Billy BONDS	Mar 02 1974	Div 1	H	Chelsea	W	3-0
3	Bobby GOULD	Sep 18 1974	FL Cup	H	Tranmere Rovers	W	6-0
3	Billy JENNINGS	Dec 20 1975	Div 1	H	Stoke City	W	3-1
3	David CROSS	Mar 24 1978	Div 1	H	Ipswich Town	W	3-0
3	David CROSS	Aug 19 1978	Div 2	H	Notts County	W	5-2
3	Bryan ROBSON	Oct 07 1978	Div 2	H	Millwall	W	3-0
3	Billy LANSDOWNE Jnr.	Oct 08 1979	FL Cup	H	Southend United	W	5-1
3	David CROSS	Oct 01 1980	ECWC 1:2	H	Castilla	W	5-1
3	Paul GODDARD	Apr 21 1981	Div 2	H	Queens Park Rangers	W	3-0
3	Paul GODDARD	Sep 22 1981	Div 1	H	Southampton	W	4-2
3	Francois Van Der ELST	Dec 07 1982	FL Cup	A	Notts County	D	3-3
3	David SWINDLEHURST	Sep 10 1983	Div 1	H	Coventry City	W	5-2
3	Paul GODDARD	Jan 05 1985	FA Cup	H	Port Vale	W	4-1
3	Tony COTTEE	Mar 06 1985	FA Cup	H	Wimbledon	W	5-1
3	Alvin MARTIN	Apr 21 1986	Div 1	H	Newcastle United	W	8-1
3	Tony COTTEE	Sep 13 1986	Div 1	A	Queens Park Rangers	W	3-2
3	Tony COTTEE	Oct 07 1986	FL Cup	H	Preston North End	W	4-1
3	Jimmy QUINN	Mar 21 1990	Div 2	H	Sheffield United	W	5-0
3	Frank McAVENNIE	May 02 1992	Div 1	H	Nottingham Forest	W	3-0
3	Tony COTTEE	Dec 17 1994	Prem	H	Manchester City	W	3-0
3	Paul KITSON	May 03 1997	Prem	H	Sheffield Wednesday	W	5-1
3	John HARTSON	Sep 29 1997	FL Cup	H	Huddersfield Town	W	3-0
3	Frank LAMPARD Jnr.	Nov 19 1997	FL Cup	H	Walsall	W	4-1
3	Paul KITSON	Nov 19 2001	Prem	A	Charlton Athletic	D	4-4
3	Jermain DEFOE	Sep 23 2003	FL Cup	A	Cardiff City	W	3-2
3	Matthew ETHERINGTON	Mar 09 2004	Champ	H	Wimbledon	W	5-0
3	Marlon HAREWOOD	Sep 12 1005	Prem	H	Aston Villa	W	4-0
3	Victor OBINNA	Jan 30 2011	FA Cup	H	Nottingham Forest	W	3-2
3	Ricardo VAZ TE	Apr 14 2012	Champ	H	Brighton & Hove Albion	W	6-0
3	Kevin NOLAN	May 19 2013	Prem	H	Reading	W	4-2

Miscellaneous
Sending offs

Player	Date		Competition	Venue	Opponents	Result	
Henry HIRD	Oct 30	1897	Lond	A	Leyton	W	3-1
Matthew KINGSLEY	Mar 25	1905	SL Div 1	A	Brighton & Hove Albion	L	1-3
Frank PIERCY	Feb 22	1908	SL Div 1	H	Millwall	L	0-2
Frederick SHREEVE	Apr 1	1911	SL Div 1	H	Bristol Rovers	D	2-2
Thomas BRANDON	Dec 27	1913	SL Div 1	A	Swindon Town	L	1-4
Jack TRESADERN	Sep 20	1919	Div 2	H	Rotherham County	W	2-1
George KAY	Feb 11	1920	Div 2	A	Bury	L	0-1
William COPE	Feb 26	1921	Div 2	A	Bristol City	L	0-1
Terry WOODGATE	Oct 6	1951	Div 2	A	Rotherham United	L	1-2
Noel CANTWELL	Dec 10	1955	Div 2	A	Bristol Rovers	D	1-1
Ken TUCKER	Jan 21	1956	Div 2	A	Fulham	L	1-3
Bobby MOORE	Nov 4	1961	Div 1	A	Manchester City	W	5-3
Harry REDKNAPP	Oct 12	1968	Div 1	A	Leeds United	L	0-2
Billy BONDS	Sep 9	1970	FLC 2	A	Hull City	W	1-0
Ted MacDOUGALL	Oct 6	1973	Div 1	H	Burnley	L	0-1
Keith ROBSON	Dec 27	1975	Div 1	H	Ipswich Town	L	1-2
Derek HALES	Mar 11	1978	Div 1	H	Wolverhampton Wanderers	L	1-2
David CROSS	Sep 16	1978	Div 2	H	Bristol Rovers	W	2-0
Billy BONDS	Apr 22	1980	Div 2	H	Birmingham City	L	1-2
Paul ALLEN	Dec 1	1981	FLC 3 2 Rep	H	West Bromwich Albion	L	0-1
Frank LAMPARD	Oct 23	1982	Div 1	A	Brighton & Hove Albion	L	1-3
Alvin MARTIN	Nov 27	1982	Div 1	H	Everton	W	2-0
Ray STEWART	Dec 4	1982	Div 1	A	Aston Villa	L	0-1
David SWINDLEHURST	Oct 27	1984	Div 1	H	Arsenal	W	3-1
Ray STEWART	Jan 18	1986	Div 1	A	Liverpool	L	1-3
Alvin MARTIN	Mar 15	1986	Div 1	A	Arsenal	L	0-1
Alvin MARTIN	Sep 20	1986	Div 1	H	Luton Town	W	2-0
Frank McAVENNIE	Feb 25	1987	FAC 5 Rep	H	Sheffield Wednesday	L	0-2
Mark WARD	Sep 12	1987	Div 1	A	Wimbledon	D	1-1
Mark WARD	Dec 5	1987	Div 1	H	Southampton	W	2-1
Leroy ROSENIOR	May 2	1988	Div 1	H	Chelsea	W	4-1
Mark WARD	Feb 18	1989	FAC 5	A	Charlton Athletic	W	1-0
David KELLY	Sep 2	1989	Div 2	A	Hull City	D	1-1
Julian DICKS	Nov 22	1989	FLC 4	H	Wimbledon	W	1-0
Martin ALLEN	Jan 17	1990	FLC 5	H	Derby County	D	1-1
Frank McAVENNIE	Mar 20	1991	Div 2	H	Bristol City	W	1-0
Tony GALE	Apr 14	1991	FAC SF	A	Nottingham Forest	L	0-4
Colin FOSTER	Sep 21	1991	Div 1	H	Manchester City	L	1-2
Tim BREACKER	Dec 7	1991	Div 1	A	Everton	L	0-4
Mike SMALL	Aug 16	1992	Div 1	A	Barnsley	W	1-0
Julian DICKS	Aug 29	1992	Div 1	A	Newcastle United	L	0-2
Julian DICKS	Oct 4	1992	Div 1	A	Wolverhampton Wanderers	D	0-0
George PARRIS	Oct 24	1992	Div 1	H	Swindon Town	L	0-1
Trevor MORLEY	Nov 24	1992	AIC Grp	H	Reggiana	W	2-0
Matthew RUSH	Dec 16	1992	AIC Grp	H	Pisa SC	D	0-0
Julian DICKS	Jan 10	1993	Div 1	A	Derby County	W	2-0
Jeroen BOERE	Sep 25	1993	Prem	A	Newcastle United	L	0-2

Player	Date		Competition	Venue	Opponents	Result	
Tony COTTEE	Sep 10	1994	Prem	A	Liverpool	D	0-0
Don HUTCHISON	Nov 5	1994	Prem	H	Leicester City	W	1-0
Alvin MARTIN *	Jan 23	1995	Prem	H	Sheffield Wednesday	L	0-2
Tim BREACKER	Jan 23	1995	Prem	H	Sheffield Wednesday	L	0-2
Martin ALLEN	May 3	1995	Prem	H	Queens Park Rangers	D	0-0
Marco BOOGERS	Aug 23	1995	Prem	A	Manchester United	L	1-2
Julian DICKS	Sep 16	1995	Prem	A	Arsenal	L	0-1
Ludek MIKLOSKO	Dec 11	1995	Prem	A	Everton	L	0-3
Steve POTTS	Mar 18	1996	Prem	A	Newcastle United	L	0-3
Marc RIEPER	Sep 21	1996	Prem	A	Nottingham Forest	W	2-0
Michael HUGHES	Mar 1	1997	Prem	A	Leeds United	L	0-1
Steve LOMAS	Dec 20	1997	Prem	A	Blackburn Rovers	L	0-3
Samassi ABOU	Jan 17	1998	Prem	A	Tottenham Hotspur	L	0-1
John HARTSON	Feb 21	1998	Prem	A	Bolton Wanderers	D	1-1
John HARTSON	Apr 11	1998	Prem	H	Derby County	D	0-0
David UNSWORTH	May 5	1998	Prem	A	Crystal Palace	D	3-3
Neil RUDDOCK	Dec 5	1998	Prem	A	Leeds United	L	0-4
John MONCUR	Apr 24	1999	Prem	A	Tottenham Hotspur	W	2-1
Ian WRIGHT	May 1	1999	Prem	H	Leeds United	L	1-5
Shaka HISLOP	May 1	1999	Prem	H	Leeds United	L	1-5
Steve LOMAS	May 1	1999	Prem	H	Leeds United	L	1-5
John MONCUR	Sep 25	1999	Prem	A	Coventry City	L	0-1
Marc-Vivien FOE	Oct 3	1999	Prem	H	Arsenal	W	2-1
Shaka HISLOP	Oct 17	1999	Prem	A	Middlesbrough	L	0-2
Javier MARGAS	Nov 7	1999	Prem	A	Chelsea	D	0-0
Steve LOMAS	Dec 6	1999	Prem	A	Tottenham Hotspur	D	0-0
Igor STIMAC	Mar 18	2000	Prem	H	Chelsea	D	0-0
Trevor SINCLAIR	May 2	2000	Prem	A	Arsenal	L	1-2
Marc-Vivien FOE	May 14	2000	Prem	H	Leeds United	D	0-0
Igor STIMAC	Aug 23	2000	Prem	H	Leicester City	L	0-1
Stuart PEARCE	Mar 31	2001	Prem	H	Everton	L	0-2
Tomas REPKA	Sep 15	2001	Prem	A	Middlesbrough	L	0-2
Tomas REPKA	Oct 14	2001	Prem	A	Blackburn Rovers	L	1-7
John MONCUR	Jan 6	2002	FAC 3	A	Macclesfield Town	W	3-0
Paolo DI CANIO	Jan 20	2002	Prem	A	Chelsea	L	1-5
Ian PEARCE	Sep 15	2002	Prem	A	Tottenham Hotspur	L	2-3
Tomas REPKA	Dec 26	2002	Prem	H	Fulham	D	1-1
Steve LOMAS	Jan 19	2003	Prem	A	Arsenal	L	1-3
Frederic KANOUTE	Feb 8	2003	Prem	A	Leeds United	L	0-1
Ian PEARCE	Apr 19	2003	Prem	A	Bolton Wanderers	L	0-1
Jermain DEFOE	Sep 20	2003	Champ	A	Gillingham	L	0-2
Jermain DEFOE	Nov 8	2003	Champ	H	West Bromwich Albion	L	3-4
Jermain DEFOE	Dec 20	2003	Champ	A	Walsall	D	1-1
Matthew ETHERINGTON	Feb 21	2004	Champ	A	Norwich City	D	1-1
Stephen BYWATER	Mar 21	2004	Champ	A	Millwall	L	1-4
David CONNOLLY	Apr 12	2004	Champ	A	Crystal Palace	L	0-1
Rufus BREVETT	Aug 7	2004	Champ	A	Leicester City	D	0-0
Chris COHEN	Aug 28	2004	Champ	H	Burnley	W	1-0
Steve LOMAS	Aug 30	2004	Champ	A	Coventry City	L	1-2
Hayden MULLINS	Nov 13	2004	Champ	H	Brighton & Hove Albion	L	0-1
Marlon HAREWOOD	Nov 21	2004	Champ	A	Millwall	L	0-1

Player	Date		Competition	Venue	Opponents	Result	
Tomas REPKA	Mar 5	2005	Champ	H	Preston North End	L	1-2
Paul KONCHESKEY *	Aug 20	2005	Prem	A	Newcastle United	D	0-0
Hayden MULLINS	Apr 26	2006	Prem	H	Liverpool	L	1-2
Paul KONCHESKEY	Dec 23	2006	Prem	A	Fulham	D	0-0
Bobby ZAMORA	Jan 13	2007	Prem	H	Fulham	D	3-3
Lee BOWYER *	Feb 9	2008	Prem	H	Birmingham City	D	1-1
Luis BOA MORTE	Mar 9	2008	Prem	A	Tottenham Hotspur	L	0-4
Mark NOBLE	Aug 24	2008	Prem	A	Manchester City	L	0-3
Carlton COLE	Oct 26	2008	Prem	H	Arsenal	L	0-2
Carlton COLE	Mar 4	2009	Prem	A	Wigan Athletic	W	1-0
James TOMKINS	May 16	2009	Prem	A	Everton	L	1-3
Scott PARKER	Oct 25	2009	Prem	H	Arsenal	D	2-2
Radoslav KOVAC	Oct 31	2009	Prem	A	Sunderland	D	2-2
Mark NOBLE	Dec 12	2009	Prem	A	Birmingham City	L	0-1
Victor OBINNA	Jan 11	2011	FLC SF:1	H	Birmingham City	W	2-1
Frederic PIQUIONNE	Jan 22	2011	Prem	A	Everton	D	2-2
Callum McNAUGHTON	Aug 24	2011	FLC 1	H	Aldershot Town	L	1-2
Frederic PIQUIONNE	Sep 10	2011	Champ	H	Portsmouth	W	4-3
Joey O'BRIEN	Dec 10	2011	Champ	A	Reading	L	0-3
Jack COLLISON	Dec 10	2011	Champ	A	Reading	L	0-3
Kevin NOLAN	Feb 4	2012	Champ	H	Millwall	W	2-1
Matthew TAYLOR	Feb 14	2012	Champ	H	Southampton	D	1-1
Robert GREEN *	Feb 21	2012	Champ	A	Blackpool	W	4-1
Carlton COLE *	Dec 22	2012	Prem	H	Everton	L	1-2
Mark NOBLE	Sep 21	2013	Prem	H	Everton	L	2-3
Kevin NOLAN	Dec 7	2013	Prem	A	Liverpool	L	1-4
Kevin NOLAN	Jan 1	2014	Prem	A	Fulham	L	1-2
James TOMKINS	Jan 11	2014	Prem	A	Cardiff City	W	2-0
Andy CARROLL	Feb 1	2014	Prem	H	Swansea City	W	2-0
James COLLINS	Aug 16	2014	Prem	H	Tottenham Hotspur	L	0-1
ADRIAN San Miguel del Castillo *	Feb 11	2015	Prem	A	Southampton	D	0-0
Morgan AMALFITANO	Feb 14	2015	FAC 5	A	West Bromwich Albion	L	0-4

* Rescinded

Miscellaneous
Ever present in League/Premier League

Season	Player	Games Played
1921-22	Percy ALLEN	42
1922-23	William MOORE	42
1923-24	William HENDERSON	42
1924-25	James RUFFELL	42
1925-26	Jim BARRETT Snr.	42
1926-27	Jim BARRETT Snr., Jimmy COLLINS, Stanley EARLE, Victor WATSON	42
1927-28	Jimmy COLLINS, Tommy YEWS	42
1933-34	Joe COCKROFT, John MORTON	42
1934-35	Alfred CHALKLEY, Joe COCKROFT, Albert WALKER	42
1935-36	Joe COCKROFT	42
1936-37	Joe COCKROFT, Len GOULDEN	42
1937-38	Charlie BICKNELL	42
1947-48	Norman CORBETT, Steve FORDE, Ernie GREGORY, Eric PARSONS	42
1948-49	Eric PARSONS	42
1949-50	Ernie GREGORY	42
1950-51	Terry WOODGATE	42
1952-53	Ernie GREGORY	42
1953-54	Malcolm ALLISON	42
1957-58	Andy MALCOLM	42
1958-59	John BOND, Ken BROWN, Noel CANTWELL, Mike GRICE, Andy MALCOLM	42
1960-61	Ken BROWN	42
1964-65	Geoff HURST, Jim STANDEN	42
1968-69	Billy BONDS, Geoff HURST, Martin PETERS, Alan STEPHENSON	42
1969-70	Billy BONDS	42
1971-72	Clyde BEST, Billy BONDS, Bryan ROBSON, Tommy TAYLOR	42
1972-73	Bobby MOORE, Bryan ROBSON	42
1973-74	Frank LAMPARD Snr.	42
1974-75	Mervyn DAY	42
1975-76	Tommy TAYLOR	42
1976-77	Trevor BROOKING, Mervyn DAY	42
1977-78	Tommy TAYLOR	42
1978-79	Paul BRUSH	42
1980-81	Phil PARKES, Geoff PIKE	42
1981-82	Ray STEWART	42
1982-83	Phil PARKES	42
1983-84	Phil PARKES, Ray STEWART	42
1985-86	Tony GALE, Phil PARKES, Mark WARD	42
1986-87	Tony COTTEE	42
1987-88	Tony COTTEE	40
1990-91	Ludek MIKLOSKO	46
1992-93	Ludek MIKLOSKO, Steve POTTS, Kevin KEEN	46
1993-94	Ludek MIKLOSKO	42
1994-95	Ludek MIKLOSKO, Steve POTTS	42
1998-99	Frank LAMPARD Jnr.	38
2001-02	Christian DAILLY	38
2002-03	David JAMES	38
2007-08	Robert GREEN, George McCARTNEY	38
2008-09	Robert GREEN	38
2009-10	Robert GREEN	38
2012-13	Jussi JAASKELAINEN	38
2013-14	Mark NOBLE	38
2014-15	Aaron CRESSWELL, ADRIAN del CASTILLO	38

Youngest / oldest debutant

Youngest debutant

	Player	Age	Opponents	Venue	Competition	Date	Result	
1	William WILLIAMS	16 yr 221 days	Blackpool	A	Div 2	06 May 1922	L	1-3
2	Chris COHEN	16 yr 283 days	Sunderland	H	Div 1	13 Dec 2003	W	3-2
3	Robert ALLEN	16 yr 363 days	Birmingham	H	Div 2	01 Nov 1919	L	1-2
4	Neil FINN	17 yr 3 days	Manchester City	A	Prem	01 Jan 1996	L	1-2
5	Paul ALLEN	17 yr 28 days	Southend United	H	FLC 3	25 Sep 1979	D	1-1
6	Joe COLE	17 yr 55 days	Swansea City	H	FAC 3	02 Jan 1999	D	1-1
7	Martin BRITT	17 yr 107 days	Blackburn Rovers	H	Div 1	04 May 1963	L	0-1
8	Mark NOBLE	17 yr 109 days	Southend United	H	FLC 2	24 Aug 2004	W	2-0
9	Reece BURKE	17 yr 124 days	Nottingham Forest	A	FAC 3	05 Jan 2014	L	0-5
10	Bobby MOORE	17 yr 149 days	Manchester United	H	Div 1	08 Sep 1958	W	3-2

Youngest Premier League

	Player	Age	Opponents	Venue	Competition	Date	Result	
1	Neil FINN	17 yr 3 days	Manchester City	A	Prem	01 Jan 1996	L	1-2
2	Joe COLE	17 yr 63 days	Manchester United	A	Prem	10 Jan 1999	L	1-4
3	Rio FERDINAND	17 yr 180 days	Sheffield Wednesday	H	Prem	05 May 1996	D	1-1
4	Frank LAMPARD Jnr	17 yr 225 days	Coventry City	H	Prem	31 Jan 1996	W	3-2
5	Frank NOUBLE	17 yr 325 days	Wolverhampton Wanderers	A	Prem	15 Aug 2009	W	2-0
6	Michael CARRICK	18 yr 31 days	Bradford City	A	Prem	28 Aug 1999	W	3-0
7	Mark NOBLE	18 yr 97 days	Blackburn Rovers	H	Prem	13 Aug 2005	W	3-1
8	Freddie SEARS	18 yr 109 days	Blackburn Rovers	H	Prem	15 Mar 2008	W	2-1
9	Josh PAYNE	18 yr 116 days	Blackburn Rovers	A	Prem	21 Mar 2009	D	1-1
10	Glen JOHNSON	18 yr 151 days	Charlton Athletic	A	Prem	22 Jan 2003	L	2-4

Oldest debutant

	Player	Age	Opponents	Venue	Competition	Date	Result	
1	Teddy SHERINGHAM	38 yr 128 days	Leicester City	A	Champ	07 Aug 2004	D	0-0
2	Les SEALEY	37 yr 352 days	Arsenal	A	Prem	16 Sep 1995	L	0-1
3	Robert LEE	37 yr 189 days	Preston North End	A	Champ	09 Aug 2003	W	2-1
4	Jussi JAASKELAINEN	37 yr 122 days	Aston Villa	H	Prem	18 Aug 2012	W	1-0
5	Stuart PEARCE	37 yr 105 days	Tottenham Hotspur	H	Prem	07 Aug 1999	W	1-0
6	Leslie BENNETT	36 yr 349 days	Derby County	H	Div 2	25 Dec 1954	W	1-0
7	Jack MORRISON	36 yr 258 days	Plymouth Argyle	A	SL Div 1	16 Sep 1911	D	0-0
8	Nigel WINTERBURN	36 yr 252 days	Chelsea	A	Prem	19 Aug 2000	L	2-4
9	Wilf PHILLIPS	36 yr 111 days	Blackburn Rovers	A	Div 1	28 Nov 1931	W	4-2
10	Les FERDINAND	36 yr 45 days	Charlton Athletic	A	Prem	22 Jan 2003	L	2-4

Oldest player in his final game

	Player	Age	Opponents	Venue	Competition	Date	Result	
1	Billy BONDS	41 yr 226 days	Southampton	A	Div 1	30 Apr 1988	L	1-2
2	Charlie BICKNELL	41 yr 59 days	Leicester City	A	Div 2	04 Jan 1947	L	0-4
3	Teddy SHERINGHAM	40 yr 300 days	Watford	H	FAC 4	27 Jan 2007	L	0-1
4	Jussi JAASKELAINEN	39 yr 298 days	Southampton	A	Prem	11 Feb 2015	D	0-0
5	Les SEALEY	39 yr 224 days	Manchester United	A	Prem	11 May 1997	L	0-2
6	Richard WALKER	39 yr 211 days	Plymouth Argyle	H	Div 2	18 Feb 1953	L	0-1
7	Phil PARKES	39 yr 190 days	Oldham Athletic	A	FLC SF:1	14 Feb 1990	L	0-6
8	Edward HUFTON	39 yr 163 days	Chelsea	A	Div 1	07 May 1932	L	2-3
9	Nigel WINTERBURN	39 yr 53 days	Liverpool	H	Prem	02 Feb 2003	L	0-3
10	Stuart PEARCE	39 yr 25 days	Middlesbrough	A	Prem	19 May 2001	L	1-2

Miscellaneous
Penalties

	Player	Scored	Missed	Taken	%
1	Ray STEWART	76	10	86	88.37
2	Julian DICKS	36	7	43	83.72
3	Mark NOBLE	23	3	26	88.46
4	Geoff HURST	22	6	28	78.57
5	Johnny BYRNE	19	2	21	90.47
6	John BOND	16	6	22	72.72
7	Paolo DI CANIO	12	1	13	92.30
8	Harry HOOPER	10	1	11	90.90
9	Marlon HAREWOOD	10	2	12	83.33
10	Bryan ROBSON	9	1	10	90.00
11	Bill ROBINSON	9	2	11	81.81
12	George HILSDON	8	2	10	80.00
13	Syd PUDDEFOOT	6	0	6	100.00
14	Danny SHEA	6	0	6	100.00
15	Teddy SHERINGHAM	6	1	7	85.71
16	Tony COTTEE	5	0	5	100.00
17	Terry WOODGATE	5	0	5	100.00
18	Frank BURTON	5	1	6	83.33
19	Malcolm ALLISON	5	1	6	83.33
20	George KITCHEN	5	3	8	62.50
21	Alessandro DIAMANTI	4	1	5	80.00
22	William McCARTNEY	4	1	5	80.00
23	Trevor MORLEY	4	1	5	80.00
24	Dave SEXTON	4	1	5	80.00
25	Frederick SHREEVE	4	3	7	57.14
26	Noel CANTWELL	3	0	3	100.00
27	Martin PETERS	3	1	4	75.00
28	James ROTHWELL	3	1	4	75.00
29	Jim BARRETT Snr	2	0	2	100.00
30	David CONNOLLY	2	0	2	100.00
31	William GRASSAM	2	0	2	100.00
32	Eddie LEWIS	2	0	2	100.00
33	Mike SMALL	2	0	2	100.00
34	Frank LAMPARD Jnr	2	1	3	66.66
35	Geoff PIKE	2	1	3	66.66
36	Ken TUCKER	2	1	3	66.66
37	Liam BRADY	2	2	4	50.00
38	Jimmy ANDREWS	1	0	1	100.00
39	Tommy ALLISON	1	0	1	100.00
40	Ian BISHOP	1	0	1	100.00
41	Andy CARROLL	1	0	1	100.00
42	Carlton COLE	1	0	1	100.00
43	Jack COLLISON	1	0	1	100.00
44	Jermain DEFOE	1	0	1	100.00
45	Don HUTCHISON	1	0	1	100.00
46	Luis JIMENEZ	1	0	1	100.00
47	Kevin KEEN	1	0	1	100.00

	Player	Scored	Missed	Taken	%
48	Harry KINSELL	1	0	1	100.00
49	Alfred LEAFE	1	0	1	100.00
50	Alvin MARTIN	1	0	1	100.00
51	Victor OBINNA	1	0	1	100.00
52	Frederic PIQUIONNE	1	0	1	100.00
53	Trevor SINCLAIR	1	0	1	100.00
54	Junior STANISLAS	1	0	1	100.00
55	Matthew TAYLOR	1	0	1	100.00
56	Tommy TAYLOR	1	0	1	100.00
57	Carlos TEVEZ	1	0	1	100.00
58	Ricardo VAZ TE	1	0	1	100.00
59	Harry WILLIAMS	1	0	1	100.00
60	Mark WARD	1	0	1	100.00
61	John HARTSON	1	1	2	50.00
62	Archie MACAULAY	1	1	2	50.00
63	James RUFFELL	1	1	2	50.00
64	Jimmy QUINN	1	2	3	33.33

his penalty listing shows every West Ham United player to have at least scored one goal from the penalty spot. In compiling this list we have trawled through nearly two thousand match reports, owever we do acknowledge the list is probably not 100% complete.

enalty Note:

penalty recorded as scored is deemed to have been converted at the first attempt, a goal scored on the rebound after a goalkeeper has made an initial save is recorded as missed.

vo of Ray Stewart's 10 missed penalties fall into this category, Luton Town (1979-80) and Lincoln City (Milk Cup 1982-83), on both occasions the goalkeepers parried his initial effort only for him followed through and score on the rebound.

here are many Hammers who have tried and failed from the spot who have not made it onto the list, some more than once, including Lionel Watson (1906-07) and Joseph Foxall (1938-39) who oth missed two spot-kicks.

PART FIVE

HONOURS
HAMMER OF THE YEAR
INTERNATIONAL HAMMERS
CLUB HONOURS
RECORDS
TRANSFERS
THE STORY OF BUBBLES
THE HISTORY OF THE WEST HAM UNITED CREST

Honours
Hammer of the Year

Since it foundation in 1957 just 36 players have been voted Hammer of the Year. It was in the 1957-58 season that members of the West Ham United Supporters' Club wanted to honour the outstanding player of the season with an official award.

The first recipient was defender Andy Malcolm, who outstanding form that season had helped Ted Fenton's side win the Second Division title on the final day of a memorable campaign.

Geoff Hurst was the first player to received the award in successive years (1966 and 1967). In 1961 Bobby Moore won the first of his four awards at the tender age of 20 and Trevor Brooking was the first to receive this accolade for three successive seasons (1976 - 1978), Brooking also holds the record for winning the most trophies, five in total between 1972 and 1984.

Year	Winner	Further information
1958	Andy Malcolm	The club's first England Youth international who helped West Ham win the Second Division title in 1957/58
1959	Ken Brown	Spent 14 seasons at the club, winning the FA Cup in 1964, European Cup Winners' Cup in 1965 and an England cap 1959
1960	Malcolm Musgrove	Left winger who scored 98 goals in 318 appearances over nine seasons between 1954 and 1962
1961	Bobby Moore	Captained West Ham and England to three successive Wembley finals, 1964 FA Cup, 1965 European Cup Winners' Cup and England' 1966 World Cup Final
1962	Lawrie Leslie	Scottish international keeper signed from Airdrieonians for £14,000, being voted Hammer of the Year in his first season
1963	Bobby Moore	
1964	Johnny Byrne	Scored 108 goals in 206 appearances in claret and blue, winning the FA Cup in 1964 and capped ten times by England whilst with the Hammers
1965	Martin Peters	Tagged "Ten years ahead of his time," by England manager Alf Ramsey the versatile player went on to play in every position - including Goalkeeper!
1966	Geoff Hurst	One of the most feared and revered strikers in World football Hurst scored 249 goals in 503 appearances for West Ham United
1967	Geoff Hurst	
1968	Bobby Moore	
1969	Geoff Hurst	
1970	Bobby Moore	
1971	Billy Bonds	Swashbuckling captain spent 21 years at the Boleyn Ground, making a club-record 793 appearances and winning FA Cup medals in 1975 and 1980
1972	Trevor Brooking	Capped 47 times by England (1974 - 1982), Brooking won the FA Cup twice during 17 seasons with the Hammers
1973	Bryan Robson	Pop' Robson spent two three-year spells with West Ham United, netting 104 goals in 255 appearances in claret and blue
1974	Billy Bonds	
1975	Billy Bonds	
1976	Trevor Brooking	
1977	Trevor Brooking	
1978	Trevor Brooking	
1979	Alan Devonshire	Devo' was signed from non League Southall for £5,000 in September 1976, winning the FA Cup in 1980 and eight England caps
1980	Alvin Martin	Centre-back joined the Hammers in 1978, going on to captain the side to a best-ever third place finish in 1985-86. Awarded two testimonial's for his 19-year service
1981	Phil Parkes	Goalkeeper who cost a world-record £565,000 in February 1979, winning the FA Cup the following season
1982	Alvin Martin	
1983	Alvin Martin	
1984	Trevor Brooking	
1985	Paul Allen	Became the youngest player ever to lift the FA Cup in 1980. He scored eleven times in 197 appearances
1986	Tony Cottee	The striker scored 26 goals as West Ham United achieved their best-ever Football League finish in 1985/86
1987	Billy Bonds	
1988	Stewart Robson	The former Arsenal midfielder marked his first full season at the Boleyn Ground by being voted Hammer of the Year 1987/88
1989	Paul Ince	Academy graduate and tough-tackling midfielder totalled 12 goals in 95 appearances for the Hammers
1990	Julian Dicks	The left-back scooped four Hammer of the Year awards and 65 goals in 326 appearances during his two spells at the club
1991	Ludek Miklosko	The giant Czech goalkeeper became a folk hero in east London, winning the Hammer of the Year in his first season at the club
1992	Julian Dicks	
1993	Steve Potts	Current Development Manager, Steve Potts came through the ranks before going on to make 505 first-team appearances, scoring a solitary goal.
1994	Trevor Morley	Hard-working forward Trevor Morley netted 70 goals in 214 senior appeances for the club
1995	Steve Potts	
1996	Julian Dicks	
1997	Julian Dicks	
1998	Rio Ferdinand	Rio Ferdinand was just 19-years-old when he was crowned Hammer of the Year for the first and only time in 1997/98

Year	Winner	Further information
1999	Shaka Hislop	The Trinidad & Tobago goalkeeper helped the Hammers secure a club-record fifth-place Premier League finish in 1998/99
2000	Paolo Di Canio	A £1.7 million pound signed from Sheffield Wednesday, the passionate Italian scored 51 goals in 141 matches for the Hammer
2001	Stuart Pearce	The former England left-back was 37 when he arrived at West Ham United in August 1999, but showed no signs of age during his time at the club
2002	Sebastien Schemmel	Originally signed for the Hammers on a temporary one-month loan, the French wing-back went on to win the accolade in his first full season with the club
2003	Joe Cole	Academy graduate Joe Cole mesmeric play helped West Ham United win the FA Youth Cup in 1999 and saw the midfielder himself crowned Hammer of the Year in 2003
2004	Matthew Etherington	Left winger who joined from Tottenham Hotspur in August 2003, Etherington was another player to win the accolade in his first full season with the club
2005	Teddy Sheringham	Sheringham won the Hammer of the Year award a month past his 39th birthday after scoring 21 goals in 36 matches.
2006	Daniel Gabbidon	Central defender who helped the Hammers to finish ninth in the Premier League and reach the FA Cup final in 2005/06
2007	Carlos Tevez	The Argentina international scored only seven goals for the Hammers, but his contribution to the 'Great Escape' was immense
2008	Robert Green	The England goalkeeper enjoyed a typically consistent 2007/08 campaign as the Hammers finished tenth in the Premier League
2009	Scott Parker	Midfielder Scott Parker became a true fans' favourite, winning three consecutive Hammer of the Year awards
2010	Scott Parker	
2011	Scott Parker	
2012	Mark Noble	Home-grown midfielder Mark Noble is West Ham United's all-time record Premier League appearance-maker
2013	Winston Reid	The New Zealand national-team captain and outstanding defender scooped the Hammer of the Year award in 20012/13
2014	Mark Noble	
2015	Aaron Cresswell	The pacey left-back joined the Hammers from Championship side Ipswich Town in July 2014. The defender's first top-flight season saw him crowned Hammer of the Year

Hammer of the Year 1963: Jim Standen runner-up, Bobby Moore winner and Ken Brown third place.

International Hammers

No.	Player	Country Debut Order	Country	Federation	Caps	Date
1	William JONES	1st	WALES	UEFA	4	1901 - 1902
2	George WEBB	1st	ENGLAND	UEFA	2	1911
3	Victor WATSON	2nd	ENGLAND	UEFA	5	1923 - 1930
4	Jack TRESADERN	3rd	ENGLAND	UEFA	2	1923
5	William MOORE	4th	ENGLAND	UEFA	1	1923
=6	Edward HUFTON	=5th	ENGLAND	UEFA	6	1923 - 1929
=6	William BROWN	=5th	ENGLAND	UEFA	1	1923
8	Dick RICHARDS	2nd	WALES	UEFA	3	1924
9	James RUFFELL	7th	ENGLAND	UEFA	6	1926 - 1929
10	Stanley EARLE	8th	ENGLAND	UEFA	1	1927
11	Jim BARRETT	9th	ENGLAND	UEFA	1	1928
12	Wilf JAMES	3rd	WALES	UEFA	2	1931
13	Len GOULDEN	10th	ENGLAND	UEFA	14	1937 - 1939
14	John MORTON	11th	ENGLAND	UEFA	1	1935
15	Charlie TURNER	1st	REPUBLIC of IRELAND	UEFA	3	1938 - 1939
16	Tommy MORONEY	2nd	REPUBLIC of IRELAND	UEFA	11	1948 - 1951
17	Danny McGOWAN	3rd	REPUBLIC of IRELAND	UEFA	3	1949
18	Frank O'FARRELL	4th	REPUBLIC of IRELAND	UEFA	7	1952 - 1956
19	Noel CANTWELL	5th	REPUBLIC of IRELAND	UEFA	17	1953 - 1960
20	Fred KEARNS	6th	REPUBLIC of IRELAND	UEFA	1	1954
21	Phil WOOSNAM	4th	WALES	UEFA	14	1958 - 1962
22	John DICK	1st	SCOTLAND	UEFA	1	1959
23	Noel DWYER	7th	REPUBLIC of IRELAND	UEFA	4	1959 - 1960
24	Ken BROWN	12th	ENGLAND	UEFA	1	1959
25	Bobby MOORE	13th	ENGLAND	UEFA	108	1962 - 1973
26	Johnny BYRNE	14th	ENGLAND	UEFA	10	1963 - 1965
27	Geoff HURST	15th	ENGLAND	UEFA	49	1966 - 1972
28	Martin PETERS	16th	ENGLAND	UEFA	33	1966 - 1970
29	Clyde BEST	1st	BERMUDA	CONCACAF	2	1968
30	Frank LAMPARD Snr.	17th	ENGLAND	UEFA	2	1972 - 1980
31	Bertie LUTTON	1st	NORTHERN IRELAND	UEFA	4	1973
32	Trevor BROOKING	18th	ENGLAND	UEFA	47	1974 - 1982
33	Alan DEVONSHIRE	19th	ENGLAND	UEFA	8	1980 - 1983
34	Ray STEWART	2nd	SCOTLAND	UEFA	10	1981 - 1987
35	Alvin MARTIN	20th	ENGLAND	UEFA	17	1981 - 1986
36	Francois VAN der ELST	1st	BELGIUM	UEFA	8	1982 - 1983
37	Paul GODDARD	21st	ENGLAND	UEFA	1	1982
38	Frank McAVENNIE	3rd	SCOTLAND	UEFA	4	1985 - 1986
39	Tony COTTEE	22nd	ENGLAND	UEFA	3	1986 - 1988
40	Liam BRADY	8th	REPUBLIC of IRELAND	UEFA	11	1987 - 1990
41	Allen McKNIGHT	2nd	NORTHERN IRELAND	UEFA	4	1988 - 1989
42	David KELLY	9th	REPUBLIC of IRELAND	UEFA	1	1988
43	Jimmy QUINN	3rd	NORTHERN IRELAND	UEFA	2	1990 - 1991
44	Ludek MIKLOSKO	1st	CZECH REPUBLIC	UEFA	9	1990 - 1997
45	Iain DOWIE	4th	NORTHERN IRELAND	UEFA	15	1991 - 1997
46	Chris HUGHTON	10th	REPUBLIC of IRELAND	UEFA	2	1991
47	Alex BUNBURY	1st	CANADA	CONCACAF	6	1993

No.	Player	Country Debut Order	Country	Federation	Caps	Date
48	Keith ROWLAND	5th	NORTHERN IRELAND	UEFA	13	1993 - 1997
49	Marc REIPER	1st	DENMARK	UEFA	23	1995 - 1997
50	John HARKES	1st	USA	CONCACAF	4	1996
51	Robbie SLATER	1st	AUSTRALIA	AFC	2	1996
52	Slaven BILIC	1st	CROATIA	UEFA	14	1996 - 1997
53	Michael HUGHES	6th	NORTHERN IRELAND	UEFA	9	1996 - 1997
54	Mark BOWEN	5th	WALES	UEFA	4	1996 -1997
55	Ilie DUMITRESCU	1st	ROMANIA	UEFA	2	1996
56	Hugo PORFIRIO	1st	PORTUGAL	UEFA	1	1996
=57	Steve LOMAS	7th	NORTHERN IRELAND	UEFA	27	1997 - 2003
=57	John HARTSON	6th	WALES	UEFA	6	1997 - 1998
59	Stan LAZARIDIS	2nd	AUSTRALIA	AFC	14	1997 - 1999
60	Craig FORREST	2nd	CANADA	CONCACAF	23	1997 - 2001
61	Rio FERDINAND	23rd	ENGLAND	UEFA	10	1997 - 2000
62	Eyal BERKOVIC	1st	ISREAL	UEFA	11	1998 - 1999
63	Bernard LAMA	1st	FRANCE	UEFA	2	1998
64	Ian WRIGHT	24th	ENGLAND	UEFA	2	1998
65	Shaka HISLOP	1st	TRINIDAD & TOBAGO	CONCACAF	18	1999 - 2006
66	Javier MARGAS	1st	CHILE	CONMEBOL	2	1999 - 2000
=67	Stuart PEARCE	25th	ENGLAND	UEFA	2	1999
=67	Igor STIMAC	2nd	CROATIA	UEFA	9	1999 - 2000
69	Frank LAMPARD Jnr.	26th	ENGLAND	UEFA	2	1999 - 2001
70	Marc VIVIAN-FOE	1st	CAMEROON	CAF	7	2000
71	Paulo WANCHOPE	1st	COSTA RICA	CONCACAF	8	2000
72	Davor SUKER	3rd	CROATIA	UEFA	6	2000 - 2001
=73	Hayden FOXE	3rd	AUSTRALIA	AFC	7	2000 - 2001
=73	Rigobert SONG	2nd	CAMEROON	CAF	22	2000 - 2002
=75	Svetoslav TODOROV	1st	BULGARIA	UEFA	6	2001
=75	Hannu TIHINEN	1st	FINLAND	UEFA	1	2001
77	Christian DAILLY	4th	SCOTLAND	UEFA	39	2001 - 2007
=78	Joe COLE	27th=	ENGLAND	UEFA	10	2001 - 2003
=78	Michael CARRICK	27th=	ENGLAND	UEFA	2	2001
80	David JAMES	29th	ENGLAND	UEFA	18	2001 - 2003
81	Don HUTCHISON	5th	SCOTLAND	UEFA	10	2001 - 2003
=82	Tomas REPKA	2nd	CZECH REPUBLIC	UEFA	2	2001
=82	Grant McCANN	8th	NORTHERN IRELAND	UEFA	5	2001 - 2002
84	Trevor SINCLAIR	30th	ENGLAND	UEFA	11	2001 - 2003
85	Vladimir LABANT	1st	SLOVAKIA	UEFA	8	2002 - 2003
86	Gary BREEN	11th	REPUBLIC of IRELAND	UEFA	9	2002 - 2003
87	Titi CAMARA	1st	GUINEA	CAF	2	2002
88	David CONNOLLY	12th	REPUBLIC of IRELAND	UEFA	3	2003
89	Andy MELVILLE	7th	WALES	UEFA	4	2004
90	Carl FLETCHER	8th	WALES	UEFA	14	2005 - 2006
91	Daniel GABBIDON	9th	WALES	UEFA	25	2005 - 2010
92	Gavin WILLIAMS	10th	WALES	UEFA	2	2005
93	Yossi BENAYOUN	2nd	ISREAL	UEFA	15	2005 - 2012
94	James COLLINS	11th	WALES	UEFA	30	2005 - 2015

No.	Player	Country Debut Order	Country	Federation	Caps	Date
95	Paul KONCHESKY	31st	ENGLAND	UEFA	1	2005
96	Yaniv KATAN	3rd	ISRAEL	UEFA	1	2006
97	Lionel SCALONI	1st	ARGENTINA	CONMEBOL	1	2006
98	John PANTSIL	1st	GHANA	CAF	20	2006 - 2008
99	Roy CARROLL	9th	NORTHERN IRELAND	UEFA	2	2006
=100	Javier MASCHERANO	2nd=	ARGENTINA	CONMEBOL	1	2006
=100	Carlos TEVEZ	2nd=	ARGENTINA	CONMEBOL	10	2006 - 2007
102	Lucas NEILL	4th	AUSTRALIA	CONMEBOL	19	2007 - 2009
103	Jonathan SPECTOR	2nd	USA	CONCACAF	28	2007 - 2011
104	George McCARTNEY	10th	NORTHERN IRELAND	UEFA	5	2007 - 2008
105	Kieron DYER	32nd	ENGLAND	UEFA	1	2007
106	Henri CAMARA	1st	SENEGAL	CAF	8	2007 - 2008
107	Nolberto SOLANO	1st	PERU	CONMEBOL	5	2007
108	Craig BELLAMY	12th	WALES	UEFA	8	2007 - 2008
109	Frederik LJUNGBERG	1st	SWEDEN	UEFA	8	2007 - 2008
110	Matthew UPSON	33rd	ENGLAND	UEFA	14	2008 - 2010
111	Jack COLLISON	13th	WALES	UEFA	16	2008 - 2014
112	Dean ASHTON	34th	ENGLAND	UEFA	1	2008
113	Valon BEHRAMI	1st	SWITZERLAND	UEFA	7	2008- 2010
114	Herita ILUNGA	1st	DR CONGO	CAF	5	2008- 2010
115	Radoslav KOVAC	3rd	CZECH REPUBLIC	UEFA	2	2009
116	Robert GREEN	35th	ENGLAND	UEFA	11	2009 - 2012
117	Carlton COLE	36th	ENGLAND	UEFA	7	2009 - 2010
118	Luis BOA-MORTE	2nd	PORTUGAL	UEFA	2	2009
119	Guillermo FRANCO	1st	MEXICO	CONCACAF	6	2009 - 2010
120	Benni McCARTHY	1st	SOUTH AFRICA	CAF	1	2010
121	Thomas HITZLSPERGER	1st	GERMANY	UEFA	1	2010
122	Pablo BARRERA	2nd	MEXICO	CONCACAF	16	2010 - 2011
123	Tal BEN-HAIM	3rd	ISRAEL	UEFA	3	2010
124	Lars JACOBSEN	2nd	DENMARK	UEFA	5	2010 - 2011
125	Winston REID	1st	NEW ZEALAND	OFC	12	2010 - 2015
126	Victor OBINNA	1st	NIGERIA	CAF	1	2010
127	Scott PARKER	37th	ENGLAND	UEFA	3	2011
=128	Demba BA	2nd	SENEGAL	CAF	1	2011
=128	Robbie KEANE	13th	REPUBLIC of IRELAND	UEFA	3	2011
130	John CAREW	1st	NORWAY	UEFA	3	2011
131	Mohamed DIAME	3rd	SENEGAL	CAF	15	2014
132	Joey O'BRIEN	14th	REPUBLIC of IRELAND	UEFA	2	2012 - 2015
133	Modibo MAIGA	1st	MALI	CAF	13	2012 - 2015
134	Andy CARROLL	38th	ENGLAND	UEFA	1	2012 - 2015
135	Frederic PIQUIONNE	1st	MARTINIQUE	CONCACAF	2	2012
136	Emanuel POGATETZ	1st	AUSTRIA	UEFA	3	2013
137	Razvan RAT	2nd	ROMANIA	UEFA	5	2013 - 2014
138	Pablo ARMERO	1st	COLOMBIA	CONMEBOL	1	2014
139	Cheikhou KOUYATE	4th	SENEGAL	CAF	9	2014 - 2015
140	Enner VALENCIA	1st	ECUADOR	CONMEBOL	9	2014 - 2015
141	Diafra SAKHO	5th	SENEGAL	CAF	1	2014 - 2015
142	Stewart DOWNING	39th	ENGLAND	UEFA	1	2014 - 2015

Club Honours
Thames Ironworks

Southern League Second Division

Winners	1898/99

West Ham United

Southern League First Division

Highest placing	3rd 1912/13

Football League (Second Tier)

Winners	1957/58, 1980/81	Runners-up	1922/23, 1990/91, 1992/93

Football League (Second Tier) Play-Off

Winners	2005	v. Preston North End (1-0)	Runners-up	2004	Crystal Palace (0-1)
Winners	2012	v. Blackpool (2-1)			

Football League (Top Tier)

Highest placing	3rd 1985/86

Premier League

Highest placing	5th 1998/99

FA Cup

Winners	1964	v. Preston North End (3-2)	Runners-up	1923	v. Bolton Wanderers (0-2)
Winners	1975	v. Fulham (2-0)	Runners-up	2006	v. Liverpool (3-3 lost 1-3 pens)
Winners	1980	v. Arsenal (1-0)			

Football League War Cup

Winners	1940	v. Blackburn Rovers (1-0)

Football League Cup

Runners-up	1966	v. West Bromwich Albion (1-4 agg)
Runners-up	1981	v. Liverpool (1-2 replay)

European Cup Winners' Cup

Winners	1965	v. TSV Munchen 1860 (2-0)	Runners-up	1976	v. Anderlecht (2-4)

UEFA Intertoto Cup

Winners	1999	v. FC Metz (3-2 agg)

Charity Shield

Shared	1964	v. Liverpool (2-2)	Runners-up	1975	v. Derby County (0-2)
			Runners-up	1981	v. Liverpool (0-1)

FA Youth Cup

Winners	1963	v. Liverpool (6-5 agg)	Runners-up	1957	v. Manchester United (2-8 agg)
Winners	1981	Tottenham Hotspur (2-1 agg)	Runners-up	1959	v. Blackburn Rovers (1-2 agg)
Winners	1999	v. Coventry City (9-0 agg)	Runners-up	1975	v. Ipswich Town (1-5 agg)
			Runners-up	1996	v. Liverpool (1-4 agg)

Records
Results

Record Premier League victories

Home	6-0	v. Barnsley, 10 January 1998
Away	5-0	v. Derby County, 10 November 2007

Record Division One victories

Home	8-0	v. Sunderland, 19 October 1968
Away	6-1	v. Manchester City, 8 September 1962

Record Division Two victories

Home	8-0	v. Rotherham United, 8 March 1958
Away	6-0	v. Leicester City, 15 February 1923

Record European victories

Home	5-1	v. Castilla (Spain) European Cup Winners' Cup, 1 October 1980
Away	3-1	v. FC Metz (France) UEFA Intertoto Cup, 24 August 1999 and v. NK Osijek UEFA Cup, 30 September 1999

Record FA Cup victories

Home	8-1	v. Chesterfield, 10 January 1914
Away	5-0	v. Chatham, 28 November 1903

Record Football League Cup victories

Home	10-0	v. Bury, 25 October 1983
Away	5-1	v. Cardiff City, 2 February 1966

Record Premier League defeats

Home	1-5	v. Leeds United, 1 May 1999
Away	1-7	v. Manchester United, 1 April 2000 and v. Blackburn Rovers, 14 October 2001

Record Division One defeats

Home	2-8	v. Blackburn Rovers, 26 December 1963
Away	0-7	v. Everton, 22 October 1927 and v. Sheffield Wednesday, 28 November 1959

Record Division Two defeats

Home	0-6	v. Sheffield Wednesday, 8 December 1951
Away	0-7	v. Barnsley, 1 September 1919

Record European defeats

Home	1-4	v. Dinamo Tbilisi, European Cup Winners' Cup, 4 March 1981
Away	0-3	v. Palermo, UEFA Cup, 28 September 2006

Record FA Cup defeats

Home	1-5	v. Huddersfield Town, 13 January 1960
Away	0-6	v. Manchester United, 26 January 2003

Record Football League Cup defeats

Home	2-5	v. Barnsley, 6 October 1987
Away	0-6	v. Oldham Athletic, 14 February 1990 and v. Manchester City, 8 January 2014

Record draws

Home	5-5	v. Aston Villa, 3 Janaruy 1931
Away	5-5	v. Newcastle United, 10 December 1960 and v. Chelsea, 17 December 1966

Transfers

Record Transfer Fee Paid	
Undisclosed	Andy Carroll from Liverpool, May 2014
Undisclosed	Enner Valencia from Pachuca, July 2014
Undisclosed	Matt Jarvis from Wolverhampton Wanderers, August 2012
Undisclosed	Savio from Fiorentina, January 2009
£7.5m	Craig Bellamy from Liverpool, July 2007

Record Transfer Fee Received	
£18m	Rio Ferdinand to Leeds United, November 2001
£14m	Craig Bellamy to Manchester City, January 2009
£11m	Frank Lampard Jnr to Chelsea, June 2001
£8.5m	Nigel Reo-Coker to Aston Villa, July 2007
£8m	Anton Ferdinand to Sunderland, August 2008

The Story of Bubbles

Generations of West Ham fans have sung 'I'm Forever Blowing Bubbles' on the terraces at Upton Park, but how many are aware of how it became a West Ham anthem?

The song was written in 1919 in the United States by joint composers and became a hit on both sides of the Atlantic. The composers were James Kendis, James Brockman and Nat Vincent who formed their names into Jaan Kenbrovin a pseudonym named on the original sheet music. The lyrics were added by John William Kellette.

How 'Bubbles' came to be associated with West Ham has been the subject of many a debate over the years. The popular theory is that the singing of the song came together with the unlikely ingredients of a soap advert, and a young curly headed footballer. In 1829 Sir John Millais painted a portrait of his grandson watching a soap bubble he had just blown through a clay pipe. The painting was exhibited at the Royal Academy. Later the Pears Soap Works used the painting as an advertisement and displayed posters throughout the East End of London. As the soap works were situated in Canning Town the West Ham supporters would have been familiar with the posters. The West Ham Boys team often played their home games at Upton Park in front of huge crowds and one of their team Will Murray having fair curly hair resembled the boy in the advert. He soon gained the nickname 'Bubbles' Murray and whenever he played the crowd would sing 'I'm Forever Blowing Bubbles' being the popular song of the day. 'Bubbles' Murray became famous and was mentioned in the programme in May 1921 when West Ham Boys played Liverpool in the English Schools Football Championship Final.

Around that time the Beckton Gas Works Band used to play 'Bubbles' before the kick off and this tradition continued up until the 1970s through the Metropolitan Police Band, the Leyton Silver Band and finally the British Legion Band. Although the song became popular all around the ground there was particular affinity with the fans who stood in what was known as the Chicken Run'. It was an encouraging sight for the team as the supporters sang 'Bubbles' and swayed from side to side. It was first believed that 'Bubbles' was sung at the 1923 FA Cup Final when the Hammers met Bolton Wanderers, but this was not the case as a souvenir leaflet issued on the day had words to be sung by the Hammers fans to the tune of 'Till We Meet Again'.

Another theory of how 'Bubbles' originated was the connection with Swansea Town Between 1920 and 1926 the Welsh fans used to sing Bubbles at their home games and this was mentioned in the history of Swansea Town, published in 1982. Various match reports mentioned the singing. A report for the home game with Bury in 1921 mentioned the ever popular singing of 'Bubbles' from the main bank with a tremendous sway. For the cup tie with Clapton Orient in 1924 it was stated that once again the crowd swayed to Bubbles. The 'Leader' in 1925 reported on the Swans trip to Southend by saying the support was considerable with lusty renderings of Bubbles. Finally the report for the FA Cup tie with Aston Villa in 1925 said that despite the rendering of 'Cwm Rhonda' and 'Bubbles' the

Villa won 3-1.

In 1922 West Ham played Swansea three times in the FA Cup with a game at both grounds and a replay at Ashton Gate in Bristol. It could be therefore that the Hammers supporters adopted the song after this. In those days of friendly rivalry it was possible that both sets of supporters would have sung Bubbles and swayed to join in the fun. There was a close affinity between the two clubs. The old grounds were similar and the areas surrounding them were industrial and working class and each could identify with the other. The author Brian Belton in doing research for his various West Ham books has put forward another interesting theory in that during the war Bubbles was sung as crowds gathered during air raids in shelters and underground stations especially in blitz torn East London. This led to a rise in communal singing both in the Forces and the general public to raise morale. The song was heard at the 1940 League Cup Final and this may mark the real beginning of the song being the West Ham theme.

The song has endured through the years to echo the hopes and disappointment of the West Ham faithful. It has been said that the words are too sentimental for a football song but tradition dies hard and the Hammers supporters would not be the same without their beloved anthem. Not only is it heard at football grounds but whenever Hammers fans get together at family gatherings and parties they request that the tune is played. One other club that has Bubbles as its signature tune is AFC Telford who have had the song for many years when they were known as Wellington Town. Back in 1990 the players approached the club chairman asking for a tune which would be more in keeping with the clubs tradition. Through the Shropshire Star the fans were asked what they would like and the older supporters indicated they would like to keep Bubbles, with the younger fans requesting a new song. A compromise was reached when West Ham sent them a more modern version of Bubbles which was recorded by the 1975 FA Cup Final squad.

A soap advert, a curly headed footballer, a popular song, the Swansea connection and the war time community singing: the true answer behind the legend probably lies somewhere in the mists of time.

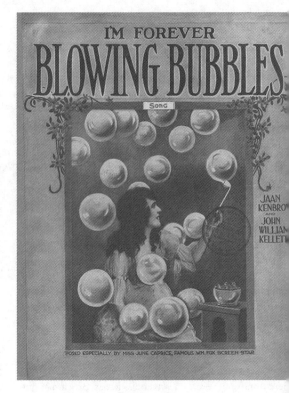

The history of the West Ham United crest

Two main features of the present day West Ham United crest are a pair of crossed hammers and a castle. The hammers were symbolic of the tools used in shipbuilding and the castle a representation of the house that stood on the present day Boleyn Ground.

But that was not always the case, when the Thames Ironworks Football Club was formed in 1895 the players wore a 'Union Jack' crest with the initials T.I.W.

There is no official evidence as to when the crossed hammers was adopted, the Thames Ironworks was wound up as a works team in 1900 and later re-born as a professional club under the name West Ham United. The earliest known publication portraying the crossed hammers motif is the official match day programmes from the 1911-12 season.

A 'castle turret' and separate 'crossed hammers' motif were a regular feature on the cover of the club programme between 1921 and 1958. The castle was traditionally believed to be connected with Henry Vlll's second Queen, Anne Boleyn. However, this was not founded on fact, as the castle was a building known as Green Street House built in 1544, eight years after the execution of the King's second wife.

A couple of turrets were added to the property two years later 'to enhance the beauty of the grounds', and one remained on the Green Street frontage and can often be seen in the background to team group photographs after the Second World War until it fell into disrepair and was demolished in 1955.

During the 1950s, the players wore West Ham United badges with the 'crossed hammers' on their playing kits, while the 'turrets' were a prominent feature on the Club's official blazer.

When West Ham were promoted as champions from the old Football League Division Two in 1958, the Club incorporated both the castle design with turrets and the symbolic crossed hammers.

As was the case with many other football clubs at the time, the badge was further refined in the early 1980s to give it a more up-to-date look and feel and to maximise its marketing potential

The crest we see today was redesigned in the late 1990s and features a wider castle with fewer cruciform 'windows' along with the peaked roofs being removed the tops of the towers. The designer also altered the shape of the hammer heads, border and other small changes in order to give a more substantial feel to the iconography.

At the start of the 2016-17 season, West Ham United will sport a newly-designed crest when they move to the Olympic Stadium. The new crest sees the castle removed from the current design with a heavier focus on the historic 'irons'. The addition of 'London' helps to focus the club's roots and status.

PART SIX

A C K N O W L E D G E M E N T S
BIBLIOGRAPHY
ROLL OF HONOUR

Acknowledgements

First of all we would like to thank James Corbett and Thomas Regan at deCoubertin Books for giving us the opportunity to write this book on our favourite club.

It is with pleasure that we would like to show appreciation to our footballing friends who have readily given assistance to help in the compilation of West Ham United The Complete Record.

Our gratitude goes to Roy Shoesmith for his assistance on the war time seasons, programme collectors Stuart Allen and Dennis Lamb for supplying war-time programme covers.

A special thank you to Barbara Shrimpton for the time she has spent trawling the Ancestry Records in providing over 150 player birth dates which until now have previously gone unrecorded.

Grateful thanks to Richard Miller for double-checking our statistics and allowing us access to his newspaper archives which would seriously rival the British Library. John Powles for allowing us to tap into his specialist knowledge on Thames Ironworks FC.

We also thank John Farley from a land far, far away (New Zealand) for his expertise in extracting sensible data from over 180 of our databases compiled over the last 40 years.

For their support and encouragement we would like to express our appreciation to Roger Hillier, Dave Alexander, the Sturton family Chas, Julie, Graham and Paul, Dave Clements, Alan Deadman, Lee Jackson, Nigel Kahn, Nigel Turner, Steve Bell, Gerald Mills, Vic Lindsell, Richard Quirk and to West Ham club historian John Helliar.

Finally we thank our wives Marian and Sally, who have made vital contributions of encouragement and practical help.

Bibliography

Charles Korr, *West Ham United, Duckworth, 1986*

Brian Belton, *Days of Iron, Breedon Books, 1999*

Kirk Blows & Tony Hogg, *The Essential History of West Ham United, Headline, 2000*

John Northcutt, *The Definitive West Ham United FC, Soccer Data, 2003*

John Powles, *Iron in the Blood, Soccer Data, 2005*

John Helliar. *West Ham United The Elite Era, Desert Island Books, 2005*

Tony Hogg, *Who's Who of West Ham United, Profile Sports Media, 2005*

Barry Hugman, *Premier and Football League Players Records, Queen Anne Press, 2005*

John Northcutt, *The Claret and Blue Book of West Ham United, Pitch Publishing, 2007*

John Powles, *Irons of the South, Soccer Data, 2008*

Websites

www.theyflysohigh.co.uk

www.whu-programmes.co.uk

www.westhamstats.info

www.11v11.com

Newspapers

Newham Recorder

East London Advertiser

Photo credits

West Ham United Football Club plc for the use of the Club Crest and access to their player portrait archives spanning the Thames Ironworks period through to the Millennium in 2000.

Photographer Rob Newell (TGS Photo and The Digital South Lt for readily agreeing to bridge the portrait gap from 2000 to 2015.

Page 599: West Ham United Supporters Club

Steve Marsh

John Northcutt

Thomas Regan

Leslie Priestley

James Corbett

Daniel Lewis

James Montague

Andrew Westlake

Archie, Leicester Hammers

Mark Ford

Paul Ford

Trevor and Jordan Poole

Andrea & Ian Nelson-Harris

Stephen Gill

Gary Bush

Colin Auchterlonie, Tommy Auchterlonie, Lottie Auchterlonie, Katie Carr

Gary Smithurst

Roger Hillier

Nigel Bailey

Simon Lord

Richard Quirk

Mark Waight

Eoin Cotter

Tony Jagger (Yorkshire Iron)

Steven Holliday

Glenn Barrett

John Reynolds

Tony the Iron

Michael Grayson

Big Al's Badges (Isle of Wight)

Richard Miller

Stuart Allen

John Farley

Nigel Turner

Sally Marsh

Holly Mills

Ryan Mills

Jasper Mills

Antony Northcutt

David Scremin

Paul Richman